May 6–11, 2017
Denver, CO, USA



Association for
Computing Machinery

*Advancing Computing as a Science & Profession*

# CHI'17

## Proceedings of the 2017 ACM SIGCHI Conference on Human Factors in Computing Systems

*Sponsored by:*

***ACM SIGCHI***

*Supported by:*

***Bloomberg, Facebook, Google, IBM Research, Microsoft, & NSF***

Association for
Computing Machinery

*Advancing Computing as a Science & Profession*

**The Association for Computing Machinery**
**2 Penn Plaza, Suite 701**
**New York, New York 10121-0701**



**ISBN:** 978-1-4503-4655-9 (Digital)

**ISBN:** 978-1-4503-5461-5 (Print)

Additional copies may be ordered prepaid from:

**ACM Order Department**
PO Box 30777
New York, NY 10087-0777, USA

Phone: 1-800-342-6626 (USA and Canada)
+1-212-626-0500 (Global)
Fax: +1-212-944-1318
E-mail: acmhelp@acm.org
Hours of Operation: 8:30 am – 4:30 pm ET

Printed in the USA

CHI 2017 is the premier international conference for the field of Human-Computer Interaction (HCI). This year it was held in Denver, bordering the beautiful Rocky Mountain region in the U.S., and reflected in our logo. The CHI 2017 conference began with two days of workshops and symposia, followed by four days of a technical program with 17 parallel sessions of provocative papers, panels, case studies, SIGs (Special Interest Groups), courses, and the popular student research, design, and game competitions. The growing alt.chi forum, now in its twelfth year, presented stimulating new ideas in HCI. The Interactivity forum showcased cutting-edge technology. For its second year, the CHI Art Exhibit merged art and technology in fascinating ways.

This innovative work can be found in the Proceedings and Extended Abstracts, archived in the ACM Digital Library. For papers, the conference received 2400 submissions which were rigorously reviewed, resulting in 600 accepted papers. To ensure a better fit with reviewers, new subcommittees were created. Across all tracks, CHI received nearly 5000 submissions and accepted over 1000.

Our conference theme this year, *Explore, Innovate, Inspire*, informed our planning process. A new venue held this year was CHI Stories. We generally know little of the personalities that drive the research presented at CHI. CHI Stories is a chance for CHI community members to share personal stories of inspiration, challenge, successes and failures, and grit. We also focused on inclusion this year. Hundreds of CHI attendees volunteered their skills in a Day of Service partnering with non-profit organizations. Inclusion was also manifest throughout the conference, for example, in the Diversity and Inclusion Lunch and by using telepresence robots to enable people with disabilities to participate remotely in the conference. Our keynote speakers were chosen to reflect our conference theme. The speakers were Neri Oxman, who combines computational design, digital fabrication, materials science and synthetic biology; Ben Shneiderman a founder of the CHI conference who, along with some key CHI personalities, gave a perspective on CHI's history and future; Wael Ghonim, credited with starting the Arab Spring and nominated for the Nobel Peace Prize; and best-selling author Nicholas Carr who challenges us to examine the unforeseen impacts of technology, particularly with automation.

The world has experienced a dramatic change this past year. We live in extraordinary times and this calls for extraordinary thinking, something that the CHI community excels at. One of the challenges the community faced this year was responding to a U.S. executive order to ban citizens of certain countries from entering the country to attend CHI. As CHI is committed to inclusion, we decided to hold events at the conference to discuss and plan how we can continue our commitment to inclusion. The conference held a panel to discuss impacts of current political events on science, and hastily organized a panel to promote a conversation of civil liberties in science and a SIG on how the CHI community can participate in change. We are proud to have expanded telepresence options through the use of robots to enable people to participate in the conference remotely if they were physically unable to enter the country. We had a keynote speaker who inspired us on the topic of Internet activism. Our art exhibit, *I'll Be Watching You,* examined the contemporary issue of surveillance.

We are extremely grateful to a legion of volunteers who made CHI 2017 possible, including over 7000 reviewers across all areas of the technical program, 254 senior members of the papers program committee, over 100 members of the CHI 2017 conference organization committee and importantly, the more than 175 student volunteers. We also thank SIGCHI (the Special Interest Group on Computer-Human Interaction of ACM) as well as the ACM itself for its continued support.

**Gloria Mark,** University of California Irvine, CHI 2017 General Conference Co-Chair

**Susan Fussell,** Cornell University, CHI 2017 General Conference Co-Chair

**Cliff Lampe,** University of Michigan, CHI 2017 Technical Program Chair

**m.c. schraefel,** University of Southampton, CHI 2017 Technical Program Chair

**Juan Pablo Hourcade,** University of Iowa, CHI 2017 Papers Co-Chair

**Caroline Appert,** Université Paris-Sud, CHI 2017 Papers Co-Chair

**Daniel Wigdor,** University of Toronto, CHI 2017 Papers Co-Chair

**Loren Terveen,** University of Minnesota, President, ACM SIGCHI Executive Committee

**Scooter Morris,** University of San Francisco, ACM SIGCHI Liaison

# Table of Contents

# Table of Contents

# Table of Contents

# Table of Contents

# Table of Contents

# Table of Contents

# Table of Contents

# Table of Contents

# Table of Contents

# Table of Contents

# Table of Contents

# Table of Contents

# Table of Contents

## Session: Mindfulness and Reflection



## Session: Supporting Low Resource Communities



## Session: Technology Augmented Driving



## Session: Autism, Disabilities and Assistive Technology

# Table of Contents

# Table of Contents

# Table of Contents

# Table of Contents

# Table of Contents

# Table of Contents

# Table of Contents

# Table of Contents

# Table of Contents

# Table of Contents

# Table of Contents

# Table of Contents

# Table of Contents

# Table of Contents

# Table of Contents

# Table of Contents

# Table of Contents

# Table of Contents

# Table of Contents

# Table of Contents

# CHI 2017 Organization

**Conference Chairs**
Gloria Mark, University of California, Irvine
Susan Fussell, Cornell University

**Assistants to General Chairs**
Yiran Wang, University of California, Irvine
Ge Gao, Cornell University

**Senior Technical Program Chair**
Cliff Lampe, University of Michigan

**Technical Program Chair**
m.c. schraefel, University of Southampton

**Assistant to the Technical Program Chairs**
Lindsay Blackwell, University of Michigan

**Papers Chairs**
Caroline Appert, Univ. Paris-Sud & CNRS
Juan Pablo Hourcade, University of Iowa
Daniel Wigdor, University of Toronto

**Assistant to Papers Chairs**
Michael Glueck, University of Toronto

**alt.chi Chairs**
Karrie Karahalios, University of Illinois at Urbana – Champaign
Jessa Lingel, University of Pennsylvania
Janet Vertesi, Princeton University

**Case Studies Chairs**
Stephen Snow, University of Southampton
Jessica Tsimeris, Google

**Courses Chairs**
Erik Andersen, Cornell University
Hilary Hutchinson, Google
Max Wilson, University of Nottingham

**Demos Chairs**
Ido Guy, Yahoo
Stephen Voida, University of Colorado Boulder

**Doctoral Consortium Chairs**
Anna Cox, University College London
Jeff Bigham, Carnegie Mellon University
Kenton O'Hara, Microsoft Research, UK

**Interactive Installations Chairs**
Adrian Friday, Lancaster University
Shengdong Zhao, National University of Singapore

**Late Breaking Work Chairs**
Sharon Ding, Fudan University
Ingrid Erikson, Rutgers University
Bryan Semaan, Syracuse University
Fanis Tsandilas, INRIA

**Panels Chairs**
Sarita Schoenebeck, University of Michigan
Jude Yew, National University of Singapore

**Student Design Competition Chairs**
Joonhwan Lee, Seoul National University
Scott Minneman, California College of Arts

**Student Game Competition Chairs**
Floyd Mueller, RMIT University
Josh Tanenbaum, University of California, Irvine

**Student Research Competition Chairs**
Jeremy Birnholtz, Northwestern University
Jenn Thom, Spotify

**Special Interest Groups Chairs**
Lindsay Reynolds, Facebook
Bert Scerbo, Disney

**Systems Chairs**
Michael Stewart, Virginia Tech
Dorota Filipczuk, University of Southampton

**Symposia Chair**
Lana Yarosh, University of Minnesota

**Video Showcase Chairs**
Danyel Fisher, Microsoft Research
Catherine Letondal, ENAC

**Workshops Chairs**
Duncan Brumby, University College London
Christopher Frauenberger, Vienna University of Technology, Austria
Shamsi Iqbal, Microsoft Research

**Art Chairs**
Jiffer Harriman, University of Colorado
Andruid Kerne, Texas A&M University
HyunJoo Oh, University of Colorado Boulder
Thecla Schiphorst, Simon Fraser University

**CHI Stories Chairs**
Nazanin Andalibi, Drexel University
Nick Diakopoulos, University of Maryland, College Park
Andrea Forte, Drexel University
Misa Maruyama, University of Hawaii at Manoa
Scott Robertson, University of Hawaii at Manoa

**Career Development Workshop Chairs**
Luigina Ciolfi, Sheffield Hallam University
Michael Muller, IBM Research

**Journals Chair**
Hrvoje Benko, Microsoft Research

**Remix Chairs**
Susan Dray, Dray & Associates
Amy Voida, University of Colorado Boulder

**Student Volunteer Chairs**
Patrick Carrington, University of Maryland, Baltimore County (UMBC)
Anna Kötteritzsch, Universität der Bundeswehr München

**Video Previews Chair**
Carla Griggio, Inria

**Awards Chair**
Steven Drucker, Microsoft

**Accessibility Chairs**
Erin Brady, Indiana University – Purdue University Indianapolis
Sean Goggins, Missouri University
Shaun Kane, University of Colorado Boulder

**Data Chair**
Boyu Gao, Konkuk University
Toni-Jan Keith Monserrat, University of the Philippines Los Baños

**Diversity and Inclusivity Lunch Chairs**
Anke Brock, Inria Bordeaux
Allison Druin, University of Maryland
Gopinaath Kannabiran, Indiana University, Bloomington

**Language Inclusion Chair**
Tilman Dingler, University of Stuttgart

**Local Arrangements Chairs**
Jed Brubaker, University of Colorado Boulder
Tom Yeh, University of Colorado Boulder

**Social Impact Chairs**
Kathy Baxter, Salesforce
Elizabeth Gerber, Northwestern University
Jill Woelfer, Google

**Social Media Chairs**
Dan Afergan, Google
Bart Knijnenburg, Clemson University
Vicky McArthur, University of Toronto Mississauga

**Telepresence Chairs**
Min Kyung Lee, Carnegie Mellon University
Carman Neustaedter, Simon Fraser University

**Translations Chairs**
Hao-Chuan Wang, National Tsing Hua University
Naomi Yamashita, Nippon Telegraph and Telephone

**Design Director**
Donghee Yvette Wohn, New Jersey Institute of Technology

**Logo Design/Artwork**
Jia Zhang, MIT Media Lab

**Web Designer**
Xiying Wang, Cornell University

**Webmaster**
Xiying Wang, Cornell University

**ACM Liaison**
Farrah Khan, ACM

**SIGCHI Liaison**
Scooter Morris, University of California, San Francisco

**Conference Management**
Paul Henning, Conference & Logistics Consultants, Inc.
Stacey Ogren, Conference & Logistics Consultants, Inc.
Lois Sarfo-Mensah, Conference & Logistics Consultants, Inc.
Michael O'Connell, Conference & Logistics Consultants, Inc.

**Registration**
Taylor Vick, Executive Events, Inc.

**Sponsorship and Exhibits**
Carol Klyver, Foundations of Excellence

**Technical Liaison**
Sara Drenner, BI WORLDWIDE

# Self-tracking for Mental Wellness: Understanding Expert Perspectives and Student Experiences

**Christina Kelley[1], Bongshin Lee[2], Lauren Wilcox[1]**

[1]School of Interactive Computing
Georgia Institute of Technology
{christina.kelley, wilcox}@gatech.edu

[2]Microsoft Research
bongshin@microsoft.com

## ABSTRACT

Previous research suggests an important role for self-tracking in promoting mental wellness. Recent studies with college student populations have examined the feasibility of collecting everyday mood, activity, and social data. However, these studies do not account for students' experiences and challenges adopting self-tracking technologies to support mental wellness goals. We present two studies conducted to better understand self-tracking for stress management and mental wellness in student populations. First, focus groups and card sorting activities with 14 student health professionals reveal expert perspectives on the usefulness of tracking for three scenarios. Second, an online survey of 297 students examines personal experiences with self-tracking and attitudes toward sharing self-tracked data with others. We draw on findings from these studies to characterize students' motivations, challenges, and preferences in collecting and viewing self-tracked data related to mental wellness, and we compare findings between students with diagnosed mental illnesses and those without. We conclude with a discussion of challenges and opportunities in leveraging self-tracking for mental wellness, highlighting several design considerations.

### Author Keywords

Self-monitoring; self-tracking; personal informatics; Quantified Self; mental health; mental wellness; health communication; patient–clinician communication.

### ACM Classification Keywords

H.5.2. Information interfaces and presentation (e.g., HCI): User-centered design; J.3. Life and medical sciences: Health.

## INTRODUCTION

Mental health and wellness concerns are a major public health issue, with an economic cost in the US of over $2.5 trillion per year [44]. Although people of all ages are affected by stress and poor mental health, these concerns are particularly rampant in undergraduate and graduate student populations. Student emotional health is at an all-time low as students face increasing stress and academic pressures [12]. In a recent national survey of college students, 85% of students reported that they felt overwhelmed by demands over the last year and 47.8% reported feeling that things were hopeless [1]. A widely-recognized college mental health crisis [5,13,34] has led to overwhelming demand on counseling services at campuses across the country [40].

A variety of efforts aim to make the identification and treatment of mental health concerns more readily accessible. Companies like Ginger.io [19] use mobile sensing to provide app-based mental health coaching at opportune moments, while Computerized Cognitive Behavioral Therapy (CCBT) allows patients to undergo remote treatment for anxiety [37], and insomnia [39]. Meanwhile, the StudentLife study at Dartmouth College [44] has demonstrated that it is possible to use automatic smartphone sensing to gather passive data corresponding to certain behaviors (e.g., attending a class or a party). By combining this passive sensing with ecological momentary assessment (EMA) responses, researchers have begun to draw correlations between tracked behaviors and self-reported indicators of mental well-being.

Understanding user preferences is crucial to the adoption of any health monitoring system [3], yet no prior studies, of which we are aware, bring to light the experiences and challenges of those who actually self-track to achieve mental wellness goals. We aim in this work to better understand both the general and mental wellness-focused practices of student self-trackers and the expert perspectives of student health professionals. Together, these viewpoints contribute to a foundational understanding of the role that self-tracking can play for the student population, and its potential to help—or hinder—stress management and mental wellness.

We focus our scope of mental wellness on the issues—both clinical and non-clinical—of stress, anxiety, and depression, as they are the three mental health concerns most prominent for students [6]. We further define stress in the context of this work as negative stress which, while sometimes adaptive, can lead to negative psychological and physical effects over time [2,28]. This definition guided our work but, importantly, we also aimed to better understand how student stress is perceived by students and clinicians; specifically, how they approach subjective evaluations of students' ability


*CHI 2017,* May 06 - 11, 2017, Denver, CO, USA

ACM 978-1-4503-4655-9/17/05...$15.00
DOI: http://dx.doi.org/10.1145/3025453.3025750

to cope with the demands posed by student life, and affective responses to that evaluation.

This paper makes the following contributions:

(1) An investigation of student health professionals' experiences with and perspectives on the role of self-tracking for student mental health and wellness, through which we identify ways that self-tracking can be particularly beneficial or harmful, and distill expert perspectives on leveraging active and passive sensing to support students' mental wellness goals.
(2) Results of a survey with 297 college and graduate students, probing their self-tracking practices, their attitudes toward the value of self-tracking for mental wellness, and their data-sharing preferences.
(3) Further investigation into how student self-trackers with and without diagnosed mental illness use self-tracked personal data to support individual mental health and wellness management.

Findings from our studies allow us to examine how student self-tracking practices compare to clinicians' recommendations. We conclude with a discussion of the challenges and opportunities we see in leveraging self-tracking for student mental wellness, highlighting several considerations for the design of self-tracking technologies.

## RELATED WORK

### Personal Informatics and Self-tracking

Personal informatics is a growing field based on *collecting* one's own personal information and *reflecting* on it [13,26]. Personal informatics systems often utilize *self-tracking* technologies, many of which include goal-setting and data review capabilities to report status and progress toward goals over time. Such self-tracking applications have been effective in promoting physical activity [27], weight loss [4], and medication adherence [25], improving use of sleep diaries [7] and productivity [24], and influencing what people attend to online [29].

### Self-tracking in Mental Health Contexts

Just as it is important to manage health behaviors such as sleep and exercise, the HCI community has long recognized the importance of tracking psychological elements of health. Work in this space has shown the potential of sensing technology to identify, track, and improve stress and mental wellness: stress has been detected through typing analysis [45] and computer mouse pressure [21], while wearable sensors such as AutoSense [16] and SPIRE [41] show potential to detect stress using physiological signals.

However, stress and mental wellness bring unique challenges to the design and evaluation of self-tracking technologies. Prior systems have largely focused on the development of psychometric sensing and self-regulation of behaviors, and there is limited understanding of how people have appropriated such systems to meet their wellness goals. We expect that those who track for mental wellness will have different experiences and encounter different challenges than those who track other types of personal information, as there are many social and environmental factors that can affect mental well-being [20,37] and make it more challenging to monitor.

Moreover, as in other health contexts, self-reflection is crucial to the tracking process for stress management and mental well-being—but holds additional challenges in this domain. People can be overwhelmed by their data [46] and ashamed of what the data reflects [20,42]. Additionally, it is non-trivial to choose when and how to display feedback. Biofeedback displays in the form of games have been found to help reduce stress levels more quickly [10], but representations matter: displaying someone's stress data does make them more aware of their stress levels, but can also exacerbate their stress [33].

### Communication, Sharing, and Privacy

Many self-trackers want not only to collect and reflect on their own data but also to share the data with others including their healthcare team, though their sharing preferences may differ based on what is shared and with whom. Sharing health information with family and friend networks is a way to control one's health identity [22], keep loved ones up-to-date [34], gain social support [32], and share experiences with others in similar situations [22]. Sharing self-tracking data can also enable shared motivation, accountability, and recommendations [15].

Sharing self-tracking data with one's healthcare team can be more challenging. Healthcare providers in primary care settings already face information overload and difficult time constraints. They may also have concerns about the quality, completeness, or relevance of patient-generated data, as well as potential legal issues [48]. Moreover, though providers may disagree, patients often believe that what they have to share is uninteresting, or that sharing certain information may not help [22]. These perceived barriers to sharing relevant data can hinder the assessment of—and discussion around—mental wellness in clinical contexts and understanding how to overcome them remains an open challenge.

## INFORMING RESEARCH DIRECTIONS

Our research began with a more general attempt to understand health-related use of self-tracking technology in student populations. To gather informal perspectives of experts, we conducted four focus groups over 11 months in 2015, with a total of 10 student health professionals (3-5 in each focus group, with some overlap between groups) at our home institution (Study 0 in Table 1). These focus groups served as a preliminary investigation into how experts perceive the role of self-tracking in improving student health. Experts emphasized students' struggles to recognize symptoms and triggers of their stress, their likelihood of engaging in negative behaviors to relieve stress, and their challenges in developing self-care skills that could mitigate chronic stress and other conditions. Student health professionals also commented on their own challenges in identifying potential mental health and wellness needs with limited information. Informed by

| Study | Methods | Analysis | Participants | Specialty |
|---|---|---|---|---|
| Study 0: Informing research directions | Focus groups | Thematic analysis | Student health professionals ($n$ = 10) | Primary care (4), psychiatry (2) women's health (2), health promotion (1), nutrition (1) |
| Study 1: Understanding clinician perspectives on self-tracking data for mental wellness in clinical contexts | Card sorting sessions | Think-aloud, inductive iterative thematic analysis, descriptive statistics | Student health professionals ($n$ = 14) | Psychiatry (9), primary care (2) women's health (2), health promotion (1) |
| Study 2: Understanding student perspectives on self-tracking for mental wellness | Online Qualtrics survey | Closed-format questions: descriptive statistics and non-parametric comparison tests; Open-format questions: inductive thematic analysis | Undergraduate and graduate students ($n$ = 297) Undergraduate ($n$ = 211), Graduate ($n$ = 86)<br><br>Male ($n$ = 185, 62.29%), Female ($n$ = 108, 36.36%) Declined to specify ($n$ = 4, 1.35%) | |

**Table 1. Study design for the focus groups, subsequent card sorting study, and student survey.**

these focus groups, we narrowed our research questions and generated student personas for our subsequent study based on recurring examples and scenarios mentioned by student health experts. The focus groups, subsequent card sorting study, and student survey were each approved by our institution's IRB; informed consent was obtained for each participant in each study.

## STUDY 1: UNDERSTANDING EXPERT PERSPECTIVES

Our first study focused on elucidating expert perspectives on the role of active (e.g., EMA) and passive sensing for mental wellness applications (Study 1 in Table 1). Human communication and expert review are still important in therapeutic contexts, so we aimed to understand how self-tracking currently alters these conversations and how this might manifest differently in the future.

We conducted study sessions with 14 student health professionals from two universities, over February–March 2016, to understand the current and future role of students' personal, self-tracking data in the context of stress management. All study participants were employed by on-campus health services and worked directly with students; seven had participated in the initial focus groups. Nine participants worked in psychiatry, two in primary care, two in women's health, and one in health promotion.

### Study Material and Procedure

Our study combined individual card sorting (Fig. 1) with note-taking and retrospective think-aloud, to structure feedback on specific data types while permitting flexibility in grouping, sorting, and noting additional information. These methods allowed us to probe what specifically experts found useful and in which scenarios, and whether considerations or concerns arose surrounding specific types of data.

Card sorting materials consisted of 26 data types from Dartmouth College's StudentLife study [43] so as to include a combination of actively- and passively-sensed data types that are geared towards student experiences. Data types included passively-sensed proxies for routines and behaviors (e.g., bed time, minutes of vigorous exercise), EMA-based health measures (e.g., Patient Health Questionnaire (PHQ-9) depression scale), and data unique to student life such as class attendance (inferred through GPS data and student schedule), dining hall visits, and workload.[1] These data are feasible to collect now, and were found to be potentially useful to clinicians during our initial focus groups.

We also created representative hypothetical situations that could be discussed in the context of stress management. Each situation was made up of a persona and a clinical scenario, based on the findings from our prior focus groups:

Persona 1: Lack of sleep

- *Assessment:* you are looking over this data in advance of a consultation with a student who is having trouble sleeping.
- *Communication:* you are discussing this data in consultation with the student.
- *Self-care planning:* you are helping the student think about strategies for managing his/her stress and sleep issues going forward.

Persona 2: Poor diet

- *Assessment:* you are looking over this data in advance of a consultation with a student who is not eating well.
- *Communication:* you are discussing this data in consultation with the student.
- *Self-care planning:* you are helping the student think about strategies for managing his/her stress and improve their nutrition going forward.

For each of the six card sorting rounds, we gave participants 26 cards—each containing the name of one StudentLife data type—and introduced a hypothetical situation (described above). In round one, for example, we told participants that

[1] The full StudentLife dataset is available at `http://student-life.cs.dartmouth.edu/dataset.html`

Figure 1. A card sorting session in progress.

they were reviewing data in advance of a consultation (assessment) with a student who had high-normal levels of stress but whose primary concern was lack of sleep. We asked participants to sort their 26 data type cards into *useful*, *maybe useful*, and *probably not useful* categories based on perceived relevance of the data type to the persona and scenario. We also encouraged participants to group data types that would be important to review together, and provided many blank cards to accommodate any additional data types that were not included. After each round, participants conducted a retrospective think-aloud about the results of their sorting, as we took notes and photographed the results. Each session lasted around 60 minutes, and all sessions were audio- and video-recorded and transcribed verbatim.

### Data Analysis and Findings

Our goal was to use the card sorting to elicit structured feedback through a think-aloud protocol. We analyzed data with descriptive statistics (illustrating usefulness of each data type across and between participants, personas, and scenarios), but the bulk of our data analysis was qualitative. Using the card sorting results as a guide, we examined session transcriptions for trends, outliers, and representative quotations. We found some trends in data usefulness overall, with a few data types considered commonly useful across all personas and scenarios. The six data types reported most frequently useful (*vigorous exercise, sleep quantity, class attendance, academic workload, bed time,* and *depression scale)* were incorporated into the design of our student survey.

Most importantly, our results showed clear differences in perceived usefulness of other data types across different personas and scenarios. In the sections below, we illuminate these differences as well as other relevant findings and expert commentary. Throughout our findings, we refer to student health professionals as "HP" (e.g., HP1).

#### *Persona 1: Lack of Sleep*

Not surprisingly, the most useful data types for understanding student stress across all scenarios for Persona 1 were related to sleep habits: *sleep quantity*, *sleep quality*, *bed time*, and *wake up time*. Despite the common high-level ranking of these data types, however, a deeper analysis revealed considerations unique to student life. Participants were especially interested in *bed time* and *wake up time* data due to a concern that sleep is happening at unusual hours, with HP4 explaining that *"for a lot of people, a lot of students... their sleep isn't always just going to be sleep at the end of the day, so that's really important."*

Most participants were also eager to assess whether Persona 1's actual behavior supported their account of it, and whether this had changed over time. They clarified the importance of elaborating on any sleep-related data to understand the context behind the numbers, noting the role that environmental factors and sleep hygiene [31] can play. Participants were interested in augmenting sleep data with *time spent on phone apps*, worrying that *"they're staring at an app instead of sleeping... [or] they're constantly checking a particular app in the middle of night... [so] they're activating their brain in a way that won't engender a rest time for the brain"* (HP8).

Most participants found *class attendance* and *academic workload* to be useful data types for Persona 1 as well. HP5 noted the importance of understanding the relationship between sleep and academic data, explaining that *"this is kind of [a] which came first, the chicken or the egg... are these [academics] being impacted because of lack of sleep or [is] this impacting sleep habits? That's important to assess."*

#### *Persona 2: Poor Diet*

The most useful data for understanding stress across scenarios for Persona 2 included *dining rate* (useful to all participants in all scenarios) and all but one participant felt similarly about *meal timing.* Dietary habits and nutritional content of consumed foods, such as calories, were missing from the dataset, and five participants commented on the importance of these data. Participants also wrote in additional data types that they found important, including *weight*, *BMI*, *substance use,* and *body image.*

We found that the use of passively-sensed proxies is much more challenging in the context of diet than sleep, and this led to more variety in data usefulness among participants and an interest in data types like *location*, which could support assumptions about eating habits (e.g., by restaurant) when nutritional data is lacking. HP4 noted, beyond asking students to keep a time-consuming food log, *"there is not much we can do objectively... so, [you] have to communicate and assess at the same time."* Many participants raised issues related to use and interpretation of data proxies in mental wellness applications. For example, HP6 worried that data on *time spent studying* might be incorrect, pointing out that *"[what seems to be] time in the library could be drinking coffee at Starbucks, which is not helping them [sleep]."*

To augment nutrition information and diet habits, *vigorous exercise* and *light exercise* were also found to be useful for Persona 2. Many participants were interested in some measure of physical activity: not as concerned with specific measures as much as a "picture" of general movement levels and exercise-related habits. Participants were also interested in understanding potential underlying psychological issues that might be contributing to poor diet. *Depression scale* was considered commonly useful here, as well as *heart rate* for identifying *"if they're having an eating disorder [or] affecting their metabolic processes"* (HP2).

#### *Scenario 1: Assessment*

Looking across student personas, we also found interesting trends in data usefulness based on scenario. For *assessment*, many participants mentioned the difficulty of drawing lines for what is "typical" or "healthy" for an individual. This difficulty complicates the design of systems that rely on specific behavioral targets—even personalized ones, and that report health status or progress toward goals based on limited behaviors. HP5 explained this disconnect in the context of social data, saying that *"we [could] have someone that spends three or four hours a day with friends and says, 'I'm lonely all the time,' [while] others would say, 'I spent three or four [hours] with friends, I wish they'd find something else to do so I can get my work done.'"*

Across personas, *depression scale* was another data type considered more useful in a diagnostic context, to help clarify or rule out the possibility of serious mental illness. Participants found the assessment phase as generally useful for understanding *"what else we'd want to screen [someone] for, depression, current well-being"* (HP7). Some participants also expressed an interest in seeing *anxiety scale* data in parallel with depression.

#### *Scenario 2: Communication*

Some participants believed that the same data would be useful for the communication scenario as the assessment scenario; still other participants focused on data that they already go over with students, explaining that it would be helpful to have concrete data to augment communication about stress, mental health, and behavior during a consultation. HP7 explained *"I do ask very specific questions about [sleep issues], so having information historically would be really useful rather than having to rely on their subjective report of their sleep."* Some participants worried about time constraints in a consultation, and wanted to focus more closely on only those data that pertain to specific consultation topics.

#### *Scenario 3: Self-care Planning*

Many participants articulated that self-care planning should be focused on directly-measured data that students have more control over to improve their stress levels and problematic behaviors. HP4 explained, for instance, that a depression scale *"gets [at] the diagnostic assessment of where they're coming [from]... but since this is self-care... this stuff, it's not going to be as useful for planning for them [though] it might... be useful for me thinking about it."*

HP10 added that *"if you are planning a conversation with a patient, you've got to focus on the things that are really concrete and practical, things that they can control themselves."*

HP13 thought that physical activity and social measures would be useful for self-care as well, elaborating that *"these are things that on a day-to-day [basis] would be helpful for them to know where their time is going... now you know I'm going to class tomorrow and spending less time on phone [apps]... self-monitoring like this can be helpful to notice."*

## STUDY 2: UNDERSTANDING STUDENT PERSPECTIVES

Our second study aimed to expand on expert perspectives by gathering data on students' current self-tracking practices (Study 2 in Table 1). We included questions about general self-tracking practices and preferences to provide important context, while incorporating focused questions on self-tracking as it relates to mental health and wellness.

### Methods

Using Qualtrics [36], we conducted an online survey of current students ($n$ = 297), probing self-tracking experiences and preferences, and perceived mental well-being. Both college and graduate students were eligible to participate as long as they were currently degree-seeking or matriculating into a degree program in the fall. Recruitment occurred for six weeks from July to August 2016, via postings to social media and online forums as well as through snowball sampling. Recruitment postings featured a link to a pre-survey in which respondents provided their email address and, if eligible (i.e., a ".edu" address was given), we emailed them a link to the consent form, which then linked to the full survey if consent was given. Participants who completed the survey received a $10 Amazon gift card as a gratuity.

All survey participants answered questions on demographics, history of chronic and mental illness, and the 10-question Perceived Stress Scale [9]. Respondents who have been self-tracking for at least three months also answered a series of questions about their motivations, preferences, and sharing habits for the data type they find most important for self-tracking. Finally, all participants (both self-trackers and non-trackers) were asked about their willingness to track and share the six data types that experts in Study 1 had found most useful across both students and all scenarios: *vigorous exercise, sleep quantity, class attendance, academic workload, bedtime, and depression scale.*

### Data Analysis and Findings

We analyzed survey questions with single-selection and multiple-selection responses using descriptive statistics, and compared responses between the group of students with mental health conditions and those without using non-parametric comparison tests. We examined responses to open-format survey questions through inductive thematic analysis (by all authors). We analyzed 13 open-ended questions for themes. For the four primary open-ended questions (see Table 2, at the end of the paper, for details), three researchers independently coded the responses using constant comparison to iteratively arrive at themes, in a bottom-up fashion, until consensus was reached [17]. Nine remaining open-ended questions were simpler elaborations, which were coded independently by one researcher.

Students from 58 institutions of higher education participated in the survey. Respondents consisted of undergraduate ($n = 211$), master's ($n = 32$), PhD ($n = 52$), and professional degree ($n = 2$) students. 185 (62.29%) respondents were male, 108 (36.36%) were female, and four (1.35%) declined to specify. Most respondents were between 18 and 24 years old. Since the survey was initially advertised to students at our home institution, most respondents were students there ($n = 190$). All respondents had Internet access in their homes, while 97.98% also had an internet-accessible mobile device. Only 5.95% of respondents reported being part of a "Quantified Self" community.

The survey collected some demographic health data to better understand the physical and mental well-being of respondents. Twelve percent of those who took the survey had been diagnosed with a chronic illness and 16.50% had been diagnosed with a mental illness; 6.73% currently see a mental health professional, and an additional 19.87% have previously seen a mental health professional but do not see one currently. For respondents with chronic or mental illness, many reported that their tracking is related to the illness (41.67% of those with chronic illnesses; 43.48% of those with mental illnesses).

Taking a closer look at respondents who had been previously diagnosed with a mental illness (*Diag* group, $n = 49$), we found that these respondents were significantly more likely to have a co-morbid chronic illness ($\chi^2 = 7.09, p = .008$) and to be female ($\chi^2 = 16.34, p < .001$). Like other differences between *Diag* and *non-Diag* respondents, the prevalence of women in the *Diag* group does not necessarily mean that women are more likely than men to have mental health issues, but could be attributed to other factors. The most common mental illnesses in the *Diag* group were anxiety ($n = 34$; 69.39% of those with mental illness) and depression ($n = 22$; 44.90%). This is consistent with prior findings that anxiety and depression are the most common mental health conditions in student populations [6]. In the remainder of the paper, we will refer to students in the *Diag* group as "PD" (e.g., PD1) and student in the *non-Diag* group as "PN" (e.g., PN2).

The PSS, a validated measure of stress with a maximum score of 40, was incorporated into the survey to gather a baseline measure of self-reported student stress levels across and between groups. While past studies have shown student PSS averages around 18 [38], our respondents had an overall average score of 16.89; however, students in the *Diag* group scored significantly higher, with an average score of 20.8 compared to 16.11 for those without mental illness ($U = 8729.5, p < .001$).

Overall, ninety percent of respondents currently self-track one or more things; see Table 3 for a complete list of items. While the survey was open to non-trackers as well, due to the nature of the survey, students who self-track would have been more likely to participate. Workouts were selected as "most important" for tracking 17.84% of the time ($n = 48$), followed by steps (14.87%), weight (14.13%), eating habits (12.64%), and sleep (9.29%). Students were most likely to use mobile apps for self-tracking (46.27%), but 17.01% used wearable devices and 12.54% used a paper journal.

| Data type | % who track | Data type (cont.) | % who track (cont.) |
|---|---|---|---|
| Steps | 48.15 | None | 9.43 |
| Workout (excluding walking) | 47.14 | Medication | 7.41 |
| Weight | 44.44 | Social interactions | 7.41 |
| Sleep | 33.33 | Caffeine | 4.71 |
| Eating habits, diet, or supplements | 30.64 | Allergies | 4.04 |
| Phone or internet usage | 29.63 | Psychometrics (e.g., mood) | 3.70 |
| Heart rate | 21.21 | Alcohol | 3.03 |
| Menstrual cycle | 20.88 | Blood pressure | 3.03 |
| Water intake | 13.47 | Other | 3.03 |
| Time spent working | 12.12 | Blood glucose | 2.36 |
| | | Migraine | 2.02 |

**Table 3. Percentage of survey respondents who track various items, ranked by their frequency.**

*Encountering Negative Data*

Thirty-six percent of respondents said that there has been a time when they felt that the data they collected reflected something negative about them. Students with mental illness were significantly more likely to report experiences with negative data (56.52%; $\chi^2 = 11.12, df = 2, p = .004$). Respondents who reported encountering negative data were then asked to explain in free text what it was that they felt reflected something negative. A main theme that emerged in our inductive qualitative analysis of these responses was the disconnect between the data itself and individual reactions to that data; students seemed to give more meaning to the data than it deserved, and often found that the representation of the data did not match their experiences. PN43 described this disconnect as *"[feeling] that the results were not to the best of my ability even though each workout was,"* while PN228 *"started questioning my physical health and wondering if there was anything wrong with my body"* since the data showed an inability to lose weight.

Thematic analysis also demonstrated that students commonly experienced personal guilt and disappointment in themselves, as well as the social pressures, stigma, and embarrassment they felt regarding their data. There was frequent description of failure to achieve goals or lack of progress towards a goal, as well as lack of self-control and, correspondingly, lack of control over the data. Some students were frustrated by inconsistency, and others feared that their data made them look lazy. As PN254 explained, *"I wasn't making progress as quickly as I would have liked... I am afraid that it shows that I am lazy (despite the fact that I know I'm not)."*

Finally, some students found that their self-tracking data revealed an *unhealthy behavior* or an *incorrect assumption.* PN102 found that the *data "shocked me at the beginning,"* and PN3 wrote that *"initially I was surprised by... how vastly I had underestimated my calorie intake... I also found my idea that [fewer] meals per day equal[s] less calorie input wasn't necessarily well-founded."*

In closed-format questions about what they did when they encountered this data they perceived as negative, students were most likely to report feeling more motivated to achieve their goals (41.24%) or that the negative data was "just another hurdle" in achieving their goals (29.90%). However, students in the *Diag* group were more likely to report feeling very demotivated and frustrated by the data (19.23% vs. 8.45%).

### Sharing Preferences

Many respondents who currently self-track reported that they share information about their tracking with others. When responding to closed-format questions probing why they share and with whom, respondents' most common reason for sharing with both family (37.17%) and friends (44.98%) was "I feel a greater sense of accomplishment when I share my success with others," while the most common reason for sharing with peers (19.70%) was "I want to help others by sharing my experiences."

In closed-format questions about sharing data with healthcare providers, 36.43% of respondents said that their tracking has in some way changed their visits with healthcare providers. Most of the remaining 63.57% who did not experience a change explained that they either do not see doctors frequently or had not shared their tracked data with one. Only one respondent said that tracking made communicating with a provider more difficult, while 27.51% said it helped them better communicate with their health care team. Over 12 percent reported that it helped them follow their provider's instructions, while 6.69% said it helped their provider make a crucial decision about their healthcare.

For those who did share data with their doctors and found it useful, our thematic analysis offers some insight into why. Students frequently mentioned satisfaction with the higher levels of detail and accuracy they were able to share with their providers, and the increased confidence they felt regarding the information they shared because it was data-driven. For instance, PN82 was *"able to give accurate and consistent data,"* while PN47 expressed that *"I am able to speak more intelligently about my health."* Other students found that the data was helpful for tailoring treatments to their individual needs or demonstrating abnormalities or irregularities in their health. PN78 noted that *"I was able to understand why [my doctor] wanted me to go on a diet."*

Students also found self-tracking data useful in showing progress between appointments with their doctors, or as proof that they are doing what they say they are doing. PN97 discussed these benefits of self-tracking for anemia, explaining that *"some people can become perfectly healthy taking a supplement, and there is this undertone that I must not be taking my pills and not eating correctly if I am still having problems... having some records help me stand up for myself [to show] that I am doing all of the things that I need to be doing and still not seeing improvements."*

To learn more about student sharing preferences and willingness, we asked all survey respondents (both current trackers and those who do not currently track) to tell us whether they would be *willing* to track and share information on the six data types that student health professionals found to be most useful (*vigorous exercise, sleep quantity, class attendance, academic workload, bedtime, and depression scale*) with student health clinicians. Due to its relationship to depression and our broader focus on mental well-being, we added a question about self-tracked mood.

On average, 69.41% of respondents do or would be willing to share these data types with clinicians. Students in the *Diag* group were *more* willing to share data with healthcare professionals than those without mental illness (81.92% vs 66.71%), and there was no single data type that *Diag* students were less willing to share than *non-Diag* students. Students in the *Diag* group were most willing to share depression scale data (87.76%) while others were most willing to share exercise data (77.42%). Overall, respondents were *least* willing to share class attendance (53.87%) and workload (62.63%).

It is useful to note that students express a willingness to share additional information beyond what they currently track and share with healthcare providers. Likewise, it is informative to see that many respondents had positive experiences sharing self-tracking data with providers, as previous research of individuals with cancer has shown that patients often believe their providers would not be interested in the data they collect [22]. Findings from Study 1 reinforced previous findings that providers are in fact interested in seeing health-related tracking data from their patients; therefore, it is useful to know that some sharing of this data happens already and that student patients have had generally positive experiences.

### Goals and Motivations

In open-format responses, students described diverse motivations for their self-tracking (Table 2). Many of these themes reflect similar motivations found in previous work, namely Epstein et al.'s Lived Informatics Model [14] and Choe et al.'s report on tracking practices of Quantified Self (QS) community members [8]. Common motivating themes emerging from our inductive qualitative analysis align especially with Choe et al.'s overarching motivation category of *improving health*, as most of our study participants were tracking health-related data. Our thematic findings also matched two of the three classes of motivations defined by

Epstein and colleagues: *behavior change goals* and *instrumental tracking goals.*

*Behavior change goals* replicated by our results include testing a hypothesis, understanding patterns, and managing goals and expectations. For instance, PN18 described a goal of *"understanding patterns of what causes me to feel the way I do and further rooting out certainties or uncertainties that drive them."* Many other students focused on the sustainability of a behavior or goal, including managing expectations and setting the right goal, as well as understanding their own limits or ranges. PD52, who has anxiety and depression, explained *"my main intentions are to keep myself from becoming addicted or dependent."* Desires to improve general health, increase physical activity, and lose or maintain weight were also commonly cited as goals.

Other students reported being motivated by what Epstein et al. refer to as *instrumental tracking* goals, such as rewards or competition with others. Some respondents felt *"encourage[d] to want to work out every day even if I don't want to because I don't like to see where I skipped a day"* (PD212) or noted how *"reaching milestones makes me feel good"* (PN73). Students were also frequently motivated by *social and appearance-related goals*, noting *"a personal drive to look my best"* (PN21) and that *"I didn't like being the one scrawny guy who wasn't good at sports"* (PD15). Interestingly, these social and appearance-related goals were absent from the QS study—for us, students' specific developmental and life stage directly shaped their goals.

Our respondents also demonstrated other motivations not captured in either prior study. Rather than being driven by *curiosity*, identified as a motivational class by Epstein et al., our respondents were instead motivated by *awareness*. Respondents noted their interest in improved awareness such as *"understand[ing] my fitness level"* (PN151), becoming *"aware of the status of my heart"* (PN231), and *"be[ing] aware of what I am eating to make healthy choices."* While QS practitioners were motivated by a desire to be mindful in their daily lives, self-trackers in our study were motivated to be more mindful specifically of their own health.

Many students in the *Diag* group were additionally motivated by a desire to improve their mental health. For some, the connection is direct, i.e., tracking is part of maintenance or treatment, e.g., PD157 noted *"tracking my food and caloric intake help[s] me manage my condition without immune suppressors/medication."* For others, tracking is related to illness in a broader sense; for mental illness especially, respondents described their tracking in ways that drew connections between their behaviors and their mental health and that focused on awareness of when something might be out of equilibrium. PD238 writes that *"tracking strength growth encourages me to continue working out, which in turn mitigates the anxiety/stress,"* while PD127, who also has anxiety, tracks *"exercise, sleep, and caffeine intake to minimize triggers."*

Some students in both the *Diag* and *non-Diag* groups also reported that their goals and motivations for tracking changed over time. For many, they started out with more specific goals which then grew more general over time. PN3 explained that, *"I'm more about keeping healthy now, getting fitter... it's less about staying below the calorie number and more about making sure I eat right."* Students found that as they grew up, their perspectives—and therefore their motivations—changed, with many gaining new knowledge or understanding through their tracking. For PN188, *"seeing qualitative progress motivates me to set more specific goals for larger achievements rather than just continued participation."* Additionally, some students moved from a *loss or gain stage* to a *maintenance stage*, or wanted to adjust their goals to challenge them more or less. As PN90 wrote, *"I have lowered my expectations a little and just want to be fit and feel healthy and active."*

## DISCUSSION

The two studies discussed in this paper give us an important foundation for understanding current self-tracking practices in student populations and the role of self-tracking in managing stress and mental wellness. Mental health brings unique challenges to designing and evaluating self-tracking technology, and we sought to better understand current experiences and perspectives as a foundation for future research in this space. Here, we discuss challenges and opportunities that stem from our research, of the *what*, *when*, and *why* of self-tracking for mental wellness.

### *Proxies for Stress Management and Mental Wellness*

While there is still much to learn regarding self-tracking for stress and mental wellness, some clear design considerations come out of this work. Understanding *what* to track to ultimately improve one's stress and mental well-being is important, but also incredibly challenging. There are fewer clear data correlates for mental than physical wellness, and understanding the interactions between behaviors and mental well-being can be its own challenge. We found in Study 2 that many students with mental illnesses made their own behavioral connections through their data collection; regardless of accuracy, drawing their own correlations between behaviors and mental health in a way that belies the difficulty of making such associations. PD235, for instance, described tracking sleep because *"I know that I feel more depressed and stressed when I am chronically tired,"* while PD279 tracks steps because *"walking and getting outside helps manage my depression."*

Interestingly, of those whose self-tracking is related to a mental illness, only one respondent reported tracking mood directly: all others tracked *behaviors* that relate to their mood or mental wellness. There are many readily-available tools for monitoring steps, weight, and other commonly-tracked physical health metrics than there are tools for tracking mental and emotional well-being, and it is therefore unsurprising that many students monitor behavioral proxies for mental wellness. Additionally, even clinical mental health treatment involves frequent use of behavioral proxies to detect, monitor, and treat mental illness; in this sense, the use of proxies by student trackers is a reasonable extension—and even a desired outcome—of clinical care for mental well-being.

The use of proxies is also a consideration not just for students with mental illnesses, but for anyone who is interested in tracking and managing their stress. Stress is difficult to track directly: more so for students who have trouble identifying when they are stressed or do not fully understand their stressors. The student health professionals in Study 1 echoed this understanding in how they defined data usefulness for stress-related self-care planning. Many encouraged the awareness of behavioral correlates of stress and mental wellness, noting that these data types are simply more "useful" in the day-to-day than many more direct measures of stress and mental health would be. Reflecting on the student who had trouble sleeping, HP6 said *"when you're actually giving treatment planning to somebody about what they're going to do, [some] things... are going to become much less useful. These things they can't control. [Those] things they may or may not be able to control. It's the stuff they can control that's useful [here], when they go to bed, when they wake up."*

While the use of behavioral proxies can be beneficial, students must be careful to draw well-founded hypotheses and conclusions, and systems should be designed to encourage and assist in these processes. Previous research has illustrated challenges with the sort of ad-hoc self-experimentation that can arise from health-related self-tracking: poor understanding of device accuracy, systematic error, and uncontrolled comparisons, for example, can lead to misguided trust in devices and misinterpretation of results [49]. As systems integrate multi-modal sensing and advancements in behavioral modeling to generate system recommendations, it will be vital to communicate not only sensed or self-tracked observations, but inferences drawn from them, while minimizing the potential for misinterpretation.

### *Helpful versus Harmful Tracking*

Understanding self-tracking for mental health is made more challenging by the fact that **close monitoring is not always beneficial as a strategy of management**. In Study 1, student health professionals offered insights into situations in which self-tracking can be detrimental to students' physical and mental well-being, with many foretelling the dangers of self-tracking in disordered eating scenarios. HP14, for instance, noted that students with *"[eating] disorders have perfectionist sort of attitude[s]"* and careful tracking can veer into obsession and worsen the problem. HP3 explained that with disordered eating *"you're going to have to take care of that psychological part first...before [nutrition] is going to get any better."*

In Study 2, we found evidence that some students had engaged in elements of this *disordered tracking*—self-tracking that promotes negative health behaviors. PD129 explained, *"I used to track my calorie intake with the intention of losing weight and would set goals for myself that were extremely low and see if I could beat them... this was a function of my eating disorder."* Similarly, PN96 was *"somewhat obsessive in tracking while I was losing weight, and can't shake the habit for fear of gaining back the weight."* For students like these, with eating disorders or obsessive weight-loss habits, self-tracking can contribute to the problem; future research is crucial to understand the boundaries between helpful and disordered tracking in these and other mental health contexts.

Our study indicates that special care must be paid to scaffolding students as they begin tracking for mental well-being. For instance, Study 2 results demonstrate that many students were more likely to track whatever the device they used recommended, which means that any device designed for tracking correlates of mental wellbeing must be deliberate in such recommendations. There must also be increased mechanisms in place for students who feel their data is reflecting something negative about them. This was more common in students with diagnosed mental illnesses, and it will be important that systems frame negative data in a way that does not further demotivate these students going forward.

### *Designing for Students' Life Stage*

Undergraduates especially have motivations unique to college life, and certain constraints and lifestyle habits (e.g., finances, homework, parties) that shape their environment, daily routines, mental health concerns, and management styles. A common theme that emerged from our focus groups was the ubiquity of *"unhealthy means of self-care"* (HP1) by students (e.g., alcohol, drugs) and the importance of elucidating for students what self-care is, which practices are helpful or harmful, and how it can help improve well-being. It is also common for mental health conditions to emerge during young adulthood [30], and many students will be managing these concerns on their own and for the first time. Tailoring self-monitoring interventions to these needs and constraints will improve adoption and increase effectiveness of future systems. We note that since we focus our considerations on university students, the implications of our work may differ for students of other ages and situations.

## CONCLUSION

Our work provides foundational insights through two studies examining student experiences of and expert perspectives on self-tracking for stress and mental wellness. These studies serve as an essential step towards advancing personal informatics systems and mobile health technology to promote mental wellness. By illuminating how students with and without mental illnesses track and share data, and comparing these experiences with the recommendations of student health experts, we can better inform the design of these technologies. Our future work will expand our focus to a wider audience, and will gather student perspectives via interviews to supplement our findings.

## ACKNOWLEDGEMENTS

We thank our study participants and Clayton Feustel. This work was funded in part by the Georgia Tech Institute for Information Security and Privacy.

| Question | Themes | Examples |
|---|---|---|
| How is your tracking related to managing or treating your mental illness? (*n* = 19) [conditional question] | Correlation between behaviors and mental illness | "I track my yoga workouts, and I do yoga specifically to help manage my anxiety and stress." (P212) |
| | Indirect measurement of mental health | "trying to understand impact of sleep; exercise diet on mood." (P232) |
| | Treatment tracking (medication, schedule) | "...I do my best to track which medications I have taken when." (P52) |
| | Adjustments | "I track my period so that I know how to increase my medication doses. About a week before my period shout start, I take a higher dose of my anxiety medication." (P243) |
| | Triggers; finding signals that something is out of equilibrium | "Tracking exercise/sleep and caffeine intake to minimize triggers." (P127) |
| How is your tracking related to managing or treating your chronic illness? (*n* = 13) [conditional question] | Measuring a physical indicator (status, progress) | "Need to track blood glucose and [blood] pressure to ensure diabetes and hypertension are both controlled." (P139) |
| | Decision-making (lifestyle, medication) | "Have to make sure my blood pressure stays below a certain number while also making healthy life decisions." (P219) |
| | Managing schedules | "Blood tests and… regular medications." (P267) |
| | Symptom control | "Checking glucose levels to ensure they remain at a normal level." (P77) |
| | Hypothesizing about triggers | "I write down all occurrences of headaches in an attempt to figure out the cause." (P14) |
| What would you consider your main goal or motivation for tracking? (*n* = 269) | Understanding personal limits or ranges | "To know how strong I am so I don't hurt myself, but keep progressing at a maximum speed toward getting stronger." (P153) |
| | Sustainability of behaviors and goals (setting the right goal, expectations, predictions) | "Figuring out what I can do to decrease my weight (i.e. what works)." (P138) |
| | Hypothesis testing & understanding relationships | "I'd like to be able to prevent migraines by understanding my set of triggers as well as possible." (P135) |
| | Motivation through data (rewards, competition, fun) | "Keeps me going to the gym so that I can fill progress bars." (P49) |
| | Performance | "Keeping track of my running pace and mileage - to get faster and go longer." (P58) |
| | Social goals | "Competition with friends." (P68) |
| | Appearance-related goals | "A personal drive to look my very best." (P21) |
| | Being mindful about health | "To…be aware of my health." (P182) |
| | Improvements vs. maintenance | "Losing weight at first, then just generally staying healthy and eating right once I noted it made me feel better in general." (P3) |
| What was it [in the data] that you felt reflected something negative about you? (*n* = 97) [conditional question] | Disconnect between data and one's reaction to the data | "I felt that the results were not to the best of my ability even though each workout was... I was disappointed in the [amount of] activity I could achieve." (P43) |
| | Social pressures and stigma; embarrassment | "At times I felt embarrassed for having to be so dependent on my large amount of medicines." (P7) |
| | Guilt and disappointment | "I felt unhappy with how I slipped into unhealthy eating habits and how it reflected in my body." (P92) |
| | Laziness (physical activity related, not productivity) | "Sometimes my weight increases (if [I] skip [going to the] gym for a while or eat a lot), so it reflects laziness/lack of seriousness on my part." (P64) |
| | Lack or reversal of progress and gains, despite effort; failure to achieve a goal | "I felt the graph of my progress showed how I reversed on my progress." (P182) |
| | Lack of control over changes; lack of self-control | "Sometimes I splurged on high-calorie food." (P63) |
| | Inconsistency | "It showed that I wasn't as active as I should be, and that I wasn't consistent in the amount of steps I got each day." (P148) |
| | Revealing an unhealthy or unexpected habit or behavior | "[I]nitially, I was surprised by how bad my eating habits were and how vastly I had underestimated my calorie intake." (P3) |

**Table 2. Themes from four open-format survey questions.**

## REFERENCES


1. American College Health Association (ACH). 2016. National College Health Assessment II: Reference Group/Executive Summary Fall 2015. Hanover, MD. Retrieved from http://www.acha-ncha.org/docs/NCHA-II%20FALL%202015%20REFERENCE%20GROUP%20EXECUTIVE%20SUMMARY.pdf
2. Steve Whittaker Artie Konrad, Vitoria Belotti, Nicole Crenshaw, Simon Tucker, Les Nelson, Honglu Du, Peter Pirolli. 2015. Finding the adaptive sweet spot: Balancing compliance and achievement in automated stress reduction. In *Proceedings of the 33rd Annual ACM Conference on Human Factors in Computing Systems* (CHI '15:), 3829–3838. http://doi.org/10.1145/2702123.2702512
3. Jennifer S. Beaudin, Stephen S. Intille, Margaret E. Morris. 2006. To track or not to track: User reactions to concepts in longitudinal health monitoring. *Journal of Medical Internet Research* 8, 4: 29. http://doi.org/10.2196/jmir.8.4.e29
4. Lora E. Burke, Valerie Swigart, Melanie Turk Warziski, Nicole Derro, Linda J. Ewing. 2009. Experiences of self-monitoring: Successes and struggles during treatment for weight loss. *Qualitative Health Research* 19, 6: 815–828.
5. Linda G. Castillo and Seth J. Schwartz. 2013. Introduction to the special issue on college student mental health. *Journal of Clinical Psychology* 69(4): 291-297.
6. Center for Collegiate Mental Health. 2015. Center for Collegiate Mental Health 2014 Annual Report. 1–44. Retrieved from http://ccmh.psu.edu/wp-content/uploads/sites/3058/2015/02/2014-CCMH-Annual-Report.pdf
7. Eun Kyoung Choe, Bongshin Lee, Matthew Kay, Wanda Pratt, Julie A. Kientz. 2015. SleepTight: Low-burden, self-monitoring technology for capturing and reflecting on sleep behaviors. In *Proceedings of the ACM International Joint Conference on Pervasive and Ubiquitous Computing* (UbiComp '15), 121–132. http://doi.org/10.1145/2750858.2804266
8. Eun Kyoung Choe, Nicole B. Lee, Bongshin Lee, Wanda Pratt, Julie A. Kientz. 2014. Understanding quantified-selfers' practices in collecting and exploring personal data. In *Proceedings of the ACM Conference on Human Factors in Computing Systems* (CHI '14), 1143–1152. http://doi.org/10.1145/2556288.2557372
9. Sheldon Cohen, Tom Kamarck, Robin Mermelstein. 1983. A global measure of perceived stress. *Journal of Health and Social Behavior* 24, 4: 385–396. http://doi.org/http://dx.doi.org/10.2307/2136404
10. Alison Dillon, Mark Kelly, Ian H Robertson, Deirdre A Robertson. 2016. Smartphone applications utilizing biofeedback can aid stress reduction. *Frontiers in Psychology* 7, June: 832. http://doi.org/10.3389/FPSYG.2016.00832
11. Gavin Doherty, David Coyle, Mark Matthews. 2010. Design and evaluation guidelines for mental health technologies. *Interacting with Computers* 22, 4: 243–252. http://doi.org/10.1016/j.intcom.2010.02.006
12. Kevin Eagan, Ellen Bara Stolzenberg, Joseph J Ramirez, Melissa C Aragon, Maria Ramirez Suchard, Sylvia Hurtado. 2016. *The American Freshman: National Norms Fall 2014*. Retrieved from http://heri.ucla.edu/monographs/TheAmericanFreshman2014.pdf
13. Daniel Eisenberg, Justin Hunt, Nicole Speer. 2012. Help seeking for mental health on college campuses: review of evidence and next steps for research and practice. *Harvard Review of Psychiatry* 20, 4: 222–232.
14. Daniel Epstein, An Ping, James Fogarty, Sean A Munson. 2015. A lived informatics model of personal informatics. In *Proceedings of the ACM International Joint Conference on Pervasive and Ubiquitous Computing* (UbiComp '15), 731–742. http://doi.org/10.1145/2750858.2804250
15. Daniel A. Epstein, Bradley H. Jacobson, Elizabeth Bales, David W. McDonald, Sean A. Munson. 2015. From "nobody cares" to "way to go!" In *Proceedings of the ACM Conference on Computer Supported Cooperative Work & Social Computing* (CSCW '15), 1622–1636. http://doi.org/10.1145/2675133.2675135
16. Emre Ertin, Nathan Stohs, Santosh Kumar, Andrew Raij, Mustafa al'Absi, Siddharth Shah. 2011. AutoSense: unobtrusively wearable sensor suite for inferring the onset, causality, and consequences of stress in the field. In *Proceedings of the ACM Conference on Embedded Networked Sensor Systems* (SenSys '11), 274–287. http://doi.org/10.1145/2070942.2070970
17. Jinjuan Feng, Jonathan Lazar, Libby Kumin. 2010. Computer usage by children with down syndrome: challenges and future research. *ACM Transactions on Accessible Computing* 2, 3: 17–61. http://doi.org/10.1145/1714458.1714460.http
18. Andrea Gaggioli and Giuseppe Riva. 2013. From mobile mental health to mobile wellbeing: opportunities and challenges. *Studies in Health Technology and Informatics* 184, February: 141–147.

http://doi.org/10.3233/978-1-61499-209-7-141

19. Ginger.io. Retrieved from https://ginger.io/
20. Christine R. Harris and Ryan S. Darby. 2009. Shame in physician-patient interactions: patient perspectives. *Basic and Applied Social Psychology* 31, 4: 325–334. http://doi.org/10.1080/01973530903316922
21. Javier Hernandez, Pablo Paredes, Asta Roseway, Mary Czerwinski. 2014. Under pressure: sensing stress of computer users. In *Proceedings of the ACM conference on Human Factors in Computing Systems* (CHI '14), 51–60. http://doi.org/10.1145/2556288.2557165
22. Maia L. Jacobs, James Clawson, Elizabeth D. Mynatt. 2015. Comparing health information sharing preferences of cancer patients, doctors, and navigators. In *Proceedings of the ACM Conference on Computer Supported Cooperative Work & Social Computing* (CSCW '15), 808–818. http://doi.org/10.1145/2675133.2675252
23. Ravi Karkar, Jasmine Zia, Roger Vilardaga, Sonali R Mishra, James Fogarty, Sean A Munson, Julie A Kientz. 2016. A framework for self-experimentation in personalized health. *Journal of the American Medical Informatics Association* 23, 3: 440–448. http://doi.org/10.1093/jamia/ocv150
24. Young-Ho Kim, Jae Ho Jeon, Eun Kyoung Choe, Bongshin Lee, Kwonhyun Kim, and Jinwook Seo. 2016. TimeAware: Leveraging framing effects to enhance personal productivity. In *Proceedings of the ACM Conference on Human Factors in Computing Systems* (CHI '16), 272–283. http://doi.org/10.1145/2858036.2858428
25. Matthew Lee and Anind Dey. 2014. Real-time feedback for improving medication taking. In *Proceedings of the ACM Conference on Human Factors in Computing Systems* (CHI '14), 2259–2268. http://doi.org/10.1145/2556288.2557210
26. Ian Li, Anind Dey, Jodi Forlizzi. 2010. A stage-based model of personal informatics systems. In *Proceedings of the ACM Conference on Human Factors in Computing Systems* (CHI '10), 557–566. http://doi.org/10.1145/1753326.1753409
27. Susan Michie, Charles Abraham, Craig Whittington, John McAteer, Sunjai Gupta. 2009. Effective techniques in healthy eating and physical activity interventions: A meta-regression. *Health Psychology* 28, 6: 690–701. http://doi.org/10.1037/a0016136
28. Neema Moraveji and Charlton Soesanto. 2012. Towards stress-less user interfaces: 10 design heuristics based on the psychophysiology of stress. In *Extended Abstracts on Human Factors in Computing Systems* (CHI EA '12), 1643–1648. http://doi.org/10.1145/2212776.2223686
29. Sean A. Munson, Hasan Cavusoglu, Larry Frisch, and Sidney Fels. 2013. Sociotechnical challenges and progress in using social media for health. *Journal of Medical Internet Research* 15, 10: 1–14. http://doi.org/10.2196/jmir.2792
30. National Alliance on Mental Illness: Teens & Young Adults. Retrieved from http://www.nami.org/Find-Support/Teens-and-Young-Adults
31. National Sleep Foundation. Sleep Hygiene. Retrieved from https://sleepfoundation.org/ask-the-expert/sleep-hygiene
32. Carolyn Pang, Carmen Neustaedter, Bernhard Riecke, Erick Oduor, and Serena Hillman. 2013. Technology preferences and routines for sharing health information during the treatment of a chronic illness. In *Proceedings of the ACM Conference on Human Factors in Computing Systems* (CHI '13), 1759–1768. http://doi.org/10.1145/2470654.2466232
33. Pablo Paredes, Ran Gilad-Bachrach, Mary Czerwinski, Asta Roseway, Kael Rowan, Javier Hernandez. 2014. PopTherapy: Coping with stress through pop-culture. In *Proceedings of the Int'l Conference on Pervasive Computing Technologies for Healthcare* (PervasiveHealth '14), 109–117. http://doi.org/10.4108/icst.pervasivehealth.2014.255070
34. Stephanie Pinder-Amaker, Catherine Bell. 2012. A bioecological systems approach for navigating the college mental health crisis. *Harvard Review of Psychiatry* 20, 4:174–188. http://doi.org/10.3109/10673229.2012.712842
35. Wanda Pratt, Kenton Unruh, Andrea Civan, and Meredith Skeels. 2006. Personal health information management. *Communications of the ACM* 49, 1: 51–55. http://doi.org/10.1145/1107458.1107490
36. Qualtrics. Retrieved from https://www.qualtrics.com/
37. Stefan Rennick-Egglestone, Sarah Knowles, Gill Toms, Penny Bee, Karina Lovell, Peter Bower. 2016. Health technologies "in the wild": experiences of engagement with computerised CBT. In *Proceedings of the ACM Conference on Human Factors in Computing Systems* (CHI '16), 2124–2135. http://doi.org/10.1145/2858036.2858128
38. Jonathan W Roberti, Lisa N Harrington, Eric A Storch. 2006. Further psychometric support for the 10-item version of the perceived stress scale. *Journal of College Counseling* 9: 135–147. http://doi.org/10.1002/j.2161-1882.2006.tb00100.x
39. Michael Seyffert, Pooja Lagisetty, Jessica Landgraf, Vineet Chopra, Paul N. Pfeiffer, Marisa L. Conte,

Mary A. M. Rogers. 2016. Internet-delivered cognitive behavioral therapy to treat insomnia: A systematic review and meta-analysis. *PLoS ONE* 11, 2: 1–21. http://doi.org/10.1371/journal.pone.0149139

40. Timothy B. Smith, Brenda Dean, Suzanne Floyd, Christopher Silva, Momoko Yamashita, Jared Durtschi, Richard A. Heaps. 2007. Pressing issues in college counseling: A survey of american college counseling association members. *Journal of College Counseling* 10, 1: 64–78.
41. Spire.io. Retrieved from https://spire.io/
42. Mark Joseph Stern. 2013. Weight, watched. *Slate*. Retrieved from http://www.slate.com/articles/technology/future_tense/2013/11/smartphone_diet_apps_are_they_helping_us_lose_weight.html
43. StudentLife Study. Retrieved from http://studentlife.cs.dartmouth.edu/
44. Sebastian Trautmann and Hans-ulrich Wittchen. 2016. Do our societies react appropriately to the burden of mental disorders? *EMBO Reports* 17, 9: 1245–1249. http://doi.org/10.15252/embr.201642951
45. Lisa M Vizer. 2009. Detecting cognitive and physical stress through typing behavior. In *Extended Abstracts on Human Factors in Computing Systems* (CHI EA '09), 3113–3116. http://doi.org/10.1145/1520340.152044040
46. Katy Waldman. 2013. The year we quantified everything and learned...anything? *Slate*. Retrieved from http://www.slate.com/blogs/xx_factor/2013/12/27/quantified_self_critique_personal_data_apps_for_calories_exercise_sleep.html
47. Rui Wang, Fanglin Chen, Zhenyu Chen, Tianxing Li, Gabriella Harari, Stefanie Tignor, Xia Zhou, Dror Ben-Zeev, and Andrew T. Campbell. 2014. StudentLife: assessing mental health, academic performance and behavioral trends of college students using smartphones. In *Proceedings of the 2014 ACM International Joint Conference on Pervasive and Ubiquitous Computing* (UbiComp '14), 3–14. http://doi.org/10.1145/2632048.2632054
48. Peter West, Richard Giordano, Max Van Kleek, Nigel Shadbolt. 2016. The quantified patient in the doctor's office: challenges & oppportunities. In *Proceedings of the ACM Conference on Human Factors in Computing Systems* (CHI '16), 3066–3078. http://doi.org/10.1145/2858036.2858445
49. Rayoung Yang, Eunice Shin, Mark W. Newman, Mark S. Ackerman. 2015. When fitness trackers don't "fit": end-user difficulties in the assessment of personal tracking device accuracy. In *Proceedings of the ACM International Joint Conference on Pervasive and Ubiquitous Computing* (UbiComp '15), 623–634. http://doi.org/10.1145/2750858.2804269

# "It's Definitely Been a Journey": A Qualitative Study on How Women with Eating Disorders Use Weight Loss Apps

Elizabeth V. Eikey
The Pennsylvania State University
University Park, PA USA
eveikey@psu.edu

Madhu C. Reddy
Northwestern University
Evanston, IL USA
mreddy@northwestern.edu

## ABSTRACT

Technology is often viewed as either positive or negative. On one hand, in HCI, weight loss apps are usually seen as a positive influence on users. From the sociocultural perspective, on the other hand, media and technology negatively impact body satisfaction and contribute to eating disorders; however, these studies fail to include weight loss apps. While these apps can be beneficial to users, they can also have negative effects on users with eating disorder behaviors. Yet few research studies have looked at weight loss apps in relation to eating disorders. In order to fill this gap, we conducted interviews with 16 women with a history of eating disorders who use(d) weight loss apps. While our findings suggest these apps can contribute to and exacerbate eating disorder behaviors, they also reveal a more complex picture of app usage. Women's use and perceptions of weight loss apps shift as they experience life and move to and from stages of change. This research troubles the binary view of technology and emphasizes the importance of looking at technology use as a dynamic process. Our study contributes to our understanding of weight loss app design.

### Author Keywords

Weight loss apps; mobile applications; eating disorders; anorexia nervosa; bulimia nervosa; qualitative; persuasive; food journal; self-tracking; quantified self

### ACM Classification Keywords

H.5.m. Information interfaces and presentation (e.g., HCI): Miscellaneous

## INTRODUCTION

Many young women use mobile health applications for weight loss (weight loss apps). As of January 2014, 51.7% of the 46 million people who used apps from the health and fitness category were women [52]. According to Neilson, the most popular health app during this time was MyFitnessPal, an app that allows users to track calories, exercise, and weight, with 8.7 million users [52].


*CHI 2017, May 06-11, 2017, Denver, CO, USA*
© 2017 ACM. ISBN 978-1-4503-4655-9/17/05...$15.00
DOI: http://dx.doi.org/10.1145/3025453.3025591.

Women's motivation for using these apps is often to lose weight even if they are technically at a healthy weight [51]. With the pressure to be thin and beautiful, some women have an unrealistic and distorted view of their bodies. In fact, in North America, there is such a pervasive body dissatisfaction and preoccupation with weight that psychologists have developed the term "normative discontent", which describes the "normalcy" of being unhappy with one's weight as a woman [39].

From the sociocultural perspective, much of this dissatisfaction is driven by the media and now technology [39]. The sociocultural model of eating disorders posits that "disordered eating is a result of internalizing the increasing pressures for women in Western society to achieve an ultra-slender figure/the thin ideal, which current cultural trends emphasize as an essential component of beauty" (p.1225) [18]. With this obsession with weight and size, women may engage in extreme and even dangerous behaviors to achieve an unattainable idea of beauty – even when losing weight is unnecessary. Some of these women develop eating disorders as a result. In fact, it is estimated that 35% of "typical dieters" develop eating disorder behaviors, and of those, 20-25% develop partial or full eating disorders [37].

Few research studies have looked at weight loss apps as a type of new media that may contribute to or exacerbate eating disorders. Yet weight loss apps often contain the same types of content as other technologies that have been shown to worsen body dissatisfaction and disordered eating. In Human-Computer Interaction (HCI), weight loss apps are often viewed as positive influence on users. In order to understand if weight loss apps contribute to eating disorders, we wanted to hear stories from women with a history of eating disorders who use or have used weight loss apps. We used semi-structured interviews with 16 participants in order to get in depth and detailed descriptions of their experiences. One primary research question guided our study: How do women with a history of eating disorders use weight loss apps?

What emerged from this data is a complex perspective of how weight loss apps are used. While there is evidence to suggest that weight loss apps, like other technologies, may contribute to and exacerbate eating disorder behaviors, how these apps are used and users' perceptions of these apps change over time. This finding "troubles" the typical binary view of technology. That is, instead of technology being seen as only positive or negative, the role of technology can shift depending on where users are in their health "journey". This should be of growing interest to the HCI community because viewing technology as just good or bad neglects the larger picture of how technology use changes depending on user needs. Specifically, our study shows women with eating disorders reflect on and use apps differently as they go through their eating disorder journey. Our research has implications for the design of more health-focused apps.

## BACKGROUND

### Eating Disorders

While it is estimated that 20 million women in the United States have an eating disorder, many more have unhealthy eating behaviors or may be undiagnosed [33,48]. It is estimated that 8%-17% of college-aged students have an eating disorder, and 20% of college students believe they have had an eating disorder in their lifetime [14,21,34].

For the purposes of our study, we focused on behaviors associated with anorexia and bulimia nervosa and other specified eating disorder/eating disorder not otherwise specified because there is some overlap between these disorders [1]. Eating disorder behaviors related to these disorders include excessive calorie or food restriction, intense fear of gaining weight, obsession with weight and consistent behavior to prevent weight gain, self-esteem overly related to body image, bingeing, feeling of being out of control during bingeing, purging, dramatic weight loss, preoccupation with weight, food, calories, fat grams, and dieting, refusal to eat certain foods, comments about feeling "fat", hunger denial, excessive exercise regimen, and development of food rituals.

Some eating disorder behaviors may be viewed as typical to achieve weight loss or not severe enough to warrant medical attention. Research has shown that even women of a healthy weight may utilize "weight loss methods" indicative of eating disorders [33]. Additionally, research has shown that 25% of college women in the United States have engaged in bingeing and purging as a weight loss method [48].

### Sociocultural Perspective of Eating Disorders

While biological and psychological factors play a role in an individual's predisposition and development of eating disorders [12], researchers in psychology have highlighted the sociocultural perspective - that social and cultural factors play a significant role in the development and prevalence of eating disorders [3]. This perspective is used to understand how social and cultural factors, such as traditional media, affect an individual's mental processes and behaviors [36]. For example, it has been used to understand the impact of media on body image and eating behaviors [3]. For quite some time, research has shown that media exposure contributes to body dissatisfaction and disordered eating [31]. However, much of this research has focused on conventional mass media, such as magazines and television.

In recent years, researchers have been calling for more work in understanding the impact of new media, such as online content, on the thin ideal, body image, and eating disorder symptomology [31]. From this perspective, technology is viewed as a negative influence on users. Recent work has shown that online content, such as social media, is associated with poor body image and eating disorders, especially among women [2,16,24,26,42]. Many online weight loss and fitness communities either overtly or subtly promote eating disorders, and this negatively affects users who are trying to address their eating disorder issues [41,45]. Researchers in psychology have recognized the importance of understanding the effects of new media on eating disorder symptomology.

However, their focus has largely been on social media. For example, using Facebook is correlated with drive for thinness in women and men [23] and body dissatisfaction [16,17,42]. Mabe et al. [24] found that frequency of Facebook use was related to disordered eating. Similarly, Stronge et al. [42] found women and men of all ages are more likely to have poorer body satisfaction if they use Facebook. Kim and Chock [23] conducted an online survey to examine Facebook's impact on users' body image attitudes. While they did not find a correlation between time spent on social media and body image concerns, they found engaging in particular social media behaviors such as checking friends' profiles, leaving messages, and commenting on profiles is correlated with a drive for thinness in both females and males.

Even HCI researchers who study eating disorders have primarily focused on social media [7,13,30]. Some researchers have found that social media promotes eating disorder behaviors. For example, Chancellor et al. [7] found that despite Instagram's strategies to reduce pro-eating disorder content, pro-eating disorder communities still exist and are thriving. Similarly, Pater et al. [30] analyzed hashtags on Tumblr, Instagram, and Twitter and found pro-eating disorder-related hashtags, images, and text. While this work is important because many people (especially young females) use social media, research is lacking on the role of weight loss apps. Additionally, this perspective only considers media and technology as a negative influence; whereas our study looks at weight loss apps as both positive and negative.

### Health Apps for Weight Loss, Diet, and Exercise

We add to the HCI literature on food journaling, self-tracking, weight loss and persuasive technology. In HCI, many researchers focus on how weight loss apps are positive influences on users. Specifically, weight loss technology is often seen as a way to help people combat obesity and obesity-related health conditions. Thus, the focus is on designing apps to motivate users to eat less or healthier, exercise more, and use the app long-term [4,6,9,10,20,22,27,35,40,46,47,49] and how this technology contributes to users' ability or their perception of their ability to achieve health goals, such as weight loss and exercising [8,28].

These apps can be useful weight loss tools [19,38], but they may also trigger unhealthy eating and exercise behaviors by creating a dependence on logging food, exercise, and weight. Tan et al. [44] found that users felt weight loss and fitness apps could be both helpful and harmful for eating disorder recovery but did not elaborate further. Prior to weight loss apps, some people (including those with eating disorders) tracked their diet and exercise on paper. While this can still negatively impact eating disorder behaviors, weight loss apps are more personalized, discreet, mobile, and quicker to use. They also provide users with precise values for food and exercise and visualizations of weight loss and calories consumed/burned with an added component of the app "rewarding" them for eating less, exercising more, and losing weight.

Recently, some HCI researchers have been challenging the narrative that quantifying behaviors and logging is always positive or appropriate. For example, Cordeiro et al. [11] considered the use and problematic aspects of food journaling for a general population, where the focus is to encourage logging. Similarly, Cordeiro et al. [10] discussed how in self-tracking, quantifying behaviors are pervasive but not always appropriate because of user goals. Purpura et al.'s [32] fictional Fit4Life is related to our work because they discussed problems of persuasive technology. They call for us to expand our criteria beyond BMI because it is not a good measure of health and explore unintended consequences.

Our study directly contributes to prior HCI work. Like other researchers, we also believe the quantification of behaviors is not always appropriate but investigate the use of *existing* self-tracking tools to understand how users' needs are not being met. Our study looks at the issues of weight loss technologies and unintended consequences but in the context of eating disorders.

## METHODS

### Participants and Recruitment

To be eligible for the study, participants (1) Had to use/have used weight loss apps, (2) Be an 18-25 year old woman, and (3) Have/had an eating disorder (symptoms related to anorexia and/or bulimia nervosa). Although eating disorders are increasing among men [43], we focused on women because they are more likely to develop eating disorders [15]. Because some people do not meet the full criteria for a specific diagnosis and because many people never seek treatment for their eating disorder, we recruited both participants who were formally diagnosed and those who were not. We posted flyers at the university and at public locations around the local town. Each participant was compensated $25.

### Data Collection Sessions

The first author conducted all data collection sessions. Each session consisted of a survey, a think-aloud exercise, and a semi-structured interview. Through the survey, we obtained demographic information as well as history and status of their eating disorders. For the think-aloud exercise, we asked participants to go through 3 tasks: (1) setting goals, (2) viewing progress visualizations, and (3) using social and community features. After the think-aloud exercise, we moved into the interview portion of the study, which focused more on their perceptions of the app and technology use in general. The think-alouds showed us how users used the app and provided us with concrete examples of goals set, calorie budgets, etc. During the interview, we asked users to reflect on how they have used the app over time, show what made them feel negative and positive emotions, explain how the app changed their behaviors, and discuss what aspects were helpful to recovery and exacerbated ED symptoms.

The think-aloud exercises were video recorded. The entire discussion was audio recorded; thus, transcriptions represent both think-alouds and interviews. Each session took anywhere between 40 minutes and 1 hour and 45 minutes. We conducted a total of 16 sessions because we saw repetitive themes in participants' responses (i.e., data saturation) [25].

### Analysis

The audio files from the data collection sessions were transcribed into electronic format (approximately 278 pages). This was appropriate because the goal was "to analyze the content of communication" to understand the participant's experience (p. 2937) [50]. Then we used thematic analysis to identify themes across the data set [5]. As participants explained their use over time, we noticed a lot of discussions about "before" and "after", so we first grouped discussions according to users' descriptions of when they first started to use the app and then after they changed their use/stopped using the app. We then developed initial codes, searched for themes, and reviewed and grouped them together, which led to the final themes.

## FINDINGS

We first present information about our participants. Then we discuss how their app use changed over time. Finally, we provide quotations from participants that exemplify their experiences. Specifically, we focus on:

1. Disordered use of weight loss apps (such as obsessive logging, need to be exact, acute awareness of numbers, restricting, manipulating the app to lose weight, compensatory behaviors, manipulating the app to avoid negative emotions),
2. Making a change (such as adding in calories and/or focusing on nutrition and taking a break from apps), and
3. Falling back into old habits.

These showcase the participants' journey of weight loss app use as many reflected on their eating disorder and app usage over time.

### Participants

Participants were ages 18-23 with the mean being 20.88 years. The majority of participants identified as White (non-Hispanic) ($n$=12) with one from Israel. Two identified as Asian, Asian American, or Pacific Islander, 1 identified as multi-racial, and 1 identified as Native American or American Indian. As shown in Table 1, most participants had not been professionally diagnosed with an eating disorder (*n*=12), and most reported being in recovery or recovered (*n*=13). Participants estimated they had an eating disorder anywhere from 2 months to 7 years, and their eating disorder behaviors included extreme restriction, obsession with "healthy" foods, bingeing, excessive and compensatory exercise, purging, and extreme anxiety and concern related to food and weight. Most (*n*=13) felt their eating disorder began before using weight loss apps. Participants reported using weight loss apps between 2 months and 8 years (mean of 35.63 months or 2.97 years with a standard deviation of 31.92 months or approximately 2 years). The most commonly used app was MyFitnessPal (*n*=15).

Founded in 2005, MyFitnessPal[1] has become one of the most popular weight loss apps [52]. It allows users to create a diet plan by entering their height, starting weight, goal weight, weekly weight loss/gain goal, and activity level. Users can enter their foods by searching the database of foods, manually entering calories, or scanning barcodes, and they can input exercise manually or by synchronizing other apps or wearables, such as Fitbit. The app also allows users to track nutrients, such as carbohydrates, and set nutrient goals. MyFitnessPal provides visualizations of calories consumed/burned, weight loss, and nutrients. Users can also choose to connect with other users through adding friends, messaging friends, participating in challenges, and posting on the MyFitnessPal forums.

### Patterns of Use

Participants discussed not only their current use of weight loss apps, but also their past use and how it has changed over time. Because many participants have been using weight loss apps for over a year (and some many years), they shared how their eating disorder influenced their app use and how the app impacted their eating disorder. Most participants also felt they were in recovery from their eating disorder, which gave them the opportunity to reflect on how they arrived at this point in their health journey. In fact, some participants actually referred to their eating disorder and subsequent app experience as a journey.

In hearing their experiences, a pattern of use began to emerge as shown in Figure 1. The lines in the figure represent bidirectional arrows. In the beginning, participants' intentions were most commonly to lose weight (whether or not they were at a healthy weight). When they first began using weight loss apps, they found them helpful in losing weight and tracking their foods even though some of their behaviors were disordered. A number of participants describe how their diet and tracking sort of "spiraled out of control". As time went on, participants began to think that they may have an eating disorder and that the app was exacerbating it. Upon this realization, participants would either decide to use the app as a tool to eat more or stop using the app altogether. However, participants often began using weight loss apps again and felt they were battling their eating disorder mindset even when recovery was the focus. We showcase their journey by providing quotations regarding their experiences of (1) using the app in a disordered way, (2) deciding to make a change, and (3) falling back into old habits.

### Disordered Use of Weight Loss Apps

During the height of their eating disorders, participants talked a lot about the ways they used weight loss apps in an unhealthy manner (even though they did not often recognize their behaviors as disordered early on) and ways the app impacted them.

#### *Obsessive logging*

A number of participants explained that they became obsessed with logging their food and began using the app multiple times a day. One participant talked about how she felt the need to log everything she ate:

*"I got more hung up on tracking everything. Before I could just eat something. I didn't have to worry about logging it into something. I didn't really keep track of it throughout the day.... Then the ability to track it only made it [eating disorder behaviors] worse... Definitely before [recovery], it was really bad. Like I would get on there [the app] a few times a day, like more than the 3, and just be very obsessive about it." [U02]*

Similarly, another participant discussed how obsessive food logging and tracking turned into an eating disorder:

*"I started to diet and that's kind of how my eating disorder manifested itself, after the diet became an obsession with tracking my food and how low I could get the number basically... When I was in the middle of my eating disorder, I would definitely use it [the app] everyday. And it was one of those things where I would pretty much try and track everything the day before." [U06]*

These participants explained that they used the app many times a day everyday to the point that they felt compelled to log and track their foods and check the app.

#### *Need to be exact*

Participants also talked about how they felt the need to be exact with recording their calories and macronutrients.

[1] https://www.myfitnesspal.com/

| ID | Professionally Diagnosed | ED[2] / ED Behaviors | Do you think you currently have an ED? | ED Length | ED Before or After App | Apps Used | App Use Length |
|---|---|---|---|---|---|---|---|
| U01 | Yes | Anorexic behaviors, binge eating | No | 2 months | After | MyFitnessPal | 2 months |
| U02 | Yes | Anorexic behaviors, orthorexia[3] | Yes | 1 year | Before | MyFitnessPal, Nike+Running | 1 year |
| U03 | No | Anorexia nervosa, exercise anorexia | No | 6 years | Before | MyFitnessPal | 8 years |
| U04 | No | Anorexic behaviors, EDNOS/OSFED[4], excessive exercise, strict diet | No | 1 year | Before | MyFitnessPal, MapMyRun | 4 years |
| U05 | No | Anorexic behaviors, back and forth between eating and not eating | No | 2 years | Before | MyFitnessPal, Fitbit, Moodnotes | 4 months |
| U06 | No | Anorexia nervosa, orthorexia, binge eating disorder | No | 3 years | After | MyFitnessPal, FitBit | 4 years |
| U07 | No | Anorexic behaviors, restriction, purging | No | 1 year | Before | MyFitnessPal | 5 months |
| U08 | No | Anorexic behaviors, barely ate, some bingeing, EDNOS/OSFED | No | 1 year | Before | MyFitnessPal, WeightWatchers, 21 Day Fix | 7 years |
| U09 | No | Anorexia nervosa | No | 2 years | Before | MyFitnessPal, Calorie Counter | 7 years |
| U10 | No | Bulimia nervosa | No | 6-7 years | Before | MyFitnessPal | 4 years |
| U11 | No | EDNOS/OSFED, binge eating-exercise/diet-binge eating, had great anxiety related to eating/dieting | No | >4 years | Before | MyFitnessPal | 8 months |
| U12 | Yes | Bulimia nervosa | No | 6 months | Before | Cronometer | 1.5 years |
| U13 | Yes | Anorexia nervosa | Yes | 3 years | After | MyFitnessPal | 5 months |
| U14 | No | EDNOS/OSFED, always thinking about food, need to track everything eaten, concern when not hitting macronutrients, restriction, bingeing | Yes | 7 years | Before | MyFitnessPal | 2 years |
| U15 | No | Anorexia nervosa | No | 1 year | Before | Lose It, Steps, MyFitnessPal | 2 years |
| U16 | No | EDNOS/OSFED, anxiety about food, afraid to eat "unhealthy" in pubic, bingeing in private, compensatory exercise, diet-bingeing cycles | No | 4 years | Before | MyFitnessPal, FitBit, Nike Running App, Nike Training App, Healthy Out, Eating Well, Spartan Race | 5 years |

**Table 1. Information about participants' eating disorder and app use**

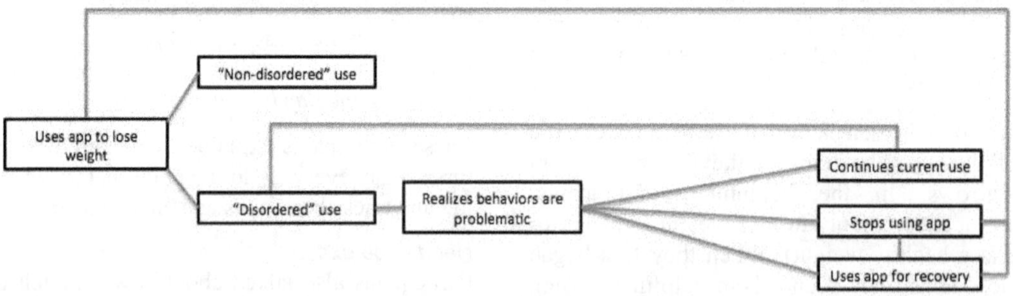


**Figure 1. Patterns of weight loss app use**

[2] ED = eating disorder

[3] Orthorexia is an obsession with eating healthy foods.

[4] EDNOS = eating disorder not otherwise specified; OSFED = other specified feeding or eating disorder

One participant explained how she would log every single piece of food even if it were only a portion of a calorie:

*"So literally, it [the app] just knew everything... It had the one tiny little morsel of food logged in there... I remember I went to church one day and I got a communion [wafer], and I even found the calories of it, which it's a half of calorie, that doesn't matter. But I think it was still in there, so I logged it... Why would you even have that in there? So that just didn't help." [U13]*

Another participant described her anxiety around needing to hit her calorie and macronutrients exactly and how that affected her ability to spend time with her family:

*"I try to get exactly on [the number]... I like having it exactly on... It [the app] made me more OCD [obsessive compulsive disorder], 'cause I'm like, 'I have to hit this number,' basically... It's made me more, very stringent on what I'm eating and making sure I hit those numbers... There was one time my parents wanted to go out to dinner... So, I called the [restaurant] so I could already track it and have it as close as possible. And then my parents get here, and they're like, 'Oh, we're going go to [this other restaurant] instead.' And I was literally having anxiety about going. I didn't want to go to dinner. I was like, 'No. I already had everything perfectly planned for my day,' and that was probably a bad moment... I feel like eating disorders stem from people trying to be perfect, and with this, you're hitting numbers trying to be perfect, so I think that could be kind of bad." [U14]*

Many participants discussed how they used the app to help them achieve exactness when tracking calories and macronutrients. Using the app fueled this desire to be exact and resulted in anxiety if they did not know the precise amount of calories and macronutrients in the foods they were eating in order to log them accurately.

#### *Acute awareness of numbers*

Weight loss apps also tend to put an emphasis on numbers associated with foods and exercise. As participants discussed, this focus on numbers worsened their eating disorder behaviors. One participant talked about how the app made her more aware of calories, which fed into her need for control:

*"I guess it [the app] has made me more aware of numbers and just trying to meet some you know, calories burned for exercise and stuff like that because it will log it in there. So getting really hung up on numbers has worsened things... like you get so fixed on controlling everything because you know it's at your hands, literally. You can control everything and then act on it. If I want to, the night before, I'll tell myself what I will eat, like I get very big on planning the meal for the next day when it's still the day before. So it's a big control thing..." [U02]*

Similarly, another participant talked about how weight loss apps can change users' relationship with food so that the food essentially boils down to its numbers. At the worst of her eating disorder, one participant talked about how every food was viewed as its calorie amount:

*"I think it's [logging food and exercise everyday] definitely very triggering because you become obsessed with food, you look at food differently. Like now when I look at food, I see like that's protein, that's fat, that's carbs instead of like that's a chicken breast, that's peanut butter, that's a piece of bread, and so it's always thinking, how can I eat these things when I only have so many carbs or I have to eat this much protein. And so it's definitely very, very triggering to be tracking it all the time. And especially back then [during my eating disorder], it was like, 'Well, that's 100 calories right there, like I need to eat broccoli instead, that's like 35 calories.' It's a number game basically." [U06]*

The heavy focus on the numbers in weight loss apps was problematic for a number of participants. By providing a way to monitor their diet so closely, the app fueled their need for control.

#### *Restricting*

One way participants maintained control was through restricting their calories. Participants described how they felt encouraged by the app to continue to restrict and accomplished when they ate under their daily calorie allotment. One participant described how she was almost in competition with herself and the app to eat fewer calories each day:

*"I kind of set it [my goal], and then it [the app] gave me a calorie count of maybe 1200 calories. But I never wanted to go above 1000 calories. I remember like coming home from the gym, and if I was around like 500 calories, like I was happy with that... so I definitely didn't want to be anywhere near the maximum. I wanted to be underneath. So that's like a negative thing, thinking back... But at the time, it was kind of like a game to beat the calories, kind of. So one day I had a 0, maybe it was like a negative calorie. I was like, 'Oh, wow, like look at me, like that's cool!' But that's not what you should be thinking [laughs]. Or the days where I was eating like above 1000, I was like, 'Oh, I ate way too much today,' just because I wanted to be like way under the like 1200... Just because like you can visualize what you're eating, so the more you don't eat, it's like, 'Oh I beat the app!'... I definitely wanted to beat the calories they gave me. I feel like that kind of does start an eating behavior where you don't want to eat anything." [U07]*

Similarly, another participant talked about how the app made it seem "good" to eat under the allotted calories and how she felt proud when she did:

*"It [the app] had you put in your weight and stuff. I think that the calories they gave you was the lowest that it would give you [laughs]. And then it just became this weird competition thing with it... [I felt] amazing [when I ate under my calorie allotment]... I just felt like I achieved my goal for the day. I just felt a sense of achievement. And then each day I would get lower and lower and lower... Because it [the*

*app] taught you that if you went over, you didn't succeed that day. But if you went under, then congrats, you're going to lose weight! You did what you were supposed to do that day... At the end of the night I would look through what I ate, and if it was mostly vegetables or something, I'd be proud, and then if it was strayed from that a little, I would probably freak out." [U13]*

Participants discussed how the apps could contribute to their restrictive behaviors by making it seem like a game to eat less than the given amount and less than the prior day. By seeing that they ate under their calorie budget, many participants would feel a sense of accomplishment, which fueled their desire to continue and even intensify their restrictive behaviors.

#### *Manipulating the app to lose weight*

Some participants talked about ways they manipulated the app so that they were actually netting less calories than the app stated. This was often achieved by not honestly reporting information about exercise and activity level. For instance, one participant talked about how she reported her activity level as "sedentary" even though she was really active so that she would lose more weight quickly:

*It [the app] only takes you as low as 1200 calories because that's a regular diet would recommend, the lowest you can go. So I would adjust my diet... I put in I wasn't active even though I was really active, so my maintenance calories were already lower than they should have been. And then if I put in like lose 2lbs per week, it would be even lower. So I feel like that can be manipulative... I think it can easily spiral into like disordered eating." [U03]*

Another participant explained how she would do a lot of calorie-burning activities and then go to the gym but never log calories burned from exercise:

*"I was dancing 4 days a week for like 2-ish hours and then I was swimming 4-5 days a week for 1-2 hours as well as thinking I needed to start lifting. So I would in between all that, go to the gym 4 times a week and lift up the 10lb dumbbells, so my calorie expenditure was probably 3000-4000 calories a day, and I was eating 1000... I didn't [record my exercise]. I don't think I ever recorded it simply because I knew I was doing so much." [U06]*

These participants manipulated their calorie budgets and expenditures by not accurately inputting their activity level and exercises. Without exercise, the app told them that they would lose weight, so being more active than reported acted as buffer or a means to more quickly achieve weight loss.

#### *Compensatory behaviors*

While participants felt rewarded by staying under their daily calorie allotment, sometimes they would exceed those budgets, and the app would reflect that. Participants often purged through exercise but sometimes vomited. Many talked about how they restricted their intake more the following days to compensate for being over budget. One participant described how she would use exercise to "get calories back" and would restrict more if she exceeded her allotment:

*"If I see the red, it's pretty much a bad day, and I feel like I have to start all over again. So then you'll probably see the next week [I'll] be super low in like everything... I used to work at [a doughnut shop], so I would snack on things there, so you can log having a [doughnut hole]... and I actually had eaten a lot of calories, and I felt like crap... And I logged it, and I think it went into the red. When I went to gym, I worked out for so long that day, and I was able to see it go back to green and still say it had remaining calories... Like to see it go back to green made me feel like, 'Ok, like I'm fine' even though in retrospect, even if I'm eating a bunch of crap and exercising, that's really not that much healthier... But I liked seeing it go from like red to green.*

Another participant discussed how she used exercise to "cancel out" calories:

*"So I kind of used this app to document like every single thing I did. So if I went for like an hour walk, I would put it in here. And like every little exercise I did to get calories out of the app, I would do that... the exercise part was kind of how I was able to get to my 500 calorie limit. Normally, I would only want to eat around 800 or 900 calories, and then after exercise, it would drop down to, I would normally burn like 300 calories, so it would get pretty low. I remember one day... after exercising, I was at 0 calories. And I was like, 'Look! Look at this! That's kind of cool.' Like thinking about it, it's like so bad, but the app's kind of designed that way, to kind of want you to cancel out your calories." [U07]*

The apps are designed in a way that allows users to "remove" calories eaten by adding in exercise. Participants often talked about how they would utilize exercise as a way to compensate for going over their calories for the day. They also would eat less in the days following exceeding their calorie budget.

#### *Manipulating the app to avoid negative emotions*

Exceeding the calorie budget almost always resulted in negative feelings, such as guilt and shame. In order to avoid those feelings, some participants would not log their food if they knew they would exceed their allotment. One participant talked about how she felt devastated when she significantly exceeded her calorie budget, so she would rather not enter it on the app:

*"Normally on my cheat days, I try not to even enter it in the app because I didn't want to see it on the app [laughs]. But I think we went to the [restaurant] with my dad, and I remember me and my sister, we split a cheesecake, and she went to enter it in the app and saw that it had 40 saturated fats! And she literally started to almost cry after seeing that 'cause like, that's just almost, it's weird to say, but it's kind of devastating just because like visually, once you start losing weight, I started to picture the food I ate on parts of my body. So I was like, 'That cheesecake's going to go right to my*

*thighs, like right to my stomach.' I didn't even enter it in the app 'cause I was like, 'I don't want to see it,' like I didn't want to know." [U07]*

Another participant also did not want to see how many calories she consumed on the app:

*"What actually happens is if it's way over, I just don't log it [because] I don't want to see the damage. So I literally won't log it... I avoid that negative emotion by just simply not logging it." [U10]*

The act of logging those foods and visualizing the calories on the app made it seem "real", which resulted in too much guilt and shame. By selectively inputting their calories, some participants were able to minimize negative emotions associated with exceeding their calorie budget.

### Making a change

Many participants explained that at some point they began to realize their behaviors and thoughts associated with food, exercise, and body image were unhealthy. When they actively decided to try to be healthier, participants would either change how they used the app or stop using the app.

#### *Adding in calories and/or focusing on nutrition*

One way participants changed their app usage and oriented their use towards recovery was by slowly adding more calories to their diet and focusing more on nutrition. Through the app, they logged additional calories as well as macronutrients. This essentially taught them that they could eat more, which reduced their fears around weight gain. One participant talked about how adding calories and tracking macronutrients helped her recover:

*"I slowly added calories, and then that's when I started tracking my macros, like my protein, carbs, and fat, to reach a certain amount to slowly gain weight, and then I guess you could say the way I use the app in recovery, like it kind of taught me how to eat again because when I would eat, it was just so disordered. I would have like 5 crackers. It was just all over the place. So I would say tracking my macros on here [the app] helped me recover because it taught me how to eat again, like a breakfast, lunch, dinner, and then snacks." [U03]*

Another participant explained how seeing that she could eat more without gaining too much weight helped her:

*"It's [the app] helped... I can fit certain things into my macros and not feel bad about it. I was fitting an Oreo everyday kind of thing and realized that there's no bad foods... It helped me eat a lot more. This past off-season I was eating so much. Honestly, I don't want get back up to that point, but it really helped my metabolism get up and so I could track it and realize, 'Oh, I can eat this much food and still stay pretty lean.'" [U14]*

While participants were still logging their foods, they began to change their perceptions around food, which helped them in their recovery.

#### *Taking a break from weight loss apps*

Sometimes participants felt the best course of action for their recovery was to stop using the app. For example, one participant talked about how ceasing use really helped her recover:

*"[sigh] I took a break from tracking, like the past year, I stopped using the app and just kind of started eating like a normal person again, and that was really nice so. I think everyone should do that, and I think that's really what has helped me." [U06]*

Another participant described how she stopped using the app when it consumed too much of her time and she was having anxiety attacks about food:

*"I went to a psychologist on campus... because I was so anxious. And if I would binge-eat, then it would have been binge-eating of vegetables because I was so anxious about gaining weight. Just something at some point after a long miserable, I think semester at least, I just said no more and this is crazy. Nothing should drive me nuts, like food. So that's when I said, 'I'm going to erase it [the app], I'll be fine.' Then I would cheat a little bit, like I would remember everything. So I would write down on a paper. I had this and this and like add it up and do a calculation in my head. But that's when I erased it [the app], when it was just occupying me and energy-wise and time-wise just to insanity really." [U12]*

At some point, many of the participants stopped using weight loss apps at least for some period of time because they thought it would help with recovery.

### Falling Back into Old Habits

Although a number of participants took a break from using weight loss apps, many of them began using weight loss apps again. Even when participants had recovery goals in mind, they wanted to use weight loss apps to keep track of their foods or to lose weight. Some participants described pressures to lose weight and be fit as a result of being athletes or fitness competitors, and they felt the app in some ways was the only way to achieve that:

*"[I started to use the app again because of] just the desire to lose the weight because I know that I can't do it on my own. I really enjoyed competing in the body building show, and I really enjoyed that experience of being on stage and it's like this very glamorous day, you've never felt prettier. You get your hair done, your makeup done, it's crazy, it's a great day. But it was the after effects that I struggled with, and so I want to do that again, but I know I'm not ready to do it if I can't lose the weight on my own and like get to a better starting point... I think that I am at a healthy weight, just not where I want to be." [U06]*

In addition to wanting to track foods, one participant explained that deleting the app caused her anxiety, so she felt compelled to use it to manage her diet:

*"Last summer, I had to delete it. I deleted it and had to get it back 'cause I was like, 'Oh, my gosh, I need to know what I'm eating.' And I'm a very scientific numbers-based person, so I like having everything on point... So, it's hard for someone to have an app like that whenever you're like that. It consumes you... I literally got anxiety, so I had to get it back... I just want to hit everything correctly." [U14]*

While participants were interested in supporting their recovery, they often felt the need to continue to use weight loss apps either to help them reach athletic and fitness goals or to relieve anxiety around food and weight.

## DISCUSSION

Our findings highlight two sides to weight loss apps, troubling the binary view of technology. On one hand, they can exacerbate and contribute to eating disorders. On the other hand, users use apps for eating disorder recovery. We further discuss how our findings trouble the binary view of technology and then provide insights from our study that are useful for designing more health-focused apps and technologies in the future.

### Troubling the Binary View of Technology

Typically, studies talk about technology as either a negative influence or a positive one. For example, from the sociocultural perspective, technology negatively impacts body image and eating disorder behaviors while much HCI research views weight loss apps as beneficial to users. Our findings show that weight loss apps can be both negative and positive. In line with the sociocultural perspective, there are aspects of weight loss apps that contribute to and exacerbate eating disorder behaviors, such as the heavy focus on numbers, which fuels obsessive logging, makes users want to be exact, changes the relationship with food, and allows them to manipulate the app to lose more weight; and calorie visualizations, which make users feel rewarded for eating under and guilty for eating over their budget and contribute to their need to exercise to compensate for calorie consumption. Therefore, some users, especially those who are still struggling with eating disorder behaviors and poor body image, can easily be triggered by using weight loss apps. In the right mindset though, users who are trying to add more calories into their diet or focus on nutrition may find it helpful to track their foods and alleviate anxiety around weight gain.

As this study demonstrates, focusing on a binary view of technology is problematic because technology is neither inherently good nor bad. Thus, the context around technology use is crucial in understanding users' needs and the effects of using health technology, particularly when talking about eating disorders. While many users believe weight loss apps can be problematic for those with eating disorders, many stated the effects of the app depend a lot of how users use them and users' own mentalities, attitudes, and motivations during use.

Users go through stages of use and report both positive and negative effects of the app at these various stages. As users reflect back on their journey, they talk a great deal about the negative effects of the app during the early stages of use. However, when they first began using the app, they often did not realize their behaviors were indicative of an eating disorder and even found the app helpful. Users then often begin to realize their behaviors are unhealthy. Sometimes users continue using the app to restrict calories or "erase" calories. However, some decide to make a change to be healthier or focus on eating disorder recovery. Users are motivated to make a change due to personal reasons, such as realizing the health implications of their eating disorder (e.g., having a low heart rate, infertility). Sometimes parents discover their daughter has an eating disorder, and they intervene by making her see a professional, ceasing use of the app, or controlling her meals and exercise. Other times, users make a change because of the social dynamics in college, which often center on food (e.g., going out to eat, eating at the dining commons, going to parties, etc.). In order to participate in the "typical" college lifestyle and maintain friendships, users decide to stop using the app, use it less frequently, or use it differently (i.e., changing calorie budget). Unfortunately, because of the way in which weight loss apps are designed and the nature of eating disorders, users sometimes revert to old habits of unhealthy eating and exercising or begin using the app when they feel it is not healthy for them. This reflects users' journey of not only how they used weight loss apps, but also how they perceived them in relation to their eating disorder.

### Weight Loss App Design

Although weight loss apps can be used in both positive and negative ways, there are certain aspects of weight loss app design that need to be reconsidered in order to focus more on promoting health. This study highlights ways weight loss apps may unintentionally promote unhealthy habits or lead to negative emotions. For instance, we found users manipulate the app to avoid negative emotions, such as guilt, when they exceed their calorie budget, which is in line with Cordeiro et al.'s [11] findings about food journaling and negative nudges.

When users exceed their calorie allotment, that number turns red. This happens regardless if the user exceeds their allotment by 1 or 1000 calories. Many participants talked about how seeing this number displayed and how "seeing the red" made them feel anxious and guilty. In order to alleviate these feelings, participants would either exercise to "get back in the green" or not log when they knew they would exceed their budget. As Cordeiro et al. [11] suggested, it is not necessary to make users feel so guilty for going over their budget, especially by little amounts, as this may actually cause users to feel badly, resort to extreme measures, or not use the app at all.

When users net fewer calories than they are budgeted, many weight loss apps show their calories remaining as a green number. We found users felt the remaining number in combination with the green color encouraged them to try to eat under their allotted calories or purge (most often through exercise) to "remove" calories from the app. Consuming fewer calories gave participants a sense of pride and achievement, which they felt was intensified because of how the app showed their food and calories. Interestingly, this is in contrast to Cordeiro et al. [11], who found general users did not feel strong positive emotions for eating under their calorie budget and seeing the green did not make them feel rewarded, which highlights how different users are impacted differently, showcasing the interaction between eating disorders and app design. Thus, we should reconsider how we visualize being over or under budget as red and green have strong emotional responses based on how they are used throughout society. These visuals need to be more nuanced, perhaps using different colors. Future work needs to explore different types of feedback and visualizations and test for their impact on different types of users, including those with eating disorders.

Our findings also show users often become obsessed with logging, which is in line with Cordeiro et al. [11]. HCI has typically viewed breaks from logging as negative or a barrier; however, we should reconsider this viewpoint as breaks can be healthy for users to eat "normally" and listen to their body's signals. For instance, users with eating disorders often find taking a break from using the app helps them in the process of recovery. However, contrary to Cordeiro et al. [11], users with eating disorders do not really "lose the habit" of logging because they feel the need have control over their food, diet, weight, etc. This begs the question of how much and how often we should tell users to log? For some, we should encourage logging breaks, monitor how often they use the app, and recommend less use.

We found weight loss apps create a need to be exact and an acute awareness of numbers. While this awareness was mentioned in Cordeiro et al. [11], it was not as extreme. In HCI, this awareness is often viewed as a positive, but our work shows that it can promote an unhealthy relationship with food. While Cordeiro et al. [11] found users were challenged to log because of the variety of foods they eat, for users with eating disorders, such an awareness is created around calories that users eat the same types of foods repetitively because they are "safe" foods. To counteract these issues, apps should focus more on healthy behaviors like eating nutrient-rich foods and a variety of foods. This number focus is not necessarily in line with healthy lifestyle promotion, as echoed in Cordeiro et al.'s [11] findings about apps being about ease of tracking (easy to log fast food and pre-made food).

Contrary to Cordeiro et al. [11] who found the eating context was a barrier to journaling, instead of not logging, users with eating disorders will preplan for or avoid social engagements or scenarios where they might be challenged to log; if they cannot preplan or avoid it, they feel anxiety, which helps to perpetuate their eating disorder.

When we try to discourage users from certain behaviors, we have to make sure we're not unintentionally encouraging negative habits. For example, users saw a warning message of eating too little as an accomplishment. It may also be helpful to eliminate the ability to cancel out calories through exercise and instead allow users to track exercise but do not show a deduction in calories consumed.

Because users manipulate the app to lose weight, perhaps we can find other ways to determine user needs besides self-entering. For instance, apps could synchronize with wearables that give users a sense of what they need but do not show the quantifications to users. This falls in line with Purpura et al. [32] who cautioned that weight technology focuses too heavily on quantitative measures and "promotes behaviors based on limited understanding of users' actual personal situations" p429.

Currently these types of apps do not support recovery goals or weight gain goals, which helps explain why users may fall back into old habits even when they have recovery goals. Some apps do not allow weight gain goals, and if they do, then they are not designed to persuade users to gain (green if under not over even if you have a weight *gain* goal). More personalization could help. For instance, if users have a weight gain goal, then when they exceed their budget, they should feel a sense of accomplishment as they are moving toward their goal. Current apps do not support this nuanced aspect of goal setting. We need to reconsider how we motivate users based on their individual needs.

There should be a shifting focus away from just weight loss as a marker for health, and we need to find ways to support this in apps. Future research needs to study the effects of design in more detail on various types of users.

## CONCLUSION

We trouble the binary view of technology by showing that as users reflect on their health journey, they report both positive and negative effects and perceptions of weight loss apps. In fact, women go through a journey of weight loss apps use as they change and go through different stages of their eating disorders. While every user's journey is somewhat different and the timeframe between disordered use and making a change varies, there are patterns of use that exist across users with eating disorders. This study demonstrates the dynamic nature of weight loss app use, which is important for designing weight loss apps that promote health.

## ACKNOWLEDGMENTS

This material is supported by the National Science Foundation under Grant #DGE1255832. Anything expressed in this does not necessarily reflect the views of the NSF.

## REFERENCES


1. American Psychiatric Association (ed.). 2013. *Diagnostic and Statistical Manual of Mental Disorders (DSM-5)*. American Psychiatric Publishing, Washington, D.C. and London, England.
2. Julie L. Andsager. 2014. Research directions in social media and body image. *Sex Roles* 71: 407–413. https://doi.org/10.1007/s11199-014-0430-4
3. Rheanna N Ata, Lauren M Schaefer, and J Kevin Thompson. 2015. Sociocultural Theories of Eating Disorders. In *The Wiley Handbook of Eating Disorders*. John Wiley & Sons, Ltd, 269–282. https://doi.org/10.1002/9781118574089.ch21
4. Shlomo Berkovsky, Jill Freyne, and Mac Coombe. 2012. Physical Activity Motivating Games. *ACM Transactions on Computer-Human Interaction* 19, 4: 1–41. https://doi.org/10.1145/2395131.2395139
5. Virginia Braun and Victoria Clarke. 2006. Using thematic analysis in psychology. *Qualitative Research in Psychology* 3, 2: 77–101. https://doi.org/10.1191/1478088706qp063oa
6. Brandon Brown, Marshini Chetty, Andrea Grimes, and Ellie Harmon. 2006. Reflecting on health. In *CHI '06 Extended Abstracts*, 1807–1812. https://doi.org/10.1145/1125451.1125794
7. S. Chancellor, Jessica Pater, T. Clear, E. Gilber, and Munmun De Choudhury. 2016. #thyghgapp: Instagram Content Moderation and Lexical Variation in Pro-Eating Disorder Communities. In *CSCW*, 1–13.
8. Eun Kyoung Choe, Bongshin Lee, Sean Munson, Wanda Pratt, and Julie A Kientz. 2013. Persuasive performance feedback: The effect of framing on self-efficacy. In *AMIA*, 1–9.
9. Eun Kyoung Choe, Nicole B. Lee, Bongshin Lee, Wanda Pratt, and Julie a. Kientz. 2014. Understanding quantified-selfers' practices in collecting and exploring personal data. In *CHI '14*, 1143–1152. https://doi.org/10.1145/2556288.2557372
10. Felicia Cordeiro, Elizabeth Bales, Erin Cherry, and James Fogarty. 2015. Rethinking the mobile food journal: Exploring opportunities for lightweight photo-based capture. In *CHI '15*, 1–10. https://doi.org/10.1145/2702123.2702154
11. Felicia Cordeiro, Daniel a Epstein, Edison Thomaz, Elizabeth Bales, Arvind K Jagannathan, Gregory D Abowd, and James Fogarty. 2015. Barriers and Negative Nudges: Exploring Challenges in Food Journaling. *Proceedings of the 33rd Annual ACM Conference on Human Factors in Computing Systems - CHI '15*: 1159–1162. https://doi.org/10.1145/2702123.2702155
12. Kristen M. Culbert, Sarah E. Racine, and Kelly L. Klump. 2015. Research Review: What we have learned about the causes of eating disorders - A synthesis of sociocultural, psychological, and biological research. *Journal of Child Psychology and Psychiatry and Allied Disciplines* 56, 11: 1141–1164. https://doi.org/10.1111/jcpp.12441
13. Elizabeth V Eikey and Kayla M Booth. Recovery and Maintenance: How Women with Eating Disorders Use Instagram. In *iConference*, 1–12.
14. D. Eisenberg, E.J. Nicklett, K. Roeder, and N.E. Kirz. 2011. Eating Disorder Symptoms Among College Students: Prevalence, Persistence, Correlates, and Treatment-Seeking. *Journal of American College Health* 59, 8: 70–707. https://doi.org/10.1038/nature13314.A
15. Christopher G. Fairburn and Paul J. Harrison. 2003. Eating disorders. *Lancet* 361, 9355: 407–416. https://doi.org/10.1016/S0140-6736(03)12378-1
16. Jasmine Fardouly, Phillippa C Diedrichs, Lenny R Vartanian, and Emma Halliwell. 2015. Social comparisons on social media: The impact of Facebook on young women's body image concerns and mood. *Body Image* 13: 38–45. https://doi.org/10.1016/j.bodyim.2014.12.002
17. Jasmine Fardouly and Lenny R. Vartanian. 2015. Negative comparisons about one's appearance mediate the relationship between Facebook usage and body image concerns. *Body Image* 12: 82–88. https://doi.org/10.1016/j.bodyim.2014.10.004
18. Ellen E. Fitzsimmons-Craft. 2011. Social psychological theories of disordered eating in college women: Review and integration. *Clinical Psychology Review* 31, 7: 1224–1237. https://doi.org/10.1016/j.cpr.2011.07.011
19. Susannah Fox and Maeve Duggan. 2012. Mobile Health 2012. *Pew Internet & American Life Project*. Retrieved from http://pewinternet.org/Reports/2012/Mobile-Health.aspx
20. Visda Goudarzi and Stanislav Tomic. 2006. PEDdo: Steps to a healthy lifestyle. In *CHI '06 Extended Abstracts*, 1825–1830. https://doi.org/10.1145/1125451.1125797
21. Sharon L Hoerr, Ronda Bokram, Brenda Lugo, Tanya Bivins, and Debra R Keast. 2002. Risk for disordered eating relates to both gender and ethnicity for college students. *Journal of the American College of Nutrition* 21, 4: 307–314. https://doi.org/10.1080/07315724.2002.10719228
22. Anne Hsu, Jing Yang, Yigit Han Yilmaz, Md Sanaul Haque, Cengiz Can, and Ann E. Blandford. 2014. Persuasive technology for overcoming food cravings and improving snack choices. In *CHI '14*, 3403–3412. https://doi.org/10.1145/2556288.2557099
23. Ji Won Kim and T Makana Chock. 2015. Body image 2.0: Associations between social grooming on Facebook and body image concerns. *Computers in Human Behavior* 48: 331–339. https://doi.org/10.1016/j.chb.2015.01.009
24. Annalise G. Mabe, K. Jean Forney, and Pamela K. Keel. 2014. Do you "like" my photo? Facebook use maintains eating disorder risk. *International Journal of Eating Disorders* 47: 516–523. https://doi.org/10.1002/eat.22254
25. M N Marshall. 1996. Sampling for qualitative research. *Family Practice* 13, 6: 522–526. Retrieved from http://www.ncbi.nlm.nih.gov/pubmed/9023528

26. Evelyn P Meier and James Gray. 2014. Facebook photo activity associated with body image disturbance in adolescent girls. *Cyberpsychology, Behavior, and Social Networking* 17, 4: 199–206. https://doi.org/10.1089/cyber.2013.0305

27. Florian Mueller, Joe Marshall, Rohit Ashok Khot, Stina Nylander, and Jakob Tholander. 2014. Jogging with technology: Interaction design supportging sport activities. *CHI '14 Extended Abstracts*: 1131–1134. https://doi.org/10.1145/2559206.2559209

28. M Neve, P J Morgan, P R Jones, and C E Collins. 2009. Effectiveness of web-based interventions in achieving weight loss and weight loss maintenance in overweight and obese adults: a systematic review with meta-analysis. *Obesity Reviews: International Association for the Study of Obesity* 11: 306–321. https://doi.org/10.1111/j.1467-789X.2009.00646.x

29. Edward Nguyen, Tanmay Modak, Elton Dias, Yang Yu, and Liang Huang. 2014. Fitnamo: Using bodydata to encourage exercise through google glass™. In *CHI '14 Extended Abstracts*, 239–244. https://doi.org/10.1145/2559206.2580933

30. Jessica Pater, Oliver Haimson, Nazanin Andalibi, and Elizabeth D Mynatt. 2016. "Hunger hurts but starving works:" characterzing the presentation of eating disorders online. In *CSCW*, 1–16. https://doi.org/10.1145/2818048.2820030

31. Richard M. Perloff. 2014. Social media effects on young women's body image concerns: Theoretical perspectives and an agenda for research. *Sex Roles*: 363–377. https://doi.org/10.1007/s11199-014-0384-6

32. Stephen Purpura, Victoria Schwanda, Kaiton Williams, William Stubler, and Phoebe Sengers. 2011. Fit4life: The design of a persuasive technology promoting healthy behavior and ideal weight. *Proceedings of the 2011 annual conference on Human factors in computing systems - CHI '11*: 423. https://doi.org/10.1145/1978942.1979003

33. L. Reba-Harrelson, A. Von Holle, R. M. Hamer, R. Swann, M. L. Reyes, and Cynthia M. Bulik. 2009. Patterns and prevalence of disordered eating and weight control behaviors in women ages 25-45. *Eating and Weight Disorders* 14, 4. https://doi.org/10.1007/BF03325116

34. Mark F Reinking, Laura E Alexander, and St Louis. 2005. Prevalence of Disordered-Eating Behaviors Athletes and Nonathletes. *Journal of Athletic Training* 40, 1: 47–51.

35. John Rooksby, Mattias Rost, Alistair Morrison, and Matthew Chalmers. 2015. Pass the ball: Enforced turn-taking in activity tracking. In *CHI '15*, 2417–2426. https://doi.org/10.1145/2702123.2702577

36. Catherine A. Sanderson. 2010. *Social Psychology*. John Wiley & Sons, Inc. https://doi.org/10.4135/9781446247198

37. C M Shisslak, M Crago, and L S Estes. 1995. The spectrum of eating disturbances. *The International Journal of Eating Disorders* 18, 3: 209–219. https://doi.org/10.1002/1098-108x(199511)18:3<209::aid-eat2260180303>3.0.co;2-e

38. Aaron Smith. 2015. U.S. Smartphone Use in 2015. *Pew Research Center*, 1–7. Retrieved November 11, 2015 from http://www.pewinternet.org/2015/04/01/us-smartphone-use-in-2015/

39. Wendy Spettigue and Katherine A Henderson. 2004. Eating disorders and the role of the media. *The Canadian Child and Adolescent Psychiatry Review* 13, 1: 16–19.

40. Katarzyna Stawarz, Anna L Cox, and Ann Blandford. 2015. Beyond self-tracking and reminders: Designing smartphone apps that support habit formation. In *CHI '15*, 2653–2662. https://doi.org/10.1145/2702123.2702230

41. Cassandra Marie Stover. 2014. Elements of a Sensibility: Fitness Blogs and Postfeminist Media Culture. The University of Texas at Austin.

42. Samantha Stronge, Lara M. Greaves, Petar Milojev, Tim West-Newman, Fiona Kate Barlow, and Chris G. Sibley. 2015. Facebook is linked to body dissatisfaction: Comparing users and non-users. *Sex Roles* 73: 200–213. https://doi.org/10.1007/s11199-015-0517-6

43. Eric Strother, Raymond Lemberg, Stevie Chariese Stanford, and Dayton Turberville. 2012. Eating Disorders in Men: Underdiagnosed, Undertreated, and Misunderstood. *Eating Disorders* 20, 5: 346–355. https://doi.org/10.1080/10640266.2012.715512

44. Tina Tan, Angeline Kuek, Shih Ee Goh, Ee Lian Lee, and Victor Kwok. 2016. Internet and smartphone application usage in eating disorders: A descriptive study in Singapore. *Asian Journal of Psychiatry* 19: 50–55. https://doi.org/10.1016/j.ajp.2015.11.007

45. Marika Tiggemann and Mia Zaccardo. 2015. "Exercise to be fit, not skinny": The effect of fitspiration imagery on women's body image. *Body Image* 15: 61–67. https://doi.org/10.1016/j.bodyim.2015.06.003

46. Tammy Toscos, Anne Faber, Shunying An, and Mona Praful Gandhi. 2006. Chick clique: Persuasive technology to motivate teenage girls to exercise. In *CHI '06 Extended Abstracts*, 1873–1878. https://doi.org/10.1145/1125451.1125805

47. Dhaval Vyas, Zachary Fitz-walter, Erica Mealy, Alessandro Soro, Jinglan Zhang, and Margot Brereton. 2015. Exploring physical activities in an employer-sponsored health program. In *CHI '15 Extended Abstracts*, 1421–1426. https://doi.org/10.1145/2702613.2732815

48. T. D. Wade, A. Keski-Rahkonen, and J. Hudson. 2011. Epidemiology of eating disorders. In *Textbook in Psychiatric Epidemiology (3rd ed.)* (M. Tsuang). Wiley, New York, 343–360. https://doi.org/10.1002/9780470976739.ch20

49. Greg Walsh and Jennifer Golbeck. 2014. StepCity: A preliminary investigation of a personal informatics-based social game on behavior change. In *CHI '14 Extended*

*Abstracts*, 2371–2376. https://doi.org/10.1145/2559206.2581326

50. Tz-Li Wang and Ya-Hui Bella Lien. 2013. The power of using video data. *Quality & Quantity* 47: 2933–2941. https://doi.org/10.1007/s11135-012-9717-0

51. Elanor H. Wertheim, Susan J. Paxton, and Simone Blaney. 2009. Body image in girls. In *Body image, eating disorders, and obesity in youth: Assessment, prevention, and treatment* (2nd ed.). American Psychological Association, Washington, D.C., 47–76.

52. 2014. Hacking Health: How Consumers Use Smartphones and Wearable Tech To Track Their Health. *Nielsen*. Retrieved August 8, 2016 from http://www.nielsen.com/us/en/insights/news/2014/hacking-health-how-consumers-use-smartphones-and-wearable-tech-to-track-their-health.html

# Conflict in Comments: Learning but Lowering Perceptions, With Limits

**W. Ben Towne, Carolyn P. Rosé, & James D. Herbsleb**
Carnegie Mellon University
Pittsburgh, Pennsylvania
{wbt, cprose, jdh}@cs.cmu.edu

## ABSTRACT
Prior work and perception theory suggests that when exposed to discussion related to a particular piece of crowdsourced text content, readers generally perceive that content to be of lower quality than readers who do not see those comments, and that the effect is stronger if the comments display conflict. This paper presents a controlled experiment with over 1000 participants testing to see if this effect carries over to other documents from the same platform, including those with similar content or by the same author. Although we do generally find that perceived quality of the commented-on document is affected, effects do not carry over to the second item and readers are able to judge the second in isolation from the comment on the first. We confirm a prior finding about the negative effects conflict can have on perceived quality but note that readers report learning more from constructive conflict comments.

### Author Keywords
Experiment; validation; social influence; comments; crowdsourcing; distributed evaluation; creative work.

### ACM Classification Keywords
H.1.2. User/Machine Systems: Human factors, Human information processing; H.5.2 Evaluation/methodology, Natural language, Interaction styles; H.5.3 Group and Organization Interfaces: Computer-supported cooperative work, Web-based interaction, Evaluation/methodology.

## INTRODUCTION
"Wicked problems" such as climate change may be more complex than any specific individual or committee is capable of completely understanding by themselves. However, evidence indicates that a large and distributed set of cognitive resources may be available to help solve such problems, if we can figure out how to use them well [22]. Addressing one set of approaches to large-scale distributed problem solving, a 2016 *Science* article by Michelucci & Dickinson asserts that human computation has "huge potential" to address wicked problems, going beyond microtask crowdsourcing to create shared online workspaces where participants "contribute, combine, revise, connect, evaluate, and integrate data and concepts" [18]. In many platforms designed to support large-scale distributed problem solving, basic ideas are crowdsourced and posted publicly, where others can evaluate the contribution and/or add comments and/or read the comments others have written. However, there are questions being raised in at least the public dialogue about the potential of spill-over effects from comments and interactions posted online to undermine the significant positive potential of Internet-based collaboration [24].

Where others' comments on or ratings of content are also visible, as is often the case, they can have an impact on the level of quality perceived by subsequent readers. Social influence on perceptions of quality could create a feedback loop that leads groups of people to irrationally herd toward large group evaluations that are path-dependent and not necessarily connected to the quality of what is being perceived [1,21]. Causes and consequences of market-based valuation bubbles and herding in asset pricing have been studied (e.g. [11]), but little is known about how much of that knowledge applies to distortions in perceptions of value when the signals and consequences are more purely social, in the absence of pricing or direct economic incentives.

Examining social influence effects in large online community platforms, Muchnik, Aral, & Taylor conducted an experiment in which fresh and unrated content, which users had posted to a social news aggregation Web site, was *randomly assigned* to an initial upvote or downvote (or control condition with neither). The random upvote increased the probability of up-voting by the first viewer by 32% without a corrective increase in down-voting; the effects of that initial manipulation persisted and increased mean ratings by 25% five months later. A random initial downvote doubled the probability of subsequent downvotes, but also significantly increased the probability of a subsequent corrective upvote. "Friends" of the commenter were more likely to upvote in response to a randomly assigned initial vote (up or down) than to a post with no random initial vote, but even when differences in the probability of voting were considered, there remained differences attributed to statistically significant opinion


*CHI 2017, May 06 - 11, 2017, Denver, CO, USA*

ACM 978-1-4503-4655-9/17/05...$15.00
DOI: http://dx.doi.org/10.1145/3025453.3025902

change resulting from the random initial vote. Their results "suggest that social influence substantially biases rating dynamics in systems designed to harness collective intelligence." That paper concludes by calling for more research exploring mechanisms driving individual and aggregate ratings, especially in real social environments, as "essential to our ability to interpret collective judgment accurately and to avoid social influence bias in collective intelligence" [19].

In the setting of Wikipedia, Towne, Kittur, Kinnaird, & Herbsleb [26] showed that when readers are exposed to discussion behind collaboratively edited content, their assessment of the quality of the content is lower than readers who do not see the discussion. The effect is stronger if the discussion contains conflict, but this strengthening can be erased if the discussion shows a Compromise or Collaboration resolution strategy from the editors involved. The effect, observed in a between-subjects experiment, was in that study counterintuitively accompanied by participants' self-reports that reading the discussion *increased* their perceptions of article quality.

The present study seeks to test the extent of that prior work's finding, using a similar methodology in a different setting and measuring the extent to which this effect might extend beyond the article being discussed directly, to other articles that are similar along a couple selected dimensions.

## METHOD OVERVIEW

In this study, we show participants a segment from each of two crowdsourced proposals entered into a platform designed to support large-scale collaboration around a complex issue, namely global climate change. Following the first proposal (only), most participants saw a comment associated with that first proposal. We experimentally varied the type of comment shown in a 3x2 full factorial design, plus a no-comment control, as described in "Experimental Conditions" below. We also independently varied the relationship between the first and second proposals (i.e. same author, similar topics, or neither) as described below. After reading each proposal (and if applicable, the comment immediately following the first proposal), participants were asked to evaluate the proposal quality with a multi-item scale. We look to see if those quality evaluations changed as a result of the experimental conditions to which participants were randomly assigned.

## HYPOTHESES

Hypotheses in this work are presented here in descriptive form, summarized in Table 2. Based on work by Towne et al. [26], we hypothesize that (H1) the presence of a comment will negatively affect participants' ratings of the first proposal's quality, and (H2) the size of the effect will depend on the type of comment, such as whether it presents conflict. The size of the effect may also depend on how that conflict is resolved [26]. This study investigates further to determine if (H3) the effect extends to other proposals (i.e. the second one participants saw) which are similar or different in certain ways.

In investigating that possible spill-over effect, we experimentally manipulate whether comments are directed at the *content* or the *author*. We hypothesize that (H4) if the comment is attributed to something about the *content* (e.g. a claim that the main idea is significantly flawed), the effects of reading that comment might extend to other topically similar proposals regardless of who wrote them, and (H5) that if the comment is something attributable to the *author*, the effects might extend to other proposals by the same author regardless of proposal topic.

Whether or not H1 and H2 were supported, we wanted to be able to better understand the processes underlying any differences in ratings between experimental conditions. If the same set of processes is at work here as observed previously [26], we hypothesize (H6) that participants would report *beliefs* that their perceptions of quality had been affected in the *opposite* direction that the between-subjects analysis showed that it had been. To explore this hypothesis, we asked participants who saw comments about the degree to which they thought reading the comments raised/lowered their quality perceptions, as two questions on a page immediately following participants' evaluations.

We also asked participants to tell us whether or not they learned anything from the comments, to investigate a potential benefit they might provide and put H2 in context, as comments offering a different perspective may provide the reader with more novel and/or useful information than comments which do not express both a conflict and resolution. This allowed us to explore the hypothesis (H7) that participants would learn most from comments containing constructive conflict.

In all conditions, content was presented in the same order. We recognize that reading the first proposal could have an order-specific effect on the rating of the second, separate from underlying differences between the proposals that might lead to rating differences between the first and second proposals. This experiment specifically investigates one hypothesized order effect, namely how reading a comment and then providing an evaluation which may be influenced by it may also influence perceptions of material read immediately after it, on the same page. Having the rating materials on the same page increases the probability of observing (and being better able to characterize) a carry-over effect if one exists. Participants are randomly assigned to a comment condition (or control condition absent any comments), and the primary analysis compares between those conditions.

## MATERIALS

### Corpus

Inspired by examples of successful large-scale collaboration elsewhere, such as Wikipedia or FoldIt, Malone et al. created the MIT Climate CoLab to be a global platform for collaboratively developing and evaluating proposals for what to do about global climate change [16]. In an annual series of contests, its members have collectively produced, commented on, and voted on over 1500 proposals, typically 1500-3000 words in length [4], on a wide range of climate-change-related topics. At the start of the main 2016 contests, the site had over 50,000 registered user accounts. We used the 1501 proposals in contests that were then completed as the documents in our model and experiment.

In recent years, several contests have been run in parallel, each addressing different subtopics (such as Transportation, Waste Management, Buildings, and Energy Supply) or calling for plans that integrate a number of other proposals [17]. Participants and problems discussed come from many countries, though most participants come from North America [6]. The interface, proposals meeting the language requirements [2], and all materials used in this experiment are in English.

We further restricted our materials to the 350 Climate CoLab proposals submitted in contests between 2011 and 2015 inclusive that made the semifinalist round as selected by expert judges. We chose semifinalist proposals (or higher) to establish a minimum degree of quality, similar to Towne et al.'s procedure for choosing high-quality articles in [26]. We set the threshold at semifinalist proposals as opposed to finalists or winners to maintain some quality while also ensuring that the pool of proposals to choose from would be sufficiently large (as in [20]).

We further eliminated proposals that could not be basically understood by the summary text, e.g. because the proposal relied heavily on reference to other proposals or documents. We removed two proposals whose content had been submitted in the form of images, and another whose latest version simply read "The new version will be posted shortly" because the text of these had not been properly captured for topic modeling.

### Experimental Conditions

Comments shown on the first proposal were randomly assigned from a 2x3 factorial design, plus a "no comment" control which helps us test H1. The three levels of the "conflict" factor (Conflict without resolution, Conflict with resolution, and Non-conflict) were chosen based on the categories distinguished by previous work [26], and help test H2. The two levels of the "direction" factor (content-directed vs. author-directed) help test H4 and H5.

The second proposal was chosen randomly from the cells in Table 1. We excluded the "Same author, similar content" cell because when observed, the proposal pairs in this cell are largely copies of each other, sometimes with little or no modification, and in allocating our budget for experimental conditions, it was least interesting to see if comments on one proposal would affect perceptions of another copy of that proposal. The relationship between proposals was

| *4 similarity types (2x2):* | *Same Author* | *Different Author* |
|---|---|---|
| *Similar Content* | ≈ Copies (not tested) | Relationship C |
| *Dissimilar Content* | Relationship A | Relationship D |

**Table 1: Relationship second proposal has to first proposal, randomly assigned. This factor crosses author and content similarity factors, a factorial design excluding one cell.**

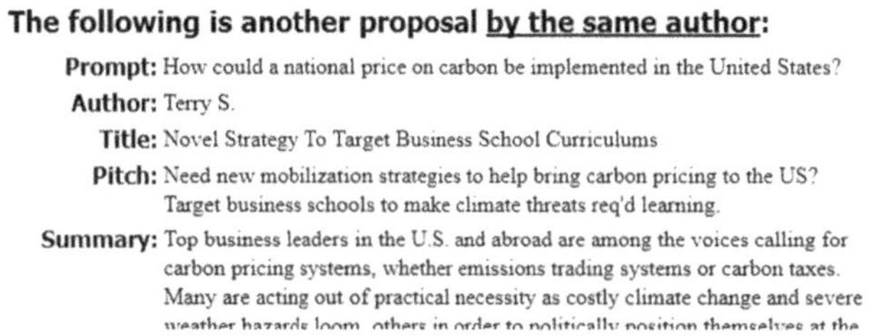


**Figure 1: The relationship between proposals was explicitly called out. This screenshot shows Relationship A from Table 1. For Relationship C, the underlined text read "about a similar topic" and for Relationship D, it read "that was submitted" without underline.**

called out in bold underlined header text just before the presentation of the second proposal, as shown in Figure 1.

### Selecting focal proposals

As potential focal proposals, we considered those where other proposals existed that fit the "same author, unrelated content" criteria described below. We selected multiple focal proposals so that our experimental results would not be too sensitive to specific details of any particular proposal, but kept the number small so that we could collect relatively robust sets of quality ratings on each and analyze aggregated results while still controlling for any real quality differences that may exist between selected proposals.

In order to better cover the space of available proposals, we used a constraint satisfaction solver to maximize diversity by selecting the set of four focal proposals by four different authors that were on average maximally different from each other according to a previously studied LDA/cosine similarity measure [27] (the same as used in "Selecting topically related proposals" below). The solver we used was Excel 2013's "Evolutionary" solver, which produced better results than its "GRG nonlinear" solver.[1]

### Selecting topically related proposals

For each focal proposal, we selected the proposal that had no overlap in author team and the greatest topical similarity to the focal proposal, operationalizing relationship "C" from Table 1. Topical similarity was measured by the cosine similarity of proposals' topic vectors according to a

[1] For more detailed citations, see http://www.solver.com/excel-solver-algorithms-and-methods-used.

Latent Dirichlet Allocation (LDA) model run over the entire corpus with program default hyperparameters.

Consistent with [27] and with Xu and Ma's goal of maximizing dissimilarity between clusters [31:303], we selected the number of topics by choosing the model with the lowest average percentage of proposals that has neither or both topics in each possible topic pair. The model was run to 1000 iterations for coarse tuning between 5 and 300 topics, and 2000 iterations for fine tuning between 50 and 60 topics, concluding with a 57-topic model, as the one which maximally separated proposals into different topics.

In a prior experiment, Towne et al. [27] found this measure to match human perceptions of which pair among three documents were most similar two-thirds to three-quarters of the time. Using this measure of topical similarity instead of the CoLab contest categories helps us generalize results beyond the Climate CoLab structure which requires manual creation of a topic hierarchy and manual assignment of proposals to those categories (here, by proposal authors who are not experts about the categorization scheme).

### Selecting topically unrelated proposals

For each focal proposal, we sorted other proposals according to the same LDA/cosine similarity scale and randomly selected from the bottom half of that distribution, ensuring that it was by a different author, operationalizing relationship "D" referenced in Table 1.

We drew proposals operationalizing relationship "A" in Table 1 from this same bottom half of the distribution. If the author had multiple proposals there, we chose the one more different from the focal proposal (this happened in only one of the four sets, and the two options were adjacent to each other in the list). In all eight cases, these proposals were from contests different than the focal proposal.

### Proposal Tweaks

Proposal summaries were modified from the originals for greater suitability for use in the experimental setting and consistency with each other in the following ways. Hyperlinks and text references to other proposals were removed, to make the summary more self-contained. Special formatting was removed. Acronyms that were not clearly introduced but discoverable in the original context (e.g. GHG) were spelled out. Spelling and grammar were cleaned up so that these attributes of writing would not dominate or interfere with perceptions of quality based on other factors, removing this potential source of variance for a cleaner experiment. One proposal summary was shortened (largely by removing redundancy) to bring its length in line with the others, appropriate for a Mechanical Turk task. After these modifications, the proposal summary lengths ranged from 168 to 350 words, with an average of 290 and standard deviation of 48. Material length was comparable with a previous study based on news articles [25].

### Selecting names

Because author attribution is a factor being explored in this experiment, we attach author names to proposals to help underscore the "same author" relationship. However, researchers presenting experimental materials with names attached need to be aware of the impact of those names, because aspects of the name (such as perceived gender) can change the way participants perceive the materials attributed to them [8].

Through a set of four studies, Fleet and Atwater [8] identify four most gender-neutral *first/given names* and of these four we chose the two most prevalent ("Expected total number alive today" male + female total) in the United States according to the Wolfram|Alpha Knowledgebase, 2016 (e.g. [29]), which were Terry and Lee respectively.

We used only a surname initial instead of a full surname according to the advice of Kasof [14:152]. The US Census publishes the frequency of *surnames* occurring >100 times, covering 90% of the population [30]; at the time of study the most recent available data is from the 2000 Census. (First name information is not available from the 2000 census.) Within this data, the most common first letter (surname initial) is M, followed closely by S.

We crossed these two for balance. In our experiment, the focal proposal was always credited to "Terry S." and the other proposal, if by a different author, was credited to "Lee M." An experiment by Howard & Kerin [12] found that *similarity* between a participant's name and the putative name of an author whose work the participant was evaluating (in the experiment, first name and last initial were shown to match or not match participants'), engages self-referencing and increases thoughtful examination. Here, we did not ask for participants' real names, but we don't expect any rare overlaps to lead to differences between the randomly assigned experimental groups.

### Dependent Measures

As in work by Towne et al. [26], we consider quality assessment criteria used in the community where the data comes from. In the Climate CoLab, proposals are assessed by expert judges along four scales: Feasibility (in four specific aspects), Novelty, Impact, and Presentation [3]. These criteria and their descriptions have been consistent through the history of the platform. We requested each participant evaluate each proposal using the following seven-point Likert items, each with {{Strongly, Moderately, Slightly} {Agree, Disagree}}, Neutral, and "I don't know" options:

*"Based on the excerpt shown above, I believe the proposal as a whole is likely to...*

*...be {technically, economically, socially, politically} feasible." (4 questions, answers averaged for feasibility)*

*...be novel, reflecting innovative thinking and originality."*

*...make an impact on the issue raised in the prompt, if it were implemented."*

*...be well-presented."*

For an overall measure of quality, on the same scale, we also asked included an item (from [15] and [26]) *"Based on the excerpt shown above, I believe this proposal should be included in a collection of high quality proposals."* This is the fifth item in a five-item perceived quality scale that is our primary dependent variable. In relatively rare cases where a participant refused to answer any particular item, that item simply carries no weight in computation of the composite (mean) rating for that participant and scale.

### Demographics & prior expertise

Before the task, participants answered questions about their educational background and level of interest and experience in the general domain area of the content material, including questions copied from prior surveys of the community where materials came from.

We recognize that prior knowledge about a topic has been identified as a potentially dominant factor in quality evaluations [25] in work that explicitly seeks follow-up studies illuminating the impact of issue familiarity on the effect of comments [25:71]. Also, people who have more prior knowledge or are more involved do more elaborate information processing, attend to more quality cues, especially intrinsic ones, and may be less extreme but possibly faster in their overall quality judgments [23:315]. Therefore, after each evaluation, we included an item "I have expertise on the topic(s) discussed in this proposal." As the final multiple-choice question in our study, we asked participants about their level of familiarity with the platform from which materials were drawn.

### Participants & Filters

We recruited participants on Amazon's Mechanical Turk paid crowdsourcing platform, in part because the population for generalizability of results is intended to broadly include those likely to visit/use crowdsourcing platforms. (Our materials come from a different crowdsourcing platform, described above.) This choice of participant pool also has several other benefits relevant to experiments exploring the impact of social information on perceptions in *CHI* [13]. Our tasks were posted midweek, on days describes as slow (with respect to the volume of tasks being posted) on the Turker Nation forum. Tasks were posted through afternoon and evening times and continued at a slower pace into the following day.

We reduced potential evaluation variance by restricting participants to those who were in the United States according to their Turk profile, and prior to analysis we filtered out any data from participants who did not have a GeoIP lookup resolving to the United States. We also restricted participation to those who had at least 500 assignments approved by other requesters and a 95% overall approval rating. (This is the same as in [27]). In the main experiment, we also excluded from analysis two participants who wrote keyboard-mashing strings in unselected "other" boxes on demographic questions, and two participants who took steps to defeat the participation limits. We filtered out those who completed the main experiment in under 2.5 minutes because less than one minute per proposal plus 30 seconds for demographic questions indicates those participants are less likely to have fully read the materials or questions.

Both usage goals and time pressure also affect perceptions of quality [23:316], and we held these constant across experimental conditions. During the task, we specified usage goals (proposal evaluation) and did not add any time pressure beyond what is self-imposed by participants independently of the task (similar to e.g. [25]), permitting an hour for a task which typically took several minutes.

At the very end of our task, participants also had an open text box to optionally provide feedback about what they had just completed. We have found this to be a best practice that can facilitate detection of certain errors in experimental setup if they exist, provide qualitative feedback that can help inform future analyses and/or task designs, and increase participant satisfaction by allowing participants to express any remaining thoughts they wanted to express. We read all feedback submitted.

## MANIPULATION CHECK ON COMMENTS

### Manipulation Check on Comments: Design

The comments for each focal proposal and experimental type were created by authors of this paper based on a review of real comments left on proposals on the site, similar to the setup in [26].

Before proceeding with the experiment, we checked to see if the differences between experimental conditions were manipulating the intended constructs. To do this, each of the 24 comments was posted to Turk along with the following 8 statements assessed on the same 7-point agree/disagree scale described above, followed by a free-text feedback field:

1. This comment is civil.

2. This comment is directed at the *author* of the proposal.

3. This comment is directed at the *content* of the proposal.

4. The author of the comment and the author of the proposal likely have some conflicting views, at least regarding what this comment is about.

5. If there is conflict present, it seems likely to have a good resolution. (If there is not conflict present, please choose "neutral.")

6. If this comment were automatically analyzed, it **should** be scored as a *negative* comment.

7. If this comment were automatically analyzed, it **should** be scored as a *positive* comment.

8. This comment is likely to be helpful to the person who wrote the proposal the comment is on.

We paid US$0.12 per comment reviewed. In this manipulation check, participants were allowed to participate up to 6 times, each time randomly selecting one of the six comment types not previously evaluated by that worker, and randomly selecting one of the four focal proposals. Participants in the manipulation check were not allowed to participate in the main experiment.

### Manipulation Check on Comments: Results

160 unique Turkers, who passed the same inclusion restrictions applying to the main experiment, completed 432 rating tasks. Based in part on the results detailed below, we believe our comment type manipulations were successful.

#### *Comparison between (focal) proposals*

We checked each of the eight questions, plus time on task, and (using an ANOVA) looked for any significant differences between the four focal proposals. In cases where the Levene statistic rejects the null hypothesis that group variances are homogeneous, we use the Welch statistic as it is more appropriate than the $F$ statistic to test for the equality of group means. We found only 3 significant differences ($\alpha$=.05), which matches the expected number of randomly significant comparisons with 6 comment types and 9 comparisons each (6*9=54 comparisons). When all comment types were aggregated together, there were no significant differences between focal proposals on any of the 9 measures.

#### *Author-directed vs. Content-directed: Questions 2 & 3*

The author-directedness of the comment (Question 2) was significantly ($p$<.0005) higher in the author-directed conditions, considering the data overall (4.09 vs. 6.22 Likert points) or each proposal set independently, or each level of the "conflict" factor independently.

The content-directedness of the comment (Question 3) was significantly ($p$<.0005) higher in the content-directed conditions, considering the data overall (4.63 vs. 6.50 Likert points) or each proposal set independently, or each level of the "conflict" factor independently.

#### *Conflict vs. non-conflict conditions: Questions 4 & 5*

The comment's level of conflict (Question 4) was significantly ($p$<.0005) higher in the conflict conditions, considering the data overall (2.49 vs 5.53 Likert points) or each proposal set independently, or each level of the "direction" factor independently. The 95% confidence intervals for the mean of this item are fully on the "disagree" side for non-conflict conditions and on the "agree" side for conflict conditions.

Excluding non-conflict comment conditions from analysis, the conflict's likelihood of a good resolution (Question 5) was significantly ($p$<.0005) higher in the constructive conflict conditions than the "no good resolution" conditions, considering the data overall (3.16 vs 5.01 Likert points) or each proposal set independently, or each level of the "direction" factor independently ($p$=.001 in content-directed conditions).

#### *Timing*

The amount of time taken to complete the rating task was not significantly different across comment types, considering the data overall or each proposal set independently.

#### *Comment type 4 more negative*

The civility, positivity, and helpfulness of the comment (Questions 1, 7, & 8) were significantly ($p$<.0005) lower, and negativity (Question 6) significantly higher, in comment type 4 (author-directed unresolved conflict) than in the other comment types, considering the data overall or each proposal set independently.

#### *Sentiment and Civility: Questions 1, 6, 7 & 8*

All four of these questions were significantly correlated with each other ($p$<.0005 by Pearson or Spearman). Questions 6 and 7 were very strongly negatively correlated (Pearson's r: -.937; Spearman's $\rho$: -.930), as expected.

Comments were rated significantly ($p$<.0005) less civil, less positive, and more negative in conflict conditions than in non-conflict conditions, considering the data overall or each proposal set independently, or each level of the "direction" factor independently. Comments were rated significantly ($p$<.0005) less civil, less positive, and more negative in the conflict than non-conflict conditions even when excluding comment type 4 from analysis, overall or considering each level of the "direction" factor independently.

There are no civility or negativity differences between the two non-conflict conditions analyzing the data overall; the author-directed non-conflict condition is significantly ($p$=.001) more positive than the content-directed non-conflict condition.

In general, comments were scored as significantly ($p$<.0005) more civil and helpful when directed at the content than when directed at the author, overall and (with $p$<.05 on "civil") considering each proposal set independently.

There were no significant differences between author-directed and content-directed comments in positivity or negativity, considering the data overall.

The helpfulness of the comment (Question 8) was significantly (.0005<$p$<.01) lower in conflict than non-conflict conditions when analyzed overall.

## MAIN EXPERIMENT RESULTS

After filtering as described above, we had 1252 responses. The median task completion time was 331.5 seconds, with an interquartile range of (246, 463) seconds.

### Multi-Item Scales

In this subsection, we describe and validate the multi-item scales used in our primary dependent measure. We provide evidence supporting the unidimensional treatment of our dependent construct "rated (or 'perceived') quality."

Cronbach's Alpha for the four-item feasibility scale is .869 (n=2391). An exploratory Principal Components analysis with these four items also showed all four loading onto a single principal component, and all four items were significantly (p<.0005) and strongly (average >0.6 by Pearson or Spearman) correlated with each other.

Cronbach's Alpha for the five-item quality scale, which includes the feasibility scale as one item, is .865 (n=2343). An exploratory Principal Components analysis with these five items also showed all five loading onto a single principal component, and all five items were significantly (p<.0005) and strongly (average >0.55 by Pearson or Spearman) correlated with each other. This is our multi-item perceived quality scale.

In order to increase comparability across the four proposal sets and reduce noise due to inherent differences in proposal quality, we compute the overall average quality rating for each proposal and compute each participant's rating as a deviation from that proposal-specific mean. This centered measure is our primary dependent variable for proposal quality evaluations discussed below. Unless otherwise noted, reported results are from planned contrast analyses within a larger ANOVA across comment types, with or without the assumption of homogeneous variances.

### Main differences in ratings of focal proposal

Differences in the type of comment shown on the focal proposal caused significant differences in how participants rated the quality of that proposal. The conflict conditions led to significantly lower ratings of quality than the non-conflict or non-comment conditions (-.3071 vs .4334 Likert points, p<.0005), replicating the negative effect of conflict observed in [26] and **supporting H2**. (Table 2 below summarizes findings for each hypothesis.)

We did not observe any significant differences in the ratings of either proposal based on conflict resolution within conflict conditions, nor between "non conflict" and "no comment" conditions. Finding no significant difference in the latter comparison means we **do not find support for H1**.

### Differences in ratings of second proposal

There was a small but significant (p<.0005, n=1249) correlation between participant's quality ratings of the first and second proposal (r=.229, ρ=.194 for deviation from proposal means as used here; r=.188, ρ=.155 for raw scale score), most likely indicating a per-rater effect that some raters were generally more generous and others more strict. Our experimental design controls for this by randomly assigning participants to experimental conditions, so we would not expect any systematic differences in rater scoring bias between the experimental conditions.

We did not find any statistically significant differences in the ratings of the second proposal caused by differences in the type of comment displayed on the first. Although differences in the rating of the first proposal based on comment type were observed, we did not find comment-caused differences in ratings of the second proposal even when the second proposal that was actually and was labeled as being by the same author or about similar topics. This is a **lack of support for H3, H4, and H5**.

### Learning from comments

Most participants (>60% at each level of the "conflict" factor) agreed with the statement "I learned something from the comments." Participants reported strongest agreement (along the same 7-point Likert scale described above) with "I learned something from the comment(s)" in the "constructive conflict" comments, followed by the "non-conflict" and then "unresolved conflict" comments (group means of 5.18, 4.85, and 4.57 Likert points respectively, all differences statistically significant even with Tukey's Honestly Significant Differences test). This provides **support for H7.**

Further, participants' self-reported learning from the comments correlates significantly (p<.0005 overall and for each conflict type) with how much they thought "reading the comments *raised* my perception of proposal quality" (r=.567, ρ=.550, n=1044 overall). The correlation was strongest (r=.768, ρ=.751, n=333) in the non-conflict condition.

As expected, the degrees to which participants thought the comments *raised* and *lowered* their perception of proposal quality were significantly (p<.0005 in each conflict condition and overall, n=1053 overall) negatively correlated with each other (r=-.427; ρ=-.449 overall). The correlation was strongest in the constructive conflict condition (r=-.689; ρ=-.697, n=375). In general, significant differences on one or both of these measures were observed alongside significant differences in actual quality ratings, in a direction consistent with the observed effect, indicating **no support for H6**.

At least half the participants (at any level of the "conflict" factor) believed that the comments did not lower their perception of proposal quality (i.e. selected a "disagree" option on the "lowered" question) and most participants believed that reading the comments raised their perception of proposal quality. This aligns with the previous finding that participants believe seeing discussion increases their perception of the quality of the material discussed [26].

### Power

Where we do not observe a difference between experimental groups, that logically means that either (A) no significant difference exists between the groups, (B) the experiment was not designed properly to detect a difference, or (C) the difference between groups was so small that our experiment did not have sufficient power to detect it. (B) seems relatively unlikely given how closely our design mirrors a design that has previously identified differences [26] as well as the results of the manipulation check above. (C) appears relatively unlikely, based on computations using G*Power 3.1.9.2 [7] to identify how small of an effect we would have still had a 95% chance of observing, if it existed. For the ANOVA used here, the effect size parameter $f$ is considered "small" at .1, "medium" at .25, and "large" at .40 [5:348].

Aggregating across relationships between proposals (Table 1 conditions) and looking for differences between second proposal ratings caused by comment types, we would have had a 95% chance of observing differences between cells with an effect size index of .13 or greater, and .10 or greater in a two-group comparison (e.g. conflict conditions vs. others). The minimum effect size observable with 95% probability is .17-.18 for a two-way comparison within any one of the Table 1 cells. The power for observing a medium size effect is 99.9% for a two-group comparison between comment types within any one of the Table 1 cells and higher for even a 7-group comparison aggregating across them.

### Demographics

Prior work demonstrates that pre-existing cultural context can impact the way readers are affected by comments [25]. We report demographics here for easier comparison to other participant populations and more detailed identification of our participant pool. The initial questions and responses were as follows, except that questions 2 and 6 also each had an infrequently used "other" option manually recoded for analysis into the most similar available listed category.

1. Do you think that global warming is happening? {Yes: 85.7%, No: 6.5%, Don't know: 7.8%, n=1237}

2. Assuming global warming is happening, do you think it is … {Caused mostly by human activities: 49.8%, Caused mostly by natural changes in the environment: 10.3%, None of the above because global warming isn't happening: 2.7%, Caused by both human activities and natural changes: 37.1%, n=1250}

3. What is your gender? {Female: 50.4%, Male: 49.6%, n=1241}

4. What is your age? {under 20: 1.4%, 21- 29: 31.0%, 30- 39: 33.9%, 40- 49: 18.3%, 50- 64: 13.3%, 65 and over: 2.1%, n=1249}

5. What is the highest level of education you have attained to date? {High school or less: 17.1%, Attending college / university: 20.6%, Graduated from college / university: 46.3%, Attending graduate or professional school: 2.8%, Completed graduate or professional school: 13.3%, n=1245}

6. What is your current situation / status? {Student: 7.6%, Employed full-time: 54.7%, Employed part-time: 14.0%, Free-lance consultant: 7.5%, Unemployed [or homemaker]: 12.9%, Retired: 3.3%, n= 1244}

Last (after task). I am familiar with the MIT Climate CoLab. {Strongly disagree: 62.8%, Moderately disagree: 21.2%, Slightly disagree: 6.6%, Neutral 4.5%, Slightly agree: 2.9%, Moderately agree 1.1%, Strongly agree 0.9%, n= 1234}

### Findings with Demographic Covariates

In addition to our primary hypotheses looking at how randomly assigned experimental conditions affect the target variables, we also did some analyses exploring how some of our observations may have interacted with demographic variables, which may help guide future research.

Among participants with no college degree, the constructive conflict led to significantly *lower* ratings than the unresolved conflict (contrast value .3865 points, p=.006-.008), while college graduates tended to rate the proposal quality significantly higher after viewing a non-conflict comment than after viewing no comment (contrast value .3141 points, p=.019-.021). Among participants reading comments illustrating unresolved conflict, college graduates rated the proposal slightly higher than non-college grads (contrast value .2950 points, p=.038), even though in the no-comment control condition college grads on average rated proposals slightly lower (contrast value .4044 points, p=.016-.022). This suggests that the more educated readers may have viewed the materials with a bit more critical and independent thinking.

Among comment conditions, the author-directed comments surprisingly led to higher quality evaluations than the content-directed comments in the "Constructive Conflict" conditions only, (-.4843 vs -.2048 Likert points, p=.017), which was enough to create an overall difference between content- and author-directed conditions (-.1564 vs. .0365 Likert points, p=.009). In further exploration, this significant difference in rating was only observed among female participants but not male participants, and among college graduates but not those without a college degree. Rater gender and college education were independent according to a chi-square test with a 95% chance of observing a "small" effect (effect size index w=.10 [7]).

### Effect of Expertise

We found a small but statistically significant correlation between self-reported expertise on a proposal's topics and participants' quality rating of that proposal, both for the first proposal (r=.078 / p=.006; ρ=.093 / p = .001, n=1242) and the second proposal (r=.103 / p<.0005; ρ=.070 / p = .013, n=1250). There was also a small correlation between self-reported expertise on the first proposal's topics and if the comments raised participants' quality perceptions (r=.142; ρ=.133, p < .0005, n=1055). In general, more than three quarters of participants' self-reported topic-specific expertise level was on the "disagree" side of the scale and less than 14% of expertise self-reports were on the "agree" side of the scale (n=2492). Especially combined with random assignment to the experimental conditions, we do not believe that pre-existing judgments about the material dominated quality evaluations (as when different materials were used in [25]).

## CONCLUSIONS

| # | Hypothesis |
|---|---|
| ~~H1~~ | Comment presence lowers 1st proposal qual. ratings |
| H2 | Comment type & conflict affects size of H1 effect |
| ~~H3~~ | H1 effect extends to other proposals from platform |
| ~~H4~~ | Content-directed comments on one proposal affect quality ratings on a topically related proposal |
| ~~H5~~ | Author-directed comments on one proposal affect quality ratings on another proposal by that author |
| ~~H6~~ | Participants report perceptions being affected by comments in opposite direction from true effect |
| H7 | Participants learn most from comments containing constructive conflict |

**Table 2: Summary of hypotheses. "No support" results where power calculations indicate a true effect would likely have been seen are indicated by ~~red strikethrough~~ on the left. Hypotheses supported by statistically significant differences are indicated by green underline in the left column.**

In this large-scale [13] experiment, we showed that when comments about crowdsourced content are presented alongside that content, the contents of the comment affect how people perceive the content. We replicated a previous finding that comments containing conflict lower perceptions of content quality more strongly than comments which do not indicate conflict, but noted that readers reported learning more from constructive conflict comments than comments without conflict or without a good resolution. Participants in this study were also aware of the effects comments had on their perceptions of proposal quality, reporting significantly different answers (in the aligned direction) about how reading comments raised and/or lowered their perception of quality, when such differences were observed between their ratings.

We also observed that although the presence of comments may affect perceptions of the proposal the comment is on, that effect **does not** carry over to a second proposal read and judged in quick succession (in this case, on the same Web page), even when the second proposal is by the same author or about a similar mix of topics, and that connection between the proposals is called out with underlined bold header font. Participants in our experiment were apparently able to evaluate the second proposal independently after whatever effects the comment may have had on their perception of the first proposal. This result is encouraging for the future development of platforms that crowdsource proposals about how to solve some particular challenge, where readers may be evaluating those proposals either as part of a platform-hosted contest or for their own reasons (e.g. deciding what proposals to back or adopt in practice).

## DISCUSSION

While large-scale observational data sets for many online interaction and content production platforms are now available, observational data does not allow us to distinguish between perceptions based on underlying qualities from those based on other factors which may affect perceptions [19:647]. Controlled experiments with random assignment of the factor being examined, as done here, allows us to draw causal conclusions about the differences between levels of the randomly assigned factor.

This study contributes to a small set of related studies in the field. For example, Steinfeld, Samuel-Azran, and Lev-On recently published what they described as the first study to examine how readers' perceptions of news articles' quality is affected by a set of comments presented below the article [25]. The study used eye trackers and post-study interviews to measure the attention users paid to the comments. Its setting intended to capture participants' common views about comments sections in online news sites, and found that most participants did not even read the comments, fewer than one in ten read any comments in detail, and even in those cases readers (undergraduates, mostly new first-years, at an Israeli college) often heavily discounted the content of the comments based on stereotypes about people who write them. As a result, that study found that the comments did not influence participants' evaluations of the articles, but drew a primary conclusion emphasizing the need to continue to "map the interplay between user comments and public opinion across various topics and domains" [25:72].

Past work at *CHI* specifically has looked at crowdsourced visual presentations of data and how comments on that data by other users affects later users' quantitative perceptions of graphical information. For example, Hullman, Adar, & Shah [13] asked Turkers to judge proportions or linear association strengths from charts, and found that these judgments were affected by a "social histogram" putatively showing prior viewers' estimates. However, the effects of biased information did not carry over to subsequent chart-perceiving tasks [13:1465]. That paper's Future Work section suggests exploring tasks more difficult than perception of quantitative information from the charts used there, where social influence is more likely to be observed. In this paper, we explored the task of evaluating the quality of a textually summarized proposal for addressing some aspect of a large, complex problem. Our results are consistent with that prior work about social influence on the perception of quantitative content [13], extending that result into more subjective judgments about content quality.

Social influence signals (e.g. comments) affect readers' perception of the content most directly related to the influence signals (e.g. proposals), as evidenced here. This experiment strengthens the call to be aware of these effects and consider them when designing such platforms and the "need to form new theories and models that explain the impact of social processes on community-driven visualization environments and lead to new systems" [13:1469].

## FUTURE WORK

### Anchor points

This experiment found results for H1 and H6 that were different from our source for those hypotheses [26], despite a strong degree of similarity in task setup and associated details. When considering differences in task setup that may have produced these differences in results, the most likely source seems to be the difference in materials used, i.e. Climate CoLab proposals (and proposal comments) compared to Wikipedia articles (and Talk page discussions).

In contrast to participants in the present study based on Climate CoLab proposals, participants in the experiment based on Wikipedia materials were generally unaware of the effect, particularly the between-subjects primary observation that the presence of even non-conflict comments (in that study) led to lower perceptions of article quality [26]. The difference in H6 suggests that a different psychological process may have been operating with the different materials, and this may have produced the difference in H1.

For example, it may be that in the previous study [26], the presence of comments caused participants to become more acutely aware of Wikipedia articles' draft-in-progress status and anchor their initial quality measurements based on that category, while participants who saw no discussion evaluated quality beginning from an anchor point more applicable to a reference work perceived as polished or complete. In the present experiment, expectation-driven anchor points for the quality of a document described only as a "proposal," even without comments, may have already been lower and perhaps more in line with a draft or work-in-progress than a well-regarded reference work, so the mere presence of comments may not have lowered an initial anchor point. This could explain our finding of no support for H1. To determine if this indeed the case, future work would need to explore how anchor points are set for evaluation and how the way people perceive discussion may differ depending on the status of the artifact being discussed.

In a set of experiments, Galak and Nelson [10] asked readers to evaluate the quality of short stories, experimentally varying the fluency of the text through presentation factors like a more compressed font or asking participants to furrow their brow while reading. They find that the quality rating effects caused by differences in fluency vary as a function of what the reader expects from the reading and the anticipated purpose of the reading (e.g. conveying information contrasted with maximizing enjoyment). It is possible that different purposes for reading cause different expectations, and thus different anchor points from which perceptions are adjusted, between Wikipedia articles and Climate CoLab proposals.

Work in this area relates to the Affective Expectation Model [28], a theory about how people's expectations affects their subjective judgments. In this theory, people who have expectations about the quality value of some content (in the original paper, the humor value of comics) quickly check for features in given material that match their expectations and if found, perceive qualities based on those expectations, even inaccurately. This is a more specific version of schema theory applied to affect [28:524]. According to this theory, people making more specific evaluations (such as with the multidimensional rating scale readers evaluated on here) are more likely to notice discrepancies between their expectations and the actual material being evaluated [28:524], so the most surprising aspects of the theory are unlikely to be responsible for the differences observed here. However, a major part of this theory is about how *quickly* and *easily* people form judgments and how deeply their thoughts are engaged in the material [28:528] and measuring this requires more detailed control over the experimental environment (e.g. lab study) as opposed to Mechanical Turk where variance in e.g. response times can be attributed to a wide variety of other causes. Further research is necessary to better understand the expectation factors that could more clearly link these results into theories that explain the results based on reader expectations.

### Larger Comment Sets

Because we used a randomized controlled experiment, we have some confidence the observed effects are *caused* by the presence and content of the comments. However, each participant saw only one comment posted on each proposal, while in real instances of the intended application environment there may be several comments posted on each proposal (as also seen in [25]), and readers may extract information from properties of the set, such as total/mean length, number of comments, unique participants, valence mean/variance, or other factors based on the interaction between commenters or between commenters and the proposal author, etc. This experiment held those factors relatively constant, and does not tell us if larger sets of comments with various properties would have led to different results. Future work would be needed to determine if more and/or more strongly critical comments have a cumulative effect.

## ACKNOWLEDGEMENTS

The authors gratefully acknowledge support from the National Science Foundation, grant #1302522. We also thank members of Daemo [9] for piloting the main experimental task, and the many Turkers who participated in either the main experiment or manipulation checks.

## REFERENCES


1. Sushil Bikhchandani, David Hirshleifer, and Ivo Welch. 1992. A Theory of Fads, Fashion, Custom, and Cultural Change as Informational Cascades. *Journal of Political Economy* 100, 5: 992–1026. Retrieved February 10, 2016 from http://www.jstor.org/stable/2138632
2. Dustin Carey. 2015. Comment 16: Language Requirement. Retrieved April 26, 2016 from http://climatecolab.org/contests/2016/shifting-behavior-for-a-changing-climate/c/proposal/1320702/tab/COMMENTS#_message_1349447
3. Climate CoLab. 2016. How will proposals be judged? Contest Rules. Retrieved March 2, 2016 from http://climatecolab.org/web/guest/resources/-/wiki/Main/contest+rules#Howwillproposalsbejudged
4. Climate CoLab. Climate CoLab Judges. Retrieved September 18, 2014 from http://climatecolab.org/resources/-/wiki/Main/Climate+CoLab+Judges
5. Jacob Cohen. 1969. *Statistical Power Analysis for the Behavioral Sciences*. Academic Press, New York.
6. Erik P. Duhaime, Gary M. Olson, and Thomas W. Malone. 2015. *Broad Participation in Collective Problem Solving Can Influence Participants and Lead to Better Solutions: Evidence from the MIT Climate CoLab*. MIT Center for Collective Intelligence, Cambridge, MA. Retrieved from http://cci.mit.edu/working_papers_2012_2013/duhaime%20colab%20wp%206-2015%20final.pdf
7. Franz Faul, Edgar Erdfelder, Axel Buchner, and Albert-Georg Lang. 2009. Statistical Power Analyses Using G*Power 3.1: Tests for Correlation and Regression Analyses. *Behavior Research Methods* 41, 4: 1149–1160. https://doi.org/10.3758/BRM.41.4.1149
8. David D. Van Fleet and Leanne Atwater. 1997. Gender Neutral Names: Don't Be So Sure! *Sex Roles* 37, 1–2: 111–123. https://doi.org/10.1023/A:1025696905342
9. S. Gaikwad, D. Morina, R. Nistala, M. Agarwal, A. Cossette, R. Bhanu, S. Savage, V. Narwal, K. Rajpal, J. Regino, A. Mithal, A. Ginzberg, A. Nath, K. R. Ziulkoski, T. Cossette, D. Gamage, A. Richmond-Fuller, R. Suzuki, J. Herrejon, K. V. Le, C. Flores-Saviaga, H. Thilakarathne, K. Gupta, W. Dai, A. Sastry, S. Goyal, T. Rajapakshe, N. Abolhassani, A. Xie, A. Reyes, S. Ingle, V. Jaramillo, M.D. Godinez, W. Angel, M. Godinez, C. Toxtli, J. Flores, A. Gupta, V. Sethia, D. Padilla, K. Milland, K. Setyadi, N. Wajirasena, M. Batagoda, R. Cruz, J. Damon, D. Nekkanti, T. Sarma, M.H. Saleh, G. Gongora-Svartzman, S. Bateni, G. Toledo-Barrera, A. Pena, R. Compton, D. Aariff, L. Palacios, M. P. Ritter, Nisha K.K., A. Kay, J. Uhrmeister, S. Nistala, M. Esfahani, E. Bakiu, C. Diemert, L. Matsumoto, M. Singh, V. Jaramillo-Lopez, K. Patel, R. Krishna, G. Kovacs, R. Vaish, and M. Bernstein. 2015. Daemo: a Self-Governed Crowdsourcing Marketplace. In *Proceedings of the 28th Annual ACM Symposium on User Interface Software & Technology* (UIST '15). Retrieved May 12, 2016 from https://uist.acm.org/uist2015/schedule#uistp142
10. Jeff Galak and Leif D. Nelson. 2011. The Virtues of Opaque Prose: How Lay Beliefs About Fluency Influence Perceptions of Quality. *Journal of Experimental Social Psychology* 47, 1: 250–253. https://doi.org/10.1016/j.jesp.2010.08.002
11. David Hirshleifer and Siew Hong Teoh. 2003. Herd Behaviour and Cascading in Capital Markets: a Review and Synthesis. *European Financial Management* 9, 1: 25–66. https://doi.org/10.1111/1468-036X.00207
12. Daniel J. Howard and Roger A. Kerin. 2011. The effects of name similarity on message processing and persuasion. *Journal of Experimental Social Psychology* 47, 1: 63–71. https://doi.org/10.1016/j.jesp.2010.08.008
13. Jessica Hullman, Eytan Adar, and Priti Shah. 2011. The Impact of Social Information on Visual Judgments. In *Proceedings of the SIGCHI Conference on Human Factors in Computing Systems* (CHI '11), 1461–1470. https://doi.org/10.1145/1978942.1979157
14. Joseph Kasof. 1993. Sex bias in the naming of stimulus persons. *Psychological Bulletin* 113, 1: 140–163. https://doi.org/10.1037/0033-2909.113.1.140
15. Aniket Kittur, Bongwon Suh, and Ed H. Chi. 2008. Can You Ever Trust a Wiki? In *Proceedings of the ACM 2008 Conference on Computer Supported Cooperative Work* (CSCW '08), 477. https://doi.org/10.1145/1460563.1460639
16. Thomas W. Malone, Robert Laubacher, and Laur Fisher. 2014. How Millions of People Can Help Solve Climate Change. *PBS NOVA Next*. Retrieved January 18, 2014 from http://www.pbs.org/wgbh/nova/next/earth/crowdsourcing-climate-change-solutions/
17. Thomas W. Malone, Jeffrey Nickerson, Robert Laubacher, Laur Fisher, Patrick de Boer, Yue Han, and W. Ben Towne. 2017. Putting the Pieces Back Together Again: Contest Webs for Large-Scale Problem Solving. In *Proceedings of the ACM 2017 Conference on Computer Supported Cooperative Work* (CSCW '17), In Press.
18. Pietro Michelucci and Janis L. Dickinson. 2016. The Power of Crowds. *Science* 351, 6268: 32–33. https://doi.org/10.1126/science.aad6499
19. Lev Muchnik, Sinan Aral, and Sean J. Taylor. 2013. Social Influence Bias: A Randomized Experiment.

*Science* 341, 6146: 647–651. https://doi.org/10.1126/science.1240466

20. Pinar Ozturk, Yue Han, W. Ben Towne, and Jeffrey V. Nickerson. 2016. Topic Prevalence and Reuse in an Open Innovation Community. In *Collective Intelligence*. Retrieved from https://sites.google.com/a/stern.nyu.edu/collective-intelligence-conference/

21. M. J Salganik, P. S Dodds, and D. J Watts. 2006. Experimental Study of Inequality and Unpredictability in an Artificial Cultural Market. *Science* 311, 5762: 854.

22. Clay Shirky. 2010. *Cognitive Surplus: Creativity and Generosity in a Connected Age*. Penguin.

23. Jan-Benedict E. M. Steenkamp. 1990. Conceptual Model of the Quality Perception Process. *Journal of Business Research* 21, 4: 309–333. https://doi.org/10.1016/0148-2963(90)90019-A

24. Joel Stein. 2016. How Trolls Are Ruining the Internet. *Time*. Retrieved September 14, 2016 from http://time.com/4457110/internet-trolls/

25. Nili Steinfeld, Tal Samuel-Azran, and Azi Lev-On. 2016. User Comments and Public Opinion: Findings from an Eye-Tracking Experiment. *Computers in Human Behavior* 61: 63–72. https://doi.org/10.1016/j.chb.2016.03.004

26. W. Ben Towne, Aniket Kittur, Peter Kinnaird, and James Herbsleb. 2013. Your Process Is Showing: Controversy Management and Perceived Quality in Wikipedia. In *Proceedings of the 2013 Conference on Computer Supported Cooperative Work* (CSCW '13), 1059–1068. https://doi.org/10.1145/2441776.2441896

27. W. Ben Towne, Carolyn P. Rosé, and James D. Herbsleb. 2016. Measuring Similarity Similarly: LDA and Human Perception. *ACM Transactions on Intelligent Systems and Technology* 8, 1: 7:1–7:28. https://doi.org/10.1145/2890510

28. Timothy D. Wilson, Douglas J. Lisle, Dolores Kraft, and Christopher G. Wetzel. 1989. Preferences as Expectation-Driven Inferences: Effects of Affective Expectations on Affective Experience. *Journal of Personality and Social Psychology* 56, 4: 519–530. https://doi.org/10.1037/0022-3514.56.4.519

29. Wolfram Alpha. 2016. Lee (given name). Retrieved April 28, 2016 from http://www.wolframalpha.com/input/?i=Lee+(given+name)

30. David L. Word, Charles D. Coleman, Robert Nunziata, and Robert Kominski. 2016. *Frequently Occurring Surnames Data*. US Census Bureau. Retrieved April 27, 2016 from http://www.census.gov/topics/population/genealogy/data.html

31. Gu Xu and Wei-Ying Ma. 2006. Building Implicit Links from Content for Forum Search. In *Proceedings of the 29th Annual International ACM SIGIR Conference on Research and Development in Information Retrieval* (SIGIR '06), 300–307. https://doi.org/10.1145/1148170.1148224

# Identification and Classification of Usage Patterns in Long-Term Activity Tracking

**Jochen Meyer**
**Merlin Wasmann, Wilko Heuten**
OFFIS Institute for Informatics
Oldenburg, Germany
{firstname.lastname}@offis.de

**Abdallah El Ali**
**Susanne C.J. Boll**
Carl von Ossietzky University
Oldenburg, Germany
{firstname.lastname@uol.de}

## ABSTRACT
Activity trackers are frequently used in health and well-being, but their application in effective interventions is challenging. While research for reasons of use and non-use is ongoing, little is known about the way activity trackers are used in everyday life and over longer periods. We analyzed data of 104 individuals over 14,413 use days, and in total over 2.5 years. We describe general tracker use, periodic changes and overall changes over time, and identify characteristic patterns. While the use of trackers shows large individual heterogeneity, from our findings we could identify and classify general patterns for activity tracker use such as try-and-drop, slow-starter, experimenter, hop-on hop-off, intermittent and power user. Our findings contribute to the body of knowledge towards the successful design of effective health technologies, health interventions, and long-term health applications.

### Author Keywords
Activity tracker; usage patterns; quantitative analysis; longitudinal use; activity monitoring

### ACM Classification Keywords
H.5.m. Information interfaces and presentation (e.g., HCI): Miscellaneous.

## INTRODUCTION
Physical activity is undoubtedly one of the most important behaviors in the prevention [33] or treatment [28] of numerous diseases such as obesity, diabetes, or cardio-vascular diseases. At the same time wellbeing and fitness are deemed socially desirable and being fit and active is part of a modern lifestyle. Within this context, activity trackers such as those from Fitbit, Garmin, Nike, Jawbone and other companies have become extremely popular.


*CHI 2017, May 06 - 11, 2017, Denver, CO, USA*

ACM 978-1-4503-4655-9/17/05...$15.00
DOI: http://dx.doi.org/10.1145/3025453.3025690

HCI research has investigated activity tracking for many years. Early systems such as UbiFit [6] or Fish-N-Steps[21] still used mobile phones as a sensing platform but already showed that interventions can successfully induce a change. While medical research has initially criticized activity trackers for their low precision in comparison to high-end accelerometers [30], they are now more and more understood as a new class of tools with distinct characteristics and acceptable precision [13] that is useful in e.g. epidemiological studies [3]. Activity trackers are used in numerous contexts such as personal wellbeing and fitness, life and health logging, but also health behavior change interventions and research studies. Despite their popularity, however, the use of activity trackers in health interventions is still challenging, and their success is not undisputed. While existing research has studied the effectiveness of activity tracker–based intervention, the reasons why people use activity trackers, and when and why they stop, the researchers have primarily looked at these subjects qualitatively [9] and only for short time periods.

To fully understand how activity trackers are used over longer periods of time, we studied long-term usage patterns across four different user cohorts in different studies. In this paper we present how activity trackers are used in different settings, in everyday life, and over prolonged periods of time. We provide an in-depth analysis of data from more than 100 users giving insights into when and how trackers are used. We identify usage patterns for short-term and long-term activity tracker users. From our observations we discuss implications for the design and utilization of activity tracker–based health interventions.

## STATE OF THE ART
Activity trackers are a billion dollar market, with 22.5 million devices shipped in Q2/2016 alone [17]. The devices are easily used in daily life [23], including by elderly persons [12] and, with proper preparation, even by very difficult target groups such as dementia patients [32]. Nevertheless, their use still imposes technical and practical problems [16] and it is not yet clear if they will be used and contribute to personal wellbeing over longer periods of time.

### Effectiveness of Activity Tracker–Based Interventions

Studies of the effectiveness of activity tracker–based interventions show mixed results. A meta-study conducted by Bravata et al. [2] showed significant increase of physical activity for pedometer users. And Connelly et al. [5] found that of 15 studies aiming to increase physical activity in type 2 diabetes patients using technology all reported an increase.

On the other hand, an analysis by Bort-Roig et al. [1] found that of 17 studies evaluating a mobile phone–based intervention to increase physical activity only 4 reported an increase in physical activity over up to six months. And in a pedometer-based intervention for elderly women conducted by McMurdo et al. [22] there was an increase after three months, but no significant difference beyond six months. Etkin [11] even found negative effects of short-term interventions: although step counting increased the participants' physical activity, it also reduced the joy of walking.

### Long-Term Use, Abandonment, and Compliance

While behavior change interventions are the most obvious use for activity trackers, the potential beyond behavior change arising from long-term use of activity trackers is now receiving more attention. Karapanos et al. [18] found that, in the long term, the user's thoughts about the behavior become less important as the incentive to continue; rather, the decision to continue is driven more by improved physical health and social relationships; rather user experience is driven by physical thriving and social relatedness. Based on interviews with 30 users of activity trackers [14] Fritz et al. suggest design implications for long-term support, including motivation to maintain gains already made, as well as to continue to change, and the need to support changes in activity and metrics.

The long-term potential of activity trackers, however, is lost by early abandonment. A market survey from 2014 found that one-third of all activity trackers are abandoned within 6 months [8]. Various research studies report similar or worse experiences: In a study by Lazar et al. [20] 80% of devices were abandoned after 2 weeks. And in a study by Shih et al. [31] 75% of 26 undergraduate students with activity trackers stopped using the tracker within four weeks.

Initial work has recently been presented discussing different types of user compliance in using activity trackers: In a long-term study, Purta et al. [29] found that users are either very compliant or not at all. Epstein et al. [10] suggest three basic types of use patterns: short use, long and consistent use, and intermittent use. While a detailed classification of use patterns has been done, e.g. for smartphone app use [35], we are not aware of similar work for activity tracker use.

### Reasons for Use and Non-Use

There is growing consent among researchers on reasons for abandonment. Shih et al. found three categories: a misfit between devices and participants' self-conceptions, the collected data not being useful, and too much effort for use. Epstein et al. [9] found six themes among the reasons: cost of collecting, cost of ownership, discomfort with information, data quality concerns, learned enough, and change in life circumstances. And Clawson et al. [4] found various detailed reasons, including expectation mismatch, technical complexity, and goal met.

Shih also found reasons for ongoing use: perceived usefulness, novelty and curiosity, hope for potential future use, and developed routine of use. Finally Gouveia et al. [15] found that activity trackers are "'deficit technologies' that 'scaffold' behavior during particular problematic moments in time, and 'transformational' technologies that instill and routinize new practices to the point that the technology is no more necessary."

## APPROACH

We contribute to the ongoing research about use and abandonment of activity trackers by analyzing actual use of activity trackers in different settings, in the long term, and in real life. Complementing the existing research on *why* people use or do not use trackers, and going beyond initial work on compliance [10,29] we investigate *how* people use the trackers. Rather than looking at outcomes such as changes, we strictly focus only on use. Our findings contribute to understanding the users' needs and thus facilitate the design of better activity tracker–based interventions. To the best of our knowledge our approach has not been pursued before. Our work is therefore also meant to explore the opportunities from these analyses and to open the door for follow-up activities to confirm and extend our findings.

### General Setup

Our analyses are based on data from more than 100 users collected in two intervention studies, one observational study, and in-the-wild data. These sources enable us to observe differences of use in different settings. In all four cases, the users tracked their physical activity in their daily lives using an off-the-shelf activity tracker. One intervention study is a short-term study of 12 weeks; the other three studies are long term, ongoing since at least 9 months and not limiting the duration of use of activity trackers, but leaving it to the user when to stop. The two intervention studies have been approved by ethical review committees and registered at public trial registers; all studies and the respective procedures have been approved by data protection officers. After receiving the users' consent we collected the data by accessing the tracker's corresponding internet service using the API provided by the manufacturers.

Depending on the study, different complementary data were available. We took into account a minimal core set that we deemed particularly relevant for activity tracker use. Not all data are available for all sources or all users, and for some data, measures are different between different sources. An

| | IPP 1YearRehab | PROMOTE 12WeekIntervention | Lotus 9MonthObservation | VitaDock LongTermInTheWild |
|---|---|---|---|---|
| **Study overview** | | | | |
| setting | Longitudinal intervention study | Short-term intervention study | Longitudinal observation study | Longitunal in-the-field use |
| duration of study | >= 1 year | 12 weeks | >=9 months | arbitrary |
| influence of study on tracker use | low to medium | high | medium | low; opt-in |
| # users w/ activity data | 43 | 17 | 5 | 39 |
| **Tools used** | | | | |
| tracker | Medisana ViFit | Fitbit Zip | Fitbit Ultra, One, Flex | Medisana ViFit |
| affinity to technology range | TA-EG 0-76 (highest) | n/a | BMTC 0-48 (highest) | self-assessed 1-5 (highest) |
| fitness, health, phys. activity; range | n/a | self-assessed health status; 1-5 (best) | IPAQ lo - med - hi | self-assessed fitness 1-5 (best) |
| **Demographics** | | | | |
| # users with demogr. | 22 | 6 | 5 | 38 |
| age | 34-74 ($\bar{x}$ 55.3, σ 11.3) | 67-70 ($\bar{x}$ 68.0, σ 1.1) | 33-56 ($\bar{x}$ 47.5, σ 9.0) | 17-80 ($\bar{x}$ 53.4, σ 13.9) |
| sex | 22 m | 3m, 3f | 2m, 3f | 26m, 10f, 2 n/a |
| affinity to technology | 5-68 ($\bar{x}$ 45.0, σ 15.7) | n/a | 30-40 ($\bar{x}$ 36.0, σ 4.2) | 3-5 ($\bar{x}$ 4.4, σ 0.7) |
| fitness, phys. activity | n/a | 1-3 ($\bar{x}$ 2.3, σ 0.8) | 2 hi, 2 med, 1 low | 1-5 ($\bar{x}$ 3.1, σ 1.0) |

**Table 1. Overview of studies and characteristics.**
**Measures used: IPAQ [7], TA-EG [19]. BMTC - Brief Measure for Technology Commitment [26]**

overview over the studies and the available data is given in Table 1. After the initial presentation we use meaningful codenames for the studies, also given in the table.

### Studies

**1YearRehab - IPP Intervention Study:** IPP[1] is a multi-centric, comparative study involving patients aged 18-75 who suffered from a myocardial infarction in the last 30 days [34]. The primary goal of IPP is to improve rehabilitation in the 12 months after the infarct using an intensive prevention program (IPP) consisting of, among others, regular coaching, education, and clinical assessments. Patients in the intervention group were offered a Medisana[2] ViFit activity tracker and access to an online portal for regular observation of their compliance to heart friendly living, replacing a subjective self-assessment of physical activity with the objective monitoring by the ViFit tracker. 43 patients in the intervention group accepted and used a tracker; their data are used in our study. Of these, 22 filled out the demographic questionnaires at the beginning of the study. The patients were invited but not obligated to use the tracker. Moreover the tracker was not the focus but merely a side-measure of the intervention, so we assume that the study's influence on tracker usage is low to medium.

**12WeekIntervention - PROMOTE Intervention Study:** The PROMOTE study[3] investigates the effects of tailored physical activity interventions for elderly persons aged 65-75 [25]. The study is conducted successively in multiple local communities. Within two intervention groups and one control group, the participants' fitness is assessed pre- and post-study. The intervention groups conduct a 12-week training program tailored to their needs and abilities according to the initial assessment. Both intervention groups have access to a web portal for an online diary of their activities and as an exchange and information platform. One intervention group self-assesses their physical activity using the diary; the other intervention group additionally uses a Fitbit Zip for objective monitoring of physical activity. This group's data from two local communities are used in our study. For this group the use of the tracker was mandatory; we therefore assume that the study's influence on tracker usage is high.

**9MonthObservation - Lotus Observation Study :** The aim of the Lotus study is to observe the long-term use of

[1] Registered at ClinicalTrials.gov; study id NCT01896765

[2] A German company manufacturing consumer health devices and operating the "Vitadock" connected health service. see www.medisana.com and https://cloud.vitadock.com/?lang=en

[3] Registered at German Clinical Trials Register. https://drks-neu.uniklinik-freiburg.de/drks_web/; study id DRKS00010052.

networked health devices by average users under real-life circumstances. Seven persons are equipped with a comprehensive set of consumer devices for tracking physical activity, sleep, and weight for at least 9 months. The participants are requested to use the devices according to their own discretion and only as they see fit. Nevertheless we found that participants felt some urge to use the tracker "to deliver proper data". We therefore assume that the study's influence on tracker usage is medium. Due to technical access problems, two persons' data had to be excluded from analysis.

**LongTermInTheWild - VitaDock Data Analysis Study:** In a fourth study we acquired data from activity tracker users in the wild. In a newsletter sent to the customers of Medisana's connected health service "VitaDock" and in the VitaDock Facebook page we invited the recipients to provide us with their activity data and pointed them to an online system that we built for this purpose. After they granted our system access to their VitaDock account, their activity data were downloaded to our database. We then presented a short questionnaire with some demographic questions and self assessments which the users could, but were not required to, fill in. As this data is collected in the wild and ex-post there is no maximum duration in this setting, and there is no influence of the study on tracker use. However the opt-in procedure for providing the data may have induced a bias towards more engaged users.

Compared to general tracker users our population is slightly older and more male: A random sample of 1,463 ViFit users (independent of our population) showed a median of 47.8 years and 53.6% male; and US data from 2015 [27] showed 36% in age group 35-54 and 25% in age group 55+, and 46% male.

## DATA PROCESSING

The activity data come as time series denoting for each user and each day the steps performed per minute (Fitbit) or per 15 minutes (Medisana ViFit). In rare cases we found some obviously wrong entries: 29 days (0.5% of the data) dated to the year 2000. And on 50 days we found 15-min intervals with more than 3,700 steps (long distance runners make less than 3,000 steps per 15 minutes). We ignored the respective days.

| Measure | Description |
|---|---|
| **use day** | a day on which a user has recorded at least 500 steps |
| **first / last day of use** | a user's temporal first/last use day |
| **duration of use** | total time from first to last use day |
| **density of period** | relation of number of use days in a period to length of period, range [0..1] |
| **total density** | density for duration of use |
| **use days per week** | Alternative measure for density per week with range [0..7] |
| **streak** | uninterrupted series of use days |
| **break** | uninterrupted series of non-use days |
| **phase** | a series of streaks interrupted by short breaks, ending with a long break |

**Table 2. Terms and measures.**

Measuring activity tracker usage is challenged by the fact that both non-use of the device and wearing the device while being inactive result in 0 steps for that time interval and cannot easily be distinguished. To the best of our knowledge this is true for all activity trackers today, and it is certainly true for the trackers used in the four studies. However, also in sufficiently long periods of inactivity some minimum number of steps is made, e.g. by moving around in the house or going to the bathroom. On the other hand we want to distinguish real use for monitoring physical activity (even if it relates only to short periods of a day) from unintended use where, e.g., the tracker is just taken from the bedside table and put into a drawer. After discussion with medical experts and after reviewing the data, we decided to use a simple threshold approach: Days with fewer than 500 steps are deemed non-use and are excluded from our analyses (8.3%, 1,320 of 15,812 days). An in-depth discussion of partial intra-day use of activity trackers with more insights is given below.

## DATA ANALYSES

In the subsequent sections we first present general characteristics of activity tracker use such as duration and frequency of use, then describe longer-term characteristics such as weekly rhythms, and finally look in more detail into how users take breaks in the long term. We use a number of – mostly canonical – terms and measures shown in Table 2 to characterize the data. Where we use thresholds to categorize the data we define them quantitatively based on the observed data; we had also experimented with other e.g. heuristically defined thresholds and found that they don't considerably change the overall picture.

We analyzed the data from 104 users. The users collected data on 14,413 use days in the time from January 16, 2014, to August 1, 2016, and recorded 113,449,034 steps.

### General Quantitative Observations

The key figures of our findings are summarized in Table 3.

#### *Active users vs past users*

Users frequently pause using the tracker and restart later. Therefore we cannot know for sure whether users are still using the tracker but are in a break, or whether they ultimately abandoned use. From our analyses of streaks and breaks – see below – we assume that a person is likely to have abandoned tracker use if that person hasn't used the tracker since 20% longer than their longest break so far, but at least for 50 days. We call these persons "past users".

With this, 66 of 104 users are active users, 38 are past users. Within the 1YearRehab study, abandonment is frequent. In contrast in the LongTermInTheWild study, most users are still active; this may be due to the opt-in

| | 1YearRehab | 12Week Intervention | 9Month Observation | LongTerm InTheWild |
|---|---|---|---|---|
| **Active and past users** | | | | |
| Still active users | 10 | 17 | 5 | 34 |
| Past users | 33 | 0 | 0 | 5 |
| **Typical duration (in days) and density** | | | | |
| Duration of active users | 102-311 (196) | defined by study settings | | 270-566 (463) |
| Duration of past users | 46-172 (125) | n/a | n/a | 16-285 (163) |
| Total density | 48-68% (59%) | 90-100% (100%) | 55-96% (91%) | 20-93% (67%) |
| **Typical streak and break lengths (in days)** | | | | |
| Streak length | 1-2 (1) | 3-17 (11) | 3-28 (12) | 2-13 (6) |
| Avg streak length per user | 1.5-4 (2.2) | 11-42 (15) | 11.3-26.4 (18.8) | 4.6-35.2 (12) |
| Max streak length | 4-9 (7) | 14-51 (15) | 34-57 (38) | 12-119 (36) |
| Break length | 1-1 (1) | 1-3 (2) | 1-2 (1) | 1-4 (1) |
| Average break length per user | 1.2-3 (1.5) | 1.3-3.9 (2.8) | 1.4-9.3 (2) | 3.4-35.4 (8.2) |
| Maximum break length | 3-14 (6) | 2-5 (4) | 3-51 (4) | 13-157 (53) |
| **Use during day** | | | | |
| Average 3-a-day-ratio | 73.6% | 92.8% | 88.2% | 78.8% |

**Table 3. Quantitative observations. Ranges indicate Inter-Quartile Range, i.e. quartiles 2 and 3, figures in brackets are median**

procedure for data acquisition that may primarily have attracted engaged users. With 12WeekIntervention being a short-term study with limited duration, past users are not relevant. Finally the 9MonthObservation study is still ongoing without dropouts.

*Use Duration by Active Users*

In the 1YearRehab study, active users are using the tracker for 3 to 10 months already, some up to 1½ years. In the LongTermInTheWild population, use durations are considerably longer up to 2.5 years. For 12WeekIntervention and 9MonthObservation, the maximum use duration is determined by the study settings.

*Abandonment by Past Users*

Abandonment in 1YearRehab happens often in the first 6 months. Of all 1YearRehab users, 11 (25.6%) definitely use or used the tracker for more than 6 months, 27 (62.8%) definitely abandoned within the first 6 months, and 5 (11.6%) are active users with a use duration of so far less than 6 months. The rate of abandonment is thus lower than found in the aforementioned studies [20,31], but higher than in the market survey [8].

In LongTermInTheWild, abandonment happened after two weeks to 13 months; again this may be influenced by the opt-in procedure for data acquisition and cannot be considered representative for the general population.

*Density*

The density, i.e. the percentage of use days in a period of time, is very different in the four settings. In the 12WeekIntervention study, it is up to 100%; this might be influenced by the high pressure induced by the study to use the tracker. In 9MonthObservation it is between 50% and close to 100%; due to the small population size this is strongly influenced by individual users' behaviors. 1YearRehab shows a fairly narrow density with typically 4.1 use days per week. In LongTermInTheWild densities are in general higher than in 1YearRehab but they are much more spread out. Some users have extremely low densities of less than 20%. We provide an explanation for the latter below.

*Streaks and Breaks*

Streaks, i.e. uninterrupted use of the tracker over successive days, in general last a few days only, with some considerable differences in the different populations and with outliers up to one year. In 1YearRehab most streaks are very short, with no more than 2 days, whereas in the more controlled 12WeekIntervention and 9MonthObservation settings streaks are much longer, often up to 3-4 weeks. The LongTermInTheWild setting is somewhere in between.

In all populations, breaks are on average shorter than streaks, and 94.8% of all breaks are one week or shorter. Outliers are more extreme, with maximum almost 2 years of break before resuming use. These long breaks are one explanation for the very low densities we observed particularly in the LongTermInTheWild population.

In each population a considerable number of users have a quite high maximum streak length. This is most visible in the LongTermInTheWild population, but can also be observed in other populations. In 1YearRehab this is least distinct, but there are outliers with longer streaks. Therefore many but not all users use the tracker at least once uninterruptedly for a longer period.

The longest break before using the tracker again is 3.5 to 53 days (median per study). With this we believe that the minimum 50-day period of non-use that we apply to estimate past users is a fair choice.

### *Usage During the Day*

Investigating tracker use throughout the day is challenging, as both non-use of the tracker and inactivity result in 0 steps for the given interval. We therefore examine on which days the tracker has been used at least once in the morning from 3 a.m. to 11 a.m, once around noon from 11 a.m. to 3 p.m., and once in the afternoon after 3 p.m. This heuristics, subsequently called "3-a-day", implies a continuity of use during the whole day. Applied to a long-term Fitbit user with known very high consistency, this measure shows 97.6%, reinforcing that the measure is a fair indicator for whole-day use: the higher the ratio of days fulfilling the 3-a-day measure in relation to all use days, the more likely it is that the user has used the tracker consistently the whole day.

With this measure we see that in all populations the tracker has been used in the morning, noon, and afternoon between 74% and 93% of all days. The 12WeekIntervention population, which in our previous measures, such as density, has already shown high engagement in wearing the tracker, scores best here, with 9MonthObservation performing only slightly worse. And the 1YearRehab population performs worst, with the LongTermInTheWild population being in between.

## Use Rhythms per Weekday, Month, Over Time

Analyzing recurring use rhythms requires sufficiently long use durations that we only find in the 1YearRehab and the LongTermInTheWild populations (N=82). We therefore exclude 12WeekIntervention and 9MonthObservation from the subsequent analyses. For specific analyses we also need to further exclude participants; we mention this in the respective sections.

### *Use per Weekday*

We observe how trackers are used on the days of the week. To mitigate the influence of the novelty effect we here take into account only users with at least 60 use days (N=62).

The distribution gives an unclear picture. In 1YearRehab (N=26) we observe a below-average use on Tuesdays and Wednesdays, and an above-average use on Saturdays and Sundays (see Fig. 1). For LongTermInTheWild users (N=27) the deviations are smaller, but the effect is somewhat reverse – less use on Saturdays and Sundays, and more during the week.

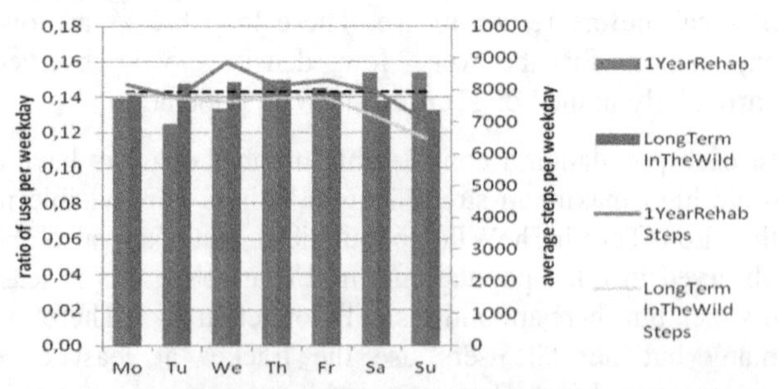


**Fig. 1: Use and average steps per week day for 1YearRehab and LongTermInTheWild. Dashed line indicates equal distribution of tracker use**

The relation between use of tracker and actual activity is subtle, as indicated by the average steps per weekday in Fig. 1. For LongTermInTheWild, use and average steps are about constant during the week, and lower on the weekend, confirmed by a strong positive correlation (Pearson's $r = 0.803$, $p = 0.0297$) between use and average steps per day. Somewhat counter-intuitive, for 1YearRehab tracker use is higher during the weekend, but again average steps are lower; indeed there is no significant correlation between use and average steps (Pearson's $r = -0.399$, $p = 0.376$). The users' choice to wear the tracker is thus independent of the activity level.

### *Use per Calendar Month*

To understand if there are periodical changes per year, we analyzed the density (measured in use days per week) per month of year, which only makes sense for users with at least one year of activity tracker use. And to avoid a bias by single users we only observe a time span with at least 10 users. This leaves us with Jan'15 to Jun'16 of the LongTermInTheWild population (N=24).

The analysis shows no obvious change of density throughout the year and no seasonal effects, e.g. during summer time or over Christmas. Wearing the tracker seems not to be influenced by, e.g., bad weather conditions or seasonally reduced activity.

### *Use over Time*

To understand whether users change their use behavior over time, we analyze the density per week after first day of use. To avoid a bias by individual users, we only observe time spans with at least 10 users. We end up with 79 weeks with LongTermInTheWild data and 32 weeks with 1YearRehab data (N=81).

We observe (see Fig. 2) that aside from some minor change in the first weeks and some fluctuation, the use over time is on average practically constant. Users use the tracker consistently until the end, and then they stop. This is in contrast to Karapanos et al. [18] who found that intensity of use decreases over time; we will discuss this finding in the

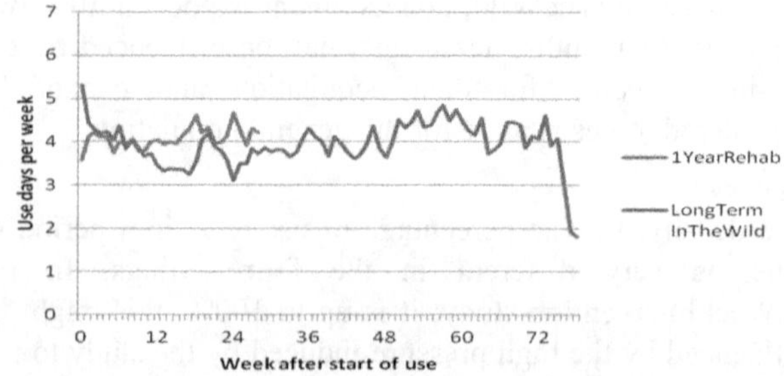


**Fig. 2: Use after start of use**

next section. The dip towards the end of LongTermInTheWild curve is an artifact caused by 5 long-term low-density users; we will explain this in the next section.

### Taking Breaks from Use

*Definition of Use Phases*

To understand how users take breaks from using the tracker, we observe *phases*, i.e. series of streaks separated by short breaks and ending with a long break, as a more relaxed measure than the streak, allowing for a couple of days off. Our definition of a *long break* separating two phases is a break of more than one week: A week is a strong cultural rhythm that is perceived and lived as a basic time structure for differentiating "recent" from "past" also in the context of reflecting health behaviors [24]. Also we saw above that 94.8% of all breaks are one week and shorter, so anything longer is indeed an exception. Finally we also experimented with other durations up to 28 days and found that the overall picture drawn below remains consistent.

*Number of Phases per User*

Our data contain 218 phases in total, of which 177 (81.2%) are finalized, and 41 are still active. The number of phases per user is often low: 57 of the 104 users have exactly one finalized or active phase; and 94 users have finalized or are still active in four phases or less. Maximum number of phases is 9, achieved by two users. 41 users are currently active in a phase, 63 users have finalized their last phase, being either past users (N=38), or being in the break towards a possible next phase (N=25). Users in the LongTermInTheWild setting have more phases than users in the other three settings; this can partially be explained by the generally longer duration.

Since the characteristics of active phases may still change, we restrict our further analyses on finalized phases. To avoid a bias by individual users, we further restrict our per-study analyses to phases where at least 10 users finalized a phase. This again excludes 12WeekIntervention and 9MonthObservation and leaves the first two phases of 1YearRehab (N=41 / 12 in phase 1 / 2) and the first four phases of LongTermInTheWild (N=34 / 20 / 17 / 13).

*Temporal Distribution of Phases*

The length of the first phase varies widely from 1 to 529 days. Median in 1YearRehab is quite high, with 125 days. For LongTermInTheWild the first phase is much shorter, with median 29.5 days (see Fig. 3). The subsequent phases decrease considerably in length. In 1YearRehab, median of phase 2 drops drastically to 23 days with outliers from 1 to 156 days. For LongTermInTheWild, variations are smaller but still show a reduction to up to half the length of the first phase. Breaks between phases are usually shorter than the phase lengths. They have typical durations of 2-3 weeks up to 2-3 months, although they can also be longer than 1.5 years.

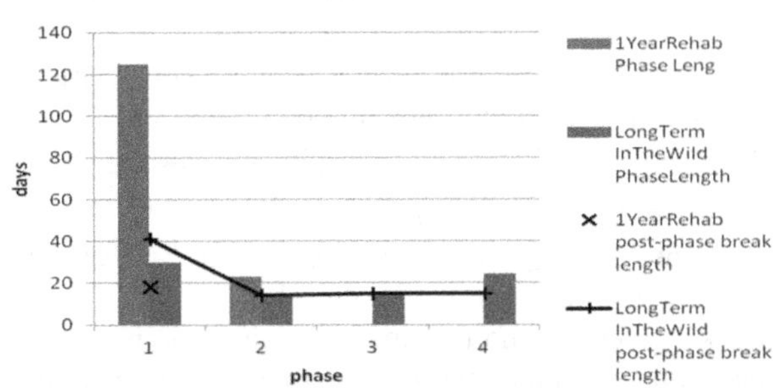


**Fig. 3: Median length of phases (bars) and breaks after phases (marker, line)**

*Characteristics of Phases*

We use four core measures to describe usage characteristics within the phases: density, average and maximum streak length, and ratio of 3-a-day use days to total use days (see Fig. 4). Median density in phase 1 is 65% to close to 100%. In 1YearRehab density is increasing from phase 1 to 2. In LongTermInTheWild we observe only a minor decrease in density from phase to phase; this is in line with our observations on use over time remaining mostly constant. We discussed above that in contrast to Karapanos et al. [18] we found on average no change of intensity over time; with this observation on use phases we now explain this contrast by the fact that per user in phases of use the density indeed stays mostly stable, but longer breaks and shorter use phases reduce the overall density. Average streak length is between 2 and 15 days in the first phase (with an impressive maximum of 179 days). In 1YearRehab there is an increase on a low level from phase 1 to 2, whereas in LongTermInTheWild there is a clear decrease from the first to the later phases. Maximum streak lengths per phase show little variation. 3-a-day ratio, i.e. intra-day use, decreases for 1YearRehab and fluctuates considerably for LongTermInTheWild.

*Changes in Use between Phases*

In general we see some tendency that the first phase has different characteristics from the subsequent ones. This might be explained in two ways: On the one hand, this might be inter-user effects caused by less than half the users entering into a second phase; this may result in a bias

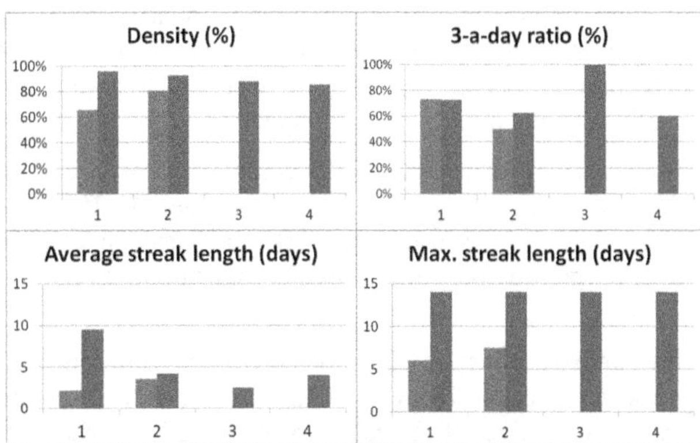


**Fig. 4: Median of key characteristics of the first phases (horizontal) for 1YearRehab (left bar, blue) and LongTermInTheWild (right bar, purple).**

towards more engaged users for later phases. On the other hand this may be intra-user changes, with the first phase possibly influenced by a novelty effect with more engagement and adherence, whereas a user's later phases may be more routine use. We discuss reasons for this in the next section.

## PATTERNS OF USE

### Approach

Based on the quantitative analysis of activity tracker use, we aim to identify patterns of use. We chose an expert driven, qualitative approach to explore our data and to identify potential patterns of use. Three HCI experts with experiences in activity tracker based health interventions, and one communication scientist with a focus on user experience and user analysis reviewed the data in a two-step process: In the first step they clustered phases based on common combinations of phases' attributes such as length and density. In the second step they identified the actual usage patterns by finding frequently occurring combinations of types of phases and other general use characteristics such as total use duration. For thresholds used to define phases and patterns, the experts discussed both, heuristic reasoning based on expert knowledge, and quantitative definitions based on observed data, and finally decided to go for quantitative definition which seemed less arbitrary and was still close to the experts' intuition. The experts individually reviewed the data and developed hypotheses for phases and patterns, taking into account their experiences from their previous work. The hypotheses were jointly discussed and the criteria applied to the data to check for occurrences of patterns, consistency with the quantitative observations such as the percentiles of the respective measures in the observed data, and ability to discriminate different usages. The process was repeated until a consensus was reached

### Types of Phases

The experts identified the following, non-disjoint characteristic types of phases (in parentheses: the number of instances found):

- **minor use phase**: a short phase (in 1$^{st}$ quartile of phase length, 10 days) with either at the most 3 use days, or 3-a-day ratio below 50%. Here the user has tried but not really used the tracker. (N=45, 20.6%)
- **long streak phase**: a phase that contains a long streak (in 4$^{th}$ quartile maximum streak length per user, 41.25 days). Here the user has used the tracker at least once for a longer period of time without interruption. (N=45, 20.6%)
- **low density phase**: a phase of significant duration (>10 days) with density below median density (64%). Here the tracker is used regularly but sparsely. (N=37, 17.0%)
- **high intensity phase**: a phase of significant duration, density in 4$^{th}$ quartile (>92%), and 3-a-day ratio in 4$^{th}$ quartile (>89.6%). Here the tracker is used on most days and consistently. (N=24, 11.0%)
- **restarting phase**: a phase starting after a break with length in 4$^{th}$ quartile of maximum break length per user (32 days). Here the user is resuming use after having taken a long break (N=41, 18.8%)
- **very long phase:** a phase in 4$^{th}$ quartile of phase length (>103 days). Here the user has used the tracker over a very long time in a row (N=54, 24.8%)
- 76 phases (34.9%) have no specific characteristic.

Other types of phases were hypothesized, such as a low density phase that also includes a long streak, indicating a change of behavior within a phase. However no significant number of occurrences could be found for such phases in the data, hence they were rejected.

### Use Patterns

The experts identified 12 non-disjoint use patterns. The number of occurrences of patterns, as well as the co-occurrences with other patterns, are reported in Table 4. Four of the patterns relate to the start of use (dotted frame top left in the table), five are relevant for longer-term use (dashed frame in the middle), two are additional attributes of other patterns, and one is without further specification.

#### *Patterns for Start of Use*

- **beginner**: *active user with short use duration (in 1$^{st}$ quartile; ≤ 62 days).* These users are still in their early days of use, so we cannot say much about them yet.
- **try-and-drop**: *past user with use duration ≤62 days and only minor use phases.* These users took the initial barrier of installing the tracker, but stopped using very fast before being able to assess the value of tracker use.
- **short-term** *past user with use duration ≤62 days.* These users tried the tracker for a short time. At some quite early point they must have made a – conscious or unconscious – evaluation of the benefits and found that they do not outweigh the perceived costs and disadvantages, in line with the reasons for abandonment already discussed [9,20,31].
- **slow-starter:** *first phase minor use, all other phases of significant duration (>10 days).* These users needed some time after setting up the tracker before going into actual use. This pattern is relatively rare; only 2 of the longer-term users are slow-starters, and 3 of the slow-starters are try-and-drop users with just the one minor use phase. So most users go into regular use right from the beginning,

#### *Patterns for Long-Term Use*

- **experimenter**: *≥ 2 minor use phases, and <90% of use days in non-minor use phases.* These users try out the tracker often for short periods of time. Experimenters can be found in both long-term settings, 1YearRehab and LongTermInTheWild. Some have very long use durations of over two years, and all have a low number of use days. These users seem to use the tracker more playfully, using it from time to time for a few days, possibly answering some very concrete question, and then stopping again.

- **hop-on hop-off**: *more than 3 phases, at least half of phases (excluding phase 1) and at least 2 phases are restarting phases.* These users often take long breaks from tracker use, but regularly resume use. We observe hop-on hop-off use in LongTermInTheWild only, but not in study and intervention-oriented settings. These users' first phase in general has a normal length (average 32 days), whereas in most cases (with two exceptions) the next phases are much shorter (average usually around 11 days). Users with this pattern have some reason to restart tracker use after some time. We hypothesize that the earlier phases help build a basic understanding, whereas later phases have a more concrete use such as re-evaluating a behavior.
- **intermittent user**: *>62 days of use and with only low density phases.* These users use the tracker consistently but sparsely. This pattern is particularly interesting. All intermittent users are in the 1YearRehab population. 3-a-day ratio is low with on average 74%, so intra-day use seems to be selective. On the other hand, use duration is relatively high; average of the intermittent users is 197 days. All but one users have only one phase; this makes most of them long-phase users. The engagement of intermittent users with trackers is therefore, although low, very consistent over a long time. It seems that intermittent users are not primarily interested in a complete logging and understanding of their activity, but have other reasons for use. This pattern seems to be related to external motivation induced by a study setting.
- **power user**: *>62 days of use and only high intensity phases.* These users use the tracker consistently and intensely. Power users appear in all but the 1YearRehab settings. All are still active; use duration is high in the open-ended LongTermInTheWild setting (average 370 days). 2 have two phases; the others have one phase only. 3 of those who are not long-phasers are in the 12WeekIntervention population, where the study is shorter than our definition of a very long phase. All have very long maximum streaks between 57 and 277 days, 3-a-day ratio is average 97%, so also intra-day use seems to be high. These users are compliant in using the tracker the whole day for a very long period of time, taking only exceptional breaks. They are found in study settings as well as in the wild, but their occurrence is relatively low.

| | beginner | try-and-drop | short-term | slow-start | experimenter | hop-on hop-off | intermittent | power use | gen con | long-phaser | health logger | other |
|---|---|---|---|---|---|---|---|---|---|---|---|---|
| beginner | 14 | | | 1 | | | | | | | 2 | |
| try-and-drop | | 4 | 4 | 3 | 1 | | | | | | | |
| short-term | | | 13 | 4 | 1 | | | | | | | |
| slow-start | | | | 7 | | | | | | 1 | 1 | |
| experimenter | | | | | 8 | 1 | | | | | | |
| hop-on hop-off | | | | | | 7 | | | | | | |
| intermittent | | | | | | | 14 | | 14 | 14 | | |
| power use | | | | | | | | 9 | 9 | 5 | 9 | |
| gen con | | | | | | | | | 50 | 38 | 19 | |
| long-phaser | | | | | | | | | | 43 | 17 | |
| health logger | | | | | | | | | | | 26 | |
| other | | | | | | | | | | | | 8 |

**Table 4. Occurrences and co-occurrences of patterns. Boxes mark patterns for start of use (left) and long-term use (right).**

- **generally consistent user**: *>62 days of use, has only phases of significant duration.* This is a "Jane and John Doe" pattern, where the tracker is used for some time with moderate requirements to consistency of use. By definition all intermittent and all power users fall in this pattern. Leaving these out, 26 generally consistent users (25%) remain. This is the largest group that we observe. These users appear in all but the 12WeekIntervention settings; 15 are still active; average use duration is 11 months, density 73%, 3-a-day ratio 80%. This pattern is pursued by many users and shows a moderate but quite long-term engagement.

### *Attributive Patterns*

The subsequent two patterns usually co-occur with other patterns. We therefore consider these to be primarily attributes of existing patterns rather than independent patterns themselves.

- **long-phase user:** *at least 75% of all use days in very long phases.* These users usually use the tracker without major interruptions for a longer period of time. This pattern overlaps particularly with generally consistent, intermittent and power users. The relatively low overlap with the latter is due to 12WeekIntervention users who cannot fulfill the long phases due to the study setting. There is no overlap with hop-on hop-off users or experimenters. Having a long phase thus seems to be a frequent behavior for users with a generally regular use.
- **health logger**: *at least one phase is a long-streak phase.* These users log complete activity data for a longer period of time. Health logging can be observed for all power users, for many generally consistent users, but only for one intermittent user and occasionally in some other patterns. Logging complete activity seems therefore to be related to generally higher engagement.

### *Miscellaneous*

- **Other**: *a user fulfilling none of the patterns above.* 8 users fall into this pattern; 4 more fulfill only the long-phase and health logging attributes. The users in this pattern are diverse. They appear in all but the 12WeekIntervention settings. Some are long-term users with high consistency that just missed one of our strict criteria for another pattern, whereas others have unique combinations of phases such as mixtures of very long and short phases, or phases without specific characteristics. With 11.6% of such non-classified users our patterns have a good coverage.

## DISCUSSION

At first glance our results may not look particularly surprising and merely give evidence to the seemingly obvious. However, looking closer our findings reveal important insights:

Most users fall in only one or two of the use patterns, and they don't change this pattern over long periods of time. Although these patterns are likely influenced by the study settings as indicated e.g. by the high density in 12WeekIntervention, they also appear across very different studies and thus also seem to be inherent to a user. We therefore conclude that a user has an individual and "natural" way of using an activity tracker.

While forcing users into other patterns may be possible, long-term interventions and studies using activity trackers are probably well advised to respect the user's natural patterns to increase adherence and reduce abandonment. Systems might even use these patterns to their advantage: If after a few weeks of use the user's pattern can be identified, interventions may adapt accordingly to the user's preferred way of tracker use. And deviations from a use pattern might indicate a change in use that makes changes in the intervention necessary.

Furthermore for the majority of users their natural way of tracker use involves regularly taking breaks. Temporary non-use is therefore not the exception but the rule and must be considered appropriately in interventions and studies.

Breaks can be as short as a couple of days or even just hours. Such breaks result in gaps in the data where the activity reported is less than the activity actually performed. This must be taken care of when analyzing the data. And in such short breaks users may be open to reminders and encouragement to use the tracker again soon.

Breaks may also be longer, covering many weeks or even months. This may be considered temporary abandonment and users may or may not resume use. Long-term interventions therefore need a great staying power when such breaks occur. Strategies to persuade the user to resume are likely different from those for short breaks. Accepting the break and waiting for the user to return on their own or using small nudges at the most may be better suited than continuously sending obtrusive reminders.

Nevertheless abandonment happens. While indeed many users stop after 3-6 months, there are individual differences ranging from a couple of days to more than a year. Reducing abandonment in early stages is particularly relevant for many interventions. Here two different challenges must be addressed: the one is the try-and-drop user; she or he must be convinced to give the tracker a fair chance. The other is the general short-term user who has tried the tracker but found no value in using it.

## LIMITATIONS AND NEXT STEPS

Our work is to the best of our knowledge the first to use quantitative analyses of tracker use to understand user interaction. It is meant to provide initial reliable insights and open the door for follow-up activities which may confirm and broaden our results and can help to overcome the limitations of our work:

The number of users per setting is small to moderate, with 5 to 43 persons. The settings and the demographic data were heterogeneous, and the influence of the study settings on tracker use is not fully understood. Therefore some findings per setting and overall statistical relevance are limited. We based our identification of patterns on qualitative analyses. Future work could be based on quantitative analyses of larger populations, also including a greater number of different settings. We investigate observed use only. Follow-up work could also use a mixed-methods approach, identifying users' motivations and relating these to observed use patterns.

Our work is descriptive. Larger data might also allow identifying predictors for patterns, e.g. based on a user's demographic data and the study setting. This would allow tailoring an intervention to the individual user's needs from the very beginning, thus better matching the intervention to the user's actual behavior, increasing compliance and hopefully intervention success.

We discuss when users abandon use, but we don't examine the non-starting users who had been invited to tracker use but chose not to do so. The try-and-drop users are one step further than the non-starters but may have similar reasons for abandonment. Understanding their reasons might also help in building interventions that are not abandoned after a few weeks.

## CONCLUSION

Our analyses provide detailed insights into activity tracker use in long-term and short-term studies. They add a quantitative perspective to the qualitative analyses of reasons for use and abandonment. The insights facilitate the design of activity tracking–based health technologies, interventions, and long-term applications better matching the users' preferences and needs.

## ACKNOWLEDGMENTS

This work would not have been possible without the work of the teams from the PROMOTE and the IPP studies. Thanks also to Medisana for the support of the data acquisition.

This work has partially been funded by the German Federal Ministry of Education and Research (Project No. 01EL1422C), by the Hewlett Packard Innovation Research Programme, and by the Stiftung Bremer Wertpapier-Börse, (Bremen Stock Exchange Foundation).

## REFERENCES


1. Judit Bort-Roig, Nicholas D Gilson, Anna Puig-Ribera, Ruth S Contreras, and Stewart G Trost. 2014. Measuring and influencing physical activity with smartphone technology: a systematic review. *Sports medicine (Auckland, N.Z.)* 44, 5: 671–86. http://doi.org/10.1007/s40279-014-0142-5
2. Dena M Bravata, Crystal Smith-Spangler, Vandana Sundaram, et al. 2007. Using pedometers to increase physical activity and improve health: a systematic review. *JAMA Journal of the American Medical Association* 298, 19: 2296–304. http://doi.org/10.1001/jama.298.19.2296
3. Steindorf K. Bruhmann B A, Schmidt M E. 2014. Assessment of physical activity in epidemiological studies : Are questionnaires obsolete in the era of accelerometry ? *GMS Med Inform Biom Epidemiol* 10, 1: 1–12. http://doi.org/10.3205/mibe000155
4. James Clawson, Jessica A. Pater, Andrew D. Miller, Elizabeth D. Mynatt, and Lena Mamykina. 2015. No longer wearing. *UbiComp '15: Proceedings of the 2015 ACM International Joint Conference on Pervasive and Ubiquitous Computing*: 647–658. http://doi.org/10.1145/2750858.2807554
5. J Connelly, A Kirk, J Masthoff, and S MacRury. 2013. The use of technology to promote physical activity in Type 2 diabetes management: a systematic review. *Diabetic medicine : a journal of the British Diabetic Association* 30, 12: 1420–32. http://doi.org/10.1111/dme.12289
6. Sunny Consolvo, David W. McDonald, Tammy Toscos, et al. 2008. Activity sensing in the wild: a field trial of ubifit garden. In *CHI '08 Proceedings of the SIGCHI Conference on Human Factors in Computing Systems*, 1797–1806. http://doi.org/10.1145/1357054.1357335
7. Cora L Craig, Alison L Marshall, Michael Sjöström, et al. 2003. International physical activity questionnaire: 12-country reliability and validity. *Medicine and science in sports and exercise* 35, 8: 1381–95. http://doi.org/10.1249/01.MSS.0000078924.61453.FB
8. Endeavour Partners LLC. 2014. *Inside Wearables - How the Science of Behavior Change Offers the Secret to Long-Term Engagement.*
9. Daniel A. Epstein, Monica Caraway, Chuck Johnston, An Ping, James Fogarty, and Sean A. Munson. 2016. Beyond Abandonment to Next Steps: Understanding and Designing for Life after Personal Informatics Tool Use. *CHI '16 Proceedings of the SIGCHI Conference on Human Factors in Computing Systems.* http://doi.org/10.1145/2858036.2858045
10. Daniel A. Epstein, Jennifer Kang, Laura R. Pina, James Fogarty, and Sean A. Munson. 2016. Reconsidering the Device in the Drawer: Lapses as a Design Opportunity in Personal Informatics. In *UbiComp '16: Proceedings of the 2016 ACM International Joint Conference on Pervasive and Ubiquitous Computing*, 829–840. http://doi.org/10.1145/2971648.2971656
11. Jordan Etkin. 2016. The Hidden Cost of Personal Quantification. *Journal of Consumer Research* 42, 6: 967–984.
12. Cara Bailey Fausset, Tracy L Mitzner, Chandler E Price, Brian D Jones, Brad W Fain, and Wendy A Rogers. 2013. Older Adults' Use of and Attitudes toward Activity Monitoring Technologies. *Proceedings of the Human Factors and Ergonomics Society Annual Meeting* 57, 1: 1683–1687. http://doi.org/10.1177/1541931213571374
13. Ty Ferguson, Alex V Rowlands, Tim Olds, and Carol Maher. 2015. The validity of consumer-level, activity monitors in healthy adults worn in free-living conditions: a cross-sectional study. *The International Journal of Behavioral Nutrition and Physical Activity* 12: 42.
14. Thomas Fritz, Elaine M Huang, Gail C Murphy, and Thomas Zimmermann. 2014. Persuasive technology in the real world: a study of long-term use of activity sensing devices for fitness. *CHI '14 Proceedings of the SIGCHI Conference on Human Factors in Computing Systems*: 487–496. http://doi.org/10.1145/2556288.2557383
15. Rúben Gouveia, Evangelos Karapanos, and Marc Hassenzahl. 2015. How do we engage with activity trackers?: a longitudinal study of Habito. In *UbiComp '15: Proceedings of the 2015 ACM International Joint Conference on Pervasive and Ubiquitous Computing*, 1305–1316. http://doi.org/10.1145/2750858.2804290
16. Daniel Harrison, Nadia Berthouze, Paul Marshall, and Jon Bird. 2014. Tracking physical activity: problems related to running longitudinal studies with commercial devices. In *UbiComp '14 Adjunct: Proceedings of the 2014 ACM International Joint Conference on Pervasive and Ubiquitous Computing: Adjunct Publication*, 699–702. http://doi.org/10.1145/2638728.2641320
17. IDC. 2016. *Worldwide Quarterly Wearable Device Tracker.*
18. Evangelos Karapanos, Rúben Gouveia, Marc Hassenzahl, and Jodi Forlizzi. 2016. Wellbeing in the making: Peoples' experiences with wearable activity trackers. *Psychology of Well-Being* 2013. http://doi.org/10.1186/s13612-016-0042-6
19. Katja Karrer, Charlotte Glaser, Caroline Clemens, and Carmen Bruder. 2009. Technikaffinität erfassen – der Fragebogen TA-EG (Assessing affinity to technology - the TA-EG questionnaire). In *Der Mensch im Mittelpunkt technischer Systeme*, 196–201.
20. Amanda Lazar, Christian Koehler, Joshua Tanenbaum, and David H. Nguyen. 2015. Why we use and abandon smart devices. *UbiComp '15: Proceedings of the 2015 ACM International Joint Conference on Pervasive and Ubiquitous Computing*: 635–646. http://doi.org/10.1145/2750858.2804288
21. James J Lin, Lena Mamykina, Silvia Lindtner, Gregory Delajoux, and Henry B Strub. 2006. Fish ' n ' Steps : Encouraging Physical Activity with an Interactive Computer Game. In *UbiComp '06 Proceedings of the 8th international conference on Ubiquitous computing*, 261–278. http://doi.org/10.1007/11853565_16

22. Marion E T McMurdo, Jacqui Sugden, Ishbel Argo, et al. 2010. Do pedometers increase physical activity in sedentary older women? A randomized controlled trial. *Journal of the American Geriatrics Society* 58, 11: 2099–106. http://doi.org/10.1111/j.1532-5415.2010.03127.x

23. Jochen Meyer, Jutta Fortmann, Merlin Wasmann, and Wilko Heuten. 2015. Making Lifelogging Usable: Design Guidelines for Activity Trackers. In *Multimedia Modeling 2015*. Sydney, NSW, Autralia, 323–334. http://doi.org/10.1007/978-3-319-14442-9_39

24. Jochen Meyer, Anastasia Kazakova, Merlin Büsing, and Susanne Boll. 2016. Visualization of Complex Health Data on Mobile Devices. In *MMHealth'16: Multimedia for personal health and health care Proceedings*. http://doi.org/10.1145/2985766.2985774

25. Saskia Muellmann, Sarah Forberger, Tobias Möllers, et al. 2016. Effectiveness of eHealth interventions for the promotion of physical activity in older adults: a systematic review protocol. *Systematic Reviews* 5, 1: 47. http://doi.org/10.1186/s13643-016-0223-7

26. Franz J. Neyer, Juliane Felber, and Claudia Gebhardt. 2012. Entwicklung und Validierung einer Kurzskala zur Erfassung von Technikbereitschaft (Development and validation of a brief measure of technology commitment). *Diagnostica* 58, 2: 87–99. http://doi.org/10.1026/0012-1924/a000067

27. NPD. 2015. *Consumers and Wearables Report*. Las Vegas.

28. Massimo F Piepoli, Ugo Corrà, François Carré, et al. 2010. Secondary prevention through cardiac rehabilitation: physical activity counselling and exercise training. *European Heart Journal* 31, 16: 1967–76. http://doi.org/10.1093/eurheartj/ehq236

29. Rachael Purta, Stephen Mattingly, Lixing Song, et al. 2016. Experiences measuring sleep and physical activity patterns across a large college cohort with fitbits. In *Proceedings of the 2016 ACM International Symposium on Wearable Computers - ISWC '16*, 28–35. http://doi.org/10.1145/2971763.2971767

30. Patrick L Schneider, Scott E Crouter, Olivera Lukajic, and David R Bassett. 2003. Accuracy and reliability of 10 pedometers for measuring steps over a 400-m walk. *Medicine and Science in Sports and Exercise* 35, 10: 1779–1784. http://doi.org/10.1249/01.MSS.0000089342.96098.C4

31. Patrick C. Shih, Kyungsik Han, Erika Shehan Poole, Mary Beth Rosson, and John M. Carroll. 2015. Use and Adoption Challenges of Wearable Activity Trackers. In *iConference 2015 Proceedings*.

32. Torben Wallbaum, Melina Frenken, Jochen Meyer, and Andreas Hein. 2014. Acceptance of sensor networks by dementia patients. In *7. Deutscher AAL-Kongress*.

33. WHO. 2011. *Global status report on noncommunicable diseases 2010*.

34. H. Wienbergen, T. Backhaus, J. Stehmeier, et al. 2016. Assessment and monitoring of physical activity with pedometers and and online documentation in secondary prevention after myocardiac infarct (Erfassung und Kontrolle körperlicher Aktivität mit Schrittzählern und Online-Dokumentation in der Sekundärprävent. In *Tagung der Deutschen Gesellschaft für Kardiologie*.

35. Sha Zhao, Julian Ramos, Jianrong Tao, et al. 2016. Discovering different kinds of smartphone users through their application usage behaviors. In *UbiComp '16: Proceedings of the 2016 ACM International Joint Conference on Pervasive and Ubiquitous Computing*, 498–509. http://doi.org/10.1145/2971648.2971696

# AirPanes: Two-Handed Around-Device Interaction for Pane Switching on Smartphones

**Khalad Hasan[1], David Ahlström[2], Junhyeok Kim[1], Pourang Irani[1]**

[1]University of Manitoba
Winnipeg, Manitoba, Canada
{Khalad, kimj3415, Irani}@cs.umanitoba.ca

[2]Alpen-Adria-Universität Klagenfurt
Klagenfurt, Austria
david.ahlstroem@aau.at

## ABSTRACT

In recent years, around device input has emerged as a complement to standard touch input, albeit in limited tasks and contexts, such as for item selection or map navigation. We push the boundaries for around device interactions to facilitate an entire smartphone application: browsing through large information lists to make a decision. To this end, we present AirPanes, a novel technique that allows two-handed in-air interactions, conjointly with touch input to perform analytic tasks, such as making a purchase decision. AirPanes resolves the inefficiencies of having to switch between multiple views or panes in common smartphone applications. We explore the design factors that make AirPanes efficient. In a controlled study, we find that AirPanes is on average 50% more efficient that standard touch input for an analytic task. We offer recommendations for implementing AirPanes in a broad range of applications.

### Author Keywords

Around-Device Interaction; In-air input; Two-handed Mobile Interaction; Analytic Interfaces; m-commerce interfaces.

### ACM Classification Keywords

H.5.2. Information interfaces and presentation (e.g., HCI): User Interfaces – Interaction styles.

## INTRODUCTION

With the rapid advances in optical sensing and finger tracking technologies [9, 37], researchers have explored the use of the in-air space around a mobile device for input. Prior studies have demonstrated the use of in-air space for fundamental on-screen interactions, such as selecting on-screen [17] and off-screen items [18], switching modes [41], text-entry [29], zooming and panning [25]. While such prior work has laid the foundation for around-device in-air input, a complete mobile application that deploys and benefits from such an input modality has yet to be demonstrated. Accordingly, our goal is to step beyond the design and study of isolated in-air alternatives for standard on-screen interactions and to explore how in-air input can enhance user performance in more complete mobile scenarios. In particular, we focus on the ability to facilitate a complex (high-level) goal, such as making a decision through information exploration and interaction.


*CHI 2017, May 06-11, 2017, Denver, CO, USA*
© 2017 ACM. ISBN 978-1-4503-4655-9/17/05...$15.00
DOI: http://dx.doi.org/10.1145/3025453.3026029

In the context of smartphone applications, GUI designers generally organize large information spaces into multiple views, or panes. Typically, each pane serves a specific function, such as providing interactive controls to query a large dataset, showing the query results, or showing details of a selected list item. This use of a multi-pane UI structure (analogous to Tabs or Windows in desktop applications) forces users to frequently switch back and forth between views, which quickly becomes tedious for even common tasks such as looking at details of items in a list.

We propose *AirPanes*, a novel strategy to structure a mobile interface, using panes located in mid-air around the device. As an example scenario we pick mobile commerce (also known as m-commerce) applications as these are used to purchase products through mobile devices by millions of users [35] and require browsing and interacting with large information content before arriving at a decision. We demonstrate the benefits of AirPanes in a scenario where the user browses products, applies filters, inspects result lists, and bookmarks interesting items before making a final purchase. Our AirPanes interface relies on two-handed in-air interaction and takes full advantage of the space around the device. It uses both the spatial region accessible by the thumb of the hand holding the device, as shown in Figure 1a, and the in-air space reachable by fingers of the non-holding hand, as shown in Figure 1b and c. Ways to leverage multiple in-

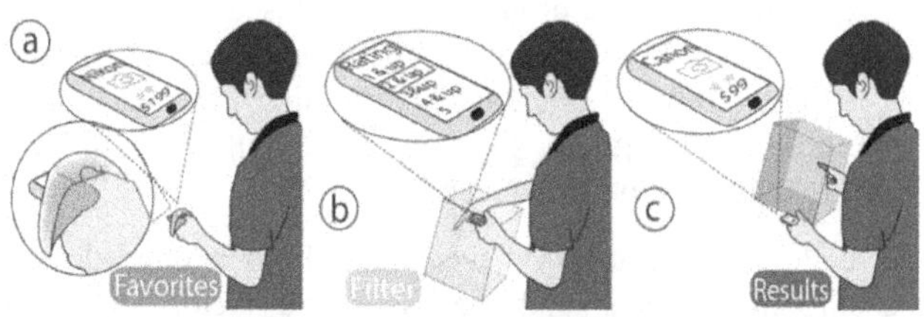


**Figure 1. Two-handed around-device interaction in an m-commerce application using AirPanes. a) Previously tagged favorite products are access in-air with the thumb of the hand holding the phone. b) Query result lists and c) filter options are accessed using in-air panes reachable with the other hand.**

air spaces to provide access to functionality in mobile applications has never been explored before.

We first investigated how the mobile application interfaces are structured to support information exploration on such small screen. Our initial investigation indicates that application interfaces use multiple panes and users required to frequently switch between the panes to access necessary information. We use this knowledge to identify how best to organize panes in mid-air around the device. We optimize design parameters for AirPanes interactions necessary for a complete application, i.e., to select items, their details, to interact with filter controls, and to switch between views. Our results reveal promising item organization and selection strategies as well as layouts to facilitate in-air pane switching. We then designed and implemented AirPanes for an m-commerce app interfaces that works with a Vicon tracking system [37]. We evaluate AirPanes with standard touch interfaces and find that AirPanes is on average 50% more efficient than the common touch interaction.

Our findings came as a result of a systematic design process leading to the following contributions: 1) AirPanes, a strategy to structure mobile interfaces using content panes located in the air around the device that leverages two-handed around-device input; 2) two studies that explore and reveal insights on key AirPanes design factors; 3) a demonstration using AirPanes in an m-commerce interface to support an analytic decision-making task that requires browsing through large item sets and frequent switching between interface views.

## RELATED WORK

We review previous work that inspired our AirPanes approach, including work on around-device interactions, in-air sensing techniques, and two-handed interactions.

### Around-Device Interactions

Prior work on around-device interaction has shown that the in-air space surrounding a mobile device can be used as an alternative to touch input. Researchers have explored the use of around-device space for many fundamental operations, such as widget manipulation [17, 30], multi-touch interaction [4], digit entry [29], and item selection [17, 18]. These operations facilitate limited activities within a complete application, such as controlling the volume of a music player, switching between images, answering and rejecting phone calls, drawing shapes, or entering text. Research also shows that mid-air space can be used for more complex tasks, such as map navigation [39], content browsing [18, 30], mode switching, zooming [25, 46], and to manipulate 3D objects that are displayed on the screen [31].

Several earlier projects have focused on around-device sensing mechanisms and the associated factors, such as hardware, software, localization and classification of detected in-air movements [30, 41, 45], but without considering realistic use cases for around-device input and how to integrate this type of interactions in a complete application.

In this paper, we explore the use of around-device space for a complete smartphone application. We consider an advanced analytic task in our application, which requires users to perform many operations, such as item selection, item browsing, and switching between multiple interface views, or panes. Some of these operations are best suited for on-screen touch, but we identify which of them can be facilitated through in-air input.

People often operate their smartphone applications with one hand while their second hand serves other activities, such as holding a shopping bag while clinging onto a handle bar in a bus [24, 26, 27]. In such one-handed situations, the thumb belonging to the hand holding the device is the digit most readily available for input purposes [24]. However, given the bio-mechanical limits of the thumb, most users cannot reach all parts of the touchscreen with the thumb without readjusting the grip of the phone. Researchers have proposed different solutions to overcome this limitation, such as using a virtual on-screen thumb [32], fisheye and zoom techniques [28], pressure sensors along the side of the device [24], and tilt [8] or back-of-device input [21]. Although the thumb can easily be moved ‘in-air’ while holding the device, in-air thumb interaction has received very little attention. To our knowledge, our work is the first to investigate the use of this in-air space for a smartphone application. Additionally, our AirPanes strategy considers using two different in-air spaces: one controlled by the thumb holding the device, the second controlled via the index finger on the hand not holding the device. To the best of our knowledge, the combined use of two in-air spaces (and operating digits) has not been previously explored.

### Around-Device Sensing Techniques

There has been substantial previous work from industry and academia investigating different sensing mechanisms to track movements around various devices. Several prior projects used industry solutions such as the Vicon [18, 19] and OptiTrack [15, 25, 42] systems, or the Microsoft Kinect [10, 22] to emulated an around-device sensing environment. Though such solutions provide precise motion capture data, miniaturizing to making them portable for mobile devices is not yet possible. Accordingly, numerous research projects have mounted external sensors to a mobile device to detect in-air hand movement in its vicinity. For example, IR sensors [4, 30, 45], depth cameras [9, 31, 44], and the use of GSM signals [47] have been promising solutions to detect in-air input. Also on-board sensors (magnetometers and cameras) in combination with external widgets, such as magnetic objects [17, 29] or an omnidirectional mirror [38, 46], have been shown to be useful for in-air tracking. Recently, Song et al. [41] showed that a smartphone's RGB camera can be used to recognize hand movement behind and in front of the camera without relying on external attachments. These efforts inspire us to count on future smartphones with advanced 3D around-device sensing technologies.

### Two-Handed Interactions

Previous work has demonstrated advantages of using two-handed input for symmetric and asymmetric bimanual tasks over one-handed input [3, 5, 7, 34]. Symmetric assignments, where both hands have a similar role and are used in parallel, have been shown to improved performance [3, 7, 34]. However, Balakrishnan and Hinckley [3] revealed that due to the lack of visual integration, symmetric role assignments could become asymmetric. In asymmetric bimanual interaction, as defined by Guiard's [13] Kinematic Chain model, the non-dominant hand provides the frame of reference and the dominant hand regulates the finer level of interaction details. AirPanes leverages asymmetric bimanual interaction: the non-dominant hand holding the device creates a reference point which the dominant hand navigates around. Additionally, the dominant hand performs fine-grained operations such as exploring items and panes, whereas the non-dominant hand (thumb) issues course-grained operations, such as making selections.

## BACKGROUND ON MULTI-PANE INTERFACES

Our AirPanes strategy to structure a mobile interface in content panes located in mid-air around the device is motivated by the frequent (and often time consuming) pane switching imposed by the interface organization used in current mobile applications.

We started our exploration on the structure and organization used in mobile applications guided by Carrascal et al. [6] who found that people use their smartphones for the following most frequent purposes: 1) phone and audio, 2) SMS/texting, 3) social networking, 4) searching and browsing, and 5) email communication. We studied two applications in each purpose-category: 1) Phone dialer and Skype, 2) Messaging and Hangout, 3) Facebook and Twitter, 4) Google and Yahoo, and 5) Gmail and Yahoo mail. Our informal study revealed that all studied interfaces use multiple panes to organize functionality and information. The number of panes that is used depends on the features supported and the amount and type of information the application contains. However, generally the contained information is broken down into several smaller units which are presented and accessed on separate panes. A master pane (i.e., the home/start screen of the application) shows snippets, or links, to these panes in a vertical scrollable list (some applications use a 'horizontal' carousel widget). A tap on a snippet/link opens a new pane, which shows the full and detailed information. For example, the home screen of the Gmail app lists a snippet of each received email. The user accesses the content of the desired email by taping on its snippet. To check the next email, the user switches back to the home screen and taps the next snippet. Few apps provide a 'Next/Previous' button. Application functionality, settings and options are organized in the same way, with access through taps on snippets/links in an overview pane.

This common multi-pane structure often requires extensive scrolling in the master pane and forces the user to frequently switch back and forth between the different panes.

We iterated through several cycles of design-test-change activities to inform our AirPanes strategy for pane switching. In the following we first present the two most central user studies and then we present our final study where we evaluated the performance of the AirPane strategy against a touch-based interfaces.

## TWO DESIGN STUDIES

In our work, we assume that robust finger tracking in 3D-space will be possible with future smartphones (as indicated by strong efforts in both industry, e.g., [33, 40, 43] and academia, e.g., [4, 17, 30]). We use a Vicon MX system to emulate a device with around-device tracking capabilities. The system tracks IR markers attached to a Google Nexus 5 phone (4.95-inch screen, 1080×1920 pixels) and to the user's left and right thumbs and right hand index finger. The four markers for each thumb and for the finger are positioned on 3D printed finger rings and the six markers for the phone are positioned on a 3D printed holder, which is attached to the top of the phone, as depicted in Figure 2a. With this arrangement of markers and with eight tracking cameras, the system provides noise- and dropout-free tracking of finger and device movements within a 3×3×2 meters large volume. Position data is sent from the Vicon system to an application (Unity+Android) on the smartphone, which interprets the data as user input and reacts with corresponding output.

People hold their smartphones and provide screen input in many ways, depending on the current task (e.g., texting vs. surfing), interaction (e.g., pinch-zooming vs. scrolling), and context (e.g., sitting vs. walking and carrying a bag). We focus on the common situation where the user holds the device in the non-preferred hand and uses the index finger on the preferred hand for input. In this constellation, the thumb of the non-preferred hand, which holds the device, is mostly passive and rests along the side of the device. However, our earlier work [20] demonstrates that an average user can easily and comfortably move the thumb of the hand that is holding the device at least 130mm sideways and 57mm up above the smartphone, as visualized in Figure 2b and c. Encouraged by this finding, we envision this accessible in-air thumb-space as being useful for triggering commands and for storing, selecting and browsing information items (much like Hasan et al.'s [18] AD-Binning concept).

Accordingly, we explored ways to arrange items (i.e., 'in-air buttons') within the accessible thumb-space and methods to select such in-air items. After pilot testing with different numbers of items and different ways to arrange items inside the thumb-space we found that a horizontal arrangement of 10 to 12 wedge-shaped items, in either two or three layers (Figure 2d and e), seems reasonable. Through pilots we also arrived at three promising selection methods: Dwell, Tilt, and Touch (Figure 2f, g, and h). To trigger a selection with Dwell, the user keeps the thumb still for 600ms within the

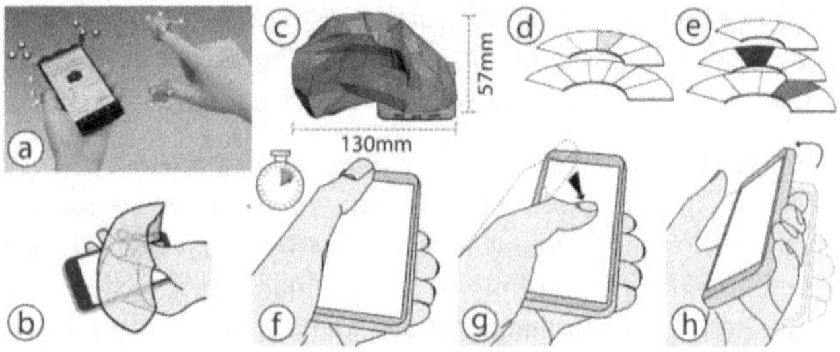


**Figure 2. a) Tracking markers. b) In-air swipe motions. c) Spatial in-air region accessible by the thumb of the hand holding the device. d) On screen visualization with a colored cursor to indicate the position of the thumb inside the in-air region in relation to the items, arranged in two and e) three layers. f) Dwell selection. g) Touch selection. h) Tilt selection.**

desired item's region. To select with Tilt, the user positions the thumb within the item's desired region and then quickly tilts (or rolls) the device sideways (we use a relative 30° threshold). The Touch method involves moving the thumb to the desired in-air region and then quickly tapping down with the thumb, anywhere, on the screen. We use a threshold to resolve situations where the thumb passes through undesired items on its way to the screen (e.g., when selecting an item in an upper layer): we ignore any items which the thumb visited for less than 250ms and treat the most recent item with a visit time greater than 250ms as the selected target.

## Study 1: Selecting In-Air Regions with the Thumb

To inform our design choices for the AirPanes design, we studied users' performance with the three selection methods and the two different item arrangements in a 3×2 within-subjects experiment. Twelve right-handed smart-phone owners participated (3 female; no participant had previously participated in any pilot or study within our AirPanes project; mean age 25.2 years, s.d. 5.5).

### Task

A start button in the middle and a 1.5×1.5cm visualization of the thumb-space (cf. Figure 2d and e) in the top-right corner of the screen are displayed at the trial start. A tap with the tracked left thumb on the button starts timing. The target item for the trial is colored red in the visualization and a blue position cursor indicates the current location of the thumb within the thumb-space. The cursor turns green when the thumb enters the target item (Figure 2d). Timing for the trial ends and the start screen for the next trial is loaded when the system detects a correctly issued selection from within the target item. An error is recorded (timing continues) if the participant performs a selection action from a non-target item.

All participants performed two series of six blocks of trials with each of the three selection methods, one series with the 2-Layer and one series with the 3-Layer arrangement. Each block contained one trial for each of the 11 item positions (presented in random order within a block). Participants were divided in six pairs, one pair for each of the six possible presentation orders of selection methods. One participant in each pair always started with the series for the 2-Layer arrangement, one started with the 3-Layer arrangement. Each participant performed a total of 396 timed trials: 3 methods × 2 arrangements × 6 blocks × 11 item positions. A study session lasted 45 min (incl. instructions, practice and breaks).

### Results

*Error trials*: In 253 of the 4,752 trials (5.32%) participants issued one or more correct selection actions in a non-target item before correctly selecting the target item. In total, 5,115 correct selection actions were registered, 363 selections were on a non-target item: 99 with Touch, 130 with Dwell, and 134 with Tilt. A Friedman Test showed no significant difference between the three methods. The number of errors for each item position in the two arrangements are shown in Figure 3a and b. In total, 192 and 171 errors were registered with the 2-Layer and 171 3-Layer arrangements, respectively. A Wilcoxon Signed-Rank test showed no difference between the two arrangements.

Although the item size was slightly smaller in the middle of the layers (cf. Figure 2d and e), we see a trend with more erroneous selections for the slightly larger items at the right and left side. A possible reason for this is that the outer items require stretching the thumb more. Possible solutions to resolve this issue could be to either use a fisheye space discretization [18] that provides more space to the currently 'touched' item or to use a more extreme angle dependent discretization to assign even more space to outer items.

*Trial time*: We only use error free trials (4,499) to analyze selection time and take the median trial time for each method × arrangement × position combination for each participant. This median time data was right skewed and we performed a logarithmic transformation (which resulted in a distribution close to normal) before analyzing the data.

The geometric mean selection time (i.e., the antilog of the mean of the log-transformed data) was similar for the three methods: Touch 1.53s, Tilt 1.56s, and Dwell 1.60s. There was also no marked difference between the two arrangements: 2-Layer 1.58s, 3-Layer 1.56s. A two-way RM-ANOVA (method × arrangement) showed no significant main or interaction effect.

Figure 3c and d show the geometric mean selection time for each item position in the two arrangements. Two separate one-way ANOVAs, one for each arrangement, showed that there was a statistically significant effect for item position on selection time (2-Layer: $F_{10,121} = 9.31$, $p < 0.0001$, $\eta^2 = 0.44$;

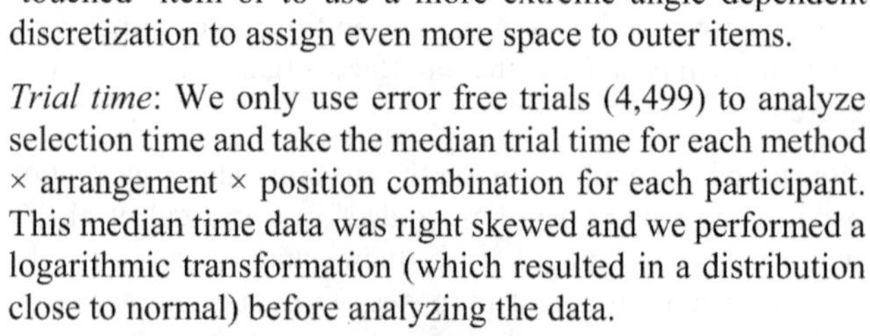


**Figure 3. a) and b) Number of errors and c) and d) geometric mean trial time for each item position (from left to right in each layer, cf. Figure 3c and d).**

3-Layer: $F_{10,121} = 6.67$, $p < 0.0001$, $\eta^2 = 0.36$). Again, as with error trials, we see a trend with more difficulties with outer items. Bonferroni adjusted post-hoc pairwise comparisons confirmed: the inner items, Item 3, 4, and 5, in the bottom layer in the 2-Layer arrangement were faster to select than the two outmost items in either layer; Item 4 in the bottom layer in the 3-Layer arrangement was faster to select than the two outmost items in either layer (all p's < 0.0009).

*Summary*: We conclude that regarding both errors and selection time, the three selection methods and the two arrangements score about equally well. The somewhat more error and slightly longer selection times for item positions at the outer ends in a layer indicate a trend suggesting that item positions at the far ends tend to be slightly more troublesome to select than items in the middle. The results regarding the three selection methods are promising and suggest that all of our three methods are suitable for in-air thumb selections, which gives the designer the flexibility to choose method as appropriate according to other factors, such as usage context or application type.

With insights about viable item arrangements and selection methods for the in-air thumb space, we move on and present a second central study we performed to inform our AirPanes apprroach.

### Study 2: AirPane Layout and Pane Switching

As we noted in our survey on mobile application interfaces, the small display sizes used on smartphones forces designers to structure their interfaces in a multiple-pane. With such a structure the user has to repeatedly tap on small UI buttons (or on other interface elements, such as entries in scrollable lists) to switch views. Our AirPane approach is based on the idea to off-load panes into around-device space. With panes residing in-air, the user can quickly switch between panes by simply moving the in-air input finger inside the desired pane's in-air area – and the pane's content is displayed on the screen. We also envision that the user interacts with pane content directly from in-air space using finger gestures.

We explored five different ways to arrange four panes in around-device space and the use of an in-air pinch-gesture to select pane content.

*Stacked layout* (Figure 4a): The four panes are stacked on top of each other to the right of the smartphone, to above the device, two below the device. Each pane's bottom-left x-y position aligns with the device's bottom-right x-y position. If the user moves the device, the panes follow to maintain their position relative to the device. With previous work [1] showing that social acceptability related concerns are raised

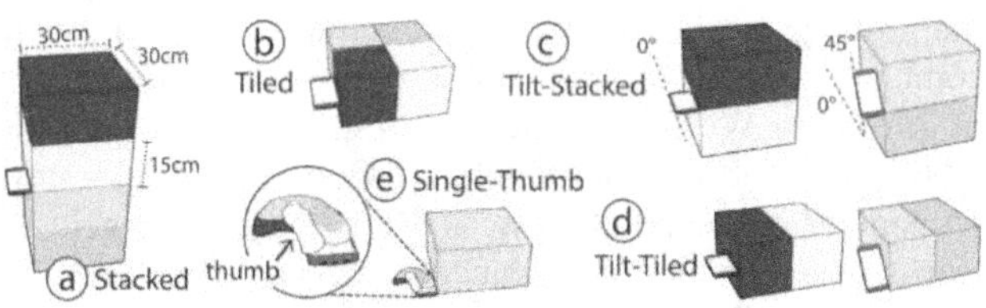


**Figure 4. Five AirPane layouts.**

for around-device gestures taking place beyond 30cm from the device, we limit our panes to a 30×30cm area. The screen's 1080×1776 pixels are mapped to 1080×1776 in-air 'pixels', each approximately 0.028×0.017cm large. The two middle panes are each 15cm high; one of our earlier studies showed this gives the user enough vertical space to perform in-air gestures inside a pane without accidentally entering (and so switching to) an adjacent pane. The top and the bottom panes extend infinitely in the upward respectively downward directions.

*Tiled layout* (Figure 4b): The four panes share the space used for a single pane in the Stacked layout. This requires less in-air hand movements for pane switching, but more precise movements when interacting with pane content. Each pane measures 15×15cm and extends infinitely upward and downward. The corresponding in-air 'pixel' measures approximately 0.014×0.008cm.

*Tilt-Stacked layout* (Figure 4c): Similar to the Stacked layout, each pane uses a 30×30cm area (the top pane extends infinitely upwards, the bottom pane downwards, in-air 'pixels' measure approx. 0.028×0.017cm). The four panes are grouped in two pairs, only one pair is accessible at a time. When the device is tilted at an angle less than 45°, the user can switch between the first pair of panes by moving the finger vertically above or below the device. When the device is titled at an angle more than 45°, the other pair is accessible. This provides a larger area for each pane and requires less vertical movements than with the Stacked layout, but introduces a tilting action.

*Tilt-Tiled layout* (Figure 4d): Again, panes are grouped in pairs and a tilt angel is used to switch between pairs. Each pane uses a 15×30cm area (extended infinitely upward and downward, in-air 'pixels' measure approximately 0.014× 0.017cm). Horizontal in-air movements are used to switch between panes in a pair.

*Single-Thumb layout* (Figure 4e): Only one 30×30cm pane (extending infinitely upwards and downwards, in-air 'pixels' measure approximately 0.028×0.017cm) is accessible at a time beside the device. The user switches between panes with in-air thumb selections using the left thumb. The in-air thumb-space is divided into four approximately equally sized regions arranged in two layers (cf. inset Figure 4e). Moving the thumb into another area and selecting with the Touch method from Study 1 switches to the selected pane.

To inform our design choices regarding pane switching for our m-commerce demonstration interface, we studied 15 right-handed smartphone owners' performance with the five AirPane layouts (2 female, no participant had previously participated in any pilot or earlier study; mean age 21.1, s.d. 1.8). We used a low-level task where participants had to switch between four panes and select items in the panes.

#### Task

A trial consists of selecting first a blue and then a yellow 'target item', positioned in two different panes. The other two panes contain one red distractor item each. The squared items are positioned at random positions inside the pane. The blue target is labelled "1", the yellow target is labelled "2". The panes are numbered 1 to 4 (to provide a clear visual identifier for each pane). A black circular cursor on the screen provides feedback about the position of the index finger inside the active in-air pane. Figure 5a and b visualize a selection of the yellow target item; when the cursor enters the target, the target is highlighted in green. With the cursor inside the target, the participant separates the pinched thumb and index finger by at least 1cm to invoke a selection.

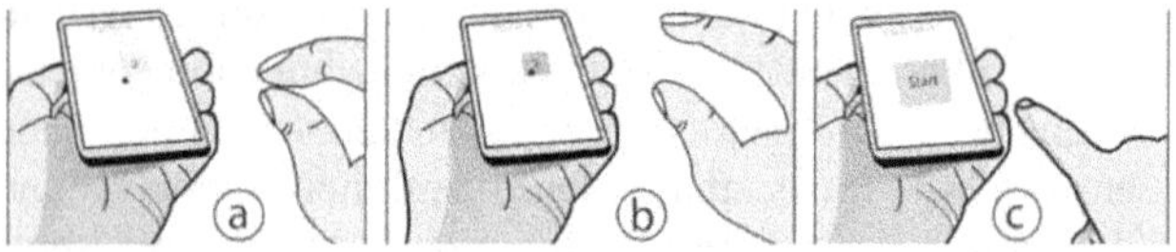

**Figure 5. a) A participant moves the 'pinched' in-air fingers to steer the on-screen cursor over the target. b) Releasing the pinch with the cursor over the target selects it. c) Start screen.**

After successfully selecting the first target the participant proceeds to find (i.e., switch to) the pane with the yellow target. Successfully selecting the yellow target ends timing and shows the start screen for the next trial (Figure 5c). An on-screen tap on the "start" button starts timing for the next trial. Selections in distractor items are ignored. Selections outside items or a selection of the yellow target before the blue target are also ignored, but the trial is marked as an error trial. Marked trials are re-queued at a random position among unfinished trials within a block of trials.

The in-air space available for an item inside a pane depends on the used pane layout. This suggests a possible trade-off between the ease and speed with which a user can switch panes and the ease and speed with which in-air items can be selected. Accordingly, we used three different on-screen item sizes to investigate such a possible trade-off: 100×100, 200×200, and 300×300 pixels.

Each participant completed a block of five (error free) trials for each of the 5×3 layout-size combinations. Participants had six practice trials with each layout before they started with the first block of timed trials. The presentation order of the five layouts were counterbalanced between participants and the three item sizes were presented in a random order within each layout. We instructed participants to finish each trial as quickly and accurately as possible. Participation lasted 45 min (incl. instruction, practice trials, and breaks).

### Results

*Error trials*: 135 trials were marked with an error. These trials were about equally distributed across participants, layouts and target sizes.

*Trial time*: For the error free trials we use the median trial time for each layout × target size combination for each participant (i.e., 15 trials). This data was right skewed and we performed a logarithmic transformation (which resulted in a distribution close to normal) before analyzing the data.

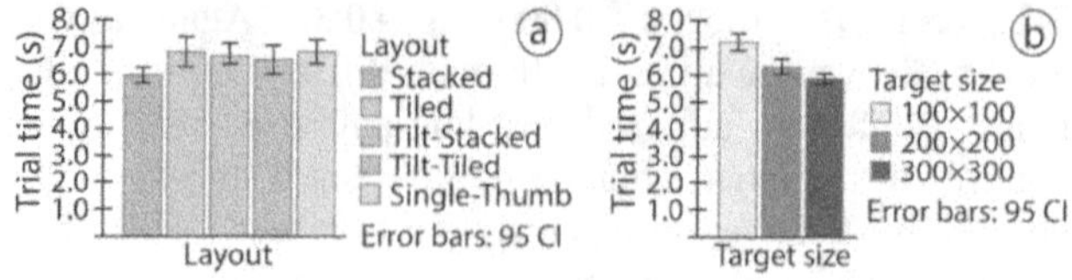


**Figure 6. Geometric mean trial times, a) layout, b) target size.**

Figure 6 shows the geometric mean selection time for the five layouts and for the three target sizes. A two-way RM-ANOVA showed significant main effects for both layout ($F_{4,56} = 2.70$, $p < 0.05$, $\eta^2 = 0.16$) and target size ($F_{2,28} = 50.7$, $p < 0.0001$, $\eta^2 = 0.78$) but not a significant interaction effect. Bonferroni corrected post-hoc pairwise comparisons of layouts showed that the Stacked layout (5.96s) was significantly faster than all other layouts (all p's < 0.005), which did not differ and were 10.7% slower (or more): Tiled 6.85s, Tilt-Stacked 6.64s, Tilt-Tiled 6.60s, Single-Thumb 6.68s.

As expected, large items are faster to select than smaller (Figure 6b, 100×100 7.40s, 200×200 6.44s, and 300×300 5.97s). Bonferroni corrected post-hoc pairwise comparisons of the three target sizes showed that each pairwise comparison was significant (all p's < 0.016) with the larger target in each comparison being faster than the smaller.

*Summary*: Our results suggest that the Stacked layout is fast since no secondary activity is needed to switch to another pane, such as tilting the device or moving a second hand, as with Single-Thumb. A vertical hand movement is enough with Stacked. Many participants commented on the convenience and ease with moving the in-air hand in vertical directions, i.e., up and down for switching panes, compared to moving the hand toward or away from the body. A few participants mentioned that they had slight difficulties getting used to tilting the device, especially in early trials, which may explain the somewhat inferior performance with the tilt-based layouts. Our results also indicate that the trial time is strongly influenced by target size. Naturally, large items are easier and faster to select than small items. The non-significant layout×size interaction effect indicates a consistency between all layouts, with no layout suffering more (or less) due to too small in-air targets. Next, we demonstrate how we used our insights about effective switching mechanisms and around-device pane layouts to design an m-commerce interface that utilizes AirPanes and two-handed interaction.

## USING AIRPANES IN AN M-COMMERCE INTERFACE

With millions of users purchasing products online from their smartphones (the number of online purchases from smartphones has steadily increased over the past years and the growing trend is expected to continue [35, 36]), an m-commerce scenario is a realistic scenario to showcase the use of AirPanes. We first studied the responsive websites and mobile apps (versions installed from Google Play [12]) from 15 popular online retail services [2] (listed in Figure 7a) to learn about common m-commerce interface structures and functionality. We found that all studied interfaces use similar

**Figure 7. a) Studied m-commerce interfaces. b) General UI structure of the surveyed interfaces. c) Filter selection pane in a mobile app. d) A responsive website's overview list. d) Detail item view in a mobile app. AirPanes interface: f) product details, g) filter options, and h) product detail view for a bookmarked item. Classic touch interface: i) scrollable overview list of search results, j) product detail view, k) filter view, and l) modal view with filter options.**

interface components to provide the necessary functionality, as summarized in Figure 7b. A text field is used for product search. Filter functionality is accessed through a "filter" button (most often positioned close to the search functionality) which opens a separate pane that displays the provided filter options (Figure 7c). Search results (filtered or unfiltered) are displayed below the search box in a scrollable overview list (Figure 7d), or in a grid. A thumbnail image and general product information are provided for each item in the list. A tap on an item opens up a new pane which shows further details about the product (Figure 7e). A tap on a "back" button displays the overview list again. From the detail pane, the user can add the item to the shopping cart (and/or favorite list) with a tap on an "add" button.

Our AirPanes interface includes the same functionality as found in conventional m-commerce interfaces. We present the design based on a scenario where the user wants to buy a camera. To issue a product query, the user enters a search text in a text field, as in conventional m-commerce interfaces. Instead of displaying overview information for each camera in the result set in a scrollable list on the screen, for the AirPane interface we off-load the result items onto a 30×30cm in-air pane to the right of the smartphone. We use the best performing Stacked layout from Study 2, and we provide access to filter functionality in a second 30×30cm pane below the results pane. The user can switch between these two panes by moving the in-air hand up and down, crossing an imaginary horizontal plane (as defined by the smartphone's touch-surface). As soon as the in-air finger enters the results pane with camera items, the user sees full information about one of the camera items on the screen, as depicted in Figure 7f. What camera is shown depends on the position of the in-air finger. The camera items in the results pane are arranged in a n×m matrix with equally sized cells filling out the pane. The size of the cells depends on the number of items in the result set. An on-screen visualization with a blue cursor (inset Figure 7f) provides feedback about the in-air finger's current position within the pane.

When the in-air finger enters the filter pane, below the results pane, the user sees filter options on the screen, as depicted in Figure 7g. The filter pane uses a Tiled layout that divides the pane in four 15×15cm large sub-panes, one for four different filter categories (Brand, User ranking, Pixels, Price). Again, the finger's position within the pane is visualized in an on-screen overview (inset Figure 7g) and the current sub-pane is marked with a blue border. The available filter options in each sub-pane are arranged top-to-bottom in the in-air sub-pane (as on the screen). Each option in a category spans horizontally across the whole in-air sub-pane (15cm), the number of options determine the 'height' of the in-air area used for each option (e.g., with five options, each in-air area measures 15×3cm). If more than five filter options are available within a filter category, as with the "Brand" category in Figure 7g, the user can move the in-air finger below the filter pane into a new 30×30 pane where the additional options are available.

The user issues a pinch gesture (as used in Study 2, Figure 5) to select filter options. The pinch gesture is also used when browsing result items inside the topmost in-air pane. With a pinch inside a camera item, the item is added to a list of favorites for later quick access and further inspection and a check mark is shown on the screen (a second pinch inside the same item removes it from the list, and the check mark from the screen). The list of bookmarked items can be inspected using the in-air thumb-space (as in Study 1, cf. Figure 2). To activate the thumb-space the user moves the right hand outside any in-air pane (e.g., moving the hand to the right thigh) and lifts the left thumb into thumb-space. Favorite items are arranged in layers inside thumb-space, as Studied in Study 1. The number of layers and the size of the items are dynamically adjusted according to the number of items that has been added to the list. When the thumb enters an item the corresponding camera information is displayed on the screen. An on-screen visualization informs about the current position within thumb-space, as shown in Figure 7h. The thumb-space is deactivated when the user moves the right hand into any in-air pane to the right of the smartphone. The results pane which is the topmost pane extends infinitely upwards. The filter pane (with its sub-panes) in the middle is 15cm high and the bottom most pane with additional filter options extends infinitely downwards.

### Study 3: AirPanes vs. Conventional Interface Design

We evaluated the efficiency of our AirPanes interface against a touch-based m-commerce interface. The touch interface provides the same functionality as the AirPanes version. The functionality is organised in multiple views, as typical for popular m-commerce interface and shown in Figure 7. Search results are presented in scrollable list with overview information for each item (Figure 7i). A tap on an item shows its detail view (Figure 7j), where the user can add the item to the favorite list. A check mark signals if the item is already in the favourite list (as in Figure 7f) and the "add" button is substituted by a "remove" button. From the view with the result list the user can tap on a "Filter" button to narrow down the result by first selecting a filter category in the filter view (Figure 7k), and then select desired filter options in a second view (Figure 7l). Access to the list of bookmarked favorites is provided from the view with the result list by tapping the "favorite" button in the top-right corner of the screen. The favorites are presented in a scrollable list with overview information for each item, exactly as in the main view with search result. A tap on an item shows its detail view. From all views, a tap on the back button in Android's navigation bar (bottom of the screen) switches back to the previous view.

Twelve right-handed male smartphone owners (age 23.2 years, s.d. 3.2) participated. All were new to the concept of around-device interactions and none had participated in any previous pilot or earlier study within our AirPanes project.

#### *Task*

The study task covers typical steps taken when searching for a camera to buy online. First, a text prompt is displayed on an external monitor, e.g., "Apply the following filters: Price between \$200 and \$400, user rating 3 and higher, then find the lightest camera with a weight between 400g and 500g" and "Apply the following filters: Brand: Nikon and Sony, Pixels: 10MP and up, then find the camera with the greatest optical zoom between 25X and 40X". The task prompt always includes two filters in varying combinations, one criteria range (*between* value X and Y for either optical zoom, LCD size, or weight), and one superlative (smallest, greatest, lightest, or heaviest). After reading the prompt (which remains visible throughout the trial), the participant taps a "start" button on the smartphone screen, this starts the trial timer. We exclude the entering of a search query from the task since this is done in the same way in the two interfaces. Instead, the task starts with a default set of 99 cameras. Now the participant needs to apply the two requested filters. After applying the filters either 10, 20, or 30 cameras remain in the results set (the number varies randomly between trials). The participant can now start inspecting the product details of the remaining cameras and can bookmark candidate cameras to "favorites" that correspond to the selection criteria (e.g., weight between 400g and 500g, 4 to 7 cameras per trial). After this, the participant accesses the favourite functionality to find the one and only camera that matches the complete task prompt. When the participant believes having found the correct camera, the trial ends with a tap on a "buy" button (when using the touch interface) or with a thumb-tap from the corresponding item inside thumb-space (when using AirPanes, cf. Study 1 and Figure 2g). If it is the correct camera trial time stops and the task prompt for the next trial is displayed on the external display. If it was incorrect, the screen flashes in red and the participant can continue the search for the correct camera.

Each participant performed nine trials with each interface (three trials per result set size (10, 20, 30) in random order). Six participants started with AirPanes, six with the touch interface. We demonstrated the two interfaces and showed how the filter functionality and the bookmarking feature would help them to speed up their searches. We instructed participants to try to finish each trial as quickly as possible. Each participant had two practice trials with each interface before starting with the timed trials. Participation lasted about 1 hour (including instructions, practice, and breaks).

#### *Results*

We analyze the trial time and the time participants spent with each of the three sub-activities: applying filters (*filter time*), inspecting items and bookmarking items in the filtered set of cameras (*results time*), and inspecting and selecting from the bookmarked favorites (*favorite time*). For each separate time measure we use the median time for each interface × results size combination for each participant. The data was right skewed and we performed logarithmic transformations (which resulted in a distribution close to normal for all four time measures) before analyzing each time measure.

*Trial time*: The trial time is shown in Figure 8a. The geometric mean trial time was 57.3s with AirPanes and 116.1s with the touch interface. The difference corresponds to 50.6%. A RM-ANOVA (interface, results size) showed a significant effect for interface ($F_{1,11} = 222.60$, $p < 0.0001$, $\eta^2 = 0.95$) and for results size ($F_{2,22} = 48.64$, $p < 0.0001$, $\eta^2 = 0.82$), but no significant interaction effect. The trial time increased with increasing results size: 63.2s with 10 items, 86.3s with 20 items, and 99.7s with 30 items. Bonferroni corrected post-hoc pairwise comparisons between results sizes showed a significant difference for each pair (all p's < 0.016).

We turn to our analyses of the three separate sub-activities the participants performed to find the explanation for the great overall difference between the two interfaces.

*Filter time*: The time spent with the first sub-activity is shown in Figure 8b. A two-way RM ANOVA showed that across the three result sizes participants needed significantly more time ($F_{1,11} = 22.80$, $p < 0.001$, $\eta^2 = 0.68$) to apply the filters using AirPanes (15.1s) than with the touch interface (11.0s). As expected, there was no significant effect for

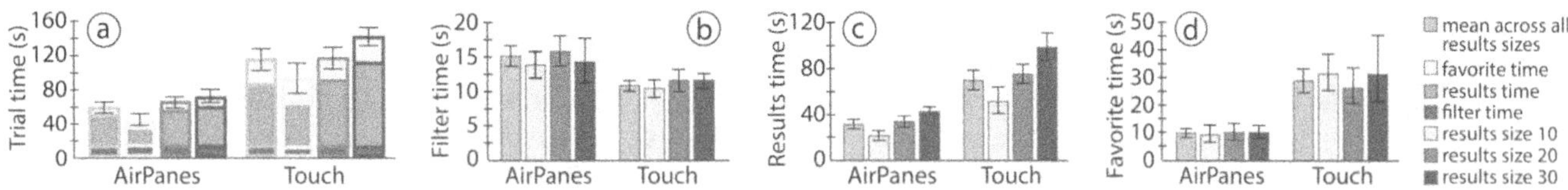


**Figure 8. Geometric mean times. a) Trial time, b) filter time, c) results time, and d) favorite time. Error bars: 95 CI.**

results size (results size 10: 11.1s, result size 20: 14.6s, results size 30: 13.0s) or a significant interaction effect. Recall that the results size was relevant only after that the filters had been applied. Accordingly, the time difference (3.9s) between the two interfaces mainly comes from selecting the filter controls, which was more challenging (and unfamiliar) with in-air pinches using AirPanes.

*Results time*: The time spent in the second sub-activity, inspecting items and bookmarking items in the filtered set of cameras, is shown in Figure 8c. Overall, across the three results sizes, participants needed significantly ($F_{1,11} = 157.4$, $p < 0.0001$, $\eta^2 = 0.94$) more time for this activity when using the touch interface (71.3s) than when using AirPanes (30.8s). There was also a significant effect for results size ($F_{2,22} = 50.8$, $p < 0.0001$, $\eta^2 = 0.82$). Comprehensibly, with more items to inspect the longer it takes (results size 10: 35.8s, results size 20: 53.7s, results size 30: 69.5s). Bonferroni adjusted post-hoc comparisons showed that all three results sizes differed (all p's < 0.016). The relative increase in results time with increasing results size was similar for both interfaces (i.e., the RM-ANOVA did not show a significant interface × results size interaction). We attribute the slow inspection and bookmarking time with the touch interface to the frequent (and tedious) switching between items in the result list and their corresponding detail views to find the necessary information. With AirPanes on the other hand, no switching is needed. Instead, the user does only need to move the in-air finger a short distance to enter a new in-air item and so call in its detail information on the screen.

*Favorites time*: The time spent in the third sub-activity, selecting from the bookmarked items, is shown in Figure 8d. Overall, across the three result sizes, participants were significantly faster ($F_{1,11} = 59.2$, $p < 0.0001$, $\eta^2 = 0.84$) selecting from the favorite set when using AirPanes (9.7s) than when using the touch interface (28.7s). As with the filtering activity, results size had no significant effect on how much time was needed to identify and select the target item from the favorites (results size 10: 17.4s, results size 20: 19.8s, results size 30: 20.8s). Again, as when involved with inspecting the filtered set of cameras, we attribute the disadvantage with the touch interface to the frequent view switching that is required to going back and forth between camera overviews and details. With AirPanes, only a small movement of the in-air thumb is necessary to view information about a new item.

### Summary

Our results show that, in comparison to touch input, in-air interactions with AirPanes reduces browsing time by taking the advantage of an in-air 'hover' state. With AirPanes, detailed item information can be inspected without having to perform an action (i.e., tapping) to open the detail view. This makes AirPanes an efficient browsing interface, which does not require frequent switching between views, as in many touch-based interfaces (where the user has to tap on an item in a list, open its details and then tap again to switch back to the list). Our results also demonstrate that users can capitalize on this in-air 'hover' state when using their thumb.

Though promising, a few participants raised concerns about arm fatigue through prolonged use of in-air movements. Furthermore, some participants indicated the possible difficulty for persons with small hands to retain a stable grip of the device while using the in-air thumb space.

## DISCUSSION

In the light of these promising results, we discuss design recommendations, potential issues regarding the integration of AirPanes in smartphone applications and present future directions to extend our work.

### Design Recommendations

Our investigation offers the following recommendations regarding around-device interactions:

*Thumb-space usage*: When complemented with in-air index finger input, the in-air thumb-space is well suited for input. It works best for short interactions involving a limited number of items. We suggest using this space to provide access to ten or less items, such as frequently used phone contacts, or to quickly load recently visited websites.

*Non-tilt based pane layout*: Several participants in Study 2 reported having felt less comfortable with the tilt-based pane layout style as it required rotating the smartphone to switch between sets of panes. This movement also caused a disturbing change in viewing angle. Accordingly, we recommend designers to consider using the Stacked and Tiled layouts for placing panes in around-device space.

*Nested pane layout*: In our AirPanes design, we used nested in-air panes to provide access to the four filter categories and their options. This nesting strategy increases the number of panes that can be used in an application. We recommend designers to adopt nesting instead of stacking several planes on top of each other which requires larger vertical movements for switching between panes.

### Considerations for Integration of AirPanes in Applications

*AirPanes scalability*: We tested AirPanes with a limited number items in a pane (e.g., a maximum of 30 cameras in the results pane). However, the design can be extended to accommodate a larger number of panes. For instance, a UI scrolling strategy could be adopted where moving the index finger to a certain in-air location would show new panes. Moreover, an AirPanes application could incorporate other strategies, such as pagination, to divide large sets of in-air items into sub-sets which could be triggered in thumb-space.

*Pane organization styles*: Our AirPanes implementation considers a mixed pane organization, the panes with filter options and the results pane are stacked. The panes with filter categories were tiled. We envision that AirPanes can work with many alternative pane organizations. For example, AirPanes could be designed for one-handed use using only stacked or tiled layout, as shown in Figure 9a respectively 9b. In these ways, all the panes would be accessible with the index finger on the free hand. Alternatively, a pane organization could leverage two-handed usage by assigning the thumb-space for triggering panes that are accessed with the other hand, as shown in Figure 9c.

*Generalization of AirPanes for other Applications*: We showed the benefit of using AirPanes for an m-commerce application scenario with a complex analytic task where users had to frequently switch between multiple panes to reach a decision. Thus, the AirPanes design can be generalized to any applications that require navigate and interact with several panes before reaching a decision. Such applications include any shopping, retails or travel booking apps. In addition, other popular apps such as search engines (e.g., Google or Yahoo) are most often displayed with headlines and snippets and the user has to open the results, one by one, which involves frequent view switching. Since AirPanes reduces the need for frequent switching through its in-air 'hover' state, we believe most applications that require view switching would benefit from an AirPanes design. Further investigation is needed to identify a generic design for AirPanes accommodating a wide range of applications.

*Usage Context*: We explored AirPanes with a task where the user was standing. However, AirPanes could also be used while sitting, or when the smartphone is laying on a flat surface. In such cases, AirPanes could use the surrounding physical surface to leverage haptic feedback into mixed physical and in-air interactions. For instance, AirPanes could use the surrounding surface (e.g., use the user's thigh, a table or a wall as shown in Figure 9d) for applying filters, and then use the in-air space for browsing results.

### Limitations and Future Work

AirPanes demands accurate and robust finger detection around the smartphone. Although current smartphones do not provide such features, in a recent study Song et al. [41] showed that a smartphone's camera can be used to recognize in-air hand movement, but in limited directions. Further such explorations are needed to make devices capable of precise around-device hand tracking.

We considered the smartphone to be in 'AirPanes' mode by default. However, further investigation is needed to develop implicit or explicit mode switching mechanisms to activate and deactivate around-device input to counter accidental in-air gesture events. For instance, air thumb input can be implicitly set into "in-air" mode by making it possible for the thumb to engage only when the in-air space is being used with the index finger. Explicit mode switching can be done, for example, with a physical button that the user presses to activate AirPanes mode.

We acknowledge that current mobile apps also support switching between views using right/left swipes, which we did not include in out last study. We believe that using such a swipe mechanism in the touch-based interface would further ascertain our claims as this approach allows only sequential access to items, which we expect to be slow.

In our AirPanes design, we consider in-air thumb-space as a complementary input region. In our future work we will focus on exploring this space for one-handed use cases such as supporting multi-touch interactions (e.g., zoom in/out a map) with thumb within this in-air space. Though the current smartphone design allows holding the device with one hand, the flat shape of the phone prohibits users from reaching the topmost regions of the screen with the thumb in a one-handed usage situation. We will also explore improved off-screen visualizations [14, 16] to manage two-handed around device input, as well as explore ways to mitigate thumb and arm fatigue [23].

## CONCLUSION

We have presented AirPanes, a novel technique that utilizes in-air spaces to organize multiple panes that are commonly seen in smartphone applications. We demonstrated the value of AirPanes for carrying out a complex task in an m-commerce application that requires users to frequently switch between multiple in-air panes, such as filters, results, and favourites to make a purchase decision. Through two initial studies, we identified properties of various design factors relevant to AirPanes. Our final study confirmed that AirPanes facilitates complex analytic tasks by reducing task time by 50% compared to a standard touch screen interface. We believe that AirPanes is the first successful step in using in-air spaces for a complete mobile application and so pushes the boundary of current around-device interactions.

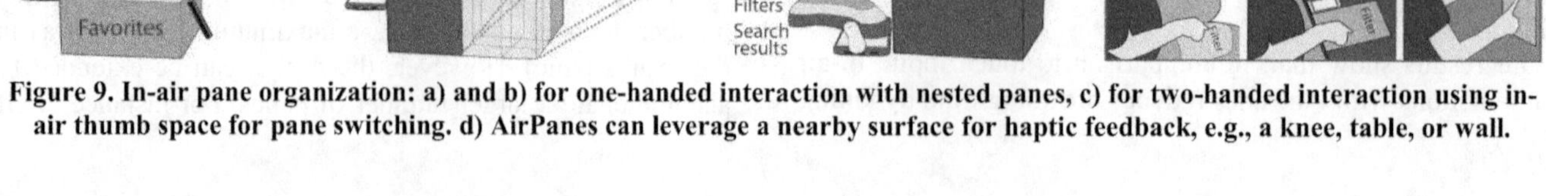


**Figure 9. In-air pane organization: a) and b) for one-handed interaction with nested panes, c) for two-handed interaction using in-air thumb space for pane switching. d) AirPanes can leverage a nearby surface for haptic feedback, e.g., a knee, table, or wall.**

## REFERENCES

1. David Ahlström, Khalad Hasan, and Pourang Irani. 2014. Are you comfortable doing that?: acceptance studies of around-device gestures in and for public settings. In *Proceedings of the 16th International Conference on Human-Computer Interaction with Mobile Devices and Services* (MobileHCI '14), 193-202. https://doi.org/10.1145/2628363.2628381
2. Alexa Top 500 Global Sites. 2017. Retrieved January 04, 2017 from http://www.alexa.com/topsites.
3. Ravin Balakrishnan and Ken Hinckley. 2000. Symmetric bimanual interaction. In *Proceedings of the SIGCHI Conference on Human Factors in Computing Systems* (CHI '00), 33–40. https://doi.org/10.1145/332040.332404
4. Alex Butler, Shahram Izadi, and Steve Hodges. 2008. SideSight: multi-"touch" interaction around small devices. In *Proceedings of the 21st Annual ACM Symposium on User Interface Software and Technology* (UIST '08), 201-204. http://dl.acm.org/citation.cfm?doid=1449715.1449746
5. W. Buxton and B. Myers. 1986. A study in two-handed input. In *Proceedings of the SIGCHI Conference on Human Factors in Computing Systems* (CHI '86), 321–326. https://doi.org/10.1145/22627.22390
6. Juan Pablo Carrascal and Karen Church. 2015. An in-situ study of mobile app & mobile search interactions. In *Proceedings of the 33rd Annual ACM Conference on Human Factors in Computing Systems* (CHI '15), 2739-2748. https://doi.org/10.1145/2702123.2702486
7. Didier Casalta, Yves Guiard, and Michel Beaudouin-Lafon. 1999. Evaluating two-handed input techniques: Rectangle editing and navigation. In *Proceedings of the CHI '99 Extended Abstracts on Human Factors in Computing Systems* (CHI EA '99), 236–237. https://doi.org/10.1145/632716.632862
8. Youli Chang, Sehi L'Yi, Kyle Koh, and Jinwook Seo. 2015. Understanding users' touch behavior on large mobile touch-screens and assisted targeting by tilting gesture. In *Proceedings of the 33rd Annual ACM Conference on Human Factors in Computing Systems* (CHI '15), 1499–1508. https://doi.org/10.1145/2702123.2702425
9. Xiang 'Anthony' Chen, Julia Schwarz, Chris Harrison, Jennifer Mankoff, and Scott E. Hudson. 2014. Air+touch: interweaving touch & in-air gestures. In *Proceedings of the 27th Annual ACM Symposium on User Interface Software and Technology* (UIST '14), 519-525. https://doi.org/10.1145/2642918.2647392
10. Euan Freeman, Stephen Brewster, and Vuokko Lantz. 2016. Do that, there: an interaction technique for addressing in-air gesture systems. In *Proceedings of the 2016 CHI Conference on Human Factors in Computing Systems* (CHI '16), 2319-2331. http://dx.doi.org/10.1145/2858036.2858308
11. Verena Giller, Rudolf Melcher, Johann Schrammel, Reinhard Sefelin, and Manfred Tscheligi. 2003. Usability evaluations for multi-device application development three example studies. In *Proceedings of Human-Computer Interaction with Mobile Devices and Services* (MobileHCI '03), 302–316. http://link.springer.com/chapter/10.1007/978-3-540-45233-1_22
12. Google Play. 2017. Retrieved January 04, 2017 from https://play.google.com/store?hl=en
13. Yves Guiard. 1987. Asymmetric division of labor in human skilled bimanual action. *Journal of Motor Behavior* 19, 4: 486–517. https://doi.org/10.1080/00222895.1987.10735426
14. Sean Gustafson, Patrick Baudisch, Carl Gutwin, and Pourang Irani. 2008. Wedge: clutter-free visualization of off-screen locations. In *Proceedings of the SIGCHI Conference on Human Factors in Computing Systems (CHI '08)*, 787-796. https://doi.org/10.1145/1357054.1357179
15. Sean Gustafson, Daniel Bierwirth, and Patrick Baudisch. 2010. Imaginary interfaces: spatial interaction with empty hands and without visual feedback. In *Proceedings of the 23nd Annual ACM Symposium on User Interface Software and Technology* (UIST '10), 3-12. http://dl.acm.org/citation.cfm?doid=1866029.1866033
16. Sean G. Gustafson and Pourang P. Irani. 2007. Comparing visualizations for tracking off-screen moving targets. In *Proceedings of the CHI '07 Extended Abstracts on Human Factors in Computing Systems (CHI EA '07)*, 2399-2404. https://doi.org/10.1145/1240866.1241014
17. Chris Harrison and Scott E. Hudson. 2009. Abracadabra: wireless, high-precision, and unpowered finger input for very small mobile devices. In *Proceedings of the 22nd Annual ACM Symposium on User Interface Software and Technology* (UIST '09), 121-124. https://doi.org/10.1145/1622176.1622199
18. Khalad Hasan, David Ahlström, and Pourang Irani. 2013. Ad-binning: leveraging around device space for storing, browsing and retrieving mobile device content. In *Proceedings of the SIGCHI Conference on Human Factors in Computing Systems* (CHI '13), 899-908. http://dl.acm.org/citation.cfm?doid=2470654.2466115
19. Khalad Hasan, David Ahlström, and Pourang Irani. 2015. SAMMI: a spatially-aware multi-mobile interface for analytic map navigation tasks. In *Proceedings of the 17th International Conference on Human-Computer Interaction with Mobile Devices and*

*Services* (MobileHCI '15), 36-45. https://doi.org/10.1145/2785830.2785850

20. Khalad Hasan, Junhyeok Kim, David Ahlström, and Pourang Irani. 2016. Thumbs-Up: 3d spatial thumb-reachable space for one-handed thumb interaction on smartphones. In *Proceedings of the 2016 Symposium on Spatial User Interaction* (SUI '16), 103-106. https://doi.org/10.1145/2983310.2985755
21. Khalad Hasan, Xing-Dong Yang, Hai-Ning Liang, and Pourang Irani. 2012. How to position the cursor?: an exploration of absolute and relative cursor positioning for back-of-device input. In *Proceedings of the 14th International Conference on Human-Computer Interaction with Mobile Devices and Services* (MobileHCI '12), 103–112. https://doi.org/10.1145/2371574.2371591
22. Doris Hausen, Sebastian Boring, and Saul Greenberg. 2013. The unadorned desk: exploiting the physical space around a display as an input canvas. In *Proceedings of the 14th IFIP TC13 Conference on Human-Computer Interaction* (INTERACT '13), 140–158. http://link.springer.com/chapter/10.1007/978-3-642-40483-2_10
23. Juan David Hincapié-Ramos, Xiang Guo, Paymahn Moghadasian, and Pourang Irani. 2014. Consumed endurance: a metric to quantify arm fatigue of mid-air interactions. In *Proceedings of the SIGCHI Conference on Human Factors in Computing Systems (CHI '14)*, 1063-1072. https://doi.org/10.1145/2556288.2557130
24. David Holman, Andreas Hollatz, Amartya Banerjee, and Roel Vertegaal. 2013. Unifone: designing for auxiliary finger input in one-handed mobile interactions. In *Proceedings of the 7th International Conference on Tangible, Embedded and Embodied Interaction* (TEI '13), 177-184. http://dx.doi.org/10.1145/2460625.2460653
25. Brett Jones, Rajinder Sodhi, David Forsyth, Brian Bailey, and Giuliano Maciocci. 2012. Around device interaction for multiscale navigation. In *Proceedings of the 14th International Conference on Human-Computer Interaction with Mobile Devices and Services* (MobileHCI '12), 83-92. https://doi.org/10.1145/2371574.2371589
26. Amy K. Karlson and Benjamin B. Bederson. 2007. ThumbSpace: generalized one-handed input for touchscreen-based mobile devices. In *Proceedings of the 11th IFIP TC 13 International Conference on Human-Computer Interaction* (INTERACT'07), 324-338. http://dx.doi.org/10.1007/978-3-540-74796-3_30
27. Amy K. Karlson, Benjamin B. Bederson, and Jose L. Contreras-Vidal. 2008. Understanding one handed use of mobile devices. In *Handbook of Research on User Interface Design and Evaluation for Mobile Technology*, 86-101.
28. Amy K. Karlson, Benjamin B. Bederson, and John SanGiovanni. 2005. AppLens and launchTile: two designs for one-handed thumb use on small devices. In *Proceedings of the SIGCHI Conference on Human Factors in Computing Systems* (CHI '05), 201–210. https://doi.org/10.1145/1054972.1055001
29. Hamed Ketabdar, Mehran Roshandel, and Kamer Ali Yüksel. 2010. MagiWrite: towards touchless digit entry using 3D space around mobile devices. In *Proceedings of the 12th International Conference on Human-Computer Interaction with Mobile Devices and Services* (MobileHCI '10), 443-446. https://doi.org/10.1145/1851600.1851701
30. Sven Kratz and Michael Rohs. 2009. Hoverflow: exploring around-device interaction with IR distance sensors. In *Proceedings of the 11th International Conference on Human-Computer Interaction with Mobile Devices and Services* (MobileHCI '09), Article 42, 4 pages. https://doi.org/10.1145/1613858.1613912
31. Sven Kratz, Michael Rohs, Dennis Guse, Jörg Müller, Gilles Bailly, and Michael Nischt. 2012. PalmSpace: continuous around-device gestures vs. multitouch for 3D rotation tasks on mobile devices. In *Proceedings of the Working Conference on Advanced Visual Interfaces* (AVI '12), 181-188. https://doi.org/10.1145/2254556.2254590
32. Jianwei Lai and Dongsong Zhang. 2014. ExtendedThumb: a motion-based virtual thumb for improving one-handed target acquisition on touch-screen mobile devices. In *Proceedings of the Extended Abstracts of the 32nd Annual ACM Conference on Human Factors in Computing Systems* (CHI EA '14), 1825–1830. https://doi.org/10.1145/2559206.2581158
33. Leap motion. 2017. Retrieved January 04, 2017 from https://www.leapmotion.com/
34. Andrea Leganchuk, Shumin Zhai, and William Buxton. 1998. Manual and cognitive benefits of two-handed input: an experimental study. *ACM Transaction on Human-Computer Interaction*. 5, 4: 326–359. https://doi.org/10.1145/300520.300522
35. Mobile eCommerce Stats in 2016 and the future. 2017. Retrieved January 04, 2017 from http://www.outerboxdesign.com/web-design-articles/mobile-ecommerce-statistics
36. Mobile Marketing Statistics Compilation. 2017. Retrieved January 04, 2017 from http://www.smartinsights.com/mobile-marketing/mobile-marketing-analytics/mobile-marketing-statistics/
37. Motion Capture System | VICON. 2017. Retrieved January 04, 2017 from https://www.vicon.com/.
38. Takehiro Niikura, Yuki Hirobe, Alvaro Cassinelli, Yoshihiro Watanabe, Takashi Komuro, and Masatoshi

Ishikawa. 2010. In-air typing interface for mobile devices with vibration feedback. In *ACM SIGGRAPH 2010 Emerging Technologies* (SIGGRAPH '10), Article 15, 1 pages. https://doi.org/10.1145/1836821.1836836

39. Michel Pahud, Ken Hinckley, Shamsi Iqbal, Abigail Sellen, and Bill Buxton. 2013. Toward compound navigation tasks on mobiles via spatial manipulation. In *Proceedings of the 15th International Conference on Human-Computer Interaction with Mobile Devices and Services* (MobileHCI '13), 113-122. https://doi.org/10.1145/2493190.2493210
40. Project Soli. 2017. Retrieved January 04, 2017 from https://atap.google.com/soli/
41. Jie Song, Gábor Sörös, Fabrizio Pece, Sean Ryan Fanello, Shahram Izadi, Cem Keskin, and Otmar Hilliges. 2014. In-air gestures around unmodified mobile devices. In *Proceedings of the 27th Annual ACM symposium on User Interface Software and Technology* (UIST '14), 319-329. https://doi.org/10.1145/2642918.2647373
42. Martin Spindler, Martin Schuessler, Marcel Martsch, and Raimund Dachselt. 2014. Pinch-drag-flick vs. spatial input: rethinking zoom & pan on mobile displays. In *Proceedings of the SIGCHI Conference on Human Factors in Computing Systems* (CHI '14), 1113-1122. https://doi.org/10.1145/2556288.2557028
43. Structure sensor. 2017. Retrieved January 04, 2017 from http://structure.io/
44. Eduardo Velloso, Jayson Turner, Jason Alexander, Andreas Bulling and Hans Gellersen. 2015. An empirical investigation of gaze selection in mid-air gestural 3d manipulation. In *Proceedings of the 15th IFIP TC13 Conference on Human-Computer Interaction* (INTERACT '13), 315-330. http://dx.doi.org/10.1007/978-3-319-22668-2_25
45. Anusha Withana, Roshan Peiris, Nipuna Samarasekara, and Suranga Nanayakkara. 2015. zSense: enabling shallow depth gesture recognition for greater input expressivity on smart wearables. In *Proceedings of the 33rd Annual ACM Conference on Human Factors in Computing Systems* (CHI '15), 3661-3670. http://dx.doi.org/10.1145/2702123.2702371
46. Xing-Dong Yang, Khalad Hasan, Neil Bruce, and Pourang Irani. 2013. Surround-see: enabling peripheral vision on smartphones during active use. In *Proceedings of the 26th Annual ACM Symposium on User Interface Software and Technology (UIST '13)*, 291-300. https://doi.org/10.1145/2501988.2502049
47. Chen Zhao, Ke-Yu Chen, Md Tanvir Islam Aumi, Shwetak Patel, and Matthew S. Reynolds. 2014. SideSwipe: detecting in-air gestures around mobile devices using actual GSM signal. In *Proceedings of the 27th Annual ACM Symposium on User Interface Software and Technology* (UIST '14), 527-534. https://doi.org/10.1145/2642918.2647380

# Float: One-Handed and Touch-Free Target Selection on Smartwatches

**Ke Sun, Yuntao Wang†, Chun Yu, Yukang Yan, Hongyi Wen, Yuanchun Shi**
Key Laboratory of Pervasive Computing, Ministry of Education
Tsinghua National Laboratory for Information Science and Technology
Department of Computer Science and Technology, Tsinghua University, Beijing, 100084, China
{k-sun14, yyk15}@mails.tsinghua.edu.cn, {yuntaowang, chunyu, shiyc}@tsinghua.edu.cn

## ABSTRACT
Touch interaction on smartwatches suffers from the awkwardness of having to use two hands and the "fat finger" problem. We present Float, a *wrist-to-finger* input approach that enables one-handed and touch-free target selection on smartwatches with high efficiency and precision using only commercially-available built-in sensors. With Float, a user tilts the wrist to *point* and performs an in-air finger tap to *click*. To realize Float, we first explore the appropriate motion space for wrist tilt and determine the *clicking* action (finger tap) through a user-elicitation study. We combine the photoplethysmogram (PPG) signal with accelerometer and gyroscope to detect finger taps with a recall of 97.9% and a false discovery rate of 0.4%. Experiments show that using just one hand, Float allows users to acquire targets with size ranging from 2mm to 10mm in less than 2s to 1s, meanwhile achieve much higher accuracy than direct touch in both stationary (>98.9%) and walking (>71.5%) contexts.

## Author Keywords
Smartwatch; one-handed interaction; tilt; finger gesture; target selection

## ACM Classification Keywords
H.5.2. Information interfaces and presentation: User interfaces; Input devices and strategies

## INTRODUCTION
Smartwatches are becoming more popular with users, providing efficient interactions on quick information access and response. Touch is still the most dominant way users interact with smartwatches, which benefits from its nature of direct input and the transfer of usage from other modern touchscreen devices. After a user survey and literature investigation, we however observe two typical problems of using touch to interact on smartwatches affecting its user experience.

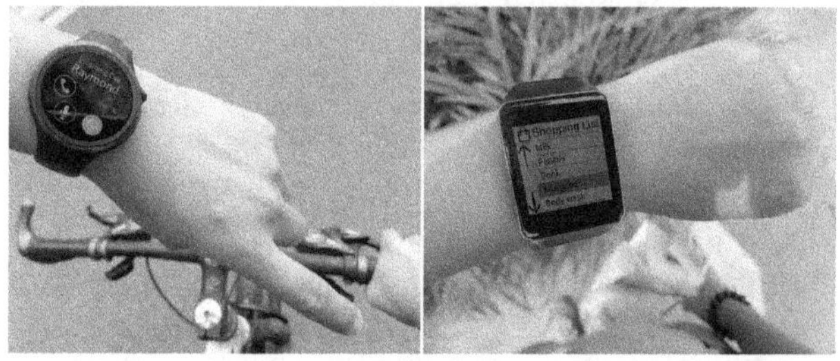

**Figure 1. Potential scenarios of Float. Left: a user handles an incoming call while riding by tilting the wrist and clicking the "message" button with a finger tap; Right: a user is checking the shopping list on a smartwatch while carrying lots of bags.**

First, touch on smartwatches always requires the "free hand" or the "other hand" on which the smartwatch is not attached. Interactions such as carrying objects, cooking, holding an umbrella, riding a bike and driving will be inconvenient when the other hand is occupied; The second drawback is that of the fat finger problem, which is exacerbated by the ultra-small display on smartwatches. The finger can easily occlude over half of the display [45]. Commercial products enlarge selectable items to ensure the accuracy, making many of the basic interactions slow and laborious with sequences of swipes and taps [21].

Based on these two limitations, we are motivated to seek out alternative input modalities that enable one-handed and non-touch interactions on smartwatches. Our goal was to provide more hands-free interactions, while improving the accuracy and efficiency of target selection beyond direct touch. In this paper, we propose Float, an interaction technique that enables one-handed and touch-free input on smartwatches based on a combination of wrist tilt and finger gestures. The basic idea is simple: a user tilts the wrist to *point* and performs an in-air finger tap to *click*. For example, a user can handle incoming calls with a single hand while riding a bicycle (Figure 1.a).

Tilt is not novel. Prior research has investigated tilt for menu navigation [40, 26], game control and text entry [32, 42] on mobile phones and tablets. Most of the work however used tilt to perform only uniaxial selection by either mapping the tilt inclination or the tilt direction. With a smartwatch on the wrist, Float explores wrist tilt as a general pointing method over the watch face. This brings two benefits: (1) One can access any location on the watch face, which can be

† denotes the corresponding author.

*CHI 2017, May 06-11, 2017, Denver, CO, USA*
 ISBN 978-1-4503-4655-9/17/05...$15.00
DOI: http://dx.doi.org/10.1145/3025453.3026027

applied directly to existing devices with-out redesigning GUI into ad-hoc forms; (2) target selection can be achieved with only one hand, which is useful when the other hand is occupied. We also present a rigorous calculation to map users' wrist tilt movement to positions on the watch face based on the intrinsic rotation matrix.

After establishing tilt as the way of *pointing*, we first conducted a pilot experiment. In the first part, we explored the appropriate rotation space when tilting a wrist-worn watch; in the second part, we performed a user-elicitation study to determine the *clicking* interaction. Finally, finger motion/gesture of the involved hand was selected from five candidates, including dwell-time, voice, gaze, etc.

To realize the interactive system, we use only commercially built-in sensors on smartwatches. When a user performs a finger tap, the joint tendons and skin will cause significant motion and strain, which can be reflected by a peak in the accelerometer and gyroscope sequence of the motion sensor after a high-pass filter and a sharp *pulse-like* pattern in the PPG signal of the heart rate monitor. We implemented a detection algorithm combining thresholding, dynamic time warping and a k-NN classifier. To our knowledge, there is no previous work that detects hand actions using the PPG signal. Evaluation showed that finger taps could be detected with a recall of 97.9% and a false discovery rate of 0.4% in standing and walking contexts.

We conducted two user studies to evaluate the performance of Float. In the first study, we investigated the effects of target location (direction and distance) on pointing speed and stability through a discrete pointing experiment. We provide implications for layout and task design. In the second study, we conducted a continuous target selection experiment in both standing and walking contexts. We found that participants could select a target within 1s ~ 2s for target size ranging from 10mm to 2mm. In addition, the occlusion avoidance benefit and real-time visual feedback enable precise target selection on smartwatches with an accuracy of 98.9% / 71.5% ~ 100%, which is much more accurate than direct touch.

In summary, the contributions of this work are: (1) presenting Float, a one-handed and touch-free input approach for smartwatches; (2) a participatory design to explore the appropriate motion space for wrist tilt and the *clicking* actions for Float; (3) an interactive implementation of Float only using sensors (motion and PPG) that are available on off-the-shelf smartwatches; (4) empirical studies comparing Float to direct touch.

## RELATED WORK

### Interaction Techniques on Smartwatches

On smartwatches, the fat finger and occlusion problems are exacerbated by the ultra-small screen. When performing touch interactions, an average of 60% of the area is occluded by the finger over the touchscreen [45]. On a two-dimensional finger touch experiment, error rates were reported ranging from 25% to 66% with target width from 4.8mm to 2.4mm [6]. Smartwatches on the market mostly use enlarged icons and a hierarchical structure for UI design, making many interactions slow and laborious with sequences of swipes and taps [21].

Numerous previous works have explored enhancing the input abilities and input space of smartwatches, such as *Beating Gestures* [28] as well as *WristTap* and *TwoTap* [21]. Ashbrook *et al.* [3] studied inter-target movements for round touchscreen wristwatch. *EdgeTouch* [27], with capacitive sensors around the edge, allows the device screen to remain clearly in view while the finger is touching on the edge. Xiao *et al.* [46] expanded the watch plate into a multi-DOF and mechanical interface. Continuous 2D panning and twist, binary tilt and click can be achieved by interaction on the edge. As for the input space, *SideSight* [7] positions optical sensors along edges of the device allowing virtual touches around the body. Researches also extended the interactive surface to the arm skin through various sensing techniques, such as *Skin Buttons* [23], *SkinWatch* [29] and *SkinTrack* [48].

Researchers have also exploited several factors to improve the pointing accuracy on smartwatches. Oney and Harrison [30] introduced *ZoomBoard*, using iterative zooming to enlarge tiny targets for comfortable sizes. Xia *et al.* [45] presented *NanoStylus*, a finger-mounted tip stylus that enables fast and accurate pointing on a smartwatch with only 16% occlusion. One notable insight is that pointing performance on a smartwatch can be largely improved simply by providing the visual feedback clearly. Ostberg and Matic [31] examined the effects of pre-selection while Yu *et al.* [47] investigated the effects of post-selection feedback for target acquisition. With a little completion time loss, the cursor feedback significantly reduced touch error rates. Float also takes such an advantage, thoroughly.

These previous works above however, all require the other hand to interact. When the other hand is occupied, it will be inconvenient for efficient interaction. We combined tilt and finger actions to overcome this issue.

### Tilt Interactions

Tilt has been investigated in a wealth of tasks such as navigating menus [40, 26], 3D rotation [34], text entry [32, 42, 17], mobile touchscreens [9] and authoring system [20]. More surveys can be found in [38]. Crossan [11] *et al.* investigated one-dimensional wrist rotation for mobile interaction with a Fitts' Law analysis. These works including ours follow a basic principle: map the tilt direction and angle to the position of a virtual or latent cursor.

Our present work builds on tilt interaction for selecting tasks in two significant ways. First, previous work primarily focused on binary, discrete or uniaxial control in rectilinear or circular form. For example, a user simply tilts by different inclinations to select an item in a list [26, 40] or simply tilts in discrete (4,8 or 12) directions to acquire an item [10, 14,

32]. Float however, establishes tilt as a more general and continuous 2D pointing method on the smartwatch screen. Second, to our knowledge, our method to calculate the tilt direction and angle is different. The previous typical method is simply computing the magnitude (angle) and arcsin (direction) of pitch and roll [24, 37, 38], which is in fact an approximate and imprecise solution. We present the rigorous calculation based on the intrinsic rotation matrix, which reflects the user's true tilt intention. Although tilt has been testified to be inferior to touch on phone-sized screens, our study showed that after careful calculation and design, tilt enables efficient and much more accurate target selection on a wristwatch than direct touch.

### Non-touchscreen and One-Handed Input

Our work is also motivated by bare-handed/non-touch interactions that are designed to mitigate touch problems on the watch face. Abracadabra [15] enables the user to input above and around the device with a high CD gain. The *Gesture Watch* [19] utilizes an array of proximity sensors to detect 10 hand gestures over the device. Shimon *et al.* [2] elicited user-defined [44] gestures for 31 smartwatch tasks. These works still need bimanual interactions, which go against our *one-handed* goal.

To address this issue, one-handed interactions have been explored. *PinchWatch* [22] invokes functions by finger-palm gestures with another camera device attached on body. *ProxiWatch* [25] provides one-handed input by moving the watch towards or away from the body. *GestureWrist* [35] is a specially designed wristband-type device that recognizes hand gestures and forearm movements. Wen *et al.* [41] recognized a set of five fine-motor finger gestures using built-in motion sensors. But the performance would fail when users are walking. More recently, Guo and Paek [14] also take one-handed input on smartwatches as the goal, exploring tilt for wrist-only interactions. The work focused on optimizing the control mechanism with an underlying physics model and presented *ObjectPoint.* They used *tilt-and-persist-to-select* as the confirming action. Although faster than *dwell-to-select*, it was still relatively slow, 1380ms per trial for four targets and 2005ms per trial for 12. In addition, they still placed only one target along a direction (1D pointing circularly). We think this is partly because the confirming action and the tilt-mapping mode are unsuitable for any-location-pointing on smartwatches.

More generally, *DigitSpace* [16] investigated touch performance for one-handed and eyes-free thumb-to-fingers interfaces. Chan *et al.* [8] performed a user-elicitation study eliciting singer-handed microgestures (SHMGs). To recognize hand gestures, previous work integrated external custom-built sensors, such as capacitive sensors [35], force sensitive sensors [12], and strain-gauge sensors [18] onto the watch. In our work, our goal was to recognize finger taps only using sensors (PPG signal from the heart rate monitor and the motion sensor) that are available on common smartwatches. In addition, the algorithm should be accurate and robust in both stationary and mobile contexts.

### Target Acquisition Techniques on Screen

Touch benefits from its nature of direct input [1]. However, precise target acquisition is limited on touch screens, especially for small targets. Researchers have developed techniques to address this issue. However, it is generally difficult to apply these techniques to smartwatches.

Earlier pixel-accuracy techniques (*Cross-Keys*, *Precision-Handle* [1], *Dual Finger Selections* [5]) mostly use two fingers and a relatively large extra surface area to possess fine motor control. The callout / popup methods (*Take-Off* [33], *Shift* [39], *TapTap* [36]) avoid occlusion underneath the finger, but meanwhile create new occlusions on other areas. In addition, callout placement on a watch-size screen is much more limited on smartwatches. Back-of-device interaction with a *pseudo-transparency* strategy [43, 4] is also not appropriate for smartwatches due to the form factor.

## FLOAT: AN OVERVIEW

Float is a *wrist-to-finger* input interaction, designed as a supplementary technique for touch in hand-busy scenarios. Figure 2 shows a walkthrough of the technique and its coexistence mechanism with touch. Scenario:

(a) **Raise-to-wake:** to interact with the smartwatch, the user raises the arm and turns the wrist so that the watch face faces their line of sight. This *raise-to-wake* action is detected to light up the screen.

(b) **Enabling Float:** The user performs the first in-air finger tap as the *enabling* command to activate the Float interactive mode, after which a (virtual) cursor appears at the center of the watch face.

(c) **Tilt to point:** To select the target, the user tilts the wrist towards a certain *direction* by a certain *angle*. The direction and angle codetermine the cursor location on the watch face.

(d) **Finger tap to select:** Once the correct position is visually verified, a finger tap as the *clicking action* causes a brief highlight and completes the selection.

(e) **Disabling Float:** Any touch event on the screen (indicating that the hand is free) or lowering the arm (indicating that tasks are over) disables Float.

The enabling and disabling commands ensure the separation and compatibility of Float with existing touch interactions on smartwatches, allowing users to explicitly switch between these two input styles.

The main difference between Float and touchscreen-based techniques is that all selecting actions occur within one hand. Float also addresses the *fat finger* problem by allowing the user to always see and verify the pointing position. All UI elements on the screen are visible to users rather than occluded by the wide finger surface or a copied callout. The second difference is that Float uses the polar coordinate system. This requires users to put in different

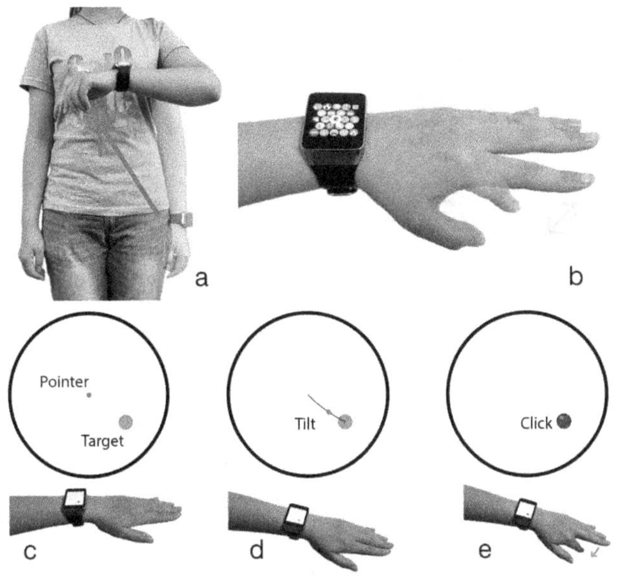


**Figure 2. Float input walkthrough. (a) A user raises and turns the wrist to *wake* up the screen; (b) The first in-air finger tap *enables* the Float interaction mode; (c-e) Then the user tilts the wrist to *point* and performs a finger tap to *click*, and continues to point to the next target.**

effort selecting targets at different locations, especially along the radial coordinate. The third difference lies in the feedback. Float mainly leverages the proprioception of wrist motion to control.

## COORDINATE CALCULATION OF TILT

Float maps wrist tilt to positions in polar coordinates on the two-dimensional watch face. When the watch face tilts to the current orientation from the initial reference, we regard the tilt direction as the cursor 's angular coordinate and map the inclination to the radial coordinate.

Suppose $C_0$ and $C_1$ are the initial and the current coordinate system of the watch face respectively. When in $C_0$, the cursor locates at the center of the watch face, $(0,0)$ on the $xy-plane$. The goal is to calculate the cursor's location after the watch face rotates to $C_1$. Say $(\alpha,\beta,\gamma)$ is the angle change of the intrinsic rotation around the $x,y,z$ axes respectively which transforms $C_0$ to $C_1$ in the order of $z \rightarrow x \rightarrow y$, and $\boldsymbol{R}$ is its corresponding rotation matrix. So, the unit outward normal vector $\boldsymbol{n_0} = (0,0,1)^T$ of the watch face rotates to (see Eq.1):

$$\boldsymbol{n_1} = (x_1, y_1, z_1)^T = (cos\alpha \ sin\,\beta, -sin\,\alpha, cos\alpha \ cos\beta)^T$$

Projecting $\boldsymbol{n_1}$ onto $xy-plane$ of $C_0$ gives the tilt direction:

$$Dir = atan2(y_1, x_1)$$

The angle between $\boldsymbol{n_1}$ and $\boldsymbol{n_0}$ gives the inclination:

$$Inc = arccos(z_1)$$

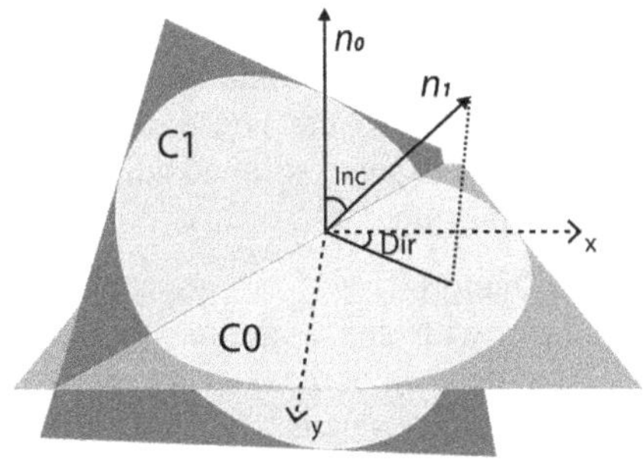


**Figure 3. Calculation of the tilt direction and angle when the watch face rotates. A rotation with $\alpha = \beta = 30^o$ results in *Inc* = 41.41° and *Dir* = 40.89°.**

Such calculation has two characteristics. First, there is a one-to-one correspondence between the wrist orientation and the cursor positions. Any target on the watch face can be reached through appropriate wrist control. Second, Float behaves as users expect. The angular and radial coordinate's mapping accords with users' intuition of locating: The tilt direction of the watch face coincides with the target's angular coordinate; and the farther away the target is located from the center, the more the wrist should tilt. Many previous works [24, 37, 38] simply computed the *magnitude* and *arcsin* of pitch and roll as the tilt direction and angle. Such computation is an approximate method because rotation angles are not equal and have specified orders in intrinsic rotations. For example, if $\alpha = \beta = 30^o$, the tilt direction will be 45° using their method. But in fact, it should be ≈ 40.89° (see Figure 3). A rigorous mapping is important for accurate pointing, especially on the ultra-small display of smartwatches.

## PARTICIPATORY EXPLORATION AND DESIGN

To better understand how users expect to use Float, we conducted a preliminary study where participants were instructed to explore the appropriate tilt space and elicit *confirming* actions themselves. Study results were used to determine the final design of Float.

### Participants

We recruited 12 volunteers (3F/9M, 1 left-handed), ranging in age from 21 to 26 from our university. All of them had experience with ordinary watches and four of them had experience with smartwatches. All participants were given $10 for their participation, which lasted about 40 minutes.

### Apparatus

We implemented the tilt calculation described above on a Samsung Galaxy Gear Live smartwatch running Android 5.1. Given the initial and current reference coordinate system, we calculated the intrinsic rotation $(\gamma,\alpha,\beta)$ through Android API `getRotationMatrix()` and `getAngleChange()`. The accelerometer and geomagnetic data were collected at

$$\boldsymbol{n_1} = \boldsymbol{R}\cdot\boldsymbol{n_0} = \begin{bmatrix} cos\beta\ cos\gamma + sin\alpha\ sin\beta\ sin\gamma & -cos\beta\ sin\gamma + sin\alpha\ sin\beta\ cos\,\gamma & cos\alpha\ sin\,\beta \\ cos\alpha\ sin\,\gamma & cos\alpha\ cos\gamma & -sin\,\alpha \\ -sin\beta\ cos\gamma + sin\alpha\ cos\beta\ sin\,\gamma & sin\beta\ sin\gamma + sin\alpha\ cos\beta\ cos\,\gamma & cos\alpha\ cos\beta \end{bmatrix} \cdot \begin{bmatrix} 0 \\ 0 \\ 1 \end{bmatrix} = \begin{bmatrix} cos\alpha\ sin\,\beta \\ -sin\,\alpha \\ cos\alpha\ cos\beta \end{bmatrix} \quad (1)$$

a frequency of 180Hz. A filter was applied for each 0.1s sliding window to smooth the white noise. The smartwatch was worn on the wrist of the non-dominant hand. Each participant was asked to stand still and adjust the arm to the most comfortable posture.

### Procedure and Design

The study began with the experimenter explaining the principle of Float and the purpose of the study. The whole procedure consisted of two parts.

In the first part, the participant completed a series of discrete *"subjective"* tilting trials. The participant was first asked to explore their own most comfortable position and orientation of the smartwatch. In each trial, the participant first adjusted the watch to the *initial* orientation, where they thought the cursor would be at the center of the watch face. The *calibrate* button was pressed to set and record the initial coordinates. Then a target on the boundary of the circular background was displayed on the watch face. During the trial, a radial cursor reflected the tilting direction. The participant was asked to tilt towards the target taking the cursor as a reference, and then inclined *subjectively* to access the target. The *'subjective'* pointing was based on three conditions: (1) physically comfortable: tilt motion must be easy without arm discomfort; (2) visually comfort-able: the whole UI can be seen and comprehended clearly; (3) they thought subjectively that the inclination angle corresponded to the tilt boundary along this direction. The task consisted of 16 trials, where the targets were arranged uniformly along the boundary of the circular watch face (Figure 4 left). Each participant repeated the task twice.

The second part included two stages. In the first stage, participants were encouraged to design *clicking actions* as much as possible that would cause the "selected" effect based on preference without concern for implementation feasibility in a 'user-defined' [44] manner. After all participants completed the first stage, we summarized all the elicited interactions. Then in the second stage, we explained each interaction to participants and asked them to rate subjective preference scores on a five-point Likert scale for all elicited candidates. Factors they considered included efficiency, comfort and operability, discrete and continuous selection tasks, stationary and mobile contexts and social acceptance. They were advised to wear a smartwatch and evaluate each *clicking action* along with wrist tilt through simulation usage.

### Results and Final Design

#### *Tilt Range Determination*

For tilt range determination, we collected and analyzed a total of 384 trials from 12 participants. Overall, the appropriate inclination area of wrist-tilt is nearly an oblique ellipse rather than a circle, with an average of 30.15°. A repeated measures ANOVA showed there was a significant effect of tilt directions on the inclination range ($F_{15,165}$=9.83, $p$<.001). The upward direction (around 90°) had the largest inclination range of 39.34°, while the lower left had the smallest range of 23.91°. The lower right range matched the perfect circle most with an average of 29.71° (SD = 0.64).

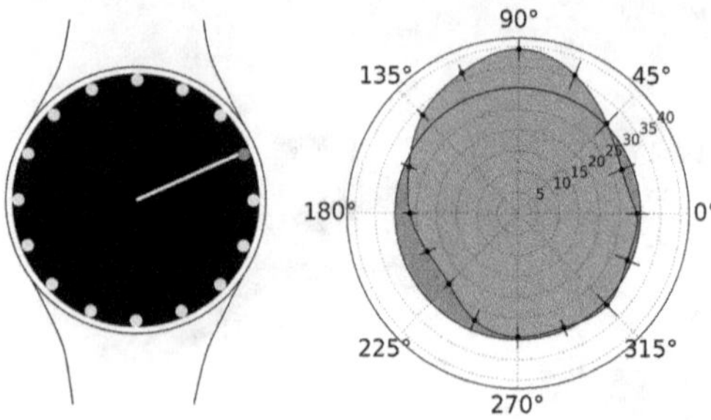


**Figure 4. Left: task in exploring the appropriate tilt space; Right: inclination range varies along different directions. The skew pattern was consistent among subjects with variance.**

The results suggested that due to the specific wrist structure, participants tended to incline by different angles along different directions. Therefore, to maximize the agreement between users' tilt-motion intention and the displayed cursor position, we scaled the inclination to different ranges as the tilt direction varies. For example, if a user tilted by 20° along the 0° direction, the cursor was located at (20/29.34, 0°) = (0.68, 0°) in polar coordinates; but a same 20°-tilt along the 90° direction would result in (20/39.34, 90°) = (0.51, 90°). The scaling factor was interpolated by a 1-D cubic spline function along 360°.

#### *Elicited Clicking Action*

For user-defined clicking actions, five interaction modalities were elicited (Figure 5). All the participants came up with using *dwell-time* to select while seven out of 12 proposed using *voice control* and *specific wrist motion*. Participants also suggested using *finger actions,* such as an in-air tap and *head / gaze* movement. In the post-rating stage, however, participants rated *finger tap* as the most recognized and appropriate interaction for pointing confirmation, with an average preference score at 4.58. Eleven out of 12 participants voted *finger air-tap* as their favorite option although it had the least elicited times in the first stage.

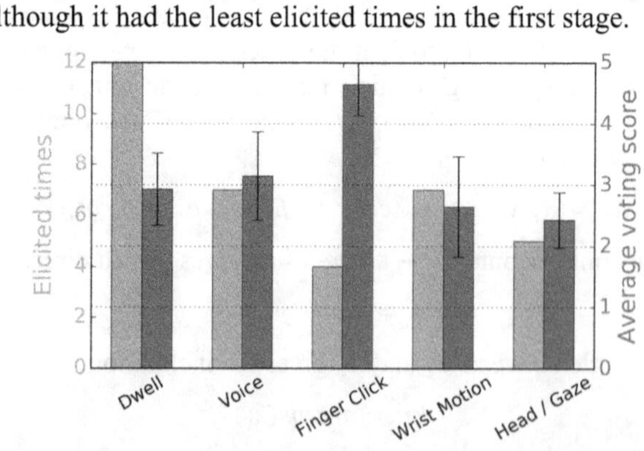


**Figure 5. Elicited times and average preference of five user-defined *clicking* interactions in the elicitation study.**

*Finger tap* was recognized as a clear, easy-to-perform and control, and relatively quick method. Participants and pilot tests reported inevitable drawbacks for other options. It is difficult for *Dwell* to be applied on real products because it "*lacks a clear clicking action (P4)*". *Dwell-time* cannot recognize whether a user is holding the wrist to browse the contents or is making selections, and it cannot distinguish between intentional and unintentional dwelling, especially in continuous selecting tasks; Specific wrist motion (e.g. a rapid rotation) would result in cursor's offset and visual interference; *Voice control* is limited due to its inherent problems such as noisy environment and social issues. Not all users are willing to 'speak out' their interactions; Predictably, wink can be faster than finger tap, but suffers from unintended activations from natural eye movements.

Therefore, we chose the *in-air finger tap* as the final design for *clicking*. The next goal was to develop techniques to enable Float interaction, especially to detect *finger taps* accurately and robustly both in stationary and mobile scenarios. We are also expecting to use sensors that have already been embedded in current smartwatches.

## TECHNICAL IMPLEMENTATION

The technical implementation of Float includes three parts corresponding to the three transitional actions in Figure 2: raise to wake, tilt and finger tap. We developed the interactive system based on an Android Wear smartwatch. Three types of sensors were used: the motion sensor (accelerometer and gyroscope), position sensor (geomagnetic field) and the heart rate monitor (HRM) sensor.

The motion sensor and the position sensor reflect users' arm and wrist movements, enabling us to recognize the *"raise to wake"* action and compute the cursor position.

The HRM sensor is located on the rear panel of the smartwatch. It detects the PPG signal which measures the amount back of IR/RED light reflected from the blood vessel in the skin. When a user performs finger gestures, significant patterns can be observed from the PPG signal due to the deformation and strain of the wrist skin. So we used the HRM sensor, combined with the motion sensor, to detect users' *clicking action* through *finger tap*. The HRM sensor has been embedded in most commercial smartwatches. But because the raw PPG signal is not open, we decided to attach a standalone HRM sensor (Pulse Sensor [52]) on the rear panel, fixed by a rigid shell by 3D printing (Figure 6.a). The data were processed by an ATmega2560 board at 102 Hz and recognition results were sent to the smartwatch through a Bluetooth module (TI CC2540). Our initial intention was to use the off-the-shelf smartwatch directly if the PPG raw data was available.

### Raise-to-Wake Detection

We asked participants to simulate raising arm and turning wrist actions as if they were using the smartwatch in real-life scenarios. Figure 6.b shows the orientation of the watch face against the horizontal ground direction. Within a three-second sliding window, if the inclination was on a declining curve in the first two seconds and stayed stabilized horizontally in the last one second (inclination $< 15^{\circ}$ and standard deviation $< 0.5^{\circ}$), a *raise-to-wake* action was detected.

### One-bit Detection of Finger Air-tap

When users perform an *air-tap* action with the finger, joint muscle and skin cause a short but significant change in both motion and PPG signal.

#### *Data Collection*

Because smartwatches are usually used in mobile contexts, we collected data in two contexts: stationary and walking (1.2m/s). We recruited 12 participants. For each context, the participant was instructed to wear the smartwatch with comfortable tightness and perform finger taps for five blocks. Each block lasted for 30 seconds with 13 ~ 16 finger taps. In total, 1782 (stationary: 894, walking: 888) trials were collected.

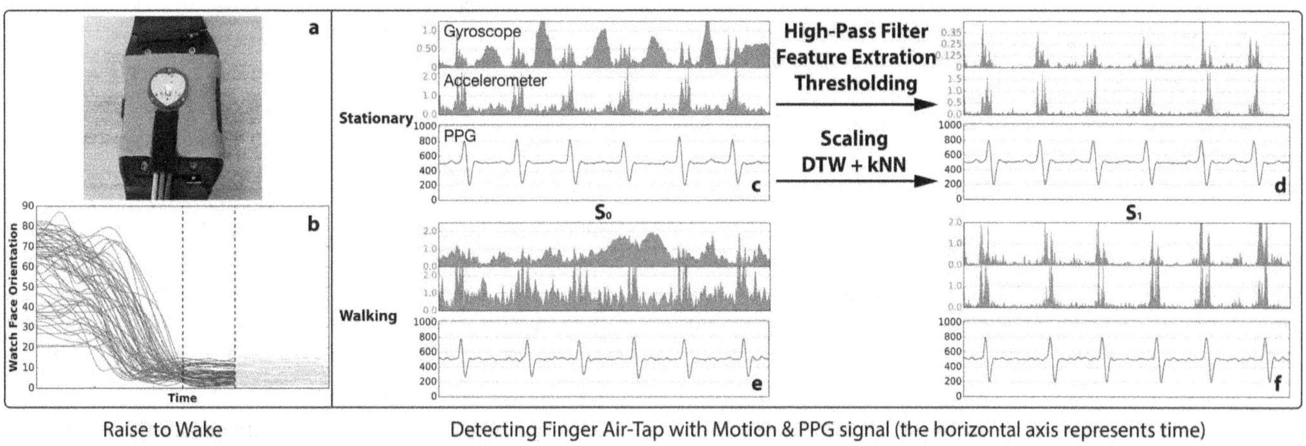


**Figure 6. Implementation of Float. (a) Pulse Sensor on the rear panel of the smartwatch; (b) Orientation change of the watch face when users raise the watch to light up the screen; (c) ~ (f) When performing finger taps, significant patterns can be observed in the PPG (green) signal and in the accelerometer (blue) and gyroscope (red) sequence after a high-pass Butterworth filter in both stationary and walking contexts.**

*Detection from Motion Signal*

Motion data was mostly full of noise, especially for the walking context (Figure 6.e). Useful information that reflects finger movements in Float needs to be extracted. We first analyzed the distribution in the frequency domain of the accelerometer data after a Fast Fourier Transform (FFT) in these two contexts. It was found that the frequency spectrum of body motion mostly concentrated below 12.4 Hz. So a high-pass Butterworth filter [49] was applied to remove the low-pass (body motion) part, with resonance $=\sqrt{2}$ and cutoff frequency $= 12.4\,Hz$. Figure 6 shows the absolute value of original signal sequence $S_0$ and the output sequence $S_1$. The finger air-tap actions resulted in bundles of significant *peaks* in data sequence. To detect such peaks, 6 statistical features were calculated from each $T_{tap}$ sliding window of $S_1$: *sum, standard deviation and 4 gtX* features. The *gtX* feature is the number of frames whose value is greater than $X$ (set by observation of data) in the window.

The same processing and calculations were performed on the gyroscope data. When and only when all 12 features satisfied certain thresholds (calculated from training data), a *finger tap* action was detected by the motion sensors. However, using only motion data for detection was not reliable. Many other casual but rapid motions, such as jitters would result in similar patterns and cause undesirable false positives, especially in mobile contexts. We combined the PPG signal to improve the robustness.

*Detection from Photoplethysmogram Signal*

For the PPG sensing data (0~1024), we adopted a Nearest Neighbor Classifier using Dynamic Time Warping (DTW) as a distance measure, which has been shown effective in mining time series data [13]. Specifically, we used the one nearest neighbor classifier on labeled data. Figure 6 shows the PPG signal of users interacting with Float while standing and walking. When performing finger taps, there was a significant pattern – first ascend, then descend, then ascend back. For each sliding window $T_{tap}$, if *max-min* is greater than a certain threshold (200 in standing context and 350 in walking context), data in the window was normalized between 200 and 800. For training, the average value of each frame of all labeled samples in the training set was computed as the template $t$. For testing, the distance of DTW between each sliding window $s$ and $t$ decided whether it was a *finger tap* action or not.

Finally, a finger *air-tap* action was detected when and only when both motion and PPG sensor returned true. This constraint was to reduce false positives as much as possible.

*Evaluation*

The average time of performing an in-air finger tap was 439.7ms (SD=32.1). We evaluated the effectiveness of our detection system through a five-fold cross-validation for each participant. In total, there were zero false positives and nine false negatives out of 894 condition positives for the stationary test while there were seven false positives and 21 false negatives out of 888 condition positives for the walking test. The recall was thus 98.9% and 96.9% respectively. The false discovery rate was 0% and 0.81%. So, it was confirmed that with only PPG and motion sensors, the finger tap actions for Float interaction could be detected accurately.

| | Stationary | | Walking | |
|---|---|---|---|---|
| | Finger tap | None | Finger tap | None |
| Finger tap | 885 | 9 | 861 | 20 |
| None | 0 | / | 7 | / |

**Table 1. Confusion matrix of finger air-tap detection: Each column represents the instances in a predicted class while each row represents the instances in an actual class.**

Above, we have designed and realized Float to enable one-handed input on smartwatches. We then conducted two user studies to investigate its feasibility and performance.

## USER STUDY 1: LOCATION EFFECTS

Float maps the tilt direction and angle of a user's wrist to the corresponding position on a watch face. Based on such a mechanism, we first investigated the effects of target location on the pointing performance.

### Task and Procedure

Participants were presented with a series of individual target selection trials. During the study, participants were asked to keep standing. Before each trial, a *calibrate* and a *start* button were displayed at the corners of the watch face, outside the circular background. Participants adjusted their wrist and the smartwatch to their own initial orientation. Participants pressed the *calibrate* button to set the initial coordinates, after which a crosshair cursor appeared at the center. Once the start button was selected by touch, a circular target (r = 0.8 mm) was displayed on the circular background. Participants tilted their wrist to guide the cursor towards and stay inside the target. The trial was completed when the cursor stayed in the target for over 0.4s. Participants were instructed to acquire these targets as accurately and quickly as possible. We did not use finger tap as the selecting action in this study because the focus was on the tilting process.

### Design

We used a repeated measures within-participant factorial design. The independent variables were *target Distance* (1/5, 2/5, …, 5/5 of the radius R) and *target Direction* (0°, 10°, …, 350°) on the watch face. Presentation of the *Distances* was counter-balanced across participants. Within each block, the 36 *Directions* were presented in random order. Overall, the experimental design was: 5 *Distances* × 2 *Blocks* × 36 *Directions* = 360 data points per participant.

### Participants and Apparatus

The 12 participants who had participated in the pilot study were recruited in this study. All participants were paid $5 for their participation, which lasted about 15 minutes. The experiment was conducted on the Gear Live smartwatch

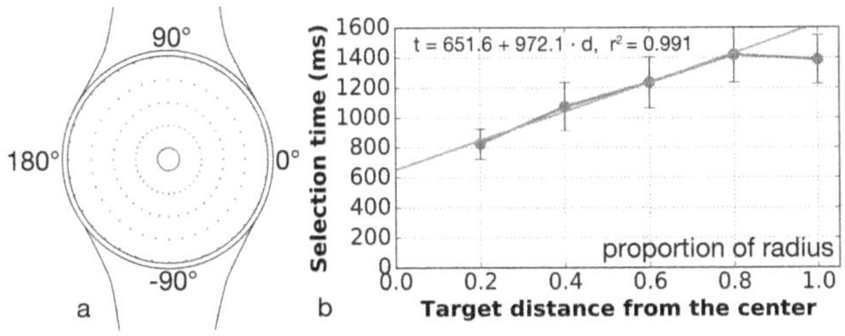


**Figure 7. Left: task in Study 1; Right: selection time with different target distances.**

described above. It has a 30.5 × 30.5mm, 320 × 320px display with an effective resolution of 10.5px/mm.

### Results

*Performance with Different Distances*

We evaluated the performance by *selection time*, which was measured from the moment the finger was lifted off the start button to the moment the target was selected. A repeated measures ANOVA (same statistical test was used hereinafter) showed that there was a significant effect of *target distance* ($F_{4,44}$=150.60, $p$<.001) on selection time. Targets at 5/5 distance were faster to acquire than targets at 4/5 because participants could directly tilt by a greater inclination than the mapping limit without much controlling along radial directions.

Considering the first four distances, there was a strong linear correlation between the *selection time* and the *target distance* (r = 0.991). This suggested that participants could guide the cursor to move uniformly by tilting the wrist with the control-display function of linearly mapping from tilt inclination to the radial coordinate on the watch face. The average speed was around 1.03 R/s. The intercept was 651.6ms, containing 251.6ms of reaction time $T_{reaction}$ at the beginning and 400ms of dwell time $T_{dwell}$ at the end.

*Performance along Different Directions*

For various directions, we measured the performance by the pointing speed, which was defined as

$$v = \frac{Distance}{T_{total} - T_{reaction} - T_{dwell}}$$

Overall, the average pointing speed is 1.12 R/s. We found a significant effect of *target direction* ($F_{35,385}$=5.71, $p$<.001) on *pointing speed.* There were two distinct speed peaks around +90° and -90°, with 1.58R/s and 1.75R/s respectively, suggesting that participants pointed fastest when tilting the wrist up and down. Another slightly faster direction was around 180° (tilt left), 1.13R/s. Somewhat surprisingly, the pointing speed around the 0° (tilt right) was the lowest, only 0.90 R/s.

We further analyzed the *offset angle* between the actual moving path of the cursor and the ideal straight path, which was defined as the angle between $\boldsymbol{p}_{target} - \boldsymbol{p}_{start}$ and $\boldsymbol{p}_{dmax} - \boldsymbol{p}_{start}$ where $\boldsymbol{p}_{dmax}$ is the point farthest from the ideal straight path. There was also a significant effect of *target direction* ($F_{35,385}$=4.86, $p$<.001) on *offset angle.* An interesting finding was that there was a strong negative correlation between *pointing speed* and *offset angle* with Pearson's Correlation Coefficient [50] $r = -0.719$, $p < .0001$. Participants guided the cursor with smaller *offset angles* along directions with faster pointing speed. For example, the *offset angle* was only 7.53° along the +80° direction. This suggested that due to the physical structure of the wrist, users have different motion and control abilities along different directions, resulting in different selecting performance.

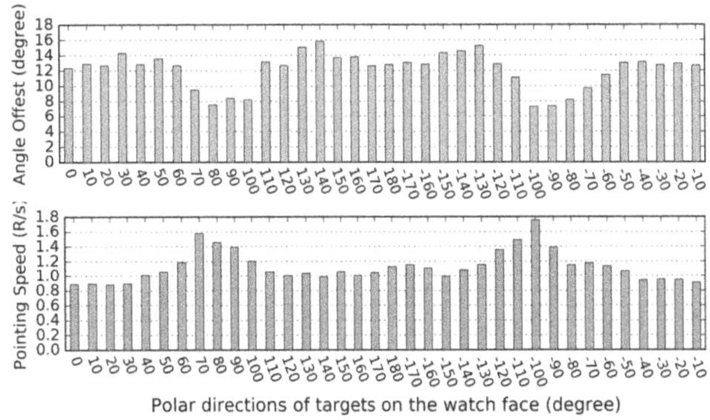


**Figure 8. Pointing speed (bottom) and offset angle (top) along different target directions.**

These results also provide implications for layout and task design of tilt interactions on smartwatches. Overall, important or frequently-accessed targets should be placed as near the center as possible. The exception is that the boundary should be considered before its inner neighboring region. For targets with the same distance from the center, we should give priority to angles around +90°, -90° and 180°.

## USER STUDY 2: CONTINUOUS POINTING

In this study, we evaluated the overall performance of Float on continuous pointing tasks.

### Task and Procedure

Participants were presented with a series of sequential target selection trials. A total of nine target sizes and two usage contexts were tested. Participants were instructed to follow the Float scenario and acquire these targets as accurately and quickly as possible.

At the beginning of each block, participants raised the arm to *wake up* the task. Then round targets were presented con-

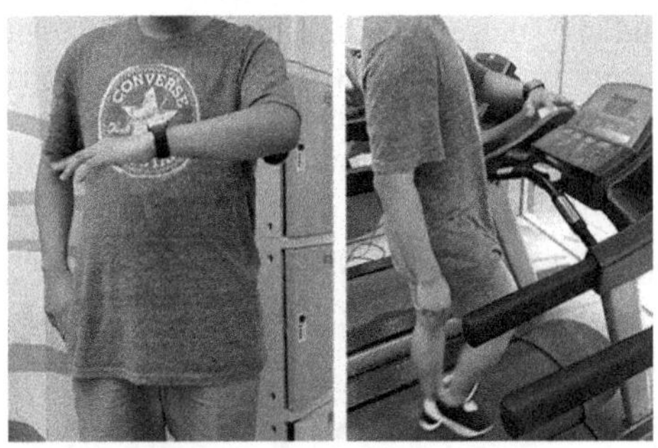

**Figure 9. Study 2 was conducted in both standing (left) and walking (right) contexts.**

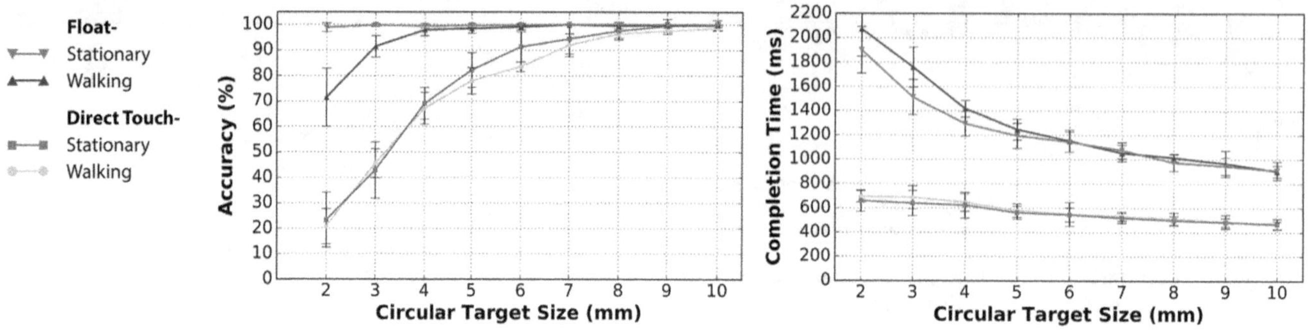


**Figure 10. Mean accuracy and completion time of continuous pointing for *Technique* and *Context* over different target sizes.**

secutively on the circular background of the watch face. Once a target appeared, participants guided a cursor in crosshair shape towards the target by tilting the wrist. When the cursor was into the target, participants performed an in-air finger tap to confirm and complete the selection. The cursor location right before the finger tap was set as the *clicking* position. Participants advanced to the next trial immediately regardless of error.

Because there is still a lack of baseline techniques for one-handed smartwatch interaction in research, in this study we compared Float with direct touch which is widely used on smartwatches. It is worth noting that Float enables input with only one hand, which is the basis of work. The exper-iment of direct touch was more concerned with providing a visual reference on performance than merely comparison.

### Design

A repeated measures within-participant factorial design was used. The independent variables were *Technique* (*Float* and *Touch*), interaction *Context* (*Stationary*, *Walking*), and *Target Size* (diameter: 2, 3, 4, 5, 6, 7, 8, 9, 10 mm). Presentation of *Technique* and *Context* was counterbalanced across participants. The target size as small as 2~5mm was to measure the precision and ability of Float. We tested the performance while *Walking* because smartwatches are usually used in wild and mobile scenarios.

The 9 *Target Sizes* were presented in random order for each participant. For each condition, participants completed 1 practice block and 5 testing blocks. Each block consisted of 10 targets whose positions were randomly generated across the watch face. The average distance between targets was around 13.8mm, 128/45π of the screen radius. The targets were randomly placed to simulate actual usage and test its average performance. We did not follow the standard Fitts' Law design in a circular form because unlike touch screen, Float is location-sensitive. Targets may appear anywhere and tilt paths mostly do not cross the center.

In summary, the experimental design was: 2 *Techniques* × 2 *Contexts* × 9 *Target Sizes* × 5 *Blocks* × 10 *Trials* = 1800 data points per participant.

### Participants and Apparatus

The 12 participants who had participated in the data collection of the implementation section were again recruited for this study. Finger taps were detected with the method above. For the *Walking* condition, participants were asked to walk on a treadmill at the speed of 1.2m/s [51] while performing selecting tasks. All participants were paid $20 for their participation, which lasted about 90 minutes.

### Results

#### Accuracy

In *stationary* context, participants achieved almost 100% of accuracy on all target sizes from 2mm to 10mm with Float. This benefited from its clear visual feedback and participants could directly verify whether the cursor was inside the target or not. In addition, a high pointing accuracy on 2mm (98.9%) suggested that participants could hold the cursor steadily by controlling the wrist.

We found a significant effect of *Context* ($F_{1,11}$=42.42, $p$<.001) on the pointing accuracy of Float. During *walking*, there was an obvious decrease on performance on *size* 2mm and 3mm with an accuracy of 71.5% and 91.5%, respectively. This was because during walking, the body movement itself had effects on the wrist movement and the accelerometer of the motion sensor, causing the cursor fluctuation on the watch face. With *size* no less than 4mm, however, participants were able to perform high-precision (> 98.0%) target selection with Float.

A repeated measures ANOVA showed that there was a significant main effect of *Technique* on *accuracy* in both *stationary* ($F_{1,11}$=68.29, $p$<.001) and *walking* contexts ($F_{1,11}$=598.77, $p$<.001). Figure 10 also demonstrates that Float was more accurate than direction touch over all target *sizes*, especially for smaller targets from 2mm (85.21%% vs 22.07%) to 6mm (99.50% vs 87.47%). Touch can only reach an accuracy of 70% at *size* 4mm and 90% at 6mm.

#### Completion Time

The completion time of Direct Touch was significantly ($F_{1,11}$=598.77, $p$<.001, 1240ms at *size* 2mm and 439ms at 10mm) smaller than Float, which benefited from its nature of direct input. For Float, there was a significant effect of *Target Size* ($F_{8,88}$=344.62, $p$<.001) on completion time. In *stationary* context, participants spent an average of 1900ms at *size* 2mm to 910ms at *size* 10mm. The completion time decreased largely (607ms) from *size* 2mm to *size* 4mm and then gradually to *size* 10mm (373ms).

There was also a significant effect of *Context* ($F_{1,11}$=11.36, $p$<.01) on the accuracy of Float. Participants spent more time (51~172ms) on selecting smaller (2~5mm) targets during *walking* than staying *stationary* due to the unstable cursor. On larger (6~10mm) targets, the completion time showed no significant difference.

## DISCUSSION AND LIMITATIONS

We wanted to explore if the combination of wrist tilt and finger tap could improve one-handed and touch-free input on smartwatches. Our experimental results support our expectation. The occlusion avoidance benefit and real-time visual feedback of Float enable precise target selection on smartwatches. In the walking context, the accuracy performance only reduced for ultra-small targets (< 4mm). To complete a selection, participants spent an average of ~1s to ~2s on targets from large (10mm) to small (2mm). The completion time of Float doubles or triples the time of touch due to the *pointing* and *clicking* processes.

Lastly, we revisit part of our work and discuss the lessons we learned and the limitations of our approach.

### Screen Visibility

In Float, the inherent issue with wrist tilt is that it changes the viewing angle and the screen visibility may be of concern. The visual ability on the tilted screen is indeed unevenly distributed. To ensure its feasibility, we have investigated the appropriate boundaries for the wrist tilt in the elicitation study so that users could see and comprehend well the entire contents over the watch face. Figure 11 illustrates the visual perception in practical experience with Float when the user tilted the watch face by the maximum angle along three typical directions. Even small texts of 2mm height near the boundary could be seen very clearly.

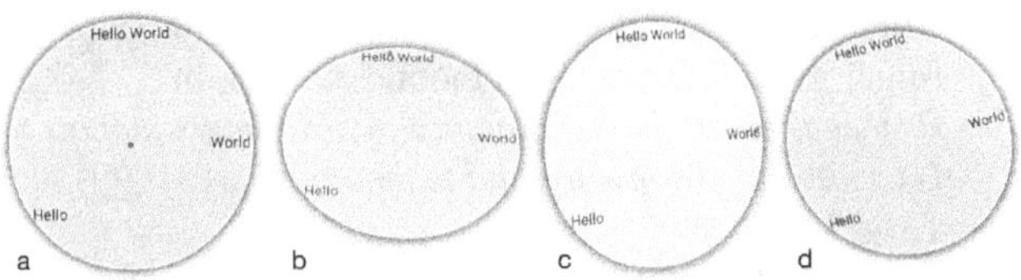


**Figure 11. Visual perception when using Float from the first perspective. The red point represents the cursor. Tilt angles are (a) 0° at the initial phase, (b) ≈40° when tilting upward, (c) ≈30° when tilting to the right, and (d) ≈25° when tilting to the lower left corresponding to the tilt ranges in Figure 4.**

Another visual limitation is that the cursor might occlude contents when interacting with Float. We think the appearance of the cursor should be content-dependent. For example, when the interface is organized as clicking objects (e.g. buttons, list items), it can hide the cursor and only highlight the target background; when the interface is for setting a specific position or value, the cursor should appear.

### Motion and Perception

The non-linear input mapping in the elicitation study and the pointing performance in study 1 reflect different motion abilities and perception of wrist tilt along directions (Figure 4, Figure 8). A significant phenomenon from observation is the subtleness of the body movement. Up/down tilts are small and discrete motions, while left/right tilts are much larger because the forearm, the elbow and sometimes even the upper arm need to jointly move. This also partly explains the unevenly distributed performance on the watch face of Float. Overall, tilting up/down achieved both faster and more stable pointing performance than that of tilting to the left/right. Participants also expressed their subjective feedback on this: *"I need to raise or lower my elbow to point to some areas." (P2)* and *"The physical cost is different but does not affect the user experience much" (P4)*. We will analyze the arm motion and examine its influence on feasibility in actual scenarios in future work.

### Finger Tap and User Evaluation

The presented user evaluation is limited because in the experiment, we only tested the performance of finger tap as the selecting action, which was derived from a user-elicitation study with usability analysis. Although finger tap performs as hypothesized, we believe other elicited input styles or their variants also have their own merits. Future work will include a statistical comparison of all mentioned techniques in Figure 5 to understand the usability and advantages of each approach in real-world practice.

### Application Examples

In study 2, we have confirmed the accuracy of Float on 2mm-10mm target sizes which are smaller than common targets on a touchscreen. This first proves that Float can be directly applied to current UIs on smartwatches. Meanwhile, Float can enable tasks that require precise pointing which are difficult to achieve on smartwatches due to the small form factor and the fat finger problem. Application examples may include specifying a location on a map, selecting color in a color picker, inserting the cursor in the text and inputting characters with a mini keyboard (< 3mm per key).

## CONCLUSION

We have explored input interactions on smartwatches when the other hand is occupied. With Float, a user tilts the wrist to *point* and performs an in-air finger tap to *click*. We have conducted a participatory study to explore the appropriate wrist tilt space and let users define the *clicking* interaction. To realize Float, we only use sensors that are commercially embedded on smartwatches. We first present how to map the wrist tilt movement to the corresponding positions on the watch face. Then we recognize finger taps robustly using the PPG signal and the motion sensor. Results from two user studies have confirmed the feasibility of Float which provides quick and high-precision target selection.

## ACKNOWLEDGEMENT

This work is supported by the National Key Research and Development Plan under Grant No. 2016YFB1001402, the Natural Science Foundation of China under Grant No. 61272230 and No. 61572276, Tsinghua University Research Funding No. 20151080408.

## REFERENCES


1. Pär-Anders Albinsson and Shumin Zhai. 2003. High precision touch screen interaction. In *Proceedings of the SIGCHI conference on Human factors in computing systems* (CHI '03), 105-112. DOI=http://dx.doi.org/10.1145/642611.642631
2. Shaikh Shawon Arefin Shimon, Courtney Lutton, Zichun Xu, Sarah Morrison-Smith, Christina Boucher and Jaime Ruiz. 2016. Exploring Non-touchscreen Gestures for Smartwatches. In *Proceedings of the SIGCHI Conference on Human Factors in Computing Systems* (CHI '16), 3822-3833. DOI=http://dx.doi.org/10.1145/2858036.2858385
3. Daniel Ashbrook, Kent Lyons and Thad Starner. 2008. An investigation into round touchscreen wristwatch interaction. In *Proceedings of the international conference on Human computer interaction with mobile devices and services* (MobileHCI '08), 311-314. DOI=http://dx.doi.org/10.1145/1409240.1409276
4. Patrick Baudisch and Gerry Chu. 2009. Back-of-device interaction allows creating very small touch devices. In *Proceedings of the SIGCHI Conference on Human Factors in Computing Systems* (CHI '09), 1923-1932. DOI=http://dx.doi.org/10.1145/1518701.1518995
5. Hrvoje Benko, Andrew D. Wilson and Patrick Baudisch. 2006. Precise selection techniques for multi-touch screens. In *Proceedings of the SIGCHI Conference on Human Factors in Computing Systems* (CHI '06), 1263-1272. DOI=http://dx.doi.org/10.1145/1124772.1124963.
6. Xiaojun Bi, Yang Li and Shumin Zhai. 2013. FFitts law: modeling finger touch with fitts' law. In *Proceedings of the SIGCHI Conference on Human Factors in Computing Systems* (CHI '13), 1363-1372. DOI=http://dx.doi.org/10.1145/2470654.2466180
7. Alex Butler, Shahram Izadi and Steve Hodges. 2008. SideSight: multi-"touch" interaction around small devices. In *Proceedings of the 21st annual ACM symposium on User interface software and technology* (UIST '08), 201-204. DOI=http://dx.doi.org/10.1145/1449715.1449746
8. Edwin Chan, Teddy Seyed, Wolfgang Stuerzlinger, Xing-Dong Yang and Frank Maurer. 2016. User Elicitation on Single-hand Microgestures. In *Proceedings of the SIGCHI Conference on Human Factors in Computing Systems* (CHI '16), 3403-3414. DOI=http://dx.doi.org/10.1145/2858036.2858589
9. Youli Chang, Sehi L'Yi, Kyle Koh and Jinwook Seo. 2015. Understanding Users' Touch Behavior on Large Mobile Touch-Screens and Assisted Targeting by Tilting Gesture. In *Proceedings of the SIGCHI Conference on Human Factors in Computing Systems* (CHI '15), 1499-1508. DOI=http://dx.doi.org/10.1145/2702123.2702425
10. Andrew Crossan and Roderick Murray-Smith. 2004. Variability in wrist-tilt accelerometer based gesture interfaces. In *Proceedings of the International Conference on Mobile Human-Computer Interaction* (MobileHCI '04), 144-155.
11. Andrew Crossan, John Williamson, Stephen Brewster and Rod Murray-Smith. 2008. Wrist rotation for interaction in mobile contexts. In *Proceedings of the international conference on Human computer interaction with mobile devices and services* (MobileHCI '08), 435-438. DOI=http://dx.doi.org/10.1145/1409240.1409307
12. Artem Dementyev and Joseph A. Paradiso. 2014. WristFlex: low-power gesture input with wrist-worn pressure sensors. In *Proceedings of the 27th annual ACM symposium on User interface software and technology* (UIST '14), 161-166. DOI=http://doi.acm.org/10.1145/2642918.2647396
13. Hui Ding, Goce Trajcevski, Peter Scheuermann, Xiaoyue Wang and Eamonn Keogh. 2008. Querying and mining of time series data: experimental comparison of representations and distance measures. In *Proceedings of the VLDB Endowment 1*, 2: 1542-1552. DOI=http://dx.doi.org/10.14778/1454159.1454226
14. Anhong Guo and Tim Paek. 2016. Exploring tilt for no-touch, wrist-only interactions on smartwatches. In *Proceedings of the International Conference on Human-Computer Interaction with Mobile Devices and Services* (MobileHCI '16), 17-28. DOI=http://dx.doi.org/10.1145/2935334.2935345
15. Chris Harrison and Scott E. Hudson. 2009. Abracadabra: wireless, high-precision, and unpowered finger input for very small mobile devices. In *Proceedings of the 22nd annual ACM symposium on User interface software and technology* (UIST '09), 121-124. DOI=http://dx.doi.org/10.1145/1622176.1622199
16. Da-Yuan Huang, Liwei Chan, Shuo Yang, Fan Wang, Rong-Hao Liang, De-Nian Yang, Yi-Ping Hung, and Bing-Yu Chen. 2016. DigitSpace: Designing Thumb-to-Fingers Touch Interfaces for One-Handed and Eyes-Free Interactions. In *Proceedings of the SIGCHI Conference on Human Factors in Computing Systems* (CHI '16), 1526-1537. DOI=http://dx.doi.org/10.1145/2858036.2858483
17. Eleanor Jones, Jason Alexander, Andreas Andreou, Pourang Irani and Sriram Subramanian. 2010. GesText: accelerometer-based gestural text-entry systems. In *Proceedings of the SIGCHI Conference on Human Factors in Computing Systems* (CHI '10), 2173-2182. DOI=http://dx.doi.org/10.1145/1753326.1753655

18. Jun Gong, Xing-Dong Yang, and Pourang Irani. 2016. WristWhirl: One-handed Continuous Smartwatch Input using Wrist Gestures. In Proceedings of the 29th Annual Symposium on User Interface Software and Technology (UIST '16), 861-872. DOI=https://doi.org/10.1145/2984511.2984563

19. Jungsoo Kim, Jiasheng He, Kent Lyons and Thad Starner. 2007. The gesture watch: A wireless contact-free gesture based wrist interface. In *Proceedings of the International Symposium on Wearable Computers* (ISWC '07), 1-8. DOI=http://dx.doi.org/10.1109/ISWC.2007.4373770

20. Ju-Whan Kim, Han-Jong Kim and Tek-Jin Nam. 2016. M. Gesture: An Acceleration-Based Gesture Authoring System on Multiple Handheld and Wearable Devices. In *Proceedings of the SIGCHI Conference on Human Factors in Computing Systems* (CHI '16), 2307-2318. DOI=http://dx.doi.org/10.1145/2858036.2858358

21. Benjamin Lafreniere, Carl Gutwin, Andy Cockburn and Tovi Grossman. 2016. Faster Command Selection on Touchscreen Watches. In *Proceedings of the SIGCHI Conference on Human Factors in Computing Systems* (CHI '16), 4663-4674. DOI=http://dx.doi.org/10.1145/2858036.2858166

22. Loclair C, Gustafson S, Baudisch P. 2010. PinchWatch: a wearable device for one-handed microinteractions. In *Proceedings of the International Conference on Human-Computer Interaction with Mobile Devices and Services* (MobileHCI '10)

23. Gierad Laput, Robert Xiao, Xiang Chen, Scott E. Hudson and Chris Harrison. 2014. Skin buttons: cheap, small, low-powered and clickable fixed-icon laser projectors. In *Proceedings of the 27th annual ACM symposium on User interface software and technology* (UIST '14), 389-394. DOI=http://dx.doi.org/10.1145/2642918.2647356

24. I. Scott MacKenzie and Robert J. Teather. 2012. FittsTilt: the application of Fitts' law to tilt-based interaction. In *Proceedings of the Nordic Conference on Human-Computer Interaction: Making Sense Through Design* (NordiCHI '12), 568-577. DOI=http://dx.doi.org/10.1145/2399016.2399103

25. Florian Müller, Sebastian Günther, Niloofar Dezfuli, Mohammadreza Khalilbeigi and Max Mühlhäuser. 2016. ProxiWatch: Enhancing Smartwatch Interaction through Proximity-based Hand Input. In *Proceedings of the SIGCHI Conference Extended Abstracts on Human Factors in Computing Systems* (CHI EA '16), 2617-2624. DOI=http://dx.doi.org/10.1145/2851581.2892450

26. Ian Oakley and Sile O'Modhrain. 2005. Tilt to scroll: evaluating a motion based vibrotactile mobile interface. In First Joint Eurohaptics Conference and Symposium on Haptic Interfaces for Virtual Environment and Teleoperator Systems. World Haptics Conference (HAPTICS '05), 40-49. DOI=http://dx.doi.org/10.1109/WHC.2005.138

27. Ian Oakley and Doyoung Lee. 2014. Interaction on the edge: offset sensing for small devices. In *Proceedings of the SIGCHI Conference on Human Factors in Computing Systems* (CHI '14), 169-178. DOI=http://dx.doi.org/10.1145/2556288.2557138

28. Ian Oakley, Doyoung Lee, M.D Rasel Islam and Augusto Esteves. 2015. Beats: Tapping Gestures for Smart Watches. In *Proceedings of the SIGCHI Conference on Human Factors in Computing Systems* (CHI '15), 1237-1246. DOI=http://dx.doi.org/10.1145/2702123.2702226

29. Masa Ogata and Michita Imai. 2015. SkinWatch: skin gesture interaction for smart watch. In *Proceedings of the Augmented Human International Conference* (AH '15), 21-24. DOI=http://dx.doi.org/10.1145/2735711.2735830

30. Stephen Oney, Chris Harrison, Amy Ogan and Jason Wiese. 2013. ZoomBoard: a diminutive qwerty soft keyboard using iterative zooming for ultra-small devices. In *Proceedings of the SIGCHI Conference on Human Factors in Computing Systems* (CHI '13), 2799-2802. DOI=http://dx.doi.org/10.1145/2470654.2481387

31. Anna Ostberg and Nada Matic. 2015. Hover cursor: Improving touchscreen acquisition of small targets with hover-enabled pre-selection. In *Proceedings of the SIGCHI Conference Extended Abstracts on Human Factors in Computing Systems* (CHI EA '15), 1723-1728. DOI=http://dx.doi.org/10.1145/2702613.2732903

32. Kurt Partridge, Saurav Chatterjee, Vibha Sazawal, Gaetano Borriello and Roy Want. 2002. TiltType: accelerometer-supported text entry for very small devices. In *Proceedings of the 15th annual ACM symposium on User interface software and technology* (UIST '02), 201-204. DOI=http://dx.doi.org/10.1145/571985.572013

33. Richard L. Potter, Linda J. Weldon and Ben Shneiderman. 1988. Improving the accuracy of touch screens: an experimental evaluation of three strategies. In *Proceedings of the SIGCHI conference on Human factors in computing systems* (CHI '88), 27-32. DOI=http://dx.doi.org/10.1145/57167.57171

34. Jun Rekimoto. 1996. Tilting operations for small screen interfaces. In *Proceedings of the 9th annual ACM symposium on User interface software and technology* (UIST '96), 167-168. DOI=http://dx.doi.org/10.1145/237091.237115

35. Jun Rekimoto. 2001. Gesturewrist and gesturepad: Unobtrusive wearable interaction devices.

In *Proceedings of the International Symposium on Wearable Computers* (ISWC '01), 21-27.

36. Anne Roudaut, Stéphane Huot and Eric Lecolinet. 2008. TapTap and MagStick: improving one-handed target acquisition on small touch-screens. In *Proceedings of the working conference on Advanced visual interfaces* (AVI '08), 146-153. DOI=http://dx.doi.org/10.1145/1385569.1385594
37. Keigo Shima, Kazusa Onishi, Ryosuke Takada, Takuya Adachi, Buntarou Shizuki and Jiro Tanaka. 2016. Investigating Accuracy of Tilting Operation on Wrist-worn Devices with Touchscreens. In *Proceedings of the SIGCHI Conference on Human Factors in Computing Systems* (CHI '16), 2705-2711. DOI=http://dx.doi.org/10.1145/2851581.2892377
38. Robert J. Teather and I. Scott MacKenzie. 2014. Position vs. velocity control for tilt-based interaction. In *Proceedings of Graphics Interface* (GI '14), 51-58.
39. Daniel Vogel, and Patrick Baudisch. 2007. Shift: a technique for operating pen-based interfaces using touch. In *Proceedings of the SIGCHI Conference on Human Factors in Computing System* (CHI '07), 657-666. DOI=http://dx.doi.org/10.1145/1240624.1240727
40. Lars Weberg, Torbjörn Brange and Åsa Wendelbo Hansson. 2001. A piece of butter on the PDA display. In *Proceedings of the SIGCHI Conference Extended Abstracts on Human Factors in Computing Systems* (CHI EA '01), 435-436. DOI=http://dx.doi.org/10.1145/1240624.1240727
41. Hongyi Wen, Julian Ramos Rojas and Anind K. Dey. 2016. Serendipity: Finger Gesture Recognition using an Off-the-Shelf Smartwatch. In *Proceedings of the SIGCHI Conference on Human Factors in Computing Systems* (CHI '16), 3847-3851. DOI=http://dx.doi.org/10.1145/2858036.2858466
42. Daniel Wigdor and Ravin Balakrishnan. 2003. TiltText: using tilt for text input to mobile phones. In *Proceedings of the 16th annual ACM symposium on User interface software and technology* (UIST '03), 81-90. DOI=http://dx.doi.org/10.1145/964696.964705
43. Daniel Wigdor, Clifton Forlines, Patrick Baudisch, John Barnwell and Chia Shen. 2007. Lucid touch: a see-through mobile device. In *Proceedings of the 20th annual ACM symposium on User interface software and technology* (UIST '07), 269-278. DOI=http://dx.doi.org/10.1145/1294211.1294259
44. Jacob O. Wobbrock, Meredith Ringel Morris and Andrew D. Wilson. 2009. User-defined gestures for surface computing. In *Proceedings of the SIGCHI Conference on Human Factors in Computing Systems* (CHI '09), 1083-1092. DOI=http://dx.doi.org/10.1145/1518701.1518866
45. Haijun Xia, Tovi Grossman and George Fitzmaurice. 2015. NanoStylus: Enhancing Input on Ultra-Small Displays with a Finger-Mounted Stylus. In *Proceedings of the 28th Annual ACM Symposium on User Interface Software and Technology* (UIST '15), 447-456. DOI=http://dx.doi.org/10.1145/2807442.2807500
46. Robert Xiao, Gierad Laput and Chris Harrison. 2014. Expanding the input expressivity of smartwatches with mechanical pan, twist, tilt and click. In *Proceedings of the SIGCHI Conference on Human Factors in Computing Systems* (CHI '14) 193-196. DOI=http://dx.doi.org/10.1145/2556288.2557017
47. Chun Yu, Hongyi Wen, Wei Xiong, Xiaojun Bi and Yuanchun Shi. 2016. Investigating Effects of Post-Selection Feedback for Acquiring Ultra-Small Targets on Touchscreen. In *Proceedings of the SIGCHI Conference on Human Factors in Computing Systems* (CHI '16), 4699-4710. DOI=http://dx.doi.org/10.1145/2858036.2858593
48. Yang Zhang, Junhan Zhou, Gierad Laput and Chris Harrison. 2016. SkinTrack: Using the Body as an Electrical Waveguide for Continuous Finger Tracking on the Skin. In *Proceedings of the SIGCHI Conference on Human Factors in Computing Systems* (CHI '16), 1491-1503. DOI=http://dx.doi.org/10.1145/2858036.2858082
49. https://en.wikipedia.org/wiki/Butterworth_filter
50. https://en.wikipedia.org/wiki/Pearson_product-moment_correlation_coefficient
51. https://en.wikipedia.org/wiki/Preferred_walking_speed
52. www.pulsesensor.com

# COMPASS: Rotational Keyboard on Non-Touch Smartwatches

**Xin Yi**[1], **Chun Yu**[1†], **Weijie Xu**[1], **Xiaojun Bi**[2], **Yuanchun Shi**[1]
[1]Key Laboratory of Pervasive Computing, Ministry of Education
Tsinghua National Laboratory for Information Science and Technology
Department of Computer Science and Technology, Tsinghua University, Beijing, 100084, China
[2]Department of Computer Science, Stony Brook University, Stony Brook, NY, United States
{yix15,xu-wj13}@mails.tsinghua.edu.cn {chunyu,shiyc}@tsinghua.edu.cn xjunbi@gmail.com

(a) (b) (c) (d) (e)

Figure 1: A storyboard illustrating a user entering "an" with *COMPASS*. (a) The keyboard shows three cursors at initial locations, the user rotates the bezel counterclockwise to hit 'a' with a nearby cursor. (b) The user presses the physical button to select 'a'. (c) Upon selection, the keyboard changes the location of the cursors so as to minimize the expected rotational distance for the next key. As there is already a cursor on 'n', the user presses again to select 'n' without rotating. The color of each key indicates the probability of it being the next selection. (d) The user long-presses the physical button to enter word selection mode. Dimmed keys are not possible for the next selection. (e) The user presses the button to select "an".

## ABSTRACT

Entering text is very challenging on smartwatches, especially on non-touch smartwatches where virtual keyboards are unavailable. In this paper, we designed and implemented *COMPASS*, a non-touch bezel-based text entry technique. *COMPASS* positions multiple cursors on a circular keyboard, with the location of each cursor dynamically optimized during typing to minimize rotational distance. To enter text, a user rotates the bezel to select keys with any nearby cursors. The design of *COMPASS* was justified by an iterative design process and user studies. Our evaluation showed that participants achieved a pick-up speed around 10 WPM and reached 12.5 WPM after 90-minute practice. *COMPASS* allows users to enter text on non-touch smartwatches, and also serves as an alternative for entering text on touch smartwatches when touch is unavailable (e.g., wearing gloves).

† denotes the corresponding author.



*CHI 2017*, May 06-11, 2017, Denver, CO, USA
© 2017 ACM ISBN 978-1-4503-4655-9/17/05...$15.00
DOI: http://dx.doi.org/10.1145/3025453.3025454

## ACM Classification Keywords

H.5.2. Information Interfaces and Presentation (e.g. HCI): User Interfaces; Input devices and strategies (e.g., mouse, touchscreen)

## Author Keywords

Text entry; smartwatch; multiple cursors; circular keyboard; non-touch.

## INTRODUCTION

Smartwatches have become increasingly popular in the Post-PC computing era. They are easy-to-access, always-on and could be fashionable decorations if well designed. To meet the diverse market demand, a variety of smartwatches have been designed and manufactured, which can be classified as either *touch* or *non-touch* smartwatches. The former has a touch-sensitive screen and supports touch interaction (e.g., Apple Watch [3]), while the latter is equipped with a non-touch display in order to reduce power consumption and to be more affordable. For example, the Pebble Time watch [6] uses a non-touch e-ink color display, with an up to 7 day battery life.

To better serve users, a smartwatch is enhanced with more and more interactive features. Entering text, which is one of the most performed tasks in mobile computing, is one of the most desired features on smartwatches. However, it has remained a big challenge, especially for non-touch smartwatches, on which the typical virtual keyboard is not supported.

One approach of entering text on non-touch smartwatches is to use speech (e.g. MOTO 360 [5]). However, it suffers from two major problems: 1) it is socially inappropriate to input with voice in some situations (e.g., at meetings or classrooms); 2) speech-based input is error-prone especially in noisy environments. Although a considerable amount of effort has been investigated in improving smartwatch text entry (e.g. [12, 16, 22, 27, 34]), very little of them is for non-touch smartwatches. In this paper, we aim to address this important but overlooked problem.

In this paper, we designed and implemented *COMPASS*, a bezel-based, multi-cursor text entry technique for non-touch smartwatches. It works for non-touch smartwatches, and also for touch smartwatches when touch input is unavailable (e.g., wearing gloves). To enter text, users rotate the bezel to hit keys on the circular keyboard with a cursor. To minimize rotational distance, the location of each cursor is dynamically optimized after each key selection according to the probability of next keys needed.

We followed an iterative design process in designing *COMPASS*. In the first user study, we compared the text entry performance and user preference with different cursor placement strategy and number of cursors. Results showed that a dynamic strategy with three cursors was optimal. We then further improved this technique according to the user behavior data, and evaluated its usability in the second user study. Users achieved a pick-up speed of 9.3 WPM, and after 90 minutes of practice, they achieved 12.5 WPM without sacrificing accuracy. Expert users even reached 15.4 WPM in the last block. We concluded that *COMPASS* is a promising text entry method for non-touch smartwatches and other rotational interfaces.

## RELATED WORK

### Interaction Techniques for Smartwatches

A number of text entry techniques have been proposed to faciliate text entry on touch smartwatches. Some techniques achieved accurate character-level input by iterative selection (e.g. ZoomBoard [27], SwipeBoard [12] and SplitBoard [19]) or using a call-out to show the finger occluded area (e.g. ZShift [22]). The text entry speed reached 9.3 WPM [27], 19.6 WPM [12], 15 WPM [19] and 9.1 WPM [22] respectively. Alternatively, some techniques provided efficient word-level input by incorporating input decoders. (e.g. VelociTap [34] and WatchWriter [16] reached 41 WPM and 22 WPM respectively). Noticeably, all these techniques adopted a QWERTY keyboard. However, the limitation of touchscreen-based techniques lies in a tradeoff between the screen occupation and input precision. Besides, touchscreens is even unavailable in certain scenarios (e.g. wearing gloves). Funk et al. [14] used a touch-sensitive wristband to support text entry on smartwatches. However, the speed reached only about 3 WPM.

To address this problem, some researchers sought to enhance the interaction capability for non-touch smartwatches. For example, Arefin et al. [8] designed a set of non-touchscreen gestures to enable interaction with the smartwatch in mid-air. Abracadabra [17] used magnetometers to enable wireless, unpowered and high fidelity finger input for smartwatches. And Serendipity [35] used the motion sensors of the smartwatch to sense finger gesture. Plaumann et al. [28] used a bezel to support list selection based on a circular alphabetical menu. Kerber et al. [20] compared bezel interaction with digital crown and touch, where the bezel showed worse performance than the latter two. Noticeably, none of these techniques has been applied to the scenario of text entry. In this regard, we seek to explore the possibility of text entry on off-the-shelf non-touch smartwatches in this paper.

### Circular Keyboard Techniques

Besides conventional QWERTY layout, there are also some keyboards that use a circular layout. Although less common, the circular layout poses some advantages in certain scenarios (e.g. rotational interfaces [29], personal area on tabletop [18], or to minimize the travelling distance [25, 32]).

Cirrin [25] used a circular keyboard to support pen input using word-level gestures. The order of the characters were optimized to minimize the stroke distance. To reduce the difficulty of selecting a letter, Cechanowicz et al. [11] modified Cirrin by expanding the characters as the stylus approached it. However, the text entry performance dropped due to a higher error rate. These two keyboards optimized the order of the characters for efficiency. However, at the same time, this would result in more cognitive load for users, which may limit the text entry speed.

Alternatively, some techniques used an alphabetic ordered list of characters to aim the pick-up speed. BubbleCircle [18] used a circular keyboard on a tabletop displays, and dynamically adjusted the key sizes according to user's input. Shoemaker et al. [32] proposed a circular keyboard for text entry on large wall displays. User moves the pointer to highlight the desired character and presses a button to select it. TUP [29] places the characters at fixed positions on the wheel, and user press a select key to select the highlighted character.

### Multi-Cursor Techniques for Target Acquisition

Using multiple cursors to assist target acquisition has been extensively studied in the scenario of Graphical User Interface (GUI). These techniques usually placed multiple cursors on the screen, which move synchronously following the mouse. A user can point to a target use the cursor that is closest to it. This posed an inherent advantage that the travel distance between targets in cursor-based interfaces can be significantly reduced. Ninja Cursors [21] uniformly distributed multiple cursors on the screen, and used a waiting queue algorithm to resolve the ambiguity. Similarly, satellite cursor [36] places a cursor in the vicinity of every target, and used an "aggregate and expand algorithm" to avoid ambiguity.

Some researchers incorporate eye-gaze to help resolve the cursor ambiguity when multiple targets were selected at the same time. Raiha et al. [31] augmented the Ninja Cursors by using eye-gaze to select the active cursor. Similarly, the Rake Cursor [10] also used a grid of cursors controlled by a mouse, and the selection of the active cursor by gaze. However, the active cursor can only change when a mouse motion event occurs.

### COMPASS: DESIGN AND IMPLEMENTATION

We implemented *COMPASS* on a Samsung Gear S2 smartwatch (see Figure 1). The watch has a 1.2" round screen, a rotational bezel and two physical buttons. The rotational bezel can detect discrete rotation events. According to our test, the rotation precision is about 24 $levels/360°$. As we focus on non-touch smartwatches, we did not leverage the touchscreen of this watch. In practice, one can also implement *COMPASS* on other hardware as long as it supports rotation and press interaction (e.g. the digital crown on Apple Watches [3] and the BMW iDrive controller [4]).

#### Keyboard Layout

We adopted a circular layout that best fits the rotation interaction paradigm. To help users locate the target keys quickly, the character keys were organized in alphabetical order [29]. Furthermore, we flipped the characters on the lower half of the keyboard inside out ('H' to 'S') to help users visually recognize these characters (see Figure 1a).

An advantage of the circular layout is that different from conventional QWERTY keyboards (e.g. [16]) and T9 keyboards (e.g. the system keyboard on Samsung Gear S2 smartwatch), it allows the remaining screen area to be in a round shape. Therefore, the screen contents can be scaled to fit in the inner area without changing the look-and-feel. We can also use a transparent keyboard to further avoid shrinking the contents.

#### Interaction Design

The design goal of *COMPASS* is to enable text entry on smartwatches without using the touchscreen. To achieve this, we displayed cursors along the circular keyboard. During text entry, users rotate the bezel of the smartwatch to move the cursors, and press the physical button to select characters and words [29, 32]. Compared to touchscreen-based keyboards, this design avoided the fat-finger problem, and provides tactile feedback during rotation. Considering that long rotations were slow and hard to perform, we employed a multi-cursor interaction paradigm, where multiple cursors move and select the characters simultaneously according to user's control. Figure 1 shows the storyboard illustrating a user entering words using *COMPASS*. The interaction is as follows:

1. Users rotate the bezel to hit the target key with any nearby cursors, and press the physical button on the side of the smartwatch to select the character.
2. Upon selection, *COMPASS* showed three candidate words according to the current input on the bottom of the inner area.
3. Users long press the physical button to switch to word selection mode, where there is only one cursor. We empirically set the time threshold of long press to be 250 ms according to our pilot study.
4. If there is only one candidate word left, the word would be automatically entered. Otherwise, users rotate the bezel to hit the target word with the cursor, and then press the button again to confirm the selection. *COMPASS* automatically appends a space after the selected word.
5. During typing, users can flick their wrists to delete the last entered word after selection, or the last character during entering a word.

#### Flicking Gesture

During text entry, we designed wrist flick as an action to trigger deletion. Flicking is a system gesture for Android Wear [7] and Tizen OS, which is natural and easy to perform.

We recognized the flick gestures based on the gyroscope data from the Samsung Gear S2 smartwatch, which reports the rotation of the wrist at about 100Hz. Figure 2 illustrates the signal during a typical flicking gesture. According to empirical evidence, we used a 500 ms time window with two thresholds ($\pm 550°/s$) on the X dimension data to recognize the gesture.

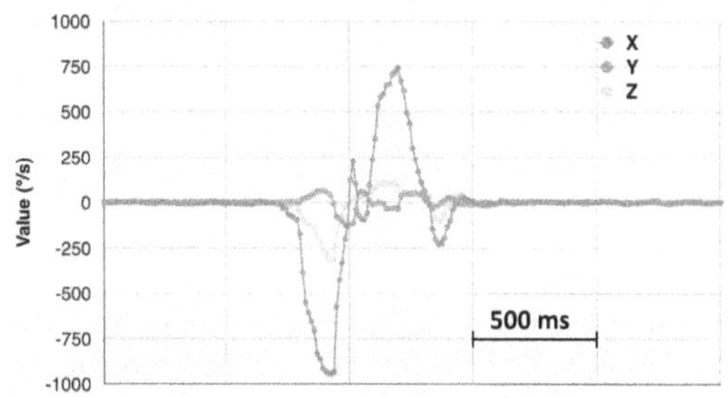


Figure 2: Illustration of the gyroscope data during a flicking gesture.

#### Prediction Algorithm and Language Model

As with any modern smart keyboards, we employed a prediction algorithm in *COMPASS* to resolve the ambiguity in user's input. We employed Goodman et al.'s Bayesian model [15] to predict the target word. Given user's input $I$, it calculates the probability of a word $W$ in a predefined dictionary as:

$$P(W|I) \propto P(I|W) \times P(W) \tag{1}$$

As *COMPASS* used multiple cursors to select characters simultaneously, we have

$$I = \begin{pmatrix} I_{11} & I_{12} & \cdots & I_{1n} \\ I_{21} & I_{22} & \cdots & I_{2n} \\ \vdots & \vdots & \ddots & \vdots \\ I_{N1} & I_{N2} & \cdots & I_{Nn} \end{pmatrix} \tag{2}$$

where $N$ is the number of cursors, and $n$ is the length of the input. As with many smart keyboard techniques, we assumes that users generate no insertion or omission errors, and we treat each input point independently (e.g. [13, 15]), therefore:

$$P(I|W) = \prod_{i=1}^{n} P(I_{\cdot i}|W_i) \tag{3}$$

where $I_{\cdot i}$ refers to the $i$th column of $I$, and $W_i$ is the $i$th character of $W$. Meanwhile, we set

$$P(I_{\cdot i}|W_i) = \begin{cases} 1 & \text{if } \exists 1 \le j \le N \quad \text{s.t.} \quad I_{ji} = W_i \\ 0 & \text{otherwise} \end{cases} \tag{4}$$

This assumption is based on the observation in pilot study that, users rarely makes mistake when selecting characters. In this way, *COMPASS* behaves similar with an ambiguous keyboard (e.g. T9 keyboard).

We used the top 15,000 words as well as their corresponding frequency in the *American National Corpus* [2] as our corpus. According to Nation et al. [26], this would be sufficient to cover over 95% of the common English words.

### Visual Hint

When entering text using *COMPASS*, one of the critical factors that affect the text entry performance is the ease to visually acquire the target key. In this regard, we designed visual cues to help users find their target keys during text entry.

Assuming the user has generated the input $I$ (see Equation 2), we denote $S(I)$ as the set of all words $W$ in the dictionary that $P(I|W_1W_2...W_n) \neq 0$. In other words, $S(I)$ contains all words whose prefix matches the input $I$. Now, for each character $c$ in the alphabet, the probability of it being the following character can be calculated as:

$$P(c) = \frac{\sum_{W \in S(I) \wedge W_{n+1}=c} P(W)}{\sum_{W \in S(I)} P(W)} \quad (5)$$

Based on $P(c)$, we designed two kinds of visual cues, as showed in Figure 3. First, the keys whose probability was zero would be dimmed to avoid distracting the user (e.g. 'F' and 'T'). Second, we adjusted the brightness of the remaining keys according to their probability. The higher the probability is, the lighter the key color would be (e.g. 'P' vs. 'A'). During text entry, the visual cues automatically updates upon each character selection. According to our interview, this design indeed helped users to find the target keys (especially those with high probability) more easily.

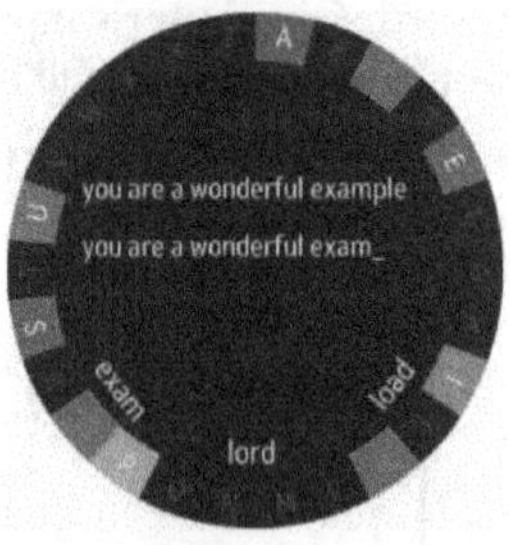


Figure 3: Visual cues to help users find the target keys. Impossible keys are dimmed, while others are highlighted according to their possibility.

### Cursor Placement Strategy

A key problem of *COMPASS* arise from the multi-cursor paradigm. On the one hand, if the relative location of the cursors keep fixed, users may be able to program their rotation behavior in advance. On the other hand, dynamically optimizing the position of the cursors could reduce the rotation distance, thus potentially increasing the text entry speed. However, this dynamic interface may introduce more cognitive load for users at the same time. Therefore, whether or not to employ a dynamic cursor placement strategy is worth exploring.

To address this problem, we designed two variations of *COMPASS*: *S-COMPASS* (*S* for *Static*) and *D-COMPASS* (*D* for *Dynamic*). The two techniques share the same design except for the cursor placement strategy.

#### *S-COMPASS*

The design goal of *S-COMPASS* is to keep a static cursor placement to reinforce users' motor programming ability, but at the cost of a presumably longer rotation distance. Consider that we used $N$ cursors, it is obvious that the cursors should be placed evenly along the keyboard to minimize the expected rotation distance. Given the static cursor placement strategy, *S-COMPASS* functions similar with an ambiguous keyboard, where there are $N$ characters on each "key".

#### *D-COMPASS*

The design goal of *D-COMPASS* is to dynamically adjust the position of the cursors according to user's input, such that the expected distance of the next rotation is minimized. During typing, the location of the cursors changed upon each character selection. Compared with *S-COMPASS*, *D-COMPASS* could potentially increase the text entry speed by reducing the rotation distance.

Each time the user selects a character, the algorithm searches all the $C_{26}^N$ possible cursor locations, and selects the one with the lowest *Expected Next Rotation Distance (ENRD)*, which was defined as:

$$ENRD = \sum_{c \in \chi} dis(c) \times P(c) \quad (6)$$

where $\chi$ is the set of all 26 characters, $P(c)$ was calculated according to Equation 5, and $dis(c)$ is the rotation distance that needed to hit key $c$ with the closest cursor. For example, in Figure 3, $dis(E) = 2$.

Ideally, the above optimization would minimize the expected distance of next rotation. However, as Equation 6 is a weighted distance, in practice, the optimization tended to place the cursors around keys with highest frequencies, and cause these keys to be selected at the same time (see Figure 4a). As a result, the number of remaining keys after each selection would not drop as fast as expected. To alleviate this problem, we adopted an intuitive method that prevents high-frequency keys to be selected at the same time: Instead of considering all $C_{26}^N$ possibilities, we pruned the candidates that would cause any two of the $N$ characters with the highest $P(c)$ to be selected at the same time (see Figure 4b).

This heuristic restriction helps the optimization procedure to avoid grouping high probability keys together. With a small sacrifice of the rotation distance, it may decrease the entropy of the remaining text, and thus increased the overall typing performance. According to our pilot study, optimizing rotation distance was also more perceived and appreciated by users than optimizing ambiguity.

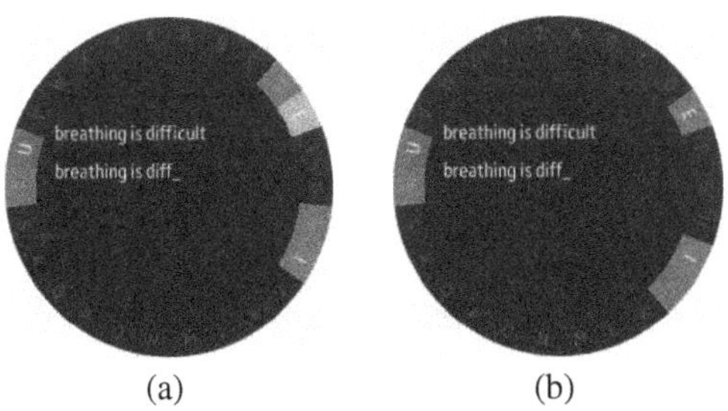


Figure 4: Example of cursor placement (a) before applying restriction, 'U', 'E' and 'I' would be selected at the same time (b) after applying restriction, 'U', 'E' and 'I' could not be selected at the same time.

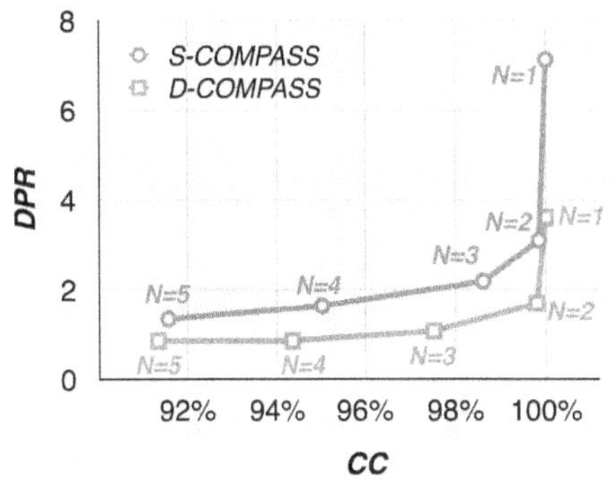


Figure 5: Simulation result. *SRD* and *CC* for each *N* and technique.

### Number of Cursors

It is intuitive that the number of cursors (*N*) is crucial for the performance of every multi-cursor techniques [21]. On the one hand, the more cursors we use, the shorter distance users would have to rotate during text entry. On the other hand, too many cursors would result in two problems: 1) as multiple characters are selected by the cursors simultaneously, this would let to input ambiguity 2) too many cursors may spam the user interface, causing visual and cognitive burden for users [30]. Therefore, we conducted a simulation to determine the range of possible *N* that is applicable. Metrics include *rotation distance*, which is indicative of the text entry speed, and *input ambiguity*, which would affect the input accuracy.

#### *Simulation Design*

We defined two metrics: 1) *Distance Per Rotation (DPR)*, which is average distance for each rotation when entering a word, normalized by key size. A greater *DPR* suggests longer distance for each rotation, and presumably longer input time. 2) *Candidate Coverage (CC)* measures the ratio of the words in the dictionary that could appear in the top three candidates given user's input. A higher *CC* implies that the technique is more accurate in input disambiguation.

We tested all words in the dictionary for both *S-COMPASS* and *D-COMPASS*. For each word, we simulated user's input by assuming that the user would always use the nearest cursor to hit the keys. We tested the number of cursors (*N*) from 1 to 5. For each level of *N*, we measured the average *DPR* of each word as well as the *CC*.

#### *Results*

Figure 5 shows the simulation results. As expected, for *S-COMPASS* and *D-COMPASS*, *DPR* and *CC* both drop monotonously with increasing *N*, suggesting a tradeoff between rotation distance and input ambiguity.

Generally, *S-COMPASS* yielded a slightly higher *CC*, but a significantly higher *DPR* than *D-COMPASS*. Interestingly, the *DPR* of *S-COMPASS* ranged from 1.34 to 3.10 for $N \geq 2$, but dynamically jumped up to 7.13 for $N = 1$, suggesting a much further rotation distance. Meanwhile, $N = 5$ only decreased *DPR* by 0.29 comparing with $N = 4$, but decreased *CC* by 3%. Therefore, we considered the applicable number of cursors for *S-COMPASS* to be from 2 to 4.

The results on *D-COMPASS* are similar. The *DPR* ranged from 0.85 to 1.69 for $N \geq 2$, and jumped up to 3.61 for $N = 1$. Meanwhile, $N = 5$ yield the same *DPR* with $N = 4$, but decreased *CC* by 3%. Therefore, the applicable number of cursors for *D-COMPASS* was also from 2 to 4.

## EXPERIMENT 1: COMPARING DIFFERENT DESIGNS

So far, we have proposed several design alternatives for *COMPASS*, each representing a tradeoff between certain design goals. In this section, we conducted a user study to compare the performance and user preference of these designs with two main goals: 1) determine the optimal number of cursors for both *S-COMPASS* and *D-COMPASS* in terms of text entry performance and user preference; 2) compare the performance and subjective feedback of *S-COMPASS* and *D-COMPASS*.

### Participants

We recruited 12 participants from the campus (8 male, 4 female), with an average age of 22.7 (SD = 2.0). None of them had used the Samsung Gear S2 smartwatch before. Each participant was compensated $12.

### Procedure

We used a within-subjects, two-factor design. One factor is *Technique* with two levels (*S-COMPASS* and *D-COMPASS*), and the other is *number of cursors* (*N*) with three levels (2, 3 and 4). Participants were seated during the experiment. They were asked to complete two sessions of text entry tasks, corresponding to *S-COMPASS* and *D-COMPASS* respectively. In each session, they completed three blocks of tasks, each corresponds to a level of *N*. The order of different *Technique* and *N* was counterbalanced. In each block, they were first allowed three minutes to familiarize themselves with the technique. They then entered 5 phrases randomly sampled from the Mackenzie and Soukoreff phrase set [24]. A two-minute break was enforced between blocks. And after the experiment, questionnaires and interviews were carried out to gather their subjective feedback.

Figure 6 shows a screenshot of the experiment platform. The task phrase was showed in the middle of the screen, with the

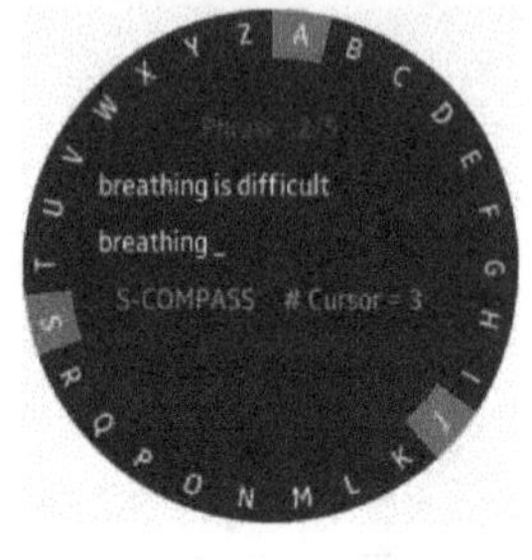


Figure 6: Experiment platform.

entered text showed below it. Participants were instructed to type "as quickly and as accurately as possible". They were free to correct the errors or leave them uncorrected. After finishing each phrase, they swipe right on the touchscreen to continue to the next phrase.

### Results

Across all participants, we gathered 2 Techniques × 3 N × 5 phrases × 12 participants = 360 phrases.

#### Speed

We calculated the text entry speed similar with Mackenzie [1]:

$$WPM = \frac{|W|-1}{T} \times 60 \times \frac{1}{5} \quad (7)$$

where $|W|$ is the length of the final transcribed string, and $T$ is the elapsed time in seconds from the first press to the selection of the last word. Figure 7a shows the text entry speed for different techniques and $N$. *RM-ANOVA* found *D-COMPASS* to be significantly faster than *S-COMPASS* ($F_{1,11} = 100.7, p < .0001$).

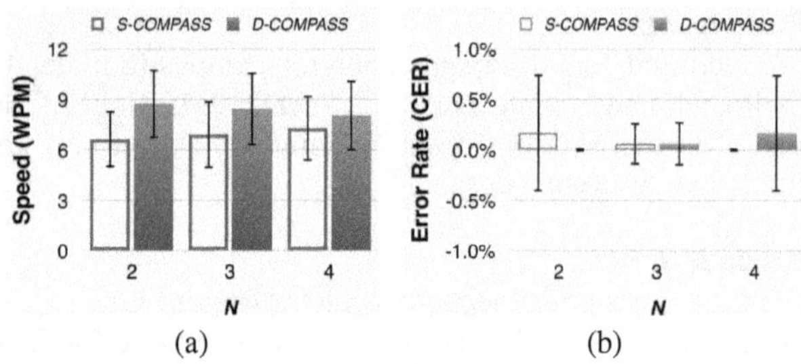


Figure 7: (a) Text entry speed and (b) error rate for different techniques and $N$, black bar indicated one standard deviation.

For *S-COMPASS*, WPM slightly increased with increasing $N$, with the average speed being 6.6 (SD = 1.7), 6.9 (SD = 2.0) and 7.3 (SD = 1.9) for $N = 2$, 3 and 4 respectively. This confirmed that with more cursors, the rotation distance could be shortened. On contrary, for *D-COMPASS*, WPM slightly drops with increasing $N$, with the average speed being 8.7 (SD = 2.0), 8.4 (SD = 2.2) and 8.0 (SD = 2.1) for $N = 2$, 3 and 4 respectively. We speculate that this was due to the extra time to locate the cursors after adaptation. A significant effect of $N$ was found on WPM for both *S-COMPASS* ($F_{2,22} = 3.42, p = .05$) and *D-COMPASS* ($F_{2,22} = 7.04, p < .01$).

#### Error Rate

We calculated error rate using CER [33], Figure 7b shows the error rate for different techniques and $N$. As with previous findings, users tended to leave few errors in the final transcribed string (e.g. [23, 33]), with the average error rate for all six conditions under 0.17%. As expected, no significant effect of *Technique* was found on CER ($F_{1,11} = 0.00, p = .99$). Moreover, no significant effect of $N$ on CER was found for either *S-COMPASS* ($F_{2,22} = 0.66, p = .52$) or *D-COMPASS* ($F_{2,22} = 1.00, p = .38$).

#### Subjective Ratings

We collected participants' subjective ratings for each condition using a 5-point Likert scale questionnaire. Dimensions included perceived speed, perceived accuracy and overall preference. Table 1 shows the average ratings. *D-COMPASS* was showed to significantly outperformed *S-COMPASS* in terms of all dimensions (perceived speed: $F_{1,11} = 12.2, p < .01$, perceived accuracy: $F_{1,11} = 11.3, p < .01$, overall preference: $F_{1,11} = 26.2, p < .001$).

| Technique | S-COMPASS | | | D-COMPASS | | |
|---|---|---|---|---|---|---|
| N | 2 | 3 | 4 | 2 | 3 | 4 |
| Perceived Speed | 2.4 (0.9) | 3.2 (0.8) | 3.7 (0.6) | 3.5 (1.1) | 4.3 (0.6) | 4.2 (0.6) |
| Perceived Accuracy | 3.6 (1.1) | 4.0 (0.8) | 3.8 (0.7) | 4.2 (0.8) | 4.5 (0.7) | 4.0 (0.8) |
| Overall Preference | 2.2 (1.1) | 3.2 (0.9) | 3.3 (0.8) | 3.3 (1.0) | 4.5 (0.5) | 3.8 (0.7) |

Table 1: Average ratings for different conditions, standard deviations showed in parenthesis. 5 means the most positive and 1 means the most negative.

For both *S-COMPASS* and *D-COMPASS*, Friedman test found a main effect of $N$ on perceived speed ($\chi^2(2) = 17.1, p < .001$ and $\chi^2(2) = 7.31, p < .05$) and overall preference ($\chi^2(2) = 8.34, p < .05$ and $\chi^2(2) = 10.3, p < .01$). However, no significant effect of $N$ was found on perceived accuracy ($\chi^2(2) = 1.92, p = .38$ and $\chi^2(2) = 2.61, p = .27$). Noticeably, for *S-COMPASS*, $N = 4$ yield the highest average score in perceived speed and overall preference, while for *D-COMPASS*, $N = 3$ yield the highest average score among all conditions.

#### Interaction Statistics

We looked more into users' text entry behavior by analyzing the interaction statistics. Figure 8 shows the average *Distance per Rotation (DPR)* for each condition. Both *Technique* ($F_{1,11} = 1957, p < .0001$) and $N$ ($F_{2,22} = 1132, p < .0001$) was found to yield significantly effect on *DPR*. Consistent with the simulation result, *DPR* decreased with increasing $N$ for both *S-COMPASS* and *D-COMPASS*. And for all $N$, the *DPR* for *D-COMPASS* was less than 50% of that for *S-COMPASS*. This confirmed that *D-COMPASS* effectively reduced the rotation distance than *S-COMPASS*.

We then analyzed which interactions takes up the most amount of time during text entry. Table 2 shows the top 3 interactions with the highest time ratio. Noticeably, for *S-COMPASS*, *Rotate-Rotate* takes up 44.6% of all interactions, which corresponds to Figure 8 that users has to rotate a relatively long distance on average. On contrast, for *D-COMPASS*, the most time-consuming interaction was *Press-Press*, which happens

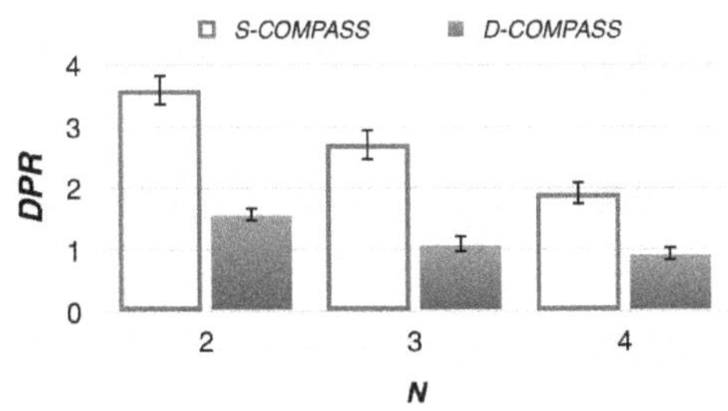


Figure 8: Average *DPR* for each condition, black bar indicates one standard deviation.

when users hit a target without rotating. This highlights that *D-COMPASS* effectively decreased the rotation frequency.

| Interaction | Average Time | Frequency | Time Ratio |
|---|---|---|---|
| Rotate - Press | 0.68 s | 21.4% | 29.0% |
| Press - Rotate | 0.84 s | 17.2% | 28.7% |
| Rotate - Rotate | 0.22 s | 44.6% | 19.0% |

(a)

| Interaction | Average Time | Frequency | Time Ratio |
|---|---|---|---|
| Press - Press | 0.92 s | 19.5% | 27.0% |
| Press - Rotate | 1.13 s | 12.4% | 21.0% |
| Rotate - Press | 0.69 s | 18.6% | 19.1% |

(b)

Table 2: Interaction statistics for (a) *S-COMPASS* and (b) *D-COMPASS*, merged from $N = 2,3$ and 4. Shows the top 3 with the highest time ratio.

## Discussion

### *Number of Cursors*

The number of cursors seemed not to affect text entry performance significantly. For *S-COMPASS*, WPM slightly increased with $N$, while for *D-COMPASS*, WPM slightly drops with $N$. Although these differences were statistically significant, in both cases, the amplitude of change was very small ($\pm 0.6$ WPM). Meanwhile, $N$ did not significantly affect the error rate or perceived accuracy.

However, subjective preference changed dramatically with $N$. For *S-COMPASS*, $N = 4$ yielded the highest score in perceived speed and overall preference, and for *D-COMPASS*, $N = 3$ yielded the highest score in all dimensions, which are all significant. Therefore, we considered 4 and 3 to be the optimal number of cursors for *S-COMPASS* and *D-COMPASS* respectively.

### *S-COMPASS vs. D-COMPASS*

Interestingly, both objective and subjective results favors *D-COMPASS* as opposed to *S-COMPASS*. The text entry speed of *D-COMPASS* was 32%, 22% and 15% higher than that of *S-COMPASS* with increasing $N$ (see Figure 7a), and there was no significant difference in error rate. Due to the dynamic cursor placement strategy, the rotation distance for *D-COMPASS* was less than 50% of that for *S-COMPASS* (see Figure 8).

In terms of subjective feedback, *D-COMPASS* significantly outperforms *S-COMPASS* in all dimensions (perceived speed, perceived accuracy and overall preference). During interview, most of the participants (11/12) preferred *D-COMPASS* to *S-COMPASS*, only 1 participant preferred *S-COMPASS*. Therefore, we considered *D-COMPASS* to be more applicable.

### *Improving COMPASS*

So far, we have showed that in terms of text entry performance and user preference, *D-COMPASS* with three cursors was the best technique among the six alternatives. However, the interaction statistics and subjective feedback suggested that there are still space for further improving the performance.

Table 2b shows that for *D-COMPASS*, *Press-Press* was the most frequent interaction, and took the most amount of time. This usually happens when there are only a few possible keys left. For example, when entered "welc" for "welcome", users has to press three times without rotating for 'o', 'm' and 'e'. And in our interview, 6/12 participants suggested that the text entry process could be accelerated in this case. To this end, we improved *D-COMPASS* by incorporating an auto-completion algorithm.

We implemented the auto-completion algorithm using a similar method as in the Android keyboard [9]. When calculating $P(I|W)$, we considered all $W$ whose length are not less than $I$, and augmented Equation 3 to the formula below:

$$P(I|W) = \prod_{i=1}^{n} P(I_{\cdot i}|W_i) \times \alpha^{m-n} \tag{8}$$

where $m$ is the length of $W$ ($m \geq n$). Here, $\alpha$ could be interpreted as the penalty to prevent long, high-frequency words from dominating short, low-frequency words. For example, if the frequency of "and" is higher than "an", "and" would always appear in front of "an". We tested alpha ranging from 0.0 to 1.0 in simulation, and set $\alpha = 0.7$ that yields the best compromise between aggressiveness and candidate coverage.

## EXPERIMENT 2: PERFORMANCE EVALUATION

In this section, we conducted a second user study to evaluate the performance of the improved *COMPASS* technique. Henceforth, we referred to *COMPASS* as the *D-COMPASS* with three cursors and auto-completion algorithm. Participants were asked to perform text entry tasks using the technique. We were interested in the pick-up usability of *COMPASS*, and the text entry performance that users could achieve with practice.

### Participants

We recruited another 10 participants from the campus, with an average age of 22.0 (SD = 1.5). None of them has experienced a rotational interface before (e.g. the smartwatch we used in this experiment). Each participant was compensated $30.

### Procedure

We used the same experiment platform as in the previous study (see Figure 6). Participants were seated in a chair during the experiment. They were first allowed up to three minutes to familiarize themselves with the technique. They then completed 8 blocks of text entry tasks. In each block, they entered 10 phrases randomly chosen from the Mackenzie and Soukoreff phrase set [24]. A three-minute break was enforced between blocks. Participants were instructed to type "as fast and as natural as possible". They were free to correct the input or leave the error uncorrected. Each block took about eight minutes, and totally, the tasks took about 90 minutes. After the final block, we carried out interviews to gather their subjective feedback.

### Results

Across all participants, we gathered 8 blocks × 10 phrases × 10 participants = 800 phrases.

#### Text Entry Speed

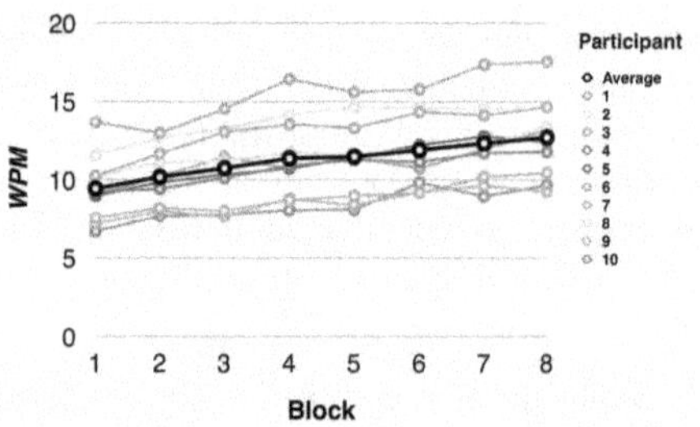


Figure 9: Text entry speed in each block, black line shows the average speed across participants.

Figure 9 shows each participant's speed and the average speed in each block. Participants' speed increased monotonously with block, suggesting a consistent learning trend. The average speed was 9.3 WPM (SD = 2.2) in block 1 and 12.5 WPM (SD = 2.5) in block 8, which was an increase of 34%. The top three participants with highest speed achieved an average of 11.9 WPM in the first block, and 15.4 WPM in the last block. A significant effect of *Block* was found on text entry speed ($F_{7,63} = 48.0, p < .0001$).

Notice that in Experiment 1, participants only reached 8.4 WPM when using *D-COMPASS* with three cursors. This improvement suggested that auto-completion may be helpful for increasing the performance of *COMPASS*. Although this speed was lower than word-level techniques using a miniature QWERTY keyboard [16]. We consider it still important as *COMPASS* used only rotation and button pressing, which is inevitably slower than using touchscreens. Moreover, WPM seemed not to stop increasing in block 8, suggesting that users may achieve higher text entry speed with more practice.

#### Error Rate

Figure 10 shows each participant's error rate and the average error rate in each block. Consistent with the result in Experiment 1, participants left few errors in the final transcribed phrase. There were an average of 4.6 (SD = 3.3) deletions for each participant in each block. In all 800 phrases, only 4 phrases yielded a CER > 0. As expected, no significant effect of *Block* was found on error rate ($F_{7,63} = 0.81, p = .58$).

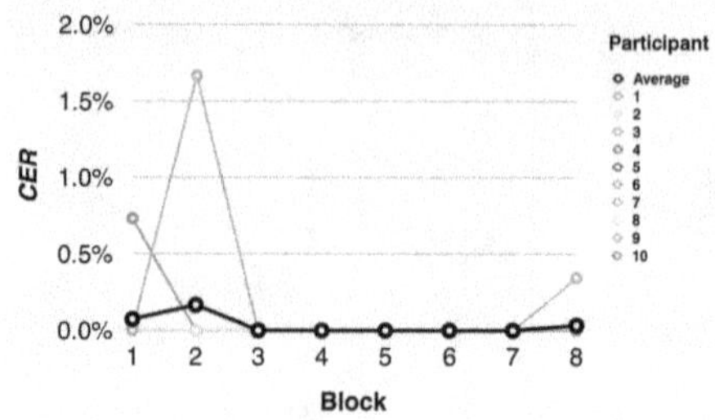


Figure 10: Error rate in each block, black line shows the average speed across participants.

#### Interaction Statistics

To examine whether user's interaction behavior evolved with practice, we analyzed the interaction statistics. We were interested in: 1) Time taken to visually acquire the target key, which is indicative of the familiarity of the keyboard layout; 2) the usage of the auto-completion feature.

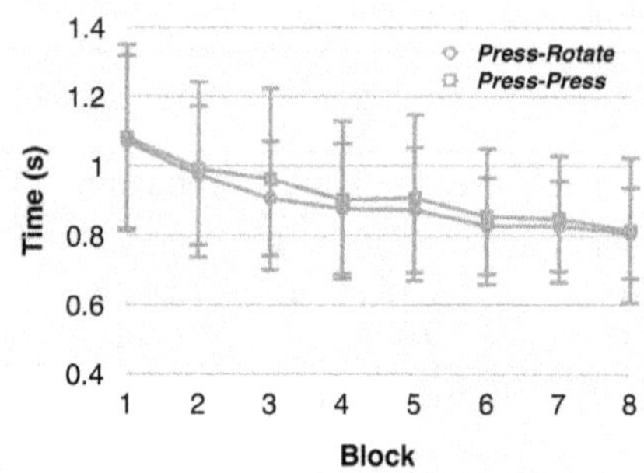


Figure 11: Average *Press-Rotate* and *Press-Press* time in each block, bar shows one standard deviation.

Ideally, the time taken to locate the target key should be measured by analyzing the eye-gaze data. Considering this impractical, we resort to use two other metrics that is measurable: the average time of *Press-Rotate* and *Press-Press*. These two values measure the time elapse from the update of the cursors to the next interaction action, which could approximate the time taken to find the target key.

Figure 11 shows the average interaction time for these two interactions in each block. Generally, the average time for *Press-Rotate* and *Press-Press* was very close, confirming the consistency of the two metrics. Both time dropped with block, suggesting that with more practice, users could spent less time searching for the target key. In the first block, the average time for *Press-Rotate* and *Press-Press* were 1.07 s (SD = 0.26) and 1.08 s (SD = 0.27) respectively. And in block 8, they dropped to 0.81 s (SD = 0.14) and 0.81 s (SD = 0.22) respectively. Significant effect of *Block* was found on both times ($F_{7,63} = 14.9, p < .0001$ and $F_{7,63} = 11.8, p < .0001$).

To quantify users' adoption of the auto-completion feature, we defined *SPC (Selection Per Character)* as a metric, which can be calculated as:

$$SPC = \frac{|N_{selection}|}{|TranscribedText|} \quad (9)$$

where $|N_{selection}|$ is the total number of *Press* and *Long Press*, and $|TranscribedText|$ is the length of the final transcribed string. A lower SPC indicates that the user used the auto-completion feature more frequently, thus spent less effort on selecting characters and words.

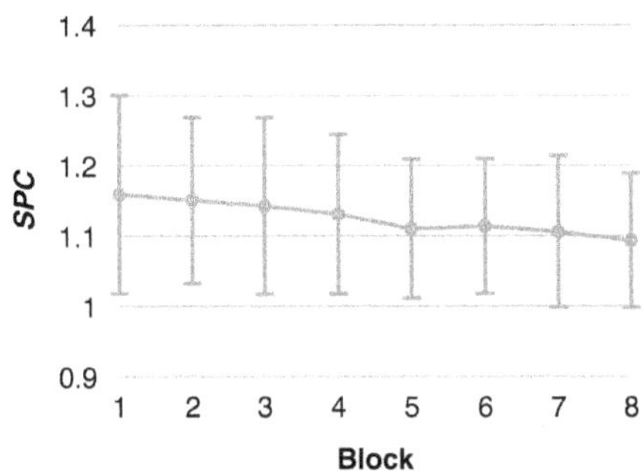


Figure 12: Average SPC in each block, bar shows one standard deviation.

Figure 12 shows the average SPC in each block. SPC dropped with block, suggesting that with more practice, participants used the auto-completion feature more frequently. In the first block, the average SPC were 1.16 (SD = 0.09). While in block 8, it dropped to 1.09 (SD = 0.05). Significant effect of *Block* was found on SPC ($F_{7,63} = 4.32, p < .001$). This result also imples that the accuracy of auto-correction was acceptable to users, and thus can increase their confidence in using it with practice.

### Subjective Feedback

We now summarize some subjective feedback from user interview. Though participants were new to the circular layout at first, they could get used to it easily with the help of the visual cues (highlight and dim).

*"The visual cues significantly reduced the effort to locate the target keys." (P6)*

The interaction design (rotation and press) was intuitive and fitted well with the form factor of the smartwatch.

*"Using rotation and press is very clever and intuitive on the rotary interface of this smartwatch." (P5)*

All participants found the auto-completion feature is helpful in increasing the text entry speed.

*"The auto-completion feature is amazing! Sometimes I only have to enter half the characters to get the word." (P10)*

After the experiment, some participants even suggested implementing *COMPASS* in more scenarios.

*"I think COMPASS is a great solution for text entry when wearing gloves. I'm also looking forward to using it with the digital crown on my Apple Watch." (P3)*

Participants felt the flicking gesture easy and accurate to perform, while some participants found the *Long Press* interaction a bit hard to perform.

*"Flick to delete seemed natural to me, but the long press interaction is a bit tiring." (P7)*

## LIMITATION AND FUTURE WORK

There are several limitations of this work, which we also see as opportunities for future work.

First, the current prototype of *COMPASS* was only designed for entering words that is in the dictionary, as it covers most of the daily text entry tasks. However, it is also worthwhile for any real text entry technique to support character-level input (e.g. passwords) and entering Out-Of-Vocabulary words. In practice, by treating each individual character as a "word" in the language model, they are both achievable using the current mechanism.

Second, the current cursor placement strategy (see Equation 6) did not fully modelled user's rotation ability. For example, during interview, some participants reported that they felt clockwise rotation easier to perform than counterclockwise rotation. We speculate this was due to they were right-handed users. It is interesting to further investigate user's rotation ability, and to further improve the algorithm of *COMPASS*. In addition, although evaluation results showed that the performance of the heuristic restriction in optimization was acceptable, it is valuable to further look into the issue of input disambiguation in a more principled way.

Third, the learning curve in Experiment 2 has not converge yet. Therefore, the results may not be representative of the final text entry performance that users could achieve with *COMPASS*. Therefore, we plan to conduct a more longitudinal study to evaluate the performance of *COMPASS* in the wild.

## CONCLUSION

In this paper, we proposed *COMPASS*, a bezel-based text entry technique for non-touch smartwatches. *COMPASS* placed multiple cursors along a circular keyboard. Users rotate the bezel and press the physical button to enter text, while the position of the cursors were dynamically adjusted to minimize rotational distance. We followed an iterative design process with two user studies. In the first experiment, we showed that dynamically adjusting the position of the cursors showed outperformed fixing their positions in terms of text entry speed and subjective preference, and the optimal number of cursors is three. In the second experiment, we showed that by incorporating auto-completion algorithms, users could reach a pick-up speed of 9.3 WPM, and they could improve to 12.5 WPM after 90 minutes of practice. Some participants even reached 15.4 WPM. *COMPASS* provides a potential solution for text entry on smartwatches without using the touchscreens, and could be implemented to other rotational interfaces.

## ACKNOWLEDGEMENTS

This work is supported by the National Key Research and Development Plan under Grant No. 2016YFB1001200, the Natural Science Foundation of China under Grant No. 61303076 and No. 61272230, Tsinghua University Research Funding No. 20151080408.

## REFERENCES

1. 2016. A note on calculating text entry speed. (2016). http://www.yorku.ca/mack/RN-TextEntrySpeed.html.

2. 2016. American National Corpus. (2016). http://www.americannationalcorpus.org/OANC/index.html.
3. 2016. Apple Watch. (2016). http://www.apple.com/watch/.
4. 2016. BMW iDrive. (2016). http://www.bmw.com/com/en/insights/technology/technology_guide/articles/controller.html.
5. 2016. Moto 360. (2016). https://www.motorola.com/us/products/moto-360.
6. 2016. Pebble Watch. (2016). https://www.pebble.com/.
7. 2016. Wrist Gestures. (2016). https://support.google.com/androidwear/answer/6312406.
8. Shaikh Shawon Arefin Shimon, Courtney Lutton, Zichun Xu, Sarah Morrison-Smith, Christina Boucher, and Jaime Ruiz. 2016. Exploring Non-touchscreen Gestures for Smartwatches. In *Proceedings of the 2016 CHI Conference on Human Factors in Computing Systems (CHI '16)*. ACM, New York, NY, USA, 3822–3833. DOI: http://dx.doi.org/10.1145/2858036.2858385
9. Xiaojun Bi, Tom Ouyang, and Shumin Zhai. 2014. Both Complete and Correct?: Multi-objective Optimization of Touchscreen Keyboard. In *Proceedings of the SIGCHI Conference on Human Factors in Computing Systems (CHI '14)*. ACM, New York, NY, USA, 2297–2306. DOI: http://dx.doi.org/10.1145/2556288.2557414
10. Renaud Blanch and Michaël Ortega. 2009. Rake Cursor: Improving Pointing Performance with Concurrent Input Channels. In *Proceedings of the SIGCHI Conference on Human Factors in Computing Systems (CHI '09)*. ACM, New York, NY, USA, 1415–1418. DOI: http://dx.doi.org/10.1145/1518701.1518914
11. Jared Cechanowicz, Steven Dawson, Matt Victor, and Sriram Subramanian. 2006. Stylus Based Text Input Using Expanding CIRRIN. In *Proceedings of the Working Conference on Advanced Visual Interfaces (AVI '06)*. ACM, New York, NY, USA, 163–166. DOI: http://dx.doi.org/10.1145/1133265.1133299
12. Xiang 'Anthony' Chen, Tovi Grossman, and George Fitzmaurice. 2014. Swipeboard: A Text Entry Technique for Ultra-small Interfaces That Supports Novice to Expert Transitions. In *Proceedings of the 27th Annual ACM Symposium on User Interface Software and Technology (UIST '14)*. ACM, New York, NY, USA, 615–620. DOI: http://dx.doi.org/10.1145/2642918.2647354
13. Leah Findlater and Jacob Wobbrock. 2012. Personalized Input: Improving Ten-finger Touchscreen Typing Through Automatic Adaptation. In *Proceedings of the SIGCHI Conference on Human Factors in Computing Systems (CHI '12)*. ACM, New York, NY, USA, 815–824. DOI:http://dx.doi.org/10.1145/2207676.2208520
14. Markus Funk, Alireza Sahami, Niels Henze, and Albrecht Schmidt. 2014. Using a Touch-sensitive Wristband for Text Entry on Smart Watches. In *CHI '14 Extended Abstracts on Human Factors in Computing Systems (CHI EA '14)*. ACM, New York, NY, USA, 2305–2310. DOI: http://dx.doi.org/10.1145/2559206.2581143
15. Joshua Goodman, Gina Venolia, Keith Steury, and Chauncey Parker. 2002. Language Modeling for Soft Keyboards. In *Proceedings of the 7th International Conference on Intelligent User Interfaces (IUI '02)*. ACM, New York, NY, USA, 194–195. DOI: http://dx.doi.org/10.1145/502716.502753
16. Mitchell Gordon, Tom Ouyang, and Shumin Zhai. 2016. WatchWriter: Tap and Gesture Typing on a Smartwatch Miniature Keyboard with Statistical Decoding. In *Proceedings of the 2016 CHI Conference on Human Factors in Computing Systems (CHI '16)*. ACM, New York, NY, USA, 3817–3821. DOI: http://dx.doi.org/10.1145/2858036.2858242
17. Chris Harrison and Scott E. Hudson. 2009. Abracadabra: Wireless, High-precision, and Unpowered Finger Input for Very Small Mobile Devices. In *Proceedings of the 22Nd Annual ACM Symposium on User Interface Software and Technology (UIST '09)*. ACM, New York, NY, USA, 121–124. DOI: http://dx.doi.org/10.1145/1622176.1622199
18. Uta Hinrichs, Holly Schmidt, Tobias Isenberg, Mark S Hancock, and Sheelagh Carpendale. 2008. Bubbletype: Enabling text entry within a walk-up tabletop installation. (2008).
19. Jonggi Hong, Seongkook Heo, Poika Isokoski, and Geehyuk Lee. 2015. SplitBoard: A Simple Split Soft Keyboard for Wristwatch-sized Touch Screens. In *Proceedings of the 33rd Annual ACM Conference on Human Factors in Computing Systems (CHI '15)*. ACM, New York, NY, USA, 1233–1236. DOI: http://dx.doi.org/10.1145/2702123.2702273
20. Frederic Kerber, Tobias Kiefer, and Markus Löchtefeld. 2016. Investigating Interaction Techniques for State-of-the-Art Smartwatches. In *Proceedings of the 2016 CHI Conference Extended Abstracts on Human Factors in Computing Systems (CHI EA '16)*. ACM, New York, NY, USA, 2540–2547. DOI: http://dx.doi.org/10.1145/2851581.2892302
21. Masatomo Kobayashi and Takeo Igarashi. 2008. Ninja Cursors: Using Multiple Cursors to Assist Target Acquisition on Large Screens. In *Proceedings of the SIGCHI Conference on Human Factors in Computing Systems (CHI '08)*. ACM, New York, NY, USA, 949–958. DOI:http://dx.doi.org/10.1145/1357054.1357201
22. Luis A. Leiva, Alireza Sahami, Alejandro Catala, Niels Henze, and Albrecht Schmidt. 2015. Text Entry on Tiny QWERTY Soft Keyboards. In *Proceedings of the 33rd Annual ACM Conference on Human Factors in Computing Systems (CHI '15)*. ACM, New York, NY, USA, 669–678. DOI: http://dx.doi.org/10.1145/2702123.2702388

23. I. Scott MacKenzie and R. William Soukoreff. 2002. A Character-level Error Analysis Technique for Evaluating Text Entry Methods. In *Proceedings of the Second Nordic Conference on Human-computer Interaction (NordiCHI '02)*. ACM, New York, NY, USA, 243–246. DOI: http://dx.doi.org/10.1145/572020.572056

24. I. Scott MacKenzie and R. William Soukoreff. 2003. Phrase Sets for Evaluating Text Entry Techniques. In *CHI '03 Extended Abstracts on Human Factors in Computing Systems (CHI EA '03)*. ACM, New York, NY, USA, 754–755. DOI: http://dx.doi.org/10.1145/765891.765971

25. Jennifer Mankoff and Gregory D. Abowd. 1998. Cirrin: A Word-level Unistroke Keyboard for Pen Input. In *Proceedings of the 11th Annual ACM Symposium on User Interface Software and Technology (UIST '98)*. ACM, New York, NY, USA, 213–214. DOI: http://dx.doi.org/10.1145/288392.288611

26. Paul Nation and Robert Waring. 1997. Vocabulary size, text coverage and word lists. *Vocabulary: Description, acquisition and pedagogy* 14 (1997), 6–19.

27. Stephen Oney, Chris Harrison, Amy Ogan, and Jason Wiese. 2013. ZoomBoard: A Diminutive Qwerty Soft Keyboard Using Iterative Zooming for Ultra-small Devices. In *Proceedings of the SIGCHI Conference on Human Factors in Computing Systems (CHI '13)*. ACM, New York, NY, USA, 2799–2802. DOI: http://dx.doi.org/10.1145/2470654.2481387

28. Katrin Plaumann, Michael Müller, and Enrico Rukzio. 2016. CircularSelection: Optimizing List Selection for Smartwatches. In *Proceedings of the 2016 ACM International Symposium on Wearable Computers (ISWC '16)*. ACM, New York, NY, USA, 128–135. DOI: http://dx.doi.org/10.1145/2971763.2971766

29. Morten Proschowsky, Nette Schultz, and Niels Ebbe Jacobsen. 2006. An Intuitive Text Input Method for Touch Wheels. In *Proceedings of the SIGCHI Conference on Human Factors in Computing Systems (CHI '06)*. ACM, New York, NY, USA, 467–470. DOI: http://dx.doi.org/10.1145/1124772.1124842

30. Philip Quinn, Andy Cockburn, and Jérôme Delamarche. 2013. Examining the costs of multiple trajectory pointing techniques. *International Journal of Human-Computer Studies* 71, 4 (2013), 492–509.

31. Kari-Jouko Räihä and Oleg Špakov. 2009. Disambiguating Ninja Cursors with Eye Gaze. In *Proceedings of the SIGCHI Conference on Human Factors in Computing Systems (CHI '09)*. ACM, New York, NY, USA, 1411–1414. DOI: http://dx.doi.org/10.1145/1518701.1518913

32. Garth Shoemaker, Leah Findlater, Jessica Q Dawson, and Kellogg S Booth. 2009. Mid-air text input techniques for very large wall displays. In *Proc. GI'09*. Canadian Information Processing Society, 231–238.

33. R. William Soukoreff and I. Scott MacKenzie. 2003. Metrics for Text Entry Research: An Evaluation of MSD and KSPC, and a New Unified Error Metric. In *Proceedings of the SIGCHI Conference on Human Factors in Computing Systems (CHI '03)*. ACM, New York, NY, USA, 113–120. DOI: http://dx.doi.org/10.1145/642611.642632

34. Keith Vertanen, Haythem Memmi, Justin Emge, Shyam Reyal, and Per Ola Kristensson. 2015. VelociTap: Investigating Fast Mobile Text Entry Using Sentence-Based Decoding of Touchscreen Keyboard Input. In *Proceedings of the 33rd Annual ACM Conference on Human Factors in Computing Systems (CHI '15)*. ACM, New York, NY, USA, 659–668. DOI: http://dx.doi.org/10.1145/2702123.2702135

35. Hongyi Wen, Julian Ramos Rojas, and Anind K. Dey. 2016. Serendipity: Finger Gesture Recognition Using an Off-the-Shelf Smartwatch. In *Proceedings of the 2016 CHI Conference on Human Factors in Computing Systems (CHI '16)*. ACM, New York, NY, USA, 3847–3851. DOI: http://dx.doi.org/10.1145/2858036.2858466

36. Chun Yu, Yuanchun Shi, Ravin Balakrishnan, Xiangliang Meng, Yue Suo, Mingming Fan, and Yongqiang Qin. 2010. The Satellite Cursor: Achieving MAGIC Pointing Without Gaze Tracking Using Multiple Cursors. In *Proceedings of the 23Nd Annual ACM Symposium on User Interface Software and Technology (UIST '10)*. ACM, New York, NY, USA, 163–172. DOI: http://dx.doi.org/10.1145/1866029.1866056

# WatchThru: Expanding Smartwatch Displays with Mid-air Visuals and Wrist-worn Augmented Reality

**Dirk Wenig**[1,2] **Johannes Schöning**[2] **Alex Olwal**[3] **Mathias Oben**[4] **Rainer Malaka**[1,2]

[1]Digital Media Lab (TZI);
[2]Computer Science Faculty
University of Bremen
{dwenig, malaka}@tzi.de,
schoening@uni-bremen.de

[3]Interaction Lab
Google, Inc.
olwal@google.com

[4]Computer Science Faculty
Hasselt University
mathias.oben@student.uhasselt.be

## ABSTRACT

We introduce WatchThru, an interactive method for extended wrist-worn display on commercially-available smartwatches. To address the limited visual and interaction space, WatchThru expands the device into 3D through a transparent display. This enables novel interactions that leverage and extend smartwatch glanceability. We describe three novel interaction techniques, *Pop-up Visuals*, *Second Perspective* and *Peek-through*, and discuss how they can complement interaction on current devices. We also describe two types of prototypes that helped us to explore standalone interactions, as well as, proof-of-concept AR interfaces using our platform.

### ACM Classification Keywords

H.5.1 Multimedia Information Systems: Artificial, augmented, and virtual realities; H.5.2 User Interfaces: Graphical user interfaces, Input devices and strategies; I.3.6 Methodology and Techniques: Interaction techniques

### Author Keywords

Smartwatches; Micro-Interaction; Wearable Devices

## INTRODUCTION

Smartwatches are designed to support micro-interactions. Their small screens enable compact form factors, but result in a limited visual and interaction space. While most work on addressing these limitations explores additional input techniques or modalities, this work focuses on the output challenges that arise from small screen sizes of currently 1.5–1.8″ (10–25% the size of typical 5″ smartphone screens).

WatchThru extends the output capabilities of current smartwatches into 3D with an additional 1.8″ transparent screen that complements the main touchscreen with graphics that can be displayed floating in mid-air (see Figure 1). WatchThru can show different information on the two screens, based on


*CHI 2017, May 6-11, 2017, Denver, CO, USA.*
ACM ISBN 978-1-4503-4655-9/17/05.
http://dx.doi.org/10.1145/3025453.3025852

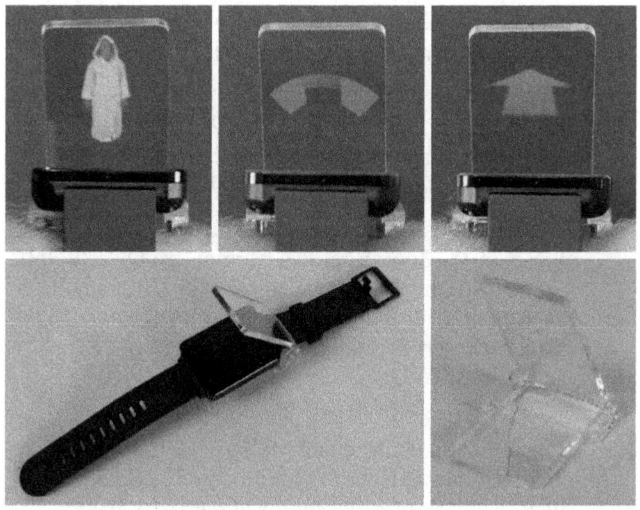

Figure 1: WatchThru is a lightweight and easy-to-build display extension for existing smartwatches.

the user's viewing direction. Additionally, by registering the display with the world (e.g., with an external tracking system or camera-based tracking on the watch), WatchThru enables lightweight, wrist-worn augmented reality (AR) capabilities.

Our contributions with WatchThru are the following:

- The concept, design and implementation of a smartwatch that is extended with a transparent display to increase the output capacity with mid-air visuals and wrist-worn AR.
- An exploration of novel interaction techniques enabled by our introduced concept that show how they can improve future interactions with smartwatches.
- Two prototypes of which we share the instructions how to replicate them, to enable others to extend our WatchThru concept. The first, demonstrating capabilities with a self-contained smartwatch. The second, using external tracking for a proof-of-concept implementation of techniques that we anticipate will be available with miniaturization of current inside-out tracking technology.

## RELATED WORK

Fitzmaurice introduced the concept of *spatially-aware displays* [4], which use motion sensing to enable viewports, or peepholes [21], into a virtual information space. WatchThru leverages recent advancements, where wearable devices embed a variety of sensors that can track device motion and orientation. WatchThru is also inspired by early mobile AR concepts like NaviCam from Rekimoto and Nagao [16], as well as, wearable magic lens interfaces [2]. This work builds on an extensive body of research into mobile AR [17, 12], but focuses on the capabilities enabled by a wrist-mounted optical see-through display.

More recently, researchers have investigated wrist-mounted displays and displays around the user's body [3]. Pohl et al. [15] used LEDs mounted at the bottom of a watch for notifications through the user's skin. Grubert el al. [6] investigated interaction with multiple displays; in one variant a HMD combined with a smartwatch. Doppio [18] is a smartwatch with two screens; one of them is reconfigurable to allow tangible interaction.

Peripheral displays has been explored with multiple displays in Facet [10] and as edge notifications on recent smartphones (e.g., Samsung Galaxy S Edge). Skin Buttons [9] use direct projection to extend the display, whereas ScatterWatch uses indirect skin illumination [15]. The WatchThru display configuration is similar to the Sonic Flashlight [19, 20], which used a half-silvered mirror to combine an ultrasound image with the view of the patient's body.

## WATCHTHRU INTERACTIONS

In this section we illustrate the interaction possibilities that arise from WatchThru. As WatchThru is focused on output, the interactions rely on known input techniques.

### Pop-up Visuals: Extended Display for Mid-Air Graphics

Our concept of *Pop-up Visuals* enables information that visually extends out from the watch face. For notifications and incoming calls, the advantage is that the users do not necessarily need to lift up their hand and twist their wrist to look at the information on their smartwatch. Because of the additional WatchThru screen, the users notice them out of the corner of their eyes while having their arms in a relaxed position, e.g., arms hanging down.

When the user is directly looking at the screen, the WatchThru prototype naturally allows for more complex information, such as numbers (e.g., remaining minutes until the next bus), short text or symbols. Figure 1 (top, right) shows a conceptual app using the WatchThru screen to display static and animated notifications.

### Second Perspective: Alternative Presentation

The *Second Perspective* enables users to quickly access alternative views on the WatchThru display. The main advantage is that additional information, e.g., navigational directions, become implicitly accessible to the user. Figure 2 shows a prototypical app with a 2D map on the main screen and an oriented 3D arrow on the WatchThru screen. It allows the user to navigate along a route on the main screen and, using the built-in compass, it shows the current direction on the WatchThru screen. Users simply orient their wrist to view the screen. When combined with pop-up visuals on the WatchThru screen, the main screen could display contextual information, e.g., for information about incoming calls. During a video call displayed on the WatchThru screen, the main screen could show the text chat window for sharing links and media.

Figure 2: *Second Perspective* navigation with a 2D map (left) and directional arrows (right).

The second perspective could also be used to display independent information. In the mobile context, the user often has to perform multiple tasks at the same time. For example, with the second perspective, the WatchThru screen could display navigational directions while the main screen is used for notifications. In addition, the transparent screen has the advantage that it also enables the combination of additional information on the WatchThru screen with the real world. This means that, e.g., the arrow shown on the WatchThru display is aligned with the real world target.

### Peek-through: Optical See-through Wrist-worn AR

The see-through display makes it possible to augment objects by overlaying registered graphics using the device. We call the interaction *Peek-through*. With peek-through, a navigation arrow on the WatchThru screen could be fully integrated in 3D into the environment. In contrast to most AR displays, this device does not obstruct the user's face, nor requires the user to bring it out and hold it (like a smartphone). It therefore has interesting potential as a wearable, unobtrusive and always-accessible AR device on the user's wrist.

For peek-through, we prototypically implemented several applications for different scenarios. Figure 3 (c, d) show a smart home scenario where objects in a room, e.g., power sockets, are augmented with information shown on the WatchThru screen. In Figure 3 (e), a learning scenario, a virtual globe is presented in the middle of a room. It could allow school children to explore the earth, including the orbiting moon, from different perspectives. Additionally, WatchThru could help children and adults learn board games, such as chess. With peek-through, the board could be overlayed with game strategies—not to cheat, but to help the player grow.

Figure 3 (f) shows an assembly scenario; WatchThru shows the user how to connect electronic components. Similarly, WatchThru could help technicians with maintenance, e.g. to repair elevators. WatchThru with a foldable display (see section on Limitations) could be a lightweight and unobtrusive add-on to (smart)watches that technicians usually wear and would not require an additional device. Additionally, similar to the Sonic Flashlight [19, 20], WatchThru could be used in a medical context to overlay the patient's body with information such as ultrasound imagery. Furthermore, we see WatchThru having the potential as an entertainment device, which could be used for location-based games with AR, such as the recently popular Pokémon GO [13].

## IMPLEMENTATION OF PROTOTYPES

We developed two interactive prototypes by extending commercial smartwatches with additional display and tracking capabilities. The first was designed to support *Pop-up Visuals* and *Second Perspective* with minimal modification, while the other allowed us to explore the *Peek-through* wrist-worn AR experiences with 3D position and orientation tracking.

### Prototype 1: Pop-up Visuals and Second Perspective

For the first WatchThru prototype screen we used a special acrylic glass (3 mm thick) with one reflective side and one transparent side, developed to enable projections on see-through materials[1]. The screen was fabricated with a laser cutter, including a mount, and bent into the right configuration while hot ($\sim$135°). Given that only one side of the acrylic glass is laminated with the reflective layer, the image quality is barely affected when viewing through the WatchThru screen. We built several versions for different Android/Android Wear smartwatches, e.g., the LG G Watch and the Samsung Gear Live (Figure 1, bottom). Modifying the design for other smartwatches usually only requires scaling of the CAD drawings so that the WatchThru screen has the same size as the main screen of the smartwatch and, if necessary, to bend the mounting part so that it fits the back of the smartwatch.

For correct display on the WatchThru screen, graphics need to be mirrored on the main screen. For the second perspective, we used the built-in inertial sensors to infer whether the user is looking at the WatchThru screen or at the main screen. In our proof-of-concept implementation, we activate WatchThru content when the smartwatch is held parallel to the ground and display main screen content otherwise. Using the built-in digital compass, we display orientation-sensitive information on the second screen.

### Prototype 2: Peek-through AR

While current smartwatches are equipped with a great variety of motion sensors, they are not sufficiently sophisticated yet to track absolute position. Therefore, to explore the peek-trough interactions, we developed a second prototype that was tracked with an external tracking system.

We used a 12-camera OptiTrack System by NaturalPoint to accurately track position and orientation of the smartwatch in our lab using infrared illumination. Five retro-reflective markers were attached to the smartwatch and to the user's head (using a cap with attached markers) to track their pose in the room (Figure 3 a,b). The 12 cameras continuously broadcast UDP packets with position and orientation of the markers at 200Hz. Packets are directly sent to the smartwatch via WiFi to

[1] http://www.holocube.eu

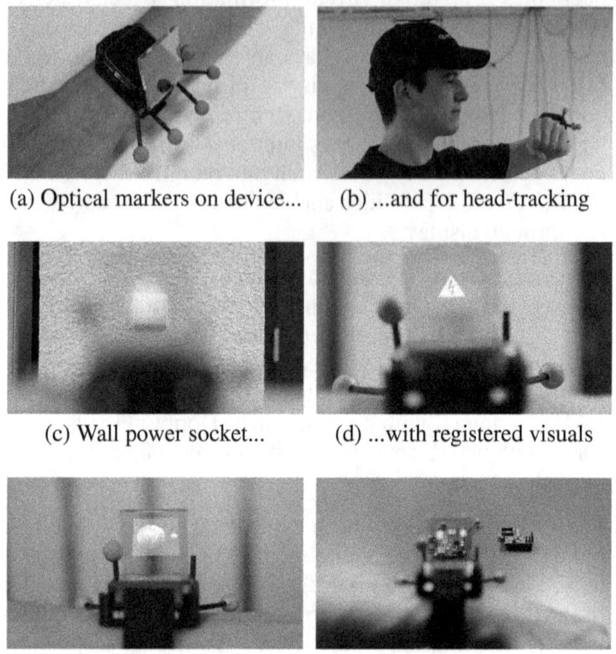

(a) Optical markers on device... (b) ...and for head-tracking

(c) Wall power socket... (d) ...with registered visuals

(e) Virtual globe (f) Electronics assembly

Figure 3: The *Peek-through* prototype uses external cameras to track retroreflective markers on the (a) device and (b) user, which enabled the several implemented AR scenarios (c–f).

reduce latency and processed by a Unity3D application that is running on the device (Simvalley Mobile AW-414 Go). The field of view (FOV) is calculated and dynamically updated using the distance between the user's eye(s) and the watch.

### Preliminary User Feedback

While developing the prototypes we continuously explored the WatchThru interactions in informal user tests with computer science students (representing early adopters) not involved in the project. For the second perspective interaction, the view switching angle of 12.5° was determined in an experiment, where participants experienced different angles of 45°, 22.5°, and 12.5°. The results indicate that when looking at the WatchThru screen, participants hold the device parallel to ground to see through the screen, such that switching to the first perspective at a flat angle is best suited. In general, participants commented that the WatchThru screen works well and is easy to recognize except under strong illumination. However, some of them criticized that the main screen can be distracting when looking at the WatchThru screen.

## LIMITATIONS AND FUTURE WORK

*World-registered graphics*

For AR experiences, absolute and accurate 6DOF tracking is required. While techniques like PTAM [8], KinectFusion [7], and Google's project Tango [5] could be used, they currently require more computational resources and power than what is currently available in wrist-worn form factors. As these techniques have moved from desktop workstations, to tablets and smartphones, we expect future availability in smaller devices.

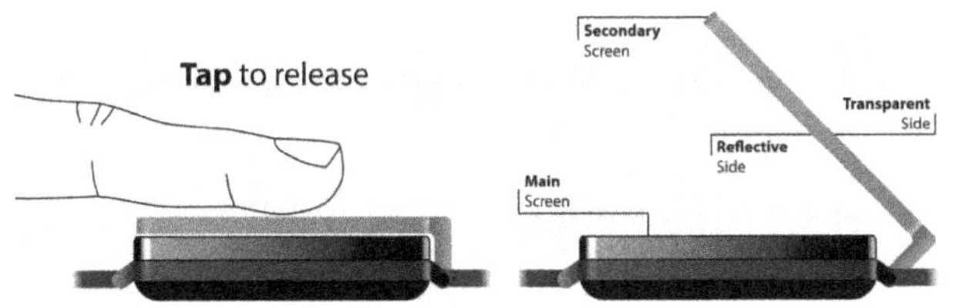


Figure 4: In the future for WatchThru, we envision a transparent screen that can be folded out when needed.

*Tracking user's perspective*

Given that the display is not co-located with the user's eyes, any AR experience need to account for the user's viewpoint. This makes WatchThru more challenging to calibrate than video see-through systems, where camera, tracking and display are combined. For peek-through AR, tracking of device and user's head are not yet solved in a practical way. In addition to perspective tracking with on-device sensing, tracking the user's head to calculate the field of view could be realized with front-facing cameras, similar to Amazon's Fire Phone [1].

*Form factor*

We chose the current transparent screen as a first step to implement the WatchThru concept, which can also be easily replicated by other researchers to explore the concept further. We are already working on iterations of the technical prototype to address some shortcomings. The current prototype requires the secondary screen to extend from the device at a 45° angle. While other display configurations are possible, e.g., using holographic optical elements, transparent LCDs or transparent OLEDs, it may still be impractical or undesirable with display components that extend out. As alternative, we could also envision an extendable screen with a mechanical folding mechanism (see Figure 4) such that the WatchThru screen could be pulled out (manually or automatically) when needed. A thin touch-friendly WatchThru screen, or increased projected capacitance sensitivity for touch through the WatchThru screen, could allow the user to interact with the smartwatch in a traditional way when the WatchThru screen is not expanded.

*Dual content—one display source*

Our current implementations are based on a passive optical combiner, which has advantages of simplicity, ease-of-fabrication, low-cost, optical see-through qualities and ease-of-integration. It works under the assumption that the user focuses on either the main or WatchThru screen, and that the device can adequately detect the user's focus to switch contents on the screen in a sufficiently responsive manner. Our prototype showed the feasibility of this idea, but also the time-sharing limitations when both displays are visible. Future implementations could address this with active translucent secondary displays, which would trade some simplicity for the ability to display simultaneous content on both screens.

*Interaction requires both hands*

While smartwatches do not occupy the hands when not in use, interacting with them requires both hands, in contrast to most current head-worn displays (e.g., Google Glass).

*Usage in complex lighting conditions*

As with other optical see-through displays, the display will have limited capability to function under strong illumination. This could be addressed with wavelength-selective and directional selective materials, such as holographic diffusers and optical elements, that only reflect light from a specific wavelength and incident angle, similar to ASTOR [14].

*Focal planes*

The semi-transparent display creates a virtual image 90° rotated from the wrist. This makes it challenging to fuse overlaid graphics with distant real-world objects. Additional optics could allow placing the virtual image at infinity, for objects that are further than a few meters away. We are also interested in close-up use cases as well as AR overlays onto paper documents and handheld equipment and tools.

*User input techniques*

The goal of WatchThru is to expand smartwatch displays, with focus on output. Therefore, in the presented use cases we used common techniques (e.g., touch and peepholes). To enable interaction with the WatchThru screen, we could use IR-based edge-lit touch-sensing (e.g., ZeroTouch [11]) or add a touch layer on top of the reflective layer (with added complexity). In the future, we will also explore input alternatives such as mid-air and around the device interaction.

## CONCLUSIONS

We introduced WatchThru, a novel interactive method for wrist-worn display using smartwatches. Based on the small display of smartwatches and the limited interaction space on the device, WatchThru extends the visualization space into the third dimension, beyond the flat watch screen, and extends the range of interaction possibilities. We have shown how such a transparent WatchThru screen could allow for *Pop-up Visuals* for ambient notifications, *Second Perspectives* that extend the display configuration, and for *Peek-through* AR scenarios.

*Pop-up Visuals* extend the passive character of the watch to an ambient notification device. We plan to do deeper explorations into additional interaction techniques, application scenarios, and user-dependent factors that are relevant for the usability and user experience of WatchThru. In the *Second Perspective* mode, turning the wrist allows switching between the displays to leverage tilt-based interaction with smartwatches, to complement gestures, buttons and on-screen widgets. With *Peek-through* AR, we show that WatchThru has the potential to act as an always-available, wrist-worn AR device.

We are currently working on a self-contained version to allow peek-through interactions also in non-instrumented environments and prototypes that allow different viewports. Thus, our minimal addition to a smartwatch opens up a whole spectrum of new interactive capabilities for wearable devices.

## ACKNOWLEDGMENTS

This work is partially founded by the Volkswagen Foundation through a Lichtenberg professorship and by a Google Faculty Research Award.

## REFERENCES


1. Amazon. 2017. Fire Phone. (3 January 2017). Retrieved January 3, 2017 from `https://amazon.com/Fire-Phone/`.
2. Eric A. Bier, Maureen C. Stone, Ken Pier, William Buxton, and Tony D. DeRose. 1993. Toolglass and Magic Lenses: The See-through Interface. In *Proceedings of the 20th Annual Conference on Computer Graphics and Interactive Techniques (SIGGRAPH '93)*. ACM, New York, NY, USA, 73–80. DOI: http://dx.doi.org/10.1145/166117.166126
3. Jesse Burstyn, Paul Strohmeier, and Roel Vertegaal. 2015. DisplaySkin: Exploring Pose-Aware Displays on a Flexible Electrophoretic Wristband. In *Proceedings of the 9th International Conference on Tangible, Embedded, and Embodied Interaction (TEI '15)*. ACM, New York, NY, USA, 165–172. DOI: http://dx.doi.org/10.1145/2677199.2680596
4. George W. Fitzmaurice. 1993. Situated Information Spaces and Spatially Aware Palmtop Computers. *Commun. ACM* 36, 7 (July 1993), 39–49. DOI: http://dx.doi.org/10.1145/159544.159566
5. Google. 2017. Tango. (3 January 2017). Retrieved January 3, 2017 from `https://get.google.com/tango/`.
6. Jens Grubert, Matthias Heinisch, Aaron Quigley, and Dieter Schmalstieg. 2015. MultiFi: Multi Fidelity Interaction with Displays On and Around the Body. In *Proceedings of the 33rd Annual ACM Conference on Human Factors in Computing Systems (CHI '15)*. ACM, New York, NY, USA, 3933–3942. DOI: http://dx.doi.org/10.1145/2702123.2702331
7. Shahram Izadi, David Kim, Otmar Hilliges, David Molyneaux, Richard Newcombe, Pushmeet Kohli, Jamie Shotton, Steve Hodges, Dustin Freeman, Andrew Davison, and Andrew Fitzgibbon. 2011. KinectFusion: Real-time 3D Reconstruction and Interaction Using a Moving Depth Camera. In *Proceedings of the 24th Annual ACM Symposium on User Interface Software and Technology (UIST '11)*. ACM, New York, NY, USA, 559–568. DOI: http://dx.doi.org/10.1145/2047196.2047270
8. Georg Klein and David Murray. 2007. Parallel Tracking and Mapping for Small AR Workspaces. In *Proceedings of the 6th IEEE/ACM International Symposium on Mixed and Augmented Reality (ISMAR '07)*. IEEE, Washington, DC, USA, 225–234. DOI: http://dx.doi.org/10.1109/ISMAR.2007.4538852
9. Gierad Laput, Robert Xiao, Xiang 'Anthony' Chen, Scott E. Hudson, and Chris Harrison. 2014. Skin Buttons: Cheap, Small, Low-powered and Clickable Fixed-icon Laser Projectors. In *Proceedings of the 27th Annual ACM Symposium on User Interface Software and Technology (UIST '14)*. ACM, New York, NY, USA, 389–394. DOI: http://dx.doi.org/10.1145/2642918.2647356
10. Kent Lyons, David Nguyen, Daniel Ashbrook, and Sean White. 2012. Facet: A Multi-segment Wrist Worn System. In *Proceedings of the 25th Annual ACM Symposium on User Interface Software and Technology (UIST '12)*. ACM, New York, NY, USA, 123–130. DOI: http://dx.doi.org/10.1145/2380116.2380134
11. Jon Moeller and Andruid Kerne. 2012. ZeroTouch: An Optical Multi-touch and Free-air Interaction Architecture. In *Proceedings of the SIGCHI Conference on Human Factors in Computing Systems (CHI '12)*. ACM, New York, NY, USA, 2165–2174. DOI: http://dx.doi.org/10.1145/2207676.2208368
12. Alessandro Mulloni, Hartmut Seichter, and Dieter Schmalstieg. 2011. Handheld Augmented Reality Indoor Navigation with Activity-based Instructions. In *Proceedings of the 13th International Conference on Human Computer Interaction with Mobile Devices and Services (MobileHCI '11)*. ACM, New York, NY, USA, 211–220. DOI: http://dx.doi.org/10.1145/2037373.2037406
13. Niantic. 2017. Pokémon GO. (3 January 2017). Retrieved January 3, 2017 from `https://pokemongo.com/`.
14. Alex Olwal, Christoffer Lindfors, Jonny Gustafsson, Torsten Kjellberg, and Lars Mattsson. 2005. ASTOR: An Autostereoscopic Optical See-through Augmented Reality System. In *Proceedings of the 4th IEEE/ACM International Symposium on Mixed and Augmented Reality (ISMAR '05)*. IEEE, Washington, DC, USA, 24–27. DOI:http://dx.doi.org/10.1109/ISMAR.2005.15
15. Henning Pohl, Justyna Medrek, and Michael Rohs. 2016. ScatterWatch: Subtle Notifications via Indirect Illumination Scattered in the Skin. In *Proceedings of the 18th International Conference on Human-Computer Interaction with Mobile Devices and Services (MobileHCI '16)*. ACM, New York, NY, USA, 7–16. DOI:http://dx.doi.org/10.1145/2935334.2935351
16. Jun Rekimoto and Katashi Nagao. 1995. The World Through the Computer: Computer Augmented Interaction with Real World Environments. In *Proceedings of the 8th Annual ACM Symposium on User Interface and Software Technology (UIST '95)*. ACM, New York, NY, USA, 29–36. DOI:http://dx.doi.org/10.1145/215585.215639
17. Dieter Schmalstieg and Daniel Wagner. 2007. Experiences with Handheld Augmented Reality. In *Proceedings of the 6th IEEE/ACM International Symposium on Mixed and Augmented Reality (ISMAR '07)*. IEEE, Washington, DC, USA, 3–18. DOI: http://dx.doi.org/10.1109/ISMAR.2007.4538819
18. Teddy Seyed, Xing-Dong Yang, and Daniel Vogel. 2016. Doppio: A Reconfigurable Dual-Face Smartwatch for Tangible Interaction. In *Proceedings of the 2016 CHI Conference on Human Factors in Computing Systems (CHI '16)*. ACM, New York, NY, USA, 4675–4686. DOI: http://dx.doi.org/10.1145/2858036.2858256
19. Damion Shelton, George Stetten, and Wilson Chang. 2002. Ultrasound Visualization with the Sonic Flashlight. In *ACM SIGGRAPH 2002 Conference Abstracts and*

*Applications (SIGGRAPH '02)*. ACM, New York, NY, USA, 82–82. DOI: http://dx.doi.org/10.1145/1242073.1242117

20. Georg Stetten, Vikram Chib, Daniel Hildebrand, and Jeannette Bursee. 2001. Real Time Tomographic Reflection: Phantoms for Calibration and Biopsy. In *Proceedings of the IEEE/ACM International Symposium on Augmented Reality (ISAR '01)*. 11–19. DOI: http://dx.doi.org/10.1109/ISAR.2001.970511

21. Ka-Ping Yee. 2003. Peephole Displays: Pen Interaction on Spatially Aware Handheld Computers. In *Proceedings of the SIGCHI Conference on Human Factors in Computing Systems (CHI '03)*. ACM, New York, NY, USA, 1–8. DOI: http://dx.doi.org/10.1145/642611.642613

# Evaluation of Korean Text Entry Methods for Smartwatches

**Ivaylo Ilinkin**
Gettysburg College
Gettysburg, USA
iilinkin@gettysburg.edu

**Sunghee Kim**
Gettysburg College
Gettysburg, USA
skim@gettysburg.edu

### ABSTRACT
This paper presents results from a user study designed to evaluate the effectiveness of Korean text entry methods for smartwatches. Specifically, the study compares the four popular text entry methods for smartphones in the context of smartwatch use (three multi-tap 3x4 keypad methods and a QWERTY-like method). A distinctive feature of text entry in Korea is that traditionally different manufacturers have developed their own text entry methods starting with particular physical layouts on feature phones that are now available as soft keypads on smartphones. This research considers the next step in this progression by studying the viability of adopting these text entry methods on smartwatches. The results from the user study indicate that existing methods can be effective for text entry on smartwatches; analysis of the data offers suggestions for improving the effectiveness of the methods.

### ACM Classification Keywords
H.5.2. User Interfaces: Evaluation/Miscellaneous,Input devices and strategies

### Author Keywords
text entry; soft keyboard; smartwatch.

### INTRODUCTION
The introduction of smartwatches has brought back the challenge of providing efficient and effective techniques for small screen sizes [1]. Recent work on text entry methods for smartwatches (e.g. DualKey [4], ZoomBoard [12], Swipeboard [3], SplitBoard [7]) has focused on adapting the QWERTY layout to the constraints of the small screen size. This work aims to evaluate the effectiveness of existing 3x4 layouts for text entry; a QWERTY-like layout was also included as a base line.

The context of this work is Korean text entry. Korean users have long faced multiple choices for text entry on their mobile devices. Starting with feature phones different manufacturers offered their own fixed keypad layouts for the traditional 3x4 keypad. This trend continued with the introduction of smartphones, with the added flexibility that the users can now choose their preferred text entry method. The larger screen size of smartphones has made it possible to adopt a QWERTY-like layout for Korean smartphones, but its effectiveness on a smartwatch has been questioned due to the limited space in which to fit 26 alphabetic keys. Previous work has studied Korean text entry on feature phones [8], which represent a significantly different form factor and mode of interaction (physical vs. soft keys, two-thumb vs. single-finger typing).

Korean text entry methods were chosen for the study, since there are multiple alternatives that have been proven effective and have been adopted by Korean users. In fact, some manufacturers are already providing a soft keyboard for a smartwatch based on one of the layouts considered in this study. While these are essentially multi-tap methods, they do have unique characteristics and offer innovative solutions to mapping an alphabet to a small set of keys. Note that Korean is an alphabetic language, so the results in this work could inform research on text entry methods for English.


*CHI 2017*, May 06–11, 2017, Denver, CO, USA.
 ISBN 978-1-4503-4655-9/17/05...$15.00.
DOI: http://dx.doi.org/10.1145/3025453.3025657

### KOREAN TEXT ENTRY
Figure 1 shows the layouts that were analyzed in this study: (*i*) Sky (SKY), which was introduced by SK Telecom; (*ii*) *Chon-Ji-In* (CJI), which was popularized by Samsung; (*iii*) *Na-Rat-Gul* (NRG), which was developed by LG; and (*iv*) *QWERTY-like* (2SET), which is the Korean layout for a standard keyboard. In the rest of the paper the term *layout* will be used for *text entry method*.

The Korean language is alphabetic and consists of 40 letters: 14 basic consonants, 5 double consonants, 10 basic vowels, and 11 vowel diphthongs. The basic forms can be seen in Fig. 1(2SET) with the vowels occupying the right half of the keypad. The 11 vowel diphthongs are typically not mapped directly to keys on a layout, but are formed by combining the basic vowels (e.g. ㅗ+ㅏ = ㅘ, ㅏ+ㅣ=ㅐ).

A unique feature of the Korean writing system is that the letters are "packed" into syllables of 2 to 4 letters, which gives Korean writing a distinctive appearance — for example, the translation of the phrase *Korean script* has the letter sequence ㅎㅏㄴㄱㅡㄹ, but is written as 한글.

Finally, Korean letters for similar sounds tend to have similar shapes: ㄱ/ㅋ (g/k), ㄷ/ㅌ (d/t), ㅏ/ㅑ (a/ya). This has offered opportunities for creative solutions of layout design.

The rest of this section introduces the 4 layouts used in this study. The key mappings and an example key sequence to enter the word 뱃속 are shown in Fig. 1 and Fig. 2, respectively.

SKY CJI NRG 2SET

| | Phrases | Words |
|---|---|---|
| total: | 400 | 1402 |
| min len: | 8 | 2 |
| max len: | 35 | 19 |
| avg len: | 25.42 | 6.54 |
| letters: 10169 | | |
| correlation with Korean: 0.993 | | |

**Figure 1. The four layouts used in this study and phrase set statistics; the numeric labels are only for reference and do not appear on the interface. The *backspace* key deletes only the last letter of the last syllable.**

SKY

| ㅃ | ㅕ | ㅅ | | ㅅ | ㅗ | ㄱ |
|---|---|---|---|---|---|---|
| 888 | 66 | 77 | ↲ | 77 | 9 | 1 |

CJI

| ㅃ | ㅕ | ㅅ | | ㅅ | ㅗ | ㄱ |
|---|---|---|---|---|---|---|
| 777 | 221 | 8 | ↲ | 8 | 23 | 4 |

NRG

| ㅃ | ㅕ | ㅅ | ㅅ | ㅗ | ㄱ |
|---|---|---|---|---|---|
| 5⊕⊗ | 33⊗ | 7 | 7 | 6 | 1 |

**Figure 2. Key sequences for the word 뼛속 assuming the standard numbering on a 3x4 keypad; ↲ is used for key segmentation in SKY and CJI.**

### SKY Layout

SKY is a 3x4 multi-tap layout. Letters are grouped on the individual keys based on similarity of sound. The vowels occupy the last column and the middle key on the top row. To enter a letter the corresponding key is tapped as many times as indicated by the position of the letter on the key (e.g. 8 (ㅂ), 88 (ㅍ), 888 (ㅃ)). SKY requires a method for segmentation when two letters on the same key need to be entered after each other. For this study the only means for key segmentation was via a single tap of the ↲ control key (timeout was not used).

### CJI Layout

CJI shares some similarities with SKY with respect to the consonants. Its distinguishing characteristic is that the vowels are not explicitly represented on the keypad. Instead they are composed with the keys on the top row [ ㅣ • — ], since each vowel either has a horizontal or a vertical main stroke. The • is used to complete a vowel by adding the shorter stroke(s) and the order relative to the main stroke is important. For example, ㅣ + • = ㅏ, but • + ㅣ = ㅓ; similarly, — + • = ㅜ, but • + — = ㅗ.

CJI also requires a means for segmentation. This layout has the advantage of reducing the number of keys required to compose the vowels. The disadvantage is that it has higher gestures per vowel and increased mental load due to the order in which the gestures are to be performed.

Note that CJI does not use the bottom-left/right letter keys. This seems rather wasteful for a smartwatch where space is limited. While it would have been possible to try a variation that uses all keys (for example, distributing ㅎ, ㅇ, ㅁ on the bottom row, so that each requires one gesture), ultimately the standard layout was used for the following reasons:

1. Manufacturers are likely to offer the standard form on a smartwatch (e.g. LUNA G from SK Telecom) and it would be useful to discover its performance characteristics.
2. The availability of the two extra keys makes it possible to have immediate access to punctuation symbols and emojis.
3. To some extent SKY is a variant of CJI that uses all keys.

In fact, the results suggest that leaving out the two keys did not affect the performance of CJI relative to the other layouts.

### NRG Layout

NRG is conceptually different from the previous layouts. Its design is inspired by the structure of Korean letters and uses the concepts of *adding a stroke* (⊕) and *doubling* (⊗), which are assigned to the bottom row [⊕ — ⊗]. Only a small subset of letters is available on the keypad and the rest are composed via these two transformations. For example:

ㅁ ⊕ = ㅂ, ㅂ ⊗ = ㅃ

ㅂ ⊕ = ㅍ

NRG does not require segmentation. It has been considered to be faster than the other layouts for expert users, but it has higher mental load due to the rules of composing the letters.

### 2SET Layout

2SET is essentially the analog of QWERTY for Korean keyboards. The letters are mapped on a regular keyboard, including 4 of the diphthongs. The 5 double consonants and 2 of the diphthongs are produced by first tapping a *shift* key (⇑).

2SET has the advantage that most letters require just one gesture and Korean users are already familiar with it. As with the QWERTY layout for English, the challenge of offering a full 2SET layout on a smartwatch is that the small size of the keys could make it impractical for text entry. 2SET was included in the study as a baseline for this and future work.

## EVALUATION

The performance characteristics of the four layouts were assessed through a formal user study that involved a text copy task. The study was conducted at a university in Seoul, Korea.

### Participants

A total of 32 participants (16 male, 16 female; age range [20, 26], $\mu$ = 22.6) were recruited for the study. All participants were native Koreans and none had used a smartwatch previously. Only one participant was left-handed.

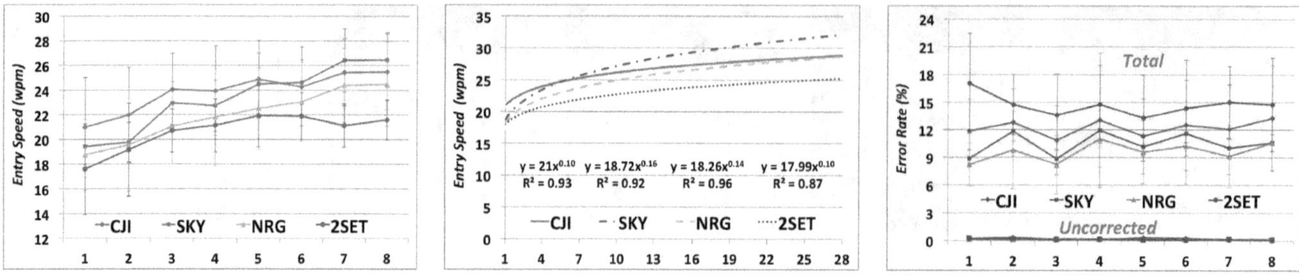


**Figure 3. Performance averaged over all users per session with 95% CI: (a) text entry speed; (b) speed extrapolated to 28 sessions; (c) error rates.**

### Apparatus

The device used was an LG G Watch with a 29.6 x 29.6 mm touchscreen. The presented phrase was shown at the top of the screen and the participants typed underneath.

### Phrase Set

The phrases used in this study were derived from the phrase set in [8], which is a translation of the phrase set in [11]. The phrases in [8] were adapted by the second author (a native Korean), so that no phrase was longer than 14 syllables. Thus, the longest presented phrase with 35 letters could fit within the screen due to the rules of the Korean script of packing letters into syllables. Figure 1 shows the phrase set statistics computed using the software in [11] and the letter frequencies reported in [9] for estimating the correlation with Korean.

### Design

The study was gender balanced and used between-subject design with 8 participants per layout. The participants were assigned a layout that they had not used previously or were least familiar with based on a self-report questionnaire. The one exception was 2SET, since all participants were familiar with it and 21 participants were using 2SET on their smartphones.

The recorded data was used to analyze text-entry speed (WPM), and total error rate (TER). Participants also completed a NASA-TLX survey [5] (Korean translation [10]).

### Procedure

Each participant attended 8 sessions over 4 consecutive days and entered 50 phrases per session for a total of 400 phrases per participant. Each day consisted of 2 sessions separated by a 5 minute break; within a session there was a forced 2 minute break after 15 minutes. A typical session lasted 15–20 minutes. The participants wore the watch on their non-dominant hand and entered the phrases with their dominant hand.

The first day included short training to familiarize the participants with their assigned layout. After the participants were briefed about the purpose of the study and signed a consent form they were given a manual describing the layout and were asked to enter 15 phrases. During training a new phrase was shown only when the previous one had been entered correctly or the participant exceeded 5 attempts.

During testing only one attempt was allowed per phrase. The participants were instructed to enter the phrases as accurately and as quickly as possible and to ignore errors beyond the last 2-3 syllables. Nevertheless, the participants tended to correct most errors as observed in [13, 14].

## RESULTS

### Text-Entry Speed

Figure 3a shows the average text-entry speed per session for each layout. 2SET is slowest across all sessions achieving 21.6 WPM by the end of the study ($\mu = 20.6, \sigma = 3.12$), while SKY starts to dominate around session 6 and achieves 26.4 WPM ($\mu = 23.4, \sigma = 3.42$). CJI is the fastest in the first half of the study, but ends up slightly behind SKY with 25.5 WPM ($\mu = 23.6, \sigma = 4.15$). Finally, NRG is ahead of 2SET achieving 24.5 WPM ($\mu = 22.0, \sigma = 4.26$).

ANOVA revealed significant effect of *layout* and *session* on *text-entry speed* (Table 1), the latter confirming the presence of learning effect. A post hoc Tukey HSD showed that CJI was faster than NRG and 2SET, and that SKY was faster than 2SET at $p < .05$. The other differences were not significant. In contrast NRG was faster than CJI and SKY on feature phones [8], which might be due to the advantage afforded by two thumb typing that is lost on a smartwatch—on average NRG requires longer travel distance with single-finger typing to compose a letter with the ⊕ and ⊗ keys.

| Source | df | *F* | *p* | *F* | *p* |
|---|---|---|---|---|---|
| layout | 3 | 10.43 | < .001 | 15.44 | < .001 |
| session | 7 | 9.91 | < .001 | 1.12 | > .05 |
| layout*session | 21 | 0.52 | > .05 | .48 | > .05 |
| Error | 224 | | | | |
| | | WPM | | TER | |

**Table 1. ANOVA results for WPM and TER.**

Figure 3b shows the learning curve extrapolated to 28 sessions. The data suggests that NRG may continue to improve and achieve performance similar to CJI. Despite the expectation that 2SET will be impractical on a smartwatch the participants achieved an average speed over 20 WPM and seemed to plateau at 21.5 WPM around session 5. This is fairly good considering the constraints on key size. Also, CJI ranked at the top even though it only uses 10 of the available 12 keys.

### Error Rate

Figure 3c shows the average TER and UER per session for each layout. As mentioned previously, despite the instructions

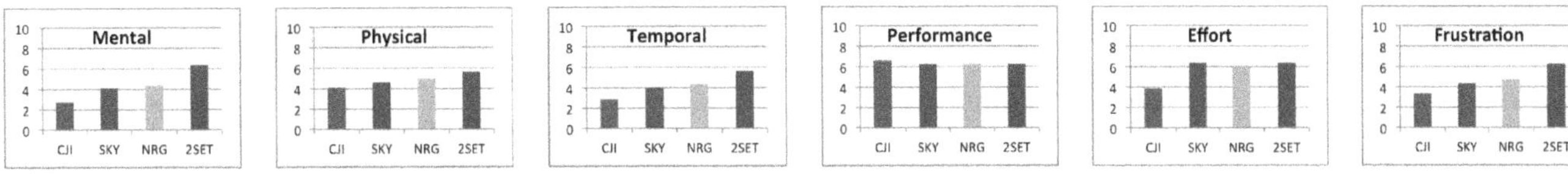


**Figure 4. Summary of the qualitative feedback from the 10-point scale NASA-TLX questionnaire.**

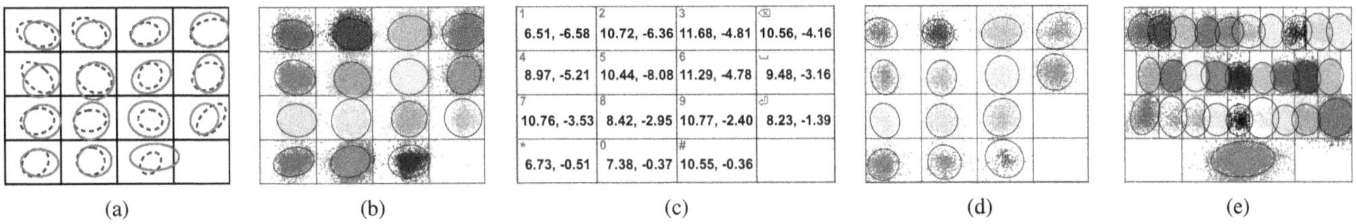


**Figure 5. Touch distributions with 95% confidence ellipses: (a) SKY session 1 (blue, dashed) and 8 (red, solid); (b) SKY all sessions; (e) average (dx, dy) offsets in pixels between key and ellipse centers for SKY; (d) NRG left-handed all sessions; (e) 2SET all sessions.**

to balance speed and accuracy the participants tended to correct most errors, which is reflected in the very low UER. As expected 2SET had the highest TER ($\mu = 15.1, \sigma = 5.31$) due to the very small key sizes. NRG had the lowest TER ($\mu = 9.6, \sigma = 4.18$) across all sessions followed by SKY ($\mu = 10.5, \sigma = 3.98$) and CJI ($\mu = 12.4, \sigma = 5.76$).

ANOVA revealed a significant effect of *layout* on *total error rate* (Table 1). A post hoc Tukey HSD showed that 2SET had higher TER than the other methods, and CJI had higher TER than NRG, and this difference was significant at $p < .05$.

### Qualitative Feedback

After the study each participant filled out a NASA-TLX questionnaire to rank the various dimensions of the task workload (Fig. 4). Of particular interest are the responses to the Mental, Temporal, and Frustration dimensions. (The responses to Performance and Effort suggest that the participants did not have a good frame of reference of what constituted good performance.) As expected 2SET had the highest expressed levels of workload, followed by NRG. Interestingly, CJI was perceived as less demanding across all dimensions, despite the reduced set of available keys and higher difficulty for composing the vowels. SKY, which is a fairly straightforward layout, was found more demanding than CJI.

### Touch Distributions

Interesting patterns were observed in the data from the touch distributions. In general, for the 3x4 layouts the spread of the distributions was larger in the last session compared to the first (Fig. 5a). The larger spread seems to correspond to faster text entry speed — in the first session the participants were slower and tentative, which resulted in a more concentrated area of touches on the keys. By the end the increase in speed resulted in less precise, though still effective, key taps.

A second observation for the 3x4 layouts is that, in general, there was a skew toward the bottom-right corner of each key (Fig. 5b,c — only SKY shown due to space constraints); for the single left-handed participant the skew was toward the bottom-left corner (Fig. 5d). This corresponds to the relative orientation between the line of sight and direction of approach to the keypad, and seems to be a result of the participants' intent to compensate for the occlusion problem. The data for 2SET showed an overall tendency to touch below the key centers (Fig. 5e), which is consistent with the findings in [6, 2].

A possible direction for future work could be to study the impact on error rate of the compensation functions described in [6] that shift the coordinates of the touch by a fixed or dynamically computed offset. The results in [6] for QWERTY layout on smartphones showed a decrease in error rate and it would be important to confirm this effect for smartwatches.

## DISCUSSION

This paper presented results from a user study on the effectiveness of 3x4 and QWERTY-like layouts for Korean text entry on smartwatches. The results show that these are viable options that achieve competitive speed at reasonable error rate.

Although the study was on Korean text entry, it could inform work on English, particularly 3x4 layouts, which have been studied less extensively. Note that the Korean layouts arrange the letters so that the consonants and vowels occupy two distinct areas (vowels in top row of CJI, right column of SKY and NRG, and right half of 2SET). This arrangement is well suited for two thumb typing on a smartphone, since within a phrase consonants and vowels alternate which generates a rhythm for typing. This might also enhance text entry on a smartwatch, since the vowels are accessible in a fixed location that facilitates recall. Here are possible modifications of the standard English layouts inspired by the consonant-vowel split with only minimal changes and treating y as a vowel:

| **ae** | **io** | **uy** |
|---|---|---|
| bc | df | gh |
| jk | lm | npq |
| rs | tvw | xz |

| q w r t **y a e u i o** |
|---|
| s d f g h j k l p |
| z x c v b n m |

Similarly, one might expect comparable performance for the English QWERTY layout. While the participants expressed higher levels of frustration with 2SET, they still achieved over 20 WPM, albeit with 14.7 TER. Since 2SET has higher demand than QWERTY (7 letters require *shift* key), it seems that QWERTY should be closer to 2SET in speed. The data reported for QWERTY [7, 12] does not support this observation, which might be due to differences in experimental setup.

## REFERENCES


1. Ahmed Sabbir Arif and Ali Mazalek. 2016. *A Survey of Text Entry Techniques for Smartwatches.* Springer International Publishing, Cham, 255–267. DOI: http://dx.doi.org/10.1007/978-3-319-39516-6_24

2. Shiri Azenkot and Shumin Zhai. 2012. Touch Behavior with Different Postures on Soft Smartphone Keyboards. In *Proceedings of the 14th International Conference on Human-computer Interaction with Mobile Devices and Services (MobileHCI '12).* ACM, New York, NY, USA, 251–260. DOI: http://dx.doi.org/10.1145/2371574.2371612

3. Xiang 'Anthony' Chen, Tovi Grossman, and George Fitzmaurice. 2014. Swipeboard: A Text Entry Technique for Ultra-small Interfaces That Supports Novice to Expert Transitions. In *Proceedings of the 27th Annual ACM Symposium on User Interface Software and Technology (UIST '14).* ACM, New York, NY, USA, 615–620. DOI: http://dx.doi.org/10.1145/2642918.2647354

4. Aakar Gupta and Ravin Balakrishnan. 2016. DualKey: Miniature Screen Text Entry via Finger Identification. In *Proceedings of the 2016 CHI Conference on Human Factors in Computing Systems (CHI '16).* ACM, New York, NY, USA, 59–70. DOI: http://dx.doi.org/10.1145/2858036.2858052

5. Sandra G. Hart and Lowell E. Staveland. 1988. Development of NASA-TLX (Task Load Index): Results of Empirical and Theoretical Research. In *Human Mental Workload*, Peter A. Hancock and Najmedin Meshkati (Eds.). Advances in Psychology, Vol. 52. North-Holland, 139 – 183. DOI: http://dx.doi.org/10.1016/S0166-4115(08)62386-9

6. Niels Henze, Enrico Rukzio, and Susanne Boll. 2012. Observational and Experimental Investigation of Typing Behaviour Using Virtual Keyboards for Mobile Devices. In *Proceedings of the SIGCHI Conference on Human Factors in Computing Systems (CHI '12).* ACM, New York, NY, USA, 2659–2668. DOI: http://dx.doi.org/10.1145/2207676.2208658

7. Jonggi Hong, Seongkook Heo, Poika Isokoski, and Geehyuk Lee. 2015. SplitBoard: A Simple Split Soft Keyboard for Wristwatch-sized Touch Screens. In *Proceedings of the 33rd Annual ACM Conference on Human Factors in Computing Systems (CHI '15).* ACM, New York, NY, USA, 1233–1236. DOI: http://dx.doi.org/10.1145/2702123.2702273

8. Ivaylo Ilinkin and Sunghee Kim. 2010. Evaluation of Text Entry Methods for Korean Mobile Phones, a User Study. In *Proceedings of the SIGCHI Conference on Human Factors in Computing Systems (CHI '10).* ACM, New York, NY, USA, 2023–2026. DOI: http://dx.doi.org/10.1145/1753326.1753633

9. H. Kim and Kang B. 1997. *Frequency analysis of Korean.* Korea University Institute of Korean Culture.

10. Wonsup Lee, Sujin Kim, Sunghye Yoon, Jangwoon Park, Dalho Lee, Seikwon Park, Byunggil Kang, Jooho Uem, and Heecheon Yoo. 2008. Development of a comprehensive pilot workload assessment model for evaluation of helicopter cockpit design. In *Proceedings of the Fall conference of the Ergonomics Society of Korea (ESK '08).* 306–309.

11. I. Scott MacKenzie and R. William Soukoreff. 2003. Phrase Sets for Evaluating Text Entry Techniques. In *CHI '03 Extended Abstracts on Human Factors in Computing Systems (CHI EA '03).* ACM, New York, NY, USA, 754–755. DOI: http://dx.doi.org/10.1145/765891.765971

12. Stephen Oney, Chris Harrison, Amy Ogan, and Jason Wiese. 2013. ZoomBoard: A Diminutive Qwerty Soft Keyboard Using Iterative Zooming for Ultra-small Devices. In *Proceedings of the SIGCHI Conference on Human Factors in Computing Systems (CHI '13).* ACM, New York, NY, USA, 2799–2802. DOI: http://dx.doi.org/10.1145/2470654.2481387

13. R. William Soukoreff and I. Scott MacKenzie. 2003. Metrics for Text Entry Research: An Evaluation of MSD and KSPC, and a New Unified Error Metric. In *Proceedings of the SIGCHI Conference on Human Factors in Computing Systems (CHI '03).* ACM, New York, NY, USA, 113–120. DOI: http://dx.doi.org/10.1145/642611.642632

14. Jacob O. Wobbrock, Brad A. Myers, and Htet Htet Aung. 2004. Writing with a Joystick: A Comparison of Date Stamp, Selection Keyboard, and EdgeWrite. In *Proceedings of Graphics Interface 2004 (GI '04).* Canadian Human-Computer Communications Society, School of Computer Science, University of Waterloo, Waterloo, Ontario, Canada, 1–8. http://dl.acm.org/citation.cfm?id=1006058.1006059

# "WhatsApp is for family; Messenger is for friends": Communication Places in App Ecosystems

Midas Nouwens Carla F. Griggio Wendy E. Mackay
LRI, Univ. Paris-Sud, CNRS,
Inria, Université Paris-Saclay
F-91400 Orsay, France
{nouwens, griggio, mackay}@lri.fr

## ABSTRACT
Today's users communicate via multiple apps, even when they offer almost identical functionality. We studied how and why users distribute their contacts within their app ecosystem. We found that the contacts in an app affect a user's conversations with other contacts, their communication patterns in the app, and the quality of their social relationships. Users appropriate the features and technical constraints of their apps to create idiosyncratic *communication places*, each with its own recursively defined membership rules, perceived purposes, and emotional connotations. Users also shift the boundaries of their communication places to accommodate changes in their contacts' behaviour, the dynamics of their relationships, and the restrictions of the technology. We argue that communication apps should support creating multiple communication places within the same app, relocating conversations across apps, and accessing functionality from other apps.

### ACM Classi cation Keywords
H.5.3. Group and Organization Interfaces: Computer-supported cooperative work.

### Author Keywords
Communication places; communication ecosystem; contact management; Instant Messaging; Computer-Mediated Communication (CMC).

## INTRODUCTION
The mediated communication landscape has expanded significantly over the past decade, from a handful of distinct forms of communication (phone calls, email, texts) to hundreds of communication apps. *Mobile Instant Messaging (MIM)* alone comprises a wide variety of apps, including *Messenger, WhatsApp, iMessage, KakaoTalk, WeChat, Line, Viber*, and more. Researchers often point to the qualities inherent in each app, such as its functionality or cost, to explain the effect of the medium on users' communication patterns. For example, Rost et al. [15] discuss the link between the presence of message history and chit-chat, and Grinter and Eldridge [6] describe how the cost of text messaging can lead to short, abbreviated, and blunt exchanges. Yet these apps are often very similar, with nearly identical functionality. Even so, Cramer and Jacobs [5] found that users consistently use equivalent apps such as *WhatsApp* and *Messenger* alongside each other, but in idiosyncratic ways. This suggests that knowing the inherent qualities of an app is insufficient for understanding how it affects communication patterns.

O'Hara et al. contend that we need to *"capture the quiddity of the experiences sought for and enabled by these applications in ways that reaches beyond economic or technological determinism"* [14]. Scissors and Gergle [16] recently argued we should consider channel selection relative to the other apps in the user's ecosystem rather than focusing on just one, and Jung and Lyytinen [10] showed how it is the ecology — the relations among the different media and their surroundings — that shapes channel choice. We believe this perspective should be extended beyond channel selection: Considering a user's ecosystem of apps should help us to better understand how use of mostly identical communication apps diverges over time, which factors create and maintain these differences, and how the ecosystem influences the relationships among communication partners.

This paper presents a qualitative study with 18 participants that explores (1) why users distribute their social relationships across different apps; (2) how individual communication apps are used with respect to other communication apps in the user's ecosystem; and (3) how users establish patterns that maintain these distributions.

## RELATED WORK

### Multiple communication apps for one contact
Research discussing multiple communication channels often focuses on how users choose among various options available. Only recently have researchers asked how users take advantage of this multiplicity and how the use of one communication app informs the use of another. Some studies describe the process of channel switching or channel blending: how one coherent conversation takes place over multiple channels. In professional contexts, Su revealed how employees go through "communication chains", i.e. interactions through different


*CHI 2017* May 6–11, 2017, Denver, CO, USA

DOI: http://dx.doi.org/10.1145/3025453.3025484

channels in rapid succession [18]. In personal contexts, Scissors and Gergle [16] described how couples switch back and forth between different channels during conflicts to leverage the particular qualities of different forms of communication. Cramer and Jacobs [5] extended this beyond conflicts and showed how couples combine different channels throughout their relationship to communicate importance or add emotional value to a message. These studies focus on the use of multiple apps for the purpose of a single conversation or contact, but leave unexplored the use of multiple apps to manage multiple relationships.

### Multiple communication apps for multiple contacts

Studies that focus on how people take advantage of multiple channels to manage multiple contacts are often related to email use. A large-scale survey with university employees by Capra et al. [2] revealed that 88% of respondents had at least two email accounts. The most common reason for having multiple email accounts is to let users separate their personal and work lives [3]. Gross and Churchill [7] expanded on these email studies and argued that research should take into account the user's full range of communication means. They examined both email and *IM (Instant Messaging)* to see how users employ multiple addresses and accounts to manage interruptions, deal with usability issues, and separate business and personal contacts. However, like most email-related research, the focus is on professional relationships rather than social communication and the many apps dedicated to its support.

### One communication app for multiple social contacts

Most studies of how users manage their social relationships are conducted in the context of social networking sites. The presence of multiple contacts in the same environment is shown to cause tension if users belong to different social spheres, with the diversity of contacts corresponding to the level of tension [1]. Shklovski et al. [17] discuss how users deal with these tensions through selective self-disclosure or each site's built-in privacy settings. These studies show that such conflicts arise because person-to-person communication is public to all other contacts in the environment. However, this does not explain why users distribute contacts across apps when information is *not* broadcast, as with most dedicated communication apps.

## METHOD

We conducted an interview study to investigate how people manage their growing collections of communication apps to manage their social relationships. We are particularly interested in why they decide to use specific apps to communicate with particular contacts or groups.

### Participants

Participants included 10 women and 8 men (n = 18) between the ages of 18 and 40 (mean = 25) who came from twelve different countries in Asia, Europe, North America and South America. They were currently living in Argentina, France, the Netherlands, Sweden, the United Kingdom, or the United States. The participants' occupational backgrounds include: clinical supervisor, student, secretary, social media manager, journalist, copywriter, lecturer, unemployed, and pre-school teacher.

### Procedure

We recruited participants through a snowballing technique and by approaching strangers in public spaces. We conducted semi-structured interviews using a variation of critical incident technique [13]. We asked participants to describe specific, recent, memorable stories about the interplay among different people (contacts) in their communication apps. Interview questions focused on who the participants communicate with, the channels they choose for their different contacts, what rules they use and how they feel about those channels, and how their use of a channel corresponds to the other channels they use.

Examples of questions include "*When was the last time you deleted someone from an app?*" and "*Did you answer someone through a different app than the one they contacted you with?*". The resulting stories served as the point of departure for learning more about their overall associations with an app and the role it plays relative to the other apps in their ecosystem. Each interview lasted between 45 and 90 minutes. Eleven interviews were conducted live; seven interviews were conducted via Skype. All interviews were recorded and transcribed.

## RESULTS AND DISCUSSION

Two researchers independently and iteratively analysed the transcribed interviews using thematic analysis [8]. Concepts were identified using open coding and grouped into categories using axial coding. Categories that emerged from stories included: feeling', rule', practice', breakdown', and workaround'. For example, one participant's *WhatsApp* felt close (feeling) which meant she only wanted people that were important to her (rule) and she reinforced this by withholding her phone number from those she did not want (practice). When the participant's father contacted her via a coworker's phone (breakdown) she blocked the co-worker and deleted the messages (workaround). The interviews were reanalysed to confirm that these categories captured all salient data points.

We found that participants communicated via a wide variety of devices, including smartphones, laptops, desktops, and tablets. They used *Messenger* (17), *WhatsApp* (15), *SMS* (15), *Skype* (13), *Snapchat* (6), *Slack* (4), *Tinder* (3), *Grindr* (2), *GChat* (2), *iMessage* (2), *Telegram* (2), *Couchsur ng Messages* (1), *GroupMe* (1), *Line* (1), and *LinkedIn Messages* (1). Participants mentioned other communication platforms, such as social networks and e-mail; our analysis here focuses on private messaging using mobile (or multi-platform) apps.

### Contacts contaminate apps

The contacts present in an app can colour other communication experiences, even if individual conversations are isolated from each other and no information is shared across contacts. Participants view apps as shared communication spaces and said that the presence of a particular contact can change the content of other conversations, such as when they copy a joke or match another person's writing style. The presence of a contact in an app can also change their emotional state during conversations. One participant, who was relaxed when talking to a friend, became stressed in the presence of a past lover.

 

Another's conversation with her partner felt intimate until she noticed a co-worker in the same app.

The contacts in a shared communication space can also indirectly affect individual communication activities by changing participants' communication patterns. For example, one participant initially used *WhatsApp* to send two friends *"whimsical"* (P5) voice messages and impersonations. As *WhatsApp* became more popular, other people started to contact him there. Their presence made him uncomfortable, so he and his two friends switched to another app:

> *I didn t really use WhatsApp in a functional way. [The app] felt sullied because those voice messages are what I used WhatsApp for. It was speci c people and it was all light hearted and fun. They just got kind of drowned out by all the other people who moved there.* (P5)

The presence of other contacts also damaged or improved relationships with other contacts in the same app. One participant avoided a channel because of a barrage of messages from a particular conversation, which angered the other contacts that she inadvertently ignored. Another participant began to spend more time on an app to keep in touch with her travelling uncle, which rekindled her friendship with another contact:

> *I ended up with my previous boyfriend because of Skype ... because I was there he started talking to me. I m pretty sure that if my uncle had never travelled the world this wouldn t have happened.* (P12)

These results suggest that a shared communication space is not just a collection of individual conversations that occur in isolation. Rather, because these contacts exist in the same environment, the user's relationships with their contacts become subtly intertwined. The addition of a single person can alter what the user talks about with the other contacts, how the user feels during the conversation, how often the user enters the communication space, and how much time is spent within it. These particular ways of interrelating ultimately make up the dynamics of each relationship, which are affected by the particular collection of contacts present in the shared communication space.

### Users control contacts

Participants were actively invested in controlling the presence of contacts in their apps, usually by leveraging and appropriating the app's technical features and constraints. We identified three primary strategies for keeping apps in their preferred state.

#### *Preventing entry*

Fourteen participants described how they tried to prevent a person from entering their app environment. Most just lied, saying either that they did not have the app, or they did not use it. Some asked their friends not to give out the identifier (such as username or phone number) without their explicit permission. One participant explained his process for deciding where to locate a contact:

> *When I meet a new person they do get a little interview like... "Would you be a psycho texter?" So I test the waters out a little bit where I m like ... "Yeah I ll give you my number." or "Let s keep you on Snapchat or on Grindr."* (P5)

#### *(Re)moving intruders*

Ten participants removed contacts from or moved contacts to an app. Participants removed contacts by blocking the person or permanently deleting the conversation. They either moved contacts implicitly, for example by replying via a different app or taking a long time to respond, or explicitly, for example by telling the contact where they should message them:

> *If [my friend] would message me on WhatsApp I would reply but I wouldn t do it myself. I would message him via Facebook Messenger. And then if he would continue to message me on WhatsApp I would tell him to not contact me on WhatsApp anymore.* (P1)

One participant went to great lengths to ensure that particular contacts were included rather than excluded in an app. When neither his closest friend nor his parents had *Snapchat*, he said it *"felt wrong"*, as if he was *"cheating them"*. He convinced his friend to buy a better phone so she could use *Snapchat*. For his parents, he *"sat them down to explain how it worked"* and *"coached"* them:

> *When people don t have a certain channel where I d like them to be in it feels like a shame and that it doesn t t that they don t have it. It s something they should have and we should communicate that way.* (P5)

#### *Tolerating outsiders*

When participants did not or could not exclude a contact from an app — either by preventing them from entering or (re)moving them after they did — they appropriated the features of the app to shape how these contacts appear:

> *If I m not comfortable with them having contacted me, I just don t add them as contacts. So that just their number comes up. It s not that I don t want any contact with them, but I obviously didn t feel comfortable with them being part of my WhatsApp. I think it is a way of reserving WhatsApp and my phone for important personal information.* (P6)

> *You can archive conversations and then they only pop up when something new happens. Or when you think to send them a new text. So I archive other people so that my close friends and family are always at the top of the chat list.* (P5)

Interestingly, the participants were aware that these practices had no impact on the contact's actual ability to communicate with them via the app. One called it *"being rude in private"* (P6), but acknowledged that it was just a way to manage the experience of the contact's presence.

In summary, these results suggest that people actively create and shape personalised communication spaces by managing contacts within and across their apps. Participants took advantage of the similar communication apps to, as one participant put it, *"build boundaries"* (P7) between social relationships.

This echoes Chalmers and Galani's [4] notion of the "seamfulness" of technology, where users appropriate its limitations to their benefit. Here, users appropriate the siloed nature of communication apps to manage and control contacts.

### De ning Communication Places

Stable patterns of contact management obtain across the different communication apps, based on how users organise and separate their contacts to manage social relationships. In addition, 13 participants attributed particular identities to specific communication apps, which fulfilled distinct roles in their everyday communication.

> *It s more likely that if someone sends me a message on Facebook and I am connected with them on WhatsApp that I will reply on WhatsApp. For some reason I associate WhatsApp with a much more easy, more immediate medium. And I have no idea why because functionality wise there is no real difference. In my mind it s just not what Facebook Messenger is about, it has nothing to do with the functionality.* (P6)

> *In my head, WhatsApp is slow and old. I m not sure why. I only really use it for groups, like the family WhatsApp group. So to talk to my friend there is weird. Whereas Facebook Messenger is white and happy and empty. It feels way more airy and I use it for all my friends.* (P7)

We call apps with particular identities *communication places* i.e. personal and idiosyncratic constructs that users build on top of communication apps, which in turn shape their subsequent communicative actions and experiences.

We define communication places according to their:

- *Membership rules*: who belongs to them,
- *Perceived purpose*: what they are for, and
- *Emotional connotations*: how they feel to the user.

Communication places are personal to the user rather than inherent to the app. The same app may have different or even contradictory rules, purposes or connotations for different users. For example, some participants found text messaging *"a little more personal"* (P16) or *"intimate"* (P5), whereas others used texting *"more for practical reasons"* (P6), or *"for logistics"* (P1). Another said: *"Texts are like gold. So I don t use it"* (P7).

Communication places affect how participants interpret the same message or behaviour:

> *I deleted this guy on Tinder. But not on WhatsApp. It feels more personal if I did it there.* (P3)

> *Someone had passed my number on and they contacted me on WhatsApp and I didn t feel comfortable with that. It would have been OK for them to contact me through Facebook, because on Facebook I am more comfortable with that type of contact.* (P6)

Communication places reflect and sometimes affect the quality of the relationship between a participant and their contact:

> *I have a friend who I talk to almost every day. We work together and we live in the same building, but if I want to talk to him I message him on Facebook Messenger. We are close, but we are not close enough for WhatsApp.* (P1)

> *I gave out my number to people on Tinder and added them on WhatsApp but then eventually that started feeling like I was letting them into my personal bubble. It s like you re setting a second step in your relationship with those people.* (P7)

Communication places are constantly redefined, not only as the user engages with the app over time, but also in response to a variety of catalysts, such as new app features, changed phone numbers or moving to a new country. Each communication place has a reciprocal relationship with its underlying app: On one hand, the user's actions and experiences with the app shape the communication place and its attributes; on the other hand, the communication place influences which actions and experiences the user permits in the app (see Figure 1).

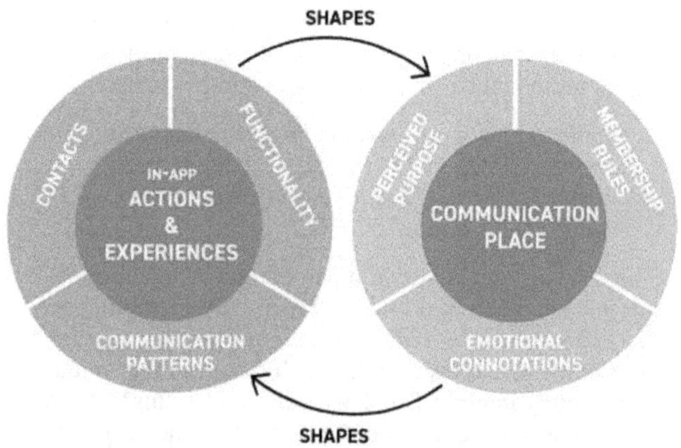


**Figure 1. The reciprocal relationship between actions and experiences in the communication app and the communication place that is created on top of it.**

Our use of the term "communication place" is influenced by Harrison and Dourish's distinction between "space" and "place". They define space as *"the structure of the world"*, in contrast to place, which they define as *"a space which is invested with understandings of behavioural appropriateness, cultural expectations, and so forth"* [9]. Our findings support this distinction: Here, communication apps provide the structure for communication, independent of the user, whereas communication places encompass the rules, roles, and feelings that users apply to their apps.

Harrison and Dourish's work addressed common practices for building *collaborative* virtual environments [9]. As such, their definition and discussion of place centres around how users create places *collectively*. Our results show how *individual* users can also create personal places. Places are not only developed together with others *through* technology, but also by individual users *with respect to* their particular use of the technology.

### Breaking Communication Places

Participants constantly tried to negotiate between the communication place they desire and the environment imposed on them by the communication app's design or their contact's behaviour. Mismatches between communication places and contacts create friction. Sometimes, users succeed in resolving them through the prevention, (re)moving, and tolerating strategies described above. However, nearly all participants experience situations where they cannot find a solution, and thus must shift the boundaries and settle for less-than-ideal communication places.

#### *Relationships are nuanced — apps are crude*

All but one participant who mentioned blocking, deleting, or preventing a contact from entering an app, also apologetically explained that it was not because of the contact, but because they were simply "out of place". The social undesirability of these boundary-building strategies was further illustrated by the fact that five participants stopped themselves from removing a contact from an app because they felt it was too rude:

> *I wasn t sure what to do, whether I should block him. Because he is a very nice person, but... he is just one of those darlings you don t want to kill that is now permanent in a sense in my WhatsApp. And so I scroll down and I see his name. And it s not that I hate him, but I just don t want to see him when I go through my contacts and have to think about him.* (P3)

One participant summarised how most participants perceived these measures:

> *It s of course very easy to ignore and block people, but those are very crude measures. It s just not very nice and not really acceptable to myself, even though it is really easy to do via these apps. So that is really a rule I create for myself, that I want to still be a good person and so I have to tell these people like "hey sorry I don t think this will work out" rather than just blocking them and being done with them. There aren t enough nuances to what is possible.* (P7)

Users can only block, remove or delete contacts to remove a contact from a communication place without talking to them, but these methods are considered too absolute. Participants want more nuanced options that range from *"I never want to see them"* to *"I just want to be less aware of them"* or *"I would like to see them once a month"*. Human relationships require more nuance than is currently offered by the design of these apps and users compromise their values or communication places as a result.

#### *Relationships are fluid — apps are inflexible*

Five participants struggled to account for the dynamic nature of their relationships. While participants may initially put a contact in the right communication place, they may become "out of place" as the relationship changes. For example, P5 had two *Snapchat* accounts: one under a fake name for online friends who knew about his bisexuality and one for offline friends who did not. These communication places were kept strictly separate so he could be open with himself *"without it being traceable back to real life"* (P5). However, over time his relationships with both groups changed:

> *When I started to come out to my friends, switching back and forth between the two accounts became hard and I started to have those people on the fake account as friends who I no longer wanted to have as just online acquaintances anymore.* (P5)

Merging them, however, required him to *"come out backwards"* to his online friends because he had to explain why they were in the *"fake account"* to begin with.

Another participant struggled to deal with the presence of a recently deceased family member in the communication place she established for close friends and work contacts: *"I didn t want to be confronted with them when I scrolled down my WhatsApp. It was a sad thing to see on a regular basis, to be reminded"* (P6). However, she felt uncomfortable deleting the contact and history because *"it felt too sudden"* and she did not want to lose her precious messages. Eventually she *"needed to confront it"* and compromised:

> *I went through all the messages and I wrote down in a book any of the ones I liked, anything they d said. I made a note of those in a little book to keep because I didn t want to lose them. Then I deleted the history.* (P6)

Contacts and message histories are currently locked inside apps, which can cause problems when relationships change. Over time, a contact's app membership might be revoked or reinstated multiple times based on the changing nature of the relationship or communication place. This fluidity is inhibited by the way history of use is coupled with the app in which it occurred. Sometimes breaking that link and abandoning the built-up history and communication habits is worth the cost, as in the two examples above. Other times, the user will choose to compromise their communication place rather than enforce its boundaries.

#### *Relationships are unique — Features are generic*

Five participants reported breakdowns caused by their need to access or escape a certain feature for a particular contact. For example, P4 has a rule to keep all *Grindr* contacts in that app. However, he often violates this rule so that he can receive notifications, a function available only in the paid version:

> *With a guy from Grindr who I only met once, I don t want to give him my number because then he has the power to show up on my lock screen and I don t trust him with that. But I still do sometimes.* (P4)

This breach makes him *"very uncomfortable"* because friends can (and did) see the explicit messages he receives.

Additionally, apps often impose the same functionality on all contacts within its boundaries. For example, P7 started to avoid *WhatsApp* after she added *Tinder* contacts there, because *WhatsApp* would tell them when she was last online — which made her anxious. However, this also meant she missed out on her family's *WhatsApp*-group conversations:

> *So I changed that feature where you can see when I was online or read the message. And that was much better*

> *because then I could respond to my family without feeling like you were online and you didn t respond, why aren t you responding . But it also meant I couldn t see if my family was online or read my messages, so eventually I switched it back on again. And it would have been better if I could have done that for individual people.* (P7)

A participant's need for a particular feature can force them to compromise their communication places in order to meet their relationship needs. Because features exist at the app-level rather than at the contact-level, participants cannot selectively apply features based on the requirements of a particular relationship. For example, users who create a communication place for their close friends and family may end up sacrificing functionality; and users who want a particular feature to communicate with one contact may end up "contaminating" a communication place that was meant for another group.

### Discussion Summary

Our findings demonstrate how mediated communication is influenced not only by each app's technical characteristics and features, but also by the *communication places* that users establish to manage their social relationships.

We show that:

- The presence of particular contacts in an app affects communication with other contacts;
- Users purposely distribute contacts across communication apps to control their impact;
- Users establish personal strategies for maintaining this distribution of contacts;
- Users construct *communication places* with membership rules, perceived purpose, and emotional connotations that affect the meaning of messages, the appropriateness of behaviour, and relationships between users and contacts.

A few participants describe the above activities as a linear process. However, most viewed them as interwoven activities with reciprocal effects. In general, the collection of individual activities and experiences within an app serves to establish the corresponding communication place, and at the same time, the communication place shapes which activities and contacts appear within its boundaries. Because the communication place affects who or what is allowed *inside*, it simultaneously pushes other contacts *outside* its boundaries. This in turn influences the "placeness" of the other apps in the participant's ecosystem (Figure 2). In other words, users not only create an ecosystem of apps, but also an ecosystem of communication places.

Although the relationship between an app and its corresponding communication place is reciprocal, the relationships among different communication places in the ecosystem may not be. Membership rules for one communication place can easily push certain contacts into other apps, but may not receive contacts in return. For example, *Telegram* may serve as the communication place for a romantic partner, and drive acquaintances to *iMessage*. If the membership rules for *iMessage* change to include 'friends and family', the *Telegram* communication place may not be modified to include them as well.

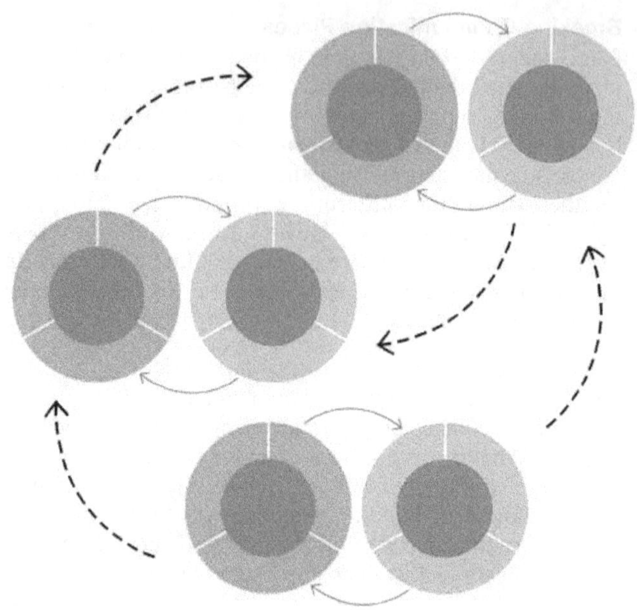

**Figure 2. A user's ecosystem of apps and communication places: each in uences the other.**

## IMPLICATIONS FOR DESIGN

Currently, communication places cannot easily be separated from the apps on top of which they are constructed. Unfortunately, communication app designers often make decisions that seriously inhibit or prevent users from creating communication places. Users are forced to make trade-offs between the features they want, the health of their social relationships and their emotional state. We propose three design directions that would permit more flexible relationships between apps and communication places, with a corresponding increase in the user's control over each communication place.

### Create multiple communication places in a single app

Apps should allow the creation of multiple communication places within the app, to alleviate breakdowns caused by the intermixing of contacts in the shared communication space. Currently, it is impossible for users to remain unaware of the other contacts in an app when communicating with a particular individual. Users are either confronted with these contacts when returning to the "home" screen, or they receive notifications from other contacts while in a conversation with someone else. Users are thus forced into zero-sum decisions: either they accept this intermixing of contacts or they have to exclude themselves or a contact entirely. For example, P7 could only avoid her *Tinder* contacts in *WhatsApp* by also missing out on the conversation within her family's group-chat; P5 felt his childhood friends were *"drowned out"* by other contacts and had to switch to a different app to compensate.

Allowing users to create multiple instantiations of the same app can support the creation of multiple communication places within it. Users can still take advantage of all the features a particular app has to offer, but their communication remains independent from contacts that belong outside that particular communication place. For example, a user could "turn off" the *Highschool Friends Telegram* during a busy day but still receive messages from the *Family Telegram*. These separate communication places could have their own distinct icons and notification badges (Figure 3), allowing users to communicate with the contacts in one communication place without being aware of contacts in another.

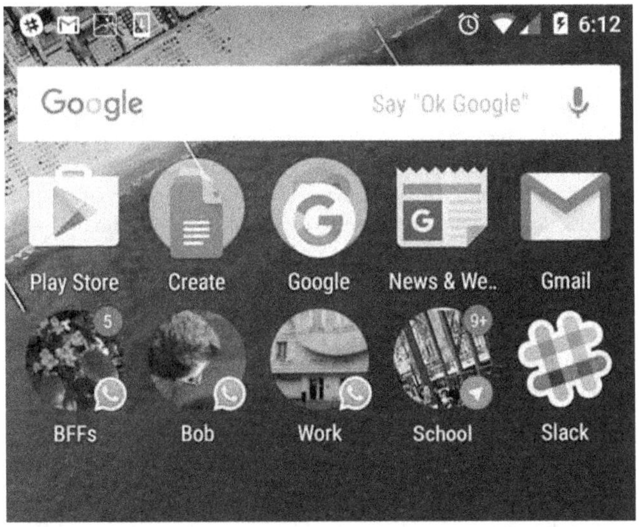


**Figure 3. A communication app ecosystem with apps containing multiple communication places. The icons are instances of *WhatsApp*. The icon is an instance of *Telegram*. Apps could still be used as we do today, as in the case of *Slack*.**

### Relocate conversations across apps

*SMS* messages can be sent and received from and to any phone model or operating system. Similarly, email can be exchanged independently of the email address provider or the email client used by the sender and recipient. By contrast, messaging apps force channel symmetry: communication partners must agree which app to use or when to switch. Although the sender might feel a contact is in the "right place", it might be "out of place" for the recipient. For example, P1's communication place for her boyfriend is *WhatsApp*, but her boyfriend prefers *Messenger* and sometimes refuses to switch channels. Allowing users to freely move their conversations across apps would address breakdowns associated with "out of place" contacts, without forcing them to resort to "rude" behaviour.

Currently, messaging apps such as *Hangouts*, *Messenger*, and *iMessage* partially support "cross-app conversations" by allowing users to send and receive *SMS* messages through them. This lets two users communicate through asymmetrical channels, e.g. to send messages from *Hangouts* to *Messenger* and vice versa (Figure 4). This gives users more freedom to construct a communication place independent of the channel used or preferred by the contact they are talking to. However, this does not fully support the creation of flexible communication places because users still cannot decide which messages are forwarded to which communication place. Instead, *all SMS* messages are just forwarded to one app. We did not observe any situations in which users took advantage of this functionality to match their conversations with a particular communication place, perhaps because the current design does not permit conversations to be distributed.

Decoupling conversations from applications opens up new opportunities but also creates new challenges. What if a *Messenger* user sent an animated sticker to an app that lacks support for animated images? To let users dynamically relocate their conversations, communication apps should support compatible media. This could be accomplished by sharing protocols across heterogeneous media types, or with a system like Webstrates, which allows the exchange of self-contained media messages that "know how to render themselves" when transcluded in the canvas of a conversation [12]. In summary, moving conversations across apps would support flexible and open-ended matching of a contact to a communication place, overcoming the channel symmetry imposed by today's messaging apps.

### Access functionality from other apps

We argue that users should be able to access functionality from other apps without compromising their communication places. Communication apps try to differentiate themselves by offering unique features. Since users appropriate multiple apps to create multiple communication places, they will have different functionality in each place. The need to access a particular feature, then, often corresponds with moving a contact from one communication place to another. For example, P17 brought a contact from *Tinder* to *Telegram* so he could share a custom-made sticker with her; and P13 used *GroupMe* to have group chats with contacts he had on *iMessage*.

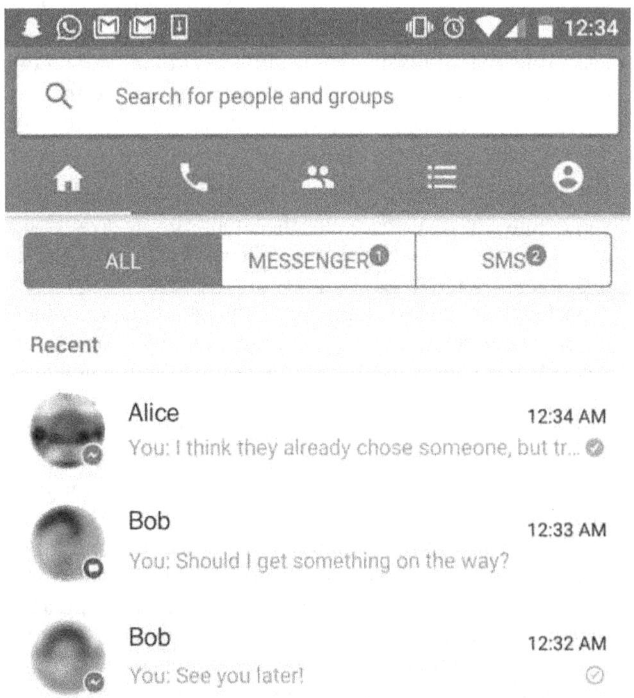


**Figure 4. Two parallel conversations with the same contact (Bob) in the same app (Android's *Messenger*). The conversation uses *SMS/MMS*, the conversation uses the "data" messages of *Messenger*.**

The idea of "breaking the silos" has been explored in the context of multi-device interactive systems [11]. We encourage app designers to also share and compose functionality across communication apps within the same device. Apps can already communicate with each other to share content, e.g. a picture taken with the *Camera* app or a location from the *Maps* app can be shared directly with any messaging app. We argue that similar mechanisms should be used to share features among communication apps themselves. For example, a user talking to her boyfriend on *Messenger* could take a picture and add *Snapchat* decorations without having to leave the app. This would support users who want to use a particular app as a communication place, based on its use history, but also take advantage of some of its features with contacts that belong somewhere else.

## LIMITATIONS AND FUTURE WORK

We do not claim that all users create communication places or manage relationship boundaries through communication apps. Nor do we believe that users are necessarily conscious of their attempts to control their communication environments. In this study, two participants did not create any rules or establish practices around their communication channels and never felt that the app environment affected their conversations. P2 communicated only with four close contacts and did not see the need to segregate them on different apps. P8, a freelance journalist, communicated with a large number of people, but used a *"hodgepodge, make-shift system"* instead of clearly delineated communication places and boundaries. For example, he freely exchanges *Skype* information with people he meets at a conference just so he can *"engineer a non-awkward end to a conversation"*, even if he has no intention of staying in touch. Despite using *Skype* daily for work, he is clearly far less protective of his communication environment than other participants. The fact that not all users create communication places, however, could be due to their lack of support in current communication apps.

The diversity of participants (in age, profession, nationality, and country of residence) plus the small sample size for each of those demographics makes it difficult to generalise the findings per subset. We selected this diverse sample because we expected the culture or subgroup of the individual to influence the practices related to a communication app. For example, *WhatsApp* is widely used in the Netherlands, but much less in France. Had we selected a homogeneous sample and found they all believed that "*WhatsApp* is for family", it would have been difficult to determine whether such connotations are inherent to the app or a subjective construction by the participant. Although these findings cannot be used to claim that specific demographics or apps correspond to particular types of communication places, the diversity of the sample helped us uncover different associations around the same app and as such provided rich insight into varied practices across cultures. Future work should address how communication places develop in different user populations, and to what extent specific apps support creation of specific communication places.

Finally, this study focuses on how users appropriate features of communication apps that exist in separate "silos" when constructing personalised communication places. Future work should explore whether communication places also emerge with more open communication technologies that can send and receive messages from any client, such as email and, to a limited extent, *SMS*.

## CONCLUSION

Users create complex, personalised app ecosystems that often include a variety of communication apps, many with highly similar features. These similar apps fulfil distinct communication roles within the ecosystem as users develop divergent use patterns for each app. We found that the presence of specific contacts within a particular app changes the use of that app, and shapes its role relative to other apps within the communication ecosystem. We also found that users carefully consider which apps to use with which contacts, based on the app's role in the ecosystem

Most users develop idiosyncratic associations with specific communication apps, based on their previous activity and experiences within the boundaries of the app. We call these *communication places*: Users appropriate the features and technical constraints of their apps to construct personal communication environments with unique membership rules, perceived purposes, and emotional connotations. Users shift the boundaries of their communication places to accommodate changes in their contacts' behaviour, the dynamics of their relationships, and the restrictions of the technology.

Users employ various strategies for managing the influence of individual contacts, including preventing certain people from joining an app, removing them from or moving them to other apps, or appropriating an app's features to affect how these contacts appear within the app. Unfortunately, current communication apps are not designed to support the creation and maintenance of communication places, and users often end up fighting the technology. Despite their best efforts, users sometimes end up with broken communication places, causing tension and damaging their personal relationships.

We offer three design suggestions to better support the creation and maintenance of communication places. Allow: creation of multiple communication places within a single app; relocation of conversations across apps; and full access to functionality from other communication apps.

Communication places can be seen as blueprints for the user's ideal communication environment. Understanding the rules and emotions associated with communication places offers insights into users' communication needs and desires, with corresponding implications for the design of effective communication technology.

## ACKNOWLEDGEMENTS

This project has received funding from the European Research Council (ERC) under the European Union's Horizon 2020 research and innovation programme (grant agreement No 321135 CREATIV: Creating Co-Adaptive Human-Computer Partnerships).

## REFERENCES


1. Jens Binder, Andrew Howes, and Alistair Sutcliffe. 2009. The Problem of Conflicting Social Spheres: Effects of Network Structure on Experienced Tension in Social Network Sites. In *Proceedings of the SIGCHI Conference on Human Factors in Computing Systems (CHI 09)*. ACM, New York, NY, USA, 965–974. DOI: http://dx.doi.org/10.1145/1518701.1518849
2. Robert Capra, Julia Khanova, and Sarah Ramdeen. 2013. Work and personal e-mail use by university employees: PIM practices across domain boundaries. *Journal of the American Society for Information Science and Technology* 64, 5 (2013), 1029–1044.
3. Marta E. Cecchinato, Abigail Sellen, Milad Shokouhi, and Gavin Smyth. 2016. Finding Email in a Multi-Account, Multi-Device World. In *Proceedings of the 2016 CHI Conference on Human Factors in Computing Systems (CHI 16)*. ACM, New York, NY, USA, 1200–1210. DOI: http://dx.doi.org/10.1145/2858036.2858473
4. Matthew Chalmers and Areti Galani. 2004. Seamful Interweaving: Heterogeneity in the Theory and Design of Interactive Systems. In *Proceedings of the 5th Conference on Designing Interactive Systems: Processes, Practices, Methods, and Techniques (DIS 04)*. ACM, New York, NY, USA, 243–252. DOI: http://dx.doi.org/10.1145/1013115.1013149
5. Henriette Cramer and Maia L. Jacobs. 2015. Couples' Communication Channels: What, When & Why?. In *Proceedings of the 33rd Annual ACM Conference on Human Factors in Computing Systems (CHI 15)*. ACM, New York, NY, USA, 709–712. DOI: http://dx.doi.org/10.1145/2702123.2702356
6. Rebecca E. Grinter and Margery A. Eldridge. 2001. Y Do Tngrs Luv 2 Txt Msg?. In *Proceedings of the Seventh Conference on European Conference on Computer Supported Cooperative Work (ECSCW 01)*. Kluwer Academic Publishers, Norwell, MA, USA, 219–238. http://dl.acm.org.focus.lib.kth.se/citation.cfm?id=1241867.1241879
7. Benjamin M. Gross and Elizabeth F. Churchill. 2007. Addressing Constraints: Multiple Usernames Task Spillage and Notions of Identity. In *CHI 07 Extended Abstracts on Human Factors in Computing Systems (CHI EA 07)*. ACM, New York, NY, USA, 2393–2398. DOI: http://dx.doi.org/10.1145/1240866.1241013
8. Greg Guest. 2012. *Applied Thematic Analysis*. Sage. DOI: http://dx.doi.org/10.1080/08870440903194015
9. Steve Harrison and Paul Dourish. 1996. Re-place-ing Space: The Roles of Place and Space in Collaborative Systems. In *Proceedings of the 1996 ACM Conference on Computer Supported Cooperative Work (CSCW 96)*. ACM, New York, NY, USA, 67–76. DOI: http://dx.doi.org/10.1145/240080.240193
10. Yusun Jung and Kalle Lyytinen. 2014. Towards an Ecological Account of Media Choice: A Case Study on Pluralistic Reasoning While Choosing Email. *Info. Sys. Jour.* 24, 3 (May 2014), 271–293. DOI: http://dx.doi.org/10.1111/isj.12024
11. Clemens Nylandsted Klokmose and Michel Beaudouin-Lafon. 2009. VIGO: Instrumental Interaction in Multi-surface Environments. In *Proceedings of the SIGCHI Conference on Human Factors in Computing Systems (CHI 09)*. ACM, New York, NY, USA, 869–878. DOI: http://dx.doi.org/10.1145/1518701.1518833
12. Clemens N. Klokmose, James Eagan, Siemen Baader, Wendy Mackay, and Michel Beaudouin-Lafon. 2016. Webstrates: Demonstrating the Potential of Shareable Dynamic Media. In *Proceedings of the 19th ACM Conference on Computer Supported Cooperative Work and Social Computing Companion (CSCW 16 Companion)*. ACM, New York, NY, USA, 61–64. DOI: http://dx.doi.org/10.1145/2818052.2874325
13. W.E. Mackay. 2002. Using Video to Suppport Interaction Design. Video Tutorial distributed at CHI'02, Directed by C. Leininger, Produced by INRIA Multimedia Services. 83 minutes.
14. Kenton P. O'Hara, Michael Massimi, Richard Harper, Simon Rubens, and Jessica Morris. 2014. Everyday Dwelling with WhatsApp. In *Proceedings of the 17th ACM Conference on Computer Supported Cooperative Work & Social Computing (CSCW 14)*. ACM, New York, NY, USA, 1131–1143. DOI: http://dx.doi.org/10.1145/2531602.2531679
15. Mattias Rost, Christos Kitsos, Alexander Morgan, Martin Podlubny, Pietro Romeo, Edoardo Russo, and Matthew Chalmers. 2016. Forget-me-not: History-less Mobile Messaging. In *Proceedings of the 2016 CHI Conference on Human Factors in Computing Systems (CHI 16)*. ACM, New York, NY, USA, 1904–1908. DOI: http://dx.doi.org/10.1145/2858036.2858347
16. Lauren E. Scissors and Darren Gergle. 2013. "Back and Forth, Back and Forth": Channel Switching in Romantic Couple Conflict. In *Proceedings of the 2013 Conference on Computer Supported Cooperative Work (CSCW 13)*. ACM, New York, NY, USA, 237–248. DOI: http://dx.doi.org/10.1145/2441776.2441804
17. Irina Shklovski, Louise Barkhuus, Nis Bornoe, and Joseph 'Jofish' Kaye. 2015. Friendship Maintenance in the Digital Age: Applying a Relational Lens to Online Social Interaction. In *Proceedings of the 18th ACM Conference on Computer Supported Cooperative Work & Social Computing (CSCW 15)*. ACM, New York, NY, USA, 1477–1487. DOI: http://dx.doi.org/10.1145/2675133.2675294
18. Norman Makoto Su. 2009. Temporal Patterns of Communication: Media Combos. In *Proceedings of the ACM 2009 International Conference on Supporting Group Work (GROUP 09)*. ACM, New York, NY, USA, 387–388. DOI: http://dx.doi.org/10.1145/1531674.1531737

# I Need Your Encouragement! Requesting Supportive Comments on Social Media Reduces Test Anxiety

**Robert Deloatch, Brian P. Bailey, Alex Kirlik, Craig Zilles**
Department of Computer Science
University of Illinois
Urbana, IL 61801
{deloatc2, bpbailey, kirlik, zilles}@illinois.edu

### ABSTRACT
Many students underperform on exams due to experiencing high test anxiety. We report on a study comparing a novel intervention of seeking support from one's social network to the more common approaches of expressive writing and studying task-relevant materials for simulated open-ended test questions. We measured in-the-moment (state) anxiety before and after each intervention, and correctness of the solutions. We also surveyed students to learn about their perceptions of the interventions. Our results showed that social support decreased the anxiety of high test-anxious students by 21% with the reduction in anxiety correlating with the number of messages received. Social support also allowed high test-anxious students to score at the level of low test-anxious students. Expressive writing showed a similar effect, but increased the anxiety of low test-anxious students by 61%. Studying task materials had no effect on anxiety and high test-anxious students performed worse than low test-anxious students. Despite benefiting from social support, we found that students were uncomfortable soliciting support from their online social network. Realizing the benefits of this approach may therefore require different formulations of social support in practice.

### Author Keywords
Anxiety; social support; expressive writing; programming.

### ACM Classification Keywords
H.5.3 [Information Interface and Presentation]: Group and Organization Interfaces--Collaborative computing.

### INTRODUCTION
Students who experience high levels of test anxiety perform worse on exams [37], and struggle with absent-mindedness, feelings of sickness, and irrelevant thinking [10, 34]. High test anxiety can also have adverse long-term effects on grade history, general anxiety, and classroom behavior [1].


*CHI 2017, May 06-11, 2017, Denver, CO, USA*
© 2017 ACM. ISBN 978-1-4503-4655-9/17/05...$15.00
DOI: http://dx.doi.org/10.1145/3025453.3025709

Test anxiety may be particularly acute for students taking exams with open-ended problems. These types of problems introduce more uncertainty over how to approach solutions, the constraints must be quickly understood, mistakes made early can inhibit later choices, and it is more difficult to guess a correct solution [41]. Open-ended problems are often encountered on exams in computing, among other disciplines. Here students must not only address the challenges of solving open-ended problems, but must also manage the uncertainty related to the use of the programming tools required to construct the solution (e.g. compilation or runtime errors).

HCI and related research offer several possible approaches to reduce test anxiety during exams. One approach is to provide test anxious students with social support. For instance, prior work has shown that facilitating group discussions before an anagram task increased the number of correct solutions for students with high test anxiety [37]. A second approach is the use of expressive writing. Expressive writing is a form of therapy where people write about a past incident by recording their thoughts and feelings [32]. Ramirez and Beilock showed that expressive writing increased exam scores for high text anxious students for a multiple choice test [34]. However, these approaches have never been empirically compared, and neither has been tested for open-ended exam questions.

We report on a study investigating a novel application of social media for reducing test anxiety. Students posted a request for encouragement to their online social network (Facebook) and read the responses prior to solving open-ended programming problems. We compared this approach to the widely studied anxiety intervention of expressive writing and a control condition (N=88). In the expressive writing condition, students wrote about their thoughts and feelings regarding the tasks they were about to perform. In the control condition, students read task-relevant material to simulate common student behavior of reviewing course notes before an exam. An incentive scheme was applied to further simulate the stress of an authentic exam situation. We measured in-the-moment (state) anxiety before and after each intervention, and the correctness of the programming solutions. The Cognitive Test Anxiety scale was used to categorize high and low test anxiety students.

Students were also surveyed to learn about their perceptions of the interventions used.

Our study produced three main findings. First, our results showed that reading supportive messages decreased the in-the-moment (state) anxiety of high test-anxious students by 21%. Supportive messages also allowed the high test-anxious students to achieve scores on the programming tasks that were similar to that of low test-anxious students. Second, we found that the number of messages received was positively correlated ($r^2$=0.30, p=0.002) with the reduction in anxiety, while less substantive interactions, such as 'likes', had a non-significant correlation ($r^2$=0.10). However, our qualitative results showed that students were reluctant to solicit supportive messages from their own social network. Therefore, realizing the benefits of this approach may require exploring different formulations of social support in practice. Third, we found that expressive writing also allowed high test-anxious students to perform similarly to low test-anxious students. However, this intervention increased the state anxiety of low test-anxious students by 61%. Taken together, our results advocate for the use of a social support intervention for those students who generally experience high text anxiety.

Our work makes three contributions to the CHI community. First, our results provide empirical understanding for using a social media intervention to lower anxiety and increase performance on a simulated exam. Second, we report how the appropriation of social media for anxiety reduction compares to the more widely studied approach of expressive writing. Third, we extend prior work on test anxiety interventions to open-ended programming problems. We believe these contributions can be applied to help students perform better in evaluative situations.

## RELATED WORK

We describe test anxiety and situate the choice of measures in our study. We also describe how social support and expressive writing have been used to reduce anxiety for various tasks, and situate these methods in the context of other possible anxiety interventions. Last, we describe the unique characteristics of open-ended questions on exams.

### Measures and Studies of Test Anxiety

Test anxiety is a combination of physiological and emotional responses that occur while preparing for and during testing situations [1]. It has been found to negatively correlate with scores on achievement tests, problem-solving and memory tasks, course grades, and cumulative GPA [18]. When test anxiety is reduced, increases in aptitude and standardized tests, as well as GPA have been observed [18].

Previous studies have found that between 25-41% of students experience test anxiety, with higher numbers reported in women and students of color [1, 27, 33]. Another recent study found 22% of high test-anxious students have no method of coping with it [15]. High test-anxious students display strong fears of negative evaluation and lower levels of self-esteem [18]. They also show an increase in the number of distracting thoughts and test-irrelevant thinking when in a testing situation [5, 20, 37].

In our study, we chose two methods to measure anxiety. We used the Cognitive Test Anxiety scale (CTA) to measure test anxiety. CTA has a rich history of being used to measure the cognitive aspects of test anxiety including task-irrelevant thinking and lapses in attention [10]. We also used the State Trait Anxiety Inventory (STAI) form. The state portion of the STAI is used to measure anxiety in the moment while the trait portion is used to measure anxiety of the person [43]. Many other measures of anxiety and test anxiety exist [6, 11, 36, 38, 39]. However, we chose the CTA and STAI because they have been validated and are relatively straightforward to administer.

### Social Support

Social support is defined as an "interpersonal transaction in which one can rely on others for information, help, and advice" [30]. It consists of several categories, including emotional support (e.g. encouragement, sympathy, love), instrumental aid (e.g. providing material aid or behavior assistance), companionship (e.g. spending time with others during leisure time), and informational support (e.g. guidance) [40]. CHI researchers have examined the effects of social support in education. For example, Saerbeck et. al. showed that a socially supportive robot helped children score higher on a language test and report higher intrinsic and task motivation than children in a neutral condition [35]. Kao and Harrell showed that an encouraging message, such as "You're doing well," shown while participants were playing a STEM learning game improved the experience of the game for players [22]. Other researchers in the HCI community have examined how social media is leveraged for support when experiencing life events, such as gender transition or job loss [9, 16]. Online health communities have also been investigated as a source of social support [26, 29, 46]. For example, Newman et al. studied how seeking social support in online health communities and social networks can provide emotional support, accountability, and motivation [29]. Wang et al. found that members of online health communities who receive emotional support participate longer than members receiving only informational support [46].

Researchers in the behavioral sciences have begun to study the impact of social support on test anxiety. For example, Sarason showed that students who participated in either a group discussion or overheard a supportive message directed toward another student before completing an anagram task, scored higher than students that did not participate in the discussion or overhear the message [37]. These effects were even more favorable for high test-anxious students. Additionally, Kimbler showed that a single emotionally supportive message before completing the Everyday Problem Solving Test reduced the number of distracting thoughts participants experienced and increased task performance [23]. The buffering hypothesis offers one explanation for how these beneficial effects are realized; social support reduces the negative emotions that occur when appraising an evaluative situation [12].

In our study, we synthesize and extend these threads of prior work by developing a novel intervention for test anxiety reduction where students request social support by leveraging their online social network. Our work is also original in that it compares this and two other interventions for anxiety reduction for open-ended programming tasks.

### Expressive Writing

Expressive writing has been widely studied as an anxiety reduction technique. McKeachie, Pollie, and Speisman conducted early research on reducing anxiety during classroom exams. By studying student performance on a multiple-choice psychology exam, they found that student scores increased when the problems contained sections for writing comments about the exam. They attributed this performance increase to a decrease in anxiety [28].

Other researchers showed that writing about one's thoughts and feelings before arithmetic problems or an exam increased math accuracy and exam scores, respectively, for students when compared to students who were asked to think about task-irrelevant topics before the same evaluation. The expressive writing task was shown to be especially beneficial for students with high test anxiety or high math anxiety [31, 34]. Lang used a writing exercise to heighten student self-perceptions of their knowledge. The writing exercise increased the scores of high test-anxious high school students on an intelligence test, while lowering the scores of low test-anxious students [25]. A proposed theory for this effect is that writing about worries before the task unburdens working memory during the task, making it available to focus on the evaluative task [31].

This prior work shows that expressive writing can reduce student test anxiety. However, the research on expressive writing as a test anxiety intervention focuses on its use in forced-choice problems. Our research extends the study of an expressive writing intervention to open-ended problems where there is more uncertainty related to solution generation [41]. We also compare expressive writing to social support and reading task-related materials for anxiety reduction, and analyze student perceptions of these interventions.

### Other Anxiety Interventions

There are approaches for anxiety reduction beyond social support and expressive writing. One approach is to work with a trained professional on relaxation and desensitization procedures [14, 49]. Hembree's meta-analytic study found that this approach reduces anxiety but found mixed results for increasing cognitive performance [18]. Another approach, cognitive behavioral therapy, can also be effective for decreasing test anxiety and raising test performance [18]. These two approaches are helpful for those experiencing severe anxiety, but the drawback is that they require working with a trained professional. A third approach is to modify the exams, such as adjusting item difficulty order or integrating humor into exam questions [6, 13, 49]. The generalizability of this approach is unclear, however, since it relies on individual interpretations of difficulty or humor.

Of the possible approaches for anxiety reduction, we chose to compare social support and expressive writing, in addition to a control condition, in the current study. We chose these approaches because they have been shown to be effective for anxiety reduction in other task situations, can be widely applied through technology, and can be implemented without training or a trained therapist.

### Anxiety and Open-ended Questions

Prior work on test anxiety interventions focused on forced-choice questions. Though often used, the limitations of this format include the inability to effectively assess problem solving and creativity [4, 17]. In contrast, open-ended questions are considered to better measure these attributes but students perceive increased anxiety and uncertainty when solving them [42, 48]. For example, Zeidner showed that students found open-ended essay exams more difficult, complex, and anxiety provoking than multiple-choice exams [48]. Additionally, Schmidt and Crocker showed that low test-anxious students performed better on open-ended exams and high test-anxious students performed better on multiple-choice exams [42]. Lastly, Deloatch et al. showed that students report moderate to high levels of anxiety when solving open-ended programming problems on exams and 21% of students reported having no method of coping [15]. Our motivation for using open-ended programming problems was due to our interest in computer science assessment and the paucity of literature on the effectiveness of anxiety reduction techniques to help students solve open-ended problems.

## RESEARCH QUESTIONS

The goal of our study was to answer the following research questions:

1. How do social support and expressive writing affect the anxiety experienced by students prior to an exam situation?
2. How does the level of student anxiety relate to the correctness of programming solutions on an exam?
3. How do students feel about seeking social support or expressive writing to reduce anxiety prior to an exam?

With these questions, we want to produce empirical knowledge for how to reduce student anxiety and increase performance for exams with open-ended problems.

*Please take the next 7 minutes to write as openly as possible about your thoughts and feelings regarding the programming problems you are about to perform. In your writing, I want you to really let yourself go and explore your emotions and thoughts, as you are getting ready to start the problems. You might relate your current thoughts to the way you have felt during other similar situations at school or in other situations in your life. Please try to be as open as possible as you write about your thoughts at this time. The text you write will only be viewed in aggregate and your response will not be evaluated. When the timer at the bottom expires you will move to the next page. Please start writing.*

**Figure 1. Prompt for the expressive writing condition.**

## METHOD

To answer these research questions, we performed a single factor between-subjects controlled experiment. The factor was Anxiety Intervention (social support vs. expressive writing vs. control). Participants were randomly split into groups representing each condition. Next, we describe the participants, programming tasks, interventions, and measures.

### Participants

Participants were recruited via an email sent to all undergraduate students in the computer science department (1,235) at a large mid-western university. Additionally, an instructor sent an email to all students currently enrolled in a Spring 2016 Data Structures course (600). Participants enrolled in the course received extra credit whereas other participants received $10. Additionally, participants were entered into a multi-winner lottery for $100. In total we had 88 participants complete all parts of the experiment.

Our participants were 78% men, 20% women, with 2% not responding. Most participants (94%) were enrolled in the Spring 2016 Data Structures course. Participants were mostly engineering students majoring in computer science (52%), computer engineering (16%), and electrical engineering (7%). Just over half (51%) of participants were in their first year, 30% in their second year, 14% in their third year, and 5% in their fourth year. About one-third (31%) of participants reported having previously used Facebook to request encouragement from their social network.

### Programming Tasks

The two programming problems chosen for this study included a binary tree task and linked list manipulation and were to be completed in C++. For the first problem, participants were asked to write a function that returns the number of nodes in a binary tree that have exactly one child. This problem was selected because it used concepts of recursion and data structures that students in our curriculum were expected to be familiar with. The second problem was a modification of a question from a prior midterm in the course. It required participants to write a

*Hi friends, I need your encouragement. I will be competing in a computer programming challenge on Monday. I will have the opportunity to view comments and likes you put on this post during the challenge. I will also be able to see private messages. I won't be able to respond to any of your messages at that time, but I will be able to read them. Any supportive comments would be great to see.*

**Figure 2. The template text participants in the social support condition adapted and posted to Facebook.**

function that removed nodes from a singly linked list if the node's string data element was longer than a given threshold. The function had to return the number of nodes removed and the resulting changed linked list. These two problems had many viable solutions in terms of memory efficiency, complexity, and choice of language constructs. No two participants produced identical solutions to either problem. Participants were provided with a source code text editor with the ability to compile and run their code. We estimated that students were expected to complete each problem within 20 minutes, so we provided participants with 40 minutes to complete the two problems. A pilot study revealed participants believed the problems were appropriate for their level of knowledge and that the amount of time provided was adequate.

### Anxiety Interventions

Our study compared two interventions, expressive writing and social support, and a control condition of reading task-relevant information. The interventions were administered prior to participants performing the programming tasks. For expressive writing, following the procedures described in prior work [31, 34], participants were given the prompt shown in Figure 1 and wrote their response into an online form. Participants in the social support condition adapted a template message and posted it to their Facebook timeline the day before the experiment (see Figure 2). They were informed that just prior to the experiment, they could view the likes, comments, and private messages associated with their post. Participants were instructed to refrain from viewing the responses until they arrived for the study. We chose to implement social support using a social media platform because the approach is scalable, accessible, and fast; features which we believe would increase the likelihood that students would use this approach in practice and receive timely responses. We chose Facebook since it's network is based on social relationships. In the control condition, participants read general information regarding computer programming data structures before completing the programming tasks. The control condition was intended to simulate common student behavior of reviewing course material immediately before an exam.

### Procedure

After informed consent, participants completed an online form asking about their years of programming experience, C++ experience, and gender. In addition, participants

**Figure 3. A summary of the experimental procedure. Participants were briefed and completed the state anxiety form. Participants then performed the assigned intervention and completed the state anxiety form again. The coding tasks were then performed, followed by a survey.**

completed the Cognitive Test Anxiety instrument and the *trait* portion of the State-Trait Anxiety Inventory (STAI).

Participants were also asked about their willingness to post a message to Facebook as part of the study and if they have ever used Facebook to solicit social support. Finally, participants completed a five-question multiple choice pre-test without any outside assistance. The pre-test focused on basic data structures, runtime complexity, and C++ syntax. The pre-test was used to ensure participants had a basic understanding of programming.

Participants assigned to the social support condition were asked to adapt a template message and post it to their Facebook timeline (Figure 2). They were informed that they could modify the text to fit their style, but any modification should still convey the message of when the programming task occurs, that they will have the opportunity to read the responses, and that supportive comments would be valued.

Upon arriving at the study location, our experiment followed the process shown in Figure 3. An experimenter instructed participants that they would have forty minutes to complete two programming problems and described the remuneration. The experimenter then presented a scenario designed to induce increased anxiety. Participants were informed that they would receive an additional \$100 for earning a perfect score on the programming problems and \$10 if each member of their assigned group, determined by arrival order, scored at least a 75% score on the problems. We believe this created an increased anxiety scenario due to previous work on simulating exam situations by using monetary incentives along with pressure to perform well relative to peers [34]. A pilot study also revealed that participants reported feeling increased anxiety if they could see the members of their group working and if they thought that they should be able to complete the problems. Thus, groups were assigned in view of participants and they were told that the programming problems were based on their expertise as measured by the pre-test problems.

After hearing this information, participants logged on to a lab computer and worked in view of other participants. This design was also employed to mimic authentic exam situations where students can see each other when working. In the lab, students first completed the *state* portion of the STAI to obtain a pre-condition state anxiety measurement.

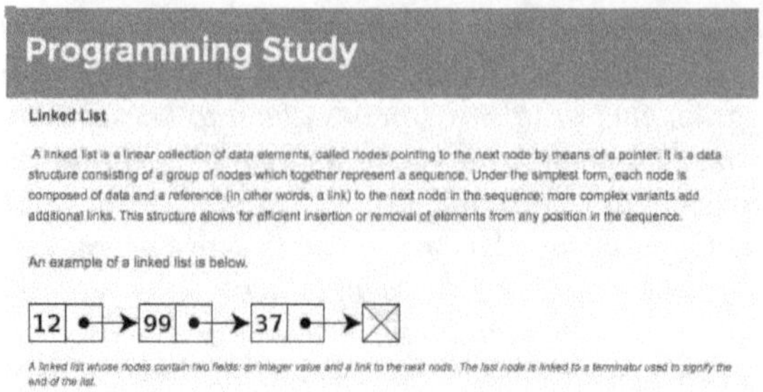


**Figure 4. The task relevant information read by participants in the control condition.**

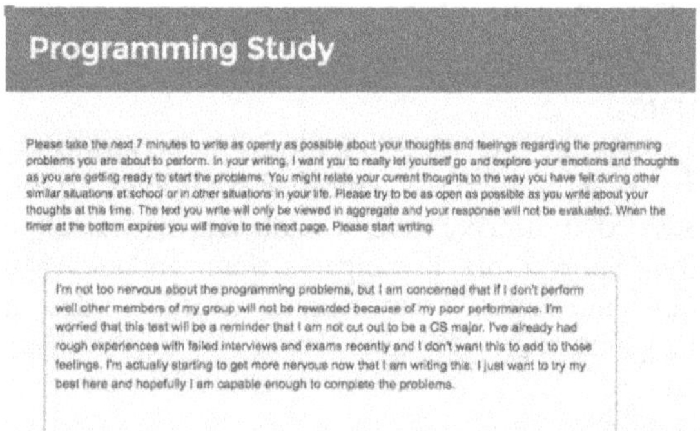


**Figure 5. The user interface and prompt for the expressive writing condition. Participants read the prompt and entered their response.**

**Figure 6. An example Facebook Timeline post made by a participant in the social support condition. The post was made to Facebook to elicit encouraging responses from friends. Names were redacted for anonymity.**

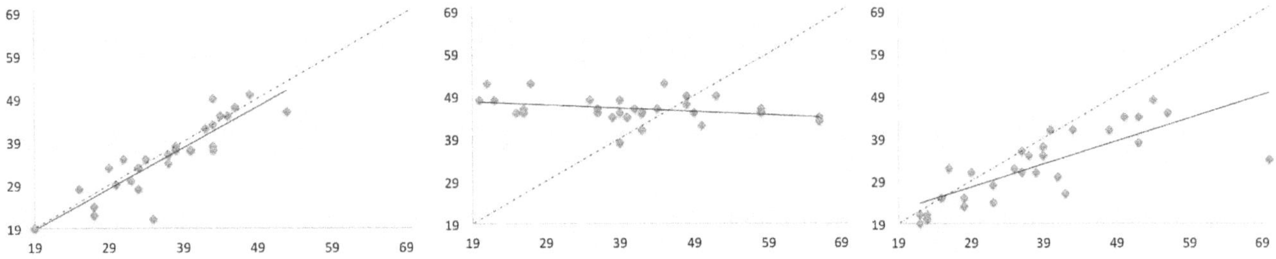

**Figure 7. State anxieties before (X-axis) and after (Y-axis) the assigned anxiety interventions. The graphs show results for the control (left), expressive writing (middle), and social support (right) conditions. The dotted line indicates perfect correlation and the solid line is the regression line for the data ($R^2$=0.8; 0.1; 0.61, respectively).**

Participants then performed a seven-minute intervention based on the assigned condition. Control group participants read relevant material on data structures and answered three questions about the text (Figure 4). Participants in the expressive writing condition were presented with the interface in Figure 5 and typed their response. Participants in the social support condition viewed the comments, likes, and private messages they received from their prior post. They were asked to report the number of responses received and which response made them feel most supported. An example post with responses is shown in Figure 6. As a manipulation check, participants reported their perception of how supportive the responses to the post were.

After completing the intervention, all participants completed the *state* portion of the STAI again to obtain a post-intervention measurement. Participants were then presented with two programming tasks and had 40 minutes to complete them. Afterward, participants completed a survey that focused on their perceptions of how the control, expressive writing, or social support activity affected their anxiety and if they would perform a similar activity before a course exam.

### Measures

The Cognitive Test Anxiety scale (CTA) and the State Trait Anxiety Inventory (STAI) were used to measure participant cognitive test, state, and trait anxieties. The CTA is a 27-item questionnaire that focuses on behaviors before and during testing, including task-irrelevant thinking, making comparisons to others, and lapses in attention. It ranges from 27 (lowest anxiety) to 108 (highest anxiety). Previous studies classify a sample of participants as low or high test-anxious based on scoring in higher or lower percentiles [10, 34]. The STAI measures state (of the moment) and trait (of the person) anxiety with two twenty-item questionnaires. Each questionnaire ranges in score from 20 (lowest anxiety) to 80 (highest anxiety). Due to experimenter oversight, the state portion of the STAI was measured using nineteen of the twenty items, adjusting the range from 19 to 76. We believe the effects of this omission on our data to be inconsequential.

The final survey consisted of two five-point Likert scale questions: "[Intervention] helped reduce my stress or anxiety" and "I would [intervention] before a course exam," where [intervention] reflected the condition. The questions ranged from 1 (Strongly Disagree) to 5 (Strongly Agree). We asked participants to explain their rating. Our goal was to gauge student perceptions of the assigned anxiety intervention. The open-ended responses were partitioned into idea units. Thematic codes were assigned to each unit on an initial pass, and subsequent passes were made to group similar themes into more abstract categories until they were reasonably exclusive. The programming problems were scored using input test cases and ranged from 0-100, with both problems weighted equally. Evaluations were performed blind to condition.

| | CTA | Trait | State |
|---|---|---|---|
| CTA | 1 | -- | -- |
| Trait Anxiety | 0.64** | 1 | -- |
| Initial State Anxiety | 0.73** | 0.60** | 1 |

**Table 1. The correlations between the anxiety metrics. The CTA, trait anxiety, and initial state anxiety had moderate positive correlations. ** Indicates significance at the p < .001 level.**

### RESULTS

ANOVAs confirmed that participants in each condition did not differ for their initial state anxiety, C++ experience, cognitive test anxiety, trait anxiety, and pre-test scores. Additionally, we found that the CTA, state, and trait anxiety metrics had moderately positive correlations, as expected, and are reported in Table 1.

A Wilcoxon signed rank test revealed that participants in the social support condition found the responses they received to be supportive, ($\mu$=4.62, $\sigma$=0.82, $p < .001$, $d$=2.80), confirming our manipulation and corroborating prior work [7]. The average number of likes, comments, and private messages per post were 41.8, 12.5, and 1.38, respectively.

Figure 7 shows the state anxiety of participants before and after the assigned anxiety intervention. From the plots, we saw that participants in the control group were largely unaffected by the task relevant reading activity. They also show that participants in the social support and expressive

| | Low CTA | High CTA | All |
|---|---|---|---|
| Control | 32 (7.9) | 39.3 (8.8) | 36.3 (8.4) |
| | 29.2 (7.1) | 38.1 (8.9) | 35.1 (8.9) |
| | 12 | 8 | 29 |
| Writing | 28.7 (7.2) | 47.7 (10.0) | 40.6 (12.3) |
| | 47 (2.9) | 44.4 (2.5) | 46 (3.1) |
| | 11 | 15 | 30 |
| Social | 28.7 (7.0) | 46.6 (10.4) | 37.9 (11.9) |
| | 26.2 (6.7) | 36.8 (6.4) | 32.3 (8.3) |
| | 11 | 12 | 29 |

**Table 2. The pre / post state anxiety scores grouped by condition and CTA cluster. For each condition, the initial state anxiety (SD) is on the top row, the post state anxiety (SD) is on the second row, and the number of participants is on the third.**

writing conditions were affected differently and we discuss these differences below.

### Effects on Anxiety

Table 2 shows the means for the initial state anxiety and the post state anxiety for each condition. We computed the difference between the two state anxiety measurements for each participant. We conducted a one-way ANCOVA with the difference scores as the dependent variable and anxiety intervention as the factor. The Cognitive Test Anxiety score was included as a covariate. Results showed a main effect ($F(2,82)=21.59$, $p < 0.001$). Post hoc comparisons showed that the social support condition (μ=5.67) had a larger decrease in anxiety than the control condition (μ=1.28). Also, the control condition had a larger decrease in anxiety than the expressive writing condition (μ=-5.3).

We performed a correlational analysis between the social media interactions (likes, comments, and private messages) and anxiety difference scores. The more substantive responses (comments and private messages), which we collectively refer to as *messages*, were compared to less substantive "likes". We found a moderately positive relationship between the number of messages received and anxiety difference scores ($r=0.55$, $p=0.002$, n=29), whereas the relationship between likes and anxiety difference scores was not significant ($r=0.32$, $p=0.09$, n=29).

Based on our main result and prior work we classified participants as "Low anxiety" if they scored in the bottom 40$^{th}$ percentile on the CTA and as "High anxiety" if they scored in the upper 40$^{th}$ percentile [10]. Table 2 shows the mean state anxiety before and after the intervention for each classification.

We performed an ANOVA with anxiety difference as the dependent variable and the CTA cluster and intervention as factors. For the control condition, we found no difference between the two CTA clusters on the difference scores, $F(1,18)=0.79$, $p=0.39$. For the social support condition, the analysis showed that the "High Anxiety" participants experienced a larger decrease in anxiety (μ=9.8) than the "Low Anxiety" participants (μ=2.5; $F(1, 21)=5.76$, $p=0.03$). For the expressive writing condition, the "Low Anxiety" participants experienced a larger increase in anxiety (μ=-18.3) than the "High Anxiety" participants (μ=3.3; $F(1,24)=30.13$, $p < 0.001$). These results indicate that social support decreased anxiety, especially for the "High Anxiety" participants, whereas expressive writing increased the anxiety for "Low Anxiety" participants.

| | Low CTA | High CTA | All |
|---|---|---|---|
| Control | 77.4 (29.8) | 38.3 (24.9) | 63.2 (30.9) |
| Writing | 74.1 (25.6) | 54.4 (28.2) | 61.2 (31.3) |
| Social | 62.7 (20.5) | 67.4 (38.1) | 67.6 (31.8) |

**Table 3. Means and (SD) of the programming task scores grouped by condition and CTA cluster.**

### Effects on Performance

To examine how the anxiety intervention affected the correctness of the programming solutions, we conducted a one-way ANCOVA using Cognitive Test Anxiety score as a covariate. Results showed an interaction between factors ($F(2,82)=3.24$, $p = 0.04$). To examine it we performed an ANOVA with correctness of solutions as the dependent variable and the CTA classification and anxiety intervention as factors. The results can be seen in Table 3.

For the social support condition, the "High Anxiety" (μ=67.4, σ=38.1) and "Low Anxiety" (μ=62.7, σ=20.5) participants showed no difference in the correctness of programming solutions (F(1,21)=0.13, $p=0.724$, $d=0.15$). Additionally, a correlational analysis between the social media interactions and performance scores revealed no significant relationships. In the expressive writing condition, our analysis showed a large noticeable difference between the means of the "High Anxiety" (μ=54.4,σ=28.2) and "Low Anxiety" (μ=74.1, σ=25.6) participants, but the analysis showed only a marginal effect (F(1,24)=3.32, $p=0.08$, $d=0.70$). Consistent with prior work, in the control condition the "High Anxiety" participants scored significantly worse on the programming solutions (μ=38.3, σ=24.9) than the "Low Anxiety" participants (μ=77.4, σ=29.8; F(1,18)=9.35, $p=0.007$, $d=1.16$). Together, these results indicate that both social support and expressive writing allowed the high test anxiety participants to perform as well as the low anxiety participants.

### Participant Perceptions

We asked participants in the social support condition to explain which post made them feel most supported. We found that the authors of the posts participants identified included close friends, family members, people they admired, and friends who the participant had not recently communicated with. For example, one participant stated,

"*One of my friends privately reached out to me to express her support. She is one of my smartest friends, and it felt comforting to have her support going into this challenge.* (P62)" We also found various reasons for why the particular post made them feel supported, including it increased their confidence, put them at ease, made them laugh, or was unexpected. Some participants stated the effort others made by writing personal responses, finding supportive quotes from noteworthy people, or praying on behalf of the participant encouraged them. For example, one participant stated that their family member said, "*You do your best work with the word 'challenge' in it. Prayers are starting as of now.*" This participant said it was "*encouraging to know that she was taking time out of her day to pray for me.* (P71)"

To evaluate responses about how participants perceived the effects of the assigned intervention on their anxiety, we conducted Wilcoxon signed rank tests on responses to the question "[Intervention] helped reduce my stress or anxiety." [Intervention] was replaced by the assigned condition. We used a Bonferroni adjustment on our significance threshold to be $p$=0.05/3=0.016. We found that the control and writing conditions had moderate effect sizes on perceived anxiety compared to a Neutral response, but were not significant: ($\mu$=3.45, $\sigma$=1.05, $p$=0.04, d=0.60) and ($\mu$=3.3, $\sigma$=0.92, $p$=0.09, $d$=0.46) respectively. In the social support condition, participants reported the responses significantly decreased their perceived anxiety ($\mu$=3.59, $\sigma$=0.63, $p < 0.001$, $d$=1.33) when compared to a Neutral response. These results are consistent with our findings using the STAI measure.

From the open-ended responses explaining their rating, the main theme from the social support condition was "Emotionally Beneficial" (n=31). The "n=" indicates how many occurrences of this theme were in the data based on our previously mentioned coding scheme. This theme focused on liking the encouragement received and its ability to help them relax and increase their confidence. One participant stated, "*They restored my self-confidence,*" (P77) when referring to the Facebook friends that left responses on their post. In the expressive writing condition, the two largest themes were "Emotionally Beneficial" and "Not Useful." The "Emotionally Beneficial" theme (n=13) stated that the activity helped them feel better, and reduced their anxiety. For example, one participant stated, "*After I write down the feeling I can calm down easier. (P45)*" The other theme was "Not useful" (n=8). Participants in this theme stated that the activity did not affect them. For example, one participant stated, "*I don't think it really helped that much with reducing any anxiety that I had.* (P34)" Finally, in the control condition, three themes emerged: "Mentally Beneficial," "Emotionally Beneficial," and "Not Useful." The "Mentally Beneficial" theme (n=11) contained responses that stated the reading helped refresh their memory or gave them an idea of what to expect. For example, one participant stated that it "*helped me gather my thoughts*" and was a "*valuable refresher that helped me to remember the general ideas which made it easier to think of the finer details later on. (P15)*" The "Emotionally Beneficial" theme (n=10) contained responses about increases in confidence and decreases in anxiety or stress. For example, one participant stated that the reading "*helped boost my confidence*, (P16)" and another stated that it "*put me at ease.* (P25)" Participants in the "Not Useful" theme (n=11) made statements such as "*It did nothing for me (P29)*" or "*I knew nearly everything that was written. (P2)*"

For the second question, "I would like to use [intervention] before a course exam," we conducted one-sample Wilcoxon signed rank tests on the responses, and adjusted our significance threshold using a Bonferroni adjustment ($p$=0.05/3=0.016). Our results showed that participants in the writing condition showed no difference from a Neutral response in how they answered the question ($\mu$=2.77, $\sigma$=1.14, $p$=0.25, $d$=0.29). Participants in the control condition strongly favored referring to notes before an exam over a Neutral option ($\mu$=4.0, $\sigma$=0.86, $p < 0.001$, $d$=1.67). Additionally, participants in the social support condition reported they would not elicit support of their Facebook friends before a course exam ($\mu$=2.34, $\sigma$=1.14, $p$=0.005, $d$=0.81).

The open-ended responses explaining the rating revealed two themes in the control condition: "Reinforcement" and "Information Dependent." For "Reinforcement" (n=15), participants stated that they would prefer to read course notes before an exam because it boosted their confidence, provided a refresher, and calmed them. One participant stated, "*I would like to read before exam. Because it helps me to review the topic in class and gives me more confidence. (P7)*" For "Information Dependent" (n=5), participants stated that they would like to review course notes before an exam only if they did not know the material. One participant stated, "*If I wasn't well versed in a topic, it would be extremely helpful to read general information before taking an exam.* (P8)"

In the writing condition, there were two major themes: "Alternative" and "Positive Experience." For "Alternative" (n=19), participants stated that they found the writing exercise ineffective and in some cases felt it increased their anxiety. Participants also stated they would rather engage in other activities, such as reviewing course notes. For example, one participant stated, "*I am just too nervous to think of doing so before taking exams. I would rather read more review materials, maybe. Lol.* (P44)" For "Positive Experience" (n=7) participants stated that expressive writing calmed them or helped them organize their thoughts. For example, one participant stated, "*I think that I may benefit from writing about thoughts before an exam.* (P55)"

The most common theme in the social support condition was "Uncomfortable" (n=29). In this theme, participants stated that they would not like to rely on others or felt it was uncharacteristic for them to broadcast messages for encouragement. For example, one participant stated, "*While I would like reading encouraging responses before an exam, I would not like posting to Facebook because this behavior seems attention seeking and slightly annoying in my opinion. (P88)*" Another participant stated, "I *would not post to Facebook like this again. It's not something that people do, and such a post is definitely out of place. I would, however, consider using a more passive and ephemeral media like Snapchat or Yik Yak. That has the benefits of not breaking social norms on FB.* (P74)"

## DISCUSSION

Our study investigated how social support and expressive writing impact the state anxiety and solution correctness of open-ended programming problems for students. The results showed that supportive messages from a student's social network decreased the state anxiety of high test-anxious students by 21% before performing a mentally stressful activity. Further, the results showed that the number of messages (comments and private messages) received correlated with the reduction in anxiety, whereas the number of 'likes' did not correlate. They also showed that when completing programming tasks under pressure, supportive messages and expressive writing allowed high test-anxious students to perform similarly to low test-anxious students. However, expressive writing increased the anxiety of low test-anxious students by 61%, whereas the social support condition did not. Additionally, studying task-relevant materials had no effect on anxiety and high test-anxious students scored lower than low test-anxious students. Though the quantitative data favored the social support intervention, all of the students reported through the surveys that they were uncomfortable leveraging their online social network to elicit support. The discomfort stemmed from the public nature of the posts and concerns about being perceived as attention seeking.

Information disclosure research has shown that disclosing private information is perceived to be inappropriate for public posts on Facebook [3]. Participants may therefore have felt that asking for encouragement was too private to post on Facebook in our study. Additionally, previous work has shown that people perceive risks of being vulnerable when disclosing private information such as negative outcomes [50]. As a majority of the participants in our study were computer science students, the competitive environment of the curriculum may also have led to concerns about how others would perceive them [2]. They may have felt that such statuses could harm relations in group project settings. Further research is needed to understand if participants were uncomfortable with the specific formulation of seeking social support in our study or with seeking social support online generally.

Different formulations of seeking social support online, such as giving users more control over the audience, ephemerality, anonymity of the requests, and rhetorical strategies should be considered. Lists with only certain members of a user's social circle could be used to better control disclosure while still reaching a wide audience. For example, Haimson found that people undergoing gender transition used lists to manage their disclosure [16]. Reducing the length of time messages are visible to a social network by controlling ephemerality could also increase comfort. For example, Xu et al. found that participants had fewer concerns over self-presentation when using Snapchat (which allows ephemeral messages) compared to other communication tools [47]. Anonymity, such as on Yik Yak or Facebook Confessions Boards, has been shown to increase comfort as people are more willing to disclose to strangers [21]. Additionally, different rhetorical strategies have been shown to effect response rates in online communities [8]. In the context of this study, different strategies could include the phrasing of the requests and how much information is revealed pertaining to the request. Future work is needed to test how these formulations would affect students' comfort levels when seeking social support online, balanced against the speed, volume, and quality of the messages received.

Instructors who prefer not to use any social media platform could write and share supportive messages with students. For instance, students could be reminded of previous assignments where their performance was commendable. Instructors could also organize course-restricted online discussions where students could exchange supportive thoughts prior to exams.

Our results also contribute to understanding how expressive writing affects the anxiety and programming correctness of students. Previous work has suggested that expressive writing increases the performance of higher test anxious participants on exams, modular arithmetic tasks, and anagram tasks [31, 34]. Our results support this and extend this finding to open-ended tasks, such as programming. We also extend prior work by showing expressive writing negatively impacts the state anxiety of lower test anxious students. By expanding the scope of measures considered in prior work to also include student perceptions, we were able to learn that students with lower test anxiety felt the expressive writing "made them aware of their own anxiety," and "amplified their nervousness."

Social association with other participants and experimenter empathy has previously been found to aid in performance on anagram tasks [37]. Our work focuses on social support from members of a student's social network. Our findings show that supportive messages from Facebook friends help high test-anxious students score similarly to low test-anxious students on programming tasks. Additionally, our findings extend the literature by showing that reading supportive messages before performing open-ended tasks under pressure decreases the state anxiety of students.

### Limitations

One limitation of this study is that all participants attended the same university and the majority were peers in the same course. Future work is needed to generalize our findings to other courses, exam formats, and university environments. It would also be interesting to test the generalizability of our findings in other evaluative situations, such as in job interviews and programming competitions. Prior work showed that women reported increased anxiety for computer-based tests, whereas men reported decreased anxiety [15]. In our present study, we were unable to examine effects of gender or race due to insufficient sample sizes in our participant pool. Further research is needed to examine how these anxiety interventions affect different demographics.

Our study design allowed participants in the social support condition to view their supportive messages before they arrived at the experiment. We asked participants to refrain from viewing these messages, but we could not be sure that the first time participants viewed the responses was in the laboratory. This could have been controlled by constructing a more artificial study, but this may have limited the ecological validity of our experimental design. Further research is needed to understand if viewing messages more than a few minutes before a testing situation affects student test anxiety and performance.

### Future Work

We see at least three additional directions of work for reducing anxiety during programming exams. One direction is investigating how anxiety affects the coding behavior of programmers at a more granular level. For example, prior work has shown the feasibility of detecting stress by analyzing mouse and keyboard interaction [19, 24, 44, 45]. Expanding this work to understand how anxiety relates to edit, compilation, and execution behavior could lead to possible targeting of anxiety reduction methods within the programming interface. A second direction for future work focuses on how sharing the benefit that supportive messages had on anxiety and solution correctness could encourage others to adopt the strategy. Tracing how student perceptions change as they view peers seeking support may lead to less reservation around using broadcast messages for support. A third direction is studying how regularly seeking social support from one's social network affects anxiety and performance, and how it affects the response rate.

## CONCLUSION

Test anxiety is pervasive and particularly acute for open-ended questions on exams. The contribution of this work was to compare how a novel intervention implemented using social media affects student anxiety and solution quality relative to expressive writing for exams with open-ended programming questions. We found that an expressive writing intervention allowed high test-anxious students to perform as well as low test-anxious students, but increased the anxiety of low test-anxious students by 61%. We also found that supportive messages from a student's own social network decreased the anxiety of high test-anxious students by 21% and allowed them to perform similarly to low test-anxious students on programming tasks. Though the effects of this intervention are promising, our results show that many students are uncomfortable requesting social support from their online social network. Realizing the benefits of this approach may therefore require different formulations of social support in practice. It is our hope that this work will inspire instructors, researchers, and practitioners to explore methods of reducing anxiety in evaluative situations, allowing each person to perform at their best.

## ACKNOWLEDGMENTS

This research project was funded in part by the Strategic Instructional Innovation Program (SIIP) in the College of Engineering at the University of Illinois.

## REFERENCES

1. Arezou Asghari, Rusnani Abdul Kadir, Habibah Elias, and Maznah Baba. 2012. Test Anxiety and It's Related Concepts: A Brief Review. *GESJ: Education Science and Psychology* 22, 3: 3-8.
2. Lecia Jane Barker, Kathy Garvin-Doxas, and Michael Jackson. 2002. Defensive Climate in the Computer Science Classroom. In *Proceedings of the 33rd ACM Technical Symposium on Computer Science Education,* 43-47. http://dx.doi.org/10.1145/563517.563354.
3. Natalya N. Bazarova. 2012. Contents and Contexts: Disclosure Perceptions on Facebook. In *Proceedings of the 15th ACM Conference on Computer Supported Cooperative Work & Social Computing,* 369-372. http://dx.doi.org/10.1145/2145204.2145262.
4. William E. Becker and Carol Johnston. 1999. The Relationship Between Multiple Choice and Essay Response Questions in Assessing Economics Understanding. *The Economic Record* 75, 231: 348-357. http://dx.doi.org/10.1111/j.1475-4932.1999.tb02571.x.
5. Jeri Benson and Nabil El-Zahhar. 1994. Further Refinement and Validation of the Revised Test Anxiety Scale. *Structural Equation Modeling: A Multidisciplinary Journal* 1, 3: 203-221. http://dx.doi.org/10.1080/10705519409539975.
6. Ronald A. Berk and Joy Nanda. 2006. A randomized trial of humor effects on test anxiety and test performance. *Humor: International Journal of Humor Research* 19, 4: 425-454. http://dx.doi.org/10.1515/humor.2006.021.
7. Moira Burke and Mike Develin. 2016. Once More with Feeling: Supportive Responses to Social Sharing on Facebook. In *Proceedings of the 19th ACM Conference on Computer Supported Cooperative Work & Social Computing,* 1460-1472. http://dx.doi.org/10.1145/2818048.2835199.
8. Moira Burke, Elisabeth Joyce, Tackjin Kim, Vivek Anand, and Robert Kraut. 2007. Introductions and Requests: Rhetorical Strategies That Elicit Response in Online Communities. *Communities and Technologies:*

21-39. http://dx.doi.org/10.1007/978-1-84628-905-7_2.

9. Moira Burke and Robert Kraut. 2013. Using Facebook after Losing a Job: Differential Benefits of Strong and Weak Ties. In *Proceedings of the 16th ACM Conference on Computer Supported Cooperative Work & Social Computing,* 1419-1429. http://dx.doi.org/10.1145/2441776.2441936.
10. Jerrell C. Cassady and Ronald E. Johnson. 2002. Cognitive Test Anxiety and Academic Performance. *Contemporary Educational Psychology* 27, 2: 270-295. http://dx.doi.org/10.1006/ceps.2001.1094.
11. Beth G. Chung, Mark G. Ehrhart, Karen Holcombe Ehrhart, Keith Hattrup, and Jerry Solamon. 2009. Stereotype Threat, State Anxiety, and Specific Self-Efficacy as Predictors of Promotion Exam Performance. *Group & Organization Management* 35, 1: 77-107. http://dx.doi.org/10.1177/1059601109354839.
12. Sheldon Cohen and Thomas Ashby Wills. 1985. Stress, Social Support, and the Buffering Hypothesis. *Psychological Bulletin* 98, 2: 310-356. http://dx.doi.org/10.1037/0033-2909.98.2.310.
13. Jerry L. Deffenbacher, Sheila R. Deitz, and Susan L. Hazaleus. 1981. Effects of Humor and Test Anxiety on Performance, Worry, and Emotionality in Naturally Occuring Exams. *Cognitive Therapy and Research* 5, 2: 225-228. http://dx.doi.org/10.2466/pr0.1999.84.3c.1203.
14. Jerry L. Deffenbacher and Richard M. Suinn. 1988. Systematic Desensitization and the Reduction of Anxiety. *The Counseling Psychologist* 16, 1: 9-30. http://dx.doi.org/10.1177/0011000088161002.
15. Robert Deloatch, Brian P. Bailey, and Alex Kirlik. 2016. Measuring Effects of Modality on Perceived Test Anxiety for Computer Programming Exams. In *Proceedings of the 47th ACM Technical Symposium on Computing Science Education,* 291-296. http://dx.doi.org/10.1145/2839509.2844604.
16. Oliver L. Haimson, Jed R. Brubaker, Lynn Dombrowski, and Gillian R. Hayes. 2015. Disclosure, Stress, and Support During Gender Transition on Facebook. In *Proceedings of the 18th ACM Conference on Computer Supported Cooperative Work & Social Computing,* 1176-1190. http://dx.doi.org/10.1145/2675133.2675152.
17. Gregory R. Hancock. 1994. Cognitive Complexity and the Comparability of Multiple-Choice and Constructed Response Test Formats. *Journal of Experimental Education* 62, 2: 143-157. http://dx.doi.org/http://dx.doi.org/10.1080/00220973.1994.9943836.
18. Ray Hembree. 1988. Correlates, Causes, Effects, and Treatment of Test Anxiety. *Review of Educational Research* 58, 1: 47-77. http://dx.doi.org/10.3102/00346543058001047.
19. Javier Hernandez, Pablo Paredes, Asta Roseway, and Mary Czerwinski. 2014. Under pressure: Sensing Stress of Computer Users. In *Proceedings of the SIGCHI Conference on Human Factors in Computing Systems,* 51-60. http://dx.doi.org/10.1145/2556288.2557165.
20. James G. Hollandsworth Jr., Robert C. Glazeski, Karl Kirkland, Gary E. Jones, and Laura R. Van Norman. 1979. An Analysis of the Nature and Effects of Test Anxiety: Cognitive, Behavioral, and Physiological Components. *Cognitive Therapy and Research* 3, 2: 165-180. http://dx.doi.org/10.1007/BF01172603.
21. Ruogu Kang, Laura A. Dabbish, and Katherine Sutton. 2016. Strangers on Your Phone: Why People Use Anonymous Communication Applications. In *Proceedings of the 19th ACM Conference on Computer Supported Cooperative Work & Social Computing,* 358-369. http://dx.doi.org/10.1145/2818048.2820081.
22. Dominic Kao and D. Fox Harrell. 2016. Exploring the Effects of Encouragement in Educational Games. In *Proceedings of the SIGCHI Conference on Human Factors in Computing Systems Extended Abstracts,* 1906-1914. http://dx.doi.org/10.1145/2851581.2892335.
23. Kristopher J. Kimbler, Jennifer A. Margrett, and Tara L. Johnson. 2012. The role of supportive messages and distracting thoughts on everyday problem-solving performance. *Experimental Aging Research* 38, 5: 537-558. http://dx.doi.org/10.1080/0361073X.2012.726158.
24. Artie Konrad, Victoria Bellotti, Nicole Crenshaw, Simon Tucker, Les Nelson, Honglu Du, Peter Pirolli, and Steve Whittaker. 2015. Finding the Adaptive Sweet Spot: Balancing Compliance and Achievement in Automated Stress Reduction. In *Proceedings of the 33rd Annual ACM Conference on Human Factors in Computing Systems,* 3829-3838. http://dx.doi.org/10.1145/2702123.2702512.
25. Jonas W.B. Lang and Jessica Lang. 2010. Priming competence diminishes the link between cognitive test anxiety and test performance. Implications for the interpretation of test scores. *Psychological Science* 21, 6: 811-819. http://dx.doi.org/10.1177/0956797610369492.
26. Michael Massimi, Jackie L. Bender, Holly O. Witteman, and Osman H. Ahmed. 2014. Life transitions and online health communities. In *Proceedings of the 17th ACM Conference on Computer Supported Cooperative Work & Social Computing,* 1491-1501. http://dx.doi.org/10.1145/2531602.2531622.
27. Angus S. Mcdonald. 2001. The Prevalence and Effects of Test Anxiety in School Children. *Educational Psychology* 21, 1: 89-101. http://dx.doi.org/10.1080/01443410020019867.
28. W.J. Mckeachie, Donald Pollie, and Joseph Speisman. 1955. Relieving Anxiety in Classroom Examinations.

*The Journal of Abnormal and Social Psychology* 50, 1: 93-98. http://dx.doi.org/http://dx.doi.org/10.1037/h0046560.
29. Mark W. Newman, Debra Lauterbach, Sean A. Munsun, Paul Resnick, and Margaret E. Morris. 2011. "It's not that I don't have problems, I'm just not putting them on Facebook": Challenges and Opportunities in Using Online Social Networks for Health. In *Proceedings of the 14th ACM Conference on Computer Supported Cooperative Work & Social Computing,* 341-350. http://dx.doi.org/10.1145/1958824.1958876.
30. Deborah A. Olson, Jeanny Liu, and Kenneth S. Shultz. 2012. The Influence of Facebook Usage on Perceptions of Social Support, Personal Efficacy, and Life Satisfaction. *Journal of Organizational Psychology* 12, 3/4: 133-144.
31. D. Park, G. Ramirez, and S. L. Beilock. 2014. The role of expressive writing in math anxiety. *Journal of Experimental Psychology: Applied* 20, 2: 103-111. http://dx.doi.org/10.1037/xap0000013.
32. James W. Pennebaker and Sandra Klihr Beall. 1986. Confronting a Traumatic Even: Toward an Understanding of Inhibition Disease. *Journal of Abnormal Psychology* 95, 3: 274-281. http://dx.doi.org/10.1037//0021-843X.95.3.274.
33. Dave Putwain and Anthony L. Daly. 2014. Test anxiety prevalence and gender differences in a sample of English secondary school students. *Educational Studies* 40, 5: 554-570. http://dx.doi.org/10.1080/03055698.2014.953914.
34. G. Ramirez and S. L. Beilock. 2011. Writing about testing worries boosts exam performance in the classroom. *Science* 331, 211: 211-213. http://dx.doi.org/10.1126/science.1199427.
35. Martin Saerbeck, Tom Schut, Christoph Bartneck, and Maddy D. Janse. 2010. Expressive Robots in Education Varying the Degree of Social Supportive Behavior of a Robotic Tutor. In *Proceedings of the SIGCHI Conference on Human Factors in Computing Systems,* 1613-1622. http://dx.doi.org/10.1145/1753326.1753567.
36. Irwin G. Sarason. 1978. The Test Anxiety Scale: Concept and Research. *in C. D. Spielberger & I. G. Sarason, (Eds.) Stress and Anxiety* 5: 193-216.
37. Irwin G. Sarason. 1981. Test Anxiety, stress, and social support. *Journal of Personality* 49, 1: 101-114. http://dx.doi.org/10.1111/j.1467-6494.1981.tb00849.x.
38. Irwin G. Sarason. 1984. Stress, Anxiety, and Cognitive Interference: Reactions to Tests. *Journal of Personality and Social Psychology* 46, 4: 929-938. http://dx.doi.org/10.1037/0022-3514.46.4.929.
39. Irwin G. Sarason, Barbara R. Sarason, Dennis E. Keefe, Bob E. Hayes, and Edward N. Shearin. 1986. Cognitive Interference: Situational Determinants and Traitlike Characteristics. *Journal of Personality and Social Psychology* 51, 1: 215-226. http://dx.doi.org/http://dx.doi.org/10.1037/0022-3514.51.1.215.
40. Cathy Donald Sherbourne and Anita L. Stewart. 1991. The MOS Social Support Survey. *Social Science and Medicine* 32, 6: 705-714. http://dx.doi.org/10.1016/0277-9536(91)90150-B.
41. Mark G. Simkin and William L. Kuechler. 2005. Multiple-Choice Tests and Student Understanding: What Is the Connection? *Decision Sciences Journal of Innovative Education* 3, 1: 73-97. http://dx.doi.org/10.1111/j.1540-4609.2005.00053.x.
42. Richard E. Snow. Construct validity and constructed-response tests. In *Construction versus choice in cognitive measurement,* W.C. Ward and R.E. Bennett Eds. Routledge,1993, Hillsdale, NJ, 45-60|.
43. Charlers D. Speilberger, Lushene R. Gorsuch, P.R. Vagg, and G.A. Jacobs. 1983. Manual for the State-Trait Anxiety Inventory. *Consulting Psychologists Press.*
44. David Sun, Pablo Paredes, and John Canny. 2014. MouStress: Detecting Stress from Mouse Motion. In *Proceedings of the SIGCHI Conference on Human Factors in Computing Systems,* 61-70. http://dx.doi.org/10.1145/2556288.2557243.
45. Lisa M. Vizer. 2009. Detecting Cognitive and Physical Stress Through Typing Behavior. In *Proceedings of the Extended Abstracts on Human Factors in Computing Systems,* 3113-3116. http://dx.doi.org/10.1145/1520340.1520440.
46. Yi-Chia Wang, Robert Kraut, and John M. Levine. 2012. To Stay or Leave? The Relationship of Emotional and Informational Support to Commitment in Online Health Support Groups. In *Proceedings of the 15th ACM Conference on Computer Supported Cooperative Work & Social Computing,* 833-842. http://dx.doi.org/10.1145/2145204.2145329.
47. Bin Xu, Pamara Chang, Christopher L. Welker, Natalya N. Bazarova, and Dan Cosley. 2016. Automatic Archiving versus Default Deletion: What Snapchat Tells Us About Ephemerality in Design. In *Proceedings of the 19th ACM Conference on Computer-Supported Cooperative Work & Social Computing,* 1660-1673. http://dx.doi.org/10.1145/2818048.2819948.
48. Moshe Zeidner. 1987. Essay versus Multiple-Choice Type Classroom Exams: The Student's Perspective. *The Journal of Educational Research* 80, 6: 352-358.
49. Moshe Zeidner. 1998. *Test Anxiety: The State of the Art.* Plenum Press.
50. Chen Zhao, Pamela Hinds, and Ge Gao. 2012. How and To Whom People Share: The Role of Culture in Self-Disclosure in Online Communities. In *Proceedings of the 15th ACM Conference on Computer Supported Cooperative Work & Social Computing,* 67-76. http://dx.doi.org/10.1145/2145204.2145219.

# Goodbye Text, Hello Emoji: Mobile Communication on WeChat in China

**Rui Zhou**
School of Interactive Computing
Georgia Institute of Technology
Atlanta, Georgia
r.zhou@gatech.edu

**Jasmine Hentschel**
THRIVE
Atlanta, Georgia
hentscj@gmail.com

**Neha Kumar**
School of International Affairs
School of Interactive Computing
Georgia Institute of Technology
Atlanta, Georgia
neha.kumar@gatech.edu

## ABSTRACT

We present a qualitative study of mobile communication via WeChat in Southern China, focusing on the rapid proliferation of emoji and stickers and the lessening dependence on text. We use interview and observation data from 30 participants to investigate how rural, small town, and urban Chinese adults creatively and innovatively balance the use of emoji, stickers, and text in their mobile communication practices. We also discuss design implications of our research for the field of HCI, offering ways of leveraging the non-textual communication practices that we uncover, in scenarios where purely text-based communication may not suffice.

### ACM Classification Keywords

H.5.m. Information Interfaces and Presentation (e.g. HCI): Miscellaneous

### Author Keywords

China; WeChat; Mobile; Emoji; Stickers; Qualitative Methods

## INTRODUCTION

> *"Emoji-mania is in full force, and we certainly aren't mad about it. We now live in a world with emoji-only restaurant menus, and very important emoji debates; and we even judge celebs on how good their own line of emoji are. So, it makes perfect sense that we would now have a convention completely devoted to all things emoji..." [9]*

Emoji are rapidly penetrating our daily communication practices. The quote above was included in the description of the very first Emojicon - *"a multi-day celebration of all-things emoji"* that took place in San Francisco in November 2016 [9]. The event was aimed at engaging people from all walks of life with different flavors and forms of emoji, through exhibitions of emoji artwork, screenings of emoji films, and more, affirming the growing hype associated with emoji-driven non-textual communication.


*CHI 2017, May 6-11, 2017, Denver, CO, USA.*
Copyright © 2017 ACM ISBN 978-1-4503-4655-9/17/05 ...$15.00.
DOI: http://dx.doi.org/10.1145/3025453.3025800

Our research provides a situated perspective of the use of non-textual elements such as emoji and stickers in mobile communication on WeChat, where they feature widely. WeChat is currently the most popular mobile instant messaging platform in China [56]. Designed, developed, and launched by Tencent, one of China's leading technology companies, WeChat started out as a lightweight instant messaging application but has evolved into much more. The Chinese use WeChat for calling taxis, making various reservations, booking flight tickets, and more. We find that WeChat is now an integral part of daily life in China and emoji/stickers are too [26].

Prior research in the fields of Computer-Mediated Communication (CMC) and Human-Computer Interaction (HCI) has taken an active interest in studying emoji as well as similar instant messaging elements such as emoticons (*e.g.,* ;-)). While CMC researchers have focused mostly on the non-verbal cues offered by emoticons [6, 30], they have also briefly examined their other illocutionary uses [8, 19]. HCI research on emoji use, by contrast, is still in nascent stages and has studied various motivations underlying sticker use [28] and by specific cultural populations (*i.e.,* Japanese teens) [53]. Our research extends prior work by studying the combined use of emoji and stickers. The former are small, rely on unicode, are available via standardized keyboards, and cannot be edited; the latter are bigger, static or animated, can be added or deleted, and must be sent separately without insertion in text messages. Our focus on China offers a novel contribution by investigating a case of previously unstudied, widespread appropriation of emoji and stickers. Our choice of qualitative methods provides, in addition, an in-depth perspective into the motivations underlying adoption and use.

Our paper is structured as follows. After conducting a comprehensive review of related work that has studied emoji in the fields of CMC and HCI, we provide background on WeChat and emoji/sticker use in China so that our readers can better understand our findings and analysis. Next we present our methodology, describing the sites we visited in Southern China and participant demographics. In our findings section, we outline our participants' adoption and use of emoji/stickers on WeChat, and how they balanced their use of text with non-textual communication. Finally, we discuss the implications of our findings for the HCI community by making design recommendations for use cases that could leverage the non-textual communication patterns we uncover.

## RELATED WORK

Below we summarize relevant literature that examines communication practices on popular mobile instant messengers (MIMs). We also discuss CMC and HCI research that studies emoji/sticker use. Finally we describe a growing line of work that examines dependence on text.

### Communication on Mobile Instant Messengers

Around fifteen years ago, researchers started examining the practice of exchanging instant messages via mobile phones. They studied how adults sent messages in the workplace [18, 39] and how teenagers engaged in this practice at home or at school [14, 15]. Later, when mobile devices became progressively smarter, research shifted to examining how MIMs played a role in people's lives. Church and Oliveira [2] discussed that people were beginning to actively use MIMs such as WhatsApp but were also using traditional SMS. O'Hara et al. [40] studied how people enjoyed WhatsApp because it offered a sense of "dwelling" – a feeling of being with people through the exchange of messages. Since then, "dwelling" has been widely researched not only in relation to WhatsApp, but also with other popular MIMs in particular cultural contexts [20, 59, 60]. We not only study how people communicate with each other through MIMs and in China, but also how this communication is mediated by the use of emoji/stickers.

### Emoji Adoption and Use

Emoji is a Japanese word made up of two parts – the *e* means "picture" and *moji* means "letter" [53]. It was originally crafted to refer to pictorial representations for expressions and other objects such as the sun [1]. Before emoji, there were emoticons – symbolic representations for facial expressions based on punctuation marks that could be covered using a standard keyboard (*e.g.,* :-)). Emoji and emoticons have been used widely by those who communicate daily using computing/mobile devices. As technologies develop, new types of emoji are coming into being. Stickers are one example. As explained, these are also pictorial representations, but are more elaborate and often animated.

CMC research examines how communication takes place and is influenced by the presence of computers. As early as 2001, researchers like Walther and D'Addario [58] started to work on learning more about emoticons. In order to understand how emotion was perceived, Derks et al. [7] reviewed relevant works in CMC and found that online communication was as emotionally rich as offline communication; that is, people still needed to express their emotions even when they were not communicating face-to-face. This study was significant because it explicitly pointed to the possible connection between emotion and emoticons in CMC. Since then, researchers have further investigated how emotions and other nonverbal cues were represented by emoticons. Both Lo [30] and Derks et al. [6] confirmed that people relied on emoticons to express nonverbal cues. Liebman and Gergle [29] studied how social reciprocity played a role when people exchanged nonverbal cues such as emoticons and punctuation in their conversations. However, Dresner and Herring [8] challenged the dominant view that emoticons were only for emotion by noting that they could also indicate other illocutionary forces. Jibril and Abdullah [19] built on this by stating emoticons were even "morpheme-like units," expanding the understanding of emoticons as solely paralinguistic elements. We also examine how non-verbal cues are employed in online communication, additionally offering a situated understanding of rampant emoji and sticker use in China. In addition, we make design recommendations for mobile communication.

The HCI community only recently came to study emoji and has chiefly been interested in how emoji are integrated into technology. Examples include how to achieve better design when integrating emoji [43, 54], how people engage with emoji via various platforms [28], if people understand the same emoji differently [36], and whether culture shapes people's understanding and use of emoji [31]. We draw directly on two recent works. In 2016, Lee et al. [28] examined their participants' motivation for using stickers and found that users not only send stickers to represent emotions, but also for strategic or functional purposes. Sugiyama [53], on the other hand, provided an in-depth, culturally situated understanding of emoji use among a specific people, asking how Japanese teens use emoji to *"manage communication climate and express their aesthetic selves."* We build on this work to cover both traditional emoji and sticker use in China, sharing findings from participants across various social strata.

### Dependence on Text

There has been a strong focus on reducing text dependence in user interfaces (UIs) in the field of Information and Communication Technologies and Development (ICTD). This is because many users, typically from underserved communities, tend to be semi-literate or illiterate, with little ability to engage with technologies that depend heavily on text-based interactions. Medhi's work discussing the need for text-free user interface design was seminal [32]. Since then, her work has been widely referenced by others aiming to develop UIs that rely less on text. One line of work that has developed in this regard is that of voice-based user interfaces and frameworks, such as Avaaj Otalo [42], "the Spoken Web" [23], and CGNet Swara [38]. Another line considers video-based approaches. Studies include Medhi and Toyama [33] and Ladeira et al. [25]. Some take a participatory video-based approach for designing UI for low-literate users, including Digital Green [10], Projecting Health [24], KrishiPustak [34], and VideoKheti [3]. In 2015, Medhi-Thies reviewed works that designed UIs for low-literate and novice users, signaling multiple design opportunities for the future [57].

These works above aim for improved and more usable UIs for low-literate users in resource-constrained regions. There are also other scenarios where users might be keen to use less text, such as in the case of aging. We address these scenarios by considering how emoji/stickers as increasingly common visual elements in online communication could assist in communication. In our design recommendations, we consider the possibilities of integrating pictorial representations such as emoji/stickers when designing user interfaces or other HCI applications for populations that are less text-friendly.

(a) Main user interface (b) Dialogue user interface

Figure 1: WeChat's UI also includes an emoji keyboard.

(a) Small built-in emoji for goodbye (b) A sticker (c) A Sticker with text: *"Kneel and call me father!"*

Figure 2: Users can send built-in emoji on WeChat.

## EMOJI IN WECHAT

WeChat was initially launched by Tencent in 2011 across China. Other similar applications (such as Feixin [4] and QQ Mobile [63]) exist, but none are used as widely as WeChat. In March 2016, there were a total of 762 million monthly active users [56], making WeChat the third-most popular instant messaging application worldwide [51]. The WeChat UI, as shown in Figure 1, is similar to other MIMs such as WhatsApp. When WeChat was first launched, it was only a messaging service and did not stand out among its competitors. It allowed users to send text and audio messages with some default emoji inherited from QQ [61], also an instant messaging software by Tencent [55]. WeChat has now successfully developed into an all-in-one mobile application. People use WeChat for a diverse set of culturally situated uses, such as sending digital red envelopes[1]. It is now an integral component of people's personal lives in China [26].

Emoji were included as soon as WeChat launched in 2011, while stickers came only 1.5 years later [37]. Although WeChat's emoji are different in appearance from those in iOS or Android, they are also small with yellow round faces showing various expressions (see Figure 2a). Additionally, they can be inserted alongside text, just as emoji in other applications. Stickers, as described earlier, are similar to yet different from emoji. They are generally bigger than regular emoji and occupy more screen space. This also means that they cannot be used within a text message, only sent as separate entities. WeChat stickers can be either static or animated, while emoji are always static. Moreover, emoji are built into WeChat and cannot be added or deleted, while stickers can. Two kinds of stickers are supported in WeChat: custom stickers and downloadable ones shown in the sticker gallery. Stickers in this gallery are presented in "sets," where each sticker set represents a cohesive theme and contains either 16 or 24 individual stickers [45]. Custom stickers are individual ones uploaded by users from other sources, such as conversations on WeChat or photos on the phone. Once uploaded, they can be shared.

[1]This is an age-old Chinese custom for gifting money.

## METHODOLOGY

Our study took place from June to August 2016 and included 30 in-depth, semi-structured interviews of individuals from field sites in rural, small town, and urban China (see Table 1). We recruited our participants using a combination of purposive and snowball sampling [13, 21]. Our study was approved by the institutional review board (IRB) at Georgia Tech.

We recruited participants from the following field sites in Southern China: Zhijiang county and Huaihua in the Hunan province, along with Shenzhen in the Guangdong province. Huaihua is a small town that lies on the western side of Hunan [17]. Zhijiang county is a part of Huaihua and covers 301 villages. We use "Zhijiang county" to refer to the three villages where we recruited our study participants. Our last site was Shenzhen, one of the most developed cities in China [49]. This selection of sites gave us a reasonable demographic spread across rural, small town, and urban China.

As is evident from Table 1, our participants were between 18 and 63 years old. This is because we were keen to study use across ages and understand whether young and old users displayed different behaviors. Our sample included 12 men and 18 women; recruiting male participants in rural/small town China proved significantly more difficult because the interviewer was female. Since WeChat only operates on smartphones, we needed to impose smartphone use as a criterion for participation in our study. This ruled out several potential participants in our rural field sites. Further, at the time of our study, smartphone penetration was largely limited to younger generations and those from higher socioeconomic strata.

The first 18 interviews were conducted in Hunan: 7 in Zhijiang and 11 in Huaihua. We then interviewed 12 participants in Shenzhen. All interviews were 30-60 minutes long and took place at participants' homes. The first author conducted all interviews; these took place in Mandarin, also her native language. During each interview, we first asked our participants for basic information, including their age, devices they used, and how long they had been using WeChat and smartphones (See Table 1). We proceeded by asking if they had used emoji on WeChat and how. We also observed the emoji on their phones and how they used them. We took notes and kept audio recordings. These recordings were transcribed in Mandarin and then translated to English for analysis.

| Participant | Gender | Age | Location* | Smartphone** | Years of Smartphone Use | Years of WeChat Use |
|---|---|---|---|---|---|---|
| 1 | F | 54 | Small town | Huawei | 2+ | 2 |
| 2 | F | 54 | Small town | Samsung | 3 | 2.5 |
| 3 | F | 52 | Small town | Samsung | 3 | 2 |
| 4 | F | 61 | Small town | Samsung | 5+ | 1.5 |
| 5 | M | 25 | Small town | iPhone | 7 | 3+ |
| 6 | M | 58 | Small town | Samsung | 4.5 | 2.5 |
| 7 | F | 52 | Small town | iPhone/Xiaomi | 4.5 | 2+ |
| 8 | F | 18 | Small town | Huawei | 4.5 | 0.5 |
| 9 | M | 42 | Rural | OUKI | 5+ | 2 |
| 10 | M | 63 | Rural | Samsung | 2+ | 2 |
| 11 | M | 27 | Small town | iPhone | 6 | 4 |
| 12 | F | 28 | Small town | Samsung | 7 | 4 |
| 13 | F | 54 | Small town | Coolpad | 1+ | 0.5 |
| 14 | F | 23 | Rural | iPhone | 2.5 | 2.5 |
| 15 | F | 25 | Rural | Oppo/Unknown | 4+ | 3 |
| 16 | M | 43 | Rural | Gionee | 4+ | 4+ |
| 17 | F | 43 | Rural | Vivo | 0.5 | 0.5 |
| 18 | F | 54 | Rural | Huawei | 3 | 1 |
| 19 | F | 26 | Urban | Hammer | 8 | 4 |
| 20 | M | 63 | Urban | iPhone | 5 | 5 |
| 21 | F | 59 | Urban | iPhone | 5+ | 4.5 |
| 22 | F | 39 | Urban | Huawei | 5 | 3.5 |
| 23 | F | 47 | Urban | Huawei | 1.5 | 1.5 |
| 24 | M | 25 | Urban | iPhone | 6 | 6 |
| 25 | M | 27 | Urban | Xiaomi | 3 | 3 |
| 26 | M | 27 | Urban | iPhone | 10 | 5 |
| 27 | M | 41 | Urban | iPhone | 10+ | 3 |
| 28 | M | 27 | Urban | iPhone | 6.5 | 4 |
| 29 | F | 26 | Urban | iPhone | 5.5 | 4.5 |
| 30 | F | 25 | Urban | Samsung | 8 | 4 |

Table 1: Participant Demographics

* Rural → Zhijiang; Small town → Huaihua; Urban → Shenzhen

** Other than Samsung and iPhone, other smartphones were all Chinese branded. P7 and P15 both owned two smartphones.

We applied interpretive qualitative analysis to all interview transcripts [35]. Our analysis began with "open coding," in which we assigned short phrases as codes. The first round of coding was done line-by-line within transcripts, so that codes stayed close to data. Examples of first-level codes include "emoji are entertaining," "using emoji for festivals and holidays," and "sending emoji according to the audience." We proceeded to analyze these codes and extracted themes for a conceptual understanding. Second-level categories included "sending emoji: audience matters," "stickers with or without texts: descriptions and understandings," and "non-use of emoji: conditions and rationales." The process of analyzing data was iterative – we continuously went back and forth between categories and data to discover patterns and subject data to further scrutiny. Finally, we arrived at distinct themes that highlight how our participants started using emoji/stickers and how they currently use or do not use these.

## FINDINGS

In this section, we structure our findings by describing how participants adopted emoji/stickers, how they used emoji/stickers to support and complement their use of text, and how these use cases have evolved over time such that emoji/stickers have taken on meanings of their own, sans text. We offer, in addition, a few cases of emoji/sticker non-use.

### Hello, Emoji!

Most participants started using emoji on WeChat around 2013. When we asked what had inspired their adoption of emoji in the first place, we discovered that it was largely because they had been introduced to it by their friends in their chats. When WeChat introduced stickers, it placed a red dot in the interface to indicate the new addition, just as it always highlights new features [62]. More savvy participants noticed this and began to use them right away, while others learned from their family and friends. P13 described how she learned to send emoji/stickers by asking her daughter-in-law to teach her. She had seen them in conversations but did not know how to save or send them. P17 mentioned that her daughter, who was still a primary school student, was much more tech-savvy than her: *"My daughter used my phone all the time. These stickers were all downloaded by her. I saw them so I used them too. She taught me how to send at the beginning."* In general, intermediaries – as described by Sambasivan et al. and others [11, 41, 46, 47] – played a significant role in expanding WeChat emoji's user base. Prior experience and familiarity with QQ also made a difference, since WeChat first inherited emoji from QQ [61].

In general, our participants shared that they had adopted emoji/stickers because text was not always sufficient. Many participants called text messages boring, dry, and limited in the expressiveness they allowed. P4, who was familiar with computers and accustomed to typing on them, said: *"It didn't look pretty when there was only text on the screen."* P11 added that text looked *"weak and powerless, whereas emoji are so much more lively."* In sections that follow, we describe how emoji/sticker adoption has led to the evolution of WeChat use as well.

### Emoji for Non-Verbal Cues

According to Dresner and Herring [8], emoticons can be used to offer non-verbal cues that are poorly conveyed by text. We found that our participants also appeared to engage with emoji for this purpose. In general, when communicating emotions, expressions, feelings, greeting, blessings, and appreciation, they used emoji extensively as non-verbal cues and as "emotion indicators" [8]. Most participants told us they send emoji when they feel happy or when they want to bless or greet someone along with words for a livelier exchange. This role of emoji also reveals how people intentionally add them to text. For instance, P22 described how she usually sends emoji at the end of a sentence to help her show happiness. Similarly, P28 indicated that he often sends a smiley at the beginning of a conversation to indicate his friendliness. P27 summarized how he adds emoji to text messages: *"After saying something, I will then add emoji in the middle or in the end. This is to assist expression; some emoji simply express a response without adding much content."* Here,

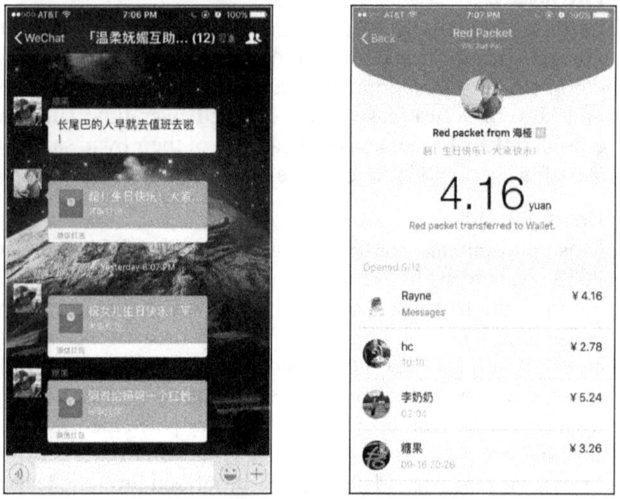


(a) Three red envelopes in one conversation

(b) Opened a Red Envelope

Figure 3: Clicking on the envelope shows money received.

emoji support text without introducing new meaning, serving a more supplementary role by adding non-verbal cues.

Stickers also serve similar function. In WeChat, stickers can either be solely graphical or contain both an image and text. Typically, there are one to ten characters in a single sticker, depending on the information it is trying to convey and whether the meanings of the text and image are aligned. A few participants believed that stickers with text are *"clear and complete,"* because they contain words that people cannot misunderstand. Their main focus was on the text and not the image, which ended up playing a supplementary role.

**Emoji/Stickers for Complementing Text**

Instead of echoing what the text represents by offering non-verbal cues, emoji/stickers also offer important information to complement the text so that emoji/stickers and words combine to form a holistic meaning. In some cases, text may not even be present.

*Emoji/Stickers for Behaviors, Actions, and Attitudes*

Certain types of messages are easier to convey when complemented by stickers than by inputting text, as discussed briefly by Lee et al. [28]. Behaviors, actions, and attitudes fall into this category. P1 shared how she often sends emoji hugs to her middle school classmates since she would really like to hug them in person. Nearly half of our participants told us they send emoji to express agreement or disagreement.

*Stickers as Connotations*

When stickers are used for adding connotative information, they complement text with meanings it failed to convey. When describing the kind of stickers he saved, P11 said: *"Some connotative stickers, such as 'give you a look and you understand it on your own.' Also ones that feature 'moral integrity shattered all over the place'.*[2]*"* Though the stickers he referred to were custom stickers, they embedded meanings that were rich, subtle, and culturally relevant, so they would likely be very hard to express through text. In these cases, a picture was indeed worth the proverbial thousand words.

*Emoji/Stickers Modify Textual Meaning*

Emoji/stickers can also modify the meaning of text. We observed and discussed with participants how they use emoji/stickers to alter the meaning of text deliberately. P1 said: *"Sometimes when it's not appropriate to say something or when you don't have a proper word in mind, stickers will help you to communicate. For example, Zhijiang people use 'the brain-chopper' to curse people. But if you really use this word, it sounds pretty serious. Use a knife [emoji], then it becomes entertaining."* This finding differs from Walther and D'Addario's [58] since they believe the negative element, whether verbal or graphical, will make the entire message negative. P1, instead, uses emoji to lighten the negative tone. P19 shared similar feelings here by telling us she makes sure to add an emoji if she believes her text could potentially hurt those on the receiving end. These examples highlight that users must understand the meanings of both the text and the emoji/stickers, and well enough, to balance their holistic meaning in diverse situations.

*Emoji/Stickers Represent Silence*

One third of our participants said they use emoji/stickers when they have nothing to say or do not know what to say. P8's reply fell into the former category: *"I usually use stickers when the conversation becomes awkward. This means there's no way to proceed. . . ."* P5 also used emoji when he did not want to talk, which happened frequently when he chatted with his older family members. He said: *"They cannot understand. I sent emoji and tried to say that, in fact, I don't want to talk to you. But it was a smiley, so the other side thought I was happy and continued talking even more."* P19 described her use of emoji when she was unsure of what to say. All these participants show that this particular use depends on specific audience and context.

**"Timing is Crucial"**

We discovered that many emoji/stickers are used only on certain occasions, such as festivals or holidays. These emoji/stickers must be understood by taking into consideration both the special contexts and the traditional cultural value ascribed to them. P9 told us he uses the rose emoji most often. When asked about when he uses it, he said: *"The flower is for festivals and for birthdays, no matter whose birthday."* P24 explained further: *"I use stickers frequently when it's Chinese New Year. I probably don't really want to send a simple 'Kung Hei Fat Choy' when it's Chinese New Year, [but] the kind that is a bit joyful and also with some patterns."* Since the New Year is meant to be a happy occasion and represents family reunions, people adhere to traditional cultural values by choosing specific stickers that match the festive atmosphere.

The digital red pocket, or red envelope, is also used on special occasions. A red envelope is a red paper envelope used to gift cash. Chinese people traditionally have given them to children as a blessing during the Chinese New Year, but nowadays they are sent in other situations as well, such as

[2]Both are phrases and jargon commonly used by Chinese youth.

(a) Expectation (b) Distribution (c) Appreciation

Figure 4: Various stickers featuring red envelopes.

weddings, birthdays, moving into new homes, and more [44]. Tencent designed a digital version of a red envelope (see Figure 3) for WeChat in January 2014 [26] in order to support an online experience of this cultural tradition. Fourteen participants told us they use emoji/stickers when expecting, sending, or receiving red envelopes and that these emoji/stickers generally take the form of stickers featuring red envelopes, similar to the examples shown in Figure 4. P23 claimed (and we confirmed) that most of her stickers featured red envelopes. P2, whose stickers were nearly all related to red envelopes, told us she saves these red envelope stickers strategically:

> *"It's not possible to send one sticker for indicating appreciation in all cases. Today I grab two [red envelopes], then I will send two "thank you" patterns. Two days later, if there are more [red envelopes], then I will just send another two [thank you stickers]. I don't want to send the same patterns in the same group."* (P2)

We can see that the use of these stickers depends on the user's understanding of red envelopes. Given the widespread nature of this tradition of sending red envelopes [44], it was unsurprising that we saw red envelope stickers being used whenever people wished to send red envelopes.

Finding the right emoji for the right occasion is not enough. They also need to be sent fast enough, we found. But what counts as "the right time" if it's not a festival or a birthday? Why does speed matter so much? P29 tried to explain:

> *"Sometimes people send messages pretty fast in groups. You need to be able to send out something fast enough for your sticker to make sense at that moment. People have already sent a few messages, and then it's awkward if you suddenly send a sticker, which shows up after someone else's message. For example, if you say something and I want to reply with a sticker, but other people are able to reply very quickly with several messages. Your message has already passed. If I still send a sticker (to your message), that will be very odd. Timing is crucial."* (P29)

In this example, the speed of replying with emoji/stickers becomes part of the context. Being able to reply in the appropriate timeframe entails digesting the entire context accurately and finding the proper emoji/sticker for a reply as soon as possible rather than spending considerable time typing long sentences. Because emoji/stickers essentially only require one click, they are much quicker to use than text. When mobile conversations move quickly, emoji/stickers trump text.

### Motivations for Sticker Use

As discussed earlier, emoji and stickers are similar but different. Our participants shared their various motivations for using stickers over emoji.

#### *All about Oneself*

Emoji/stickers are not used just for communication; they are also representations of oneself. Sugiyama discusses the interpretation of "*kawaii*[3] aesthetics" among Japanese teens' use of emoji [53]. Our research confirms these findings with stickers but also finds that participants used stickers as a part of their personal identity, regardless of age and location. For example, P11 shared that after becoming a cop, he had become much more aware of his occupation and was keen that his online communication preserve his professional image. Some of his contacts on WeChat were strangers who only talked to him when they wanted his help. He showed us multiple saved stickers that featured cops and told us that he had gotten these from his colleagues.

Other than profession, participants showed awareness of their personality traits and how they conveyed these using stickers. P8, who had just graduated from high school, told us she liked stickers that were *"silly and also a bit funny,"* which (to her) meant that they looked simple and straightforward. When asked why she chose those stickers, she answered: *"Probably because my personality is like them, and I like this simple style since I was very young. Truly simple."* These stickers spoke to her because they resonated with how she understood herself. P12 said she sent a particular set of stickers to her female friends in which the characters looked *"capricious and unhappy,"* because she felt free with these friends. Here, stickers were used with the intention of revealing aspects of oneself with different audiences – this is also how people act in the real world [12]. If the audiences know the sender, they will be able to understand the connection between the sender and the stickers. Otherwise, the audiences can get to know the sender through these stickers, making stickers even more crucial in this communication.

Finally, users also choose stickers because they resemble their physical features. P5, for example, used a sticker just because people thought he looked like the character in the sticker. He provided more details:

> *"Whenever I send this sticker, particularly smiling like this at the end a conversation, people will say 'hey this guy really looks like you' or ask me 'are you this guy?' Later I even imitated this sticker! Then people will respond: 'OMG, is this you?' "* (P5)

All in all, these participants were naturally drawn to stickers that they could relate to for a variety of reasons. They were aware of these tendencies and more than happy to integrate these stickers into their communication, with the hope of constructing a desirable and fitting online image for themselves. We find that as mobile communication develops, sticker use is coming increasingly into focus, both for non-verbal communication and for identity management.

[3]Cute in the context of Japanese popular culture [27].

#### *When Love Matters more than Time*

We mentioned earlier that time matters a lot – however, some participants seemed to care more for stickers than for time. Two participants, P6 and P12, shared that they used stickers all the time. We confirmed this by looking over their WeChat conversations, which revealed high sticker use. Both sent stickers and really seemed to enjoy these graphical dimensions to their communication. P6, who was more than 60 years old and lived in a small town, loved stickers so much that he downloaded 56 sticker sets – even more than P5, a young man who saved 33 sticker sets and saw himself as a "heavy sticker user." We asked P6 why he had so many sticker sets and didn't delete any of them. He laughed and answered: *"Because they are good. It's better to have a hundred sets. That will be the best."* He went on and on about how he liked stickers better than text:

> *"I think it's better to use stickers. Writing, first, is too slow. Second, if I'm happy, it will be better to hop and jump like [the bunny] in the sticker. I also like the stickers without text. If there are images, then perhaps it's better to use them as often as possible since text messages may cause misunderstanding. Some text may not express the meaning completely."* (P6)

P12 also uses sticker extensively: *"I send stickers to my boss."* She used stickers even if she did not quite understand their meanings – she saved a sticker set which featured NBA stars, only because her husband was a huge fan of NBA, so she could send them to him. She did not really know the basketball stars or what the animations meant. She just liked using them: *"When I see a sticker, I will think about if this one is interesting and if it can be sent to somebody. Then I will look for it – to see whether it's there [in the sticker gallery]."*

In the cases above, participants took time to pick and choose their stickers, searching for them actively. Stickers played a major role in their mobile communication on WeChat by shaping their patterns of communication so that they turned to stickers before turning to text. P6 was so used to stickers that he would only think about how stickers could correctly illustrate his feelings. Similarly, P12 cared about her husband and, on encountering the NBA sticker set, thoughts of her husband first came to mind.

### Emoji/Sticker Subcultures

Subculture, as defined by Dick Hebdige, is "a subversion to normalcy" [16]. We talk about emoji/sticker subcultures by pointing out how our participants' novel use of emoji/stickers cultivated smaller groups of users that shared distinct beliefs towards emoji/stickers, when compared against the larger user population. We present two examples below.

#### *The "Mysterious Smile"*

All emoji/stickers on WeChat have a label. People generally become familiar with underlying meanings of them by looking at their graphical representations and names before sending them out, particularly for new and unfamiliar stickers. It is therefore not surprising that our participants used emoji/stickers as the names suggested, such as using a crying face to illustrate sadness. Nevertheless, this is not always the case. Younger participants from the city or small town appropriated emoji by assigning unconventional meanings to them. The first emoji, the ordinary smiley: ☺, was originally designed and understood to be a genuine smile [1]. However, our young participants (P5, P25, and P30) rejected this convention and insisted that it was a *"mysterious smile"* that covered all kinds of connotations, such as sarcasm or speechlessness, even though they knew that it was mostly used to indicate an ordinary smile. P5 told us he sent this smiley when he did not really have anything to say or when he did not know how to reply – but surely it was not meant to be a genuine smile. Similarly, P24 saw this smiley as *"a fake smile."* We found that this alternative interpretation was widely known and accepted among younger participants but not among older users. Older participants, such as P20 and P21, shared that they used this smiley when they wanted to smile or show friendliness. The "mysterious smile" interpretation for this particular smiley was likely determined by age, since participants like P5 and P30 told us that they would not send it to their older family members since *"they won't understand."* For P8, P24, and P25, even though they used the smiley as a "mysterious smile" in their family groups, they did not bother to explain this connotation and did not care if their families understood.

#### *"Sticker Competitions"*

A special practice that has evolved in the case of sticker use is the *sticker competition,* when users exchange stickers for the sake of exchanging them, for showing off the stickers they have, or for collectively putting together a story using stickers only. Three of our participants, P8, P19, and P25, whose ages ranged from 18 to 27, mentioned that they occasionally engaged in sticker competitions. P19, who was a graduate student, described how she and her roommate used to compete with stickers in 2015:

> *"We had a WeChat group for the four of us in our dorm. So sometimes we would chat if there was nothing urgent to do for our labs. Since we all had other groups, we saved stickers from here and there, so we would communicate in our group. In general, it was between the two of us, myself and a roommate. The other two girls just watched. Basically, when we two received any interesting stickers, we sent them in the group and then started showing off. We would show off when we were terribly bored - 'Hey I saved so many new stickers today' and send tons of them. Then she would say: 'Hey this is interesting. I have received these ones', then she would send tons of other stickers. It was like that. Back and forth we both saved many, many stickers. We sent stickers for the sake of sending them."* (P19)

Instead of sending stickers for nothing in particular, P25 competed with stickers with his friend and they crafted stories without using any text: *"We only sent stickers, yes, but stickers could form some stories. For example, I sent this 'eating shit' sticker, she would reply with shit covering the face [sic]. This is actually very funny."* We proceeded by asking him if they were showing off, and he answered:

> *"Not really showing off. It was just a particular type of humor. Sometimes you don't want to talk and when you send stickers, you feel entertained. This is especially the case when I can connect the stickers together, creatively, connect them as a story – it becomes really fun."* (P25)

During sticker competitions, the phone screen fills with all kinds of stickers but zero text. Because all these three participants were recalling past experiences when referring to sticker competitions, we were unable to investigate this practice real-time. According to their descriptions, however, we can see the potential for mobile communication to involve mainly stickers, without explicit need for text. We note, however, that such sticker competitions need users to be relatively familiar with the stickers he or she has. Of course, users must also be fans of stickers for this level of use.

### Democratized Stickers

Stickers, unlike emoji, have greater flexibility. As mentioned in the previous section, WeChat supports users in creating custom stickers elsewhere and uploading to WeChat for communication and exchange. Therefore, the content and design of these custom stickers is entirely under the creator's control, not WeChat's. A few participants took advantage of this flexibility and democratized stickers in one form or other.

#### *Creating One's Own Stickers*

Two male participants, P24 and P25, were so enthusiastic about using stickers that they started creating their own stickers. P24, who likes to build things, made a custom sticker to create an animation of his work, so he could share it with others more easily. He used a mobile application called *Meitu Xiuxiu* to shoot a short video and transmit it as a gif. After that, he imported the gif as a custom sticker into WeChat, a process he described as *"convenient."* P25, somewhat differently from P24, made multiple stickers based on the ordinary smiley that we discussed above as the "mysterious smile." In fact, P25's idea of creating his own stickers came from the alternative interpretation of "mysterious smile." He explained:

> *"This emoji is very magical, this 'mysterious smile.' All the ones I created were based on it. There are plenty of resources online, so I just downloaded the first emoji and used it as a base and then worked on it in Meitu Xiuxiu (a mobile application for editing images)."* (P25)

He told us how he did not expect people to use his stickers at the beginning, but found that they were soon being circulated by his friends. Together, these examples demonstrate how when users have been actively engaged in using stickers, they turn to creatively making their own and find ways to replace textual representations with their own creations.

#### *Erotic Stickers*

Sometimes during an interview, we would request or be given a chance to take a look at the stickers participants used and saved. When scanning their lists of custom stickers, we occasionally found them saving erotic stickers that presented pornographic visual elements in one way or another. For instance, some of them included graphic representations of a penis, while others were snippets of adult videos. P5, P25, and P26 were the only participants that were willing to openly discuss erotic stickers with us. While P5 initially hesitated to show his custom erotic stickers, he eventually opened up and handed us his phone. P25 claimed he did not save any erotic stickers, while P26 said he saved them just for keeping them – not for circulating them, the same as P24. While most of these participants were young men in their 20s, there was one exception: P16, a rural villager in his 40s, told us that most of his custom stickers were saved by his daughter. There was a visible gender divide here, since not a single female participant saved erotic stickers. P1, who had recently retired as a teacher, told us how disgusting it was when her male peers sent erotic stickers in WeChat groups: *"Only those naughty guys send them."* (P1)

Because the dissemination of pornographic content is not allowed in China, either online or offline, it can only exist in the form of custom stickers that are made, uploaded, and disseminated by individual users. To the best of our knowledge, these custom stickers are not monitored by Tencent and are thus freely circulated on WeChat, allowing enthusiastic users the freedom to create and share stickers of their choice. P12 mentioned that there were groups in which people would exchange erotic stickers without using a single word – *"Why bother, since no text is needed?"* The use of custom stickers for pornographic communication is apt since they offer versatile pictorial representations.

#### *A Magical Custom Sticker*

One rural participant, a young woman (P15), was happy to talk to us and told us she owned two smartphones. While one was on charging, she showed us the other one. She mentioned that she was not very into stickers but often used emoji: *"I'm a mother and I don't have time to play around with those stickers."* She also described how she conducted her small business via WeChat. We noticed that the last custom sticker on her list looked more like a screenshot than a regular sticker. When we asked what it was, she clicked on it to show us that it was in fact an instructional sticker for teaching people how to change an iPhone setting: *"Some iPhone users don't know how to add the platform (an application her business used), so we will send it to them, as it illustrates the procedure for changing the setting pretty clearly."* We present an example here with this instructional sticker, demonstrating that these graphical representations embedded in online communication can effectively convey information without relying excessively on text. This is also an area that we believe future HCI research could focus on.

### Non-Use of Emoji

Two interview participants told us that they did not use emoji. P7 and P10, both retired, chatted daily with friends and family on WeChat. Even though we found that they both had saved stickers on their phone, they told us firmly that they did not like emoji and refused to use any:

> *"Texts and audio messages in WeChat already convey meaning. To add emoji is redundant, not necessary. I like brevity. Many of these emoji are small, crammed in a single screen. Their differences are nuanced, so sometimes they may be used wrongly. With just a round*

> *face, they are also monotonous without much novelty. Audio and text can express meanings completely. They are not necessary."* (P10)

P7's attitude towards emoji was similar. She told us she never liked using emoji. She used text to communicate for any formal communication because it was clearer. Apart from P7 and P10, some younger participants also shared that though they still used emoji, they had started using some stickers. P29, a user experience designer, had a lot of stickers on her phone, but said she could not figure out which to use:

> *"Whenever I want to send a sticker, it takes me such a long time. If they are convenient to manage or if I'm able to find the sticker very quickly, then I will probably use them. It doesn't do a good job right now so I don't want to use them. The order of these custom stickers cannot be rearranged. If I use these ten stickers very often, I should be able to move them to the top."* (P29)

P25 echoed P29's views by adding that it could be troublesome to locate a sticker, because one page could only show eight stickers but 23 smaller emoji. In addition, emoji were more straightforward and widely understood, while stickers were too diverse and often required context.

## DISCUSSION

Our findings highlighted the widespread adoption of emoji and stickers in WeChat and how the use of these non-textual elements in mobile communication also signals the lessening dependence on text. Although some of our findings are consistent with prior studies that show emoji/stickers to supplement text [8, 30], we also highlight how these embed additional rich and culturally relevant information. This rapid and multi-faceted proliferation of emoji/stickers in mobile communication carries important implications for several areas of interest within HCI, as we discuss below.

### In Support of Text

We discussed earlier that emoji are frequently used to display non-verbal clues and supplement text. Our study participants mentioned how emoji helped them to better express their emotions and supported the text in their messages for more accurate and effective communication. Scholars including Derks et al. [7], Lo [30], and Dresner and Herring [8] have argued for giving importance to non-verbal cues in online communication. In addition, there is P15's example of a custom sticker used for its instructional value. Given prior work and our findings, we believe that emoji/stickers might be leveraged to compensate for the lack of non-verbal cues in text-based exchanges and/or to simply convey meaning more effectively. HCI research addressing the design of user interfaces for populations that are less literate, such as Medhi's [57], could build on our findings to examine the role that emoji/stickers might play to augment text-based communication among this population by allowing for diverse pictorial representations. With the gradually lessening dependence on text that we found in our study, and rapidly growing penetration of smartphones worldwide [50], leveraging emoji/sticker use might carry powerful implications for a growing group of users. This is an area we intend to explore with future work.

### When Text is Incomplete

Our participants discussed how emoji/stickers could complement text to convey behaviors, actions, and attitudes, *e.g.*, for modulating tone. In these cases, a complete intended meaning is only conveyed when pictorial elements are included. We saw several instances of this. For example, P19 shared that she added emoji to ensure that her texts were correctly understood by her audience. Also, since the Chinese language is complex and nuanced [5], the presence of emoji/stickers can compensate for the subtlety of messages, particularly on a text-based communication medium. Several languages other than Chinese, such as Indic languages, tend to require considerable effort from the user for the input of text. Aging users might also find it challenging to enter text on small phone screens. In these scenarios, emoji/stickers could be leveraged for a smoother user experience.

Sometimes, less text may be preferred. In the case of certain vulnerable populations operating amidst significant social stigma, such as people living with HIV or sex workers, pictorial representations can help to make communication more palatable and less intrusive as necessary. Sambasivan et al. described a deployment that sent medical testing advertisements to urban sex workers [48]. In contexts such as these, since the content of these messages is sensitive, exchanges must take place in discrete fashion and with regard for the comfort levels of the audience. Sorcar et al.'s approach in [52] highlights the value of carefully designed pictorial representations in communicating taboo topics.

Certain emoji are already commonly used in research and feedback instruments such as surveys, forms, and diary studies to make responding easier [9, 22]. This practice could draw on our findings to design instruments that make the process of data collection less tedious by including more pictorial representations that are familiar, diverse, and packed with meaning. This might mitigate barriers that hinder reporting.

### Outside of Text

There are multiple facets to communication that lie beyond the realm of text. We found our participants took great pleasure in using emoji/stickers for personalizing their communication or for cultural exchanges in ways that would not have been possible with text. The sticker competitions highlighted an extreme scenario of how these exchanges could take place entirely without the use of text. The most active exchange of "red envelopes" that we witnessed also attests to high levels of engagement during acts of cultural production. Our participants also derived happiness from generating and/or appropriating pictorial representations that allowed them to develop their own identities in ways that they valued.

There are real-world scenarios where communication may need to convey silence and individuals may wish to convey silent consent or silent dissent to avoid uncomfortable situations. Young adults might be expected or feel pressure to listen to elders without stating their opinions. This might also be true for work scenarios where junior employees need to show deference to higher authorities. In such cases, emoji/stickers may be actively leveraged to add nuance to communication and fill in for the absence of appropriate words.

Our research highlights these prevalent, non-textual dimensions to mobile communication and how examining user-generated and/or culturally relevant emoji and stickers could bring additional, desirable meaning to communication that is primarily text-based. Appropriately factoring these dimensions into technology design within HCI could make interactions more rich and meaningful, as our findings demonstrate.

## CONCLUSION

We presented a qualitative study of non-textual mobile communication practices in Southern China. Studying the rapid proliferation of emoji and stickers in WeChat use, we also examined the trend of lessening dependence on text. Using interview and observation data from 30 participants, we investigated how rural, small town, and urban Chinese adults creatively and innovatively use non-textual elements in their communication. We drew on our findings to discuss implications of our research for mobile-communication focused technology design in the field of HCI. These include considerations for scenarios in which emoji and stickers could be leveraged to augment existing text, compensate for text that is incomplete either due to concerns around social stigma or because it is tedious to type in certain languages, or replace text altogether. Our study is the first to qualitatively examine in-depth the widespread adoption and appropriation of both emoji and sticker use in a particular cultural context. Future work could explore this phenomenon in disparate contexts and go deeper to focus on incorporating these non-textual elements into technology design, possibly in tandem with audio and/or other modalities as well.

## ACKNOWLEDGMENTS

We thank all the participants. We are sincerely grateful to the feedback offered by Maia Jacobs, Marisol Wong-Villacres, and all the anonymous reviewers on this paper. We would also like to thank Fengze Jiang for his invaluable support.

## REFERENCES

1. Jeff Blagdon. 2013. How emoji conquered the world: The story of the smiley face from the man who invented it. *The Verge* (March 2013). `http://www.theverge.com/2013/3/4/3966140/how-emoji-conquered-the-world`.
2. Karen Church and Rodrigo de Oliveira. 2013. What's up with WhatsApp? Comparing Mobile Instant Messaging Behaviors with Traditional SMS. In *Proc. MobileHCI 2013*. ACM Press, 352–361.
3. Sebastien Cuendet, Indrani Medhi, Kalika Bali, and Edward Cutrell. 2013. VideoKheti: Making Video Content Accessible to Low-Literate and Novice Users. In *Proc. CHI 2013*. ACM Press, 2833–2842.
4. C. Custer. 2013. WeChat Competitor Feixin: 100 Million Users, But Low Activity Levels. *Tech in Asia* (June 2013). `https://www.techinasia.com/wechat-fetion-feixin-100-million-users`.
5. John DeFrancis. 1984. *The Chinese Language: Fact and Fantasy*. University of Hawaii Press.
6. Daantje Derks, Arjan E.R. Bos, and Jasper Von Grumbkow. 2008a. Emoticons in Computer-Mediated Communication: Social Motives and Social Context. *CyberPsychology and Behavior* 11, 1 (2008), 99–101. DOI: `http://dx.doi.org/10.1089/cpb.2007.9926`
7. Daantje Derks, Agneta H. Fischer, , and Arjan E.R. Bos. 2008b. The Role of Emotion in Computer-Mediated Communication: A Review. *Computers in Human Behavior* 24, 3 (2008), 766–785. DOI: `http://dx.doi.org/10.1016/j.chb.2007.04.004`
8. Eli Dresner and Susan C. Herring. 2010. Functions of the Nonverbal in CMC: Emoticons and Illocutionary Force. *Communication Theory* 20, 4 (2010), 249–268. DOI: `http://dx.doi.org/10.1111/j.1468-2885.2010.01362.x`
9. Emojicon 2016. `http://www.emojicon.co/` Accessed September 20, 2016.
10. Rikin Gandhi, Rajesh Veeraraghavan, Kentaro Toyama, , and Vanaja Ramprasad. 2009. Digital Green: Participatory Video and Mediated Instruction for Agricultural Extension. *Information Technologies and International Development* 5, 1 (2009), 1–15.
11. Ishita Ghosh. 2016. Contextualizing Intermediated Use in the Developing World: Findings from India and Ghana. In *Proc. CHI 2016*. ACM Press, 355–359.
12. Erving Goffman. 1959. *The Presentation of Self in Everyday Life*. Anchor Books.
13. Leo A. Goodman. 1961. Snowball Sampling. *The Annals of Mathematical Statistics* 32, 1 (1961), 148–170.
14. Rebecca E. Grinter and Margery Eldridge. 2003. Wan2tlk?: Everyday Text Messaging. In *Proc. CHI 2003*. ACM Press, 441–448.
15. Rebecca E. Grinter and Leysia Palen. 2002. Instant messaging in teen life. In *Proc. CSCW 2002*. ACM Press, 21–30.
16. Dick Hebdige. 1979. *Subculture: The Meaning of Style*. Routledge.
17. Huaihua Government Online: Overview 2016. `http://www.huaihua.gov.cn/hhgk/hhgk.htm/` Accessed September 20, 2016.
18. Ellen Isaacs, Alan Walendowski, Steve Whittaker, Diane J. Schiano, and Candace Kamm. 2002. The character, functions, and styles of instant messaging in the workplace. In *Proc. CSCW 2002*. ACM Press, 11–20.
19. Tanimu Ahmed Jibril and Mardziah Hayati Abdullah. 2013. Relevance of Emoticons in Computer-Mediated Communication Contexts: An Overview. *Asian Social Science* 9, 4 (2013), 201–207. DOI: `http://dx.doi.org/10.5539/ass.v9n4p201`
20. Da jung Kim and Youn kyung Lim. 2015. Dwelling Places in KakaoTalk: Understanding the Roles and Meanings of Chatrooms in Mobile Instant Messengers. In *Proc. CSCW 2015*. ACM Press, 775–784.

21. Victor Jupp. 2006. *The SAGE Dictionary of Social Research Methods*. SAGE Publications Ltd.
22. Sin-Hwa Kang and Jacquelyn Fort Morie. 2013. Users' Socially Desirable Responding with Computer Interviewers. In *Proc. CHI EA 2013*. ACM Press, 229–234.
23. Arun Kumar, Sheetal K. Agarwal, and Priyanka Manwani. 2010. The Spoken Web Application Framework - User Generated Content and Service Creation through low-end mobiles. In *Proc. W4A 2010*. ACM Press, Article No. 2.
24. Neha Kumar, Trevor Perrier, Michelle Desmond, Kiersten Israel-Ballard, Vikrant Kumar, Sudip Mahapatra, Anil Mishra, Shreya Agarwa, Rikin Gandhi, Pallavi Lal, and Richard Anderson. 2015. Projecting Health: Community-Led Video Education for Maternal Health. In *Proc. ICTD 2015*. ACM Press, Article No. 17.
25. Ilda Ladeira and Edward Cutrell. 2010. Teaching with Storytelling: An Investigation of Narrative Videos for Skills Training. In *Proc. ICTD 2010*. IEEE, Article No. 22.
26. Dune Lawrence. 2016. Life in the People's Republic of WeChat. *BloombergBusinessweek* (June 2016). `http://www.bloomberg.com/news/articles/2016-06-09/life-in-the-people-s-republic-of-wechat`.
27. Takie Sugiyama Lebra. 2004. *The Japanese Self in Cultural Logic*. University of Hawaii Press.
28. Joon Young Lee, Nahi Hong, Soomin Kim, Jonghwan Oh, and Joonhwan Lee. 2016. Smiley face: why we use emoticon stickers in mobile messaging. In *Proc. MobileHCI 2016*. ACM Press, 760–766.
29. Noah Liebman and Darren Gergle. 2016. It's (Not) Simply a Matter of Time: The Relationship Between CMC Cues and Interpersonal Affinity. In *Proc. CSCW 2016*. ACM Press, 570–581.
30. Shao-Kang Lo. 2008. The Nonverbal Communication Functions of Emoticons in Computer-Mediated Communication. *CyberPsychology and Behavior* 11, 5 (2008), 766–785. DOI: `http://dx.doi.org/10.1089/cpb.2007.0132`
31. Xuan Lu, Wei Ai, Xuanzhe Liu, Qian Li, Ning Wang, Gang Huang, and Qiaozhu Mei. 2016. Learning from the ubiquitous language: an empirical analysis of emoji usage of smartphone users. In *Proc. UbiComp 2016*. ACM Press, 770–780.
32. Indrani Medhi, Aman Sagar, and Kentaro Toyama. 2006. Text-Free User Interfaces for Illiterate and Semi-Literate Users. In *Proc. ICTD 2006*. IEEE, 72–82.
33. Indrani Medhi and Kentaro Toyama. 2007. Full-Context Videos for First-Time, Non-Literate PC Users. In *Proc. ICTD 2007*. IEEE, unknown.
34. Indrani Medhi-Thies, Pedro Ferreira, Nakull Gupta, Jacki O'Neill, and Edward Cutrell. 2013. KrishiPustak: A Social Networking System for Low-Literate Farmers. In *Proc. CSCW 2015*. ACM Press, 1670–1681.
35. Sharan B. Merriam. 2002. *Qualitative Research in Practice: Examples for Discussion and Analysis*. Jossey-Bass.
36. Hannah Miller, Jacob Thebault-Spieker, Shuo Chang, Isaac Johnson, Loren Terveen, and Brent Hecht. 2016. "Blissfully happy" or "ready to fight": Varying Interpretations of Emoji. In *Proc. ICWSM 2016*. AAAI Press.
37. Steven Millward. 2016. WeChat is 5 years old. Heres how its grown. *TechinAsia* (Jan. 2016). `https://www.techinasia.com/5-years-of-wechat/`.
38. Preeti Mudliar, Jonathan Donner, and William Thies. 2012. Emergent Practices Around CGNet Swara: A Voice Forum for Citizen Journalism in Rural India. *Information Technologies and International Development* 9, 2 (2012), 65–79.
39. Bonnie A. Nardi, Steve Whittaker, and Erin Bradner. 2000. Interaction and outeraction: instant messaging in action. In *Proc. CSCW 2000*. ACM Press, 79–88.
40. Kenton O'Hara, Michael Massimi, Richard Harper, Simon Rubens, , and Jessica Morris. 2014. Everyday Dwelling with WhatsApp. In *Proc. CSCW 2014*. ACM Press, 1131–1143.
41. Elisa Oreglia, Ying Liu, and Wei Zhao. 2011. Designing for Emerging Rural Users: Experiences from China. In *Proc. CHI 2011*. ACM Press, 1433–1436.
42. Neil Patel, Deepti Chittamuru, Anupam Jain, Paresh Dave, , and Tapan S. Parikh. 2010. Avaaj Otalo - A Field Study of an Interactive Voice Forum for Small Farmers in Rural India. In *Proc. CHI 2010*. ACM Press, 733–742.
43. Henning Pohl, Dennis Stanke, and Michael Rohs. 2016. EmojiZoom: emoji entry via large overview maps. In *Proc. MobileHCI 2016*. ACM Press, 510–517.
44. Red Envelope 2014. `http://traditions.cultural-china.com/en/214Traditions11960.html/` Accessed September 20, 2016.
45. Regulations for Creating Stickers on WeChat Sticker Open Platform 2016. `https://sticker.weixin.qq.com/cgi-bin/mmemoticon-bin/readtemplate?t=guide/index/` Accessed September 20, 2016.
46. Nithya Sambasivan, Ed Cutrell, Kentaro Toyama, , and Bonnie Nardi. 2010. Intermediated Technology Use in Developing COmmunities. In *Proc. CHI 2010*. ACM Press, 2583–2592.
47. Nithya Sambasivan and Thomas Smyth. 2010. The Human Infrastructure of ICTD. In *Proc. ICTD 2010*. ACM Press, Article No. 40.
48. Nithya Sambasivan, Julie Sage Weber, and Edward Cutrell. 2011. Designing a Phone Broadcasting System for Urban Sex Workers in India. In *Proc. CHI 2011*. ACM Press, 267–276.

49. Shenzhen Government Online: General Info 2016. http://english.sz.gov.cn/gi/ Accessed September 20, 2016.

50. Smartphone user penetration as percentage of total global population from 2014 to 2020 2017. https://www.statista.com/statistics/203734/global-smartphone-penetration-per-capita-since-2005/ Accessed January 5, 2017.

51. Craig Smith. 2016. How Many Users Do Skype, WhatsApp, WeChat, LINE, Facebook Messenger and Other Top Chat Apps Have? *DMR* (July 2016). http://expandedramblings.com/index.php/how-many-people-use-chat-apps/.

52. Piya Sorcar, Benjamin Strauber, Prashant Loyalka, Neha Kumar, and Shelley Goldman. 2017. Sidestepping the Elephant in the Classroom: Using Culturally Localized Technology to Teach Around Taboos. In *Proc. CHI 2017*. ACM Press.

53. Satomi Sugiyama. 2015. Kawaii meiru and Maroyaka neko: Mobile emoji for relationship maintenance and aesthetic expressions among Japanese teens. *First Monday* 20, 10 (2015). http://journals.uic.edu/ojs/index.php/fm/article/view/5826.

54. Channary Tauch and Eiman Kanjo. 2016. The roles of emojis in mobile phone notifications. In *Proc. UbiComp 2016*. ACM Press, 1560–1565.

55. Tencent - Products and Services 2016. http://www.tencent.com/en-us/ps/ Accessed September 20, 2016.

56. Tencent 2016 first quarter total revenue reached 31.995 billion yuan: An increase of 43 percent 2016. http://tech.qq.com/a/20160518/067853.htm/ Accessed September 20, 2016.

57. Indrani Medhi Thies. 2015. User Interface Design for Low-literate and Novice Users: Past, Present and Future. *Foundations and Trends in Human-Computer Interaction* 8, 1 (2015), 1–72. DOI: http://dx.doi.org/10.1561/1100000047

58. Joseph B. Walther and Kyle P. D'Addario. 2001. The Impacts of Emoticons on Message Interpretation in Computer-Mediated Communication. *Social Science Computer Review* 19, 3 (2001), 324–347.

59. Yang Wang, Yao Li, Bryan Semaan, and Jian Tang. 2016. Space Collapse: Reinforcing , Reconfiguring and Enhancing Chinese Social Practices through WeChat. In *Proc. ICWSM 2016*. AAAI, 427–435.

60. Yang Wang, Yao Li, and Jian Tang. 2015. Dwelling and Fleeting Encounters: Exploring Why People Use WeChat - A Mobile Instant Messenger. In *Proc. CHI EA 2015*. ACM Press, 1543–1548.

61. WeChat Report: Understanding WeChat's Five Top Businesses through 47 PPT Slides 2016. http://tech.qq.com/a/20160321/007049.htm/ Accessed September 20, 2016.

62. What does the red dot mean when chatting on WeChat 2016. http://www.88868889.cc/a/thread-28647.htm/ Accessed September 20, 2016.

63. Wireless Internet Value-Added Services 2016. https://www.tencent.com/en-us/ps/mtservices.shtml Accessed Jan 5, 2017.

# A Kaleidoscope of Languages: When and How Non-Native English Speakers Shift between English and Their Native Language during Multilingual Teamwork

**Ge Gao[1], Susan R. Fussell[1,2]**
[1]Department of Communication, [2]Department of Information Science
Cornell University
Ithaca NY 14850 USA
[gg365, sfussell]@cornell.edu

### ABSTRACT
Multilingual teams often include subgroups of members who share a native language different from the team's common language. Linguistic choices by members of these subgroups can have implications for information exchange at the team level. We reported a field study of language use in 3 multilingual teams, each of which consisted of some native English speakers (NS) and some non-native English speakers (NNS) who shared a native language with at least one other team member. We found that NNS often shifted between English and their native language. The way language shift happened differed for formal meetings, informal conversations, and instant messaging. Language variation was often associated with shifts in content, participants, and communication medium. Further analysis indicated that language shift had both benefits and costs for team communication, depending on the context in which it happened. Based on these findings, we outline suggestions for designing multilingual collaboration systems.

### Author Keywords
Language shift; multilingual communication; diverse team; computer-supported cooperative work (CSCW).

### ACM Classification Keywords
H.5.3. Group and Organization Interface: Computer-supported cooperative work.

### INTRODUCTION
Multilingual teams in which people speaking different native languages work together are common in modern organizations [22]. Despite the promise of multilingual teams for integrating diverse expertise on a global scale, this potential is often hindered by problems regarding the use of a common language (e.g., English) to communicate [12]. For example, in teams that use English as a common language, Non-native English speakers (NNS) are sometimes less active during meetings because they are concerned about their imperfect fluency [39], and native English speakers (NS) face challenges making themselves understood by NNS colleagues [20]. Differences in fluency in a team's common language may further contribute to the emergence of language-based subgroups that distance team members from each other [22, 40].


*CHI 2017*, May 06 - 11, 2017, Denver, CO, USA

ACM 978-1-4503-4655-9/17/05…$15.00
DOI: http://dx.doi.org/10.1145/3025453.3025839

Native English Speaker

Native Chinese Speaker

Native Chinese Speaker

**Figure 1. An example of communication conducted via mixed languages. One native English speaker and two native Chinese speakers are having a discussion in English. Among them, the two Chinese speakers may use either English or their native language to communicate.**

Using one's native language can help NNS alleviate the burdens of communicating in English. When the team consists of a subset of NNS who share the same native language, they sometimes interact in their native language rather than in English (see Figure 1). Hinds and colleagues [22], for instance, documented cases in which native German speakers temporarily switched to German during English meetings when they felt it was clearer and more efficient to do so. Lønsmann [31] further observed that NNS in multinational organizations that use English as the official working language sometimes talked to each other in their native languages during informal chat. This use of multiple languages had complicated impacts on communication at the team level. On the positive side, speaking in their native language allowed NNS to participate in work discussions more efficiently [1]; on the negative side, NS often reported feeling excluded when they could not comprehend and engage in conversations in the NNS's native language [4].

Researchers have argued that work communication would be most effective if multilingual teams could draw on the benefits of their members' various languages while minimizing the costs [27, 42]. With this goal in mind, a number of investigators have designed and evaluated tools to facilitate multilingual teamwork using either a common language or everybody's native language [e.g., 14, 15, 16, 19, 37, 42, 44]. For example, Gao and colleagues [15, 16] found that showing Japanese speakers automated transcripts of English speech improved conversational grounding during English-based meetings. Wang et al. [42] found that machine translation tools helped NNS speakers formulate messages during text-based conversations, though they hindered comprehension by both NNS and NS. Hara and Iqbal [19] found that speech translation tools enabled participants with various native languages to have oral conversations, but people needed to adapt their speech production and comprehension styles to compensate for errors induced through the speech recognition and translation processes.

While previous tools to support multilingual teams have sometimes been modestly successful, no tools to date allow for multilingual interaction that is as fluid and natural as that of conversations among native speakers of the same language. One reason for this may be that the tools have taken an "all or nothing" approach; either all text/speech is translated or transcribed, or none of it is [e.g., 19, 42]. However, studies of multilingual teams [e.g.,22, 31] suggest the process of switching among languages is much more subtle than this and that NNS may want or need different levels of support at different points in a conversation.

The goal of the current paper is to understand when and why members of multilingual teams shift between English as a common language and their native language, with the goal of informing the design of tools to better support multilingual teams. We present an in-depth field study of three multilingual teams that aims to understand people's actual practices of language use during teamwork. All teams consisted of both NS and NNS team members. Among the NNS, each person shared a native language with at least another member of the team.

Through extended observation of the team and interviews with team members we identified language shift, the practice through which people move back and forth between using English and non-English, as a central element in multilingual teamwork. These shifts in language use revealed how people drew on their mundane wisdom to balance values and costs of using multiple languages at work. More specifically, NNS team members reported that they constantly negotiated between using different languages. They conducted language shift as this negotiation was happening. They also developed strategies to cope with potential tensions, if any, that arose from language shifts. Our observation data further showed that the ways people shifted between languages differed depending on whether communication occurred in formal meetings, informal face-to-face conversation, or over computer-mediated communication channels.

Our findings provide an anchor for HCI researchers to reflect on the design of collaboration systems that support multilingual teamwork, and suggest strategies to maximize the value of having multilingual teams. We propose design suggestions regarding when and how technology could support teamwork by facilitating language shift.

## RELATED WORK AND RESEARCH QUESTIONS

In this section, we first review literature on the complexity of language use in multilingual teams. We then describe techniques developed by HCI scholars that have the potential to facilitate teamwork conducted in multiple languages. Based on the review of these two bodies of work, we outline research questions concerning an important yet missing piece of knowledge for both understanding and facilitating multilingual teamwork.

### The Multilingual Reality of Multilingual Teamwork

Multilingual teams usually adopt a common working language (e.g., English) that enables communication among all members. Having a common language, however, does not turn all work conversations into monolingual events [1]. People in multilingual workplaces may interact in a variety of languages depending on the situation [2, 4]. Barner-Rasmussen and Aarnio [4], for example, interviewed employees in Finnish subunits of English-speaking multinational companies and found that participants reported communicating frequently in both their native languages and in English. Peltokorpi and Vaara [38] similarly interviewed employees from Western subsidiaries in Japan and found that people conducted a considerable amount of work in their native languages rather than the common language. Tange and Lauring [40] interviewed employees from 14 multinational organizations in Denmark and found that communication, especially spontaneous chat, often occurred in a mixture of English, Danish, and several other languages.

Code-switching, or shifting from one language to another during the same conversation [2], has also been observed in multilingual teams. Ethnographic research has found this specific form of language use during both formal meetings [e.g., 22] and informal chat [e.g., 31] in multilingual workplaces. According to self-report data, NNS and NS who attended the same English conversation usually held different views of code-switching. While NNS reported switching to their native languages to reduce anxiety about speaking English and to make better arguments for their perspectives, NS colleagues reported feeling disconcerted and excluded when code-switching occurred [22].

### Techniques to Support Multilingual Teamwork

A number of scholars have designed and evaluated tools to enhance multilingual teamwork [e.g., 14, 15, 16, 19, 37, 42, 44]. In general, this work has taken one of two approaches:

maximizing the value of communicating in a common language or facilitating the use of multiple native languages.

In the first line of work, researchers have tried to improve the quality of English communication at meetings between NNS and NS of English. For example, Yamashita and colleagues helped NNS follow an English conversation by applying a variety of speech processing techniques, such as inserting artificial transmission lags between NS's utterances [44], showing automated transcripts of everyone's speech [15], and providing NS with information about how NNS interacted with automated transcripts [16].

In the second line of research, a number of techniques have been explored to support entire conversations in each person's own native language. For example, machine translation (MT) tools have been used to mediate various types of conversations between multilingual dyads, including text-based brain-storming [42], text-based hidden profile tasks [14, 45], and oral chats on casual topics [19]. NNS of English were found to be more talkative when they could communicate in their native language rather than in English, although message comprehension was sometimes challenged by translation errors [e.g., 42].

These two lines of work have achieved modest success at supporting multilingual teamwork but have rarely been able to support conversation that is as fluid and comprehensible as conversation among native speakers of a language. In part we argue that it is because researchers have generally taken an "all or nothing" approach such that either all messages were transcribed and/or translated or none of them were. However, as the field studies discussed earlier in this section suggest [e.g., 22, 31], NNS speakers in multilingual groups shift back and forth between the common language and their native language depending on the current context and goals.. To make multilingual collaboration systems more successful, we argue that these systems need to consider the contextual aspects of language use: when and why NNS shift between the team's common language and their native languages. The goal of this study is to provide an in-depth understanding of these processes in order to inform the design of future multilingual communication tools.

*RQ1. When and why do members of multilingual teams use their native language instead of a common language (e.g., English), and vice versa, at work?*

*RQ2. How do members of multilingual teams balance the value and the cost, if any, of using their native language vs. a common language?*

In the rest of this paper, we present a field study that aims to answer these research questions.

## METHOD

We conducted a field study of multilingual teams from a university in the United States. Following the theoretical sampling process suggested by grounded theory [18], we iterated through generating codes from collected data and checking and elaborating these codes by collecting more data. We stopped our data collection once all the core variables were saturated and checked. The final dataset consisted of observations and interviews with three multilingual teams, each of which was observed and interviewed for about 100 hours. All three teams yielded similar insights, which provided a robust, in-depth view of language practices for this type of team.

### Basic Information of Selected Teams

To best capture the dynamics of language use, we looked for teams that met the following requirements:

1) The team must include 4 or more members;
2) The team must use English as its only common language;
3) There should be at least 2 different native languages (including English), each spoken by a subset of members within the team;
4) The team had at least 1 ongoing project that required communication between multiple members of the team.

We started with an initial set of three teams that met these requirements. Each included several PhD students and one advisor who conducted research in an engineering and technology field. Two teams also had senior undergraduate and/or master's research assistants (RAs) who were involved in idea development, technical execution, and paper writing. All teams had a similar collaboration structure: The PhDs led each research project working with each other and RAs directly, and the advisor supervised all projects using a hands-off style.

All NNS of English in these teams passed the language exams for entering graduate school in the U.S. (e.g., TOEFL and GRE). Their self-reported level of fluency in English as described in the Interagency Language Roundtable (ILR) scale [25] was above professional working proficiency but below native proficiency. The composition of each team is summarized in Table 1.

| Team | Distribution of NS and NNS of English | |
|---|---|---|
| A | NS | 4 native speakers of English (1 advisor, 3 RAs) |
| | NNS | 2 native speakers of C (2 PhDs) |
| | | 2 native speakers of H (1 PhD, 1 RA ) |
| B | NS | 2 native speakers of English (2 PhDs) |
| | NNS | 2 native speakers of C (1 PhD, 1 RA) |
| | | 2 native speakers of K (1 PhD, 1 RA) |
| | | 2 native speakers of H (1 advisor, 1 PhD) |
| C | NS | 3 native speakers of English (1 advisor, 2 PhDs) |
| | NNS | 2 native speakers of C (2 PhDs) |

**Table 1. The linguistic composition of observed multilingual teams (the names of languages spoken by NNS were replaced by randomly assigned letters C, K, and H).**

Each team had its own workspace where all members sat either side-by-side or back-to-back and worked together. Near each team's workspace there were conference rooms for formal meetings. A sketch of the physical space each team was located in is given in Figure 2.

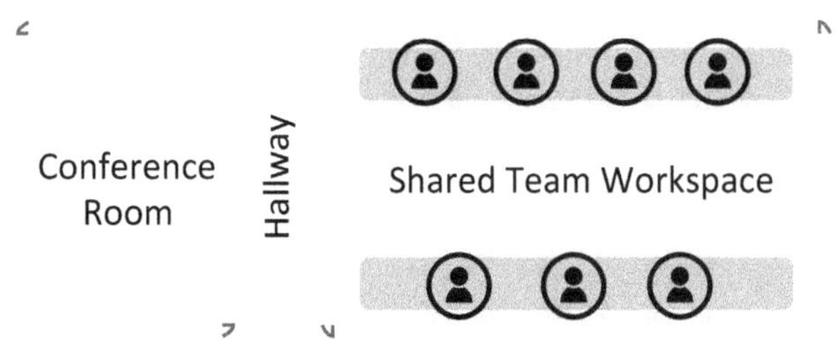


**Figure 2. A sketch of each observed team's physical spaces. All teams had similar spatial arrangements.**

### Data Collection

The first author of this paper, a bilingual English-Mandarin Chinese speaker, conducted on-site observations and interviews with each team between July and November of 2015. The full dataset consists of observation notes and interview transcripts generated from about 100 hours of field work for each team. The use of multiple sources of data deepens our understanding of people's language use through a process of triangulation [10].

During the observation phase, the first author stayed in the same workspace as a team and took notes on communication events as they happened. The notes documented multiple aspects of the conversation [24], including: the physical environment, the participants, the topic, the form of turn-taking, gestures and facial expressions, the medium (e.g., face-to-face vs. online), and the language (e.g., English vs. Mandarin). When the conversation was conducted in a language that we didn't understand, we sought clarification from participants afterwards. No audio or video recording was conducted due to team concerns over the proprietary nature of their topics of conversation.

Whenever possible, we asked people to reflect immediately after a communication event they just participated in. This retrospection allowed us to understand how people interpreted key aspects of the conversation such as the context, the perceived norms, people's motivations for using a particular language, and people's reactions to others' language choices [24].

In addition to the observations and the immediate retrospections, we performed semi-structured interviews with each member of the team. The interview included questions about (a) the interviewees' native language and cultural background; (b) the work s/he was doing in the team; (c) his/her general reflections on how and why s/he used each language; (d) perceived benefits and costs when using a common language vs. his/her native language; and (e) the role of technology in team communication.

### Analysis

We followed an inductive approach guided by grounded theory [10] to analyze all of our data. To maintain the natural structure of the data, we linked observation notes and interview transcripts by putting everything related to the same communication event together. Through multiple iterations of open coding, we identified language shift as a strong and central theme emerging from the data. We then conducted selective coding to explore the connection between language shift and other emerged categories. Finally, we iterated through both the data and related literatures, reflecting on the role of language shift within the entire communication flow at the team level. Our detailed findings are presented in the following section.

## FINDINGS

Our data suggested that NNS in the observed teams often shifted between English and their native language. Among all the communication events that included subsets of NNS who share the same native language, we witnessed different patterns of language shift in different communicative contexts including formal meetings, informal conversations, and instant messaging (IM). People's demographic background (e.g., gender and age) and roles in a team did not show clear association with the shift of language.

In the next four sections, we first describe in detail how and why NNS shifted languages in these three contexts (formal meetings, informal conversations and IM conversations). For each context, we draw on observation notes and/or interview data to examine the norms of language use, language shifts and their association with other shift(s) in the conversation, and other team members' reactions to language shift. After this, we present findings regarding the role of language shifts within the flow of team communication across contexts. For anonymization purposes, we recode part of the information in observation and interview quotes: the names of languages spoken by NNS were replaced by randomly assigned letters (e.g., C refers to language C), and name of participants were replaced by IDs linked to native language (e.g., C1 and C2 refer to different NNS speaking language C).

### Language Shift at Formal Meetings

In each team, we observed several formal meetings. Some were general group meetings at which one person presented on his or her work and received feedback from the rest of the team. Others were project meetings at which a subset of team members discussed specific issues regarding that project. These meetings always required advance preparation, including setting an agenda, negotiating a meeting time, and booking a conference room. Finalized information was announced to all participants via group email or online messages. Through this process, people inferred that these meetings were formal and only for work discussions. As one of our interviewees described:

*At the meetings, we really need to discuss the research and stay focused. That time is not reserved for a random friendly conversation. That time is reserved to figure out the research and see how we can make it as good as possible.* [E7, NS, Team C]

*Norms of Language Use*

When participants spoke up at formal meetings, they stated that their language use was subtly guided by their perception of the interpersonal and physical atmosphere of these meetings:

*Everybody is expected to speak English at formal meetings, because we need to make sure our thoughts are shared with everybody in this room. Sometimes when I speak, I know maybe I'm not using the best way to express an idea in English, but I just try my best.* [C1, NNS, Team A]

*At meetings, my rule of thumb is that everyone in this meeting room should understand what I say. There won't be the situation where someone is excluded just because of the language. We share professional discussions, and we use English.* [H3, NNS, Team B]

As indicated by the quotes given above, the use of English was perceived as a norm at formal meetings and it was respected by all members of these multilingual teams. Our observation on the actual language use at meetings further confirmed the adoption of this norm.

*Language Shift and Its Association with Content Shift*

We witnessed language shift at a very small proportion of formal meetings. The following segment of our observation notes documents a typical case of this kind of shift:

*At some point, H1 tried to make a comment on the idea C2 just proposed. H1 said "so maybe we can first make a prototype with the…". H1 made a pause here while looking toward H2. H1 then said something in [H] using a rising tone. H2 replied "oh, you mean Play-doh" and smiled. H1 nodded and said "oh, with the Play-doh" and continued to the next speech.* [Group meeting, Team A]

During the immediate retrospection afterwards, H1 gave a detailed explanation of his/her language shift:

*I didn't finish that sentence in English, because I didn't know the exact word in English. I got stuck there. So I asked H2 for help and explained what I wanted to say in [H]. If it is in writing, I usually stop and Google it. But when talking in person, I ask the question out because it keeps the flow of the conversation. My question is very short anyway.* [H1, NNS, Team A]

The above case of language shift, consistent with other cases we observed, showed that NNS may use their native languages when they encounter speech content that they cannot accurately express in English. This content, as we observed and heard from interviewees, usually referred to non-academic vocabularies and/or knowledge that was initially adopted in non-English education.

Language shift at formal meetings usually ended within just one or two speaking turns. Through the shifts, NNS tried to solve potential grounding problems [7] collaboratively with people who shared their native language. Once this goal was achieved, they shifted back to English immediately. Figure 3 illustrates the general pattern of language shift we observed at formal meetings.

*Reactions to Language Shift*

In all the cases we observed, there were no negative reactions from other participants to language shifts at formal meetings. People reported that they were fine with this temporary use of an unknown language, because "*it's short and it's clear from the context that they are trying to figure out something we all understand* [E9, NS, Team C]".

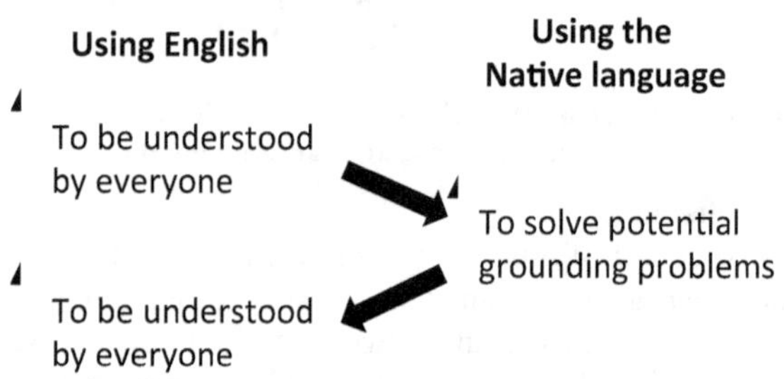


**Figure 3. The general pattern of NNS's language shift at formal meetings.**

### Language Shift at Informal Conversations

Informal conversations were mostly conducted in a team's workspace rather than the conference room, and they comprised the vast majority of communication in all observed teams. Spontaneity was identified as the most important feature of informal conversations by almost all interviewees:

*When we talk at our seats, the conversation could be about everything. It could be I run into a problem about work, so I ask another person a question. It could also be random chat, or many things mixed together. This is why I feel it's different from conversations at formal meetings. There is a lot of freedom. Other people can join and leave your conversation at any time.* [C1, NNS, Team A]

*Most of the time, we just turn to each other and say hey and we start talking. It's more like spontaneous interactions, like talking about something that we are doing at the moment. I just sit there and I spontaneously decide I may need someone's input on this or I'm going to use something for the next step.* [E8, NS, Team C]

*Norms of Language Use*

When people initiated an information conversation, they usually started by picking one specific addressee rather than talking to a whole group of people as they did at formal meetings. The addressee was usually claimed through either gestures (e.g., tapping a shoulder, gazing at someone) or verbal announcement (e.g., calling one's name). When the speaker and the addressee spoke different native languages, they used English as a common language to communicate. When the conversation happened between NNS with a shared native language, however, they often started the conversation in their native language rather than English. Our interviews indicated that NNS, regardless of which native language they spoke, were highly aware of this norm. NNS interviewees described their native language as the default way to communicate with one another:

*I think [C] is the default language for me to have face-to-face conversation with another [C] speaker. It's just our natural way of talking. It is the language for us to best express ourselves and understand others.* [C2, NNS, Team A]

*When I talk to K2 in the office, we usually talk in [K]. It's natural and it's more intimate and efficient. We chat about research and we chat about life. Everything in our one-on-one conversation is in [K].* [K1, NNS, Team B]

One interesting observation regarding NNS' language use was that they often inserted English words or phrases into their speech although the main body of their conversation was in their native language. These inserted words were always theoretical concepts and/or technical terms. NNS reported that they kept these words in English because they could not find equivalents in their native language. As one of the interviewees said:

*When H3 comes to my seat, we often talk in [H] because it's easier to build your speech. But technical terms are a little bit awkward to translate. There might be counterparts of them in [H]? But I don't know what they are. So we say them in English and insert that into [H] conversations.* [H4, NNS, Team B]

### Language Shift and Its Association with Participant Shift

Although informal conversations between NNS often started in their native language, we saw many cases in which NNS shifted back and forth between their native language and English during the conversation. Our data analysis indicated a close association between NNS' language shift and shifts in conversation participants. More specifically, since informal settings in the workspace do not set a clear boundary of who can or cannot participate in a conversation, the same participant may play different roles as the conversation goes on. Here, we adopt vocabulary from previous literature (e.g., [9], [8], [17]) to differentiate four basic types of participants:

- The **speaker** who makes the speech;
- **Addressee(s)** to whom the speaker's speech is directed;
- **Side participants** who are not addressees but who are perceived by the speaker as a part of the conversation;
- **Overhearers** who listen in on a conversation but are not considered by the speaker to be participants in the conversation.

Building on this vocabulary, we analyzed three selected examples from the observation notes, each of which described language shift in association with one specific form of participant shift.

***Example 1: Overhearers vs. Addressees***

*C5 and C6 were having a casual chat at their seats in [C]. In the middle of this conversation, E8 walked into the office, sat down, and said "hey guys, how are you doing?" in English. The three people then started chatting about each other's research and life, all in English. This conversation lasts for about 4 minutes. Then E8 took out a laptop and started replying to emails. Soon after this, C5 said something short to C6 in [C]. C6 replied a short sentence also in [C]. The conversation ended after C5 left the office.* [Informal conversation among 1NS and 2NNS who speak language C, Team C]

In the above example, the two NNS shifted languages when E8 entered the conversation. During the immediate retrospection, *C6* reported that they shifted from language C to English because "*E8 said hi to us, so we felt maybe we should include E8 into our conversation*". Their use of English stopped once E8 distanced himself from the conversation and became just an overhearer.

***Example 2: Overhearers vs. Side-Participants***

*H3 walked to H4's seat and initiated a conversation in [H]. H4 replied, also in [H]. While they were talking, they faced each other and exchanged gaze. After three rounds of turn-taking, H4 suddenly said something in English, "You know there will be a talk this week, right? It's about X (the research topic). I feel it's very related to your project and maybe also others' in our group". H3 replied, "cool, I will check that", also in English. This whole conversation lasted for just a few minutes. It ended when H3 walked away. While this conversation was happening, most people in this team were just seating in the workspace and working on their own stuff.* [Informal conversation between 2NNS who speak language H, Team B]

This example showed an interesting case in which the speaker used different languages as s/he assigned different roles to people who are not the direct addressee of a speech. As H4 reported in the immediate retrospection, they used language H during the first part of the conversation because "*we were talking about one of H3's papers, so it's not related to others. I don't think it deserves other's attention. They may not even care about it*". However, as the conversation went on, they mentioned a talk that was related to not only H3's work but also other people's research in this team. H4 then shifted to respond in English, with the consideration that "*other people might find that information useful as well*". Here, people who were initially overhearers could become side-participants and share the information exchanged in the team's common language.

***Example 3: Addressees vs. Side-Participants***

*E1 and C2 were having an English conversation at their seat about a technical problem they encountered while working on a project. After 3 minutes of talking, they went to C1 for some suggestions. The three people then stood in a circle and continued the conversation, still in English. At some point, C2 looked at E1 and said "give us one minute, we will discuss this [refers to several candidate solutions] in [C]". E1 smiled and said "okay". C2 and C1 then shifted to [C] to continue the discussion. Both people talked much faster than when they were talking in English. E1 stood there quietly looking at them talking. After about 2 minutes, they shifted back to English and said "okay, we found a solution". They then explained the solution in English to E1 in two sentences. While this whole conversation was happening, E2 and H1 were sitting in the workspace working on with their laptops.* [Informal conversation among 1NS and 2NNS who speak language C, Team A]

Different from the other two examples, this is a case in which NNS switched to their native language in the middle of an English conversation. As we found across all cases similar to this, the segment of native language communication was usually separated from the rest of English communication by a shift-beginning marker and a shift-ending marker. In Example 3, specifically, C2 marked the beginning of language shift by giving E1 a heads-up in English (e.g., "*give us one minute, we will discuss this in [C]*"), and the ending of this shift was marked by the two NNS indicating a closure of their conversation in language C (e.g., "*okay, we found a solution*"). These markers were provided intentionally for "*being polite*" to other participants in the conversation. During the immediate retrospection, C1 and C2 both reported that they shifted to language C for improving the efficiency of the technical discussion. As C2 described:

*We used [C] because it's way more efficient for problem solving. That discussion was about a lot of very detailed things, like many possible methods and also many terms. There were things that I didn't know if I could express precisely in English, and I believe it's the same for C1. But we have no problem getting everything clear in [C].* [C2, NNS, Team A]

While the two NNS talked in their native language, E1 was turned from a direct addressee to a side-participant because of the language shift. Both C1 and C2 were aware of the shift of E1's role. Once they finished the discussion in their native language, they included E1 as an addressee again by shifting back to English and updating him/her on what had been discussed in C. However, it is worth noting that the update was given as a summary rather than in detail. C1 explained that they omitted the details because "*the solution itself was what really mattered for all of us*".

Taken together, our analysis shows that NNS's language shift in informal conversations is closely associated with shifts in perceived conversational participants. Figure 4 diagrams the general pattern of language shift we observed in informal conversations.

*Reactions to Language Shift*

Overhearers of these informal conversations reported a mixed feeling toward NNS's language shift. All interviewees reported that they wouldn't mind their colleagues speaking a different language for making the conversation more efficiently. However, many of them also expressed the concern of getting excluded from discussions that they should have been included:

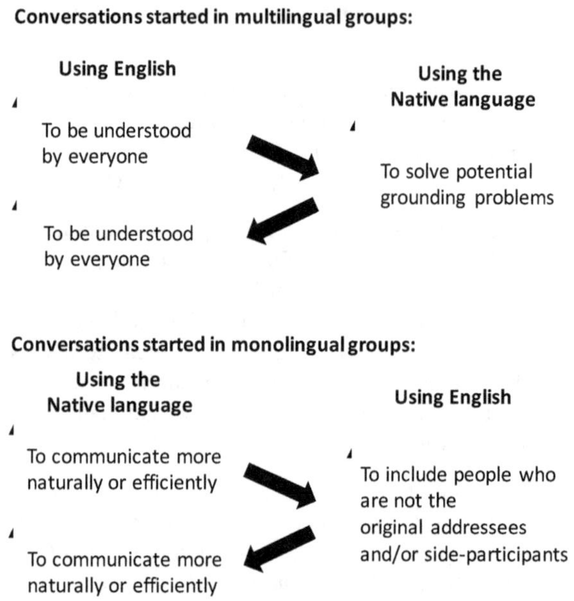


**Figure 4. The general pattern of NNS's language shift in informal conversations. NNS start a conversation in English or their native languages in multilingual (as example 3) or monolingual groups (as example 1 and 2), respectively. They shift between English and their native language as they assign different roles to other participants in the conversation.**

*I would prefer people in the lab to speak a language that we all understand, because, you know, sometimes that makes me feel excluded. I don't mind if they are just talking about their personal stuff. There is no reason for me to be involved in those conversations. But I would like to be involved in work related conversations. Maybe I could contribute something to those conversations, you know. But again, I feel it would be rude to say 'hey, please speak English'.* [E8, NS, Team C]

This interviewee pointed out an important issue that was confirmed by most other interviewees across the three teams: understanding the main topic of a conversation matters a lot to overhearers. People would love to understand research discussions that are related to the shared interests of the team, but they usually did not mind others talking about minor details of their own project or their personal life in a different language. Thus, when NNS were willing to explain the main topic of their work-related conversations, as what we saw in Example 3, other people always reported this as something they highly appreciated.

When NNS would not share the topic of their native language conversation voluntarily, other people sometimes relied on certain cues to guess the topic of the conversation. A primary cue mentioned by most interviewees was English loan words inserted in non-English conversations. People reported that these English words enable them to get a sense of the conversation: *"(I can) sort of say they are talking about this or that, even though I don't really understand what they are talking about* [E5, NS, Team B]".

### Language Shift at Instant Messaging (IM)

We also looked at how people conducted online communication through IM. Two of the teams we observed relied on Slack[1] to set up online communication. On the Slack page of these teams, there are a number of group channels built for sending out announcements to the whole team or having project-centered discussions among specific subsets of people. People could also set up one-on-one chat on Slack by clicking another person's name and creating a private channel.

For the team that didn't use Slack, online communication was mainly conducted via Google Hangout. All team members had Google accounts associated with their working email addresses assigned by the university. People could sign into Google Hangout by opening either the client-side application or the Gmail webpage.

During our observations, we saw people keep their Slack or Hangout window open once they arrived at the office. Some people also installed the mobile application of these IM platforms, so that they could receive messages even without a laptop. People perceived both Slack and Google Hangout as communication platforms specifically for the team's work conversations. As some of our interviewees said:

*Slack is the place where we talk about work coordination, or ask research related questions, or many other things about working in this group. All the people you can see on this Slack page are people you work with here. You won't add your friends out of work into this channel. Also, all conversations here are organized under themes, that's usually the name of each project. It helps us structure the messages, and it's good.* [H2, NNS, Team A]

*We use Google Hangout to discuss about work online. For example, I get an idea for the next step of the research, so I send it to other people through Hangout. We also talk on Hangout to discuss the time for a meeting. It's mostly only for work, maybe because it's connecting with your work Email. The whole network here is your professional network.* [C5, NNS, Team C]

#### *Norms of Language Use*

We asked people to open their Slack or Hangout conversation history and reflect on their language use. Interestingly, the conversation history showed that NNS rarely exchanged messages in their native language on either platform.

During the interview, many NNS reported that they used English for these IM conversations intentionally, so that messages could be found more easily in the future:

*I try to use as much English as possible here (refers to Slack), because we are talking about the research and these messages are archived. I may want to review or even copy some of this content when I write papers in the future. That will be in English. I don't do publications in [K]. Face-to-face conversations don't have such record, so there is no other use of a conversation outside the current physical environment.* [K1, NNS, Team B]

*On Hangout I only text in English. I know my English is not perfect, but conversations here are always about work and they are archived. There is a benefit of using English here. When I go back and search for stuff using keywords, it's always easy to do it in English. I'm actually not sure how the search would work in [C]. It's like when you are using Google scholar, you never search a keyword using [C].* [C6, NNS, Team C].

In addition to concerns about the long-term functionality of messages, some NNS interviewees further pointed out that IM allowed them to "*double check the grammar and adjust the wording with the help of online dictionaries before a message was sent out* [C1, NNS, Team A]". Thus, they usually felt it was easier to use English at IM conversations than in face-to-face conversations.

#### *Language Shift and Its Association with Medium Shift*

Slack and Hangout were online platforms used by NNS to have work discussions in English, but they were not the only platforms for these discussions. We witnessed many cases in which NNS used their personal IM platforms, such as WhatsApp or Facebook messenger, to have both work-related and personal conversations. On these platforms, NNS always shifted to their native language to communicate with other NNS. NNS explained during interviews that these local IM platforms "*were initially set up for contacting friends rather than colleagues, so there is little sense of obligation to use English* [C3, NNS, Team B]".

#### *Reactions to Language Shift*

Our interviews indicated that people were usually not aware of others' online conversations outside Slack or Google Hangout. However, some interviewees reported that there was reason to expect NNS with the same language use their local platforms to communicate. One of the interviewees said:

*They (refers to NNS who share the same native language) probably communicate to each other through other channels, and I will never be a part of those conversations. I don't know if that's actually true or not, but that's the expectation.* [E5, NS, Team B]

[1] https://slack.com/is

### Language Shift within The Whole Flow of Team Communication

Language shift not only complicated the communication in each specific context (formal meetings, informal chat, and online communication), but also had complex influences on the whole flow of communication across contexts. During the observations and interviews, we found cases in which NNS conducted informal conversations in their native languages and took advantage of these discussions to improve their later participation in formal English meetings. People reported that these informal conversations allowed them "*to polish the ideas better beforehand and they make the later English meetings way more efficient* [H1, NNS, Team A]". However, we also witnessed cases in which NNS set up a series of conversations on the same research idea across different languages and mediums. As a result, it usually "*requires extra effort to translate all the information between languages and integrate them together, so that the information could be shared with the whole group at the later stage (of the research)* [C4, NNS, Team B]".

In sum, our data showed that language shift has both benefits and costs for team communication, depending on the context in which it happened.

## DISCUSSION

Consistent with previous research [e.g., 12, 31], our findings showed that NNS did not use the team's common language or their own native language for all conversations. Instead, they chose between different languages based on the context. In the rest of the discussion, we considered the association between NNS's language shift and their interpretation of the most salient need under each context.

Formal meetings set up the context in which a whole group seeks to establish common ground. The use of English, as indicated by the interviews, enabled both NS and NNS to satisfy this contextual need. Previous work on bilingualism found that bilingual speakers temporarily switched to another language to clarify content that could not be grounded in the current language [13]. The NNS in our study used a similar practice as a strategy for building common ground in English conversations with a multilingual audience. Furthermore, we found that NNS tried to minimize the salience of their language shifts during formal meetings. They shifted to their native language for just one or two turns and then shifted back to English immediately; or, they had informal discussions in their native languages prior to formal meetings.

Although some research on multilingual teams reported cases in which NNS had lengthy discussions in their native language at English meetings or even converted the rest of the meeting into their native language [e.g., 22, 31], we did not see similar cases during our study. One possible explanation of this difference is the macro language environment where these multilingual teams immersed in. Since previous research [e.g., 4, 22, 31, 38] was often conducted in multinational organizations located in non-English speaking countries, NNS of English may perceive their local language as having equal legitimacy in the workplace as English [31]. In our study, however, all teams were from a university in the United States where the local language is English. Our study, along with previous research, indicated that language shift is a common practice of communication in multilingual teams regardless of what the dominant language is at the societal level.

Besides formal meetings, informal conversations also play a crucial role in teamwork especially at executing work-related tasks and sharing knowledge between co-workers [26, 43]. Previous CSCW research has indicated that NNS of English living in English-speaking countries prefer to communicate with fellow speakers using their native language during informal conversations [46]. Our study extends this work by digging deeper into how NNS use different languages to communicate in the workplace. Specifically, we found that NNS often perceived two different but interlaced needs during informal conversations: to properly include certain participants in a conversation, and to maximize conversational grounding efficiency. Linguistic choices that addressed one need might fail to fulfill the other [5]. As we demonstrated through some examples, two NNS can communicate most efficiently in their native language, but this excludes others from the conversation; speaking English allows both NS and NNS to be included in the same conversation, but it hinders NNS's ability to express complicated thoughts. Every time NNS opted for English vs. his/her native language, this choice generated ripple effects on later stages of the conversation. NNS then made further language shifts as these rippled effects happened. They used shift-markers as a technique to help balance benefits and costs associated with their choosing and re-choosing on language.

When NNS communicate using work-focused IM platforms, their language use is closely associated with contextual needs guaranteed by the "perceived affordance [36]" of the medium. More specifically, since messages exchanged via IM are usually archived, it offers the potential for people to review, search, and reuse the content of their earlier conversations. The use of English further consolidates the long-term functionality of IM messages by simplifying the process of information retrieval. In the field of HCI and CSCW, substantial research has examined the use of IM for lightweight communication [e.g., 6], work coordination [e.g., 33], and multitasking [e.g., 26]. While these studies emphasized the immediate delivery of IM messages, little research has examined the "archiveabilty" of IM messages and its influence on teamwork. The current study helps address this question by connecting the archiving of messages and NNS's language use in multilingual teams. Further, our observations showed that NNS usually shift to their native language when having work-related conversations on personal IM platforms that are not always noticed by others. This use of hidden platforms can decrease the communication visibility at the team level [11, 29]. Using NNS's native languages on these platforms can further intensify the lack of communication visibility between subsets of people who speak different languages.

It is worth noting that people's contextual use of language as we discussed here was qualified by certain attributes of our observed teams. These attributes include but may not limited to: collocated, research-oriented, non-industrial and requiring high English language competence. Future research will be needed to verify to what extent our findings can be transferred to other forms of multilingual teams.

## DESIGN IMPLICATIONS

Findings from this study provide insights for the design of multilingual collaboration systems. These insights concern how technology could be applied to facilitate multilingual communication based on the context in which it happens.

### Machine Translation (MT) Tools and Formal Meetings

Formal meetings are usually dominated by English conversations. NNS may shift to their native languages, but only temporarily, in order to translate words and expressions. This suggests a new way to incorporate MT modules into multilingual meeting systems. Instead of using MT to translate all messages, as most previous research has done [e.g., 19, 42], tool designers should consider giving users full control over when to turn the MT module on or off. Moreover, interviewees in our study mentioned that interacting with translation tools can break the natural flow of an oral conversation. To address this concern, automatic language identification (LID) could be implemented into the MT module. When NNS choose to turn the MT module on, the system could detect language shift and provide MT output automatically.

### Non-Human Agents and Informal Conversations

NNS's language use in informal communication was closely associated with their perception of who was participating in a conversation. NS who are perceived as overhearers may want to join in but they cannot do so if the conversation is conducted in an unknown language. Based on this finding, we suggest that a system might sense the environment and prompt users with information about the context of conversation. More specifically, systems may help speakers stay aware of the potential participants and what roles each participant may take over the conversation [20, 32]. Systems might also increase speakers' awareness of different value interpretations held by different participants.

Further, our interviewees reported that it would be rude to ask others to shift to English. They also did not want to interrupt others if the topic of the conversation was about personal matters. Based on this finding, we suggest using non-human agents to alleviate the social awkwardness associated with language shift. Research in human-robot interaction has demonstrated how interpersonal interactions that are problematic between people could be facilitated by the use of robots and agents [e.g., 3, 23, 41]. Following this line of thoughts, we propose implementing non-human agents, such as desktop robots or intelligent avatars on tablets, into the physical workspace to facilitate interactions between speakers of different native languages. When an agent detects conversations in a language that is not understood by overhearers, it could ask the speaker whether s/he would like to explain the topic of the conversation using the common language. In this way, the speaker could be reminded to reflect on their language choice based on the current context. Overhearers would benefit from this reflection without interrupting others abruptly.

### Text Annotation Tools and Instant Messaging (IM)

We found that NNS hold work-related conversations not only on work-focused IM platforms (e.g., Slack) but also on personal IM platforms. The languages they chose to use on different platforms were often different, requiring extra effort to integrate and translate all the information surrounding a single work task. Previous work has shown how text annotation tools can help NNS better process and structure information in English IM conversations [e.g., 30]. We propose implementing similar tools in IM platforms used by NNS. Annotation tools could automatically generate English tags based on the text exchanged in IM chat. Once key words, such as a particular technical term, are detected, the annotation tool could mark this part of the conversation and categorize it into a note. It might also generate auto-reminders to NNS to ask if they would like to move the conversation to a work-focused platform or summarize the conversation in English. When NNS need to integrate information across IM platforms and languages, they could use the automated tags to organize and/or translate these conversations with less effort.

## CONCLUSION

To better understand and facilitate communication in teams consisting of speakers of multiple native languages, we conducted a field study of language use in three multilingual teams. Each team consisted of some native English speakers (NS) and some non-native English speakers (NNS) who shared a native language with at least one other team member. We found that NNS in these teams often moved back and forth between using English and using their native language. This shift of language may happen in different ways and serve for different purposes under various contexts of communication. Our analysis also showed that language shift can have complicated impacts on communication at the team level, depending on the context in which it happened. Based on these findings, we propose design ideas for facilitating communication in multilingual teams during formal meetings, informal conversations, and instant messaging, respectively.

## ACKNOWLEDGMENTS

This research was funded in part by National Science Foundation grants #1421929 and #1318899. We thank Leslie Setlock, Sun-Young Hwang, and Alexandra Hinck for their assistance. We also thank all the anonymous teams for their support and the reviewers for their valuable comments.

## REFERENCES

1. Jo Angouri. 2013. The multilingual reality of the multinational workplace: Language policy and language use. *Journal of Multilingual and Multicultural Development* 34, 6: 564-581.
2. Peter Auer. 1988. A conversation analytic approach to codeswitching. In *Codeswitching: Anthropological and Sociolinguistic Perspectives*, Monica Heller (eds.). Berlin: Mouton Publishers, Berlin, 187 – 214.
3. Wilma A. Bainbridge, Justin Hart, Elizabeth S. Kim, and Brian Scassellati. 2008. The effect of presence on human-robot interaction. In *Proceedings of the IEEE International Symposium on Robot and Human Interactive Communication* (RO-MAN' 08). IEEE, 701-706.
4. Wilhelm Barner-Rasmussen and Christoffer Aarnio. 2011. Shifting the faultlines of language: A quantitative functional-level exploration of language use in MNC subsidiaries. *Journal of World Business* 46, 3: 288-295.
5. Allan Bell. 1984. Language style as audience design. *Language in Society* 13, 2: 145-204.
6. Jeremy P. Birnholtz, Thomas A. Finholt, Daniel B. Horn, and Sung Joo Bae. 2005. Grounding needs: achieving common ground via lightweight chat in large, distributed, ad-hoc groups. In *Proceedings of the SIGCHI Conference on Human Factors in Computing Systems* (CHI '05). ACM, New York, NY, USA, 21-30. DOI=http://dx.doi.org/10.1145/1054972.1054976
7. Herbert H. Clark. 1996. Using Language. Cambridge: Cambridge University Press.
8. Herbert H. Clark and Edward F. Schaefer. 1987. Concealing one's meaning from overhearers. *Journal of Memory and Language* 26, 2: 209-225.
9. Herbert H. Clark and Thomas B. Carlson. 1982. Hearers and speech acts. *Language* 58, 2: 332-373.
10. Juliet Corbin and Anselm Strauss. 1990. Basics of Qualitative Research: Grounded Theory Procedures and Techniques. Newbury Park, CA: Sage Publications, Inc.
11. Alan R. Dennis, Julie A. Rennecker, and Sean Hansen. 2010. Invisible whispering: Restructuring collaborative decision making with instant messaging. *Decision Sciences* 41, 4: 845-886.
12. Alan J. Feely, and Anne-Wil Harzing. 2002. *Forgotten and Neglected: Language the Orphan of International Business Research.* Aston Business School.
13. Joseph Gafaranga. 2000. Medium repair vs. other-language repair: Telling the medium of a bilingual conversation. *International Journal of Bilingualism* 4, 3: 327-350.
14. Ge Gao, Bin Xu, David C. Hau, Zheng Yao, Dan Cosley, and Susan R. Fussell. 2015. Two is better than one: Improving multilingual collaboration by giving two machine translation outputs. In *Proceedings of the ACM Conference on Computer Supported Cooperative Work & Social Computing* (CSCW '15). ACM, New York, NY, USA, 852-863. DOI: http://dx.doi.org/10.1145/2675133.2675197
15. Ge Gao, Naomi Yamashita, Ari MJ Hautasaari, Andy Echenique, and Susan R. Fussell. 2014. Effects of public vs. private automated transcripts on multiparty communication between native and non-native English speakers. In *Proceedings of the SIGCHI Conference on Human Factors in Computing Systems* (CHI '14). ACM, New York, NY, USA, 843-852. DOI: http://dx.doi.org/10.1145/2556288.2557303
16. Ge Gao, Naomi Yamashita, Ari M.J. Hautasaari, and Susan R. Fussell. 2015. Improving multilingual collaboration by displaying how non-native speakers use automated transcripts and bilingual dictionaries. In *Proceedings of the SIGCHI Conference on Human Factors in Computing Systems* (CHI '15). ACM, New York, NY, USA, 3463-3472. DOI: http://dx.doi.org/10.1145/2702123.2702498
17. David R. Gibson. 2003. Participation shifts: Order and differentiation in group conversation. *Social Forces* 81, 4: 1335-1380.
18. Barney G. Glaser. 1978. Advances in the Methodology of Grounded Theory: Theoretical Sensitivity. San Francisco, CA: The Sociology Press.
19. Kotaro Hara and Shamsi T. Iqbal. 2015. Effect of machine translation in interlingual conversation: Lessons from a formative study. In *Proceedings of the SIGCHI Conference on Human Factors in Computing Systems* (CHI '15). ACM, New York, NY, USA, 3473-3482. DOI: http://dx.doi.org/10.1145/2702123.2702407
20. Christian Heath and Paul Luff. 1992. Collaboration and control: Crisis management and multimedia technology in London underground line control rooms. *Computer Supported Cooperative Work* 1, 1-2: 69-94.
21. Jane K. Henderson. 2005. Language diversity in international management teams. *International Studies of Management & Organization* 35, 1: 66-82.
22. Pamela J. Hinds, Tsedal B. Neeley, and Catherine D. Cramton. 2014. Language as a lightning rod: Power

contests, emotion regulation, and subgroup dynamics in global teams. *Journal of International Business Studies* 45, 5: 536-561.

23. Guy Hoffman, Oren Zuckerman, Gilad Hirschberger, Michal Luria, and Tal Shani Sherman. 2015. Design and evaluation of a peripheral robotic conversation companion. In *Proceedings of the Tenth Annual ACM International Conference on Human-Robot Interaction* (HRI'15). ACM, New York, NY, USA, 3-10.
24. Dell Hymes. 1967. Models of the interaction of language and social setting. *Journal of Social Issues* 23, 2: 8-28.
25. Interagency Language Roundtable (ILR). ILR Scale: https://en.wikipedia.org/wiki/ILR_scale
26. Ellen Isaacs, Alan Walendowski, Steve Whittaker, Diane J. Schiano, and Candace Kamm. 2002. The character, functions, and styles of instant messaging in the workplace. In *Proceedings of the ACM Conference on Computer Supported Cooperative Work* (CSCW '02). ACM, New York, NY, USA, 11-20. DOI=http://dx.doi.org/10.1145/587078.587081
27. Torum Ishida. 2011. The Language Grid: Service-Oriented Collective Intelligence for Language Resource Interoperability. Springer Science & Business Media.
28. Steinar Kristoffersen and Fredrik Ljungberg. 1999. An empirical study of how people establish interaction: implications for CSCW session management models. In *Proceedings of the SIGCHI Conference on Human Factors in Computing Systems* (CHI '99). ACM, New York, NY, USA, 1-8. DOI=http://dx.doi.org/10.1145/302979.302980
29. Paul M. Leonardi. 2014. Social media, knowledge sharing, and innovation: Toward a theory of communication visibility. *Information Systems Research* 25, 4: 796-816.
30. Na Li and Mary Beth Rosson. 2014. Using annotations in online group chats. In *Proceedings of the SIGCHI Conference on Human Factors in Computing Systems* (CHI '14). ACM, New York, NY, USA, 863-866. DOI: http://dx.doi.org/10.1145/2556288.2557209
31. Dorte Lønsmann. 2014. Linguistic diversity in the international workplace: Language ideologies and processes of exclusion. *Multilingua* 33, 1-2: 89-116.
32. Andrew Monk and Leon Watts. 2000. Peripheral participation in video-mediated communication. *International Journal of Human-Computer Studies* 52, 5: 933-958.
33. Bonnie A. Nardi, Steve Whittaker, and Erin Bradner. 2000. Interaction and outeraction: instant messaging in action. In *Proceedings of the ACM Conference on Computer Supported Cooperative Work* (CSCW '00). ACM, New York, NY, USA, 79-88. DOI=http://dx.doi.org/10.1145/358916.358975
34. Clifford Nass, Jonathan Steuer, Ellen Tauber, and Heidi Reeder. 1993. Anthropomorphism, agency, and ethopoeia: computers as social actors. In *Proceedings of the SIGCHI Conference on Human Factors in Computing Systems* (CHI '93). ACM, New York, NY, USA, 111-112. DOI=http://dx.doi.org/10.1145/259964.260137
35. Clifford Nass and Youngme Moon. 200. Machines and mindlessness: Social responses to computers. *Journal of social issues* 56, 1: 81-103.
36. Donald A. Norman. 1999. Affordance, conventions, and design. *Interactions* 6, 3 (May 1999), 38-43. DOI=http://dx.doi.org/10.1145/301153.301168
37. Yingxin Pan, Danning Jiang, Michael Picheny, and Yong Qin. 2009. Effects of real-time transcription on non-native speaker's comprehension in computer-mediated communications. In *Proceedings of the SIGCHI Conference on Human Factors in Computing Systems* (CHI '09). ACM, New York, NY, USA, 2353-2356. DOI=http://dx.doi.org/10.1145/1518701.1519061
38. Vesa Peltokorpi and Eero Vaara. 2012. Language policies and practices in wholly owned foreign subsidiaries: A recontextualization perspective. *Journal of International Business Studies* 43, 9: 808-833.
39. Pemela Rogerson-Revell. 2008. Participation and performance in international business meetings. *English for Specific Purposes* 27, 3: 338-360.
40. Hanne Tange and Jakob Lauring. 2009. Language management and social interaction within the multilingual workplace. *Journal of Communication Management* 13, 3: 218-232.
41. Brett Stoll, Chad Edwards, and Autumn Edwards. 2016. "Why aren't you a sassy little thing": The effects of robot-enacted guilt trips on credibility and consensus in a negotiation. *Communication Studies*. DOI: 10.1080/10510974.2016.1215339
42. Hao-Chuan Wang, Susan Fussell, and Dan Cosley. 2013. Machine translation vs. common language: effects on idea exchange in cross-lingual groups. In *Proceedings of the ACM Conference on Computer Supported Cooperative Work* (CSCW '13). ACM, New York, NY, USA, 935-944. DOI=http://dx.doi.org/10.1145/2441776.2441882
43. Steve Whittaker, David Frohlich, and Owen Daly-Jones. 1994. Informal workplace communication: what is it like and how might we support it?. In *Proceedings of the SIGCHI Conference on Human Factors in Computing Systems* (CHI '94). ACM, New York, NY, USA, 131-137. DOI=http://dx.doi.org/10.1145/191666.191726

44. Naomi Yamashita, Andy Echenique, Toru Ishida, and Ari Hautasaari. 2013. Lost in transmittance: how transmission lag enhances and deteriorates multilingual collaboration. In *Proceedings of the ACM Conference on Computer Supported Cooperative Work* (CSCW '13). ACM, New York, NY, USA, 923-934. DOI=http://dx.doi.org/10.1145/2441776.2441881

45. Naomi Yamashita, Rieko Inaba, Hideaki Kuzuoka, and Toru Ishida. 2009. Difficulties in establishing common ground in multiparty groups using machine translation. In *Proceedings of the SIGCHI Conference on Human Factors in Computing Systems* (CHI '09). ACM, New York, NY, USA, 679-688. DOI=http://dx.doi.org/10.1145/1518701.1518807

46. Chien Wen Yuan, Leslie D. Setlock, Dan Cosley, and Susan R. Fussell. 2013. Understanding informal communication in multilingual contexts. In *Proceedings of the ACM Conference on Computer Supported Cooperative Work* (CSCW '13). ACM, New York, NY, USA, 909-922. DOI=http://dx.doi.org/10.1145/2441776.2441880

# The (Un)sustainability of Imagined Future Information Societies

**Daniel Pargman[1], Elina Eriksson[1], Mattias Höjer[2], Ulrika Gunnarsson Östling[2], Luciane Aguiar Borges[2]**

[1]School of Computer Science and Communication, KTH Royal Institute of Technology, Sweden, {pargman, elina}@kth.se

[2]School of Architecture and the Built Environment, KTH Royal Institute of Technology, Sweden, {mattias.hojer, ulrika.ostling, luciane.borges}@abe.kth.se

## ABSTRACT
The pathway to a sustainable society is not clear, and we need to consider different developmental possibilities. This paper describes the results of a research project in the intersection of HCI and Futures Studies as well as in the intersection between "the future information society" and sustainability.

We here present parts of the body of materials that were developed in a multi-year research project with the aim of describing and evaluating the sustainability impact of possible future information societies. We also discuss some of the lessons learned and what HCI and design fiction can learn from Futures Studies in general and from this project in particular. The main stakeholders in this project have been city administrators and corporate partners, and the overarching goal has primarily been to influence planning processes at the regional (Stockholm, Sweden) level.

### Author Keywords
Design fiction; Futures studies; Scenarios; Sustainability

## INTRODUCTION
Societies change. Sometimes imperceptibly and sometimes in great leaps – or at least so it seems in hindsight. Contemporary societies are struggling with numerous predicaments and sustainability is one of them. These predicaments – unlike simpler more straightforward problems – cannot once and for all be "solved," but they still need to be addressed in the present. The particular ways in which our modern societies develop are not set in stone and we *do* have the potential to avoid certain futures, choose between other futures and attempt to shape futures chosen in directions we deem desirable. Little can be changed in the short term, but more can be changed in the long term since both uncertainty and degree of freedom increases over time. But *how* can we do that? How do we *practically* think about the future and weigh different options against each other?


*CHI 2017, May 06 - 11, 2017, Denver, CO, USA*

ACM 978-1-4503-4655-9/17/05...$15.00
DOI: http://dx.doi.org/10.1145/3025453.3025858

There are many examples of how researchers and scientists have been inspired by science fiction literature and of how ideas from science fiction currently are shaping our future [7, 11, 24, 28, 53]. There are also numerous examples of science fiction authors who are also researchers, e.g. professor of mathematics Vernor Vinge, space scientist Alastair Reynolds, professor of linguistics Suzette Haden Elgin, professor of biology Joan Slonczewski, professor of physics Gregory Benford, etc. The border between fact and fiction, between inspiration and aspiration, and between science and speculation is not always clear-cut.

Within the field of human-computer interaction (HCI), the future is always ever present since typically the underlying aim is to influence the design and development of future computer systems. However, there has been a recent and increasing interest within both design and HCI in exploring more alternative futures through, for example, design fiction [11, 12, 51].

This paper does not however take its starting point in HCI, but rather in the adjacent academic field of futures studies, which for decades has worked with *possible*, *probable*, and *preferable* futures [see further 1, 8, 9]. In this paper, we describe the results of a research project that examined the intersection of "the future information society" and sustainability. While the theoretical framework and the selected research methods primarily come from futures studies, there is nothing that inherently makes this study or its results *essentially* different from a project that could have emanated from within HCI.

One major difference however is that the project we describe below has (as apart from a typical HCI project) not had as its purpose an attempt to suggest, influence, or steer processes of innovation in terms of designing or developing interactive digital technologies, systems, or services. While such technologies, systems and services in fact *have* been "designed" (or conjured up) in the project, this has not been a *goal* but rather a *means* for reaching project goals. The research project has instead had city administrators (bureaucrats, planners, and policymakers) and private companies (corporate partners) as its primary audiences. The ulterior purpose has not been to influence design, but rather to influence the civil servants who already draw up the *actual* plans and policy documents that will shape the future of our (information) society for decades to come. The civil servants in question primarily work in the Stockholm region of Sweden.

While many of these city administrators are very interested in the idea of using Big Data as a tool for (policy) modeling [30, 34, 35], only recently have they awoken to the fact that they should also more generally take ICT developments into consideration more generally when planning for future needs in terms of roads, public transportation, housing, school, health care, jobs, leisure, etc. While digital technologies advance at a rapid pace, changes in infrastructure are by contrast slow and cumbersome.

## BACKGROUND

Few dispute that we have left "industrial society" behind and now live in an "information society." Many researchers and pundits have attempted to identify this shift and place it in the past, the present, or the near future. Thirty years ago, James Beniger [10, p.4-5] enumerated no less than 75 "*modern societal transformations identified since 1950.*" Many of these specifically treated a shift to a future "information society" and it seems each researcher felt compelled to propose a more or less fanciful term for the future societies they had identified[1]. Google's Ngram Viewer, an online search engine that specifically looks for the frequency of a specified term in printed sources[2], shows that the use of the term "information society" started to rise slowly in the beginning, and then more rapidly at the end of the 1970s before peaking 30 years later, in the early 2000s.

Numerous visions of the future information society have consequently been formulated during the last few decades [22, 27, 57]. In parallel, other visions also exist of future *sustainable* societies [18, 31]. There is however a dearth of visions that take both these notions into consideration by trying to combine them so as to imagine *future sustainable information societies*, or, *the sustainability* (or the lack thereof) *of imagined future information societies*. That was the purpose of the research project we report upon here: "*Scenarios and sustainability impacts in information societies.*" What could future information societies look like? What would be the impact in terms of the sustainability (or not) of such a society? By asking and by exploring these questions, and by working both towards and together with city administrators as well as private companies, the purpose of the research project was to influence planning processes and/or raise sustainability and ICT as topics that (preferably together) should be taken into account by public policies and industrial strategies.

## FUTURES STUDIES

Even though people have always been thinking of the future, futures studies as an academic field emerged in the mid-1960s [2, 8], initially focusing on technological developments with implications for national security [21]. The use of futures studies methodologies subsequently spread to the private sector as a way to cope with uncertainty [58]. Futures studies has become a tool to support decision-making in different sectors of society such as transportation [63], environmental policy-making [49] and climate change [40], as well as informing debate surrounding them.

Futures studies posit images, or stories about the future, while including an analysis of how those prospective futures relate to the current state [50]. They can thus help us prepare for different futures, including aiming for certain futures and avoiding others. The plural term 'futures' highlights that the future is uncertain and opens up for several parallel stories about the future rather than only one. Futures studies do not regard the future as a disconnected end-state, but rather as rooted in both the past and the present [8, 37]. This means that even though there are some future events that we can be rather certain about, the future is on the whole shaped by us, together. This means that we *can* influence the future, which seems like a rather obvious statement when taken at face value. It should however be remembered that it is not uncommon in decision making to only refer to "what *will* happen" (for example "*you can't stop innovation so you shouldn't even try*"), as if it was impossible to decide *what future we want* and try to influence events by working towards the realization of particular futures.

The field of futures studies uses a plurality of research approaches that typically lead to some kind of description of a scenario. Even if the term "scenario" can be used in several different ways, scenarios all refer to the future, and there are ways in which they can be classified [17]. One useful classification is based on what question the scenario is supposed to respond to [17]; *predictive scenarios* respond to the question '*what will happen?*', *explorative scenarios* respond to '*what can happen?*' and *normative scenarios* respond to '*how can a specific target be reached?*'.

In *predictive scenarios*, the future derives from assumptions that are based on historical and current developments.

[1] For example "Computer revolution" (Berkeley 1962), "Computerized society (Martin & Norman 1970), "Age of information" (Helvey 1971), "Compunications" (Oettinger 1971), "Information revolution" (Lamberton 1974), "Communications age" (Phillips 1975), "Electronics revolution" (Evans 1977), "Information economy" (Porat 1977), "Network nation" (Hiltz & Turoff 1978), "Telematic society" (Nora & Minc 1978), "Wired society" (Martin 1978), "Computer age (Dertouzos & Moses 1979), "Microelectronics revolution" (Forester 1980), "Network marketplace" (Dordick 1981), "Communications revolution" (Williams 1982), "Information age" (Dizard 1982), "Computer state" (Burnham 1983).

[2] https://books.google.com/ngrams/info

These scenarios thereby avoid challenging existing power structures and configurations. In a context where we strive for sustainability, [48] argues that these kinds of scenarios are useful as eye-openers that indicate how past and current development paths must be changed to pursue more sustainable futures. They can also be used to adapt decisions to a future that seems to be difficult or impossible to influence. Even though these types of predictions can be called scenarios, [50] do not include them in the futures studies field. This is mainly because they typically do not include any developed descriptions of a future state but merely contend with extending current trends. This activity is important for futures studies work, but is traditionally not seen as futures studies per se.

*Explorative scenarios* instead create images of a variety of expectations of future developments and aim at analyzing current structures. They typically illustrate a major change in society without focusing on *how* this change came about. Explorative scenarios harbor a kind of relativization of the future, which thus becomes negotiable, open, and unpredictable [33]. While these scenarios can be normatively charged (e.g. explicitly or implicitly embody various values), the term "normative" has a special and different meaning in futures studies, as described below.

*Normative scenarios* finally take as a starting point a goal that should be reached in the future. Such scenarios are created with the explicit purpose of fulfilling certain targets and they can be either *preservative* or *transformative*. In the first case, the target can be reached through the prevalence of current structures. In the second case, the target-fulfilling scenario demands structural changes beyond the validity of existing models [17]. When working with *transformative* normative scenarios, a key element is thus to develop images of a future that fulfills the chosen targets. In *preservative* normative scenarios, focus is instead spent on strategies and policies for reaching targets. Just as explorative scenarios can be "normative" (normatively charged), normative scenarios are also "explorative" in the sense that they explore futures that do not yet exist – futures in which particular targets have been fulfilled.

Explorative and normative scenarios in futures studies typically work with changes on a *societal* and *structural* level. This distinguishes futures studies from design fiction, which instead often has a different aim and to a greater extent focuses on concrete artifacts and activities at the level of individuals or small groups.

## DESIGN FICTION

There has been an increased interest within Human-Computer Interaction (HCI) of envisioning the future through (using the terminology from futures studies) *explorative* scenarios. Such scenarios can be seen as proposals that answer the question "*what can happen in the future?*". Design fiction can in this context be used to envision the future by way of creating semi-fictional narratives, concepts, prototypes, or movies [11, 52, 59]. Some HCI predecessors to design fiction are 1) simple fictional vignettes to frame research [20], 2) scenarios that illustrate the practical use of soon-to-be-developed technologies [62] and 3) fictive, made up "personas" (prototype users) with designated gender, age, professions and habits [25].

More than 45 years ago, computer scientist Alan Kay said that "*the best way to predict the future is to invent it*" [see also 15]. Design fiction does not live up to Kay's benchmark of inventing and building the technical systems that "everybody" will (or might) use in the future, but instead explore *multiple* possible futures through the immensely less costly use of combining fiction with various supporting media (e.g. texts, sketches, images, movies, prototypes). However, "*the striking feature of the future imagined by HCI researchers and practitioners is that it is often simplistic, short term, and focused on utility*" [41].

The use of design fiction within HCI is hence often geared towards the design of *concrete* (future) technologies and artifacts, and the effects such artifacts could have in the future. This kind of "solutionist" stance has also been criticized [13]. The nebulous entity called "the future" is often treated cursorily, including basic questions such as *when* the future in question is supposed to happen (with some notable exceptions, e.g. [6, 14, 45]). While there are exceptions (e.g. [29]), Bleecker recurrently and emphatically emphasizes the strong connection between design fiction and the *near* future, e.g. "*Designed fictions are projections and extrapolations meant to explore possible near futures*" [11, p.25].

While there can be normative overtones in some design fiction research, e.g. designing a technology that works towards certain goals that are external to the technology in question (e.g. "sustainability," see further [46]), the focus is seldom on *reaching* specific goals, but rather on raising matters of concern [23, 36]. This differs from how normative (goal-fulfilling) scenarios are used in futures studies where much work is put into defining the goals that should be fulfilled. Use of such goal-fulfilling scenarios in HCI/design fiction would start with the statement "we want *this* to happen" and then ask what technologies we would need to invent or develop so as to reach that particular goal. The hard part then becomes figuring out suitable metrics that would be useful in order to evaluate if said technologies could lead to the desired goal being achieved. We know of no case where such an approach has been applied rigorously within HCI/design fiction.

## METHODS

The scenarios presented in this paper are part of the results of a three-year research project. The project involved around 15 researchers. Most of the researchers came from KTH Royal Institute of Technology in Stockholm, Sweden, but there were also participants from Ericsson, the City of Stockholm, Interactive Swedish ICT, Stockholm County Council and Telia.

A starting point of the project was while there are visions of future information societies and visions of future sustainable societies, there are few visions that combine these two notions and attempt to evaluate future information societies in terms of sustainability (or unsustainability). Generating a variety of scenarios and evaluating them in terms of opportunities and risks would help towards having informed discussions about the future. The work of *generating* scenarios and of *evaluating* their impact in terms of sustainability was partly separated in the project. This paper is primarily concerned with the process of generating the scenarios, with presenting the resulting scenarios, and with describing how these scenarios were used. For more about the methodology for evaluating the scenarios, see [3, 5] and for more about the actual results of the evaluations of the scenarios, see [4].

There are several ways of generating and presenting sets of scenarios and the most well-known is to use a "scenario cross" with four alternative scenarios that are the product of combining "high" and "low" characteristics in a two-dimensional space [54]. However, this reduces the scenarios so that they relate heavily on *exactly these two* particular dimensions (disregarding many other relevant factors that might exist). The futures studies researchers in this project instead developed a method based on "leading ideas." The strength of this approach is that interesting and potentially important developments could be explored without being forced to relate to only two specific and pre-specified dimensions. The main point of developing "leading ideas" scenarios was to be able visualize the existence of major differences and to open up space for discussions about risks and opportunities, and of what constitutes desirable futures in the first place. Working towards this goal, the exact and particular choice of scenarios may in retrospect not have been as important as it was to develop a set of scenarios that highlighted ideas and thoughts that needed to be debated.

The identification of leading ideas started in late 2012 with a half-day workshop with ten participants from corporate and public partners that were affiliated with the research project. By using a variety of brainstorming techniques, a number of factors relating to present/future societies, as well as what the role of ICT could be, were identified. Identified factors were summarized throughout the session and developed back-office into a number of leading ideas. One such leading idea was based on the fact that we spend more and more time online, staring into computer screens, tablets and smartphones [19, 55, 56, 60]. During the spring of 2013, similar workshops were organized parallel to several internal KTH project meetings and these activities later resulted in the choice of five leading ideas. These five leading ideas were:

1. Economic decline – the European economy is in decline but ICT use is still highly prioritized.

2. Trusted communities – segregation increases online and especially offline (gated communities, etc.).

3. Life online – people lead full lives online while the physical environment for the most part is neglected.

4. Controlled convenience – people trade away their integrity in exchange for a supremely convenient life.

5. Valued environment – development and implementation of ICT is dedicated to solving environmental problems.

The leading ideas were then developed into half-page long "scenario skeletons" that were then discussed and fleshed out in workshops with partners, policy makers, students, researchers, and once (October 2013) with attendees at a sci-fi-convention in Stockholm. The five leading ideas evolved during these activities, and all but one changed their names at one point or another during this period. Using the futures studies terminology presented above, the first four scenarios are explorative, while the fifth scenario is normative (e.g., goal-fulfilling). The goal to be fulfilled for the fifth scenario was to describe a society that would attain all of Sweden's 16 environmental quality objectives[3] (as adopted by the Swedish Parliament in 1999).

At the same time, several parallel sub-projects explored various aspects of (both present and future) society, e.g., "Work", "Space"[4], "Things", "ICT", "Media" etc. The choice of sub-projects was based on the results of project workshops and on identifying crucial dimensions of information societies *and* of arenas with large implications for sustainability. The sub-projects were thus focused on central societal themes; how they have evolved historically, how they can be characterized at the present, and what futures can be identified and imagined for each both in terms of main trends but also in terms of identifying more small-scale, potentially transformative forces acting in the here and now.

The scenarios skeletons developed into considerably longer descriptions over time and after many rounds of redesign. The evolution of the scenarios was based both on input from altogether 17 workshops and 10 in-depth interviews with project participants from businesses and public authorities, as well as from the results of the sub-projects. The process of developing the scenarios included many workshops where participants (typically) were presented with short versions of the scenarios and were then tasked with working in groups to develop, criticize, or reflect upon them.

The project aimed at describing Sweden sometime between 2050 and 2060, i.e., 35-45 years into the future. Robinson

[3] Sweden's Environmental Objectives – An Introduction. http://www.miljomal.se/Global/24_las_mer/broschyrer/Swedens-environmental-objectives.pdf

[4] "Space" here refers to the built environment and the use of public and private space in urban environments.

[47, p.852] mentions that 40 years represents a time frame that is appealing because "*many users care about a time frame that is roughly the working life of their children, or their own working life if they are too young to have children.*" "Prototyping the Future" [32] is another example of a research project where futures studies and design fiction have been used to project a sustainable future society in the year 2053, i.e., equally far into the future.

Four decades is a very long perspective from an ICT point of view, but not particularly long when it comes to planning the physical infrastructure of a city in terms of the lifespan of buildings, urban structures, and general transportation networks. This presented us with certain challenges. The chosen time scale ("a generation") conforms to the time scales that the target groups (city administrators; bureaucrats, planners, and policymakers) work with, but the actual "future ICT" that is imagined and described in the scenarios could easily be perceived as tame or perhaps even "limp" in comparison to stock HCI design fiction exercises that often describe wildly exciting "near-future" scenarios [6, 14, 45]. If we on the other hand had extrapolated from such imaginative "near-future" design fiction scenarios, we would have had to develop almost otherworldly future technologies for our 40-year time scale and this would neither have worked with the target group nor with the intended purpose of the research project. It is to be expected that city administrators who strive to make well-grounded decisions *today* would not seriously entertain the idea of the singularity [38, 39], nor would it be possible for them to relate to or to slot in effects of the singularity into their current planning practices.

In the end, we felt that we did not have any other choice but to invent (or prescribe) future technologies that were indeed tame, but that would be compatible with the persons and the practices we worked towards. It should also be noted that we spent considerably more time imagining and discussing social implications of various kinds of technological developments than we spent on doing research on the feasibility of specific near-future or over-the-horizon technologies. All scenarios had some – but not an exclusive – focus on describing how ICT was used in our imagined futures. The technical descriptions of "future ICT" were, in the end, relatively limited. The focus of the research project has to a much greater extent been on describing how ICT was/could be *used* and its (social, everyday, spatial, industrial) *effects* on future information societies.

## THE SCENARIOS

We have chosen to present shortened descriptions (around 200 words each) of each of the five scenarios together with an "avatar story" for each scenario (ca 400-600 words each). There also exists a longer, more thorough description for each scenario (ca 3750 worlds each). An avatar story instantiates a scenario and provides a glimpse into the lives of the people who live in that particular society. The most important purposes for creating avatar stories were:

- To flesh out the scenarios and give them flavor.
- To explain high-level trends through concrete examples, i.e., as a tool to communicate results [52].
- To "test" the scenarios; is it even possible to describe a day in the life of an individual who lives in a specific imagined future information society?
- To describe a *normal* day (rather than an unusual day that is characterized by breakdowns or by untypical interactions).

Some other decisions that were made in relation to the avatar stories were 1) to make sure that ICT use played a relatively prominent role in each scenario, 2) to find both positive and negative aspects on life in each scenario (so each scenarios would have the potential to gladden and gall different readers) and, 3) to try to convey what is taken-for-granted by the people who live in a particular world. After describing the five resulting scenarios, we will discuss aspects and implications.

### 1. Economic Decline

For a long time, Sweden has struggled with negative economic growth, lackluster technological developments, and a high unemployment rate. This situation is occurring in most first industrialized countries (FICs), resulting in lesser economic variance between countries globally. In this economic environment, the Swedish population has less money, but they tend to value – and are prepared to pay for – maintenance and access to digital technologies. There is still a belief that the government should be responsible for fundamental services such as education and health, but the standards have declined and not everyone is guaranteed a consistent and high level of service. Instead, a more divided class society has developed in which a smaller, wealthier, and well-connected group of the population has access to a high level of human welfare services such as well-functioning private healthcare. This has led to a decline in the general population's trust in the government, the differing political parties and their political 'solutions,' and an increase in social unrest, especially among the younger demographic. People have been forced to care for and to take more responsibility for their lives and the lives of others. Although arising from a negative situation, this has also led to the positive outcome of many people feeling more alive, self-sufficient and responsible. They experience feeling satisfied by knowing they can manage and make a difference in the lives of their friends and family.

#### *Economic Decline – avatar story*

Kim wipes the sweat from his forehead and swears at the thickets that grow on the hard land. Despite hours of work with the shovel, he has hardly gotten anywhere. Kim brushes off the worst of the dirt and goes into the apartment he shares with his partner Lo and Lo's parents. On a discussion forum about small-scale farming, he learns that he needs a rototill to make the soil cultivable. He finds instructions for how to build one at a low cost and with stuff many people might have at home and starts to think about procuring usable parts. Kim is fortunate to be able to borrow many of the tools he needs from the neighborhood utility pool. Kim shuts down the computer and unplugs the power even though this model is supposed to never go into power hungry standby mode.

-The crisis meeting! Kim rushes off, shouting to Lo's parents to take care of the children. The municipality has threatened to remove the nearest bus stop, but that would make it more difficult for residents to get to work and school. Kim is ready to battle for the bus stop, the most recent symbol of a crumbling welfare system. Kim angrily wonders if anyone in the neighborhood is ready to pay even a single Swedish krona in tax if they won't even have a bus stop nearby - not to mention the substandard medical care and the decreasing standard of the schools nowadays...

In the afternoon Kim does wage work. He feels privileged to have found a well-paid job where he can use his professional training as a nurse. He analyzes X-ray images at the family's computer and sends the results back to different hospitals. He is indeed pleased that the extended family has a computer, but annoyed about the quickly depleting batteries.

In the evening, the whole family goes to the local soup kitchen: a communal kitchen where members take turns at cooking. Kim and his family help themselves and then settle down to eat among friends. The soup is delicious, but Kim longs for spring vegetables. - Jeez, it is high time to sow the seeds! Kim gets into a discussion about the rototill and soon finds more people who are interested in helping out - and Larry has some of the special tools you need!

After dinner, the kids lounge on the couch with their grandparents and watch cartoons on the tablet computer. Downloading large files is cumbersome but Kim usually carries around a memory stick that can be filled with fun stuff for the kids when the opportunity arises (sharing is caring!). The kids know to be careful of the tablet since it has just been repaired at the corner shop and they don't want to hear Kim and Lo argue about the expense again.

**2. Trust in local and digital communities**

Europe is now a mosaic of subcultures. People put a high value on their relationships with family, their close friends, in their neighborhoods, and in online groups. Most local communities are based on interests, socioeconomic factors, culture, religion, or ethnicity. As people remain within the boundaries of their physical or online communities, trust in politics and in public social life in Sweden is low. Growing gaps between local communities have led to a diversification of norms and values – with people in different communities valuing different things in different ways. There is no consensus across the country on what is a fair and appropriate way to organize society.

Despite the lack of trust in society – with communities organizing their own education, and basic elder and health care – society is highly regulated in many ways. Sweden functions in a 'night-watchman' state, where the government's role is mostly limited to maintaining internal and external security. As a response to the public's distrust, surveillance has become omnipresent. Advanced systems are used to identify people, objects, and actions that do not belong or are under suspicion of breaking community rules or regulations. People feel safe and secure within their (enclosed) communities. These communities do their best to protect their members, even when they venture outside their community's physical or digital boundaries. People conduct almost all of their social activities within the borders of their online or local communities.

*Trust in local and digital communities – avatar story*

Amalia is one of many people waiting for the bus. The bus station is located in a 'transition space' used by members of several different communities. Conflicts are rare, but being in a transition space is often tense. Amalia calms her mind by thinking about how lucky she is to have a good job, a husband, children, and to belong to the 'Solsidan' community. Staying alert to her surroundings, Amalia checks this week's schedule at the hospital where she works as a nurse.

This week is packed with activities and extra work. Tomorrow evening it is Amalia's turn to help clean her kids' classrooms and she's also to attend a local meeting to discuss new subjects in the fifth year curriculum (which her eldest daughter will start next spring). Some people grumble about the high taxes in Solsidan, but Amalia is happy. It is priceless to know that her kids are being educated by members of the community and in accordance with the values she cherishes. Moreover, the communitarian work is a way of getting closer to other members and to have a voice in decisions.

Meeting a plurality of people from different communities at work has convinced Amaila that she belongs to one of the best communities. Last week Amalia treated a patient who had been roughed up by a burglar. Poor man! This never happens in Solsidan. Amalia believes her job would be even more arduous if communities were open for strangers to enter. There would be more assaults, conflicts and violence, but only the other week Amalia heard someone at the hospital complain about segregation. He said that the surveillance threatens privacy and violates individuals' rights. Of course, Amalia did not get into a discussion but thought to herself, "Get real … if someone has something to hide, then there must be something seriously wrong!"

In the evening, after eating dinner with her husband and children, Amalia sits in front of the computer to research 'first aid' subjects. She wants to be prepared for the school meeting and argue for the inclusion of emergency care in the curriculum. She always surfs the Net with utmost caution, scared that her computer could be hacked. Amalia's community cannot afford a premium Internet provider and her search is annoyingly slow. She decides to instead continue the search at the hospital tomorrow.

Amalia hears steps outside. It is out of the ordinary and her heart starts racing. She slowly pulls the window curtain back and is relieved to realize that the man standing outside is an officer from her community's militia. He has just found her neighbor's missing cat.

While preparing to go to bed, Amalia thinks about the community gathering next Saturday. A movie will be screened at the main square, and her friend Jane who lives in a twin 'Solsidan' community will watch it simultaneously. So exciting! Amalia and Jane will be able to talk about the movie through the new 'Solsidan chat site' that links their communities. Yes, the whole family will definitely have a great time! The movie might not be that interesting for the kids, but they will be able to play perfectly safely with other kids from the community. Her last thought before she falls asleep is a wish for good weather.

**3. Life Online**

Physical space, physical objects, and physical interactions have – to a large extent – lost their meaning in people's everyday lives. Instead, people spend most of their time online. Information is not only consumed through screens, but also in other, more immersive ways. The main driving force behind the "exodus to online worlds" is the fact that reality leaves many people disillusioned compared to the designed and much-improved virtual worlds that motivate, stimulate, and satisfy. Online, suitably large tasks and challenges *can be solved.* 'Gamified' interaction and short feedback loops reward desirable behavior. Consequences of climate change are becoming increasingly evident and people have taken refuge in the safe and predictable life online.

In an online world, anything can happen – but only if, and when, the individual wants it to. In addition, human bodies are being 'upgraded' to enable enhanced participation in life online. This started as a bio-hacking movement in the beginning of the 2010s, and human bodies are gradually becoming 'machine-enhanced' to various degrees.

*Life Online – avatar story*

After a quick breakfast, Lisa is finally online again! She is keen to find out what has happened with the online art exhibition project since she went to sleep nine hours ago. Yayanta, her Indian colleague has done a great job. Lisa continues where he left off and gets in touch with Weng to finalize the artists' conditions for inclusion. Then Lisa enters the political discussions she is currently engaged in at www.politico.org. While typing, her eyes occasionally wander to the park outside her window. Her discussion forum opponent has a point – the park does look a little shabby nowadays, but who wants to spend more time working offline and less time playing online anyway?

Lisa's lightbulbs burn out too often and she has booked an electrician (of sorts) for today. She thus has to be offline and she and her home have to be presentable for the upcoming 'probably-sometime-before-noon' visit. Having to get dressed despite today not being her workday is annoying, but having to change the lightbulb every other day is even more annoying.

Fortunately, the electrician comes before lunch and Lisa can enter her four-hour afternoon session as her long-time alter ego, space captain Li Sa. The everyday boredom of being a recruiter for the Sargon faction has now been replaced with the exciting task of infiltrating the competing Nine Worlds faction. The complex plan is moving ahead and four months of planning, followed by 18 months of work seems to pay off. In a best-case scenario, the Sargon faction will obliterate its long-time competitor and take control of the entire space quadrant. Who would have guessed, based on her faction's humble beginnings twelve years ago? Life is so satisfying when things go your way!

Lisa's gaming session is followed by a dinner with her Thursday night friendship circle. It is always nice to enjoy an intimate dinner with friends, but tonight Arne has a problem with his video link and has to withdraw. The end of the Thursday dinner can be an anticlimax as Friday is Lisa's weekly workday.

Lisa does not regularly call her mother, but the real-time health feed indicates that her mother's cholesterol values have been too high recently. Lisa calls her mother on her mobile phone. She really loves her mother, but it would be so much more convenient to get in touch with her online while multi-tasking! She wishes her mother was not so old fashioned and that her mother was not so good at noticing when Lisa starts doing something else while talking.

**4. Controlled convenience**

Development within the ICT sector has and is the driver of societal change. 'Derived choice' is the key concept of the day and it means that people are given advanced support in making everyday choices, of which many are externalized to a system that knows their individual preferences just as well, or better, then they do themselves. People and objects are connected symbiotically in real-time and ICT systems are constantly processing huge amounts of data. Technology has not only moved closer to people's physical bodies, but has also *entered* people's physical bodies (contact lenses that can overlay or display information, sensors that measure and intercept internal bodily processes, implanted chips) by working as personal identification and providers of information. Virtually everything is connected to provide enhanced functionality and experience as well as to feed data into ICT systems to further optimize each aspect of life. The interaction with connected objects is seamless, and screens and other distinct user interfaces are no longer common.

The public's trust in the government is high. Convenience and well-being compensates for the government's knowledge (and to some extent, control) about individuals' actions and choices. An increase in economic growth and technological developments since the mid-2010s supports the belief that technology will solve the environmental problems caused by climate change, which are now more obvious than at any time during the last 50 years. The mood in Swedish society is optimistic and it is supported by an efficient marriage between government and technology to ensures that individuals can live a comfortable life.

*Controlled convenience – avatar story*

On the way to the lunch restaurant picked by PONG, a subtle alarm informs Stina to sales of a new model of her phone. Her phone battery has gotten weak even though it is only six months old, and Stina decides to go have a look. The new colors are attractive and she leaves the store with a shiny new phone feeling satisfied and happy. Her old phone had suddenly felt old-fashioned and she can barely believe that she only recently showed it off to everyone – it's frankly embarrassing!

It is three o'clock and it is time for coffee break at Stina's job. Stina receives notices from PONG on all work-related devices and is informed that there will be a cake that has been cross-checked with her food allergies, containing nothing that she is allergic to. Many people turn up and an agreeable chatter fills the room until Anna starts talking about sustainability and an uncomfortable silence spreads. She thinks it is irresponsible to live too spaciously. Stina and others feel hurt, believing that her way of living should be her private concern. Someone says in an angry voice: - This is not *our* problem, it must be adjusted by the Political Algorithm! Everyone agrees and the pleasant chitchat resumes.

Lisa forgot to change PONG to work mode and an alarm beeps, reminding her that her dad who lives in the countryside is getting old and decrepit: she ought to talk to him about his future. Either he must equip himself with the latest monitoring technology within his body (measuring cholesterol, blood pressure, etc., and communicating any deviation to his doctor) and have a robot help him at home, or he must move to a high-tech elderly home. He would never accept a big-city retirement home, but maybe one in the nearest village? The message stresses Lisa, but she asks PONG to announce appropriate times for this talk when nothing ails her father and he feels reasonably good.

At home, Lisa gets an impulse to go to the theater. She loves the old-fashioned atmosphere, the set design (especially when it is hand crafted instead of only projected), and to drink a glass of wine in the lobby bar. However, she has no clue about what to see or with whom. She asks PONG to choose a suitable theatre play and synchronize the playing time with her friends' calendars. PONG soon finds a new version of an Ibsen play that has received good reviews. Lisa's friend Svante is free and could be interested, so PONG recommends she call him. As she hasn't met him for a few months, it feels a bit too intimate and she instead sends a text message.

On the way to the theater a heavy rain falls and Lisa wonders swiftly if the weather has become strange, but pushes away these thoughts and tells herself that things will work out as they always do. She is also distracted by a notification from PONG (monitoring her body) that she should buy some cough drops in the next block since that is her last chance before she reaches the theatre. She is happy that PONG knows her body even better than she does, and follows the advice.

**5. Valued environment**

A strong environmental policy, supported by citizens and industry, has enabled Sweden to finally reach the environmental objectives developed in the mid-2010s. The ICT sector in particular has focused its development on solving important environmental problems, with technology developed to reduce resource usage in everyday life. Trust in the government and in other people is high, with people engaged and interested in politics and especially in areas concerning environmental issues. Global cooperation and trade in virtual and digital products is high, with ICT companies playing an important role alongside non-government organizations and open licenses. Environmentally conscious values permeate society, with society giving greater respect and standing to individuals and groups who use fewer resources, and especially to those who invent and develop solutions that diminish resource use for everyday tasks.

*Valued environment – avatar story*

"Darling, I love Lisa, but she gives me a hard time even though their Spartan lifestyle is partly made possible by us!" Erik grumbles to Airi. "You and I both work hard, we deserve our salaries, and still they donate their surplus environrights to some 'worthwhile cause' instead of accepting our hard-earned cash for them!" Airi agrees with Erik and tries to calm him down. Meeting Erik's sister and her holier-than-thou husband often turn into a tense low-key verbal battle. But Lisa's small farm is lovely in the summer, and their children really enjoy the countryside and spending a full month at the farm with their cousins. The squash, potatoes, and beets that Lisa insisted they bring with them to the city look lovely, and will last for quite some time. Yet Lisa's strict ultra-low-carbon-emissions lifestyle makes it hard for her family to get by without a helping hand from her brother.

Erik and Airi's own summer cottage is even more unassuming. It is not practical to heat the house during the winter, but they spend a lot of time there in the summer. At the first trip of the year, the children are like frisky calves let out to pasture after a long winter indoors. It is easy to book a large vehicle through the carpool and transport everything door-to-door, but they have to pay through the nose. Worse still, the cost of private transportation goes up every year as the individual carbon allowances continue to shrink. Still, Erik and Airi do not complain much. It's the same for everyone else and they still have more than most others, and (after all) Sweden is on target to meet its carbon emission reduction goals.

For five years, Erik and Airi have had a plan that is unknown to most of their friends. Their goal is to save environrights, and to use their high incomes to buy extra environrights on the open market. They plan to spend them all visiting Airi's relatives in Australia next year. It will be a wonderful trip and something they hope their children will remember for the rest of their lives. While they regularly talk to their Australian relatives, only Airi has met them in person. It might very well be the last intercontinental flight any of them ever makes. Boats take an eternity to cover that distance, but with their comparatively low carbon footprint and low environrights price tag they continue to capture market shares.

Saving up environrights has forced them to make many small changes in their lifestyle. Their oldest son wanted to practice karate, but they did not want to use money and environrights to book a car to take him there. Instead he started to practice judo at the local club, and made new friends they sometimes run into. When you know people in the area you feel more settled and invested in the local community. He can switch to karate if he really wants to when he is old enough to use public transport by himself.

Their biggest decision has been the change of diet. As Erik and Airi have decent incomes, it makes sense for them to spend more money and fewer environrights on products with a lower ecological footprint. They always try to buy wild game meat, like boar, instead of industrially produced pork. Their children rarely eat dairy products and the milk has been replaced with oat milk. To always look for locally produced food, food in season, and alternative sources of protein (the kids love beans) is now second nature to them.

## DISCUSSION

This paper does not describe a research project that self-identifies as being about Human-Computer Interaction or design fiction. The primary theoretical and methodological difference is that the project and the scenarios described above come out of the area of futures studies. We might then ask how the end results – including the scenarios themselves – differ in comparison to how design fiction is used within HCI.

Going back to the origins of these approaches and examining their respective intended purposes, there are large differences between design fiction and futures studies despite the fact that both are focused on the relation between the present and the future. Bleecker [11], in his original 2009 essay about design fiction, sees design fiction as a method for envisioning new kinds of near future environments, artifacts and practices. By encouraging cross-pollination between ideas from design, science fact and science fiction, his wish is for new, better and more interesting design ideas to materialize. Despite giving prominence to "environments" and "practices", it is clear that the main emphasis of design fiction was on imagining/designing near future artifacts. Futures studies on the other hand has traditionally not paid any special attention to invention, to design, or to imagining specific (future) artifacts. Futures studies has instead originally been about planning, e.g., for an uncertain future and by trying to decrease uncertainty (business risks, etc.).

Both futures studies and design fiction have however developed in ways that it is possible to imagine that they to a certain extent can overlap, e.g., with futures studies engaging in design through explorative scenarios and backcasting [61] and with design fiction increasingly positioning itself in terms of possible societal impacts of technology and at lager scales than at the level of individual artifacts [36]. We hope that this paper has made those connections clearer and that we have helped guide interested HCI researchers to relevant futures studies literature, as did [42] in a previous paper that also introduced futures studies (primarily the Dephi method) to an HCI audience. While similarities can be traced between this project and HCI/design fiction, there are also significant differences, including in terms of research methods, stakeholders, and project goals.

One major difference is that the (heavily abbreviated) scenarios presented here have been developed iteratively and in cooperation with other societal actors over a period spanning years. It is in fact hard to differ 1) the process of developing the scenarios together with various stakeholders (e.g., public authorities and corporations) from 2) using the scenarios to engage stakeholders and elicit feedback from them (e.g., through workshops, interviews) and 3) iteratively incorporating stakeholders' feedback to further develop the scenarios.

Consequently, the scenarios are not end products but should rather be seen as tools for communicating and collaborating with different actors. In this project, the purpose of the intensive collaboration with the stakeholders was both to learn from their practices and to provide a framework for discussing long-term development and planning processes at the regional (Stockholm) level with various actors who had differing backgrounds and knowledge about ICT and sustainable development. Starting with the framework provided by the scenarios, a future-oriented discussion on policy measures and instruments (etc.) could then be held.

Yet another difference is that the scenarios are not very focused on gadgets and on maximizing the "wow factor." We were not primarily interested in the future technologies in and of themselves as much as we were interested in thinking through possible effects of ICT *on the rest of society*, for example in terms of production, transportation, consumption, work, leisure, education, time use, etc. Thus, our scenarios were elaborated based on a rather long-term perspective and with the intention of allowing for (profound) structural changes.

The last difference we point out here is the project's emphasis on *actually* assessing sustainability aspects of the five scenarios – although not elaborated on in this paper due space limitations. The assessment has been published elsewhere [3, 4, 5], but it can be noted that the scenario which is closest to the futures that the HCI community "as a whole" works towards, "Controlled Convenience," *is hardly a sustainable society* when assessed in terms of (among other factors) land use, mineral use, energy use, greenhouse gas emissions, participation and influence in society, equity and justice, social cohesion, etc. [3, 5]. The scenario "Economic Decline" is on the other hand one of two scenarios that have the highest chance of being environmentally sustainable [4], but that scenario implies that much current work in HCI misses the target *if the goal is an environmentally sustainable society*.

One important lesson from this project is that actors such as local government early on expressed the opinion that "ICT developments are not something that can be steered or influenced (and certainly not by us)," but after participating in workshops they realized that ICT and its use is malleable. Contrary to their original beliefs, local government has, through the procurer role, ample opportunities to influence which technologies they want and to shape how they want them to be used (and how they want them *not* to be used). Instead of seeing ICT developments as a juggernaut or an irresistible force, they started to discuss how ICT can be contextualized and used in urban developments. For example, it became possible to discuss how ICT can influence travel habits and be used for reaching important targets like decreased emissions of $CO_2$ through decreased car travel. This exemplifies a lesson that is often an outcome of futures studies scenario projects, i.e., that different stories about the future help us pluralize the future and decisively establish that more than one future is possible, and perhaps that some futures are equally possible based on what we know today. When that realization has been socially established, it then becomes possible to choose or to influence which future(s) to aim for.

What then are the take-away lessons from the project and what can HCI and design fiction learn from this? Comparing this futures studies project with design fiction, we posit some notable differences between these two approaches:

**Time span**. If sustainability spans geology, resource use, and meeting "*the needs of the present without compromising the ability of future generations to meet their own needs*" [16] while HCI typically spans only the near future in terms research, innovation, development, and productions cycles (as well as writing up a paper for next year's CHI conference), then this research project straddles the middle ground by working with time spans of decades: which are more commensurable with the rate a city or a society changes.

**Real-world grounding**. While different strands of design (as practiced in HCI) can be effective for generating new ideas and for uncovering that which is taken for granted, our research project also points at the power of developing scenarios that specifically and explicitly aim at exploring a specific normative issue – in our case "sustainability" in relation to regional development. How could design fictions be crafted towards other outcomes, for example towards sharing, encouraging pro-social behaviors, or to fulfill the United Nations' Sustainable Development Goals [26]?

**Goal-fulfilling scenarios.** Design fiction has thus far primarily worked only with explorative scenarios. We hope to see examples also of goal-fulfilling design fiction scenarios. While only cursorily mentioned here, the real-world assessment of the resulting scenarios could also be a fruitful venue to further explore within HCI.

**Changing society "for real"**. While the focus of design fiction oftentimes seems to be to imagine or develop futuristic technologies, this project instead emphasized working with stakeholders whose work consists of actually planning for, and building the future society we will live in during the coming decades. The scenarios developed harbor the potential of having direct implications for policy.

**Radical transformation**. Having to repeatedly negotiate with various stakeholders tends to put a drag on imaginative suggestions (c.f., "design by committee"). It is probably the case that we over time toned down the most original parts of the scenarios, ostensibly to make them more "useful" for various stakeholders [43]. For truly groundbreaking ideas and critique of different phenomena, design fiction might be a more promising approach, e.g., [13].

The aim of this project has been to explore what future information societies could look like and assess their impacts in terms of (primarily ecological) sustainability. The goal has been to work both towards, and together with city administrators and private companies to raise ICT and sustainability as topics that (preferably together) should be taken into account by public policies and industrial strategies. While we have primarily used futures studies methodologies, we believe that developments in design fiction could benefit futures studies, for example in terms of tools and sophisticated methods of situating imagined technologies not yet developed into fictional frameworks as a way to explore or advance arguments about futures. We also believe that a better understanding of futures studies methods and perspectives could benefit HCI in general and design fiction in particular.

## ACKNOWLEDGEMENTS

We would like to thank Marcel Pufal for detailed comments about language.

## REFERENCES


1. Amara, A. (1981). The futures field: searching for definitions and boundaries, *The Futurist* 15 (1), 25–29.
2. Andersson, J. (2006). Choosing Futures: Alva Myrdal and the Construction of Swedish Futures Studies, 1967 – 1972. *Int Review of Social History* 51:277-295.
3. Arushanyan, Y., Ekener Petersen, E., Moberg, A., & Coroama, V. C. (2015). A framework for sustainability assessment of ICT futures Scenarios and sustainability impacts of future ICT-societies. In *Proc ICT4S'15*. Atlantis Press, 1-9.
4. Arushanyan, Y. (2016). *Environmental impacts of ICT: present and future*. PhD thesis, KTH Royal Institute of Technology, Stockholm, Sweden.
5. Arushanyan, Y., Ekener, E., & Moberg, Å. (2017). Sustainability assessment framework for scenarios–SAFS. *Env Impact Assessment Review*, 63, 23-34.
6. Baumer, E.P., Ahn, J., Bie, M., Bonsignore, B., Borutecene, A., Buruk, O.T., Clegg, T., Druin, A., Echtler, F., Gruen, D., Guha, M. L., Hordatt, C., Kruger, A., Maidenbaum, S., Malu, M., McNally, B., Muller, M., Norooz, L., Norton, J., Özcan, O., Patterson, D., Riener, A., Ross, S., Rust, K., Schoening, J., Silberman, M. S., Tomlinson, B., and Yip, J. (2014). CHI 2039: Speculative Research Visions. In *Proc CHI'14*. ACM, 761-770.
7. Bell, G., & Dourish, P. (2007). Yesterday's tomorrows: notes on ubiquitous computing's dominant vision. *Personal and ubiquitous computing*, 11(2), 133-143.
8. Bell, W. (2003) *Foundations of futures studies: human science for a new era. vol. 1, History, purposes, and knowledge*. New Brunswick, NJ Transaction Publishers.
9. Bell, W. and Olick, J.K. (1989) An epistemology for the future field: problems and possibilities of prediction. *Futures* 21 (2): 115-135.
10. Beniger, J.R. (1986). *The control revolution: Technological and economic origins of the information society*. Harvard University Press.
11. Bleecker, J. (2009). *Design Fiction: A short essay on design, science, fact and fiction*. Near Future Laboratory, 29.
12. Blythe, M. (2014). Research through design fiction: narrative in real and imaginary abstracts. In *Proc. CHI'14*. ACM, 703-712.
13. Blythe, M., Andersen, K., Clarke, R., and Wright, P. (2016). Anti-Solutionist Strategies: Seriously Silly Design Fiction. In *Proc. CHI'16*. ACM, 4968-4978.
14. Blythe, M., & Buie, E. (2014). Chatbots of the gods: imaginary abstracts for techno-spirituality research. In *Proc of NordiCHI'14*. ACM, 227-236.
15. Brand, S. (1988). *The Media Lab: Inventing the future at M.I.T.* New York: Penguin Books.
16. Brundtland, G. (1987). *Our common future: The world commission on environment and development*. Oxford: Oxford University Press
17. Börjeson, L., M. Höjer, K.-H. Dreborg, T. Ekvall and G. Finnveden (2006). Scenario types and techniques: Towards a user's guide. *Futures* 38:723-739.
18. Carlsson-Kanyama, A., Dreborg, K.-H., Eenkhorn, B. R., Engström, R., Falkena, H. J., Gatersleben, B., et al. (2003). *Images of everyday life in the future sustainable city: experiences of back-casting with stakeholders in five European cities*. FMS Report 182.
19. Carr, N. (2010). *The Shallows: What the Internet Is Doing to Our Brains*. W. W. Norton.
20. Carroll, J.M. in Helander, M., Landauer, T.K. and Prabhu, P., eds., (1999). *Handbook of Human-Computer Interaction*. Amsterdam: Elsevier.
21. Cornish, E. (1977). *The study of the Future – An Introduction to the Art and Science of Understanding and Shaping Tomorrow's Worlds*. World Future Society.
22. Denning, P. J., & Metcalfe, R. M. (1998). Beyond calculation: The next fifty years of computing. Springer Science & Business Media.
23. DiSalvo, C., Lukens, J., Lodato, T., Jenkins, T., and Kim, T. (2014). Making public things: how HCI design can express matters of concern. In *Proc. CHI'14*. ACM, 2397-2406.
24. Dourish, P., & Bell, G. (2014). "Resistance is futile": reading science fiction alongside ubiquitous computing. *Personal and Ubiquitous Computing*, 18(4), 769-778.
25. Eriksson, E., Artman, H. and Swartling, A. (2013). The secret life of a persona: When the personal becomes private. In *Proc. CHI'13*. ACM, 2677-2686.
26. Eriksson, E., Pargman, D., Bates, O., Normark, M., Gulliksen, J., Anneroth, M., & Berndtsson, J. (2016). HCI and UN's Sustainable Development Goals: Responsibilities, Barriers and Opportunities. In *Proc NordiCHI'14*. ACM, Article No. 140.
27. Gershenfeld, N. (1999). *When things start to think*. Macmillan.
28. Gunn, E. (2014). How America's leading science fiction authors are shaping your future. *Smithsonian Magazine*.
29. Hauser, S., Desjardins, A., and Wakkary, R. SFUture: envisioning a sustainable university campus in 2065. (2014). In *Proc. DIS'14*. ACM, 29-32.
30. Helbing, D. (2014). *Crystal Ball and Magic Wand - the Dangerous Promise of Big Data* (Chapter 3 of Digital

Society. Digital Society, Forthcoming. Available at SSRN: http://ssrn.com/abstract=2502561

31. Höjer, M., Gullberg, A., and Pettersson, R. (2011). *Images of the future city – time and space for sustainable development.* Springer.
32. Ilstedt, S. and Wangel, J. Altering expectations: how design fictions and backcasting can leverage sustainable lifestyles. (2014). In *Proc DRS 2014.*
33. Inayatullah, S., (1990). Deconstructing and Reconstructing the Future: Predictive, Cultural and Critical Epistemologies. *Futures*, 22(2), 115-141.
34. Janssen, M., Matheus, R., & Zuiderwijk, A. (2015). Big and Open Linked Data (BOLD) to Create Smart Cities and Citizens: Insights from Smart Energy and Mobility Cases: In *Int Conf on Electronic Government.* Springer International Publishing, 79-90.
35. Joshi, S., Cerratto Pargman, T., Gazis, A. and Pargman, D. (2016). Whose future is it anyway?: Limits within Policy Modeling. In *Proc. LIMITS'16.* ACM.
36. Kirman, B., Linehan, C., Lawson, S., & O'Hara, D. (2013). CHI and the future robot enslavement of humankind: a retrospective. In *CHI'13 Extended Abstracts.* ACM, 2199-2208.
37. Koselleck, R. (1979/2004). *Futures past: on the semantics of historical time.* New York: Columbia University Press.
38. Kurzweil, R. (2000). *The age of spiritual machines: When computers exceed human intelligence.* Penguin.
39. Kurzweil, R. (2005). *The singularity is near: When humans transcend biology.* Penguin.
40. Larsen, K. & Gunnarsson-Östling, U. (2009). Climate change scenarios and citizen-participation: Mitigation and adaptation perspectives in constructing sustainable futures. *Habitat International* 33(3), 260-266.
41. Linehan, C., Kirman, B.J., Reeves, S., Blythe, M.A., Tanenbaum, J.G., Desjardins, A., and Wakkary, R. (2014). Alternate endings: using fiction to explore design futures. In *Proc. CHI'14.* ACM, 45-48.
42. Mankoff, J., Rode, J. A., & Faste, H. (2013). Looking past yesterday's tomorrow: using futures studies methods to extend the research horizon. In *Proc CHI'13.* ACM, 1629-1638.
43. Meyerson, D. E., & Scully, M. A. (1995). Tempered radicalism and the politics of ambivalence and change. *Organization Science*, 6(5), 585-600
44. Pargman, D., & Raghavan, B. (2014). Rethinking sustainability in computing: From buzzword to non-negotiable limits. In *Proc NordiCHI'14.* ACM, 638-647.
45. Penzenstadler, B., Tomlinson, B., Baumer, E., Pufal, M., Raturi, A., Richardson, D., Cakici, B., Chitchyan, R., Da Costa, B., Dombrowski, L., Picha Edwardsson, M., Eriksson, E., Franch, X., Hayes, G.R., Herzog, C., Lohmann, W., Mahaux, M., Mavin, A., Mazmanian, M., Nayebaziz, S., Norton, J., Pargman, D., Patterson, D.J., Pierson, J, Roher, K., Silberman, M.S., Simonson, K., Torrance, A.W., and van der Hoek, A. (2014). ICT4S 2029: What will be the systems supporting sustainability in 15 years? In *Proc ICT4S'14.* Atlantis Press.
46. Prost, S., Mattheiss, E., and Tscheligi, M. From Awareness to Empowerment: Using Design Fiction to Explore Paths towards a Sustainable Energy Future. (2015). In *Proc CSCW'15.* ACM,1649-1658.
47. Robinson, J. (2003). Future subjunctive: backcasting as social learning. *Futures*, 35(8), 839-856.
48. Svenfelt, Å. (2010). *Two strategies to deal with uncertainty in social-ecological systems.* PhD thesis, KTH Royal Institute of Technology, Stockholm, Sweden.
49. Svenfelt, Å. Engström, R., & Höjer, M. (2010). Use of explorative scenarios in environmental policy-making—Evaluation of policy instruments for management of land, water and built environment. *Futures* 42(10), 1166-1175.
50. Svenfelt Å. and Höjer, M. (2012) Framtidsstudier och osäkerheter [Futures studies and uncertanties]. In Alm, S., Westholm, E. and Palme, J. (eds) *Att utforska framtiden* [Exploring the future]. Dialogos, Stockholm
51. Tanenbaum, J., Tanenbaum, K., & Wakkary, R. (2012). Design fictions. In *Proc TEI'12.* ACM, 347-350.
52. Tanenbaum, J. (2014). Design fictional interactions: why HCI should care about stories. *Interactions*, 21(5), 22-23.
53. Tanenbaum, J., Pufal, M. and Tanenbaum, K. (2016). The Limits of Our Imagination: Design Fiction As a Strategy for Engaging with Dystopian Futures. In *Proc LIMITS'16.* ACM.
54. Tapio, P., Höjer, M., Svenfelt, Å., & Varho, V. (2014) Exploring the space of alternatives: Heuristics in sustainability scenarios. In Huutoniemi, K. and Tapio, P. (Eds) *Transdisciplinary Sustainability Studies: A Heuristic Approach.* Routledge.
55. Turkle, S. (1995). *Life on the Screen: Identity in the Age of the Internet.* Simon & Schuster.
56. Turkle, S. (2011). *Alone together: Why we expect more from technology and less from each other.* Basic books.
57. Turoff, M., & Hiltz, S. R. (1978). *The network nation: Human communication via computer.* Reading, PA: Addison-Wesley.
58. Wack, P. (1985). Scenarios: shooting the rapids. *Harvard Business Review*, 63(6), 139-150.

59. Wakkary, R., Desjardins, A., Hauser, S., & Maestri, L. (2013). A sustainable design fiction: Green practices. *ACM TOCHI*, 20(4), 23.

60. Wallace, P. (2015). *The psychology of the Internet*. Cambridge University Press.

61. Wangel, J. (2012). *Making futures: on targets, measures and governance in backcasting and planning*. Doctoral Thesis. KTH Royal Institute of Technology.

62. Weiser, M. (1991). The computer for the 21st century. *Scientific American*, 265 (3), 66-75.

63. Åkerman, J. and Höjer, M. (2006). How much transport can the climate stand?—Sweden on a sustainable path in 2050. *Energy Policy* 34(14), 1944-1957.

# Means and Ends in Human-Computer Interaction: Sustainability through Disintermediation

**Barath Raghavan**
ICSI
barath@icsi.berkeley.edu

**Daniel Pargman**
KTH Royal Institute of Technology
pargman@kth.se

## ABSTRACT

There has been an increased interest in broader contexts from ecology and economics within the HCI community in recent years. These developments suggest that the HCI community should engage with and respond to concerns that are external to computing yet profoundly impact human society. In this paper we observe that taking these broader contexts into account yields a fundamentally different way to think about sustainable interaction design, one in which the designer's focus must be on a) ecological limits, b) creating designs and artifacts that do not further a cornucopian paradigm, and c) fundamental human needs.

It can be hard to be responsive to these contexts in practical HCI work. To address this, we propose that the design rubric of disintermediation can serve as a unifying approach for work that aims to meet the ecological and economic challenges outlined in the literature. After discussing the potential use and impact of disintermedation, we perform an analysis using this design rubric to several key application areas.

### Author Keywords

Sustainable computing; Sustainable HCI, Sustainability; Complexity; Disintermediation

### ACM Classification Keywords

H.5.m Information interfaces and presentation (e.g., HCI): Miscellaneous

## INTRODUCTION

Concern about environmental sustainability has motivated significant work in the area of Sustainable HCI and Sustainable Interaction Design over the past decade. Beginning with the work of Blevis [6] and Mankoff et. al. [51], there has been an increasing interest in the overlap of computing generally and HCI specifically with sustainability. This interest has grown for years both among HCI researchers [19, 29, 43, 83] and in computing in general [38]. There has been a recognition of the need to integrate sustainability goals into the process of user-centered design along with analyzing the role of computing within a broader ecological scope.


*CHI 2017, May 6-11, 2017, Denver, CO, USA.*

ACM ISBN 978-1-4503-4655-9/17/05 ...$15.00.
http://dx.doi.org/10.1145/3025453.3025542

However, the Sustainable HCI perspective is one that is challenging to engage with, as it is difficult to strike the right balance. Some work tends to address sustainability concerns only superficially while other work delves so deeply into ecology that the HCI questions are lost, as we noted previously [67]. Nevertheless, strong work on this topic manages to avoid these pitfalls and advances our understanding of design criteria that have often been ignored in the past [3, 11, 24, 31, 41, 61, 93].

Recently, three works have challenged our collective thinking about HCI in regard to broader contexts from ecology and economics. Our prior work [67] identified ecological limits as key to selecting appropriate problems and responses in the area of Sustainable HCI. Preist, Schien, and Blevis [69] analyzed the unsustainable cornucopian paradigm and its often-implicit implications for design. Ekbia and Nardi [23, 24] identified political economy generally and inequality specifically as oft-ignored sources of concern that demand a shift in thinking in HCI.

In this paper we observe that combining these three important threads of thought leads to a fundamentally different set of goals for user-centered design, one in which the designer's focus must be on a) fundamental human needs (per Ekbia and Nardi), b) designs and artifacts that do not further the unsustainable growth-based cornucopian paradigm (per Preist et al.), and c) designs that are responsive to ecological limits (our prior work).

However one might note that this new perspective appears on its surface awfully limiting, and, further, lacking cohesion, as these mandates may appear too dissimilar and too broad to be useful in guiding system design. That is, how would a designer go about leveraging the insights of these works—regarding economics, ecology, and unsustainable practices—in practical HCI work? Our aim in this paper is to answer this question: we propose a design rubric—*disintermediation*—that can unify these themes and provide practical direction.

Disintermediation involves the re-engagement of entities—removing intermediaries—in a human-computer system. It is more accurately viewed as a *re*-design approach, since it focuses on redesigning existing systems that have potentially-undesirable layers. Thus applied in user-centered design, the role of disintermediation is to identify layers within a system that can be removed while retaining the key functionality of the system, and without diminishing the system's usability or usefulness to the user. However, at this abstract level it may not be apparent how disintermediation can unify these disparate threads of thought.

Our aim is to extract lessons from these three prior works, show how they argue for a new perspective in user-centered design, and show how the idea of and practice around disintermediation could unify this new direction. Specifically, they indicate that for human society to be sustainable, it must remain within planetary boundaries—impacting natural systems in ways that to not exceed their replenishment or repair; this is the core of what we mean by sustainability in this paper. However, the cornucopian paradigm [69] is part of a growth-based economic system, something that cannot continue on a finite planet, especially given that many planetary boundaries have already been exceeded by human society. At the same time, given that human well-being and human needs are not directly tied to such growth, we can then seek technological responses that meet those needs *without* growth (and therefore without increasing humanity's ecological impact) while taking care to meet other important economic challenges such as inequality. After we discuss this basic narrative that follows from prior work, we then perform a critical analysis and redesign of several categories of systems that are user-centered but fail to meet these new objectives. Finally, we discuss how disintermediation can help us achieve sustainability goals.

## LESSONS FROM SUSTAINABLE HCI

The alluring promise of Sustainable HCI is to decrease the ecological impact of current unsustainable social practices by using interactive digital technologies to change human-computer systems and to ambiently increase people's awareness, to persuade, sense, nudge, challenge, convince, confront, design or in general to bring a critical sustainability lens to user-centered design [19, 29, 43, 83]. In this section we review the relevant lessons from Preist *et al.* [69], from our prior work [67], and from other Sustainable HCI work in the literature.

### Fundamentals

Sustainability is a concept about the journey of human societies towards a stable equilibrium with the natural world [79]. It is impossible to precisely pinpoint when a society crosses the boundary from sustainable to unsustainable—that is, when its use of and impact on natural systems exceeds their natural replenishment and remediation—nor would it be possible to pinpoint when an unsustainable society has sufficiently adjusted its practices to be characterized as "sustainable". However since the concept of sustainability, at its core, captures a trajectory rather than a position, it is possible for a society to "overshoot"—to be on an unsustainable trajectory without having yet faced the consequences of that overshoot [12, 77, 99–101]. We cannot know where modern technological society resides in such an arc, but scientific evidence indicates *both* that overshoot began some time ago—likely 2-3 decades ago [56, 100]—and that consequences are becoming ever more apparent [33, 36, 37, 55, 80, 87, 88].

The goal of much sustainability research is to respond to the urgent challenges identified in the research literature in the natural sciences, which indicate that many important biophysical limits have been exceeded by global human society [80, 88]. We are living in an age of ecological overshoot [12, 100] and are in a mad dash appropriating resources from all other species on Earth as well as appropriating "phantom carrying capacity", e.g. imports from else*where* (foodstuff from other places, so-called "ghost acreage") [8] and imports from else*when* ("fossil acreage", energy from prehistoric sources in the form fossil fuels) [12, 34]. This cannot be sustained indefinitely, and this overshoot is manifested not by just one dimension of unsustainable practices, but dozens—from carbon emissions to aquifer depletion to eutrophication to species loss [88]. The literature outside of computing is clear: massive deleterious changes in the global ecosystem are taking place due to human actions, and little has been put into place to prevent the situation from escalating. In a worst-case scenario, we could very well pass various tipping points that trigger self-reinforcing feedback loops in the global ecosystem, with severe consequences for life on the planet [48, 55].

It is these challenges that Sustainable HCI researchers are responding to. However, as we noted in prior work [67], sometimes this perspective can be too narrowly applied in research, yielding analyses and systems that do not engage with the global ecological challenges we face, and rather focus on small, incremental, and peripheral issues. Instead of aiming to incrementally improve the efficiency of computing systems, for example, we argued that we should instead evaluate global ecological limits and keep those boundaries in mind when doing design, aiming to build systems that do not contribute to overshoot. After discussing prior work that was purportedly sustainable, we discussed the importance of choosing appropriate (not too narrow) system boundaries when evaluating the sustainability of a system, as well as the importance of having a holistic approach to the challenges of sustainability.

### Computing's Role

In a society that is technologically dominated and mediated, computing has a large role to play in the future of societal sustainability. This is not only due computing's impact on the global ecosystem (e.g., due to power consumption, e-waste, etc.) but also due to the patterns of human-computing behavior that trace out the path of much that takes place in industrial economies today.

Sustainable HCI research encompasses two subfields: sustainable computing and computing for sustainability. The former aims to decrease the footprint of computing itself while the latter broadens the target and examines the role of computing in improving the sustainability in other societal sectors.

Despite many years of work on the subject, the former has remained tractable and yet insufficiently broad or impactful—as computing has a limited, though increasing, impact globally relative to other sectors [50, 72, 73, 96]—while the latter has remained hopelessly daunting and complex—as improving societal sustainability easily runs aground due to economic, political, cultural, biophysical, and other factors that are far beyond the ken of computing researchers.

Preist, Schien, and Blevis [69] dissect the cornucopian paradigm, its implications for the design of computing infrastructure, and the consequent (un)sustainability that results from following the current trajectory. Through various examples, they show how current design practices and technical and business drivers together further the expansion of networks, services, data centers, traffic, devices, and the like. These trends naturally increase the environmental footprint of computing at a rapid pace and follow a trajectory of an ever-expanding unsustainable cornucopian bonanza.

### Impact of Sustainable HCI

While it is important, necessary, and laudable to work on lowering the environmental footprint of computing itself, such work is ultimately too narrow and will remain insufficient. This is for two reasons. The first is that the footprint of computing, while growing, still represents only about 2 percent of global energy use and a comparable amount of materials [50,71,72,96]. The second reason is that proposed efficiency gains easily evaporate due to various rebound effects [30,65,78] such as Jevons's paradox [40]. Thus while we believe it is important to make computing more efficient, and to power computing infrastructure using energy from renewable sources, the impact of such work on societal sustainability will remain small.

The other direction that Sustainable HCI (and the larger non-HCI field of ICT for Sustainability more generally) offers is to utilize and leverage the potentially beneficial effects of digital technologies in such a way that its footprint is more than compensated by carbon emission reductions and similar sustainability improvements in *other* parts of industry and society. A paradigmatic example is to decrease travel by using digital technologies for videoconferencing. Another is to use use digital and various concordant technologies (sensors, Internet of Things, etc.) to increase the "smartness" and efficiency in other sectors of society, for example by deploying smart grids, smart home technologies, and through smart cities initiatives [7].

This approach promises to have larger impacts (see [28]) but will also have to bear increased costs both in terms of money (investments), efforts, and complexity. This approach also tries to reform the system incrementally "from the inside" but it is far from certain that emissions, pollution, or resource throughput can shrink/decrease as much and as quickly as is needed.

Our aim in this paper is largely with respect to the latter thread of Sustainable HCI—computing for sustainability—and later we detail how we view disintermediation as a key design rubric to that end.

### Growth and its Impacts

All industrial and post-industrial economies are organized around the concept of economic growth, which is seen as a universal aim for national policy. However, as Daly has observed, in our current situation, this growth has become "uneconomic"; that is, the marginal benefits of the growth in production and consumption are outweighed by the marginal costs of growth, when including external costs such as negative effects on the environment [15]. These negative externalities are largely due to ecological impacts.

We begin from the observation that growth—economic and material—is central to this cornucopian paradigm, and that it is a core challenge in sustainability research. While in theory it is possible for economic growth to decouple from material growth, and have no negative sustainability impact, in the history of the past century there are no known instances of this happening in a sustained fashion, except for narrow examples limited to a product or sector. Thus economic growth and material resource consumption proceed in tandem, along with the arc of cornucopian technologies.

With GDP as a measure and with GDP growth as a national (and international) policy goal, and given the ecological impacts that research indicates are taking place as a result of the expansion of societal demands on the ecosystem, the concept of uneconomic growth becomes harder to ignore.

However, another key observation of Daly (and others) is that GDP growth is not supposed to be an end, but a means to an end: increased human well-being. It has long been recognized that growth is not fundamental, but rather something that arises out of policy goals and the structure of financial systems in the economy [14]. Therefore, if GDP growth and human well-being decouple then we can pursue the latter without the former. A corollary is that if we can decouple growth from human well-being we can be less concerned if GDP actually declines (i.e., degrowth [13]) as long as well-being stays the same or improves. Human well-being is of course much more challenging to measure than GDP, but with the urgent need to address sustainability issues today this is a challenge worth addressing head on.

Economic growth generally, and GDP growth specifically, is key to how we evaluate economies. The theory goes that if we have economic growth then people are wealthier, and this enables them to meet their needs better, increasing overall welfare. One key source of growth is monetization of goods and services that were previously outside the money economy. In recent decades, this happened in many economic sectors. For example, in the food industry there has been a dramatic increase in the packaging of fresh and prepared foods rather than simply selling basics that must be cooked at home; in doing so, the work involved in food preparation is monetized. By monetizing, these economic interactions can be easily measured, but that is not the only consequence: they are expressed in terms of a money whose supply is dominated by debt (e.g., the vast gulf between M3 and M0 money supplies), which must grow [46]. As a result, there are increasing claims on underlying real natural resources, which in turn must be extracted at a greater rate to keep up with demand, furthering ecological overshoot.

Thus for the rest of this paper we will concern ourselves with the end goal of improving human well-being without regard to growth.

### Responses to Unsustainable Growth

A natural strategy for fixing the unsustainability of industrial society is at the policy level. Indeed, it has been argued for decades that the right set of policy responses can remedy the sustainability challenges we face [56]. We do not disagree. However, despite the awareness of these challenges for quite some time, few nations have implemented sufficient policy changes to achieve sustainability. As a result, while we do view policy changes as the ideal remedy for sustainability challenges, such changes are challenging to achieve through computing research and HCI research specifically.

Instead, we can reflect on the fact that computing today is pervasive and is the organizing technology that both drives much growth and is driven itself by growth. As a result, computing can itself affect the sustainability of society as we as researchers can help change the plumbing and the windows through which we examine the world, even without directly making policy changes. It is this ability and centrality of computing that Sustainable HCI research can leverage.

### Intermediation

There has long been a search for an all-encompassing explanation for today's unsustainability and for a silver bullet solution to remedy it. We do not believe either exists. Here we focus on one explanation—intermediation—and one response—disintermediation—that have significant merits.

Much of the GDP growth that takes place in today's global economy stems from intermediation, as much of the new monetary wealth being generated today involves the abstraction of some resource (e.g., previously-unacknowledged labor, natural resources and ecosystems, etc.) and the addition of layers of social, technological, and economic intermediation to control the flow of that resource and bring it within the money system. Often these layers of intermediation are tightly woven together using new technological systems (e.g., complex just-in-time global supply chains).

A complete analysis of intermediation in the global economic system is far beyond the scope of this paper, so for the sake of space we give two short (non-computing) examples of where intermediation has led to unsustainable practices in recent decades.

First, consider the industrial food system and specifically the raising of grazing animals in concentrated animal feeding operations [68]. What was once universally a simple and relatively sustainable practice—as grazers fed on grass and their manure helped build the soil—was turned into a wholly unsustainable practice through intermediation. The grazing animals were separated from the grassland and a feeding operation was placed in between the animals and their food source. The feeding operation was tasked with providing high quantities of calorie-dense, non-perishable food (e.g., corn) which had to be grown elsewhere and transported, and further required synthetic fertilizer inputs (from fossil fuels) as no manure was present to nourish the plants and pesticides, herbicides, and other chemicals (also from fossil fuels) to maintain the crop. The manure from the grazing animals then had to be collected and disposed of in some way. As Wendell Berry puts it, "[t]he genius of American farm experts is very well demonstrated here: they can take a solution and divide it neatly into two problems." [5].

Second, consider the transformation of the global manufacturing system over the last four decades. Industrial production has rapidly become globalized, with material resources abstracted and intermediated in a global just-in-time supply chain built by large multinational corporations that source resources where they can find them the cheapest, employ labor where the labor is cheapest, and take advantage of the relatively low cost of fossil fuels for the transportation of materials and products [49]. This intermediation hides the true ecological and human cost of the products, as resources are sourced where they are cheapest and unregulated, and the ease with which global resources are made available via modern information systems hide the true impact of their use (and later, their disposal).

### Disintermediation and Sustainable HCI

Thus far we have argued that: 1) sustainable HCI research is likely to be most impactful when addressing societal sustainability challenges, 2) as long as growth and its attendant impacts continue, it will likely be difficult for sustainable HCI research to increase societal sustainability, and 3) examining the factors involved in the global economy today, specifically the process of intermediation, provides a promising new avenue for a broad range of sustainable HCI research. These observations lead us to conclude that disintermediation—the redesign of systems to remove intermediaries—can be applied in many specific applications of computing and can serve as a key technique for Sustainable HCI.

In line with Joseph Tainter's work [91, 92], we argue that (increasing) complexity in itself is unsustainable as more resources have to be diverted to maintain (the increasingly complex) system itself *and* the marginal utility of solving the next (and the next and the next) problem diminishes over time (e.g., low-hanging fruits tend to be picked first as the costs are low and the benefits are high).

It thus follows that ever-increasing complexity is deeply problematic from a sustainability point of view [66]. What would be desirable is instead to decrease complexity down to a level that retains most of the benefits of complexity but with much lower costs. This would entail seeking solutions in the process of disintermediation, which involves removing intermediaries to simplify a system while simultaneously maintaining most or all of the system's benefits; in prior work we analogized this process to that of refactoring software and other computing systems [75].

## POLITICAL ECONOMY

In a pair of papers, Ekbia and Nardi introduced the connections between political economy and HCI [23, 24]. Their observations mirror those in the sustainability discourse: that important questions are being ignored and moreover by choosing to ignore political economy we are not neutral, but instead are perpetuating a set of values, assumptions, and perspectives that in recent times have led to greater social inequality:

> *Our contention is not that HCI researchers and practitioners are unaware of the relationship between economy and technology; rather, that this does not typically figure in any deep way into our theories, practice, and*

> *designs. We in HCI face the reality of the larger economic system and its impact on our daily life and work, but we do not incorporate these understandings into our research and practice to the extent that we perhaps should.* [23].

Ekbia and Nardi argue for a focus on more fundamental human needs and on human well-being as a design goal. They also exhort designers to be conscious of value, class, labor, and social control. To our surprise, and as we briefly examine in this section, the strategy of disintermediaion is responsive to all of these concepts of political economy and, even better, in exactly the ways that Ekbia and Nardi identify.

In this section we outline some of their arguments, and then connect those arguments to the rubric of disintermediation.

### Value

Ekbia and Nardi, in line with Preist et al., observe that value and the production of wealth have become inextricably linked to a growth-based economic system that does not know any limits and in which money is the primary store of value to be sought. Given the hyper-growth of computing and technology sectors over the last three decades, economic growth at large is increasingly linked to the development of new digital technologies.

Given that the size of the economy depends on both the amount of money in circulation and the velocity of said money (e.g., the pace at which it circulates in the economy), it is possible to increase profits in financial markets and elsewhere by increasing the velocity of money flowing through the system. Information technologies have been very helpful in this regard by lowering barriers and increasing the speed of transactions. This also means that today's financial system favors investment in technologies that specifically aim to further increase the velocity of money (e.g., to service the needs of financial markets and actors).

### Class

At its core, class is about economic differentiation: placing the control of economic systems in the hands of some (few) and not in the hands of (many) others. The creation of increasing levels of intermediation in complex economies presents more opportunities for economic differentiation and class structures, as does the concentration of wealth through these structures.

Ekbia and Nardi [23] argue that the computing systems we design often disproportionately benefit the comfortable middle class (which makes sense economically according to a capitalist logic) while the needs of low-income communities [16], disadvantaged communities [18], disadvantaged job seekers [17], or the homeless [102, 103] are less often served by the systems we develop. The same is of course also true for systems developed to serve the impoverished in the global South [104, 105].

### Labor

Much labor in the digital economy is unacknowledged, unpaid labor that is done by many for the benefit of the few (platform owners) [22, 44], such as filling social platforms with contents [47], developing a computer game mod [84], or by producing a cultural product (e.g., a documentary movie) without being sufficiently rewarded to be able to get by without a second job [94]. Some tasks that do receive monetary remuneration do so at a level far below the legislated minimum wage [39] or below what is needed even to just get by [20, 42]. The wealth that is created in many technology companies, and the astronomical valuation that companies with a few dozen employees can have, comes from the free distributed work of the users of those services.

### Social Control

Technologies that purport to be human-centric have just as often created means for social control, as Ekbia and Nardi observe, in that they enable surveillance and disconnection:

> *Although technologies such as the Internet are used for emancipatory purposes, they have also turned into instruments of surveillance, control, and coercion. Many technologies provide effective control and surveillance mechanisms for the organizations that employ or provide services to us. [...] Thanks to digital technologies, what is lost to reduced bureaucratic control is more than rebalanced in capital's favor by continuous access and surveillance.* [24].

The often-repeated adage "if you're not paying for it, you are the product" is backed up by numerous examples of how collected data has been shared, used in ways not advertised or intended, sold or stolen [10, 25, 95].

### Disintermediation and Political Economy

As we mention above, disintermediation is, surprisingly, an appropriate and direct methodological response to these four axes of political economy (and their impacts) described by Ekbia and Nardi. That is, not only does disintermediation have the potential to help achieve societal sustainability, but some of those very properties of the approach also serve to address the political economy concerns outlined by Ekbia and Nardi. It is important that this is the case, as it would be unfortunate for a design technique that improves sustainability to simultaneously increase inequality.

#### *Value*

A disintermediated system is one in which we have removed economic mechanisms designed to extract wealth from existing flows of goods and services. Moreover, disintermediation taken to the extreme can serve to eliminate the possibility of wealth extraction. This occurs in a way that is almost definitional, but also true: by virtue of removing intermediaries in an economic system (e.g., financial institutions) between two parties, those intermediaries lose the ability to take a cut of the wealth flow. In doing so, we enable a more ecologically-based accounting of value (donor value) as it is easier to trace value to its ecological root (i.e., the ecosystem services that underlie the human economy), as opposed to conventional receiver (market) measures of value [64].

#### *Class*

System structures that entail more layers of indirection, especially in the form of hierarchies, create more chances for class structures to strongly emerge. This is due to the fact that each layer of intermediation must be controlled by some party, and thus each layer can be controlled by a different party than the end user. Fundamentally, disintermediation tends to have the effect of deconstructing hierarchies and empowering each entity in a system to have the power of choice and control, thereby hindering class differentiation.

*Labor*
Intermediaries in digitally-mediated labor can leverage such layers to benefit from the labor (often free labor) of others. By disintermediating we can avoid this problem (though other graph structures may emerge over time).

*Social Control*
One of the most insidious effects of the proliferation of cloud-based services—those rightly scorned by Preist *et al.*—is not just the obscuring of where resources come from and the furtherance of the cornucopian paradigm. It is that a system with many intermediaries, especially where those intermediaries concentrate power (per the challenges above), is one in which social control can be exerted via those powerful intermediaries. This has appeared in its most extreme form in recent years in countries that suppress free speech online (e.g., in online social networks), as these online services now function as gatekeepers of communication between people in a way that did not exist in the past [59]. A disintermediated system, on the other hand, is one in which there is less room for centralized social control, manipulation, or censorship.

## IMPLICATIONS FOR DESIGN

In this section we examine the intersection of increasing human well-being, HCI research, and the implications of the application of disintermediation as a design rubric. We here exemplify the principle of disintermediation by applying it to few areas of daily life: food, work, communication, and transportation.

To keep our discussion concrete, we focus on *both* commercial systems, such as online social networks, and non-commerical systems, such as grassroots instances of "collaborative consumption" [9], and will refer (primarily) to HCI research that delves into and analyzes such work [4, 32, 90]. Our examples are chosen to illustrate how the design rubric of disintermediation could be applied to areas that correlate with increasing human well-being in modern society, such as meeting primary human needs such as food and transportation and secondary needs such as communication and employment.

### Food

Today's global industrial food system has supplanted traditional, more sustainable methods. In part this is because industrial agriculture leverages mechanization, chemical fertilizers and pesticides, and genetic engineering, all of which have decreased costs and increased efficiency. However the purported cost and efficiency gains have only held true in a narrow accounting; the environmental and social impacts of this approach to agriculture have been devastating [2, 27, 68, 86, 97]. The woes of industrial agriculture can be seen as a consequence of the abstraction of plants as machines that take water, N-P-K, and sunlight and turn it into food. Indeed, industrial agriculture companies such as John Deere now say this explicitly, as they claim that "a farm is a factory in a remote area" [98]. This also involves the intermediation of natural processes that enable the decomposition of animal and plant wastes to replenish the soil, whereas sustainable, disintermediated, perennial crop systems help stabilize the soil and increase fertility (vs. tilling, which provides a short-term boost in soil fertility with long-term consequences), as do similar natural methods that ensure the sustainability of a natural system of food production.

Many of the computing systems that have been developed for agriculture have remained within this industrial food paradigm, and so have served to further it (and amplify its intermediation) rather than reforming the system structure itself. There has, for example, been substantial work on the Internet of Things in the context of agriculture, placing sensors and actuators throughout a farm to increase the efficiency of the system to increase yields and/or decrease costs. However, as Odom and others observed [63], this is not a clear win.

Not only have the processes of food production become intermediated, but so have the processes of bringing that food to people. An extreme example of this is soylent [21], in which food is processed to the extreme to produce a single synthesized product that in concept has all the nutrients required to sustain a person. In addition to the food products themselves, the distribution channels for food have only recently begun to revert to older, localized practices, such as farmers markets and community gardens [45].

In recent years there have been a few proposals for alternatives to this industrial food system and the role that Sustainable HCI research can play. One example is our work on Computational Agroecology [74], which focuses on the planning, implementation, and management of alternative, complex agroecosystems that are modeled after natural systems and aim to produce high yields while ensuring sustainability. Farms based upon agroecology are in effect disintermediating relative to the industrial food system: they no longer require much or any external or synthetic inputs, and instead leverage natural ecosystem services to create a sustainable food system [62]. Community-supported agriculture extends this model to the process of farm financing and food distribution.

This disintermediated model could be extended to one in which a network of local agroecology-based farms supply food, along with local community gardens and individual backyards, and users use computational tools to gather together this food from these disparate, local, and direct sources. In this model, while technology would be adding some amount of intermediation (to help find the food locally), this would be replacing other intermediaries (e.g., large grocery stores and their long-distance supply chains) and doing so in a way that connects people directly to their food's source.

### Workplace

Hoffice ("home office") is a disintermediated solution to having (access to) a workplace without having an outside firm (e.g., an ordinary employer or a coworking firm) to provide that workplace. Hoffice consists of a network of members who organize and offer up one-day pop-up workspaces to the other members in the network. In essence, Hoffice enables the creation of ad-hoc, peer-to-peer coworking spaces. Members ("hosts") offer other members ("guests") the use of their kitchen (and/or living room, balcony, kitchen, etc.) as a temporary office for, typically, 4-10 people for a day. Due to the founder's strong philosophical convictions about the value of gift economies, it is unlikely that Hoffice would become a commercial service—the idea of offering up one's kitchen for free to others is a central part of the Hoffice concept.

Hoffice was started in 2013 in Stockholm by the founder and a small group of self-employed social entrepreneurs who lacked a functioning structure for their workdays. Hoffice currently has thousands of members and events are organized daily. There are also numerous smaller Hoffice groups in other Swedish cities as well as in dozens of countries on several continents.

The structure of a Hoffice workspace is interesting in that it is not the disintermediation that directly provides sustainability benefits: instead, it is what the disintermediation enables. Many of those that participate in Hoffice are self-employed and would otherwise be using their own facilities (e.g., heating their homes to work at home, renting commercial office space which then must be maintained, etc.) which comes with its own financial and environmental costs. By consolidating workspaces together via Hoffice, the participants better share resources. Since Hoffice is held largely in Swedish cities with excellent public transportation systems that are widely used, most Hoffice participants have little transportation energy footprint for traveling to their destinations.

Hoffice currently piggybacks on social media for coordination; this could itself use a disintermediated solution, as we discuss below. There is no central clearinghouse for events, though any member can post a note about an upcoming Hoffice event in their home. While there have not been any scientific research papers written about Hoffice, there has been research on related topics within mobility and work, for example "nomadic work" [52, 81, 89] and in the utilization of ad-hoc coworking spaces [26, 85].

### Communication

Earlier we noted that many services, even disintermediated ones, may need centralized services (e.g., web-based services or app backend infrastructure). The most common computing services that users interact with today are web-based services that are run by large service providers. Some of these services, such as social networks, are focused on the interactions of users who want to communicate with one another for personal, business, or other reasons. Other services provide a focal point for user collaboration, storing their context and content, providing means for sharing and editing data, and controlling access to that data.

A key aim of cloud systems is the presentation of a unified view of the data stored in the systems from the user's perspective. In most modern cloud-based services the systems are indeed administratively centralized (i.e., stored on systems owned by one company) even if many different physical computers are used in a data center to store the data. In systems terminology, the backend cloud systems in data centers are "scale out" but the administrative control adheres to the older, now-archaic model of "scale up", as we discuss in prior work [70].[1]

The technical structure of these systems has direct impact on the axes identified by Preist *et al.* and Ekbia and Nardi—that of the cornucopian paradigm and of issues of labor. Labor is often provided by users for free while the company who owns the technical infrastructure harvests the monetary values that are created by this arrangement [44]. Ekbia and Nardi use the term *heteromation* [22] to describe:

> *...a labor relation in which humans and machines collaborate (hence "heteromation" vs automation), but where the human occupies a marginal role computationally or organizationally. Heteromation is digitally mediated labor that involves the extraction of economic benefit for someone other than the laborer. The labor is uncompensated or very low cost.* [60]

Several examples of heteromation have been studied in the HCI field but the most well-known and well-researched example is Amazon's Mechanical Turk service [39, 53, 82] which has numerous downsides with regard to labor relations, surveillance, and social control.

Applying the disintermediation rubric to the context of cloud computing, we can decentralize the systems while still providing a coherent view to users. It is the latter that users want, while the former is typically entirely incidental to users (i.e., users wouldn't mind it if Facebook were to no longer run Facebook). While there are numerous technical details that must be addressed to achieve a fully decentralized computing infrastructure that provides similar functionality to cloud-based services, the technical challenges in building such systems are relatively straightforward. However, the HCI challenges that are entailed in building user-acceptable cloud-like services are numerous, as users have come to expect the illusion of infinite computing resources that are transparently and instantaneously available everywhere.

### Transportation

There are numerous technologically-mediated transportation services and ride-sharing intiatives today such as Uber, Lyft, Wingz, BlaBlaCar (France and more than 20 other countries), Haxi (primarily Norway) and Skjutsgruppen (Sweden). These services have been studied from an ICTD perspective [1], in terms of labor practice in ridesharing [76], personal ride sharing experiences [58] and for supporting the transportation needs of the elderly [57] in the HCI literature.

This topic area is challenging to analyze in terms of its intermediation. While a service such as Uber is problematic due to the reasons enumerated above (see "Communication"), so are traditional taxi services with a centralized switchboard and cars aimlessly circling around the city. Thus while non-profit, grassroots ridesharing services attempt to service

[1] In scale-up systems a single node is made more powerful to meet demand rather than increasing the number of small systems to meet the demand in aggregate.

human needs without furthering the unsustainable growth-based cornucopian paradigm, an ideal system would be to a) better make use of the hundreds of millions of half-empty cars that traverse cities and highways, b) support car-free transportation (e.g. walking, biking, buses, subways) in such a way that car transportation needs decrease, or c) to build cities in such a way that transportation needs in general decrease [35]; these ideal solutions are in fact disintermediated forms—either due to their self-sufficient nature or due to the elimination of prior intermediaries—relative to today's common practices.

## DISCUSSION

In analyzing existing work in Sustainable HCI and evaluating possibilities for disintermediation, we found that three key qualities consistently arose: decentralization, decommercialization, and decomplexification. Decentralization removes a possible intermediary, decreasing the potential harmful economic challenges that might arise. Decommercialization decreases the growth incentive. Decomplexification decreases the cost of maintaining the system. All three lead to decreased economic growth as it is currently conceived, and as a result have the potential to benefit sustainability while simultaneously not harming (or even improving) human well-being. However we must note that not all approaches to disintermediate will achieve all three qualities in an ideal fashion, and each solution is context specific and comparative.

The concept of disintermediation is at once esoteric and mundane: esoteric because it has seldom been discussed let alone used yet mundane because once explained it is easily applied in many different contexts. However it is both of these qualities of disintermediation as a design rubric that make it potentially impactful, as there is significant low-hanging fruit ripe for disintermediation in many human-computer systems as it does not require specialized knowledge to apply.

Moreover, the potential impact it has as a technique can be seen more clearly from a distance. Returning to our earlier discussion of the implicit and often unquestioned linkage of GDP growth and human well-being, we are reminded that most actions we take in society, even purportedly sustainable ones (e.g., purchasing "green" products), further the growth-based economic system. Thus all evidence from daily life reaffirms that linkage. Disintermediation provides a direct means of severing that linkage: it enables increased well-being without growth, as it disentangles economic relationships, and in doing so has the potential to even decrease GDP. This latter concept is decidedly non-mainstream as an objective, but that is only because of its implicit linkage—that is, it is assumed that decreased GDP, such as in a recession, is always coupled with decreased well-being. What we argue here is that this is not fundamental and thus it is acceptable and perhaps even desirable from an ecological and economic standpoint to encourage disintermediated economic *de*growth rather than intermediated *un*economic growth.

The idea of taking actions to *shrink* the economy as we understand it today might be seen as a radical notion, a far cry from something as seemingly mundane as cutting out the intermediaries in some computing system. However, in doing so we are not arguing for a neo-luddite perspective that eschews new technology. Rather, we are arguing for the design of disintermediated human-computer systems that currently have little financial incentive to be built (thus are less likely to be built by the private sector) but can have the dual benefit of improving societal sustainability while decreasing inequality and the political economy problems that are prevalent today.

In addition to its direct effects on the economic system and growth, and thus on the flow of natural resources through the economy and the structure of the economy with respect to political economy concerns, disintermediation has the side effect that it is likely to enable more sustainable practices. Specifically, a significant cause of the unsustainability of today's global society is the material footprint of goods and their transportation. Intermediaries are more likely to increase the distance goods must travel, involve greater complexity, and source materials based on cost rather than sustainability. Relocalized, disintermediated manufacturing, for example, has the potential to relocalize material sources, transmit information not physical matter over long distances, and produce only what needs to be built.[2]

## CONCLUSION

Once an afterthought, HCI is now central to the success of many if not most computer systems. We argue that to the extent that the computing in general and HCI in particular has engaged with sustainability, it has often been treated as a peripheral concern rather than as a central requirement. The exception has been the small body of work on Sustainable HCI and Sustainable Computing. While some of this work has offered well-grounded critique, it has often fallen short on practical advice and on suitable techniques that are concrete enough to be actionable.

In this paper, we have placed sustainability at the center and asked what kinds of computer systems we need to develop to move towards a sustainable society. To this end, we have proposed disintermediation—the removal of intermediaries while retaining the key functionality of a system—as a strategy to decrease complexity, costs, and material throughput in society.

## ACKNOWLEDGEMENTS

We greatly appreciate the thoughtful feedback we received from Daniel Berg, Tomas Hahn, Hanna Hasseqvist, Samantha McDonald, Bonnie Nardi, Erica Öhlund, Bill Tomlinson, and the anonymous reviewers.

[2]On the flip side there is debate in the community about the sustainability benefits and drawbacks of processes such as 3D printing, as it localizes material inputs but does not benefit from manufacturing economies of scale [54].

## REFERENCES


1. S. I. Ahmed, N. Bidwell, H. Zade, S. Muralidhar, A. Dhareshwar, C. T. Baneen Karachiwala, and J. ONeill. Peer-to-peer in the workplace: A view from the road. In *Proceedings of CHI*, pages 7–12, 2016.
2. M. Altieri. Agroecology: the science of natural resource management for poor farmers in marginal environments. *Agriculture, ecosystems & environment*, 93(1):1–24, 2002.
3. E. P. Baumer and M. Silberman. When the implication is not to design (technology). In *Proceedings of the SIGCHI Conference on Human Factors in Computing Systems*, pages 2271–2274. ACM, 2011.
4. V. Bellotti, A. Ambard, D. Turner, C. Gossmann, K. Demkova, and J. M. Carroll. A muddle of models of motivation for using peer-to-peer economy systems. In *Proceedings of the 33rd Annual ACM Conference on Human Factors in Computing Systems*, pages 1085–1094. ACM, 2015.
5. W. Berry. *The unsettling of America: Culture & agriculture.* Counterpoint, 2015.
6. E. Blevis. Sustainable interaction design: invention & disposal, renewal & reuse. In *Proceedings of the SIGCHI conference on Human factors in computing systems*, pages 503–512. ACM, 2007.
7. M. Blumendorf. Building sustainable smart homes. In *Proceedings of the 1st International Conference on Information and Communication Technologies for Sustainability*, pages 151–158, 2013.
8. G. Borgstrom. hungry planet; the modern world at the edge of famine. 1965.
9. R. Botsman and R. Rogers. *What's mine is yours: how collaborative consumption is changing the way we live.* Collins London, 2011.
10. I. Brown. Social media surveillance. *The International Encyclopedia of Digital Communication and Society*, 2014.
11. H. Brynjarsdottir, M. Håkansson, J. Pierce, E. Baumer, C. DiSalvo, and P. Sengers. Sustainably unpersuaded: how persuasion narrows our vision of sustainability. In *Proceedings of the SIGCHI Conference on Human Factors in Computing Systems*, pages 947–956. ACM, 2012.
12. W. R. Catton. *Overshoot: The ecological basis of revolutionary change.* University of Illinois Press, 1982.
13. G. D'Alisa, F. Demaria, and G. Kallis. *Degrowth: a vocabulary for a new era.* Routledge, 2014.
14. H. E. Daly. *Steady-state economics: with new essays.* Island Press, 1991.
15. H. E. Daly. Uneconomic growth: in theory, in fact, in history, and in relation to globalization. *Clemens Lecture Series. Paper 10*, 1999.
16. T. Dillahunt, J. Mankoff, E. Paulos, and S. Fussell. It's not all about green: Energy use in low-income communities. In *Proceedings of the 11th international conference on Ubiquitous computing*, pages 255–264. ACM, 2009.
17. T. R. Dillahunt, N. Bose, S. Diwan, and A. Chen-Phang. Designing for disadvantaged job seekers: Insights from early investigations. In *Proceedings of the 2016 ACM Conference on Designing Interactive Systems*, pages 905–910. ACM, 2016.
18. T. R. Dillahunt and A. R. Malone. The promise of the sharing economy among disadvantaged communities. In *Proceedings of the 33rd Annual ACM Conference on Human Factors in Computing Systems*, pages 2285–2294. ACM, 2015.
19. C. DiSalvo, P. Sengers, and H. Brynjarsdóttir. Mapping the landscape of sustainable hci. In *Proceedings of the SIGCHI Conference on Human Factors in Computing Systems*, pages 1975–1984. ACM, 2010.
20. C. Doctorow, M. Harris, and N. Gorenflo. *Share or die: Voices of the get lost generation in the age of crisis.* New Society Publishers, 2012.
21. M. Dolejšová. Deciphering a meal through open source standards: Soylent and the rise of diet hackers. In *Proceedings of the 2016 CHI Conference Extended Abstracts on Human Factors in Computing Systems*, pages 436–448. ACM, 2016.
22. H. Ekbia and B. Nardi. Heteromation and its (dis) contents: The invisible division of labor between humans and machines. *First Monday*, 19(6), 2014.
23. H. Ekbia and B. Nardi. The political economy of computing: the elephant in the hci room. *interactions*, 22(6):46–49, 2015.
24. H. Ekbia and B. Nardi. Social Inequality and HCI: The View from Political Economy. In *Proceedings of the 2016 CHI Conference on Human Factors in Computing Systems*, pages 4997–5002. ACM, 2016.
25. C. Fuchs, K. Boersma, A. Albrechtslund, and M. Sandoval. *Internet and surveillance: The challenges of Web 2.0 and social media*, volume 16. Routledge, 2013.
26. A. Gandini. The rise of coworking spaces: A literature review. *ephemera*, 15(1):193, 2015.
27. S. Gliessman. *Agroecology: researching the ecological basis for sustainable agriculture.* Springer, 1990.
28. Global e-Sustainability Initiative. Gesi smarter 2020: the role of ict in driving a sustainable future. *Global e-Sustainability Initiative, Brussels, Belgium*, 2012.
29. E. Goodman. Three environmental discourses in human-computer interaction. In *CHI'09 Extended Abstracts on Human Factors in Computing Systems*, pages 2535–2544. ACM, 2009.
30. C. Håkansson and G. Finnveden. Indirect rebound and reverse rebound effects in the ict-sector and emissions of co2. In *Joint Conference on 29th International Conference on Informatics for Environmental Protection/3rd International Conference on ICT for Sustainability (EnviroInfo and ICT4S), SEP 07-09, 2015, Univ Copenhagen, Copenhagen, DENMARK*, pages 66–73, 2015.
31. M. Håkansson and P. Sengers. Beyond being green: simple living families and ict. In *Proceedings of the SIGCHI Conference on Human Factors in Computing Systems*, pages 2725–2734. ACM, 2013.
32. J. Hamari, M. Sjöklint, and A. Ukkonen. The sharing economy: Why people participate in collaborative consumption. *Journal of the Association for Information Science and Technology*, 2015.
33. J. Hansen. *Storms of my grandchildren: the truth about the coming climate catastrophe and our last chance to save humanity.* Bloomsbury Publishing USA, 2010.
34. T. Hartmann. *The last hours of ancient sunlight: Waking up to personal and global transformation.* Hachette UK, 2009.
35. H. Hasselqvist, M. Hesselgren, and C. Bogdan. Challenging the car norm: Opportunities for ict to support sustainable transportation practices. In *Proceedings of the 2016 CHI Conference on Human Factors in Computing Systems*, pages 1300–1311. ACM, 2016.
36. R. Heinberg. *Peak everything: waking up to the century of declines.* New Society Publishers, 2010.
37. R. Heinberg. *The end of growth: Adapting to our new economic reality.* New Society Publishers, 2011.
38. L. M. Hilty and B. Aebischer. *ICT innovations for sustainability*, volume 310. Springer, 2015.
39. L. C. Irani and M. Silberman. Turkopticon: interrupting worker invisibility in amazon mechanical turk. In *Proceedings of the SIGCHI Conference on Human Factors in Computing Systems*, pages 611–620. ACM, 2013.

40. W. S. Jevons. *The coal question: an inquiry concerning the progress of the nation, and the probable exhaustion of our coal-mines*. Macmillan, 1906.

41. S. Joshi and T. Cerratto-Pargman. On fairness & sustainability: Motivating change in the networked society. *Advances in Computer Science Research*, 2015.

42. S. Kessler. Pixel and dimed: On (not) getting by in the gig economy. *Fast Company*, 18, 2014.

43. B. Knowles, L. Blair, M. Hazas, and S. Walker. Exploring sustainability research in computing: where we are and where we go next. In *Proceedings of the 2013 ACM international joint conference on Pervasive and ubiquitous computing*, pages 305–314. ACM, 2013.

44. J. Lanier. *Who owns the future?* Simon and Schuster, 2014.

45. L. Li, N. Chen, W. Wang, and J. Baty. Localbuy: a system for serving communities with local food. In *CHI'09 Extended Abstracts on Human Factors in Computing Systems*, pages 2823–2828. ACM, 2009.

46. B. Lietaer. *The future of money*. Random House, 2013.

47. G. Lovink, M. Rasch, et al. *Unlike us reader: Social media monopolies and their alternatives*. Number 8. Institute of Network Cultures, 2013.

48. M. Lynas. *Six degrees: Our future on a hotter planet*. National Geographic Books, 2008.

49. A. Malm. *Fossil capital: The rise of steam power and the roots of global warming*. Verso Books, 2016.

50. J. Malmodin, P. Bergmark, and D. Lundén. The future carbon footprint of the ICT and E&M sectors. *on Information and Communication Technologies*, page 12, 2013.

51. J. C. Mankoff, E. Blevis, A. Borning, B. Friedman, S. R. Fussell, J. Hasbrouck, A. Woodruff, and P. Sengers. Environmental sustainability and interaction. In *CHI'07 extended abstracts on Human factors in computing systems*, pages 2121–2124. ACM, 2007.

52. G. Mark and N. M. Su. Making infrastructure visible for nomadic work. *Pervasive and Mobile Computing*, 6(3):312–323, 2010.

53. D. Martin, B. V. Hanrahan, J. O'Neill, and N. Gupta. Being a turker. In *Proceedings of the 17th ACM conference on Computer supported cooperative work & social computing*, pages 224–235. ACM, 2014.

54. S. McDonald. 3d printing: A future collapse-compliant means of production. In *Proceedings of LIMITS*. ACM, 2016.

55. B. McKibben and S. D. S. B. McKibben. *Eaarth: Making a life on a tough new planet*. Vintage Books Canada, 2011.

56. D. Meadows, J. Randers, and D. Meadows. *Limits to growth: The 30-year update*. Chelsea Green Publishing, 2004.

57. J. Meurer, M. Stein, D. Randall, M. Rohde, and V. Wulf. Social dependency and mobile autonomy: supporting older adults' mobility with ridesharing ict. In *Proceedings of the 32nd annual ACM conference on Human factors in computing systems*, pages 1923–1932. ACM, 2014.

58. J. Meurer, M. Stein, and V. Wulf. Designing cooperation for sustainable mobility: Mobile methods in ridesharing contexts. In *COOP 2014-Proceedings of the 11th International Conference on the Design of Cooperative Systems, 27-30 May 2014, Nice (France)*, pages 345–359. Springer, 2014.

59. E. Morozov. *The net delusion: The dark side of Internet freedom*. PublicAffairs, 2012.

60. B. Nardi. Inequality and limits. *First Monday*, 20(8), 2015.

61. L. P. Nathan. Ecovillages, values, and interactive technology: balancing sustainability with daily life in 21st century america. In *CHI'08 Extended Abstracts on Human Factors in Computing Systems*, pages 3723–3728. ACM, 2008.

62. J. Norton, S. Nayebaziz, S. Burke, B. J. Pan, and B. Tomlinson. Plant guild composer: an interactive online system to support back yard food production. In *CHI'14 Extended Abstracts on Human Factors in Computing Systems*, pages 523–526. ACM, 2014.

63. W. Odom. Mate, we don't need a chip to tell us the soil's dry: opportunities for designing interactive systems to support urban food production. In *Proceedings of the 8th ACM Conference on Designing Interactive Systems*, pages 232–235. ACM, 2010.

64. H. Odum. *Environmental accounting: emergy and environmental decision making*. John Wiley & Sons, 1996.

65. D. Owen. *The conundrum*. Penguin, 2012.

66. D. Pargman, E. Ahlsén, and C. Engelbert. Designing for sustainability: Breakthrough or suboptimisation? In *4th International Conference ICT for Sustainability (ICT4S)*. Atlantis Press, 2016.

67. D. Pargman and B. Raghavan. Rethinking Sustainability in Computing: From Buzzword to Non-negotiable Limits. In *Proceedings of ACM NordiCHI*, 2014.

68. M. Pollan. *The omnivore's dilemma: A natural history of four meals*. Penguin, 2006.

69. C. Preist, D. Schien, and E. Blevis. Understanding and mitigating the effects of device and cloud service design decisions on the environmental footprint of digital infrastructure. In *Proceedings of the 2016 CHI Conference on Human Factors in Computing Systems*, pages 1324–1337. ACM, 2016.

70. B. Raghavan. Abstraction, Indirection, and Sevareid's Law: Towards Benign Computing. In *Proceedings of LIMITS*, 2015.

71. B. Raghavan and S. Hasan. Macroscopically Sustainable Networking: On Internet Quines. In *Proceedings of LIMITS*, 2016.

72. B. Raghavan and J. Ma. The energy and emergy of the internet. In *Proceedings of the 10th ACM Workshop on Hot Topics in Networks*, 2011.

73. B. Raghavan and J. Ma. Networking in the Long Emergency. In *Proceedings of the ACM SIGCOMM Workshop on Green Networking*, 2011.

74. B. Raghavan, B. Nardi, S. T. Lovell, J. Norton, B. Tomlinson, and D. J. Patterson. Computational Agroecology: Sustainable Food Ecosystem Design. In *Proceedings of ACM CHI alt.chi*, 2016.

75. B. Raghavan and D. Pargman. Refactoring society: systems complexity in an age of limits. In *Proceedings of LIMITS*. ACM, 2016.

76. N. Raval and P. Dourish. Standing out from the crowd: Emotional labor, body labor, and temporal labor in ridesharing. In *Proceedings of the 19th ACM Conference on Computer-Supported Cooperative Work & Social Computing*, pages 97–107. ACM, 2016.

77. W. E. Rees. Achieving sustainability: reform or transformation? *Journal of planning literature*, 9(4):343–361, 1995.

78. M. B. Rivera, C. Håkansson, Å. Svenfelt, and G. Finnveden. Including second order effects in environmental assessments of ict. *Environmental Modelling & Software*, 56:105–115, 2014.

79. J. Robinson. Squaring the circle? some thoughts on the idea of sustainable development. *Ecological economics*, 48(4):369–384, 2004.

80. J. Rockström, W. Steffen, K. Noone, Å. Persson, F. S. Chapin, E. F. Lambin, T. M. Lenton, M. Scheffer, C. Folke, H. J. Schellnhuber, et al. A safe operating space for humanity. *Nature*, 461(7263):472–475, 2009.

81. C. Rossitto, C. Bogdan, and K. Severinson-Eklundh. Understanding constellations of technologies in use in a collaborative nomadic setting. *Computer Supported Cooperative Work (CSCW)*, 23(2):137–161, 2014.

82. M. Silberman, L. Irani, and J. Ross. Ethics and tactics of professional crowdwork. *XRDS: Crossroads, The ACM Magazine for Students*, 17(2):39–43, 2010.

83. M. Silberman, L. Nathan, B. Knowles, R. Bendor, A. Clear, M. Håkansson, T. Dillahunt, and J. Mankoff. Next steps for sustainable hci. *interactions*, 21(5):66–69, 2014.

84. O. Sotamaa. On modder labour, commodification of play, and mod competitions. *First Monday*, 12(9), 2007.

85. C. Spinuzzi. Working alone together coworking as emergent collaborative activity. *Journal of Business and Technical Communication*, 26(4):399–441, 2012.

86. L. Starke. State of the world. innovations that nourish the planet. *Worldwatch Institute*, 2011.

87. W. Steffen, P. J. Crutzen, and J. R. McNeill. The anthropocene: are humans now overwhelming the great forces of nature. *AMBIO: A Journal of the Human Environment*, 36(8):614–621, 2007.

88. W. Steffen, K. Richardson, J. Rockström, S. E. Cornell, I. Fetzer, E. M. Bennett, R. Biggs, S. R. Carpenter, W. de Vries, C. A. de Wit, et al. Planetary boundaries: Guiding human development on a changing planet. *Science*, 347(6223):1259855, 2015.

89. N. M. Su and G. Mark. Designing for nomadic work. In *Proceedings of the 7th ACM conference on Designing interactive systems*, pages 305–314. ACM, 2008.

90. E. Suhonen, A. Lampinen, C. Cheshire, and J. Antin. Everyday favors: a case study of a local online gift exchange system. In *Proceedings of the 16th ACM international conference on Supporting group work*, pages 11–20. ACM, 2010.

91. J. Tainter. *The collapse of complex societies*. Cambridge University Press, 1990.

92. J. Tainter. Resources and cultural complexity: Implications for sustainability. *Critical reviews in plant sciences*, 30(1-2):24–34, 2011.

93. J. Tanenbaum, M. Pufal, and K. Tanenbaum. The limits of our imagination: design fiction as a strategy for engaging with dystopian futures. In *Proceedings of LIMITS*. ACM, 2016.

94. A. Taylor. *The people's platform: Taking back power and culture in the digital age*. Macmillan, 2014.

95. D. Trottier and D. Lyon. Key features of social media surveillance. *Internet and Surveillance: the challenges of Web 2.0 and social media*, 16:89–105, 2012.

96. W. Van Heddeghem, S. Lambert, B. Lannoo, D. Colle, M. Pickavet, and P. Demeester. Trends in worldwide ict electricity consumption from 2007 to 2012. *Computer Communications*, 50:64–76, 2014.

97. J. Vandermeer. *The Ecology of Agroecosystems*. Jones & Bartlett, 2011.

98. M. von Pentz. Precision Farming's Global Future. `http://www.dtnpf.com/go/agsummit/agsummit2016/presentations/mon_gen_precision_farming_vonpentz.pdf`.

99. M. Wackernagel and W. Rees. *Our ecological footprint: reducing human impact on the earth*. Number 9. New Society Publishers, 1998.

100. M. Wackernagel, N. B. Schulz, D. Deumling, A. C. Linares, M. Jenkins, V. Kapos, C. Monfreda, J. Loh, N. Myers, R. Norgaard, et al. Tracking the ecological overshoot of the human economy. *Proceedings of the national Academy of Sciences*, 99(14):9266–9271, 2002.

101. E. O. Wilson. *The future of life*. Vintage, 2002.

102. J. P. Woelfer and D. G. Hendry. Designing ubiquitous information systems for a community of homeless young people: precaution and a way forward. *Personal and Ubiquitous Computing*, 15(6):565–573, 2011.

103. J. P. Woelfer, A. Iverson, D. G. Hendry, B. Friedman, and B. T. Gill. Improving the safety of homeless young people with mobile phones: values, form and function. In *Proceedings of the SIGCHI Conference on Human Factors in Computing Systems*, pages 1707–1716. ACM, 2011.

104. S. P. Wyche, A. Forte, and S. Yardi Schoenebeck. Hustling online: understanding consolidated facebook use in an informal settlement in Nairobi. In *Proceedings of the SIGCHI Conference on Human Factors in Computing Systems*, pages 2823–2832. ACM, 2013.

105. S. P. Wyche and L. L. Murphy. Powering the cellphone revolution: findings from mobile phone charging trials in off-grid Kenya. In *Proceedings of the SIGCHI Conference on Human Factors in Computing Systems*, pages 1959–1968. ACM, 2013.

# Crowdfunding Platforms and the Design of Paying Publics

**Ann Light**
School of Engineering and Informatics
University of Sussex, Falmer, UK
Ann.Light@sussex.ac.uk

**Jo Briggs**
School of Design
University of Northumbria at Newcastle
Jo.Briggs@northumbria.ac.uk

## ABSTRACT
Crowdfunding enables groups to self-fund the changes they want to make in the world. In other words, digital financial platforms are proving capable of supporting new relations between groups of people as well as offering new ways to organize money. Taking an HCI lens, we look at how some crowdfunding platform owners are approaching social innovation, not only at the level of supporting individual community initiatives, but at the broader level of using their platform to change societal behavior. Through four case studies, we show how crowdfunding has been chosen as a tool to redesign society by promoting environmental or social sustainability. We argue that the groups constituted through these interactions are not merely 'crowds', but deliberate constellations built round a thing of interest (or 'paying publics'). Our interviews with managers and owners explore how interactions with and around platforms work to achieve these ends and we conclude with design considerations.

### Keywords
Digital platforms; sustainability; platform design; social innovation; paying publics; business models; infrastructure.

### ACM Classification Keywords
H.5.m. Information interfaces and presentation (e.g., HCI): Miscellaneous.

## INTRODUCTION
New peer-to-peer (P2P) platforms offer new arrangements for financing, using new digital aggregation and network tools. The range stretches from quasi-banks (e.g Zopa.com), to campaign fundraising for enterprises or causes (e.g. Kickstarter.com) to charitable giving (e.g. JustGiving.com). Inevitably, connecting up people and money in new ways leads to changes of practice. However, little attention has been paid to crowdfunding innovators hoping to change, not just individual aspects of a community or business fundraising campaign, but how the world works. Noting that money sits at the heart of much of society and its interactions, we use this paper to present the ambitions of four UK crowdfunding platforms with social change goals. (For reasons of space and focus, we are neither attempting to validate their achievements here, nor take the views of campaign organizers and funders into account.) We wish to bring before CHI a look at the potential crowdfunding offers to change societal relations at a fundamental level and make social as well as financial innovation.


*CHI 2017*, May 06-11, 2017, Denver, CO, USA
ACM 978-1-4503-4655-9/17/05.
http://dx.doi.org/10.1145/3025453.3025979.



Our contribution is to reveal how platform owners are experimenting to restructure people's socio-economic relations through payments and to ask in which ways platforms might be seen to configure publics. In doing this, we show the link these producers are making between financial models and the nature of future society. And we challenge the use of the term 'crowd' to capture the subtlety of the relationships that platform design can support, arguing instead for a class of DIY 'paying publics'.

To achieve this, we share excerpts from interviews with platform owners and their teams in which they articulate their ambitions over several years, and how they hope to achieve them. We present four case studies – two with an environmental sustainability angle and two focusing on social sustainability. We are not asking readers to judge the success of the platforms, one of which has already closed to new business, but to consider with us what the implications of bringing people together around a collective issue may be and how this might be regarded as both a new path to funding and a significant evolution in societal relations. We are using examples from the UK, which is world-leading in its variety of crowdfunding initiatives [40].

We begin with an overview of where crowdfunding sits as a money management system. We draw on social science and recent HCI work on the formation of crowds and publics (c.f. [14,29]) to establish a position on the constellations of people and groups within which crowdfunding platforms operate. We then present four crowdfunding platforms, picked because of their owners' intentions to make social change. We close with analysis of the connection between these societal ambitions and design choices, exploring the idea of paying publics as a series of design considerations.

## BACKGROUND
Crowdfunding brings distinct but interdependent markets together to co-create value in new ways [43]. Especially for social innovation undertakings, it offers a welcome new approach at a time of shrinking state support.

The innovation hinges on the potential of digital platforms. Gawer [18] defines a digital platform as 'a building block, providing an essential function to a technological system – which acts as a foundation upon which other firms can develop complementary products, technologies or services' (p2). In other words, a platform is infrastructure, something to be built on, and its design will influence, but not determine, what can be built on it [6]. Working alongside the design features of the platform are the social, economic and legal aspects of financial systems that evolve over time and also constrain what platforms can enable.

Is the co-shaping of social and financial structures new? Society has long had mechanisms for both redistributing wealth and payment for services and other societal goods. These vary from intensely local, (neighborhood lending circles and subscription activities for clubs) to global, (the banking system), including the establishment of local authorities to manage resource distribution. Each culture has shaped and been shaped by how transaction is managed (e.g. [5,36]). In the UK, where this study took place, banks, and mutual initiatives, such as credit unions and building societies, provide management for finances. Taxation by the state and municipality pays for collective services and redistributes some wealth. These tools of collaborative living evolved over centuries, responding to political conditions. Crowdfunding is one of a long line of devices for managing the movement and exchange of value, now part of the "collaborative economy" (e.g. timebanking [3,7,8], sharing services [31,32]), in which networks change potential. Particularly when we look at crowdfunding for social innovation, we see a new socio-economic mechanism with a long history of collective funding activity behind it.

So, what is new? The Web brings connections between 'the many and the many' [42:111], allowing scaling of systems globally through distributed participants. Digital micro-payments on an industrial scale are possible, meaning new interactions can be monetized and individual small returns can be amassed. Platforms are low cost to run, needing comparatively little support. They can act as brokers or trading partners using algorithms that handle matchmaking, data aggregation and other decisions. They evolve fast in response to new technical opportunities, usage patterns and legal and regulatory issues.

At the same time, driving innovation in the arts, state and voluntary sectors in Britain, and elsewhere, is the loss of much public funding and the prospect of more cuts. A neoliberal agenda is promoting market mechanisms at the expense of interventionist and more collectivist approaches and new network paradigms may feed into this trend [21]. Though individual countries have different stories based on their economic orientations, there is an overall shift toward self-help at community level and away from government support. Despite old policies of state provision, there is, more recently, growing inequality in income and wealth accompanying a shrinking tax base as the population ages. UK municipalities are struggling to be the providers they became in the 20th century, taking instead enabling roles like place-shaping [34].

Crowdfunding has drawn considerable recent research [e.g 1,2,12,13,19,23,37,38,39,41,50,54,55] along with design for crowds [49]. Of relevance to this paper is the growing field of civic crowdfunding [13,50] where crowdfunding acts as service design for mobilizing social innovation, generating value through 'community or quasi-public assets' ([13: 342]). Early on, Murray et al [42] observed potential for collective funding that was still nascent in 2009: 'A group with a shared interest may want to act collectively as consumers, or workers, or investors in a project. ... But in that they are acting collectively, they are part of the social economy in a way that is distinct both from the private economy, and from charities. ...For all those investing, it is a particular form of collective financing and ownership' (p113). More recently, some literature sets up a contrast between philanthropic motivations and those focused on capital-raising. Agrawal et al [1] describe funder motivation as quite binary: giving for the common good or for a good return. However, others (e.g. [50]) detail a more symbiotic relationship, with a measure of self-interest apparent among those who donate to local social projects. Investing money as crowdfunding can reinforce commitment to an activity, being qualitatively different from voting to give go-ahead [41] and more like participatory budgeting [44]. And success with platforms draws repeat borrowers away from banks and towards P2P lending [47].

### Types of Crowdfunding

The UK is a major center for crowdfunding expertise and activities [40], supported by light-touch regulation and government investment. Part of the reason for the UK's leadership is that, till May 2016 and implementation of the JOBS Act (with a subsection on crowdfunding) [24], *equity* crowdfunding was not legal in the US, so major innovation as well as less commercial projects had to take a *rewards* route, on platforms such as Kickstarter [27].

UK platforms come in many shapes that we can expect to see propagate. Research [2] and practice (e.g. database for UK founders [11]) has adopted a four-part classification:

- *Donation-based:* philanthropically and socio-politically motivated and no tangible goods are exchanged.
- *Rewards-based*: fundraisers solicit money within a time-limit in return for a tangible reward: All Or Nothing: fundraisers must reach a pre-agreed funding goal to claim pledged money; Keep It All: they take any money raised.
- *Equity*: funders enter formal agreements with business start-ups or other enterprises in exchange for equity and with a view to realizing a profit over time.
- *Loan-based* or *P2P*: platforms broker deals; funders lend to fundraisers for a pre-agreed period and interest rate.

Design research has largely followed US commercial and legal contingencies, so much existing work focuses on reward-based campaigns, their motivations [e.g. 19] and how to make them effective [e.g.12,23,37,38,54,55]. The Kickstarter platform has garnered most HCI research (e.g. [2,19,38]), not least because its campaigns remain public even after closure, providing a ready corpus of data, at scale. More challenging is acquiring access to P2P and equity platforms' data, such as these here, as these platforms often keep campaigns private. But these data point the way to concerns that are now going worldwide.

Of particular relevance here is research showing the impact of campaign organizers' use of platform messaging tools at campaign milestones in facilitating a completed campaign [54], the effect of language in soliciting additional pledges [37], ideas of community among fundraisers and supporters, and how creatives support each other through the social functions of online tools [23]. These suggest the importance of the interface, but also of the design of the process that platforms offer campaign organizers to engage, update, keep on board and build up their sponsors.

## CROWDS VS PUBLICS

In addressing crowdfunding, we cannot miss the word *crowd*. We suggest that, in looking at activity with and round platforms, we are not served well by this term. Instead, we argue that participants in a crowdfunding ecosystem for social innovation meet the definition of *public* (cf [14,29]), with common interests growing through an investment of time and/or resources in related outcomes.

### Constellations

Platforms link many types of people, each with a different stake in what is being brokered and/or paid for. Designers provide the platform that allows transactions between groups and/or individuals. Campaign organizers use these sites to collect money/promote their ambitions. Sponsors and investors choose to put their money in, for a reward, a dividend or other return, such as feeling good. The platforms mediate interactions between these primary users (fundraisers and sponsors) and third parties, including platform owners, who may levy a fee for each transaction, online payment companies, which take a small cut of transactions (a 2-5% fee) and crowdfunding support companies (e.g. Kicktraq.com). Last, there are also beneficiaries, who have no direct engagement with the platform, such as the people that community or arts-based campaigns go on to involve and influence. These groups of people can all be understood as collaborating in the production of the socio-technical system of crowdfunding.

This means that platforms innovators sit at the center of a complex system of interrelations when they consider what the purpose, value and values of a crowdfunding system should be. We have chosen examples of crowdfunding with a social innovation angle, i.e. they are explicit about changing the world in some way. This enables us to see most clearly the kinds of change crowdfunding platforms could usher in and discuss how new publics might be created as part of this. To date, most research has focused on campaigns [e.g. 38] and organizer/sponsor relations [e.g 19], whereas we look at the underlying platform and the constellations that can be generated through design choices.

### Crowd

*Crowd* in online activity dates to *Wired* magazine in 2006 and refers to a 'network of people' responding to an open call, either in 'the form of peer-production (when the job is performed collaboratively)' or, 'often undertaken by sole individuals' [22 n.p.]. These individuals form as a crowd through engaging with the platform, rather than having the collective and co-located status that has historically been intrinsic to crowds (though see Gupta for how 'turkers' find mutual support in crowdsourcing [20] and Hui on strategic support for self-help amongst crowdfunders [23]).

Historically, crowds are a problem. Sociologist Borch [4] says 'Due to the central role that the problem of crowds occupied in the early sociological thinking, it is virtually impossible to map out every account and discussion' (p8). Till recently, crowds drew theoretical attention for being unruly and challenging to social order. Park epitomizes this in distinguishing between crowds as emotional on the one hand, and publics as reasonable on the other [45].

In crowdfunding, multiple individuals co-fund ventures, just as, in crowdsourcing, many individuals co-source answers, solve problems and offer the wisdom of the crowd [22,39]. They may know each other or not, act in concert or not, but that is not their dominant characteristic – they are *the help*. In fact, we can be quite precise about who the individual members of a crowd contributing through a particular platform to a specific campaign might be, from friends and family to international networks of funders. But the term un-differentiates them and lumps them together.

### Publics

We now turn to Dewey's work on how publics form round issues [14], drawing a parallel in how people gather with a common focus in the crowdfunding ecosystems we have been studying. In gathering, they form interest groups, more or less explicitly, contributing towards something being funded. We are not the first to use the idea of publics in HCI and design (e.g.[15,29,33,52]). In talking about publics, we refer here to the way that groups round platforms may be constituted by the actions of the platform. Where people related through platforms are not aware of each other at outset, the platforms (and campaign organisers) may work to build this awareness. Clearly, it is unnecessary to generate this level of collective sensibility for all crowdfunding, but we are looking at instances when such constellations can be usefully mobilized. We will look more closely at characteristics of building this awareness.

We note Le Dantec and DiSalvo's comments [29] on 'the contention, unevenness, and permeability of a public', saying that a public 'is usefully understood as a plurality of voices, opinions, and positions' and 'no single public, but rather a multitude of publics' [p243]. They embrace Dewey's public, 'not as a single generic a priori mass of people, but as a particular configuration of individuals bound by common cause in confronting a shared issue' [29: 243]. Further, Marres [35] argues that publics arise through (and can be seen in) how objects are constituted. So we might see crowdfunding platforms as materializing types of publics and being materialized by them.

Karasti [26] notes that 'Dewey's "publics" is a state-level concept', whereas she uses it for community-level activity in participatory design [p147]. Similarly, we can regard collecting, loaning and giving money for a particular social end as the construction of community-level publics round an issue. 'The public' is identified and constituted by an issue *outside its immediate control* [14]. In crowdfunding, possible engagement is determined by design factors in the hands of the platform-makers and in regulatory frameworks such as UK financial legislation, so participants have little control over the form of their engagement. Yet, these local publics can exert influence and play a part in enacting or resisting the goals of those setting the agenda. Murray et al [42] note the impact of/on an early group of funders: 'In February 2008, 26,000 people, responding to a web call, each put £35 into a newly formed co-op and bought a football club, Ebbsfleet United. Two months later many of the members – pioneers of a new form of financial collaboration – travelled to Wembley and saw their side win the FA trophy' [p112]. Similarly, the first community pub bought under the 2011 Localism Act in the UK was part-funded by 371 community shares, many in the hands of local people who drink there now with greater pride [31].

## METHODS OF DATA COLLECTION

We interviewed the people behind several crowdfunding platforms with an interest in social innovation, to learn of their motivations and their ensuing design choices. By learning about their intentions and looking at how these are embodied in the platform, we can begin to discuss relations between design and configuring socio-economic activity. All our samples are from the UK. This does not affect the generalizability of our headline findings, since the overall relations we describe hold for other circumstances, but it may affect the detail, such as the regulatory framework and what counts as social innovation in a region.

We chose the sample presented here from a wider pool of interviews, some of which span several years, selecting those where the interviewees exhibited a clear intention to change social practice as well as raise money through crowdfunding. Light has, since 2004 (e.g. [30]), been following the progress of several activists using digital technology to solve social problems, some of whom run platforms. Another part of the motivation for the interviews was to gather qualitative data for UK research council funded projects on the sharing economy and crowdfunding led by the two authors. As mentioned, we have limited the sample to the UK, where we can talk within a common regulatory framework and one that allows a wide diversity of crowdfunding to flourish. We selected the cases, for variety and relevance, from our samples (~15 long-term studies by Light and ~15 more cross-sectional interviews by Briggs), choosing to feature four examples with related themes to make the points in this paper. Given there is no stable sample in such an entrepreneurial environment, we accept the inevitability of non-systematic sampling – this is not a complete overview, but examples chosen to show the new relations we observed. We have picked cases of innovators with social change ambitions that pair well to draw contrasts and find common ground: two attempting to change societal environmental behavior through providing a new financial mechanism and two that speak to a more general socio-economic trend in reconfiguring local relations (see table 1). We are not claiming all platforms show these characteristics, merely that attempting to shape social behavior is a discernible phenomenon. Within interviews, we paid rigorous attention to claims interviewees made for their platforms and design choices; *how* they spoke about goals and what support was given to enacting these goals as they pertained to social organization. We recorded all interviews, transcribed and analyzed them (see [48] on discourse analysis for process).

Our first interviews specific to digital platforms were conducted in 2009. Those we use come from between 2012 and 2016. Access to interviewees came through personal relationships and intermediary introductions over many years of participating in business, social and activist networks, and government forums. The benefit of coming in at the start with several initiatives, before launch, is that we have been able to trace progress and draw on it. In other words, long exposure to the sector informs our conclusions. We note the details in each sub-section.

## FOUR EXAMPLES OF DIGITAL CROWDFUNDING

The descriptions here are drawn from the extended semi-structured interviews with those in charge of (or acting as spokesperson for) a platform, interwoven with observations from watching their progress. In all cases, we asked our interviewees about why and how the platform got started, about opportunities and challenges in developing, launching and running it and about their plans for the future. Each interview covered aspects of motivation, beliefs, ethical orientation and ambitions for the platform, but we only draw on a narrow cross-section here to discuss social change elements and how these fit with choices and outcomes. As noted, we do not include material from users, either as fundraisers or funders, limiting this discussion to the ambitions of those behind the platforms for purposes of brevity and focus. Our goal is to map intention to design and offer initial thoughts on aspirations for crowdfunding. We have presented the studies in two pairs to reflect similarities between goals (see table 1): first, two platforms that engage with worldwide environmental sustainability in their choice of services, and then another two that seek to make more generic socio-economic change toward regional social and economic sustainability.

| Platform | Trillion Fund | Patchwork Present | Newcastle CC (Funding Circle) | Crowdfunder |
|---|---|---|---|---|
| | *Driving new societal environmental behavior* | | *Changing local socio-economic configurations* | |
| **Description** | Ltd. company - renewable energy investments | Ltd. company - coordinated gift-giving | Local authority working with Ltd. company | Ltd. company - mobilizing grassroots |
| **Motivation beyond profit** | Environmental sustainability by moving investment into green fuels | Minimizing waste through coordinated gift-buying | Fast finance for local firms by networking local investors | Support for groups, start-ups and causes to raise project funds |
| **Products** | P2P lending<br>Community shares<br>Bonds, Equity, etc | Customized donation-reward system for aggregating presents | P2P lending | Reward<br>Donation<br>Community shares |

**Table 1: Summary of characteristics of our four case studies**

## CASE STUDY: THE TRILLION FUND

*Trillion Fund* claimed to be '*the UK's largest social crowdfunding platform*' in April 2015 (video [53]), with a turnover in millions and 7000 members. The material here is taken partly from interviews with Julia Groves, the former CEO in 2012 before the service was launched, further conversations through the life of the platform (not cited directly), and from the platform website, as noted.

The platform is principally a P2P loan, rather than an equity model, enabling the spreading of investments and a range of 'raises' to support. However, there are some opportunities that involve issuing community shares: '*By joining, you are becoming part of a community that has a broader objective than just maximizing returns for investors*' [52]. The team that set up *Trillion Fund* ('*crowdfunding for people, planet and profit*' [52] was motivated by the need for large loans and advances to small energy companies wanting to innovate with renewables. They were already successful entrepreneurs and the target (in the name) was to help generate the '*$1 trillion of annual global investment required to reach the scale of clean energy generation needed to prevent further global warming*' [52]. Motivation was commercial and environmental, a business to make money for the platform owners while diverting existing funding to greater global ecological wellbeing. This mix of missions ran through all aspects, informed by the belief that investors tend to look at returns first: '*I don't care immediately why people are investing in renewables. I want them to invest in renewables and then make money. Profit is the motivation that breaks down barriers and makes people aware. We have to preach to the unconverted because that is the majority.*' (Groves, interview). The owners felt it important that the model did not rely on the ethical commitments of its investors; instead, investors agree a rate of return on their loan, made directly to any company trying to raise funds, but brokered by the site. The platform acts as a two-sided market, allowing investors to search for and manage opportunities that range from supporting major energy infrastructure projects to social enterprises, and providing companies seeking funds with investment. The team promotes their featured energy companies, both on the site and beyond, and campaign for more funding and subsidy for the renewables sector. This is to be witnessed in the blog accompanying the platform, and has included a high-profile celebrity party to encourage awareness and investment. This promotion can be seen as part of making the site commercially successful, but also as a pragmatic strategy to promote renewable investment.

In a shock move, the platform closed to all future business in September 2015. The service was like many P2P lending platforms, but, in specializing in the renewable sector that was made viable by government subsidy, it became vulnerable to changes in national funding policy. '*Most renewable energy projects in the UK are dependent on subsidies to provide returns to lenders. The level of subsidy is dropping rapidly and it is not clear what projects will be seeking funding going forward. As a business, Trillion incurs significant costs in marketing new loans and the Board has decided it is not prudent to continue to offer loans without visibility of future funding and project opportunities*' [53]. Existing clients, based on more than 120 capital 'raises' in the area of renewable energy, continue to borrow/lend through the site but there are no new campaigns. Instead, the company is developing its technology and crowdfunding administration services and Groves has left to pursue energy initiatives elsewhere.

## CASE STUDY: PATCHWORK PRESENT

The second study in this pair involves a gift-aggregation platform. An interview with platform designer and business owner Olivia Knight was conducted shortly after it went live in 2014. Knight left a job at an environmental charity to set up the platform, which she runs from a shop in South London, stressing both local presence and green ambitions: '*The principles are about being resourceful, using our money wisely to invest in things that are wanted and needed and not buying each other a ton of crap that we don't need, that ends up in landfill*'.

*Patchwork Present* [46], with the styling of a rewards-based service but the function of a donation system, supports groups of people buying a single collective present. An item, like a bicycle, or series of elements, like those for a honeymoon, are divided into manageably-priced bundles, shown in a patchwork image on the website, under the slogan: '*Get friends and family together to fund one gift that's really wanted – piece by piece*'. Then each donor pays for a part, directly into the recipient's *Paypal* account, and the site levies a fraction of the cost. Knight raised the money to fund the project through patchwork principles, involving 25 individual investors who all have 1% of the business. The company raised £250,000 in 20 days.

She says that the idea came to her as she planned her own honeymoon, worrying about the taboo of asking for money: '*gift giving should have some element of ritual to it and it shouldn't just be a financial transaction.*' She created a website with imagery suggesting the things she wanted to buy and a rough price, directing friends and family to this instead of a wedding list. '*So they could choose a physical thing like two beers in a bar or a night in a hotel.*'

The platform allows for customization, in choosing images, prices, etc. and in then allowing you to send a personal "thank you" to the individuals who bought each piece. '*So you can send pictures of you drinking your beer on the beach to all the people who bought the beer.*' The effort people put in has impressed Knight. There are ready-made patchworks for use, but people go further, for instance the couple getting married, who not only made a patchwork themselves, but staged what they wanted to do, took pictures of themselves doing it and uploaded the images.

The site takes 3% of each contribution. This contrasts with other platforms, such as *Kickstarter* [27] and *Just Giving* [25], which charge more, or *Taskrabbit* [51] with a 20% service levy. '*In terms of competition, our commission is quite low. That will be one of the things we will have to look at - the sharing economy only really works when you reach scale. So there won't really be any money to be made until we reach real scale.*' This figure was chosen from a user's point of view '*and just intuitively what feels right. What's quite nice is, on the average wedding gift, it works out at the same price as a piece of wrapping paper.*' Knight points out an advertising-supported model would not work, nor would affiliation to retailers, but even in 2017, it remains early days in terms of financial viability.

## CASE STUDY: NEWCASTLE CITY COUNCIL

This loan platform and portfolio shows the working, for mutual benefit, of branded 'white label' platform products (i.e. developed to be branded by others) in a partnership between a council and a technology provider. The account is based on interviews in 2014 with Cllr Michael Johnson, an elected member who instigated the initiative at this northern English council, and with Sophie Chappelow, senior marketing and partnership manager at P2P platform *Funding Circle* [17]. The interviews were conducted a few weeks after the launch of the new council-backed lending scheme. Briggs also then ran a series of crowdfunding workshops and roundtable events in northeast England.

Newcastle City Council is supporting the supply side of business finance, because '*traditional methods of raising capital were no longer working for companies*' (Johnson, interview). The council believes lending decisions should be based on flexible criteria, with a quicker turnaround than that of traditional banks, which can take months to respond to a loan request (by which time opportunities have often passed). The elected member, who works as a professional business consultant, was aware of people locally '*who didn't have experience of investing in businesses and who didn't have sufficient capital to become Angel investors, but who had enough money to be managing their personal investments*'. Johnson judges that, being risk averse, these individuals are unlikely to invest in businesses directly, but are '*probably socially motivated*'. These characteristics, and Johnson's own interest in P2P lending prompted him to find a way to '*provide them with an investment product that not only presents itself as a lower risk option [but] also has a social benefit of restricted investment criteria – so it has to give back locally, perhaps introduce a premium to firms that invest in apprenticeships or that pay a living wage.*'

A policy was introduced enabling the city council to co-design a product with *Funding Circle.* Previously, '*[the council] would have taken on a fund to do that and ... it might be the cost of hiring three or four people to manage this pot of money*' (Chappelow, interview). The partnership is intended to enable council and lenders to benefit through the low cost of each financial transaction and, overall, a fast, easy and inexpensive business loan supply service.

Funders make loans from 6 months to 5 years. They select companies to invest in based on the credit model given a proposal (banded A+ to C- depending on risk) and offer loans in return for annual interest of between 6% and 15%. Investors can assess the viability of a loan request by conducting online searches and the platform facilitates queries via direct communication with those seeking funds. Alternatively, the platform 'auto-bid' function auto-matches an investor to suitable investments, based on their appetite for risk and desired interest-rate reward. Like *Trillion Fund*, all money is held by clients rather than with the platform and investors make their own decisions. This puts financial risk with investors (including the council which is a lender), rather than with the platform makers.

*Funding Circle* promotes itself as a technology company (not as crowdfunding or finance), designing and managing all the algorithms that support bidding (Chappelow). It views its partnership with a local authority as building '*an element of trust. We know we're trustworthy, but conveying that? People will go: "Oh, well I probably wouldn't have trusted them before but if the council is involved...". Trust is a big element of it.*' (Chappelow). In this way, the partnership operates as advocacy not only for the platform but also for the P2P sector.

There are, however, tensions specific to the ambitions of the council in using networked finance. The council wants to keep invested money local, whereas the platform auto-bid algorithms factor in 'diversification' (of sector and geography) to mitigate, or, at least, spread, investment risk for funders. And, anecdotally, take-up of council loans on *Funding Circle* has been slow; several months into the scheme only one had been authorized and problems persist, with low take-up across northeast England [56]. Marketing at launch was hampered by timing, running into constraints on public communication in the lead up to elections. Other issues concern eligibility, with applicant companies not having a requisite Newcastle postcode; and companies finding the credit requirements of the platform as onerous as conventional bank loans, requiring two years' accounts.

### CASE STUDY: CROWDFUNDER

The UK's nearest equivalent to *Kickstarter* is *Crowdfunder*, Britain's major rewards-based platform, which supports community enterprise, charitable donation and product generation. Material comes from conversation and collaboration with the platform [10] in 2014-5, and a 2016 interview with *Crowdfunder*'s fund manager Jason Nuttall.

*Crowdfunder* focuses on social issues, partly organized by geographical location. This is counter-intuitive given the scaling potential of automated platforms, but works to grow audience for local activity. 'Crowdfunder Local' on the platform website features area-specific campaigns to show off campaigns, e.g. '*Crowdfund Somerset showcases the best crowdfunding projects in the county. If you have a community group, business, charity or other great idea then add your project today.*' [10d]. The platform is very active in scouting for and helping to encourage both new projects and new partnerships. '*The team has taken an entrepreneurial approach to developing new partnerships*' (website). For instance, *Crowdfunder* works with several UK universities running micro-crowdfunding sites [10b]. It fosters small, located enterprises such as *Leeds Bread Cooperative* (LBC), which used the platform to raise money to buy ovens to set up a business. Their campaign raised £8,690 in 42 days from 114 backers. In the process, the bakery built an online local public that converted to a customer base beyond the campaign [10c]. LBC then received grant funding from a cooperative legacy fund and other business loans in what Chappelow (at *Funding Circle*) refers to as the '*multiplier effect... making that money work a lot harder*' (interview) and aggregating sources of finance beyond that sourced via the platform. Funding manager Nuttall visits traditional funders to explain how match-funding funds communities are managing to collect can improve impact for their budgets and these projects' reach.

Nuttall is personally interested in developing the platform to gather and redistribute resources beyond money, such as gifts-in-kind and time. These forms of exchange are useful to social enterprises, building up support around them. He points to the novel structures that have been enabled by the platform's support, such as a community-owned distillery (which asked for £1.5M, received £2.5M and is building a visitor center with the extra money: growing tourism and further including its funders). Nuttall points to the value gained in organizing a social initiative with a campaign: it builds long-term engagement, extending first commitments with news, encouragement and more opportunity. The campaign structure provides the frame for a relationship between those running a campaign and those sponsoring it. '*It can show what that project goes on to do. And, if there's a delay, people are more forgiving as they understand the dynamics and are being kept up to date. It makes for better publicity for any hazards.*' (Nuttall, interview). He suggests that people are not merely sponsoring, shopping or even building a brand; they are in the process of becoming the network through which the aims of enterprises are realized.

*Crowdfunder's* P2P relations mean that projects need to deliver, producing tangible assets that can be witnessed by these networks. Much support goes into helping organizers choose a suitable project, plan and schedule: '*to do X by Y with Z*' (Nuttall). Would-be founders struggle with this and lack the confidence to tackle the necessary practical skills, especially making a video. *Crowdfunder* provides coaching to people starting out on the platform.

The platform's lineage already tells a story of constellation, emerging at scale through mergers and acquisitions of small, novel and innovative (if less sustainable) platforms, and partnerships with government departments and an equity platform. A platform was launched in 2011 as *Peoplefund.it*, which, in 2012, merged with *WeDidThis* – a platform specializing in arts funding through collective sponsorship. The platform then merged with *Crowdfunder*, a small rewards-based site that had been set up by the equity platform *Crowdcube*. Together, the merger launched as *Crowdfunder.co.uk* with a greatly expanded network [10b]. Plymouth University came on board as co-owner to promote education in enterprise. In 2014, *Crowdfunder* ran a campaign on its partner platform *Crowdcube* raising £650k in one morning, and, in late 2015, ran another campaign raising more than £1.3M, for nearly 9% of *Crowdfunder's* equity [9]. This period also marked the beginning of government and charity-backed match-funding community crowdfunding schemes to promote local impact of social change projects [10d]. In June 2015, *Crowdfunder* began offering community share partnerships. At time of writing, more than £32.5M (~US$40M) had been raised for projects across the UK [10].

### DISCUSSION

We have presented some key platform types – equity, donation, rewards, loan – and begun to link structure to socio-economic goals. There are features common to all our examples, such as using algorithms to manage transactions and networks to connect up markets. And there are marked differences, such as how campaigns are built and how they anticipate long-term viability. But we do not want to limit our discussion to such features here. Instead, we want to address questions about how relations are managed and, thus, how *paying publics* are brought into being.

### Ambitions for Social Outcomes

Our interviews with platforms makers show that socio-economic intentions informed the design of each, with a goal of assembling people to a specified societal end.

'*Trillion Fund* is changing money' says the platform's site. Accompanying the owners' aims to capitalize for profit on new forms of financial mechanism are social, political and environmental ambitions. Their aim was to mobilize the huge sums needed to secure enough renewable energy to impact climate change. Within their strategy, they knew a competitive rate of return on investment was non-negotiable: it would be impossible to woo investors on the strength of a green portfolio alone. Nonetheless, their marketing and careful vetting of portfolio speak to their concern to use the platform to enable green initiatives to compete with existing forms of energy generation and replace them. Talking to the CEO and other team members reveals a passion to change not financial relations, but directions of funding and a pragmatic goal of using a financial tool to do so. They hoped that people would come for the profits and stay for the politics, intending to form a public who is increasingly interested in renewable energy because they have invested in it. Ironically, their most effective move to generate collective interest may have been to suspend new schemes (after change in subsidy policy), arousing group concern from platform investors about the safety of their investments. But here too they attempted to turn investor and media attention into fuel for a campaign on subsidies and change from traditional energy sources, using the interest to make their point and unite their investors. The headline on site remains 'Why pull money out of coal, oil and gas?' Existing investment shows that ethical products with good returns can appeal, belying Agrawal et al's [1] finding that giving for the common good and for a good return are mutually incompatible. What may be true at individual level looks different when viewed as a commercial strategy intended to make social and political change. However, without government renewables subsidy the platform itself becomes less viable.

Patchwork Present also aims to have positive environmental impact, changing social practice and enabling personalized services that are more than a sum of its parts. Here, the mechanism for bringing this about is offering a new, easy way for gift-giving, using the power of the network to communicate, connect, broker and to manage and aggregate money. Knight can point to the elaborate creative work done by users as an endorsement of the effort she put into devising a clear and configurable set of interactive visual elements. The effect of success would be to cut down on poor resource use (unwanted gifts), whether or not her customers use the service because of green principles.

But it is when we turn to *Crowdfunder* and the 'white-label' council platform that we see intended societal remodeling most nakedly. Agnostic about what kind of campaign they support, as long as they are legitimate, both the reward- and loan-based platform stress their potential to move money into enterprises that (increasingly) struggle to find flexible support elsewhere, creating a new wave of entrepreneurship funded collectively by individuals. Both want to work at a local level and *Crowdfunder* is able to link fundraising with community generation, witnessed here in the new market for artisan bread in Leeds born of the campaign to launch it.

The other platforms are not as successful as the last. They may be assembling people around them, but not always at a scale that offsets the cost of doing so. We are not discussing tactics for running a viable service, but looking at the world-changing ambitions of the platforms and how these aspects are enacted. Although still seen as a novelty by many users, the platforms regard their mission as changing the whole way society distributes and/or makes money (and/or what it lends on). We note that everything from government policy to onerous authentication requirements to lack of advertising opportunity can hamper development. These aspects have discernible impact on viability, i.e. parts of the constellation create challenges, but it does not negate the potential to meet these challenges and make big change. All four sites have engaged people in crowdfunding in ways that the owners have chosen, so as to make societal change.

### Publics: Mutual Awareness and Trust Issues

Publics form round issues [14] and objects representing issues [35], and mutual awareness grows through issue formation. Only one of our studies presupposes existing relations. *Patchwork Present* provides the means to join people in a collaborative act where mutual awareness is already high. It brings together people who wish to do something for someone else and many will be known to each other as the recipient's friends. Often friends do support campaigns and the outcome is an aggregation of resources that collectively supports individuals. *Patchwork Present*, in making a *present*, does not need to bring people into contact, but it does involve them in an activity that would not happen without a sense of collective connection and loyalty to the gift's recipient. Most platforms do not assume loyalty from anyone, even if individual campaigns may depend on family and friends.

Nonetheless, other people's behavior is an influential factor across platforms in attracting funders and giving them confidence to invest. People need to see others taking a risk and making it work. Conversations in 'how to' workshops co-run by Briggs for would-be campaign fundraisers suggest crowdfunding is about authenticity, trust and where money has come from, also, crucially, being able to signal and assess these online. Making enough money to sustain platforms' business may be paramount, but a prerequisite is making crowdfunding socially acceptable.

As noted, the *Crowdfunder Local* pages make destination campaigns for many cities and regions to promote clusters of people and activities. Local clustering can create what Light and Miskelly call 'a relational asset' in an area [32: 55] where 'no one is working in isolation. Borrowing goes on between projects and the effort to find materials, support and funds is often shared'. This kind of environment makes a fertile bed for crowdfunding, drawing in new adherents as the idea becomes more integrated and a more *usual* way to raise funds or offer support. We can see a zone of influence constructed beyond immediate actions on the platform.

Thus, Murray and colleagues [42] propose that the act of giving in crowdfunding 'is not the transfer of funds for a good cause, but a gateway to greater engagement. ...It provides a micro thread for continuing civic involvement.' [42:114]. Relatedly, partnerships are about supplying traffic and signaling trust, shown in the gratitude *Funding Circle* has for its council partner in Newcastle. The partnership is significant for how the platform is accepted, beyond any individual campaign. It is interesting that a council is acting as the face of the new mechanism, showing an ability to reinvent itself, but also the complexity of the journey for new financial instruments if they are to be taken up by all echelons in society and all areas of the country/world.

### Rewards and Returns

If ambitions and team involvement shape the service round a platform (and so the nascent social outcomes), so does the reward. The time-sensitive group pledge model (All or Nothing), when a minimum must be reached by a fixed date, is more likely to activate a community round a campaign than a slow climb to funding would [54].

The effect noted here is broader-brush. For instance, *Patchwork Present* uses a donation-reward hybrid model with particular challenges. The design is more elaborate than most donation platforms because it has to deal with the fact that, at root, the user may be asking for money for their personal gain, unlike charities or sponsored activities. In this, it is closer to art and social enterprise platforms, which have to convince potential funders that something exciting is to be done with their money. Thus, the platform offers creative tools and resists the disembodiment of a virtual present by making it 'real'. Money, the shared commodity, is rendered material through design that uses images to present a patchwork of items; offers a 'thank you' mechanism that reinforces the idea of actual goods; and equates the cost of the service to the wrapping paper round a present. The payback may be the fun of using the site and the talking point created in the present-giving network.

There is also clearly a difference between supporting a bakery, from which you can buy bread afterwards, or a distillery, when your shares come with a favorite drink, and lending only for promised income. Loan models are not intrinsically social and the rewards they promise are profit. They are more likely to have users who remain remote from each other, making it harder to create publics. (That is, until a platform is threatened or legislation changes dramatically, when, like *Trillion Fund*, there is collective interest in future activities and the safety of lender money.) Yet *Trillion Fund* celebrity shareholder Vivienne Westwood held a party to attract investors and raise awareness of renewables, a specifically social occasion for a service that does not need to bring its users into contact. While this is good business and promotion, there is also a rationale for the particular choice of engagement that draws on their social mission to accumulate a constellation around them.

Other intermediaries are rewarded by even a small amount of paying business. This is clearest in *Patchwork Present* using *Paypal* as a platform for its own service; payments collected contain a levy for this third party. And all income contributes to paying shareholder dividends. In fact, the constellations that *Patchwork Present* is configuring are far from straightforward and, as a consequence, there is no single public. They include a patchwork of investors, its campaign focus on a recipient known to all the funders, and the visible use of third-party technology products (unlike the 'white-labeling' described in the council study), This hybridity is visible to some degree across all our examples, with no simple meeting of markets, publics, or both.

## DESIGNING PAYING PUBLICS

We have argued that platforms can be used to configure the constellations of people that are involved in crowdfunding by bringing them into being in particular relations round socio-economic issues (and objects that represent issues, such as the platforms themselves). We have likened this to publics as they are discussed by Dewey [14] and in HCI and design [15,29,33,52]. The particular character of these interactions is financial, because of the financial nature of direct engagement with the platform. All the focus is on the movement and redistribution of funds and what they will buy. This is why we have talked about 'paying publics' in our title, drawing attention to the way that crowdfunding platforms create interests of an economic kind. Yet, we are not just talking about new markets.

Markets are full of crowds, masses of people who happen to be together. We make the distinction between markets, which are purely economic, and publics, which are social and political; between crowds, which are happenstance, and publics, which evolve and shape (as well as being shaped). We can make this distinction since each platform described here has a goal beyond making money through bringing together types of market; it has sought to provide social and ethical interests of the kind that configure publics. There is awareness of contributing to, and benefitting from, building new types of financial mechanism that may change societal relations, albeit within a global context where neoliberalism has depoliticized finance. But there is also awareness of the potential for impact in/on a particular sector through new relations, be that renewable energy or local business. No platform is redesigning economic life, despite *Trillion Fund's* claim it is 'changing money'. However, each offers possibilities for linking private, public and personal money and services in new ways round issues of concern, and, together, that signals societal as well as financial change.

In our first pair, the publics constituted are global, united by use of a platform to drive new collective environmental behavior and, as such, less obviously social in an immediate sense. In the second, concerns are defined as local (part of a localism agenda) and publics are thus geographical, where new relations among communities are an expected outcome as well as higher-level societal structures. We have given two examples of each to show that platforms can work in quite different ways to effect social change - and the related *paying publics* look different too.

### Design of Paying Publics

We have shown four ways that crowdfunding platforms can operate with articulated areas of concern. For each, the owner/designer talks of a desire for transformation: forms of financial human-computer interaction that enable new opportunities for local and global groups with evolving common interest. We have called constellations round these sites 'paying publics' to express the new financial and socio-economic structures of the arrangement.

Platforms can be easy to build – an off-the-shelf payment system, content management system and a fairly standard interface design. This makes the generosity and size of a platform's publics key to its effectiveness and this hinges on its unique design. *Crowdfunder,* the UK rewards-based platform, in many ways closely resembles the standardized design of world leader *Kickstarter* (video, text campaign message below, ladder of increasingly expensive rewards in a right-hand column). Yet, *Crowdfunder*'s business model and design of services (such as coaching to potential founders) is significantly different. *Crowdfunder* is actively shaping publics through partnerships and local engagement. Nuttall is teaching would-be founders what a campaign is, securing match funding for these enterprises, helping them build take-up of services as well as campaigns and so changing how such organizations operate.

The design *round* the platform, of relations built with each neighborhood and wider social structures, becomes key to gathering and shaping a paying public. This may also be key to the platform's viability: the ability to attract users. But we hope to have shown that something more than mere use can take place in engaging in the new forms of financial practice now available with crowdfunding.

A crowd uses a platform. A *paying public* emerges as it develops a collective sense as an interest group able to fund particular outcomes through placing its money. As these publics evolve, platforms become more than infrastructural, they are a support, a magnet and a focus for societal trends and what it is possible to enact with a popular groundswell. We are watching a vanguard, using algorithms to enable and automate interactions. Yet we may be reminded of the subscription models used in the 18$^{th}$-19$^{th}$ century in Britain and other parts, when people provided and shared activities and resources without state or local government mediation.

We can point to the work of active public-building that our studied platforms engage in: promoting mutual awareness by showing user activities on site, in newsletters and blogs; flagging up campaigns (particularly successes) and listing numbers of pledges as well as pledged amounts; running events round campaigns; teaching founders how to organize campaigns and tell a compelling story about their goals; showing how to turn a public into customers and realigning organizations to benefit from match-funding initiatives and crowdfunded outcomes; thinking geographically as well as thematically about who the public might be. We can also note that legal and regulatory matters shape what platforms can do; and changes in financial and political climate have an impact on how publics form and what concerns them. The sector will continue to change fast. For instance, the new act in the US means a range of start-ups and businesses that were constrained to using rewards-based platforms can now access professional investment.

Last, we can ask, speculatively, what impact the growth of these new formations could have. Locality has not been written out, despite the global reach of networks, but new forms of public commissioning raise questions of justice, equity and inclusion. We cannot predict if these variants on subscription will provide service for all, or just subscribers. Loans continue to define a borrower and a lender, even if the lending is distributed, but there is social import to this change. Murray et al's [42] football fans buying their club, then going to support it, or the drinkers in the community-owned pub are potentially the start of a more profound trend that the platforms here are seeking to contribute to.

Should we predict the reinvention of publics as *paying publics* round hundreds of new transaction mechanisms and their shapes? Design considerations for these interventions go beyond interface and interaction design, on one hand, and shaping viable business, on the other, to consider how we want our societies organized and funded and how we acknowledge social justice issues [16] in making financial choices. Crowdfunding platforms collectively change the economic landscape and could enfranchise new pockets of society to contribute and see their choices enacted - in ways defined by the subtleties of each platform's design - but only if they are designed to do so.

## ACKNOWLEDGEMENTS

We are grateful for support from multiple grants: EPSRC [EP/K003593/1] and ESRC [ES/M00371X/1]. We thank our interviewees, collaborators and the CHI reviewers for their comments. Due to ethical concerns, some supporting data cannot be made available. See [31] for data in the public domain; or check with the authors (emails above).

## REFERENCES


1. Ajay Agrawal, Christian Catalini and Abi Goldfarb, 2010 (online version). The Geography of Crowdfunding. *NBER Working Paper* No. 16820 http://www.nber.org/papers/w16820.pdf
2. Paul Belleflamme and Thomas Lambert. 2014. Crowdfunding: Some Empirical Findings and Microeconomic Underpinnings. *SSRN Electron. J.* doi:10.2139/ssrn.2437786
3. Victoria Bellotti, Sara Cambridge, Karen Hoy, Patrick Shih, Lisa Handalian, Kyungsik Han and John Carroll. 2014. Towards Community-Centred Support for Peer-to-Peer Service Exchange: Rethinking the Timebanking Metaphor. In *Proceedings of the 2014 SIGCHI Conference on Human Factors in Computing Systems* (CHI'14). New York: ACM Press, 2975-2984. http://dx.doi.org/10.1145/2556288.2557061
4. Christian Borch. 2012. *The Politics of Crowds: An Alternative History of Sociology.* Cambridge University Press.
5. Pierre Bourdieu. 2005. *The Social Structures of the Economy*. Polity Press.
6. Geoffrey C. Bowker and Susan Leigh Star. 2000. *Sorting Things Out: Classification and Its Consequences*. MIT Press.
7. Jo Briggs, Celia Lury and Sarah Teasley. 2015. *Creative Temporal Costings: A ProtoPublics Research Project with Leeds Creative Timebank.* http://nrl.northumbria.ac.uk/24800/
8. Ed Collom, Judith Lasker, and Corinne Kyriacou (eds.) 2012. *Equal Time, Equal Value: Community Currencies and Time Banking in the US*, Burlington VT: Ashgate.
9. *Crowdcube* (crowdfunding campaign, no date) www.crowdcube.com/investment/crowdfunder-19203
10. *Crowdfunder* (website) http://www.crowdfunder.co.uk
    b. http://www.crowdfunder.co.uk/blog/crowdfunding-went-mainstream-crowdfunder-story/
    c. http://www.crowdfunder.co.uk/leeds-bread-coop
    d. http://www.crowdfunder.co.uk/campaigns/local
11. *CrowdingIn: Crowdfunding in the UK* (website) http://crowdingin.com/platforms/all/all#
12. Roel Davidson and Nathaniel Poor. 2016. Factors for success in repeat crowdfunding: why sugar daddies are only good for Bar-Mitzvahs, *Information, Communication & Society*, 19:1, 127-139 DOI=http://dx.doi.org/10.1080/1369118X.2015.10935 33
13. Rodrigo Davies. 2014. Three provocations for civic crowdfunding. In *Information, Communication & Society*. 18 (3). http://dx.doi.org/10.1080/1369118X.2014.989878
14. John Dewey. 1927. *The Public and its Problems*. New York: Holt.
15. Carl DiSalvo, Jonathan Lukens, Thomas Lodato, Tom Jenkins, Tanyoung Kim. 2014. Making public things: How HCI design can express matters of concern. In *Proceedings of the 2014 SIGCHI Conference on Human Factors in Computing Systems* (CHI'14). ACM, New York, NY, USA, 2397-2406. http://dx.doi.org/_10.1145/2556288.2557359
16. Lynn Dombrowski, Ellie Harmon, and Sarah Fox. 2016. Social Justice-Oriented Interaction Design: Outlining Key Design Strategies and Commitments. In *Proceedings of the 2016 ACM Conference on Designing Interactive Systems* (DIS '16). ACM, New York, NY, USA, 656-671. http://dx.doi.org/10.1145/2901790.2901861
17. *Funding Circle* (website) https://www.fundingcircle.com/uk/
18. Annabelle Gawer. 2009. Platforms, Markets and Innovation: An Introduction. In *Platforms, Markets and Innovation.* Annabelle Gawer ed. 2009. Edward Elgar, 1-16.
19. Elizabeth Gerber and Julie Hui. 2013. Crowdfunding: Motivations and deterrents for participation. In *ACM Transactions on Computer-Human Interaction* (TOCHI) 20 (6): article no. 34. http://doi.acm.org/10.1145/2530540
20. Neha Gupta, David Martin, Benjamin V. Hanrahan, Jacki O'Neill. 2014. Turk-life in India. In *Proceedings of the 18th International Conference on Supporting Group Work* (GROUP '14), 1-11. http://doi.acm.org/10.1145/2660398.2660403
21. David Hakken, Maurizio Teli, Barbara Andrews. 2016. *Beyond Capital: Values, Commons, Computing, and the Search for a Viable Future*, Routledge
22. Jeff Howe. June 2, 2006. *Crowdsourcing: A Definition*. Crowdsourcing Blog.
23. Julie S. Hui, Michael D. Greenberg, Elizabeth M. Gerber. 2014. Understanding the role of community in crowdfunding work. In *Proceedings of the 17th ACM conference on Computer supported cooperative work & social computing* (CSCW '14), 62-74. http://dx.doi.org/10.1145/2531602.2531715
24. Jumpstart Your Business Startups Act *Wikipedia* https://en.wikipedia.org/wiki/Jumpstart_Our_Business_Startups_Act
25. *JustGiving* (website) www.justgiving.com
26. Helena Karasti. 2014. Infrastructuring in participatory design. In *Proceeding of the Participatory Design Conference*, (PDC 2014), p142-150. http://doi.acm.org/10.1145/2661435.2661450
27. *Kickstarter* (website) https://www.kickstarter.com/

28. *Kicktraq* (website) https://www.kicktraq.com
29. Christopher Le Dantec and Carl DiSalvo. 2013. Infrastructuring and the formation of publics in participatory design. In *Social Studies of Science* 43(2) 241–264. DOI: 10.1177/0306312712471581
30. Ann Light and Clodagh Miskelly, (2008) Brokering between Heads and Hearts: an analysis of designing for social change, *Proc. Design Research Society* 2008 (DRS '08).
31. Ann Light and Clodagh Miskelly. 2014. *Design for Sharing*, Sustainable Society Network+: https://designforsharingdotcom.files.wordpress.com/2014/09/design-for-sharing-webversion.pdf
32. Ann Light and Clodagh Miskelly. 2015. Sharing Economy vs Sharing Cultures? Designing for social, economic and environmental good, *IxD&A*, 49-62 http://www.mifav.uniroma2.it/inevent/events/idea2010/doc/24_3.pdf
33. Silvia Lindtner, Judy Chen, Gillian R. Hayes and Paul Dourish. 2011. Towards a Framework of Publics: Re-encountering Media Sharing and its User, ACM *Transactions on Human-Computer Interaction* (ToCHI), 18 (2) Article 5. http://doi.acm.org/10.1145/1970378.1970379
34. John Lyons. 2007. *Place-Shaping: A shared ambition for the future of local government*, HMSO, London
35. Noortje Marres. 2007. The issues deserve more credit: Pragmatist contributions to the study of public involvement in controversy. In *Social Studies of Science* 37(5): 759–780. http://sss.sagepub.com/content/37/5/759.full.pdf+html
36. Doreen B. Massey. 1995 (2nd edn). *Spatial Divisions of Labor: Social Structures and the Geography of Production*, Psychology Press.
37. Tanushree Mitra and Eric Gilbert. 2014. The Language that Gets People to Give: Phrases that Predict Success on Kickstarter. In *Proceedings of Computer Supported Cooperative Work* (CSCW'14), 49-61. http://dx.doi.org/10.1145/2531602.2531656
38. Ethan Mollick. 2014. The Dynamics of Crowdfunding: An exploratory study. In *The Journal of Business Venturing,* 29 (1), 1–16. http://dx.doi.org/10.1016/j.jbusvent.2013.06.005
39. Ethan Mollick and Ramana Nanda. 2016. Wisdom or Madness? Comparing Crowds with Expert Evaluation in Funding the Arts. In *Management Science* 62(6):1533-1553. DOI: 10.1287/mnsc.2015.2207
40. Jonathan Moules. 2014. London emerging as world leader in crowd-funding. *Financial Times*, 15 August 2014: http://on.ft.com/1uJ5ujJ
41. Michael Muller, Werner Geyer, Todd Soule, Steven Daniels and Li-Te Cheng. 2014. Crowdfunding inside the Enterprise: Employee-Initiatives for Innovation and Collaboration. In *Proceedings of the SIGCHI Conference on Human Factors in Computing Systems* (CHI '14), 503-512. http://doi.acm.org/10.1145/2470654.2470727.
42. Robin Murray, Julie Caulier-Grice and Geoff Mulgan. 2009. *Ways to Design, Develop and Grow Social Innovation: Social Venturing*. Nesta and the Young Foundation. http://www.nesta.org.uk/sites/default/files/social_venturing.pdf
43. Laurent Muzellec, Sébastien Ronteau and Mary Lambkin. 2015. Two-sided Internet Platforms: A Business Model Lifecycle Perspective. In *Industrial Marketing Management*, 44 (2), 139-150. http://dx.doi.org/10.1016/j.indmarman.2015.02.012
44. Andreas Novy and Bernhard Leubolt. 2005. Participatory budgeting in Porto Alegre: Social innovation and the dialectical relationship of state and civil society. *Urban Studies* 42, 11: 2023–2036. http://doi.org/10.1080/00420980500279828
45. Robert E. Park. 1975. *The Crowd and the Public and Other Essays*. University of Chicago Press.
46. *Patchwork Present* (website) www.patchworkpresent.com
47. Yannis Pierrakis and Liam Collins. 2013. *Banking on Each Other: Peer-to-peer lending to business: evidence from funding circle.* Nesta.
48. Jonathan Potter and Margaret Wetherell. *Discourse and social psychology: beyond attitudes and behaviour.* London Newbury Park, California: Sage. 1987
49. Stuart Reeves, Scott Sherwood and Barry Brown. 2010. Designing for Crowds. In *Proceedings of the 6th Nordic Conference on Human-Computer Interaction* (NordiCHI '10), 393-402 http://doi.acm.org/10.1145/1868914.1868960
50. Alexandra Stiver, Leonor Barroca, Shailey Minocha, Mike Richards and Dave Roberts. 2015. Civic crowdfunding research: Challenges, opportunities, and future agenda *New Media & Society*, 17 (2), 249-271. doi: 10.1177/1461444814558914
51. *Taskrabbit* (website) www.taskrabbit.com
52. Teli, Maurizio, Silvia Bordin, María Menéndez Blanco, Giusi Orabona, and Antonella De Angeli. 2015. 'Public Design of Digital Commons in Urban Places: A Case Study'. Int. J. of Human-Computer Studies 81: 17–30.
53. *Trillion Fund* (website) https://www.trillionfund.com
54. Rick Wash and Jacob Solomon. 2014. Coordinating Donors on Crowdfunding Websites. In *Proceedings of Computer Supported Cooperative Work* (CSCW'14) http://dx.doi.org/10.1145/2531602.2531678

55. Anbang Xu, Xiao Yang, Huaming Rao, Wai-Tat Fu, Shih-Wen Huang and Brian P. Bailey. 2014. Show Me the Money! An Analysis of Project Updates during Crowdfunding Campaigns. *Proceedings of the SIGCHI Conference on Human Factors in Computing Systems* (CHI '14), 591-600. http://doi.acm.org/10.1145/2556288.255704

56. Bryan Zhang, Peter Baeck, Tania Ziegler, Jonathan Bone and Kieran Garvey 2016. *Pushing Boundaries: The 2015 UK Alternative Finance Industry Report*, Nesta and Cambridge University https://www.nesta.org.uk/sites/default/files/pushing_boundaries_0.pdf

# Reappropriating Hackathons: The Production Work of the CHI4Good Day of Service

**Emily Porter[1], Chris Bopp[1], Elizabeth Gerber[2], Amy Voida[3]**

[1]ATLAS Institute
University of Colorado Boulder
{empo0270, chris.bopp}@colorado.edu

[2]Segal Design Institute
Northwestern University
egerber@northwestern.edu

[3]Dept. of Information Science
University of Colorado Boulder
amy.voida@colorado.edu

## ABSTRACT
The popularity of hackathons has increased as technology pervades more facets of our lives. Originally designed for programmers, hackathons are now being appropriated by new stakeholders across diverse sectors. Yet with this evolution in hackathons, we no longer adequately understand what is produced and, thereby, the value of these events. We conducted an interview study with 22 stakeholders—participants, representatives of nonprofit organizations, and organizers—of the CHI4Good Day of Service to understand what is produced through philanthropic hackathons. Whereas traditional hackathons are oriented around the production of code or prototypes, our analysis of interview data suggests that the production work of philanthropic hackathons also includes technical capacity and expertise, expanded social networks, an exposure to design process, affective experiences, and an opportunity for participants to shape their identities against a cross-sectoral, interdisciplinary backdrop. We conclude by reflecting on implications for the CHI community in carrying out philanthropic events styled after hackathons.

### Author Keywords
Hackathon; Social-issue; Civic; Material Production; Social Networks; Design Process

### ACM Classification Keywords
H.5.3. [Information Interfaces and Presentation]: Group and Organization Interfaces—Collaborative Computing

## INTRODUCTION
Hackathons bring together participants from different backgrounds to address a problem through the creation of a computational intervention over the course of a day or two. Historically, hackathons have been recognized as a site for the development of prototypes in the form of code or other physical artifacts. More recently, however, diverse stakeholders across sectors have begun appropriating hackathons to address their own challenges, resulting in hackathons newly-dubbed as "civic" [3] or "social-issue" hackathons [7]. These new styles of hackathons have been described as "addressing social conditions and their consequences" [3] and marketed as "coding for change[1]". With this evolution in hackathons, however, it is no longer clear what the hackathon genre produces.

As these new styles of hackathons increase in popularity, it has become clear that the production work of these events extends beyond that of the distinct digital artifact of code or a prototype [3, 5, 6, 7, 8]. Irani notes that sometimes no artifact is produced at all [6]. And indeed, Gregg has criticized hackathons for their lack of deep engagement with social issues, shifting quickly from often-complex issues to a simplified, technical solution. Her criticism draws from the cultural exaltation of the Silicon Valley entrepreneur as a more valuable citizen, bypassing administrative bureaucracy and skipping right to action [5]. It is even more important, then, to understand what other forms of value might be produced through the work of philanthropic hackathons. If hackathons can be restructured to further facilitate and produce a broader spectrum of valuable outcomes in this context, we might better support the goals of nonprofit and civic organizations alongside the philanthropic goals of programmers, designers, and user experience researchers. To this end, this research seeks to provide a more comprehensive understanding of what is produced as a result of applying a hackathon-style event in a philanthropic context. Broadening our understanding of production work to include both the tangible and intangible outcomes of philanthropic hackathons provides a unique lens through which we can begin to understand what these experiences produce for the diversity of stakeholders.

Our research seeks to understand what is produced when the genre of a hackathon is appropriated in philanthropic contexts. Through interviews with 22 stakeholders of the CHI4Good Day of Service, we learn that in addition to artifacts, philanthropic hackathons produce technical expertise, expanded social networks, an exposure to design process, affective experiences, and an opportunity for participants to shape their identity against a cross-sectoral,


CHI 2017, May 06 - 11, 2017, Denver, CO, USA

ACM 978-1-4503-4655-9/17/05□$15.00
DOI: http://dx.doi.org/10.1145/3025453.3025637

[1] https://www.whitehouse.gov/blog/2016/06/03/open-data and-innovation-national-day-civic-hacking-2016

interdisciplinary backdrop. By understanding these alternative outcomes, we help position the HCI community to better plan and set expectations for Day of Service events styled after hackathons.

## RELATED LITERATURE

Hackathons allegedly originated in Silicon Valley during the late 1990's as internal prototyping and problem-solving events for large technology companies [7]. Most hackathons last one to two days and are characterized by the formation of small groups to address a particular challenge through the production of a digital or physical prototype [3, 4, 5, 6, 7, 8, 10]. In some cases, hackathon organizers incentivize participants by presenting a prize to the team that implements the most innovative solution [7].

In recent years, hackathons have been appropriated by governments, international institutions, and nonprofits to address societal or "social-issue" challenges with pro-bono work [3, 5, 6, 7]. These philanthropic hackathons are generally understood by researchers as more complex forms of the conventional hackathon. Multiple researchers have independently observed that philanthropic hackathons accomplish more than the physical outcomes typically associated with traditional hackathons, suggesting that these events also provide a venue for knowledge exchange, public relations opportunities, and citizen engagement [3, 5, 6, 7]. The emergent understanding that philanthropic hackathons engender new forms of production work prompts the question: *what is the breadth of production work for the diversity of stakeholders when traditional hackathons are appropriated in a philanthropic context*?

## RESEARCH METHODS

### Research Context

The CHI4Good Day of Service was promoted as a volunteer opportunity for individuals attending the 2016 ACM SIGCHI Conference on Human Factors in Computing Systems to "enable CHI attendees to leverage their skills to make an impact."[2] Held for eight hours on the Saturday preceding the conference, three conference co-chairs and a consultant event organizer brought together 34 non-profit organizations from the Bay Area and approximately 100 volunteers for a hackathon-style event hosted at the Convention Center in San Jose, California.

### Data Collection & Analysis

Researchers conducted semi-structured interviews using an interview protocol customized to the role of the participant. Each protocol explored the following areas: motivations for participating or not participating, preparation work before the event, and perceptions of the event's "success" as operationalized by each participant. A total of 22 individuals—representative of the diversity of the event's stakeholders—participated in the research:

- 4 event organizers, referenced with an anonymous participant number O1–O4;
- 5 representatives of nonprofit organizations who attended the event (N1–N5);
- 1 representative of a nonprofit organization who applied to participate but was never matched with a volunteer group (AN1);
- 8 volunteers who attended the event (V1–V8);
- 3 volunteers who originally RSVP'd but did not attend the event (AV1–AV3); and
- 1 individual who purposefully chose not to participate in the event (C1).

A researcher interviewed all organizers during the event or within the following month. Nonprofit representatives were interviewed during the event's breaks, with two of the five also participating in follow-up interviews three months later. Researchers received contact information for AN1 through event organizers; she was interviewed two months following the event. All volunteers, whether they attended or not, were recruited through a series of emails sent by event organizers after the event. Interviews with individuals in attendance lasted 33 minutes, on average, and interviews with individuals who did not attend lasted an average of 18 minutes.

Researchers transcribed and inductively coded all interviewers. In moving back and forth between the research literature and this initial coding, researchers developed a guiding question that drove subsequent rounds of analysis: "What was produced (or not produced) in this experience for this individual?" Relevant sections of transcripts were printed and clustered during collaborative analysis sessions to identify the variety of outputs and their context.

## RESULTS: WHAT IS PRODUCED?

### Artifacts

Similar to a traditional hackathon, most participants noted contributing to a digital artifact that was handed over to the nonprofits after the Day of Service concluded. While a few of these artifacts were prototypes (e.g., a digitized "re-entry" guide for those exiting the American prison system), they were the minority of digital artifacts created during the Day of Service. More frequently, teams implemented small improvements for the nonprofits' existing websites or they produced wireframes and visual mockups. In some cases, the artifact was actually a draft document detailing important "next steps" for the nonprofits. As V6 explained:

> *[We] summarized this in the PowerPoint presentation…and include[d] other things like examples of other great nonprofit websites, some things about payment services and tools to collect donations, and articles on good design for nonprofit websites as well as hosting options especially targeted to nonprofits, so at the end we didn't code anything. (V6)*

[2] https://chi2016.acm.org/wp/day-of-service/

Yet, despite the broad-based interest in producing digital artifacts, participants reported mismatches in expectations and needs, particularly between volunteers and nonprofit representatives. One nonprofit representative explained:

> *...we're moving to WordPress but it doesn't seem like something a lot of these volunteers use. They prefer... Bootstrap, probably, or... HTML. So there's platforms that seem more user friendly but... pure technical people don't want to use [them]... (N1)*

### Technical Expertise

Almost all nonprofit representatives interviewed discussed being unsure of what skills or tools would be needed to accomplish the project they had proposed for the event. Most agreed that participation in the event led to a better understanding of their baseline project needs, an awareness of existing technologies that might satisfy these needs, and their organization's potential capacity to fulfill these needs. N5 discusses the production of technical expertise:

> *I now know more than I did this morning...like how much will it cost me to by a Google App engine. I have leads of places where either I can get it for free or somebody will pay for it. (N5)*

The lack of technical expertise among nonprofit representatives going into the event was a central theme among all stakeholder groups. In a minority of cases, participants suggested that technical expertise may not yet have been produced for nonprofits in ways that would cultivate long-term impact.

> *... for a nonprofit that's done at least two or three of these [events], after about three, they're over it because they realize they really are investing more money in coming to these than they're getting out of them. (O2)*

### Design Process Experience

Most projects proposed for the event were ill-suited for either the timeline of the day or the expertise of the volunteers. Many projects, then, required restructuring or adaptation; in some cases, the entire proposal was scrapped by volunteers. One nonprofit representative suggested that the lack of a streamlined process for defining not only technical needs, but also for monitoring the progress of the project might contribute to the discontinuity: "...sometimes it comes down to an individual in a nonprofit taking the initiative…there aren't any best practices." (N1)

Yet as teams restructured project proposals or, in some cases, developed totally new ones, there was a discernable shift towards user-centered design methods to reshape the plans. In one project team, the user-centered design processes used during the event influenced changes in the organization:

> *I think the framework of user experience has been helpful... pushing how to get people to change their minds about the role of technology. I stress that internally within our organization because I think we're having to change the mindset of what that is for folks internally. My [Day of Service] team is a strategic partner [now]... (N3)*

### Social Networks

Individuals in all stakeholder groups were motivated to attend the event by the potential to produce larger social networks. Participants reported developing new ties between nonprofit organizations and volunteers, among volunteers, between organizers and nonprofit organizations, and between organizers and volunteers. Participants found different kinds of ties more or less valuable based on perceived need at a personal or organizational level. AV9, for example, valued the opportunity to meet other volunteers:

> *I thought it would be an amazing networking opportunity...just to kind of meet people who do similar things and also people who just care about different things... (AV9)*

Participants believed that these new network ties would lead to possible job or volunteer opportunities, new volunteers for their organization, or increased understanding of the value of individuals with different disciplinary backgrounds. O4 discusses one instance in which this outcome was produced: "One [nonprofit] is now going to hire a [UX] designer, that will be employee two or three for [them]…" (O4)

### Affect

Affect emerged as a more abstract product of the Day of Service—an unexpected but significant theme across stakeholder groups. Both volunteers and nonprofit representatives alluded to emotional changes throughout the day brought about by social interactions, event logistics, and perceptions of progress (or the lack thereof). Terms like "energy," "fun," and "good feeling" were used to describe positive affect while "awkward," "uncomfortable," and "frustration" were used to describe negative affect. Many individuals mentioned that their intention to participate in the event was largely motivated by the idea that some sort of positive affect would be produced:

> *... it was a social thing that beforehand a lot of my friends said that they were all going to volunteer, as well. I was like 'this is going to be great, we're going to work on different projects but we're all going to go there together and it's going to be a blast.' (AV2)*

### Hackathon Identity

The work of navigating the diverse backgrounds and varied levels expertise of team members within each hackathon team afforded an opportunity for individuals to explore and construct their hackathon identity, much in the same way that Arrow and McGrath find that processes created in small group settings are fundamental to establishing the identity of the group as well as the individuals within the group [2]. By understanding the goals, motivations, and other information about team members, participants worked out their identity with respect to the role they might play and what they might contribute to the project at hand:

> *The first project was interesting... I thought that I had a lot to contribute to it. The second one... I was familiar with the process of identifying the appropriate web design but I haven't a lot of experience with that in a long time. I was kind of learning on the way... (V2)*

Numerous participants noted that skill matching with projects was of particular importance to the production of their hackathon identity. Additionally, unlike typical hackathons, volunteers at the Day of Service were able to rotate through the event based on personal preference or schedule. Some volunteers took part in a project for no more than two hours while others stayed for the entire eight-hour period. Participants commented that the fluid group composition created a context for the continual renegotiation of one's hackathon identity:

> *The new person... came in kind of fresh and not knowing what was going on so her role kind of turned out to be usability participant... (V1)*

As the production of one's hackathon identity played out over the course of the day, the diversity within teams—both disciplinarily and reflecting varied levels of expertise—created significant tensions. Some participants described difficulty merging the ideas of different team members due to differences in disciplinary approaches and expectations. V3 describes how identities within her team were constructed in response to a hierarchy of expertise:

> *I worked with a woman that is a manager [at a software company] so it was like I'm a student and she has all this experience and I think with that dynamic she felt that she had the final say in a lot of things. (V3)*

## DISCUSSION

Results of this research, systematically explore what is produced for the diversity of stakeholders involved in these events, suggest that the products of philanthropic hackathons are not limited to prototypes or even other tangible artifacts but include the production of a diversity of more abstract and immaterial items, as well. Irani suggests that hackathons may favor "quick and forceful action" over "the slow construction of coalition across difference" [6]. Gregg and Toyama raise similar concerns about whether hackathon-style events may move too quickly from complex social issues to overly simplistic technical solutions [4, 9]. A more robust understanding of the non-technical products of philanthropic hackathons, then, stands to be an important step towards mitigating these important concerns. We turn, then, to consider how we might better design philanthropic hackathons to help form and foster meaningful connections among the stakeholders of the event and to encourage teams to engage more deeply with social issues, moving less quickly, if at all, to technical solutions.

### Design Implications for Philanthropic Hackathons

By foregrounding and providing scaffolding to better support the diversity of what is produced by hackathons—beyond digital artifacts—we speculate that the hackathon genre might be productively restructured to benefit the breadth of stakeholders. Based on our empirical data, we suggest several implications for the redesign of philanthropic hackathons. Organizers might better support technical capacity building and expertise by offering repurposeable templates or design patterns (e.g., for setting up databases, creating websites, or developing mobile applications) (see also [8]). Organizers might better support the expansion of social networks by connecting participants before the hackathon to start building connections and after the hackathon to support potential follow-up communication and collaboration. To support an exposure to design process, organizers might offer nonprofit representatives step-by-step guidance through a flexible design process, producing user needs' assessments and workflows prior to attendance at the event (see also [8]). As affect has been found to accompany creative activity [1], organizers might support the expression of both positive and negative affect through opportunities for active reflection throughout the day. Lastly, to support occasions for shaping identities for collaboration, organizers might propose distinct roles and responsibilities for participants to achieve shared goals.

## CONCLUSION

As HCI researchers, we are committed to understanding new ways to practice, develop, and improve methods in HCI. In this research, we have developed a richer understanding of how philanthropic hackathons go beyond creating digital artifacts—to support technical expertise, design process, social networks, affect, and identity. Understanding the value in the breadth of what is produced by philanthropic hackathons will enable us to rethink the design of these events and will, we hope, spark a conversation about how the HCI community can best reappropriate hackathons for societal good.

## ACKNOWLEDGEMENTS

We thank our participants for sharing their time and experiences with us. We are particularly indebted to the CHI4Good Day of Service co-chairs—Kathy Baxter, Liz Gerber, and Dan Russell—for their support of this research.

This material is based upon work supported by the National Science Foundation under Grant Number 1602660. Any opinions, findings, and conclusions or recommendations expressed in this material are those of the authors and do not necessarily reflect the views of the National Science Foundation.

## REFERENCES

1. Teresa M. Amabile, Sigal G. Barsade, Jennifer S. Mueller, and Barry M. Staw. 2005. Affect and

Creativity at Work. *Administrative Science Quarterly* 50, 3: 367-403.

2. Holly Arrow and Joseph E. McGrath. 1993. Membership Matters How Member Change and Continuity Affect Small Group Structure. *Small Group Research* 24, 3: 334-361.
3. Catherine D'Ignazio, Alexis Hope, Becky Michelson, Robyn Churchill, and Ethan Zuckerman. 2016. A Feminist HCI Approach to Designing Postpartum Technologies: "When I first saw a breast pump I was wondering if it was a joke." In *Proceedings of the SIGCHI Conference on Human Factors in Computing Systems* (CHI '16), 2612-2622.
4. Carl DiSalvo, Melissa Gregg, and Thomas Lodato. 2014. Building Belonging. *Interactions* 21,4: 58-61.
5. Melissa Gregg. 2015. Hack for Good: Speculative Labour, App Development and the Burden of Austerity. *The Fibreculture Journal* 25, 186: 183-201.
6. Lilly Irani. 2015. Hackathons and the Making of Entrepreneurial Citizenship. *Science Technology & Human Values* 40, 5: 799-824.
7. Thomas J. Lodato and Carl DiSalvo. 2016. Issue-Oriented Hackathons as Material Participation. *New Media & Society* 18, 4: 539-557.
8. Andrea K. Thomer, Michael B. Twidale, Jinlong Guo, and Matthew J. Yoder. 2016. Co-designing Scientific Software: Hackathons for Participatory Interface Design. In *Proceedings of the SIGCHI Conference on Human Factors in Computing Systems* (CHI '16), 3219-3226.
9. Kentaro Toyama. 2015. *Geek Heresy: Rescuing Social Change from the Cult of Technology.* PublicAffairs.
10. Eric H. Trainer, Arun Kalyanasundaram, Chalalai Chaihirunkarn, and James D. Herbsleb. 2016. How to Hackathon: Socio-technical Tradeoffs in Brief, Intensive Collocation. In *Proceedings of the ACM Conference on Computer-Supported Cooperative Work & Social Computing* (CSCW '16), 1118-1130.

# Understanding Concept Maps: A Closer Look at How People Organise Ideas

**Stefano Padilla, Thomas S. Methven, David A. Robb, Mike J. Chantler**
School of Mathematical and Computer Sciences, Heriot-Watt University
Edinburgh, Scotland, UK EH14 4AS
{s.padilla, t.methven, d.a.robb, m.j.chantler}@hw.ac.uk

## ABSTRACT
Research into creating visualisations that organise ideas into concise concept maps often focuses on implicit mathematical and statistical theories which are built around algorithmic efficacy or visual complexity. Although there are multiple techniques which attempt to mathematically optimise this multi-dimensional problem, it is still unknown how to create concept maps that are immediately understandable to people. In this paper, we present an in-depth qualitative study observing the behaviour and discussing the strategy used by non-expert participants to create, interact, update and communicate a concept map that represents a collection of research ideas. Our results show non-expert individuals create concept maps differently to visualisation algorithms. We found that our participants prioritised narrative, landmarks, abstraction, clarity, and simplicity. Finally, we derive design recommendations from our results which we hope will inspire future algorithms that automatically create more usable and compelling concept maps better suited to the natural behaviours and needs of users.

### Author Keywords
Design; Interfaces; Information; Visualisation; Data; Interaction; Concept Maps; Knowledge; Organisation.

### ACM Classification Keywords
H.5.2. Information interfaces and presentation (e.g., HCI): User Interfaces: User-cantered Design.

## INTRODUCTION
The organisation and representation of knowledge is an important area of visualisations. These serve as a common medium to explore, explain, and communicate information produced in medicine, the sciences, engineering, humanities, and between individuals as described by Bigelow et al. [6] and Heer et al. [28]. A few example applications of these type of visualisations which organise and represent knowledge are concept maps [22], mind maps [20], and scientific overviews [47, 51]. Information in these maps usually consists of various abstract ideas (Figure 1) that link together to represent a high level multi-dimensional concept, topic, or query [13, 29, 36, 54].


*CHI 2017,* May 06-11, 2017, Denver, CO, USA
 ISBN 978-1-4503-4655-9/17/05...$15.00
DOI: http://dx.doi.org/10.1145/3025453.3025977

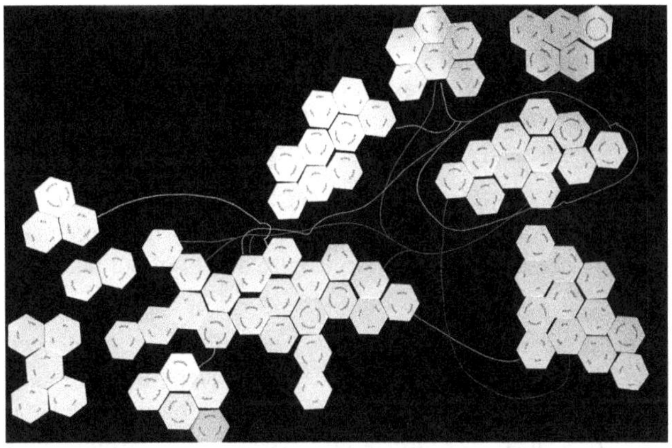

**Figure 1. Example of ideas organised by one of our pilot participants {Pp}.**

Concept maps have no simple or optimal solution to represent and structure their information either by conventional theory, mathematical algorithms, or evaluation methods [50, 63] due to their complex multi-dimensional nature [61]. Individuals, however, can come up with a satisfactory solution quickly and effortlessly. As a result, we believe this is an interesting problem to observe and explore from a non-expert perspective as it will help us inspire designers and create novel algorithm of concept maps that are immediately understandable to people.

Early research focused on building these maps either using simple visual theories (such as the Gestalt Laws) or by using mathematical rules to define and organise the ideas into a Euclidean space [65, 66]. These earlier visualisations were also evaluated using traditional usability metrics such as efficiency, effectiveness, and satisfaction as described by O'Connell [50]. Recent research, however, has begun to observe novice users and expert designers create visualisations either with physical objects, or on a screen [6, 26, 55]. Furthermore, there has been a drive to explore how humans interact with visualisations using various novel techniques including physicalisation [30, 33].

In this paper we present an in-depth study that examines how non-experts create physical concept maps, and their experience of doing so, by conducting extensive semi-structured interviews afterwards. Our main aim is to understand how people organise ideas in concept maps.

In particular, we focus on the four main aspects found in visualisations: how people *create* visualisations to map information, how they *interact* with them once created, how they would *update* their visualisations with new information, and how they *communicate* the concepts within their maps to others [66].

Our primary contributions from our study are that we:

- document how people create, interact, update, communicate, and feel about how successfully their concept maps convey the information contained within;
- analyse how people create concept maps using content and thematic analysis to formulate design considerations; and
- discuss new general design approaches that can be applied to concept maps and suggest opportunities for future research and creation of algorithms and tools.

## RELATED WORK AND DESIGN CHALLENGES

In this section, we review the related work of the three main areas of research which informed the design of our study.

### Information mapping

The process for information visualisation has been previously modelled as a sequence of steps starting with data and finishing with interactions. The main model has been described by Card et al [7] where they explain how visualisations are created in four steps (data, tables, structures and views) and how the user interprets and interacts with the visualisations. Card's model was extended by Chi et al. [9] to allow for multiple pipelines and later it was further refined [8] and extended again by Jansen et al. [33]. For our study, we are focusing on the *visual mappings* and *structures* required to create *views* (Figure 2 highlights these sections).

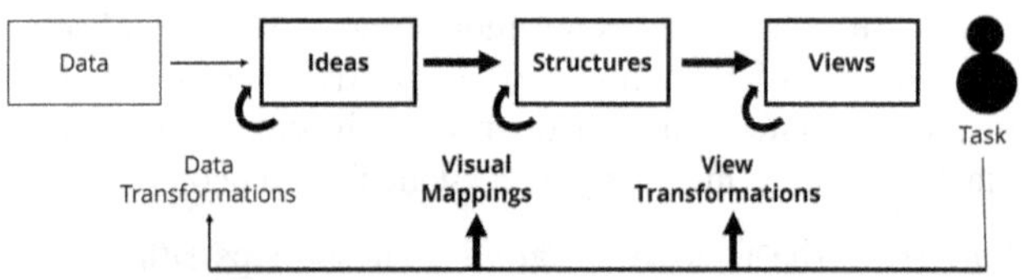


**Figure 2. Visual reference model by Card et al. [7]. We have slightly modified the model to highlight sections of our study.**

While several aspects of the models have been researched in depth, including interactions of views and analytical processes [2, 24, 37, 58, 70], relatively few studies show how visualisations are created from the point of view of those who are actually going to use them [6, 14, 29, 55, 69]. In addition, understanding how users map and communicate multi-dimensional information remains quite limited [3].

This paper, therefore, aims to shed some light on these less researched areas and find out how non-experts would organise and visualise information if given the chance.

### Visual mapping

Various studies have been produced in the area of human vision exploring how our visual system organises elements into groups [4, 5, 27, 53]. In psychology, the pioneering Gestalt theory enlightens our understanding in terms of organisational principles for visualisations [4, 38, 66, 68].

There are 8 commonly defined Gestalt laws [4, 68]. Two are outside the scope of this study as they are concern with motion perception which we are not planning to investigate at this stage. The remaining 6 laws can be summarised as:

- *Proximity*: things closer together are perceptually grouped together.
- *Similarity*: similar elements tend to be grouped together.
- *Connectedness*: expressing relationship between objects by entities (e.g. lines).
- *Continuity*: well aligned contours are perceived as to be grouped.
- *Closure*: closed contours are to be grouped.
- *Symmetry*: symmetrically arranged pairs of elements are perceived as a group.

Some research has explored the use of these theories for human interaction [25, 39, 42, 64]. Our motivation and challenge, however, is to understand if participants use vision fundamentals and Gestalt laws to map information and how the results of our study can influence the development of design recommendations.

### Human perspective

Novak et al introduced the theoretical foundations and psychology advantages behind concept maps [49], while Ruiz-Primo studied concept maps when looking at student assessment [57]. Markham et al also studied concept maps in the domain of research and evaluation tools [43] while Sims-Knight et al explored them in the design domain [59]. While these studies present glimmers of insight into the creation of concept maps by participants, they have not explored the process itself with the aim of discovering the insights into the aspects of visualisation, usability and communication of concept maps.

The process of organising ideas into groups has been researched extensively using methods like card sorting, which has been used in a wide variety of ways, from organising web sites [48] to clinical application design [60], both locally or using remote card sorting tools [10, 44]. While card sorting resembles the process, however, it does not work well for concept maps as ideas in groups do not overlap, there are no links, and they do not provide concise concepts.

Finally, constructive visualisations are an innovative paradigm that can aid the creation of flexible and dynamic visualisations. They rely on elementary building blocks to allow non-experts to create simple, expressive and dynamic visualisations as described by Huron et al. [31]. This new trend has a few advantages over digital representations: it enhances cognition, communication, learning, problem solving, and decision making [26, 41, 33, 61] while avoiding the creation of complex interfaces with possible confounding factors. As a result, we decided to exploit the advantages of physical elements to allows us to comprehensively study the key behaviours of how our participants organise and represent knowledge using concept maps without adding any complexity from visual interfaces.

## STUDY METHOD

The aim of this study is to observe the behaviour and discuss the strategy used by non-expert participants to create, interact, update, and communicate a concept map that represents a collection of ideas. We designed our study to consider the organisation of specific ideas, as described in the next sub-sections, as this is performed almost daily in companies, research organisations, and at the individual level for various tasks.

### Dataset

For our study, we chose research information as the main data source for the ideas. Previous studies have tried to organise and evaluate visualisations of this information using mathematical models [47, 52], but to our knowledge none of these studies involved feedback from individuals. Furthermore, visualising this type of information has been identified as a major challenge by various national research organisations, as they believe there are important gains in inter-disciplinary collaboration and research to be had. Just three of the research organisations concerned with this challenge are the NIH/NSF [34], RCUK [17] and Europe H2020 [19].

The raw data for our study was acquired from a national research organisation [56] and it consisted of a portfolio of accepted research grant ideas from all research areas at the national level. These data were suited for our study as it is possible to extract ideas that can be encapsulated into *units*, are *comprehensible* without further need to explain them, occupy a *multi-dimensional* space, have known *links* between ideas, and can be *abstracted* into an overview, or visualisation.

Our raw data consisted of 42,861 descriptions of research grants with an estimated value of over £3.0 billion GBP (approximately $4.5 billion USD at time of writing). We used topic modelling to encapsulate the grant descriptions into 100 unit ideas using a similar process to that described by Padilla et al. in their work to map the HCI area [51]; specifically, we used Latent Dirichlet Allocation as defined by McCallum [35]. We set our model parameters (beta = 0.01) to benefit from the natural structure of the data, and to allow the necessary coverage and overlap in the portfolio.

The output from the topic model was 100 individual topics, each of which consisted of a distribution of terms. To further encapsulate these ideas, we used just the most important term for each topic. Finally, we removed repeated and meaningless terms. Our final set of unit ideas consisted of 79 words representing the whole research portfolio as shown in Table 1.

| aerosol | design | ice | patient | simulation |
|---|---|---|---|---|
| africa | dna | image | people | site |
| algorithm | drug | imaging | plant | social |
| animal | earth | language | policy | solar |
| arctic | earthquake | laser | population | sound |
| art | energy | magnetic | program | species |
| bacterium | evolution | market | protein | star |
| blood | fat | material | public | structure |
| brain | film | measurement | quantum | technology |
| carbon | flow | muscle | reaction | text |
| cell | food | music | religious | theory |
| child | fuel | network | school | universe |
| climate | gene | nuclear | security | virus |
| community | health | ocean | sediment | war |
| cultural | history | optical | sensor | water |
| data | hormone | particle | service | |

**Table 1. List of ideas used in the study.**

By using the techniques previously described, we processed our dataset into ideas that do not only fit the design challenges for our study, but also have the advantage of representing a real problem rather than a synthetic one. This was to allow us to observe how non-experts react to and solve some of the problems found in real, complex, and often contradictory information datasets.

### Data representation

Each idea was represented as a unit on white card inspired by the work from Huron et al. [31] and described in the previous section. Care was taken to print the label of each idea onto the cards so it could be read in any orientation to avoid any possible orientation biases. As a result, the word was printed three times, following the circumference of a circle inside the hexagonal card shape.

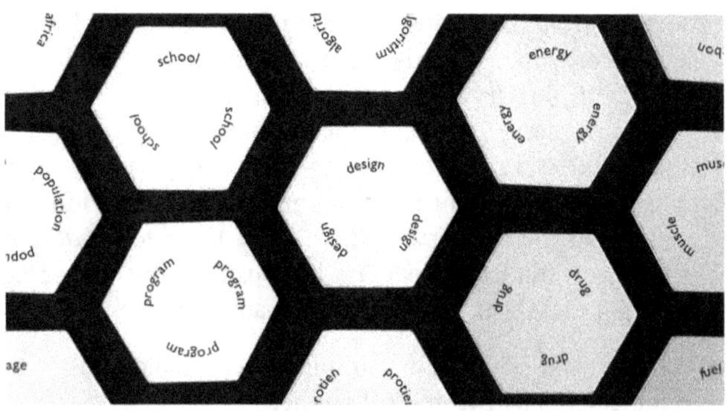


**Figure 3. Ideas were represented as hexagonal cards to allow connections, easy handling, placement, and to maximise the possible area for each idea. The cards were machine cut, white, 4.5 cm in width and 300 GMS in weight.**

The white cards were hexagonal (see Figure 3) in shape to allow for naturally accessible *structure* and *connections* between ideas which is commonly used in concept maps [49]. Also, hexagons are the most optimal shape to minimise wasted space between items while maximising the area inside it. Thanks to these advantages, hexagons are fairly common in nature, further enhancing the *aesthetic quality*, *familiarity*, and *acceptance* from our participants as described by Emmer [16]. Finally, hexagons allow some immediate perceptual affordances, in particular their *symmetry* and *tiling* properties that would benefit our context and task without over-restricting it or over-complicating it.

The physical space was restricted to a board of 76.0 cm by 47.0 cm (30.0 in by 18.5 in), denoted by a black card background to further highlight the ideas and task. The specific dimensions were calculated to allow 3 times more empty space than the total area the cards would occupy. A Golden ratio was used to maintain a familiar and also natural appearance. This is a well know ratio common in nature and devices like monitors and portable devices [16].

**Figure 4. A lab member demonstrating the study. The experimental setup includes the hexagonal ideas, markers, board and video recorder.**

## Task

Our task was inspired by evaluation patterns [15], reflections on scenarios [40], and methods [63] for visualisations. In our study we used a similar technique to the *Once Upon A Time* method, where we provided a fictional scenario for our participants to solve [15]. Participants were asked to imagine they were new employees at the organisation in charge of research in their country, and their supervisor had asked them to *create an overview* of funded research ideas using only 75 ideas (keeping 4 ideas). In addition, participants were asked to:

- make the overview simple, clear, and easy to understand by the general public,
- ensure the overview gave a complete view of all the ideas funded by the organisation,
- design the overview so it could be reproduced on paper, and
- fit the overview within the designated black card area.

At a later stage participants were asked to think about how they would update their visualisation if they had to add the 4 remaining ideas [40, 63]. Users were also able to annotate their visualisations with three colour markers, either by drawing on the card, or by using extra blank cards if desired. By defining the task in this manner, it allowed us to probe the thoughts and reactions of participants when they were *creating*, *interacting*, *updating*, and *communicating* their visualisations.

## Procedure

The study was carried out in a controlled environment. The set up consisted of a table with a sheet of black card in front of the participant. In addition, a box containing 75 of the hexagonal cards (in random order), a box with three markers of different colours, and a box with blank tiles were placed above and outside the black card, but within the view of the participants. The missing 4 cards (75 + 4 = 79) were hidden from the participant until they were asked to think about how they would update their visualisation with these new ideas.

A video camera was used to record the actions of the participants when they were creating their visualisations as shown in Figure 4. Care was taken to only record the experiment area to maintain as much anonymity as possible. Participants were allowed two hours to complete the experiment and they were given a voucher worth £20 GBP (approximately $30 USD) for their time.

| | Aspect | Examples |
|---|---|---|
| Semi-Structured Interview | **Creation** | Gestalt Structures<br>Links<br>Abstractions<br>Strategies<br>Annotations |
| | **Interaction** | Possibilities<br>Physicality<br>Engagement |
| | **Update** | Strategies<br>Reorganisation |
| | **Communication** | Confidence<br>Problems<br>Memory |

**Table 2. Example aspects covered in the semi-structured interviews.**

We conducted semi-structured interviews after a participant had finished creating their visualisation to investigate the thought processes and decisions they underwent while they were creating, and later, explaining their visualisations. We decided to use semi-structured interviews as our main data collection method, instead of other methods like recording participants thinking out loud, as the former allowed us to investigate more complex issues and strategies. Furthermore, the interviews were conducted shortly after the creation process allowing us to capture the participants' immediate recollections and avoid biases due to fatigue and self-awareness issues. These concerns are highlighted in Ericsson and Simon's work [18]. Moreover, in our pilot we observed that participants did not find it natural to talk out loud during the creation task. We believe the main reason was that the task is an automated and rapid process that hinders out loud reporting from participants.

The semi-structured interviews were organised based on the four aspects of visualisations (*creation*, *interaction*, *update* and *communication*). In addition, these aspects were extended as shown in Table 2 to get a deeper understanding into the participants' thoughts and actions in the semi-structured interviews. These are based on insights from

Ware [66] and the research literature as described in the previous sections.

A senior researcher running the study was present in the room throughout the duration of the experiment to aid and answer any questions from the participants about the procedure. Finally, the interview was carried out after the visualisation was completed. The same video camera which recorded the construction of the visualisation was also used to record the participants' answers during the semi-structured interview, which consisted of both audio of their answers and video of the gestures towards their creation.

## RESULTS

In total, 14 subjects {P1 – P14} agreed to participate in our study (including 1 pilot participant {Pp}), Figure 6 presents photographs of all the visualisations (high res versions available here: dx.doi.org/10.6084/m9.figshare.c.3658130). Our participants were recruited across departments in our institution and from external companies. We recruited a varied group of participants comprising of 9 male and 5 female participants with an age range of 20-40 years. Professions included creative to mathematical sectors. All participants declared they had no professional experience with concept maps, apart from creating the occasional Excel or Matlab chart in their daily work. Ethical approval was granted from our institution before proceeding with the study. All participants stated that they would allow themselves to be recorded, and have their post-study interview recorded and transcribed for this study, as long as their results were anonymised.

Content and thematic analysis was used to discover and conceptualise the structures, patterns, insights, recommendations and interests from the interview data. We followed standard guidelines to code our themes, as described by Wengraf [67] and Corbin and Strauss [11]. In our analysis we found saturation for our themes, therefore, we believe the sample size in our study was appropriate. Finally, the visuals of their videos were coded and analysed to gather further insight into the creation process.

As show in the time column of Table 3, participants took between 11 and 64 minutes to complete the experiment, with the interviews afterwards taking, on average, 30 minutes. Participants were allowed as much time as they felt necessary to familiarise themselves with the task instructions, and to then create their visualisations. In total, more than 20 hours of video was recorded and analysed. Analysis and coding of the results data took approximately 100 researcher-hours in total, and more than 2,500 coding instances were compiled. In addition, we are making the transcribed interviews and analysed data open for future research (dx.doi.org/10.6084/m9.figshare.c.3658130).

### Resulting concept maps

First we present some simple metrics collected from the concept maps created by our participants (Table 3 and Figure 6). We can conclude from these collected statistics that:

- On average, participants took 36 minutes to *create* their concept maps from the 75 supplied ideas.
- These ranged from having a *single connected* group, to 20 *distinct groups*.
- Participants used *grouping* (a collection of ideas), *narrative* (connecting ideas using a story), or *both* to communicate their visualisation to others.
- Participants that created a single connected group {P5, P13} did not feel *confidence* communicating it.
- Only half of the participants felt the need to *annotate* their concept map.
- In addition, *annotations* did not improve {P5}'s confidence to communicate their concept map.
- 12 out of 14 participants used groupings as their main *strategy* to create and communicate their maps.
- Finally, participants struggle the most with *singletons* (groups with only one idea).

| | Time (hh:mm:ss) | Number of groups | Annotations | Singletons | Communication Confidence | Style of communication | |
|---|---|---|---|---|---|---|---|
| P1 | 0:16:21 | 9 | No | 0 | Yes | Groups | |
| P2 | 0:44:05 | 17 | Yes | 1 | Yes | Groups | |
| P3 | 0:33:59 | 10 | No | 0 | Yes | Both | |
| P4 | 0:57:44 | 9 | No | 10 | Yes | Both | |
| P5 | 0:51:10 | 1 | Yes | 0 | No | None | |
| P6 | 0:26:55 | 6 | Yes | 1 | No | Both | |
| P7 | 0:27:01 | 13 | Yes | 10 | Yes | Both | |
| P8 | 0:27:56 | 20 | No | 0 | Yes | Groups | |
| P9 | 0:38:17 | 10 | No | 0 | Yes | Both | |
| P10 | 0:20:09 | 9 | Yes | 0 | Yes | Both | |
| P11 | 0:53:07 | 10 | No | 0 | Yes | Both | |
| P12 | 0:39:31 | 5 | Yes | 0 | Yes | Both | * |
| P13 | 0:10:56 | 1 | No | 0 | No | Narrative | |
| Pp | 1:04:05 | 10 | Yes | 0 | Yes | Groups | |

**Table 3. General statistics of all participants' visualisations. N.B. The starred participant created a single island, but elucidated separate groups in the post-study interview.**

In the next section we discuss the data from the post-creation semi-structured interviews and our design recommendations derived from our study.

## DISCUSSION AND DESIGN RECOMMENDATIONS

Insights were discovered after analysing the information from our semi-structured interviews. In total 28 sub-themes reoccurred in the interviews, these were organised into 4 over-arching themes as previously discussed:

1. ***Creation***: the *strategies* of how non-experts created their concept maps and the *structures* used during creation (Gestalt laws).
2. ***Interaction***: how they *interacted* with the physical elements provided, and their enjoyment of the process.
3. ***Update***: strategies used when *adding* new ideas.

4. *Communication*: how *confident* they would be communicating the visualisation and the strategies they would use to do so.

For each theme we will discuss the design implications including the sub-themes, the frequency of the sub-themes (Tables 4 to 7), and discuss various design recommendations in the form of questions and answers highlighted by borders in the text.

### Creation

First, we will discuss what techniques and common *strategies* our participants used in order to build their visualisations from the basic elements. Second, we will discuss the use of *structures* and Gestalt laws by our participants.

#### *Creation strategy*

Participants started creating their visualisations by either reading all the ideas first, or by taking the ideas one by one from the box of ideas. In either case, the next step for 12 of our participants was to create groups which contained ideas of a similar nature. e.g. *"...I have just tried to group them into like groups which kind of relate to some general theme"* {P1}. The remaining 2 participants just connected ideas together to create either a narrative only visualisation {P13} or an aesthetically packed mass of linked ideas {P5} (see Figure 6 Participant 5). E.g. *"...I sort of started connecting... things [ideas] that related, that depended on each other... And then connect to the next [idea] to the next to the next to next..."* {P12}.

From the 12 participants that created groups, all of them abstracted their groups by adding a notion of a *core idea* or unique abstracting concept for each group. Participants reported that having this 'core' allowed them to remember and communicate their groups more easily, e.g. *"P11: I tried to relate the research ideas so that the audience can easily understand [them]. So, what I did here. I wanted to group the related ideas together so that if someone reads these they could easy grasp the idea. Interviewer: So each group had a main core idea? P11: Yes, the universe here, public, and service, and here policy, here ..."* {P11}.

**What strategies do people use to create their concept maps?**

In our study it was discovered that participants were using *groups defined by a core idea, narrative*, or *both* to simplify the ideas into a more memorable number of abstract concepts (1-20). The best strategy was to use both narrative and core concepts to aid the communication of the visualisation. The participant that created a visualisation using only narrative {P13} commented that they thought they would be the only one who could understand their visualisation, while the participant with all the ideas in a single, contiguous island, rather than as separate groups, {P5} commented that they would not be confident if asked to explain or remember his visualisation. As a result, we believe narrative by itself is not enough, while abstraction into core concepts is always needed to create successful visualisations of this type.

***Design Recommendation**: Use groups and narrative to simplify abstraction and enhance the communication of your concept maps.*

Several participants (5) gave more prominence to certain hexagons, using them as *landmarks*, to aid the understanding and communication of their visualisation, e.g. *"So what I was thinking was... what people are most going to be interested in are themselves. So I put people at the centre, and then we branch off into things people are concerned about"* {P4}, *"the main purpose is the 'people' which is why I put it in the middle"* {P7}, and "*child is basically where all ideas centre around*" {P13}.

From all the participants, half of them (7) *annotated* their visualisations using the provided pens. The annotations were used to enhance their visualisation e.g. *"This (annotation) was just to make it a little bit more exciting"* {P12}, and to strengthen the groups and their core idea, e.g. *"You'll notice I've labelled them. So this is 'technology island', 'material island', 'earth island', this is 'health and patient island', that's 'art island' ..."* {P6}. Contrary to popular visualisation techniques (e.g.. spider diagrams, network diagrams, or concept maps) participants did not use annotations to link ideas, however, three participants {P2, P6, and Pp} did use annotations to create links between groups of ideas instead.

**How can I enhance the main ideas in my visualisations?**

We observed two techniques commonly used by our participants to enhance their maps. *Landmarks* and/or *annotations* aid the understanding of the core narrative, and groupings in their visualisations. This result confirms what has also been found by Gansner [21]. We believe these two techniques are currently under used and if investigated further could lead to more understandable mapping of information in concept maps.

***Design Recommendation**: Use landmarks and annotations, if possible, in your visualisations to strengthen core ideas to help people remember and communicate it at a later date.*

Most of our participants were aware that ideas next to each other were conceptually linked together. If an idea did not match their neighbours they relocated it to a different section of the group, "*the connections were much more if the tile should be touching other tiles*" {P5}. Only one participant {P7} matched all of the ideas to the core of the group, similar to card sorting, effectively creating piles of ideas represented by the one on top, their aim to simplify the communication task, "*the purpose was ... because people don't spend much time looking at things ... one concept, that would kind of summarise (the group)*" {P7}.

Only two participants {P5 and P13} thought of links between ideas expanding further than their immediate neighbours "*maybe, like... two-levels I guess*" {P5}. The rest of the participants only linked the ideas to their immediate neighbours and to the essence of the group. However, participants did discuss an implicit, transitive relationship between ideas in groups e.g. "*Yes they are related because this one [1st idea] here is related to this one [2nd idea] - what I thought is this one [3rd idea next to 2nd idea] is related to this one [1st idea]*" {P11}. Furthermore, no participant used distance to quantify connection, "*it is just the same group, being far off it, no [it makes no difference]*" {P9}.

**How aware are non-experts of long distance interactions between ideas in their visualisations?**
The similarities and connections from non-neighbouring ideas were mostly transitive and, as a result, the long distance relationships were mostly between the core concepts and not between individual ideas. In addition, our participants stated that the similarity of items beyond neighbours was non-linear. For example, none of our participants through that an item being twice as far from another item made it twice as dissimilar. We therefore suggest that non-experts might not have a notion of long-distance information or similarity. As a result, we believe that the distance similarity data created by dimensionality reductions algorithms, such as Multi-Dimensional Scaling, might be overlooked by users.

***Design Recommendation:*** *Use local similarity information in preference to long-distance similarity when designing or creating algorithms for visualisations.*

Less than half of the participants (6) were aware of the need to or did actually pack and optimise their space. Mostly the packing was concerned with joining groups together into bigger groups (11), e.g. *"Yes, I think I joined two groups together. I think this one was two groups. The first one was... the social service, for example, and then I combined it with the school.*" {P3}, or *"That is what I do and at the beginning I had many groups... I did tried to join some of the groups to minimise the category or classification"* {P11}. Even though some participants were aware of packing, almost all of the participants (12) agreed with the notion of needing empty spaces to differentiate groups, e.g. "*there was a kind of general concept of the islands being all related to each other ... But then... I think there is a need to separate this island off [with a space], because having these two connected is making it too confused*" {P5}, "*I wanted spaces so it was not a complete mass*" {P12}.

**Do we need to optimise space and efficiency in our visualisations?**
Most of our participants (12) expressed a preference for having blank spaces between groups of items and did not feel the need to pack these groups efficiently, nor keep them on the grid implied by the ideas being presented as hexagons. Most visualisation algorithms, however, are optimised to reduce spaces and use the available space efficiently. We believe new algorithms in visualisations could incorporate blank spaces as a metric.

***Design Recommendation:*** *Allow blank spaces between groups to signify breaks and groups don't necessarily need to be aligned on an underlying grid.*

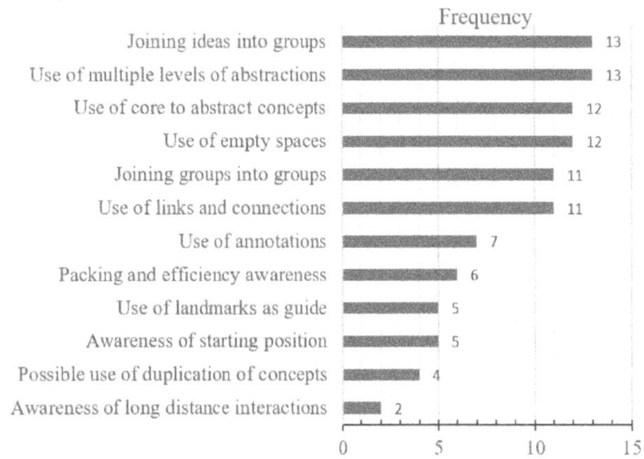


**Table 4. Creation strategy sub-themes from our interviews.**

*Creation Structures*

The creation structures results are linked to the 6 Gestalt laws (proximity, similarity, connectedness, continuity, closure, and symmetry) explained in the previous section.

Our analysis showed that almost all of our participants used proximity and similarity while creating their visualisations. Only participant {P13}, who created their visualisation based only on narrative and storytelling, did not used these two Gestalt laws, however, they were still aware of similarity by means of connection, e.g. *"It's a bunch of ideas connected"* {P13}.

Connectedness was expressed in terms of annotations, and links between ideas and groups as previously described in the creation strategies subsection. Connectedness was also expressed by participants {P6 and P12} by connecting groups using ideas that were of a higher level of abstraction or of ambiguous nature (for example *'site'*, *'technology'* or *'Africa'*). *"You could then just connect it [an idea] to anything [the rest of the group], really"* {P6}.

A few participants use continuity (5), closure (3), and symmetry (3). Most participants did not focus on these three laws, but instead concentrated on the connections and similarities of the groups, e.g. "*...the shape is dependent on the criteria we considered when grouping.*" {P11}. Even so, almost all participants (13) expressed that symmetry would probably have improved their map, e.g. "*That would be nicer. I haven't got it symmetrical at all. But yeah, I'd prefer it to be more symmetrical, that's why I'm not happy with the shape. ... some work would have to be done with the jigsaw puzzle because there were some things that could fit different ways... made it a bit more symmetrical ..., or more the shape of something particular.*" {P12}

**Should we care about Gestalt?**
The laws of *proximity (13)*, *similarity (13)*, and *connectedness* (12) were observed in the majority of our

participants' visualisations. To a lesser extent *continuity* (5), *closure* (3), *and symmetry* (3) were used by participants. Most participants thought these laws would enhance their visualisations but most of them (11) did not actually use or were unaware of them whilst creating their own visualisations.

***Design Recommendation:*** *Use proximity, similarity, and connectedness in your visualisation. In addition, use continuity, closure, and symmetry only to improve the aesthetic nature of the visualisation.*

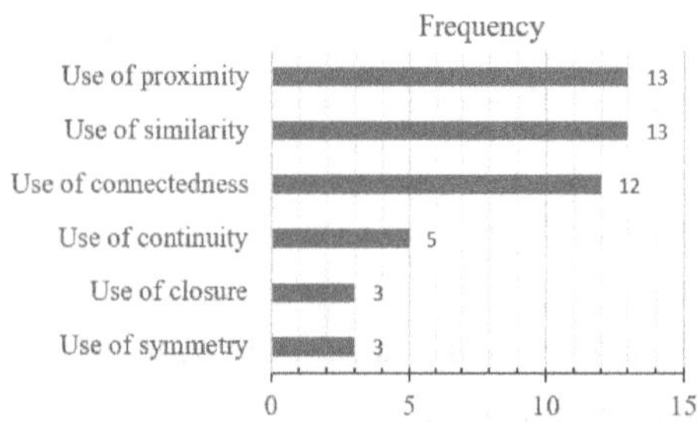


**Table 5. Creation structures sub-themes from our interviews.**

### Interaction

Participants expressed various possible interactions that could be applied to the visualisations. These include the ability to colour the core idea of a group, or colouring individual groups in different colours, e.g. "*What might have been an interesting idea is if certain ones could have been color-coded*" {P4}.

An interesting interaction from participant {P1} was to perfectly tessellate ideas with strong relationships while more loosely arranging ideas when there was not a strong link. "*All these words are quite strongly related. I was able to kind of make it [the groups] quite nicely...*" {P1}. We believe this interaction can be replicated in digital interfaces using positioning or some kind of subtle wobbling animation to indicate uncertainty.

Almost all participants enjoyed the physicality of the study. They could easy organise, pile, and think about the task in hand, e.g. "*It's easier for me to think if I can build... so what I did at the start, was I took them all out and went 'right, let's first of all just throw them into piles*" {P6}. Some participants, however, mentioned a few advantages a digital study could allow, compared to the physical study. These included easier reorganization {P4}, zoom capabilities {P2}, and cleaner placement of ideas {P8}.

**Did people enjoy the physical side of the study?**

Almost all the participants enjoyed the physicality of the task. They asserted that having the ideas as physical items allowed them to reflect longer on them, handle the ideas in ways not possible on computer screens (e.g. piling), and concentrate more on the task in hand. We believe this physicality could allow for interesting research in the areas of communication, collaborations, and the networking of people using physical and digital visualisations. These avenues of research are already being explored in some human computer interaction workshops [1]. In addition, our results and observations can also be applied to other areas, including information communication using interactive walls [12], interactive networking tools [45], and table top collaboration [62].

In addition, we believe that by freeing our participants from the various aspects of interfaces (like menus, commands, buttons or instructions), we can investigate more in-depth the natural behaviours from our participants when creating their concept maps. Furthermore, we can later apply our finding to digital interfaces.

***Design Recommendation:*** *Paper prototype your design using simple materials and discover the possible advantages to it. You can also use colours, groups, tessellations, positioning and tightness to enhance interaction in your digital designs.*

The biggest annoyance identified by all participants (14) was that some ideas were too ambiguous or at a different level of abstraction (for example *'site'* and *'technology'*) and these were difficult to place. Some participants just separated these ideas into singletons {P6} while others used these ideas as links between groups {P12}. Participant {P10} suggested an interesting solution to this ambiguity problem by adding descriptions of the idea to the back of the hexagon to disambiguate singletons: "*... there were a few that I thought they were quite general and it was not quite clear to me ... maybe if I had the whole description [on the back – the participant points]*" {P10}.

**What got in the way of creating the visualisations?**

While participants abstracted the ideas into groups we noticed that all participants found it difficult to group the ideas that they saw as ambiguous. We believe the main reason for their difficulties was that the ambiguous ideas were at *different levels of abstraction* from the other ideas in a group. For example, *health* is a more general concept than *brain, cell, DNA, fat,* or *gene,* making it difficult to link the general and more specific ideas into a single group. We believe abstraction levels can solve these problems, similar to Scheiderman's recommendations [58].

***Design Recommendation:*** *If possible, ensure that the ideas or concepts represented in your visualisation are at the same level of abstraction.*

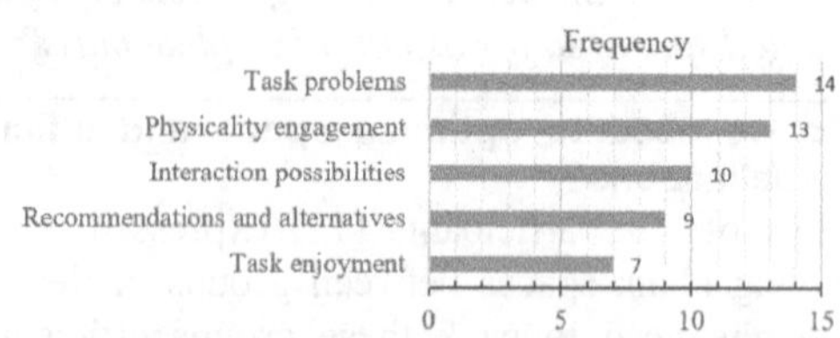


**Table 6. Interaction sub-themes from our interviews.**

### Update

On further inspection of the video recordings, along with analysis of the interviews, only three participants {P1, P3 and P13} reorganised a group when adding new ideas to their visualisations. It was apparent that once the groups and/or narrative was defined the participants were unwilling to change the fundamental structure of it by changing the number of groups.

Almost all participants just attached the new ideas to existing groups, or narrative chains, e.g. "*In general yes [I would attach them]. When they became too many or clearly they are completely different then I would create the new [group]*" {P10}, "*I'd have preferred to put them into the design I already [have]*" {P4}.

**What can we learn from non-experts updating their concept maps?**

As mentioned before participants were reluctant to update their main group structures. We assume the cognitive effort to re-abstract, re-organise and re-learn new group structures constrained participants. Instead the simplest strategy for them was to simply attach ideas to their previous groups.

***Design Recommendation:*** *When updating the main structures or groups think of the cognitive effort from users to understand, memorise and abstract your new structures.*

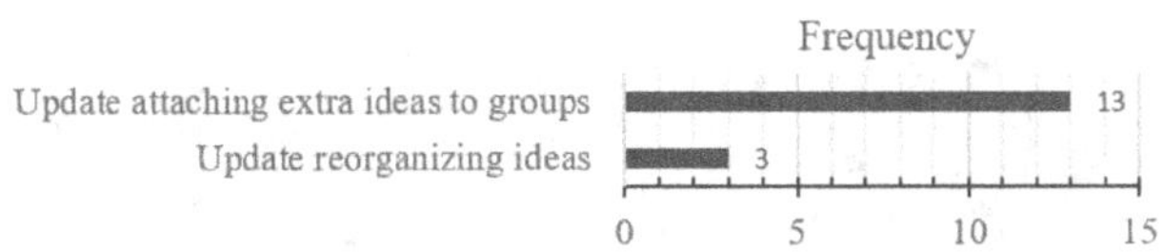


**Table 7. Update sub-themes from our interviews.**

### Communication

From our participants, 11 of them reported feeling confident enough to communicate their visualisations in terms of a general overview of core ideas, or the narrative they'd created, but not the individual ideas, e.g. "*Yes, I think I could give them an overview of the general things in [it]*" {P12}, "*yeah I think so, maybe, I don't know if I would remember these small things [ideas]. But as a general idea I think so*" {P10}.

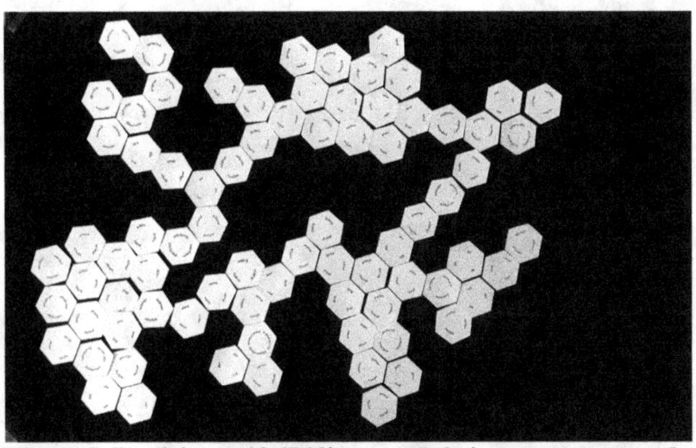

**Figure 5. Participant 13 {P13} created their concept map only using narrative. They later expressed their concern about communicating their concept map.**

Participant {P6} expressed concerns about how the many permutations of the visualisation could affect their ability to communicate it, however, they were quite pleased that their visualisation reflected their personal opinion, "*My brain was arguing with me that there were other ways of doing it... and there are very different ways of grouping these together. These ones reflect 'me'... so I'm happy in that respect, I'm happy that this reflects my opinion of them, and how they relate to each other.*" {P6}.

Participant {P5} argued they could not communicate it at all, "*I doubt it'd be very clear to the public*" {P5} while participant {P13} also expressed concern about other people understanding their visualisation, "*No, because the words are too limited to explain my ideas*" {P13}. We argue that the blocking factor for both participants is that neither of them abstracted the ideas into different groups, each containing a core idea. In the case of {P5} there is no distinction of core groups, instead they relied on a single contiguous island containing all the ideas, while in the case of {P13} they decided to create their visualisation using only narrative, therefore missing the abstraction provided by separating the ideas into thematic groups.

**How do people think about and communicate their visualisations after they've finished creating them?**

It is important to note that most participants could remember the abstractions of their groups easily, but struggled with the individual ideas. We believe *memory* plays a crucial role as people can only keep a limited amount of things in their working memory [46]. As a result, participants found it natural to abstract the 75 ideas into a smaller number of memorable concepts. We believe visualisations can benefit from this by allowing users to abstract the visualisation at different levels. For example, Google Maps [23] allows users to start from one simple concept, the Earth, and then zoom in to a more detailed level, continents, then zoom in again to another level, countries, and so on.

***Design Recommendation:*** *Allow users to customise the complexity of the visualisation, so they can see a simple overview of the ideas, memorise the main structures, and navigate into the detail if they want to.*

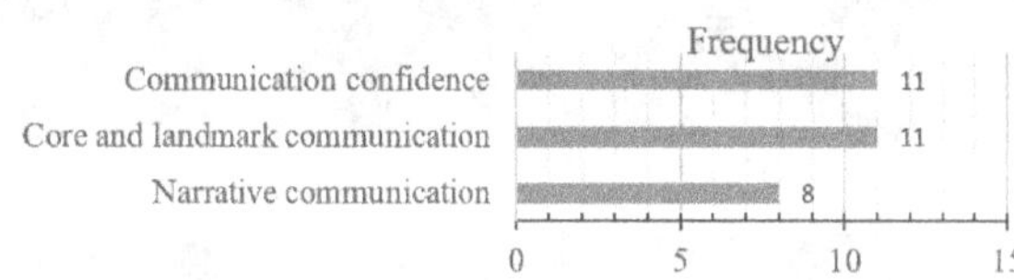


**Table 7. Communication sub-themes from our interviews.**

## CONCLUSIONS AND FUTURE WORK

In this paper we presented a comprehensive study designed to help understand how non-experts create, interact, update, and communicate information using concept maps. We asked 14 participants to organise 79 ideas into a single visual overview. Insights into the thoughts of the participants were collected by recording their actions and by analysing post-study, semi-structured interviews.

By analysing their actions and responses, we deconstructed the process into 28 sub-themes, to understand how they organised separate ideas into cohesive concept maps. These sub-themes are explained in detailed in our *Results* and *Discussion* section. In addition, we defined 9 design recommendations distilled from our results, which we hope will inspire future algorithms that automatically create usable concept maps better suited to the natural behaviours and needs of users.

The main implications from our study is that non-experts appreciate narrative, landmarks, abstraction, blank space, and groups of items related to a core concept, instead of algorithmic optimisation and space efficiency. Furthermore, we think our study can be extended by future work which explores wider issues including communication confidence metrics, scale, training, strategies, and additional applications of our recommendations. Finally, we believe that understanding and researching the needs and behaviours of non-experts will improve the way we design and implement visualisations like concept maps.

## ADDITIONAL MATERIALS

Data, including high resolution images, animations, transcriptions and interview coding available here: dx.doi.org/10.6084/m9.figshare.c.3658130.

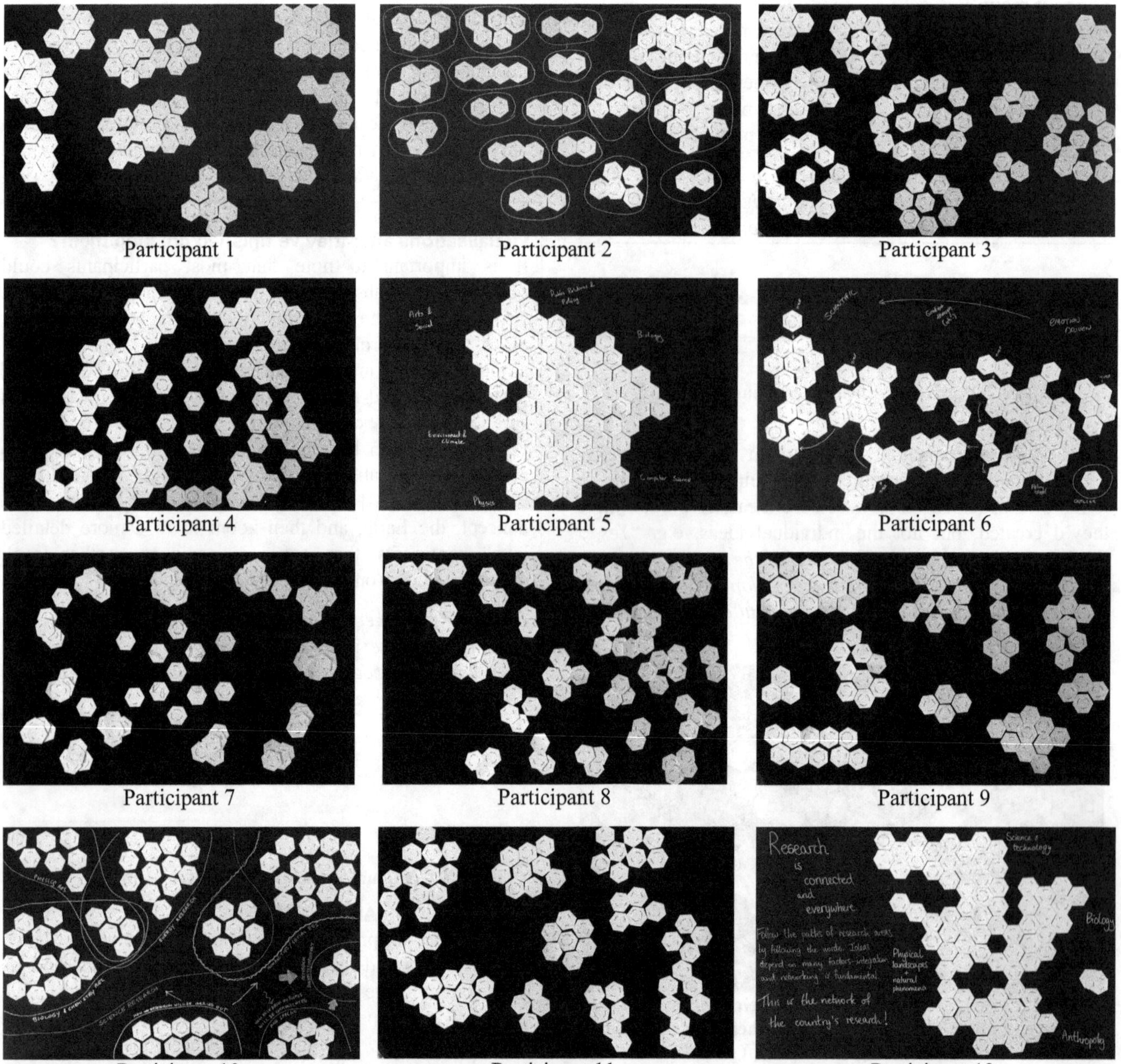


**Figure 6. The visualisations created by our participants for the study. Participant 13 and pilot results are shown in figure 1 and 5 respectively. High resolution images and animated GIFs available from our public research repository (dx.doi.org/10.6084/m9.figshare.c.3658130).**

## REFERENCES


1. Jason Alexander, Yvonne Jansen, Kasper Hornbæk, Johan Kildal, and Abhijit Karnik. 2015. Exploring the Challenges of Making Data Physical. In *Proceedings of the 33rd Annual ACM Conference Extended Abstracts on Human Factors in Computing Systems (CHI EA '15).* ACM, New York, NY, USA, 2417-2420. http://doi.acm.org/10.1145/2702613.2702659
2. Robert Amar, James Eagan, and John Stasko. 2005. Low-Level Components of Analytic Activity in Information Visualization. In *Proceedings of the 2005 IEEE Symposium on Information Visualization (INFOVIS '05).* IEEE Computer Society, Washington, DC, USA, 15.
3. Christopher Andrews, and Chris North. 2012. Analyst's Workspace: An embodied sensemaking environment for large, high-resolution displays. In *Visual analytics science and technology (vast), 2012 ieee conference on*, pp. 123-131. IEEE.
4. Juhee Bae and Benjamin Watson. 2014. Towards a Better Understanding and Application of the Principles of Visual Communication. In *Handbook of Human Centric Visualization*, 179-201. Springer New York.
5. Mercedes B. Ben-Av and Dov Sagi. 1995. Perceptual grouping by similarity and proximity: Experimental results can be predicted by intensity autocorrelations. *Vision research* 35, no. 6: 853-866.
6. Alex Bigelow, Steven Drucker, Danyel Fisher, and Miriah Meyer. 2014. Reflections on how designers design with data. In *Proceedings of the 2014 International Working Conference on Advanced Visual Interfaces (AVI '14).* ACM, New York, NY, USA, 17-24. http://doi.acm.org/10.1145/2598153.2598175
7. Stuart K. Card, Jock D. Mackinlay, and Ben Shneiderman (Eds.). 1999. *Readings in Information Visualization: Using Vision to Think.* Morgan Kaufmann Publishers Inc., San Francisco, CA, USA.
8. Marianne Sheelagh Therese Carpendale. 1999. A Framework for Elastic Presentation Space. Ph.D. Dissertation. Simon Fraser University, Burnaby, BC, Canada, Canada. AAINQ51848.
9. Ed Huai-hsin Chi and John Riedl. 1998. An Operator Interaction Framework for Visualization Systems. In *Proceedings of the 1998 IEEE Symposium on Information Visualization (INFOVIS '98).* IEEE Computer Society, Washington, DC, USA, 63-70.
10. Lydia B. Chilton, Juho Kim, Paul André, Felicia Cordeiro, James A. Landay, Daniel S. Weld, Steven P. Dow, Robert C. Miller, and Haoqi Zhang. 2014. Frenzy: collaborative data organization for creating conference sessions. *In Proceedings of the 32nd annual ACM conference on Human factors in computing systems (CHI '14).* ACM, New York, NY, USA, 1255-1264. DOI=10.1145/2556288.2557375 http://doi.acm.org/10.1145/2556288.2557375.
11. Juliet Corbin and Anselm Strauss. 2014. *Basics of qualitative research: Techniques and procedures for developing grounded theory.* Sage publications.
12. Kelly L. Dempski and Brandon L. Harvey. 2005. Touchable interactive walls: opportunities and challenges. In *Proceedings of the 4th international conference on Entertainment Computing (ICEC'05).* Springer-Verlag, Berlin, Heidelberg, 192-202. http://dx.doi.org/10.1007/11558651_19
13. Stephen G. Eick. 2000. Visualizing multi-dimensional data. *ACM SIGGRAPH computer graphics* 34, no. 1: 61-67.
14. Micheline Elias and Anastasia Bezerianos. 2011. Exploration views: understanding dashboard creation and customization for visualization novices. In *Proceedings of the 13th IFIP TC 13 international conference on Human-computer interaction - Volume Part IV (INTERACT'11),* Vol. Part IV. Springer-Verlag, Berlin, Heidelberg, 274-291.
15. Niklas Elmqvist and Ji Soo Yi. 2012. Patterns for visualization evaluation. In *Proceedings of the 2012 BELIV Workshop: Beyond Time and Errors - Novel Evaluation Methods for Visualization (BELIV '12).* ACM, New York, NY, USA, Article 12, 8 pages. http://doi.acm.org/10.1145/2442576.2442588
16. Michele Emmer. 2005. *The visual mind II.* MIT press.
17. EPSRC Working together theme. Retrieved on 23 of September 2015 from https://www.epsrc.ac.uk/research/ourportfolio/themes/ict/introduction/workingtogether/
18. Anders K. Ericsson, and Simon A. Herbert. 1980. Verbal reports as data. *Psychological review* 87, no. 3:215.
19. The European Union Framework Programme for Research and Innovation. Retrieved 23 of September 2015 from http://ec.europa.eu/programmes/horizon2020/
20. Haakon Faste and Honray Lin. 2012. The untapped promise of digital mind maps. In *Proceedings of the SIGCHI Conference on Human Factors in Computing Systems (CHI '12).* ACM, New York, NY, USA, 1017-1026. http://doi.acm.org/10.1145/2207676.2208548
21. Emden R. Gansner, Yifan Hu, and Stephen G. Kobourov. 2014. Viewing Abstract Data as Maps. In *Handbook of Human Centric Visualization*, pp. 63-89. Springer New York.
22. Jens Gerken, Hans-Christian Jetter, and Harald Reiterer. 2010. Using concept maps to evaluate the usability of APIs. In *CHI '10 Extended Abstracts on Human Factors in Computing Systems (CHI EA '10).* ACM, New York, NY, USA, 3937-3942.

23. Google Maps API. Retrieved 25th of September 2015 from https://developers.google.com/maps

24. David Gotz and Michelle X. Zhou. 2009. Characterizing users' visual analytic activity for insight provenance. *Information Visualization* 8, no. 1: 42-55.

25. Scott R. Grabinger. 1993. Computer screen designs: Viewer judgments. *Educational Technology Research and Development* 41, no. 2: 35-73.

26. Lars Grammel, Melanie Tory, and Margaret-Anne Storey. 2010. How Information Visualization Novices Construct Visualizations. *IEEE Transactions on Visualization and Computer Graphics* 16, 6 (November 2010), 943-952.

27. Shihui Han, Glyn W. Humphreys, and Lin Chen. "Uniform connectedness and classical Gestalt principles of perceptual grouping." *Perception & psychophysics* 61, no. 4 (1999): 661-674.

28. Jeffrey Heer, Frank Ham, Sheelagh Carpendale, Chris Weaver, and Petra Isenberg. 2008. Creation and Collaboration: Engaging New Audiences for Information Visualization. In *Information Visualization*, Lecture Notes In Computer Science, Vol. 4950. Springer-Verlag, Berlin, Heidelberg 92-133.

29. Catherine B. Hurley. 2004. Clustering visualizations of multidimensional data. *Journal of Computational and Graphical Statistics* 13, no. 4.

30. Samuel Huron, Sheelagh Carpendale, Alice Thudt, Anthony Tang, and Michael Mauerer. 2014. Constructive visualization. In *Proceedings of the 2014 conference on Designing interactive systems (DIS '14).* ACM, New York, NY, USA, 433-442. http://doi.acm.org/10.1145/2598510.2598566

31. Samuel Huron, Yvonne Jansen, and Sheelagh Carpendale. 2014. Constructing visual representations: Investigating the use of tangible tokens. *Visualization and Computer Graphics*, IEEE Transactions on 20, no. 12: 2102-2111.

32. Yvonne Jansen and Pierre Dragicevic. 2013. An interaction model for visualizations beyond the desktop. *Visualization and Computer Graphics*, IEEE Transactions on 19, no. 12: 2396-2405

33. Yvonne Jansen, Pierre Dragicevic, Petra Isenberg, Jason Alexander, Abhijit Karnik, Johan Kildal, Sriram Subramanian, and Kasper Hornbæk. 2015. Opportunities and Challenges for Data Physicalization. In *Proceedings of the 33rd Annual ACM Conference on Human Factors in Computing Systems (CHI '15).* ACM, New York, NY, USA, 3227-3236.

34. Chris Johnson, Robert Moorhead, Tamara Munzner, Hanspeter Pfister, Penny Rheingans, and Terry S. Yoo. 2006. NIH/NSF visualization research challenges report. In *Los Alamitos*, Ca: IEEE Computing Society.

35. Andrew Kachites McCallum. 2002. *Mallet: A machine learning for language toolkit.*

36. Samuel Kaski. 1997. Data exploration using self-organizing maps. In *Acta polytechnica scandinavica: mathematics, computing and management in engineering series.* no. 82.

37. Alfred Kobsa. 2001. An Empirical Comparison of Three Commercial Information Visualization Systems. In *Proceedings of the IEEE Symposium on Information Visualization 2001 (INFOVIS'01).* IEEE Computer Society, Washington, DC, USA, 123.

38. Kurt Koffka. 2013. *Principles of Gestalt psychology.* Vol. 44. Routledge.

39. Christopher Kurtz. 2011. Code Gestalt: a software visualization tool for human beings. In *CHI '11 Extended Abstracts on Human Factors in Computing Systems (CHI EA '11).* ACM, New York, NY, USA, 929-934. http://doi.acm.org/10.1145/1979742.1979518

40. Heidi Lam, Enrico Bertini, Petra Isenberg, Catherine Plaisant, and Sheelagh Carpendale. 2012. Empirical studies in information visualization: Seven scenarios. *Visualization and Computer Graphics*, IEEE Transactions on 18, no. 9: 1520-1536.

41. Mathieu Le Goc, Pierre Dragicevic, Samuel Huron, and Jean-Daniel Fekete. 2015. Design Considerations for Composite Physical Visualizations. In *Proceedings of the CHI Workshop on Exploring the Challenges of Making Data Physical.*

42. David Chek Ling Ngo, Lian Seng Teo, and John G. Byrne. 2002. Evaluating interface esthetics. *Knowledge and Information Systems* 4, no. 1: 46-79.

43. Kimberly M. Markham, Joel J. Mintzes, and M. Gail Jones. 1994. The concept map as a research and evaluation tool: Further evidence of validity. *Journal of research in science teaching* 31, no. 1: 91-101.

44. Thomas Methven, Stefano Padilla, David W. Corne, Mike J. Chantler. Research Strategy Generation: Avoiding Academic 'Animal Farm'. 2014. Proceedings of the companion publication of the 17th ACM conference on Computer supported cooperative work & social computing. ACM. http://dx.doi.org/10.1145/2556420.2556785

45. Thomas S. Methven, Stefano Padilla, and Mike J. Chantler. 2015. I Don't Think We've Met: Encouraging Collaboration via Topic-Based Search. In *Proceedings of the 18th ACM Conference Companion on Computer Supported Cooperative Work & Social Computing (CSCW'15 Companion).* ACM, New York, NY, USA, http://doi.acm.org/10.1145/2685553.2702678

46. George A. Miller. 1956. The magical number seven, plus or minus two: some limits on our capacity for processing information. *Psychological review* 63, no. 2: 81

47. Lisa J. Miller, Rich Gazan, and Susanne Still. 2014. Unsupervised classification and visualization of unstructured text for the support of interdisciplinary collaboration. In *Proceedings of the 17th ACM conference on Computer supported cooperative work & social computing (CSCW '14)*. ACM, New York, NY, USA, 1033-1042.
48. Jakob Nielsen. 1995. Card sorting to discover the users' model of the information space. *Obtained from: http://www.useit.com/papers/sun/cardsort*
49. Joseph D. Novak, and Alberto J. Cañas. 2006. The theory underlying concept maps and how to construct them. *Florida Institute for Human and Machine Cognition* 1: 2006-2001.
50. Theresa A. O'Connell, and Yee-Yin Choong. 2008. Metrics for measuring human interaction with interactive visualizations for information analysis. In *Proceedings of the SIGCHI Conference on Human Factors in Computing Systems (CHI '08)*. ACM, New York, NY, USA, 1493-1496.
51. Stefano Padilla, Thomas S. Methven, David W. Corne, and Mike J. Chantler. 2014. Hot topics in CHI: trend maps for visualising research. In *CHI '14 Extended Abstracts on Human Factors in Computing Systems (CHI EA '14)*. ACM, New York, NY, USA, 815-824. http://doi.acm.org/10.1145/2559206.2578867
52. Stefano Padilla, Thomas S. Methven, David A. Robb, Mike J. Chantler. 2015. What to Study in HCI? A Reflection Based on CHI and UK Research Data. In *Proceedings of the CHI workshop What to Study in HCI?,* Seoul, Korea. http://dx.doi.org/10.13140/RG.2.1.5169.2969
53. Stephen E. Palmer. 1992. Common region: A new principle of perceptual grouping. *Cognitive psychology* 24, no. 3: 436-447.
54. Ronald M. Pickett and Georges G. Grinstein. 1988. Iconographic displays for visualizing multidimensional data. In *Proceedings of the 1988 IEEE Conference on Systems, Man, and Cybernetics*, vol. 514, p. 519.
55. Zachary Pousman, John T. Stasko, and Michael Mateas. 2007. Casual information visualization: Depictions of data in everyday life. *Visualization and Computer Graphics,* IEEE Transactions on 13, no. 6: 1145-1152.
56. Research Councils UK, Gateway to Research API. Retrieved on 23 of September 2015from http://gtr.rcuk.ac.uk/resources/api.html
57. Maria Araceli Ruiz-Primo, and Richard J. Shavelson. 1996. Problems and issues in the use of concept maps in science assessment. *Journal of research in science teaching 33*, no. 6: 569-600.
58. Ben Shneiderman. 1996. The Eyes Have It: A Task by Data Type Taxonomy for Information Visualizations. In *Proceedings of the 1996 IEEE Symposium on Visual Languages (VL '96)*. IEEE Computer Society, Washington, DC, USA, 336.
59. Judith E. Sims-Knight, Richard L. Upchurch, Nixon Pendergrass, Tesfay Meressi, Paul Fortier, Plamen Tchimev, Rebecca VonderHeide, and Madeleine Page. 2004. Using concept maps to assess design process knowledge. In *Frontiers in Education, 2004. FIE 2004. 34th Annual*, pp. F1G-6. IEEE.
60. Nancy Staggers and Michelle R. Troseth. 2011. Usability and clinical application design. *Nursing Informatics*. Springer London, 2011.
61. Faisal Taher, John Hardy, Abhijit Karnik, Christian Weichel, Yvonne Jansen, Kasper Hornbæk, and Jason Alexander. 2015. Exploring Interactions with Physically Dynamic Bar Charts. In *33rd Annual ACM Conference on Human Factors in Computing Systems (CHI '15)*. ACM, New York, NY, USA, 3237-3246. http://doi.acm.org/10.1145/2702123.2702604
62. John C. Tang. 1991. Findings from observational studies of collaborative work. Int. J. Man-Mach. Stud. 34, 2 (February 1991), 143-160. http://dx.doi.org/10.1016/0020-7373(91)90039-A
63. Melanie Tory. 2014. User studies in visualization: A reflection on methods. In *Handbook of Human Centric Visualization*, pp. 411-426. Springer New York.
64. Thomas S Tullis. 1988. A system for evaluating screen formats: Research and application. *Advances in human-computer interaction* 2: 214-286.
65. Barbara Tversky. 2011. Visualizing thought. *Topics in Cognitive Science* 3, no. 3: 499-535.
66. Colin Ware. 2012. *Information visualization: perception for design*. 3rd Edition, 978-0123814647, Elsevier.
67. Tom Wengraf. 2001. *Qualitative research interviewing*. London: Sage.
68. Max Wertheimer and Kurt Riezler. 1944. Gestalt theory. *Social Research* (1944): 78-99.
69. Ji Soo Yi, Youn-ah Kang, John T. Stasko, and Julie A. Jacko. 2008. Understanding and characterizing insights: how do people gain insights using information visualization?. In *Proceedings of the 2008 Workshop on BEyond time and errors: novel evaLuation methods for Information Visualization (BELIV '08)*. ACM, New York, NY, USA, Article 4, 6 pages. http://doi.acm.org/10.1145/1377966.1377971
70. Jian Zhao, Zhicheng Liu, Mira Dontcheva, Aaron Hertzmann, and Alan Wilson. 2015. MatrixWave: Visual Comparison of Event Sequence Data. In *Proceedings of the 33rd Annual ACM Conference on Human Factors in Computing Systems (CHI '15)*. ACM, New York, NY, USA, 259-268.

# Increasing Users' Confidence in Uncertain Data by Aggregating Data from Multiple Sources

**Miriam Greis, Emre Avci, Albrecht Schmidt, Tonja Machulla**
VIS, University of Stuttgart, Germany
{firstname.lastname}@vis.uni-stuttgart.de

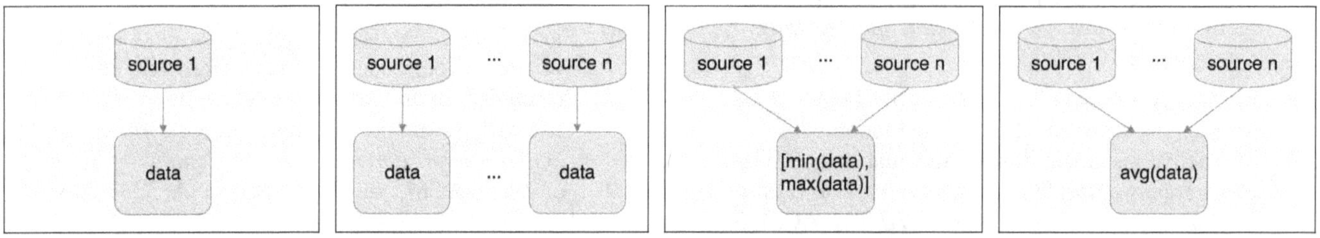


(a) Single source (b) Direct comparison (c) Range aggregation (d) Average aggregation

**Figure 1. Many interactive systems, for example weather applications, show uncertain data from a single source (see a). To encourage the design of interactive applications that show uncertain data from multiple sources, we identified three aggregation mechanisms. The direct comparison allows users to look at data from multiple sources at the same time introducing mental workload to aggregate the data. The range and average aggregation provide computationally aggregated data which reduces the mental workload for the user.**

## ABSTRACT
We often base our decisions on uncertain data - for instance, when consulting the weather forecast before deciding what to wear. Due to their uncertainty, such forecasts can differ by provider. To make an informed decision, many people compare several forecasts, which is a time-consuming and cumbersome task. To facilitate comparison, we identified three aggregation mechanisms for forecasts: manual comparison and two mechanisms of computational aggregation. In a survey, we compared the mechanisms using different representations. We then developed a weather application to evaluate the most promising candidates in a real-world study. Our results show that aggregation increases users' confidence in uncertain data, independent of the type of representation. Further, we find that for daily events, users prefer to use computationally aggregated forecasts. However, for high-stakes events, they prefer manual comparison. We discuss how our findings inform the design of improved interfaces for comparison of uncertain data, including non-weather purposes.

## ACM Classification Keywords
H.5.2 Information Interfaces and Presentation (e.g. HCI): User Interfaces


ACM 978-1-4503-4655-9/17/05...$15.00.
DOI: http://dx.doi.org/10.1145/3025453.3025998

## Author Keywords
Uncertainty; Aggregation; Multiple Sources; Comparison; Weather Forecast

## INTRODUCTION
People have to deal with uncertain data in their everyday lives and understanding it correctly can be crucial. For example, the misinterpretation of a long-term forecast of a financial market trend can lead to negative consequences for the individual. Most of the time, people however use short-term predictions such as arrival time or calorie expenditure predictions. The most prominent examples for such a short-term prediction are weather forecasts. Here, people are usually aware of the uncertainty in the prediction [22] and take it into account (e.g., by bringing an umbrella even though the chance for rain may be low).

For many forecasts, users can choose between different providers. The information between providers may differ as they use different models as basis for their forecasts. In informal interviews in the context of a former study, we found that a large percentage of people compare forecasts from different providers since they do not have sufficient trust in a single source. For example, people will consult several weather forecast providers before going on a hike in the mountains as the weather can change quickly and facing a thunderstorm in the mountains can have deadly consequences. However, the comparison of multiple sources of information can be tedious and cumbersome. For example, many people reported that they open several tabs, each for one weather website, and then manually switched between them while trying to remember what values the other forecasts showed. This approach requires mental effort. High-level services that combine multiple forecasts from different sources could support comparison. The demand for such services for easy comparison is clearly given as some applications[1] supporting weather forecast comparison recently entered the market. What is still missing, is a theoretical underpinning of how to design for easy comparison of weather forecasts, and for uncertain data in general.

The main goal of our work is to understand how services that aggregate and display multiple forecasts should be designed to be most useful for users and increase their confidence in the uncertain data depicted. Therefore we compare three aggregation mechanisms: two mechanisms that computationally aggregate the data (see Figure 1c and Figure 1d) and one mechanism that supports manual comparison (i.e., the user can directly compare the data from separate sources without having to switch between applications or websites; see Figure 1b). Computational and manual aggregation are likely to differ with regards to the amount of mental workload they induce and the amount of perceived control, as in one case the computer aggregates the data for the users and in the other the users have to aggregate the data on their own.

In a first step, we evaluated the aggregation mechanisms using an online survey. We used three different visual and one textual representation as well as three scenarios to understand whether and how they influence the preference for one aggregation method over another. We then conducted a real-world study using a custom Android application that supports manual and computational comparison.

Our three contributions aligned to the goals of our research are as follows:

1. We present **aggregation mechanisms for uncertain data from multiple sources** spanning the range from automatic to manual aggregation.
2. We show that the **aggregation of multiple sources is preferred to single source forecasts**, independent of the type of representation. However, the preference depends on the importance of the scenario, for which the weather forecast is consulted. Additionally, we show that **people place higher confidence in aggregated forecasts**.
3. We provide **implications for the development of applications that support comparison**.

Our results demonstrate that designing for comparison increases users' confidence in uncertain data. We specifically recommend to use direct comparison when the potential negative consequences associated with an uncertain event are essential for a user and to introduce computational aggregation when the negative consequences are rather negligable.

## BACKGROUND & RELATED WORK

As basis for our work, we build on previous work on uncertainty of different fields including psychology, HCI, visualization, and meteorology.

[1]Climendo: `http://climendo.com/`, WeatherXM: `http://weatherxm.exm.gr/`

### Definitions of Uncertainty

Most work on uncertainty is domain-specific, which leads to manifold definitions and references of the term uncertainty. Because each domain focuses on their research independently, the term 'uncertainty' is used inconsistently [21]. This leads to specialized typologies, for example for geospatial information [37] that only work in the context of one domain. One of the earliest classifications for visualizations of uncertain data focuses on the data type and the visualization extent [27]. Potter et al. [29] recently proposed another taxonomy focusing on to-date visualization approaches for uncertain data that takes into account the data dimension and the data uncertainty dimension. Broader classifications focus on the level of the data [34] or the sources of uncertainty [29]. In our work, we focus on implicit uncertainty induced from using multiple sources rather than on statistical uncertainty. Each source of uncertain data may include statistical uncertainty, however, it is often not communicated by providers.

### Uncertainty in Psychology and HCI

A multitude of psychological studies show that humans struggle with probabilistic information. When they judge uncertain information, humans are prone to biases and heuristics [38]. Humans also have difficulties to integrate information to make binary decisions [14]. These findings are particularly important for the field of risk perception to understand how to communicate, for example, information about a hazard [35].

In HCI, there has been a recent increase in the interest in uncertainty visualization and communication, such as in the case of the exploration of personal genomics data [32], data analysis [8], machine learning [17, 41], bus arrival predictions [15], or range anxiety in electric cars [13]. Kay et al. [16] reported that missing uncertainty information decreased trust for body weight measurements. In all of these application areas in HCI it is possible to use aggregated forecasts if multiple predictions from different sources are available and they may therefore benefit from our findings.

### Visualization of Uncertainty

A large number of previous publications have focused on the visualization of uncertain data. Glyphs [27, 42] are for example heavily studied for visualizing uncertainty for experts. Other visualization methods such as line graphs [36], box plots [28], or bar charts [3] have been studied as well. Other research focuses on a specific type of uncertainty and compares different approaches, e.g., for bounded uncertainty [26]. For laymen, either quantitative or qualitative approaches can be used to communicate uncertain data. Both approaches have considerable drawbacks. On one hand, understanding quantitative information can be difficult as studies showed that even well-educated adults have difficulties in solving easy probability questions [20]. On the other hand, qualitative information can be misleading due to different perceptions of terms such as "low risk" or "low uncertainty" [39].

In spite of this wealth of findings regarding uncertainty visualization, there are no clear guidelines for which visualizations to use in which context. One more main challenge in uncertainty visualization is the quantification of the uncertainty.

The uncertainty has to be captured and modeled accurately to ensure correctness of the data displayed in the visualization [1]. As quantification of uncertainty is difficult, comparing outcomes from different models (in our case different providers) can be used to implicitly get information about the uncertainty of the models.

### Uncertainty in Weather Forecasts

Already several years ago, the National Research Council [5, 6] and the American Meteorological Society [4] highlighted the importance and value of communicating uncertainty to the public. This has raised an interest in research in uncertainty communication [2, 7]. In a nationwide survey in the US, Morss et al. [22] found that 96% of the participants use weather forecasts more than three times per day. People are also aware that weather forecasts are uncertain [11, 19, 22, 23]. Multiple studies conducted by researchers in the field of meteorology and psychology showed that people prefer forecasts with uncertain information to deterministic ones [22] and additionally make better decisions [10, 24, 30, 31].

Adding uncertainty increases perceived transparency and reliability, probably by increasing the trust in a forecast [12, 30]. Joslyn et al. [12] also found that showing explicit hints regarding how to make a decision did not help people. Mostly, they wanted to do a self-informed decision and did not have confidence in the forecast of the system. Siegrist [33] describes the concept of general confidence in risk perception as the feeling that everything is under control and that uncertainty is low, which is what should be achieved by systems communicating uncertain data.

Although much research exists regarding how to communicate and visualize uncertainty in the weather domain, current forecasts seldom communicate uncertainty beyond the probability of precipitation. This is mainly the case because there is still the perception that the general public does not understand probabilities [18, 25]. Additionally, quantification of the uncertainty is not a trivial task. One interesting approach has been developed by Frick et al. [9] who presented the predictions of different models in an ensemble flood warning system. Here, participants preferred more detailed information after using the system for a while to make an informed decision on their own. We see a connection to people looking at multiple weather forecasts and comparing them. As different forecast providers use different weather models and data, the easy comparison of these forecasts could support people in their feeling of making a more informed decision.

## DESIGN RATIONALE FOR AGGREGATION MECHANISMS

Supporting the comparison of forecasts can be achieved in two ways. First, manual comparison of forecasts could be supported by reducing the mental workload and the tedious switching between providers. Second, the data could be aggregated by the computer to decrease the mental challenge even further. However, this second approach may result in a feeling of loosing control as people do not necessarily follow given advice and decision aids [12]. To compare a wide range of possible mechanisms, we use the direct comparison as a mechanism that still requires a high mental workload

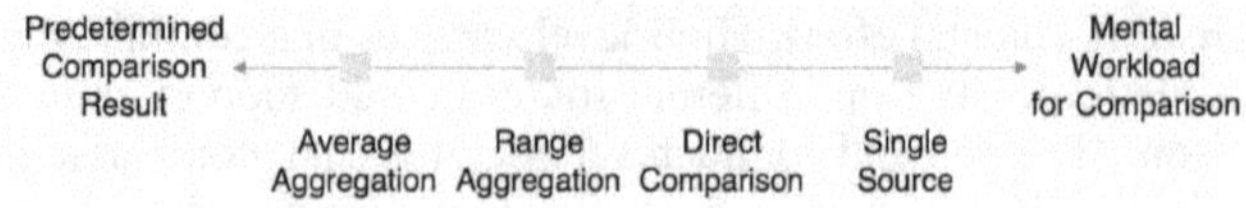


**Figure 2. The Aggregation Mechanisms differ on the amount of mental workload needed for comparison by presenting less predetermined comparison results (from left to right).**

from users as they have to aggregate the data on their own. This is in contrast to the average aggregation where the comparison is completely pre-defined. The range aggregation is in-between these two mechanisms as it computationally aggregates data, but still allows for users' own judgment (see Figure 2).

We describe the mechanisms in more detailed in the following sections and also include the a baseline "Single Source". To identify the ideal number of sources that people normally compare, we conducted a short informal survey with six participants where five out of six participants stated that three sources are the optimal number, and one participant stated that two sources would be optimal. Therefore, we decided to use three sources in all our design considerations and sketches.

### Single Source

A single source forecast (see Figure 1a) is how many current weather forecasts are displayed – i.e., the weather forecast shows the weather data of one source. We mainly use this as a baseline for comparing the other aggregation mechanisms against the current state of weather applications. The single source induces the highest mental workload in the user when comparing different forecasts as the user has to open different sources and potentially remember them if they cannot be shown next to each other (for example due to small screen size on a mobile phone).

### Direct Comparison

Direct or manual comparison (see Figure 1b) is similar to having several single source forecasts in one system such that they can be perceived in one glance (similar to the approach used by Frick et al. [9]). This reduces the mental workload on comparison as values can be compared directly without remembering them. It also reduces the time and effort of finding multiple sources, but the comparison and interpretation of the data itself still needs to be done "manually" by the user. The effectiveness of this aggregation mechanism also depends highly on the number of sources for information and screen constraints. On a small screen of a mobile phone for example, only a few sources can be shown next to each other without scrolling.

### Range Aggregation

The range aggregation (see Figure 1c) is a computational aggregation mechanism that still enables users to make some comparison on their own. A range representation was already suggested by Morss et al. [23] for showing weather forecast uncertainty. In contrast to their visualization, our aggregation mechanism does not take the values from the same weather source but shows the minimum and maximum values from across multiple sources of information. This gives the user the possibility to judge by how much sources vary without having to compare all values manually. On the downside, having one source with an extreme erroneous value would affect the outcome of this aggregation mechanism significantly.

### Average Aggregation

The average aggregation mechanism (see Figure 1d) is identical to the information provided by the single source mechanism, except that the values are averages across multiple sources. It reduces multiple values into a single, easy to interpret value. The mechanism therefore keeps the simplicity of a single source forecast, but at the same time contains information from multiple sources. In our case, the average is computed by equally weighting the sources, but it could also be computed as a weighted average based on the accuracy or on the uncertainty spans of the forecast providers, if available. When an average is used, this has to be communicated very clearly to users as it may otherwise be interpreted as a single forecast, as these two mechanism are indistinguishable without additional information. Although average aggregation is simple, users do not have the possibility to make an informed decision on their own as the data is aggregated into a single value, which may give them a feeling of loosing control.

## RESEARCH QUESTIONS

Our main goal is to understand the influence of aggregated forecasts on people. We broke this goal down into five concrete research questions (RQ1 to RQ5), each with one associated hypothesis regarding what we expect to find.

*RQ1: Does the aggregation of multiple forecasts change the users' confidence in uncertain data?* We assume that aggregation increases users' confidence in uncertain data. Especially for weather forecasts, where model uncertainty is seldom presented to the public, users are able to get a better understanding for their uncertainty by comparing them. This leads to *H1: People are more confident regarding aggregated forecasts than single source forecasts.*

*RQ2: Do people prefer aggregated forecasts to single source forecasts?* We assume that people generally prefer forecasts with aggregation as aggregation adds more information and lets them do a more informed decision. Also weather applications that recently entered the market support aggregation. This leads to *H2: People prefer aggregated forecasts to single source forecasts.*

*RQ3: Do people prefer different aggregation mechanisms (manual vs. computational aggregation) according to the importance of a scenario?* Aggregation mechanisms can provide a different amount of data. Either the computer can aggregate the data in a meaningful way or the computer can help the user to aggregate the data in a meaningful way. The latter induces a higher mental workload. We assume that whether users prefer full computational aggregation or rather would like to aggregate the data themselves depends on the importance of a scenario and on context. This leads to *H3: People prefer manual aggregation for important events because this gives them a feeling of control.*

*RQ4: Do people prefer different aggregation mechanisms depending on the type of visual or textual representation?* Aggregated forecasts can be shown with a multitude of visual and textual representations. These representations may have certain criteria which make them more suitable for a specific aggregation mechanism. This leads to *H4: People prefer different aggregation mechanisms depending on the type of visual or textual representation.*

*RQ5: Can the theoretical findings be transferred to real world application usage?* We want to transfer the theoretical finding to a real world application to better understand whether our hypotheses do also apply in real world usage.

## EXPERIMENT 1: ONLINE SURVEY

We evaluated the three aggregation mechanisms and the single source baseline by conducting an online survey.

### Design

We used a 4 x 4 x 3 within-subject design with three independent variables: *Aggregation mechanism* (with the four levels single source, direct comparison, range, average), *representation* (with the four levels text, pictogram, bar, line), and *scenario* (with the three levels daily dress code, outdoor BBQ party, outdoor wedding). For each combination of aggregation mechanism and representation, we measured participants' general confidence and their preference regarding all scenarios using a 7-point Likert item.

We decided to focus on the three most reported weather properties: temperature, chance of rain, and rain amount.

#### *Representations*

Since weather providers use different representations for weather forecasts, we included multiple representations in our survey. To identify suitable representations, we looked at existing weather applications, which mainly use pictograms with numbers or line graphs. We additionally introduced bar graphs and a textual representation to cover a span of different representations. Although the uncertainty in our study is not stochastic, but instead stems from the divergence of information from different sources, we treat it as model uncertainty. For the bar charts and line charts we use the ambiguation methods developed by Olston et al. [26] to show a range aggregation.

All representations show the following information: the location of the weather station, a pictogram of the current weather (e.g., a sun for sunshine) and numeric values for the weather properties temperature (current temperature as well as predicted daily minimum and maximum), chance of rain, and amount of rain. The pictogram representation (see Figure 3a) is dominated by a large pictogram of the current weather (e.g., a sun or a cloud). Other weather properties are presented numerically. The bar representation (see Figure 3b) shows (partially) filled bars with adjacent numeric values. The line representation (see Figure 3c) shows a line chart for each of the weather properties and a line to indicate the current hour of the day. The text representation (see Figure 3d) reports the weather verbally, with the numeric values for different weather properties emphasized by using colored font.

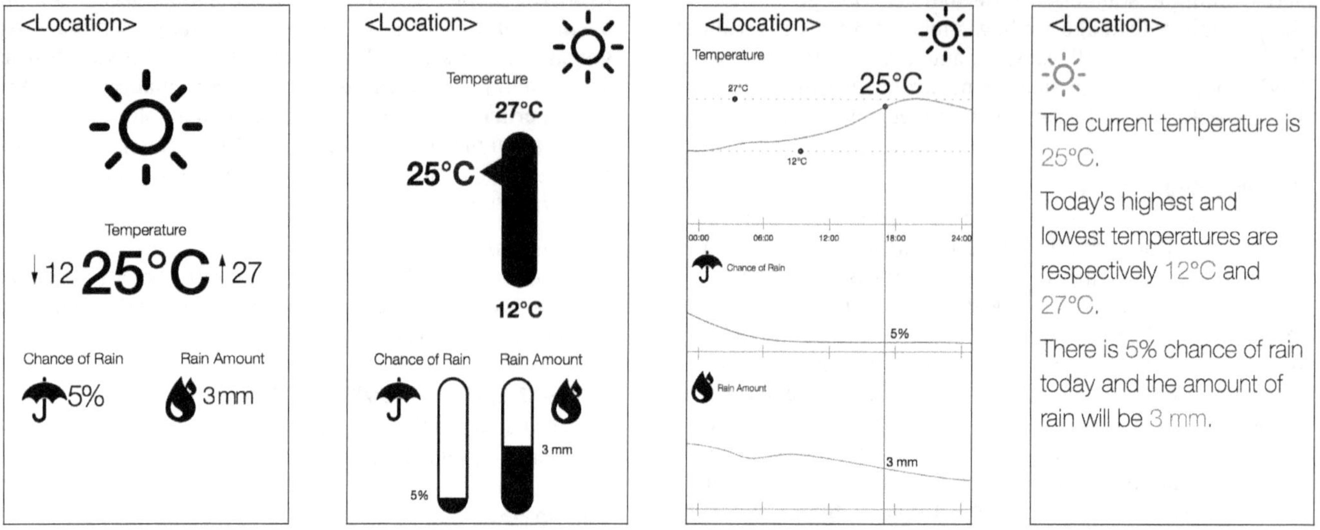


(a) Pictogram (b) Bar graph (c) Line graph (d) Text

**Figure 3. Exemplary sketches for the representation methods used in the online survey displaying a single source or average aggregation forecast.**

*Scenarios*

To obtain scenarios for our study, we assembled a list of 12 scenarios, in which weather conditions may influence people's behavior: (1) What to wear when going to work, (2) Whether to take the train or bike to work, (3) Outdoor soccer viewing event with friends, (4) Camping trip, (5) Outdoor wedding, (6) Packing for a trip, (7) You are going to do outdoor sports (e.g., swimming, hiking), (8) Planning an outdoor barbecue party, (9) Harvest as farmer, (10) Garden work, (11) Whale watch, (12) Attending outdoor concert.

We perceived the time of the event as an important factor as people know that the accuracy of weather forecasts decreases with time. In order to eliminate the time factor from our scenarios, we decided to address all of them as being "tomorrow".

In a short hallway questionnaire, we asked 15 people to decide whether a scenario was casual important, somewhat important, or very important for them. From the answers of participants, we selected three scenarios of varying importance were most participants agreed on the importance. This resulted in the scenario with the least importance (10 participants chose "casual important"), one with medium importance (11 participants chose "somewhat important") and the one with the highest importance (13 participants chose "very important"): (1) Daily Dress Choice: You are going to work/school tomorrow morning on a regular day and you need to decide what to wear., (2) Outdoor BBQ Party: You are planning a BBQ party for tomorrow and you want to know whether the weather will be good for having a party outdoors., (3) Outdoor Wedding: You have your wedding tomorrow and it is an outdoor wedding. You need to decide whether you should make changes in the organization (like arranging a tent, or moving the wedding indoors).

With this range of scenarios, we made sure to expose participants to scenarios with a varying amount of importance.

### Participants

In total, 71 participants (37 male, 33 female) between an age of 19 and 77 years ($M = 24.8, SD = 7.0$) completed our online survey. We recruited them via social networks and our University mailing list. The majority of the participants had either a completed high school diploma (26.8%) or a completed university degree (59.1%). As compensation, participants had the possibility to be part of a raffle of two vouchers worth 20€.

Most of our participants (70.4%) stated that they consult the weather forecast multiple times a week. Further, participants reported that they use the weather forecast more or less frequently depending on the season (*"Especially in summer because the weather changes very often."*), events (*"I always check it before going to swim outside, and a barbecue, or a festival (everything outside where it could be fatal to wear the wrong clothes or the event is not appropriate for rainy weather)."*), travel plans, location (*"It usually depends if I am going somewhere where the weather patterns are unfamiliar to me."*), and specific weather conditions (*"Especially when the weather doesn't seem to be stable."*).

The majority (52.1%) of our participants reported using more than two weather providers regularly ($M = 1.68, SD = 0.92$). They picked their weather providers due to the perceived reliability and accuracy, usability, fast and easy access, and amount of information. Several participants stated that they discontinued using weather sources before either because they were inaccurate or not easily available. Participants reported to compare sources for several reasons: to find out whether the sources provided consistent information (*"If I really need to know the weather I look at all of them to see if they match."*), to compute the average (*"I find they never agree with one another so I always try to find multiple sources and average them out (informally)."*), or estimate the worst possible scenario (*"I usually estimate the worst possible weather for a given scenario and prepare accordingly."*).

### Tasks

The online survey comprised the evaluation of sketches of several potential interfaces. Each sketch depicted the combination of one representation with one aggregation mechanism. Therefore, the total number of tasks was 16: four aggregation mechanisms x four representations. For each sketch, participants first rated their confidence in the depicted weather forecast on a 7-point Likert-type item (*"I feel confident that this will be the tomorrow's weather."*) ranging from *completely disagree* to *completely agree*. Participants were aware that the depicted weather forecast was hypothetical, i.e., it did not veridically display the weather of the next day. Subsequently, participants rated their preference for the sketch on three 7-point Likert-type items, each for using the depicted interface in one of the three possible scenarios (e.g., *"I would like to use this representation for the scenario: Daily Dress Choice"*). For every task, we additionally gave participants the possibility to provide qualitative feedback in the form of a text field.

### Procedure

Participants began the survey by filling in their demographic information and relation to weather forecasts. They then navigated through four pages (one per representation). The order of presentation of the four representations was randomized across participants. On each of the pages, participants received an explanation of the representation, all aggregation mechanisms and the scenarios. Additionally, they completed the four tasks for the shown representation. At the end, participants who wanted to be part of the voucher raffle could enter their email address.

### Results

We performed two linear mixed-effects model analyses on the aligned-rank transformed Likert item data [40], one for participants preference ratings and one for participants confidence ratings. In the first analysis, we added the fixed factors *aggregation method*, *representation*, and *scenario* as well as the random factor *participant*. In the second analysis, we added the fixed factors *aggregation method* and *representation* as well as the random factor participant. Significant effects were further explored using post hoc pair-wise comparisons with Bonferroni corrections. Only significant effects of interest are reported.

#### *Aggregation method*

*Range* received the highest mean rating ($M = 4.85, SD = 1.73$), followed by *direct* ($M = 4.51, SD = 1.9$), *mean* ($M = 4.22, SD = 1.82$), and *single* ($M = 4.13, SD = 1.72$). Figure 4a shows participants overall **preference ratings** for each of the four aggregation methods as a function of the representation method (error bars represent standard errors of the mean). The mixed-effects analysis revealed a main effect of aggregation method on participants preference ratings ($F(3, 3290) = 37.78, p < 0.001$). Pair-wise comparisons showed that participants preferred *range* over the other three methods (range vs. direct: $t(3290) = 5.55, p < 0.001$; range vs. mean: $t(3290) = 7.69, p < 0.001$; range vs. single: $t(3290) = 10.21, p < 0.001$), as well as *direct* over *single* (direct vs. single: $t(3290) = 4.66, p < 0.001$).

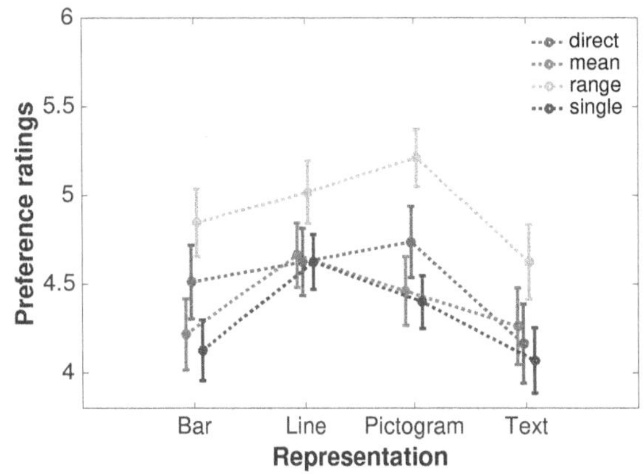


(a) Preference ratings for the aggregation mechanisms as a function of representation

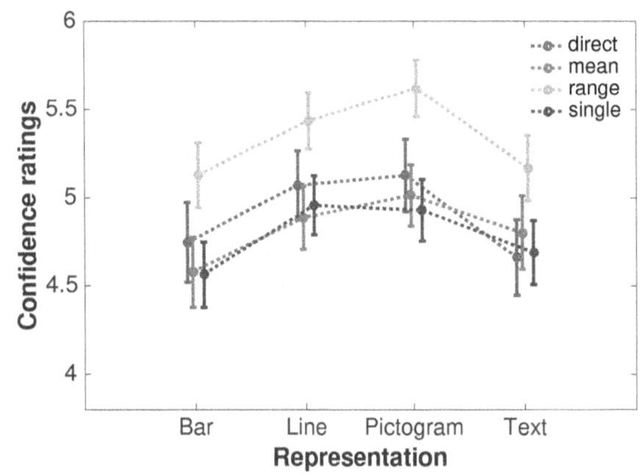


(b) Confidence ratings for the aggregation mechanisms as a function of representation

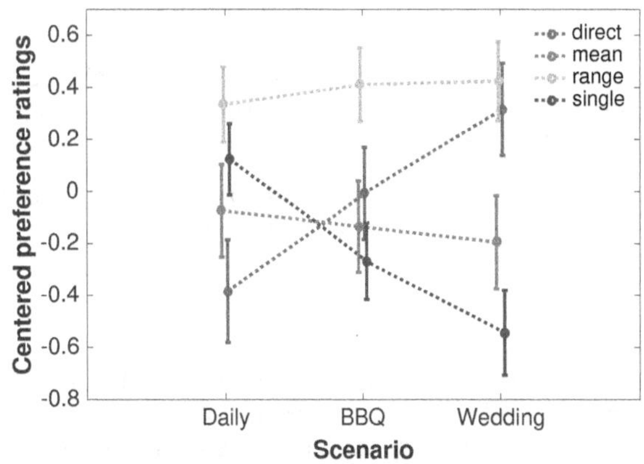


(c) Preference ratings for the aggregation mechanisms as a function of scenario

**Figure 4. Participants' mean preference and confidence ratings (measured on a 7-point Likert-type item with 1 corresponding to completely disagree and 7 corresponding to completely agree); error bars represent standard errors of the mean. Figure 4c depicts centered mean ratings, i.e., the main effect of scenario has been removed to improve the perceptibility of the interaction effect.**

Figure 4b shows participants mean **confidence ratings** for each of the four aggregation methods as a function of the different representations (error bars represent standard errors of the mean). Mean ratings were highest for *range* ($M = 5.34, SD = 1.46$), followed by *direct* ($M = 4.9, SD = 1.75$), *mean* ($M = 4.83, SD = 1.6$), and *single* ($M = 4.79, SD = 1.5$). The linear mixed effects analysis revealed a main effect of aggregation method on participants confidence ratings ($F(3, 1050) = 13.5, p < 0.001$). In particular, pair-wise comparisons showed that participants indicated higher confidence in *range* compared to the other three methods (range vs. direct: $t(1050) = 3.48, p < 0.01$; range vs. mean: $t(1050) = 4.85, p < 0.001$; range vs. single: $t(1050) = 6.0, p < 0.001$).

These results provide support for our hypothesis H2 that people generally prefer to receive more rather than less information with regards to the weather (i.e., they prefer aggregated presentations over single source presentations) and for hypothesis H1 that they place higher confidence in aggregated data, specifically in the form of aggregation into a range.

### Representations

*Line* received the highest mean preference rating ($M = 4.73, SD = 1.67$), followed by *pictogram* ($M = 4.7, SD = 1.73$), *bar* ($M = 4.42, SD = 1.81$), and *text* ($M = 4.28, SD = 1.88$). The mixed-effects analysis revealed a main effect of representation on participants preference rankings ($F(3, 3290) = 16.48, p < 0.001$). Pair-wise comparisons indicated that participants preferred *line* and *pictogram* over *bar* and *text* (line vs. bar: $t(3290) = 4.17, p < 0.001$; line vs. text: $t(3290) = 5.92, p < 0.001$; pictogram vs. bar: $t(3290) = 3.682, p < 0.001$; pictogram vs. text: $t(3290) = 5.436, p < 0.001$).

Mean **confidence ratings** were highest for *pictogram* ($M = 5.17, SD = 1.53$), followed by *line* ($M = 5.09, SD = 1.49$), *text* ($M = 4.83, SD = 1.67$), and *bar* ($M = 4.7, SD = 1.69$). The linear mixed effects analysis revealed a main effect of representation ($F(3, 1050) = 7.27, p < 0.001$). Pair-wise comparisons showed that *pictogram* received higher confidence ratings than *bar* ($t(1050) = 4.08, p < 0.001$) and *text* ($t(1050) = 3.8, p < 0.001$).

In sum, our results indicate that participants preferred the representations *line* and *pictogram*. The latter also receives a confidence bonus.

### Interactions

Of the three possible two-way interactions and the one three-way interaction between the three factors in the three-way analysis of **preference ratings**, only the interaction between *aggregation method* and *scenario* is significant ($F(6, 3290) = 11.71, p < 0.001$). Figure 4c shows the mean preferences for each of the four aggregation methods as a function of the scenario (error bars represent standard errors of the mean). For illustration purposes, the data of each scenario was centered on the scenario's overall mean. This was done since preference differences between the three scenarios are of no interest to us (i.e., the main effect of scenario) and may mask trends in preference ratings across the three scenarios.

| Contrast | | df | $\chi^2$ | p-value |
|---|---|---|---|---|
| **Direct-Single** | **BBQ-Daily** | 1 | 22.47 | < 0.001 |
| **Range-Single** | **BBQ-Daily** | 1 | 10.35 | 0.023 |
| **Direct-Single** | **BBQ-Wedding** | 1 | 11.37 | 0.013 |
| **Direct-Mean** | **Daily-Wedding** | 1 | 25.24 | < 0.001 |
| **Direct-Range** | **Daily-Wedding** | 1 | 10.23 | 0.025 |
| **Direct-Single** | **Daily-Wedding** | 1 | 65.81 | < 0.001 |
| **Mean-Single** | **Daily-Wedding** | 1 | 9.54 | 0.036 |
| **Range-Single** | **Daily-Wedding** | 1 | 24.15 | < 0.001 |

**Table 1. Difference of the *differences* between two aggregation methods across two scenarios (e.g., is the difference between Direct and Single larger in the BBQ or in the Daily scenario).**

As the figure illustrates, a main source of the interaction effect is the increase in the preference ratings for the *direct* aggregation method as the importance of the scenario increases. Five of nine pairwise comparisons involving the *direct* aggregation method show significant differences of the difference of participants preference ratings between the *direct* aggregation method and one of the other methods across two levels of the factor scenario (e.g., for the daily scenario *single* presentation is preferred over the *direct* aggregation while the situation is reversed for the wedding scenario; see Table 1 for test statistics and p-values for all significant contrasts). This partially confirms our hypothesis H3 that the willingness to perform aggregation manually increases with the importance of the scenario (though aggregation into a *range* remains the overall preferred method).

A secondary source of interaction results from the stronger decrease in preference of the *single* source as compared to the other aggregation methods as importance of scenario increases (e.g., the difference between *single* and *range* is larger for the wedding scenario then for the daily scenario).

We find no interaction effect between aggregation method and representation. In other words, there is not sufficient evidence in favor of hypothesis H4 that users have different preferences regarding the aggregation method, depending on which representation is provided. Rather, users show an overall preference for *range*.

### Qualitative Feedback

We additionally collected some qualitative feedback about the aggregation mechanisms. People mostly stated that the single source (especially the pictogram representation) "*seems like enough information for daily dress choice, and it is a similar representation to what [they] usually use. However, [they] would like a more detailed forecast for event planning.*"

As expected, participants preferred the direct comparison as they felt able to make an informed decision: "*I like having control and letting me make the decisions. I am informed of all possibilities, and it is up to me to come to a decision.*"

Participants also positively expressed that they liked the range aggregation: "*I like this representation because it provides almost as much information as the side-by-side comparison, but is much easier to see and interpret. It seems more trustworthy because it provides a range rather than a single value for temperature and rainfall. This acts as a margin of error, which means it is more likely to be correct.*"

For the average aggregation, most participants stated that it "*does not represent the variation in forecasts between different weather providers, and it also (probably) does not provide the exact values reported by any one provider [and it] seems untrustworthy.*" In contrast to this, one participants also stated that he does not "*see the different temperature and so on, but [he] know[s] that it's an average of some forecast sources, that's why [he] trust[s] the forecast.*"

### Discussion

The results of our survey show that participants generally preferred to receive information of multiple sources since single source obtained the lowest ratings. The average aggregation however did not receive significantly better ratings. Instead, participants preferred range aggregation and direct comparison, which are the mechanisms that support an informed decision and provide at least some transparency on the individual sources. This also illustrates that computational aggregation does not necessarily increase trust significantly as it does not provide any additional information beyond the single source. The sheer knowledge of having multiple sources apparently is not enough to increase confidence.

Regarding the representation, participants preferred the line and the pictogram. We assume that they were preferred due to being the standard representations in most common weather applications.

We did not find any interaction effect between representations and aggregation mechanisms. This indicates that users do not exhibit differential preferences of for one or the other aggregation method depending on the representation. This allowed us to chose the aggregation and representation for the application depending on users' overall preferences. In general, this also suggests that aggregation mechanisms are generally preferred no matter what representations are used and that aggregation mechanisms are not tied to specific representations.

The interaction effect between the aggregation mechanism and the scenario shows that with increasing importance of the scenario, users exhibit a slight increase in preference for range and a large increase in preference for direct comparison, while the preference for single source drops below all aggregation mechanisms. This indicates that people prefer more control over decisions in important scenarios. Interestingly, this also applies for the range aggregation, which apparently provides enough details to give users this feeling of control.

## EXPERIMENT 2: "WEATHER COMPARE" APPLICATION

Based on the results of the online survey, we developed the weather application "Weather Compare", which we evaluated in an in-the-wild study.

### Apparatus

We developed an Android application named "Weather Compare" to further evaluate the most promising aggregation mechanisms. Based on the results of the online survey we decided to implement the pictogram representation. The online survey did not reveal a significant difference to the line representation for preference, however the pictogram representation received a confidence bonus and better ratings for the most promising aggregation mechanisms. To improve the representation, we added hourly information, which participants had stated to be important in their comments.

For the aggregation mechanisms, we decided to implement the range aggregation and the direct comparison as these two were preferred in the online survey. Users of the application are able to toggle between the two aggregation methods on demand. The range aggregation is the default view of the application. By tapping the details button, a user can switch to the details view for direct comparison.

We looked at existing weather APIs to identify those that fulfill the following requirements: (1) Hourly weather data for 72 hours, (2) Temperature, chance of rain, amount of rain, and pictogram included, (3) Reasonable number of API calls per day, (4) Free to use for non-commercial/research purposes. We only found two APIs that fulfilled all requirements: Apixu [2] and Wunderground [3]. We picked Forecast.io [4] as a third API although it only included weather data for the next 48 hours. As all our scenarios were directed at the next day, 48 hours seemed to be enough.

The application required users to turn on their location data as it would automatically fetch the location of the user and show the corresponding weather. For the final design of the application, we built upon the layout of the existing sketches used in the survey. We added the hourly information as vertical scroll bar at the bottom of the screen and polished the application to make it look professional.

### Participants

23 participants (12 male, 10 female, 1 preferred not to say) between the age of 19 and 57 ($M = 30.0, SD = 11.3$) installed the application and participated in the study. All participants were regular users of weather applications and did use the application in everyday life. We invited them by sharing the news about the application on the social media channels and the e-mail list of the University.

### Procedure

We sent all participants a detailed explanation of how the application works and an apk file to install the application on their phone. We then asked them to use the application instead of their normal weather application for the course of at least one week. Afterwards, participants filled in an online questionnaire with free text questions. The free text questions asked for the following feedback: (1) Advantages/Disadvantages compared to the application normally used, (2) Feature requests, (3) Future usage of "Weather Compare", (4) Opinion about having data from multiple sources, (5) Usage of range vs. details view, (6) Potential change in confidence due to the aggregation.

[2]Apixu: `http://www.apixu.com/`

[3]Wunderground: `https://www.wunderground.com/weather/api`

[4]Forecast.io `https://darksky.net/dev/`

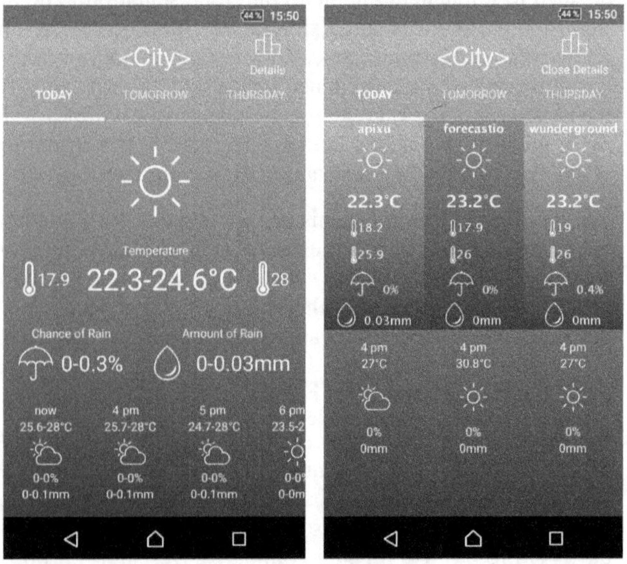


(a) App - Range aggregation (b) App - Direct comparison

**Figure 5. Screenshots of the weather application "Weather Compare" with the main screen showing the range aggregation and the details screen showing the direct comparison of in total 3 different weather providers.**

### Results

During the week of the user study, participants opened the application on average 17.95 (+/ − 5.72) times. The details view, which corresponds to our manual aggregation condition in Experiment 1, was used on average 6.14 (+/ − 2.69) times, i.e., in approximately one-third of cases.

In the following, we present the qualitative feedback of participants regarding general feedback about the application and the aggregation.

#### *General Feedback about the Application*

We collected general feedback such as differences to the applications normally used and feature requests on the first page of the questionnaire.

**Advantages/Disadvantages compared to the application normally used.** Participants mainly stated that the differences between "Weather Compare" and the application they normally use are the GPS location feature and the hourly forecasts. Other participants mentioned that they see a disadvantages in the small range of the forecast (only 48 hours) and that there was no wind forecast. On the positive side, eight participants liked the range representation with multiple sources. One participant also positively mentioned the hourly forecast, and another participant found the forecast very reliable and accurate.

**Feature requests.** Function and feature requests mainly covered the disadvantages and suggestions for including well-known features from other applications. Additionally, one participant asked to be able to choose sources and one participant suggested to show a range for the lowest and highest temperature.

**Future usage of "Weather Compare".** Besides three participants, who would like to prefer using their normal application in the future, all participants stated that they would like to use "Weather Compare" in the future if the experienced issues would be fixed.

#### *Specific Feedback about the Aggregation*

We collected more specific feedback about the aggregation mechanisms and data from multiple sources on the second page of the questionnaire.

**Opinion about having data from multiple sources.** 14 participants explicitly stated that having data from multiple sources *"is the main thing that [they] liked about the app"*. The aggregation helped them to better judge the forecast: *"I liked it because since this is a forecast, one provider is not really reliable but when you see that 3 different providers agree on something, it is more convincing."* Only one participant did not appreciate the aggregation and stated *"that the cognitive load is too high when making the effort and actually comparing the values in contrast to just looking at a yellow sun or grey cloud."*

**Usage of range aggregation vs. direct comparison.** Six participants stated that they *"always used the range representation and used the detailed view only out of curiosity."* In contrast, three participants only used the details view. As one participant explained: *"I usually used the details view everyday, because normally I would check at least 2 different sources to be sure about the weather, thus, I would like to know what each source says rather than seeing an average of them."* One participant regularly used both views. Six other participant stated that they used the details view if *"the range of values [was] too wide, I checked the details page."* or *"before I spent a longer time outside"*.

**Influence of aggregation on confidence.** 12 participants stated that the application increased their confidence as they felt that the forecast was more detailed and having multiple sources made them trust the forecast more. Only one participant stated that *"the range was typical only 2-3 degrees, in which case it does not influence [his] decision in any way."* One participant did not think that having forecasts from multiple sources increased her confidence, *"because when they differ [she] kind of feel[s] like [she] lose[s] trust in all of them."*

### Discussion

With the help of the qualitative feedback, we were able to identify the biggest disadvantages that people experienced. First, the weather APIs provided a limited amount of information that we were able to access and show in the application. Second, participants missed a certain feature (e.g., typing in a location) or a certain information (e.g., wind forecast) that they were used to from former usage. We assume that these problems could be solved by providing more features and specific settings allowing users to individualize the application.

Although for most participants, it was not important which APIs we used, one participants wanted to choose the sources to be shown in the application. Increasing transparency by providing more sources and additional information on what exact data the APIs provide could help users to understand the prerequisites of the weather providers. By choosing a number of providers, they would be able to specify the requirements for the weather forecast on their own (e.g., time of forecast period, additional wind forecast).

Surprisingly, some participants exclusively used the range or the detailed view. From our online survey, we mainly expected participants to use the range aggregation for everyday usage and the detailed view for important events as six participants reported. We assume that although all our participant beforehand stated to use weather forecasts everyday, the weather forecast generally was of different importance to them. Participants that only used the range view apparently had no strong interest in weather forecasts in general while participants that only used the detailed view enjoyed to have the details to be more confident about the forecast. These three participants in general commented highly positively about the application, which shows that they liked using the application as it reduced the time they need for comparing forecasts.

In line with these findings, the majority of participants stated that the aggregation of forecasts from different sources increased their confidence in the forecast and that they would like to continue using this type of service. Interestingly, one participant mentioned that seeing how the forecasts disagree rather makes her lose trust in the forecasts. It seems that although research suggests otherwise, some people are not aware of the uncertainty in weather forecasts or perceive it to be lower than the actual difference between different weather providers. It would be interesting to investigate whether this opinion changes after using the application long-term or when switching back to the weather application used before the study (as this is now maybe also perceived to be more uncertain).

## IMPLICATIONS FOR DESIGN AND FUTURE WORK

Based on the results of our online survey and the in-the-wild study, we identified five implications for future work on designing for comparison of uncertain data. These implications do not only apply for weather-related purposes and could help to inform the design of interactive systems in other application areas, for example for arrival time prediction or health predictions.

### Support contexts with different importance

Applications should support range aggregation and direct comparison to adapt to contexts with different importance. Although people like aggregated data, experiment 1 showed that users still want to make an informed decision on their own judgment if something is important for them.

### Support perception at a glance

For applications such as weather applications, it is crucial to support an aggregation mechanism in combination with a representation that can be perceived at a glance. In experiment 2, users expressed that they do not want to spend too much time with the application in everyday use or even felt that the cognitive load was too high.

### Support different types of users

Applications should make switching between aggregation mechanisms easy and give people the choice for what they want to have as standard view. Experiment 2 showed that people have different tolerances for giving control to an application and prefer different aggregation mechanisms as their standard. They may even only use one mechanism.

### Give opportunities for choice

Applications should offer users a list of many providers to choose a default number of sources (e.g., 3) to be displayed. This increases the feeling of control as users have a choice to make their own decision on which providers they want to rely on. In experiment 2, users stated that they would like to have a choice or include their current source.

### Establish transparency

In experiment 2, users requested a longer range of the forecast and specific information (e.g., wind forecast). By providing details on what data the original sources provide and how this data is aggregated in the application, users would better understand the requirements of the application. In combination with giving users the opportunity to select their sources, users can fulfill their specific requirements by only picking matching sources.

## CONCLUSION

In this paper, we identified and evaluated aggregation mechanisms for uncertain data from multiple sources using an online survey and an in-the-wild study. As uncertainty is difficult to quantify and often not communicated at all, users compare multiple sources as a workaround to assess the uncertainty. We demonstrated that interactive applications can help to make comparison easier and less cumbersome.

Our results show that aggregation of uncertain data is generally preferred and increases users' confidence, independent of the type of representation used for the data. Computationally aggregated forecasts are more suited for everyday events while manual aggregation is preferred for high-stakes events. Nevertheless, certain types of users prefer to always use one or the other aggregation mechanism based on the personal importance of the topic 'weather'. To satisfy all users' needs, both computational and manual aggregation should be supported. Additionally, computationally aggregated data has to be easily comprehensible. Lastly, transparency of the origin of the data (for example the name of the sources) and choice of sources is an important factor of success.

In future work, these mechanisms could also be applied to non-weather related purposes as for example arrival time predictions, health predictions, or contradicting sensor measurements. We also plan to study the long-term usage behavior of such mechanisms and the influence of long-term usage on users' confidence.

## ACKNOWLEDGEMENTS

The authors would like to thank the German Research Foundation (DFG) for financial support of the project within the Cluster of Excellence in Simulation Technology (EXC 310/2) at the University of Stuttgart.

## REFERENCES


1. Nadia Boukhelifa and David J. Duke. 2009. Uncertainty Visualization: Why Might It Fail?. In *CHI '09 Extended Abstracts on Human Factors in Computing Systems*. ACM, New York, NY, USA, 4051–4056. DOI: http://dx.doi.org/10.1145/1520340.1520616

2. David V. Budescu, Stephen Broomell, and Han-Hui Por. 2009. Improving Communication of Uncertainty in the Reports of the Intergovernmental Panel on Climate Change. *Psychological Science* 20, 3 (2009), 299–308. DOI: http://dx.doi.org/10.1111/j.1467-9280.2009.02284.x

3. Michael Correll and Michael Gleicher. 2014. Error Bars Considered Harmful: Exploring Alternate Encodings for Mean and Error. *Visualization and Computer Graphics, IEEE Transactions on* 20, 12 (Dec 2014), 2142–2151. DOI: http://dx.doi.org/10.1109/TVCG.2014.2346298

4. AMS Council. 2008. Enhancing weather information with probability forecasts. *Bulletin of the American Meteorological Society* 89 (2008), 1049–1053.

5. National Research Council. 2003. *Communicating Uncertainties in Weather and Climate Information: A Workshop Summary*. The National Academies Press. DOI: http://dx.doi.org/10.17226/10597

6. National Research Council. 2006. *Completing the Forecast: Characterizing and Communicating Uncertainty for Better Decisions Using Weather and Climate Forecasts*. The National Academies Press. DOI: http://dx.doi.org/10.17226/11699

7. David Demeritt, Hannah Cloke, Florian Pappenberger, Jutta Thielen, Jens Bartholmes, and Maria-Helena Ramos. 2007. Ensemble predictions and perceptions of risk, uncertainty, and error in flood forecasting. *Environmental Hazards* 7, 2 (2007), 115 – 127. DOI: http://dx.doi.org/10.1016/j.envhaz.2007.05.001

8. Nivan Ferreira, Danyel Fisher, and Arnd C. Konig. 2014. Sample-oriented Task-driven Visualizations: Allowing Users to Make Better, More Confident Decisions. In *Proceedings of the SIGCHI Conference on Human Factors in Computing Systems (CHI '14)*. ACM, New York, NY, USA, 571–580. DOI: http://dx.doi.org/10.1145/2556288.2557131

9. J. Frick and C. Hegg. 2011. Can end-users' flood management decision making be improved by information about forecast uncertainty? *Atmospheric Research* 100, 23 (2011), 296 – 303. DOI: http://dx.doi.org/10.1016/j.atmosres.2010.12.006

10. Susan Joslyn, Karla Pak, David Jones, John Pyles, and Earl Hunt. 2007. The effect of probabilistic information on threshold forecasts. *Weather and Forecasting* 22, 4 (2007), 804–812. DOI: http://dx.doi.org/10.1175/WAF1020.1

11. Susan Joslyn and Sonia Savelli. 2010. Communicating forecast uncertainty: public perception of weather forecast uncertainty. *Meteorological Applications* 17, 2 (2010), 180–195. DOI: http://dx.doi.org/10.1002/met.190

12. Susan L. Joslyn and Jared E. LeClerc. 2012. Uncertainty forecasts improve weather-related decisions and attenuate the effects of forecast error. *Journal of Experimental Psychology: Applied* 18, 1 (2012), 126–140. DOI: http://dx.doi.org/10.1037/a0025185

13. Malte F. Jung, David Sirkin, Turgut M. Gür, and Martin Steinert. 2015. Displayed Uncertainty Improves Driving Experience and Behavior: The Case of Range Anxiety in an Electric Car. In *Proceedings of the 33rd Annual ACM Conference on Human Factors in Computing Systems (CHI '15)*. ACM, New York, NY, USA, 2201–2210. DOI: http://dx.doi.org/10.1145/2702123.2702479

14. Daniel Kahneman and Amos Tversky. 1979. Prospect Theory: An Analysis of Decision under Risk. *Econometrica* 47, 2 (1979), 263–291. DOI: http://dx.doi.org/10.2307/1914185

15. Matthew Kay, Tara Kola, Jessica R. Hullman, and Sean A. Munson. 2016. When (Ish) is My Bus?: User-centered Visualizations of Uncertainty in Everyday, Mobile Predictive Systems. In *Proceedings of the 2016 CHI Conference on Human Factors in Computing Systems (CHI '16)*. ACM, New York, NY, USA, 5092–5103. DOI: http://dx.doi.org/10.1145/2858036.2858558

16. Matthew Kay, Dan Morris, M.C. Schraefel, and Julie A. Kientz. 2013. There's No Such Thing As Gaining a Pound: Reconsidering the Bathroom Scale User Interface. In *Proceedings of the 2013 ACM International Joint Conference on Pervasive and Ubiquitous Computing (UbiComp '13)*. ACM, New York, NY, USA, 401–410. DOI: http://dx.doi.org/10.1145/2493432.2493456

17. Matthew Kay, Shwetak N. Patel, and Julie A. Kientz. 2015. How Good is 85Classifier Evaluation to Acceptability of Accuracy. In *Proceedings of the 33rd Annual ACM Conference on Human Factors in Computing Systems (CHI '15)*. ACM, New York, NY, USA, 347–356. DOI: http://dx.doi.org/10.1145/2702123.2702603

18. H. Kootval. 2008. Guidelines on communicating forecast uncertainty. *World Meteorological Organization/Technical Document* 4122 (2008).

19. Jeffrey K. Lazo, Rebecca E. Morss, and Julie L. Demuth. 2009. 300 Billion Served. *Bulletin of the American Meteorological Society* 90, 6 (2009), 785–798. DOI: http://dx.doi.org/10.1175/2008BAMS2604.1

20. Isaac M. Lipkus, Greg Samsa, and Barbara K. Rimer. 2001. General Performance on a Numeracy Scale among Highly Educated Samples. *Medical Decision Making* 21, 1 (2001), 37–44. DOI: http://dx.doi.org/10.1177/0272989X0102100105

21. Alan M. MacEachren, Anthony Robinson, Susan Hopper, Steven Gardner, Robert Murray, Mark Gahegan, and Elisabeth Hetzler. 2005. Visualizing Geospatial Information Uncertainty: What We Know and What We Need to Know. *Cartography and Geographic Information Science* 32, 3 (2005), 139–160. DOI:http://dx.doi.org/10.1559/1523040054738936

22. Rebecca E. Morss, Julie L. Demuth, and Jeffrey K. Lazo. 2008. Communicating Uncertainty in Weather Forecasts: A Survey of the U.S. Public. *Weather and forecasting* 23, 5 (2008), 974–991. DOI: http://dx.doi.org/10.1175/2008WAF2007088.1

23. Rebecca E. Morss, Jeffrey K. Lazo, and Julie L. Demuth. 2010. Examining the use of weather forecasts in decision scenarios: results from a US survey with implications for uncertainty communication. *Meteorological Applications* 17, 2 (2010), 149–162. DOI:http://dx.doi.org/10.1002/met.196

24. Limor Nadav-Greenberg and Susan L. Joslyn. 2009. Uncertainty Forecasts Improve Decision Making Among Nonexperts. *Journal of Cognitive Engineering and Decision Making* 3, 3 (2009), 209–227. DOI: http://dx.doi.org/10.1518/155534309X474460

25. Neville Nicholls. 1999. Cognitive Illusions, Heuristics, and Climate Prediction. *Bulletin of the American Meteorological Society* 80, 7 (1999), 1385–1397. DOI: http://dx.doi.org/10.1175/1520-0477(1999)080<1385:CIHACP>2.0.CO;2

26. Chris Olston and Jock D. Mackinlay. 2002. Visualizing data with bounded uncertainty. In *Information Visualization, 2002. INFOVIS 2002. IEEE Symposium on*. 37–40. DOI: http://dx.doi.org/10.1109/INFVIS.2002.1173145

27. Alex T. Pang, Craig M. Wittenbrink, and Suresh K. Lodha. 1997. Approaches to uncertainty visualization. *The Visual Computer* 13, 8 (1997), 370–390. DOI: http://dx.doi.org/10.1007/s003710050111

28. Kristin Potter, Joe Kniss, Richard Riesenfeld, and Chris.R. Johnson. 2010. Visualizing Summary Statistics and Uncertainty. *Computer Graphics Forum* 29, 3 (2010), 823–832. DOI:http://dx.doi.org/10.1111/j.1467-8659.2009.01677.x

29. Kristin Potter, Paul Rosen, and Chris R. Johnson. 2012. From quantification to visualization: A taxonomy of uncertainty visualization approaches. In *Uncertainty Quantification in Scientific Computing*. Vol. 377. Springer, 226–249. DOI: http://dx.doi.org/10.1007/978-3-642-32677-6_15

30. Mark S. Roulston, Gary E. Bolton, Andrew N. Kleit, and Addison L. Sears-Collins. 2006. A laboratory study of the benefits of including uncertainty information in weather forecasts. *Weather and Forecasting* 21, 1 (2006), 116–122. DOI: http://dx.doi.org/10.1175/WAF887.1

31. Mark S. Roulston and Todd R. Kaplan. 2009. A laboratory-based study of understanding of uncertainty in 5-day site-specific temperature forecasts. *Meteorological Applications* 16, 2 (2009), 237–244. DOI:http://dx.doi.org/10.1002/met.113

32. Orit Shaer, Oded Nov, Johanna Okerlund, Martina Balestra, Elizabeth Stowell, Lauren Westendorf, Christina Pollalis, Jasmine Davis, Liliana Westort, and Madeleine Ball. 2016. GenomiX: A Novel Interaction Tool for Self-Exploration of Personal Genomic Data. In *Proceedings of the 2016 CHI Conference on Human Factors in Computing Systems (CHI '16)*. ACM, New York, NY, USA, 661–672. DOI: http://dx.doi.org/10.1145/2858036.2858397

33. Michael Siegrist, Heinz Gutscher, and Timothy C. Earle. 2005. Perception of risk: the influence of general trust, and general confidence. *Journal of Risk Research* 8, 2 (2005), 145–156. DOI: http://dx.doi.org/10.1080/1366987032000105315

34. Meredith Skeels, Bongshin Lee, Greg Smith, and George G. Robertson. 2010. Revealing Uncertainty for Information Visualization. *Information Visualization* 9, 1 (2010), 70–81. DOI: http://dx.doi.org/10.1057/ivs.2009.1

35. Paul Slovic. 1987. Perception of risk. *Science (Washington, D.C.); (United States)* 236 (Apr 1987). DOI:http://dx.doi.org/10.1126/science.3563507

36. Susanne Tak, Alexander Toet, and Jan van Erp. 2014. The Perception of Visual Uncertainty Representation by Non-Experts. *Visualization and Computer Graphics, IEEE Transactions on* 20, 6 (June 2014), 935–943. DOI:http://dx.doi.org/10.1109/TVCG.2013.247

37. Judi Thomson, Elizabeth Hetzler, Alan MacEachren, Mark Gahegan, and Misha Pavel. 2005. A typology for visualizing uncertainty. In *Electronic imaging 2005*. International Society for Optics and Photonics, 146–157. DOI:http://dx.doi.org/10.1117/12.587254

38. Amos Tversky and Daniel Kahneman. 1974. Judgment under Uncertainty: Heuristics and Biases. *Science* 185, 4157 (1974), 1124–1131. http://www.jstor.org/stable/1738360

39. Thomas S. Wallsten, David V. Budescu, Amnon Rapoport, Rami Zwick, and Barbara Forsyth. 1986. Measuring the vague meanings of probability terms. *Journal of Experimental Psychology: General* 115, 4 (1986), 348–365. DOI: http://dx.doi.org/10.1037/0096-3445.115.4.348

40. Jacob O. Wobbrock, Leah Findlater, Darren Gergle, and James J. Higgins. 2011. The aligned rank transform for nonparametric factorial analyses using only anova procedures. In *Proceedings of the SIGCHI Conference on Human Factors in Computing Systems*. ACM, 143–146.

41. Jianlong Zhou, Constant Bridon, Fang Chen, Ahmad Khawaji, and Yang Wang. 2015. Be Informed and Be Involved: Effects of Uncertainty and Correlation on User's Confidence in Decision Making. In *Proceedings of the 33rd Annual ACM Conference Extended Abstracts on Human Factors in Computing Systems (CHI EA '15)*. ACM, New York, NY, USA, 923–928. DOI: http://dx.doi.org/10.1145/2702613.2732769

42. Torre Zuk and Sheelagh Carpendale. 2006. Theoretical analysis of uncertainty visualizations. *Proc. SPIE* 6060 (2006), 606007–606007–14. DOI: http://dx.doi.org/10.1117/12.643631

# Bottom-up vs. Top-down: Trade-offs in Efficiency, Understanding, Freedom and Creativity with InfoVis Tools

Gonzalo Gabriel Méndez[†*] Uta Hinrichs[†] Miguel A. Nacenta[†]
[†]SACHI, University of St Andrews, UK {ggm, uh3, mans}@st-andrews.ac.uk
[*]Escuela Superior Politécnica del Litoral, Ecuador gmendez@espol.edu.ec

## ABSTRACT
The emergence of tools that support fast-and-easy visualization creation by non-experts has made the benefits of InfoVis widely accessible. Key features of these tools include attribute-level operations, automated mappings, and visualization templates. However, these features shield people from lower-level visualization design steps, such as the specific mapping of data points to visuals. In contrast, recent research promotes constructive visualization where individual data units and visuals are directly manipulated. We present a qualitative study comparing people's visualization processes using two visualization tools: one promoting a top-down approach to visualization construction (Tableau Desktop) and one implementing a bottom-up constructive visualization approach (iVoLVER). Our results show how the two approaches influence: 1) the visualization process, 2) decisions on the visualization design, 3) the feeling of control and authorship, and 4) the willingness to explore alternative designs. We discuss the complex trade-offs between the two approaches and outline considerations for designing better visualization tools.

### Author Keywords
Information Visualization; Tableau Desktop; iVoLVER.

### ACM Classification Keywords
H.5.m Information Interfaces and Presentation (e.g. HCI): Miscellaneous; D.1.7 Software: Visual Programming

## INTRODUCTION
Visualization tools for non-experts—people with no formal training on visualization concepts—are increasingly popular, and allow millions to create their own visual data representations for a multitude of purposes. However, to create effective visualizations people still need to learn the principles of visualization design (e.g., what data types should be mapped to which visual attributes).

The gateway to this knowledge is usually the same digital tool that is used to create the visualization. People will therefore learn as they experiment with an interface which might not have been designed for supporting an understanding of effective visualization design. To better support non-experts vis designers to leverage the power of visualization it is important to understand how they go about creating visualizations and how the tools themselves affect this process.

We explore these questions by comparing the use of Tableau Desktop, a heavily automated visualization tool, with iVoLVER, a digital tool based on the philosophy of constructive visualization as proposed by Huron et al. [24]. We present a qualitative study investigating how these tools influence non-experts' approaches to the visualization process, the differences in the resulting visualizations, design choices, low-level visual mappings, and justifications of these approaches. Our findings show trade-offs between these visualization construction approaches. In our study, Tableau enabled the speedy exploration of visualization solutions with minimum input from the user, yet it did not promote a critical understanding and reflection on the visualization process and outcomes. As a constructive tool iVoLVER required initial thinking about the intended visualizations and a hands-on, sometimes tedious procedure of mapping data to visuals. This resulted, however, in a transparent, flexible visualization process facilitating creative and critical thinking as well as a feeling of control and authorship.

With our study results we contribute: 1) a characterization of non-expert visualization processes comparing two tools with different approaches to visualization construction; 2) a discussion of how these tools' paradigms influence non-expert's visualization design decisions; and 3) a reflection on the complex set of trade-offs we found between the two studied approaches. Our findings provide guidance on designing tools that support the development of visualizations as well as learning the principles of visualization design.

## RELATED WORK
Three research areas are relevant to our study: the fundamentals of the InfoVis design process, existing vis tools, and empirical studies on visualization construction.

### The Visualization Design Process
Several authors have discussed the different stages and key elements of visualization design (e.g., [5, 11, 15, 36, 39]). Card et al. [10] describe the process of creating visual data representations as a set of four steps: 1) data analysis, 2) filtering, 3) mapping, and 4) rendering. Step 3—the creation of mappings between visual properties and data attributes—is one of the most important and well researched elements of visualization design. Much of the InfoVis research of the last 50 years focuses on the perceptual properties of visual elements [13] and the fit between the data types and the marks


*CHI 2017*, May 06 - 11, 2017, Denver, CO, USA.

ACM 978-1-4503-4655-9/17/05 $15.00
DOI: http://dx.doi.org/10.1145/3025453.3025942

and visual properties to represent them (e.g., [3, 4, 32, 43]). We are interested in representational mapping as an important part of the process. In particular, our focus is on the types of mappings that people come up with when designing their own visualizations. This relates to recent research on how people sketch data representations. Walny et al. [42] describe a "representation continuum" that shows a wide range of levels of abstraction when people sketch up representations of small datasets by hand, from *countable* (concrete and numeric) to *pictorial* (abstract) representations.

### Visualization Tool Types

Visualizations are typically built using digital tools, and a large variety of these tools exists [9, 17, 33]. Many tools allow to produce similar outcomes with different interfaces. Based on Grammel et al.'s categorization [17], three types are most relevant to our work: template editors, shelf configuration tools, and visual dataflow programming tools.

According to Grammel et al., in ***template editors*** *"the user selects some data and then picks a pre-defined visual structure in which to represent it. The distinguishing criteria of this approach are the separation between the initial visualization selection steps and the refinement of the selected visualization"* [17]. A related concept is "using tools" as described by Victor [40]. Examples of template tools are Many Eyes [41] and MS Excel. Tableau Desktop's "Show me" pane is a template feature within what is mostly a shelf configuration tool.

***Shelf configuration*** tools allow the specification of mappings through simple GUI operations on collections of visual properties and data attributes that are presented visually. Customization—typically based on cursor operations (e.g., drag-and-drop) or menues and dialogs—requires additional steps. Tableau Desktop and Lyra [37] (a more recent research prototype) fall within this category.

***Visual Dataflow Programming*** tools enable designers to specify visualizations by connecting elements (nodes) through links. The graph of connected components defines the dataflow and the characteristics of the visualization. This approach has a long history (e.g., [1, 29]) but is also present in more recent tools such as ExPlates [27], DataMeadow [16], and iVoLVER [31].

Besides Grammel et al.'s categorization [17] of visualization tools we can also distinguish between more high-level approaches to vis construction: bottom-up and top-down.

In a ***bottom-up*** approach one starts at a low level of abstraction, by manipulating individual data points and attributes to incrementally generate the overall visualization. Related to bottom-up approaches is the idea of *constructive visualization*, which Huron et al. define as *"the act of constructing a visualization by assembling blocks, that have previously been assigned a data unit through a mapping."* [23, pp. 436]. Constructive visualization is grounded in educational theories such as Papert's Constructionism [34] and Piaget's constructivism [2, 35]. Because of their educational roots, constructive tools might be more accessible to non-experts [24, 25] and appropriate for teaching visualization. Visualization tools implementing constructive principles can be considered bottom-up. We consider iVoLVER an example of both.

In contrast to tools applying a bottom-up approach, in ***top-down*** tools decisions about the visual representation of data happen at an attribute level. Template-based and shelf configuration tools inherently follow this approach—they focus on the overall mapping between attributes and visuals first. Customizations can be applied only after the initial attribute-level mappings are created. Data mappings performed in this way typically include all data points of an attribute, or even the entire dataset. The manipulation of the visual representation at an individual data point level is generally not possible (e.g., in Tableau visual mapping actions include all data points associated to a single attribute).

The tool categories and approaches to vis construction can potentially lead to different outcomes and design processes—a relevant issue for designers of visualization authoring tools.

### Previous Empirical Findings

Grammel et al. [18] studied how novices indirectly designed visualizations by instructing a Tableau expert to create the visualizations according to their specifications. Although participants did not directly use Tableau, the study findings are valuable and relevant, since data attribute selection, template selection, and visual mapping were identified as the main activities of the process. The study also showed that participants often missed relevant steps and specifications (e.g., specific mappings) when communicating with the expert.

Wun et al. [44] compared building bar charts using MS Excel vs. a set of physical tiles. They found that the building process was very different for the two tools. Our research complements and expands theirs in that we compare two digital tools (eliminating the possible physicality confound), and we do not restrict the visualization designs to bar charts.

## TWO VISUALIZATION TOOLS

To investigate the virtues and problems of bottom-up and top-down approaches to visualization design, we chose two tools that represent two ends of this continuum. This section discusses the two tools and their differences.

On the top-down end of the continuum we have traditional shelf configuration and template-based tools (as defined in [17, 40]). Tableau Desktop[1], a current leader in the visualization tool market, is a shelf configuration tool and therefore a representative of the top-down approach. Tableau's main interface is divided into rectangular panes. Once the data is loaded the user can see a pane containing the different data attributes (A in Fig. 1). Dragging and dropping attributes from this data pane onto the columns and rows shelves (B in Fig. 1) triggers a separate visualization pane (C in Fig. 1) to display a default data representation that is automatically selected by the system according to the selected attributes. An additional pane enables adjustments of the marks' visual properties by dropping data attributes to other shelves of the interface (D in Fig. 1). A further pane, "Show-me" (E in Fig. 1), provides a gallery with several visualization templates (e.g., choropleth map, area charts). The templates that are not available with the current attribute selection are automatically grayed out.

On the opposite end of the spectrum we have tools that support a bottom-up approach to visualization construction

[1] `http://www.tableau.com`

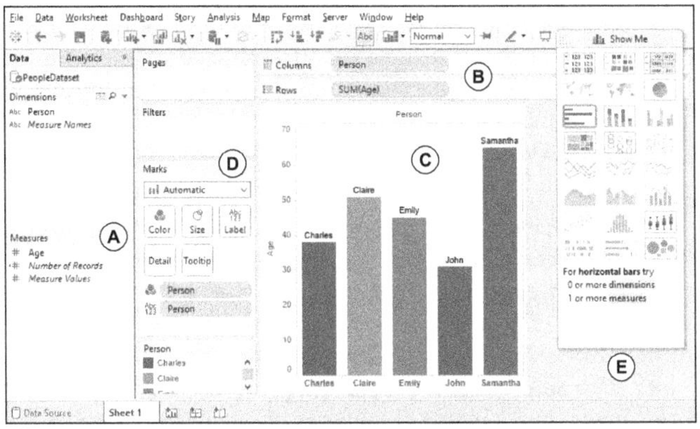


**Figure 1. Tableau Desktop Interface.**

such as those implementing *constructive visualization* principles [22, 23, 24, 25]. In bottom-up tools people explicitly establish mappings between individual data points and the graphical elements that represent them. The final visualization emerges as the result of many small-scale decisions and manipulations. As representative of this approach we selected iVoLVER [31], the **I**nteractive **V**isual **L**anguage for **V**isualization **E**xtraction and **R**econstruction, because it is digital as Tableau Desktop and the code is recent, open, and available on-line.[2] iVoLVER is based on an infinite zoomable canvas interface. On opening the tool the user imports the data which appears directly on the canvas (e.g., a table of data will be composed by numbers and lines that are canvas objects; see A in Fig. 2). In addition to the data there are other objects such as marks or positioner widgets, that can be dragged from a palette (B in Fig. 2) into any position on the canvas and subsequently be linked to the data or to each other. A toolbar on top provides access to global options such as selecting the data to import or showing or hiding the connections between canvas objects (C in Fig. 2).

Tableau Desktop and iVoLVER are both digital tools and share the use of marks (as defined by Bertin [4]) and visual properties [12, 13] as central concepts in visualization design. Additionally, neither of the tools requires textual programming and both support dragging and dropping interactions; however, the two fundamentally differ in their underlying design approach, which results in important differences that motivate our study, as discussed below.

[2] `http://ivolver.cs.st-andrews.ac.uk`

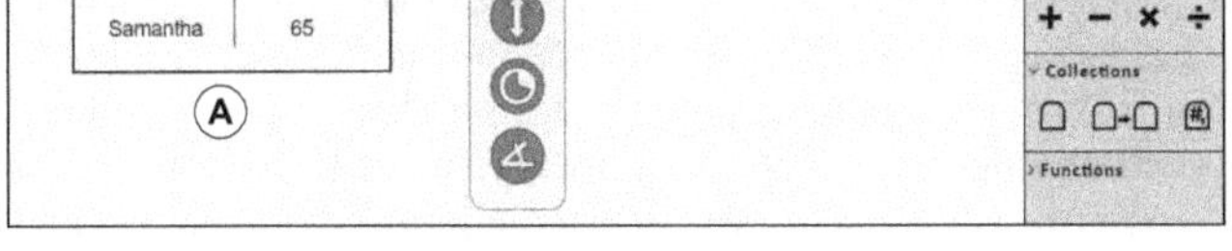


**Figure 2. iVoLVER Interface.**

*Data Granularity and Operation Repetition*

The main activity of designing visualizations in Tableau Desktop consists of the assignment (through drag-and-drop), of a data attribute to a visual dimension (row or column) or a visual property. A key point here is that Tableau users do not have the option to manipulate individual data points, but instead deal with the full range of data by attribute. Interactions happen at an attribute-level, including all the corresponding values in the dataset. This enables fast construction of visualizations. In constrast, iVoLVER operates at the level of individual data points, a lower level of data abstraction. With iVoLVER users are responsible for defining what is a data point, how it is mapped to a specific visual property, and how it is to be interpreted (e.g., as categorical or numerical data).

In Tableau, a single action typically affects all elements of the visualization regardless of whether the dataset contains a handful or millions of rows. Thus, Tableau typically does not require repeated interaction steps. In contrast, iVoLVER's paradigm of bottom-up construction forces users to apply operations per data value. Although it could be feasible to implement mechanisms to eliminate repetition through automation in constructive approaches (à la *programming by example* [6, 14, 28]), iVoLVER does not currently allow this.

*Visual Representations as Controllers*

iVoLVER is designed to blur the line between visual representations and their control and configuration. The dataset, controls, configurations, and visual elements all reside in an infinite canvas, and most widgets are both representations of data *and* allow its manipulation. In contrast, Tableau's pane-based interface separates manipulation and representation: the central visualization pane shows the results of operations spatially separated from the configuration areas of the interface. Access to some functionality takes place through menus.

To investigate the consequences of these two differing interface approaches we conducted two studies with non-experts: an in-classroom pilot study and a more in-depth lab study.

## IN-CLASSROOM PILOT STUDY

Our pilot study was run as part of an introductory university course on information visualization. As part of this within-subjects study students were introduced to Tableau Desktop and iVoLVER in two subsequent tutorials that took place in weeks three and four of the 11-week course, immediately after a lecture on marks, visual variables, and mappings. Students completed three visualization exercises using each of the tools and provided feedback about their process, the character of visualizations they built, and their general experience with the tools. We describe the methodology, which is shared with our main study, in detail below.

### Participants

Out of 36 students enrolled in the class, 19 volunteered to participate in the study. Of these, eight did not complete both study sessions, leaving us with 11 participants (7 male, 4 female; age 21–26, median 22). Only data from these students was considered in our analysis of findings. Participants had backgrounds in computer science, information technology, language & culture, and statistics. All of them were novices in InfoVis with varying self-reported expertise: four had no prior knowledge about information visualization; four were aware of InfoVis through the web and/or magazines without knowledge about its theory; and three had been actively following visualization topics but did not have practical application experience.

### Study Procedure

The study was divided into two sessions. In Session 1 all students of the course were split into two groups. One group was introduced to Tableau Desktop and the other to iVoLVER. In Session 2 (the following week), students switched tools. Each study session started with an introduction to Tableau Desktop or iVoLVER to the respective groups. Students then completed a set of tasks with the corresponding tool and dataset. We used one dataset on oil production and consumption levels and another about movies; each with five data points and five attributes. The tasks were to create three different visualizations addressing different aspects of the data. For the oil dataset we asked for visualizations about: oil production levels by country (V1); the countries and their regions (V2); the oil production, consumption and population by country (V3). The tasks for the movies dataset were equivalent in the type and number of attributes: V1 was about displaying the budget of each movie; V2 about genre; and V3 was about budget, world-wide gross revenue, and duration (see auxiliary material for the datasets and tasks). Students had 30 minutes to complete the tasks. To balance tasks, datasets and tools, participants in both groups saw the same datasets and tasks in the first session, and different (but equivalent in size and difficulty) datasets and tasks in the second.

After completing the tasks, participants filled out questionnaires about their satisfaction with the tool, the visualizations they created, and the rationale for their representation choices. They also rated the process of constructing visualizations with the tool and listed its most useful and problematic features. At the end of Session 2 we conducted a group discussion with all students, who compared their experiences with each tool and perceived benefits and drawbacks.

### Data Collection & Analysis

We recorded 650 minutes of participants' visualization processes in the form of video screen captures. We analyzed the video through a qualitative video coding process as proposed by Heath et al. [19]. Specifically, we coded for visualization types, selected mappings, exploration of alternative designs, experimentation with features of the tool, and problems observed during the construction process.

Similarly, participants' statements from the questionnaires were categorized and analyzed using qualitative coding. Codes focused on design approaches, satisfaction level rationale, useful and problematic features, and benefits and limitations of the tools. The 17-minute group discussion at the end of Session 2 was audio-recorded and transcribed. The qualitative analysis of discussion statements focused on perceived differences, benefits and limitations of the tools.

### Pilot Study Results

The analysis of the screen recordings gave us an initial understanding of the common sequences of actions participants carried out, the tool features they had problems with, and the extent to which they explored alternative designs. We found that participants using Tableau Desktop explored more alternative designs than those using iVoLVER, but almost exclusively through the "Show-me" pane in something that appeared to be a trial-and-error approach. Also, the visualizations constructed in iVoLVER were more diverse than those created in Tableau and included non-standard visualizations.

Some of participants' motivations behind their design decisions can be inferred through their questionnaire responses: *"I just dragged and dropped the attributes and Tableau did the rest and I just kept moving them around until I found one I liked."* [s7], *"by exploring available chart types and then selecting them depending on the available properties/measures."* [s8, commenting about her vis approach in Tableau]. While these responses and our video analysis suggested a fundamental difference in both tools regarding how students' approached their visualization design, the brief nature and vagueness of the students' written comments in the questionnaire did not provide enough context for an in-depth analysis of the nature of these differences. For example, when asked how they decided on the visual mappings, one student answered *"Messing around."* [s9], and another wrote *"Different shapes, I like circles."* [s2].

During the group discussion conducted at the end of Session 2 students highlighted the benefits and limitations of both tools. In particular, they identified trade-offs, for example, between the level of automation (as provided by Tableau) and flexibility (provided by iVoLVER) and the interplay between these features. However, only six students actively contributed to this discussion, so this data is not representative.

Perhaps more importantly than its results, the pilot helped motivate and focus our research on several key questions: What characterizes and drives the overall visualization design process using the two tools? Do top-down and bottom-up construction approaches influence the visualization design decisions and the exploration of alternative designs and if so, how? How do non-experts experience these two approaches in comparison? Following up on this pilot, we conducted a study to explore these questions more in-depth.

## IN-DEPTH COMPARISON OF IVOLVER & TABLEAU

Our in-depth comparative study of iVoLVER and Tableau Desktop followed a similar procedure as the pilot, but focused more on eliciting participants' individual perspectives on the tools which required one-on-one open-ended interviews. This study is therefore based on individual sessions, rather than an in-classroom setting.

### Participants

We recruited ten participants (3 female, 7 male, 20–46 years old—median 28) from our university via word-of-mouth. None of them had participated in the pilot or ever taken an InfoVis course or any other training in visualization. Seven were undergrad or graduate students enrolled in computer science, mathematics, or physics; three were professionals with experience in teaching and/or researching in topics related to information technology, computer science, physics, and medical engineering. Two participants stated to have no knowledge of visualization, six reported having come across visualizations on the web and/or in magazines, but never considered visualization concepts. One participant had been actively following and reading about visualization-related topics, but did not have any practical experience. Finally, one participant had been actively reading about the topic, and had experience in creating visualizations for at least one year. All participants stated to be familiar with reading graphs and charts, with six stating to have created some, and one stating to be frequently involved in creating graphs and charts and to be quite comfortable with it. Some participants had experience with common visualization tools—such as MS Excel (10), D3.js (1), and Processing (1)—and programming languages, such as Matlab (4) and Python (5). None of the ten participants had used Tableau Desktop before the study, but four had heard of it. One participant had used iVoLVER once, six had heard of it but never used it, and three did not know it at all. No participant had ever received formal instruction on visualization concepts such as marks and visual properties. Even the participant who had used D3.js, stated to have sparse conceptual knowledge on InfoVis. Participants received a £10 gift voucher.

### Study Procedure

Each study session consisted of the following activities:

***Introduction to Visualization Concepts.*** After filling out a questionnaire about their demographics and visualization expertise, each participant watched a 4-minute video[3] explaining the fundamentals of the process of creating visual representations. The video explained the concepts of marks and visual variables and their relevance in the design and construction of visualizations. It also discussed how some visual variables are more (or less) effective for certain data attribute types. The video ended with a slide showing several standard visualizations encouraging participants to think about the composition of marks and their visual properties in these representations. Participants kept a printout summarizing the video to have at hand during the tasks (see auxiliary material for details). This stage ensured that all participants had at least some minimum knowledge on basic visualization concepts, similar to participants in the pilot who had seen these concepts as part of their InfoVis course.

***Introduction to Tool.*** A 20-minute tool introduction session followed for the first tool (iVoLVER or Tableau Desktop) that included an overview of its interface features and a demonstration of how the tool implements the concepts of marks and visual variables, as well as the interactions steps required to map data to visuals. This live demonstration showed participants how the tool was used to create a visualization of a small dataset. Participants were provided with a printed "tool cheatsheet" (see auxiliary material for details) to help them in the subsequent visualization tasks.

***Visualization Task.*** Participants received a dataset and tasks to complete identical to those in the pilot study (same data and tasks–see pilot above and the auxiliary material). Participants had 30 minutes to complete the tasks.

***Feedback on Tool.*** Participants filled out a questionnaire rating their experience with the visualization tool, their satisfaction with the resulting visualizations, and their understanding on the dataset after interacting with the tool. An open-ended interview followed where they described their visualizations, their creation process, their mapping choices, and their general experience and satisfaction with the tool and its features.

Participants went again through the sequence of intro-to-tool, visualization task, and feedback session with the second tool and the second set of data and tasks. Tool order was counterbalanced across participants to reduce learning effects and assure that each tool was tested the same number of times on each dataset and task. The study session concluded with a final interview where participants compared how iVoLVER and Tableau Desktop supported the visualization process and listed their perspectives on benefits and limitations of each tool. We also asked them if they would use any of the tools in the future and if so, for what types of visualization tasks. Each study session took approximately two hours.

### Data Collection & Analysis

We used questionnaires to collect participant demographic and background information as well as their ratings of the visualization process and results. Questionnaire answers were coded and categorized according to themes such as design ideas, rationale for the choice of visualization type, visual mapping strategies, identified benefits and limitations of each tool, and potential usage scenarios.

We took written notes of participants' interaction processes with the tools and video captures of all on-screen activities. In total, 415 minutes of video data were analyzed using qualitative methods as proposed by Heath et al. [19]. This included a characterization of the individual visualization steps and a detailed analysis of particularly interesting episodes flagged by the experimenter in the observational notes (e.g., patterns in the use of specific functionality and problematic interaction paths). We also collected the visualization outcomes (30 in Tableau and 28 in iVoLVER—two participants did not complete all tasks due to time constraints).

All interviews were audio recorded, fully transcribed and qualitatively coded by two researchers independently following a thematic analysis approach [8]. Initial coding focused on themes from the interview questions such as the visual mapping process and the benefits and limitations of the tools. From there, higher-level themes emerged, for example, suitable usage scenarios for each tool, and perceived ownership of the process and results. The scheme evolved through regular meetings of the researchers who discussed and refined the codes until the scheme stabilized.

## FINDINGS

Figure 3 shows an overview of the visualizations created with both tools. Visual inspection supports an overall difference in the range of visualization types created with each tool.

***iVoLVER.*** Participants created a large variety of visualization types for the three tasks. For V1, most participants (8/10) produced bar charts; two participants created a bubble chart. For V2 there was a strong preference for representing qualitative attributes with changes in shape and color (6/10); other visualization approaches included a Venn diagram (p1), a graph representation (p2), a table (p8), and a cluster-based visualization (p10). For V3, scatter plots constitute half of the vi-

[3]Available at `http://ivolver.cs.st-andrews.ac.uk/study`

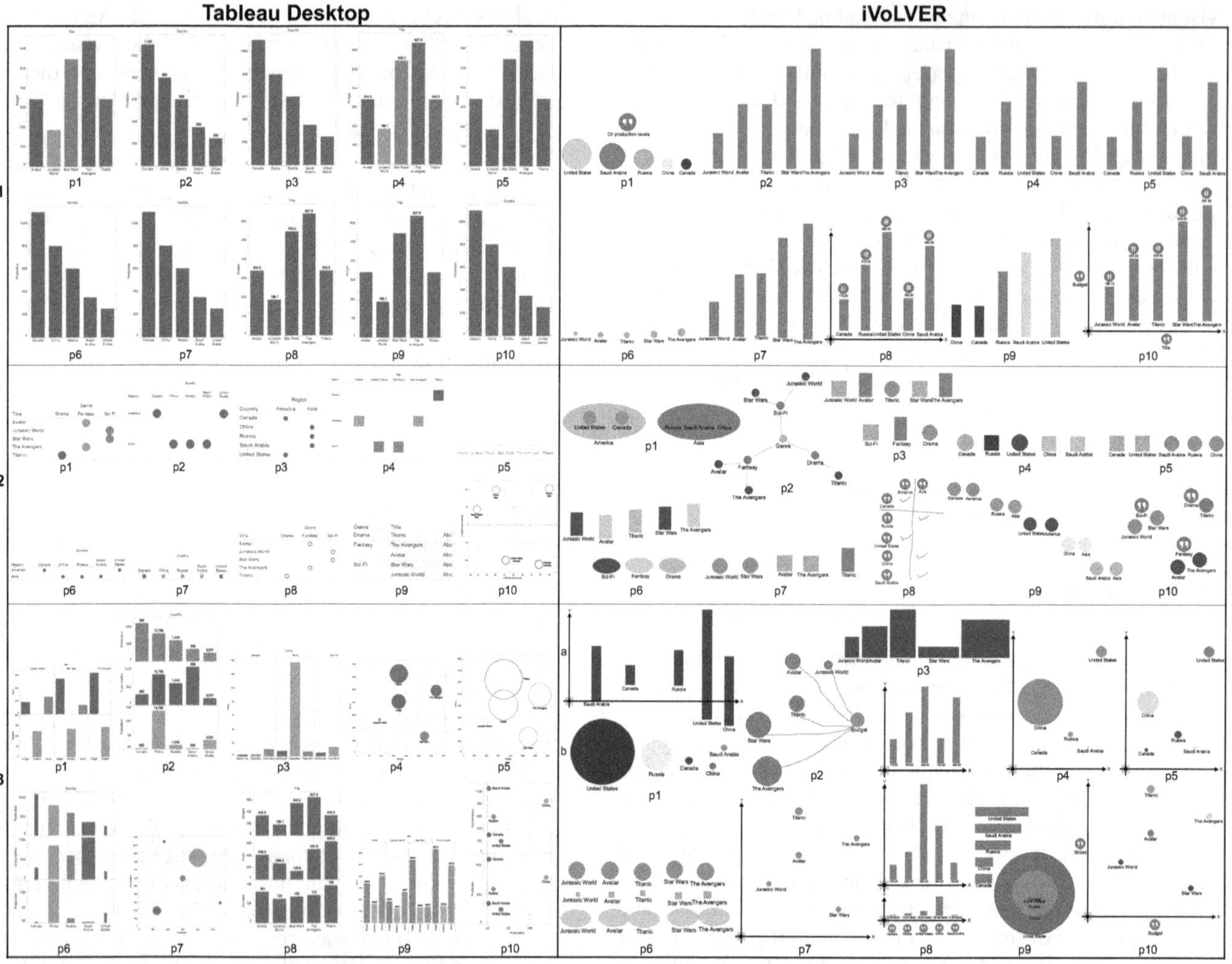


**Figure 3. The visualizations built by participants of the main study, per task and tool, labelled according to participant number.**

sualizations, together with one multi-bar chart (i.e., one bar chart for each attribute—p8), one unfinished graph representation (p2), and three non-standard visualizations where attributes were mapped to shape, color, and/or the width and height of rectangular marks (p3, p6, p9).

***Tableau Desktop.*** Visualizations created in Tableau Desktop form a less heterogeneous set. All participants created bar charts for V1. The majority of visualization types created for V2 are matrix-like representations with marks located in cells (7/10), with the exception of one visualization containing colored text marks (p5), one text table (p9), and a scatter plot where the latitude and longitude auto-generated by Tableau were used to position circular colored marks to represent different countries (p10). V3 visualizations were split between multi-bar charts (6/10) and scatter plots (4/10).

The popularity of bar-based constructions visible in the visualization results of both tools is consistent with previous findings of novices constructing visualizations in Tableau with the assistance of an expert [18]. The entire set of designs also resembles the *representation continuum* discussed by Walny et al. in the context of data sketching [42], but our participants did not create line graphs or pictorial representations.

### The Visualization Construction Process

The video and interview analyses revealed that participants approached their visualization construction process differently in iVoLVER and Tableau Desktop, as summarized in the sequence diagrams of Figure 4.

In ***iVoLVER***, participants followed a mostly linear process (see Fig. 4.A). They reported that they first identified the *data attributes* relevant for the given task and then tried to come up with an *idea* of the type of visualization they wanted to build (e.g., a bar chart) or the types of marks they would use to represent the data (e.g., circles): *"For the first design I just thought about all the general bar graphs that we see all the time in, you know, publications and stuff like that."* [p3].

Participants would then engage in a *representation process* trying to realize their initial idea. This process typically involved extracting relevant data points from the data table and mapping them directly onto the marks' properties. However, some participants also reported creating first some marks and assigning them colors or labels, before connecting these marks to data points: *"It's like you're pulling shapes into the thing in the same way you might in a drawing package. And only then are you kind of introducing data aspects."* [p5].

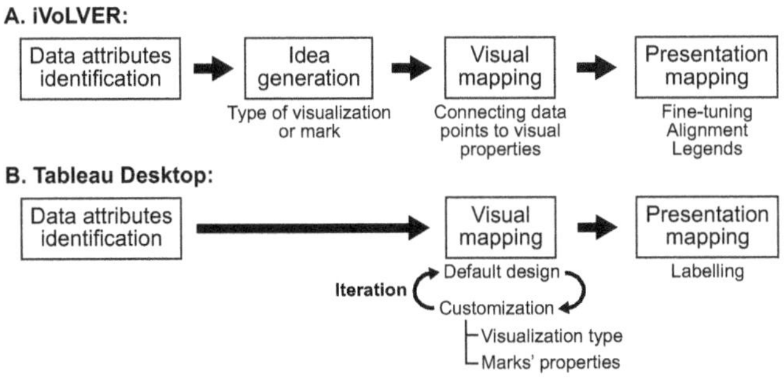


**Figure 4. Stages of the observed visualization construction processes performed with iVoLVER (A) and Tableau Desktop (B).**

Applying textual labels to marks referring on their corresponding data—typically discussed as a step of presentation mapping [26]—was an integral part of the representation process, as it allowed participants to keep track of what mark represented which data point. Participants would also position, align, or group their marks intentionally. Final layout adjustments and the creation of legends (2/10) concluded participants' visualization construction process in iVoLVER.

What stands out in this process is its linearity. The exploration of alternative visualization designs or iterating on initial ideas was rare with only one participant attempting to construct different designs in iVoLVER (see p1 for V3 in Fig. 3). Exploration was mostly done in the context of testing the suitability of a representation idea, for example, a particular mapping using a single data point and a single mark. Participants' statements indicate that it was the elaborate construction process that prevented them from further design iterations or explorations in iVoLVER: *"Many things need to be manually done. For example, even for these five marks I need to drag fifteen times. [...] But if, after I drag fifteen times, I realize 'no, a bar chart is not good' and I need to change. Then, probably it would be quite difficult to change at that time."* [p8].

In ***Tableau Desktop***, as with iVoLVER, participants first identified the *data attributes* relevant to their task. However, they then typically started the *representation process* right away, dragging the attributes of interest into the rows and columns shelves, even if they did not have an idea in mind about how to represent these attributes. Only two participants reported having an initial idea before they started to explore visualization types in Tableau Desktop. Participants typically followed Tableau's default suggestions for their initial visualization design (visible in the Tableau visualizations for V1 and V2 in Fig. 3) and spent most of their representation process customizing this design (e.g., changing shapes or colors).

In contrast to iVoLVER, we found the representation process in Tableau Desktop to be more iterative, with participants experimenting with the mapping of attributes to visual elements and rearranging the attributes in the rows and column shelves to redefine existing mappings. Many participants also made use of the "Show me" pane to explore alternative visualization types, however, we observed this type of exploration much less frequently than in the classroom context of the pilot study. These notable differences in the sequence of actions confirm the results of previous studies that compared approaches of constructing bar charts using template-based digital tools and physical tiles [44].

### The Tools' Influence on the Design Approach

When it comes to constructing visualizations, coming up with ideas on how to visually encode data is key. During the interviews, we prompted participants to comment on how they carried out their mappings and what drove this process. As shown in Figure 3, we found that the two tools heavily influenced participants' approaches to visualization design.

With ***iVoLVER*** participants typically reported to have a design idea in mind and only then to start the practical process of mapping data to visuals. They often mentioned the need to plan and/or think before engaging into the representation process—this was experienced as challenging, but also encouraged creativity: *"In iVoLVER there is sort of an extra step where you actually have to come up with the plot itself and the strategy to build it. [...] When you say 'I wanna do bar charts' in iVoLVER, you have to think of stuff like 'OK, so. How am I going to order the bars?', 'How am I gonna connect?' It's up to you, all kind of different things: 'Am I gonna scale the data?'"* [p2]; *"[In iVoLVER] you have to think about the properties in one sense but also the marks. And it's slightly more creative because you are making that selection, before you're seeing a bar chart or a graph or something that's quite default and typical."* [p9].

In contrast, the exploration of designs in ***Tableau Desktop*** was tool-driven, as shown by the video analysis and interviews. The process was characterized by participants following Tableau's design lead in the absence of an initial idea or reflection on adequate data mappings: *"I mean, I don't really have to think about it [the design] in any way. I just put the title in one column and the value in the rows and, you know, that automatically created the bar chart, which is perfectly adequate. [...] I didn't necessarily have a bar chart in mind. I just wanted to put it there and decide later on how it's best represented depending on what the program does. [...] And then see where to go from there."* [p1].

Six participants mentioned or suggested this notion of "no-need-to-think" when working in Tableau: *"I was just dragging values around like 'Oh, I'll put this in the columns', 'I'll put this in the rows', 'I'll change this mapping from this thing', but without really thinking about it."* [p5]; *"It feels like a very quick and easy way of presenting some simple data if you don't have time to think about how you want to do it in a different way."* [p9]. One participant directly compared the design process of the two tools—their conclusions are representative: *"I really, really, liked the way that I can very quickly get something going [in Tableau]. I felt that [...] I didn't have to think as much about how to implement it, as I did in iVoLVER."* [p5]. These statements confirm what our video analyses of the construction processes in both the pilot and the main study hinted at: with Tableau Desktop participants experimented rapidly with a range of different design approaches, but typically without much critical reflection.

The impact of this tool-driven approach seen with Tableau should not be underestimated; we have evidence that it can fundamentally influence the way in which people think about visualization design—even if they do not use the tool any longer. Three out of five participants who worked first with Tableau stated that their decisions on visualizations types in iVoLVER were based on what they did with Tableau: *"Because I did the previous experiment using Tableau. The datasets are quite similar, so I already had in my mind, it should be something like a bar chart, because I did the previous experiment."* [p8]. In fact, when working with iVoLVER, this participant replicated all the visualizations he previously built with Tableau Desktop. We did not find any evidence that working with iVoLVER influenced design choices in Tableau.

#### Design Exploration

The fundamentally different approaches to visualization design represented by the tools also have an influence on how and how much participants explored alternative design ideas. The speedy, tool-driven process in ***Tableau Desktop*** promoted the exploration of multiple mappings as indicated by the following statements: *"Since there are so many options, you want to try putting data in different slots and try different kinds of graphs in order to see what looks better. In a way that's good because you get to explore more stuff."* [p3]; *"I can change from bars to other things quite easily. [...] so, I can quickly experiment with different charts and see the final one. But for iVoLVER I need to decide first and then I choose the bar chart."* [p8]. As mentioned earlier, with iVoLVER participants typically did not iterate on their visualization designs once they had built them, neither did they explore different visualization types (see Fig. 4).

However, the type of exploration promoted by Tableau seems less in-depth compared to iVoLVER, with participants not critically reflecting on the meaning and potential impact of their explorations: *"There wasn't any need to do anything else because what [Tableau] did automatically was what I should have done, I suppose."* [p1]; *"Because it takes care of so much for you, you sort of have to build up a good set of experience to use it. You know, to just be able to expect what it will do."* [p2]. Furthermore, the tool-driven exploration hampered participants' experimentation with their own ideas: *"I think because it's quite automated, sometimes it's perhaps a bit more difficult to customize things in the way that you want to."* [p1]; *"It felt like I wasn't really composing the thing. I was kind of putting stuff into pre-canned visualizations."* [p5]. While design explorations can be laborious in iVoLVER, they allow for more free-form, creative experimentation and critical reflection. With iVoLVER we observed a more "thoughtful" approach to visualization design exploration: *"And I think the process [in iVoLVER] is very much an atomic thing. So, you do know 'OK, this one is bigger than this one', because you're dragging it and you're doing it. And so you're thinking about the values of each thing you are putting on consciously rather than just assuming."* [p10].

#### Deciding on Visual Mappings

The visualization design process not only includes coming up with an idea of how to represent the data as a whole (e.g., the type of visualization) but also how to encode particular attributes using visual variables such as size, color, or shape. According to participants' statements these low-level visual mappings were typically a consequence of the visualization type chosen: *"I chose bar charts and, of course, the height is the suitable [visual variable]."* [p8, about his process with iVoLVER]. However, most participants, regardless of the tool, were able to justify their decisions on visual mappings by reflecting on the suitability of certain visual variables to encode particular attribute types. For example, working with Tableau, participants stated things like: *"The budget is quantitative, so I used length."* [p4]. Statements after using iVoLVER go in a similar direction: *"I decided on color because it seemed like a good way to represent categorical data."* [p5]. These statements, which link to what participants learnt through our introductory video, indicate that in both tools they were able to apply visual mappings they came up with for their visualization.

### Manipulating Data and Associated Visual Elements

iVoLVER and Tableau Desktop represent opposite extremes in the bottom-up/top-down vis construction spectrum, and the consequences are reflected in the interviews. Participants discussed iVoLVER's bottom-up strategy as laborious because it requires manipulating every single data value: *"For every circle I had to do the same, the same, the same thing. So, if there was a way I just do it for one circle, and it automatically does it for all the circles around—it would be perfect."* [p7]. However, they also highlighted flexibility and freedom as benefits of the bottom-up approach: *"Because of the way iVoLVER presents all the values you can change all of the direct mappings. I can kind of be a bit more creative with them. [...] Perhaps a good example would be that in the case of the third activity it was very, very easy to see that I could map one value to the height and one value to the width."* [p3]; *"[iVoLVER] was actually much more free and helped me come up with new ideas. In Tableau I had no idea what to do with that type of [categorical] data and there wasn't a huge amount of freedom to play. Whereas here [in iVoLVER], moving the actual atomic data points and figuring out 'OK, this isn't linear [...] How do I move them and group them?'"* [p10].

The above statements highlight what we believe is an important trade-off: Tableau's top-down approach results in very few required interactions allowing for the speedy creation and exploration of different visualization types. However, this comes at the cost of transparency of the visualization process. When working with Tableau, it was sometimes difficult for participants to follow how data was mapped to the visual properties of marks, in contrast to iVoLVER where this connection is clearly visible. Along these lines, one participant stated: *"iVoLVER is better for design because you actually get to see what works, what doesn't work and why. Whereas in Tableau I don't think you get to see what works and doesn't work and why [...] because it's generated so quickly that you don't get the sense of something building up. Whereas in iVoLVER you've built something up from a quite low level. Whereas in Tableau you just come in and something is created. You don't see how it is created or why."* [p10].

In general, most visualization features in Tableau are connected on an attribute-level; manipulating them can introduce fundamental changes in the visualization that can be difficult to follow. Commenting on their experience with the "Show me" pane, one participant stated: *"At one point I clicked on it, and it changed everything. I was like 'This is a disaster!' [...] I was just not quite sure what it was going to do once I put genre in columns. It was just very abstract."* [p4]. This, along with previous statements, makes clear that predicting, keeping track of, and interpreting exactly how Tableau Desktop maps data to visual properties was often difficult for participants due to the speed and the attribute-level scale in which things change based on user's interactions. That being said, the links that show the mappings between data and visuals in iVoLVER, while adding transparency, also frequently cluttered the interface and, therefore, hampered the visualization process. Four participants mentioned this explicitly: *"You get to a certain level of complexity, it becomes very hard to manage all connections."* [p5]; *"You have the connections, which, again, are quite confusing sometimes. Again, you have to keep good track of what you have done so far."* [p1].

### Control and Authorship

The type of words participants used when describing their visualization process in Tableau vs. iVoLVER further indicates that the visualization process in Tableau is largely tool-driven. When explaining their iVoLVER constructions, all participants assumed authorship of the process and outcomes. This was visible in the use of first person singular personal pronouns (e.g., *"I did"*, *"I mapped"*), as the following statement illustrates: *"And the third [vis] I'm satisfied with because I showed different data in, like, a readable way."* [p4]. Across all interviews, in just a single instance was iVoLVER credited with a design decision: when a participant released a connection on top of a circular mark and iVoLVER associated this to the mark's radius property (its default behavior). In contrast, in their descriptions of the process with Tableau most participants (8/10) at some point accredited Tableau the responsibility for certain design decisions: *"Tableau did a very good job of ordering them. For example, now we know what Canada produces."* [p6]. It was also common for participants to describe their visualization results as a consequence of a mix of their own and Tableau's actions which they clearly separated, as illustrated in this exemplary statement: *"I dragged the title and I dragged the gross here. Then it automatically generated this [vis], which I think is good enough. I can understand this already and, again, I wanted to add the labels to make it easier to read. [...] So, I tried to drag the label."* [p8]).

Authorship was also explicitly commented on (unprompted by us) by six participants when summarizing their experience with the two tools: *"[In] Tableau you just throw it at the system; throw everything and then it generates for you"* [p8]. And commenting on iVoLVER: *"I'd say that the process [in iVoLVER] is definitely more involved in that you have to actually interact with that data instead of just throwing the idea of a column into a thing and having it built for you. [...] Because designing is something that you need to be involved in, and you need to understand what's happening with the data for you to show what's happening with the data."* [p4].

### Overall Preferences

At the end of each study session, we asked participants' what tool they preferred overall. Most of them favored Tableau Desktop (7/10) because of the speed of construction. However, two of these seven also mentioned a trade-off between speed and: 1) opportunities to explore (*"I did everything quicker in Tableau, even though there was less space for exploration."* [p3]; and 2) experiencing the process (*"Because I am writing papers, I just want to see the result; I don't need the process. So, Tableau would be better. But if sometimes I need the process I might choose iVoLVER."* [p8]). One participant preferred iVoLVER because of its flexibility, but considered Tableau her default option because of its speed: *"I'm a very visual user. So, although I got a bit stuck with iVoLVER, I would probably persevere with it just because it let me drag and play around and I could quickly see changing shapes and objects and things like that. But I could see me defaulting to Tableau if I have to quickly create a graph."* [p9].

As indicated by these statements, all participants found the tools' suitability to be context dependent. Tableau is convenient when dealing with large datasets: *"I'd probably prefer Tableau because I generally use large datasets, and in a large dataset iVoLVER is just not gonna handle it. And so, Tableau would be the only viable option."* [p10]. iVoLVER was considered useful for prototyping, for exploring unfamiliar datasets, and for more creative approaches to visualization: *"iVoLVER could be a really powerful tool to prototype visualizations because of its generality and because it's really convenient and really transparent."* [p2]; *"I would say [iVoLVER] is much more useful probably with more unique types of visualizations. Something that isn't just a standard chart; something where you want to have that fine grained control; and something where you aren't super familiar with the dataset and you want to figure it out as you go."* [p4].

Two participants mentioned a hybrid approach using both tools. They identified iVoLVER as a good starting point to experiment with potential designs and Tableau Desktop as preferable for implementing the visualization once the design has been decided: *"If I don't know what I want yet, I would prefer to try iVoLVER first to see in how many ways I can design the visualization. And then, if I know what I actually want already, I would just put it on Tableau because it's faster."* [p7]; *"I would use iVoLVER for quick drafts of data visualizations. And then if I had to do maybe a more professional one, then maybe move to Tableau."* [p3].

### Teaching and Learning InfoVis

Because of its predefined templates, one participant mentioned Tableau as a good tool to teach people the design space of standard visualizations: *"If you're sort of learning a taxonomy of different types of visualizations, Tableau is probably better because they already exist, and you can experiment very quickly by just moving a few things around."* [p5].

Conversely, iVoLVER was mentioned as useful to train beginners because of its transparency regarding the visualization process which brings across basic visualization concepts: *"If I was trying to show people the ideas and the intuition and the motivation behind visualizing things, definitely iVoLVER. Once again, the triviality and the transparency [of the process] are the two winning factors."* [p2]; *"Because it's more intuitive. At least I believe that in order to learn something, you have to get your hands dirty; you actually have to go and see. The level of automation of Tableau is very high. It's just like drag, and then you have no idea what would happen. For iVoLVER you can influence directly what will happen. [...] I believe that for a beginner iVoLVER is better than*

*Tableau."* [p7]; *"Tableau does it for you, which isn't helpful at any kind of education system. Because you don't have to figure out what specifically is happening and how position works and how area works. It's just sort of you drag it into size and—whoop!—it does it. Whereas in iVoLVER you need to actually pay attention."* [p4].

## DISCUSSION

Our findings show important differences between the two tools in outcomes, process, design approach, authorship, and preference. Participants recognized Tableau Desktop as an efficient tool, but often used it in a haphazard way—"no thinking required". Although the visualization process in Tableau Desktop included more alternatives, visualization outcomes were also more homogeneous. The analysis also shows that participants using iVoLVER initiated the design process with their own ideas whereas Tableau users were strongly led by this tool's design suggestions. Although most participants preferred Tableau Desktop for its speed (7/10), the consensus was that iVoLVER facilitated an understanding of the visualization process and promoted a feeling of authorship.

### Efficiency vs. Understanding, Freedom and Creativity

The comparison of the two tools highlights the consequences of bottom-up and top-down visualization construction approaches on process and outcomes, which is relevant for designers of visualization tools for non-experts. The trade-offs are remarkably tricky; Tableau's top-down approach allows people to quickly explore many alternative designs compared to the more laborious bottom-up constructive process in iVoLVER. This reflects the tension between magic and literalism identified long ago by Smith [38], but it goes further: the efficiency of the top-down template-based or shelf configuration approaches might come at the cost of thoughtfulness and affect the transparency of the process. When participants are forced to construct a visualization from the ground up (i.e., from the level of data points), they seem to be involved in a deeper process that results in a better understanding of how the visualization evolves and in a feeling of control, ultimately leading to more creative and varied designs and a stronger experience of authorship.

In many situations tools need to be, first and foremost, quick and efficient; however, it is important to recognize that visualization design is also a creative task. There is value in enhancing the breadth of people's explorations for visualizations that support their own purposes. Similarly, promoting "thoughtful exploration" and a thorough understanding of the consequences of representation design decisions is more in line with the goals of visual literacy [7, 20, 30], and is an important part in educational contexts. This is in stark contrast to "black boxing" functionality that might leave important decisions to the software.

### The Space in Between

Tableau Desktop and iVoLVER represent two extremes of the spectrum of vis construction approaches. Tools that allow "mode switches" between these two philosophies, or hybrid approaches that bridge the idea of template-based, shelf configuration and constructive approaches may maximize the benefits and overcome the disadvantages of each approach. However, finding a sweet spot that balances the trade-offs we have described requires more research; although it would be relatively easily to speed up iVoLVER with more abstract dataset operations, this very act of repetitive hands-on data mapping might be what provides the sense of thoughtfulness, creativity and authorship we observed. Additionally, increasing automation might reduce the transparency of the process and harm its understanding [21]. Exploring the design space in-between seems a promising avenue for future research.

## LIMITATIONS AND OPEN QUESTIONS

The design choices of our studies obviously impact the generalizability and validity of the presented results. First, we have studied only two particular tools with their own idiosyncrasies and workflows that we believe represent two ends of the top-down/bottom-up spectrum. Second, carrying out a controlled experiment in which we imposed particular datasets and tasks may have affected participants' process and visualization approach. While this effect has to be considered when extrapolating our findings, we believe that most of our observations can be linked to the tools' general approach rather than the specifics of our study. For example, our participants highlighted the importance of the visibility and flexibility of the visualization design process regardless of the particular implementation of each tool. Without prompting participants commented on how the tools would scale (or not) with bigger datasets. Nevertheless, additional studies are required that investigate our research questions considering additional visualization tools and different (sizes of) datasets and analysis tasks.

We must also highlight that our participants all had a science background and therefore arguably an affinity to quantitative data analysis, which may have influenced our findings. Additional studies should investigate if and how our findings expand to different populations (e.g., with a background in the arts or humanities) and age groups (e.g., teenagers and seniors). We believe that these new questions need to be addressed through further studies which, in combination with advances in the design and implementation of new visualization tools, will offer a more definitive emerging picture.

## CONCLUSION

We have presented a qualitative study that compared how non-experts design and implement visual representations with a top-down and a bottom-up visualization tool. We identified differences in how these approaches shape people's visualization process, decisions and justifications regarding the visual representation of data, and people's experience and their feeling of control and authorship toward the visualization outcomes. Our insights inform the design of future visualization tools that are fast and easy to use but also empower people to create effective visualizations and promote critical thinking on their design.

## ACKNOWLEDGMENTS

We thank the study participants, the reviewers, and SACHI members for their feedback and help. The Ecuadorian Government supports Gonzalo Gabriel Méndez through a SENESCYT scholarship.

## REFERENCES


1. Greg Abram and Lloyd Treinish. 1995. An Extended Data-Flow Architecture for Data Analysis and Visualization. In *Proceedings of the 6th Conference on Visualization '95 (VIS '95)*. IEEE Computer Society, Washington, DC, USA, 263–. http://dl.acm.org/citation.cfm?id=832271.833845
2. Edith Ackermann. 2001. Piagets constructivism, Paperts constructionism: Whats the difference. *Future of learning group publication* 5, 3 (2001), 438.
3. Jaques Bertin. 1999. Readings in Information Visualization. Morgan Kaufmann Publishers Inc., San Francisco, CA, USA, Chapter Graphics and Graphic Information Processing, 62–65. http://dl.acm.org/citation.cfm?id=300679.300683
4. Jacques Bertin. 2010. *Semiology of Graphics: Diagrams, Networks, Maps* (1 edition ed.). ESRI Press, Redlands, Calif.
5. Alex Bigelow, Steven Drucker, Danyel Fisher, and Miriah Meyer. 2014. Reflections on How Designers Design with Data. In *Proceedings of the 2014 International Working Conference on Advanced Visual Interfaces (AVI '14)*. ACM, New York, NY, USA, 17–24. DOI:http://dx.doi.org/10.1145/2598153.2598175
6. Alan F. Blackwell. 2006. *Psychological Issues in End-User Programming*. Springer Netherlands, Dordrecht, 9–30. DOI: http://dx.doi.org/10.1007/1-4020-5386-X_2
7. Jeremy Boy, Ronald A. Rensink, Enrico Bertini, and Jean-Daniel Fekete. 2014. A Principled Way of Assessing Visualization Literacy. *IEEE Transactions on Visualization and Computer Graphics* 20, 12 (Dec 2014), 1963–1972. DOI: http://dx.doi.org/10.1109/TVCG.2014.2346984
8. Richard E Boyatzis. 1998. *Transforming qualitative information: Thematic analysis and code development.* Sage.
9. Stuart K. Card and Jock Mackinlay. 1997. The structure of the information visualization design space. In *Information Visualization, 1997. Proceedings., IEEE Symposium on.* 92–99. DOI: http://dx.doi.org/10.1109/INFVIS.1997.636792
10. Stuart K Card, Jock D Mackinlay, and Ben Shneiderman. 1999. *Readings in information visualization: using vision to think.* Morgan Kaufmann.
11. Ed H. Chi. 2000. A taxonomy of visualization techniques using the data state reference model. In *Information Visualization, 2000. InfoVis 2000. IEEE Symposium on.* 69–75. DOI: http://dx.doi.org/10.1109/INFVIS.2000.885092
12. William S Cleveland and Robert McGill. 1984. Graphical Perception: Theory, Experimentation, and Application to the Development of Graphical Methods. *J. Amer. Statist. Assoc.* 79, 387 (1984), 531–554. DOI: http://dx.doi.org/10.2307/2288400
13. William S. Cleveland and Robert McGill. 1987. Graphical Perception: The Visual Decoding of Quantitative Information on Graphical Displays of Data. *Journal of the Royal Statistical Society. Series A (General)* 150, 3 (1987), pp. 192–229. http://www.jstor.org/stable/2981473
14. Allen Cypher and Daniel Conrad Halbert. 1993. *Watch what I do: programming by demonstration.* MIT press.
15. Selan dos Santos and Ken Brodlie. 2004. Gaining understanding of multivariate and multidimensional data through visualization. *Computers & Graphics* 28, 3 (2004), 311 – 325. DOI: http://dx.doi.org/10.1016/j.cag.2004.03.013
16. Niklas Elmqvist, John Stasko, and Philippas Tsigas. 2008. DataMeadow: A Visual Canvas for Analysis of Large-scale Multivariate Data. *Information Visualization* 7, 1 (March 2008), 18–33. DOI: http://dx.doi.org/10.1145/1391107.1391110
17. Lars Grammel, Chris Bennett, Melanie Tory, and Margaret-Anne Storey. 2013. A Survey of Visualization Construction User Interfaces. In *EuroVis - Short Papers*, Mario Hlawitschka and Tino Weinkauf (Eds.). The Eurographics Association. DOI: http://dx.doi.org/10.2312/PE.EuroVisShort.EuroVisShort2013.019-023
18. Lars Grammel, Melanie Tory, and Margaret-Anne Storey. 2010. How Information Visualization Novices Construct Visualizations. *IEEE Transactions on Visualization and Computer Graphics* 16, 6 (Nov 2010), 943–952. DOI: http://dx.doi.org/10.1109/TVCG.2010.164
19. Christian Heath, Jon Hindmarsh, and Paul Luff. 2010. *Video in qualitative research.* Sage Publications.
20. John A Hortin. 1980. Visual Literacy and Visual Thinking. (1980).
21. Jessica Hullman, Eytan Adar, and Priti Shah. 2011. Benefitting InfoVis with Visual Difficulties. *IEEE Transactions on Visualization and Computer Graphics* 17, 12 (Dec 2011), 2213–2222. DOI: http://dx.doi.org/10.1109/TVCG.2011.175
22. Samuel Huron. 2014. *Constructive Visualization : A token-based paradigm allowing to assemble dynamic visual representation for non-experts.* Theses. Université Paris Sud - Paris XI. https://tel.archives-ouvertes.fr/tel-01126892
23. Samuel Huron, Sheelagh Carpendale, Alice Thudt, Anthony Tang, and Michael Mauerer. 2014a. Constructive Visualization. In *Proceedings of the 2014 Conference on Designing Interactive Systems (DIS '14)*. ACM, New York, NY, USA, 433–442. DOI: http://dx.doi.org/10.1145/2598510.2598566

24. Samuel Huron, Yvonne Jansen, and Sheelagh Carpendale. 2014b. Constructing Visual Representations: Investigating the Use of Tangible Tokens. *Visualization and Computer Graphics, IEEE Transactions on* 20, 12 (Dec 2014), 2102–2111. DOI: http://dx.doi.org/10.1109/TVCG.2014.2346292

25. Samuel Huron, Alice Thudt, Bon Adriel Aseniero, Anthony Tang, and Sheelagh Carpendale. 2016. Constructive Visualization: A New Paradigm to Empower People to Author Visualization. In *SURFNET / Designing Digital Surface Applications*, Frank Maurer (Ed.). NSERC Surfnet, University of Calgary, Chapter 9, 169–191. http://dspace.ucalgary.ca/handle/1880/50450

26. Yvonne Jansen and Pierre Dragicevic. 2013. An Interaction Model for Visualizations Beyond The Desktop. *IEEE Transactions on Visualization and Computer Graphics* 19, 12 (Dec 2013), 2396–2405. DOI: http://dx.doi.org/10.1109/TVCG.2013.134

27. Waqas Javed and Niklas Elmqvist. 2013. ExPlates: Spatializing Interactive Analysis to Scaffold Visual Exploration. *Computer Graphics Forum* 32, 3pt4 (2013), 441–450. DOI: http://dx.doi.org/10.1111/cgf.12131

28. Henry Lieberman. 2000. Your wish is my command: Giving users the power to instruct their software. *Morgen Kaufmann* (2000).

29. Kwan-Liu Ma. 1999. Image Graphs - a Novel Approach to Visual Data Exploration. In *Proceedings of the Conference on Visualization '99: Celebrating Ten Years (VIS '99)*. IEEE Computer Society Press, Los Alamitos, CA, USA, 81–88. http://dl.acm.org/citation.cfm?id=319351.319360

30. Adam V Maltese, Joseph A Harsh, and Dubravka Svetina. 2015. Data visualization literacy: investigating data interpretation along the novice–expert continuum. *Journal of College Science Teaching* 45, 1 (2015), 84.

31. Gonzalo Gabriel Méndez, Miguel A. Nacenta, and Sebastien Vandenheste. 2016. iVoLVER: Interactive Visual Language for Visualization Extraction and Reconstruction. In *Proceedings of the 2016 CHI Conference on Human Factors in Computing Systems (CHI '16)*. ACM, New York, NY, USA, 4073–4085. DOI: http://dx.doi.org/10.1145/2858036.2858435

32. Tamara Munzner. 2014. *Visualization Analysis and Design* (har/psc edition ed.). A K Peters/CRC Press, Boca Raton. http://www.cs.ubc.ca/~tmm/vadbook

33. Kostas Pantazos and Søren Lauesen. 2012. Constructing Visualizations with InfoVis Tools-An Evaluation from a user Perspective. *GRAPP/IVAPP* 2012 (2012), 731–736.

34. Seymour Papert and Idit Harel. 1991. Situating Constructionism. In *Constructionism*. Ablex Publishing Corporation.

35. Jean Piaget. 2013. *Child's Conception of Space: Selected Works*. Vol. 4. Routledge.

36. Jonathan C. Roberts, Chris Headleand, and Panagiotis D. Ritsos. 2016. Sketching Designs Using the Five Design-Sheet Methodology. *IEEE Transactions on Visualization and Computer Graphics* 22, 1 (Jan 2016), 419–428. DOI: http://dx.doi.org/10.1109/TVCG.2015.2467271

37. Arvind Satyanarayan and Jeffrey Heer. 2014. Lyra: An Interactive Visualization Design Environment. *Computer Graphics Forum* 33, 3 (June 2014), 351–360. DOI: http://dx.doi.org/10.1111/cgf.12391

38. Randall B. Smith. 1987. Experiences with the Alternate Reality Kit: An Example of the Tension Between Literalism and Magic. In *Proceedings of the SIGCHI/GI Conference on Human Factors in Computing Systems and Graphics Interface (CHI '87)*. ACM, New York, NY, USA, 61–67. DOI: http://dx.doi.org/10.1145/29933.30861

39. Robert Spence. 2001. *Information visualization*. Vol. 1. Springer.

40. Bret Victor. 2013. Drawing Dynamic Visualizations. Recorded at the Stanford HCI seminar. (2013). https://vimeo.com/66085662

41. Fernanda B. Viegas, Martin Wattenberg, Frank van Ham, Jesse Kriss, and Matt McKeon. 2007. ManyEyes: a Site for Visualization at Internet Scale. *IEEE Transactions on Visualization and Computer Graphics* 13, 6 (Nov. 2007), 1121–1128. DOI: http://dx.doi.org/10.1109/TVCG.2007.70577

42. Jagoda Walny, Samuel Huron, and Sheelagh Carpendale. 2015. An Exploratory Study of Data Sketching for Visual Representation. *Computer Graphics Forum* 34, 3 (2015), 231–240. DOI: http://dx.doi.org/10.1111/cgf.12635

43. Colin Ware. 2010. *Visual thinking: For design*. Morgan Kaufmann.

44. Tiffany Wun, Jennifer Payne, Samuel Huron, and Sheelagh Carpendale. 2016. Comparing Bar Chart Authoring with Microsoft Excel and Tangible Tiles. *Computer Graphics Forum* (2016). DOI: http://dx.doi.org/10.1111/cgf.12887

# What Happened in my Home?: An End-User Development Approach for Smart Home Data Visualization

Nico Castelli[1,2], Corinna Ogonowski[2], Timo Jakobi[1,2], Martin Stein[2,3], Gunnar Stevens[1,2], Volker Wulf[2,3]

[1]Bonn-Rhein-Sieg University of Applied Science, Sankt Augustin, Germany

[2] University of Siegen, Siegen Germany

[3]Fraunhofer Institute for Applied Information Technology, Sankt Augustin, Germany

**Figure 1. (a)** ***open.DASH*** **dashboard interface (b) households create paper-based smart home visualizations (design-workshop) (c) creating a new visualization with the EUD environment (d) usability test of** ***open.DASH*** **with participants**

## ABSTRACT

Smart home systems change the way we experience the home. While there are established research fields within HCI for visualizing specific use cases of a smart home, studies targeting user demands on visualizations spanning across multiple use cases are rare. Especially, individual data-related demands pose a challenge for usable visualizations. To investigate potentials of an end-user development (EUD) approach for flexibly supporting such demands, we developed a smart home system featuring both pre-defined visualizations and a visualization creation tool. To evaluate our concept, we installed our prototype in 12 households as part of a Living Lab study. Results are based on three interview studies, a design workshop and system log data. We identified eight overarching interests in home data and show how participants used pre-defined visualizations to get an overview and the creation tool to not only address specific use cases but also to answer questions by creating temporary visualizations.

### Author Keywords

Smart Home; Qualitative Study; Data Visualization; domestic routines; Living Lab; Interface Design.

### ACM Classification Keywords

H.5.2. User interfaces - User-centered design


ACM 978-1-4503-4655-9/17/05...$15.00
DOI: http://dx.doi.org/10.1145/3025453.3025485

## INTRODUCTION

Smart home systems and smart devices have become increasingly available and affordable. These smart home technologies are collecting large amounts of data (e.g. on brightness, temperature, humidity, energy consumption and movement) through a wide variety of sensors, actors and other Internet of Things (IoT) devices within the home. Data include comprehensive information about the habits and routines of people and information about the current and historical status of the personal home itself [26]. Visualizing this data appropriately enables people to discover more about themselves and their homes and allows them to satisfy data-related requirements.

There are established research fields within human computer interaction (HCI) that deal with the visualization of individual use cases for the domestic context (e.g. eco-feedback and ambient-assisted living) and that uncover highly individual information demands. However, so far, research on integrated smart home systems has focused more on enabling technologies and automation, thereby ignoring potential to make home data accountable.

To close this gap, we conducted an 18-month qualitative study with 12 Living Lab households equipped with smart home technology. Our objective was to understand what specific data-related use cases our participants were interested in. Furthermore, we developed a flexible smart home interface that allows users to build customized and personalized visualization dashboards based on their needs and to evaluate our prototype over a period of three months.

Our main contributions in this paper are:

- to provide data-related use cases and related information necessary for a user to satisfy a specific need;
- to demonstrate the concept and development of a hybrid interface that includes pre-defined

visualizations and a visualization creation tool that lets users without programming skills extend the system (end-user development);

- to provide information on using and integrating the *open.DASH* prototype and on the appropriation of our approach for visualizing smart home data.

## RELATED WORK

Research into the topic of home automation or smart homes that support their inhabitants in their daily lives through the use of technology has been available for several years [3]. Smart home research addresses various issues at different levels of abstraction [46]. Since we cannot give a complete overview of all smart home and home automation research, we focus on studies related to our work and give a brief overview of enabling technology, smart home usage and visualization of domestic sensor data research.

### Enabling Technology (Data and Infrastructure)

Smart home research has a long tradition that focuses on enabling technology, including smart home hardware and infrastructure to collect and transfer data and to set up a smart home.

In the last few years, new developments, especially in the field of wireless network technologies and IoT, have prompted new research. These new technologies and the increasing availability of sensors for retrofitting have also introduced new challenges, e.g. the complexity of, and technical challenges to, running a smart home network or the inflexibility of commercial systems that limit usage [22,32,48]. Thus, research has focused on ensuring that technology is in line with daily routines and habits by simplifying the installation and administration of IoT for the home and on customizing the technology to support experimentation and innovation [46]. Along with these efforts, there are an increasing number of do-it-yourself (DIY) solutions for hardware and infrastructure [48]. This trend is facilitated by advances in affordable microcontrollers, such as the Arduino and by DIY platforms such as LilyPad [12]. These advances enable users to create their own systems. Mennicken and Huang [46] state the importance of supporting these tech-savvy users, who are willing to program and create custom solutions that fit to the existing infrastructure and the needs of individual households.

### Smart Home Usage (Configuration and Processing)

Another popular smart home research agenda deals with the control and processing of smart home data e.g. by focusing on tools that enable users to configure their smart homes [46].

Brush et al. [11] observed two levels of configuration required to automate actions in the smart home. The first level is the combination of different actions that are executed when the user manually carries out one specific action (e.g. a switch for turning on all lights). The second level involves rule-based systems to define conditional rules based on contextual events. Several studies deal with tools that let users define rules and scenarios when customizing the behavior of their smart home (e.g. [19,20,37]). In this area, end-user development (EUD) is one of the most relevant research topics, letting end-users define their own rules for their smart home [39,72]. The most popular example of a rule-based system (that includes home automation) is *if-this-then-that* [38] (IFTTT). IFTTT allows users to create programs that perform actions when a certain event occurs. Another prominent example is iCAP [20], a rule-based system for smart environments, where users can build trigger-action programs.

### Designing for the Smart Home Context (Visualization)

A third category deals with representing and monitoring smart home sensor data and the role of data visualization. So far, little research has been conducted in this area [9] even though informing inhabitants about the collected data and executed events play a major role in context-aware systems [5,47].

Unlike in the other two categories (enabling technology and automation), up to now, there is no EUD or DIY community dealing with visualizing smart home data. Although there are approaches, e.g. by the Information Visualization community, to support the user in creating visualizations for different applications [35] (e.g. the InfoVis Toolkit by Fekete [24], the XML Toolkit by Borner et al. [8] or Prefuse by Heer et al. [35]), they are very generic and aimed at programmers. This is also true for visualization tools such as Grafana [52], which require an understanding of databases.

Currently, commercial smart home interfaces often provide user interfaces with static elements that display raw data as numbers, text, tables or log entries [47] and focus on data that are isolated per device and not linkable to other data [68]. These deficits can lead to a loss of user trust and of acceptance of smart home systems [44] and, moreover to unused system potential [36]. Recently, more advanced smart home visualizations have been developed, e.g. by Mennicken et al. [47], who integrated smart home data into a digital calendar to improve the linking and contextualization of domestic data with everyday activities. Related work revealed that users' motivation for the smart home differs as well as their technical background, and the resulting different requirements have to be considered in the design of smart home interfaces [46,47,76]. Other work on the visualization of domestic sensor data has otherwise typically been conducted separately for two specific use cases, outlined in the following.

#### *Eco-Feedback*

There is a long tradition in HCI research looking at the effects of eco-feedback in supporting energy-efficient behavior by raising awareness of energy consumption (e.g. [7,14,18,30,58,59]). Early systems for presenting energy consumption data were simple energy monitors that displayed raw consumption data of the whole household on a Screen [40]. More sophisticated feedback systems use smart plugs to provide consumption data at a device level and therefore allow the visualization of different aggregation levels [57]. Today's feedback systems are more advanced and aesthetically pleasing as design-centric surveys (e.g. [29,55]) show. Additionally, a series of design studies have elaborated guidelines [34,45] and suggest design frameworks [7,27,56] for visualizing consumption data.

A major trend in eco-feedback design is to draw attention to user diversity, taking gender [2], age [56], motivation type [54,60,66], attitudes [31], prior knowledge [33], saving experience [17,54], and energy awareness [42,75] into account. All these factors seem to affect both the effectiveness of feedback as well as the users' preferences and needs. Kirman et al. [41] stress therefore that persuasion design could benefit from adapting to individual preferences.

#### *Ambient Assisted Living and Aging*

Ambient Assisted Living technology (AAL) is another active community dealing with technological support for a comfortable and independent life of elderly people in the home [16,65]. The overall framing for such systems is highly dependent on the user, user groups and their role, which influence the motivation for such systems. Primary users are the care recipients themselves, but the user list also includes formal care givers, remote care givers and family, neighbors and friends [49]. Furthermore, Stein et al. [63] show that, within the different user groups, there are still more finely categorized use cases that have to be considered, when designing smart home systems for elderly people, e.g. awareness, safety, health, emergency and enhancing of wellbeing.

The consideration of these factors can be seen more easily in the progress of systems that have evolved from simple telecare systems to more sophisticated ones. Takács and Hanák [67] developed an ambient facial interface (a digital human face) that used facial expressions to display emotional information about the current state of care recipients or of information on products they interacted with. Truong et al. [70] presented a more user-centered and interactive system that allowed users to write their own applications for scenarios in daily life. Mulvenna et al. [49] support this effort and suggest developing adaptive interfaces that target the specific needs of different users.

### Challenges for Visualizing Smart Home Data

The known issues in the design of interfaces and the visualization of domestic sensor data call for human-centered approaches. Research in smart home enabling technologies (including hardware and infrastructure) as well as in smart home usage (including configuration and processing) tend towards customizable and DIY approaches, such as EUD, that let users adjust the smart home to their needs and ensure an inhabitant-centered design [19]. According to Newman [50], end-user configuration capability is a key factor in smart home systems. On the visualization level of smart home data, no EUD approach has yet been discussed in literature, but much work deals with static visualization elements. These studies provide best practices and design implications mostly for specific use cases (e.g. energy, security, health, etc.) or for specific users. These works highlight that visualization play a crucial role in domestic systems. Furthermore, research shows that, even in these specific use cases, the needs, interests, capabilities and goals differ between users ("one size does not fit all" [34]). These needs and interests could also change over time with the use of such systems, and they depend on the user's current situation [42]. This variety of parameters is challenging when designing smart home visualization. Users need flexible tools for customization, data comparison and annotations that make the data understandable and to support sense-making [4].

Our *open.DASH* system (see Fig. 1a) combines these two approaches: integrating pre-defined visualizations based on gained insights and experience in specific domestic areas and additionally allowing free customization based on an EUD approach [43]. Our goal is to provide tools that allow users both to explore their smart home to gain further insights into their routines, habits and the home itself and to adjust their smart home interface to fit their specific needs.

## METHODOLOGY

In our study, we followed the user-driven design approach proposed by Stevens et al. [64] and Wulf et al. [73,74] to inform the design of our smart home interface. Thus, we applied a Living Lab approach to understand users and their contexts and to investigate the use of smart home systems in real-life environments [23,28]. With this approach, it is possible to bring users and technology together with different stakeholders from research and design in an open design process [28]. Living Labs support long-term cooperation, co-design and in-situ exploration and therefore the integration of users into a continuous evaluation of the designed artefacts from the very beginning [6]. They also allow early discussions of new concepts, testing not fully operative prototypes and field tests for long-term appropriation of new smart home systems. Especially for the smart home, it is important to investigate users' needs and the contexts for which systems should be designed [53].

### User Sample

We focused on gaining a heterogeneous user sample to have as many different users and types of households as possible. After a multi-stage recruitment process, including newspaper ads, local radio features, etc., we made a pre-selection based on spatial proximity and conducted telephone interviews with 63 interested households (from over 100 registrations) to gather an impression regarding motivation for participation, willingness to actively participate in the project and technical and smart home related foreknowledge. Twelve households with a total of

29 inhabitants were selected, varying in terms of age, living style (rented or owned home, house or flat), rural or urban residential area as well as technical level (see Table 1).

| # | household size, living style, location | tech. knowledge |
|---|---|---|
| H1 | 2-pers. household, apartment, city | Yes |
| H2 | 3-pers. household, house, rural area | Yes |
| H3 | 3-pers. household, house, rural area | Yes |
| H4 | 3-pers. household, house, rural area | Yes |
| H5 | 4-pers. household, house, rural area | Yes |
| H6 | 2-pers. household, house, rural area | Yes |
| H7 | 2-pers. household, apartment, city | No |
| H8 | 1-pers. household, house, rural area | No |
| H9 | 3-pers. household, house, rural area | No |
| H10 | 2-pers. household, apartment, city | No |
| H11 | 1-pers. household, house, city | No |
| H12 | 3-pers. household, house, rural area | No |

**Table 1. Overview of Living Lab user sample**

### Study Design and Data Collection

We conducted a two-stage qualitative empirical study, which is illustrated in Fig. 2. All interviews were audio-recorded and transcribed verbatim. In addition, the design workshop and usability evaluation were video-recorded to facilitate subsequent analysis.

#### *Phase 1: Understanding and Requirements*

We started with an explorative on-site study with a semi-structured interview (**T0**). Our main goal was to gain an understanding of the participants' homes, their daily routines and habits as well as their information needs, interests and ideas for use cases of a smart home system. Afterwards, we provided them with an "off-the-shelf" smart home solution that is currently available on the market. This Z-Wave-based (wireless communication protocol) plug'n'play smart home platform system was used as a technological probe (consisting of 6-36 components per household, selected from a wish list). Three months after the installation, we conducted a second interview study gathering experiences, demands, limitations and gained insights when using the smart home system in participants' everyday life (**T1**). After a further three month period, we conducted a design workshop with five households with the goal to validate requirements identified in T0 and T1 and to gain insights about the design needs. The gained understanding (T0), the mentioned experience and demands (T1) and the design needs from the workshop drew a first set of requirements for our *open.DASH* prototype.

#### *Phase 2: Evaluation and System Usage*

After the development, we conducted a three-stage usability evaluation to ensure that the prototype was usable during the households' everyday life (see Fig. 1d). In this evaluation, users had to perform two scenarios based on T0 and T1 with overall 12 tasks. We first conducted a heuristic usability evaluation with three usability experts from within the university, using Nielsen's usability heuristics [51]. Afterwards, we repeated our usability evaluation first with five and then again with six participants from our Living Lab. We used thinking-aloud to see how users interact with our developed interface [51]. Having addressed all problems mentioned, we rolled out the prototype in 10 out of our 12 Living Lab households (due to sickness and to technical problems, we were unable to install/run our developed interface in two households). Our system was installed as a supplement to the commercial smart home system and was connected to the same sensors and actors, thus used the same data. The participants used the *open.DASH* interface over a period of almost three months. Subsequently, we conducted a third interview study (**T2**) to gather experiences regarding the use, limits and desired extensions of our *open.DASH* interface.

### Data Analysis

Our analysis is based on all Living Lab research activities during the 18 months, including T0, T1, and T2 interviews, design workshop results and field notes from visiting the households. All transcripts were analyzed by two researchers independently using thematic analysis with an inductive coding process [10]. After each of these research activities, code categories were consolidated and developed iteratively. We also internally discussed gained insights with researchers not involved in the project. We recognized the need for some degree of inter-rater reliability and so enlisted other internal researchers that are not involved in the project to check our coding decisions. Additionally, for the evaluation of our developed prototype, we collected quantitative data on the number of site visits, visiting time, duration and customization activities.

In the analysis, we looked for common information needs and interests, actions related to information provided through the system and how the participants configured their smart home. Furthermore, we looked at the integration of smart home data into everyday life especially when users were interested in smart home data, and what questions they wanted to be answered. All quotes in our findings section were translated from the German by the authors.

**Figure 2. Methodology timeline**

## INFORMATION DEMANDS ON SMART HOME DATA

In this section, we present findings from the analysis of Phase 1 that resulted in requirements for the first prototype of our *open.DASH* interface.

### Information Needs and Scenarios

Our analysis resulted in three overall topics for the use of smart home sensor data, which are outlined below.

#### *Events and Home-Status*

A frequent information need was about the current status of the home, especially in the *"leaving-home"* scenario. The participants wanted to know if they had forgotten something such as electric devices or radiators that were still on or open windows and doors: *"Is everything O.K. when I am not at home? Did I forget something?"* (H8, T0). Although motivation varied, nearly all participants mentioned that immediate information about the current status of the home would give them a feeling of security. Another related demand dealt with situations where the participants were *away from home for a longer time*, e.g. when on vacation. Here, the focus shifted, and it was more important for participants to get information on events that happened in the home than on the home's status: *"When we are on vacation, the events are more important, for example if there is movement or if a window or door was opened"* (H8, T0). After installing the commercial smart home system, some participants mentioned that they looked regularly at their event diary, even if they were at home, to get a feeling about what was happening in the home.

#### *Energy and Performance*

Another recurring demand of households dealt with energy efficiency and performance. Before the installation of the commercial smart home system, there was a great need to check whether the devices in the home were energy efficient or not: *"I don't know how much energy is consumed by my devices, I have no possibility to check it"* (H9, T0). *"It is interesting to track what we have to pay for energy every week"* (H7, T0). *"I want to track my standby consumption"* (H12, T0). Most participants mentioned interest in feedback on energy consumption data. With the commercial system installed, requirements towards consumption data tracking and visualization turned out to be very individual. While some participants continuously tracked their consumption, a few households would only check consumption data occasionally, i.e. when they got a *new device* or when *receiving their electricity bill*: *"[Energy] is only interesting if we have a new device"* (H6, T1).

Besides electricity, heating was a very personal topic for the participants because most participants had their own "feel-good" temperature and it sometimes was difficult to quantify this optimum temperature: "*What is the real temperature? [...] How does the sun influence the inside temperature? [...] What effect does an open window have?*" (H9, T0). Therefore, it was also difficult for them to define criteria for performance or efficiency of their heating routines: *"For example, when I have invested, let's say into my heating, I want to know: Does it pay off?"* (H9, T0). *"I don't know what the influence of my heating routine is"* (H8, T1). When the participants could see the real temperature in their rooms, they developed an awareness and could identify *anomalies* by looking at the current temperature. That was also true for energy consumption. After gaining an awareness of energy consumption and temperature levels, participants looked at the data to see whether everything was o.k. and, if not, they tried to find reasons: *"If the [energy] trend is negative then I want to check why"* (H6, T1).

#### *Awareness of my Smart Home*

The installation of the commercial smart home system also resulted in new requirements related to the configuration and automation of the smart home. Because the participants initially lacked trust in the system, they were concerned about false behavior of the smart home and checked the information on the smart home interface to see if their configuration and defined rules were working properly (this is also mentioned by Mennicken et al. [47]): *"I check the system to see if something has failed, like my heating control at the beginning"* (H3, T1)

Furthermore, data served as information about the right configuration, e.g. if the defined rules worked the way the user wanted them to. The information was also used to gain awareness and for participants to build their perfect configuration: Which brightness level is enough and when should the light automatically turn on? How long does it take for the rooms to heat up? Generally, the households used a trial-and-error approach to adjust the settings step-by-step until they were satisfied with the result.

### Implications

The findings so far have shown numerous overlaps of needs and interests between participants, but also some opposing opinions. Overall, we identified eight questions that our participants had for smart home data visualization:

- What (has) happened in my home?
- Did I forget something?
- Are my devices energy efficient?
- Am I energy efficient?
- Is everything o.k.?
- What is the current status of my home?
- Does my smart home work as expected?
- Is my configuration appropriate?

Although, these questions were not always applicable, they were a good starting point to categorize use cases for home data. Not all participants were interested in all of this information, and the information needs could change over time. Besides personal interest, there were multiple other factors that influenced the information needs such as when the participants were on vacation or by seasonal effects: *"[interests in] brightness in winter [its getting dark earlier] and the window status in summer [for fresh air]"* (H1, T1).

Therefore we can further divide information needs into *long-term information needs* and *temporary (short-term) information needs*. Long-term information needs are interesting for participants over a longer period of time, e.g. for the routine to check if something was forgotten in the leaving-home scenario. Temporary information needs are irregular needs that only come up at specific times, e.g. when getting the electricity bill to check what devices are responsible for the consumption.

Especially after installing the commercial smart home, new requirements for smart home data monitoring were identified. The ability to collect data raised interest e.g. in long-term analysis of energy consumption or the combination of multiple devices for comparison or identification of relations between them (which was not fully supported by the commercial smart home system): *"For me, smart home is the connection of multiple devices [...] I don't want a single view, but to see things together, combine things and to visualize them."* (H8, T1).

In general, we can confirm findings from the literature insofar as our participants had individual and personally-motivated information needs [34,56,63]. But we could further see that our participants had also overlapping data-related interests and use-cases. To validate our findings and to identify these mutual information needs, we conducted a creative design workshop, where participants could develop their own paper-based smart home interfaces (see Fig. 1b). In the workshop, we could see that the participants were generally interested in overviews on the topics of energy, temperature and security. Furthermore, we found that people also wanted further, external information implemented into their smart home interface, such as information about the weather or a news feed. Additionally, the workshop revealed preliminary insights into exchange of experience between participants and participant interested in use cases from other participants, to develop new ideas. The concurrency of mutual interest in information, as well as the individual interest in specific information, suggest a hybrid system that includes (1) pre-defined visualizations that can be configured by users and (2) a custom tool for building custom visualizations, fitting needs and interests and allowing a detailed view of the collected data.

## DESIGN AND IMPLEMENTATION OF *OPEN.DASH*

Based on these findings and on relevant literature, we designed a flexible and highly customizable prototype to gain insights about how people use smart home data with our system in real scenarios (Fig. 3).

The system is based on a dashboard concept, allowing us to realize our general idea of multiple visualizations for the participants' needs and use cases as single web components that could easily be exchanged or configured during runtime. The header section allows direct access to the menu and customization settings. The blue-colored area shows real-time information on room level. We chose rooms as a structure because studies show that rooms build an appropriate ordering of the home [15]. A single click allows the navigation between rooms. Overall, this header section allows values in different rooms to be compared and provides an overview of the *current status*, *if everything is o.k.* or *if something was forgotten.* The customizable widget section begins under this blue-colored area. Widgets can be dynamically added, rearranged, changed in size or deleted.

### Pre-Defined Visualizations

Pre-defined widgets can be dynamically added through a widget-chooser in the side-menu. In the first draft, we included five pre-defined widgets that were inspired by the design workshop, including a news widget where an RSS-feed can be included to get current news of the preferred news portal. The development of the pre-defined visualizations was steered by the Visual Information Seeking Mantra by Shneiderman [61] to first provide an overview of the related topics and filtering and details on demand.

The energy widget provides information about the current consumption level of all devices, the current amount of money for this week's energy consumption, a trend indicator that shows if the consumption of this week has a positive or negative trend in contrast to an average weekly consumption and abstract indicators that showing the consumption for up to five single devices. Thus, this widget provides quick information about devices that are currently consuming energy (*Did I forget something?*), about the relation of consumption between devices (*Are my devices energy efficient?*) and about the usage of devices (*Am I energy efficient?).*

The temperature widget indicates the current average temperature of the home. The user can individually configure which sensors should be included in this calculation (e.g. to exclude sensors in the basement).

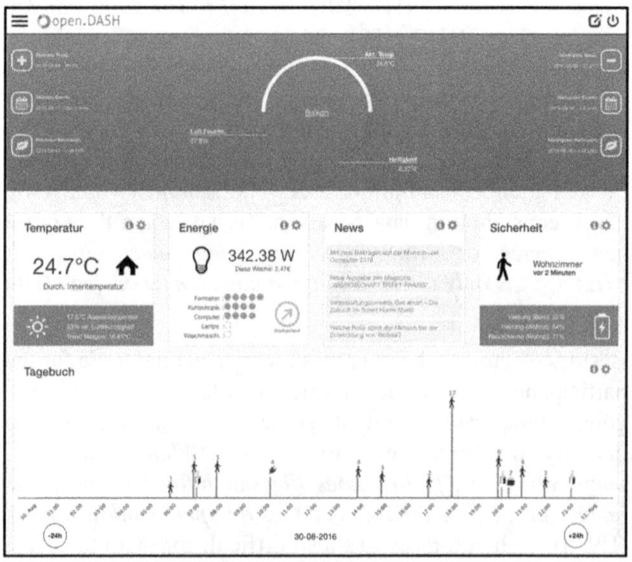


**Figure 3.** ***open.DASH*** **- interface.**

Additionally, the outside weather and the forecast of tomorrow's weather is shown. The close link between inside and outside temperature allows a quick comparison and an overview of the *current status*. Furthermore, the user can see whether the minimum temperature is maintained (*Does my smart home work as expected? Is my configuration appropriate?*).

The security widgets provide an overview of the last (security-related) event and the time it occurred. As participants mentioned that events are more important when not at home, especially movement and door/window status, this widget shows only the last movement or door/window status event, including whether it was an opening or closing event (*What (has) happened in my home?).*

The diary widget shows information about every single event that has occurred in the home, without any historical limitation. The events are placed on a time-series of one day (00:00 to 23:59), and the user can click through each day. To improve readability, the events are aggregated on an hourly level and the number of times an event has occurred is mapped through the height of the bar (*What (has) happened in my home?*). Additionally, events from configured rules or time control are visible, allowing users to check whether the smart home works properly (*Does my smart home work as expected?*).

### End-User-Development Visualization Tool

To allow a very personal customization and a detailed exploration of smart home data on demand [61], we developed an EUD environment to create custom visualizations of smart home data. As EUD for the smart home is currently a highly topical theme, we developed our environment with consideration of best practices from the literature. Therefore, we developed a guided step-by-step creation mechanism that supports the users. Furthermore, we provide simple click/touch interactions instead of more complex operations such as drag & drop [19].

Our visualization creation process consists of five-steps (see Fig. 1c,4), following the visualization pipeline by Card [13]: selecting data (Data Analysis), selecting time (Filtering), selecting chart, configuration (Mapping) and adaption (Rendering). The first step is to choose which data should be visualized. The user can choose one or many devices and sensors from the list, which contains all of the installed sensors in the home. The second step is about when the data is aggregated. The user can choose between an absolute timespan (e.g. for the exploration of a specific billing period) or a relative timespan (e.g. the last four months). After these two steps, the user can select how the data should be visualized. We implemented an algorithm that analyzes the selected data source and timespan to automatically suggest appropriate chart types. The algorithm is based on Aigner et al.'s [1] characterization of time-oriented data, and checks whether the data are univariate or multivariate, interval or point-based and whether cyclic time domains exist (e.g. for univariate data

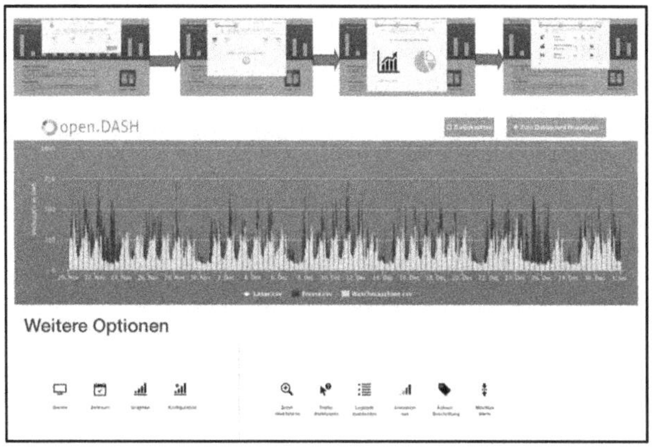


**Figure 4. Five-step process for creating an own visualization.**

the system would not suggest a pie chart). Additionally, it checks whether data could be easily summed up (energy consumption could be aggregated to hour values by summing minute-based values). The fourth step contains the special configuration for the selected chart type, e.g. whether data should be mapped on lines, points etc. on a timeline chart. After these four steps, the user gets a preview of the chart, where interaction such as zooming or selecting or hovering over points to get a tooltip with information is possible. This step mainly supports task-driven adjustments, e.g. for localizing or identifying data [69]. From this step, the user can go back to the four previous steps to change the settings or can configure the interaction or layout of the chart (e.g. changing animation settings, allow/disallow zoom). The user can decide whether the chart should be added to a dashboard as a widget or discarded. If the user wants to add it to a dashboard, a title can be added and the size defined.

By using the flexible tool, participants were able to get detailed information on questions concerning *are my devices and I energy efficient, what has happened in the home, does my smart home work as expected and is the configuration appropriate or not.*

## RESULTS

In this section, we present the results of our Phase 2 studies. Before we installed our *open.DASH* interface in the Living Lab households, we conducted a three-step usability test to minimize system usability or acceptance issues that could have influenced its usage. The heuristic usability evaluation showed some issues regarding the navigation inside the page, the wording of some features and labels, the font-size and the choice of symbols. Additionally, some parts of the EUD assistant were too complex and not clearly understandable. To overcome these issues, we implemented more filters to the interface elements to automatically hide unnecessary items. Overall, we reduced the number of symbols and text, ensuring a clearer interaction design.

### User Experience, Appropriation and Use

After three months of use, we had a total of 1,394 page visits of the *open.DASH* interface, with 70.09% from a desktop computer, 24.10% from smartphones and 5.81% from tablet PCs. In the first two weeks, the average visit duration was significantly longer than in the remaining time, which could be explained by the novelty factor and the testing of all functions. Overall, 60.47% of the visit duration was under 10 seconds and 28.43% were over three minutes.

From the T2 interviews, we found that the first impression of *open.DASH* was consistently positive. The participants liked the design and its simplicity: *"The design is very good, very clear [...] I can also customize and set up many different things [...] Here you can do that intuitively and very quickly"* (H10, T2).

Participants reported that they liked the room-based overview, allowing them to look into every room and get aggregated information about its current status. We found that aggregation of data (to the total amount or into smaller units such as rooms) was perceived as useful (in the commercial system, the devices are isolated and participants had up to ten sensors measuring temperature and 20 sockets that measured energy consumption). This aggregation improved the ability to quickly "*get an overview*". Additionally, it reduced the amount of information displayed to the user: *"I had no total consumption with the [commercial] system, I had to sum up the single values manually"* (H3, T2).

The graphical visualization of sensor events in the diary widget not only made patterns and regular times of action visible but was also used to clarify the information value of smart home data, thus, letting people think about the effect of the digitalization: *"After looking at the diary widget, I realized what information the smart home collected. Especially, in terms of motion profiles, because this is safety-critical information"* (H7, T2).

The hourly aggregation of event data within our diary widget was experienced as an obstacle for some participants, as it allowed neither a fine-grained retrospective of action nor, especially, whether the configured rules were working properly. Another drawback to our system was the missing ability to switch devices directly from the interface, which meant that if a participant recognized some energy wastage, he or she could not act directly.

## How People Customize Their *open.DASH*

As He et al. [34] mention, there is no system that fits to the needs of all users. We thus were interested in how people customized their *open.DASH* to fit their needs and to get (only) the information they were interested in.

### *Customize the Pre-defined Visualizations*

Nearly all (9/10) households adjusted their starting dashboard in some way. This also included configuring pre-defined widgets and deleting or moving existing widgets. Households deselected devices for the average temperature calculation to only include "*important rooms*" (H2, T2) and entered their city details to get weather information for their location. Three participants also reconfigured the news-feed to get news from their preferred news portal (the initial news feed was the one from the project itself). The households also rearranged widgets to see their most important information first. Some households also deleted pre-defined widgets because they were not interested in that kind of information or because they did not have enough sensors in their home to get an added value from the generated information: *"Temperature is not interesting for me neither is the news-feed."* (H6, T2). *"I've deleted the security-widget, because I have too few sensors for this widget"* (H3, T2). *"There is information about energy consumption and a diary of smart home events, I don't need more for this household"* (H1, T2).

Overall, the participants liked the idea of the temperature widget and excluding specific sensors for the calculation of the average temperature, but they also would have liked to see this configuration ability in all other pre-defined widgets. For example, two participants used a motion sensor at their television that detects whether a person was sitting in front of it. As long as a person is in front of the television the system kept the lights on. In this example, the motion detector was partly triggered over 200 times in one hour, which had a negative influence on the diary visualization. Thus, the households in question wanted to exclude this sensor from their diary widget.

### *Making Own Visualizations*

During the three months with *open.DASH* the participants created 203 charts with the EUD environment. 55 of these created visualizations were added to the dashboard. Most of the visualizations were created at the beginning and the end of the study.

Participants mentioned that they first used the EUD environment to play around with the data. They created charts, e.g. for temperature data, consumption data, etc., to get a feeling for smart home data and to explore possibilities for useful extensions for their dashboard. *"[At the beginning] I created some graphs, e.g. with the temperature curve, but they were not yet useful enough for us"* (H1, T2). After getting a feeling about the tool and its possibilities, the tool was used explicitly for individual use cases, e.g. for verification of configuration: *"I have created some [new widgets – saved to dashboard] [...] to check if rules work properly"* (H3, T2), the monitoring of specific devices in terms of energy consumption and temperature profiles: *"During a vacation, we could check if it was too hot for the cats at home."* (H1, T2). The visualizations of energy consumption data, especially, changed over the three-month usage. In most cases, the energy consumption visualization became more specific by displaying fewer devices in a chart, or it was removed completely after the first weeks. Another interesting usage scenario was that, for specific rooms participants sometimes created charts where they combined consumption data, temperature data, brightness data and event data to learn about what was going on in the room.

Additionally, participants used the creation tool to temporarily create visualizations to satisfy urgent questions and requirements or simply for "*looking into the data*". These visualizations were typically not added to the dashboard; only the preview was used to get the needed insights from the data. For example in the situation where something was considered as abnormal, participants looked into multiple data for the current day to find reasons. Another example was looking for changes in consumption behavior. If participants bought a new device or changed something in their smart home settings (e.g. cutting standby consumption off at night automatically) or their behavior, they created a time chart to compare current consumption levels with past consumption levels.

Overall, the participants stated that they liked being able to check and analyze their data spontaneously and flexibly. It allowed them to learn from the data and to continuously adjust their smart home. Yet, for some participants it was difficult for them to find any use cases themselves and especially for their set of sensors: "*I could not create any useful visualizations because we have not enough devices [sensors] installed.*" (H4, T2). The lack of ideas was also identified as a barrier for using the tool to explore data. The same household mentioned that "[…] *a source for ideas would be interesting*" (H4, T2).

### Limitations

For the evaluation of our *open.DASH* interface, we used the sensors available in the households from the commercial system (see methodology section), which lead to a few limitations. The main use cases for these sensors are: energy consumption, temperature, brightness, motion, door/window status. The evaluation of our *open.DASH* interface was conducted during the summer months, where households mentioned that temperature and brightness are not that relevant when dealing with a smart home system. Therefore, we could not investigate all usage areas for our developed system. Additionally, some households had only a few sensors installed and, as a result, little data were collected. The households mentioned use cases that they would like to uncover but, because of the limited number of sensors available, the participants were unable to realize them in an appropriate and sense-giving manner.

## DISCUSSION AND IMPLICATIONS

In this section, we discuss our results and provide implications that aim to support the design of future systems dealing with the visualization of smart home data.

### *Pre-Defined Visualizations vs. Visualization Creation Tool*

We could see that pre-defined visualizations are important in allowing the participants to have a starting point in dealing with smart home data. The participants configured and used these pre-defined visualizations to gain awareness of the data and to get an overview of the current status of their (smart) home. Topic-based widgets with aggregated data, which can be selected and (re-)arranged on the dashboard freely, seem promising in this regard [25]. Additionally, when aggregating data, it is important to empower the user to select which sensors should be included in the calculation/aggregation process to exclude data from specific sensors that are (not) relevant for specific use cases.

The EUD environment enabled participants to get more detailed information about their smart home in a flexible manner. Particularly with regard to very individual requirements and use cases, the creation tool was helpful for the households as it allows non-programming users to query their data in an understandable way. Participants explored the tool and their data to get inspiration for new use cases or information within the data. The deployment of *open.DASH* in the Living Labs showed that the *combination of customizable pre-defined visualizations and creation tools for individual visualizations* could address different information needs and interests.

Based on our results, pre-defined visualizations therefore could be informed by existing research in special topics such as eco-feedback or AAL to extend the possible fields of application. As they are a good entry point, they should be designed to provide an overview on a specific topic, letting users check on the current status and whether further details are needed [61]. However, future systems should also enable users to create complementary visualizations that go beyond universal visualizations. These could take their individual interests more into account.

### *Supporting Short-Term and Long-Term Needs*

We were able to identify that participants used *open.DASH* differently according to their changing interests over time. Users addressed specific long-term interests that occurred or were monitored regularly by creating new visualizations with the creation tool and afterwards saving them on the dashboard. In contrast, short-term interests were mainly realized by creating new mappings of data, but without saving them, and therefore allowing "on-demand" requests for temporal requirements.

Our findings suggest that smart home systems should allow users to quickly and easily map data to different kind of charts, text and symbols, thus fitting to users' different needs [62] and furthermore, enabling the user to create on demand visualization that are not permanently displayed on the dashboard. This separation in regard to the design of the dashboard also simplifies the overview page by reducing the risk of information overload on the first view.

It will be interesting to see how users deal with recurring short-term needs, e.g. checking energy consumption when a new bill arrives, and whether the creation tool is used in the same way every time. So far the system does not allow the history of self-created visualization to be stored, and users have to build the visualization from scratch every time.

*Community and Sharing*
Our participants had different knowledge about the potential of data. Some participants reported that they had several specific use cases at hand; others found it difficult to find new use cases or even one use case. During the workshops (where participants came together), we could see that there was considerable interest in finding out how other participants used their smart home. In the interviews (T2), the participants mentioned that it would be interesting to see what other households did with the visualization creation tool.

For the working context there is growing body of work that deals with the socially based tailoring of a flexible software systems to enable users to adapt the tools to achieve a specific work task [21,71]. For private flexible smart home systems therefore, we argue for allowing creation tool configurations (e.g. for a visualization that showing the correlation of outside and inside temperature) to be shared, thus addressing both the inspiring of other participants and sharing the "how to" for creation of visualizations for specific use cases with an "over-the-shoulder-learning" approach [71]. Following the IFTTT approach could make it possible to share configurations for specific use cases on a platform that other users can configure and integrate into their interface.

*(Flexible) Smart Home Data and Visualization Matters?*
From our study, we learned that the participants had varying requirements regarding smart home data. Some requirements are superficial, some are very detailed, some demands overlap between participants, some are very specific and some participants are not very interested in smart home data. However, *open.DASH* gave us first insights of participants' usage and how they customize their dashboard.

Dynamic visualization tools allow people to create different views on domestic data which allow them to gain further insights into their (smart) home: "[Only after looking at the data did I] *realize what information the smart home collected"* (H7, T2). Especially, the flexibility enables the user to adapt the system according to changing needs. This is further supported by three participants who used a wall-mounted tablet as a public display where they used our *open.DASH* or other sites that were relevant for them. We agree with Mennicken et al. [47] that it would be promising to integrate smart home data into already used tools. But we could also identify that participants wanted to integrate other data into their smart home dashboard, for instance information from social media, timetable inquiries, activity and health data or the TV program. The design workshop, where some participants asked for a newsfeed to be integrated, showed that participants are interested in making the smart home interface a place where all interesting information is shown at a look.

In this vein, especially when dealing with multiple smart components and systems we argue that future private information systems should provide a single unified interface, similar to what Few [25] description for business dashboards. Scattered access points with their own login-mechanism and incoherence in styling and control present obstacles for current smart systems. On a middleware-level open source projects, such as openHAB [77], already enable unified control from different smart components. Currently, advanced approaches for visualization and monitoring are still largely neglected. As we have shown, however, the combination of smart home data enables new applications of smart home systems and additionally offers opportunities to tap into the full potential of exploring the own home. Going a step further, we believe that creating a user-centered information portal that combines all smart home data with other relevant information could be an interesting topic for future research.

## CONCLUSION
While smart home enabling technology is continually developing and smart home configuration research is increasingly integrating the end-user with EUD rule editors or DIY hardware, research dealing with visualizing integrated smart home data is rare. As specific smart home use cases, eco-feedback and AAL research have shown that the user needs for, and interests in, domestic data differ, thus demanding more flexible tools to display sensor data. Our study shows that this view is also true for the integrated smart home case. We identified eight requirement categories that include overlapping and individual data-related use cases. To address these individuality of data demands, we developed a flexible dashboard system, including configurable pre-defined widgets and an EUD environment, allowing users to create data visualizations themselves. We tested our interface in 12 Living Lab households for three months to examine the usage and appropriation of such a flexible system. We found that participants configured and used the pre-defined widgets to get an overview of interesting topics (energy, comfort, safety, etc.). The EUD environment was used to create charts for specific use cases (e.g. temperature curve, consumption baseline) to extend dashboards individually. We also found that the EUD environment was used for urgent demands e.g. to obtain detailed information on anomalies. We think that such hybrid interfaces for smart home data visualizations are a promising approach to addressing the users' varying information demands and to supporting the development of consciousness through data exploration.

## ACKNOWLEDGMENTS
This work was funded by the Federal Ministry for Economic Affairs and Energy, Germany (funding number: 01MU14001) and Ministry for Climate Protection, Environment, Agriculture, Conservation and Consumer Protection of the State of North Rhine-Westphalia, Germany (funding number: 64.65.69-PRO-0056).

## REFERENCES


1. Wolfgang Aigner, Silvia Miksch, Heidrun Schumann, and Christian Tominski. 2011. *Visualization of Time-Oriented Data*. Springer London, London.

2. Abdullah Al Mahmud, Omar Mubin, Suleman Shahid, James F. Juola, and Boris de Ruyter. 2008. EZ phone: persuading mobile users to conserve energy. In *Proceedings of the 22nd British HCI Group Annual Conference on People and Computers: Culture, Creativity, Interaction-Volume 2*, 7–10.

3. Frances K. Aldrich. 2003. Smart Homes: Past, Present and Future. In *Inside the Smart Home*, Richard Harper (ed.). Springer London, 17–39. https://doi.org/10.1007/1-85233-854-7_2

4. M. Balestrini, T. Diez, P. Marshall, A. Gluhak, and Y. Rogers. 2015. IoT Community Technologies: Leaving Users to Their Own Devices or Orchestration of Engagement? *EAI Endorsed Transactions on Internet of Things* 1, 1: 150601. https://doi.org/10.4108/eai.26-10-2015.150601

5. Victoria Bellotti and Keith Edwards. 2001. Intelligibility and Accountability: Human Considerations in Context-aware Systems. *Hum.-Comput. Interact.* 16, 2: 193–212. https://doi.org/10.1207/S15327051HCI16234_05

6. Regina Bernhaupt, Marianna Obrist, Astrid Weiss, Elke Beck, and Manfred Tscheligi. 2008. Trends in the living room and beyond: results from ethnographic studies using creative and playful probing. *Computers in Entertainment (CIE)* 6, 1: 5.

7. Christoffer Björkskog, Giulio Jacucci, Topi Mikkola, Massimo Bertoncini, Luciano Gamberini, Carin Torstensson, Tatu Nieminen, Luigi Briguglio, Pasquale Andriani, and Giampaolo Fiorentino. 2010. Beaware: A framework for residential services on energy awareness. In *UBICOMM 2010, The Fourth International Conference on Mobile Ubiquitous Computing, Systems, Services and Technologies*, 294–300.

8. K. Borner, Unkown, and Unknown. InfoVis CyberInfrastructure- Spring Embedding Algorithm. Retrieved September 5, 2016 from http://iv.slis.indiana.edu/sw/toolkit.html

9. L. Borodulkin, H. Ruser, and H. R. Trankler. 2002. 3D virtual "smart home" user interface. In *2002 IEEE International Symposium on Virtual and Intelligent Measurement Systems, 2002. VIMS '02*, 111–115. https://doi.org/10.1109/VIMS.2002.1009367

10. Virginia Braun and Victoria Clarke. 2006. Using thematic analysis in psychology. *Qualitative research in psychology* 3, 2: 77–101.

11. A.J. Bernheim Brush, Bongshin Lee, Ratul Mahajan, Sharad Agarwal, Stefan Saroiu, and Colin Dixon. 2011. Home Automation in the Wild: Challenges and Opportunities. In *Proceedings of the SIGCHI Conference on Human Factors in Computing Systems* (CHI '11), 2115–2124. https://doi.org/10.1145/1978942.1979249

12. Leah Buechley, Mike Eisenberg, Jaime Catchen, and Ali Crockett. 2008. The LilyPad Arduino: Using Computational Textiles to Investigate Engagement, Aesthetics, and Diversity in Computer Science Education. In *Proceedings of the SIGCHI Conference on Human Factors in Computing Systems* (CHI '08), 423–432. https://doi.org/10.1145/1357054.1357123

13. Stuart K. Card, Jock D. Mackinlay, and Ben Shneiderman. 1999. *Readings in Information Visualization: Using Vision to Think*. Morgan Kaufmann.

14. Nico Castelli, Gunnar Stevens, Timo Jakobi, and Niko Schönau. 2016. Beyond Eco-feedback: Using Room as a Context to Design New Eco-support Features at Home. In *Advances and New Trends in Environmental and Energy Informatics*, Jorge Marx Gomez, Michael Sonnenschein, Ute Vogel, Andreas Winter, Barbara Rapp and Nils Giesen (eds.). Springer International Publishing, 177–195. https://doi.org/10.1007/978-3-319-23455-7_10

15. Marshini Chetty, Ja-Young Sung, and Rebecca E. Grinter. 2007. How Smart Homes Learn: The Evolution of the Networked Home and Household. In *Proceedings of the 9th International Conference on Ubiquitous Computing* (UbiComp '07), 127–144.

16. Ricardo Costa, Davide Carneiro, Paulo Novais, Luís Lima, José Machado, Alberto Marques, and José Neves. 2009. Ambient assisted living. In *3rd Symposium of Ubiquitous Computing and Ambient Intelligence 2008*, 86–94.

17. Enrico Costanza, Sarvapali D. Ramchurn, and Nicholas R. Jennings. 2012. Understanding domestic energy consumption through interactive visualisation: a field study. In *Proceedings of the 2012 ACM Conference on Ubiquitous Computing*, 216–225.

18. Sarah Darby. 2006. The effectiveness of feedback on energy consumption. *A Review for DEFRA of the Literature on Metering, Billing and direct Displays* 486: 2006.

19. Luigi De Russis and Fulvio Corno. 2015. HomeRules: A Tangible End-User Programming Interface for Smart Homes. 2109–2114. https://doi.org/10.1145/2702613.2732795

20. Anind K. Dey, Timothy Sohn, Sara Streng, and Justin Kodama. 2006. iCAP: Interactive Prototyping of Context-Aware Applications. In *Pervasive Computing*, Kenneth P. Fishkin, Bernt Schiele, Paddy Nixon and Aaron Quigley (eds.). Springer Berlin Heidelberg, 254–271. https://doi.org/10.1007/11748625_16

21. Sebastian Draxler, Gunnar Stevens, Martin Stein, Alexander Boden, and David Randall. 2012. Supporting the social context of technology appropriation: on a synthesis

of sharing tools and tool knowledge. In *Proceedings of the SIGCHI Conference on Human Factors in Computing Systems*, 2835–2844.

22. W. Keith Edwards and Rebecca E. Grinter. 2001. At Home with Ubiquitous Computing: Seven Challenges. In *Proceedings of the 3rd International Conference on Ubiquitous Computing* (UbiComp '01), 256–272.

23. Mats Eriksson and Seija Kulkki. 2005. State-of-the-Art in Utilizing Living Labs Approach to User-centric ICT innovation – a European approach. *ResearchGate* 15.

24. Jean-Daniel Fekete. 2004. The InfoVis Toolkit. In *Proceedings of the IEEE Symposium on Information Visualization* (INFOVIS '04), 167–174. https://doi.org/10.1109/INFOVIS.2004.64

25. Stephen Few. 2006. *Information Dashboard Design: The Effective Visual Communication of Data*. O'Reilly Media, Beijing ; Cambride MA.

26. Joel E. Fischer, Andy Crabtree, Tom Rodden, James A. Colley, Enrico Costanza, Michael O. Jewell, and Sarvapali D. Ramchurn. 2016. "Just Whack It on Until It Gets Hot": Working with IoT Data in the Home. In *Proceedings of the 2016 CHI Conference on Human Factors in Computing Systems* (CHI '16), 5933–5944. https://doi.org/10.1145/2858036.2858518

27. Geraldine Fitzpatrick and Greg Smith. 2009. Technology-enabled feedback on domestic energy consumption: Articulating a set of design concerns. *Pervasive Computing, IEEE* 8, 1: 37–44.

28. Asbjørn Følstad, Petter Bae Brandtzæg, Jan Gulliksen, Mikael Börjeson, and Pirjo Näkki. 2009. Towards a Manifesto for Living Lab Co-creation. In *Human-Computer Interaction – INTERACT 2009*, Tom Gross, Jan Gulliksen, Paula Kotzé, Lars Oestreicher, Philippe Palanque, Raquel Oliveira Prates and Marco Winckler (eds.). Springer Berlin Heidelberg, 979–980. https://doi.org/10.1007/978-3-642-03658-3_140

29. Jon Froehlich. 2011. Sensing and Feedback of Everyday Activities to Promote Environmental Behaviors. University of Washington.

30. Jon Froehlich, Leah Findlater, and James Landay. 2010. The Design of Eco-feedback Technology. In *Proceedings of the SIGCHI Conference on Human Factors in Computing Systems* (CHI '10), 1999–2008. https://doi.org/10.1145/1753326.1753629

31. Catherine Grevet, Jennifer Mankoff, and Scott D. Anderson. 2010. Design and evaluation of a social visualization aimed at encouraging sustainable behavior. In *System Sciences (HICSS), 2010 43rd Hawaii International Conference on*, 1–8.

32. Rebecca E. Grinter, W. Keith Edwards, Mark W. Newman, and Nicolas Ducheneaut. 2005. The Work to Make a Home Network Work. In *Proceedings of the Ninth Conference on European Conference on Computer Supported Cooperative Work* (ECSCW'05), 469–488.

33. Yukang Guo, Matt Jones, Benjamin Cowan, and Russell Beale. 2013. Take it personally: personal accountability and energy consumption in domestic households. In *CHI'13 Extended Abstracts on Human Factors in Computing Systems*, 1467–1472.

34. Helen Ai He, Saul Greenberg, and Elaine M. Huang. 2010. One size does not fit all: applying the transtheoretical model to energy feedback technology design. In *Proceedings of the SIGCHI Conference on Human Factors in Computing Systems*, 927–936.

35. Jeffrey Heer, Stuart K. Card, and James A. Landay. 2005. Prefuse: A Toolkit for Interactive Information Visualization. In *Proceedings of the SIGCHI Conference on Human Factors in Computing Systems* (CHI '05), 421–430. https://doi.org/10.1145/1054972.1055031

36. Steven Houben, Connie Golsteijn, Sarah Gallacher, Rose Johnson, Saskia Bakker, Nicolai Marquardt, Licia Capra, and Yvonne Rogers. 2016. Physikit: Data Engagement Through Physical Ambient Visualizations in the Home. 1608–1619. https://doi.org/10.1145/2858036.2858059

37. Jan Humble, Andy Crabtree, Terry Hemmings, Karl-Petter Åkesson, Boriana Koleva, Tom Rodden, and Pär Hansson. 2003. "Playing with the Bits" User-Configuration of Ubiquitous Domestic Environments. In *UbiComp 2003: Ubiquitous Computing*, Anind K. Dey, Albrecht Schmidt and Joseph F. McCarthy (eds.). Springer Berlin Heidelberg, 256–263. https://doi.org/10.1007/978-3-540-39653-6_20

38. IFTTT. IFTTT. *IFTTT / Connect the apps you love.* Retrieved September 18, 2016 from https://ifttt.com/recipes

39. T. Jakobi and T. Schwartz. 2012. Putting the user in charge: End user development for eco-feedback technologies. In *Sustainable Internet and ICT for Sustainability (SustainIT), 2012*, 1–4.

40. Li Jönsson, Loove Broms, and Cecilia Katzeff. 2010. Watt-Lite: Energy Statistics Made Tangible. In *Proceedings of the 8th ACM Conference on Designing Interactive Systems* (DIS '10), 240–243. https://doi.org/10.1145/1858171.1858214

41. Ben Kirman, Conor Linehan, Shaun Lawson, Derek Foster, and Mark Doughty. 2010. There's a monster in my kitchen: using aversive feedback to motivate behaviour change. In *CHI'10 Extended Abstracts on Human Factors in Computing Systems*, 2685–2694.

42. Jesper Kjeldskov, Mikael B. Skov, Jeni Paay, and Rahuvaran Pathmanathan. 2012. Using mobile phones to support sustainability: a field study of residential electricity consumption.

In *Proceedings of the 2012 ACM annual conference on Human Factors in Computing Systems*, 2347–2356.

43. Henry Lieberman, Fabio Paternò, Markus Klann, and Volker Wulf. 2006. End-User Development: An Emerging Paradigm. In *End User Development*, Henry Lieberman, Fabio Paternò and Volker Wulf (eds.). Springer Netherlands, 1–8. https://doi.org/10.1007/1-4020-5386-X_1

44. Brian Y. Lim, Anind K. Dey, and Daniel Avrahami. 2009. Why and Why Not Explanations Improve the Intelligibility of Context-aware Intelligent Systems. In *Proceedings of the SIGCHI Conference on Human Factors in Computing Systems* (CHI '09), 2119–2128. https://doi.org/10.1145/1518701.1519023

45. Jörn Loviscach. 2011. The design space of personal energy conservation assistants. *PsychNology Journal* 9, 1: 29–41.

46. Sarah Mennicken and Elaine M. Huang. 2012. Hacking the Natural Habitat: An In-the-wild Study of Smart Homes, Their Development, and the People Who Live in Them. In *Proceedings of the 10th International Conference on Pervasive Computing* (Pervasive'12), 143–160. https://doi.org/10.1007/978-3-642-31205-2_10

47. Sarah Mennicken, David Kim, and Elaine May Huang. 2016. Integrating the Smart Home into the Digital Calendar. In *Proceedings of the 2016 CHI Conference on Human Factors in Computing Systems* (CHI '16), 5958–5969. https://doi.org/10.1145/2858036.2858168

48. Sarah Mennicken, Jo Vermeulen, and Elaine M. Huang. 2014. From Today's Augmented Houses to Tomorrow's Smart Homes: New Directions for Home Automation Research. In *Proceedings of the 2014 ACM International Joint Conference on Pervasive and Ubiquitous Computing* (UbiComp '14), 105–115. https://doi.org/10.1145/2632048.2636076

49. Maurice Mulvenna, William Carswell, Paul Mccullagh, Juan Augusto, Huiru Zheng, Paul Jeffers, Haiying Wang, and Suzanne Martin. 2011. Visualization of data for ambient assisted living services. *IEEE Communications Magazine* 49, 1: 110–117. https://doi.org/10.1109/MCOM.2011.5681023

50. Mark W. Newman. Now We're Cooking: Recipes for End-User Service Composition in the Digital Home. *ResearchGate*.

51. Jakob Nielsen. 1994. *Usability engineering*. Morgan Kaufmann Publishers, San Francisco, Calif.

52. Torkel Ödegaard. The leading graph and dashboard builder for visualizing time series metrics. *Grafana.org*. Retrieved September 18, 2016 from http://grafana.org/

53. Corinna Ogonowski, Benedikt Ley, and Jan Hess. 2013. Designing for the living room: long-term user involvement in a living lab. *Proceedings of the SIGCHI Conference on Human Factors in Computing Systems*.

54. Petromil Petkov, Felix Köbler, Marcus Foth, and Helmut Krcmar. 2011. Motivating domestic energy conservation through comparative, community-based feedback in mobile and social media. In *Proceedings of the 5th International Conference on Communities and Technologies*, 21–30.

55. James Pierce, William Odom, and Eli Blevis. 2008. Energy Aware Dwelling: A Critical Survey of Interaction Design for Eco-visualizations. In *Proceedings of the 20th Australasian Conference on Computer-Human Interaction: Designing for Habitus and Habitat* (OZCHI '08), 1–8. https://doi.org/10.1145/1517744.1517746

56. J. Rodgers and L. Bartram. 2011. Exploring Ambient and Artistic Visualization for Residential Energy Use Feedback. *IEEE Transactions on Visualization and Computer Graphics* 17, 12: 2489–2497. https://doi.org/10.1109/TVCG.2011.196

57. Ana Rosselló-Busquet and José Soler. Towards Efficient Energy Management: Defining HEMS and Smart Grid Objectives. *ResearchGate.*

58. Tobias Schwartz, Sebastian Denef, Gunnar Stevens, Timo Jakobi, Volker Wulf, and Leonardo Ramirez. 2014. What People Do with Consumption Feedback: A Long-Term Living Lab Study of a Home Energy Management System, in: Interacting with Computers, 27 (6), 2015, 551-576

59. Tobias Schwartz, Sebastian Denef, Gunnar Stevens, Leonardo Ramirez, and Volker Wulf. 2013. Cultivating energy literacy: results from a longitudinal living lab study of a home energy management system. In *Proceedings of the SIGCHI Conference on Human Factors in Computing Systems* (CHI '13), 1193–1202. https://doi.org/10.1145/2470654.2466154

60. Anneli Selvefors, M. Karlsson, and Ulrike Rahe. 2013. Use and Adoption of Interactive Energy Feedback Systems. *Proceedings of IASDR*: 1771–1782.

61. Ben Shneiderman. 1996. The Eyes Have It: A Task by Data Type Taxonomy for Information Visualizations. In *Proceedings of the 1996 IEEE Symposium on Visual Languages* (VL '96), 336–.

62. Ben Shneiderman. 2004. *Designing the User Interface: Strategies for Effective Human-Computer Interaction.* Addison Wesley, Boston.

63. Martin Stein, Alexander Boden, Dominik Hornung, and Volker Wulf. 2016. Third Spaces in the Age of IoT: A Study on Participatory Design of Complex Systems. In *Symposium on Challenges and experiences in designing for an ageing society, 12th International Conference on Designing Interactive Systems (COOP).*

64. Gunnar Stevens, Volkmar Pipek, and Volker Wulf. 2009. Appropriation Infrastructure: Supporting the Design of Usages. . Springer Berlin Heidelberg, 50–69.

65. Hong Sun, Vincenzo De Florio, Ning Gui, and Chris Blondia. 2009. Promises and challenges of ambient assisted living systems. In *Information Technology: New Generations, 2009. ITNG'09. Sixth International Conference on*, 1201–1207.

66. Vasughi Sundramoorthy, Qi Liu, Grahame Cooper, Nigel Linge, and Joshua Cooper. 2010. DEHEMS: A user-driven domestic energy monitoring system. In *Internet of Things (IOT), 2010*, 1–8.

67. Barnabás Takács and Dávid Hanák. 2006. A mobile system for assisted living with ambient facial interfaces. *ResearchGate* 2: 33–50.

68. Peter Tolmie, Andy Crabtree, Tom Rodden, James Colley, and Ewa Luger. 2016. "This Has to Be the Cats": Personal Data Legibility in Networked Sensing Systems. In *Proceedings of the 19th ACM Conference on Computer-Supported Cooperative Work & Social Computing* (CSCW '16), 491–502. https://doi.org/10.1145/2818048.2819992

69. C. Tominski, G. Fuchs, and H. Schumann. 2008. Task-Driven Color Coding. In *Information Visualisation, 2008. IV '08. 12th International Conference*, 373–380. https://doi.org/10.1109/IV.2008.24

70. Khai N. Truong, Elaine M. Huang, and Gregory D. Abowd. 2004. CAMP: A Magnetic Poetry Interface for End-User Programming of Capture Applications for the Home. In *UbiComp 2004: Ubiquitous Computing*, Nigel Davies, Elizabeth D. Mynatt and Itiro Siio (eds.). Springer Berlin Heidelberg, 143–160. https://doi.org/10.1007/978-3-540-30119-6_9

71. Michael B. Twidale. 2005. Over the Shoulder Learning: Supporting Brief Informal Learning. *Computer Supported Cooperative Work (CSCW)* 14, 6: 505–547. https://doi.org/10.1007/s10606-005-9007-7

72. Jong-bum Woo and Youn-kyung Lim. 2015. User Experience in Do-it-yourself-style Smart Homes. In *Proceedings of the 2015 ACM International Joint Conference on Pervasive and Ubiquitous Computing* (UbiComp '15), 779–790. https://doi.org/10.1145/2750858.2806063

73. Volker Wulf, Claudia Müller, Volkmar Pipek, David Randall, Markus Rohde, and Gunnar Stevens. 2015. Practice-Based Computing: Empirically Grounded Conceptualizations Derived from Design Case Studies. In *Designing Socially Embedded Technologies in the Real-World.* Springer London, 111–150.

74. Volker Wulf, Markus Rohde, V Pipek, and G Stevens. 2011. Engaging with practices: design case studies as a research framework in CSCW. *Proceedings of the ACM 2011 conference on Computer supported cooperative work*: 505–512.

75. Tae-Jung Yun. 2009. Investigating the impact of a minimalist in-home energy consumption display. In *CHI'09 Extended Abstracts on Human Factors in Computing Systems*, 4417–4422.

76. Bin Zhang, Pei-Luen Patrick Rau, and Gavriel Salvendy. 2009. Design and evaluation of smart home user interface: effects of age, tasks and intelligence level. *Behaviour & Information Technology* 28, 3: 239–249. https://doi.org/10.1080/01449290701573978

77. openHAB. Retrieved January 1, 2017 from http://www.openhab.org/

# Opportunities and Design Considerations for Peer Support in a Hospital Setting

Shefali Haldar[1], Sonali R. Mishra[2], Maher Khelifi[1], Ari H. Pollack[3,4], Wanda Pratt[2]
{shaldar, srmishra, khelifi, apollack, wpratt}@uw.edu

[1]Biomedical & Health Informatics
University of Washington
Seattle, WA, USA

[2]The Information School
University of Washington
Seattle, WA, USA

[3]Department of Pediatrics
University of Washington
Seattle, WA, USA

[4]Division of Nephrology
Seattle Children's Hospital
Seattle, WA, USA

## ABSTRACT
Although research has demonstrated improved outcomes for outpatients who receive peer support—such as through online health communities, support groups, and mentoring systems—hospitalized patients have few mechanisms to receive such valuable support. To explore the opportunities for a hospital-based peer support system, we administered a survey to 146 pediatric patients and caregivers, and conducted semi-structured interviews with twelve patients and three caregivers in a children's hospital. Our analysis revealed that hospitalized individuals need peer support for five key purposes: (1) to ask about medical details—such as procedures, treatments, and medications; (2) to learn about healthcare providers; (3) to report and prevent medical errors; (4) to exchange emotional support; and (5) to manage their time in the hospital. In this paper, we examine these themes and describe potential barriers to using a hospital-based peer support system. We then discuss the unique opportunities and challenges that the hospital environment presents when designing for peer support in this setting.

### Author Keywords
Health informatics; pediatric; hospital; patient; caregiver; peer-to-peer; peer support.

### ACM Classification Keywords
J.3 Life and Medical Sciences, Health, Medical Information Systems; H.5.m. Information interfaces and presentation.

## INTRODUCTION
In the United States, over 34 million hospital admissions occurred in 2014 [52]. For many hospitalized individuals, their time spent between admission and discharge becomes extremely overwhelming and difficult to navigate. Patients and their caregivers must learn the intricate details of the care they are receiving and the complicated structure of the hospital hierarchy. They must also monitor information handoffs among their healthcare providers and remain vigilant due to the high risk of experiencing a preventable medical error [33]. On top of this work, they need to manage the symptoms, stress, and anxiety that emerge as a result of being in the hospital. One way to alleviate these health, information, and emotional burdens is to offer patients and caregivers the support of their peers, who can guide them through the many challenges of an unfamiliar hospital environment.


*CHI 2017, May 06-11, 2017, Denver, CO, USA*

ISBN 978-1-4503-4655-9/17/05...$15.00
DOI: http://dx.doi.org/10.1145/3025453.3026040

Evidence indicates that patients who participate in such peer support programs experience health benefits, such as increased adherence to medication, and improved clinical outcomes [3,9,20,47]. Technology-based peer support also provides an easily accessible medium for patients to find specific, tailored information related to their experience, to increase their knowledge, to strengthen their social bonds, and to feel a sense of belonging to a community [14,38,50]. A combination of these benefits and resources can lead to increased self-management, efficacy, and empowerment in their care [21,31]. However, research in the medical and HCI fields has typically focused on peer support for patients and caregivers with chronic conditions, who manage their care activities at home or in a clinic, instead of in the hospital.

To understand the opportunities and barriers for a peer support system in a hospital setting, we conducted two studies with pediatric patients and their caregivers. The first was a survey to identify the types of advice the participants wanted to share with others who have similar hospital experiences. These results served as the foundation for our second study: semi-structured interviews that incorporated "feature cards" of a hypothetical, hospital-based peer support system. Participants reacted to these features and provided their perspectives on exchanging information and interacting with peers during their time in the hospital.

In this paper, we describe five major types of information and support that hospitalized patients and caregivers want to exchange with their peers, and examine the potential barriers to using a peer support system in the hospital. Our primary contributions consist of:

- Providing a deep understanding of the informational and emotional peer support needs that patients and caregivers have, but are not currently supported during hospitalization, and
- Identifying opportunities, barriers, and design considerations for a peer support system to be used in the hospital.

These contributions have implications for peer support systems to increase engagement, reduce errors, and improve health outcomes for patients and caregivers in the hospital.

## BACKGROUND

When patients and caregivers are seeking knowledge and support about their health, many turn to online resources [8,12]. Tools such as mobile applications, social media, and online communities help these individuals to find relevant medical information, share ideas about managing their care, and gather the strength needed to cope with their illness [42,44]. These manifestations of informational and emotional support are valuable and distinct from the resources given by their healthcare provider [7,19].

Many types of options exist to facilitate peer support for a wide range of healthcare settings and patients, but hospital-based interventions do not always employ digital solutions. Rather, dyads of current and previous patients typically meet face-to-face for mentoring sessions [27,45]. Additionally, Jacobs and colleagues describe the role of cancer navigators, who assist cancer patients during different stages of their illness and treatment by answering questions, providing emotional support, and helping the patient apply for resources. These support services are nearly always provided in-person [24].

As one type of option outside the hospital, text messaging has been used to engage patients with their peers, especially with individuals managing chronic conditions at home, sometimes in low resource settings. For example, Franklin et al. implemented a mobile, text message support system called *Sweet Talk* for young patients living with type 1 diabetes to exchange "information, tips, and reminders", customize the timing of messages to appear before a clinic visit, and establish personal goals—such as regular insulin injections, blood glucose testing, healthy eating, and exercise [13]. A similar strategy by Rotheram-Borus et al. was conducted by linking women who have diabetes with a "buddy" via text message for 12 weeks. The pairs encouraged each other's adherence to their disease management tasks at home [43]. Both studies resulted in participants who engaged with their newfound community, and who demonstrated improved clinical outcomes.

Using increasingly popular smartphones, patients who are managing diabetes or obesity symptoms at home and between clinic visits can use dedicated mobile applications. These tools allow peers to share their daily fitness data and participate in a larger social network to promote healthy lifestyle changes—such as losing weight, exercising more, or improving eating habits [4,10].

A less common but appealing option, multi-user environments, have been explored by Bers et al., with the development of *Zora*, a three-dimensional environment where pediatric patients can create their own artifacts and form characters that interact with other users. Intended to help peers build a network and improve their medical adherence, this tool was designed for both diabetic patients to pass time during clinic visits, and for patients who were home from the hospital after receiving a solid organ transplant [1,2]. Similarly, Chin and Tsuei made a multi-user system for hospitalized patients with chronic illness to create narrative stories and share them with peers [5].

Websites and online forums provide additional means of support for patients and caregivers affected by a number of health issues, most notably chronic conditions—such as diabetes, obesity, cancer, and mental illness [22,28,51]. *Reach Out!* is one example that provides a place for young people with mental illness to discuss information and help-seeking strategies, with input and moderation by trained professionals. This program particularly helps reduce isolation of individuals who do not seek face-to-face support from their healthcare provider [48].

More recently, social media has emerged as a way to find people dealing with similar health-related problems. Facebook has allowed people to document their experiences, communicate with others through personal profiles, and create specialized "groups" [15,40]. Researchers have also analyzed YouTube-hosted health vlogs generated by patients diagnosed with cancer, HIV, and diabetes. This platform is used to document vloggers clinic or hospital visits, discuss their treatments and day-to-day management of their chronic illness, and share emotional struggles experienced at each significant point of their care process [23,29]. Additionally, Liu et al. found that chronically ill pediatric patients use a combination of social media, video chat, and texting to maintain a degree of normalcy, social support, and emotional support with existing friends [30]. Yet, we know little about how these tools can help hospitalized patients support each other.

In summary, the examples mentioned here represent a broad spectrum of solutions that make it easier for people to access the informational and emotional support they need, as well as share experiences and expertise acquired over time. Although some of these technologies are accessible to hospitalized patients, less is known about how the successful models of peer support tools translate to the hospital environment. Questions still remain about what the nature of peer support is among patients who share a similar hospital experience, and how to tailor this support to the specific needs of these individuals. Our research fills this knowledge gap and builds on prior work by uncovering the specific types of support that hospitalized patients and caregivers want during their stay, and are willing to share with their peers.

## METHODS

In this paper, we report and discuss findings from two studies: (1) a survey, and (2) semi-structured interviews, including feedback on feature cards of a hypothetical, hospital-based peer support system. We define **peers** in this context as people with similar health and hospital experiences. This work was conducted with hospitalized patients and caregivers, and is part of a larger study to identify opportunities for patients and caregivers to increase engagement in their care and prevent medical errors during their hospital stay [26,35–37,41]. Results from the survey informed the development of the "feature cards" used in the interviews. Each study was approved by the authors' Institutional Review Board.

### Study Site and Consent Process

Both the surveys and interviews were conducted at Seattle Children's Hospital in Seattle, WA. The hospital serves a broad geographic region, with pediatric patient demographics being slightly more diverse than the surrounding area's population. This organization manages approximately 300 beds and admits over 15,000 patients per year.

For each study, consent was obtained for all participants. If the participant was between 7 and 13 years old, the caregiver—usually a parent—provided written consent, followed by verbal assent from the pediatric patient. For patients aged 14 or above, parental consent was not required, and the patients provided written assent. Patients and caregivers were often, but not always, co-present while the studies were conducted.

### Survey

We developed a web-based survey instrument hosted by SurveyGizmo, which asked patients and caregivers about their experiences with an **undesirable event**, which we explicitly defined as an event that (1) was a small or big concern, (2) was unpleasant or caused harm, and (3) could have been avoided. Examples include: sleeping in an uncomfortable bed, experiencing a communication problem with their doctor, or receiving the wrong medication. The survey instrument went through several rounds of editing and pilot testing to ensure the questions and format were at an appropriate reading and comprehension level for eligible respondents. The final version consisted of 30 closed- and open-ended questions asking details about the event (e.g., *When did the event happen? Were you a patient or caregiver at the time of the event? Please describe the event in your own words*).

Recruitment occurred over a five-month period between February 2016 – July 2016. Our research team approached patients and caregivers in the hospital's acute and intensive care units. They were considered eligible for the study if they met the following criteria: were at least 7 years old, were well enough to provide informed consent, were comfortable reading and writing in English, had spent at least one night in the hospital as part of their current stay, and had experienced an undesirable event during either the current or a previous hospital visit. A research team member would administer the survey to the consented individuals on an iPad, and was available to answer questions or help the respondent take the survey if necessary. The iPad was cleaned with sanitizing wipes before and after each use to prevent hospital infection. More information about this study and preliminary results can be read elsewhere [16].

Unlike the other survey questions that asked specific details about the participant's undesirable event, only one question focused on peer support: "*What advice would you give to others who might have had an [undesirable] event like this in the hospital?*" This question was intended to elicit the respondent's knowledge gained through their hospital experience, and explore their willingness to share this knowledge with their peers. Of the 146 survey responses, 131 (89.7%) provided a free text answer to this question. We report these answers in addition to the results of our semi-structured interviews.

### Semi-Structured Interviews

To further explore perspectives that patients and caregivers have on receiving information and communicating with their peers in a broader context than hospital safety, we conducted semi-structured interviews with 15 hospitalized patients and caregivers. The interview consisted of an activity to design a patient-facing mobile application. This design activity involved multiple sets of "feature cards" inspired by envisioning cards, to draw out the values and preferences of patients and caregivers.

The themes that emerged from the survey analysis gave preliminary indications of the types of advice hospitalized individuals were compelled to share with their peers. To better understand *what* participants want to exchange with their peers, *how* they want to interact, and *why* they want to connect, we developed a subset of 6 feature cards that represented hypothetical components of a hospital-based peer support tool: (1) "Advice about being in the hospital" (2) "What to do when you notice a problem" (3) "Share your advice with others" (4) "Chat with another patient" (5) "Read other patient stories" and (6) "Filter patients by age, similar health issue, currently in the hospital, or other". Examples are shown in Figure 1.

The research team member conducting the interview asked participants to respond to the feature cards and explain their reasoning or thought process behind their response. For example, if patients said they were interested in chatting with another patient, we would follow up by asking why they were interested and what they would want to chat with the other patient about. All interviews took place between

July 2016 – August 2016 and were audio recorded and transcribed for analysis.

### Participants

#### *Survey Respondents*

Demographics of the 131 survey responses we received for the question, *"What advice would you give to others who might have had an [undesirable] event like this in the hospital?"* are provided in Table 1. Most respondents identified as White/Caucasian and Female. One hundred twenty-three (94.6%) reported using a smartphone, tablet, or laptop device during their most recent hospital stay. Fifty-three respondents indicated that they (either as a patient or caregiver) had at least 10 overnight hospital stays in the last 5 years.

#### *Interview Participants*

We interviewed a total of 15 individuals. Twelve were pediatric patients, ranging in age from 7-17, divided equally between males and females. The remaining 3 were caregivers of pediatric patients between the ages of 30-39 years old, consisting of one male and two females. Race and ethnicity of these participants were as follows: 11 White/Caucasian, 1 Black/African American, 3 Hispanic/Latin American, 1 Native Hawaiian/Pacific Islander, 1 Asian. Twelve people (80%) indicated that they owned a smartphone. Three of our 15 participants had never visited the hospital before their current admission.

### Data Analysis

We used a grounded theory approach to analyze both the survey and interview data [46]. The first author (SH) served as the primary coder for the survey responses. After each round of coding, SH met with the rest of the research team to discuss emergent themes, discrepancies, and codebook revisions. While interviews were conducted, three members of the research team (SH, SRM, MK) met regularly to iteratively develop a codebook based on emerging themes. After reaching saturation, SH, SRM, and MK independently coded interview transcripts. SH then compared the common threads and distinct themes of both data sets.

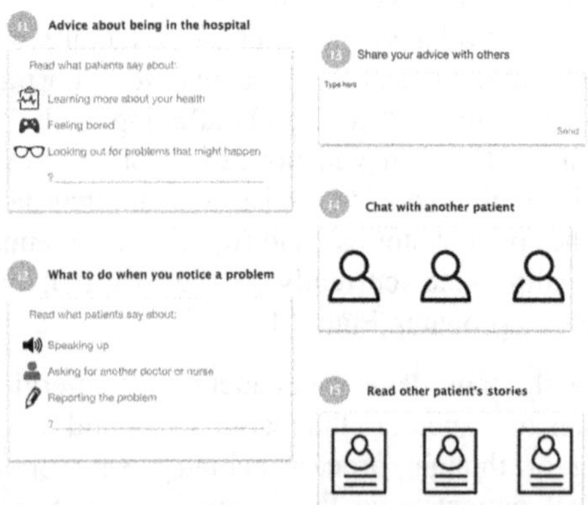


**Figure 1. Examples of cards we showed to participants during semi-structured interviews. Each contains one or more prompts related to content or features of a hospital-based peer support system.**

| | n | % |
|---|---|---|
| Total survey responses | 146 | - |
| Responses to *"advice"* question | 131 | 89.7 |
| Patients | 51 | 38.9 |
| Caregivers | 80 | 61.1 |
| Gender (F/M) | 98/33 | 74.8/25.2 |
| Age* | - | - |
| 7-13 years | 23 | 17.6 |
| 14-18 years | 21 | 16.0 |
| 19+ years | 87 | 66.4 |
| Education | - | - |
| 8th Grade | 14 | 10.9 |
| High School/GED | 22 | 17.1 |
| Some College | 16 | 12.4 |
| 2 or 4 Year Degree | 39 | 30.3 |
| Graduate/Professional | 16 | 12.4 |
| None/No Answer | 22 | 17.1 |
| Race/Ethnicity** | - | - |
| White/Caucasian | 98 | 76.0 |
| Black/African American | 8 | 6.2 |
| Hispanic/Latin American | 16 | 12.2 |
| Asian | 17 | 13.2 |
| Native American/ Pacific Islander | 11 | 8.5 |
| Other/No Answer | 12 | 9.4 |

*three caregivers selected their child's age instead of their own
**respondents could select multiple categories

**Table 1. Demographic summary of survey respondents who answered, *"What advice would you give to others who might have had an [undesirable] event like this in the hospital?"***

## RESULTS

Our analysis revealed five primary themes that were consistent across our survey and interview results: (1) asking about medical details—such as procedures, treatments, or medications, (2) learning about providers, (3) reporting and preventing medical errors, (4) exchanging emotional support, and (5) managing time in the hospital. In addition, we describe potential barriers to using a hospital-based peer support system, which include (1) synchronous vs. asynchronous communication, and (2) preferences for viewing and sharing content.

To differentiate between the participants in each study discussed in this paper, we refer to survey responses as S# and interview participants as I#, followed by their status as either a patient or caregiver. During survey data collection, we assigned unique identifiers to each survey initiated, even if the response was never completed. Therefore, some S# values are greater than the number of complete responses.

### Asking about Procedures, Treatments, or Medications

Patients and caregiver emphasized the importance of getting information about the patient's care, from their healthcare providers as well as their peers. Survey respondents repeatedly encouraged their peer counterparts to ask questions and request follow-up information from doctors and nurses. S94, a pediatric patient who had unexpected complications during a surgery and whose providers did not properly follow post-surgery instructions, wanted other patients to feel comfortable requesting information about procedures and complicated medical terminology:

*Don't be afraid to ask questions before, after, or during the procedure. If you don't understand the medical terms ask them to explain it in layman terms. Learn more of the risks involved and complications that can happen afterwards. –S94, Patient*

A caregiver, whose son experienced extreme discomfort due to an incorrectly inserted feeding tube, thought that knowledge from other patients would have been useful in identifying the source of her son's distress. She recommended other caregivers ask for this information specifically:

*Ask more questions about the tools and side effects and what other patient feedback has been. –S212, Caregiver*

When talking about information they wanted to learn from other patients, interview participants expressed interest in posing questions about procedures, treatments, and medications to patients that were currently going through or had already completed the process. I04, a patient, wanted to ask others with her same diagnosis about surgeries they had to undergo, and how well certain drugs worked. Another patient, I07, was waiting to undergo a transplant at the time we spoke to him. He also thought it was important to hear from other patients about their experiences firsthand:

*Like I'm going through transplant. If there was another kid who was going through transplants, which there is, you could ask them okay, so how did it kind of feel like when you went through the transplant? –I07, Patient*

One caregiver was also interested in learning this type of information from other parents of children with the same health condition, so her own daughter's health and symptom triggers could be normalized:

*If some parents can also share that okay, this many times in a year we have to visit because of this reason, and my kid is around this age, right? So this kind of information helps in coming up with a pattern and some kind of satisfaction that okay, this is what has happened with...most other folks, it's not only me who's having this problem. –I15, Caregiver*

Participants in each study identified both their providers and peers as valuable sources of information. By encouraging each other to actively seek information and ask about care details, patients and caregivers can increase their knowledge, prepare for their upcoming experience, and maintain a realistic perspective of the patient's health status.

### Learning about Providers

Some of our survey respondents and interview participants wanted to talk about their healthcare providers with peers. Providers were a common topic of discussion among those who had a chronic or rare health condition, and wanted to know more information about the doctors who specialize in their care. I04, a patient, said this when talking about advice she would want to read from other patients:

*I04: You could also say advice about doctors.*

*Interviewer: Like which doctor you have.*

*I04: Yeah, this doctor was better for me, this doctor I switched out because this happened. Like this doctor seemed to really know what they were doing, this doctor's already seen what I have, has the most experience with what we have. So that would be good.*

Similarly, many survey respondents shared advice for what to do when a patient's or caregiver's relationship with their provider is difficult. Through their own hospital experiences, respondents described the options available to a patient and caregiver that might not be commonly known. For example, one caregiver described receiving unsatisfactory care from a provider, which caused her to ask for a different doctor:

*When your child is in the hospital, ask to speak to a pediatrician immediately. I didn't know I had to request that, I assumed that since he was a child, we would of course speak to a Dr. for children. –S228, Caregiver*

Respondents also encouraged other patients to facilitate communication among providers (i.e., asking providers if they had spoken to another provider), to avoid communication problems, and involve a third party such as a second opinion, hospital staff supervisor, social worker, family advocate, or legal advisor if disagreements start to affect the patient's quality of care.

The quality of a patient or caregiver's relationship with their provider can greatly affect their experience in the hospital. Advice on how to evaluate and maintain this relationship proved to be important for many participants, because they wanted to avoid potential conflicts and receive the best care possible.

### Reporting and Preventing Medical Errors

Alerting someone to a serious problem was another consistent theme in both survey responses and interviews with patients and caregivers. One survey respondent, who was mistakenly administered too much laughing gas before a procedure, discussed the importance of reporting medical errors such as hers:

*Report what happened to you. I wonder all the time if the anesthesiologist has done this to other children, especially children younger than I am who had no way of knowing what was happening to them. –S129, Patient*

Information from other patients about methods for identifying and preventing errors in the hospital was also valuable for many of the pediatric patients we interviewed. For example, when I07 was asked about what advice he would want from other patients regarding their hospital stay, said: *"because that way you can know what's happening and any problems."* I12 wanted other patients' guidance so he could consult with his doctors on how best to fix an issue. A third patient, I11, was interested in finding out what errors patients had experienced, so if she had a similar problem or noticed someone who needed medical help, she would know what to do.

In addition to these examples, advice on how to avoid errors mainly came from our survey respondents, who offered strategies such as remaining alert, paying attention to details of their care, keeping track of lab tests, and following up with their healthcare providers if needed. Many respondents also emphasized double checking medicine labels to help prevent drug-related errors such as giving a medication known to cause an allergic reaction, providing an incorrect dose, or administering the drug inappropriately.

Due to the prevalence and danger of preventable medical errors in the hospital setting, patients were aware of the need for constant vigilance and prompt reporting. Increased awareness among peers about the risks and types of error also has the potential to improve early detection and prevention.

### Exchanging Emotional Support

Patients from each study discussed the idea of giving to and receiving support from their peers, by means of forming friendships, talking about their general health experiences, and offering encouragement.

Connecting with other patients who were of the same age range, health condition, or hospital was frequently mentioned as an important aspect of communicating with their peers. For many participants, this potential interaction was an opportunity to establish friendships and share mutual hospital experiences. One example was I09, a patient who traveled from out of state to be treated at the hospital. She only knew of one other person in her home state with the same diagnosis, and was excited at the prospect of talking with others like her. S233, also a pediatric patient, said she would be willing to share information about her hospital experience with another patient like herself. *"I will just talk about my stay and learn about hers/his."*

I10, another patient, wanted to ask about others' health progress and hospital stay, providing support to those who need someone to listen to them:

*Interviewer: What kinds of things would you want to ask [other patients]?*

*I10: How they're feeling and was it hard. And what they are going through.*

Beyond sharing information about general hospital experiences, participants in both studies were compelled to offer comfort to others who go through difficult times. I12, a patient diagnosed with epilepsy, offered support to other patients struggling to manage the resulting emotional impact of having this condition:

*I would say that it's okay to have epilepsy, even though you might feel like the odd one out, you could still be a perfect person in your own way. –I12, Patient*

Sentiments like this were especially evident among survey respondents. Phrases such as "don't be afraid", "stay calm", and "be strong" were frequent. Many respondents wrote messages that encouraged self-advocacy, including advice to be persistent when following up with healthcare providers, know their rights to request or turn down additional tests if needed, and to speak up when they feel uncomfortable. Others acknowledged and sympathized with the emotional impact of a stressful hospital visit:

*It's easy to feel unimportant to your doctors, especially when requests are not being acknowledged. Be your own best advocate. –S89, Patient*

When the status of the patient's health is uncertain, both the patient and caregiver can feel increased tension, anxiety, and stress. By forming strong connections and offering reassurance, these individuals can find a way to relieve their emotional burdens with others who have gone through the same difficult situations.

### Managing Time in the Hospital

During a typical hospital stay, patients and caregivers spend long stretches of time waiting for a provider to visit their room, anticipating a procedure, or recovering from treatment. Patients who responded to our survey and participated in interviews discussed advice about how to fill this time and prevent boredom. As I04 told us, *"It's a hospital, it's not exactly Disney World."* One of our interview participants, I11, was interested in finding out more information from patients who have more hospital experience than herself:

*Maybe other kids have been here longer than me and I don't know all the places or where you can find things to do. And they could share advice about what to do in the hospital. –I11, Patient*

Patients with previous hospital experiences recommended taking advantage of existing resources to rent books, movies, television shows, or board games to play with visiting friends or family. When one of our patient participants, I05, was asked about what he would want to talk with other patients about, he responded, *"Games and stuff. And like your cousins [could] play with you. And when you're bored, you can go – some people get iPad or VS."* Alternatively, mental and physical exercises were mentioned as possible ways to avoid monotony:

*Try to keep your mind busy with productive things...walk as much as possible to feel like you are doing something helpful instead of watching tv or playing on a screen. –S137, Patient*

Our participants wanted to know how to occupy their minds to distract from the physical pain and separation from family or friends. Informing patients about the resources available to them, (e.g., renting an Xbox, watching a movie) encourages these people to engage in activities outside their care and could improve their overall experience during hospitalization.

### Barriers to Using a Peer Support System

The combination of survey and interview results gave us a deeper understanding of the informational and emotional peer support that hospitalized patients and caregivers need. During the interviews with our 15 participants, we also explored their perspectives about using a hospital-based peer support system. Although all participants expressed some level of interest in such a system, they also brought up concerns, which we discuss in this section.

#### *Synchronous vs. Asynchronous Communication*

During our interviews, we asked participants how they would prefer to communicate with other patients and caregivers. Several individuals wanted to interact with one or more of their peers in real time, because it was thought to be a more personal, private, and effective method of communication. Although some patients struggled to articulate why this real-time connection was important to them, it was particularly evident among patients who were interested in connecting with others experiencing similar health issues to share relevant information:

*Interviewer: Would you want [communication] to be in real time?*

*I12: Yes. [...]*

*Interviewer: You'd be okay with [sharing your advice with others]?*

*I12: Yes, because I think if I find something and others don't, I think it would be a good thing to put out there, so other people can read about it in case they didn't know what to do or what's going on.*

*Interviewer: [...] Can I ask why it being in real time would be important to you?*

*I12: Because, I think that in real time, it would be a lot better than any other time, because – I just don't know.*

*Interviewer: You just like it better that way?*

*I12: Yeah.*

Another patient we interviewed was under isolation protocol, which prevented her from leaving her hospital room. Physical interactions with other patients were not an option. To overcome this challenge, she mentioned the use of existing video chat tools:

*Sometimes I can't come out of my room because I'm in isolation...maybe the other kid [and me] wouldn't be able to actually see each other physically, so you could Facetime or something like that. –I02, Patient*

In contrast, a few participants explicitly mentioned their desire for asynchronous communication. I11, a younger pediatric patient, did not feel comfortable chatting with people that she did not already know in person, and preferred reading information from other patients outside of a real-time environment. One caregiver expressed some reluctance toward a live chat because it can be inconvenient when the patient needs attention:

*I think real-time chat would be difficult, being in hospital, because you don't know if your kid is upset or still recovering. If they had time and their kid is ok, then they can do real-time. –I15, Caregiver*

#### *Preferences for Viewing and Sharing Content*

Despite feeling nervous about reading potentially negative hospital experiences, most interview participants still thought it was important to know this information. However, one pediatric patient preferred avoiding messages from other patients that might cause anxiety or sadness:

*I01: I wouldn't want to see that.*

*Interviewer: [...] How come?*

*I01: I don't know. Some of them are pretty sad.*

*Interviewer: You don't want to see the bad [stories]?*

*I01: No.*

Some information was also viewed as better suited for discussion with a healthcare provider instead of with another patient. For example, I04 was a patient who already felt comfortable speaking up and asking her doctor questions, so advice from other patients on doing these activities was not useful to her. I02, another pediatric patient, told us that patients should not discuss unexpected health problems with other patients, but rather with their providers or caregivers, *"because they would probably know what [the] symptoms could be or any treatment or medicine you're getting."*

Maintaining privacy was extremely valuable for caregivers. During their interviews, I14 and I15 expressed unease regarding the ability for their peers to identify them through virtual interactions. I14, who was initially not interested in exchanging information with peers, described his hesitation to communicate with other parents:

*I mean you run into people in the elevators grabbing coffee and if you feel like it you socialize, but if you don't, you just don't, right? Yeah, I would stay anonymous. Personally, I would. –I14, Caregiver*

Later in the interview, however, I14 said he was more agreeable to anonymously engaging with content from other caregivers. I15 also positively responded to the idea of anonymous interactions because it would allow people to honestly disclose information about medications or treatments without the risk of being identified.

These differing opinions about how and what to communicate with other patients begin to reveal the unique challenges that a hospital environment presents to designers of a peer support system. In the following section, we discuss opportunities and examine these challenges in more detail.

## DISCUSSION

Our research builds on previous findings that examine the roles patients and caregivers take on during their hospital visits, their degree of involvement in activities related to their care, as well as their unsupported informational and emotional needs [25,26,34,35,37,41]. The results from our two studies, surveys and semi-structured interviews, identify the specific informational and emotional needs that these hospitalized individuals are willing to exchange with their peers.

Based on these findings, we describe three design considerations for a hospital-based peer support system: (1) leveraging the Electronic Health Record to match peers, (2) protecting privacy and anonymity, and (3) accommodating dynamic interactions and needs.

In the following sections, we also briefly compare two existing tools used for peer support, to demonstrate how hospital-based systems can adopt their benefits and improve upon their limitations. The first, PatientsLikeMe, is an online community that offers a place for patients and caregivers to share experiential knowledge among members. The second, Facebook, is a social media site that allows people to form groups about various health topics. Although these examples were chosen due to their recognition and previous research, we acknowledge that other technologies are currently used for the same reasons and are relevant to this work.

### Leveraging the Electronic Health Record to Match Peers

Many of our survey respondents and interview participants strongly desired an open dialogue with their peers, especially with those who had similar health and hospital experiences. Properly aligning the interests and common attributes of peers is critical when forming quality interactions, and can be difficult to accomplish with existing tools. Facebook users must spend time independently seeking other individuals and groups related to their interests; the user sometimes may not know of or have access to a group, unless they receive an invitation from another group member. PatientsLikeMe forums are organized by chronic illness diagnosis, so those with similar experiences across diagnoses may be harder to identify.

Research on how to improve this process and match peers effectively is ongoing. For example, Hartzler et al. have used profiles and posts extracted from online health communities to optimize peer mentor recommendations [17,18]. In conjunction with solutions like this, a hospital-based peer support system can leverage information from the Electronic Health Record (EHR) to successfully match individuals with each other. Age, diagnosis, medications, procedures, treatment plans, and current physical location in the hospital are all examples of information stored with in the EHR. Thus, it would be possible to quickly match individuals who are interested in connecting with peers during their hospital stay by identifying their similar characteristics across these dimensions. One of our interview participants, I04, said she wanted to use a peer system that would help her find other patients of doctors who specialized in treating her rare condition, so she could speak to them in detail about the quality of care and differences in treatment protocols across providers. A system using information from the EHR could accomplish this by identifying groups of patients with the same diagnosis, healthcare provider, or hospital unit, who have also indicated an interest in connecting with peers. This would facilitate the exchange of expertise that I04 can use to further engage in her care.

### Protecting Privacy and Anonymity

People have varying opinions on privacy and anonymity, as well as a range of preferences for sharing their personal health information. Success of a system used in a hospital setting is dependent on supporting these preferences. Most of our interview participants were comfortable sharing their information with others, but a few specifically mentioned their desire to only interact with a peer system anonymously. These individuals are interested in the benefits of learning from other patients and caregivers without sharing their own information; I15 also thought that having the option of anonymity would increase the value of such support by allowing peers to express more honest opinions about their hospital experiences. Although existing tools like Facebook have the option for health-related groups to be closed or open to the public, there is currently no way for users to interact with these groups anonymously.

To be sensitive to individual preferences for sharing personal and potentially identifiable health information, a hospital-based system should use an opt-in model, rather than opt-out. Users must be properly informed about the risks of sharing their information with others, and safeguards for situations that result in potentially negative consequences should also be incorporated. Possible solutions can involve the system having different levels of anonymity, customizable user profiles, or icons to represent higher-level information such as health status or hospital service (e.g., surgical, oncology, transplant), so the user can selectively choose what information they are willing to share with others. At present, Facebook incorporates selective sharing preferences, that allows users to choose what audience has access to information such as their birth date, or phone number. Having flexible security settings like Facebook helps to accommodate the broad range of preferences that might also change over time, as patients and caregivers become more familiar with their peers.

### Accommodating Dynamic Interactions and Needs

The findings from our interview participants demonstrated a need to support many levels of engagement in a hospital-based peer support system. Patients like I02 and I12 valued real-time interactions with their peers, while others like I11 and I15 preferred to read content at their own time or interact with others in an asynchronous manner.

Our results also demonstrated a variety of peer support needs about the patients' health, the hospital, and emotional support. Facilitating this support while recognizing that these needs can change over the course of a hospital stay is also important. For example, a patient might need information from peers about what to expect before a procedure, or what potential errors they need to watch for. After diagnosis or treatment, this patient might want to seek or share emotional support. During recovery, while the patient rests and waits for follow-up care, information about how to pass the time and hasten discharge might take precedence. We saw these changing needs among our study participants; I07 described wanting to know information and potential problems about his upcoming transplant, and S212 encouraged others to ask questions before undergoing a procedure. I12 was compelled to exchange emotional support after his recent epilepsy treatment. Following their surgical procedures, I11 and I04 wanted advice from peers about how to minimize boredom while confined to their hospital room.

Although some research on cancer patients have also noted differing information needs over time [11], such dynamism isn't typically considered by peer tools. To support these various levels of interaction and peer support needs, researchers have emphasized the importance of designing for passive and active involvement in a system [32]. Although PatientsLikeMe and Facebook users can communicate synchronously or asynchronously via private messaging and timeline posts, finding relevant and accurate information across many resources and at different points of the care process poses many challenges. Prior work has also explored the use of virtual spaces where patients can access a repository of advice organized by symptom, treatment, or common struggle [6,49]. However, the cognitive and physical effort required to navigate and find relevant support is something that patients and caregivers in the hospital are not always not capable of due to medications or treatments [39]. In addition, such mappings by medical categories—such as symptoms—neglect the important dynamism during a hospital stay.

Providing synchronous features like text or video chat, coupled with a knowledge base to be accessed when convenient, would be particularly beneficial for hospitalized individuals. Users in the hospital could have the option of connecting with other patients currently in the hospital, or reading and contributing information to a knowledge base of patient and caregiver expertise. Individuals who were previously hospitalized and wanted to share their experiences could also add information by responding to a questionnaire after discharge. Allowing for multiple modes of interaction could increase the peer resources available to current patients, while supporting individual preferences for engaging in the system.

Adapting to peer support needs as they change over time, and reducing the user burden for finding relevant support are other critical components of a peer support system in the hospital environment. One way to accomplish this adaptation would be to have a user answer a series of prompts such as "do you want to learn from others about your upcoming procedure?" or "do you feel like playing a game with someone?" Based on their responses, the user could be automatically referred to the appropriate resource for information or emotional support. EHR data about diagnoses, medications, or procedures could be another way to direct the individual to appropriate peer information. This may reduce the burden for patients and caregivers to search for information on their own, across thousands of existing platforms. Topics or people of interest to the user could also be featured prominently within a tool and support easy navigation. A patient should be able to search, save, and organize information from their peers in a simple and efficient way. The type of content displayed could be adjusted based on their mood, health status, or current phase of their hospital stay. This capability would let individuals like I01, who only want to see positive experiences from other similar patients, avoid finding negative patient stories and still participate in other aspects of the peer support system.

## LIMITATIONS AND FUTURE WORK

Our work provides new perspectives and opportunities for peer support in a hospital setting, but we also recognize the limitations of our studies. Because our survey purposefully included people who had experienced an undesirable event, safety issues naturally were a focus of their advice to peers. Both studies were conducted at a single pediatric hospital site in an urban setting in the United States, and might not account for the perspectives of a rural or community-hospital based population. Therefore, an important next step will be to validate these findings at different hospitals and geographic regions. In the future, we also would like to seek the opinions of healthcare providers, to explore their perspective and possible interaction with such a hospital-based peer support system. Additionally, future work should understand how the use of this system may affects patients' engagement in their care.

## CONCLUSION

In this paper, we explore the possibility of a hospital-based peer support system. Our survey with pediatric patients and caregivers offered insight into hospital safety, patient expertise, and the opportunities for a peer support system in a hospital setting. Through semi-structured interviews with hospitalized patients, and their reactions to feature cards representing aspects of a peer system, we examined the specific informational and emotional needs that a hospital-based system should support.

We conclude that supporting the specific needs and values of hospitalized individuals is essential for the success of a hospital-based peer support system. More research is needed to understand how existing peer support tools do, or do not, meet these needs. Existing non-hospital-based solutions—such as PatientsLikeMe and Facebook—have components of useful features for this patient population, including synchronous or asynchronous communication options, and customizable privacy settings. However, the hospital environment presents additional design opportunities and considerations.

A future hospital-based peer support system should consist of: (1) leveraging of EHR data for high-quality peer matches and tailored content for users, (2) allowing for opt-in privacy preferences of individuals who prefer to share or hide their personal health information, (3) providing synchronous, asynchronous, active, and passive interaction, and (4) accommodating informational and emotional needs that are likely to change over the course of a hospital stay, while ensuring the support is accessible without increasing user burden. Our design considerations should help guide technological systems and maximize the benefits of peer support networks for hospitalized patients and caregivers. Ultimately, such peer support could lead to increased empowerment, engagement, and safety for these individuals.

## ACKNOWLEDGMENTS

We would like to thank our survey respondents and interview participants, who took time out of their hospital visits to contribute to our research studies. Thank you also to Kathryn Nickel, members of the Outcomes Assessment Program at Seattle Children's Hospital, and the *Patients as Safeguards* research team, including Andrew Miller, Alex Filipkowski, Cory Brown, Kelsey Aiello, and Rashmi Elera. This work was primarily funded by the Agency for Healthcare Research and Quality, grant #1R01HS022894, with additional support from the National Library of Medicine Biomedical and Health Informatics Training Grant #T15LM007442.

## REFERENCES

1. Marina Bers, Clement Chau, Keiko Satoh, and Laura Beals. 2007. *Virtual Communities of Care: Online Peer Networks with Post-Organ Transplant Youth.* International Society of the Learning Sciences.
2. Marina U. Bers, Joseph Gonzalez-Heydrich, and David Ray DeMaso. 2001. Identity construction environments: supporting a virtual therapeutic community of pediatric patients undergoing dialysis. In *Proceedings of the SIGCHI conference on Human factors in computing systems - CHI '01*, 380–387. http://doi.org/10.1145/365024.365302
3. Sharon H. Campbell, Marie Rose Phaneuf, and Karen Deane. 2004. Cancer peer support programs—do they work? *Patient Education and Counseling* 55, 1: 3–15. http://doi.org/10.1016/j.pec.2003.10.001
4. Yu Chen, Mirana E. Randriambelonoro, Antoine Geissbuhler, and Pearl Pu. 2016. Social Incentives in Pervasive Fitness Apps for Obese and Diabetic patients. In *Proceedings of the 19th ACM Conference on Computer Supported Cooperative Work and Social Computing Companion - CSCW '16 Companion*, 245–248. http://doi.org/10.1145/2818052.2869093
5. Jui-Chih Chin and Mengping Tsuei. 2009. Multi-user Narrative Sharing System for Children with Chronic Illness. In *2009 Ninth IEEE International Conference on Advanced Learning Technologies*, 479–481. http://doi.org/10.1109/ICALT.2009.154
6. Andrea Civan, David W. McDonald, Kenton T. Unruh, and Wanda Pratt. 2009. Locating patient expertise in everyday life. *Proceedings of the ACM 2009 International Conference on Supporting Group Work - GROUP '09*: 291–300. http://doi.org/10.1145/1531674.1531718
7. Andrea Civan and Wanda Pratt. 2007. Threading together patient expertise. *Proceedings of the American Medical Informatics Association Annual Symposium*: 140–144. Retrieved from https://www.semanticscholar.org/paper/Threading-Together-Patient-Expertise-Hartzler-Pratt/64eed14b34218d8626d5411c0af9e8bd4630179c/pdf
8. R J Cline and K M Haynes. 2001. Consumer health information seeking on the Internet: the state of the art. *Health Education Research* 16, 6: 671–92. http://doi.org/10.1093/HER/16.6.671
9. J. R. Dale, S. M. Williams, and V. Bowyer. 2012. What is the effect of peer support on diabetes outcomes in adults? A systematic review. *Diabetic Medicine* 29, 11: 1361–1377. http://doi.org/10.1111/j.1464-5491.2012.03749.x

10. Honglu Du, Michael G. Youngblood, and Peter Pirolli. 2014. Efficacy of a Smartphone System to Support Groups in Behavior Change Programs. In *Proceedings of the Wireless Health 2014 on National Institutes of Health - WH '14*, 1–8. http://doi.org/10.1145/2668883.2668887
11. Jordan Eschler, Zakariya Dehlawi, and Wanda Pratt. 2015. Self-Characterized Illness Phase and Information Needs of Participants in an Online Cancer Forum. *Ninth International AAAI Conference on Web and Social Media*: 101–109.
12. Susannah Fox and Sydney Jones. 2009. The social life of health information. *Washington, DC: Pew Internet & American Life Project*: 2009–12.
13. Victoria Louise Franklin, Alexandra Greene, Annalu Waller, Stephen Alan Greene, and Claudia Pagliari. 2008. Patients' Engagement with "Sweet Talk" - A Text Messaging Support System for Young People with Diabetes. *Journal of Medical Internet Research* 10, 2: e20. http://doi.org/10.2196/jmir.962
14. Jeana H Frost and Michael P Massagli. 2008. Social Uses of Personal Health Information Within PatientsLikeMe, an Online Patient Community: What Can Happen When Patients Have Access to One Another's Data. *Journal of Medical Internet Research* 10, 3. http://doi.org/10.2196/jmir.1053
15. Jeremy A. Greene, Niteesh K. Choudhry, Elaine Kilabuk, and William H. Shrank. 2011. Online Social Networking by Patients with Diabetes: A Qualitative Evaluation of Communication with Facebook. *Journal of General Internal Medicine* 26, 3: 287–292. http://doi.org/10.1007/s11606-010-1526-3
16. Shefali Haldar, Alex Filipkowski, Sonali R Mishra, et al. 2016. "Scared to go to the Hospital": Inpatient Experiences with Undesirable Events. *Proceedings of the American Medical Informatics Association Annual Symposium* 2016: 609–617.
17. Andrea L. Hartzler, Megan N. Taylor, Albert Park, et al. 2016. Leveraging cues from person-generated health data for peer matching in online communities. *Journal of the American Medical Informatics Association* 23, 3: 496–507. http://doi.org/10.1093/jamia/ocv175
18. Andrea L Hartzler, David W Mcdonald, Albert Park, Jina Huh, Charles Weaver, and Wanda Pratt. 2014. Evaluating Health Interest Profiles Extracted from Patient-Generated Data. *Proceedings of the American Medical Informatics Association Annual Symposium* 2014: 626–635.
19. Andrea Hartzler and Wanda Pratt. 2011. Managing the Personal Side of Health: How Patient Expertise Differs from the Expertise of Clinicians. *Journal of Medical Internet Research* 13, 3: e62. http://doi.org/10.2196/jmir.1728
20. Michele Heisler, Sandeep Vijan, Fatima Makki, and John D. Piette. 2010. Diabetes Control With Reciprocal Peer Support Versus Nurse Care Management: A Randomized Trial. *Annals of Internal Medicine* 153, 8: 507–515. http://doi.org/10.7326/0003-4819-153-8-201010190-00007
21. Mette Terp Høybye, Christoffer Johansen, and Tine Tjørnhøj-Thomsen. 2005. Online interaction. Effects of storytelling in an internet breast cancer support group. *Psycho-Oncology* 14, 3: 211–220. http://doi.org/10.1002/pon.837
22. Jina Huh and Mark S. Ackerman. 2012. Collaborative help in chronic disease management. *Proceedings of the ACM 2012 conference on Computer Supported Cooperative Work - CSCW '12*: 853. http://doi.org/10.1145/2145204.2145331
23. Jina Huh, Leslie S Liu, Tina Neogi, Kori Inkpen, and Wanda Pratt. 2014. Health Vlogs as Social Support for Chronic Illness Management. *ACM Transactions on Computer-Human Interaction* 21, 4: 23. http://doi.org/10.1145/2630067
24. Maia Jacobs, James Clawson, and Elizabeth D. Mynatt. 2014. Cancer Navigation: Opportunities and Challenges for Facilitating the Breast Cancer Journey. *Proceedings of the 17th ACM Conference on Computer Supported Cooperative Work & Social Computing - CSCW '14*: 1467–1478. http://doi.org/10.1145/2531602.2531645
25. Elizabeth Kaziunas, Ayse G Buyuktur, Jasmine Jones, et al. 2015. Transition and Reflection in the Use of Health Information : The Case of Pediatric Bone Marrow Transplant Caregivers. *Proceedings of the 18th ACM Conference on Computer Supported Cooperative Work & Social Computing - CSCW '15*: 1763–1774.
26. Logan Kendall, Sonali R Mishra, Ari Pollack, Barry Aaronson, and Wanda Pratt. 2015. Making background work visible: opportunities to address patient information needs in the hospital. *Proceedings of the American Medical Informatics Association Annual Symposium* 2015: 1957–66. Retrieved from http://www.ncbi.nlm.nih.gov/pubmed/26958295
27. Sharon Lawn, Ann Smith, and Kelly Hunter. 2008. Mental health peer support for hospital avoidance and early discharge: An Australian example of consumer driven and operated service. *Journal of Mental Health* 17, 5: 498–508. http://doi.org/10.1080/09638230701530242
28. Victor Li, David W. McDonald, Elizabeth V. Eikey, et al. 2014. Losing It Online: Characterizing

Participation in an Online Weight Loss Community. In *Proceedings of the 18th International Conference on Supporting Group Work - GROUP '14*, 35–45. http://doi.org/10.1145/2660398.2660416

29. Leslie S Liu, Jina Huh, Tina Neogi, Kori Inkpen, and Wanda Pratt. 2013. Health Vlogger-Viewer Interaction in Chronic Illness Management. *Proceedings of the SIGCHI Conference on Human Factors in Computing Systems - CHI '13*: 49–58. http://doi.org/10.1145/2470654.2470663

30. Leslie S Liu, Kori M. Inkpen, and Wanda Pratt. 2015. "I'm Not Like My Friends": Understanding How Children with a Chronic Illness Use Technology to Maintain Normalcy. *Proceedings of the 18th ACM Conference on Computer Supported Cooperative Work & Social Computing - CSCW '15*: 1527–1539. http://doi.org/10.1145/2675133.2675201

31. Kate Lorig, Philip L. Ritter, Diana D. Laurent, et al. 2010. Online Diabetes Self-Management Program: a randomized study. *Diabetes Care* 33, 6: 1275–1281.

32. Julie Maitland and Matthew Chalmers. 2011. Designing for peer involvement in weight management. *Proceedings of the SIGCHI Conference on Human Factors in Computing Systems - CHI '11*: 315–324. http://doi.org/10.1145/1978942.1978988

33. Martin A Makary and Michael Daniel. 2016. Medical error—the third leading cause of death in the US. *BMJ* 353: i2139. http://doi.org/10.1136/bmj.i2139

34. Danielle M. McCarthy, Emily P. Ellison, Arjun K. Venkatesh, et al. 2013. Emergency department team communication with the patient: The patient's perspective. *Journal of Emergency Medicine* 45, 2: 262–270. http://doi.org/10.1016/j.jemermed.2012.07.052

35. Andrew D Miller, Sonali R Mishra, Logan Kendall, Shefali Haldar, Ari H Pollack, and Wanda Pratt. 2016. Partners in Care: Design Considerations for Caregivers and Patients During a Hospital Stay. *Proceedings of the 19th ACM Conference on Computer Supported Cooperative Work and Social Computing Companion - CSCW '16*. http://doi.org/10.1145/2818048.2819983

36. Andrew D Miller, Ari H Pollack, Wanda Pratt, and Seattle Children. 2016. Bursting the Information Bubble : Identifying Opportunities for Pediatric Patient-Centered Technology. *Proceedings of the American Medical Informatics Association Annual Symposium*: 894–903.

37. Sonali R Mishra, Shefali Haldar, Ari H Pollack, et al. 2016. "Not Just a Receiver": Understanding Patient Behavior in the Hospital Environment. *Proceedings of the 2016 CHI Conference on Human Factors in Computing Systems - CHI '16*: 3103–3114. http://doi.org/10.1145/2858036.2858167

38. S Anne Moorhead, Diane E Hazlett, Laura Harrison, Jennifer K Carroll, Anthea Irwin, and Ciska Hoving. 2013. A New Dimension of Health Care: Systematic Review of the Uses, Benefits, and Limitations of Social Media for Health Communication. *Journal of Medical Internet Research* 15, 4. http://doi.org/10.2196/jmir.1933

39. Dan Morris and Amy Karlson. 2011. Dynamic Accessibility Requirements for Hospital Patients. *Human Factors*: 1–5.

40. Mark W. Newman, Debra Lauterbach, Sean A. Munson, Paul Resnick, and Margaret E. Morris. 2011. It's not that i don't have problems, i'm just not putting them on facebook. *Proceedings of the ACM conference on Computer supported cooperative work - CSCW '11*: 341. http://doi.org/10.1145/1958824.1958876

41. Ari H Pollack, Uba Backonja, Andrew D Miller, et al. 2016. Closing the Gap: Supporting Patients' Transition to Self-Management after Hospitalization. *Proceedings of the 2016 CHI Conference on Human Factors in Computing Systems - CHI '16*: 5324–5336. http://doi.org/10.1145/2858036.2858240

42. Jenny Preece. 1998. Empathic communities: reaching out across the Web. *Interactions* 5, 2: 32–43. http://doi.org/10.1145/274430.274435

43. Mary Jane Rotheram-Borus, Mark Tomlinson, Margaret Gwegwe, W Scott Comulada, Neal Kaufman, and Marion Keim. 2012. Diabetes buddies: peer support through a mobile phone buddy system. *The Diabetes educator* 38, 3: 357–65. http://doi.org/10.1177/0145721712444617

44. J. Sarasohn-Kahn and California Healthcare Foundation. 2008. The Wisdom of Patients: Health Care Meets Online Social Media. *California HealthCare Foundation*, April. Retrieved from http://www.chcf.org/publications/2008/04/the-wisdom-of-patients-health-care-meets-online-social-media

45. William H. Sledge, Martha Lawless, David Sells, Melissa Wieland, Maria J. O'Connell, and Larry Davidson. 2011. Effectiveness of Peer Support in Reducing Readmissions of Persons With Multiple Psychiatric Hospitalizations. *Psychiatric Services* 62, 5: 541–544. http://doi.org/10.1176/ps.62.5.pss6205_0541

46. Juliet M. Strauss, Anselm L.; Corbin. 1998. *Basics*

*of Qualitative Research: Techniques and Procedures for Developing Grounded Theory.* http://doi.org/10.1017/CBO9781107415324.004

47. M W Verheijden, J C Bakx, C van Weel, M A Koelen, and W A van Staveren. 2005. Role of social support in lifestyle-focused weight management interventions. *European Journal of Clinical Nutrition* 59: S179–S186. http://doi.org/10.1038/sj.ejcn.1602194

48. Marianne Webb, Jane Burns, and Philippa Collin. 2008. Providing online support for young people with mental health difficulties: challenges and opportunities explored. *Early Intervention in Psychiatry* 2, 2: 108–113. http://doi.org/10.1111/j.1751-7893.2008.00066.x

49. Mary Webster, Emma Foster, Rob Comber, Simon Bowen, Tim Cheetham, and Madeline Balaam. 2015. Understanding the lived experience of adolescents with type 1 diabetes. *Proceedings of the 14th International Conference on Interaction Design and Children - IDC '15*: 140–149. http://doi.org/10.1145/2771839.2771854

50. M White and S M Dorman. 2001. Receiving social support online: implications for health education. *Health Education Research* 16, 6: 693–707. http://doi.org/10.1093/HER/16.6.693

51. Andrew J. Winzelberg, Catherine Classen, Georg W. Alpers, et al. 2003. Evaluation of an internet support group for women with primary breast cancer. *Cancer* 97, 5: 1164–1173. http://doi.org/10.1002/cncr.11174

52. 2014. Fast Facts on US Hospitals. Retrieved from http://www.aha.org/research/rc/stat-studies/fast-facts.shtml

# Patient Strategies as Active Adaptation: Understanding Patient Behaviors During an Emergency Visit

**Sun Young Park**
Stamps School of Art & Design,
School of Information
University of Michigan
sunypark@umich.edu

**Yunan Chen**
Bren School of Information and
Computer Science
University of California Irvine
yunanc@ics.uci.edu

## ABSTRACT
Although the ability of patients to access their health information during ongoing care is considered crucial for better health outcomes and increased satisfaction, the current care model places patients in a passive role. To investigate the patient experience in the hospital environment where information is lacking and in accessible, we conducted an ethnographic study with patients, caregivers, and healthcare providers in the emergency care setting. We report the three types of information breakdowns ED patients encountered during their emergency visits and the strategies they developed to cope. Our findings reveal a rich picture of the coping mechanisms ED patients use to proactively adapt to the nature of the ED care context. This work expands upon our understanding of the unique information challenges ED patients face, as well as the important adapting behaviors they engage in; it also uncovers design opportunities for supporting crucial, yet unmet, patient information needs.

### Author Keywords
Health informatics; hospital; patient coping strategies; adaptation; information technology; HCI.

### ACM Classification Keywords
H.5.m. Information interfaces and presentation; J.3 Life and Medical Sciences, Health, Medical Information Systems.

## INTRODUCTION
Although recent healthcare technologies, such as online patient portals and mobile health applications [1,4,41], have enabled patients to access, track, review, and manage their health-related information in domestic or general care settings [5,34], providing real-time care-related information to patients during their ongoing medical visits is not supported in current clinical settings. A previous study found that the information patients needed regarding their ongoing care processes was not readily available to them; instead, patients had to wait for information to be delivered, cope with complex terminology, and go through unfamiliar procedures[37]. Thus, the lack of information in the clinical environment often puts patients in a passive role; patients are unable to be engaged and empowered actors who can make informed decisions and contribute to their care process [37]. In contrast, encouraging patients to seek more information and actively ask questions during clinical visits has been shown to reduce anxiety [35], improve compliance with instructions [31], and improve patient satisfaction [30].

The lack of information access for patients is especially serious in urgent care environments, such as an Emergency Department (ED). A large number of prior studies has shown that patients experience various difficulties in the ED care context, including the lack of prior acquaintance with healthcare providers, the short duration of clinical encounters, frequent staff changes, feelings of uncertainty, and overcrowding in the environment [21,22]. These problems, in turn, may negatively affect the patients' medical experience, as well as care quality. The unique challenges of the ED call for an in-depth study of the types of information breakdowns that occur during patient visits, and the ways in which patients cope with a lack of information in such an interruptive and complex environment.

In the HCI and Health Informatics communities, many have studied different health technologies that enhance access to information for patients, and found that better information access leads to better patient empowerment and engagement [2,7,37]. Recently, researchers have illustrated the potential for technologies to support the information needs of patients and caregivers in hospital settings [3,19,37]. Researchers have also begun to study the behaviors and roles of hospitalized patients and their caregivers during their hospital stay [23,24,28] For instance, Mishra et al. have reported on five roles that patients and caregivers take on when interacting with their healthcare providers [24]. Yet, we still know little about what motivates or triggers patient engagement [13], how patients and caregivers become engaged in their behaviors and roles, and the detailed process of how they actually develop these behaviors, particularly during ED visits.


*CHI 2017,* May 06-11, 2017, Denver, CO, USA
© 2017 ACM. ISBN 978-1-4503-4655-9/17/05 $15.00
DOI: http://dx.doi.org/10.1145/3025453.3025978

Building on these prior works on patient behaviors and roles, in this paper, we report findings from an ethnographic study conducted with patients and their caregivers during emergency visits. Specifically, the findings of our study identify three types of information breakdowns ED patients face in the process of receiving their care, and the corresponding strategies they develop to cope with these breakdowns and to assist with their own care. We then look at the patients' creation of the coping strategies as a) a process of active patient engagement and b) as a proactive adaptation to the unique characteristics of the ED care context. Finally, we offer suggestions for the design of a sociotechnical care environment that can serve patient information needs and behaviors, promote patient engagement in their care, and improve the overall patient experience during their clinical stays.

## RELATED WORK

The need for patients to access their health-related information has been widely studied in prior research. Many studies have investigated the information needs of health consumers and shown that patients desire more educational materials regarding their illnesses and more information about possible treatments and alternatives plans than they typically receive during clinical visits [32,34,36]. A variety of health IT systems have also been developed to address patient information needs, such as online patient portals, Personal Health Records (PHR), and mobile health apps [2,5,34,41] It is reported that these systems bring in many of the benefits of health information access, such as better patient satisfaction [1,4], reduced conflicts in decision-making [17], increased adherence to care [17], and increased patient empowerment [39]. Yet, these previous works have primarily focused on the information needs of chronically ill patients in the outpatient setting, rather than addressing the needs of patients in ongoing care during their hospital visits.

In HCI, CSCW, and Health Informatics communities, there has been an increased attention toward acknowledging the need to support patients and their caregivers during their ongoing care. Researchers have investigated the role of novel technologies, such as information wall displays, tablets, kiosks, and mobile apps [15,19,29,37,38] to provide care-related information to patients to enhance their engagement and improve their communication with healthcare providers. For instance, Bickmore et al. designed the virtual nurse agents system that guides patients through their discharge paperwork. They found that this system effectively improves patients' comprehension of discharge instructions and increases patient satisfaction [3]. Tablet computers, mobile applications, and kiosks have also been offered to facilitate patient access to information regarding medication, and other care-related and educational information during their hospital visits 15,29,37,39].

In addition, few recent studies have examined the behaviors and roles patients and caregivers participate in, in the inpatient setting [18,23,24]. Similar to the work of Mishra et al.[24], Miller et al. [23] has described the five active roles of caregivers at hospitals by examining the interactions between patients and caregivers. These studies suggest that patients and caregivers can play an active role in their own care process.

During an emergency visit, patients suffer from an urgent and serious medical condition in an unfamiliar, stressful environment. They face difficulties getting basic information about their care, unable to find out about the expected duration of their wait time, when they will see their doctor, and what care procedures will be coming next [40]. Prior studies have also mentioned the communication challenges most ED patients face and their struggles with being acknowledged by providers and having their psychosocial and emotional needs met through quality interactions [12]. Despite the need, the ED has not been studied much [29,37]. Recently, studies have offered insight into the three types of information patients need [26] and the barriers and the barriers' causing factors in patient-provider communication in ED care [27]. These studies illustrate the need to understand how patients deal with the complexities of the ED care context.

In this study, we build on these prior works to identify the information breakdowns patients face in the ED and examine how they deal with the situations. We believe this ethnographic study can offer useful insights into when and how ED patients get actively involved in their own care, and show how information breakdowns can be turned into opportunities for active patient engagement.

## METHODS

We conducted an ethnographic study in an ED affiliated with a large urban hospital in the US. The ED has nearly 50,000 patient visits each year, and approximately half of the patient population is covered by private insurance. The authors' institutional review board approved this study.

Our study included in-depth observations and interviews with ED patients and their caregivers over a five-month period between January 2015 and May 2015. Observation was used to understand the patients' experiences, and the interactions among the patient, their caregiver(s), and their healthcare providers in the ED. Our observations totaled 230 hours and each session lasted roughly two to six hours. All observation data was collected by two researchers. The researchers followed the entire journey of a patient visit from the waiting room to the discharge/admission, if possible. Our observational activities also involved following key care team members, asking clarifying questions, and taking field notes and photos. During the observations, we paid careful attention to discussions about the patient's care; any information exchanged among patients, caregivers, and providers; any information they needed and any information they wished to have; any information sources they used, including artifacts and technology use in the patient rooms; and the behaviors patients, caregivers, and providers engaged in throughout the entire ED care process. In addition, we performed informal interviews with patient participants and their caregivers during, or after observations, to gain a better understanding of the perceptions, feelings, and questions they had during their ED stay.

Our site selection and sampling criteria allowed us to recruit patients with a wide variety of ages and medical conditions. We recruited a total of 35 patients to participate. In terms of the patient selection for our observation, we tried to maximize the diversity of patients. We selected patients based on age, gender, ethnicity, and disease complexity. Following the ED rules, we excluded trauma patients, patients with contagious diseases, and psychiatric patients from our study. Patient participants had diverse medical complaints that related to various levels of complexity and urgency, different lengths of hospital stay, and varied medical conditions (ranging from migraines to congenital cerebral palsy to cancer). The patients' ages[*] ranged from 4 months to 90, and the majority were accompanied by caregivers, including family and friends. Patients were ethnically diverse: 16 were Caucasian, 1 African-American, 8 Hispanic, 7 Asian, and 3 American Indian/Alaska Native. Half of the patients were male, and half were female. The patients' health or computer literacy was not measured in this study; however, we found that even when patients have a higher health and computer literacy (based on their medical history and occupation), they still engaged in the same information behaviors during actual care situations in the ED.

### Data Analysis

While observations and informal interviews were being conducted, the research group met regularly to discuss preliminary findings and identify themes in the data. After the data collection was completed, three researchers coded the field notes from the observations and the informal interviews in an iterative coding process, using the open coding method from the grounded theory approach [11]. Each of the three researchers coded the same data to look for predominant concepts. Through several rounds of coding, the research team identified emerging themes, such as the various information breakdowns participants experienced while they were in the ED. The list of breakdowns was then used by two researchers to code all the data to explore what behaviors participants engaged in during their ED stay and what underlying factors and issues influenced their behaviors. During the analysis, the two researchers discussed the preliminary findings to determine how the various patient behaviors fit into coping strategies, and revised iteratively until agreement was reached among all researchers. Although we mainly focused on patients, we analyzed both patients and caregivers because their behaviors complemented each other.

[*] For the patients younger than 18, we followed their caregivers.

## OVERVIEW OF PATIENT CARE IN THE ED

Our observation showed that despite patients' desire to know and manage health information during care, most of the existing information technologies available at our field site did not offer information access to patients. First, the Electronic Health Records (EHR) system, the primary information infrastructure in the hospital, is mainly designed for healthcare providers and administrative staff as their working system. The EHR would appear to be an ideal resource for patients to access information as it contains all the patient information generated in the care process; yet, patients currently lack direct access to EHR data during their care.

In addition to the EHR, other information media in the patient room are a whiteboard (physical displays presenting basic patient care information, such as body temperatures, and tests orders) and a vital sign monitor (display for blood pressure and heart rate). Despite their physical accessibility, the patients we studied did not consider them to be beneficial or useful. The whiteboards were often found to be empty or to contain outdated information due to the busy bedside nurses who could not manually keep them updated, and the information on the vital sign monitor was not easy to read for ED patients who lacked medical knowledge. Thus, without proper system support, the current ED becomes an information-lacking environment for patients and makes the healthcare providers the only available information source for patients during their ED care stay.

While healthcare providers were expected to deliver care information to patients in the ED, we found that the patients in our study were not satisfied with the information they received, and often experienced information breakdowns. At our field site, especially during busy times, patients and caregivers often had to wait for providers to drop by and/or wait for tests results. These information breakdowns caused patients frustration. A few mentioned that the lengthy waits and information delays made them feel like they never got proper answers to their questions. These breakdowns more seriously led to unexpected care treatment changes, such as not getting a medication properly due to time delay, which can affect a patient's health and health care quality. To further understand this issue, we analyzed the information breakdowns experienced by ED patients, the causing factors, and how patients handled these breakdowns and the information-lacking environment of the ED.

## INFORMATION BREAKDOWNS AND PATIENTS COPING STRATEGIES WITH THEM

While the work practices of ED providers are well-supported by health IT systems, such as the EHR, the current ED practice does not provide patients access to their care-related information nor consider their need to access such information during their hospital stays. In this section, we report on three types of information breakdowns resulting from the patients' lack of information access and information support in the ED. We chose these three breakdowns and their corresponding strategies as they represent the common information behaviors that patients engage in to adapt to the challenges of the ED.

### Information Delay and Unavailability

The first type of information breakdown patients commonly experienced in the ED was the delay in receiving their care-related information. Resonating with many ED studies [18,19,23], delayed information delivery was one of the prevalent information breakdowns in our field site. Delays in receiving information induced lengthy wait times, increased patients' anxiety, and even led to information failure or loss in the middle of delivery to patients.

Information delays were caused by multiple factors related to ED work processes. First, the nature of the ED providers' work is very impromptu and must respond to emergent situations, instead of being pre-organized. Unlike other typical care settings, the ED deals with patients whose conditions span different levels of severity and urgency. Dependent on the patient cases and the numbers of patients the providers are taking care of, care priorities can be altered at any minute. Even with patient updates available on the EHR or reminders from the bedside nurses, providers might be caught up caring for trauma cases, or patients with higher care priority, for hours before providing necessary information to other patients in person; such information would not be available to those patients till then.

Second, the other reason for information to be delayed was because of the fallout of the temporal dependency in the collaborative ED care process. The medical care activities are temporally dependent on the previous ones in the patient care trajectory, since information only becomes available after the execution of prior care activities. For instance, after the initial clinical consultation, physicians mainly provide clinical updates to patients. Only after all of the orders for a patient are executed and the results are successfully collected from the lab, the physicians properly decide on a next step. Bedside nurses are not allowed to quickly deliver information to patients, since they are required to wait until the physicians communicate the lab results to patients since such information often needs to be provided with detailed medical explanations. Thus, information get delayed meanwhile. In addition, at times, care activities, such as a consultation with an admitting resident or surgeon, may require orders or care tasks to be completed by other departments, which can cause further delays due to the workloads in other departments.

In our study, we often observed many cases where ED providers were stuck waiting in the treatment process for, among other things, a consultation from an admitting resident, a confirmation from a surgeon, a pharmacy approval, or a bed availability from an inpatient unit. In these cases, patients had to simply wait for hours, suffering with their pain without a proper information update. The lag and wait between care activities often induced a delay in notifying the patient about their care progress. This delay and unavailability of information eventually led to extra stress, frustration, and anxiety for patients and caregivers, and more seriously, potential effects to patient health and health care quality.

#### *Strategy to cope with information delays*

Most patients felt that their ED care providers were usually preoccupied with other care tasks, and proactively followed up for updates on their care to prevent further delays or unexplained waits. Specifically, the patient participants in our study approached their providers or any other available provider they could find for information. For instance, patients approached providers passing by to ask when they could expect to hear updates about the next procedure. Patients also reminded providers that they were waiting for information in order to make sure their providers were aware of their need to receive updates. Most participants started engaging in these strategies by observing situations (e.g., counting the number of sicker patients to find out their turn to see doctors), as well as the behaviors of other patients and caregivers in the hallways. By doing this, patients tried to figure out the reason why information was delayed and what they could do. At our fieldsite, we observed a patient with an eye infection reached out to her providers to remind them that she was waiting.

*Yasmine, a female patient came in the ED for an eye infection. After having multiple clinical consultations and examinations with ED providers and an ophthalmologist, she was informed that she would be discharged once she took the prescribed medication. After that, Yasmine had to wait for the medication for a couple of hours in the eye-exam room. Then, she was asked to leave since another patient needed the exam room, and she was in the process of being discharged anyway. However, her lengthy wait for the medication continued even in the waiting room. After another two hours of waiting, Yasmine started worrying that her care team members might have forgotten her, as there were more trauma patients coming into the ED. So, she decided to approach an ED staff member who was passing in the hallway to remind her previous bedside nurse that she was still waiting for the medication. After some time, Yasmine finally received information that her medication had to be compounded by the pharmacy, which was more time-consuming than simply getting it from the shelf. It turned out that the bedside nurse, who was occupied with several incoming patients, did not receive this information from the resident, who was also busy with multiple trauma patients until Yasmine asked for it.*

In the case of Yasmine, the information that the medication would take a longer time to be made because of a fallout of the temporal dependency of the care process, thus require a longer wait time should have been provided to her. This information should have been delivered from the pharmacy to the physician, to the bedside nurse, and finally, to the patient; however, the information had gotten lost in the middle due to the busy schedule of the physician, and then the bedside nurse almost forgot that Yasmine was waiting since she was busy with her other patients. As seen here, Yasmine's strategy of approaching and reminding her healthcare providers facilitated her receiving the update regarding her ongoing care process and helped relieve some of her anxiety about not getting the proper care from her providers. More importantly, she prevented further delays by reminding her providers of her incomplete care process (i.e., her medication) and helped to avoid the possibility of being forgotten or having a missed medication order.

We also found similar patient coping behaviors aimed at preventing further information delays and potential errors, such as proactively reporting their own condition changes while waiting. By frequently approaching their nurse to report their condition changes or any updates, patients and caregivers believed it would make their existence more visible in the face of the providers' busy workload, and eventually help them receive updates from their providers.

As seen in this section, strategies were created and utilized by patients and caregivers to facilitate their information access and awareness of their ongoing care situation when information was not timely delivered. These strategies emerged from the patients' active efforts to recognize breakdowns, cope with not getting their ongoing care information, and prevent further information delays. Ultimately, by employing these coping strategies, patients were able to prevent potential errors, such as forgotten or missed orders, and to improve their own care quality. Furthermore, these strategies helped to expedite the patient care processes by helping to maintain the providers' focus; without these strategies, it is possible that their care processes could have been further slowed down.

#### Information Overload

Most of the patients and caregivers in our study suffered from a lack of information most of times, as seen in the previous section. However, the amount of information delivered and the ways in which it was delivered frequently raised problems for patients. Our patient participants often received a great amount of information all at once within the short period of a physician consultation and were often unable to fully process, comprehend and remember the information they received. Having information delivered in a way they could process was important for ED patients who were experiencing high levels of stress and anxiety, yet needed to understand their medical condition in order to be involved in their own care. Although providers were usually very careful about the types of information they provided, taking care not to frighten patients or subject them to undue stress, providers did not necessarily deliver information in an appropriate manner. This was particularly true at busy times when providers had to see multiple patients in a row; then, they sometimes poured out a torrent of difficult terminologies at top speed, without taking the time to clarify or explain the information to patients at a more detailed level. Since it often took some time for many patients and caregivers to actually process, reflect, and understand the information in order to raise relevant questions, even when physicians tried to check up on patients' comprehension by asking, "*Do you have any questions?*" many patients and caregivers often sat there, looking blank, still processing the information, and not yet at the point of formulating thought.

This was common at the end of the initial consultation, in particular, when physicians usually communicated care plans by rapidly listing possible diagnoses and the tests or procedures they planned to perform. As a result, after the consultation, patients often felt overwhelmed; however, it was not easy to hold their physician back since the physician was so busy. It became even worse when more than one physician was involved in a consultation, such as when a specialist came with his resident and medical students. Thus, patients experienced long and silent bedside wait times followed by a period of intense information overload. This is demonstrated in the example that follows.

*An 18 year old patient, Lee, was brought in by his parents after having black stools for two days. Lee is deaf and suffers from cerebral palsy, so his parents are in charge of his care, directly communicating with providers. A while after they waited for a doctor consultation at bedside, a resident finally came for the medical screening and asked questions about his last admission, medical history, and symptoms to Lee's mom. In the middle of the resident's consultation, an attending physician joined and asked more specific questions about Lee's current symptoms, while discussing the case with the resident simultaneously. After asking several questions, at the end of the consultation, the attending discussed a plan with the mother, speaking at a very fast pace: "he [Lee] may need a transfusion. We will do some IV and lab tests and then see the GI doc. He probably needs to be admitted again, but we will see. The blood might, probably have been from Tuesday and left out, or it may be new blood. Anyhow, we have to get rid of it. We will start with the rectal exam." Both physicians then ran out in the direction of the trauma room in response to an overhead page about two incoming trauma patients. The mother responded, "oh, okay..." and stood there with a puzzled expression. A minute later, Lee's dad came back from getting a snack.*

In the case above, although the attending physician disclosed all the available information about Lee's care plan during the consultation, receiving all the information at once caused a sudden information overload for Lee's mother. She was not able to follow the information given by the physician, let alone comprehend its meaning and raise any questions that she may have. There were simply too many items on the care plan for a layperson to properly understand and remember in a few seconds. When her husband returned and asked what the doctor said, she was only able to briefly mention the chance of re-admission, but not the other items the physician had mentioned. After the consultation, we saw the mother persistently ask a bedside nurse about what kinds of tests they would do and what the next step would be. Even for Lee's parents, who have been exposed to and prepared for frequent medical visits, and who are somewhat knowledgeable about general healthcare information, it was still challenging to handle the overload of information during their ED visit.

Apart from some chronic illness patients, a majority of the ED patients had a relatively low health literacy and were not familiar with diagnostic terms and clinical procedures. During the interviews, we discovered that several patients did not even understand the roles or names of the medical professionals, such as ophthalmologist, and had to guess or make assumptions along the way regarding what roles these professionals might have and what medical diagnoses they could have based on these roles; half of the patients we spoke with could not even remember the names of their diagnosis and the procedures they had had in the ED.

*Strategy to cope with information overload*

To address the information overload issue and to understand the unfamiliar terminologies, many patients and caregivers developed strategies during their ED stays. First, most patients tried to keep records of their care information by asking for printouts of images and lab results. Many patients and caregivers asked their bedside nurses to write down medication names or requested treatment procedure details right after consulting with physicians in order to fill in any blanks they may have had after their clinical consultation and to confirm the information they had received. Experienced chronic illness patients wanted to review the number values of test results and carry records with them, actively asking for paper copies of any test results they had. Through requesting, documenting, and keeping their own records, patients were not only able to capture missed information, but to gather and keep necessary information for themselves for later use. It also enabled them to remember the information, prepare appropriate questions, or discuss any concerns with their healthcare providers during the next consultation. This strategy was also beneficial for follow-up care because patients could provide better ED information to their family doctors or other specialists.

In addition, patients often engaged in looking up additional information, such as information related to their diagnosis or visuals of physical symptoms, to aid their own comprehension. They call their friends and family or browsed their smart phones. For instance, a patient who had come to the ER the night before because of an insect sting, came back again for the same, though not improved, symptom. To process all the information he heard from the physician consultation, he first tried to look for relevant images of the area on his arm stung by a bee. He then compared them with other images found on the web, based on potential diagnoses the physician mentioned so that he could ask the physician questions and make sure to receive the proper treatment this time.

To summarize, experiencing information overload at certain information peak times was another type of information breakdown for patients and caregivers at the ED, hindering their understanding, as well as their engagement in ED care. To deal with this breakdown, patients developed various strategies for documenting and keeping records based on the information they got from providers, and searching for relevant information in order to comprehend it. In the study, we found these strategies were not only beneficial for patients by helping them actively engage in their ED care, but also valuable for their own health as they were more able to understand and follow care instructions.

### Inconsistent Information among Multiple Care Team Members

The last type of information breakdown identified in our study was the problem of inconsistent information, where different providers involved in a single patient case may not have the same level of information. In the ED, patients have to interact with multiple healthcare providers (up to 8-10), care team members who come and go during different phases of the care process.

When communicating information at the bedside, patients and caregivers sometimes found gaps in the information that different team members had. First, because of the number of team members, and the complexity of each member's tasks and expertise, it was challenging for every member to be on the same page all the time, as different members have different professional backgrounds and focus on different aspects of care. As a result, information inconsistencies often occurred. For example, when a patient who had a history of kidney failure came into the ED for a severe migraine as his chief complaint, the patient realized that not every care team member knew the medical history related to his kidney failure and was bothered by this fact.

Second, the urgent nature of the ED care work constrains the information shared among care members. With heavy and dynamic workflows, ED care team members did not have sufficient time to check the EHR or have a chance to update and verbally communicate with each other. For instance, in our study, many physicians could not have all the information up to date for every one of their patient cases because they had to watch out for critical patients or incoming trauma patients. As the physicians could not enter the patient data into the EHR in a timely manner, the EHR did not always contain the most up-to-date information, even though it was supposed to have a real-time information-feed for the other team members. Consequently, some (often physicians) might have the most updated information, while others, such as bedside nurses, float nurses, or technicians, might not get updated, or might only get partially updated, based on the frequency of their verbal interactions with physicians.

Inconsistent information among the providers sometimes introduced the possibility of potential errors to the medical care activities. This made the patients become more concerned about the quality of the care they received. In the example of the migraine patient who had previously had a history of kidney failure, one of the float nurses accidentally brought an IV fluid without properly knowing the patient's medical history. The patient recalls this moment:" *I do not think the first nurse communicated with the doctor because if she did, she wouldn't have been trying to give me IV fluids, knowing I'm a kidney patient."* In this case, the float nurse, who was working on four different patients, as she was assisting two other busy bedside nurses, did not have the right information due to her busy workload. Since there were two other new patients incoming at the same time, and fluids were often ordered early in the care process for new patients, the float nurse, who was in a hurry, brought fluids without properly checking the medical orders for each patients and without knowing each patient's medical history details.

### *Strategies to facilitate efficient information-sharing*

While interacting with multiple care team members, patients were repeatedly asked questions about information they had already provided, and they also often received unclear answers from each team member when requesting same information. In these interactions, patient participants recognized inconsistencies in the information shared among the care team members. They then developed several coping strategies. First, the majority of the patients and caregivers we observed started carefully monitoring all of the medical activities providers performed at the bedside and requested detailed information. Before providers performed the tasks, patients verbally requested detailed information from the healthcare providers, such as what drug was being given, why they were getting an IV, what it would do to them, etc. The patients' close observations and information requests enabled the patients to become more attentive to the care process, and forced their providers be more aware of their tasks, reducing any potential medical errors, such as putting in the wrong IV fluids, overdosing, or doing unnecessary test preparation.

Second, once patients received information from their caregivers, patient participants proactively passed along such information to each incoming provider, thereby hoping to avoid any information inconsistency among team members. The information they passed along ranged from the names of medications, the names of the tests were being ordered, results of tests and labs, documents they received, updates on their care plan, and even care activities they observed at the bedside. By doing this, patients and caregivers serve as gatekeepers, maintaining information quality among the different care team members interacting at the bedsides.

Later on, some of the patients even purposely asked the same questions to each incoming provider as a way of proactively finding out whether each provider carried the same understanding of the care plan. They often asked questions, such as "*what is next after this [procedure]?*" or "*what [medication] are you giving me?*" When patients found discrepancies, like omitted details on the kidney failure, they actively reported them, and repeated the necessary information to the other providers. The strategy of asking repeated questions was perceived to be very useful because it allowed patients to discover the inconsistent or missing information, if there was any, as well as to make sure the multiple providers remained on the same page. The following vignette from our observations illustrates one caregiver proactively checking and providing information updates of a change in his father-in-law's care plan to incoming care team members in order to eliminate any information gaps.

*A 68 year-old male patient who had an issue with high potassium for the hyperkalemia came in to the ED with his son-in-law, Paul, as a caregiver. Over the time patient went through tests and waited for the results, Paul had interacted with several different care team members – bedside nurse, two float nurses, two technicians, a resident and an attending physician. After more than a two hour wait, a resident came to the room to inform Paul that they would keep the patient in the hospital overnight and consider admission since his potassium level was still too high for unknown reasons, and left the room. After 10 min, two float nurses came in to the room with medications and fluids.*

***Paul:** (scanning what nurses were bringing with) Are you giving him [a med name]?*
***Float nurse**: Yes, we are going to give him [the med name] that will make him want to poop. He will mostly have to go alone if none of us are around. [Speaking to the patient] You have to drink it...*
***Paul**: What about after that?*
***Float nurse**: I am not sure... I will have to speak to the doctor about it.*
***Paul**: I think they're admitting him. I just spoke to the doctor. He will be admitted. Could you check?*
***Float nurse**: Oh, really? Alright.*

*The float nurse left to check with the bedside nurse and the EHR to see if there's any new order based on the decision made for his admission, and the other float nurse carried on the task in the patient room.*

As seen above, the caregiver, Paul, actively monitored the incoming providers' activities and requested information about what providers would be doing to the patient and what the next step would be. Doing so, he could make sure that not only was he receiving information updates from providers, but also ensuring each provider had the same information update regarding the care procedure and plan. In this case, the admitting decision was made, but not all the care team members had been notified. When Paul asked the float nurse about the next step ("*what about after that?*"), this information was already given to him by two other providers, but he wanted to keep the float nurse updated if needed, and prevent any potential mistakes, such as not getting properly informed about an admitting procedure.

In responding to information discrepancies among multiple ED care team members, patients and caregivers gradually developed and refined their information strategies, such as deliberately checking up on all incoming care members by asking them the same questions to maintain the shared information amongst providers. These strategies enabled patients and caregivers to monitor their own care and ensure its quality. They were able to address potential concerns arising from the information inconsistency and help facilitate care team members' information-sharing and overall level of awareness. Of course, not all the patients and caregivers were as active as Paul, and there were patients we observed who did not engage with these proactive strategies nor even notice the information inconsistencies. In such cases, without the patients' active involvement, the risk of having breakdowns was higher and the patients may not have felt as satisfied or safe as when they were more engaged with their own care.

## DISCUSSION

The findings of our study indicate that while patients developed strategies in order to accommodate their basic information needs during breakdowns, these strategies later improved the overall care process of the ED by expediting information delivery during patient care, aiding providers' information sharing, and potentially enhancing patient safety. In this section, we first present the coping mechanisms that ED patients developed to deal with information breakdowns as an active engagement process. We then look at the design needs for the patients' adaptations to the ED care context.

### Patients' Coping Strategies as Active Engagement

In the ED, the time-critical and heavy workloads of the current ED work practice often places patients in a passive role and imposes challenges to receiving proper information, by forcing ED providers primarily focus on performing care tasks and limiting information support for patients. Our study has shown that nonetheless, many ED patients and caregivers are, in fact, active actors who have developed various strategies to cope with the information breakdowns they experience during their care. The coping strategies the patients created can be seen as an active engagement process of realizing problems, altering expectations and behaviors, and devising new ways of accessing and managing information.

Coping has been one of the key concepts for theory and research on engagement and health. Coping strategies are cognitive and behavioral efforts an individual takes to reduce stress caused by environmental change [20]. In the theory of coping as a process by Lazarus [20], coping changes over time and in accordance with the situational contexts in which it occurs. Coping strategies are looked at through two approaches – *emotion-focused* and *problem-focused*. Emotion-focused coping looks at an individual's emotion regulation as a means of adapting to environmental change. Problem-focused coping strategies tend to be action-based and externally focused on trying to find ways to change the environment to suit the individual's needs. Therefore, coping strategies are essentially a means of negotiating a balance between the individual and the environment as a way to reduce stress.

In coping theory, coping mechanisms are created through two assessment stages: *primary appraisal* and *secondary appraisal* [20]. When a change occurs, an individual performs a primary appraisal of the situation, by asking himself or herself, "*How does this change affect me?*" If the result of the assessment is stressful and not positive, the next secondary appraisal is performed with the individual asking, "*What can I do about this change?*" Then, based on the level of perceived control that the individual has in a specific situation, i.e., whether they possess the necessary resources to address a change in the environment or not, they take the appropriate approach (either emotion or problem-focused) to develop a coping mechanism.

Soon after entering the ED, most of the patient participants and their caregivers realized that both the ED providers and the ED environment did not properly support their information needs. Patients and caregivers experienced frequent information delays, overloads, and inconsistency rather than timely updates. To cope with the problem, patients began wondering how these breakdowns would affect their care process (*primary appraisal*). In the specific case of Yasmine, the patient with the eye infection, when she did not get any updates on her medication and had to wait hours, she started worrying, not just about the lengthy wait, but the possibility that her physician or nurse had forgotten about her, or that her medication order had gotten lost. Her medication's information delay frustrated her and had a potentially negative impact on her health. As a result, she tried to figure out what to do to better handle the problem (*secondary appraisal*). Yasmine began to actively watch how other patients requested updates in the hallways and started approaching any ED staff passing by, to figure out what was going on and what she should do next. Since she had to wait in the waiting room, outside of the bedside area, Yasmine had to think about how to effectively reach out to the bedside nurse who had taken care of her two hours prior and remind her about the medication order. After a few attempts, she learned what resources were available and what worked (i.e., who to turn to and who to ask), and she approached the appropriate personnel to contact her care team and remind them of her ongoing wait for the medication (*problem-focused*).

The process of identifying the problem, assessing the current situation, and iteratively finding the best workable solution until the goal is achieved can be considered the patients' active engagement in their own care. Since the information breakdowns they identified had immediate impacts on their care process and the quality of their care, the patients had to change their passive behaviors and actively seek information.

Patient engagement has been studied extensively in medical literature, and many frameworks have been suggested [8,13]. Carman et al.'s framework [8] presents the forms patient engagement can take, with passive consultation at the lower end of the spectrum to shared partnership, including decision-making, at the other end. Positioning what this study discovered about the adaptive behaviors of ED patients and caregivers within this framework, patient and caregiver engagement in the ED begins at the passive consultation end, where patients reply to ED providers during short consultations. However, with the active efforts of creating coping mechanisms, the level of engagement eventually moves to the partnership end of the spectrum, where patients share information with their providers, and through gathering and managing information, eventually take responsibility for their own care. A systematic review study on patient engagement [13] indicates that despite a large body of studies on patient engagement, it is difficult to identify where and how patient engagement can be introduced into routine clinical settings, and what methods would be best for doing so. Our study indicates that patients' active involvement with creating various coping mechanisms is active engagement, and shows the detailed process of how patients become actively engaged in their care as active partners in the information-lacking environment of the ED.

We suggest that the information breakdowns in the ED care process be utilized as an opportunity for engaging patients and caregivers. As discussed in our study, when developing strategies to cope with the breakdowns, patients began to actively engage in, and become responsible for, their care. The previous literature [13] has pointed out how essential introducing patient engagement into clinical routines is, but how difficult it is to actually do. In our study, we have found that patient engagement can be triggered, not only by motivating patients or encouraging healthcare providers to invite patients to engage in their care, but though the introduction of potential problems that can impact patients' perceptions and satisfaction, and the quality of care. We believe that designing health IT systems, such as a patient-facing system, to improve the ED care experience should go beyond the conventional approach of simply providing information access. Providing patients access to their care-related information at bedsides could solve some of the breakdowns identified in this study, but would not engage patients to actively be involved in the problem-solving process. Also, information breakdowns are contextual and *in situ,* and the nature of breakdowns might vary in different care situations and inevitable in reality. Thus, finding and suggesting ways to facilitate patients to become active problem solvers would be a better approach.

Utilizing the information breakdowns identified in the study, we suggest having design sessions and inviting patients to cope with various breakdown issues in order to come up with a system based on actual care situations and actual patient needs and goals [42]. For instance, through a speed-dating technique [9], the multiple stakeholders can experience the set of situated breakdowns we identified in our study and explore and discuss design solutions together. We think that this participatory design session can help guide designers to the preferred state [33] at which patients can actively engage in their ongoing care without being burdened, and to provide effective ways for patients to approach complex, real world care situations.

We argue that the kinds of coping strategies that the patients develop in the sessions, how the strategies are developed, what resources or tools are needed for the strategies, and what specific situations the strategies are used in, should be used to inform the design practices of future systems or policies for emergency care or other similar care environments.

### Adapting to the Nature of the ED Care Context and Healthcare Practice

The coping strategies the patients in our study developed have two distinct goals – one is to *address immediate information breakdowns* and meet information needs, and the other is to *proactively prevent potential breakdowns* by addressing safety and efficiency concerns specific to ED care practice. The former goal is the direct motivation for developing coping strategies, wherein patients and caregivers attempt to deal with the problems that occur when receiving care-related information. As discussed in the previous section, patients and caregivers are forced to cope with the breakdowns (e.g., information delays) because they have direct impact on their care process, causing lengthy waits, forgotten or incomplete orders, and can potentially damage their health.

Although patients develop strategies for their own care concerns, these strategies are, at the same time, adapted as a way to meet and sustain the specific care goals of the ED. This latter underlying goal for patient coping strategies is about proactively anticipating and preventing any possible breakdowns during their care. For example, in the case of having multiple healthcare providers involved in the same patient's care, patients recognized that different care team members did not always have consistent information updates because of their busy, complicated workflows and multiple patient care demands (e.g., a float nurse did not have updates on a care plan that a physician had already updated a patient on). When patients realized the information inconsistency among the team members, they could gain a sense of how ED care work is performed, which includes having multiple providers with different roles. After acquiring the basic knowledge of team-based work, patients proactively began creating ways to bridge the information gap among the different providers, since not having consistent information could affect the providers' clinical collaboration, possibly jeopardizing the care they were receiving. To maintain information consistency among care team members, as well as to address safety concerns, patients strived to proactively anticipate any potential problems by monitoring and updating every piece of information between providers. They also asked providers probing questions to check up on their information updated. Patients developed these strategies as a way to address the unique nature of the ED care context, ultimately preventing potential breakdowns that put care quality at risk. We argue that the process of proactively foreseeing and preparing for potential breakdowns, as well as seeking the most appropriate method that would work for the particular care context and its particular needs, goals, and work efficiency can be considered *patient adaptation*.

This adaptation was developed by patients through learning that patient care is done by multiple care team members who are required to work collaboratively and efficiently. However, it is challenging to have everyone updated in *actual* practice, and patients and caregivers had to modify their own expectations and behaviors accordingly – i.e. bridge the information gap by reporting and checking up on each provider about the most updated information, at the patient's bedside. This proactive adaptation behavior further facilitated not only providers' information work but also expedited the next ED care process by picking up what the providers might have left out and helping them fill the gap among the team. Therefore, this second goal of addressing the specific needs of the ED care practice is devised on a higher level and within a broader perspective than the first, adapting to a complex sociotechnical healthcare environment [16,25]; it reflects a concern for maintaining care quality, care goals, and the needs of the healthcare practice, deploying the patients and caregivers' own strategies to ensure care safety, as well as to make the healthcare practice more reliable and efficient.

We suggest that system design utilize the patient adaptations of the clinical workflow and the patient care environment. We argue that these patient adaptations are driven by design thinking efforts in the complex ED care context. To adjust to the complexity of ED care, patients engaged in design thinking [6] – the activity of learning and understanding the current situation, identifying the best solution, and iteratively looking for alternative solutions until the goal is achieved. Design thinking enables patients to proactively adapt to their sociotechnical care environment, because they are forced to create their own coping strategies and eventually redesign their own care environment through creating their own tools and learning to understand the resources and the physical space within their situated contexts. We argue that this adaptation process, driven by design thinking, can offer a valuable insight to the design community to improve or redesign the patient care environment, or even compatible patient clinical workflows, since the ways that patients reconfigure and redesign their care environment can complement design insights in a way that designers cannot predict [10].

As shown in the study, the active adaptation of patients relies heavily on the recognition of the sociotechnical context that is often new or unfamiliar to them. Even under the same ED care context, figuring out and understanding local factors, such as the team-based or mobile workflow, the roles of care team members, the accessibility of resources, and the physical layout of the ED unit, can appear differently, dependent on an individual's ability to do design-thinking. In the study, we notice that not all the patients have the ability to engage in design-thinking and adapt to their care, due to the lack of proper knowledge, experience, and/or skills. Thus, we suggest providing mediatory support to foster better adaptation, offering necessary knowledge about the care environment (e.g., how the ED functions, the ED work structure, physical layouts, or the overall characteristics of ED care). Currently, this role is supported by the bedside nurses who are always occupied with numerous tasks; thus, we see this as an appropriate function for a new supportive intermediary system support.

The mediatory support could, for instance, provide patients with guidelines to help identify any breakdowns and/or assess current care situations, provide cues for where to find necessary information, and share proactive patient-safety behavior suggestions that are tailored to each patient case. This knowledge would help patients to proactively address potential, unexpected problems by offering appropriate information access and information delivery to patients. Furthermore, this will provide ED care team members with a common information channel that can improve their limited interactions with patients. We think that having this mediatory support is important because while it may not provide a perfect solution to every breakdown, it can give better, or more appropriate, workaround/solutions, given the existing care circumstances. Without this knowledge, it may take longer, or may even be impossible, for some patients to come up with adaptation strategies, particularly those without proper medical support or insurance, but make up a good part of the ED population currently.

## CONCLUSION

We have described the experiences of patients and caregivers in ED care through the identification of three types of information breakdowns and their coping mechanisms. Our study indicates that the development of these strategies is an adaptive behavior that patients use to proactively adjust to the ED, a place where there is limited information support to address their needs. Our findings suggest that the design of a patient-facing system in a sociotechnical environment should consider patient adaptation as an active engagement process driven by design-thinking. Design support for patient adaptation behaviors should enhance patient engagement, potentially improving clinical outcomes and contributing to the quality control of care in the healthcare practice.

## ACKNOWLEDGMENTS

This work was supported by the National Science Foundation under grant HCC-1219197. We thank the ED providers and patient participants for their incredible support.

## REFERENCES

1. Jakob E. Bardram, Mads Frost, Károly Szántó, Maria Faurholt-Jepsen, Maj Vinberg, and Lars Vedel Kessing. 2013. Designing mobile health technology for bipolar disorder: a field trial of the monarca system. In *Proceedings of the SIGCHI Conference on Human Factors in Computing Systems*, 2627–2636. Retrieved January 20, 2016 from http://dl.acm.org/citation.cfm?id=2481364

2. Jared S. Bauer, Sunny Consolvo, Benjamin Greenstein, et al. 2012. ShutEye: encouraging awareness of healthy sleep recommendations with a mobile, peripheral display. In *Proceedings of the SIGCHI Conference on Human Factors in Computing Systems*, 1401–1410. Retrieved September 21, 2016 from http://dl.acm.org/citation.cfm?id=2208600

3. Timothy W. Bickmore, Laura M. Pfeifer, and Brian W. Jack. 2009. Taking the time to care: empowering low health literacy hospital patients with virtual nurse agents. In *Proceedings of the SIGCHI Conference on Human Factors in Computing Systems*, 1265–1274. Retrieved February 10, 2014 from http://dl.acm.org/citation.cfm?id=1518891

4. Katherine Blondon, Msc1 Predrag Klasnja, and M. H. A. Logan Kendall. 2013. Long–term engagement with health–management technology: a dynamic process in diabetes1. *Katherine S Blondon*: 37. Retrieved January 20, 2016 from https://digital.lib.washington.edu/researchworks/bitstream/handle/1773/23784/Blondon_washington_0250E_11783.pdf?sequence=1&isAllowed=y#page=44

5. Bernard S. Bloom. 2002. Crossing the quality chasm: a new health system for the 21st century. *JAMA: The Journal of the American Medical Association* 287, 5: 646–647. Retrieved October 22, 2015 from http://jama.ama-assn.org/content/287/5/646.2.short

6. Tim Brown. 2009. Change by design: How design thinking transforms organizations and inspires innovation. New York: HarperBusiness.

7. Christine A. Caligtan, Diane L. Carroll, Ann C. Hurley, Ronna Gersh-Zaremski, and Patricia C. Dykes. 2012. Bedside information technology to support patient-centered care. *International journal of medical informatics* 81, 7: 442–451. Retrieved September 21, 2016 from http://www.sciencedirect.com/science/article/pii/S1386505611002656

8. Kristin L. Carman, Pam Dardess, Maureen Maurer, et al. 2013. Patient and family engagement: a framework for understanding the elements and developing interventions and policies. *Health Affairs* 32, 2: 223–231. Retrieved September 21, 2016 from http://content.healthaffairs.org/content/32/2/223.short

9. Scott Davidoff, Min Kyung Lee, Anind K. Dey, and John Zimmerman. 2007. Rapidly exploring application design through speed dating. *In International Conference on Ubiquitous Computing,* 429-446. *Springer Berlin Heidelberg.*

10. Pelle Ehn. 2008. Participation in design things. *In Proceedings of the tenth anniversary Conference on Participatory Design,* 92-101. *Indiana University.*

11. Barney Glaser and Anselm Strauss. 1967. The discovery grounded theory: strategies for qualitative inquiry. *Aldin, Chicago.*

12. Jane Gorden, Lorraine A. Sheppard, and Sophie Anaf. 2010. The patient experience in the emergency department: A systematic synthesis of qualitative research. *International Emergency Nursing* 18, 2: 80-88.

13. Stuart W. Grande, Marjan J. Faber, Marie-Anne Durand, Rachel Thompson, and Glyn Elwyn. 2014. A classification model of patient engagement methods and assessment of their feasibility in real-world settings. *Patient education and counseling* 95, 2: 281–287. Retrieved September 21, 2016 from http://www.sciencedirect.com/science/article/pii/S0738399114000512

14. Sheldon Greenfield, Sherrie Kaplan, and John E. Ware. 1985. Expanding patient involvement in care: effects on patient outcomes. *Annals of internal medicine* 102, 4: 520–528. Retrieved September 21, 2016 from http://annals.org/article.aspx?articleid=699554

15. S. Ryan Greysen, Raman R. Khanna, Ronald Jacolbia, Herman M. Lee, and Andrew D. Auerbach. 2014. Tablet computers for hospitalized patients: A pilot study to improve inpatient engagement. *Journal of Hospital Medicine* 9, 6: 396–399. Retrieved January 20, 2016 from http://onlinelibrary.wiley.com/doi/10.1002/jhm.2169/full

16. Juran Joseph and A. Blanton Godfrey. 1999. *Juran's quality handbook.* McGraw Hill, New York.

17. Sherrie H. Kaplan, Barbara Gandek, Sheldon Greenfield, William Rogers, and John E. Ware. 1995. Patient and Visit Characteristics Related to Physicians' Participatory Decision-Making Style: Results from the Medical Outcomes Study. *Medical Care* 33, 12: 1176–1187. Retrieved February 10, 2014 from http://www.jstor.org/stable/3766817

18. Elizabeth Kaziunas, David A. Hanauer, Mark S. Ackerman, and Sung Won Choi. 2015. Identifying unmet informational needs in the inpatient setting to increase patient and caregiver engagement in the context of pediatric hematopoietic stem cell transplantation. *Journal of the American Medical Informatics Association*: ocv116. Retrieved September 21, 2016 from

http://jamia.oxfordjournals.org/content/early/2015/10/27/jamia.ocv116.abstract

19. Logan Kendall, Sonali R. Mishra, Ari Pollack, Barry Aaronson, and Wanda Pratt. 2015. Making background work visible: opportunities to address patient information needs in the hospital. In *AMIA Annual Symposium Proceedings*, 1957. Retrieved September 21, 2016 from http://www.ncbi.nlm.nih.gov/pmc/articles/PMC4765671/

20. Richard S. Lazarus. 1993. Coping theory and research: past, present, and future. *Psychosomatic medicine* 55, 3: 234–247. Retrieved September 21, 2016 from http://journals.lww.com/psychosomaticmedicine/Citation/1993/05000/Coping_theory_and_research__past,_present,_and.2.aspx

21. Danielle M. McCarthy, Kenzie A. Cameron, D. Mark Courtney, and John A. Vozenilek. 2012. Self-Reported Use of Communication Techniques in the Emergency Department. *The Journal of Emergency Medicine* 43, 5: e355–e361. http://doi.org/10.1016/j.jemermed.2012.02.033

22. Danielle M. McCarthy, Emily P. Ellison, Arjun K. Venkatesh, et al. 2013. Emergency Department Team Communication with the Patient: The Patient's Perspective. *The Journal of Emergency Medicine* 45, 2: 262–270. http://doi.org/10.1016/j.jemermed.2012.07.052

23. Andrew D. Miller, Sonali R. Mishra, Logan Kendall, Shefali Haldar, Ari H. Pollack, and Wanda Pratt. 2016. Partners in care: design considerations for caregivers and patients during a hospital stay. In *Proceedings of the 19th ACM Conference on Computer-Supported Cooperative Work & Social Computing*, 756–769. Retrieved September 21, 2016 from http://dl.acm.org/citation.cfm?id=2819983

24. Sonali R. Mishra, Shefali Haldar, Ari H. Pollack, et al. 2016. "Not Just a Receiver": Understanding Patient Behavior in the Hospital Environment. In *Proceedings of the 2016 CHI Conference on Human Factors in Computing Systems*, 3103–3114. Retrieved September 21, 2016 from http://www.shaldar.com/s/p3103-mishra.pdf

25. Laurie Lovett Novak, Richard J. Holden, Shilo H. Anders, Jennifer Y. Hong, and Ben-Tzion Karsh. 2013. Using a sociotechnical framework to understand adaptations in health IT implementation. *International Journal of Medical Informatics*. http://doi.org/10.1016/j.ijmedinf.2013.01.009

26. Sun Young Park and Yunan Chen. 2016. Design implications for technology to address patient information needs during an emergency visit. *Pervasive Computing Technologies for Healthcare (PervasiveHealth), 10th International Conference on. IEEE.*

27. Sun Young Park, Shriti Raj, and Yunan Chen. 2016. Beyond health literacy: supporting patient-provider communication during an emergency visit. *In Proceedings of the ACM Conference on Computer-Supported Cooperative Work and Social Computing (CSCW 2017). In Press.*

28. Jonathan Michael Pell, Mary Mancuso, Shelly Limon, Kathy Oman, and Chen-Tan Lin. 2015. Patient access to electronic health records during hospitalization. *JAMA internal medicine* 175, 5: 856–858. Retrieved September 21, 2016 from http://archinte.jamanetwork.com/article.aspx?articleID=2174938

29. Stephen C. Porter, Zhaohui Cai, William Gribbons, Donald A. Goldmann, and Isaac S. Kohane. 2004. The Asthma Kiosk: A Patient-centered Technology for Collaborative Decision Support in the Emergency Department. *Journal of the American Medical Informatics Association* 11, 6: 458–467. From http://doi.org/10.1197/jamia.M1569

30. Jennifer E. Prey, Janet Woollen, Lauren Wilcox, Alexander D. Sackeim, George Hripcsak, Suzanne Bakken, Susan Restaino, Steven Feiner, and David K. Vawdrey. 2013. Patient engagement in the inpatient setting: a systematic review. *Journal of the American Medical Informatics Association 21, 4: 742-750.* From http://doi.org/10.1136/amiajnl-2013-002141

31. Debra L. Roter. 1977. Patient participation in the patient-provider interaction: the effects of patient question asking on the quality of interaction, satisfaction and compliance. *Health Education & Behavior* 5, 4: 281–315. Retrieved September 21, 2016 from http://heb.sagepub.com/content/5/4/281.short

32. Lila J. Finney Rutten, Neeraj K. Arora, Alexis D. Bakos, Noreen Aziz, and Julia Rowland. 2005. Information needs and sources of information among cancer patients: a systematic review of research (1980–2003). *Patient education and counseling* 57, 3: 250–261. Retrieved January 20, 2016 from http://www.sciencedirect.com/science/article/pii/S0738399104001983

33. Herbert A. Simon. 1996. *The sciences of the artificial.* MIT press. Retrieved September 21, 2016 from https://books.google.com/books?hl=en&lr=&id=k5Sr0nFw7psC&oi=fnd&pg=PR9&dq=The+Sciences+of+the+Artificial&ots=-v2JlGIFJx&sig=x_blo4mJ1B3NOt4TEsD5BfLoSOY

34. Paul. C. Tang, Joan S. Ash, David. W. Bates, J. Mark Overhage, and Daniel Z. Sands. 2006. Personal Health Records: Definitions, Benefits, and Strategies for Overcoming Barriers to Adoption. *Journal of the American Medical Informatics Association* 13, 2: 121–126. From http://doi.org/10.1197/jamia.M2025

35. Suzanne C. Thompson, Christopher Nanni, and Lenore Schwankovsky. 1990. Patient-oriented interventions to improve communication in a medical office visit. *Health*

*Psychology* 9, 4: 390. Retrieved September 21, 2016 from http://psycnet.apa.org/journals/hea/9/4/390/

36. Kenton T. Unruh, Meredith Skeels, Andrea Civan-Hartzler, and Wanda Pratt. 2010. Transforming clinic environments into information workspaces for patients. In *Proceedings of the SIGCHI Conference on Human Factors in Computing Systems*, 183–192. Retrieved April 23, 2014 from http://dl.acm.org/citation.cfm?id=1753354

37. Laura Pfeifer Vardoulakis, Amy Karlson, Dan Morris, Greg Smith, Justin Gatewood, and Desney Tan. 2012. Using mobile phones to present medical information to hospital patients. In *Proceedings of the 2012 ACM annual conference on Human Factors in Computing Systems*, 1411–1420. Retrieved February 10, 2014 from http://dl.acm.org/citation.cfm?id=2208601

38. David K. Vawdrey, Lauren G. Wilcox, Sarah A. Collins, et al. 2011. A Tablet Computer Application for Patients to Participate in Their Hospital Care. *AMIA Annual Symposium Proceedings* 2011: 1428–1435. Retrieved February 10, 2014 from http://www.ncbi.nlm.nih.gov/pmc/articles/PMC3243172/

39. Lauren Wilcox, Steven Feiner, Andy Liu, Susan Restaino, Sarah Collins, and David Vawdrey. 2012. Designing inpatient technology to meet the medication information needs of cardiology patients. In *Proceedings of the 2nd ACM SIGHIT International Health Informatics Symposium*, 831–836. Retrieved February 10, 2014 from http://dl.acm.org/citation.cfm?id=2110466

40. Lauren Wilcox, Dan Morris, Desney Tan, and Justin Gatewood. 2010. Designing patient-centric information displays for hospitals. In *Proceedings of the SIGCHI Conference on Human Factors in Computing Systems*, 2123–2132. Retrieved February 10, 2014 from http://dl.acm.org/citation.cfm?id=1753650

41. Tae-Jung Yun, Hee Young Jeong, Tanisha D. Hill, et al. 2012. Using SMS to provide continuous assessment and improve health outcomes for children with asthma. In *Proceedings of the 2nd ACM SIGHIT International Health Informatics Symposium*, 621–630. Retrieved January 20, 2016 from http://dl.acm.org/citation.cfm?id=2110432

42. John Zimmerman, Erik Stolterman, and Jodi Forlizzi. 2010. An analysis and critique of Research through Design: towards a formalization of a research approach. In *Proceedings of the 8th ACM Conference on Designing Interactive Systems*, 310–319. Retrieved September 21, 2016 from http://dl.acm.org/citation.cfm?id=1858228

# Itchtector: A Wearable-based Mobile System for Managing Itching Conditions

Jongin Lee[1], Daeki Cho[2], Junhong Kim[1], Eunji Im[1], JinYeong Bak[1], Kyung Ho Lee[3], Kwan Hong Lee[4], John Kim[1]
[1]School of Computing, KAIST, [2]NEC Laboratories America,
[3]Department of Dermatology, The Catholic University of Korea, [4]AcademicMerit
{jongin.lee, jh15, imej, jy.bak, jjk12}@kaist.ac.kr
[2]dkcho@nec-labs.com, [3]beauty4u@catholic.ac.kr, [4]kwan@academicmerit.com

## ABSTRACT
Severe itching conditions such as eczema or atopic dermatitis can have a significant impact on one's quality of life. Unfortunately, many of these conditions cannot be cured, and the focus is often on properly controlling or managing the condition. Thus, it is important to understand or objectively monitor how one's scratching behavior changes, based on medication or treatment or environmental conditions. In this work, we explore how wearable devices can support people with itching conditions to better manage their conditions. We carried out a three-phase study with 40 participants and 2 dermatologists to understand the implications of various system features and designs. Based on interviews with patients and doctors, we incorporated medical guidelines for treatment and patients' needs in the proposed Itchtector – a smartwatch-based mobile system to monitor itching behaviors and provide objective information about the user's scratching behaviors. Using the Itchtector prototype, we evaluated performance and possible acceptance with subjects.

## ACM Classification Keywords
J.3 Life and Medical Sciences: Health; H.5.3 Group and Organization Interfaces: Computer-supported cooperative work

## Author Keywords
Itching management; mobile system; nocturnal scratching

## INTRODUCTION
Patients with chronic itching diseases such as atopic dermatitis and eczema need to manage their itching symptoms since the severe itching can affect their quality of life. In particular, atopic dermatitis (AD) is common among children, and its prevalence has increased, especially in developed countries [22]. Parents of the afflicted child can suffer from parental anxiety and psychological distress when managing the child's symptoms [41]. Adult patients with AD also have difficulty managing their symptoms because of environmental conditions (e.g., temperature, humidity, etc.) as well as genetic factors, all of which need to be considered when managing their itching conditions [1]. When the condition worsens, patients often visit a doctor or a dermatologist; however, since the causes of atopic dermatitis can vary significantly, even doctors can have a difficult time identifying which factors are affecting the patient's itching condition, and as a result, trial-and-error approach to treatment is commonly used [3].

Consequently, patients with severe itching conditions are often left to manage their own itching symptoms by themselves, avoiding exacerbating factors when possible. For this purpose, keeping a diary [24] is encouraged as a method to help manage symptoms – including keeping track of the foods they eat, any medication or treatment that they receive, any exacerbating factors, etc. The purpose of the diary is to help identify factors that affect their symptoms so that they can be avoided. However, maintaining a daily diary can be very difficult and in particular, representing one's condition (e.g., how severe is your current condition? has the condition improved?, etc.) can be very subjective and difficult to quantify [44]. To help patients manage their conditions more effectively, the Patient-Oriented SCORAD (PO-SCORAD) index [37] was introduced to better understand the itching severity of patients. However, this index also relies on subjective input from the patients, which can be affected by their mental state. In this work, we explore opportunities to support patients with itching conditions to better manage and control their conditions, using wearable mobile systems and services.

In this paper, we propose a new opportunity for wearable computing to help better manage itching conditions The proposed system can provide a number of benefits, including better communication with doctors, help in establishing an objective understanding of a patient's itching condition, and automatic tracking of external environmental factors that might affect their itching conditions. By conducting extensive interviews with subjects who have itching conditions as well as dermatologists, we identified how the lack of an objective metric or system to track subjects' condition can cause frustration and difficulty in managing their itching conditions. These difficulties extend to when subjects communicate with their doctors during medical visits, since they had a hard time expressing how their conditions have changed (e.g., has my condition improved since taking the new medication?). Based on the preliminary study, we propose *Itchtector* – a mobile system that measures the scratching behavior of users, using sensor data from smartwatches. The system quantifies and measures a number of scratch events to provide accurate feedback about


*CHI '17*, May 06 - 11, 2017, Denver, CO, USA

ACM 978-1-4503-4655-9/17/05...$15.00
DOI: http://dx.doi.org/10.1145/3025453.3025569

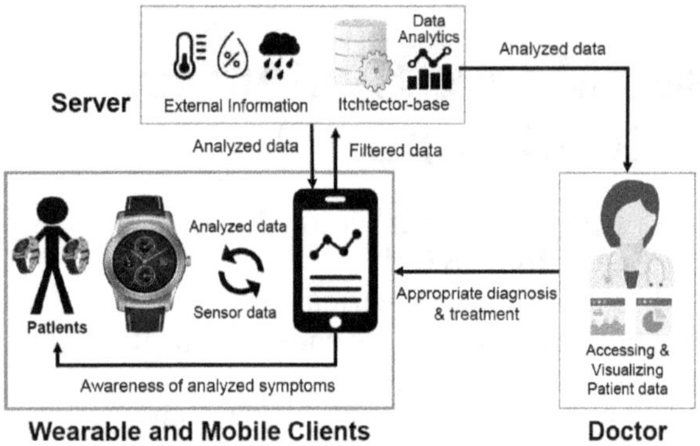


**Figure 1. A high-level overview of a system that we proposed for maintaining itching conditions.**

their itching condition. We first carefully designed a basic service flow and the key functionalities of the Itchtector using various mockup applications, and then explored subject's acceptance and the implications of the service and system. The final component of the study included development of an initial Itchtector prototype and an evaluation of its performance for tracking nocturnal scratching in a separate user study.

Figure 1 provides an overview of the possible scenarios that we envision for the Itchtector. The system consists of a mobile client and a server. The mobile client aggregates sensor data from the smartwatch and uploads the data to a server after preprocessing (e.g., noise filtering). When the server receives the data, it analyzes the data and stores the results in the database called Itchtector-base. When the results are available on the server, a doctor can access and interpret the results using the system to provide appropriate diagnosis and treatment. The Itchtector prototype in this study does not fully implement all of the components of this vision yet. However, this paper is a first step towards such a system, which can be beneficial to both doctors and patients. We also discuss how the Itchtector system can be extended in a field study, to communicate more accurate information about the patient's conditions to their doctors, possible user experience to control their chronic disease, as well as system challenges in the implementation.

## RELATED WORK

### Nocturnal Scratches in Medical Applications

Although the most accurate method for recording scratching behavior is to use an infrared video and manual labeling, it is very time consuming to manually inspect several hours of recordings. In addition, attempting to record scratching when the hands are poorly positioned or hidden (e.g., the hands are covered with a blanket) makes it even more difficult to identify scratching behaviors [17]. Actigraphy [14] and Actiwatch [15] devices (watch-type bands with an accelerometer sensor) have previously been used to measure nocturnal scratching in medical applications. Benjamin et al. [8] showed that the mean value of accelerometers is positively correlated to scratching behaviors, compared to data from an infrared camera. Other prior works [21, 7] have also shown that objective clinical scores, including SCORAD, TST%, and SASSAD, are correlated with wrist activities. However, these prior works still have limited accuracy, since they have a tendency to identify other body movements (e.g., turning over while sleeping, etc.) as scratches. Accelerometer threshold values are commonly used to determine scratching events, however, some non-scratch movements are still identified as scratches, and result in false-positive detection. A recent work [45] showed the limitations of using just the threshold values to detect scratching behaviors, and demonstrated that other body movements can cause noise in the data.

### Sensor Analysis Algorithms for Scratch Detection

Recently, alternative approaches for detecting nocturnal scratching using machine learning algorithms have been suggested [18, 32, 39]. A number of activities (i.e., walking, scratching and restless movements) can be differently clustered using $K$-means [18], and among these activities, logistic regression has also been used for scratch detection [32]. However, these works use the averaging of the $X$, $Y$, and $Z$ acceleration vectors, which weakens the periodic pattern of a scratching signal. Moreover, these studies did not consider scratching signals during real sleep (i.e., they only simulated the scratching data for scratch model validation). Although HealthSense [39] uses 3 vectors of acceleration for scratch detection with three different machine-learning techniques (Naive Bayes, C4.5, and a neural network method), they do not consider wrist orientation during scratching. Our work differs from the above works in that the Itchtector system not only uses orientation-invariant analysis to maintain the periodicity of scratching movements, but also builds scratching models that are consistent with the unconscious scratching that occurs in real sleep.

### Mobile based Healthcare Systems

While a significant amount of research has been conducted on combining mobile systems and healthcare, to the best of our knowledge, very few studies have actually looked at leveraging mobile systems to monitor the behavior of patients that experience itching problems. Although dermatological systems such as skin cancer detection [34] and monitoring newborn jaundice [12] have been suggested, they did not focus on itching or scratching. HealthSense [39] described the possibility of using sensors to detect scratch motions but they did not implement a full system and did not apply the system to patients with itching conditions.

Most of the healthcare mobile systems are proposed to improve the self-management ability of patients or caregivers [33, 11] or the communication process between patients and clinicians [20, 35, 30]. Recently, Kim et al. [23] and Chung et al. [11] have studied the feasibility of applying patient's data (e.g., food intakes, symptom logs) into the clinical context. Our proposed system makes improvements of both the self-management ability and the communication between patient and clinician by automatically quantifying the scratching behavior based on the machine learning technology.

Mobile wellness diaries or loggers are used as a self-monitoring system to manage chronic symptoms such as diabetes [4], chronic heart failure [16], and sleep disorders [27]. The early stage of those systems has required the user to manually input the data. However, recent systems automate these manual processes using the various sensors in the mobile [29, 27] that can potentially make the data collection more reliable and objective. Similar to these, our system also takes minimal input from the user and automates the data collection and the scratch behavior analysis.

## STUDY PROCEDURE AND METHOD

### Study Procedure Overview

Figure 2 illustrates our overall study procedures and methods, which consisted of three phases. Phase 1 was used to investigate the high-level motivation of subjects, as well as to obtain medical guidelines or approaches for itching diseases from dermatologists for our service design. Based on these motivations and guidelines, we designed the Itchtector service to help doctors and people who have chronic itching conditions to better manage their itching conditions. To study the implications of the Itchtector, a two-step user study was conducted in Phase 2. In the first step, a mockup-driven user study was conducted using mockup smartphone and smartwatch interfaces to provide a realistic user experience and obtain feedback from both the subjects and doctors. A scenario-driven user study was also performed within Phase 2 to obtain feedback on the different service usage scenarios. As a final part of our study, we implemented a system prototype of our system and evaluated its performance.

**Participants:** Table 1 summarizes the participants for the three phases of this study. Proper IRB permission was obtained for all phases of this study. We recruited participants with chronic itching, and also included the parents of a child with atopic dermatitis (AD). For Phase 1, we recruited the parents of 2 female children (9 years and 5 years) with AD and 12 other participants (mean = 26 years, sd = 10, 6 male and 6 female). Their skin diseases varied but the prevalent disease was AD. For Phase 2, to avoid potential bias from Phase 1, we separately recruited the parents of 1 female child (2 years) with AD and 10 other participants (mean = 24 years, sd = 9, 7 females, 3 males). 15 subjects (mean = 23 years, sd = 4, 8 males, 7 females) were also recruited in Phase 3. We also conducted a pre-survey to understand patients' current conditions, including demographics and the Patient-Oriented SCORAD (PO-SCORAD) index [37], a self-assessment tool that represents the severity and extent of itching conditions.

**Phase 1** was conducted to understand current medical approaches being used to treat or alleviate itching conditions, and the subjects' own difficulties when managing their itching conditions. We first consulted two dermatologists separately in one time face-to-face meetings of one hour. Based on these consultations, we established guidelines to be used in our service, so that the doctors who use the proposed system can provide a better diagnosis.

In parallel with the expert study with dermatologists, we conducted a semi-structured interview with the 12 participants and 2 parents of the child with AD, via a one hour face-to-face meeting. We asked them about the approaches they used to manage their itching conditions, and their difficulties they encountered. To analyze the qualitative data from the interview transcripts, two researchers segmented the direct quotes which represented a single idea, and iteratively clustered the segmented quotes into high-level categories, until arriving at broad themes.

**Phase 2** consisted of designing the Itchtector service and mockup, including a mockup-driven user study and a scenario-driven user study. Based on the findings in Phase 1, we designed Itchtector – a wearable system in which sensor data

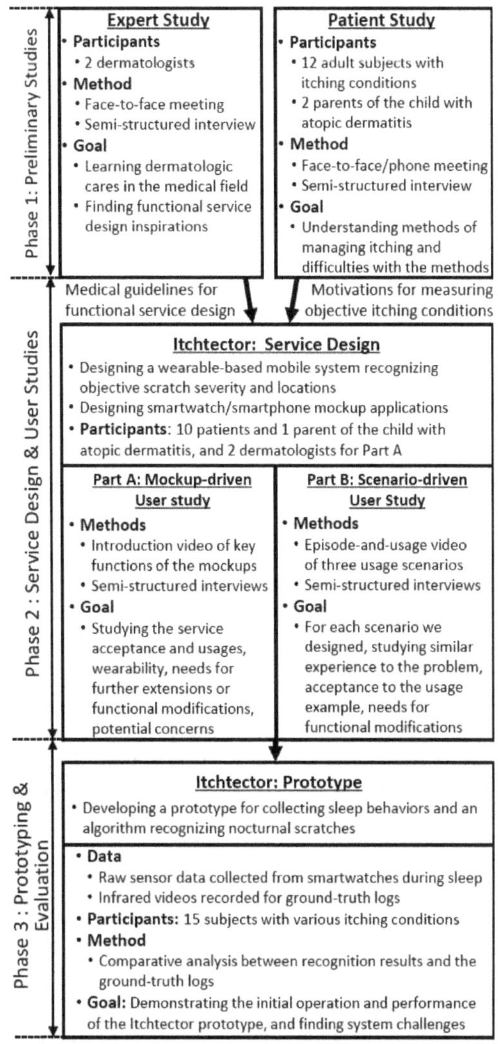


**Figure 2. Overall study procedure for Itchtector system.**

is collected by smartwatches and then analyzed to recognize scratching counts/location. The analyzed data can be used by patients to better manage their itching conditions and can also be provided to their doctors for improved treatment. External sensor data was also collected and combined with the scratch data to provide a better understanding of the influence of external factors on the severity of itching.

To investigate the potential usages of Itchtector with doctors and subjects, we conducted a two-part user study through individual face-to-face interviews. In the first part, we showed videos of mockup Itchtector functions to explore potential usages of our designed system, as well as service acceptance, the usability of the wearable device, possible extensions or functional modifications, and potential concerns. Another part of Phase 2 was a scenario-driven user study that consisted of three different application scenarios identified in Phase 1. User scenario videos were created which used the mockup interface to demonstrate how Itchtector could be used in different patient scenarios, and feedback was obtained for each scenario. Since the scenarios were based on subjects' experiences, we did not interview doctors for this part of the study. The first part of Phase 2 was done separately from the second part in order to obtain feedback from the participants

| P# | Gender | Age | Diagonosis | Period (years) of disease |
|---|---|---|---|---|
| P1 | F | 25 | AD | 20 |
| P2 | F | 30 | SD | 5 |
| P3 | M | 29 | PS, SD | 4 |
| P4 | F | 31 | AD | 26 |
| P5 | F | 25 | AD, Urticaria | 18 |
| P6 | M | 21 | AD | 16 |
| P7 | F | 30 | Urticaria | 2 |
| P8 | M | 26 | AD | 26 |
| P9 | M | 25 | AD | 12 |
| P10 | M | 24 | AD | 18 |
| P11 | M | 40 | AD, Heat rash | 29 |
| P12 | F | 43 | AD | 43 |
| P13 | F | 9 (child) | AD | 9 |
| P14 | F | 5 (child) | AD | 5 |

(a) List of participants in Phase 1

| P# | Gender | Age | Diagonosis | Period (years) of disease |
|---|---|---|---|---|
| P15 | F | 30 | AD | 25 |
| P16 | F | 22 | Urticaria | 12 |
| P17 | F | 21 | AD, CD | 26 |
| P18 | M | 30 | AD | 21 |
| P19 | F | 27 | NE, AD | 26 |
| P20 | M | 37 | AD | 12 |
| P21 | F | 25 | Eczema | 1 |
| P22 | M | 29 | AD, SD, Eczema | 24 |
| P23 | F | 20 | AD | 15 |
| P24 | F | 26 | AD, DU, Eczema | 24 |
| P25 | F | 2 (child) | AD | 2 |

(b) List of participants in Phase 2

| P# | Gender | Age | Diagnosis |
|---|---|---|---|
| P26 | F | 20 | AD, Allergy |
| P27 | F | 26 | AD |
| P28 | F | 22 | Urticaria |
| P29 | M | 35 | Urticaria, Allergy |
| P30 | M | 21 | Shingles, Eczema |
| P31 | M | 21 | AD |
| P32 | M | 21 | AD, Eczema |
| P33 | F | 26 | AD, PS, Angioma |
| P34 | M | 27 | AD |
| P35 | M | 27 | AD |
| P36 | F | 19 | AD, Heat rash |
| P37 | M | 21 | SD |
| P38 | F | 20 | AD |
| P39 | M | 24 | AD |
| P40 | M | 20 | AD, Eczema |

(c) List of participants in Phase 3.

AD: Atopic dermatitis, CD: Contact dermatitis, DU: Dermatographic urticaria, NE: nummular eczema, SD: Seborrheic dermatitis, PS: Psoriasis

**Table 1. Lists of participants for the three phases of this study.**

regarding the system and interface, without biasing them with the scenarios that we had developed.

**Phase 3** focused on developing an algorithm to recognize nocturnal scratching using an Itchtector prototype and evaluating the initial performance. We focused on nocturnal scratching, since participants are not necessarily aware of their scratching behaviors while sleeping. The Itchtector prototype was implemented to collect various scratching and non-scratching behaviors during the entire sleeping period, from subjects who had various itching conditions. Then, an Itchtector algorithm was designed to reflect the periodic patterns of nocturnal scratching.

## PHASE 1: PRELIMINARY STUDIES

### Medical Approaches to Itching Diseases

We interviewed two dermatologists to learn and understand the methods for diagnosing skin diseases that cause severe itching (e.g., atopic dermatitis), and medical approaches used to measure itching conditions.

The dermatologists stated that the process of diagnosing skin diseases that cause severe itching, such as atopic dermatitis, is mainly based on examining skin lesion, as well as patients' comments and any historical diseases the patient might have had. With visible skin lesions, doctors can better evaluate skin conditions and determine a diagnosis for treatments since the diagnosis of skin disease is fundamentally based on the physical distribution, character, and shape of the skin lesions [19]. Accordingly, when there is no skin lesion, it makes diagnosis more difficult, and the doctors often try to find other aspects that can possibly affect the itching, such as internal secretions, psychiatry, nervous systems, environmental factors, etc. Patients' comments about the symptoms they experience are also considered part of the diagnosis, but these comments are not completely reliable, since the diagnosis needs to be primarily based on objective information [38].

Dermatologists also noted that the medical indexes [1](e.g., SCORAD, EASI, etc.) that are commonly used are not practical in many clinical settings since the methods require significantly more consultation hours, and can create privacy issues, since the skin condition of the patient's entire body needs to be examined. Instead, the examination is often limited to the skin lesions that the patients present.

### Patients' Experiences in Managing Itching

We interviewed 12 participants with itching conditions and 2 parents of the child with AD. Table 1(a) summarizes the participants. We first asked each a broad question regarding how they managed their itching condition. Most of the participants commonly used medicines (e.g., topical steroids) when their itching symptoms became worse. They commonly used moisturizers (e.g., lotions) to manage their itching conditions. While foods and environmental factors (especially temperature and humidity) could impact their itching condition, most of the participants felt that it was difficult to control such factors. Most of the participants felt that maintaining a healthy lifestyle (e.g., getting enough sleep, avoiding fast food, minimizing stress, etc.) was important to minimize their itching condition. Because of the difficulties in managing their conditions, some participants (P4, P7, P12) also spent significant effort to research itching symptoms on their own, through the Internet and books, while trying to share information with others that have similar conditions. We categorized the difficulties as well as their hardships in managing their itching symptoms, using the six categories below.

*Difficulties in communicating with doctors*

**1. Explaining scratching severity and locations of itching:** Some subjects pointed out how difficult it was to explain their itching symptoms when they visited the doctor, and in particular, when the appearance of their skin lesions did not reflect the itching severity. (P7) *"My skin lesions are severe every night. (...) however, I could not show the doctor the skin lesions in the evening. I felt like I was a liar in front of the doctor. (...) Doctors did not seem to understand my symptoms."* The parent of the child with AD (P14) also complained about the diagnosis from the doctor: *"I thought that my child's itching symptoms were severe. But whenever we consulted with the doctor, my child's symptoms seemed to get better at the time of our doctor's visit and the doctor did not understand my child's severe symptoms."*

*Difficulties in managing their own itching conditions*

**2. Late recognition of worsening itching severity and sites:** We also found that some subjects were slow to recognize the growing severity of their itching: (P5) *"I was not aware of my severe itching condition since the condition worsened very*

[1] SCORAD (SCORing Atopic Dermatitis) and EASI (Eczema Area and Severity Index) are survey-based medical tools used to measure the extent and severity of atopic dermatitis or eczema, including the location of where the skin conditions occur.

*slowly. I only recognized the severity of my condition when I noticed the large skin lesion with a wound."* (P6) *"My symptom sometimes got worse gradually. (...) It was very difficult to recognize that my symptoms were getting worse. I became aware of my severe symptom after the symptom had become totally severe and needed medical cares from doctors."*

**3. Understanding external factors affecting itching:** All subjects were aware that external factors (e.g., temperature, season, locations, etc.) can affect their itching conditions. Some participants (P4, P5, P10) became familiar with which particular factors affected them only because they have had the itching condition for a very long period of time (e.g., 15 years). However, many participants did not know exactly which factors had a serious impact on their itching conditions: (P1) *"My itching symptoms were sometimes severe, but I did not know the reason. (...) I thought the temperature or humidity were not strongly related to my symptoms, but I am not sure about that either."* In particular, P2 stated difficulties in identifying geographical location effect. *"I recently determined that my itching symptom got worse whenever I visited a room with old books. The air quality in the rooms might affect my itching symptoms."* Some patients mentioned seasonal or long-term effect: (P8) *"My symptom seemed to get severe during the winter. I also thought that humidity might affect my itching symptom"* (P9) *"I felt my itching seemed to be severe every other year, but doctors did not agree with my opinion."*

**4. Careful use of steroids or antihistaminic medicines:** All subjects including the parents expressed concerns about the side effects of the medicines that they used. The concern was most severe for the child's parents: (P13, child) *"When I used steroid ointment on my child, the itching condition definitely improved. However, I have heard that too many steroids can lead to early puberty. (...) Because my child is young and a female, I make a big effort to avoid using steroid ointments when possible."* Most of the adult participants stated that steroid ointment was only used when their symptoms became very severe: (P4) *"I try to avoid using steroid ointment more than once a day since I know the side effects of the ointment. Instead, I tried to treat my itching sites with Vaseline or saline solutions."*

#### *Psychological and social difficulties*

**5. The anxiety produced by forthcoming severe itching:** We found that some of the participants who suffered from severe itching had anxieties about severe scratching that would occur during sleep: (P7) *"I had some anxiety around sleeping due to the severe itching and that led to insomnia. (...) If I have a meeting in the morning, I am very anxious about my poor sleep quality and dozing off during the meeting. As a result, I had to have sleep medication before going to sleep."* In spite of the anxiety, some subjects pointed out they worried about whether to use the medicine or not, due to the risk of overdose. (P5) *"Because of my severe itching experiences, I used a steroid ointment whenever I felt my itching was getting worse. (...) I always worried whether my use of steroids could cause an overdose."*

**6. Difficulties maintaining a normal social life:** Nearly all of the participants expressed frustrations about how the itching affected their social lives. (P4) *"Since I felt sleeping helped to alleviate my itching, I always went to sleep whenever I felt my itching was severe. (...) So, I did not do my homework sometimes and finally gave up the class for my health."* (P5) *"If my severe itching starts, I even do not think any social activities. (...) I could not wear tight-fitting clothes but always wore clothes with cotton. (...) I was not able to take a shower with hot water for a long time. I felt frustrated because I could not enjoy a normal social life."*

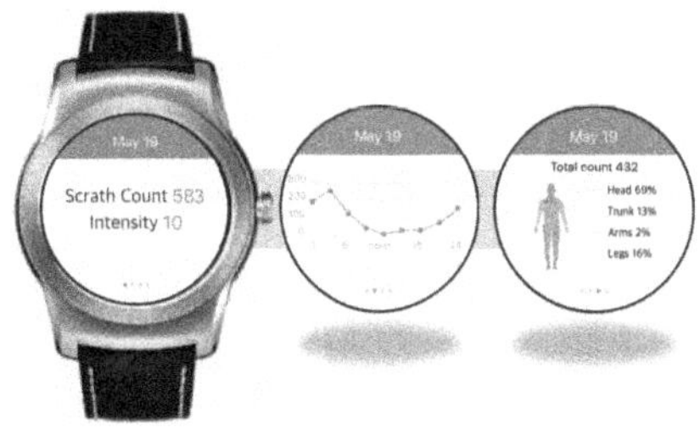


**Figure 3. Smartwatch mockup interface.**

## PHASE 2: SERVICE DESIGN OF ITCHTECTOR

Based on the findings in Phase 1, we defined three high-level opportunities for the wearable devices.

The first opportunity was to improve the communication between the doctors and the patients in conveying the patient's itching conditions. Since the communication between doctors and patients primarily occurs in a clinical setting, doctors often do not completely understand their patient's itching condition. Thus, properly recognizing scratching behaviors (and how that behavior changes) will be helpful for both doctors and patients.

The second opportunity was to provide an objective feedback to the subject on their itching conditions, to allow them to better manage their itching symptoms. In particular, an accurate awareness of the current itching condition can help the subject avoid the overuse of medications.

The third identified opportunity was to connect the scratching behaviors with various exacerbating factors, so that information could be used to help determine which factors were negatively affecting the subjects. Patients often rely on their own subjective experiences to understand the exacerbating factors. However, knowing which factors were actually associated with severe scratching behaviors can provide an objective consideration of how the external factors may influence itching for each individual subject.

### Service Design and the Key Functions of Mockups

We implemented mockup applications for both smartwatches and a smartphone, which included three key functions that satisfied the three opportunities discovered in Phase 1. The reason for implementing the mockups was to obtain early feedback from users about our initial service concept [13], before fully implementing our system or service. Figure 3 and Figure 4 show the smartwatch and smartphone mockup interface, respectively. The key functions of the mockups are to display 1) trends in scratching count/locations according to the time/month/year, and 2) scratching count in relation to exacerbating factors. Scratch behaviors were defined as periodic movements lasting longer than 3 seconds [6, 18], and scratch locations were carefully divided with doctors' consultation before designing the mockup interfaces, and the external factors were also carefully selected based on the patients' experiences we obtained in Phase 1.

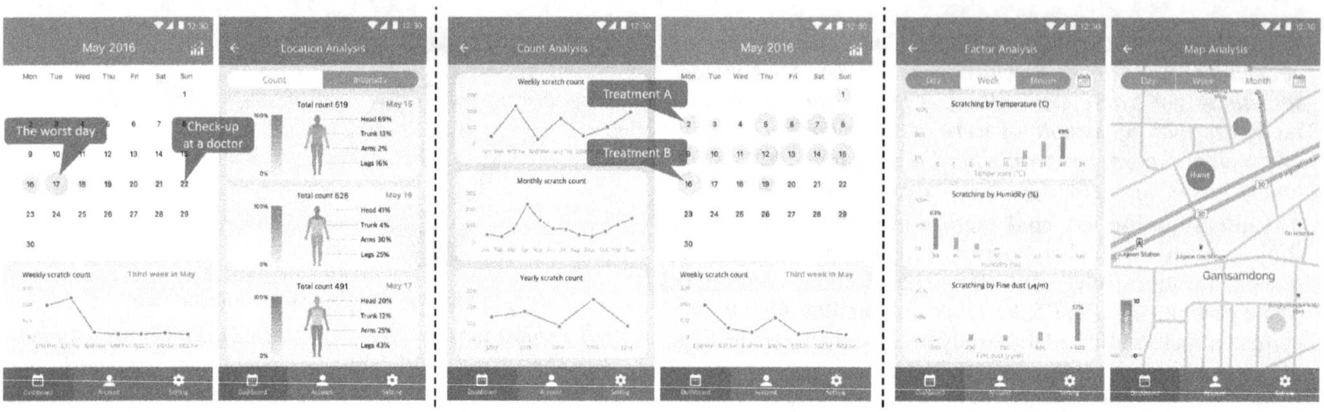


(a) (b) (c)

**Figure 4. Smartphone mockup interfaces for the 3 different scenarios: (a) Scenario 1 interface showing information on scratch count and location, (b) Scenario 2 interface shows how scratch behavior changes over time and how it might correlate with different treatments used, and (c) Scenario 3 used to better understand objective external factors that might affect itching conditions. The information in Scenario 2 showed an example with significant long-term usage. However, long-term use of wearables is a challenge [2] and needs to be addressed for Itchtector as well.**

## Part A: Mockup-driven User Study

The first part of the user study was performed with mockups that we designed, and the goal of the user study was to determine service acceptance, wearability as well as to identify any potential concerns or possible extensions or modifications. The participants were shown the mockup application on both the smartwatch and the smartphone devices; in addition, a video was also shown that introduced the functionality of the applications. The mockup-driven study was conducted with both the doctors and the subjects.

### *Doctor's Feedback*

We interviewed two dermatologists individually, with each interview lasting for approximately one hour. The questions were mainly about how the functions in the mockup could be used to improve diagnosis.

**Additional information for better diagnosis:** The doctors indicated that the information on scratching counts and scratching locations could be used for better diagnosis, since some skin conditions do not have any visible appearance on the skin. The "itch-scratch" cycle [46] behavior can also result in the temporary disappearance of the itching condition: *"If the doctor can observe scratch counts over time, we can determine whether the symptom has gotten worse or not. Normally, we are limited to checking secondary scratch marks on the skin lesion for the diagnosis."* Doctors also stated that an objective scratch count information could be used to understand the effect of medication, since the medications can often take up to two weeks to have an effect on the skin [9].

**Better communication with patients:** Both doctors also stated that knowing how the scratching behaviors change can help them communicate with their patients: *"I sometimes argue with my patients when I insist the wounded skin lesions are from scratching* (i.e., factitial dermatitis [36]) *while the patient might insist they did not scratch that particular location. If an objective record of scratch count and location are available, this type of miscommunication can be resolved."*

### *Patient's Feedback*

We also individually interviewed 10 subjects and 1 parent of the child with AD. Each interview lasted for approximately 30 minutes, and the results are summarized in Table 2. To provide details from their feedback, we include some representative quotes below.

| P# | Service acceptance | Wearability problem | Privacy problem |
|---|---|---|---|
| P15 | N | Y | N |
| P16 | Y | N(c) | Y |
| P17 | Y | N(c) | N |
| P18 | Y | N(c) | N |
| P19 | Y | Y | Y |
| P20 | Y(c) | N | N(c) |
| P21 | N | Y | N |
| P22 | Y | N(c) | N |
| P23 | Y | N(c) | N |
| P24 | Y | N(c) | N(c) |
| P25 | Y | Y | N |

**Table 2. A summary of the mockup-driven user study in Phase 2. (Y: yes, N: no, (c): conditional response)**

**Service acceptance of Itchtector:** Eight participants and one parent showed interest in using our service to manage their itching conditions: (P22) *"If I had it[Itchtector], I could be aware of my itching condition more objectively. (...) Since I am used to my itching, I think it is very difficult to recognize when it is getting worse. (...) I always become aware that my itching conditions have become severe after my symptoms have gotten too bad. "* The parent (P25) also stated: *"Since I cannot always be with my child because of my job, if I have it[Itchtector], it would help me better understand my child's itching conditions."* P16 really wanted to use our service to find factors that were affecting her itching condition. *" Since the doctors do not know the cause of my itching, I think I should avoid* any *factors that could affect my itching. As a result, it[Itchtector] would be very helpful to me. (...) How much is it?"* Interestingly, P22 and P23 pointed out that the information provided by the system could provide some reassurance: (P23) *"I currently do not have a good understanding of my itching symptoms. (...) I would be more reassured and comforted if I had some understanding of the changes in my itching condition."* P23's comment provided a new opportunity for our service design – some people have psychological difficulties because of their itching conditions, and a system like Itchtector can help provide some sense of reassurance. P17 liked having the ability to know how their scratching location changed over time: *"It would be very useful to know the scratching locations.*

*In my case, I am only aware of the scratching locations when they start to bleed from excessive scratching."*

P20 agreed about the usefulness of our service but expressed concerns about the technical feasibility of the system. P20 strongly agreed with our service, suggesting that the service could be used to complement his current treatment diary to find and avoid exacerbating factors that were affecting his itching condition. *"I think that [Itchtector] would be better for my current diary since it can automate the process of recording much of the information that would go into a treatment diary. (...) Is it technically feasible to recognize scratching behaviors?"*

P15 and P21 declined our service because their itching symptoms were near their wrists. P15 could not wear regular watches because of her itching condition. P21 stated that her itching symptoms were mainly located on both of her hands and that would make it difficult to use smartwatches.

**Functional Extensions to the Service:** Four subjects and one parent suggested extensions to our service based on their experiences. P17 and P20 wanted an 'alert' function if their itching symptom became too severe, based on collected data. P17 even wanted the device to wake her up if this happened during sleep: *"I can control my scratching during the day but cannot control the behavior while sleep. If my symptoms get worse while I am asleep, I would like the system to wake me up – perhaps through a smartwatch alarm."* P18 would have liked the service better if it could provide guidance or additional information on how to alleviate his itching condition if it got worse. *"I felt most of the information provided was simply 'data'. (...) I would have preferred if the service could perform all of the analysis and provide some treatment guidelines to me."* Interestingly, P22, who is a software developer, suggested developing a smartwatch widget that always showed up on the screen, as it would easily help him to better understand his condition – e.g., similar to a weather widget. The parent (P25) of the child with AD wanted to see whether food information of what food the child has eaten could also be displayed on the calendar, to understand the impact of food on the itching conditions.

**Wearability of the smartwatch:** Eight subjects (out of 11) felt that wearing smartwatches before going sleep would be acceptable and not cause any inconvenience. However, four female participants (P16, P17, P23, P24) suggested using alternative devices that were smaller and weighed less – such as Jawbone or Mi-Band. P18 and P22 also preferred to change to another lighter devices since they already had previous experiences with lightweight healthcare devices during sleep. P24 commented that wearing two smartwatches would look "weird" during the day, but she would wear two smartwatches if it helped her in managing her itching condition. P19 was skeptical about using smartwatches because she was very negative about devices collecting her biometric data. As mentioned earlier, P15 and P21 did not want to wear watches at all because of their itching symptoms on their wrist, near where the smartwatches would be worn. The parent of P25 accepted the service but pointed out that smartwatches would be too big for her child.

| | Similar experience to the episode in scenarios | | | Acceptance to the usage in scenarios | | |
|---|---|---|---|---|---|---|
| P# | Scenario 1 | Scenario 2 | Scenario 3 | Scenario 1 | Scenario 2 | Scenario 3 |
| P15 | O | O | O | Y | Y | Y |
| P16 | O | O | X | Y | Y | Y |
| P17 | O | O | O | Y | Y | Y(c) |
| P18 | O | O | O | Y(c) | Y | Y(c) |
| P19 | X | O | O | Y | Y | Y(c) |
| P20 | O | O | O | Y | Y | Y |
| P21 | O | O | X | N | Y | Y |
| P22 | O | O | O | Y | Y(c) | N |
| P23 | O | O | O | Y | Y(c) | Y(c) |
| P24 | O | O | O | Y | Y | Y(c) |
| P25 | O | O | O | Y | Y | Y |

**Table 3. A summary of the scenario-driven user study in Phase 2. (O: suffered the similar experience, X: no suffered the similar experience, Y: yes, N: no, (c): conditional response)**

**Privacy concerns:** Overall, eight subjects and one parent expressed that our service would not create any privacy concerns if the information collected was only used for better diagnosis from their doctors. P20 and P24 raised potential privacy concerns based on geographical location information, but they also agreed to share information with just the doctor. P16 stated that she did not want to expose her sleep behaviors through that sensor data to anyone. P19 was very sensitive to having her biometric information stored on any devices. *"I do not want my personal biometric data to be collected and analyzed somewhere. It makes me feel uncomfortable."*

### Part B: Scenario-driven User Study

We also conducted a scenario-driven user study to obtain feedback on the different scenarios that we designed, as well as to determine whether the subjects experienced similar scenarios and service acceptance. The three usage scenarios were based on the opportunities identified in Phase 1. For this step of our study, we individually interviewed the same participants as those in Part A of Phase 2 (10 adult participants and 1 parent of the child with AD). Each interview lasted for approximately 30 minutes and Table 3 summarizes the results.

The scenario-driven study was conducted by having subjects view a separate video for each scenario. Each video first explained a difficulty faced by someone with an itching condition, and then, demonstrated an example of how our service could be leveraged to help control such a problem, which including a demonstration of the smartwatch and smartphone mockup interfaces (Figure 3 and Figure 4). The following three usage scenarios were evaluated.

- **Usage scenario 1:**
  *Episode* – A patient wants to explain his itching intensity, but the doctor is unable to understand the itching symptom since there are no visible skin lesions.
  *Example of Itchtector Usage* – The trends in scratching counts/locations shown in Figure 4(a) are provided to help the doctor make a better diagnosis.
- **Usage scenario 2:**
  *Episode* – A patient asks another patient about how he manages his itching condition. However, he is worried that another person's approach would not necessarily work for him.
  *Example of Itchtector Usage* – The different trends in

scratching counts related to different management methods are shown, as in Figure 4(b), for better management of their conditions.

- **Usage scenario 3:**
  *Episode* – A patient cannot determine what factors may be exacerbating their itching condition because there are numerous possible factors such as fine dust, humidity, and geographical locations that could be affecting the patient.
  *Example of Itchtector Usage* – The sensitivity to certain scratching conditions based on correlation with external factors are shown, as in Figure 4(c), to provide better understanding and help with avoiding exacerbating factors.

*Usage scenario 1*

**Experiences similar to the episode:** Nine subjects and one parent had experiences similar to the problem presented in this scenario: (P22) *"When my symptoms were severe at night, I did everything including taking a shower to alleviate my itching. Next day, I visited my doctor and my symptoms had disappeared."* P16 also strongly agreed: *"My allergy reaction mainly appears in the evening. (...) When I visited my doctor, my allergy disappeared."* However, P19 expressed that he did not have any similar experiences since he only visits his doctor when his symptoms are very severe.

**Acceptance of the usage example:** Nine subjects and one parent agreed with the usefulness of solving the problem in the episode: (P20) *"I think Itchtector would definitely help me convey my itching conditions to the doctors."* P18 raised a question about whether doctors really needed the scratching information or not, while agreeing with the effectiveness of the Itchtector. P21 disagreed with the usage while raising a skeptical question: *"I do not think Itchtector can help discover the reasons for my itching."*

**Need for functional modifications:** Some subjects (P16, P18, P23, P24) wanted more than four parts (head, arms, trunks, and legs) of their body to be recognized, because their itching locations mainly occurred at folds on their body. In particular, P23 wanted to separate the right and left sides of her body, since whenever her itching was severe, the itching locations often changed from one side to the other.

*Usage scenario 2*

**Experiences similar to the episode:** Surprisingly, all the subjects agreed that they have had experiences similar to the episode. They had suffered from trying to find itching management methods that worked for them. For example, P22 stated, *"I did everything that I could for my itching. (...) I even went to a sulfur spa, but my symptoms got worse because of the residue from the sulfur."* P23 also stated, *"I used a moisturizer that my friend recommended, but it did not work for me. I usually try to select a moisturizer based on my experience."*

**Acceptance of the usage example:** All the subjects showed interest in this particular usage and use of the system to objectively check on their itching condition. In particular, P23 totally agreed with the usage, with the comment: *"It would help me find the management method which is effective for me. (...) If I had Itchtector, I wouldn't have to use other subjective management methods with anxiety."* Interestingly, P22 pointed out that the functions are more appropriate for younger subjects who might not have enough experiences in managing their itching while agreeing with the effectiveness of Itchtector. P23 even suggested a future function: *"It would be good to use the service at home since I really would not want to go outside if my symptoms were severe"*

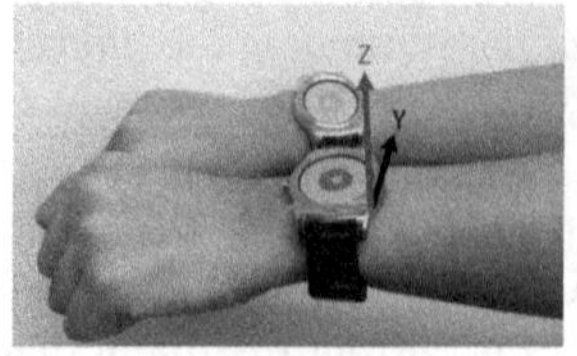

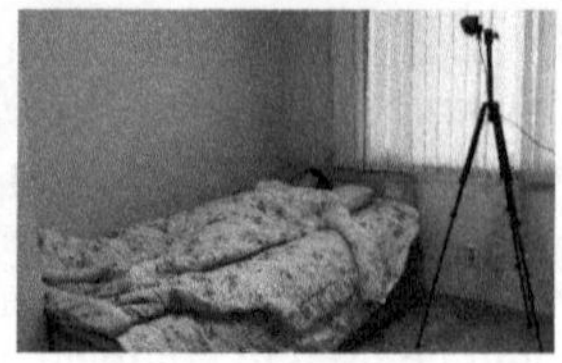

(a) (b)

**Figure 5. (a) Smartwatches used in our study and (b) experiment setting with an infrared camera to evaluate nocturnal scratching.**

**Need for functional modifications:** Some subjects (P18, P20, P25, P22) wanted to add some text to the calendar interface as a reminder, such as a managing method or treatment. P20 stated that since more than two management methods could be used, writing text in the calendar interface would be better. P21 even wanted to share her scratching information with others to find a treatment which fits her.

*Usage scenario 3*

**Experiences similar to the episode:** Eight subjects and one parent had experiences similar to the episode. They had difficulty in determining whether some external factors were affecting their itching or not. P23 stated *"I thought that my symptoms became severe when I moved to college. (...) When I came back home, the symptoms did not get better."* P17 commented about temperature and humidity: *"I first thought that the temperature and humidity did not affect my itching but I am not so sure about that these days."* Interestingly, P15 and P20, who experienced itching symptoms for 25 and 12 years, respectively, pointed out that they didn't even know about new external factors, like fine dust, because the fine dust has only occurred in the last 5 years

**Acceptance of the usage example:** Nine subjects and one parent agreed with the usefulness of Itchtector. Most of them showed interest in tracking environmental factors such as humidity or fine dust. P23 even wanted to add other environmental sensors, such as for endocrine disruptors for future usages. P19 wanted to use it but also suggested adding other external factors, such as wearing certain clothes, because environmental factors such as temperature could not be controlled by her. However, P22 did not want to use the usage functions because he believed he already understands the environmental factors affecting his itching, based on his long experiences.

**Need for functional modifications:** Some subjects (P17, P18, P24) raised questions about providing geographical information, while agreeing on the usefulness of tracking temperature, humidity, and fine dust. Because different locations might have many different factors, they felt tracking scratching behaviors based on the location might not be sufficient for understanding the external factors that affect their itching. P19 and P25 suggested that tracking environmental factors such as temperature and humidity for different locations would help determine the impact of location.

## PHASE 3: ITCHTECTOR PROTOTYPE

Based on user feedback in Phase 2, an Itchtector prototype was designed, and evaluated through a user study to measure

| Subject Information | | | | Diagnosis | Scratch Count |
|---|---|---|---|---|---|
| P# | Sex | Age | PO-SCO | (Pruritus) | All (seconds) |
| P26 | F | 20 | 28.3 | AD, Allergy | 15 (47.6) |
| P27 | F | 26 | 19.6 | AD | 10 (60.9) |
| P28 | F | 22 | 23.5 | Urticaria | 41 (126.5) |
| P29 | M | 35 | 34.3 | Urticaria, Allergy | 26 (133.3) |
| P30 | M | 21 | 15.0 | Shingles, Eczema | 37 (122.6) |
| ~~P31~~ | ~~M~~ | ~~21~~ | ~~25.3~~ | ~~AD~~ | |
| P32 | M | 21 | 31.0 | AD, Eczema | 12 (39.6) |
| P33 | F | 26 | 43.2 | AD, PS, Angioma | 97 (565.6) |
| P34 | M | 27 | 33.5 | AD | 141 (3337.9) |
| ~~P35~~ | ~~M~~ | ~~27~~ | ~~31.9~~ | ~~AD~~ | |
| P36 | F | 19 | 19.1 | AD, Heat rash | 43 (141.4) |
| P37 | M | 21 | 12.2 | SD | 4 (11.7) |
| P38 | F | 20 | 25.9 | AD | 12 (25.3) |
| P39 | M | 24 | 29.2 | AD | 62 (550.6) |
| P40 | M | 20 | 16.1 | AD, Eczema | 39 (142.1) |

PO-SCO: Patient-Oriented SCORAD (SCORing Atopic Dermatitis),
AD: Atopic dermatitis, SD: Seborrheic dermatitis, PS: Psoriasis

**Table 4. List of subjects who participated in Phase 3. In Scratch Count column, 'All' means all scratch events which are labeled with an infrared camera based on medical research [6, 18]. Because of poor video recording quality (P31) and difficulty in analyzing wrist movements hidden by blanket for ground truth analysis (P35), the data collected from P31 and P35 could not be used.**

the participants' nocturnal scratching during sleep. For the prototype, an LG Watch Urbane smartwatch was used since it has a relatively low weight and long battery life, compared to other alternative smartwatches. [2] It also supports a gyroscope and linear accelerometer sensors for detecting periodic movements. The gyroscope is used to identify very small scratching behaviors (e.g., scratching with fingers only) while the accelerometer sensor is more effective for sensing scratching behaviors that have high amplitudes.

### User Study

The experiment was carried out in the subjects' bedrooms using an infrared camera. To ensure privacy, a researcher (of the same sex as the subject) visits the room to install the infrared camera (Figure 5(b)). Each subject was provided with two smartwatches (one for each wrist) to collect data while the subject was sleeping. The subjects were also requested to sleep for more than 6 hours in order to obtain sufficient amount of data. Table 4 shows the subjects participated in Phase 3.

Once the data was collected, the recorded video was analyzed manually to identify both scratching and non-scratching behaviors. Other meta information was also collected, including start/end time of the scratching behaviors, whether the left or right wrist was involved, and the scratch location. The labeling for each patient was very time-consuming and often lasted up to 10 hours. In addition, two researchers independently labeled sleep movements for cross-validation. Some of the data was excluded if the subject's hand disappeared in the infrared video (e.g., hidden from the blanket) since the ground truth could not be obtained. The sensor data from two smartwatches were synchronized with the video recording to properly correlate the sensor movements with the ground truth.

### Scratch Recognition Algorithm

Figure 6 presents a high-level overview of the Itchtector algorithm. The first stage is **Sensing**, where the 3-axis linear-acceleration and 3-axis gyroscope data are collected at a 50Hz sampling rate. The next stage includes **Preprocessing** and **Window Classification**.

[2]Other smartwatches or health bands are considered that provide longer battery life and/or lower weight; however, many of the alternatives do not provide direct access to the raw sensor data.

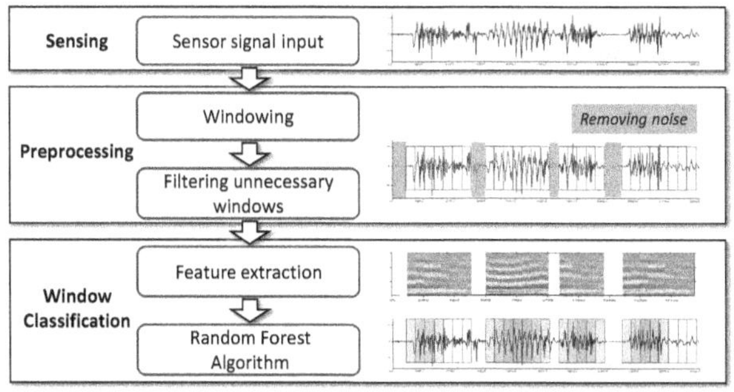


**Figure 6. A high-level overview of the algorithm in Itchtector.**

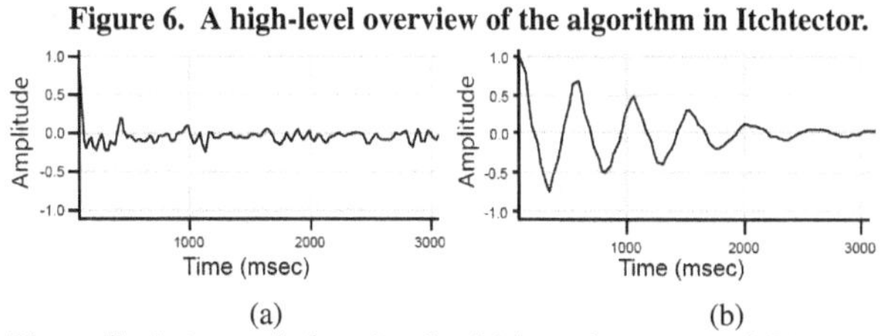


**Figure 7. Autocorrelation signals of (a) turning over and (b) nocturnal scratches. Periodic patterns are obviously shown in the autocorrelation signal of real nocturnal scratches.**

**Preprocessing:** The first step in the preprocessing is to partition the time-series sensor data into processable units called windows, which are often used in detecting human activities [10, 5]. The windows are shifted by 1 second, such that the last 2 seconds of the current window are used as part of the next window. We also removed windows that had little or no movement since people often spend a significant amount of their time sleeping without movement.

**Window Classification:** Based on the preprocessed windows, we extracted features reflecting the periodic movement of nocturnal scratching, and these features were used as an input to our machine learning algorithm for detecting windows containing scratching behavior. We first converted the 3-axis sensor data into the 1-axis sensor to reflect orientation-invariant signals as follows:

- *Mag*: The magnitude (i.e., $\sqrt{x(t)^2+y(t)^2+z(t)^2}$) of the 3-axis data, which is used in the previous work [28, 32].
- *PC1*: The first component (*PC1*) after the PCA analysis of the 3-axis sensor data. If the scratching had an obvious direction in the movement, *PC1* will reflect the periodic patterns of the scratching, regardless of wrist orientations.

Then, the two 1-axis signals (*Mag*, *PC1*) from each sensor were converted into the autocorrelation signals. This step was the noise reduction. In this study, we found that the data contained weak periodic signal noises in many places, which were mostly produced by sleep movements such as turning over. To mitigate these noises, we leveraged the autocorrelation function [42] to amplify only periodic signals in the sleep movements, without other non-periodic signals, which enables our classifier to focus only on periodic signals in the movements. An example of the converted autocorrelation signals is shown in Figure 7 for non-periodic and periodic movements. The energy of the periodic fluctuations is measured in the autocorrelation signal; this was inspired by the work to capture musical rhythmic patterns [26]. The highest peaks and lowest valleys were also extracted to reflect the periodic powers, and prominent/weak peaks were also extracted to reflect the periodicity in the autocorrelation signals [31]. With these features, each window was classified with a random forest algorithm, which is known to be effective in human activity recognition [10].

### Scratch Recognition Result

A 10-fold cross-validation [25] was used to evaluate the performance of the Itchtector algorithm. We defined *precision* as the fraction of predicted scratching behaviors that correspond to actual scratching behaviors, and *recall* as the fraction of actual scratching behaviors recognized as scratching behaviors. Overall, our Itchtector algorithm shows the performance for accuracy (nearly 90%), precision (74%) and recall (75%). In this experiment, we observed that the scratch movement are more accurately detected when the movement was continued for a longer time since those movements tend to have clear periodic movements. We leave the comparison of our proposed algorithms with alternative algorithms [28, 32, 39] as future work.

## DISCUSSION

In this section, we discuss some of the challenges of the Itchtector system, as well as other possible opportunities and applications.

**Challenge 1: Detecting nocturnal scratching:** In the nocturnal scratching data that we collected in Phase 3, we observed that some periodic movements during sleep were not necessarily scratching behaviors. For example, continuous leg cramps were identified as periodic movements, and sleep disorders, such as shaking hands in the air, were falsely identified as scratches. In addition, we found that some scratching behaviors do not necessarily show periodic movements. For example, continuous scratching with several body parts moving at the same time did not result in a clear periodic pattern. The algorithm used in Itchtector needs to be improved to decrease both false-positives and false-negatives, and to increase overall accuracy. We also expect that the algorithm can be personalized since each user tends to have differences in their scratching behaviors.

**Challenge 2: Extending Itchtector to Field Study:** The Itchtector prototype was used to conduct nocturnal scratching evaluations. However, skin conditions often change over a long period of time (e.g., one or two weeks). Thus, a longer field study can provide the historical changes in a patient's condition. Extending this work to a long-term field study presents additional challenges, including the need to improve the energy efficiency of the mobile devices, as well as further improvements in the scratch recognition algorithm, to differentiate other movements during the day time from scratching.

**Opportunity 1: Itchtector for Children:** The Itchtector system can be very beneficial for young children who suffer from chronic itching conditions. A large proportion of atopic dermatitis patients is children before their 5th birthday [40]. Unlike adults, young children often cannot clearly or accurately communicate their conditions, and often cannot control scratching their body. As a result, Itchtector can be very beneficial to young children and their doctors. However, the smartwatch used for the current prototype is likely too heavy for children. Many of the current smart bands (e.g., Fitbit, Nike Fuelband, etc.) are smaller in size and likely more suitable for children. It remains to be seen if Itchtector can be implemented on these devices.

**Opportunity 2: Collaborative data sharing for better management:** While this work focused on the treatment of individual patients and their communication with their doctors, another possible application of this work includes extending the services so that subjects can share their information with others, similar to PatientsLikeMe [43]. The absolute amount of scratching might not be directly comparable between patients, since each subject may respond to similar itching symptoms with different amounts of scratching. However, historical data and the relative change in the amount of scratching can be a useful metric to compare across different subjects. Thus, users can explore alternative treatments as well as perhaps better understand which factors aggravate their conditions.

**Opportunity 3: Curing psychological fears:** We summarized difficulties from Phase 1 into six categories, but we did not consider psychological factors in designing our service. However, as was noted earlier in Phase 2, a few of the participants provided positive feedback, indicating our service could potentially provide some "reassurance" to them by observing their behaviors over an extended period of time and maintaining historical data. In addition, P23 stated that a very serious bout of itching condition that had happened to him, had left a significant mental trauma because of the hardship it caused. Thus, we expect that Itchtector can be extended to help alleviate such psychological concerns for patients.

## CONCLUSION

Various skin conditions require proper management or control, to minimize worsening of the condition, and thus, it is important to accurately understand the current condition and how it responds to different medications or changes in the environment. In this work, we present new opportunities with wearable devices for subjects with chronic itching conditions, which can be used to improve how they manage their itching condition, as well as enable better communication with their doctors through more objective feedback. Based on extensive user studies with doctors and subjects with various itching conditions, we designed Itchtector – a wearable-based mobile system that is capable of recognizing scratching behaviors to improve the management of itching conditions. A mockup of the Itchtector was designed and its ability to enhance subjects' effort to manage their itching conditions was evaluated. The Itchtector prototype described and evaluated in this work is the first step in providing an overall system. Both doctors and patients can benefit from having an accurate analysis of the patient's itching condition.

## ACKNOWLEDGMENTS

We would like the to thank the anonymous reviewers for their comments and feedback. This research was supported by Next-Generation Information Computing Development Program through the National Research Foundation of Korea (NRF) funded by the Ministry of Science, ICT & Future Plannig (2015M3C4A7065647).

## REFERENCES


1. Cezmi A Akdis, Mübeccel Akdis, Thomas Bieber, Carsten Bindslev-Jensen, Mark Boguniewicz, Philippe Eigenmann, Qutayba Hamid, Alexander Kapp, Donald YM Leung, Jasna Lipozencic, and others. 2006. Diagnosis and treatment of atopic dermatitis in children and adults: European Academy of Allergology and Clinical Immunology/American Academy of Allergy, Asthma and Immunology/PRACTALL Consensus Report. *Allergy* 61, 8 (2006), 969–987. DOI: http://dx.doi.org/10.1016/j.jaci.2006.03.045

2. Elske Ammenwerth, Stefan Gräber, Gabriele Herrmann, Thomas Bürkle, and Jochem König. 2003. Evaluation of health information systems—problems and challenges. *International journal of medical informatics* 71, 2 (2003), 125–135. DOI: http://dx.doi.org/10.1016/S1386-5056(03)00131-X

3. Peter D. Arkwright, Cassim Motala, Hamsa Subramanian, Jonathan Spergel, Lynda C. Schneider, and Andreas Wollenberg. 2013. Management of difficult-to-treat atopic dermatitis. *Journal of Allergy and Clinical Immunology: In Practice* 1, 2 (2013), 142–151. DOI: http://dx.doi.org/10.1016/j.jaip.2012.09.002

4. Eirik Arsand, Ragnhild Varmedal, and Gunnar Hartvigsen. 2007. Usability of a mobile self-help tool for people with diabetes: the easy health diary. In *2007 IEEE International Conference on Automation Science and Engineering*. IEEE, 863–868. DOI: http://dx.doi.org/10.1109/COASE.2007.4341807

5. Oresti Banos, Juan-Manuel Galvez, Miguel Damas, Hector Pomares, and Ignacio Rojas. 2014. Window size impact in human activity recognition. *Sensors (Basel, Switzerland)* 14, 4 (2014), 6474–99. DOI: http://dx.doi.org/10.3390/s140406474

6. Bruce G. Bender, Robert Ballard, Beth Canono, James R. Murphy, and Donald Y M Leung. 2008. Disease severity, scratching, and sleep quality in patients with atopic dermatitis. *Journal of the American Academy of Dermatology* 58, 3 (2008), 415–420. DOI: http://dx.doi.org/10.1016/j.jaad.2007.10.010

7. Bruce G. Bender, Susan B. Leung, and D. Y M Leung. 2003. Actigraphy assessment of sleep disturbance in patients with atopic dermatitis: An objective life quality measure. *Journal of Allergy and Clinical Immunology* 111, 3 (2003), 598–602. DOI: http://dx.doi.org/10.1067/mai.2003.174

8. Kenneth Benjamin, Karen Waterston, Margaret Russell, Olivia Schofield, Brian Diffey, and Jonathan L. Rees. 2004. The development of an objective method for measuring scratch in children with atopic dermatitis suitable for clinical use. *Journal of the American Academy of Dermatology* 50, 1 (2004), 33–40. DOI: http://dx.doi.org/10.1016/S0190-9622(03)02480-0

9. Bruce R Bistrian, George L Blackburn, NS Scrimshaw, and JP Flatt. 1975. Cellular immunity in semistarved states in hospitalized adults. *The American journal of clinical nutrition* 28, 10 (1975), 1148–1155.

10. Pierluigi Casale, Oriol Pujol, and Petia Radeva. 2011. Human activity recognition from accelerometer data using a wearable device. In *Iberian Conference on Pattern Recognition and Image Analysis*. Springer, 289–296. DOI: http://dx.doi.org/10.1007/978-3-642-21257-4_36

11. Chia-Fang Chung, Jonathan Cook, Elizabeth Bales, Jasmine Zia, and Sean A Munson. 2015. More than telemonitoring: Health provider use and nonuse of life-log data in irritable bowel syndrome and weight management. *Journal of medical Internet research* 17, 8 (2015), e203. DOI: http://dx.doi.org/10.2196/jmir.4364

12. Lilian de Greef, Mayank Goel, Min Joon Seo, Eric C Larson, James W. Stout, James A Taylor, and Shwetak N Patel. 2014. Bilicam: Using Mobile Phones to Monitor Newborn Jaundice. In *Proceedings of the 2014 ACM International Joint Conference on Pervasive and Ubiquitous Computing - UbiComp '14 Adjunct*. 331–342. DOI: http://dx.doi.org/10.1145/2632048.2632076

13. Marco de Sá and Luís Carriço. 2008. Lessons from early stages design of mobile applications. In *Proceedings of the 10th international conference on Human computer interaction with mobile devices and services*. ACM, 127–136. DOI: http://dx.doi.org/10.1145/1409240.1409255

14. ActiGraph Devices. 2016a. (Sept. 2016). Retrieved August 22, 2014 from http://actigraphcorp.com.

15. Actiwatch Devices. 2016b. (Sept. 2016). Retrieved August 22, 2014 from http://www.usa.philips.com/.

16. Cathy A Eastwood, Lucille Travis, Tanya T Morgenstern, and Erin K Donaho. 2007. Weight and symptom diary for self-monitoring in heart failure clinic patients. *Journal of Cardiovascular Nursing* 22, 5 (2007), 382–389. DOI: http://dx.doi.org/10.1097/01.JCN.0000287027.49628.a7

17. Toshiya Ebata, H. Aizawa, R. Kamide, and M. Niimura. 1999. The characteristics of nocturnal scratching in adults with atopic dermatitis. *British Journal of Dermatology* 141, 1 (1999), 82–86. DOI: http://dx.doi.org/10.1046/j.1365-2133.1999.02924.x

18. Johanna Feuerstein, Daniel Austin, Robert Sack, and Tamara L. Hayes. 2011. Wrist actigraphy for scratch detection in the presence of confounding activities. In *Proceedings of the Annual International Conference of the IEEE Engineering in Medicine and Biology Society, EMBS*. 3652–3655. DOI: http://dx.doi.org/10.1109/IEMBS.2011.6090615

19. Rebat Halder. 2005. *Dermatology and dermatological therapy of pigmented skins*. CRC Press.

20. Sen H Hirano, Karen P Tang, Karen G Cheng, and Gillian R Hayes. 2012. The estrellita system: A health informatics tool to support caregivers of preterm infants. In *2012 6th International Conference on Pervasive Computing Technologies for Healthcare (PervasiveHealth) and Workshops*. IEEE, 195–196. DOI: http://dx.doi.org/10.4108/icst.pervasivehealth.2012.248718

21. K. L E Hon, M. C A Lam, T. F. Leung, W. Y C Kam, K. C K Lee, M. C A Li, T. F. Fok, and P. C. Ng. 2006. Nocturnal wrist movements are correlated with objective clinical scores and plasma chemokine levels in children with atopic dermatitis. *British Journal of Dermatology* 154, 4 (2006), 629–635. DOI: http://dx.doi.org/10.1111/j.1365-2133.2006.07213.x

22. JM Hopkin. 1997. Mechanisms of enhanced prevalence of asthma and atopy in developed countries. *Current opinion in immunology* 9, 6 (1997), 788–792. DOI: http://dx.doi.org/10.1016/S0952-7915(97)80179-3

23. Yoojung Kim, Sookyoung Ji, Hyunjeong Lee, Jeong-Whun Kim, Sooyoung Yoo, and Joongseek Lee. 2016. My Doctor is Keeping an Eye on Me!: Exploring the Clinical Applicability of a Mobile Food Logger. In *Proceedings of the 2016 CHI Conference on Human Factors in Computing Systems*. ACM, 5620–5631. DOI: http://dx.doi.org/10.1145/2858036.2858145

24. Ross M King and George V Wilson. 1991. Use of a diary technique to investigate psychosomatic relations in atopic dermatitis. *Journal of psychosomatic research* 35, 6 (1991), 697–706. DOI: http://dx.doi.org/10.1016/0022-3999(91)90120-D

25. Sotiris B. Kotsiantis. 2007. Supervised machine learning: A review of classification techniques. *Informatica* 31 (2007), 249–268. DOI: http://dx.doi.org/10.1115/1.1559160

26. Olivier Lartillot, Tuomas Eerola, Petri Toiviainen, and Jose Fornari. 2008. Multi-feature modeling of pulse clarity: design, validation, and optimization. In *The International Society of Music Information Retrieval - ISMIR 2008*. 521–526. http://ismir2008.ismir.net/papers/ISMIR2008

27. Shaun Lawson, Sue Jamison-Powell, Andrew Garbett, Conor Linehan, Erica Kucharczyk, Sanne Verbaan, Duncan A Rowland, and Kevin Morgan. 2013. Validating a mobile phone application for the everyday, unobtrusive, objective measurement of sleep. In *Proceedings of the SIGCHI Conference on Human Factors in Computing Systems*. ACM, 2497–2506. DOI: http://dx.doi.org/10.1145/2470654.2481345

28. Jongin Lee, Dae-ki Cho, Seokwoo Song, SeungHo Kim, Eunji Im, and John Kim. 2015. Mobile System Design for Scratch Recognition. In *Extended Abstracts of the ACM CHI'15 Conference on Human Factors in Computing Systems*, Vol. 2. 1567–1572. DOI: http://dx.doi.org/10.1145/2702613.2732820

29. Elina Mattila, Juha Pärkkä, Marion Hermersdorf, Jussi Kaasinen, Janne Vainio, Kai Samposalo, Juho Merilahti, Juha Kolari, Minna Kulju, Raimo Lappalainen, and others. 2008. Mobile diary for wellness management—results on usage and usability in two user studies. *IEEE Transactions on information technology in biomedicine* 12, 4 (2008), 501–512. DOI: http://dx.doi.org/10.1109/TITB.2007.908237

30. Andrew D Miller, Sonali R Mishra, Logan Kendall, Shefali Haldar, Ari H Pollack, and Wanda Pratt. 2016. Partners in care: design considerations for caregivers and patients during a hospital stay. In *Proceedings of the 19th ACM Conference on Computer-Supported Cooperative Work & Social Computing*. ACM, 756–769. DOI: http://dx.doi.org/10.1145/2818048.2819983

31. Dan Morris, T Scott Saponas, Andrew Guillory, and Ilya Kelner. 2014. RecoFit: using a wearable sensor to find, recognize, and count repetitive exercises. *Proceedings of the 32nd annual ACM conference on Human factors in computing systems - CHI '14* (2014), 3225–3234. DOI: http://dx.doi.org/10.1145/2556288.2557116

32. Johanna Petersen, Daniel Austin, Robert Sack, and Tamara L. Hayes. 2013. Actigraphy-based scratch detection using logistic regression. *IEEE Journal of Biomedical and Health Informatics* 17, 2 (2013), 277–283. DOI: http://dx.doi.org/10.1109/TITB.2012.2204761

33. Health Data Exploration Project. 2014. Personal Data for the Public Good: New Opportunities to Enrich Understanding of Individual and Population Health. In *Calit2, San Diego*. Calit2, San Diego. Retrieved Dec. 18, 2016 from http://www.rwjf.org/content/dam/farm/reports/reports/2014/rwjf411080.

34. Luís Rosado, Maria João M Vasconcelos, Fernando Correia, and Nuno Costa. 2015. A novel framework for supervised mobile assessment and risk triage of skin lesions. In *Proceedings of the 9th International Conference on Pervasive Computing Technologies for Healthcare*. 266–267. http://dl.acm.org/citation.cfm?id=2826165.2826213

35. PC Sanger, Andrea Hartzler, William B Lober, Heather L Evans, and Wanda Pratt. 2014. Design considerations for post-acute care mHealth: patient perspectives. In *Proceedings of AMIA Annual Symposium*. 1920–1929.

36. Walter B Shelley. 1981. Dermatitis artefacta induced in a patient by one of her multiple personalities. *British Journal of Dermatology* 105, 5 (1981), 587–589.

37. J-F Stalder, S Barbarot, A Wollenberg, EA Holm, L De Raeve, S Seidenari, Arnold Oranje, M Deleuran, F Cambazard, A Svensson, and others. 2011. Patient-Oriented SCORAD (PO-SCORAD): a new self-assessment scale in atopic dermatitis validated in Europe. *Allergy* 66, 8 (2011), 1114–1121. DOI: http://dx.doi.org/10.1111/j.1398-9995.2011.02577.x

38. Dennis L Stevens, Alan L Bisno, Henry F Chambers, E Dale Everett, Patchen Dellinger, Ellie JC Goldstein, Sherwood L Gorbach, Jan V Hirschmann, Edward L Kaplan, Jose G Montoya, and others. 2005. Practice guidelines for the diagnosis and management of skin and soft-tissue infections. *Clinical Infectious Diseases* 41, 10 (2005), 1373–1406. DOI: http://dx.doi.org/10.1086/497143

39. Erich P Stuntebeck, John S Davis Ii, Gregory D Abowd, and Marion Blount. 2008. HealthSense : Classification of Health-related Sensor Data through User-Assisted Machine Learning. *Hotmobile 2008* (2008), 1–5. DOI: http://dx.doi.org/10.1145/1411759.1411761

40. M. M. Tollefson and a. L. Bruckner. 2014. Atopic Dermatitis: Skin-Directed Management. *Pediatrics* 134, 6 (2014), e1735–e1744. DOI: http://dx.doi.org/10.1542/peds.2014-2812

41. P Warschburger, H Buchholz, and F Petermann. 2004. Psychological adjustment in parents of young children with atopic dermatitis: which factors predict parental quality of life? *British Journal of Dermatology* 150, 2 (2004), 304–311. DOI: http://dx.doi.org/10.1111/j.1365-2133.2004.05743.x

42. William Wu-Shyong Wei. 1994. *Time series analysis.* Addison-Wesley publ Reading.

43. Paul Wicks, Michael Massagli, Jeana Frost, Catherine Brownstein, Sally Okun, Timothy Vaughan, Richard Bradley, and James Heywood. 2010. Sharing health data for better outcomes on PatientsLikeMe. *Journal of medical Internet research* 12, 2 (2010), e19. DOI: http://dx.doi.org/10.2196/jmir.1549

44. Anja Wittkowski, Helen L Richards, Christopher EM Griffiths, and Chris J Main. 2004. The impact of psychological and clinical factors on quality of life in individuals with atopic dermatitis. *Journal of psychosomatic research* 57, 2 (2004), 195–200. DOI: http://dx.doi.org/10.1016/S0022-3999(03)00572-5

45. CI Wootton, K Koller, S Lawton, C O'Leary, and KS Thomas. 2012. Are accelerometers a useful tool for measuring disease activity in children with eczema? Validity, responsiveness to change, and acceptability of use in a clinical trial setting. *British Journal of Dermatology* 167, 5 (2012), 1131–1137. DOI: http://dx.doi.org/10.1111/j.1365-2133.2012.11184.x

46. Gil Yosipovitch and Alexandru DP Papoiu. 2008. What causes itch in atopic dermatitis? *Current allergy and asthma reports* 8, 4 (2008), 306–311. DOI: http://dx.doi.org/10.1007/s11882-008-0049-z

# Privacy, Security, and Surveillance in the Global South: A Study of Biometric Mobile SIM Registration in Bangladesh

**Syed Ishtiaque Ahmed[1], Md. Romael Hoque[2], Shion Guha[3], Md. Rashidujjaman Rifat[4], Nicola Dell[5]**
[1] Department of Information Science, Cornell University, Ithaca, NY, USA,
[2]Bangladesh University of Engineering and Technology (BUET), Dhaka, Bangladesh,
[3] Mathematics, Statistics and Computer Science, Marquette University, Milwaukee, WI, USA
[4]Department of Information Science, University of Colorado Boulder, CO, USA
[5]The Jacobs Institute, Cornell Tech, NY, USA
{sa738, nixdell}@cornell.edu, shion.guha@marquette.edu, rashidujjaman.rifat@colorado.edu

## ABSTRACT
With the rapid growth of ICT adoption in the Global South, crimes over and through digital technologies have also increased. Consequently, governments have begun to undertake a variety of different surveillance programs, which in turn provoke questions regarding citizens' privacy rights. However, both the concepts of privacy and of citizens' corresponding political rights have not been well-developed in HCI for non-Western contexts. This paper presents findings from a three-month long ethnography and online survey (n=606) conducted in Bangladesh, where the government recently imposed mandatory biometric registration for every mobile phone user. Our analysis surfaces important privacy and safety concerns regarding identity, ownership, and trust, and reveals the cultural and political challenges of imposing biometric registration program in Bangladesh. We also discuss how alternative designs of infrastructure, technology, and policy may better meet stakeholders' competing needs in the Global South.

### Author Keywords
Privacy; security; surveillance; HCI4D; ICTD; Bangladesh.

### ACM Classification Keywords
K.6.5 Security and Protection; H.1.2 User/Machine Systems

## INTRODUCTION
Information and Communication Technologies (ICTs) have often been considered a major vehicle for socioeconomic development in low-resource countries. Today, more than 4.6 billion people around the world have mobile phones, and 52.7% of them browse Internet with their phones [62]. Although mobile technologies have the potential to positively contribute to a range of different development initiatives in the Global South, crimes that make use of these technologies have also become a big concern for these countries. Cybercrimes, including hacking, identity theft, harassment, stalking, and revenge porn, are increasing day by day [35]. At the same time, mobile phones are used by terrorists and other criminal groups to communicate and organize crimes [49]. To combat these crimes, many countries, including Bangladesh, have created surveillance programs that monitor citizens' mobile phone usage [40]. In addition, Bangladesh is the second country in the world (after Pakistan) to deploy nationwide surveillance that relies on citizens' biometric identities: their fingerprints. The collection, storage, and usage of this biometric data has resulted a new set of privacy, security, and safety concerns that are not yet well understood.

The Bangladeshi government initiated this surveillance program in the context of a sudden rise of hate crimes coupled with an alarming rate of terrorism inside and outside the country. The trials of several political leaders for war crimes had created a nation-wide debate [11,57], and caused various political and religious tensions. In addition, militant groups, inter alia, ISIS, JMB, and Ansarullah Bangla announced their violent missions that threatened law and order in the country [8]. Since 2013, extremist groups have killed more than ten progressive writers, bloggers, and publishers in the country [56]. These murders were further punctuated by several violent attacks on religious minorities. When investigating these attacks, the government found that many extremist groups were spreading anti-government news and propaganda, and communicating using the Internet and mobile phones. In August 2013, the government passed an ICT law that enabled them to arrest individuals based on their online activities, which many people considered to be a threat to citizens' freedom of speech [60], and which has since been used to arrest several political activists. In addition to terrorism, other kinds of crimes including political killings, gender violence, corruption, and robbery have also been increasing substantially throughout the country.

Against this backdrop, at a press conference in September 2015, the State Minister of Post and Telecommunication in Bangladesh said, *"We have found that mobile connections*


*CHI 2017, May 06 - 11, 2017, Denver, CO, USA*

ACM 978-1-4503-4655-9/17/05…$15.00
DOI: http://dx.doi.org/10.1145/3025453.3025961

*are the source of all criminal activities like militancy and abduction"* [29]. According to the government, in August 2015 more than 130 million of Bangladesh's 160 million people had mobile phone SIM cards, and the Minister announced the launch of a mandatory, nationwide biometric mobile SIM registration program. In 2008, the election commission in Bangladesh created a database of citizens' fingerprints as a part of a project to issue a National ID to every citizen. The new biometric registration program stipulated that mobile phone operators were required to collect the fingerprints of every customer who owned a mobile SIM that connected to their network. This fingerprint data is then sent to the existing database for verification, after which the customer's registration is considered validated. The biometric SIM registration program formally began in December, 2015 [61].

The Minister later explained the objective of biometric SIM registration, "*The biometric verification of the mobile phone SIM has created an opportunity to verify the real owner of the mobile SIM with the information of his own National Identity (NID) and the system would help law enforcement to unearth the real crime perpetrators*" [69]. This statement suggests that the biometric data will enable law enforcement to track down individuals based on their use of mobile phones. However, almost immediately after the launch of the program, it became clear that people were confused and suspicious of the registration process, and protests began to take place across the country. Citizen groups also voiced concerns surrounding the impact that the program had on people's privacy rights [53]. In March 2016, the High Court challenged the legality of biometric SIM registration [63] and, in response, the mobile operators explained that although they were extracting data from people's fingerprints, they were not actually storing the fingerprints themselves. Following this legal challenge, the High Court cleared the way for mobile operators to continue biometric registration of SIM cards [64]. The registration process was scheduled to be completed by April 30, 2016, after which all unregistered SIMs would become non-functional. However, this deadline was subsequently extended for one month since, on the day of the deadline, the majority of SIM cards were still not registered [65].

The main contribution of this paper is to describe findings from a three-month long ethnographic study and online survey that show the tensions, complexities, and challenges surrounding the biometric SIM registration program in Bangladesh. Our findings highlight important nuances in people's conceptual understanding of ownership and identity that further the situated understanding of privacy in Bangladesh. We also show the infrastructural, social, and cultural challenges that impact biometric-based surveillance of mobile phone usage and reveal the political implications of such surveillance for the Bangladeshi people. Taken together, our findings yield valuable new insights that further existing knowledge of digital privacy, safety, and surveillance in the Global South.

## RELATED WORK

### Privacy, Ownership, and Culture

With the proliferation of computing technologies around the globe, people in all countries are increasingly exposed to risks associated with digital privacy. There have been numerous efforts to understand and mitigate these risks, including password construction and use [14], inferring preferences from social network behavior [24], supporting privacy through design [39], and understanding privacy on mobile devices [48]. However, the majority of these studies focus on the Western world and are based on Western ideas of privacy. In an effort to incorporate other contexts, Nissenbaum [44] argues that notions of privacy change with place, people, culture, and context. Her argument explains why findings of studies done in the West cannot necessarily be extended to non-Western contexts and points out a lack of HCI scholarship investigating privacy outside the West.

Recently, a small amount of HCI research has started looking at privacy in the Global South. Abokhodair et al. [1,2] reported that privacy in the Middle East is dominated by religious practices around intimacy and freedom of speech. Kumaraguru et al. described notions of privacy among Indian populations using communication media [38]. Ahmed et al. reported on notions of privacy in mobile repair markets in Bangladesh [4]. Our work builds on this nascent literature by examining concepts of ownership and identity, two of the core components of privacy [54].

Existing notions of identity and ownership are based primarily on an individualistic Western value system that often conflicts with the values of many collectivist societies in the Global South [26]. Several studies have demonstrated how technologies that are considered to be 'personal' in the West have shared and intermediated usage models in collectivist societies that challenge Western notions of 'personal computing' [13,22,37,46,50]. In addition, the prevalence of informal second-hand markets further complicates the one-to-one relationship between a user and a device [4,6,30,31]. Thus the concepts of identity and ownership often take on a different meaning in the Global South. Our paper contributes to this literature by developing a nuanced understanding of identity and ownership in Bangladesh, and their impact on digital privacy and safety.

### Surveillance, Voice, and Democracy

Lyon [41,59] defines surveillance as a "*focused, systematic and routine attention to personal details for purposes of influence, management, protection or direction*". Our focus in this paper is on government-imposed mass surveillance. In recent years, these kind of surveillance programs have focused primarily on monitoring communication media to track suspicious activities. China, Russia, Germany, Australia, the United Kingdom, the United States, India, and many other countries have dedicated projects for eavesdropping on their citizens' Internet traffic and mobile communication [70]. To be effective, many of these programs need to collect and monitor citizens' private information. Biometric identifiers are one of the most effective ways to uniquely identify a person. For example, fingerprints and retina have been used to track individuals crossing national borders or to register people for citizenship [9]. At least 25 countries in sub-Saharan Africa and South Asia have already held elections that use biometric voter IDs [18]. However, biometric surveillance of mobile phone usage is fairly new. Only Pakistan, Bangladesh, Nigeria, UAE, and a few other countries have recently launched these programs, and there has thus far been little work that seeks to understand their impact.

Regardless of how important surveillance is for national security, from the citizens' point of view these programs can be interpreted as being authoritarian or exploitative [20,23,51,58]. In addition, surveillance programs can be used to diminish political voice [23]. A person develops a political opinion through their social values, observations, readings, discussions, and debates. Surveillance can curtail the freedom with which people are able to share their ideas and opinions and reduce the diversity of public opinion and competing voices [20]. Thus, privacy is considered important in most democratic theories [12,25,42], suggesting that democratic governments need to draw and maintain a line between what data should or should not be collected. In many Western countries, constitutions have also been established that protect certain privacy rights [15]. Similarly, different citizen groups monitor and criticize government surveillance programs [45]. However, many countries in the Global South are struggling to maintain a stable democracy and are embarking on mass surveillance programs with little external oversight.

*Aadhar*, India's biometric identification project, is one of the most studied biometric identification schemes in the Global South. From the inception of this project, it received harsh criticism from activists who pointed out the potential risks regarding security, privacy, and corruption [21,34,43,47]. Johri et al. reported how Aadhar's narrow focus on data forcefully aligned technology and people and ignored many important broader aspects of identity by "viewing citizens as numbers" [33]. Jacobson reported that the Indian government is more interested in controlling citizens than ensuring their security [32]. Despite these concerns, Aadhar's data has not (yet) been used by the Indian government to track citizens' communications. Our study on the biometric mobile phone registration program in Bangladesh contributes to the growing amount of research that focuses on biometric data and further adds important elements of privacy and security in the context of the Global South.

## METHODS

We conducted a three-month ethnographic study in Dhaka, Bangladesh to study the biometric mobile registration program. The first author was born and raised in Dhaka and is a fluent speaker of Bengali. From March to June 2016, he visited 30 biometric registration points in a variety of Dhaka neighborhoods. Although the neighborhoods were chosen based in part on convenience and the ethnographer's familiarity with the area, we ensured that we covered a wide variety of registration points, including formal service centers, local shops, and temporary booths, that serviced a diverse range of people. At each of the registration points, the researcher conducted two hours of observation, resulting in a total of 60 hours of observational data. The researcher also conducted semi-structured interviews with people in charge of the registration points and in situ interviews with customers who were willing to participate in the study. In total, we performed 30 interviews with registration operators and 34 interviews with customers. All interviews were voluntary, roughly 15 minutes long, and audio recorded. Observational data was recorded in the researcher's notebook. We also took over 200 photos during our observations.

The first and second authors (both of whom are Bangladeshi) also visited the homes of 30 families in Dhaka and conducted semi-structured interviews with 52 participants at these homes. We used snowball sampling, starting with a set of families that we knew, and expanding based on suggestions for participants, stopping when we reached theoretical saturation. We tried to visit families from different socioeconomic classes to achieve diverse viewpoints. Ten families were selected from each of low, middle, and high income ranges (low-income is <10,000 Taka/month, middle-income is 10,000-20,000 Taka/month, and high-income is >20,000 Taka/month)[1]. Each of the home visits lasted approximately one hour and discussed the participants' backgrounds, mobile phone use, their experience with the biometric registration process (if any), and their thoughts on the program. Finally, we also posted flyers at three local universities and invited interested students to participant in interviews. A total of 30 students (15 males, 15 females) were recruited through this process. All interviews were voluntary, 10 to 15 minutes long, audio-recorded, and they were conducted in Bengali. All interview data was later translated into English, and transcribed by two different coders, both of whom have bilingual expertise in Bengali and English.

In addition to our ethnographic and interview data, we also conducted an anonymous online survey. The survey was in Bengali and asked questions regarding participants' demographic information, biometric registration, and their opinions about the registration program. Although most of the questions were structured checkboxes or multiple-choice questions, the survey also included an optional open-ended textbox where participants could freely express their opinions, concerns, or suggestions about the biometric SIM registration. The survey was publicized through two public posts on the ethnographer's Facebook page between March

[1] 80 Bangladeshi taka is roughly equivalent to 1.00 USD.

1st and 10th 2016. The survey was left open until April 30, 2016. A total of 606 participants completed the survey.

In total, our ethnography produced 60 hours of observational data and over 150 hours of interview data. The data was separately translated to English by two native Bengali speaking researchers and cross-checked for validation. The translated data was then coded by the team following the Grounded Theory method [16], and labeled with emerging themes. The survey data was processed similarly but separately from the ethnography data.

## THE BIOMETRIC REGISTRATION PROCESS

The biometric SIM registration process took place in three main settings: a) formal service centers, b) informal shops, and c) temporary registration booths. We discuss each of these contexts before describing the registration process.

### Formal Service Centers

The formal service centers were usually located in shopping malls and were owned and operators by large mobile phone companies. The primary goal of the centers was to provide customer service and assistance to people who were experiencing issues or having trouble with their mobile phone service. Since SIM card registration was not their main function, we found that staff at the service centers would only help people to register their SIM cards if the SIM cards were from the network of that operator.

All of the staff at the service center were highly educated (possessing at least a college degree) and well-trained on the registration process. They were also experienced with technology and capable of using computers, laptops, and tablets. They were dressed in uniforms and communicated with customers in accordance with established rules laid out by their employers. These staff reported that the majority of the customers they served were from middle or upper class communities, with one telling us:

*"Everybody knows that these places are for gentlemen. Also, people who come here ... they don't want to take risk by going to a roadside shop and doing their registration in a sloppy fashion. They want confirmation from a reliable authority." – (Formal Service Provider, male, 32 years)*

The customers at the service centers shared similar views, with one saying, *"Here you don't have to encounter foul people. Also, I don't want to risk my registration, my business is relying on this."* (Businessman, male, 45 years)

### Informal Shops

In contrast to the formal service centers, the informal shops were typically local, road-side shops that were frequented by a diverse range of people from a variety of backgrounds. These shops, which included grocery stores, laundromats, hair dressers, pharmacies, and CD/DVD shops, offered SIM card registration service in addition to their usual business. Nine out of the ten shopkeepers that we interviewed had low levels of education, with four completing elementary school and five not finishing elementary school. Only one

**Figure 1. A grocery shopkeeper is helping a customer with biometric SIM registration.**

shopkeeper was currently studying at a local university for an undergraduate degree in accounting. None of the shopkeepers were familiar with computers or the Internet. However, they all used mobile phones for sending money.

The shops were chosen to be biometric registration points by agents who worked for the mobile phone operators, often based on their existing relationship with the agents or following a previous contract with the operators for mobile-money transfers. The shopkeepers were given the equipment necessary to do the registration and received one day of training at the operator's office. Since the device used to do the registration was different for each operator, a shopkeeper could only register customers for the specific operators that had trained them. The shopkeepers would often post flyers that indicated the operators that they were authorized to serve. For each registration, the shopkeepers would receive 1.80 Taka (approx. 0.01 USD) before tax.

### Temporary Registration Booths

Temporary registration booths took a variety of different forms. Some of these booths consisted simply of a colorful umbrella on the side of the road under which a person would sit with a chair and table offering a registration service. Frequently, these booths would be located in a public place, like a road-crossing or the corner of a market. The mobile phone operators employed temporary staff to provide the registration service at these booths, with the length of the employment contract ranging from two to six months. All the staff employed had a minimum of high school education and were trained on registration process by the operators. These temporary booths aimed to serve customers from a variety of socioeconomic backgrounds. The booths would open as early as 7am and stay open until 10pm, with the staff taking only short breaks for meals.

### Completing the Registration Process

Completing the registration process would typically take about 10 minutes. Although different mobile phone operators used different equipment for the registration, they were all tablet-based systems. Some operators provided a separate fingerprint reading device that needed to be connected by wires to the tablet, while others augmented the tablet with fingerprint reading capabilities. Figure 1 shows how a customer providing his fingerprints on a tablet device for biometric SIM registration at an informal grocery shop in Dhaka.

To begin the registration process, the customer had to provide their mobile phone number and national ID document. The registration person would then give the customer a paper form to fill out that required them to provide their name, age, gender, date of birth, etc. The customer filled out the form and gave it to the registration person, who then entered relevant information into an app running on the tablet and set up the fingerprint equipment. Next, the customer had to provide fingerprints of their thumb and index finger of each hand. The device provided a notification that indicated when each fingerprint was successfully captured, prompting the customer to move on to the next fingerprint. After the fingerprints had been captured, the device would send, via text message, a unique passcode to the customer's phone. The customer then needed to enter the passcode into the system (or the registration person would help them to enter the passcode). If the passcode was correct, the registration was complete and the customer would receive confirmation that they had completed the registration process. However, after completing the registration process, the customer had to wait up to two days to know whether the registration was actually successful. During this time, the customer's data was transmitted to a central database and analyzed. The customer would then receive a text message that informed them if the registration was successful.

Although the cost of registration process was borne by the mobile phone operators and was supposed to be free for customers, during the last week of mandatory SIM registration, we found 5 informal and temporary registration centers who were illegally charging customers 20 Taka (0.25 USD) to complete the registration process.

## TENSIONS SURROUNDING BIOMETRIC REGISTRATION

This section discusses several major themes, challenges, and complexities associated with the biometric registration process that emerged during our analysis of our data.

### Ownership

Our findings reveal that the concept of ownership of the mobile phone and the SIM card was complex and not well-aligned with the 'one SIM card, one owner' model that the registration process assumed. In addition, there were many occasions where tensions surrounding ownership resulted in additional challenges for both customers and registration booth staff. For example, the separate identity of the phone and the SIM card was not clear to many customers. Seven of the people that we talked to at the registration booths said that they had come to register their "mobile phone", which they had bought somewhere else. However, it turned out that their SIM card was already registered to another person that the customer usually did not know. One told us:

*"I bought this phone 2 months ago ... in exchange for my own money, my hard-earned money. You can ask my fellow rickshaw drivers in the garage about this. They all know I bought this. Now, this registration guy is saying that this is not my phone. Why? Because I am poor?"* (Rickshaw driver, male, 40 years).

Another of our interview participants, who worked as a domestic helper, explained how she would always buy phones from other people or from the second-hand mobile phone market. She knew about the difference between the body of the mobile phone and the SIM card, but said that her husband and son did not understand this difference. She had to explain the difference to them before they went for the biometric registration. Moreover, since the SIM card in her mobile phone was not originally registered in her name, she had to buy a new SIM card, which cost her 50 Taka (approx. 0.7 USD). She said, *"I find this a new kind of business by the phone company. All they want is to drink our blood"* (Domestic helper, female, 45 years). It quickly became clear to us that the majority of mobile phone users in Bangladesh depend on the second-hand mobile phone market, where they not only trade their old phone, but also their SIM cards. As a result, associating one's identity with a SIM card is challenging. One of our participants asked us, *"What will happen when I will sell this phone to someone else, and buy a new phone?"* (Night Guard, male, 35 years)

Further tension concerning ownership arose due to the hierarchical power structure of the society, and our findings showed that in many communities the ownership of mobile phones (and SIMs) is determined by power relationships. For example, we encountered nine cases, where the senior male person of a family came to register all the SIMs for his family members in his name. One of these participants said:

*"I am the person who earns money and buys things for my family. I am responsible for anything that happens with these phones. So, who else do you think will register the SIMs?"* – (Service holder, male, 52 years).

There were six adult members in his family including his wife, three sons, and daughter. Each of them used a separate mobile phone. His elder son even paid for his phone from his own salary. However, all of the phones were 'owned' and registered in the father's name since, as he said, *"As long as they are staying in my family, I am responsible for everything they do."*

Our visits to other local families revealed many similar stories regardless of the socioeconomic status of the families. For example, we encountered five low-income families in which the women did not own their SIM cards and their husbands were in charge of registration. In three other middle-income families, the women identified the registration as the *"men's task"*, while in two more the women did not know who owned the SIM cards. In four high-income families, the women did not own their SIM cards. In total, we found only one family in which the wife had done her own registration by herself. One senior male member of a middle income family told us:

*"When you are a grown up man and you have a family, you need to know what your responsibilities are. Whenever you buy something, that may cause legal trouble at some point, and you may need to run here and there. It is always safe that men take that responsibility"*- (Pharmacist, male, 68).

Beyond families, we also encountered issues of ownership in informal business settings. For example, one customer that we spoke to at a registration booth had brought about 70 mobile phones with him, wanting to register all the phones in his name. However, the national rules say that each person can only register a maximum of 20 SIM cards. This scenario resulted in a big discussion between the customer and the registration person. The customer described himself as the owner of a rickshaw garage who had bought the mobile phones for the rickshaw drivers that worked under him. He argued that the registration needed to be in his name because he was the one who had paid for the phones. He further said that he often discharged his workers and needed to keep the phones for the new workers. The registration person argued that the situation could only be handled under "corporate registration" of the garage, which the customer did not have since the garage was his informal family business. Finally, they decided that the customer would bring his wife, brother, and son to the booth the next day and have them register 20 SIM cards each. Similar issues of ownership arose in several other cases, including owners of other informal businesses, leaders of religious institutions, or leaders of local sports teams that wanted to register SIM cards for the people working under them. In general, the power hierarchy associated with these informal organizations was not well aligned with the concept of 'ownership' that the registration process assumed.

### Identity and Identification

Another major set of challenges that were revealed by our analysis concerned the concept of identity and the process of identification. For example, the registration system required that the owner of a SIM card identify themselves with a valid ID, which could be their national ID card or passport. However, in several cases we found that people came to the registration booth with the ID of another person, and the registration person had to explain them that they should bring their own ID. One such customer told us:

*"I do not remember if I ever had an ID. Some people came to our village before the election and gave us some cards. That happened several years ago. Now I have moved to Dhaka and I do not know where those are."* – (Rickshaw Driver, male, 25 years)

Since he did not have his own ID, he brought the ID of his aunt who lived nearby, arguing, *"This is a genuine ID. Why doesn't he use this for registration? I took my aunt's permission. She considers me as her son. What is the problem?"* In addition to this participant, we found 15 other people at different booths who did not have their own IDs. Unable to register these customers, the registration person suggested that they go and talk to their Ward Commissioners[2] to obtain new IDs. However, several people reported that they had already talked to their Ward Commissioners but had failed to get new ID cards since they were not originally registered in their current Wards. Instead, they were told to travel to their villages to collect their new IDs, which they were unable to do at that time of the year. Five people said that they had never received an ID card. All of these stories highlight the challenges associated with requiring that people possess valid ID cards before they are able to register their SIM cards.

A serious challenge associated with the identification and registration process arose when several customers did not have clear lines on their fingerprints. We observed four cases where, even though the registration agents were forcefully pressing the thumbs of the customers against the machine's surface, no fingerprint lines were being captured. At one point, the agent had to apologize to the customers. When we checked the fingers of the customers in question, we found that the lines were not very clearly visible on their fingers. All four of the people that this happened to were day laborers. One explained that he did not have lines on his fingers because he regularly used hard hammers to break bricks. Another said that he burnt his hand working with hot oil. We also found one participant who had lost his thumb in an accident, and the lack of a thumb made it impossible for him to complete the registration.

Finally, we encountered a number of issues associated with identity and gender. For example, many women were concerned that the registration process would allow them to be identified as women. In one of these cases, a woman showed us her earlier registration papers, that had a man's name written on the form that did not match her name on her ID card. She argued that she had preferred to use a male name to avoid being harassed over the phone. She asked, *"Why do I have to tell them if I am a man or a woman? So that they can arrange harassments for me?"* - (University student, female, 23 years). In another case, one woman came with her husband's ID and refused to show her own ID for the SIM registration, saying, *"I do not trust these people with my information."* - (House wife, female, 30 years). Many more of our interview participants reported that the registration booths were operated by male staff members who would need to touch the customers' hands to take their fingerprints. However, the women did not like to be touched by an unknown male person, which prevented many female participants from doing the registration.

---

[2] Commissioners are elected public representatives in Wards, the smallest administrative units in Bangladeshi cities.

### Exploitation

Many of our participants were concerned that the biometric registration system would be used to facilitate exploitation of people by the Government and mobile phone operators. For example, several participants expressed that the justification for the biometric registration process – to enable the Government to track criminal behavior – was a farce. One participant described:

*"Do you think police do not know who the criminals are in a neighborhood? Of course, they know! Everybody knows. Even the children of the neighborhood know. But they will never arrest the criminals, because they take bribes from them. And now they have made this excuse of identifying the criminals for taking our fingerprints?!"*- (Retired Banker, male, 68 years).

The concern that the system would be used to exploit people was reinforced when many participants were forced to purchase new SIM cards because the SIM cards that they had bought on the second-hand market turned out to already be registered to other people. Moreover, although it was illegal, we found several registration people who were charging customers extra money to perform the registration. When we asked the customers why they paid this extra money, all of them replied that they did it because they felt that they had no other option.

The decision by the informal registration staff to risk punishment by charging extra money for the registration process [68] stemmed in part from the fact that the staff also felt exploited by the system. In particular, the staff felt that the amount of money that they earned from registering people was not sufficient to justify the amount of work that they were doing. The minimum commission that the staff were paid was 1.80 Taka excluding tax (approx. 0.016 USD) for each biometric SIM registration. Since each SIM registration took them approximately 15 minutes, if they worked solidly for 8 hours in a day, they would only be able to register about 33 SIMs for which they would earn a total of about 66 Taka (approx. 0.8 USD), which they claimed was exploitative. In response to these concerns, Bangladesh Tele Recharge and Mobile Banking Business Association held a press conference in April 2016 to present their case for increasing the commission paid for each biometric registration. They stated that they were strictly opposed to the minimum commission paid by mobile phone operators for biometric SIM registration.

### Security, Safety, and Resistance

Our analysis also revealed a wide variety of concerns and issues surrounding the safety and security of the biometric SIM registration process. For example, the security of the biometric data relied heavily on the integrity and honesty of the registration staff. However, the registration staff in the informal shops were chosen based on their relationship with the mobile phone operators, which resulted in a potential threat to the system. Although the software that they were using for data entry was not necessarily compromised, a dishonest registration person could run separate software in the background to surreptitiously capture the fingerprint data that could then be used to register duplicate SIM cards in a customer's name without informing them. Although not part of our study, such an incident was reported in June 2016 in Mymensingh, a large city in Bangladesh. A registration person was arrested with two thousand illegal duplicate sims [66]. Similarly, in May 2015 the police arrested two people who had been collecting duplicate copies of other people's SIM cards from retailers, saying that they had lost their original ones [67]. In reality, they had been collecting mobile money sent to those numbers.

In addition to the potential threat posed by the registration staff, many of our participants expressed confusion and suspicion regarding the registration process, and our conversations with participants revealed that this lack of trust was in part due to a scarcity of information that explained the process. Many participants were concerned about where their fingerprint data would be stored and how it might be used in the future. One participant said:

*"Once the Government said that the fingerprints would not be saved anywhere. Now they are saying that they will fine the mobile phone operators if they leak the fingerprints. This means, our fingerprints are being saved somewhere by the mobile phone operators. This is very unfortunate."* - (Businessman, male, 42)

Another participant was concerned about the technical knowledge of the Government saying:

*"I don't think our Government is aware of the technical flaws that may occur. I even don't think that any system is safe to keep those biometric data. Government is overconfident, but they don't even know any of the technical aspects of biometric data collection and its safety. It's undoubtedly a violation of human rights."* – (Service holder, female, 38 years)

These suspicions were accompanied by people's fear that their stolen fingerprints could be used to harm them. One participant said, *"If you have somebody's fingerprints, you can basically make papers to grab all their properties."* – (Night Guard, male, 40 years). However, other participants were less concerned about this, with one describing:

*"I know that it is possible to snatch away one's properties with their fingerprints, but I am not afraid. Because, I am a poor man and I do not have anything to lose. The rich people should be bothered about this."* – (Rickshaw Driver, male, 35 years).

In addition to theft of property, several participants raised concerns regarding their responsibility for whatever their phone might be used for. One housewife explained,

*"My husband uses my phone all the time. If he does something wrong, or talks to a criminal over my phone, why should I be responsible for that?"* - (Housewife, 55 years).

A local rickshaw garage owner expressed a similar fear concerning the phones that he provided to his drivers,

*"Look, I give my phones to the rickshaw drivers so that they can communicate with me while they are out to work. How do I know why else they are using those phones? Now, if police arrest me for that, is this a justice?"* – (Rickshaw Garage owner, male, 40 years)

A total of seven participants reported that they did not feel comfortable sharing their personal data with the government, and felt pressured to do so, with one saying,

"*I feel pressurized to share my personal information, because if I don't give away my biometric data, I have to stop using mobile phones.*" (Student, male, 22 years)

Another participant called the program a breach of privacy saying, "*Why do I have to tell them everything anyway? Then where is my privacy?*" (Housewife, female, 40 years)

In general, the security concerns, suspicions, and fears associated with the process often led people to resist the requirement to participate in the biometric registration system. Ten of our participants said that they would not register their SIM, believing that the project would finally fail. Eleven participants said they would wait until the end of the deadline to see what happened to other people who did not register. They all believed that it would be impossible for the Government to register all mobile phone users in Bangladesh, and hoped that the project would fail so that they would not have to register their information.

## FINDINGS FROM THE ONLINE SURVEY

Our online survey was designed specifically to further the understanding of our ethnographic findings. Our anonymous online survey asked participants about their demographic data and whether they supported the biometric SIM registration [71]. In addition, we provided an optional, open-ended comment box that enabled participants to share their opinions. We received 606 survey responses, from which a number of themes arose.

First, the majority (77%) of our survey participants said that they did not like the biometric SIM registration system. Only 15% supported the program and 4% said that they did not care (the rest preferred not to comment). The survey asked participants why they were dissatisfied with the biometric registration, and three answers stood out. 62% participants said they were not happy with the biometric registration because they believed that they were going to lose their personal security through this process. 55% participants said that they did not like the fact that they were being forced to give away their fingerprints. 15% thought the system could probably improve national security, but they still did not like the process of registration. Out of our 606 survey responses, 172 participants chose to use the open-ended comment box to tell us their personal opinions regarding biometric registration. We summarize the main findings from these responses below.

### Support for the Biometric Registration System

A total of 36 people (20.9% of comments in the open-ended box) said that they supported the biometric registration program. They acknowledged the infrastructural challenges associated with implementing the program, but said that such systems were necessary to reduce crime. One participant wrote:

"*If you go to USA, you don't mind giving your fingerprints to the embassy, but here you don't want to give those to your own Government. This is hypocrisy.*" – (Businessman, male, 30 years).

Another participant said, "*The Government already has our fingerprints. We gave those to them when they made the voter registration cards. If they wanted to do any harm to us, they could do that by now.*" - (Student, female, 22 years).

Some people who supported the registration process not only defended the biometric registration system, but also attacked the people who were protesting the program. For example, one comment said,

"*Some people do not like the Government, and they will protest any Government initiative. To be honest, only the people who do illegal things will be concerned of such a surveillance system.*" – (Software engineer, male, 32 years).

### Concern about Government or Political Exploitation

Of the 172 comments that we received, 73 (42.4%) did not support the biometric registration system because they thought that the Government would exploit this system later for their own political interest. One participant connected biometric surveillance with the Section 57 of ICT Law that the Bangladesh Government had imposed a few years ago, to control people's online behavior. According to the rule, the Government has the power to punish a citizen for their online activities if they are deemed to be threatening to the Government, and the Government have arrested a number of political activists in last few years through that rule [27]. The participant wrote:

"*The Government just does not want us to criticize them. The ICT law suppressed our voice online, and now this biometric surveillance will suppress our voice even over day-to-day communication. We are slowly moving to a police state.*" – (University professor, male, 54).

Many other participants also expressed fear that the system could be used for political exploitation. Some participants believed that the Government would be able to listen to their conversations and track who they talked to, saying:

*"Now you have to be careful whenever you talk to somebody through your mobile phone. Because if the (Government) don't like him, you are going to jail."* – (University student, male, 23 years).

Another participant pointed out that even if the current Government did not exploit the system, future Governments would still be able to do so:

*"Even if this Government is so good that they are not going to exploit this information, how do you know the next Government will not do that? This system is going to exist forever. The Government has just given birth to a monster."* – (University professor, male, 42 years)

### Exploitation by the Mobile Phone Operators

Of the 172 comments that we received, 28 (16.3%) said that they did not like the biometric registration process because the mobile phone operators would be able to obtain and keep their fingerprint data. One participant wrote,

*"What is the point of giving our fingerprints to some commercial company? So that they can make a business out of those?"*- (Housewife, female, 31 years).

Other participants mentioned how their fingerprints could be potentially be exploited for profit-making purposes and described how companies would be able to exercise power over them by having their fingerprint data. Eight participants were further concerned because five out of six mobile phone operators in Bangladesh were actually foreign companies, with one participant commenting,

*"This means we are basically selling our fingerprints to other nations. No sane person can support this."* (Software engineer, male, 30 years)

### Concerns about Privacy Rights

Finally, 41 out of our 172 comments (23.8%) did not like the biometric registration system because they thought that it was violating their right to privacy. Participants in this group described how they viewed their fingerprints as their personal property, that the Government had no right to force them to give that away. Several participants expressed grief, frustration, and fear regarding this issue. One participant wrote, *"This is my fingerprint, and I do not want to give this to anyone. This is my right"* (College student, female, 20 years). Another participant said, *"I am just not comfortable sharing my personal information with some people I do not know. I don't want to hear whether they are good or bad, I just don't like this."* -(Businessman, male, 54 years). Several participants also did not like the fact that they were being forced to participate in the process. One of them said, *"I just don't like to be forced. Is this why we live in an independent country?"* - (Banker, male, 38 years).

## DISCUSSION

The sections above present a qualitative analysis of our ethnographic findings and key observations from our online survey. In addition to developing a rich, field-level understanding regarding the implementation of the biometric SIM registration program in Bangladesh, our ethnography has demonstrated how the local and situated values and practices around ownership, identity, exploitation, and security and safety concerns challenged the biometric registration program. Furthermore, our online survey revealed substantial dissatisfaction with the biometric SIM registration process. Our participants expressed their fear of political exploitation, commercial use, and invasion into their privacy. These findings help us conceptualize some of the core challenges associated with imposing a biometric surveillance in Bangladesh.

However, before synthesizing our findings into a set of key takeaways, we want to acknowledge that there are a number of limitations to our study. The biometric SIM registration program is a nation-wide campaign in Bangladesh, and our research only reveals a subset of the challenges encountered in part of the capital city, Dhaka. The registration points and the families that were studied were chosen based on convenience and participant availability. Hence, the findings of our study should not be generalized over the entire country. Instead, our study relies on the strength of ethnography that, instead of capturing a general picture, reveals rich nuances and a deep understanding of situated practices. In addition, the participants in our online survey represent only a small portion of the Bangladeshi population, and those that have Internet access. As such, the survey should be viewed as collecting data to validate findings from our ethnography and to accumulate a diverse set of opinions. Combining two different kinds of data (ethnography and an online survey) was also a methodological challenge that we confronted in this study. However, we decided that both kinds of data were important in explicating the nuances associated with the biometric registration program. Despite these limitations, our research offers several key insights and takeaways that will be beneficial for the HCI community at large.

First, the core idea of biometric SIM registration was based on an assumption of individual ownership and personal use of mobile phones, which conflicted with local practices in several ways. Our ethnography revealed how mobile SIM cards frequently changed owners over time without any formal records, how the ownership of a phone in a family or a group was dominated by power relationships rather than use, and how a single device was shared among multiple people in a variety of settings. Those practices not only complicated the process of biometric SIM registration, but also challenged its main objective: that the person who 'owns' a SIM is responsible for its use. Furthermore, the mismatch between the assumptions of the registration system and local practices also created fear among the people who were being forced to register their SIM cards. Our findings suggest that a more successful registration model might focus more on actual use of the SIM card rather than relying on ownership of a SIM.

Second, the success of creating and implementing a surveillance system like Bangladesh's biometric registration program largely depends on having a functioning and robust infrastructure that is difficult to guarantee in a developing country. As we have seen in our ethnography, the informal registration points were vulnerable to data leaking, corruption, and exploitation. There were gender and economic concerns that affected the success of the registration system. In light of these concerns, we observe that securely collecting, transmitting, and storing large amounts of sensitive biometric data requires infrastructural strength that may quickly become a burden for a Government in a low-resource country. The complications that arose during the implementation of the biometric registration system suggest that biometric surveillance is resource-hungry, and without having proper infrastructural support, launching such a program should not be recommended.

Third, the success of a surveillance program may be heavily dependent on the extent to which people trust the entity responsible for the surveillance. Our ethnography and online survey both demonstrate that many people were suspicious of the motives of the Government and mobile phone operators. Although people's political beliefs undoubtedly shape part of this suspicion, it is undeniable that such a surveillance tool provides the Government with substantial power that could be used to exploit people. Many developing countries suffer from poor governance, and such surveillance tools have the potential to make the situation worse. We suggest that any action based on surveillance be made transparent to the country's citizens, so that the government cannot lie or misuse people's data. This would require that every access to the biometric database be publicly logged and justified. At the same time, an autonomous and unbiased civil society needs to be developed that will monitor and sanction access to the biometric database.

Beyond these implementation-level challenges, there are also several broader lessons from this study that are important to HCI scholarship in the "developing world". The growing enthusiasm for ICT-based "development" programs around the globe often ignores the potential negative consequences of introducing ICTs in low-resource settings. However, the prevalence of ICT-based crimes has already been a big concern for many countries, including Bangladesh, and these countries are now taking steps launch costly monitoring and surveillance systems that, due to technical, cultural, and infrastructural challenges, are likely to fail. Although we are not advocating that ICT-based solutions in these countries be discouraged, we do highlight the need for carefully considered policies, laws, and robust security infrastructure before embarking on large-scale, public ICT initiatives. Although recent HCI scholarship has critically analyzed ICT-based development programs through the lenses of postcolonial computing [28], residuality [7,52], and sustainability [17], we suggest that HCI and ICTD scholars consider the issues of infrastructural breakdown, and potentially negative consequences as important aspects for evaluating technology in development contexts. At the same time, our study highlights a need for innovations in low-cost technologies to fight ICT-based crimes in the Global South.

Another key issue that our work raises is the need for notions of privacy that better fit the contexts, values, and local practices that are prevalent in the Global South. Our data shows that the situated idea of privacy among participants often made them resist the biometric registration program. However, the origin, nature, and characteristics of privacy in the Bangladeshi context has not been studied enough to explicate this resistance. The challenges in aligning the Western notion of privacy with notions of shared use, complex ownership, and communal identity, as reported in this paper, demonstrate the dearth of knowledge in this area. With the rapid adoption of technologies worldwide, people of different cultures are exposed to technologies that are embedded with Western privacy values [19] and this issue is becoming increasingly important. Our study reveals tensions between the shared use of mobile phones and individual privacy, and between ownership and gender – both of which are culturally constructed but technology mediated. Several studies on technology and gender in the Global South have shown how the relationship between technology and women is affected by the male-dominated cultural norms [3,5,36]. However, we know little about their impact on the notion of privacy and implications for biometric identification. Hence, the gender, power, and economic dynamics that we reveal in this paper open a new space in which HCI designers can create mechanisms that preserve privacy in contexts outside the West.

Finally, our analysis reveals a tension between notions of voice and surveillance in Bangladesh. The historical conflict between surveillance and privacy in the Western world has been shaped by laws that preserve an individual's privacy rights [10,41,55,59]. However, many countries in the Global South, including Bangladesh, do not have these privacy rights protected by their constitutions. As a result, enactment of a surveillance law carries the risk of suppressing individuals' voices, and may eventually destroy the democratic environment in a country. Hence, an individual's right to privacy is inevitably associated with the democratic development of a country. This broad conceptualization of privacy allows us to perceive how the design of different privacy features in our day-to-day devices actually "function" in the Western world because of the stable democratic environment. However, when the devices leave these stable environments, a whole new set of designs and policies are required to understand "privacy" in different scenarios. As a result, in addition to understanding privacy as it relates to different social and cultural norms, it also needs to be studied in a diverse range of political environments and settings.

## REFERENCES

1. Norah Abokhodair. 2015. Transmigrant Saudi Arabian Youth and Social Media: Privacy, Intimacy and

Freedom of Expression. 187–190. Retrieved from http://dx.doi.org/10.1145/2702613.2702629
2. Norah Abokhodair and Sarah Vieweg. 2016. Privacy & Social Media in the Context of the Arab Gulf. In *Proceedings of the 2016 ACM Conference on Designing Interactive Systems.*, 672–683. Retrieved from http://dx.doi.org/10.1145/2901790.2901873
3. Syed Ishtiaque Ahmed, Nova Ahmed, Faheem Hussain, and Neha Kumar. 2016. Computing beyond gender-imposed limits. In *In Proc. LIMITS'16*, Article No. 6.
4. Syed Ishtiaque Ahmed, Shion Guha, Md. Rashidujjaman Rifat, Md. Foysal Hossain, and Nicola Dell. Privacy in Repair: An Analysis of the Privacy Challenges Surrounding Broken Digital Artifacts in Bangladesh. In *In Proceedings of the Eighth International Conference on Information and Communication Technologies and Development*, Article No. 11. Retrieved from http://dx.doi.org/10.1145/2909609.2909661
5. Syed Ishtiaque Ahmed, Steven J Jackson, Nova Ahmed, Hasan Shahid Ferdous, Md. Rashidujjaman Rifat, A. S. M. Rizvi, Shamir Ahmed, and Rifat Sabbir Mansur. 2014. Protibadi: A Platform for Fighting Sexual Harassment in Urban Bangladesh. In *In Proc. CHI'14*, 2695–2704.
6. Syed Ishtiaque Ahmed, Steven J Jackson, and Md. Rashidujjaman Rifat. 2015. Learning to fix: knowledge, collaboration and mobile phone repair in Dhaka, Bangladesh. In *In Proc. ICTD'15*, 4:1-4:10.
7. Syed Ishtiaque Ahmed, Nusrat Jahan Mim, and Steven J Jackson. 2015. Residual Mobilities: Infrastructural Displacement and Post-Colonial Computing in Bangladesh. In *In Proc. CHI'15*, 437–446.
8. Joseph Allchin. *The Rise of Extremism in Bangladesh.* Foreign Affairs. Retrieved from https://www.foreignaffairs.com/articles/bangladesh/2016-06-09/rise-extremism-bangladesh
9. Louise Amoore. 2006. Biometric borders: Governing mobilities in the war on terror. *Political geography* 25, 3: 336–351.
10. George J Annas. 2003. HIPAA regulations-a new era of medical-record privacy? *New England Journal of Medicine* 138, 15: 1486–1490.
11. BBC News. *Bangladesh war crimes trial: Key accused.* Retrieved from http://www.bbc.com/news/world-asia-20970123
12. Seyla Benhabib. 2002. *The claims of culture: Equality and diversity in the global era.* Princeton University Press.
13. Jenna Burrell. 2010. Evaluating Shared Access: social equality and the circulation of mobile phones in rural Uganda. *Journal of Computer Mediated Communication* 15, 2: 230–250.
14. Sonia Chiasson, Paul C van Oorschot, and Robert Biddle. 2007. Graphical password authentication using cued click points. In *In Proc. Computer Security-ESORICS*, 359–374.
15. Julie E. Cohen. What privacy is for. *Harvard Law Review* 125: 1904.
16. Juliet Corbin and Anselm Strauss. 1994. Grounded theory methodology. *Handbook of qualitative research*: 273–285.
17. Carl DiSalvo, Phoebe Sengers, and Hrönn Brynjarsdóttir. 2010. Mapping the landscape of sustainable HCI. In *Proceedings of the SIGCHI Conference on Human Factors in Computing Systems*, 1975–1984.
18. Kevin P. Donovan and Aaron K. Martin. 2014. The rise of African SIM registration: The emerging dynamics of regulatory change. *First Monday* Speccial Issue. Retrieved from http://firstmonday.org/ojs/index.php/fm/article/view/4351/3820
19. Mary Flanagan, Daniel C. Howe, and Helen Nissenbaum. 2008. Embodying Values in Technology: Theory and Practice. In *Information Technology and Moral Philosophy*, John Weckert (ed.). Cambridge University Press, 322–353. Retrieved from http://www.nyu.edu/projects/nissenbaum/papers/Flanagan,%20Howe%20&%20Nissenbaum%20-%20Embodying%20Values.pdf
20. Michel Foucault. 1977. *Discipline and punish: The birth of the prison.* Vintage.
21. Mehboob Geelani. 2011. Numbers and NREGA. *The Caravan.*
22. Koushik Ghosh, Tapan S Parikh, and Apala Lahiri Chavan. 2003. Design considerations for a financial management system for rural, semi-literate users. In *In Proc CHI EA'03*, 824–825.
23. Henry A Giroux. 2015. Totalitarian paranoia in the post-Orwellian surveillance state. *Cultural Studies* 29, 2: 108–140.
24. Ralph Gross and Alessandro Acquisti. 2005. Information revelation and privacy in online social networks. In *In Proceedings of the 2005 ACM workshop on Privacy in the electronic society*, 71–80.
25. Jürgen Habermas. 1991. *The structural transformation of the public sphere: An inquiry into a category of bourgeois society.* MIT Press.
26. Geert Hofstede. 1984. The cultural relativity of the quality of life concept. *Academy of Management Review* 9, 3: 389–398.
27. Faheem Hussain and Mashiat Mostafa. 2016. Digital Contradictions in Bangladesh: Encouragement and Deterrence of Citizen Engagement via ICTs. *Information Technologies & International Development* 12, 2: 47.
28. Lilly Irani, Janet Vertesi, Paul Dourish, Kavita Philip, and Rebecca E Grinter. 2010. Postcolonial computing: a lens on design and development. In *Proceedings of the SIGCHI Conference on Human Factors in Computing Systems*, 1311–1320.
29. Muhammad Zahidul Islam. 2015. *SIM re-registration a must in Bangladesh.* The Daily Star. Retrieved from

http://www.thedailystar.net/frontpage/sim-re-registration-must-139189
30. Steven J Jackson, Syed Ishtiaque Ahmed, and Md. Rashidujjaman Rifat. 2014. Learning, innovation, and sustainability among mobile phone repairers in Dhaka, Bangladesh. In *In Proc. DIS'14*, 905–914.
31. Steven J Jackson, Alex Pompe, and Gabriel Krieshok. 2012. Repair worlds: maintenance, repair, and ICT for development in rural Namibia. In *Proceedings of the ACM 2012 conference on Computer Supported Cooperative Work*, 107–116.
32. Elida KU Jacobsen. 2012. Unique Identification: Inclusion and surveillance in the Indian biometric assemblage. *Security Dialogue* 43, 5: 457–474.
33. Aditya Johri and Janaki Srinivasan. 2014. The role of data in aligning the "unique identity"infrastructure in India. In *Proceedings of the 17th ACM conference on Computer supported cooperative work & social computing*, 697–709.
34. Reetika Khera. 2011. The UID Project and Welfare Schemes. *Economic and Political Weekly* XLVI, 9.
35. Nir Kshetri. 2015. Cybercrime and Cybersecurity Issues in the BRICS Economies. *Journal of Global Information Technology Management* 18, 4: 245–249.
36. Neha Kumar. 2015. The gender-technology divide or perceptions of non-use. *First Monday* 20, 11.
37. Neha Kumar and Tapan Parikh. 2013. Mobiles, music, and materiality. In *In Proc. CHI'13*, 2863–2872.
38. Ponnurangam Kumaraguru and Lorrie F Cranor. 2006. Privacy in India: Attitudes and awareness. *Privacy Enhancing Technologies*: 243–258.
39. Heather R Lipford, Gordon Hull, Celine Latulipe, Andrew Besmer, and Jason Watson. Visible flows: Contextual integrity and the design of privacy mechanisms on social network sites. In *In Computational Science and Engineering, 2009. CSE'09. International Conference*, 985–989.
40. David Lyon. 2003. Technology vs "terrorism": circuits of city surveillance since September 11th. *International Journal of Urban and Regional Research* 27, 3: 666–678.
41. David Lyon. 2007. *Surveillance studies: An overview.* Polity.
42. Jane Mansbridge. 1983. *Beyond adversary democracy.* University of Chicago Press.
43. Arindam Mukherjee. 2011. *Aadhar, A Few Basic Issues.* Outlook.
44. Helen Nissenbaum. 2004. Privacy as contextual integrity. *Wash L. Rev* 79, 119.
45. Helen Nissenbaum. 2015. *Obfuscation: A User's Guide for Privacy and Protest.* MIT Press. Retrieved from https://mitpress.mit.edu/books/obfuscation
46. Nimmi Rangaswamy and Sumitra Nair. 2010. The mobile phone store ecology in a Mumbai slum community: Hybrid networks for enterprise. *Information technologies & international development* 6, 3: pp–51.
47. Aruna Roy. 2011. *Aadhaar Bound to Fail.* The Hindu, Kochi Edition.
48. Norman Sadeh, Jason Hong, Lorrie F Cranor, Ian Fette, Patrick Kelley, Madhu Prabakar, and Jinghai Rao. 2009. Understanding and capturing people's privacy policies in a mobile social networking application. *Personal and Ubiquitous Computing* 13, 6: 401–412.
49. Yasar Guneri Sahin and Tuncay Ercan. 2008. Detection of hidden hostile/terrorist groups in harsh territories by using animals as mobile biological sensors. *Sensors* 8, 7: 4365–4383.
50. Nithya Sambasivan, Ed Cutrell, Kentaro Toyama, and Bonnie Nardi. 2010. Intermediated technology use in developing communities. In *In Proc. CHI'10*, 2583–2592.
51. Daniel J. Solove. 2011. Why privacy matters even if you have "nothing to hide." *Chronicle of Higher Education* 15. Retrieved from http://www.chronicle.com/article/Why-Privacy-Matters-Even-if/127461
52. Susan Leigh Star and Geoffrey C Bowker. 2007. Enacting silence: Residual categories as a challenge for ethics, information systems, and communication. *Ethics and Information Technology* 9, 4: 273–280.
53. Arifuzzaman Tuhin. 2016. Fear around filgerprints for SIM registration. *NTV Opinions*. Retrieved from http://www.ntvbd.com/opinion/39175/%E0%A6%B8%E0%A6%BF%E0%A6%AE-%E0%A6%A8%E0%A6%BF%E0%A6%AC%E0%A6%A8%E0%A7%8D%E0%A6%A7%E0%A6%A8%E0%A7%87-%E0%A6%86%E0%A6%99%E0%A7%81%E0%A6%B2%E0%A7%87%E0%A6%B0-%E0%A6%9B%E0%A6%BE%E0%A6%AA-%E0%A6%A8%E0%A6%BF%E0%A7%9F%E0%A7%87-%E0%A6%AD%E0%A7%9F
54. Samuel D Warren and Louis D Brandeis. 1890. The right to privacy. *Harvard Law Review*: 193–220.
55. Alan F Westin. 1968. Privacy and Freedom. *Washington and Lee Law Review* 25, 1: 166.
56. Wikipedia Aricle. *Attacks by Islamic extremists in Bangladesh*. Retrieved from https://en.wikipedia.org/wiki/Attacks_by_Islamic_extremists_in_Bangladesh
57. Wikipedia Article. *International Crimes Tribunal (Bangladesh)*. Retrieved from https://en.wikipedia.org/wiki/International_Crimes_Tribunal_(Bangladesh)
58. David Murakami Wood. 2007. Beyond the Panopticon? Foucault and surveillance studies. *Space, knowledge and power: Foucault and geography*: 245–263.
59. Bauman Zygmunt and David Lyon. 2013. *Liquid Surveillance: A Conversation.* John Wiley & Sons.
60. 2013. *Bangladesh's ICT Act Stoops to New Lows.* Global Voices. Retrieved from https://advox.globalvoices.org/2013/09/18/bangladeshs-ict-act-stoops-to-new-lows/

61. 2015. *Trial biometric SIM registration begins Wednesday*. Dhaka Tribune. Retrieved from http://www.dhakatribune.com/bangladesh/2015/oct/20/trial-biometric-sim-registration-begins-wednesday
62. 2016. Statistics and facts on mobile internet usage. *Statista: The Statistical Portal*. Retrieved from https://www.statista.com/topics/779/mobile-internet/
63. 2016. *HC questions legality of biometric SIM registration*. The Daily Star. Retrieved from http://www.thedailystar.net/country/hc-questions-legality-biometric-sim-registration-791002
64. 2016. *HC okays biometric SIM registration*. The Daily Star. Retrieved from http://www.thedailystar.net/country/hc-okays-biometric-registration-sim-1208071
65. 2016. *Deadline for biometric re-registration of SIM cards extended by a month*. bdnews24.com. Retrieved from http://bdnews24.com/bangladesh/2016/04/30/deadline-for-biometric-re-registration-of-sim-cards-extended-by-a-month
66. 2016. *"Biometrically registered Robi SIMs" used in fraud, money stolen from bKash accounts: Chittagong police*. bdnews24.com. Retrieved from http://bdnews24.com/bangladesh/2016/05/23/biometrically-registered-robi-sims-used-in-fraud-money-stolen-from-bkash-accounts-chittagong-police
67. 2016. *Retailers bio-metrically registering SIMs without users' knowledge: BTRC*. The Daily Ittefaq. Retrieved from http://www.clickittefaq.com/retailers-bio-metrically-registering-sims-without-users-knowledge-btrc/
68. 2016. *BIOMETRIC SIM REGISTRATION : Retailers to face punishment for fee collection*. New Age. Retrieved from http://newagebd.net/197633/biometric-sim-registration-retailers-to-face-punishment-for-fee-collection/
69. *"Biometric SIM registration to help identify criminals."* The Daily Samakal. Retrieved from http://www.samakal.net/2016/05/02/5392
70. Mass Surveillance. *Wikipedia Article*. Retrieved from https://en.wikipedia.org/wiki/Mass_surveillance
71. *Online Survey on Biometric SIM registration in Bangladesh*. Retrieved from https://docs.google.com/a/csebuet.org/forms/d/1H3EhWnmAS1tgbrFKNYilpqNH4RaNtwMCqFp7CDeXpq8/edit?usp=drive_web

# Youth Perspectives on Critical Data Literacies

**Samantha Hautea*** **Sayamindu Dasgupta*†** **Benjamin Mako Hill***

*University of Washington
Seattle, WA, 98195
{smhautea,sdg1,makohill}@uw.edu

†MIT Media Lab
Cambridge, MA, 02142
sayamindu@media.mit.edu

## ABSTRACT
As contemporary youth learn, play, and socialize online, their activities are often being recorded and analyzed. What should young people know about these data collection and analysis efforts? Although critiques of these new forms of data collection and analysis have grown increasingly loud, the voices of users, and particularly youth, have largely been absent. This paper explores the critical perspectives of youth who are programming with public data about their own learning and social interaction in the Scratch online community. Using a bottom-up approach based on ethnographic observation of discussions among these young users, we identify a series of themes in how these youth critique, question, and debate the implications of data analytics. We connect these themes—framed in terms of critical data literacies—to expert critiques and discuss the implications of these findings for education and design.

### Author Keywords
critical data literacy; data literacy; youth; learning; big data; data science

### ACM Classification Keywords
K.3.2 Computers and Education: Computer and Information Science Education; H.5.m Information Interfaces and Presentation (e.g., HCI): Miscellaneous

## INTRODUCTION
As technology's ability to save and store information has increased, the creation and analysis of large-scale datasets has grown. In 2013, a study estimated that more than 90 percent of the data in the world had been produced over the last ten years, and that the world was generating 2.5 quintillion bytes of data daily. Moreover, this number is rapidly increasing [16].

The collection, management, and analysis of these rapidly expanding datasets are often described as issues of "big data" [28, 21] and "data science" [53, 49]. Although the sources of these new large datasets vary, many of the most popular accounts of the growing importance of data have focused on "digital footprints" [35, 26], "digital traces" [32], or "digital exhaust" [38]: data created as a side effect of human interaction with computing systems [19]. Quantitative analysis of these social and behavioral data is used to uncover hidden patterns and correlations, which can then be used to inform design, decision making, and policy setting [1, 47].


*CHI 2017*, May 06–11, 2017, Denver, CO, USA
ACM 978-1-4503-4655-9/17/05.
http://dx.doi.org/10.1145/3025453.3025823

Some of the excitement about data is directed at the potential to collect and analyze information about the activities of youth. As youth flock to online systems to play, learn, and socialize, their activities are measured, recorded, quantified, tracked, and analyzed in unprecedented ways.[1] In the field of digital learning systems, there is broad interest in new possibilities for digital data about youth, including using data for "personalizing instruction, improving student learning, improving student engagement, and providing rapid feedback to learners" [17, 2].

Recently, several scholars have begun to advance a critical discourse around data and its limitations. In particular, these critiques have emphasized the challenges associated with drawing valid conclusions from online behavioral data and the need for researchers and educators to reflect on the ethics of how data is acquired, interpreted, and utilized [5, 33, 34, 41]. These critiques suggest that the contemporary public discourse about data has an element of mythology embedded in it, causing "widespread belief that large data sets offer a higher form of intelligence and knowledge that can generate insights that were previously impossible, with the aura of truth, objectivity, and accuracy" [5].

Within these critical conversations, the voices and accounts of end users who are the subject of data collection are rare, with several notable exceptions (e.g. [9, 7, 44]). As individuals at the leading edge of new data collection efforts, understanding the implications of new forms of digital data collection and analysis is particularly important for youth. What should young people know about the data being collected about them and about the attempts to analyze and understand these data in ways that can shape their experience? What are the skills they require to approach the subject of data critically?

In this paper, we present a bottom-up approach that attempts to highlight youths' voices in this broader conversation about data and data literacy. In the following background section, we introduce several important concepts from prior research as a way of defining our terms. Next, we briefly introduce our empirical setting: a novel system built on top of Scratch called *Scratch Community Blocks*. Subsequently, we describe our own data and methodology. We present a unique dataset

[1] Although it is outside the scope of this paper, the legal and regulatory environment relating to collecting data on the online activities of children under 13 is complex and shifting. See boyd, Gasser, and Palfrey [6] for an overview of some of these issues.

of user discussions, ethnographic field notes, interviews, survey responses, and more than 1,600 creative artifacts that we collected over an approximately four-month period observing over 700 young programmers working with behavioral and social data in the Scratch online community. Using a grounded theory-based approach, we systematically coded and analyzed these qualitative data.

We reserve the bulk of this paper for discussing our findings. These findings are organized into five themes that reflect critical features of contemporary online data collection and analysis identified by the young people in our sample. We present these as youth perspectives on critical data literacies: (1) data collection and retention has privacy implications, (2) data analysis requires skepticism and interpretation, (3) data can come with assumptions and hidden decisions, (4) data-driven algorithms cause exclusion, and (5) measuring and reporting on data can affect the system that created the data. We use quotes and creative artifacts from youth to explicate each of these themes in detail. Furthermore, we connect these concerns to broader questions about data raised by researchers, critics, and educators. Based on these findings, we offer several suggestions for designers and educators on possible strategies for engaging youth in critically thinking about the role of data in their lives and in their world.

## BACKGROUND

Although our research design takes a bottom-up approach that is primarily grounded in the data we have collected, our work is deeply informed by previous research. First, the way in which we attempt to theorize how youth understand data is informed by Papert's theory of *constructionism*. Second, the way we understand and frame our findings is informed both by recent attempts to understand "big data" as well as related literature on *data literacies*. Finally, our desire to support youth in critically engaging in the process of meaning creation and learning is informed by Freire's concept of *critical pedagogy*.

*Constructionism* is a theory proposed by Seymour Papert and others [43, 30] that builds on Jean Piaget's theory of constructivism [46], where the learner is seen as an active constructor of knowledge rather than being a passive recipient of information. Papert argued that this process happens in a more "felicitous" way when the learner is actively engaged in constructing an entity (physical, or virtual). This entity could then be used as an "object to think with." An example of such an object is a set of differential gears that helped a young Papert grasp ideas from mathematics [42]. Our approach is informed by constructionism in that we have sought to understand youths' conceptions of data and its limitations by looking at the ways in which youth engage in the construction of data artifacts in a social context.

The topic of *data literacy* has been defined in a number of ways by educators and education researchers. We follow the Oceans of Data Institute in using the term to describe the ability to "access, interpret, critically assess, manage, handle, and ethically use data" [40]. We believe that the term "critically" is central. Our definition of *critical* is drawn from Freire, who advocated learning processes in which learners would be enabled to critically perceive "the way they exist in the world with which and in which they find themselves" [23]. Following Freire, our work seeks to contribute to the emerging literature on *critical data literacies* [20, 45]. This conversation has focused on calls for the cultivation of an understanding of the implications of large-scale data collection and analysis, which necessitates critical thinking about data, including issues of privacy, surveillance, and the power structures that enable data-driven processes to affect people's lives.

Although literacy is often conceived of as being top-down—that is, defined by educators and policymakers—our approach is fundamentally bottom-up. We do not claim that the critical data literacies described by the youth in our paper are perspectives that all youth will, or should, share. Rather, we present these youths' perspectives on critical data literacies as a way of including their voices in the emerging scholarly dialog around what data literacies might involve and what strategies may be of value to designers and educators in this space.

## EMPIRICAL SETTING

Our empirical setting is the Scratch online community. Scratch is a block-based visual programming language designed for youth aged 8–16 years old [50]. Interactive programs are constructed by dragging and dropping visual blocks together where blocks are roughly analogous to tokens in text-based programming languages. Scratch is embedded within an online social community with over 15 million registered users who can share projects, comment on each others' work, follow each others' activity, bookmark projects, and so on [37].

In early 2016, an experimental feature called *Scratch Community Blocks* was introduced to a subset of active Scratch users [15]. *Scratch Community Blocks* adds a new set of blocks to Scratch that allow users to access public metadata on users and projects from the Scratch website. The goal of the system is to engage Scratch users in programmatically accessing and analyzing these data. In particular, *Scratch Community Blocks* gives users access to the data about users' followers, followees, shared projects, and favorited (bookmarked) projects. For each of these projects, it provides access to data including the number of views received, the number of "love-its" (similar to "likes" in other social media platforms), and code metadata, such as whether the project uses blocks that play music.

A sample project illustrating how *Scratch Community Blocks* can be used is shown in Figure 1. The code shown in Figure 1a calculates the total number of followers of the user who is viewing the project (using the "`username`" block embedded inside the "for each" block) as well as the total number of followers who are from outside the United States. Once the calculation of these numbers is complete, a graphical character on the screen "says" the result using a speech bubble (Figure 1b).

*Scratch Community Blocks* was beta tested on a fully functional copy of the Scratch website. Users with access to the beta site could create and publish projects that were visible to other invitees. Although the system was deployed on a separate website, the data fetched by the system was from the main Scratch website. Unless disabled by a project's creators, users could leave comments on projects in a threaded discus-

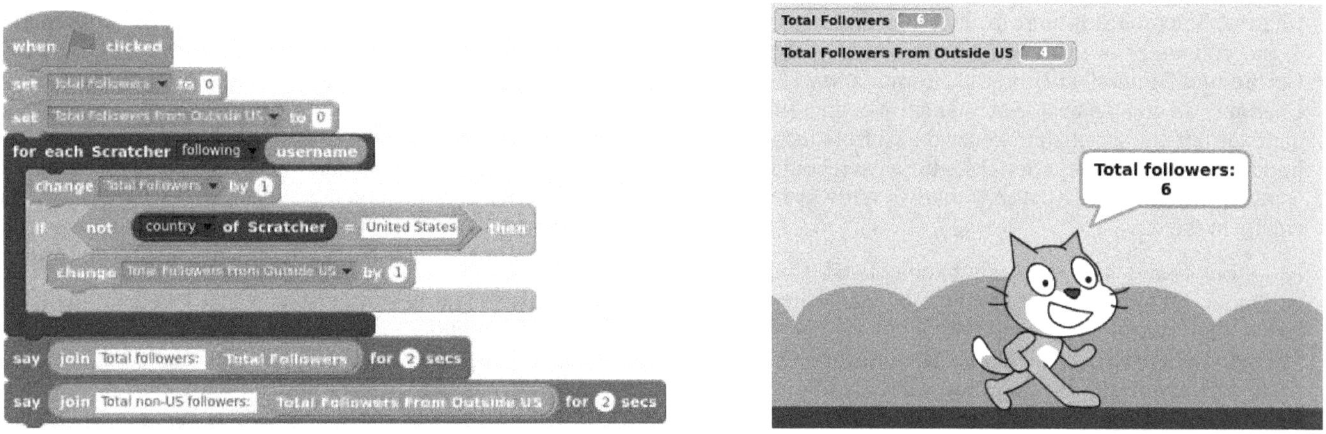


(a) Code to access and process social data (b) Results of running the code

Figure 1: Example of *Scratch Community Blocks* code. The code calculates the total number of followers of the viewer of the project and how many of them are from outside the United States.

sion area associated with each project. Additionally, there was a special threaded sub-forum in the main Scratch discussion forums dedicated to the community blocks and only accessible to invitees.

The system was beta tested over several months. Beta testers were drawn from a pool of Scratch users who had been active for at least six months and who had shared at least four projects. The self-reported age distribution of these users was close to that in the Scratch community in general—with the median age being 12 years, and with more than half being between 11 and 15. The gender ratio was approximately 48% male, 47% female, and 5% other. Selected users were given access to a separate instance of the Scratch website set up exclusively for trying out *Scratch Community Blocks*. Prior to the users being invited, the beta site did not have any content except for a few sample projects. A total of 2,500 Scratch users were invited in three stages. Over 700 of these users shared over 1,600 projects and 1,000 comments on the site. As the beta site became active, its landing page was populated with projects created by users. As with the main Scratch website, the source code for every project shared on the site could be viewed and remixed by any user.

## DATA AND METHODOLOGY

Our data was drawn from several sources, and our methodology consisted of a grounded theory-based ethnographic approach. Our primary source of data was ethnographic observation of users in the *Scratch Community Blocks* website during a four-month period of beta testing. All three authors visited both the *Scratch Community Blocks* website and forum frequently to browse projects, read comments, and to follow discussions in the special forum. Though primarily observers, we also participated by experimenting with the blocks ourselves, publishing several of our projects, and engaging in several discussions. Two of the authors played an active role in the design of the blocks, and one led the implementation. The first author exclusively focused on ethnographic observation. As a group, we attempted to be comprehensive in our coverage of activity on the site and to view projects as they were published and discussions as they were ongoing.

The time that our team spent "in the field" was between February and July 2016 and varied day-to-day with activity on the site. The site saw more posts and projects during the days immediately following each wave of invitations and then slowly returned to a low level of activity. During the most active periods, our team members visited the site and forums several times a day. Over the course of our observations, we took copious field notes, which both quoted from discussions and included our own interpretations, feelings, and reactions.

We systematically collected the full text of the *Scratch Community Blocks* forums, which included 936 distinct messages left on 42 threads. We also drew from the more than 1,000 comments left on over 1,600 projects shared by users on the site (over 200 projects received comments). Additionally, we conducted five interviews with users of the system in which we discussed the blocks and the projects they had created. Three of these interviews were conducted with active users of the beta site over voice or video chat. The remaining two interviews were conducted face-to-face after the workshop described below. These interviews lasted a total of approximately three hours.

We also distributed a survey to users of the system in June 2016. All 2,500 users who were invited to the site were asked to participate in the survey, and over 400 responded. In this paper, we draw from eight open-ended questions that probed respondents' reactions to and feelings about the blocks. We have included these questions in an online supplement. Finally, the team organized a three-hour face-to-face workshop where a total of 12 Scratch users were introduced to the blocks and then encouraged to explore, create, and discuss the blocks with the team and each other. Detailed notes were taken by the workshop facilitators.

We followed Charmaz's [11] approach to grounded theory to code and analyze these various sources of data. One feature of

Charmaz's approach is more explicit direction for researchers to incorporate prior ideas and existing theory, compared to Corbin and Strauss' [12] original formulation. Following Charmaz, we complemented our inductive coding (the bulk of our codes) with "sensitizing" codes drawn from theory during initial coding as well as later-stage iterative recoding of data using codes informed by theory that we felt was relevant to emergent themes.

All of our coding and analysis was completed using the collaborative QDA software package Dedoose using a single codebook. Following Charmaz, we iteratively completed the following analytic cycle: coding data, discussing codes as a team, grouping similar codes together, identifying themes of interest, writing and revising memos, and recoding data. We coded and analyzed data continuously. As a result, data collected in the first month of the study (field notes, forums conversations, records of projects, and comments) were coded more openly to generate a large set of initial codes. This was intended to provide a basis for grouping and identifying themes that could be further explored. Data collected later in the study (such as the survey responses) were coded less openly.

Codes included phrases such as "user stalking," "conflicts with other Scratchers," "cyber-bullying,", and "too personal." These codes, and many others, were collapsed into themes, such as "concerns about user behavior" or "concerns about privacy." At the end of this process, we found that our themes and memos were largely focused on five key features of data collection and analysis identified by youth. We present these features as perspectives on critical data literacies.

## FINDINGS

In this section, each theme is framed with a brief introduction of the critical data literacy in question. We summarize youth's perspectives on the issue they emerged in our analysis and provide evidence to support these summaries using quotes and examples from our fieldwork. We conclude each section by relating youth's perspectives to existing scholarly criticism.

We have tried to provide context for quotes without revealing the identity of any users. We indicate the self-reported age of the Scratch user wherever possible but have altered all usernames. Because our survey was anonymous and all questions were optional, we have no identifiable or demographic information on survey respondents.

### Data collection and retention has privacy implications

A primary source of excitement about new forms of data collection is the growing ability to continually record data about individuals' interactions and actions. However, because online data collection is passive, the subjects of observation are often not aware of it. Scholars have described this as "epistemic asymmetry" [9] because users are not aware that data collection, retention, and analysis is happening. Even though *Scratch Community Blocks* provides access to data that is public, the surfacing of this data collection caused many users to raise concerns. These concerns constitute our first critical data literacy: that data collection and retention has privacy implications.

Many of the projects on the beta site utilized blocks that automatically detected the username of the viewer. One project greeted users by asking them if they remember their first project before reciting that project's title and a few statistics about it. This comparatively simple demonstration of the persistent nature of retained data was evocative for a number of users. In one comment on the project, a 10-year-old user said that she found it "creepy and very cool." Another comment used the terms "scary" but "cool" to voice a similar sentiment.

The ability to retrieve information that had been published but forgotten about clearly surprised and intrigued Scratch users. Although they may have been aware that their activities were being recorded in some abstract sense, and although they explicitly chose to make their activities public by publishing their projects, *Scratch Community Blocks* revealed how easily this information could be retrieved computationally. Through comments on projects, survey responses, forum posts, and interviews, we observed how Scratch users struggled with the implications of what it means to have this data out there.

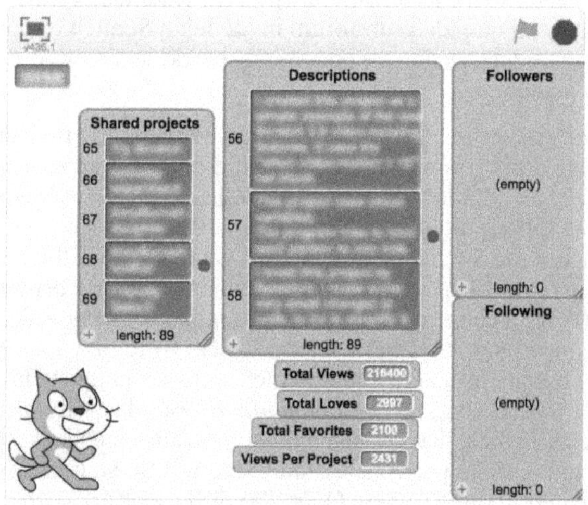


Figure 2: This "information retrieval" project calculates the cumulative number of views, loveits, and favorites received by a user over their entire trajectory. Textual data in the image has been blurred to preserve anonymity.

Some Scratch users quickly realized that computational access to their data enabled new possibilities. For example, although one can see the number of projects a user has created and their titles on the main Scratch website, calculating the cumulative views, comments, and loveits across all of a user's projects without *Scratch Community Blocks* would involve clicking on each project individually and manually calculating the sums. With the new system, users could do so with a few blocks of code. An example created by a user is shown in Figure 2.

However, some Scratch users expressed concern about the retrieval of historical information and the potential for the blocks to enable "stalking." Although the blocks only revealed information that was public, several Scratch users felt that the ability to programmatically retrieve information from anyone was invasive.

On the discussion forums, a 14-year-old user expressed concern that data about anyone on Scratch can be retrieved through the system:

> If I had to say one thing, it may be a bit personal, considering you can type in ANYONE's username, but it's still great! That's only a minor flaw that can easily be fixed.

Another user (15 years old) echoed a similar sentiment in a forum post. She pointed out that programmatic access to public data makes it easier to actively monitor someone:

> I will, however, add, that it does feel like a bit of a way to stalk Scratchers from a project. Though I suppose it doesn't make much of a difference since a stalker could always just stalk them on the site, but you get what I mean. Someone could set themselves up with some of these blocks and get themselves a constant relay of the person's activity.

Although she acknowledged that people are already looking at other user profiles and could "stalk" with or without the blocks, she also felt that programmatic access to data represented an important qualitative difference. In a survey response, a third user suggested that there should be a system that would ask for permission from a user before their data was accessed:

> The blocks are a little personal; for example someone can find out anyone's follower account, views, loves, favorites, etc., so there should be something that asks for permission from the user.

Not everyone was concerned. When presented with the concerns that other users raised about privacy, one workshop participant (11 years old) provided a passionate defense of the use of the community blocks to retrieve information

> I think that easier is never a problem. In fact, in our entire world..., everywhere in history, if you look around, technology upgrades either make our world easier, funner, or safer. Right? I mean like, vaccines, safer. Roller-coasters, funner. Computers, easier. And these Community Blocks definitely fall under easier and funner. It makes Scratch projects more diverse, which is great because projects are already diverse, and it makes it easier because you can access the information anyway. There's not any sort of privacy issues—but it makes it so much more easier and elegant to access.

The lack of consensus among the young users of *Scratch Community Blocks* on the privacy implications of new forms of data collection and new programmatic forms of data analysis mirrors disagreements among adults. boyd, et al. [7, 4], while describing teenagers' attitudes toward privacy in social media, describe *privacy* as, "both a social norm and a process," where privacy is "negotiated." Nissenbaum [39] argues for the development of "contextual" norms for data use and reuse. In other words, data collected for a stated use should not be used for another purpose unless permission is given.

What we observed through the conversation and feedback from Scratch users was essentially the process of privacy being "negotiated" (in the sense used by boyd et al.), as the socio-technical system forming the contextual backdrop for data collection and reuse added a new affordance. The ability to recognize and navigate the often messy relationship between the details of data collection, access, and analysis with privacy reflects our first critical data literacy.

### Data analysis requires skepticism and interpretation

Though data can be a powerful tool for gaining insights, there are inherent challenges to data analysis as a means to understand the world. Data can be error prone and requires interpretation. Statistics educators developing curricula for elementary school students have described the "uncertainty and intrigue of real mathematics" [51] and have highlighted the need to have students discuss, debate, and argue as they conduct data analysis. Our observations indicate that youth using *Scratch Community Blocks* encountered these challenges in various ways. The examples that we provide in this section reflect the second critical data literacy—that data analysis requires skepticism and interpretation.

In our survey, we asked Scratch users what they liked best about the community blocks. Several users commented that they felt the blocks allowed for greater precision and confidence in the accuracy of information. For example, one respondent commented that the blocks made it possible to eliminate human error when retrieving the number of page views:

> I found one project on the Scratch website (main) that added up your total views, but it required you to look through your projects and type in the number of views. This could easily result in human error, in a way that the community blocks won't [be] doing the same thing.

Another respondent echoed a similar opinion:

> I think it's a pretty neat addition to the existing blocks. I am the kind of person who loves to know the exact numbers when it comes to stats. It honestly is an amazing idea; learning about how many people were on Scratch and etc. blew my mind.

Other Scratch users pointed out that the blocks occasionally appeared to report inaccurate information. For example, one interviewee described an inconsistency with data reported by the system:

> At one point the follower blocks, it said I have slightly more followers than I do. And, that was kind of confusing when I was trying to make the project. [...] I pulled up a second [browser] tab and compared the [data from *Scratch Community Blocks* and the data in my profile].

Upon investigation, we established that the source of this discrepancy was a bug in *Scratch Community Blocks* where the block iterating over followers included users who had disabled their accounts. For users without visibility into the implementation of the system, the numbers returned simply appeared wrong.

These "incorrect" numbers were discussed by users because they did not match the numbers on the public user profiles. Through these discussions, we saw Scratch users engaging

Figure 3: The formula for 'Total Scratcher Awesomeness'—an example of a project that uses a model to score and rate users.

in what has been described in a recently released workshop report on data literacy as data skepticism, or "questioning when something doesn't make sense, particularly regarding the data sets and what they do/do not represent" [40]. Of course, *Scratch Community Blocks* provided access to some data that could not be validated. In many cases, such as the total number of Scratch projects, users had no way to know if data were wrong.

Moreover, many users aimed to measure less objectively quantifiable variables, such as "awesomeness" or "the best project." To do so, Scratch users came up with models that combined a number of more accessible variables to represent what they thought was a reasonable proxy for the concept they were interested in. In this process, they drew on their knowledge of the community and their own values to make judgments about how to use the data they have access to.

For example, one user modeled "Total Scratcher Awesomeness" of a Scratch user by adding followers with cumulative loves, favorites, and views and subtracting the number of projects created. The Scratch code to perform this calculation is shown in Figure 3.

O'Neil [41] described models such as these as "opinions embedded in mathematics" and suggested that they are often very dangerous—particularly when they are opaque and unchangeable. Scratch users were expressing their opinion on what they think is an "awesome" Scratch user through the mathematics in the code shown in Figure 3. In this case, however, the model itself was both transparent and remixable, allowing other users to see what was incorporated and to offer their own suggestions. Indeed, we saw the author of this project incorporate feedback that suggested adding number of followers and total views to show how these models can potentially evolve to represent collective opinion. One such interaction is reproduced below:

> **Commenter:** You should add how many people follow you and the total views! Cool idea!
> **Creator:** good idea! I think i will add that...

Though we observed a number of "scoring" projects, and though these projects received a considerable amount of attention as measured by views and comments, we observed comparatively little concern or discussion about opinions being expressed through the models. On some of these projects, community members left comments to ask the project creators their reasoning behind the formulas they created. Creator responses were frequently variations on "I made it up." What users chose to include and exclude in their models reveals some insight into their perceptions and beliefs. Several projects placed prominence on statistics that came out of interactions (such as likes and favorites) over those that came from user activity (such as projects created). We feel that exploring ways to foster these discussions and how youth develop these models is a promising avenue for future work.

O'Neil argues that the process of interpreting data requires a thorough knowledge of context. The importance of context was clear among the youth we observed, not only in model building, but in other discussions as well. The culture of the Scratch community can skew certain variables. For example, a common cultural practice in Scratch involves users reporting their scores in game projects through the comments section. This means that games in Scratch often have more comments. This fact was not lost on the young data analysts we observed. In one project that attempted to identify the viewer's most viewed and and most loved project, a commenter offered a suggestion to, among other things, display the viewer's project with the most comments. The 11-year-old creator of the project responded positively but added that he felt that the number of comments might be more representative of genre than popularity.

> **Commenter:** Woah, neat! A few ideas I have: Most commented on (as that may not be the same as most loved), newest project, and random project.
> **Creator:** Nice ideas! Although, the most commented might end up being a game where there is a high-score system, as everyone comments their scores.

boyd and Crawford argue that without context, data can "lose meaning and value" [5]. Definitions of "data science" (e.g., [29]) also highlight the need for domain knowledge or subject expertise to understand the "why" of data as opposed to the "what" [48]. In the example above, we see Scratch users not only engaging in analyzing data but also doing so in a manner that indicates that they are aware of the mechanism through which this data is generated. This skepticism and knowledge that data must be put into context and interpreted reflects our second data literacy.

### Data comes with assumptions and hidden decisions

Although data can have obvious errors, there are also more subtle issues that can cause the end result of data analysis to be biased or incorrect. Some scholars have framed this by suggesting that "raw data is an oxymoron" [25] or that raw data needs to be "cooked with care" [3]. The point of these critiques is that data is always shaped by decisions and assumptions made during the process of data collection, processing, and analysis. For example, if a surveyor decides to conduct a national poll over landline telephones, it will be biased toward a certain demographic. Any interpretation of the results of that poll should keep this potential source of bias in mind. Understanding the assumptions and decisions that accompany data is a critical step for consumers and purveyors of data science tools. This constitutes our third critical data literacy: that data comes with assumptions and hidden decisions.

In conversations involving projects created with *Scratch Community Blocks*, we saw that becoming fluent in this literacy is not always a straightforward process. For example, one project showed the cumulative views received by the viewer's projects as a percentage of the total number of users in Scratch. This led to some confusion as some users assumed that the project calculated what percentage of users in Scratch had viewed the project. The resultant conversation happened in the comment thread on the project page:

> **Commenter A:** that's so cool! almost 00.5% of all the users on scratch have viewed my projects and that's a lot :B but crossstitch's[2] results are indeed slightly dubious... over 100% of people have viewed his projects which is awesome but impossible - love the project!! ^o^
> **Commenter B:** @CommenterA I think it's because its based on views, not each specific player.
> **Commenter A:** @CommenterB that's awesome :D people who haven't registered on scratch have viewed a significant amount of his projects yes
> **Project Creator:** @CommenterA Yeah what @CommenterB said is correct.

Here we see an example of collective sense-making. Commenter A began by questioning the validity of a result and pointing out a discrepancy. In the following discussion, users tried to puzzle through the ways in which this discrepancy could have occurred. The creator of the project in question was aware of this particular quirk of the project, and when sharing the project, he had added the following note to the project description:

> This project does not and cannot calculate unique viewers. So some views can be the exact same person who viewed the project earlier.

The discussion above reflects a broader issue in interpreting data made available by centralized socio-technical systems such as social networks. While data may be publicly viewable, the decisions, processes, and algorithms behind the construction of this data are not. Although the project creator expressed some confidence in the fact that the project view count returned by *Scratch Community Blocks* double-counted at least some users, the details of how this number is created is not public or known. The full answer is very complicated and the author of the system that computes the view count struggled to explain it to our team. In absence of documentation from the team implementing and running the Scratch website, understanding the mechanism of how this particular variable is constructed is difficult.

This issue is not specific to Scratch. YouTube's support page on view counts state:

> Video views are algorithmically validated to maintain fair and positive experiences for content creators, advertisers, and users. To verify that views are real and accurate, YouTube may temporarily slow down, freeze, or adjust the view count, as well as discard low-quality playbacks.[3]

It is not clear what is meant by fair, positive, or a low-quality playback. While there may be reasons for Scratch and YouTube's creators to not divulge the way views are counted, the result is that users make assumptions and guesses, often without realizing they are doing so. Numbers are treated as neutral and unproblematic facts. In the conversation above, Scratch users realized that even a simple number may have a complex story behind it and began reverse-engineering the process that created it.

In grappling with the often opaque nature of data, many Scratch users created projects that sought to add context and meaning to data. When asked what they liked best about the new blocks, one survey respondent said,

> I really liked the possibility of creating a more meaningful high score list. Using an existing cloud high score list and being able to include a user's country and about me section would really be cool.

In this case, the survey respondent recognized that the existing high score systems in Scratch games provided an incomplete picture. By constructing a high score system that provided additional context, they were able to make sense of the data in a way they considered meaningful. In these conversations about context, assumptions, and hidden decisions, these users helped build toward an important critical data literacy.

### Data-driven algorithms can cause exclusion

Data and data-driven algorithms can be used for discrimination and for exclusion [13]. The potential for data-driven decisions to result in exclusion was recognized in a 2014 report to the office of the US president, which stated:

> A significant finding of this report is that recent changes in data collection and analysis have the potential to eclipse longstanding civil rights protections in how personal information is used in housing, credit, employment, health, education, and the marketplace. [47]

This represents our fourth critical data literacy: that data-driven algorithms can lead to exclusion.

The possibility of discrimination based on data was recognized by Scratch users, and it was a frequent theme in their concerns and critiques. In a forum post, one 13-year-old pointed out that since it was possible to detect how many followers the viewer of a project had, users could create code to prevent users with a low follower count from accessing a project:

> I love these new Scratch Blocks! However I did notice that they could be used to exclude new scratchers or scratchers with not a lot of followers by using a code: like this:
>     when flag clicked
>     if then user's followers <300
>         stop all.
> I do not think this a big problem as it would be easy to

[2] crossstitch is the creator of some of the most popular projects on Scratch.

[3] `https://support.google.com/youtube/answer/2991785` (accessed in September 2016)

> remove this code, but I did just want to bring this to your attention in case this not what you would want the blocks to be used for.

Although often more subtle and complex than described here, algorithmic discrimination has received significant attention among scholars [24] and in the popular press [31]. *Scratch Community Blocks* offered an opportunity for Scratch users to grapple with this debate. The user quoted above was concerned about algorithms designed to exclude users who are new to the community or less popular than their peers. He also suggested that it would be possible to "remove this code"—hinting at the possibility for oversight or monitoring mechanisms that could address such discrimination.

In the conversations around this type of code, not all comments were expressions of concern. A number of users saw the new affordance as adding new possibilities for incentives in games built with Scratch:

> You know how in certain apps, they have things like "like us on [Facebook], and get 3 coins" I could do something like "follow WillTheSuperman, and get 25 more power-ups" or something like that.

This quote, which describes a potential incentive system for gaining followers, shows how Scratch users built on their experience on platforms outside Scratch that use data to implement similar types of incentives. Scratch users recognized that they could use data to shape their peers' behavior. Not all users agreed that such incentive mechanisms would be a positive addition to what is possible in Scratch. One 16-year-old wrote:

> People can use these new blocks so that people are forced to follow them. I know, this could be a way for them to get followers, but I think it could go out of hand. Say, they were making a story, they post one chapter. They are hooked, so they go onto the next chapter. Then, on the second chapter, it says: "You have to follow me to read this chapter!" It's forcing upon them to follow this user in order to read the next chapter. I mean, this is a effective way to get followers, but it just doesn't seem right.

Using a concrete example of a hypothetical project that forces Scratch users to follow the creator to continue accessing the project, this Scratch user expressed her concern that an algorithm with access to behavioral data could intentionally shape user behavior.

While several users recognized problems, others articulated potential solutions like the first user quoted in this section. One survey respondent suggested that this would be a method of editing out the discriminatory algorithm:

> I thought that this community blocks idea might lead to some exclusion. Some people might start using the code to only let popular people play their games. This won't be too much of a problem though, because people can still edit the code and make it playable.

That said, this particular workaround is possible only because Scratch code is always open, visible, and editable by any user. Even then, it is only possible when a Scratch user has the necessary skills to make the changes to the discriminating code.

Outside Scratch, most algorithms are inaccessible. They are typically considered trade secrets or are too complicated for non-specialists to understand, let alone modify [41]. The need for technical sophistication to address this issue was not lost upon Scratch users—a 16-year-old community member wrote in a forum post:

> Just as a few others mentioned already though, we should make sure that it is not used to discriminate New Scratchers who not only likely not have many followers, projects, and comments, but also likely have a more limited knowledge of the technology, so they might not know how to change the project inside. I know that I wouldn't have.

These comments reflect sophisticated views about how access to data could affect the experience of individual Scratch users. Scratch users were able to imagine ways to use data in ways they considered both desirable and undesirable. They could conceptualize the potential effects of data discrimination on both an individual and at the community level.

In the report to the US president cited earlier, the authors raise concerns about "digital redlining," data-driven practices that may cause exclusion in the same way that banks refused to give loans to customers from certain neighborhoods during the first half of the 20th century. In the comments above, we see similar concerns within the context of Scratch, acknowledging that while data is a powerful means to understand the world, it can also establish new forms of discrimination and exclusion. In their discussion of digital exclusion and potential responses to it, Scratch users provided insight into a fourth critical data literacy.

### Measuring and reporting data can affect the system that created the data

In trying to understand and evaluate a system and its effects, there is often a tendency to value measures that are easily quantifiable. Because of their increased value, these measures are often used to evaluate performance. As a result of this process, the system that produces the underlying data can become distorted. This phenomenon of quantitative indicators ending up distorting the process or the system was noticed and documented by Campbell [10]. A classic example of this can be seen in formal educational contexts where quantifiable test scores get more attention than may be warranted. Scholars and educators such as Holt [27] have argued that education as a field has become overly focused on test scores with teachers teaching specifically for tests and ignoring less quantifiable components of education such as fostering expression and enabling creative solutions to unanticipated problems. This represents the fifth and final youth-identified critical data literacy—that measuring and reporting data can affect the systems creating the data.

Some of this information made accessible by *Scratch Community Blocks* was not easily accessible otherwise. This was particularly the case with code metadata in Scratch projects.

Using *Scratch Community Blocks*, a number of projects represented and visualized code metadata from users' trajectories in different ways. These visualizations caused some users who viewed these projects to look back on their participation and to reflect on the type of blocks they tended to use more, and the types they used less. Fostering self-reflection through data was an explicit design goal of *Scratch Community Blocks* [15].

However, this affordance also introduced the risk of an unanticipated consequence. The original design goals of Scratch [50, 52] treated creativity, collaboration, and respect for one's peers as paramount. In such a context, there is a risk that users of *Scratch Community Blocks* could shift behaviors in Scratch in deleterious ways by highlighting and incentivizing behaviors—such as attracting large number of followers—that are easy to measure and report but are, at best, orthogonal to Scratch's goals.

One survey respondent, when prompted for any additional comments on the community blocks, stated their belief that the projects created with the blocks had the potential to affect what people perceived as important:

> I am just a bit worried that people will make these projects and take it the wrong way, saying that followers are the most important thing on Scratch.

Echoing a similar concern, a 12-year-old user wrote in the forums that this can lead to disagreements and conflict within the community:

> These new features are really helpful! However, I think that it would have a possibility to leading to flame wars or fights about followers.

Similarly, another 12 year old user imagined that users with a smaller number of followers could be made fun of and harassed:

> But a few things, you can easily make fun of someone for example, "You only have 2 followers! Ha! Well I have 10!"

These concerns were not totally unfounded. We found that users were treating number outputs by projects (e.g., the Scratcher awesomeness calculator described earlier, which took into account number of followers) as scores and reporting them (sometimes competitively) as project comments. For example, in one comment, a user wrote "9189. ITS OVER NINE THOOOUUUUSAAAAAND!!!!!!" We also found a few instances of users creating projects that would generate mocking comments for users with a smaller number of projects and followers.

boyd and Crawford, quoting Du Gay and Pryke [18], note that, like accounting tools, data analysts "'do not simply aid the measurement of economic activity, they shape the reality they measure,' so Big Data stakes out new terrains of objects, methods of knowing, and definitions of social life" [5]. Similarly, the introduction of new affordances around data into Scratch can have far-reaching consequences.

The problems youth observed and described are not entirely new to Scratch. Indeed, incentivizing following behavior existed in Scratch before the introduction of *Scratch Community Blocks*. That said, Scratch users recognized that as collecting and using data became easier, it could influence behavior and, ultimately, the nature of the data itself. The ability of youth to recognize the way these blocks could affect the community in which they participate is a manifestation of a final critical data literacy.

## DISCUSSION

Our findings show that the way that youth critique, question, and debate the implications of data analytics reflects some of the existing critical discourse pertaining to data. That said, not all themes explored by scholars were raised by youth. Two notable critiques that were absent from the conversations are the point that larger data sets may not necessarily mean better data and the point that new forms of data collection and analysis can create new types of digital divides by enabling only a handful of organizations and individuals with significant resources to perform data collection and analysis [5]. We feel that these topics did not come up because they pertain more to "big data" than the types of social media analytics supported by *Scratch Community Blocks*. Moreover, youth using *Scratch Community Blocks* had little say in what data was being collected or presented to them. Relatedly, we do not know whether the critical perspectives that we described in the context of Scratch translate into insights about data practices in other social networks (e.g., Facebook or Snapchat). Understanding and addressing these gaps remain a topic for future work.

Another limitation of our approach was that although *Scratch Community Blocks* was based on Scratch, our setting was a context where we explicitly encouraged the use of data. We know from previous work by Dasgupta et al. [14] that a majority of Scratch users use only a subset of the approximately 130 code blocks that are available to them. We do not know what patterns of engagement would have emerged if these were introduced in the larger Scratch community. Strategies to engage larger groups in discussions of these questions remain an open challenge.

Even within this limited setting, discussions were driven by the agency of the Scratch users concerned. Users encountered and explored the five critical data literacies described in this paper on their own. These users were operating within the culture of Scratch, a familiar context, as they engaged in the discussions and sense-making that we have highlighted in this paper. Bruner describes the importance of such contexts in meaning making as follows:

> Meaning making involves situating encounters with the world in their appropriate cultural contexts in order to know "what they are about." Although meanings are "in the mind," they have their origins and their significance in the culture in which they are created.[8]

In a similar vein, Papert and his collaborators have described the idea of Mathland, a cognitive space where mathematical ideas are encountered naturally by the inhabitants [42]. Learning mathematics in Mathland, constructionists argue, should be similar to the experience of a child learning French in France.

In light of these theories, we can see that as the young people using *Scratch Community Blocks* grappled with the implications of social data analytics, they were supported by the fact that their encounters were situated in an appropriate and familiar cultural context. As educators consider a critical pedagogy of data, our work shows that situating the learning experience in a familiar cultural context can play an important role. Our work points to the possibility that enabling learners to analyze social and behavioral data can spark conversations that explore critical data literacies.

In May 2016, *Science* magazine published an article [36] describing the long-term vision for "big ideas" at the US National Science Foundation. One of the specific research areas constituted the development of "learning opportunities and educational pathways" driven by an "understanding of the knowledge and skill demands needed by a 21st century data-capable workforce." Earlier during the year in January 2016, the US Federal Trade Commission released a report with the title "Big Data: A Tool for Inclusion or Exclusion? Understanding the Issues" [22]. These acknowledgements, along with the concerns raised by academics and advocates, indicate that an essential piece of a "data-capable workforce" are critical data literacies of the kinds we have described here. These reports suggest that what may be at stake is not just economic productivity and competitiveness but also some of our core democratic and civic values.

In this paper, we show that it is possible for young people to discover, critique, and question the implications of digital data collection in their lives, frequently echoing the concerns raised by academic scholars. Defining critical data literacies is still a topic of ongoing conversation. We hope that the young people's perspectives presented here can contribute to this discussion. We show that not only are youth receptive to discussions about critical data literacies, they also have something to teach us as well.

## ACKNOWLEDGMENTS

Parts of this paper are included in Dasgupta's PhD dissertation, and some of the text and images in the paper appear in his thesis. We would like to thank members of the Scratch community for their time and for inspiring us with their creative work. We would also like to acknowledge Mitchel Resnick, Natalie Rusk, Hal Abelson, and our anonymous reviewers for their support and thoughtful feedback. Financial support for this work came from the National Science Foundation (grants DRL-1417663 and DRL-1417952).

## REFERENCES

1. Hal Abelson, Ken Ledeen, and Harry Lewis. 2008. *Blown to Bits: Your Life, Liberty, and Happiness After the Digital Explosion* (1 edition ed.). Addison-Wesley Professional, Upper Saddle River, NJ.
2. Marie Bienkowski, Minguy Feng, and Barbara Means. 2012. *Enhancing teaching and learning through educational data mining and learning analytics: An issue brief.* Technical Report. US Department of Education, Office of Educational Technology.
3. Geoffrey C. Bowker. 2005. *Memory Practices in the Sciences.* MIT Press.
4. danah boyd. 2014. *It's Complicated: The Social Lives of Networked Teens.* Yale University Press.
5. danah boyd and Kate Crawford. 2012. Critical Questions for Big Data. *Information, Communication & Society* 15, 5 (2012), 662–679. DOI: http://dx.doi.org/10.1080/1369118X.2012.678878
6. danah boyd, Urs Gasser, and John Palfrey. 2010. How the COPPA, as Implemented, Is Misinterpreted by the Public: A Research Perspective. (April 2010). http://cyber.harvard.edu/sites/cyber.harvard.edu/files/COPPA_Hearing_Statement_boyd_Gasser_Palfrey_4-29-10.pdf
7. danah boyd, Alice Marwick, and others. 2011. Social Privacy in Networked Publics: Teens Attitudes, Practices, and Strategies. (2011).
8. Jerome S. Bruner. 1996. *The Culture of Education.* Harvard University Press.
9. Finn Brunton and Helen Nissenbaum. 2011. Vernacular resistance to data collection and analysis: A political theory of obfuscation. *First Monday* 16, 5 (2011).
10. Donald T. Campbell. 1979. Assessing the impact of planned social change. *Evaluation and Program Planning* 2, 1 (Jan. 1979), 67–90. DOI: http://dx.doi.org/10.1016/0149-7189(79)90048-X
11. Kathy Charmaz. 2006. *Constructing Grounded Theory: A Practical Guide Through Qualitative Analysis.* Sage Publications, London.
12. Juliet M. Corbin and Anselm C. Strauss. 2007. *Basics of Qualitative Research: Techniques and Procedures for Developing Grounded Theory* (3rd ed.). Sage Publications, Inc.
13. Kate Crawford, Mary Gray, and Kate Miltner. 2014. Big Data| Critiquing Big Data: Politics, Ethics, Epistemology | Special Section Introduction. *International Journal of Communication* 8, 0 (2014). http://ijoc.org/index.php/ijoc/article/view/2167
14. Sayamindu Dasgupta, William Hale, Andrés Monroy-Hernández, and Benjamin Mako Hill. 2016. Remixing as a Pathway to Computational Thinking. In *Proceedings of the 19th Conference on Computer Supported Cooperative Work & Social Computing (CSCW '16).* ACM.
15. Sayamindu Dasgupta and Benjamin Mako Hill. 2017. Scratch Community Blocks: Supporting Children as Data Scientists. In *Proceedings of the 2017 CHI Conference on Human Factors in Computing Systems (CHI '17).* ACM, New York, NY, USA. DOI: http://dx.doi.org/10.1145/3025453.3025847 (forthcoming).

16. Åse Dragland. 2013. *Big Data–for better or worse.* Technical Report. Sintef. http://www.sintef.no/en/latest-news/big-data--for-better-or-worse/

17. DRL. 2013. *Data-Intensive Research to Improve Teaching and Learning - An Ideas Lab to Foster Transformative Approaches to Teaching and Learning.* Program Solicitation 13-565. National Science Foundation. https://www.nsf.gov/pubs/2013/nsf13565/nsf13565.htm

18. Paul du Gay and Michael Pryke. 2002. Cultural Economy: An Introduction. In *Cultural Economy: Cultural Analysis and Commercial Life Cultural economy: Cultural analysis and commercial life.* SAGE Publications Ltd, London, UK, 1–20. http://sk.sagepub.com/books/cultural-economy/n12.xml

19. Elizabeth Dwoskin. 2014. Big Data's High-Priests of Algorithms; 'Data Scientists' Meld Statistics and Software for Find Lucrative High-Tech Jobs. *Wall Street Journal (Online)* (Aug. 2014). http://search.proquest.com/newsstand/docview/1552020409/abstract/D70B27FC5DA74D5APQ/1

20. Catherine D'Ignazio and Rahul Bhargava. 2015. Approaches to Building Big Data Literacy. In *Proceedings of the Bloomberg Data for Good Exchange Conference 2015.* New York, N.Y. https://dam-prod.media.mit.edu/x/2016/10/20/Edu_D'Ignazio_52.pdf

21. Liran Einav and Jonathan D. Levin. 2013. *The Data Revolution and Economic Analysis.* Working Paper 19035. National Bureau of Economic Research. http://www.nber.org/papers/w19035

22. Federal Trade Commission. 2016. *Big Data: A Tool for Inclusion or Exclusion? Understanding the Issues.* Technical Report. https://www.ftc.gov/system/files/documents/reports/big-data-tool-inclusion-or-exclusion-understanding-issues/160106big-data-rpt.pdf

23. Paulo Freire. 2000. *Pedagogy of the oppressed.* Bloomsbury Publishing.

24. Tarleton Gillespie. 2014. The Relevance of Algorithms. In *Media technologies: Essays on communication, materiality, and society*, Pablo J. Boczkowski and Kirsten A. Foot Tarleton Gillespie (Ed.). MIT Press, Cambridge, MA, 167.

25. Lisa Gitelman. 2013. *Raw Data Is an Oxymoron.* MIT Press.

26. Scott A. Golder and Michael W. Macy. 2014. Digital Footprints: Opportunities and Challenges for Online Social Research. *Annual Review of Sociology* 40, 1 (July 2014), 129–152. DOI:http://dx.doi.org/10.1146/annurev-soc-071913-043145

27. John Caldwell Holt. 1982. *How Children Fail.* Da Capo Press.

28. NSF-NIH Interagency Initiative and others. 2012. *Core techniques and technologies for advancing big data science and engineering (BIGDATA).*

29. Iain Johnstone and Fred Roberts. 2014. *Data Science at NSF.* Technical Report. National Science Foundation. http://www.nsf.gov/attachments/129788/public/Final_StatSNSFJan14.pdf

30. Yasmin B. Kafai. 2006. Constructionism. In *The Cambridge Handbook of the Learning Sciences* (1st ed.), Keith R. Sawyer (Ed.). Cambridge University Press, 35–46.

31. Lauren Kirchner. 2015. When Discrimination Is Baked Into Algorithms. *The Atlantic* (Sept. 2015). http://www.theatlantic.com/business/archive/2015/09/discrimination-algorithms-disparate-impact/403969/

32. Bruno Latour. 2007. Beware, your imagination leaves digital traces. *Times Higher Literary Supplement* (April 2007). http://bruno-latour.fr/sites/default/files/P-129-THES-GB.pdf

33. David Lazer, Ryan Kennedy, Gary King, and Alessandro Vespignani. 2014. The Parable of Google Flu: Traps in Big Data Analysis. *Science* 343, 6176 (March 2014), 1203–1205. DOI: http://dx.doi.org/10.1126/science.1248506

34. Caitlin Lustig, Katie Pine, Bonnie Nardi, Lilly Irani, Min Kyung Lee, Dawn Nafus, and Christian Sandvig. 2016. Algorithmic Authority: The Ethics, Politics, and Economics of Algorithms That Interpret, Decide, and Manage. In *Proceedings of the 2016 CHI Conference Extended Abstracts on Human Factors in Computing Systems (CHI EA '16).* ACM, New York, NY, USA, 1057–1062. DOI: http://dx.doi.org/10.1145/2851581.2886426

35. Mary Madden, Susannah Fox, Aaron Smith, and Jessica Vitak. 2007. *Digital Footprints: Online identity management and search in the age of transparency.* Pew Internet & American Life Project, Washington, DC. http://www.pewinternet.org/files/old-media/Files/Reports/2007/PIP_Digital_Footprints.pdf.pdf

36. Jeffrey Mervis. 2016. NSF director unveils big ideas, with an eye on the next president and Congress. *Science* (May 2016). DOI: http://dx.doi.org/10.1126/science.aaf5713

37. Andrés Monroy-Hernández. 2007. ScratchR: sharing user-generated programmable media. In *Proceedings of the 6th international conference on Interaction design and children (IDC '07).* ACM, New York, NY, USA, 167–168. DOI: http://dx.doi.org/10.1145/1297277.1297315

38. Dale Neef. 2014. *Digital Exhaust: What Everyone Should Know About Big Data, Digitization and Digitally Driven Innovation* (1 edition ed.). Pearson FT Press, Indianapolis, IN.

39. Helen Nissenbaum. 2009. *Privacy in context: Technology, policy, and the integrity of social life*. Stanford University Press.
40. Oceans of Data Institute staff. 2016. *Building Global Interest in Data Literacy: A Dialogue*. Technical Report. Oceans of Data Institute, Education Development Center, Inc. 24 pages. http://oceansofdata.org/our-work/building-global-interest-data-literacy-dialogue-workshop-report
41. Cathy O'Neil. 2016. *Weapons of Math Destruction: How Big Data Increases Inequality and Threatens Democracy*. Crown/Archetype.
42. Seymour Papert. 1980. *Mindstorms: Children, Computers, and Powerful Ideas*. Basic Books, Inc., New York, NY, USA.
43. Seymour Papert and Idit Harel. 1991. Situating constructionism. In *Constructionism*. Vol. 36. Ablex Publishing, New York, NY, US, 1–11.
44. Chanda Phelan, Cliff Lampe, and Paul Resnick. 2016. It's Creepy, But It Doesn't Bother Me. In *Proceedings of the 2016 CHI Conference on Human Factors in Computing Systems (CHI '16)*. ACM, New York, NY, USA, 5240–5251. DOI: http://dx.doi.org/10.1145/2858036.2858381
45. Thomas M. Philip, Sarah Schuler-Brown, and Winmar Way. 2013. A Framework for Learning About Big Data with Mobile Technologies for Democratic Participation: Possibilities, Limitations, and Unanticipated Obstacles. *Technology, Knowledge and Learning* 18, 3 (2013), 103–120. DOI: http://dx.doi.org/10.1007/s10758-013-9202-4
46. Jean Piaget. 1970. *Genetic epistemology. Trans. E. Duckworth*. Columbia University Press, New York, NY, US.
47. John Podesta. 2014. *Big Data: Seizing Opportunities, Preserving Values*. Technical Report. Executive Office of the President, United States of America.
48. Jake Porway. 2013. You can't just hack your way to social change. *Harvard Business Review* 7 (2013).
49. Foster Provost and Tom Fawcett. 2013. Data Science and its Relationship to Big Data and Data-Driven Decision Making. *Big Data* 1, 1 (Feb. 2013), 51–59. DOI: http://dx.doi.org/10.1089/big.2013.1508
50. Mitchel Resnick, John Maloney, Andrés Monroy-Hernández, Natalie Rusk, Evelyn Eastmond, Karen Brennan, Amon Millner, Eric Rosenbaum, Jay Silver, Brian Silverman, and Yasmin Kafai. 2009. Scratch: programming for all. *Commun. ACM* 52, 11 (2009), 60–67. DOI: http://dx.doi.org/10.1145/1592761.1592779
51. Susan Jo Russell and Rebecca B. Corwin. 1989. *Statistics: The Shape of the Data. Used Numbers: Real Data in the Classroom. Grades 4-6.* Dale Seymour Publications, Palo Alto, CA. http://eric.ed.gov/?id=ED328451
52. Douglas Thomas and John Seely Brown. 2011. *A New Culture of Learning: Cultivating the Imagination for a World of Constant Change* (1 edition ed.). CreateSpace Independent Publishing Platform, Lexington, Ky.
53. Matthew A. Waller and Stanley E. Fawcett. 2013. Data Science, Predictive Analytics, and Big Data: A Revolution That Will Transform Supply Chain Design and Management. *Journal of Business Logistics* 34, 2 (June 2013), 77–84. DOI: http://dx.doi.org/10.1111/jbl.12010

# Where is the Digital Divide? A Survey of Security, Privacy, and Socioeconomics

**Elissa M. Redmiles**
University of Maryland
eredmiles@cs.umd.edu

**Sean Kross**
Johns Hopkins University
kross@jhu.edu

**Michelle L. Mazurek**
University of Maryland
mmazurek@cs.umd.edu

## ABSTRACT

The behavior of the least-secure user can influence security and privacy outcomes for everyone else. Thus, it is important to understand the factors that influence the security and privacy of a broad variety of people. Prior work has suggested that users with differing socioeconomic status (SES) may behave differently; however, no research has examined how SES, advice sources, and resources relate to the security and privacy incidents users report. To address this question, we analyze a 3,000 respondent, census-representative telephone survey. We find that, contrary to prior assumptions, people with lower educational attainment report equal or fewer incidents as more educated people, and that users' experiences are significantly correlated with their advice sources, regardless of SES or resources.

## ACM Classification Keywords

H.1.2 User/Machine Systems: Human factors

## Author Keywords

usable security, digital divide, computer science education

## INTRODUCTION AND BACKGROUND

Security and privacy are intrinsically collective behaviors—one person who clicks on a malicious email may spread that email to their entire network. As such, it is important to understand how differing knowledge, habits, and priorities can shape security behavior and associated experiences across a broad range of people.

Previous research has established the existence of a *digital divide*: an access, skill, and knowledge gap in digital literacy between lower- and higher-socioeconomic status (SES) populations [11, 12, 14, 28, 32, 33]. However, the bulk of research on this topic has not directly addressed security and privacy. Some researchers have theorized that low-income users "do not value their data as highly," that low-SES users may experience discrimination as a result of differing privacy norms, or may be unable to pay for the increasingly monetized privilege of privacy, leading to worse outcomes [9, 18, 19]. Empirically, we know that variation in SES, along with differences in skills and advice sources that may be partially correlated with SES, are associated with differences in users' security and privacy beliefs and behaviors [10, 13, 23–25, 27, 31, 34]. No prior work, however, has examined how users' SES, advice sources, and resources relate to each other and to the security and privacy experiences that users report.

To better understand this intersection of demographics, information, and experiences—particularly with respect to low-SES users—we analyzed data from a probabilistic, census-representative, telephone survey of 3,000 U.S. respondents, which we received through a data grant from Data&Society. The survey over-sampled from the low-SES population. The thoroughly pretested survey queried respondents' security and privacy experiences, including becoming the victim of a scam, having your identity stolen, having an email or social media account compromised, losing a job or other opportunity as a result of something posted online, and having someone post something about you online without consent; other questions examined respondents' advice sources, available internet resources, and demographics. The relationships identified in our analysis, and the prevalence of the experiences reported by respondents, are accurate within 2.7% of their true values in the entire U.S. population.

In line with prior work, we find that less educated users have different sources of security advice than more educated users. Contrary to prior assumptions, however, we find that low-education users report equal or lower prevalence of negative security and privacy incidents as compared to higher-education users, that there is no relationship between prevalence of reported incidents and income, and that users' reported experiences are related to their advice sources, regardless of their SES or resources. These findings have important implications for how we develop, distribute, and evaluate security and privacy advice, as well as how we think about the digital divide from a security and privacy perspective.

## METHODOLOGY

To examine the relationship between SES, advice sources, resources, and self-reported security and privacy incidents, we modeled the results of a 3,000-respondent telephone survey using binary logistic regression. Our Institutional Review Board (IRB) determined that our analysis of existing data did not constitute human subjects research. Below, we discuss the dataset and survey development process, sampling procedure, details of our statistical analysis, and limitations of our work.


*CHI 2017, May 06 - 11, 2017, Denver, CO, USA*

ACM 978-1-4503-4655-9/17/05...$15.00
DOI: http://dx.doi.org/10.1145/3025453.3025673

### Dataset

The dataset was collected by Princeton Survey Research Associates International (PSRAI) for Data&Society via a computer-assisted-telephone-interview (CATI), random digit dial (RDD) census-representative survey of 3,000 respondents from November 18 to December 23, 2015. We received this dataset through a Data Grant from Data&Society (funded by the Digital Trust Foundation). [1]

The survey was developed by a senior researcher at Data&Society with the intent of releasing the data for analysis regarding the impact of SES on security and privacy. She assembled the survey both by authoring and pre-testing new items and by leveraging a number of pre-tested questions from surveys conducted by Pew and Reason-Rupe [3, 5–7]. The survey asks questions regarding respondents' security and privacy experiences including their advice sources, their prior negative experiences, and the resources available to them, as well as standard demographic questions. The order in which the questions were asked was randomized to prevent order bias [21]. Additionally, demographic questions were placed at the end of the questionnaire to minimize sensitivity and bias, as per expert recommendations and best practices [29].

Prior to deployment, the questionnaire was pretested with a small number of respondents. These interviews were monitored by PSRAI and conducted by experienced interviewers to ensure that respondents understood the questions.

The survey was administered via CATI by professionally trained interviewers in both English and Spanish. Calls were made throughout the day, on multiple days to both landline and cell phones to maximize the chance of connecting with different respondents. Every person in the United States had a non-zero chance of being selected for the survey. [2] This was a probabilistic survey, the dataset was weighted to be representative of the U.S. population, and the findings we report are accurate within 2.7% of the true prevalence in the population. A full outline of the survey items, weighting methodology, and analysis code can be found at `go.umd.edu/2124`.

### Analysis

We built two sets of binary logistic regression models in our analysis, using the survey R library to incorporate the survey weights [22]. The first set of models was used to predict the odds of an individual reporting having experienced a security or privacy incident: one model included respondents' advice sources, another included SES status, and the third combined both. The second set of models predicted the likelihood that respondents with different SES used particular advice sources. We chose a simple grouped model rather than five individual models for ease of interpretability.

To reduce the chance of overfitting our data, we deliberately chose parsimonious models with input factors based on prior work [26]. To further prevent over fitting, we performed 5-fold cross validation in line with commonly used classification and regression practices [15]. We calculated the Akaike Information Criterion (AIC) [8] across five folds for each model, and we found that the AIC values for each fold were within an average of 3% of each other. For each model, we present the outcome variable, including factors, log-adjusted regression coefficients (*odds ratios*), 95% confidence intervals (moderated by the survey design effect [20]), and *p*-values.

[1]The survey development and deployment portion of this study was approved by Chesapeake IRB [4].

[2]Those who did not have a telephone were contacted via mail and, if interested, were provided with a phone to use for the survey.

### Limitations

Self-reported surveys have several common limitations, chiefly related to under- and over-reporting, which may be caused by satisficing (selecting the first satisfactory answer without thinking deeply) [17], recall bias (misremembering experiences), desirability bias (selecting a socially desirable rather than honest answer), and the potential for questions to be misinterpreted. These were mitigated by using thorough question-development and pre-testing processes and by interviewers reminding respondents to answer thoroughly and honestly. The survey was brief, minimizing respondent fatigue.

This survey measures only whether respondents have ever used certain advice sources or had certain negative experiences. As a result, we cannot determine how often a particular advice source was consulted or how many negative experiences a respondent had; nor can we determine whether an advice source was consulted before or after any negative event. Thus, we report our findings together with several hypothetical explanations and suggest that future work should investigate these relationships further. In addition, we did not conduct a controlled experiment, and thus these results should not be interpreted as implying causality.

## RESULTS

Below, we describe the survey sample and the factors that relate to users' security and privacy experiences.

### Sample

Our unweighted sample was nearly representative of the U.S. population with respect to gender, age, education, geographic region, number of adults in the household, population density, household phone usage, and race/ethnicity. The weighted sample is fully representative of the population, such that the 95% confidence interval for this survey is 2.7 points. This confidence interval is calculated based on the survey design effect, which represents the loss in statistical efficiency that results from a disproportionate sample design and systematic non-response. Table 1 compares a subset of the demographics of our weighted and unweighted sample to the 2013 American Community Survey [2]. Further, the prevalence of negative experiences in our data is in line with prior work. [3]

### Security and Privacy Incidents

All internet-using respondents were asked questions regarding negative security and privacy incidents that they had experienced, such as "Have you ever had important personal information stolen, such as your Social Security Number, your credit card, or bank account information?" We find that 49% of all respondents in the weighted data reported at least one of

[3]See `go.umd.edu/2124` for a comparison with Pew 2013 data [1].

| Metric | Unweighted | Weighted | Census |
|---|---|---|---|
| Male | 52.4% | 48.7% | 48.2% |
| Female | 47.6% | 51.3% | 51.8% |
| Caucasian | 58.1% | 62.8% | 65.8% |
| Hispanic | 18.6% | 15.6% | 15% |
| African American | 14.0% | 11.8% | 11.5% |
| Other | 6.7% | 7.4% | 7.6% |
| LT H.S. | 12.8% | 12.6% | 13.3% |
| H.S. grad | 27.4% | 27.8% | 28.0% |
| Some college | 24.0% | 30.0% | 31.0% |
| B.S. or above | 34.6% | 28.7% | 27.7% |
| 18-29 years | 16.3% | 20.1% | 20.9% |
| 30-49 years | 24.6% | 32.6% | 34.7% |
| 50-64 years | 28.8% | 25.4% | 26.0% |
| 65+ years | 27.0% | 18.6% | 18.4% |
| <$20k | 20% | *NA* | 32% |
| $20k-$40k | 21% | *NA* | 19% |
| $40k-$75k | 18% | *NA* | 18% |
| $75k-$100k | 10% | *NA* | 11% |
| $100k-$150k | 8% | *NA* | 12% |
| $150k+ | 7% | *NA* | 8% |

**Table 1. Sample demographics, percentages may not add to 100% due to non-response. Income was the unweighted variable of interest.**

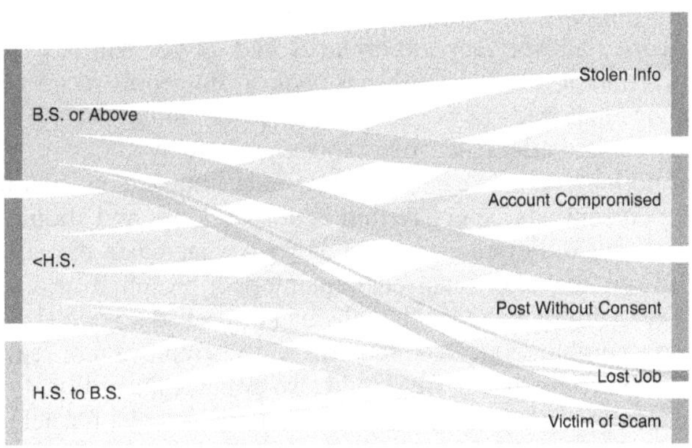


**Figure 1. Prevalence of those who reported a negative experience by education level. Interactive diagram:** `jsfiddle.net/5orqbkp4/3/`.

the negative experiences shown in Figure 1. To determine how these reported incidents relate to respondents' SES, advice sources, and resources, we utilized binary logistic regression models to predict a participant's likelihood of reporting one or more of these experiences. We created three models, detailed below. The results of all three models are presented in Table 2.

First, to understand how SES related to respondents' reported security and privacy incidents, we modeled these incidents as a function only of SES factors. In this model, we find that education is the only factor significantly related to a respondent's likelihood of reporting a negative experience (income was not correlated). Surprisingly, we find that those with lower levels of education—less than a high school diploma, and less than a bachelor's—are 60% and 35% *less* likely, respectively, to report at least one of the five negative experiences (Table 2). While 53% of those in the weighted dataset who hold a bachelor's or above reported a negative experience, only 47% of those who had less than a bachelor's reported such an incident.

| Model | Factor | OR | CI | *p*-value |
|---|---|---|---|---|
| SES & Resources Only | <H.S. | 0.40 | [0.2, 0.81] | 0.01* |
| | H.S. to B.S. | 0.65 | [0.44, 0.97] | 0.03* |
| | <$20K | 1.09 | [0.69, 1.74] | 0.71 |
| | $20-$40K | 1.20 | [0.79, 1.84] | 0.39 |
| | R: Cell only | 0.74 | [0.52, 1.06] | 0.11 |
| | R: Home internet | 1.94 | [0.87, 4.32] | 0.1 |
| Advice Only | A: Friend | 1.85 | [1.25, 2.73] | < 0.01* |
| | A: Website | 1.92 | [1.15, 3.21] | 0.01* |
| | A: Coworker | 1.59 | [0.98, 2.58] | 0.06 |
| | A: Gov. Website | 1.59 | [0.87, 2.88] | 0.13 |
| | A: Librarian | 1.73 | [0.75, 4.02] | 0.2 |
| | A: Teacher | 0.95 | [0.45, 2.01] | 0.9 |
| Advice & SES | A: Friend | 1.84 | [1.24, 2.72] | < 0.01* |
| | A: Website | 1.76 | [1.06, 2.94] | 0.03* |
| | A: Coworker | 1.53 | [0.95, 2.46] | 0.08 |
| | A: Gov. Website | 1.52 | [0.85, 2.74] | 0.16 |
| | A: Librarian | 1.88 | [0.82, 4.31] | 0.14 |
| | A: Teacher | 0.92 | [0.44, 1.96] | 0.83 |
| | <$20K | 1.09 | [0.68, 1.76] | 0.72 |
| | $20-$40K | 1.19 | [0.77, 1.83] | 0.44 |
| | <H.S. | 0.53 | [0.25, 1.09] | 0.09 |
| | H.S. to B.S. | 0.75 | [0.5, 1.13] | 0.17 |
| | R: Mostly cell | 0.77 | [0.53, 1.12] | 0.17 |
| | R: Home internet | 1.73 | [0.77, 3.88] | 0.18 |

**Table 2. Regression results for three different models of reporting at least one negative experience (binary). 'A' and 'R' indicated boolean advice sources and resources, respectively. "Mostly cell" indicates primary internet access via mobile, and "Home internet" means internet at home. Baseline for the categorical household income factor is >$40K; baseline for education is a bachelor's or above. OR is the odds ratio between the given factor and the baseline; CI is the 95% confidence interval.**

Figure 1 illustrates that negative experiences were unevenly distributed across educational groups; 32% of those holding a bachelor's or above reported having information stolen, compared to 20% of those with less than a bachelor's. There are several potential explanations for this finding, which should be explored in future work: less-educated users may be targeted less frequently for scams or identity theft, they may have more difficulty recognizing or recalling negative events, or they may have protective skills or resources not measured in this survey.

Prior work suggests that advice sources are related to users' security behaviors, and therefore potentially to their security experiences [24–26]. Thus, our second model evaluates whether the likelihood of reporting at least one negative incident is significantly related to advice sources. We find that respondents who take advice from friends and websites are 85% and 92% more likely to report at least one negative experience, respectively. Of those who took advice from friends, 49% reported a negative experience, compared to 25% of those who took advice from a co-worker, 21% from a non-governmental website, 14% from a government website, and 8% from a teacher or librarian. This may indicate that respondents more often seek advice from certain sources after a negative experience, that librarians and teachers give particularly good advice, or that respondents are receiving detrimental or difficult to interpret advice from friends, coworkers, and websites. .

Finally, we wanted to understand whether advice and SES were both related to the security and privacy incidents that users report, or whether if we controlled for both variables, only one would remain significant. We therefore constructed

| Factor | OR | CI | $p$-value |
|---|---|---|---|
| <H.S. | 0.01 | [0, 0.06] | $< 0.01$* |
| H.S. to B.S. | 0.49 | [0.31, 0.79] | $< 0.01$* |
| <$20K | 0.86 | [0.42, 1.73] | 0.66 |
| $20-$40K | 0.66 | [0.36, 1.22] | 0.19 |
| R: Cell only | 0.69 | [0.4, 1.18] | 0.17 |
| R: Home Internet | 1.62 | [0.5, 5.24] | 0.42 |

**Table 3. Regression results for website advice source model. Tables for all advice sources: go.umd.edu/2124.**

a third model containing both advice and SES as explanatory factors. We find that only advice sources are significant factors. Using a likelihood ratio test [30], we find that this combined model has a goodness of fit significantly better than the SES-only model ($X^2$=45.09, $p < 0.001$, $df = 1164$) and not significantly different from the advice-only model ($X^2$=7.33 $p = 0.29$, $df = 1164$). This suggests that users' negative experiences relate to their advice sources, regardless of SES.

### Advice, SES, and Resources

While we find that privacy and security incidents are related to respondents' advice sources, rather than their SES, we were curious to determine whether our prior finding—that there is an SES gap in advice sources [25]—held true in our sample. To do so, we constructed logistic regression models with users' advice sources as outcome variables and SES factors as inputs.

Our results show that users' advice sources are related to their level of education; Figure 2 provides an overview of respondents' reported advice sources organized by education. We find that users who hold less than a high school diploma are 99% less likely to report a coworker as an advice source, and those who hold less than a bachelor's degree, but who completed high school, are 51% less likely (Table 3). Similarly, those who held a high school diploma were 50% less likely to report coworkers and those with under a high school education were 73% less likely to report using government websites. Perhaps surprisingly, there was no significant difference in the SES or resources of respondents who reported taking advice from librarians, friends, and teachers. Overall, these results confirm our prior findings.

We hypothesize that these findings relate to less-educated users having different job roles, possessing relatively fewer internet skills [14], and distrusting websites that provide general advice without a clear source [26]. We also hypothesize that advice from websites may be more difficult to read and interpret than advice from other sources. Of note, there was no relationship between available internet resources and advice sources, implying that accessibility of advice related to devices and internet access may not be a problem.

## DISCUSSION AND FUTURE WORK

In this study, we used logistic regression to investigate how users' advice sources, SES, and resources relate to the security and privacy experiences they report. Our findings, accurate within 2.7% of the true prevalence in the U.S. population, suggest first that advice is significantly correlated with security and privacy incidents; second, that reported incidents are not directly tied to SES but to a divide in where users of differing

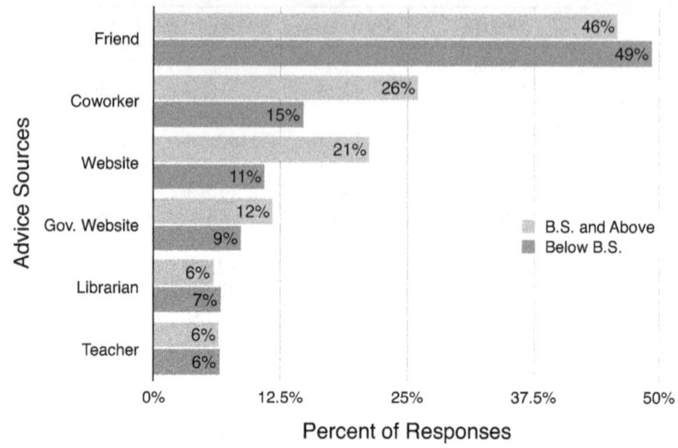


**Figure 2. Respondents' advice sources by education (weighted).**

educational attainment seek advice; and third, that less educated users report equal or fewer security and privacy incidents as more educated users. Below, we place our results in context and provide suggestions for future work.

### Advice Matters

Our findings show a clear relationship between respondents' security and privacy experiences and advice sources. The direction of this relationship is unclear: do people receive bad advice that leads to worse experiences, or do they wait to seek advice until after a negative experience? We hypothesize some of both. In either case, however, this finding confirms that the current advice ecosystem is not working, and should be reevaluated. Future work should revisit what makes bad advice bad—outdated or incorrect content, poor presentation, a lack of readability, belief in the talisman of useless advice [16], or some combination—and look for ways to remove it or replace it with better advice. We should also evaluate the utility of new channels, such as public service announcements, for helping users find good advice.

### Redefining the Digital Divide

Researchers have previously identified differences in skills, resources, and advice sources between lower- and higher-SES users. Our findings challenge the assumption that these differences lead to worse security and privacy outcomes for low-SES users. In particular, we find that income and available resources, such as in-home internet, have no impact on reported incidents. In line with prior work [25], we find that less educated users rely on less traditionally authoritative advice sources, such as friends and family. Unexpectedly, this difference is correlated with reporting slightly fewer negative incidents; further study is required to understand the causes of this result. There may be valuable lessons to learn from how less-educated users transmit security and privacy skills.

## ACKNOWLEDGEMENTS

Our thanks to Cody Buntain, Tamara Clegg, Jon Froehlich, Mary Madden, and Brenna McNally. This work was supported by Data&Society and by Maryland Procurement Office contract no. H98230-14-C-013.

## REFERENCES


1. 2013. Anonymity Omnibus Dataset. (2013). http://www.pewinternet.org/datasets/july-2013-anonymity-omnibus/
2. 2014. American Community Survey 5-Year Estimates. (2014). http://www.census.gov/programs-surveys/acs/news/data-releases/2014/release.html
3. 2015. National Cybersecurity Alliance. (2015). https://staysafeonline.org/
4. 2016. Chesapeake IRB. (2016). https://www.chesapeakeirb.com/
5. 2016a. Pew American Trends Panel. (2016). http://www.pewresearch.org/methodology/u-s-survey-research/american-trends-panel/
6. 2016b. Pew Internet and American Life Project. (2016). http://www.pewinternet.org/
7. 2016. Reason-Rupe Surveys. (2016). http://reason.com/poll
8. H. Akaike. 1974. A new look at the statistical model identification. *IEEE Trans. Automat. Control* (1974). DOI: http://dx.doi.org/10.1109/TAC.1974.1100705
9. boyd D., Levy K., and Arwick A. 2013. The Networked Nature of Algorithmic Discrimination. Data and Discrimination: Collected Essays. (2013). http://newamerica.org/downloads/OTI-Data-an-Discrimination-FINAL-small.pdf
10. C. Ciampa. 2013. A comparison of password feedback mechanisms and their impact on password entropy. *Information Management & Computer Security* (2013). DOI:http://dx.doi.org/10.1108/IMCS-12-2012-0072
11. E. Hargittai. 2002. Second-Level Digital Divide: Mapping Differences in People's Online Skills. *First Monday* (2002). http://arxiv.org/abs/cs.CY/0109068
12. E. Hargittai. 2003. *The Digital Divide and What to Do About It.* http://www.eszter.com/research/pubs/hargittai-digitaldivide.pdf
13. E. Hargittai. 2007. Whose Space? Differences Among Users and Non-Users of Social Network Sites. *Journal of Computer-Mediated Communication* 13, 1 (2007), 276–297. DOI: http://dx.doi.org/10.1111/j.1083-6101.2007.00396.x
14. E. Hargittai and Y.P. Hsieh. 2012. Succinct Survey Measures of Web-Use Skills. *Soc. Sci. Comput. Rev.* (2012). DOI: http://dx.doi.org/10.1177/0894439310397146
15. T. Hastie, R. Tibshirani, and J. Friedman. 2009. *The Elements of Statistical Learning: Data Mining, Inference, and Prediction, Second Edition.* Springer New York. http://www.springer.com/us/book/9780387848570
16. C. Herley. 2016. The Unfalsifiability of Security Claims. (2016). https://www.usenix.org/conference/usenixsecurity16/technical-sessions/presentation/herley
17. A. L. Holbrook, M. C. Green, and J. A. Krosnick. 2003. Telephone versus Face-to-Face Interviewing of National Probability Samples with Long Questionnaires: Comparisons of Respondent Satisficing and Social Desirability Response Bias. *Public Opinion Quarterly* (2003). http://poq.oxfordjournals.org/cgi/citmgr?gca=pubopq;67/1/79
18. A. E. Howe, I. Ray, M. Roberts, M. Urbanska, and Z. Byrne. 2012. The Psychology of Security for the Home Computer User.. In *IEEE S&P.* http://www.ieee-security.org/TC/SP2012/papers/4681a209.pdf
19. J. Jerome. 2013. Buying and Selling Privacy: Big Data's Different Burdens and Benefits. *Stanford Law Review* (2013). http://www.stanfordlawreview.org/online/privacy-and-big-data/buying-and-selling-privacy
20. L. Kish. 1965. *Survey sampling.* http://www.wiley.com/WileyCDA/WileyTitle/productCd-0471109495.html
21. J. A. Krosnick. 2010. *Handbook of Survey Research.* http://www.sciencedirect.com/science/book/9780125982269
22. T. Lumley. 2016. R 'survey': Analysis of Complex Survey Samples. (2016). https://cran.r-project.org/web/packages/survey/survey.pdf
23. M. Micheli. 2016. Social networking sites and low-income teenagers: between opportunity and inequality. *Information, Communication & Society* (2016). DOI: http://dx.doi.org/10.1080/1369118X.2016.1139614
24. E. Rader, R. Wash, and B. Brooks. 2012. Stories As Informal Lessons About Security. In *SOUPS.* DOI: http://dx.doi.org/10.1145/2335356.2335364
25. E.M. Redmiles, S. Kross, and M. L. Mazurek. 2016a. How I Learned to be Secure: a Census-Representative Survey of Security Advice Sources and Behavior. In *CCS.* http://dl.acm.org/citation.cfm?id=2978307
26. E.M. Redmiles, A. R. Malone, and M. L. Mazurek. 2016b. I Think They're Trying to Tell Me Something: Advice Sources and Selection in Digital Security. In *IEEE S&P.* http://www.ieee-security.org/TC/SP2016/papers/0824a272.pdf
27. E.M. Redmiles, S. Silverstein, W. Bai, and M. L. Mazurek. 2016c. More Skilled Internet Users Behave (A Little) More Securely. In *SOUPS.* https://www.usenix.org/sites/default/files/SOUPS16poster20-redmiles.pdf
28. R. E. Rice. 2006. Influences, usage, and outcomes of Internet health information searching: Multivariate results from the Pew surveys. *International J. Medical Informatics* (2006). DOI: http://dx.doi.org/10.1016/j.ijmedinf.2005.07.032
29. N.C. Schaeffer and S. Presser. 2003. The Science of Asking Questions. *Annual Review of Sociology* (2003). DOI: http://dx.doi.org/10.1146/annurev.soc.29.110702.110112

30. A.J. Scott and J.N.K. Rao. 1984. On Chi-squared Tests For Multiway Contingency Tables with Proportions Estimated From Survey Data. *Annals of Statistics* (1984). https://www.jstor.org/stable/2241033

31. S. Sheng, M. Holbrook, P. Kumaraguru, L. F. Cranor, and J. Downs. 2010. Who Falls for Phish?: A Demographic Analysis of Phishing Susceptibility and Effectiveness of Interventions. In *CHI*. http://doi.acm.org/10.1145/1753326.1753383

32. L.D. Stanley. 2003. Beyond Access: Psychosocial Barriers to Computer Literacy Special Issue: ICTs and Community Networking. *The Information Society* (2003). DOI:http://dx.doi.org/10.1080/715720560

33. J. van Dijk and K. Hacker. 2003. The Digital Divide as a Complex and Dynamic Phenomenon. *The Information Society* (2003). DOI: http://dx.doi.org/10.1080/01972240309487

34. R. Wash and E. Rader. 2015. Too Much Knowledge? Security Beliefs and Protective Behaviors Among United States Internet Users. In *SOUPS*. https://www.usenix.org/conference/SOUPS2015/proceedings/presentation/wash

# A Unified Framework for Knowledge Assessment and Progression Analysis and Design

**Shuhan Wang[1], Fang He[2], and Erik Andersen[1]**

[1]Department of Computer Science
Cornell University
{forsona, eland}@cs.cornell.edu

[2]Department of Computer Science
Peking University
wh27hf@gmail.com

## ABSTRACT

Designing engaging learning content is important but difficult, and typically involves a lot of manual specification. We present a unified framework that utilizes automatic problem decomposition and partial ordering graph construction to facilitate multiple workflows: knowledge assessment and progression analysis and design. We present results from a study with 847 participants in an online Japanese-language assessment tool demonstrating that our framework can efficiently measure student ability and predict student performance on specific problems. We also present results from analysis of curricula showing that the progressions of two different textbooks are surprisingly similar, and that our framework can lead to the discovery of general principles of expert progression design. Finally, we demonstrate automatic progression generation with desired sequencing and pacing, allowing for tailoring of progressions and mapping of parameters extracted from one curriculum onto another.

## ACM Classification Keywords

H.5.0 Information Interfaces and Presentation: General

## Author Keywords

education; automatic problem decomposition; knowledge assessment; progression analysis and design

## INTRODUCTION

A key challenge in education is keeping students engaged, and a primary consideration is the optimal sequence of knowledge to present to a particular student. One challenge is ordering: which knowledge should be introduced first? Another is speed: how quickly should the progression get more difficult? Although there are guiding principles from education and psychology [15, 55, 59] that can help design progressions, we lack pragmatic and automatic ways to bridge the gap between educational theory and practice, especially at the scale of an entire curriculum. The difficulty of designing and optimizing progressions also limits the ability of curricula to adapt to the needs of each student.



*CHI 2017*, May 06 - 11, 2017, Denver, CO, USA



ISBN 978-1-4503-4655-9/17/05. . . $15.00

DOI: http://dx.doi.org/10.1145/3025453.3025841

In HCI, this problem is relevant to the design of educational software [7, 14], video games [11, 22, 33, 37, 45], and software learnability [25, 31]. We currently design progressions mostly by hand, which is expensive and limits our ability of experimenting to find the best progressions. Recently, there has been some work in automatic progression design [6, 11]. Although this work is capable of organizing content automatically, it only addressed procedural topics and video game level design. We still lack a general framework of characterizing educational progressions capable of handling some non-procedural topics like language learning. Furthermore, we need a formal way to assess a student's knowledge using the same framework, so that we can tailor the learning progression and pace for that student. Ideally, we would be able to build adaptive progressions for a wide range of educational domains, with a minimum of effort.

In this paper, we present a framework that allows for automatic problem decomposition and partial ordering graph construction for non-procedural tasks. This framework facilitates multiple workflows. It builds upon item response theory [53], knowledge space theory [28], and knowledge tracing [14] to create multidimensional metrics of student knowledge and problem difficulty, which allows for rapid assessment and prediction of performance. It also defines a parameter space of pacing and other progression parameters, and provides a way to characterize and compare progressions as well as design new progressions that conform to desired parameters.

We present multiple evaluations of our framework. First, we present theoretical contributions for automatic problem decomposition and partial ordering graph construction for grammatical understanding in a foreign language, an important non-procedural topic. We then discuss a user evaluation of a Japanese language assessment tool with 847 participants, demonstrating that our automatic assessment algorithms can lead to accurate measurement of ability and predictions of performance according to item response theory. We also present results for automatic analysis of language learning progressions, showing that two textbooks for learning Japanese have surprisingly similar pacing and other progression characteristics, and that two online language learning tools have very different progression design strategies. Finally, we demonstrate that our framework can automatically generate progressions with desired characteristics, such as the learning pace and the proportion of learning and review. This allows for insights gained from progression analysis to be directly applied to progression design and individual progression tailoring.

## RELATED WORK

### Intelligent Tutoring Systems

There are successful adaptive learning systems such as Cognitive Tutors [7]. Some of this work has focused on language learning specifically [63, 65]. Cognitive Tutors utilize knowledge tracing [14] to track knowledge acquisition and provide tailored instruction, by tracking performance on individual production rules in a cognitive model [14, 39]. This model has been extended in several ways, including estimating of the initial probability that the student knows a skill [49], estimating of the impact of help features on probability of acquisition [10], and integrating with models of item difficulty [50]. Another method is logistic regression, which is particularly efficient for tasks involving multiple skills [64]. However, these approaches typically do not consider pacing. Instead, they continually give problems that exercise a specific production rule until a Hidden Markov Model has achieved 95% confidence that the student has learned that rule, and then move on to the next concept. Furthermore, Cognitive Tutors are difficult to construct. It has been estimated that as much as 200-300 hours of expert design effort are required to design a single hour of content [3], although newer design techniques have reduced this to 50-100 hours [4]. Our work seeks to develop automatic ways of analyzing and optimizing educational progressions.

### Education and Psychology

Many theories support the idea that *moderate difficulty* is important for engagement [1, 8, 16, 20, 34, 47]. Chess players are happiest when playing players ranked slightly above them [1]. Analyses of progressions in non-competitive games also support the use of moderate difficulty [44]. Csikszentmihalyi's theory of flow stipulates that people are most engaged when the challenge is neither too high or too low [16]. Vygotsky's zone of proximal development [59] stipulates that there is a set of concepts that a learner can acquire next with some guidance, and educational content should continually target this set. Reigeluth and Stein's Elaboration Theory [55] argues that the simplest version of a task should be taught first, followed by progressively more complex tasks that elaborate on the original task. Li et al. studied problem orderings by examining them with a machine learning agent, finding that interleaved problem orderings led to faster learning than blocked orderings [43]. We currently lack pragmatic and automatic ways to quantitatively describe these principles and apply them to real progressions, and our work aims to do this.

### Language education

Krashen [42] proposed that concepts are learned in a predictable order (the *natural order hypothesis*), and that language acquisition occurs when a learner is exposed to language that is just beyond the edge of what he or she can understand (the *input hypothesis*). There is widespread evidence in the language learning literature that learners progress through distinct stages in their use of grammatical morphemes [30], verb negation [13, 62], questions [52], possessive determiners [61, 66], relative clauses [29, 38], and temporal reference [48]. Our work seeks to create a platform that can evaluate these theories and determine if they can motivate grounded learning progressions that lead to increased learning and engagement.

### Trace-based partial orderings

Andersen et al. proposed a technique for automatically exploring the space of task progressions through static analysis of the procedure to be learned [6]. This technique characterizes tasks by analyzing the *execution trace* obtained by running the procedure on that task. By characterizing each task as a sequence of basic operations, one can specify a *partial ordering* that ranks the difficulty of problems. This partial ordering has been experimentally confirmed to match well with users' perceptions of difficulty in an educational algebra game [6]. The trace-based framework has been applied to math [6], video game level design [11], and teaching the Thai alphabet [5]. This work also used test-input generation tools like Pex [58] and FShell [36], which systematically create test case suites with high code coverage, to generate problems for all possible traces (within certain bounds). However, this framework cannot be applied to non-procedural topics. For example, it is unclear how to analyze the execution trace of how a human understands natural language. We build on this work by proposing a general framework of problem decomposition and organization, which can be applied to non-procedural educational domains such as language learning. Within this framework, we can measure a student's ability and predict the student's performance on new problems.

### Knowledge Assessment: IRT and KST

Item Response Theory (IRT) provides a framework for knowledge assessment [26, 27, 54]. IRT argues that the probability of a correct response to an item is a function of item parameters and individual ability [32]. Lord et al. proposed the 3PL model [46], which takes three item parameters into consideration: item difficulty, item discrimination, and the probability of guessing. A simpler model was proposed by Rasch [53], which stipulates that the probability of a correct response is determined only by the difference between the student's ability and the difficulty of the item. However, a common drawback of IRT models is that they measure student ability and item difficulty with unidimensional numeric scores [28], which does not reflect that students may find varying subsets of problems to be difficult depending on what they have mastered. We propose a novel way of measuring the difference between a student's ability and the difficulty of a problem that captures such variations. We validate this model with user data collected from an online knowledge assessment platform.

Knowledge Space Theory (KST) is a well-established perspective for studying the hierarchical structure of knowledge and a powerful tool for knowledge assessment [23, 24]. There are several tutoring systems based on KST, such as Alexs [28], RATH [35] and one for learning organic chemistry [57]. According to KST, a student's knowledge is represented as a knowledge state, the set of the problems that the student can solve. Problems are organized into a knowledge structure, which contains all possible knowledge states as well as the connections between these states [2, 40, 41]. Researchers have proposed approaches for building knowledge structures, such as querying experts [41] and Bayesian inference [21]. Due to the complexity of representing a knowledge state, Falmagne et al. introduced the idea of a "fringe" to characterize a student's knowledge, which can be calculated by an "entropy"-based approach [28]. We build on this work by proposing an automatic framework that can decompose a problem into its prerequisite basic skills and builds the hierarchical structure for a set of problems. Then, our framework can predict a student's performance on new problems by measuring the relationship of the student's ability to the problem within this structure.

## PARTIAL ORDERINGS FOR NON-PROCEDURAL SKILLS

In order to select practice problems at an appropriate difficult level for each student, we need a hierarchical structure that encodes difficulty relationships between problems. One straightforward way to do this is to ask experts to specify these relationships. However, this becomes prohibitively difficult as the size of the problem set grows larger. Ideally, we would have automatic methods of problem organization.

In previous work [6, 12], researchers built partial ordering graphs for procedural tasks. This work used procedural execution traces to organize content and partial orderings over those traces to create hierarchical content structures. For example, one can identify at least four basic skills that may be required to solve an integer addition problem: one-digit addition without a carry (A), one-digit addition with a carry (B), writing a carry (C), and bringing down a final carry (D). As an example, problems can be decomposed into basic skills as follows:

| Problem | 2+3 | 15+18 | 93+15 | 298+865 |
|---|---|---|---|---|
| Trace | A | ACB | AACD | ACBCBD |

However, in some domains, such as language learning, the target knowledge cannot easily be modeled as a single procedure. To induce hierarchical knowledge structures in such domains, we need to generalize beyond procedural domains. To do this, our framework takes advantage of *compositionality*, the idea that problems can be broken down into smaller conceptual units. This is well-studied in some semi-procedural domains such as math and language learning [6, 60].

For instance, a Japanese sentence can be decomposed into *grammatical templates*, units of grammar that expert language instructors and linguists have identified as the most important grammatical knowledge, and that students actually study in language lessons. These templates have proved to be beneficial for text difficulty evaluation for language learners [60]. We found that the specific task of grammatically understanding a Japanese sentence can be decomposed into a (multi)set of grammatical templates. For example, here are three Japanese sentences and their grammatical templates:

S1: 私 の 先生
I of teacher
" my teacher "
Templates: (– の)

S2: 私 の 先生 は 忙しい
I of teacher (topic) busy
" my teacher is busy "
Templates: (– の) (– は)

S3: 私 の 先生 の 名前
I of teacher of name
" my teacher's name "
Templates: (– の) (– の)

We can see that S1 has only one grammatical template: (– の). For a Japanese learner, S2 is harder than S1 since it has not only (– の), but also another template (– は). S3 repeats the same template (– の) twice hence is also harder than S1. These relationships cannot be captured by the partial ordering in [6] since it is unclear how to proceduralize the process of how a human understands these sentences. However, by considering multisets of concepts rather than execution traces, we can accommodate them as follows:

**Definition 1a.** A problem $s$ can be decomposed into a series of concepts (basic skills) required by problem $s$. Since problems may require students to repeat some skills one or more times, we use a *multiset* of basic skills, indicated as $p(s)$, to characterize the difficulty of a problem.

**Definition 1b.** We say problem $s_1$ is *at least as hard as* $s_2$, indicated as $s_1 \geq s_2$, if and only if $p(s_1) \sqsupseteq p(s_2)$. This implies that if a student can solve $s_1$, he/she must be able to solve $s_2$ as well [6].

Here $\sqsupseteq$ denotes the superset relation between multisets. If $p(s_1) \sqsupseteq p(s_2)$, then for any concept $c$ that is required by problem $s_2$ $n$ times, $c$ must also be required by $s_1$ at least $n$ times. For example, AABC $\sqsupseteq$ ABC is true, while AABCC $\sqsupseteq$ ABBC is not true since ABBC has two "B"s while AABCC has only one.

**Definition 1c.** The strict partial order $s_1 > s_2$ is defined as $s_1 \geq s_2 \wedge s_2 \ngeq s_1$, which means $s_1$ is *(strictly) harder than* $s_2$.

**Definition 1d.** We say problem $s_1$ is *directly harder than* $s_2$, if and only if $s_1 > s_2$ and there is no other problem $s_3$ such that $s_1 > s_3 > s_2$.

Using Definition 1d, we build the hierarchical structure for a set of problems as follows:

**Definition 2.** We organize a set of problems $S = \{s_1, s_2, \cdots\}$ (we call $S$ the *universal problem set*) as a *partial ordering graph* $G = \langle S, E \rangle$, where

$$E = \{(s_i, s_j) | s_i, s_j \in S \wedge s_j \text{ is directly harder than } s_i\} \quad (1)$$

Namely, there is an (directed) edge from problem $s_i$ to $s_j$ in the partial ordering graph if and only if $s_j$ is directly harder than $s_i$. An example of a partial ordering graph is shown in Figure 1.

## THE KNOWLEDGE BOUNDARY

Up until now, we have described how to build a partial ordering graph. In order to give practice problems that are at the appropriate difficulty level we need to assess students' knowledge. This is challenging because every student will understand a different subset of the problems. Therefore, we introduce the idea of the *knowledge boundary*, the "fringe" of knowledge that we use to characterize a student's ability in the partial ordering graph[1].

[1] Knowledge Space Theory defined the fringe of knowledge as a simpler representation of a student's knowledge state. However, we define the knowledge boundary in a partial ordering graph, which provides a way to measure how far away a problem is from what a student currently knows.

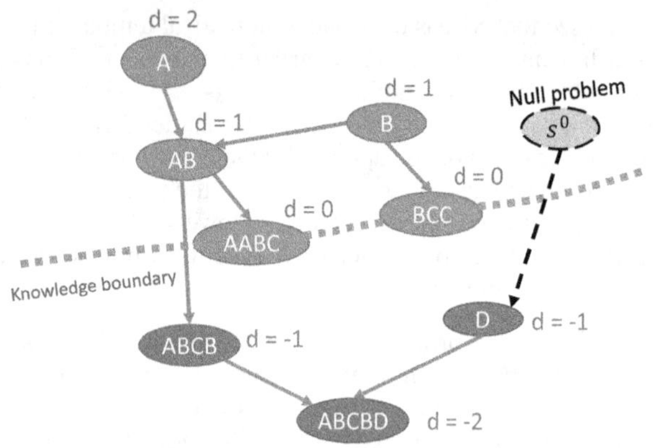


**Figure 1. A Student's Knowledge boundary in the partial orderi graph. Uppercase letters represent concepts and the nodes with strin represent problems. The student can solve the green problems while ca not solve the red ones. The distances form each problem to the kno edge boundary are indicated as $d$. The null problem $s^0$ is an anxio problem that is added to help us compute the distances.**

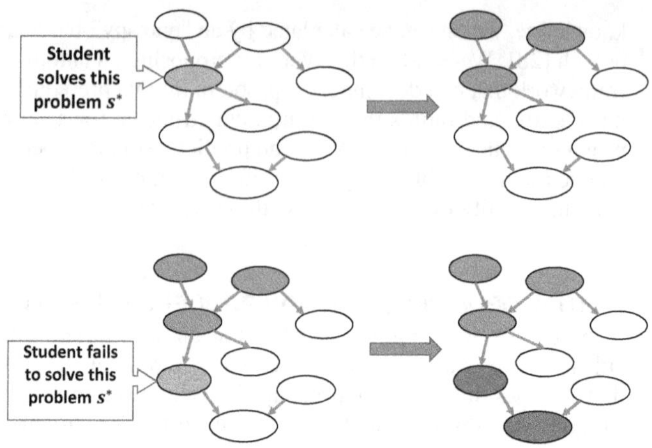


**Figure 2. Coloring the partial ordering graph based on the student's response. If the student solves $s^*$, all the nodes that are at most as hard as $s^*$ (including $s^*$ itself) will be colored 'solvable' (green); if the student fails to solve $s^*$, all the nodes that are at least as hard as $s^*$ (including $s^*$ it self) will be colored 'unsolvable' (red).**

**Definition 3.** We measure a student's ability with the *knowledge boundary K*, which is defined as the hardest problems that the student can solve. Formally, if $T$ is the set of the problems that the student can solve, then:

$$K = \{s|s \in T \wedge \nexists\, s' \in T \text{ such that } s' > s\} \tag{2}$$

Consider the partial ordering graph in Figure 1 as an example. Assume a student can solve problems A, AB, B, AABC and BCC (the green nodes in the graph), and cannot solve ABCB, D or ABCBD (the red nodes in the graph). Then the knowledge boundary consists of only two problems: AABC and BCC, since there are no other "green" problems that are harder than AABC or BCC. The knowledge boundary does not include A, AB or B since there is a "green" problem AABC that is harder than all of them.

## CALCULATING THE KNOWLEDGE BOUNDARY

We present a graph coloring algorithm of calculating a student's knowledge boundary in the partial ordering graph. This algorithm is based on two properties of the partial ordering: if a student can solve problem $s$, he must be able to solve any problem $s'$ that is at most as hard as $s$ ($s \geq s'$); if a student cannot solve problem $s$, he must not be able to solve any problem $s'$ that is at least as hard as $s$ ($s' \geq s$). For example, if a student can solve problem AB, he/she can also solve problems A and B; if a student cannot solve problem ABCB, then he/she cannot solve problem ABCBD either.

At the start of the algorithm, all the problems (nodes) in the partial ordering graph are uncolored. The algorithm asks the student whether he/she can solve some problem $s^*$. If the student can solve $s^*$, all the nodes that are at most as hard as $s^*$ (including $s^*$ itself) will be colored 'solvable'; if the student cannot solve $s^*$, all the nodes that are at least as hard as $s^*$ (including $s^*$ it self) will be colored 'unsolvable'. Figure 2 shows how this coloring process works.

The algorithm repeatedly selects an uncolored problem $s^*$ from the partial ordering graph, asks the student to solve it, and then updates the coloring of the graph based on the response. This is a greedy algorithm designed to minimize the number of problems that must be given to the student. Formally, if $n_s^+$ denotes the number of the uncolored problems that are at most as hard as $s$, and $n_s^-$ denotes the number of the uncolored problems that are at least as hard as $s$, then we can maximize the number of problems that can be colored based on the student's response by greedily selecting a problem $s^*$ as follows:

$$s^* = \underset{s \text{ is uncolored}}{\arg\max}\ \min(n_s^+, n_s^-) \tag{3}$$

## PREDICTING PERFORMANCE ON SPECIFIC PROBLEMS

### Distance to Knowledge Boundary

In order to recommend problems at appropriate difficulty levels to the students, we need to predict students' performance on problems. Existing IRT studies have proposed several popular models stipulating how student performance is related to student ability [46, 53]. However, they measure a student's ability and the difficulty of a problem using unidimensional numeric scores, which is incomprehensive [28].

Ideally, prediction of a student's performance would utilize multidimensional metrics to measure the distance between a problem and what a student already knows. The key technical challenge in the design of multidimensional metrics is that it is impossible to measure this distance without taking into account the hierarchical structure of the problem space. In our framework, we can measure this as the distance from the problem to the knowledge boundary in the partial ordering graph. We use signed numbers to distinguish which 'side' of the knowledge boundary a problem is on: problems 'inside' the boundary (which the student can solve) have positive distances while problems 'outside' the boundary (which the student cannot solve) have negative distances. Using this distance, we can leverage IRT models to predict a student's performance on new problems.

Here, we give the definition of this distance together with the examples in Figure 1. Assume we have the universal problem set $S$, and a student can solve a subset of problems $T$. For example, in Figure 1, $S =$ {A, AB, B, AABC, BCC, ABCB, D, ABCBD}, $T =$ {A, AB, B, AABC, BCC}, and the knowledge boundary $K =$ {AABC, BCC}. We calculate the distance from any problem $s \in S$ to the knowledge boundary $K$, indicated as $d(s,K)$, following the steps below:

*Step 1: Calculate distances for problems on the boundary*
For any problem $s$ such that $s \in K$, $d(s,K) = 0$.

For example, the distance of problems AABC and BCC is 0.

*Step 2: Calculate distances for problems inside the boundary*
For any problem $s$ such that $s \in T - K$, based on the definition of $K$, there must be one or more $s' \in K$ such that $s' \geq s$ (otherwise, $s$ should be contained in $K$) , and

$$d(s,K) = \min_{s' \in K} dis(s,s') \tag{4}$$

where $dis(s,s')$ indicates the length of the shortest directed path from $s$ to $s'$ in the partial ordering graph. If there is no directed path from $s$ to $s'$, $dis(s,s') = \infty$. Note that if $s' \geq s$, then there must exist at least one directed path from $s'$ to $s$.

For example, the distance of problem AB is 1, since problem AABC, which is on the knowlegde boundary, is directly harder than AB. Similar for problem B (BCC is direclty harder than B). The distance of problem A is 2, since the shortest directed path from A to any problem on the knowledge boundary (which is A→AB→AABC) has length 2.

*Step 3: Calculate distances for problems outside the boundary*
In a hierarchical knowledge structure, it follows intuitively that problems that are further away from the boundary will be more difficult to the student. Therefore, for any problem $s$ such that $s \in S - T$, we define the distance $d(s,K)$ to be shortest directed path from any problem in $T$ to $s$. Note that this distance also has a teaching interpretation: if easier problems should always be taught before harder problems [55], then this distance also measures the number of problems that need to be taught before teaching $s$.

Since there are some basic problems that have no problems easier than them, and thus have no incoming edges in the partial ordering graph, there is not always a path from a problem in $T$ to $s$. For instance, there is no directed path from any problem in $T$ to problem $D$ in Figure 1. To resolve this, we add a *null problem* $s^0$, the pseudo problem with no prerequisite concepts, to $T$. For any problem $s \in S - T$, if there is no other problem $s'$ such that $s$ is directly harder than $s'$ (namely, $s$ has no incoming edges), we add an edge $(s^0, s)$ to the partial ordering graph.

Now there is at least one directed path from the null problem $s^0$ or some problem in $T$ to $s$. We can define the distance as:

$$d(s,K) = - \min_{s' \in T \cup \{s^0\}} dis(s',s) \tag{5}$$

Note that $d(s,K)$ is negative if and only if $s$ is outside the knowledge boundary.

For example, the distance of problem ABCB is -1, since it is directly harder than the "green" problem AB. Problem D has no incoming edges in the partial ordering graph, hence we add an edge from the null problem $s^0$ to D, and the distance of problem D is -1 since the path $s^0$ →D has length 1. Lastly, the distance of problem ABCBD is -2. Actually, there are two shortest paths with length 2: AB→ABCB→ABCBD and $s^0$ →D→ABCBD.

The metric of distance is dependent on the density of the partial-ordering graph. This is inevitable since the measurement is based on the hierarchical structure of the problem space. We believe that for most well-defined problem spaces, it is a reasonable assumption that the partial ordering graph will be sufficiently dense. We will demonstrate this metric works well for a well-built Japanese language learning corpus in the next section.

In the later part of this paper, we will use $d$ to denote $d(s,K)$ for convenience.

### Adapted Rasch model

In this section, we describe how we can adapt existing unidimensional IRT models to build a multidimensional metric that leverages the partial ordering graph and the distance $d$ calculated in the previous section in order to predict student performance. One of the most famous models of IRT, the Rasch model [53], stipulates that a student's performance $P$ is a function of the difference between the student's ability $\theta$ and the problem's difficulty $b$:

$$P(\theta,b) = \frac{e^{\theta-b}}{1+e^{\theta-b}} \tag{6}$$

In the Rasch model, $\theta - b$ measures the difference between the student's ability and the difficulty of the problem. In our framework, we use $d$ to measure this, hence we want to replace $\theta - b$ with $d$. It is also common to add a *discrimination* parameter $a$, which represents the degree to which the task discriminates between students [19]. In addition, we have found in practice that we need to add an additional parameter $c$, which measures how 'comfortable' the students feel with the problems on the knowledge boundary (any problem $s$ such that $s \in K$). Ideally, students should be able to solve the problems on the boundary. However, in reality, students may still experience some difficulty with these problems. We can thus replace $\theta - b$ with $ad + c$.

This brings us to an adapted Rasch model, which stipulates how student performance $P$ is related to the distance $d$:

$$P(d) = \frac{e^{ad+c}}{1+e^{ad+c}} \tag{7}$$

In the next section, we will demonstrate that this adapted model nicely fits the data collected from our knowledge assessment platform.

## EVALUATION OF KNOWLEDGE ASSESSMENT

In this section, we will the evaluate our calculation of the knowledge boundary and the distance presented in the previous section by applying it to a Japanese language learning domain.

**Figure 3. Screenshot of J100 Platform (Assessment Stage)**

### J100: A Language Assessment Platform

J100 is a language assessment platform that evaluates how well a user understands the grammatical knowledge in *Genki I* [9] (JLPT level N5[2]). It is designed for Japanese beginners who have learned Japanese for less than 1 year. As the platform starts, users view 15-18 Japanese sentences as well as corresponding vocabulary explanations and sentence translations[3]. The J100 platform will ask users to judge how well they understand each sentence. All of the test sentences were collected from *Genki I*. Figure 3 shows a screenshot of the J100 platform.

J100 has 2 stages: *assessment* and *evaluation*. In the assessment stage, users view 10 sentences and respond whether they understand each sentence ('Yes' or 'No'). Using the graph-coloring algorithm, we calculate a user's knowledge boundary based on his or her responses in this stage. In the evaluation stage, users view 5-8 additional sentences and are asked to indicate how well they understand each sentence ('Yes', 'Almost', 'Somewhat', 'Little', or 'No'). Sentences used in the assessment stage are not repeated in the evaluation stage. The responses in the evaluation stage are used to validate the knowledge boundary calculated in the assessment stage.

### Reddit Deployment

We recruited users through the Japanese Learning sub-Reddit[4]. The deployment was very successful: 847 users finished the J100 'test', and our post received an up-vote/down-vote score of 145 (for comparison, the other posts on the same page have an average score of 12). We received about 50 comments from J100 users, and most of the comments are supportive *"This is ideal. Especially good for learners like myself who tend to forget bits and details of older lessons, and just good in general for testing your progress."* Many users even expressed a future interest in our platform and requested that we make it work for higher levels (N4-N1): *"My friends love this. If you could make some intuitive tests for N4-N1 I'd pay money if I could take tests that could also adapt to my level. Making me learn little by little what I need improving on."*

### Validating the Knowledge Boundary and Distance Metric

In order to validate our calculation of the knowledge boundary and the distance metric, we will demonstrate that the user data collected from J100 nicely fits the adapted Rasch Model. We calculate a user's knowledge boundary $K$ based on his/her responses to the problems in the assessment stage, and for each problem $s$ responded in the evaluation stage, we measure the distance from the problem $s$ to the knowledge boundary $K$. The user responses in the evaluation stage can be regarded as users' self-estimation of their performance, and we score the five possible responses uniformly from 1 to 0:

| Response | Yes | Almost | Somewhat | Little | No |
|---|---|---|---|---|---|
| Score | 1 | 0.75 | 0.5 | 0.25 | 0 |

We would like to test if the relationship between the distance and user response matches the adapted Rasch model (Equation 7). If it it does match, then this result will verify our calculation of the knowledge boundary as an effective measurement of a student's knowledge. Additionally, we can utilize the distance from a problem to the student's knowledge boundary to predict the student's performance on that problem.

We calculate each user's knowledge boundary after the assessment stage, and calculate the distance to each problem given in the evaluation stage to that knowledge boundary. Then we group these problems by these distances and calculate the the average and standard deviation of the user responses when given problems with the same distance (Table 1).

We use non-linear regression to estimate the parameters $a$ and $c$, and show the results in Figure 4. The results suggest that the adapted Rasch model fits our user data fairly well ($R^2 = 0.992$). There are some imperfections in the top-right corner of the figure, where users tended to indicate less confidence in their understanding of the sentence than would have been expected. This may be because users find it hard to judge whether they 'understand' or 'almost understand' a sentence, and may have slightly underestimated their ability. It could also result from the gap between the scores of 'Yes' (1) and 'Almost' (0.75) - if a user wanted to indicate something in between, such as 0.9, no such response was available.

There is another interesting phenomenon: the standard deviation of the user responses (in Table 1) is maximized where the distance is at some point between -2 and -3, and the slope of the curve in Figure 4 is also maximized where the distance is at some similar point between -2 and -3. According to IRT, the

[2]Japanese Language Proficiency Test (JLPT) has 5 levels: from N1 (advanced) to N5 (beginner). You can see a summary of JLPT levels here: `http://www.jlpt.jp/e/about/levelsummary.html`

[3]The vocabulary explanations are provided to users since J100 is focusing on grammatical knowledge only, while users are not recommended to read sentence translations unless they are not sure whether their understanding of the sentence is correct.

[4]`www.reddit.com/r/LearnJapanese`

| Distance | User Response | |
|---|---|---|
| | Average | StdDev. |
| -4 | 0.125 | 0.11547 |
| -3 | 0.279412 | 0.329654 |
| -2 | 0.638037 | 0.40631 |
| -1 | 0.861589 | 0.266999 |
| 0 | 0.913887 | 0.198634 |
| 1 | 0.940882 | 0.171181 |
| 2 | 0.959838 | 0.144577 |
| 3 | 0.983871 | 0.11543 |

**Table 1. The average and standard deviation of J100 user responses, grouped by the calculated distance from the knowledge boundary. Note that the standard deviation of the user responses is maximized where the distance is at some point between -2 and -3, indicating that users are most unsure of their ability at this distance.**

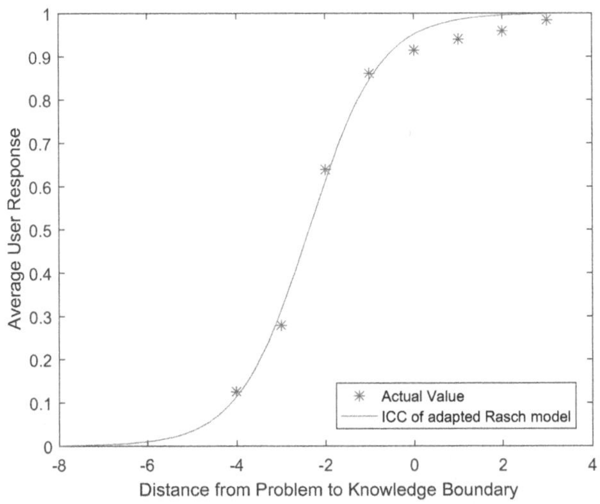


**Figure 4. The adapted Rasch model nicely fits the J100 user data. The blue data points show the average user response to problems with the same distance from the knowledge boundary, and the red curve is the *Item Characteristic Curve* (ICC) calculated based on the adapted Rasch model.**

problems that are at the difficulty level that corresponds to the maximum slope of the curve are the most discriminative, and the J100 data shows that users are most unsure of their ability at this distance. This makes sense and is further evidence that the adapted Rasch model fits the J100 user data well.

In conclusion, these results validate that our framework can efficiently measure students' ability with the knowledge boundary and predict student performance on specific problems. Since our formalism is inspired by both Item Response Theory (IRT) and Knowledge Space Theory (KST), the idea of the knowledge boundary and the distance may contribute to the unification of these two theories.

## PROGRESSION ANALYSIS

Good progressions enhance students' engagement of the curriculum [43,56], and our work aims to discover general characteristics of good progressions. In this section, we will leverage our framework to analyze educational progressions, and introduce two significant features of a good progression: composition and pace. We study existing curricula and demonstrate some striking similarities in expert-designed progressions.

### Composition: The Balance of Learning and Review

When designing an educational progression, a key consideration is how much time one should spend reinforcing previously-introduced knowledge as opposed to introducing new knowledge. Another consideration is whether the progression should grow in complexity by combining concepts together in new ways. Ideally, we would be able txo define a progression parameter space that can concisely capture these important aspects.

In our framework, for any problem $s$ that the student is about to learn, we classify $s$, with respect to the current knowledge boundary $K$, as:

*reinforcement*, if $\exists s' \in K$ s.t. $s' \geq s$;

*recombination*, if $\nexists s' \in K$ s.t. $s' \geq s$, and for any concept $c$ that is required by $s$, $\exists s' \in K$ s.t. $s'$ also requires concept $c$.

*introduction*, if there exists some concept $c$ s.t. $c$ is required by $s$ but is not required by any problem in $K$.

In other words, the next problem in the progression will be classified as reinforcement if the student has learned some problem that is at least as hard as it, as introduction if it requires any new concepts (basic skills) that the student has never learned, and as recombination if it combines together previously learned concepts in a new way.

For example, if the current knowledge boundary is:

$K = \{A, BCD, AFFD, BBECC\}$

The following problems will be classified as:

reinforcement: $A, BD, AFD, BBEC$

recombination: $AB, BFE, BBEECC, AFDD$

intruduction: $G, BHD, BBEGC, GH$

We can think of reinforcement as the review of learned knowledge, introduction as pure learning, and recombination as a mixture of both. The designer's strategy of balancing learning and review in an educational progression is revealed by the proportions of these three types, which we refer to as *progression composition*.

### Pace: The Growth Rate of Knowledge

We would like to know if the difficulty of lessons (chapters, units, etc.) in a progression grows at a consistent speed such that students can learn smoothly. Instead of numerically measuring the difficulty of each lesson, we calculate the *knowledge size*, the total number of problems that have been introduced up until each lesson. This can be measured as the number of the problems in the universal problem set[5] $S$ that are classified as reinforcement by the student's knowledge boundary $K$ after mastering all the knowledge from the start to the current lesson. The knowledge size $|K|$ is therefore the number of such problems:

$$|K| = |\{s \in S \wedge \exists s' \in K \text{ s.t. } s' \geq s\}| \quad (8)$$

[5]The universal problem set $S$ contains all the practice problems we have for an educational task.

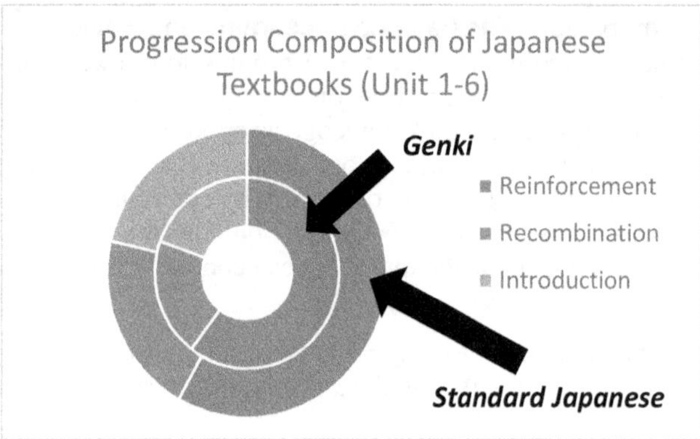


**Figure 5. Progression composition of two Japanese textbooks: *Standard Japanese* and *Genki*. The proportions are fairly similar. Note that it usually takes a student 2 semesters to learn units 1-6.**

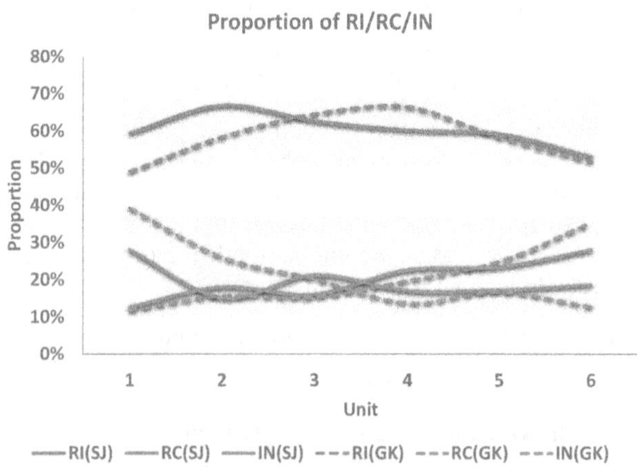


**Figure 6. Proportion of reinforcement(RI), recombination(RC) and Introduction(IN) in two series of Japanese textbooks: *Standard Japanese* (SJ) and *Genki*(GK). Here x-axis represents the learning progress: unit 1-6, and y-axis demonstrates the proportions.**

The *pace* is the ratio between knowledge growth (change of knowledge size $\Delta|K|$) and time. Assuming that the number of problems that students learn is directly proportional to the amount of expended time, we can use the length of the lesson $|L|$, which measures the number of practice problems in it, to represent time. Hence, the pace of lesson $i$ can be measured as:

$$Pace_i = \frac{|K_i| - |K_{i-1}|}{|L_i|} \quad (9)$$

where $|K_i|$ and $|K_{i-1}|$ indicate the knowledge sizes after lesson $i$ and lesson $i-1$.

For example, assume the knowledge size after lesson 5 is 110, and the knowledge size after lesson 6 is 134. If lesson 6 has 8 problems, then the pace of lesson 6 is (134-110)/8 = 3.

## EVALUATION OF PROGRESSION ANALYSIS

### Studies on Textbooks

To validate our work, we study two popular Japanese textbooks: *Standard Japanese* [51] and *Genki* [9]. Note that in language learning, 'problems' are the practice sentences that are introduced throughout the curriculum. Our goal is to find out if the progressions of both textbooks have similar pace and composition.

#### *Both Textbook Progressions Have Similar Composition*

Figure 5 shows the progression compositions of the first 6 units (which usually takes a student two semesters to learn) in these two Japanese textbooks. Clearly, both textbook progressions have a similar composition, possibly revealing that the experts who designed these two books arrived at similar conclusions.

To analyze how the progression composition changes over time, we calculate the proportions of reinforcement, recombination and introduction of each unit of both textbooks. For the proportions of unit $i$, we generate the knowledge boundary $K_{i-1}$ based on unit 1 to unit $i-1$, and classify all sentences in unit $i$ based on $K_{i-1}$.

Figure 6 shows how the composition of these two textbook progressions changes over time. Clearly, there are some striking similarities between the curves of reinforcement, recombination and introduction: for both series of books, the proportion of reinforcement increases to 70% then drops to 50%, the proportion of recombination increases from 10% to 30%-35%, and the proportion of introduction decreases from 30%-40% to 15%-20%. This validates the usefulness of characterizing progression composition, as there may be general principles of balancing learning and review that can be learned from existing textbooks.

#### *Both Textbook Progressions Have a Similar, Steady Pace*

Figure 7a shows the pace of both textbooks. Clearly, they both introduce the same amount of knowledge over the same period of time, which demonstrates they use a steady pace. This fits our intuition that learning is most comfortable with a steady pace.

To test if other reasonable progressions also have this property, we generate two alternate progressions by shuffling the sentences. The first alternate progression is generated randomly, and the second follows a topological sort. The topological sort ensures that any sentence $s$ is put before all sentences that are harder than $s$. We compare the textbook progressions with the progressions generated by the random algorithm and topological sort (Figure 7b and Figure 7c). The random progression is too difficult at the beginning because hard and easy sentences are equally likely to be selected. This may cause students to become discouraged by hard sentences at the beginning. On the other hand, the topological sort is too easy at the beginning because all of the easy sentences are put first. This results in an increase of difficulty that is initially too slow. As can be seen from our analyses of these two textbooks, steady pacing may be an important characteristic of a good progression.

### Studies on Online Language Learning Tools

We also analyze the progressions used by two online Spanish learning tools: Duolingo[6] and Language Zen[7]. We observed that some of the interesting differences in these two language

[6] https://www.duolingo.com/course/es/en/Learn-Spanish-Online
[7] www.languagezen.com

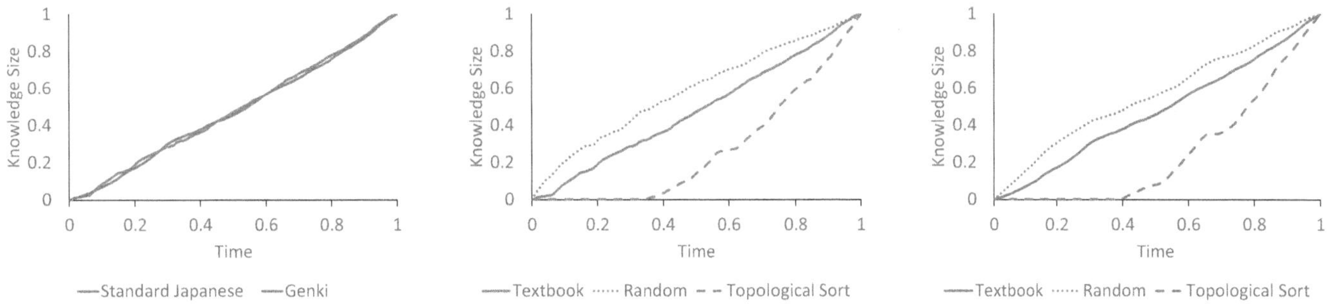


(a) Paces of Textbook Progressions: *Standard Japanese* and *Genki*.

(b) Standard Japanese Texts: Paces of textbook progression, and the progressions generated by the random algorithm and topological sort.

(c) Genki Texts: Paces of textbook progression, and the progressions generated by the random algorithm and topological sort.

**Figure 7. Pace of various progressions. Here, the x-axis represents the normalized learning time (namely, the normalized number of sentences learned), and the y-axis demonstrates the normalized knowledge size. (a) shows that both textbooks introduce the same amount of knowledge over the same period of time, which indicates that they use a steady pace. (b) and (c) compare the textbook progression to other baseline progressions. When compared with the textbook progression, random progressions are too difficult at the beginning, and progressions generated by a topological sort are too easy at the beginning.**

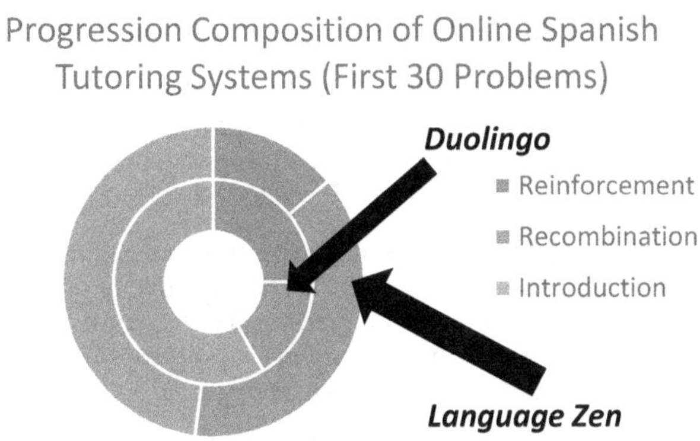


**Figure 8. Progression composition of two online Spanish learning tools: Duolingo and Language Zen. Compared with Duolingo, Language Zen has less reinforcement and less introduction, but much more recombination. Note that it usually takes a student a couple of days to learn 30 problems.**

learning progressions resulted from how they introduce vocabulary. Therefore, instead of using grammatical templates for Spanish, we treated each unique word as its own concept, and calculated the knowledge boundary and progression parameters using vocabulary.

The progression compositions of the first 30 problems (which usually take a student a couple of days to learn) introduced in these two tools are shown in Figure 8. Compared with Duolingo, Language Zen has less reinforcement and less introduction, but much more recombination. It has been claimed[8] that Language Zen is 1.5 times faster than Duolingo. We speculate that the higher proportion of recombination may contribute to this difference.

One may also notice that Figure 5 has a higher proportion of reinforcement and a lower proportion of introduction than Figure 8. There are three factors we believe that could contribute to these differences. One factor is the learning method. Textbooks are typically used in classroom learning and are thus not necessarily intended to be the only learning material that students are using. They are typically combined with lectures and assignments. However, online language learning tools such as Duolingo and Language Zen are more self-contained. Therefore, these textbooks may have a higher proportion of reinforcement (review) than these online tutoring systems.

The second factor is the difference of the learning period. The texts in Figure 5 are usually taught over two semesters, while Figure 8 only shows the sentences that are taught in the first couple of days of the online learning tools. The differences in progression composition in the two figures imply that these expert-designed progressions tend to focus more on introduction than reinforcement at the very beginning of the progression. This is also consistent with Figure 6, where the proportion of introduction is the highest at the beginning then drops afterwards.

The third factor is that Figure 5 examines grammar and Figure 8 examines vocabulary, which could imply that grammar needs more reinforcement than vocabulary.

## AUTOMATIC PROGRESSION SYNTHESIS

We have discussed two features of an educational progression: composition and pace. In this section, we will demonstrate that educational progressions can be automatically synthesized according to specific composition and pace parameters. To be more precise, a progression can be characterized as three numeric parameters: overall pace (*pace*), proportion of reinforcement (*ri*), and proportion of introduction (*in*). The proportion of recombination (*rc*) is redundant since $ri + rc + in = 1$.

We use a greedy algorithm to synthesize progressions. The algorithm starts with an empty progression, repeatedly selects the next problem that minimizes the following error function

[8] `http://elmodenafrontline.com/8825/feature/language-zen-the-new-and-coming/`

| Progression Name | Desired Progression Parameters | Synthesized Progression |
|---|---|---|
| *Genki* Simulation | pace = 0.5, ri = 0.6, in = 0.2 | DG B DG DG DG BG BG B BD B |
| Reinforcement-biased | pace=0.3, ri = 0.7, in = 0.2 | C C C C C A C A AC A |
| Recombination-biased | pace =1.2, ri = 0.2, in = 0.3 | G G AB BG AG BG EF BE AE BF |
| Introduction-biased | pace = 1.6, ri = 0.2, in = 0.5 | EF EF AB BF ABC AF CDE AF BCD DG |

**Table 2. Synthesized progressions with desired parameters. The '*Genki* Simulation' progression is synthesized with parameters extracted from the textbook. The other three progressions are generated with specific parameter settings. This demonstrates the potential of our progression synthesis framework to map characteristics of one progression onto another, and to create progressions that are tailored to the needs of an individual student.**

and appends it to the progression:

$$Error = (pace - pace^*)^2 + (ri - ri^*)^2 + (in - in^*)^2 \quad (10)$$

where $pace, ri, in$ are the actual progression characteristics, and $pace^*, ri^*, in^*$ are the desired progression parameters. Note that there may be multiple available problems with minimal error. In that case, our algorithm randomly selects one from them as the next problem.

This greedy algorithm does not always generate progressions with the exact desired parameters. However, it runs very fast. For a universal problem set of 25 problems, it can synthesize over 100 progressions (with 10 problems each) in one second. Therefore, we can run this greedy algorithm many times in order to synthesize progressions with desired characteristics.

Table 2 shows four examples of synthesized progressions. We extracted the following parameters from the *Genki* progression: $pace = 0.465, ri = 0.582, in = 0.214$. We then used these parameters (approximately) to synthesize the '*Genki* Simulation' progression. We also generated three other progressions with tailored parameter settings, which are biased towards reinforcement, recombination and introduction. Theses results demonstrate that we can not only utilize the principles of expert progression design and synthesize progressions with parameters that are good for most students, but also tailor progressions for students with specific preferences.

## CONCLUSIONS AND FUTURE WORK

Learnability is important for many aspects of HCI: user interfaces, learning tools, video games, and software usability. In this paper, we defined a framework that utilizes automatic problem decomposition and partial ordering graph construction to facilitate multiple workflows related to education: assessment of a student's knowledge, identifying and describing the learning strategies of a curriculum, and designing new learning progressions. We evaluated this framework in multiple ways: through an online deployment of a Japanese-language assessment tool, automatic extraction of pacing parameters from existing curricula, and assembly of problems into new progressions that adhere to desired pacing characteristics.

We hope to utilize our framework for several educational domains, especially computer-assisted language education. For example, we plan to leverage our framework to recommend appropriate reading materials to second language learners and improve educational games for language learning [17, 18]. In the future, we will apply our framework not only to grammatical knowledge, but also other aspects of language learning, such as vocabulary and semantics.

We hope that these ideas will enable a science of progression analysis, in which sequencing and pacing parameters are extracted from progressions across a wide variety of topics to identify the best principles. Furthermore, we hope to extend this framework so that it can automatically build adaptive learning systems that are capable of both rapid initial assessment and progression tailoring.

## REFERENCES

1. Sami Abuhamdeh and Mihaly Csikszentmihalyi. 2012. The importance of challenge for the enjoyment of intrinsically motivated, goal-directed activities. *Personality and Social Psychology Bulletin* 38, 3 (2012), 317–330.

2. Dietrich Albert and Theo Held. 1994. Establishing knowledge spaces by systematical problem construction. In *Knowledge structures*. Springer, 81–115.

3. Vincent Aleven, Bruce M McLaren, Jonathan Sewall, and Kenneth R Koedinger. 2006. The cognitive tutor authoring tools (CTAT): preliminary evaluation of efficiency gains. In *International Conference on Intelligent Tutoring Systems*. Springer, 61–70.

4. Vincent Aleven, Bruce M Mclaren, Jonathan Sewall, and Kenneth R Koedinger. 2009. A new paradigm for intelligent tutoring systems: Example-tracing tutors. *International Journal of Artificial Intelligence in Education* 19, 2 (2009), 105–154.

5. Erik Andersen. 2014. *Automatic Scaffolding for Procedural Learning*. Ph.D. Dissertation.

6. Erik Andersen, Sumit Gulwani, and Zoran Popovic. 2013. A trace-based framework for analyzing and synthesizing educational progressions. In *Proceedings of the SIGCHI Conference on Human Factors in Computing Systems*. ACM, 773–782.

7. John R Anderson, Albert T Corbett, Kenneth R Koedinger, and Ray Pelletier. 1995. Cognitive tutors: Lessons learned. *The journal of the learning sciences* 4, 2 (1995), 167–207.

8. John W Atkinson, Jarvis R Bastian, Robert W Earl, and George H Litwin. 1960. The achievement motive, goal setting, and probability preferences. *The Journal of Abnormal and Social Psychology* 60, 1 (1960), 27.

9. Eri Banno, Yoko Ikeda, and Yutaka Ohno. 2011. *GENKI: An Integrated Course in Elementary Japanese*. Japan Times and Tsai Fong Books.

10. Joseph E Beck, Kai-min Chang, Jack Mostow, and Albert Corbett. 2008. Does help help? Introducing the Bayesian Evaluation and Assessment methodology. In *International Conference on Intelligent Tutoring Systems*. Springer, 383–394.

11. Eric Butler, Erik Andersen, Adam M Smith, Sumit Gulwani, Zoran Popovic, and WA Redmond. 2015. Automatic Game Progression Design through Analysis of Solution Features. In *Proc. of the SIGCHI Conf. on Human Factors in Computing (CHI 2015)*.

12. Eric Butler, Adam M Smith, Yun-En Liu, and Zoran Popovic. 2013. A mixed-initiative tool for designing level progressions in games. In *Proceedings of the 26th annual ACM symposium on User interface software and technology*. ACM, 377–386.

13. Herlinda Cancino, Ellen Rosansky, and John Schumann. 1978. The acquisition of English negatives and interrogatives by native Spanish speakers. *Second language acquisition: A book of readings* (1978), 207–230.

14. Albert T Corbett and John R Anderson. 1994. Knowledge tracing: Modeling the acquisition of procedural knowledge. *User modeling and user-adapted interaction* 4, 4 (1994), 253–278.

15. Mihaly Csikszentmihalyi. 1990. *Flow: The Psychology of Optimal Experience*. Harper & Row Publishers, Inc., New York, NY, USA. 49 pages.

16. Mihaly Csikszentmihalyi. 1991. *Flow: The psychology of optimal experience*. Vol. 41. HarperPerennial New York.

17. Gabriel Culbertson, Erik Andersen, Walker White, Daniel Zhang, and Malte Jung. 2016a. Crystallize: An Immersive, Collaborative Game for Second Language Learning. In *Proceedings of the 19th ACM Conference on Computer-Supported Cooperative Work & Social Computing*. ACM, 636–647.

18. Gabriel Culbertson, Shiyu Wang, Malte Jung, and Erik Andersen. 2016b. Social Situational Language Learning through an Online 3D Game. In *Proceedings of the 2016 CHI Conference on Human Factors in Computing Systems*. ACM, 957–968.

19. Rafael Jaime De Ayala. 2013. *The theory and practice of item response theory*. Guilford Publications.

20. Edward L Deci and Richard M Ryan. 2000. The "what" and "why" of goal pursuits: Human needs and the self-determination of behavior. *Psychological inquiry* 11, 4 (2000), 227–268.

21. Michel C Desmarais, Peyman Meshkinfam, and Michel Gagnon. 2006. Learned student models with item to item knowledge structures. *User Modeling and User-Adapted Interaction* 16, 5 (2006), 403–434.

22. Sebastian Deterding, Miguel Sicart, Lennart Nacke, Kenton O'Hara, and Dan Dixon. 2011. Gamification. using game-design elements in non-gaming contexts. In *CHI'11 Extended Abstracts on Human Factors in Computing Systems*. ACM, 2425–2428.

23. Jean-Paul Doignon and Jean-Claude Falmagne. 1985. Spaces for the assessment of knowledge. *International journal of man-machine studies* 23, 2 (1985), 175–196.

24. Jean-Paul Doignon and Jean-Claude Falmagne. 2012. *Knowledge spaces*. Springer Science & Business Media.

25. Tao Dong, Mira Dontcheva, Diana Joseph, Karrie Karahalios, Mark Newman, and Mark Ackerman. 2012. Discovery-based games for learning software. In *Proceedings of the SIGCHI Conference on Human Factors in Computing Systems*. ACM, 2083–2086.

26. Fritz Drasgow and Charles L Hulin. 1990. Item response theory. (1990).

27. Susan E Embretson and Steven P Reise. 2013. *Item response theory*. Psychology Press.

28. Jean-Claude Falmagne, Eric Cosyn, Jean-Paul Doignon, and Nicolas Thiéry. 2006. The assessment of knowledge, in theory and in practice. In *Formal concept analysis*. Springer, 61–79.

29. Susan Gass. 1982. From Theory to Practice. (1982).

30. Jennifer M Goldschneider and Robert M DeKeyser. 2001. Explaining the "Natural Order of L2 Morpheme Acquisition" in English: A Meta-analysis of multiple determinants. *Language learning* 51, 1 (2001), 1–50.

31. Floraine Grabler, Maneesh Agrawala, Wilmot Li, Mira Dontcheva, and Takeo Igarashi. 2009. Generating photo manipulation tutorials by demonstration. *ACM Transactions on Graphics (TOG)* 28, 3 (2009), 66.

32. Ronald K Hambleton. 1991. *Fundamentals of item response theory*. Vol. 2. Sage publications.

33. Erik Harpstead, Brad A Myers, and Vincent Aleven. 2013. In search of learning: facilitating data analysis in educational games. In *Proceedings of the SIGCHI conference on human factors in computing systems*. ACM, 79–88.

34. Susan Harter. 1978. Effectance motivation reconsidered. Toward a developmental model. *Human development* 21, 1 (1978), 34–64.

35. Cord Hockemeyer, Theo Held, and Dietrich Albert. 1997. RATH-A relational adaptive tutoring hypertext WWW-environment based on knowledge space theory. (1997).

36. Andreas Holzer, Christian Schallhart, Michael Tautschnig, and Helmut Veith. 2008. Fshell: Systematic test case generation for dynamic analysis and measurement. In *International Conference on Computer Aided Verification*. Springer, 209–213.

37. Katherine Isbister, Mary Flanagan, and Chelsea Hash. 2010. Designing games for learning: insights from conversations with designers. In *Proceedings of the SIGCHI Conference on Human Factors in Computing Systems*. ACM, 2041–2044.

38. Edward L Keenan and Bernard Comrie. 1977. Noun phrase accessibility and universal grammar. *Linguistic inquiry* 8, 1 (1977), 63–99.
39. Kenneth R Koedinger, John R Anderson, William H Hadley, and Mary A Mark. 1997. Intelligent tutoring goes to school in the big city. (1997).
40. Mathieu Koppen. 1993. Extracting human expertise for constructing knowledge spaces: An algorithm. *Journal of mathematical psychology* 37, 1 (1993), 1–20.
41. Mathieu Koppen and Jean-Paul Doignon. 1990. How to build a knowledge space by querying an expert. *Journal of Mathematical Psychology* 34, 3 (1990), 311–331.
42. Stephen D Krashen. 1985. *The input hypothesis: Issues and implications*. Addison-Wesley Longman Ltd.
43. Nan Li, William W Cohen, and Kenneth R Koedinger. 2012. Problem order implications for learning transfer. In *Intelligent Tutoring Systems*. Springer, 185–194.
44. Conor Linehan, George Bellord, Ben Kirman, Zachary H Morford, and Bryan Roche. 2014. Learning curves: analysing pace and challenge in four successful puzzle games. In *Proceedings of the first ACM SIGCHI annual symposium on Computer-human interaction in play*. ACM, 181–190.
45. Derek Lomas, Kishan Patel, Jodi L Forlizzi, and Kenneth R Koedinger. 2013. Optimizing challenge in an educational game using large-scale design experiments. In *Proceedings of the SIGCHI Conference on Human Factors in Computing Systems*. ACM, 89–98.
46. Frederic M Lord. 1980. *Applications of item response theory to practical testing problems*. Routledge.
47. Thomas W Malone. 1980. What makes things fun to learn? Heuristics for designing instructional computer games. In *Proceedings of the 3rd ACM SIGSMALL symposium and the first SIGPC symposium on Small systems*. ACM, 162–169.
48. Jürgen Meisel. 1987. Reference to past events and actions in the development of natural second language acquisition. *First and second language acquisition processes* (1987), 206–224.
49. Zachary Pardos and Neil Heffernan. 2010. Navigating the parameter space of Bayesian Knowledge Tracing models: Visualizations of the convergence of the Expectation Maximization algorithm. In *Educational Data Mining 2010*.
50. Zachary A Pardos and Neil T Heffernan. 2011. KT-IDEM: Introducing item difficulty to the knowledge tracing model. In *International Conference on User Modeling, Adaptation, and Personalization*. Springer, 243–254.
51. People's Education Press. 2013. *Standard Japanese of China-Japan Exchanges for Beginners*. Mitsumura Tosho Publishing Co.Ltd.
52. Manfred Pienemann, Malcolm Johnston, and Geoff Brindley. 1988. Constructing an acquisition-based procedure for second language assessment. *Studies in second language acquisition* 10, 02 (1988), 217–243.
53. Georg Rasch. 1993. *Probabilistic models for some intelligence and attainment tests*. ERIC.
54. Mark Reckase. 2009. *Multidimensional item response theory*. Vol. 150. Springer.
55. C Reigeluth and R Stein. 1983. Elaboration theory. *Instructional-design theories and models: An overview of their current status* (1983), 335–381.
56. Charles M Reigeluth. 2013. *Instructional design theories and models: An overview of their current status*. Routledge.
57. Mare Taagepera and S Noori. 2000. Mapping students' thinking patterns in learning organic chemistry by the use of knowledge space theory. *J. Chem. Educ* 77, 9 (2000), 1224.
58. Nikolai Tillmann and Jonathan De Halleux. 2008. Pex–white box test generation for. net. In *International conference on tests and proofs*. Springer, 134–153.
59. Lev Semenovich Vygotsky. 1980. *Mind in society: The development of higher psychological processes*. Harvard university press.
60. Shuhan Wang and Erik Andersen. 2016. Grammatical Templates: Improving Text Difficulty Evaluation for Language Learners. In *Proceedings of COLING 2016, the 26th International Conference on Computational Linguistics*. 1692–1702.
61. Joanna White. 1998. Getting the learners' attention: A typographical input enhancement study. *Focus on form in classroom second language acquisition* (1998), 85–113.
62. Henning Wode. 1981. LANGUAGE-ACQUISITIONAL UNIVERSALS: A UNIFIED VIEW OF LANGUAGE ACQUISITION. *Annals of the New York Academy of Sciences* 379, 1 (1981), 218–234.
63. Ruth Wylie, Kenneth Koedinger, and Teruko Mitamura. 2010. Analogies, explanations, and practice: examining how task types affect second language grammar learning. In *International Conference on Intelligent Tutoring Systems*. Springer, 214–223.
64. Yanbo Xu and Jack Mostow. 2010. Using logistic regression to trace multiple sub-skills in a dynamic bayes net. In *Educational Data Mining 2011*.
65. Helen Zhao, Kenneth Koedinger, and John Kowalski. 2013. Knowledge tracing and cue contrast: Second language English grammar instruction. In *Proceedings of the 35th Annual Conference of the Cognitive Science Society*.
66. Helmut Zobl. 1984. The wave model of linguistic change and the naturalness of interlanguage. *Studies in Second Language Acquisition* 6, 02 (1984), 160–185.

# HOBIT: Hybrid Optical Bench for Innovative Teaching

**David Furió**
Université de Bordeaux
David.Furio@inria.fr

**Stéphanie Fleck**
Université de Lorraine
stephanie.fleck@univ-lorraine.fr

**Bruno Bousquet**
Université de Bordeaux
bruno.bousquet@u-bordeaux.fr

**Jean-Paul Guillet**
Université de Bordeaux
jean-paul.guillet@u-bordeaux.fr

**Lionel Canioni**
Université de Bordeaux
lionel.canioni@u-bordeaux.fr

**Martin Hachet**
Inria
Martin.Hachet@inria.fr

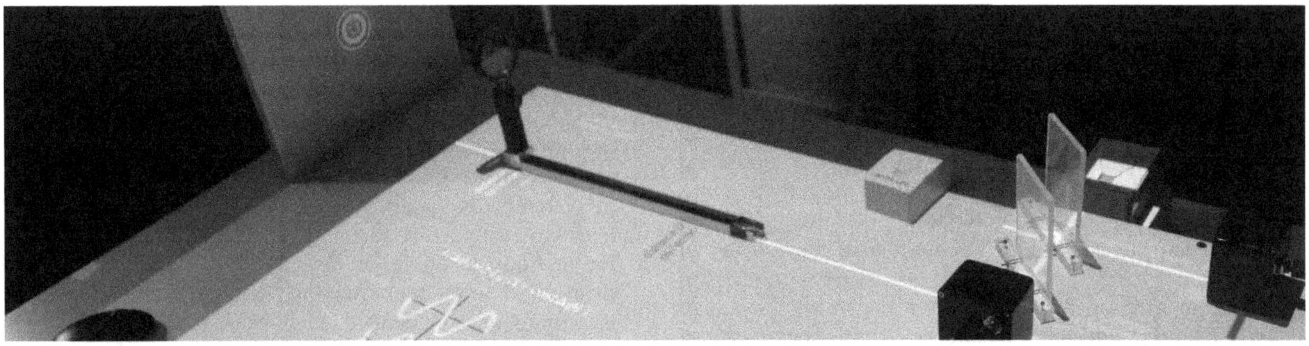

**Figure 1. Simulation and augmentation of a Michelson interferometer experiment. Physical and digital content are merged in a unique environment.**

## ABSTRACT
Practical work in optics allows supporting the construction of knowledge, in particular when the concept to be learned remains diffuse. To overcome the limitations of the current experimental setups, we have designed a hybrid system that combines physical interaction and numerical simulation. This system relies on 3D-printed replicas of optical elements, which are augmented with pedagogical information. In this paper, we focus on the well-known Michelson interferometer experiment, widely studied in undergraduate programs of Science. A 3-months user study with 101 students and 6 teachers showed that, beyond the practical aspects offered by this system, such an approach enhances the technical and scientific learning compared to a standard Michelson interferometer experiment.

### ACM Classification Keywords
H.5.2. Information Interfaces and Presentation (e.g., HCI): User Interfaces; K.3.1. Computers and Education: Computer Uses in Education

### Author Keywords
Education and Training; Optics; Augmented Reality; Simulation; Michelson interferometer


*CHI 2017, May 6-11, 2017, Denver, CO, USA.*

ACM ISBN 978-1-4503-4655-9/17/05...$15.00.
http://dx.doi.org/10.1145/3025453.3025789

## INTRODUCTION
In optics, many concepts and phenomena are difficult to perceive and understand. This is particularly true with wave optics where phenomena may appear as counterintuitive [14]. Hence, universities and schools generally reinforce theoretical courses with physical experiments where students manipulate the concepts to be learned. The integration of laboratory activities into the classroom is an essential part of science education [19] since it allows students to observe, test hypotheses, and apply their understanding of the physical world [2, 16]. Furthermore, the observation, testing and experimentation found in experimental physics have a positive impact on the students' motivation [25, 26].

However, current experimental setups suffer from several limitations, as reported by the optics teachers with whom we have worked (see *Evaluation* section). First, from a practical point of view, setting up and maintaining optics experiments may be time consuming (in particular in the case of wave optics). The required material is generally expensive and fragile. This limits the number of experiments that can be run. Experiments can be dangerous too, in particular as soon as laser sources are used. These observations were also reported in the literature [15, 22, 4].

Second, from a pedagogical point of view, the teachers as well as other prior work [27] reported that traditional experiments were not always sufficient for transmitting knowledge. Students often have difficulties to develop an understanding of the complexity and ambiguity of empirical work. They may also fail to acquire the skills needed to calibrate and troubleshoot setups used to make observations, whereas this learning is the main objective of practical works [17].

All these issues prompt to upgrade traditional optics experiments by i) overcoming the practical limitations of the current experimental setups and ii) providing pedagogical supports aiming to help the understanding of the studied phenomena. To this end, we propose HOBIT, an interactive system which stands for Hybrid Optical Bench for Innovative Teaching. Our goal is to let students operate as if they were working with a real optics experiment, but where the observed phenomenon comes from a numerical simulation. Beyond the simulation, this system allows augmenting the experiment with co-located pedagogical supports (see Figure 1).

In a first step, we focused on the Michelson interferometer, which is used in numerous applications (e.g. Fourier Transform Spectroscopy, Laser Interferometer Gravitational-Wave Observatory, and so on). Consequently, the Michelson interferometer (Figure 2) is one of the most popular optics experiments. It is based upon the division of a light wave into two beams that reflects on two separate plane mirrors before merging back into a combined beam whose projection can be observed on a projection screen. By slightly modifying the axial position or the orientation of the mirrors, one can observe resulting interference patterns—fringes or rings—on the screen (See Figure 5(a)). Various experiments can be performed with a Michelson interferometer, such as the measurement of wavelengths (e.g. Helium-Neon Laser), precise distance, or refractive indexes of transparent materials. Therefore, it is fundamental that, during lab work sessions, students familiarize themselves with the setup adjustments. They also need to translate their theoretical background into practice and understand causal effects of their direct manipulations on optical interferences phenomena.

Our contributions for this work are

- the design of a new interactive system that simulates and augments a Michelson interferometer
- a study that assesses the pedagogical relevance of the proposed approach in an ecological situation.

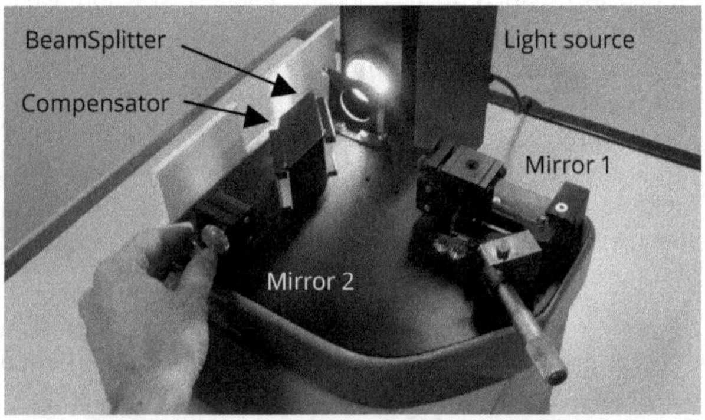


**Figure 2. A picture of a standard Michelson interferometer where a user is moving the orientation of one of the mirrors. The interference pattern is projected on a screen located on the left of the interferometer (not visible in this image).**

## RELATED WORK

Due to the abstract nature of the studied concepts, optics is one of the fields where many works were conducted to improve educational approaches and tools. Many authors emphasize the importance of Hands-on learning experience, as we do in our approach. This is notably the case of the workshop carried out by Takayama et al. [24]. During two hours, basic optics concepts (e.g. polarization and wavelength) were introduced to high school students who performed the experiments themselves, guided by two experts. Despite direct manipulations, such traditional experiments may suffer from a disconnection between the theoretical concepts to learn and the actual handling, since students can not observe the phenomena and the underlying theoretical concepts at the same time.

Beyond standard experiments, authors have explored alternative technologies to improve the teaching of physics (and optics) concepts. For example, Rodrigues and Carvalho [20] developed video-based experimental activities. Real experiments were recorded and students had to answer questions by watching and analyzing the videos. Such multimedia systems have interesting advantages over traditional experiments. Beyond cost and safety considerations, videos can be freely distributed on the web, making possible to spread them to a large number of students that can work with them at any time, and as many times they want. On the other hand, physical investigations are not possible with such intangible approaches. This can maintain misconceptions [29]. To overcome this, our work supports physical interaction.

In past few years, new approaches based on Virtual Reality (VR) have emerged with the popularization of the related technologies. These approaches rely on the immersion of users in an interactive virtual environment. Related with optics education, Hayes et al. [11] developed a VR educational module that implements a virtual laboratory with realistic models of optical devices. In this virtual lab, students can set up and perform an optical experiment, e.g. dealing with laser diode characteristics and fiber coupling. The module was composed of three levels with a short quiz at the end of each one to measure the student's understanding of the subject. Such VR environments are very flexible, and numerous experiments, which could be potentially dangerous or expensive in reality, can be built. On the other hand, pure VR approaches suffer from limitations. In particular, when equipped with a Head-Mounted-Display, the student is isolated in a virtual world, and the communication with other students and teachers is harder. This contradicts pedagogical principles that emphasis the importance of social interaction in learning [12, 5]. Moreover, the way the student manipulates virtual optics components is very far from what she or he would do during a real experiment. Consequently, the transition from the virtual to the real environment might be a problem. At the opposite, with HOBIT, students and teachers interact around a tangible experiment that is very close to the true experiment.

Related to VR, Augmented Reality (AR) has grown in importance in the last years. By superimposing virtual elements to real ones, AR allows enriching the real world with additional information. In education, this can help students to understand abstract concepts that may not be visible in real life (e.g. [8, 23]). With regard to optics education, a few AR experiments have been carried out. Yamaguchi and Yoshikawa [32] developed a system for the construction of an optical holography setup. The virtual optics components (e.g. lenses, and mirrors) were displayed on a screen on top of filmed markers. The students had to build an optical holography experiment by manipulating the markers in front of a camera. Compared to this approach where the augmentation is observed through a screen, with HOBIT, virtual information is directly projected onto the physical environment, using Spatial Augmented Reality [1].

Some authors like Underkoffler and Ishii [28], or Falcão and Price [9] had followed an approach similar to ours where projection is used to combine real and virtual information within a same physical space. Underkoffler and Ishii system aimed at simulating the interaction of laser light with various optical components in holographic setups. A projector situated above a table allows displaying augmented information (light path) around physical objects that are tracked thanks to a video/markers system. Similarly, the system of Falcão and Price consisted in an interactive tabletop environment for simulating some basic optics phenomena and was targeted at children. A projector situated on top of the table displayed the augmented information and the different physical objects were tracked from below the table thanks to a video/markers system. Continuing with AR, Yoon and Wang [33] developed a system to observe and manipulate magnetic fileds in real-time. A camera placed above the working area tracked the magnets and the augmented information (magnetic fields) was displayed on a screen situated in front of the user. These systems reproduce conceptual and simplified optics or magnetics experiments. In our case, with HOBIT, our goal is to mimic as much as possible true experiments, and to augment them with pedagogical supports.

Another interesting project related to HOBIT is *TinkerLamp*, developed by Do-Lenh et al. [7]. *TinkerLamp* tries to help logistics students learn the theoretical concepts through experimentation and AR in a scaled-down model of a warehouse. It is composed of an interactive tabletop, a projector and a camera placed above the tabletop, and a series of physical elements (sheets, models, cards, etc.) that can be tracked thanks to markers. HOBIT shares some of the ideas presented in *TinkerLamp* and some of the aforementioned projects. This notably includes tabletop configurations, top projectors, tangible interaction, and control cards.

Despite the effort that has been put to build these new educational tools, few studies have been conducted to assess the learning outcomes. Underkoffler and Ishii [28] performed a qualitative user study with 8 students. This study notably showed that the students were pleased with the fast prototyping capabilities provided by the system, but no learning outcomes were studied. In their study, Hayes et al. [11] showed that the VR module they proposed improved significantly the initial knowledge of the targeted pedagogical content. On the other hand, no comparison with a baseline condition was performed. The studies of Falcão and Price [9], and Yoon and Wang [33] were focused on children and the main goals focused on studying the collaboration between them. The results showed that AR and tangible interaction increased the teamwork of the children, but no learning outcomes were studied. Do-Lenh et al. [7] carried out a study to evaluate the learning outcomes of *TinkerLamp*. The authors suggest that *TinkerLamp* improved the learning outcomes compared to the other conditions.

In this paper, beyond describing the HOBIT platform, we report an experiment whose goal is to explore how a hybrid system as the one we propose impacts the building of new knowledge and skills. To this end, we conducted a study with a large number of participants (N = 101), and we compared HOBIT to a standard Michelson interferometer (see section *Evaluation*).

## TECHNICAL DESCRIPTION

### System Overview

HOBIT is an interactive platform dedicated to the simulation and the augmentation of optics experiments. The main components of the system are:

- A set of optical replicas whose goals is to mimic true optical elements (e.g. lenses and mirrors mounted on mechanical holders).
- A numerical simulation that computes in real-time interference patterns from a physical model, and for which the result is projected on a screen.
- An augmentation of the board by way of a second projector located on top of the experiment.

Users modify the parameters of the simulation by manipulating the optical replicas. As they would do with a real experiment, they can observe the result of their action on the projection screen. The augmentation aims at co-locating additional information within the physical experiment. Figure 3 illustrates the

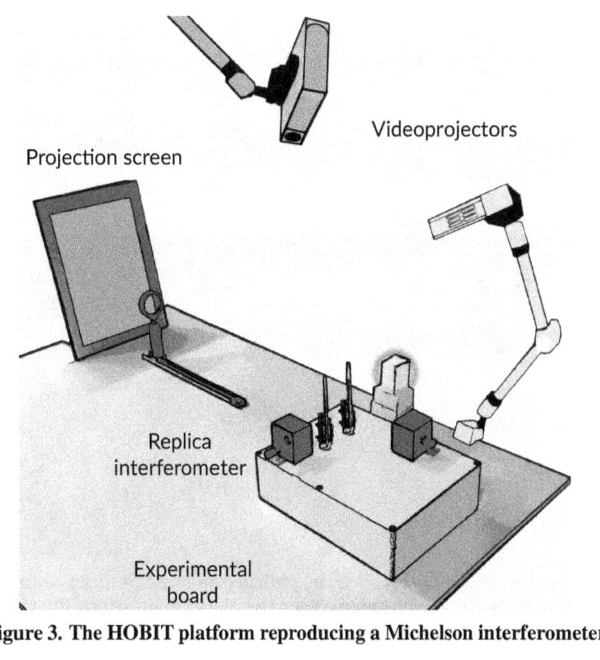


**Figure 3. The HOBIT platform reproducing a Michelson interferometer.**

HOBIT platform in a configuration that reproduces a Michelson interferometer.

The total cost of the components required to build the platform (laptop, videoprojectors, and sensors) is about four times cheaper than a standard Michelson interferometer, and several experiments can be built from the same platform. With HOBIT, the experiment is much faster to set up than with traditional optics experiments. Moreover, because the light sources are not real, HOBIT prevents from safety issues, in particular in the case of laser sources.

### Optical replicas

Optical replicas are 3D printed objects equipped with electronic sensors. For the Michelson interferometer, we built the following components.

**2 light sources** (low-pressure sodium lamp and white LED) are plastic boxes with RFID tags. A stand equipped with a RFID reader allows detecting which light source is experimented.

**2 mirror holders** are equipped with knobs that mimic micrometric screws, which are used to control the position and orientation of mirrors in real experiments. One of them (mirror 1, see Figure 4) is equipped with one knob dedicated to control the axial translation of the (virtual) mirror. The other one (Mirror 2) is equipped with two knobs dedicated to the orientation of the mirror. It is worth noticing that translation and orientation changes on mirrors in reality are not perceptible. Hence, replicas appear as true mirror holders in the simulator. The resolution of the knobs is adjusted to mimic those installed in the real setup. In particular, for the axial translation, 1 full turn of the knob was set to induce a 500 μm translation. The same happens with the knobs of the Mirror 2 where one full turn of the knob is mapped to 1°.

**1 movable lens** mounted on a linear potentiometer allows simulating the modification of the lens-to-screen distance. One step of this sensor corresponds approximately to 0.29 cm.

**2 passive elements** mimic the role of the beam splitter and the compensator.

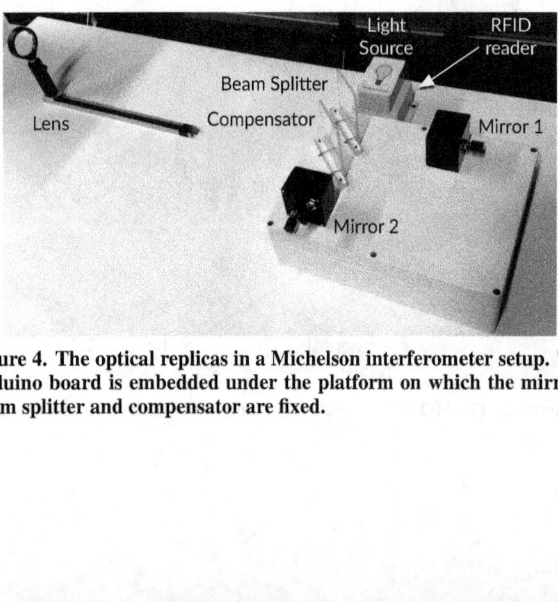


**Figure 4. The optical replicas in a Michelson interferometer setup. The Arduino board is embedded under the platform on which the mirrors, beam splitter and compensator are fixed.**

Figure 4 illustrates the optical replicas we build for the Michelson interferometer.

The RFID reader as well as all the sensors are connected to an Arduino board located under the platform where the mirrors, beam splitter and compensator are fixed. This board detects all the changes in the sensors states and sends them to the computer via an USB connection. The data is transmitted every 50ms.

### Numerical simulation

The numerical simulation computes the interference pattern from the characteristics of the light source and the position and orientation of the mirrors and lens. The intensity of a point on the screen is computed based on the theory of interference involving two waves. The detailed model that is used to compute the interference patterns is described in the accompanying complementary file for reproducibility purposes.

At the end, the obtained interference patterns are very close to the ones that are obtained from a true Michelson interferometer, as depicted in Figure 5.

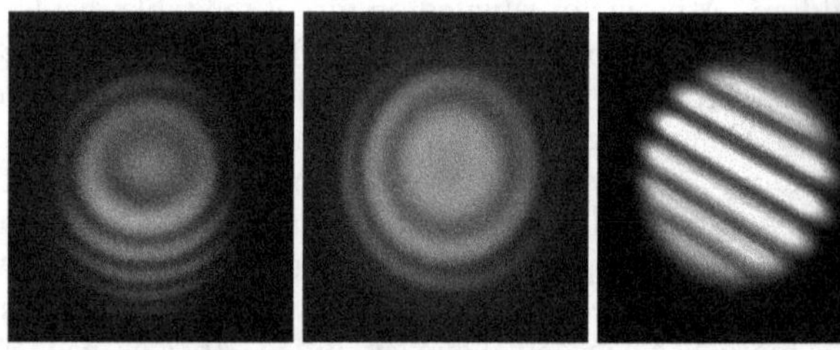

(a) (b) (c)

**Figure 5. Examples of ring interference patterns of the low pressure sodium lamp from (a) a standard Michelson interferometer and from (b) the numerical simulation of HOBIT. (c) White light fringes interference pattern obtained with HOBIT.**

### Augmentation

The augmentation consists in projecting pedagogical information into the experiment. This information (e.g. texts, drawings, and animations) have been designed to support the students' needs. For example, with a standard Michelson, students may often be lost because they have no idea of what is happening when manipulating a mirror. Have they turned too much the screw? Or not enough? At the end, they may observe nothing without knowing why. With HOBIT, a schematic representation of the current state of the optical elements can be displayed next to them, as illustrated in Figure 6(a). This may help students to understand how their actions impact the observed phenomenon. Such an augmentation would not have been possible with a standard Michelson interferometer. Indeed, the precise state of the system needs to be known, which is not the case with a standard version.

Animations may also help students to understand how light propagates. To this end, we propose the option to launch an animation that highlights the light path, and that shows how the waves coming from the two mirrors superimpose together. This is illustrated in Figure 6(b).

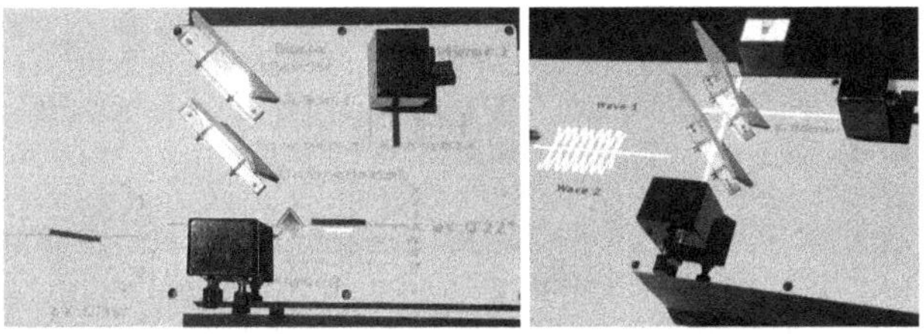

(a) (b)

**Figure 6. (a) Augmented information displayed next to the mirrors. The blue arrow indicates that Mirror 2 is being tilted forward, and the current angle is $0'22''$. The drawing on the left gives an indication of the $x$ orientation of Mirror 2, and the graduated linear scale on top magnifies the current position of Mirror 1. (b) Light path and waves combination.**

Similarly, advanced pedagogical supports can be displayed directly onto the experimental board. For example, Figure 7(a) and 7(b), illustrates two representations of the signal that could be measured at a specific point of the visualized interference pattern. This point can be selected by way of a mouse input. Such representations aims for helping students to understand how the two waves combine together and, consequently, why a resulting intensity is observed at the selected location. They also provide explanation on the changing contrast that is observed in the case of low-pressure sodium lamp, which spectrum is characterized by two wavelengths very close one to the other. Formulas related with these phenomena can be displayed, too (see Figure 6). The parameters of these formulas are updated in real-time according to the actions performed by the students. This may help the students to strengthen the link between the observed phenomena, various representations, and the underlying concepts, all of them in a unique environment.

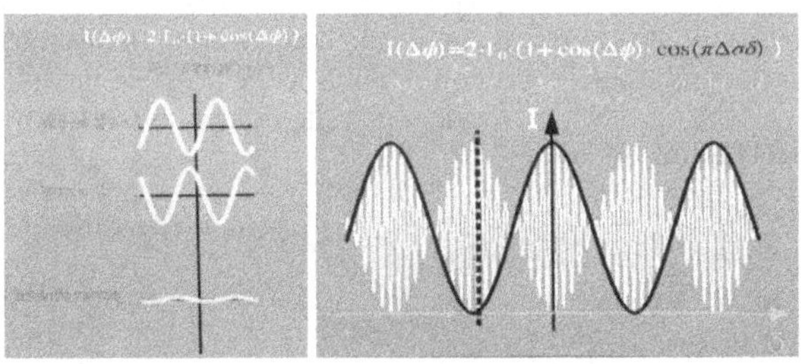

(a) (b)

**Figure 7. Intensity of the interference pattern at a given location (a) and modulation of contrast (b) can be displayed close to the observed phenomena.**

It is worth noting that all the augmentations and visual feedback features can be activated on demand. They are toggled from a keypad that stands next to the experiment. This keypad is active only when the *option* card equipped with a RFID tag is in contact with a dedicated RFID reader. A *start* card can also be used to instantly put the system back to an initial state, which is not possible with a standard Michelson interferometer. These cards give the teacher control over the application and the different pedagogical supports. At any moment, the teacher can place one of the cards in the RFID reader to enable or disable the privileges the card gives. For example, students are not able to run the simulation until the teacher has given them permission to do it by using the *start* card. The *option* card lets the teacher enable or disable the keypad in order to display or hide the augmented feedback. This notably gives the professor the ability to support his or her explanation of the theoretical concepts during the experiment. It also enables the teacher to control the difficulty of the experiment. Of course, the teacher can also decide to let the students manipulate the keypad by themselves, so they can experience, test, and discuss about the experiment.

## EXAMPLE OF PRACTICAL WORK WITH HOBIT

After having switched on the computer and the two video-projectors, the teacher runs the application. It will remain in a "stand by" mode until the teacher uses the *start* card on the RFID. Then, she or he provides an exercise form to the group composed of, typically, two or three students. The students have to experiment with the system to answer this form. For example, they have to find the right configuration of the setup for obtaining interference fringes with a sodium lamp. First, they place the (fake) sodium light on the dedicated stand. Then, they can manipulate the optical elements in order to find the concrete configurations that were theoretically presented during the lecture courses. If students encounter difficulties, the teacher can decide to display additional information like the current state of the mirror (see Figure 6(a)) and the place where the lens should be positioned to ensure adequate imaging conditions. To do so, the teacher just needs to activate the keypad with the *option* card, and toggle the corresponding option by pressing the associated key. Once the students have managed to obtain the expected interference pattern, they can physically measure the period of the fringes to determine the angle value of the mirror, directly on the projection screen (see Figure 8(a)), as they would do with a real Michelson interferometer. After the students have modified the system in order to observe rings on the screen, the teacher wants now to explain the modulation of contrast that can be observed on the pattern. The teacher decides to display a new visual feedback to support her or his explanation (see Figure 8(b)). Finally, the students have to observe what happens with a white light. Students just need to swap the sodium light box with the white light box, and they can now continue experimenting. After the experiment finishes, the teacher uses the *start* card to reset the system and begin a new experiment with the predefined conditions.

(a) (b)

**Figure 8. Example scenarios. (a) A student measures physically the period of the fringes on the projection screen. (b) Teacher explaining the modulation of contrast.**

## EVALUATION

We conducted a user study to evaluate HOBIT in a real experimental class similar to the one described in the previous section. Our main objective was to explore how this system impacts scientific and technical learning compared to a standard corresponding experiment. We also explored the user experience and attractiveness of the system.

### Subjects and apparatus

A total of 101 students (82 males and 19 females; mean age: 19.16±0.82 years old) and 6 teachers (5 males and 1 female; mean seniority in teaching position: 18.2±6.2 years old) participated to the study. The students were second-year students of a University institute of technology in optics. The teachers (3 assistant professors, 2 associate professors and 1 university professor) were those in charge of the optics lab work training program. All the teachers were experienced with standard Michelson interferometer teaching. They were all motivated by teaching in practical sessions and confident in their professional skills. All of them declared a professional use of standard digital technologies (e.g. creation of their teaching contents or their presentation slides). On the other hand, they were novice with emerging technologies (e.g. augmented reality and virtual reality). Before the experiment, the 6 teachers were invited to participate to a presentation and regulation session of the study methods. In order to get familiar with HOBIT, they first experimented with the system, guided by the research team, and they completed the problem-solving task corresponding to the upcoming students lab works. This took approximately 1 hour. After this training time, the mean perception of their *a priori* capability to use HOBIT during a lab work session was 5.1±2.2 on a Likert scale in 7 levels.

The study took place directly at the University of Bordeaux, during 3 months. Three conditions were tested:

- MI, a standard Michelson Interferometer
- SMI, a Simulator of a Michelson Interferometer, as described previously, but with no pedagogical augmentations. The SMI condition is thus a pure simulation of MI.
- ASMI, corresponding to the SMI condition, plus the pedagogical augmentations.

Our hypotheses were that

**H1:** replacing a real experiment (MI) by a simulated one (SMI) does not decrease the learning performance

**H2:** an augmented condition (ASMI) improves the learning compared to non-augmented ones (MI and SMI),

**H3:** the students who have learned with HOBIT (SMI and ASMI conditions) are able to transfer their knowledge to a real condition (MI).

MI and [A]SMI were installed in two separate rooms of the training lab, with similar setups (comparable room size, similar tables and chairs, similar lighting conditions).

### Experimental protocol

One month before the lab work sessions, all students answered a pre-test questionnaire PT0 (see description in the *Results* section). This allowed us to estimate their preliminary knowledge on Michelson interferometer after the lecture courses period. Then, the students were divided into four homogeneous groups (see Table 1). The training sessions were carried out in pairs and lasted four hours (two hours per condition). The members of group A1 and A2 used SMI (resp. ASMI) first, and then MI. The members of group B1 and B2 used first MI and then SMI (resp ASMI). Students from each group were assigned to each teacher in order to limit a "teacher effect" (see [18]). During the first two-hours session, students had to solve a set of problems involving interferometry technical skills and knowledges. After the session, the students filled out a post-test learning assessment (PT1), and they swapped with the group having done the other condition. During the second two-hours session, students had to solve similar problems as in the first session. At the end of the second session, they answered a new post-test learning assessment (PT2), and they filled out a user experience questionnaire (UX) including the french translation of the simplified Attrakdiff survey [13]. The questions we asked in this UX questionnaire were oriented towards pedagogical needs, i.e. referring on usability, usefulness, and meaningfulness. Indeed, the personal perception of a pedagogical support could influence the learning quality, as it play a role in the extrinsic motivation of the user [21].

The pedagogical content, the training goals and the related exercises were prepared by the teachers team (see Table 2). A total of 95 students' forms were analyzed (4 students did not fill the forms, and 2 of them provided non-exploitable documents). Figure 9 summarizes the whole protocol. It is worth noting that in each session teachers explained how to use the system, either [A]SMI or MI. They were also available to clarify any doubts the students had, as done in ordinary lab work conditions. In order not to introduce possible inequity between the groups, no academic grade related to the Michelson interferometer was given.

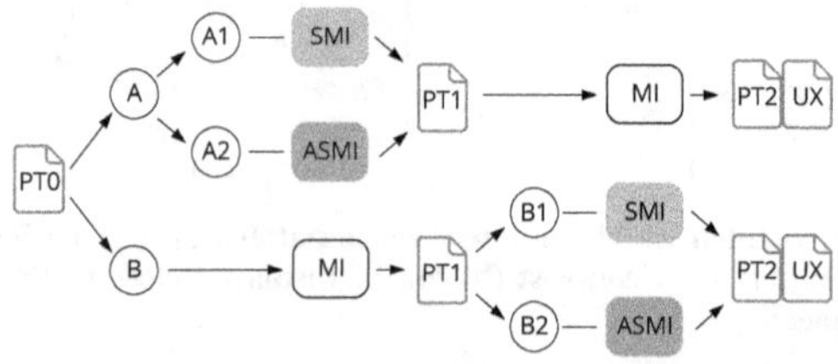


**Figure 9. Summary of the protocol. A1, A2, B1, and B2 are the groups of students, PT0 refers to the pre-test, PT1 and PT2 to the post-tests, and UX to the user experience questionnaire. MI refers to the real Michelson interferometer; SMI refers to the Michelson interferometer simulator; and ASMI refers to the interferometer simulator with augmentation.**

| Groups | A1 | A2 | B1 | B2 |
|---|---|---|---|---|
| *Number of participants* | 19 | 27 | 22 | 27 |
| *Mean±SD age* | 19.00±0.75 | 19.04±0.81 | 18.95±0.90 | 19.46±0.71 |
| *Male/Female* | 13/6 | 21/6 | 20/2 | 22/5 |

**Table 1. Distribution of the groups.**

| | |
|---|---|
| Training goals | Wave optics: Michelson interferometry |
| Learning content | Origin of interference fringes and rings<br>Role of the optical components<br>Influence of the light source (mono or polychromatic) |
| Technical skills | Mobilize precise adjustments<br>Identify and set up a technical configuration for various interference phenomena |

**Table 2. Pedagogical objectives of the lab work training program**

### Global reliability and design relevance

Overall, the subjects found that HOBIT *worked well* (mean and SD score on a 7 points Likert scale: 5.73±1.57; 7 being *"fully agree"*). During their manipulations, the students declared that they were not disturbed by occlusion problems (1.74±1.14, 7 being *"fully disturbed"*) nor by problems of delay between their actions and the resulting system reaction (2.05±1.31). They globally felt that the operating mode of HOBIT (SMI and ASMI conditions) was *close* to a standard Michelson interferometer (5.09±1.48, 7 being *"fully agree"*). These declarative results tend to show that the physical proximity of HOBIT with a standard Michelson experiment is meaningful.

### Results on learning

In order to estimate the pedagogical relevance of HOBIT, we assessed its effectiveness in regard to the achievement of the learning goals described in Table 2. This assessment focused on the students capability to schematize and to explain scientifically an interferometer configuration and the related observable phenomena (e.g. Figure 2). In the pre-test (PT0), the students had to report how to obtain interference fringes with a monochromatic light source. In PT1, they had to explain how to obtain interference rings with a monochromatic light source. Finally, in PT2, we assessed their ability to explain how to obtain interference fringes, as in PT0, but with a polychromatic light source (see Figure 5(c)). Competency is effective for a learner when the integrated set of knowledges, skills and judgment enable her or him to effectively perform in various situations [3]. Slight variation between the tests ensures that the students have to think again about the correct answer. These tests allow us to estimate the impact of the condition (MI, SMI or ASMI) on the evolution of the learning and on its stabilization.

In addition to these tests, we also asked the students to answer a set of questions referring to general definitions and mathematical exercises about interferometry. These questions were asked after PT0, PT1, and PT2. They were related to previous courses (e.g. "definition of the parameters of an optics formula") and the corresponding skills were not targeted during the lab sessions (See Table 2). The assessment of these questions showed no differences between the groups, for each test. This allows us to verify that the observed learning evolutions were due to the learning condition only, and not to a group effect. Indeed, practical work may reactivate previous knowledge, and re-introduce non homogeneity concerning the initial knowledge of the groups.

The answers to the tests and the diagrams produced by the students were scored by a teacher and a researcher of the project team, using a scale from 0 to 5. The teacher and the researcher first scored 50 tests in a double-blind approach, with harmonization steps after 10, 30 and 50 assessments to validate the scoring scale. Then, i) the researcher assessed all the remaining tests and ii) the teacher checked the results in order to validate the scoring. Less than 10 equivocal tests were discussed. This analysis of the type of answers enabled us to estimate the learning level for each student after each session. The score of 5 was given to diagrams that were fully correct and adequately annotated. In this case, the learning is considered as acquired. The score of 4 corresponds to correct but partial answers with small omissions or broad wording. The score of 3 corresponds to correct but partial answers with notable omissions (i.e., optical element, angle, etc.) and confused explanations (i.e., lack of scientific vocabulary). Both 4 and 3 scores were counted as an underway learning. Finally, the scores of 2, 1, and 0 were given in case of wrong answers (diagram without any of the expected elements and/or conflicting explanations), off-topics, or blank answers, respectively. This refers to not acquired knowledge. Figure 10 illustrates an example of diagram.

It is worth to mention that all the analyzes carried out for the learning data as well as the UX data use the Aligned Rank Transform for nonparametric factorial ANOVAs as described by Wobbrock et al. [30]. After the Aligned Rank Transform processes the data, ANOVA tests can be performed. One advantage of using the Aligned Rank Transform with ANOVAs over common nonparametric tests is that we can analyze multiple factors and their interactions.

#### *Pre-test PT0*

The scoring of PT0 showed that 94% of the students were not proficient in schematization and explanation of interferometer configuration before starting the lab work training session (mean score of the whole cohort: 2.52±1.21, see Table 3 and Figure 11). Most of their mistakes were linked to inappropri-

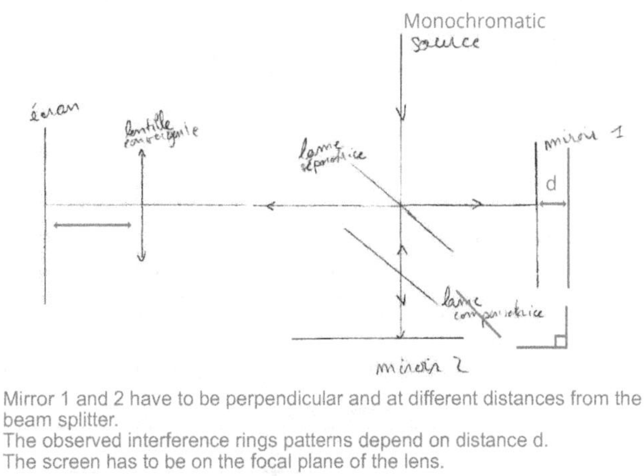


**Figure 10. Example of diagram produced by a student at PT1. She was asked to explain the configuration in which interference rings can be observed. This diagram has been marked as "under way". Indeed, the overall structure is correct, but important information is missing (e.g. lack of the shift distance d).**

ate positioning or omissions of optical components, lack of relevant annotations, or confusions with other configurations or with other interferometer (e.g. Young's interferometer). It confirms previous studies indicating that university students do not easily understand the physical models and have many difficulties to construct mental images only with a theoretical approach (see e.g. [6]). A one-way ANOVA revealed no significant differences between the four groups ($F[3, 87]=1.33$, $p=0.27$, $\eta_G^2=0.04$; see also PT0 in Table 3).

*Post-test PT1*

A two-factor mixed ANOVA showed that after the first two-hours training sessions, the overall knowledge about the interferometer configurations has improved significantly ($F[1,86]=61.94$, $p<0.01$, $\eta_G^2=0.26$ / PT0: 2.48±1.21; PT1: 3.88±1.17). The ratio of students with insufficient knowledge decreased in all groups, as illustrated in Figure 11.

The ANOVA also revealed that there is an effect of the learning condition on the scores obtained in PT1 ($F[2,86]=3.51$, $p=0.03$, $\eta_G^2=0.04$). A Tukey's pairwise test showed that the scores obtained in the ASMI condition (4.44±0.77) are significantly higher than the ones obtained in the other conditions (MI: 3.67±1.26 (p=0.02) —SMI: 3.63±1.16 (p=0.05)). This confirms that augmentations enhance the building of the targeted knowledge (**H2**). On the other hand, no significant differences were found between SMI and MI (p=0.99), which does not contradict **H1**. The ratio of students having acquired the knowledge is comparable in both conditions (Figure 11, second line). The typologies of errors were very similar (e.g. error of mirror angulation and error of distance between the beam splitter and the mirrors). This tends to show that the SMI condition reproduces closely the MI one.

*Post-test PT2*

We observed the evolution of the scores from PT1 to PT2 (see Table 3 and Figure 11). A two-factor mixed ANOVA showed that, for group A2, no significant differences were found ($F[1, 24]=0.88$, $p=0.36$, $\eta_G^2=0.04$). This tends to indicate that the students who have learned with ASMI did not decrease their performance when moving to MI. Their scores remain higher than any other conditions. These students gained most of the understanding and skills required to calibrate and troubleshoot

| Groups | A1 | A2 | B1 | B2 |
|---|---|---|---|---|
| **PT0** | (Mean±SD score, max=5) | | | |
| Target knowledge | 2.63±1.21 | 2.59±1.12 | 2.86±1.25 | 2.11±1.28 |
| *General definitions* | 1.66±0.69 | 1.81±0.95 | 1.86±0.68 | 1.51±0.79 |
| **PT1** | (Mean±SD score, max=5) | | | |
| Target knowledge | 3.63±1.16 | 4.44±0.77 | 3.72±0.89 | 3.63±1.47 |
| *General definitions* | 3.18±0.68 | 3.28±0.68 | 3.39±0.46 | 2.92±0.71 |
| **PT2** | (Mean±SD score, max=5) | | | |
| Target knowledge | 2.32±1.38 | 4.12±1.13 | 3.11±1.49 | 3.48±1.55 |
| *General definitions* | 3.58±1.09 | 3.97±0.88 | 3.92±0.81 | 3.81±1.00 |

**Table 3. Knowledge scores for the pre-test (PT0), and the post-tests (PT1 and PT2).**

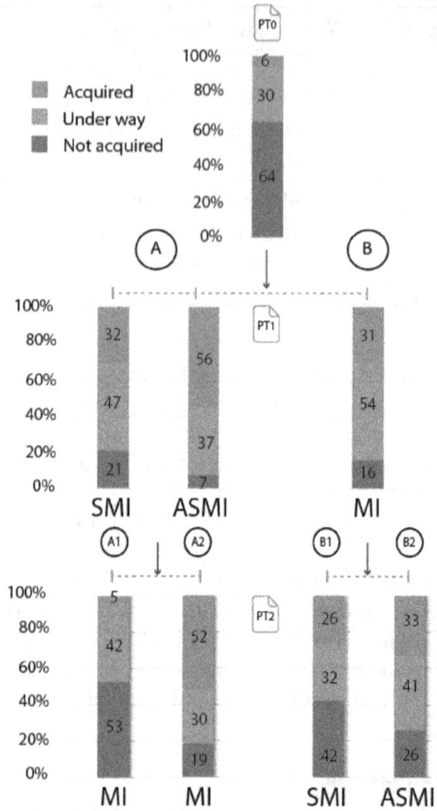


**Figure 11. Learning results as ratios of students being at different levels of knowledge and skills acquisition—before the experiment (first line), after the first training session (second line), and after the second training session (third line)**

setups used to make interferometry observations. It seems to indicate a stabilization of their learning; the knowledge that has been built with ASMI could be reinvested effectively with a classical interferometer. This would go in the direction of **H3**.

On the other hand, for group A1, i.e. the students who experienced with MI after having learned with SMI, a two-factor mixed ANOVA highlighted an unexpected result. In this group, the learning achievement significantly decreased ($F[1, 18]=8.92$, $p=0.01$, $\eta_G^2=0.33$, see Table 3). This partly refutes **H3**. The amount of students who were underway or without any clear acquisition was quite similar to those noticed in PT0. We observed that 20% of the A1 students did not answer to all the questions of PT2. They rushed their work or did a lot of basic mistakes. In comparison, this ratio was between 2 and 6% for all the other groups. A1 was the group that indicated the lowest motivational advantage to use a hybrid system compared to a standard Michelson interferometer in their UX results (see next section). Therefore, it appears as if they were demotivated. That leads us to the idea that these results could probably be linked to the hope the students put in simulator to support their learning. It might destabilize their first understanding noticed in PT1 and act as a disruption in the learning process by stating that they still had some difficulties to setup the classical Michelson interferometer even if they trained on a simulator just before. This needs to be confirmed by further analyzes and replications of the experiment. However, it opens the question of the students representation of the role of a simulator in educational context.

For the groups that have initially started with MI, no noticeable improvement can be observed after using SMI (B1) nor ASMI (B2). It tends to show that the augmentations that have shown undeniable benefits after PT1 (group A2), have little impact when activated in a second round of training session. Students may mainly built their knowledge during the first training session, where no augmentation were available. However, it worth noting that the typology of mistakes were different between the two groups. For instance, in the group using SMI at the second round (B1), 37% of the students forget to position the lens and the compensator. This indicates that they did not perceive the role of these components. At the opposite, with ASMI (B2), most of the mistakes were only due to incomplete annotations of the diagrams.

The results obtained for the questions that were not directly linked to the targeted knowledge and skills (i.e. general definition and mathematical exercises) for each step of the learning process (PT0/PT1/PT2) did not show any significant differences between the four groups. Additionally, all teachers confirmed the absence of notable modifications on their teaching practices induced by the study conditions (5.83±1.60; 7 being "fully similar"). Moreover, the participants declared that they were not stressed during the study (students: 1.21±0.63; teachers: 1.66±0.81, 7 being "fully stressed"). All these results allow us to exclude a group effect; the observed learning evolutions are due to the system only.

### Understanding the role of the augmentations

To gain insight on the relevance of the augmentations, we have looked at the declared perceptions of the ASMI users (groups A2 and B2) and the declared perception of the SMI ones (groups A1 and B1). A one-way ANOVA was performed for each of the asked questions. The ASMI users perceived the tool as less complex to operate than the SMI users, in comparison with the MI condition ($F[1, 92]=12.66$, $p<0.01$, $\eta_G^2=0.12$ - see Figure 12). Similarly, the augmented version was perceived as more motivating ($F[1, 91]=10.98$, $p<0.01$, $\eta_G^2=0.11$), and more efficient ($F[1, 74]=25.80$, $p<0.01$, $\eta_G^2=0.26$) than a tool without augmentation (see Figure 12).

Among the augmentations, the indications displaying the state of the manipulated components (Figure 6(a)) were the ones that the ASMI students cited first (69% of the them). 5 of the 6 teachers reported that they considered this augmentation as the most important. The students and the teachers also endorsed the schematic projections of the wave interferences (Figures 6(b) and 7).

A large majority of the ASMI users (91%) declared that the system they used have met or totally met their needs to their learning goals (5.95±1.15, 7 being *"fully agree"*). In comparison, the mean score for the SMI users is 4.19±1.54. About this question, the open-ended spontaneous answers (multiple answers were possible) of the ASMI users were that the system i) helped them to understand the theoretical aspect of the interferometry phenomena (49% of the answers), ii) supported

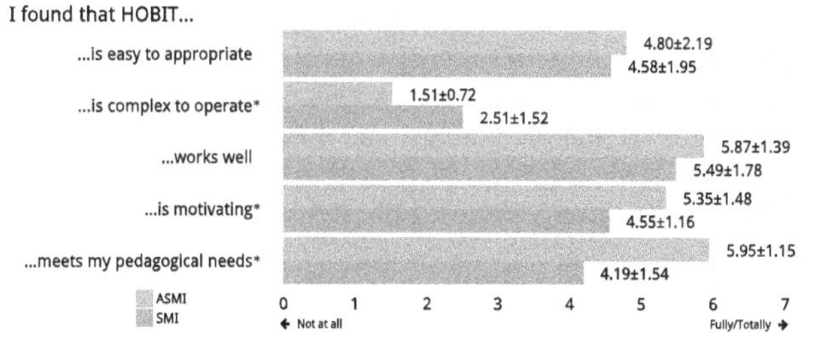


**Figure 12. Results of the UX questionnaire (selected questions). The symbol * indicates statistical significant differences between SMI and ASMI.**

or enhanced their cognitive conception (conceptualization) of the wave phenomena (32%), iii) highlighted the causal effect between their interferometer adjustments and the observed interference patterns (20%), and iv) supported or enhanced their understanding of technical adjustments of an interferometer (14%).

At the opposite, the answers of the SMI users were more neutral. They rarely declared pedagogical gains compared to the MI condition, except for the *restart* functionality.

Regarding the perceived attractiveness, the students of the ASMI condition found the system really appealing both for its pragmatic and hedonist attributes. Based on the Hassenzhal's model [10] applied on the Attrakdif results, the augmented version of HOBIT appears as a desirable pedagogical tool (see Figure 13). In contrast, the students of groups A1 and B1 who did not experienced augmentations were a bit less enthusiastic.

The answers of the students are in line with the teachers comments. Teachers reported that the ASMI students were more motivated and engaged than the SMI ones. Three of them indicated that many of the SMI students did not perceived the added value of a simulated system without augmentations. All the teachers agree that the augmented version of HOBIT is much more interesting than a version without augmentations.

The pedagogical augmentation seems to be necessary to support students in their understanding of technical specificities of the interferometer configurations and on their adjustments.

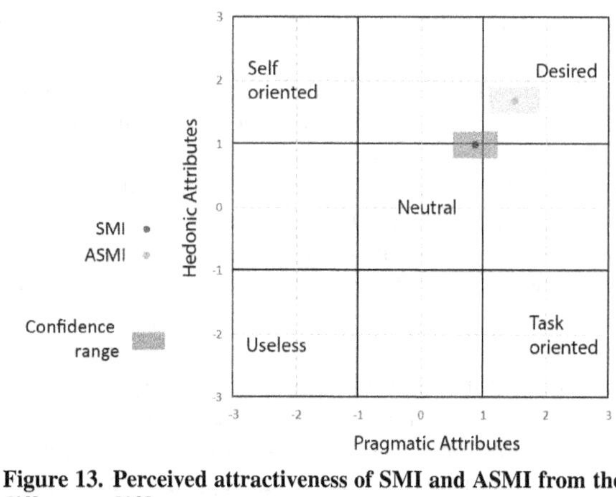


**Figure 13. Perceived attractiveness of SMI and ASMI from the Attrakdiff survey [10].**

Each user constructs his or her personal representation of the system by defining (consciously or not) various attributes. The high perception of usefulness and attractiveness provided by the pedagogical augmentations, and the perception of the users that the system addresses their needs, could explain the fact that the ASMI group obtained the best learning results.

To strengthen these results, new experiments should be conducted to assess how the acquired knowledge stabilizes over long periods of time.

## DISCUSSION AND CONCLUSION

To overcome the limitations of standard setups, we developed a hybrid platform, HOBIT, which allows us to mimick true optics experiments. This platform reduces the cost as well the setup and maintenance time as no real optical components are used. Beyond the simulation, we showed that HOBIT offers the opportunity to augment the experiment with pedagogical supports. A study conducted in an ecological situation allowed us to demonstrate that such an approach, which mixes simulation of the real phenomena and virtual augmentations, enhances the learning of students compared to traditional setups. HOBIT does not aim at fully replacing true optics experiments. Similarly to a flight simulator, this platform makes training sessions more convenient. Because we took care to mimic as much as possible the real condition, and because we embed relevant augmentations within the simulation, the good transfer to the real condition is favored.

In this work we focused on the Michelson interferometer experiment. HOBIT is not limited to this particular experiment. Numerous other augmented optics experiments can be designed from this platform. As an example, we are currently building new pedagogical activities for simulating and augmenting Young's interferometer and polarization experiments. Beyond optics, a similar approach could benefit other domains. This is notably the case of scientific fields were the visualization of abstract concepts is important. With augmented information it is possible to create new representations that can help students to observe those abstract concepts or invisible phenomena [31]. For example, in the electronics field, an efficient learning and understanding of complex concepts remains a challenge.

We hope that our work will help practitioners to design new relevant learning environments in a variety of fields. To this end, we would like to remind the importance of taking into account the nature of the scientific knowledge and the pedagogical orchestration of practical works at the early stages of the technological design process. Co-design with experts and teachers of the targeted field is a key element for the design of meaningfulness systems that remain as close as possible to the real experiences. We also encourage evaluations in ecological situations, as we did with HOBIT. Both quantitative comparative studies and UX surveys help gaining insights about the factors that play significant roles in learning. Finally, we would like to remind that a technological enhanced tool in and of itself is not necessarily a golden bullet that enhances learning. Without proper pedagogical support, it can actually backfire, as we have shown in our study.

In this paper, we have focused on the evaluation of the learning efficacy by looking at the individual performances of the students. Beyond these performances, it would be interesting to explore how a system like HOBIT modifies the interactions between the students, and how it impacts teaching practices. Indeed, education has to be considered in a larger spectrum than learning performance only. This is one axis of development of our current work.

We hope that the approach we have described in this paper will open the way to a new generation of hybrid pedagogical systems used in real conditions at schools or at Universities.

## ACKNOWLEDGMENTS

The authors would like to thank the persons who participated to this project (Benoit Coulais, Jérémy Bergognat, Patrick Reuter, David Lacoste) as well as the teachers and students who participated to the study. This work was financially supported by Idex Bordeaux (CPU and LAPHIA) and Inria.

## REFERENCES

1. Oliver Bimber and Ramesh Raskar. 2005. *Spatial Augmented Reality: Merging Real and Virtual Worlds*. A. K. Peters, Ltd., Natick, MA, USA.
2. Chris Chiaverina and Michael Vollmer. 2005. Learning Physics from the experiments. In *Informal Learning and Public Understanding of Physics, Selected Contributions of the 3rd International Girep Seminar.* 185–190.
3. Vernon Curran, Lynn Casimiro, Valerie Banfield, Pippa Hall, Kelly Lackie, Brian Simmons, Manon Tremblay, Susan J Wagner, and Ivy Oandasan. 2009. Research for Interprofessional Competency-Based Evaluation (RICE). *Journal of Interprofessional Care* 23, 3 (2009), 297–300.
4. Debnath D, Barthakur N. K, Baruah R. S, and Goswami P. K. 2012. Problems of Teaching Optics in Middle School: A Survey in Batadraba Education Block of Nagaon District, Assam, India. *International Journal of Scientific and Research Publications* 2, 8 (2012).
5. Pierre Dillenbourg, Michael J Baker, Agnes Blaye, and Claire O'Malley. 1995. The evolution of research on collaborative learning. *Learning in Humans and Machine: Towards an interdisciplinary learning science.* (1995), 189–211.
6. Blizak Djanette and Chafiqi Fouad. 2014. Determination of University Students' Misconceptions about Light Using Concept Maps. *Procedia - Social and Behavioral Sciences* 152 (2014), 582–589.
7. Son Do-Lenh, Patrick Jermann, Amanda Legge, Guillaume Zufferey, and Pierre Dillenbourg. 2012. *TinkerLamp 2.0: Designing and Evaluating Orchestration Technologies for the Classroom.* Springer, Berlin, Heidelberg, 65–78.
8. Andreas Dünser, Lawrence Walker, Heather Horner, and Daniel Bentall. 2012. Creating interactive physics education books with augmented reality. In *Proceedings of OzCHI '12*. 107–114.

9. Taciana Pontual Falcão and Sara Price. 2009. What Have You Done! The Role of 'Interference' in Tangible Environments for Supporting Collaborative Learning. In *Proceedings of CSCL'09 - Volume 1*. 325–334.

10. Marc Hassenzahl. 2005. *The Thing and I: Understanding the Relationship Between User and Product*. Springer Netherlands, Dordrecht, 31–42.

11. Dana Hayes, Craig Turczynski, Jonny Rice, and Michael Kozhevnikov. 2013. Virtual-Reality-Based Educational Laboratories in Fiber Optic Engineering. In *ETOP 2013 Proceedings*. EWP40.

12. Edwin Hutchins. 2000. Distributed cognition. *International Encyclopedia of the Social and Behavioral Sciences. Elsevier Science* (2000).

13. Carine Lallemand, Vincent Koenig, Guillaume Gronier, and Romain Martin. 2015. Création et validation d'une version française du questionnaire AttrakDiff pour l'évaluation de l'expérience utilisateur des systèmes interactifs. *Revue Européenne de Psychologie Appliquée/European Review of Applied Psychology* 65, 5 (2015), 239–252.

14. Xiaolai Liu and Qinghuai Li. 2011. Combination of the Research-Based Learning Method with the Modern Physics Experiment Course Teaching. *International Education Studies* 4, 1 (2011), 101–104.

15. Xiangchun Ma, Shaochun Zhong, Da Xu, and Chunhong Zhang. 2010. The Design and Implementation of Middle School Physics Optical Simulation Experiment Platform. In *Entertainment for Education. Digital Techniques and Systems: 5th International Conference on E-learning and Games, Edutainment*. Springer Berlin Heidelberg, Berlin, Heidelberg, 84–91.

16. Robin Millar. 1987. Towards a Role for Experiment in the Science Teaching Laboratory. *Studies in Science Education* 14, 1 (1987), 109–118.

17. Robin Millar. 2004. *The role of practical work in the teaching and learning of science. Paper prepared for the Committee on High School Science Laboratories: Role and Vision*. National Academy of Sciences.

18. Barbara Nye, Spyros Konstantopoulos, and Larry V. Hedges. 2004. How Large Are Teacher Effects? *Educational Evaluation and Policy Analysis* 26, 3 (2004), 237–257.

19. Gorazd Planinsic. 2010. Stimulating scientific reasoning through explorations of simple experiments. In *Proceedings of selected papers of the GIREP - ICPE-MPTL International conference*. 34–42.

20. Marcelo Rodrigues and Paulo Simeão Carvalho. 2014. Teaching optical phenomena with Tracker. *Physics Education* 49, 6 (2014), 671.

21. Richard M. Ryan and Edward L. Deci. 2000. Intrinsic and Extrinsic Motivations: Classic Definitions and New Directions. *Contemporary Educational Psychology* 25, 1 (2000), 54–67.

22. Magdalena Sadowska and Anna Kamińska. 2010. Problems in teaching physics in primary and secondary school, as seen by young Polish she-teachers. In *Proceedings of selected papers of the GIREP - ICPE-MPTL International conference*. 180–185.

23. Brett E. Shelton and Nicholas R. Hedley. 2004. Exploring a Cognitive Basis for Learning Spatial Relationships with Augmented Reality. *Technology Instruction Cognition and Learning* 1, 4 (2004), 323 – 357.

24. Osamu Takayama, Armand Niederberger, Petru Ghenuche, Manoj Mathew, and Giovanni Volpe. 2007. El Día de la Luz (the Day of Light): two hours optics demonstration for secondary school students. In *Tenth International Topical Meeting on Education and Training in Optics and Photonics*. 96650K–96650K.

25. Josef Trna. 2005. Motivation and Hands-on Experiments. In *Proceedings of the 2nd International Conference on Hands-on Science*. 169–174.

26. Josef Trna and Petr Novak. 2010. Motivational Effectiveness of Experiments in Physics Education. In *Proceedings of selected papers of the GIREP - ICPE-MPTL International conference*. 409–417.

27. Josef Trna, Eva Trnova, and Petr Novak. 2010. Improvement of science and technology literacy by means of ICT-based collaborative action research including hands-on experiments. In *Proceedings of the 7th International Conference on Hands-on Science*. 131–137.

28. John Underkoffler and Hiroshi Ishii. 1998. Illuminating light: an optical design tool with a luminous-tangible interface. In *Proceedings of the SIGCHI conference on Human factors in computing systems - CHI '98*. 542–549.

29. Stella Vosniadou, Christos Ioannides, Aggeliki Dimitrakopoulou, and Efi Papademetriou. 2001. Designing learning environments to promote conceptual change in science. *Learning and Instruction* 11, 4 (2001), 381–419.

30. Jacob O. Wobbrock, Leah Findlater, Darren Gergle, and James J. Higgins. 2011. The Aligned Rank Transform for Nonparametric Factorial Analyses Using Only Anova Procedures. In *Proceedings of the SIGCHI Conference on Human Factors in Computing Systems (CHI '11)*. 143–146.

31. Hsin-Kai Wu, Silvia Wen-Yu Lee, Hsin-Yi Chang, and Jyh-Chong Liang. 2013. Current status, opportunities and challenges of augmented reality in education. *Computers & Education* 62 (2013), 41–49.

32. Takeshi Yamaguchi and Hiroshi Yoshikawa. 2013. New education system for construction of optical holography setup - Tangible learning with Augmented Reality. *Journal of Physics: Conference Series* 415, 1 (2013), 12064.

33. Susan A Yoon and Joyce Wang. 2014. Making the Invisible Visible in Science Museums Through Augmented Reality Devices. *TechTrends* 58, 1 (2014), 49–55.

# PathViewer: Visualizing Pathways through Student Data

**Yiting Wang, Walker M. White, and Erik Andersen**
Department of Computer Science, Cornell University
{yw428, wmw2, ela63}@cornell.edu

## ABSTRACT

Analysis of student data is critical for improving education. In particular, educators need to understand what approaches their students are taking to solve a problem. However, identifying student strategies and discovering areas of confusion is difficult because an educator may not know what queries to ask or what patterns to look for in the data. In this paper, we present a visualization tool, PathViewer, to model the paths that students follow when solving a problem. PathViewer leverages ideas from flow diagrams and natural language processing to visualize the sequences of intermediate steps that students take. Using PathViewer, we analyzed how several students solved a Python assignment, discovering interesting and unexpected patterns. Our results suggest that PathViewer can allow educators to quickly identify areas of interest, drill down into specific areas, and identify student approaches to the problem as well as misconceptions they may have.

### Author Keywords

data visualization; programming education

### ACM Classification Keywords

H.5.0. Information Interfaces and Presentation: General

## INTRODUCTION

Analysis of student data is critical for improving education. Educators need to understand what approaches their students are taking to solve problems. These insights help educators understand the patterns in what students are doing and how they are confused, so they can drill down into areas of interest and modify their approach. There has recently been a lot of interest in using visual data mining to look at student data for programming [14, 10, 13]. These studies analyzed changes in students' programs over time by tracking the addition of conceptual components or modeling the stages of program construction as a finite state machine. However, we still lack tools for rapid visual assessment and comparison of the pathways that large numbers of students are taking.

Ideally, we would have visualizations that allow educators to triage their class and identify the primary ways in which students are confused. This would help them direct their effort towards resolving those specific sources of confusion. In this paper, we present a visualization tool, PathViewer, to model the paths students take when solving a problem. PathViewer visualizes intermediate stages of students' solutions as sequences of discrete states, building on work in education and video games [14, 10, 2, 17]. It innovates by using Sankey diagrams [15] to visualize how students "flow" from one state to the next, and n-grams [6] to visualize specific state sequences.


*CHI 2017*, May 06 - 11, 2017, Denver, CO, USA

ACM 978-1-4503-4655-9/17/05...$15.00
DOI: http://dx.doi.org/10.1145/3025453.3025819

We evaluated PathViewer by visualizing how a large group of students solved an assignment in a Cornell introductory programming course. By visualizing state transitions and the proportion of students who made each transition, we were able to search for interesting patterns such as loops and common state sequences. We found that students frequently do not move in one direction towards a solution, and instead loop back and forth as they experiment with various ways to solve the problem. We also found that the test cases that were provided to the students did not fully assess whether students had correctly implemented a particular function, since some incorrect implementations also passed all of the test cases. Furthermore, we observed that students are likely to follow patterns they have seen previously when tackling a new problem, and that they often get stuck if this pattern is incorrect.

Our results suggest that PathViewer can allow educators to quickly identify high-level solution patterns that are are particularly interesting and then drill down into specific areas of interest. In doing so, they can identify the key approaches that students are taking and misconceptions that students may have. These techniques are potentially useful not just for education, but also other areas of HCI, since they can help visualize how large groups of participants use an interface.

The main contributions of this paper are:

- A novel technique for visualizing the solution pathways that many students take to solve a problem.
- A case study using this technique in an introductory programming class to identify interesting patterns.

## RELATED WORK

Various researchers have tacked the problem of visualizing student data using visual data mining. Hosseini et al. [10] modeled intermediate steps of students' programs by analyzing changes in programming concepts that are reflected in the program and whether these changes increased or decreased the correctness of the program. Although this representation captured changes to the correctness of a student's program, it did not fully capture the number of students in one particular state, nor the paths the students took to solve a problem.

Another approach is finite state machines. Piech et al. [14] took snapshots of students' code during construction, and used a Hidden Markov Model to discover "sink states", or states that the students had high probability of remaining in for several code updates. Although this kind of visualization captures state transitions between solutions and the number of people that reach a particular state, it does not visualize how many people transition from one state to another. Furthermore, although the state diagram includes transitions to the same state as well as loops, the visualization does not display these loops. Berland et al. [3] also uses a state-based visualization to track sequences of students' programs. They label the edges between states with the percentage of participants who make that transition. In contrast, PathViewer uses these ratios to set the width of the Sankey diagram edges, rapidly drawing visual attention to the most prevalent pathways and facilitating comparison between pathways. In addition, the n-gram mode helps identify common sequences and loops, which conveys useful information about students' problem-solving strategies.

The problem of visualizing pathways in student's data is similar to a problem studied in video games, namely how to visualize the pathways that large groups of players take as they play a game. The Playtracer tool used by Andersen et al. [2] and Liu et al. [12] and the spatiotemporal tool used by Wallner et al. [17] both visualize the states that players go through when playing a level of a game. These approaches produce a state transition model that captures the number of people who reached a particular state, and displays similar states close to each other. However, these approaches do not quite capture the complete paths that people take to reach a particular state, nor the loops that frequently occur.

## PATHVIEWER

PathViewer visualizes the pathways that students take through the intermediate stages of solving a problem. The user can provide a set of equivalence classes in order to group similar states together. Paths are visualized using a Sankey diagram [15], a common way to visualize a large amount of data flowing in a particular direction. The visualization was implemented using the d3.js [5] Javascript library, the open source d3.chart.js library, and the d3.chart.sankey.js library.

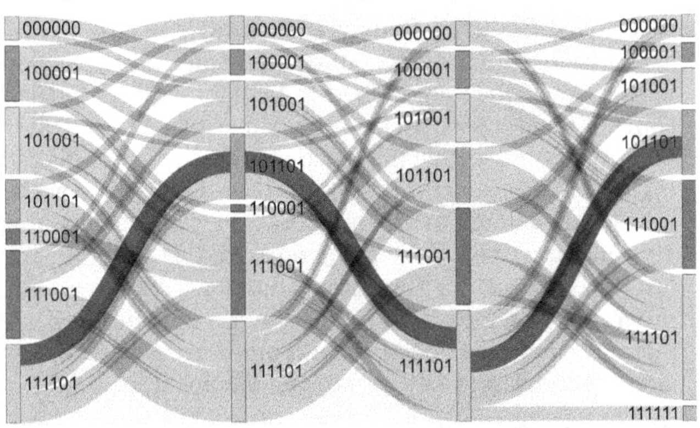


**Figure 1. This is a 4-gram visualization of paths students took when solving programming exercises. Paths with fewer than five students are hidden. Each node is a six-character string of "0"s and "1"s that indicates the specific test cases the program passed. For example, the state 111011 holds programs that passed all of the test cases except the fourth one. This visualization displays the proportion of students who take particular paths. For example, the blue path shows a loop in which students move back and forth between states 111101 and 110101.**

A common visual data mining workflow is to identify the most common patterns of pathways through solution states. To visualize and compare pathways, the tool borrows the idea of n-grams from natural language processing to visualize transitions through sequences of a specific length. To visualize this, the tool has an n-gram mode where the path can be displayed in bigrams (Figure 2), trigrams or four-grams (Figure 1). To identify which states and edges are most commonly visited, the weight of both the nodes and the edges is drawn proportionally to the number of students who took this particular path. In this mode, clicking on a particular edge of the graph highlights the path as well as students' solutions that correspond to the states along the path, as depicted in Figure 1. This allows instructors to browse through specific state sequences, and compare these sequences to look for interesting patterns.

Another useful way to analyze student paths is to look at the full path and try to see the bigger picture of where students are headed. Therefore, the tool has another mode, the full path mode, which allows for visualization of the complete paths through all the student solutions. To make visualizing paths easier, the tool supports alternate color schemes and sorting of state nodes within columns. The last three states of the full path are displayed in Figure 3.

## EVALUATION

We used PathViewer to visualize how students completed a Python assignment in Cornell's introductory programming course, CS1110.

### Data Collection

We first collected data on the intermediate stages that students' programs went through as they completed assignments. To do this, we adapted the Online Python Tutor [9] to record a snapshot of the code every time the student ran it. Students used the tool for multiple short lab exercises. The tool recorded data anonymously, and students could use it multiple times, each time resulting in a new interaction sequence. 545 students were enrolled in the class. Throughout the semester, we gathered about 400,000 snapshots of students' programs.

### Data Analysis

We used PathViewer to analyze how students wrote a specific function, *removeDups*. It is a recursive function that returns a copy of the input list with adjacent duplicates removed. We collected 757 program states for this function.

We first defined equivalence classes that would group similar programs together into the same state. Various methods have been used to compare and classify students' code. Glassman et al. [8] reformatted the solutions to remove elements such as extra white space, used an execution trace to rename the variables, then compared the resulting code for identical lines of code. Huang et al. [11] used the Abstract Syntax Trees of students' code and calculated the editing distance [16] between them to compare for similarity between programs. Other equivalence class definitions that have been used for students' programs include program size [7], a combination of code size and frequency [4], and API Call Dissimilarity [14].

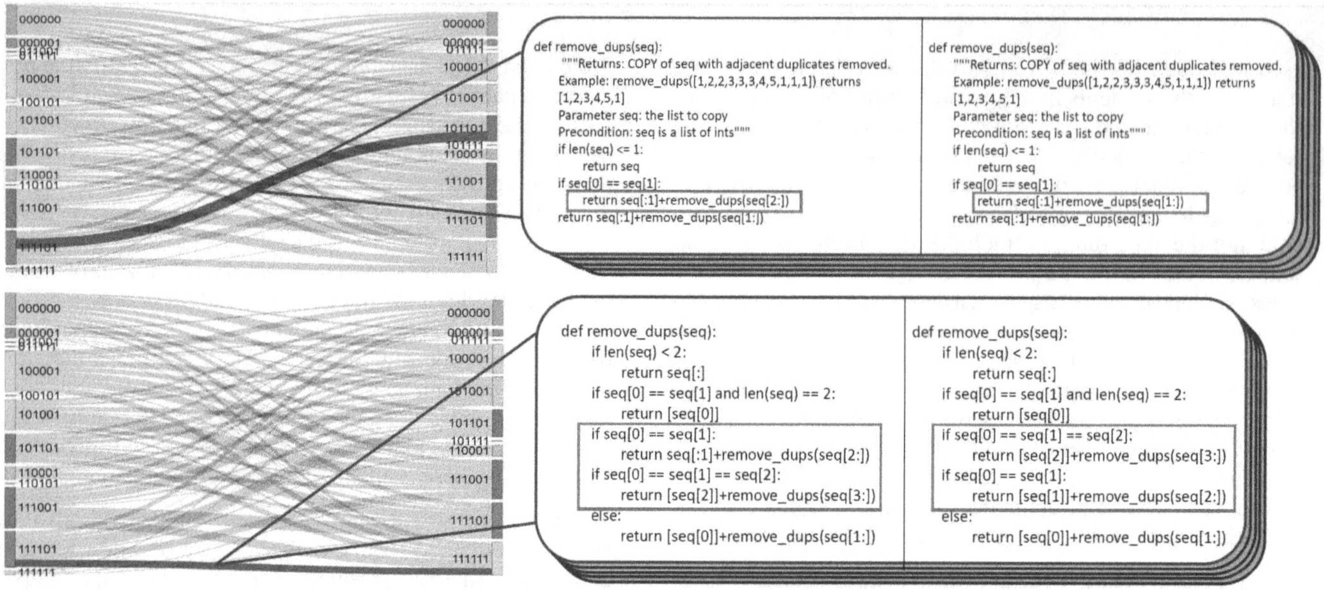


**Figure 2. These two images show how the tool can be used to investigate code transitions by displaying code samples when a particular path is clicked. From the code sample, the highlighted line of code is modified from one state to another. In the top image, the particular change in the function is not correct, which resulted in failing a test case that the code shown on the left has originally passed. The bottom image displays a transition that resulted in a piece of code (the code on the right side) that passed all 6 test cases, but is not actually correct as it only works under certain conditions.**

For this evaluation, we defined the equivalence classes to be the set of test cases that the students' program passed. This is because test cases are expert-defined equivalence classes that have been used historically to validate a piece of software [1], and are easy to execute on a large data set of student solutions. Six test cases provided feedback to the students while they implemented the function *removeDups*. We grouped programs by success on individual test cases and used binary strings to represent them. The $n^{th}$ bit is "1" if the program passed the $n^{th}$ test case, and zero if not. For example, programs in the state 111011 passed all test cases but the fourth one.

### Identifying Sequential Patterns through n-grams

Using PathViewer to view 4-grams, as shown in Figure 1, we noticed that students' solutions often do not progress linearly and revisit certain states. The highlighted blue path is one particular cycle involving the states 101101 and 111101. The transition from 101101 to 111101 is easy to explain: the program passed an additional test case. However, the transition from 111101 to 101101 was surprising because the student did made a change that failed a previously passed test case.

Figure 2 shows a bigram visualization we used to explore this abnormal but popular pattern further. To compare with successful students, we also visualized the code for the transition 111101 to 111111, displayed in the bottom of Figure 2. Roughly 60% of students who reached the state 111101 did something wrong and ended up in state 101101, while roughly 40% then passed all test cases.

We also discovered that of the 155 students who reached state 111101 and moved on to one of the two states above, 76 of them had code similar to the following:

```
if seq[0]==seq[1]:
    return [seq[0]] + remove_dups(seq[2:])
return [seq[0]] + remove_dups(seq[1:])}
```

Of those 76 students, 42 moved on to state 111111, but 34 moved on to another state 101101. The second failed test case removed duplicates from a list with two identical elements (e.g. [3,3]). 30 of these students used an approach similar to:

```
if seq[0]==seq[1]:
    return [seq[0]] + remove_dups(seq[1:])
return [seq[0]] + remove_dups(seq[1:])
```

This code is displayed in the top of Figure 2. From this visualization we discovered that the failed test cases were because of a common pattern. In this pattern, students took the head of the list, recursed on the rest, and glued them back together. This pattern was shown for a different problem in the course, but was not correct for this function. This suggests that students are likely to imitate patterns from class, especially if they have just learned a topic that is unfamiliar to them. Therefore, when the instructor is introducing a new problem to students, the instruction should present several ways to solve it.

### Identifying Common Causes of Failure

When we used PathViewer to examine the code of students with the transition from 111101 to 111111, we discovered that some of them passed all the provided test cases, but still did not actually implement the function correctly. The bottom of Figure 2 is one example of this. The code displayed shows that it had been tailored to the six test cases given, and would fail any other test case. This finding reflected that the original six test cases we had for the students did not accurately capture program correctness. To see how many students bypassed our test cases, we added three more test cases so that the equivalence classes were now based on nine test cases.

We used the full path mode in PathViewer with an alternate color scheme to depict two categories of students:

- Green: correctly implemented the function in the end
- Blue: passed all given test cases but program was incorrect

This categorization removes the students who gave up before passing all the test cases.

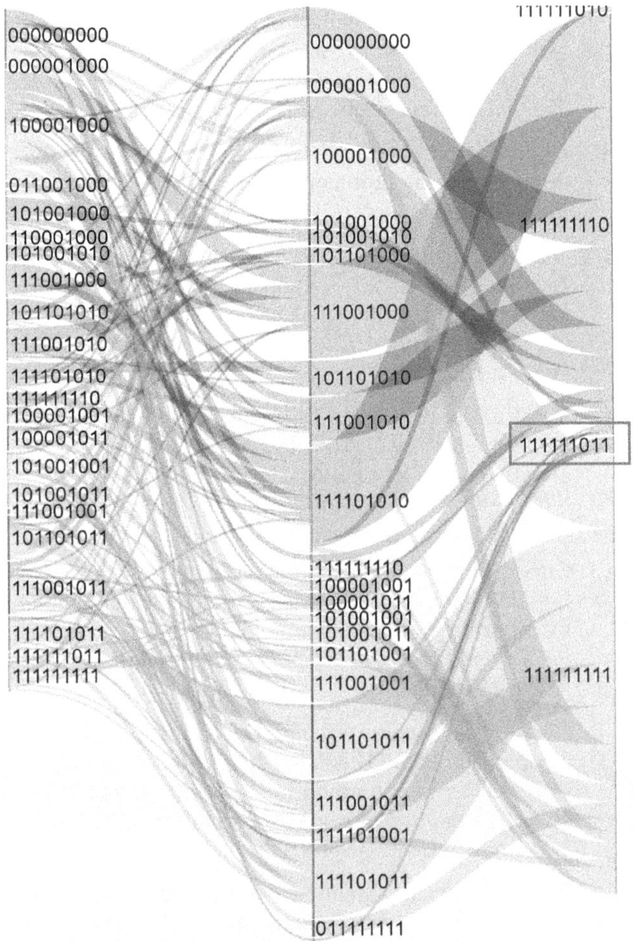


**Figure 3. This is a visualization of the last three steps in students' paths, with nodes that have fewer than eight students removed. States are now expressed as binary strings of length nine because we added three more test cases to check for code correctness in addition to the original six. Blue paths indicate programs that passed the original six test cases but did not pass some of the additional three test cases. Green paths show correct solutions. The red box shows the proportion of students who did not pass the seventh test case, suggesting they wrote their code specifically to satisfy the six test cases originally provided.**

In Figure 3, we displayed the last three steps of students in the full path mode. From the graph, it is apparent that the number of students ending in state `111111110` and the number of students in the correct state `111111111` was similar. The last test case tested whether students copied the empty list, because the function specification required students to return a copy of the original list. We can see from the pattern of the final transitions in this diagram that success or failure on this test was independent from success or failure on the other tests. Therefore, students' understanding of this step was independent of their understanding of recursion.

In addition, one can see from the state `111111011`, which highlighted by the red box, that 15 students did not pass the seventh test case. This case tested for the correctness of the function using a more complicated input than the previous six test cases. This suggests that these students did not write a correct function, but tailored their code to pass the provided six test cases. An example of one of the programs is shown in the bottom of Figure 2. This suggests (perhaps unsurprisingly) that if test cases are provided to the students, they may write their programs just to satisfy those test cases.

## DISCUSSION

PathViewer had an impact on subsequent instruction of the class. The analysis revealed that the original set test of cases for the assignment did not fully capture program correctness and more test cases were added. In the following semester, the instructor continued to use the larger set of test cases. Additionally, the instructor taught an additional recursive programming pattern (divide and conquer) in the following semester because the tool revealed that students were overusing a particular pattern (pull one element off).

However, there are still usability challenges and limitations of PathViewer, due to the preliminary status of the tool. One challenge is working with a large number of states. The user can address this by defining broader equivalence classes to group similar states and pathways together, or by displaying only the most common states and paths. Another challenge is how to define good equivalence classes. This depends somewhat on what the user intends to investigate. For example, we examined program correctness by using the set of passing test cases as an equivalence class. A third challenge is what value of "n" to use for viewing n-grams. We suggest two strategies: 1) start from bigrams and then increase to trigrams to see if there are any interesting loops or other patterns that can be found and 2) use the full graph to identify patterns and then pick "n" to dig down into those patterns. Two additional limitations are that an educator will always need to analyze the graph and find useful patterns, and the quality of analysis will always depend on the choice of equivalence classes.

In the future, we are particularly interested in how an instructor can use PathViewer to improve course materials so that students take more desirable pathways. Ideally, an instructor would use PathViewer to analyze a previous semester's data, identify problematic strategies used by students, improve lesson plans to preempt those strategies, and then use PathViewer to determine if the modifications had the desired effect.

## CONCLUSIONS

We presented a way to visualize students' solutions that helps an instructor view how large groups of students progress as they solve a problem. Our tool draws upon ideas such as n-grams and Sankey diagrams to provide a visualization that not only displays the states students solutions are going through, but also the proportion of students that take a particular path. We used this tool to analyze students' programs in introductory computer science class and uncover patterns that would be hard to identify otherwise. There is still a lot of work to be done in creating efficient visualizations of progressions of students' solutions to understand their performance. In future work, we hope to apply this approach to topics other than computer science. We also hope that analysis of intermediate stages of problem solving may make it easier to identify the students who are having the most trouble, and that this can help design early notification systems to alert teachers.

## REFERENCES


1. W Richards Adrion, Martha A Branstad, and John C Cherniavsky. 1982. Validation, verification, and testing of computer software. *ACM Computing Surveys (CSUR)* 14, 2 (1982), 159–192.
2. Erik Andersen, Yun-En Liu, Ethan Apter, François Boucher-Genesse, and Zoran Popović. 2010. Gameplay analysis through state projection. In *Proceedings of the fifth international conference on the foundations of digital games*. ACM, 1–8.
3. Matthew Berland, Taylor Martin, Tom Benton, Carmen Petrick Smith, and Don Davis. 2013. Using learning analytics to understand the learning pathways of novice programmers. *Journal of the Learning Sciences* 22, 4 (2013), 564–599.
4. Paulo Blikstein, Marcelo Worsley, Chris Piech, Mehran Sahami, Steven Cooper, and Daphne Koller. 2014. Programming pluralism: Using learning analytics to detect patterns in the learning of computer programming. *Journal of the Learning Sciences* 23, 4 (2014), 561–599.
5. Michael Bostock, Vadim Ogievetsky, and Jeffrey Heer. 2011. $D^3$ data-driven documents. *IEEE transactions on visualization and computer graphics* 17, 12 (2011), 2301–2309.
6. Peter F Brown, Peter V Desouza, Robert L Mercer, Vincent J Della Pietra, and Jenifer C Lai. 1992. Class-based n-gram models of natural language. *Computational linguistics* 18, 4 (1992), 467–479.
7. Elena L Glassman, Ned Gulley, and Robert C Miller. 2013. Toward facilitating assistance to students attempting engineering design problems. In *Proceedings of the ninth annual international ACM conference on International computing education research*. ACM, 41–46.
8. Elena L Glassman, Jeremy Scott, Rishabh Singh, Philip J Guo, and Robert C Miller. 2015. OverCode: Visualizing variation in student solutions to programming problems at scale. *ACM Transactions on Computer-Human Interaction (TOCHI)* 22, 2 (2015), 7.
9. Philip J Guo. 2013. Online python tutor: embeddable web-based program visualization for cs education. In *Proceeding of the 44th ACM technical symposium on Computer science education*. ACM, 579–584.
10. Roya Hosseini, Arto Vihavainen, and Peter Brusilovsky. 2014. Exploring problem solving paths in a Java programming course. (2014).
11. Jonathan Huang, Chris Piech, Andy Nguyen, and Leonidas Guibas. 2013. Syntactic and functional variability of a million code submissions in a machine learning mooc. In *AIED 2013 Workshops Proceedings Volume*. Citeseer, 25.
12. Yun-En Liu, Erik Andersen, Richard Snider, Seth Cooper, and Zoran Popović. 2011. Feature-based projections for effective playtrace analysis. In *Proceedings of the 6th international conference on foundations of digital games*. ACM, 69–76.
13. Chris Piech, Mehran Sahami, Jonathan Huang, and Leonidas Guibas. 2015. Autonomously generating hints by inferring problem solving policies. In *Proceedings of the Second (2015) ACM Conference on Learning@ Scale*. ACM, 195–204.
14. Chris Piech, Mehran Sahami, Daphne Koller, Steve Cooper, and Paulo Blikstein. 2012. Modeling how students learn to program. In *Proceedings of the 43rd ACM technical symposium on Computer Science Education*. ACM, 153–160.
15. Patrick Riehmann, Manfred Hanfler, and Bernd Froehlich. 2005. Interactive sankey diagrams. In *IEEE Symposium on Information Visualization, 2005. INFOVIS 2005*. IEEE, 233–240.
16. Dennis Shasha, JT-L Wang, Kaizhong Zhang, and Frank Y Shih. 1994. Exact and approximate algorithms for unordered tree matching. *IEEE Transactions on Systems, Man, and Cybernetics* 24, 4 (1994), 668–678.
17. Günter Wallner and Simone Kriglstein. 2012. A spatiotemporal visualization approach for the analysis of gameplay data. In *Proceedings of the SIGCHI conference on human factors in computing systems*. ACM, 1115–1124.

# WireFab: Mix-Dimensional Modeling and Fabrication for 3D Mesh Models

[1]Min Liu*, [1]Yunbo Zhang*, [3]Jing Bai, [1]Yuanzhi Cao, [1]Jeffrey M. Alperovich, [1,2]Karthik Ramani
[1]School of Mechanical Engineering, Purdue University, West Lafayette, IN 47907 USA
[2]School of Electrical and Computer Engineering†, Purdue University, West Lafayette, IN 47907 USA
{liu66, zhan2014, cao158, jalper, ramani} @purdue.edu
[3]School of Computer Science and Engineering, Beifang University of Nationalities, Yinchuan, China
baijing_nun@163.com

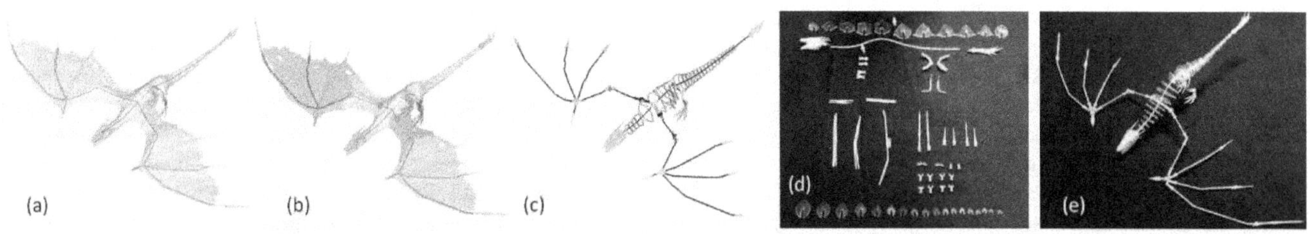


**Figure 1. The building pipeline using WireFab: Given a 3D mesh Gringotts Dragon model, WireFab allows the user to (a) generate a smooth 1D inner skeleton and (b) customize the segmentations at the locations where the inner skeleton and the part are desired to be articulated, and (c) specify the corresponding rigid body appearances of different dimensionalities, joint types and motion ranges. Also the fabrication files of all appearances and joints are generated for the user to (d) quickly prototype and (e) assemble and pose the articulated character (fabricated Gringotts Dragon with 78 parts in total).**

## ABSTRACT

Many rapid fabrication technologies are directed towards layer wise printing or laser based prototyping. We propose WireFab, a rapid modeling and prototyping system that uses bent metal wires as the structure framework. WireFab approximates both the skeletal articulation and the skin appearance of the corresponding virtual skin meshes, and it allows users to personalize the designs by (1) specifying joint positions and part segmentations, (2) defining joint types and motion ranges to build a wire-based skeletal model, and (3) abstracting the segmented meshes into mixed-dimensional appearance patterns or attachments.

The WireFab is designed to allow the user to choose how to best preserve the fidelity of the topological structure and articulation motion while selectively maintaining the fidelity of the geometric appearance. Compared to 3D-printing based high-fidelity fabrication systems, WireFab increases prototyping speed by ignoring unnecessary geometric details while preserving structural integrity and articulation motion. In addition, other rapid or low-fidelity fabrication systems produce only static models, while WireFab produces posable articulated models and has the potential to enable personalized functional products larger than the machines that produce them.

*Min Liu and Yunbo Zhang contributed equally to this paper.
†By courtesy


*CHI 2017*, May 06–11, 2017, Denver, CO. USA

DOI: http://dx.doi.org/10.1145/3025453.3025619

## ACM Classification Keywords

H.5.2. [**Information Interfaces and Presentation**]: User Interface

## Author Keywords

Mix-dimensional fabrication; shape abstraction; interactive curve modeling; skeletal deformation, physical prototyping

## INTRODUCTION

In recent years, personal design and fabrication have been enabled by the development of both hardware and software. People tend to design and fabricate 3D models based on their own ideas and in a variety of forms, such as origami, planar cross-section assembly, or 3D printing. The increasing popularity of 3D modeling software and personal fabrication devices has fueled a flurry of recent research towards seamlessly merging functional design and personal fabrication [23].

While tools and services that map static properties of a designed model to fabrication exist, constructing posable articulated models remains a difficult problem. Recent works [3, 7, 35] are proposed to tackle this issue using 3D printed parts and joints. In this paper, we propose WireFab, a new system that supports wire-based multi-dimensional modeling and rapid fabrication for articulated models. WireFab utilizes the popular personal fabrication technologies such as 3D printing, and 2D laser cutting, and integrates them with newly available desktop wire bending technology [18]. Several geometric algorithms and corresponding interaction operations have been developed to enable the embedding of 3D static meshes with wire-based custom articulation, versatile appearance attachments and parameterized joints and connectors, leading to a flexible design and prototyping system for articulated models.

We aim to lower the barriers to both design and fabrication so that designers who lack specialized knowledge can quickly prototype posable objects. To this end, we propose an intuitive workflow that takes as input a static 3D mesh model (see Fig. 1(a)) which could either be downloaded from online design repositories (e.g., http://www.thingiverse.com) or created using scanning systems such as Kinnect Fusion or Autodesk 123D Catch. The user designs an articulation model from the static mesh by first abstracting a smooth curve inner skeleton (Fig. 1(a)) that represents its skeletal structure. Using the inner skeleton as the rig, the input mesh is segmented by users at points where they desire individual parts and skeletons to be articulated (Fig. 1(b)). Users' design intent is further realized by allowing them to interactively specify the corresponding rotational joint motion constraints, as well as the appearance of the segmented parts. WireFab allows users to balance fidelity and speed to best preserve the topological structure while selectively maintaining the fidelity of the geometric appearance by combining auto-generated 3D printable joints, 1D bendable skeletal wires, and user designed appearance attachments of various forms (see Fig. 1 (c)). This framework enables users to achieve the desired prototyping speed, kinematic motion, and aesthetic outlook of 3D models.

## RELATED WORK

We broadly classify the related work into functional design and fabrication, mixed 3D fabrication, fabrication-aware shape design, and articulated object modeling and fabrication.

**Functional design and fabrication:** One of the trends we notice in the recent work on personal design and fabrication is the introduction of functionality into the fabrication process in order to allow non-expert users to create functional objects. Tubes and cuboids are embedded into given sculptural 3D models to house functionality and articulation in [29, 11] and are fabricated by low cost 3D printing processes. Prévost et al. [28] proposed an approach to generating models which can stand alone by deforming the initial inputs, while Spin-it [4] converts a given 3D model into a spinnable toy. Umentani et al. [34] proposed a method to deal with the flyability of laser cut paper airplanes. Other interesting works involve building working prototypes of mechanical designs for testing [16], printing mechanical toys [40] and characters with designable motions [33]. Most of these methods are based on 3D printing and suffer from the problems of slow processing time and extra post processing for support structures. The scale of objects generated by 3D printing is also constrained by the size of the printer.

**Mixed 3D fabrication:** Some recent works from the human-computer interaction community have begun to explore the use of other fabrication methods together with 3D printing. By introducing intermediate low-fidelity fabrication into the traditional slow but high-fidelity 3D printing process, Mueller et al. and Beyer et al. proposed a variety of alternative fabrication methods to speed-up 3D printing, such as printing a wireframe mesh of an object [25], and substituting sub-volumes of a model with standard Lego building blocks [26] or laser-cut Platener [5]. Recent work CofiFab [32] combines 3D printing and 2D laser cutting to support the fabrication of large 3D objects, while WrapIt [14] generates 3D printed support structure to help users bend the wire into appropriate shape for jewelry making. These different approaches effectively reduced the fabricating time while preserving the shape of a static model, but none of them dealt with articulation deformations of posable objects.

**Fabrication-aware shape design:** Lau et al. [19] presented a formal grammar combined with lexical and structural analysis to generate fabricatable parts and connectors from a 3D furniture model. Another study focuses on the constraints and sequences of assemblies by creating geometric puzzles, such as Polyomino [22] and Burr puzzles [37]. Li et al. [20] developed an algorithm for computing paper architecture using pop-ups. Megaro et al. [24] and Coros et al. [9] proposed interactive systems for designing animated mechanical characters. A recent work AutoConnect [17] generates connectors between different objects based on their shapes at connection points. Our WireFab is the first attempt, to the best of our knowledge, to focus on the automatic generation of both 3D-printed static connectors and motion joints specifically designed for wire connections and wire-based articulation.

**Articulated object modeling and fabrication** Recent work on mapping 3D meshes to 3D-printable, jointed models either assumes that the input mesh is associated with linear blend skinning (LBS) [3], or manually inserts a classical animation rig into the input mesh [7]. However, the skinning weights or the animation rigs might not be directly available to naive users. The proposed WireFab takes advantage of recent advances in automatic curve skeleton abstraction, and interactive mesh segmentation to further simplify the process of creating ready-to-articulate and ready-to-fabricate 3D models with 3D static mesh input. In a related work, CarboardiZer [38] also takes a 3D static mesh as the input, but it focuses on generating planar foldable patterns for each rigid body and the joint type is restricted to a 1DOF (degree of freedom) hinge joint. In WireFab, the segmented rigid bodies may have different appearances, and it supports many joint types: 1D hinge, 2D universal, or 3D ball-and-socket joints. These joints enable more articulation functionalities in the design and fabrication space.

Observing existing tools for the fabrication of articulated objects, it becomes apparent that most of them only allow for the fabrication of static models, though, some of them support articulated objects using 3D printing [3, 7] or 2D die cutting [38]. They are further limited by the size of the fabrication machines, the printing speed, or the types of motion achievable. The main contributions of WireFab are:

1) A new work-flow based on bent metal wires where inner skeletons of 3D models serve as the structural framework to which the appearances are attached;

2) 3D printed joint and connector primitives are automatically generated and are parameterized based on posability calculations with minimal user input; and

3) Multi-form appearance modeling and fabrication, including 3D printed detailed parts, 2D laser-cut planar cross-sections and 1D bent wires, which allows for a rich expressiveness.

## OVERVIEW

WireFab produces customizable articulated prototypes directly from digital 3D models. As shown in Fig. 2 , our computational design platform work-flow unfolds as follows: the designer (1) inputs a desired 3D mesh model, (2) edits the automatically generated inner curve skeleton to the desired structure and shape, (3) customizes the segmented parts and inner skeleton joint placement within the model to be articulated, (4) interactively designs the appearance of each part using a 3D solid object, 2D cross sections, or 1D wires, and (5) interactively designs the joint types, motion axes and motion ranges which define the articulation properties. The system then generates all the connectors, joints and appearances according to the fabrication model. Users are able to express their creativity and intent by controlling the number of articulated parts, appearance details, and the complexity of the articulation motion.

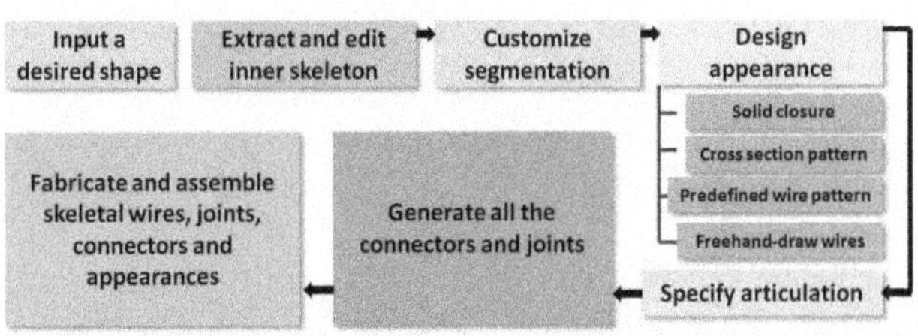


Figure 2. Pipeline process of WireFab.

## SKELETON DRIVEN ARTICULATION MODELING

The articulated behavior of a posable object is modeled from a static mesh. A Skeleton is first extracted, edited and then the set of articulated joints are defined on it so that to separate the input model into joints and rigid bodies.

### Skeletal wire extraction and editing

WireFab assumes no animation rig associated with the input mesh and it starts by extracting 1D curve skeleton of every input 3D model to capture the structural information and support articulation motion. A digital curve skeleton have been computed by thinning from a volumetric model [31] or guided by a force field [8]. Geometric methods also exist for automatic skeletonization from surface meshes, which include mesh contraction [2], computing the Reeb graph [27], or surface inflation [30]. In order not to restrict our WireFab framework, we remain agnostic as to which skeletonization method is used. In the implementation, the medial geodesic function [10] based 1D curve skeleton was used as it is topology-preserving and stable against small changes.

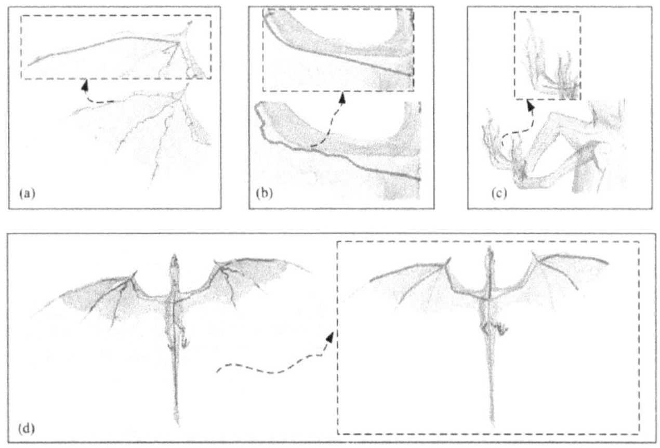

Figure 3. Some examples of skeleton editing tools and the final skeleton of the Gringotts Dragon model: (a) merging all skeletons between two junction points into one skeleton, (b) smoothing a skeleton, (c) deleting boundary segments, (d) final skeleton after editing with provided tools.

The inner curve skeleton is related but does not directly correspond to the rig required in articulation modeling; hence there is a need for editing curve skeletons to represent articulation rigs according to users' intent. The edit operation is usually required when 3D models are noisy and complex with small features, the extracted skeleton may appear zig-zag and contain numerous small branches. Some skeleton details represent tiny topological structure variations but do not affect the overall articulation. Accordingly, we developed a set of interactive tools for users to generate smooth and compact skeleton-based rig, functions including merging multiple skeletons into one using the shortest curve path; deleting boundary skeletons according to the depths of connected junction points; and smoothing skeletons via linear, conic or cubic smoothing functions. Fig. 3 gives some examples of the editing capabilities and the final skeleton for the Gringotts Dragon model.

### Customizable segmentation for rigid parts and joint placement

In WireFab, we adapt "dot scissor" [39] to capture local concave shape features using concavity-aware harmonic fields, and to select the best cutting boundaries using a voting scheme. The designer first specifies a stroke on the model surface (rendered as a small circle with the stroke as the diameter) through which the partitioning curves are expected to pass. The view direction vector and the stroke give a cutting plane which first creates a potential joint placement position on the inner skeleton. A concavity-aware harmonic field is then computed by using the user's specified stroke as a constraint. A set of candidate curves are computed upon the harmonic field by extracting iso-value curves. The voting scheme as [39] is adapted to select the best partitioning curves according to their concavity, tightness, and proximity to the potential joint on the inner skeleton. The last term is measured as the average distance of the potential joint position $c$ to $k$ sampled points $p_1, p_2, \cdots, p_k$ -on an iso-value curve. Our system with single stroke rather than dots representation, allows more of the user intent to be captured by the design process than the "dot scissor" approach. If required, the user can undo this step, redraw the stroke, and re-run the segmentation, and the user has meanwhile an option of repositioning a potential joint along the inner curve skeleton.

### Joint specification

It is not possible to estimate automatically joint types, ranges and motion axes from a character's skin model since the required explicit user inputs. Therefore, for each potential joint generated during skeleton segmentation, we give the user options to specify its articulation joint type, the corresponding rotation axes and their motion ranges. Three revolute joint types are supported in WireFab, which are: 3-DOF (degrees of freedom) ball-and-socket joints, 2-DOF universal joints and 1-DOF hinge joints as shown in Fig. 4.

*Ball-and-socket joints* associate a cone axis vector $\mathbf{n}_b$ and a socket opening angle $\theta_b$ as their motion range parameters. These joints span a wide range of angles and allow for intuitive free-form constraints on rotations away from the center axis (or cone axis) by shaping the socket opening. *Universal joints* associate two rotational axes ($\mathbf{n}_{u1}, \mathbf{n}_{u2}$) and block in-axis rotation. Each rotational axis further associates two motion range parameters: forward swing angle $\theta_{max1}, \theta_{max2}$ and backward swing angle $\theta_{min1}, \theta_{min2}$. Universal joints are common in the elbows and shoulders of characters but due to the difficulty in designing the gimbal lock configuration, this type of joint is seldom supported by previous work (see [3, 7, 38] ). In WireFab, the universal joint template is designed using the gimbal lock configuration with two rotational axes offset from each other by a small distance. This design frees a degree of restriction on the intersected rotational axes while also allowing for motion range restriction features incorporated into the design. *Hinge joints* have only one rotational axis $\mathbf{n}_h$ and a motion range containing a forward swing angle and a backward swing angle ($\theta_{max}, \theta_{min}$).

In the joint templates developed in WireFab, both universal and hinge joints are coupled with a parametric motion range restriction feature which is automatically generated according to the users' specifications on motion ranges. All motion axes are generated with their default directions based on the incident inner skeletons' configuration. Specifically, a Frenet frame is calculated for each joint located on the inner curve skeleton, and this right-handed, orthogonal frame is used as the default joint frame for motion axis specification. Users are allowed to change the default motion axis and its default motion range using a simple widget-based joint specfication tool.

## APPEARANCE MODELING

### Solid appearance

A partitioned segment of the model can be represented as a solid part so that it can be 3D printed to retain the highest shape fidelity. The original segmentation results in a set of open surfaces, therefore a solid closure operation is applied to guarantee that all the segmented parts are water-tight and 3D printable. We adopted a dynamic programming based hole filling algorithm [21] as it is efficient and easy to implement. However, directly applying hole filling on the segment parts can be troublesome and not aesthetically appealing due to the irregular boundaries of the holes (see Fig. 5 (a)). Therefore, a geodesic curve stretching method [36] is applied to the original boundary curves of segments and the smoothed boundary curves are obtained after stretching (shown in Fig. 5 (b)). Consequently, the resultant solid model after hole filling has more aesthetic shapes with the smoothed boundary curves (see Fig. 5 (b)).

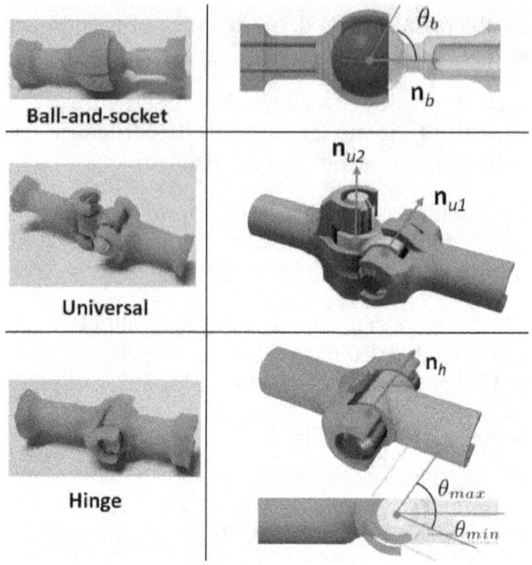


**Figure 4. Three types of revolute joints hinge, universal and ball-and-socket, from bottom to top, and their user specified joint parameters are illustrated in the right-hand column.**

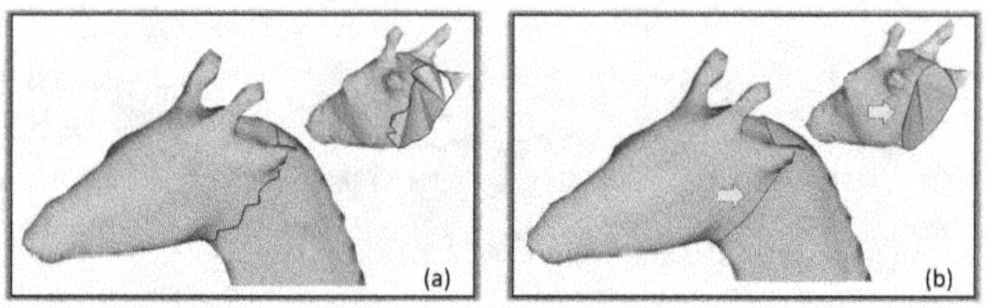


**Figure 5. The boundary curves and resultant models before (a) and after (b) geodesic curve stretching.**

### Cross section and silhouette contours

Planar contours are the basic representation of an object's shape as they contain explicit and dominant characteristics for determining an object's appearance. We provide a planar section extraction tool in our platform to cut each partitioned rigid body with a set of cutting planes and obtain the resultant cross-sectional or silhouette contours. For cross-section contours, the user has the control either to cut a segmented part according to the tangential directions of the inner skeleton (normal-to-spine option), or to use a constant normal direction. To generate the initial cutting plane direction for constant normal cutting planes, the system applies principal component analysis (PCA) to the segment so that the cutting planes are created by taking the principal axis as the normal. Initial constant cross sectional contours take the principle axis with the largest eigenvalue as the direction while silhouette wire appearance takes the smallest one as the cutting plane normal. For the normal-to-spine type of cross-sections, we calculate the pair-wise projected graph distance (the length of projected edge onto the first principal axis) and pick the one with the longest distance as the main spine. Fig. 6 gives an example of different planar contours generated automatically for user to use as appearance embodiment. For open contours, users are given the options to close them according to the solid closure or to manipulate the connection or closeness interactively.

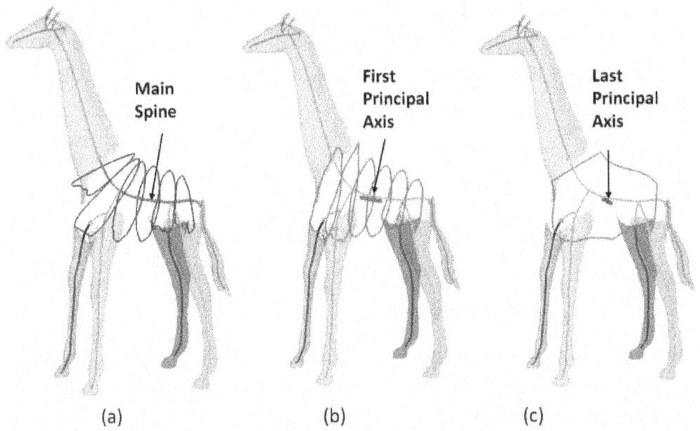


**Figure 6. The planar contour tools that allow users to generate different 2D appearance patterns: (a) normal-to-spine cross section contours, (b) constant normal cross section contours with cutting planes normal to the first principal axis of a segment, and (c) silhouette contour with cutting plane normal to the last principal axis of a segment.**

If the initial cutting plane setting is not satisfactory, a widget tool can be used to manipulate the cutting plane direction, offset the distances, or both, until it represents the desired cutting direction and offset. Furthermore, a snap fit pattern is added to each cross section plate so that it can be assembled and fit onto the skeletal wire. And silhouette contours adjust itself and intersect with the inner skeleton so that the connectedness is satisfied.

### Helix wires

Helix wire presents a segment portion of the object using 1D appearance and the least number of wire pieces; it contains only one continuous curve without self-intersection and it represents shape appearance information in a very compact way. Helix wire is computed based on the cross section contours. First, the set of cross section contours is analyzed for intersection if they were generated as normal-to-spine option. The intersecting sections will be removed from the set before they are referenced in the helix computation. Constant normal cross-sectional contours do not need to go through intersection testing as they are always parallel to each other. All the non-intersecting cross sections are then parameterized, from aligned starting points, using the arc length to the total contour length ratio as the parameter $t$ (see Fig. 7 for example). The starting point of the parametrization is located at the intersection point of a planar contour and a silhouette contour. The points on the $i$th section are moved towards the corresponding points on the $(i+1)$th section with the same arc length ratio $t$. When $t$ changes from 0 to 1, the helix wire of one coil is formed in between the $i$th and the $(i+1)$th sections. The helix wire is connected at one or both ends to the nearest point on the inner skeleton wire to ensure connectedness. If the helix wire is to be located at the bottom of a model, a flat end can also be added to the appearance to increase the stability of the structure, as shown in the example given in Fig. 7.

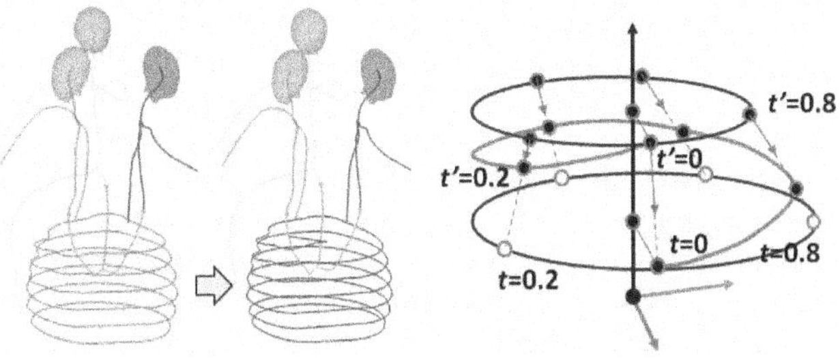


**Figure 7. Helix wire is generated from cross section contours through arc length parametrization, neighboring contour alignment and point shifting.**

### Free-hand-draw wires

For users who have patience and hand dexterity, WireFab's free-hand-draw module enables the user to define complex wire patterns on the object's surfaces. We developed a set of interactive tools including curve creation, editing and clipping. Fig. 8 shows a curve editing tool which allows the user to modify the existing curve's shape by dragging control points on the curve. During the whole process of curve creation and editing, all the points are snapped continuously onto the surfaces of a 3D model to make sure the curves perfectly follow the input model's shape. The snapping of points onto surface is done by querying the closest point on the surface of input model for each point on the curve. This query can be done efficiently by adopting a *bounding volume hierarchy* structure on the input model.

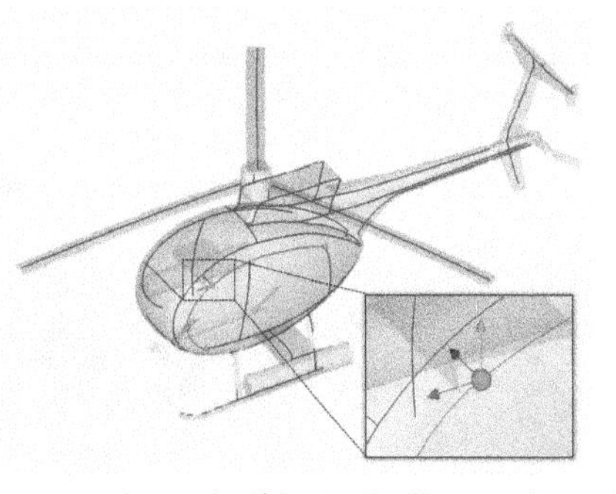

**Figure 8. Curve creating and editing tools allow on-the-surface operations.**

A design is composed of many curves and most of them are connected to each other, but the curve drawing and editing tool creates and edits a single curve individually without considering the interference between the curves. An interactive clipping tool is developed for the user to remove certain portion of the curve split by intersections with other curves.

## JOINT PARAMETRIZATION FOR POSABILITY

In the WireFab work-flow, all joints and connectors are designed to be 3D printed parts. One functional requirement for fabricated models is that the printed joints have to be tight enough to resist gravity and allow for static poses in the whole articulation motion space. Adding friction to the contacting elements of joints is the most common way to achieve posability for articulated models. The friction can be introduced using bump features [3], tolerances [7], or locking fasteners [15]. Among these methods, bump features are less suitable for our purposes as they are susceptible to wear and tear due to the small feature size and the constraints of the plastic material used in most desktop 3D printing processes. Locking fasteners is the safest way to obtain the desired friction but they require extra parts, extra processing, or assembling time, and a more complicated joint shape. We therefore use the tolerance method, which enables a very compact design to obtain the desired friction force and to hold all static poses.

**Calibration** The tolerance-based friction methods use interference fit between shafts and holes (or ball and socket in terms of ball-and-socket joint) to withstand the torques. Given any joint with its type and motion range specification, tolerances and dimensions have to be chosen to provide the desired degree of friction or torque. In theory, these joint parameters may be derived from known material properties, the specification of the 3D printing process, and the contact area of the joint. However, it is observed that even the same process may lead to different results and individual printers may vary. Thus, we leave the determination of joint dimensions and tolerances to a calibration process that we run on each printer before the joint synthesis. For this purpose, we created several data sets that are used for calibration by varying two different joint parameters: interference fit tolerance and joint diameter. For the 1DOF hinge and the 2DOF universal joint, the joint diameter is set as the inner diameter of the holes in contact with the standard size metal shaft. For 3DOF ball-and-socket joint, the joint diameter is set as the outer diameter of the ball part. By default, the joint shaft size is as same as the bent metal wire diameter and the shaft length is a dependent variable and is scaled in proportion to the shaft diameter. A calibration set example is given in Fig. 9. Based on the calibration test and theoretical torque calculation, the minimum size for a printable and functional joint can then be determined.

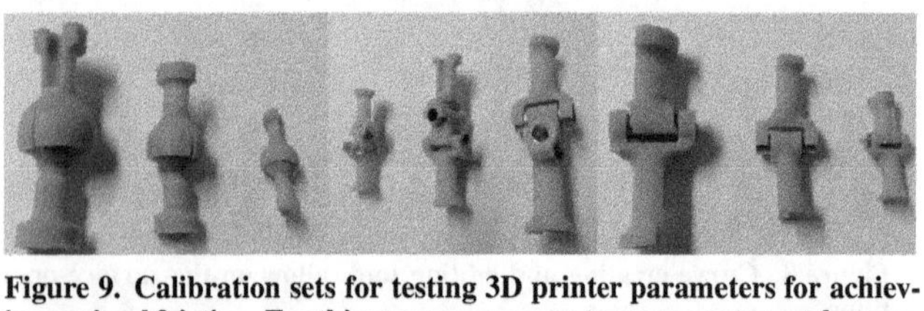

**Figure 9. Calibration sets for testing 3D printer parameters for achieving optimal friction. For this purpose we vary two parameters: tolerance and joint size. Note that the tolerance variation is not shown here since the interference value is too small to be visible.**

**Theoretical torque calculation** The theoretical torque a joint needs to hold has to be calculated for each joint. It is the sum of all the torques generated by the gravities of all child segments of the focusing joint, and it can be calculated as follows:

$$\tau_j = \sum V_k \rho_k g l_k \tag{1}$$

where $\tau_j$ is the desired torque that $j$th joint needs to hold, and $V_k$ is the total volume of the $k$th child segment and $\rho_k$ is its material density; $l_k$ is the corresponding maximum level arm distance from the centroid of $k$th child segment to the motion axis of $j$th joint in its motion space.

Of the three types of segment representation: 1D wire, 2D plate and 3D solid, the computation for the total volume of a child segment represented with wires and planar contour appearance is straightforward. Solid appearances are all represented as sets of triangular facets. It is a linear computation to calculate the interior volume of a mesh solid, done by summing the volumes of all the oriented pyramid centers at a point in 3D space (the origin, for instance) and taking a triangular facet for the base. The expression of the volume calculation of a meshed solid segment $S$ is given in the following equation:

$$V_S = \frac{1}{6} \sum_{k=1}^{|F|} g_k \cdot N_k \tag{2}$$

where $|F|$ is the number of triangles in $S$, $g_k = (x_k^1 + x_k^2 + x_k^3)/3$ and $N_k = \vec{x_k^1 x_k^2} \times \vec{x_k^1 x_k^3}$. $x_k^1, x_k^2$ and $x_k^3$ are the three vertices of the $k$th triangular facet.

In the torque equation (1), the level arm distance from the centroid of the $k$th child segment to the motion axis of a joint varies with different poses in the articulation space. We estimate a maximum torque in the motion space by sampling the motion space of all child segments to find out the maximum level arm distance. With the required torque calculated, the joint size and tolerance parameters can then be chosen based on the calibration test.

## FABRICATION DETAILS

**Snap fit design of 3D printed part to metal wire** The basic connection of 3D printed parts (joints, connectors or solid appearances) to metal wire is shown in Fig. 10. A snap fit feature design is applied to all connections between metal wire and 3D printed parts. By default $D_h$ will be a value smaller than the metal wire diameter for a tight fit or interference fit that prevents undesired movement. The user can redefine the tightness of the connection, then the diameter of the connection holder $D_h$ will change accordingly.

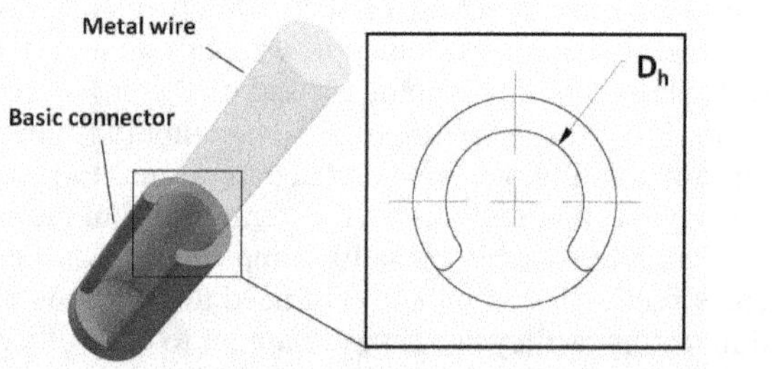


**Figure 10. The geometric feature for a basic element, to connect 3D printed parts to metal wire. $D_h$ is the inner diameter of the connector holder and it can affect the tightness of the fitting.**

**Wire-to-wire rigid connector** We have classified three basic cases for rigid connectors that connect wire to wire with no motion. *Case 1*: Two or more wires intersect at one point (Fig. 11(a)); *Case* 2: One or more wires intersect at a point on another wire (Fig. 11(b)); and *Case 3*: Two or more wires are connected together in an envelope, but they do not necessarily intersect at one point and need to be rigidly connected (Fig. 11(c)).

The first two types of rigid connectors are generated automatically based on the wire configuration at junction points. The case three connectors, however, are defined through the user interaction.

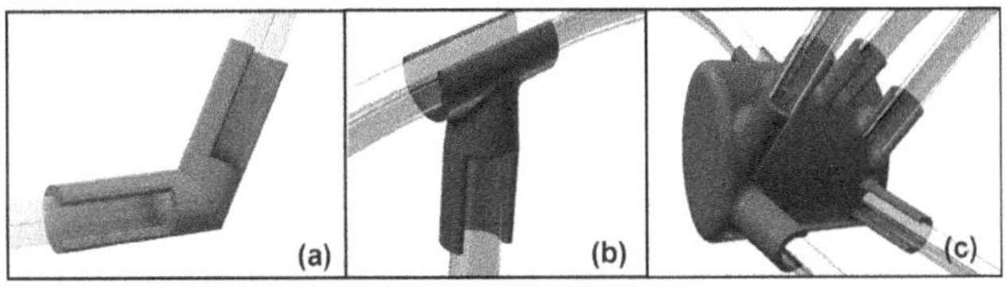


**Figure 11. Three types of rigid connectors.**

**Laser cut cross-sectional appearances** One of the appearance options is to use laser cutting to acquire planar sheets that have the shape of the model's cross-sections, and which snap fit onto the inner skeleton metal wire. WireFab has the ability to generate cross sections from the rigid parts and to apply the automatically generated snap-fit-to-wire pattern. Please refer to Fig. 12 for the cut-out pattern implemented in the current system. Each cross-section is assigned a sequence number that is included in the cutting pattern for identification during the assembly process. These patterns can then be sent to a laser cutter in DXF format to acquire the planar parts. A example DXF file for the Gringotts Dragon is shown partially in Fig. 12, where all ready-to-cut cross section plates with cut-out patterns are aligned inside the region corresponding to the sheet size specified by the user.

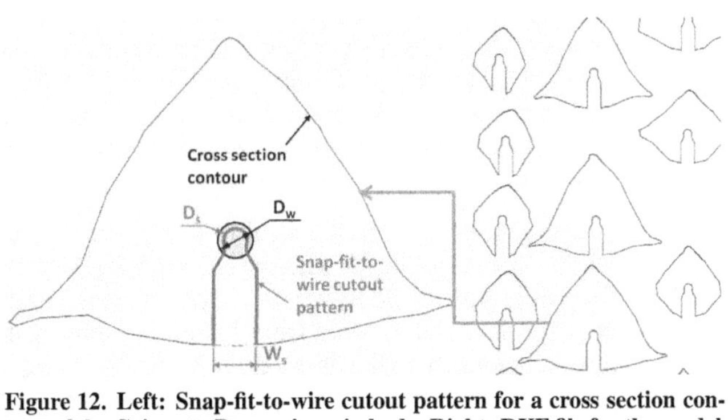


**Figure 12. Left: Snap-fit-to-wire cutout pattern for a cross section contour of the Gringotts Dragon's main body. Right: DXF file for the model (portion of the whole drawing is shown here due to the size limit). $D_W$ is the metal wire diameter specified by the user, $D_S$ is cut-out hole diameter, and there is a tight clearance $(D_W - D_S)/2$ designed for the snap fit functionality. A slot of width $W_S$ which is incremented from $D_W$ by a small amount is added to enable a smooth assembly of the metal wire with the laser cut sheet.**

**3D wire bending** Pensa Labs [18] has a commercial desktop bender available that is capable of bending wires in 2D. While still available, the open source information regarding Pensa's original 3D bender is now unsupported and has much left to be determined by the machine builder. The available information was taken and used to build a fully 3D wire bender to pair with WireFab (see Fig. 13 for the prototype). This bender is capable of bending any length of wire, and of straightening wires as they are fed through the machine. Its 3D wire bending capability is implemented by adding an additional out-of-plane rotation onto the in-plane bending. It has bend angle and feed length limitations due to the constraints of the components, however, these limitations do not inhibit creating complex models. The bend limit is 90 degrees in-plane and the minimum wire feed length is 5mm. Our software system automatically enforces the feed length constraints and splits the wire where the turning angle exceeds the bending angle limit. To avoid collision, WireFab simulates bending toolpath, detects possible collisions, and splits wires into two at where collision is detected. For helix shapes shown in Fig.7, collisions between bending machine and helix wires can be avoided by setting a minimum pitch of the helix wire. The bender uses an Arduino to output commands to 3 step motors that control the feed, bend, and rotation about the z-axis. The commands are generated by WireFab in the form of a text file containing feed length, *xy* bend angle, and *z* bend angle. These commands are run through the processing software which couples to the Arduino, sending the appropriate signals to the 3D bender's step motors.

**Figure 13. The 3D desktop wire bender prototype built for WireFab.**

**Part labeling and assembly guidance** Using WireFab's interactive tools, users could generate quite complex designs. For example, the Gringotts Dragon shown in Fig. 1 has in total 78 parts including 3D printed parts, laser cut parts, and wire segments. To ease the effort of users, WireFab automatically adds numbers on the model of connectors and appearances, and these numbers can either be printed (3D printing) or carved (laser cutting) on the parts. Wires are bent in the order set by WireFab and labeled by attaching stickers on. The numbers are displayed around all parts and wires in the software when users assemble them.

## RESULTS AND DISCUSSION

### Prototypical results

We have first tested WireFab ourselves on a number of humanoid, animal and man-made 3D objects, and Fig. 14 demonstrates the design and fabrication results with some examples. Testing cases vary in complexity and include some sculptural models (e.g. dragon, giraffe and hand) and some real life objects (e.g. memento, glasses and helicopter), all downloaded from the internet. The glasses are modeled with two hinges and the appearances include solid, inner skeleton and silhouette wire. The memento is modeled as a static model with a helix appearance as it base. The giraffe has a bendable neck which is designed and fabricated with a series of 3DOF ball-and-socket joints. The hand model is fabricated with five universal joints and ten hinges, simulating the DOF of a real hand. The modeling for the helicopter involves a set of freeform hand-draw curves, and all rigid connectors are generated automatically by WireFab.

In the experiment, the joints, connectors and solid appearances are all printed using an EnvisionTEC Xtreme 3SP printer that has a resolution of 0.1mm along both the horizontal and the vertical directions. All planar cross sectional plates are fabricated with a CO2 golden laser cutter using acrylic sheets, and all metal wires are bent using our prototyped 3D wire bender, which supports three different wire diameters in the current implementation. All fabricated models are fully functional and easy to manipulate while maintaining a balanced level of friction to allow for posing. Fig. 15 shows the results for hand and giraffe models articulated in different poses. A common issue with 3D printed joints is their durability. Depending on the printing processes, continued manipulation of a joint can lead to reduced friction due to wear and tear. However, since one of the friction elements in our joint template for universal and hinge joints is a metal shaft, the issue is less serious compared with in the pure 3D printed ball-and-socket joints.

### Preliminary user study

In order to verify the usability and the expressiveness of our system, we have invited 12 users to participate in our user study. All of them were engineering college students and none of them had any prior experience of using our system. We divided all the participants randomly into 4 groups, 3 users for each group. All the users in the same group were given the same model to process. Each user's study consisted of two sessions, the design session and the physical assembly session. During the first session, the users received a 10 minute tutorial on how to use our software. Then the users would be given a model to process with the software. Based on the users' input, all the physical parts including the metal wires, joints and connectors, and acrylic cross-sections were fabricated for the second session. During the physical assembly session, the users also received a 10 minute tutorial about handling the physical parts before they started assembling. A virtual 3D model with all required assembly information (e.g. the labeling of wires, joints and connectors and their configuration in 3D space) is given to user as an instruction of assembly. And then the users would perform hands-on assembly to produce the prototype based on the virtual model they processed during the first session.

The primary users' prototyping results are shown in Fig. 16. The expressiveness of users using our system is demonstrated directly by the end results. We can observe a variety of different expressions designed by the users who started with the same model (please refer to Fig. 16). For group 1-3, we can observe the choice of different appearances as well as user-defined functional joints. For group 4, we intentionally tested a conical shape which is not a typical articulated shape. All users processed it successfully with a static model using hand-draw surface wire tool. The users came up with various artistic surface patterns that already transcend the original conical geometry.

During the user study, every user was asked to fill out a questionnaire designed based on the system usability scale (SUS) [6]. The primary survey results are given in Fig. 17. The average SUS score was 82 (SD - 9.64). Each user took the same questionnaire twice after both the design and assembly sessions and therefore a total of 24 survey results has been collected. In Fig. 17, we sorted the survey results separately for each session and plotted their SUS scores. We observe that the average SUS score after the first session (interactive design) was 79 (SD-9.07), while the average SUS score after the second session (hands-on assembly) increased to 85 (SD-9.59).

### Discussion

We benchmarked the efficiency of WireFab by comparing the total time using WireFab with the printing time using 3D printer (EnvisionTEC Xtreme 3SP) for the same set of tested models. There are three main parts where the users spend their time within the work-flow: (1) Interacting with the WireFab software, (2) waiting for physical parts to be fabricated by the authors. and (3) assembling the physical parts into the final prototypes. We have recorded the time spent on all the models demonstrated in our paper. In the time statistic, the fabrication time are included, but the overhead time for preparing the machines and operating associated software are excluded. To fit the size constraint of 3D printer, all tested models are scaled such that their largest dimensions are in the range of 200-300 mm. To 3D print any of those models would take more than 10 hours, while using our system, we spend less than 2 hours on any of the model except the model (3) in Fig.16 presented in the paper. It took around 4 hours for that model since the user chose to use solid appearance for the main body of the model. The overall fabrication time is greatly shortened compared to 3D printing the whole model. The users spend most of their time doing the interactive design and hands-on assembly, rather than waiting idly for the fabrication. The time it takes to advance an idea from the 3D model to the physical prototype which also includes all the articulation is better using the wire bending tools and methods we present here.

Another divergence between 3D printing and WireFab is the fidelity of the products. The process developed using WireFab allows for a multitude of fidelity options, based on the user's preferences for time and appearance. This mix of fidelity not only caters more closely to the user's desires (whether it be for a time sensitive shape model or an appearance reliant structural element) but it is also able to match the fidelity of 3d printing. The mixed medium modeling capabilities of WireFab also serve to maintain and highlight the articulation of the joints, a feature that adds additional processing options that are outside the capabilities of the common user. But it is fair to point out that the shape fidelity is sacrificed in terms of build appearance if the user desires a full shape reproduction as designed. In addition the rigidity is replaced by an articulated model.

For the usability of the proposed system, the above SUS scores indicated a good usability of our system, that within a total of less than 2 hours, the users could produce a new prototype that was very different from the model they started with. Besides quantitative evaluation using SUS scores, we also collected users' qualitative feedback during and after user study. For the simplicity of notation, we label users according to

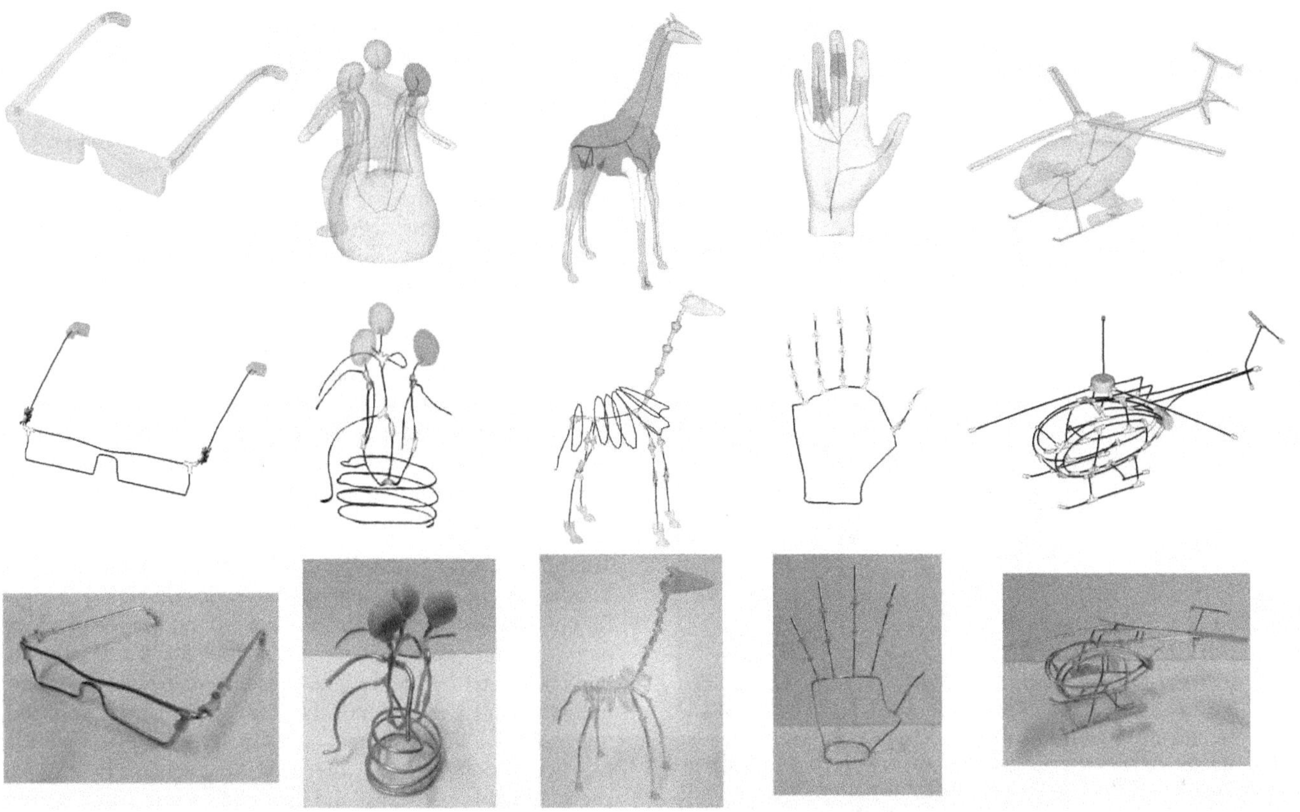

**Figure 14. Prototypical results generated by WireFab. The first row from left to right shows input models for: Glasses, Memento, Giraffe, Hand and Helicopter and their initial segmentation with potential joints. The second row shows the appearances design using different forms and the corresponding virtual fabrication models which incorporate all connectors and joints. In the last row, all finished physical prototypes are shown (from left to right, each fabricated model consists of 12, 24, 56, 46, and 72 parts respectively.).**

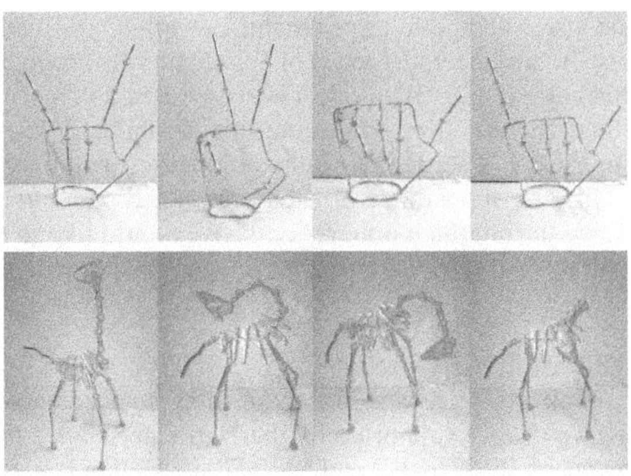

**Figure 15. Photographs of hand and giraffe models articulated in different poses.**

which model they designed and assembled (shown in Fig. 16 (1)-(12)). In general, users appreciated WireFab's interactive tools to be "*easy to learn and use*" (user 12). User 2 found WireFab's appearance modeling tools invaluable for better expressing their design intent: "*it was easy for me to create the prototype as I expected.*" As user 1 expressed, "*(appearance modeling tools) were really interesting for me as I could see how the part was going to look like after assembled, depending on the choice of the manufacturing methods.*" It is also noted that most users chose to first go through all possible appearances in the WireFab and then made their decision based on their aesthetic preferences. User 1 particularly enjoyed WireFab's customized segmentation and joint specification tools, as they "*were the easiest tools to use for generating movable objects among all software (he used)*". WireFab's joint parameterization greatly supported the generation of movable joints, as "*(users) just specified the type of motion/degrees of freedom between 2 parts and the system automatically did the rest*" (user 1). We also found that users tended to segment the model and put the joints based on their understanding of its semantic components and intent to articulate. Another important observation is that the tangibility of assembly greatly affects users' experience. The SUS score in Fig. 17 shows a significant increasing before and after users' hands-on assembly (79 with SD-9.07 vs. 85 with SD-9.59). The users were generally more satisfied with the system after the second session where they get to assemble the prototype themselves. We have observed great satisfaction among the users upon finishing assembling their models, many of the users were excited enough to take out their camera and took pictures of their models. They felt that they have actually created something new. The user who did model 7 in Fig. 16 said this after the second session : "*I didn't know it was going to be this cool when I did it on the computer.*" Another user who did model 10 said: "*I think this kind of hands-on practice is really helpful*

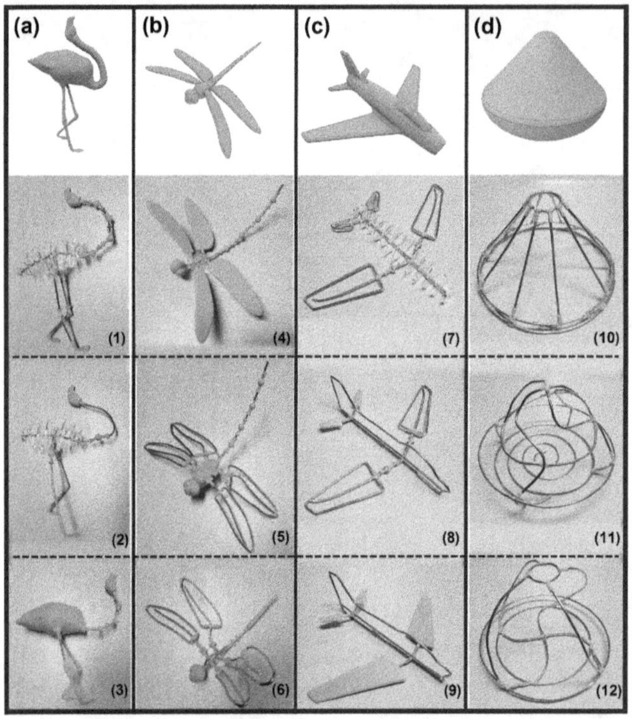


**Figure 16. Results from the user study. The first row shows the four testing models and the second to fourth rows show different articulation models built by different users. (a) Group 1 users were given a crane model to process (from top to bottom, the fabricated objects consists of 40, 23, and 16 parts). (b) Group 2 users were given a dragonfly model (from top to bottom, the fabricated objects consists of 24, 26, and 28 parts). (c) Group 3 users were given a air plane model (from top to bottom, the fabricated objects consists of 33, 21, and 12 parts). And (d), group 4 users were given a conical shaped model to process (from top to bottom, the fabricated objects consists of 63, 27, and 28 parts).**

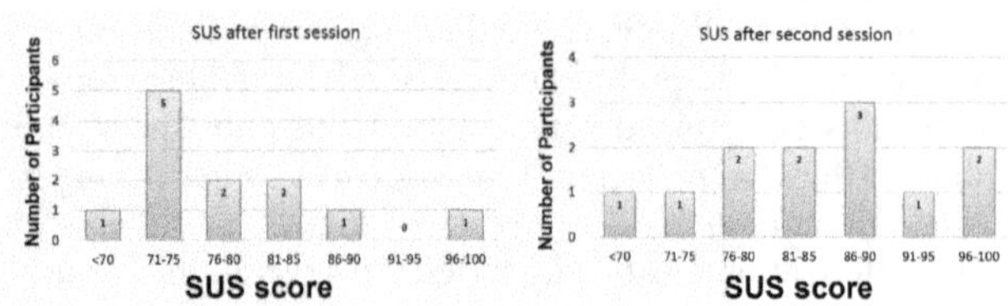


**Figure 17. (a) Results of the SUS survey after the first session(b) Results of the SUS survey after the second session.**

*to promote motivation in learning.*" The hands-on assembly helped users to "*understand the software (of WireFab) from a perspective of hands-on activity*" (user 5). This tells us just how important physical user interaction really is, especially in the personalized fabrication area. User constructed objects have been shown to promote self-extension into them and to be more engaging [13]. Prior studies [1, 13, 12] have indicated that the design, fabrication and assembly process is enjoyable and self actualizing, and computer supported creative design and fabrication processes requires further understanding as a means for engaging and embodied learning experiences. From users' feedback, WireFab has several limitations. One user found it was difficult to assemble when "*3 or more wires are connected to one connector*" (user 12). Users also pointed out the joints "*were a little weak and fragile*" (user 5), thus "*they were easy to break*" (user 7). This problem could be addressed in the future by choosing stronger materials for joint fabrication.

## CONCLUSION AND FUTURE WORK

In this paper we present WireFab, a rapid design and prototyping system that allows makers to customize and articulate everyday sculptural models by extracting a skeletal wire, adding joints and attaching various appearances to segmented rigid parts. The computational design platform and prototyping pipeline are explicitly constructed to ensure a rapid design and digital fabrication system based on a semi-automatic process, limited interactive modeling and multiple personal fabrication tools. The mixed dimensionality of the system gives novice, as well as expert designers more flexibility towards modeling and prototyping posable models. Our primary results and users' study show that our method can handle different types of input meshes in terms of geometrical complexity and variety and number of articulations.

There are several remaining challenges which may direct our future work. Currently, our system relies on visual feedback for collision detection in the relative motion between two rigid parts. An automatic collision test and feedback will help users to make more feasible designs and achieve the desired articulation range in real world models. Reducing the number of wires makes fabricating some specific shapes very efficient with less number of connectors. Currently this decision is left to the users, but it is helpful if the users had some computational guidance. Structural stability analysis would further enhance the usability of the tool. Another expansion option is towards systematic electromechanical embedding strategies so that modular electronic components can be pre-assembled with the motion joints. To further enhance the value of WireFab, we could also extend it to large structures with 3D fortified metal joints. In this paper, the focus of WireFab is the new workflow of turning existing 3D models into articulated mixed-fidelity objects. Therefore, we constrained the capability of interactive shape design. The shapes of input models remain unchanged, but only the appearance of each segmented part can be customized during the whole process. We would like to further extend this work by exploring the shape design freedom in the future.

## ACKNOWLEDGMENTS

We thank the reviewers for their valuable feedback. This work was partly supported by the National Science Foundation Award 1632154 IIP and 1329979 CPS. Jing Bai was supported by the National Natural Science Foundation of China (No. 61163016) and University Scientific Research Projects of Ningxia Province (NGY2015161). Any opinions, findings, and conclusions or recommendations expressed in this material are those of the author(s) and do not necessarily reflect the views of NSF.

## REFERENCES

1. Eric Almquist, John Senior, and Nicolas Bloch. 2016. The Elements of Value. *Harvard Business Review* (2016), 47–52.
2. Oscar Kin-Chung Au, Chiew-Lan Tai, Hung-Kuo Chu, Daniel Cohen-Or, and Tong-Yee Lee. 2008. Skeleton

extraction by mesh contraction. In *ACM Trans. Graph.*, Vol. 27. 44.

3. Moritz Bächer, Bernd Bickel, Doug L. James, and Hanspeter Pfister. 2012. Fabricating Articulated Characters from Skinned Meshes. *ACM Trans. Graph.* 31, 4 (July 2012), 47:1–47:9.
4. Moritz Bächer, Emily Whiting, Bernd Bickel, and Olga Sorkine-Hornung. 2014. Spin-it: Optimizing moment of inertia for spinnable objects. *ACM Transactions on Graphics (TOG)* 33, 4 (2014), 96:1–96:10.
5. Dustin Beyer, Serafima Gurevich, Stefanie Mueller, Hsiang-Ting Chen, and Patrick Baudisch. 2015. Platener: Low-Fidelity Fabrication of 3D Objects by Substituting 3D Print with Laser-Cut Plates. In *Proceedings of the SIGCHI Conference on Human Factors in Computing Systems (CHI '15)*. ACM Press, 1799–1806.
6. John Brooke. 1996. SUS: A quick and dirty usability scale. (1996).
7. Jacques Calì, Dan A. Calian, Cristina Amati, Rebecca Kleinberger, Anthony Steed, Jan Kautz, and Tim Weyrich. 2012. 3D-printing of Non-assembly, Articulated Models. *ACM Trans. Graph.* 31, 6 (Nov. 2012), 130:1–130:8.
8. Jen-Hi Chuang, Chi-Hao Tsai, and Min-Chi Ko. 2000. Skeletonization of Three-Dimensional Object Using Generalized Potential Field. *IEEE Trans. Pattern Anal. Mach. Intell.* 22, 11 (Nov. 2000), 1241–1251.
9. Stelian Coros, Bernhard Thomaszewski, Gioacchino Noris, Shinjiro Sueda, Moira Forberg, Robert W. Sumner, Wojciech Matusik, and Bernd Bickel. 2013. Computational Design of Mechanical Characters. *ACM Trans. Graph.* 32, 4 (2013), 83:1–83:12.
10. Tamal K. Dey and Jian Sun. 2006. Defining and Computing Curve-skeletons with Medial Geodesic Function. In *Proceedings of the Fourth Eurographics Symposium on Geometry Processing (SGP '06)*. 143–152.
11. Wei Gao, Yunbo Zhang, Diogo C. Nazzetta, Karthik Ramani, and Raymond J. Cipra. 2015. RevoMaker: Enabling Multi-directional and Functionally-embedded 3D Printing Using a Rotational Cuboidal Platform. In *Proceedings of the 28th Annual ACM Symposium on User Interface Software & Technology (UIST '15)*. 437–446.
12. Victoria Groom, Leila Takayama, Paloma Ochi, and Clifford Nass. 2009. I am my robot: the impact of robot-building and robot form on operators. In *Proceedings of the 4th ACM/IEEE international conference on Human robot interaction*. ACM, 31–36.
13. Imre Horváth. 2004. On some crucial issues of computer support of conceptual design. In *Product Engineering*. Springer, 123–142.
14. Emmanuel Iarussi, Wilmot Li, and Adrien Bousseau. 2015. WrapIt: Computer-assisted Crafting of Wire Wrapped Jewelry. *ACM Trans. Graph.* 34, 6 (2015), 221:1–221:8.
15. Alec Jacobson, Daniele Panozzo, Oliver Glauser, Cédric Pradalier, Otmar Hilliges, and Olga Sorkine-Hornung. 2014. Tangible and Modular Input Device for Character Articulation. *ACM Trans. Graph.* 33, 4 (2014), 82:1–82:12.
16. Bongjin Koo, Wilmot Li, JiaXian Yao, Maneesh Agrawala, and Niloy J Mitra. 2014. Creating works-like prototypes of mechanical objects. *ACM Trans. Graph.* 33, 6 (2014), 217:1–217:9.
17. Yuki Koyama, Shinjiro Sueda, Emma Steinhardt, Takeo Igarashi, Ariel Shamir, and Wojciech Matusik. 2015. AutoConnect: Computational Design of 3D-printable Connectors. *ACM Trans. Graph.* 34, 6 (2015), 231:1–231:11.
18. Pensa Labs. 2016. DiWire-Pensa Labs. (2016). `http://www.pensalabs.com/diwire-overview/`.
19. Manfred Lau, Akira Ohgawara, Jun Mitani, and Takeo Igarashi. 2011. Converting 3D Furniture Models to Fabricatable Parts and Connectors. *ACM Trans. Graph.* 30, 4 (July 2011), 85:1–85:6.
20. Xian-Ying Li, Chao-Hui Shen, Shi-Sheng Huang, Tao Ju, and Shi-Min Hu. 2010. Popup: Automatic Paper Architectures from 3D Models. In *ACM SIGGRAPH 2010 Papers (SIGGRAPH '10)*. 111:1–111:9.
21. Peter Liepa. 2003. Filling Holes in Meshes. In *Proceedings of the 2003 Eurographics (SGP '03)*. 200–205.
22. Kui-Yip Lo, Chi-Wing Fu, and Hongwei Li. 2009. 3D Polyomino Puzzle. *ACM Trans. Graph.* 28, 5 (Dec. 2009), 157:1–157:8.
23. James McCrae, Nobuyuki Umetani, and Karan Singh. 2014. FlatFitFab: Interactive Modeling with Planar Sections. In *Proceedings of the 27th Annual ACM Symposium on User Interface Software and Technology (UIST '14)*. 13–22.
24. Vittorio Megaro, Bernhard Thomaszewski, Damien Gauge, Eitan Grinspun, Stelian Coros, and Markus Gross. 2014. ChaCra: An Interactive Design System for Rapid Character Crafting. In *ACM SIGGRAPH/Eurographics Symposium on Computer Animation (SCA'14)*. 123–130.
25. Stefanie Mueller, Sangha Im, Serafima Gurevich, Alexander Teibrich, Lisa Pfisterer, François Guimbretière, and Patrick Baudisch. 2014a. WirePrint: 3D Printed Previews for Fast Prototyping. In *Proceedings of the 27th Annual ACM Symposium on User Interface Software and Technology (UIST '14)*. 273–280.
26. Stefanie Mueller, Tobias Mohr, Kerstin Guenther, Johannes Frohnhofen, Kai-Adrian Rollmann, and Patrick Baudisch. 2014b. faBrickation: Fast 3D Printing of Functional Objects by Integrating Construction Kit Building Blocks. In *CHI '14 Extended Abstracts on Human Factors in Computing Systems (CHI EA '14)*. 527–530.

27. Valerio Pascucci, Giorgio Scorzelli, Peer-Timo Bremer, and Ajith Mascarenhas. 2007. Robust On-line Computation of Reeb Graphs: Simplicity and Speed. *ACM Trans. Graph.* 26, 3 (2007).
28. Romain Prévost, Emily Whiting, Sylvain Lefebvre, and Olga Sorkine-Hornung. 2013. Make It Stand: Balancing Shapes for 3D Fabrication. *ACM Trans. Graph.* 32, 4 (July 2013), 81:1–81:10.
29. Valkyrie Savage, Ryan Schmidt, Tovi Grossman, George Fitzmaurice, and Björn Hartmann. 2014. A Series of Tubes: Adding Interactivity to 3D Prints Using Internal Pipes. In *Proceedings of the 27th Annual ACM Symposium on User Interface Software and Technology (UIST '14)*. 3–12.
30. Andrei Sharf, Thomas Lewiner, Ariel Shamir, and Leif Kobbelt. 2007. On-the-fly curve-skeleton computation for 3D shapes. *ACM Trans. Graph.* 26, 3 (2007), 323–328.
31. André Sobiecki, Andrei Jalba, and Alexandru Telea. 2014. Comparison of curve and surface skeletonization methods for voxel shapes. *Pattern Recognition Letters* 47 (2014), 147–156.
32. Peng Song, Bailin Deng, Ziqi Wang, Zhichao Dong, Wei Li, Chi-Wing Fu, and Ligang Liu. 2016. CofiFab: Coarse-to-Fine Fabrication of Large 3D Objects. *ACM Trans. Graph.* 35, 4 (2016).
33. Bernhard Thomaszewski, Stelian Coros, Damien Gauge, Vittorio Megaro, Eitan Grinspun, and Markus Gross. 2014. Computational Design of Linkage-based Characters. *ACM Trans. Graph.* 33, 4 (2014), 64:1–64:9.
34. Nobuyuki Umetani, Yuki Koyama, Ryan Schmidt, and Takeo Igarashi. 2014. Pteromys: Interactive Design and Optimization of Free-formed Free-flight Model Airplanes. *ACM Trans. Graph.* 33, 4 (July 2014), 65:1–65:10.
35. Francisca Gil Ureta, Chelsea Tymms, and Denis Zorin. 2016. Interactive Modeling of Mechanical Objects. In *Computer Graphics Forum*, Vol. 35. Wiley Online Library, 145–155.
36. Charlie CL Wang. 2004. CyberTape: an interactive measurement tool on polyhedral surface. *Computers & Graphics* 28, 5 (2004), 731–745.
37. Shiqing Xin, Chi-Fu Lai, Chi-Wing Fu, Tien-Tsin Wong, Ying He, and Daniel Cohen-Or. 2011. Making Burr Puzzles from 3D Models. In *ACM SIGGRAPH 2011 Papers (SIGGRAPH '11)*. 97:1–97:8.
38. Yunbo Zhang, Wei Gao, Luis Paredes, and Karthik Ramani. 2016. CardBoardiZer: creatively customize, articulate and fold 3D Mesh Models. In *Proceedings of the SIGCHI Conference on Human Factors in Computing Systems (CHI '16)*. 897–907.
39. Youyi Zheng, Chiew-Lan Tai, and Oscar Kin-Chung Au. 2012. Dot scissor: a single-click interface for mesh segmentation. *Visualization and Computer Graphics, IEEE Transactions on* 18, 8 (2012), 1304–1312.
40. Lifeng Zhu, Weiwei Xu, John Snyder, Yang Liu, Guoping Wang, and Baining Guo. 2012. Motion-guided Mechanical Toy Modeling. *ACM Trans. Graph.* 31, 6 (Nov. 2012), 127:1–127:10.

# Digital Mechanical Metamaterials

**Alexandra Ion, Ludwig Wall, Robert Kovacs, and Patrick Baudisch**
Hasso Plattner Institute, Potsdam, Germany
{firstname.lastname}@hpi.de

## ABSTRACT
In this paper, we explore how to embody *mechanical* computation into 3D printed objects, i.e., without electronic sensors, actuators, or controllers typically used for this purpose. A key benefit of our approach is that the resulting objects can be 3D printed in one piece and thus do not require assembly. We are building on 3D printed cell structures, also known as *metamaterials*. We introduce a new type of cell that propagates a digital mechanical signal using an embedded bistable spring. When triggered, the embedded spring discharges and the resulting impulse triggers one or more neighboring cells, resulting in signal propagation. We extend this basic mechanism to implement simple logic functions. We demonstrate interactive objects based on this concept, such as a combination lock. We present a custom editor that allows users to model 3D objects, route signals, simulate signal flow, and synthesize cell patterns.

### Author Keywords
Metamaterials; Fabrication; Programmable Matter

### ACM Classification Keywords
H.5.m. [Information interfaces and presentation] Misc.

## INTRODUCTION
Personal fabrication machines, such as 3D printers, allow users to make custom objects. While early work on 3D printing revolved around designing the outside of such objects [24, 32], recently researchers started exploring 3D printing as a means to design the *inside* of objects. Applications include moving objects' centers of gravity so as to make them stand [20] or spin [1].

Pushing this further, researchers created objects that consist internally of a large number of 3D cells arranged on a regular grid [15]. Since each cell is designed to perform a specific deformation, objects that entirely consist of such cells literally offer thousands of degrees of freedom. Such structures are also known as *metamaterials* [18].



*CHI 2017,* May 06 - 11, 2017, Denver, CO, USA

ACM 978-1-4503-4655-9/17/05...$15.00
DOI: http://dx.doi.org/10.1145/3025453.3025624

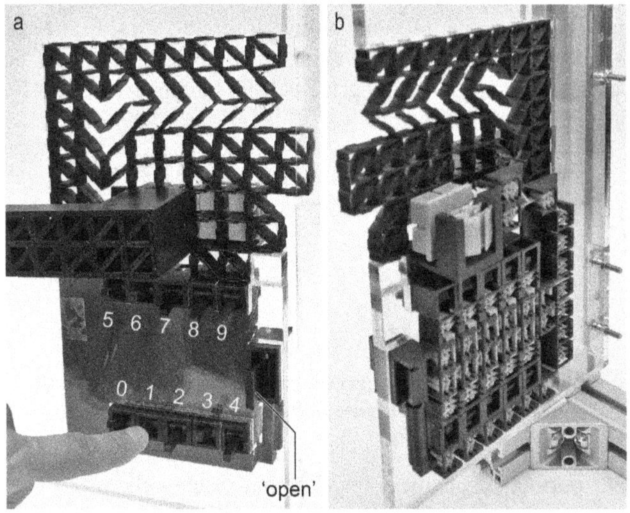


**Figure 1: (a) This combination door lock is implemented as a *digital mechanical metamaterial*, i.e., a single block of material based on a regular grid of cells. It allows users to input a numeric code, it processes the code, checks its correctness, and unlocks the latch. (b) Under the hood, the lock consists of an array of cells that transmit and process a mechanical signal.**

While metamaterials were initially understood as materials, we recently proposed to think of them as *machines;* such metamaterial mechanisms [10] consist of a single block of material, the cells of which play together in a well-defined way in order to achieve macroscopic movement. We used this principle previously to implement simple mechanical objects, such as a door latch (Figure 7).

Such *analog* machines, however, are limited in terms of complexity. As forces are passed on from one cell to the next, they are damped and the activation energy dissipates, causing the mechanical "signal" to decay exponentially. This limits the number of mechanisms that can be concatenated and therefore the complexity of the machine.

In this paper, we explore how to extend this concept towards *digital* mechanisms. Combining metamaterial mechanisms [10] with concepts from mechanical computing and mechanical signal propagation [16, 23], we introduce a new type of cell that propagates a digital mechanical signal, i.e., it counteracts signal decay and thus allows signals to pass through an *arbitrary* number of cells. We extend this basic mechanism to implement simple logic functions.

To illustrate this concept, Figure 1 shows a combination lock implemented using digital metamaterials. The device offers ten digit buttons on the front. Users tap these buttons to enter their code, then press the 'open' button to unlock the door.

## BASICS OF DIGITAL MECHANICAL METAMATERIALS

Digital metamaterials are based on a new type of cell that propagates a mechanical signal reinforced by an embedded bistable spring.

### The *bit cell* is the main underlying mechanism

Figure 2 shows the key element behind digital metamaterials, which we call *bit cell*. Bit cells contain a bistable spring, which allows them to take on two discrete states. Figure 2a shows the bit cell in its *tense* state. (b) When triggered, the spring discharges, causing the cell to switch from its *tense* state to its *relaxed* state.

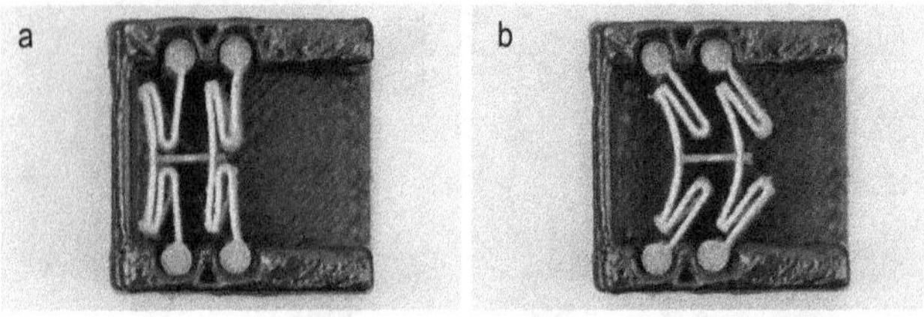


**Figure 2: (a) When triggered, this *bit cell* changes its state from tense to (b) relaxed.**

As shown in Figure 3, bit cells feature an input port and output port. A mechanical impulse that reaches the input port triggers the cell, which creates an impulse at the output port. Because discharging the spring releases mechanical energy, the impulse at the output port is larger than the required trigger impulse at the input port.

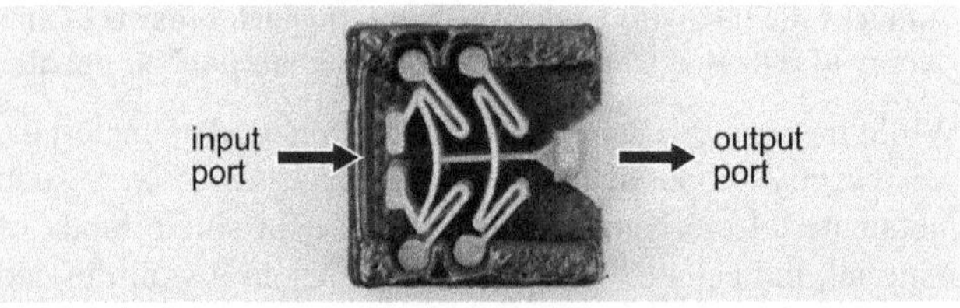


**Figure 3: Bit cells offer an input and an output port.**

As illustrated by Figure 4, this allows us to concatenate bit cells in a way that allows cells to trigger their immediate neighbors, resulting in a simple signal propagation mechanism similar to [23].

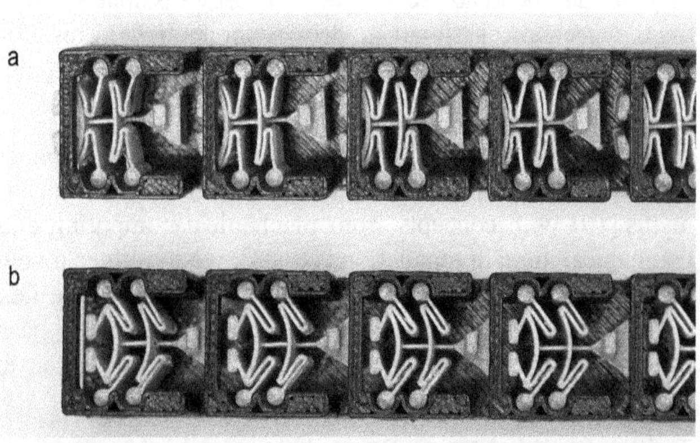


**Figure 4: Concatenating bit cells creates a signal transmission. (a) Initially all bit cells are in their tense position. (b) Triggering the leftmost cell causes the signal to propagate through all cells from left to right.**

### The combination lock example

Bit cells and the resulting concept of signal propagation allow us to implement a hierarchy of digital mechanisms of increasing complexity. We discuss these logic functions and mechanisms in full detail later in this paper, as well as a simple manual recharge mechanism to set discharged springs back into their tense state. However, Figure 5 provides a rough overview of the different elements that implement the combination lock.

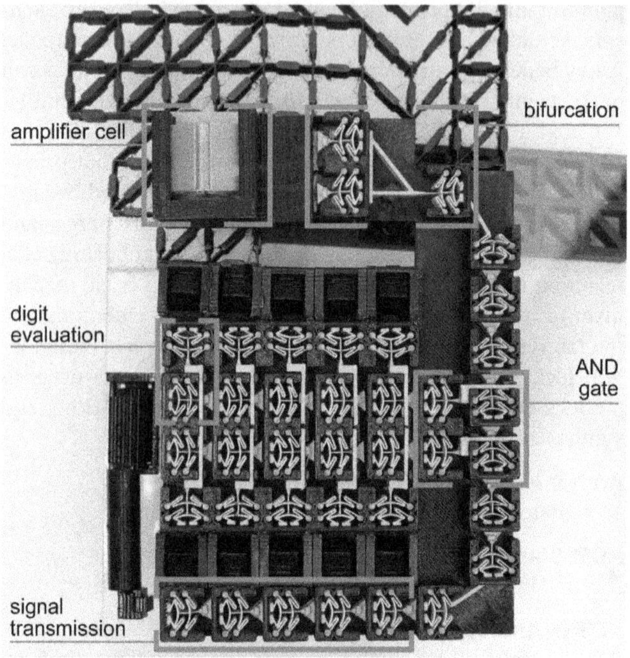


**Figure 5: Our door lock consists of 82 cells, which implement the signal transmisison, the evaluation of each digit input by the user, an AND gate, and one amplifier cell with a pre-amplification step to move the blocking bolts sufficiently.**

(1) To input the code, users tap one of the digit buttons on the front, which changes the state of the *digit evaluation* cells. The device contains 10 of these—one for each possible digit. (2) When the user pushes the 'open' button, three signal transmission lines are set off simultaneously; two of which run through the digit evaluation units and (3) set the state of the *AND gate*. The AND gate evaluates the correctness of the code by computing a logical AND the two rows of digits input by the user. The third signal transmission line runs from the bottom left towards the right, around the corner, and upwards where (4) the signal is *bifurcated*. This allows triggering (5) a double-sized *amplifier cell* that actuates the bolts to unblock the door.

Figure 6 shows a close-up of these bolts. (a) As long as the bolts are in place, they prevent the shearing cells in the middle from shearing, thereby blocking the door. (b) When the bolts are retracted, the shearing cells can shear and pushing down the handle retracts the latch—as discussed in [10]. This is where our digital metamaterials connect to the analog metamaterial door latch mechanism.

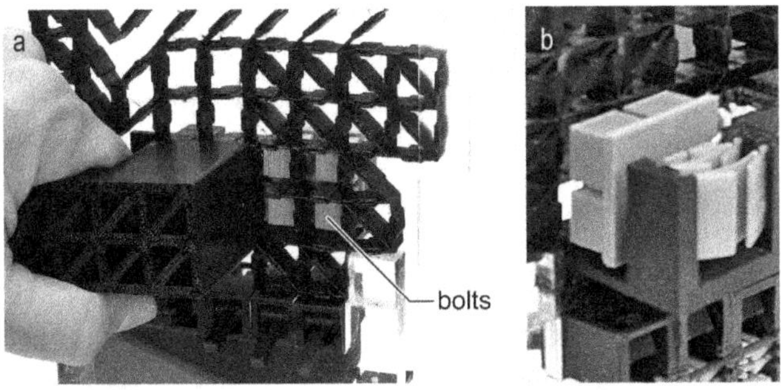


**Figure 6: We effectively lock the latch mechanism by stiffening the shearing area that enables it. We do so by inserting bolts. Once users entered the key code correctly, our lock signal retracts the bolt and enables the latch mechanism.**

## CONTRIBUTION, BENEFITS & LIMITATIONS

Our main contribution is the concept of digital mechanical metamaterials. They allow integrating computational abilities into the structure of 3D printed objects. We provide a modular system consisting of digital cells (hardware) and an editor (software) that provides a toolkit to users, enabling them to create new digital mechanisms.

While analog metamaterial mechanisms are subject to damping, which causes the mechanical "signal" to decay exponentially and limits the number of 'steps' that can be performed, *digital* mechanical metamaterials enable transmitting signals through an *arbitrary* number of cells.

When we contrast digital mechanical metamaterials to the traditional approach of augmenting objects with electronic microcontrollers, sensors, and actuators [26, 31], our approach results in an entirely mechanical solution and can be produced entirely using a 3D printer. However, since our approach lacks loops, clocks, and memory, our approach is limited to much simpler devices.

## RELATED WORK

We build on previous work in interactive personal fabrication, mechanical metamaterials, and analog computers.

### Personal fabrication

3D printers and other personal fabrication machines simplify the process for users to make custom objects. Besides printing decorative object, users often create functional objects the functionality of which is determined by their external shape [32, 14, 7]. Integrating heating elements during the print process allows to change the shape after the fabrication process to adapt, e.g. to users' bodies [9].

To fabricate mechanical assemblies, users can print the structural parts from rigid plastic (e.g., links, axles, bearings, gears, etc.) and assemble them to construct machines [2]. Such assemblies can also be printed in one process [6]. The usability of existing mechanical objects can be enhanced by fabricating additional handles or contraption using personal fabrication machines [7].

To allow users to go beyond mechanical systems made on their personal fabrication machines, researchers proposed techniques to integrate sensors and microcontrollers into objects. They range from (capacitive) position sensing [11, 29, 26] to sensing light beams for detecting user interaction [33], to complex systems like integrating a camera to track markers [25]. Adding sensors to 3D printed parts after they were fabricated even enables users to make adaptations to their everyday objects and to effectively customize the way they, for example, interact with their toaster [22]. Peng et al. recently demonstrated the idea of 3D printing motors, which allows fabricating arbitrary objects with integrated motors in the same process, enabling complex interactive objects with actuation capabilities [19].

While complex tasks, such as image processing are not possible in purely mechanical systems, we argue that we can integrate mechanical *and* simple information processing capabilities within a 3D printed object to alter its properties. To do so, we design the internal structure of 3D printed objects.

### Designing the internal structure

Researchers in HCI and computer graphics started to alter the internal structure of 3D printed objects to, e.g., optimize their strength-to-weight ratio [12], to move their center of gravity in order to balance objects [20], or to allow arbitrary shapes to spin [3]. Vidimce et al. recently proposed a system that allows users to create and edit the internal structure and material distribution of 3D printed objects [30].

### Mechanical metamaterials

Metamaterials are "artificial structures with mechanical properties that are defined by their usually repetitive cell patterns, rather than the material they are made of [18]. Metamaterials consist of large numbers of 3D cells organized on a regular grid. Since each cell can be designed to deform in a specific way [17, 27], they literally offer thousands of degrees of freedom.

Based on this concept, researchers have created objects with unusual behavior, such as objects that collapse abruptly when compressed [15], that shrink in two dimensions upon one-dimensional compression [8], or objects that combine layers of different degrees of stiffness (i.e., soft and hard cells) in order to emulate different materials, such as leather or felt [4].

However, metamaterials are usually seen as materials. In [10], we proposed thinking of metamaterials as *machines* instead. Figure 7 shows one of the objects we demonstrated—a door latch implemented as a single part.

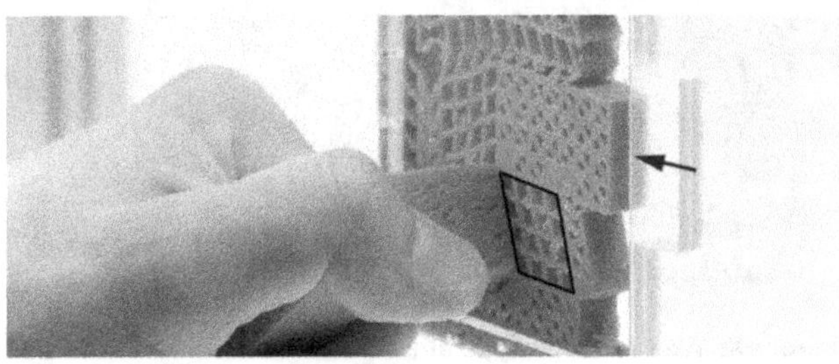

**Figure 7: Metamaterial mechanisms [10].**

In this paper, we extend on the concept of metamaterial mechanisms by introducing the notion digital signal processing, which allows us to produce more complex mechanisms, such as the combination lock shown in Figure 1. Our hardware design is inspired by mechanical wave propagation using bistable springs [16, 23].

### Mechanical logic systems

Our work combines metamaterials with concepts from mechanical computing. Since we use bistable springs for storing energy, we build our logic based on three-state logic [28], which assumes the additional output state 'high impedance'. This allows us to distinguish a cell being in its tense state from when it is in its relaxed state.

One approach to implement mechanical logic systems is dual rail logic [5]. It duplicates the signal path to provide a distinct 0-signal. However, this comes at the cost of space. Rod logic presents an interesting system that can scale to nanotechnology [13]. It is based on rods that can let signals pass, or block them. We build our signal transmission on this work.

## ROUTING SIGNALS BASED ON CELLS

In this and the following section, we now show the individual cells that implement the combination door lock we showed in Figure 5. We begin with the cell types that allow us to route signals through 3D objects. We already looked at signal propagation along a straight line (Figure 4); in this section, we demonstrate how to route signals around corners, across other signal lines, and how to bifurcate signals.

Routing signals is important because 3D printed objects can have arbitrary shape and routing allows transmitting a signal from where it emerges to where the information is needed. For the door lock, for example, we route users input from the digit inputs to the door latch mechanism—which is located elsewhere in our object.

The more specialized routing cells are all based on *bit cells.* However, we position their output ports to be oriented towards the neighbor cell we want to trigger. So while the bit cells in Figure 4 feature an output port on the side opposite to the input port, the cell shown in Figure 8 redirects the signal by 90° by adding a beam to the arm of our bistable spring. This beam rotates with the arm of the spring, allowing it to tap the input port of the rotated cell on the top right.

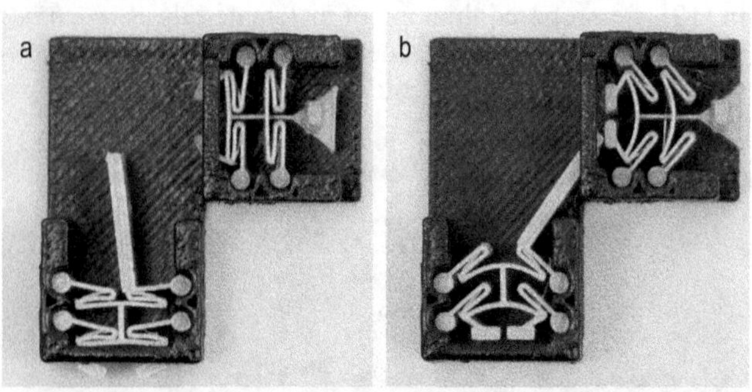


**Figure 8: We use a new type of output port to redirect the signal by 90°. We exploit the rotational movement of the spring and attach a beam that taps its neighboring cell.**

As illustrated by Figure 9, we can route signals in 3 dimensions by concatenating multiple such mechanisms. Here we route the signal from the x/y plane to the x/z plane to the y/z plane.

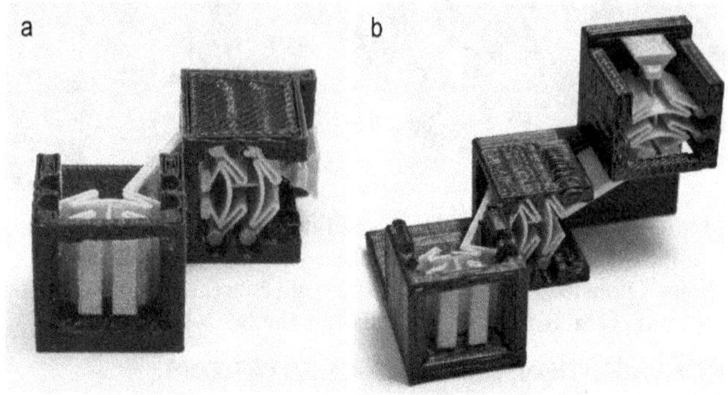


**Figure 9: (a) Rotating the receiving cell allows us to redirect signals from one plane to another. (b) Concatenating three assemblies allows us to route signals in 3D.**

Figure 10 shows a specialized three-cell mechanism that allows two signals to pass each other in minimal space. We use a crossbar that reaches from the output port of the left cell to the input port of the right cell that spans across the middle cell.

**Figure 10: We cross signals by running a crossbar across another cell.**

Figure 11 shows two mechanisms that bifurcate signals. The design shown in (a) triggers two parallel signal lines. The design shown in (b) triggers two signal lines oriented in opposite directions. Both designs exploit the fact that our bistable springs require less energy to be triggered than they output, which allows triggering two cells from one.

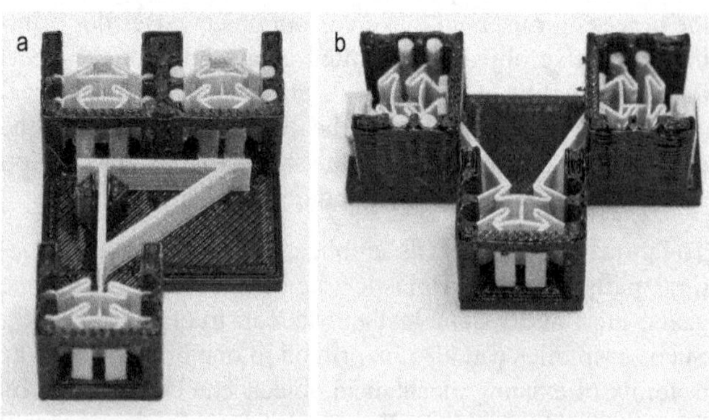


**Figure 11: We can bifurcate signals (a) in a parallel manner or (b) let the two signals run in opposite directions.**

Figure 12 shows how we merge two signals. This is an interesting construct, because it implements an OR gate.

**Figure 12: We use the opposite assembly to merge signal as we did to bifurcate them. This implements an OR gate.**

## LOGIC FUNCTIONS

To implement logic functions, we need to go beyond merely transmitting signals to also evaluating signals, which we achieve by blocking them. In the combination lock from Figure 5, we block signals for wrong digit inputs so that the door stays blocked. Later in this section, we present cell arrangements that implement basic logic, such as AND or NAND.

### Blocking signals using gate cells

To allow for asynchronous input, we have designed cells capable of storing the first input that reaches them and do not act until the last signal has been received. We call these cells *gate cells*. Our approach is based on rod logic [13].

As illustrated by Figure 13a these cells work by placing a "blocker" across their neighboring cell. When the cell on the right is triggered before the cell on the left, the blocker is aligned with the output port of the right cell so that it cannot pass and signal is blocked. However, triggering the left cell, as shown in Figure 13b, moves the blocker out of the way and the signal can pass through. The position of the blocker can also be defined to initially let signals through and only after actuation to block signals, as shown in Figure 13c–d.

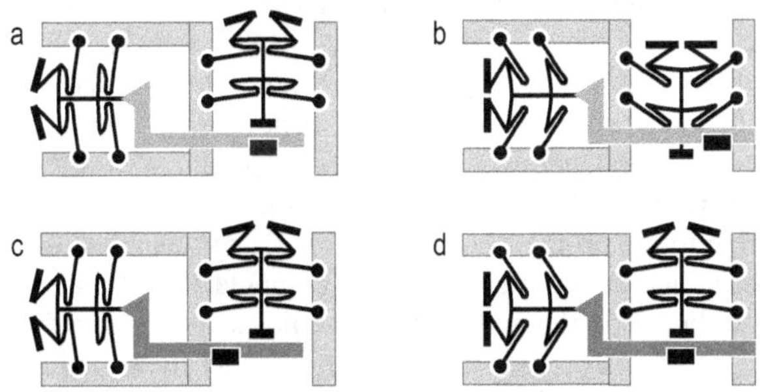


**Figure 13: *Gate cells* validate signals and can be configures to block signals (a-b) or let signals pass (c-d) in their tense state.**

Figure 14 shows the design of the two cells that form the gate cell. Each crossbar has a blocker attached on its underside.

**Figure 14: We position a blocking element that is intended to either block the signal output or let it pass.**

### Logic functions based on gate cells

We can concatenate multiple gate cells to create combinational logic functions. Figure 15 uses simplified symbols to illustrate how the positions of the blockers are configured to implement the function A ∧ ¬B ∧ C ∧ D ∧ ¬E. The positive input cells A, C, and D need to be triggered to move the blocker out of the way and let the signal pass. The negated inputs B and E are implemented by positioning the blocker so that they let the signal pass when they are *not* triggered and block the signal otherwise.

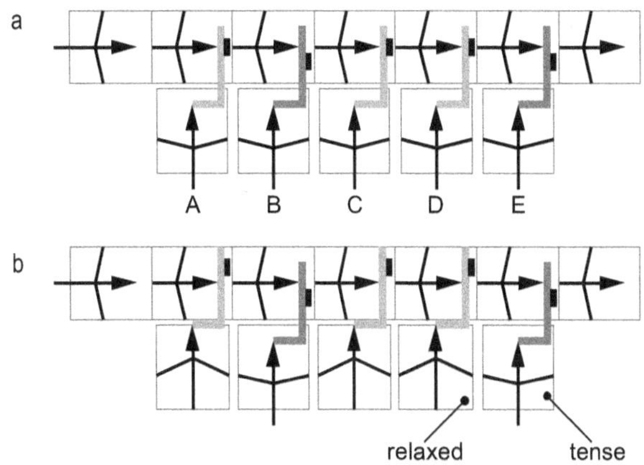


**Figure 15: (a) When all inputs are tense, the signal cannot pass. (b) Triggering the correct inputs, here A, C, and D, moves the blockers so that the signal can pass.**

If we rename the inputs of the logic function that is shown in Figure 15 from A–E to 0–4, it implements a 5-digit code evaluation. To implement the combination lock with 10 digits, we add a second row of inputs. Now we have two logic functions (one in each row), which both need to be correct, thus we add an AND gate. Figure 16 illustrates that the key code is '0 2 3 8'.

Again, we use our *gate cells* to employ the AND gate. Each code evaluation row has a gate cell at the end. Only if all the inputs of the corresponding row were correct, the blocker is moved out of the way for a third signal to pass, the *evaluation signal*.

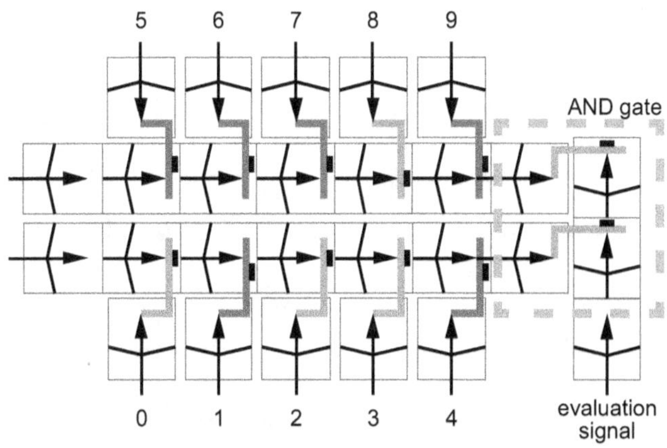


**Figure 16: We add an AND gate to validate the two rows that yield the 10-digit.**

### Combinational logic using an evaluation signal

Our implementation of the AND gate has three inputs, namely two values and one additional *evaluation signal*. We add this additional signal because our mechanical computation is fundamentally different from electronic circuits, yet adding only one single signal allows us to implement any Boolean predicate without any electronics.

A 'signal' within our system is not an applied voltage, but an *impulse*, i.e., a mechanical force within the object. This impulse *changes the system state* by changing physical properties of the material, such as the position of the blockers. Since we block invalid signals, the output of gate cells is no signal instead of a 0-signal (logical low). However, not receiving a signal is indistinguishable from a dormant system. This means that we cannot provide an 0-signal that can serve as an input to the next gate, as in classical electronic circuits.

Despite this, we are still able to employ combinational logic within our materials. The most space efficient way is to integrate the inversion into logic functions, e.g., by using a NOR instead of an OR. Figure 17 illustrates a selection of logic gates implemented with our digital cells. Note that we show a different OR gate compared to the one shown in Figure 12. The one shown here uses the general-purpose assembly that is also used in the NOT and NAND gate.

We add the additional evaluation signal as a second computation step. After the inputs are provided to the system, we send a signal off that evaluates the inputs in order to produce output. Independent of the complexity of the logic, only one single evaluation signal is necessary, since it can be furcated, merged, and routed through the material. Race conditions within operations can be resolved by adapting the length of signal paths.

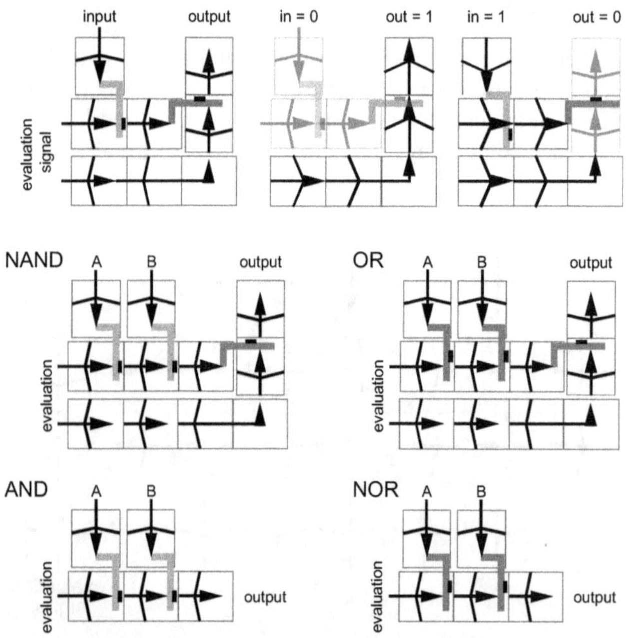


**Figure 17: Only one additional signal allows us to implement combinational logic, despite not having a traditional 0-signal.**

## AMPLIFYING THE OUTPUT

While the cells that implement the signal transmission can be arbitrarily small, the *output* cells that move material to change the material properties might need to produce a certain amount of movement or force.

In the example of the door lock, we need to move the bolts sufficiently far into the door latch's structure to stiffen it. We use what we call an *amplifier cell*, which is inspired by the metaphor of operational amplifiers in the electronics domain. Such an *amplifier cell*, as shown in Figure 18, is a cell that is doubled in size. This allows us to add a larger spring to produce more stroke length.

**Figure 18: We amplify the stroke length of our output by going from small cells to a double-sized cell.**

To transition from small cells to bigger cells, we bifurcate the signal. This gives us the energy of two cells, which together trigger the spring within the *amplifier cell*. In our door lock example, our 30 mm *amplifier cell* moves the bolts by 6 mm as compared to the stroke length of 3 mm of the 15 mm bit cells.

## RECHARGING

After the springs were triggered and they are in their relaxed state, they need to be reset to their tense state before the computation can be run again. To do so, we designed a small lid on top of each cell, which uses the cell's third dimension to recharge the spring. Figure 19 shows how as the lid is pushed down, the attached wedges move the spring backward to its tense position. We use an additional plate to push multiple recharge lids at the same time. This design enables one recharge action for every plane of computation. We added a small bump on the underside of the lid, which causes the lid to spring back upward in order to not hinder the signal transmission between the cells.

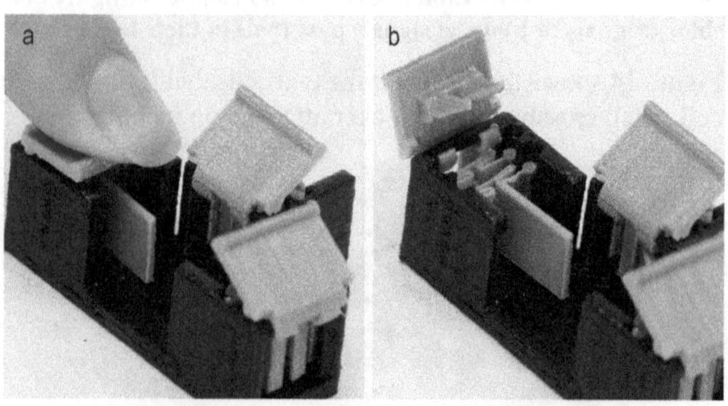


**Figure 19: (a) Each cell features a lid with wedges, pushing it (b) recharges the spring underneath.**

## ADDITIONAL APPLICATION EXAMPLE

We see digital mechanical metamaterials being particularly useful for objects that have (1) many mechanical inputs (e.g., the code lock), and/or (2) many mechanical outputs (e.g., the following example of a plant pot), and (3) which are not frequently reconfigured. For example, the density plant pot might be reconfigured when seasons change, or the door might be locked once a day. In contrast, for objects that require frequent updates (e.g., displays) or more complex programming involving loops, etc., we recommend traditional electronics.

### Example: plant pot

Figure 20 shows an example of a plant pot, where (a) users input the plant's size (small–large) and its water demands (little–much) using sliders. This triggers the computation in the bottom layer of the pot, which determines (b) how many *density cells* will be closed. After users configured the pot's density, (c) they place it into a cachepot with water. The density of the plant pot now determines how fast water can pass through to the plant.

**Figure 20: We implement a plant pot that changes its density based on user input of the plant's size and water demands.**

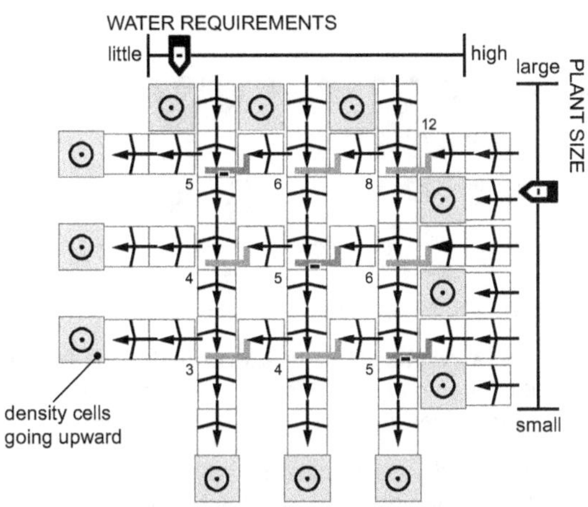


**Figure 21: The weighted computation of the plant pot's density ensures that small plants get enough water by preventing some density cells from closing. The numbers indicate how many density cells are open for each parameter combination.**

We use *gate cells* to change the weight of the parameters of the plant pot example. Figure 21 shows that by simply placing gate cells along the diagonal, we give more weight to the low values of the parameters. Since the gate cells prevent the signal from passing through, they prevent all density cells from closing, so that even for a small plant with little water demand the plant pot's permeability is 25% (3 out of 12 density cell rows remain open).

## FABRICATION OF CELLS

We print our prototypes from the commonly available filaments ABS and PLA. While our cells are designed to be printed in an assembled state, we tend to print the parts of our prototypes separately. This allows us to print all elements without support material, which tends to be faster than the single-part design that requires dissolving the support material. We printed the springs from PLA using the *Ultimaker 2+* 3D printer, and the frames that hold the springs from ABS on our *Dimension SST 1200es*. Our cell size is 15 mm for all our prototypes with a printed spring thickness of 0.4 mm.

The cell shown in Figure 22 is printed in an assembled state. We had it made at *shapeways* using their "frosted detail plastic" material, which is a UV cured acrylic polymer that is printed using the MultiJet Modeling process.

**Figure 22: A cell printed fully assembled using shapeways' "frosted detail plastic" material.**

We empirically tested how the cells miniaturize while retaining the same stress values using Autodesk Fusion's simulation. The results showed that reducing the spring thickness to ½ allows it to be shortened to ¼ of its length, i.e., to $^1/_{64}$ of the cell volume. For example, a 0.2 mm thick spring allows for a cell size of 3.75 mm, which is a matter of printer resolution.

## BISTABLE SPRING DESIGN

The bistable spring in our cells differs from a typical bistable spring that is shown in Figure 23b, which is a simple pre-bent beam that is fixed within rigid walls [21]. However, such designs have very high width-to-length ratios, which do not utilize the space within a rotation-invariant cubic cell well.

**Figure 23: (a) The spring we use in our bit cells is longer and thus weaker than (b) conventional bistable springs. Or, for the same force, our cells produce more stroke length.**

Figure 23 illustrates that our spring design includes an additional 'loop', which prolongs the beam and therefore makes it weaker, i.e., it requires less force to be triggered and charged. We measured 45% less force required to charge our type of spring compared to the conventional spring. Another way to view it is that our longer springs produce more output length (by 23% according our measurements) while requiring similar force.

Note that our cells incorporate two connected springs. This is a common technique [21] for increasing the stability of bistable springs during the so-called 'snap-through', i.e., the point where the spring is compressed the most as it is forced to its other second position.

## TECHNICAL EVALUATION

The geometry of our spring allows us to make limited changes in stroke length and force by varying the spring parameters. For example, we used slightly stronger springs in the plant pot example to compensate for the higher density of water. While the output of bit cells usually needs to be only strong and far enough to trigger the neighbor cell, the output cells may have to meet specific requirements in terms of amount of force or stroke length.

Our evaluation informs the geometrical spring parameters for achieving bistability and the maximum possible fan-out of a cell, i.e., how many cells can be triggered by one single cell.

**Independent variables:** We compared a total of 75 springs of our design where we varied three parameters independently: (1) the arm angle, (2) the length of the bent bridge in the middle, and (3) the strength of the bridge, varied trough changing its buckling magnitude and its thickness concurrently. We varied the values for the bridge strength from 1.05 times the normal spring thickness to 1.85 times, and a buckle distance from 8% of the bridge length to 40%. The spring thickness is limited by the 3D printer's resolution; we use 0.18 mm. Bridge length values ranged from 45% to 85% the total distance between the walls. We tested these values for 20°, 30° and 40° arm angles. This yields 25 springs for each arm angle.

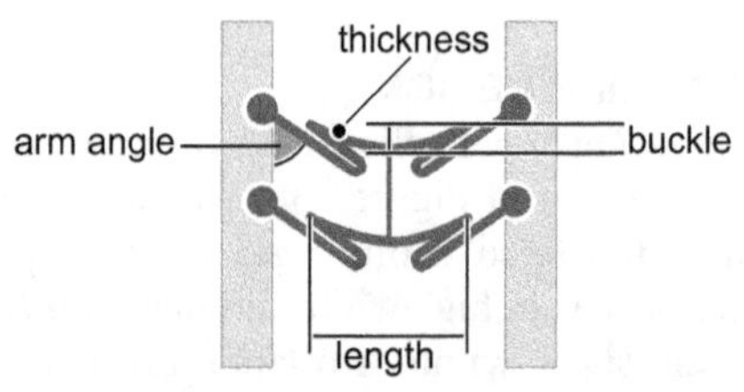


**Figure 24: We vary the parameters of bridge length and bridge strength for three different arm angles each. We measure the stroke length and the forces for charging and triggering the springs, as well as their output energy.**

**Dependent variables:** We measured (1) the force it takes to push a spring to its tense position, (2) the force necessary to trigger the spring, (3) its stroke length, and (4) the force it outputs when triggered.

**Test setup:** Figure 25 shows our test setup. We placed a ruler (error 0.5 mm) under the spring to measure the stroke length. We used a force gauge with an error of 0.05 N, which was constrained to linear movement centered to the spring and precisely moved by a threaded rod. We pushed the force gauge against the spring to measure the charge energy, we released the pressure while slowly moving the force gauge backward to measure the output energy, and we measured the trigger energy by pushing the rotated spring.

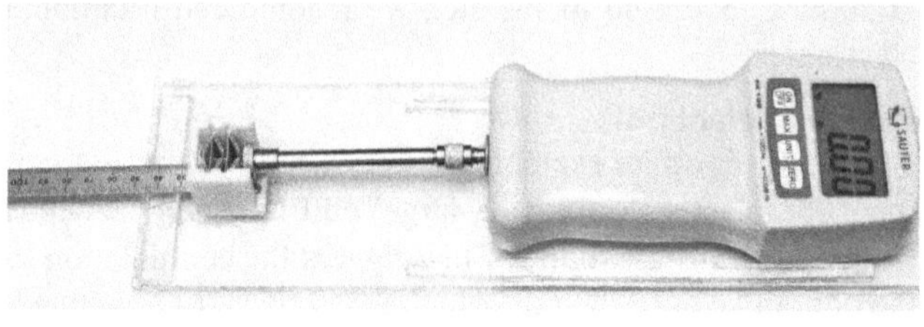

**Figure 25: We measure the forces using a force gauge (error 0.05 N), and the stroke length using a ruler (error 0.5 mm).**

### Results

Figure 26 shows charge, output, and trigger energy and stroke lengths for 50 springs. Empty fields denote springs that were not bistable. The results for springs with a 20° arm angle were omitted since only 2 of them were bistable.

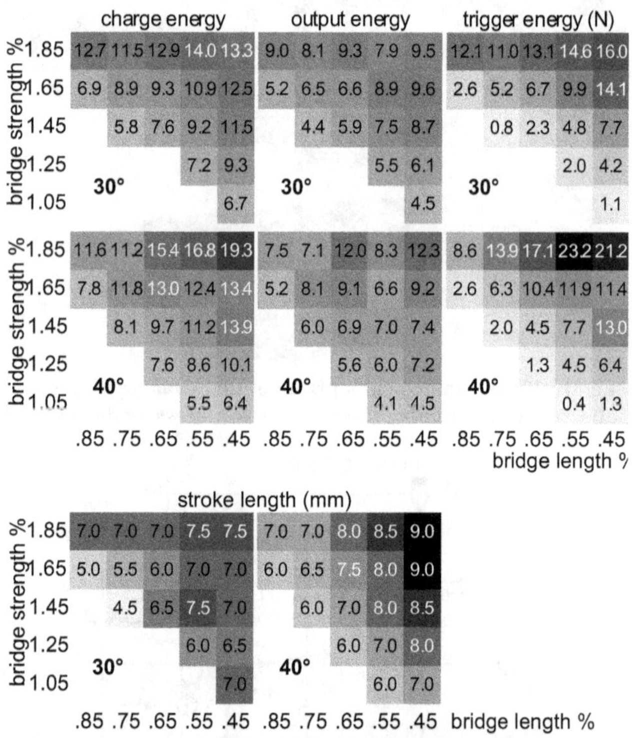


**Figure 26: Raw results of our technical evaluation for charge, output and trigger energy in N and stroke length in mm. Missing values indicate non-bistable springs.**

All four measured values increase when increasing the arm angle or the bridge strength, or when decreasing the length of the bridge. The *output energy* was on average 73% of the charge energy for 30° springs and 66% for 40° springs.

The difference between output energy and *trigger energy* is greatest right when the springs start becoming bistable. The ratio between the two decides the maximum possible fan-out of the springs, thus a 2:1 ratio is necessary for bifurcation. Choosing a higher trigger energy however increases the fault-tolerance of the system with regards to unwanted activation, e.g., by dropping the object.

*Stroke length* is affected most by the arm angle, i.e., the stroke length increases with the arm angle. Stroke is least affected by the strength of the bridge.

In contrast, *charge energy* of the spring is affected most by the strength of the bridge and least by the arm angle, which can also be seen from Figure 26 in the rapid changes along the y-axis.

Choosing appropriate values for each can tune the spring toward a longer stroke or a higher output energy without changes to its bistability. Note that these values apply to the springs we tested with and that due to differences in manufacturing they might vary slightly.

## EDITOR

To allow expert users to create and fabricate objects from digital metamaterials, we implemented a specialized 3D voxel-style editor, which is based on the editor for metamaterial mechanisms [10]. The main intent is to allow users to draw signal paths and verify them within the editor (Figure 27). We support users by allowing them to enter simple logic functions, which our editor converts to cell arrangements that implement that function.

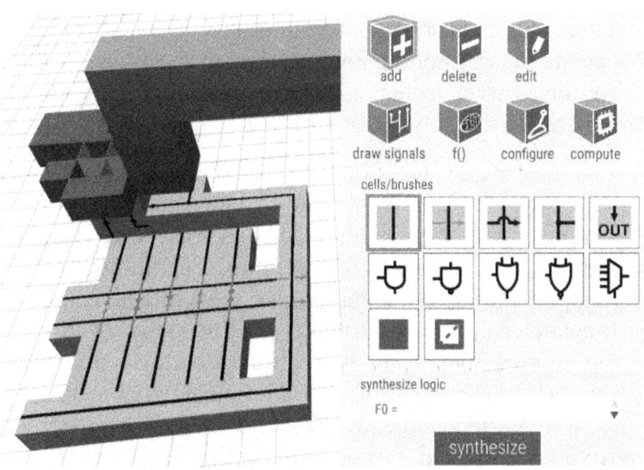


**Figure 27: Our editor helps users create digital metamaterials.**

While the editor is built to help users design digital metamaterials efficiently, knowledge about signals and logic remains necessary, i.e., this editor is for expert users.

### Walkthrough

Figure 28 illustrates how users create the door lock example from Figure 1. (a) They first draw the signal line that evaluates the upper 5 digits by dragging over the ground plane using our "draw signals" tool. (b) Then, using the same tool, they draw signals perpendicular to the first signal line. (c) When the two signals cross, the editor automatically draws a gate cell. (d) They do the same for the lower row of digits. (e) In this example, users manually configure the gate cells using the "configure", i.e., they change the initial state of 5 gate cells from initially 'pass' to 'block' by clicking on the respective gate cell. (f) The configured gate cells implement the key code for the lock.

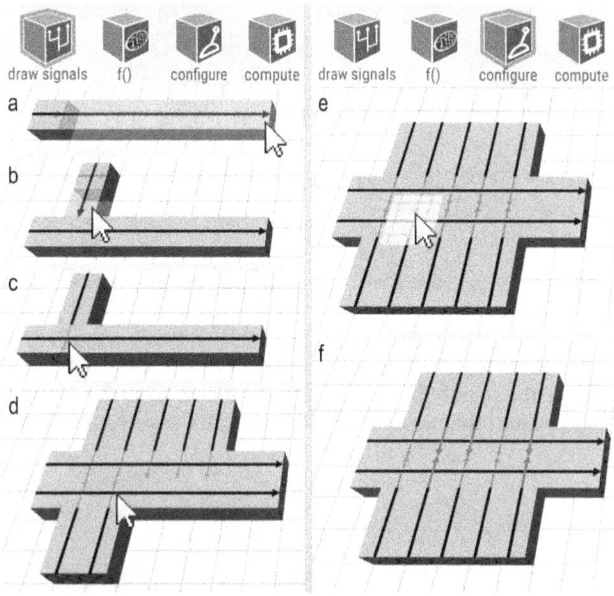


**Figure 28: (a) Users draw the signal routing using the "draw signals" tool. (b) Once they cross an existing signal route, (c) the editor automatically draws a gate cell. (d) After creating all cells for the digit evaluation, (e) users set the initial states of the gate cells using the "configure" tool (f) to define the key code.**

Users continue by adding the evaluation line, the AND gate and the output cells, which will move the bolts. Finally, they model the analog door latch mechanism on top of the digital metamaterial.

Figure 29 shows how users verify the signal transmission in our custom editor. They first charge the cells by selecting the "compute" tool. The editor visualizes charged cells by turning the signal lines blue. Clicking on a cell, as shown in Figure 29a, sets a signal off. The impulse runs through the cells, being visualized in yellow at the currently active cell. After the impulse has passed a cell, the signal path is shown in black again, because the cell is back in its relaxed state (Figure 29b). To verify the whole computational assembly, users trigger the inputs first and then the evaluation signal, as they do on the 3D printed object. They subsequently watch if the signal runs all the way through to the door. If not, they see where the signal stopped and can correct the error.

To help users create logic functions efficiently, e.g., by avoiding the need for manual configuration of cells, we allow users to input logic functions. Figure 30 shows an example, where users enter the function 'A & ~B & C & D & ~E' and click 'synthesize'. Then, they indicate where the synthesized cell arrangement shall be positioned by simply clicking on the grid. Our editor automatically synthesizes the cells that implement the entered logic functions.

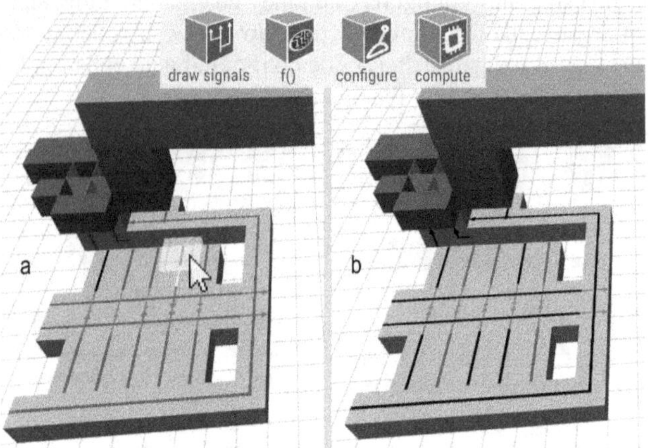


**Figure 29: Users can verify their logic and signal routing. They first charge all springs, then (a) they click the inputs to trigger the signal there, and lastly (b) they trigger the evaluation line and find that the signal passes all the way through to the latch.**

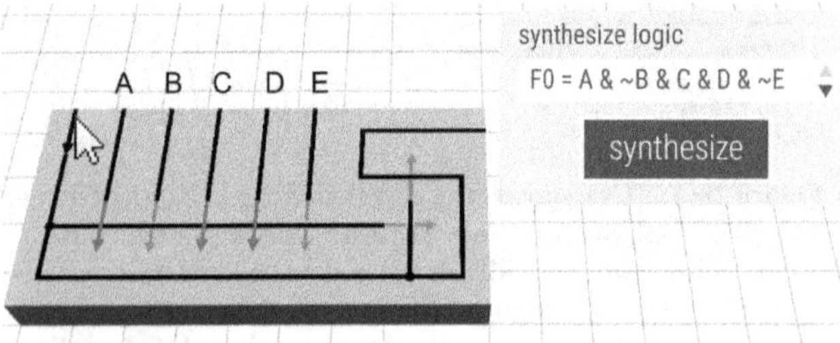


**Figure 30: Users enter the function 'A & ~B & C & D & ~E', and indicates the location by clicking on the grid. Our editor responds by automatically inserting the corresponding cells.**

## Implementation

We build on the metamaterial mechanisms voxel-style editor [10] and extend it to allow users to draw signal routes and to input logic functions. Our extension of the editor is based on a node.js javascript framework, using the three.js graphics framework and WebGL for rendering the basic geometries.

Rendering of 3D-printable .stl files was done in modular hierarchical OpenSCAD script files. The editor simply exports the cell geometries as OpenSCAD script commands to render a cell with the specific parameters.

### *Drawing signal paths*

Drawing with signal paths is realized through a freeform line tool that places appropriately connected cells following the cursor. We use a pathfinding library for 3D[1] that provides the A* pathfinding algorithm to simplify connecting cells via a signal line by finding the shortest available path while crossing existing signals where necessary.

### *Synthesizing cell arrangements*

To generate cell arrangements of minimal size that implement a user-defined logic function, we use a version of the Espresso heuristic logic minimizer[2].

The logic minimizer parses the user text input, minimizes the described input function and returns it in its disjunctive normal form. This minimized DNF is parsed a second time by our editor to identify its terms and literals, which are used to create a very compact cell arrangement that forms a disjunction of minterm conjunctions. A minterm is a minimal conjunction of the input literals that returns true. This means that an array of signals representing the disjunctions of the function is run in parallel. All input variables of the function intersect and potentially block these lines, forming conjunctions along each of the parallel lines. The combined arrangement implements the function as a whole. To choose the most succinct cell representation of the function, we also minimize the negated input function and negate its result again directly on the cell level. The cell arrangement variant that requires the least cells to implement the input function is constructed and placed in the editor at the last user-selected cell location.

The logic minimizer runs in a separate python virtual environment using the PyEDA[3] library for electronic design automation. This python server is queried via HTTP requests to a REST architecture and replies with minimized functions to logic functions encoded in the request-URL.

## CONCLUSIONS

We presented digital mechanical metamaterials. While (analog) metamaterial mechanisms suffer from signal decay, digital metamaterials are not subject to such decay, allowing us to create larger/more complex objects. Unlike solutions based on sensors, actuators, and microcontrollers, our approach still is entirely mechanical.

We showed the design of bit cells, which are the key element for the signal transmission. They contain bistable springs, which have two states, the relaxed and tense state. We also presented cells that allow for routing signals in 2D and 3D. To employ simple computation, we showed gate cells. We demonstrated our approach at the example of two prototypes: a digital door lock without electronics and a configurable plant pot. To help expert users create such digital metamaterials, we contribute an editor that allows for routing signals, verifying them, and synthesizing cell arrangements from user-defined logic functions.

For future work, we plan to explore cells that have the ability to shear *and* transmit signals, which would allow us to change the properties of every single cell within an object.

## Acknowledgements

We want to thank David Lindlbauer, Pedro Lopes, Stefanie Müller, and Willi Müller for their help and feedback.

[1] https://github.com/schteppe/PathFinding3D.js

[2] https://embedded.eecs.berkeley.edu/pubs/downloads/espresso/index.htm

[3] http://pyeda.readthedocs.io/en/latest/index.html

## REFERENCES


1. Jeffrey K. Anderson, Larry L. Howell, Jonathan W. Wittwer, and Timothy W. McLain. 2006. Piezoresistive sensing of bistable micro mechanism state. *Journal of Micromechanics and Microengineering* 16.5 (2006): 943. http://dx.doi.org/10.1088/0960-1317/16/5/010
2. Moritz Bächer, Stelian Coros, and Bernhard Thomaszewski. 2015. LinkEdit: interactive linkage editing using symbolic kinematics *ACM Transactions on Graphics* 34, 4, Article 99 (July 2015), 8 pages. http://dx.doi.org/10.1145/2766985
3. Moritz Bächer, Emily Whiting, Bernd Bickel, and Olga Sorkine-Hornung. 2014. Spin-it: optimizing moment of inertia for spinnable objects. *ACM Transactions on Graphics* 33, 4. http://dx.doi.org/10.1145/2601097.2601157
4. Bernd Bickel, Moritz Bächer, Miguel A. Otaduy, Hyunho Richard Lee, Hanspeter Pfister, Markus Gross, and Wojciech Matusik. 2010. Design and fabrication of materials with desired deformation behavior. *ACM Transactions on Graphics* 29, 4, Article 63 (July 2010), 10 pages. http://dx.doi.org/10.1145/1778765.1778800
5. Marco Bucci, Luca Giancane, Raimondo Luzzi, and Alessandro Trifiletti. 2006. Three-phase dual-rail precharge logic. In *International Workshop on Cryptographic Hardware and Embedded Systems*, pp. 232-241. Springer Berlin Heidelberg, 2006.
6. Jacques Calì, Dan A. Calian, Cristina Amati, Rebecca Kleinberger, Anthony Steed, Jan Kautz, and Tim Weyrich. 2012. 3D-printing of non-assembly, articulated models. *ACM Transactions on Graphics* 31, 6, Article 130 (November 2012), 8 pages. http://dx.doi.org/10.1145/2366145.2366149
7. Xiang 'Anthony' Chen, Jeeeun Kim, Jennifer Mankoff, Tovi Grossman, Stelian Coros, and Scott E. Hudson. 2016. Reprise: A Design Tool for Specifying, Generating, and Customizing 3D Printable Adaptations on Everyday Objects. In *Proceedings of the 29th Annual Symposium on User Interface Software and Technology* (UIST '16). ACM, New York, NY, USA, 29-39. DOI: https://doi.org/10.1145/2984511.2984512
8. Juan Carlos Álvarez Elipe, and Andrés Díaz Lantada. 2012. Comparative study of auxetic geometries by means of computer-aided design and engineering. *Smart Materials and Structures* 21.10 (2012): 105004.
9. Daniel Groeger, Elena Chong Loo, and Jürgen Steimle. 2016. HotFlex: Post-print Customization of 3D Prints Using Embedded State Change. In *Proceedings of the SIGCHI Conference on Human Factors in Computing Systems* (CHI '16). ACM, New York, NY, USA, 420-432. DOI: https://doi.org/10.1145/2858036.2858191
10. Alexandra Ion, Johannes Frohnhofen, Ludwig Wall, Robert Kovacs, Mirela Alistar, Jack Lindsay, Pedro Lopes, Hsiang-Ting Chen, and Patrick Baudisch. 2016. Metamaterial Mechanisms. In *Proceedings of the annual ACM symposium on User interface software and technology* (UIST '16). ACM, New York, NY, USA, 529-539. DOI: https://doi.org/10.1145/2984511.2984540
11. Yuichiro Katsumoto, Satoru Tokuhisa, and Masa Inakage. 2013. Ninja track: design of electronic toy variable in shape and flexibility. In *Proceedings of the 7th International Conference on Tangible, Embedded and Embodied Interaction* (TEI '13). ACM, New York, NY, USA, 17-24. http://dx.doi.org/10.1145/2460625.2460628
12. Lin Lu, Andrei Sharf, Haisen Zhao, Yuan Wei, Qingnan Fan, Xuelin Chen, Yann Savoye, Changhe Tu, Daniel Cohen-Or, and Baoquan Chen. 2014. Build-to-last: strength to weight 3D printed objects. *ACM Transactions on Graphics* 33, 4. http://dx.doi.org/10.1145/2601097.2601168
13. Merkle, Ralph C. 1993. Two types of mechanical reversible logic. *Nanotechnology* 4.2 (1993): 114.
14. Stefanie Mueller, Tobias Mohr, Kerstin Guenther, Johannes Frohnhofen, and Patrick Baudisch. 2014. faBrickation: fast 3D printing of functional objects by integrating construction kit building blocks. In *Proceedings of the SIGCHI Conference on Human Factors in Computing Systems* (CHI '14). ACM, New York, NY, USA, 3827-3834. http://dx.doi.org/10.1145/2556288.2557005
15. Tom Mullin, S. Deschanel, Katia Bertoldi, and Mary C. Boyce. 2007. Pattern transformation triggered by deformation. *Physical review letters* 99, no. 8 (2007): 084301. http://dx.doi.org/10.1103/PhysRevLett.99.084301
16. Nadkarni, Neel, Chiara Daraio, and Dennis M. Kochmann. 2014. Dynamics of periodic mechanical structures containing bistable elastic elements: From elastic to solitary wave propagation. *Physical Review E* 90.2 (2014): 023204.
17. Julian Panetta, Qingnan Zhou, Luigi Malomo, Nico Pietroni, Paolo Cignoni, and Denis Zorin. 2015. Elastic textures for additive fabrication. *ACM Transactions on Graphics* 34, 4. http://dx.doi.org/10.1145/2766937
18. Jayson Paulose, Anne S. Meeussen, and Vincenzo Vitelli. 2015. Selective buckling via states of self-stress in topological metamaterials. In *Proceedings of the National Academy of Sciences*, 112(25), 7639-7644.
19. Huaishu Peng, François Guimbretière, James McCann, and Scott Hudson. 2016. A 3D Printer for Interactive Electromagnetic Devices. In *Proceedings of the 29th Annual Symposium on User Interface Software and Technology* (UIST '16). ACM, New York, NY, USA, 553-562. DOI: https://doi.org/10.1145/2984511.2984523

20. Romain Prévost, Emily Whiting, Sylvain Lefebvre, and Olga Sorkine-Hornung. 2013. Make it stand: balancing shapes for 3D fabrication. *ACM Transactions on Graphics* 32, 4. http://dx.doi.org/10.1145/2461912.2461957

21. Jin Qiu, Jeffrey H. Lang, and Alexander H. Slocum. 2004. A curved-beam bistable mechanism. *Journal of microelectromechanical systems* 13.2 (2004): 137-146.

22. Raf Ramakers, Fraser Anderson, Tovi Grossman, and George Fitzmaurice. 2016. RetroFab: A Design Tool for Retrofitting Physical Interfaces using Actuators, Sensors and 3D Printing. In *Proceedings of the SIGCHI Conference on Human Factors in Computing Systems* (CHI '16). ACM, New York, NY, USA, 409-419. DOI: https://doi.org/10.1145/2858036.2858485

23. Jordan R. Raney, Neel Nadkarni, Chiara Daraio, Dennis M. Kochmann, Jennifer A. Lewis, and Katia Bertoldi. 2016. Stable propagation of mechanical signals in soft media using stored elastic energy. In *Proceedings of the National Academy of Sciences* (2016): 201604838.

24. Greg Saul, Manfred Lau, Jun Mitani, and Takeo Igarashi. 2010. SketchChair: an all-in-one chair design system for end users. In *Proceedings of the fifth international conference on Tangible, embedded, and embodied interaction* (TEI '11). ACM, New York, NY, USA, 73-80. DOI: http://dx.doi.org/10.1145/1935701.1935717

25. Valkyrie Savage, Colin Chang, and Björn Hartmann. 2013. Sauron: embedded single-camera sensing of printed physical user interfaces. In *Proceedings of the 26th annual ACM symposium on User interface software and technology* (UIST '13). ACM, New York, NY, USA, 447-456. http://dx.doi.org/10.1145/2501988.2501992

26. Valkyrie Savage, Ryan Schmidt, Tovi Grossman, George Fitzmaurice, and Björn Hartmann. 2014. A series of tubes: adding interactivity to 3D prints using internal pipes. In *Proceedings of the 27th annual ACM symposium on User interface software and technology* (UIST '14). ACM, New York, NY, USA, 3-12. http://dx.doi.org/10.1145/2642918.2647374

27. Christian Schumacher, Bernd Bickel, Jan Rys, Steve Marschner, Chiara Daraio, and Markus Gross. 2015. Microstructures to control elasticity in 3D printing. *ACM Transactions on Graphics* 34, 4. http://dx.doi.org/10.1145/2766926

28. Three-state logic. https://en.wikipedia.org/wiki/Three-state_logic#Tri-state_Buffer Retrieved on September 21st, 2016

29. Tatyana Vasilevitsky and Amit Zoran. 2016. Steel-Sense: Integrating Machine Elements with Sensors by Additive Manufacturing. In *Proceedings of the SIGCHI Conference on Human Factors in Computing Systems* (CHI '16). ACM, New York, NY, USA, 5731-5742. http://dx.doi.org/10.1145/2858036.2858309

30. Kiril Vidimce, Alexandre Kaspar, Ye Wang, and Wojciech Matusik. 2016. Foundry: Hierarchical Material Design for Multi-Material Fabrication. In *Proceedings of the 29th Annual Symposium on User Interface Software and Technology* (UIST '16). ACM, New York, NY, USA, 563-574. DOI: https://doi.org/10.1145/2984511.2984516

31. Voxel8. http://www.voxel8.co/ Retrieved on September 21st, 2016

32. Christian Weichel, Manfred Lau, David Kim, Nicolas Villar, and Hans W. Gellersen. 2014. MixFab: a mixed-reality environment for personal fabrication. In *Proceedings of the SIGCHI Conference on Human Factors in Computing Systems* (CHI '14). ACM, New York, NY, USA, 3855-3864. http://dx.doi.org/10.1145/2556288.2557090

33. Karl Willis, Eric Brockmeyer, Scott Hudson, and Ivan Poupyrev. 2012. Printed optics: 3D printing of embedded optical elements for interactive devices. In *Proceedings of the 25th annual ACM symposium on User interface software and technology* (UIST '12). ACM, New York, NY, USA, 589-598. http://dx.doi.org/10.1145/2380116.2380190

# Organic Primitives: Synthesis and Design of pH-Reactive Materials using Molecular I/O for Sensing, Actuation, and Interaction

**Viirj Kan[1], Emma Vargo[1], Noa Machover[1], Hiroshi Ishii[1], Serena Pan[1], Weixuan Chen[1], Yasuaki Kakehi[1,2]**
[1]MIT Media Lab, Cambridge, USA [2]Keio University, Fujisawa, Japan
Viirj@media.mit.edu, {evargo, noamori}@mit.edu, ishii@media.mit.edu, pan27@mit.edu, cvx@media.mit.edu, ykakehi@sfc.keio.ac.jp

**Figure 1. Application prototypes and scenarios using *Organic Primitives*: (left to right) acid rain sensing umbrella; color changing cosmetics; saliva sensing toothbrush; apple as sensor and display; flavor augmenting utensil; flower tattoo; bionic fruit.**

## ABSTRACT

In this paper we present *Organic Primitives*, an enabling toolbox that expands upon the library of input-output devices in HCI and facilitates the design of interactions with organic, fluid-based systems. We formulated color, odor and shape changing material primitives which act as sensor-actuators that convert pH signals into human-readable outputs. Food-grade organic molecules anthocyanin, vanillin, and chitosan were employed as dopants to synthesize materials which output a spectrum of colors, degrees of shape deformation, and switch between odorous and non-odorous states. We evaluated the individual output properties of our sensor-actuators to assess the rate, range, and reversibility of the changes as a function of pH 2-10. We present a design space with techniques for enhancing the functionality of the material primitives, and offer passive and computational methods for controlling the material interfaces. Finally, we explore applications enabled by *Organic Primitives* under four contexts: environmental, cosmetic, edible, and interspecies.

### ACM Classification Keywords

H.5.m Information interfaces and presentation (e.g., HCI): Miscellaneous

### Author Keywords

Molecular Design Interactions; pH-reactive; edible materials; microfluidics; droplets; programmable food; chemical sensing; multi-modal output; color, odor, shape change


*CHI 2017, May 06 - 11, 2017, Denver, CO, USA*

ACM ISBN 978-1-4503-4655-9/17/05 ...$15.00.
DOI: http://dx.doi.org/10.1145/3025453.3025952

## INTRODUCTION

Whether it be the information embodied within the rain, the ocean, a dinner plate, or in human tears, the flow of information through fluids provides us a glimpse into the biological and chemical states of systems. A large part of our everyday experience with natural systems is inaccessible to HCI designers and engineers for user interaction design. The challenge of programming interactive experience within the realm of food, personal care, and other organic systems lies largely in the limitations of conventional tools in HCI, as they are incompatible with these soft, fluid-based systems. The dialects required to manipulate such systems are mediated by chemical codes, which control the most complex machine we know —life. In order to open up possibilities for interacting with organic systems in HCI, an accessible, biocompatible toolbox and design process is essential. This paper offers a set of combinable material-based sensor-actuators termed *Organic Primitives*, enabling non-Chemists to design for fluid inputs.

The toolbox consists of color, odor and shape changing material primitives that sense contents within fluids and convert them into sensory information. The material primitives can output a spectrum of colors, different degrees of shape deformation, and switch between odorous and non-odorous states based on pH value. The scope of this paper focuses on sensing pH in fluid as a starting point, with the goal of developing a model methodology for future sensor-actuator development. The motivation for this toolbox is to enable designers without extensive chemistry backgrounds to create a variety of multi-modal composites by simply selecting and combining responsivities of interest. The design of our toolbox addresses five key criteria: 1) Solid-State: liquid state pH-reactive phenomena of the molecules must be synthesized into solid state materials; 2) Flexibility: materials should have the ability to be synthesized into a range of form factors, without drastically differing in their fabrication processes; 3) Accessibility: they should be safe for handling, producible in a kitchen environment and utilize reagents that are easy to attain; 4) Human-Readable: output properties should be within receptive fields and thresholds of human perception; 5) Combinability: material primitives should be compatible with one another to yield multi-property inheritances. In this paper, we demonstrate how we address these criterias through the development of our material primitives.

The sensor-actuators were synthesized by doping select biopolymers with organic molecules which offer optimal flexibility for synthesis across a range of forms. Food-grade organic compounds anthocyanin, vanillin, and chitosan were employed as accessible dopants to formulate materials which output a spectrum of colors, degrees of shape deformation, and a switch between odorous and non-odorous states. Their molecular reaction to pH enables pH information to be both sensed and communicated to the user. We present methods for how we bring these liquid-state pH reaction mechanisms into solid-state material primitives in order to be used as sensor-actuators for HCI. We evaluated the individual output properties of our primitives within this toolbox to exhibit the human-readable rate, range, and reversibility of the changes as a function of pH 2 to 10. The activation and control section exhibits how computational systems can be integrated with the material primitives. We demonstrate the primitives are self-compatible and can be combined with one another to form multi-inherited property outputs in the Design Implications section. We showcase techniques for how the primitives can transcend beyond mere input-output devices to achieve higher order complexity in the Design Space. Finally, we present Molecular Design Interactions in four application contexts to demonstrate the possibilities enabled by this toolbox for human interaction with the environment, body, food and interspecies (figure 1).

## RELATED WORK

### Interfacing with Biological and Chemical systems

Biocompatible materials for sensing and actuation are becoming increasingly relevant for the HCI community with the rise of research towards soft, low power devices that operate close to and within the human body[20]. Recent developments like bionic contact lenses leverage information excreted from the body such as the composition of tears, for medical diagnosis [13]. Ingestible devices such as Google X's pill-based authentication use stomach acids to power the biodegradable device as a temporary key for unlocking devices [32]. These research contributions typically require a background in chemistry or biology. There have been efforts to increase accessibility of synthetic biology through standardized DNA building blocks called BioBricks and miniaturized lab equipment such as the Amino[33][24]. However, genetically engineering organisms for sensing and actuation currently remains difficult in practice, as methods are often irreproducible due to variability across organisms[36][4][17]. To advance the interests of HCI and facilitate human interaction with biological and chemical systems, an accessible toolbox of input-output devices can be achieved through molecules synthesized into material primitives.

### Molecules for Sensing and Actuation

The complexity of biomolecules makes detection using modern electronic chemical sensors a challenge. Researchers in chemical and biological engineering fields often rely on chemical mechanisms and reactions for sensing and analysis. Bicinchoninic acid assay is an analytical procedure utilizing molecules copper(II) sulfate pentahydrate and bicinchoninic acid to form reactions to determine the concentration of proteins in solution[37]. The physical nature of a compound's composition can lend itself to complex reactions, offering capabilities to sense and move based on physical property gradients. Water droplets mixed with food dye have exhibited sensing and motility behaviors, termed *artificial chemotaxis*, due to the relative evaporation rates and surface tension of two-component fluids. Researchers have exploited these properties to create autonomous fluidic machines [8]. While there has been little emphasis within these fields to develop input-output devices that cater to the interests of HCI for interface design, these molecular techniques for chemical sensing and analysis can be leveraged.

### Material-Mediated Interface Design

*"The most profound technologies are those that disappear. They weave themselves into the fabric of everyday life until they are indistinguishable from it." - Mark Weiser*[40]

Recent developments in HCI and robotics have sought to achieve seamless technological devices by incorporating sensing, information processing, and actuation within a unitary material[21] [27]. The development of wearable technologies that are compact, mobile, and conform to the body demonstrate a growing value in material and molecular-based interfaces [9] [25] [35] [39]. Researchers have investigated soft, compliant methods such as thin-film electronics in Unimorph, silicone rubber in the Harvard Soft Robotics Toolkit and bacterial spores in bioLogic to create compact interactions [19][1][45]. The notion of interfaces which can deliver color change [22], odor release [23] and shape transformation [30] have been individually explored. However, compact interfaces with sensing and multiple output functionality remains a challenge due to limited tools in HCI. *Organic Primitives* offers an adaptable, molecular scale method to facilitate HCI researchers in exploring such design possibilities.

## DESIGNING PH-REACTIVE MATERIAL PRIMITIVES

To enable user interaction with organic systems, we propose utilizing the sensing-actuation capabilities of food-grade flavor molecules and edible materials, by employing them as molecular I/O mechanisms to build input-output devices for HCI. These molecules are encountered daily in food, but their stimuli-responsive properties are generally overlooked. Such renewable sensor-actuators are inexpensive to produce, safe to ingest, and offer complex multi-modal capabilities. They can be used as independent material sensor-actuators or supplemented by integrating with traditional electronic devices.

pH value is an intrinsic attribute among all fluids and serves as an important indicator in a broad range of systems, from nanoscale microbial systems to planetary-scale marine ecosystems. For this reason, we begin our material sensor-actuator development with pH-reactive primitives. Chemically, pH is the measure of the acidity and alkalinity with the relative amount of free hydrogen and hydroxyl ions in a fluid. It is an important health indicator for many complex chemical and biological processes in, out, and on the human body, from food to personal care. pH also serves as a critical environmental indicator for processes such as ocean acidification and atmospheric contamination. Many organic molecules respond to pH, but only a subset of these are edible and yield human-readable changes like color, odor, shape, and taste. Our material-based sensor-actuators begin with the selection of dopants and biopolymer substrates. Within our approach, we utilize the Brønsted-Lowry acid-base reaction as a core driver of our material transformations due to the rapid, reversible, and bidirectional nature of the reaction. In this section, we introduce pH-reactive organic molecules anthocyanin, vanillin and chitosan as color, shape and odor changing dopants, along with kappa-carageenan and sodium alginate as biopolymer substrates for material synthesis.

## Molecular Dopant Selection

In this section, we discuss the chemistry of the pH-reactive compounds. These molecules were selected for their safety, accessibility, and biocompatibility, so researchers can develop their own pH-responsive material interfaces without special tools or facilities.

### *Anthocyanin: Color-Changing Reconfigurable Molecule*

All tissues of vascular plants contain the flavonoid anthocyanin, a pigment that changes color under varying pH solutions. In the 1664 book *Experiments and Considerations Touching Colours* by chemist Robert Boyle, various edible plants are reported as visual pH indicators due to pH-responsive mechanisms in their tissues [6]. Anthocyanin is commonly used as a food colorant in the food and beverage industry, and has been found to possess anti-inflammatory antioxidant properties[18]. It has also been researched for use as an indicator for packaging applications to detect spoilage in pork and fish products[46].

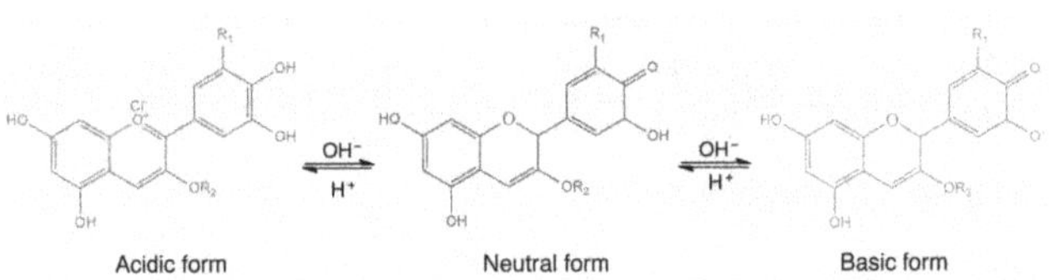


**Figure 2. Chemical diagram of color-changing anthocyanin pH reaction**

Under different pH conditions, the hydroxyl (OH) and/or methyl ether (O-$CH_3$) groups attached to the carbon rings (figure 2) undergo reversible structural transformations and ionizations. Restructuring a molecule changes the way it absorbs light, giving rise to color changes [3] [31].

### *Vanillin: Odor-Switching Flavor Molecule*

Vanillin is a flavor molecule found in vanilla beans, contributing to their characteristic aroma. The smell of vanillin has been found to elicit feelings of relaxation [38], offering potential uses for interface design. The effect of pH on vanillin stability was first characterized by food scientists in the early 1970s [42]. In 1990, Flair and Setzer determined vanillin could be used as an olfactory titration indicator for blind students [15]. Vanillin is prevalent as a flavoring for food products such as chocolate and ice-cream[5].

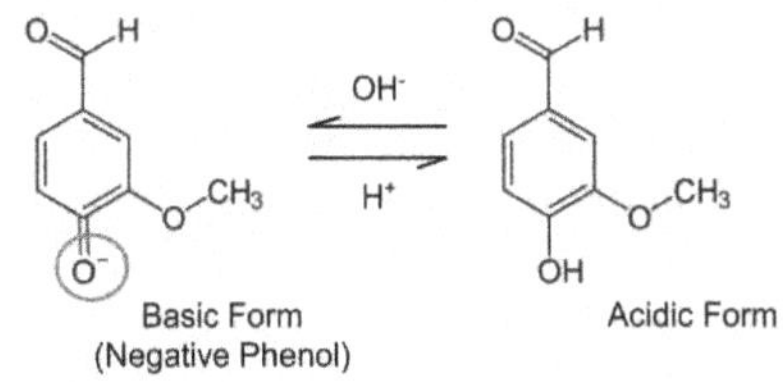


**Figure 3. Chemical diagram of vanillin pH reaction**

The smell of vanillin is elicited at pH 2-8 and suppressed at pH 9 and 10. We hypothesize that the elimination of odor at high pH is due to vanillin's phenol group pKa value of 7.38, such that it becomes negatively charged, and therefore less volatile, under basic conditions (figure 3) [10].

### *Chitosan: Swelling and Shape-Memory Macromolecule*

Chitosan is a polysaccharide derived from the exoskeletons of shrimp and crustaceans, widely studied due to its abundant and biocompatible nature [12] [29] [16]. The pH-responsive swelling of chitosan hydrogels was first characterized in publications from the 1980s [44]. It has been researched for drug delivery applications, such as to target tumor tissues through the release of drugs at specific pH[2]. The tunability and shape memory characteristics of chitosan have been studied in tissue engineering to create scaffolds with impregnated bioactive agents for guiding cellular growth towards generation of new tissue[26].

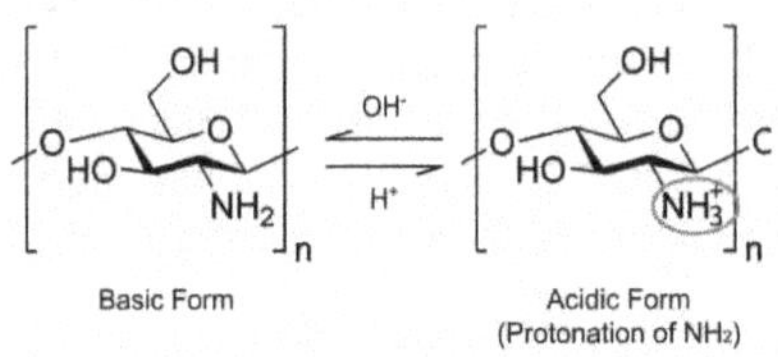


**Figure 4. Chemical diagram of chitosan pH reaction**

Illustrated in figure 4, its $NH_2$ amino functional group is protonated in low pH conditions, causing the polymer to swell due to charge repulsion; if the pH becomes high, chitosan returns to its collapsed state.

## Material Synthesis

In order to utilize the pH-reactive properties of the molecules, the chemical phenomenon must be materialized from a liquid into a solid state. We have found sodium alginate and kappa-carrageenan to be good biopolymer substrates for the pH-responsive molecules due to their semi-permeable structures, consistent behavior, rapid diffusion rates, and relatively neutral pH. Primitive subsets with different range, rate and reversibility of change can be generated by tuning synthesis parameters such as cross-linkers, co-polymers and concentrations. Kappa-carrageenan was used as the base material for our anthocyanin color-changing films. Electrostatic interactions between the two molecules allow them to create a stable compound; kappa-carrageenan is an anionic polysaccharide, while anthocyanin is cationic[14]. To synthesize an odor-changing film, vanillin was encapsulated in an alginate gel to form our scent-changing solution. Sodium alginate was cross-linked with calcium sulfate right before mixing, creating a tangled matrix to hold the vanillin molecules. Chitosan is a structural material and does not require a matrix. We synthesized shape-changing films by dissolving dried chitosan powder in 3% acetic acid and drying it in sheets. Higher concentrations of chitosan result in thicker, stiffer sheets. Concentrations of the three materials and dopants should be tuned for the application; an example composition of each material is given in the next section.

## OUTPUT CHARACTERIZATION

In order to evaluate the human-readability and assess the design parameters of our color, odor and shape changing sensor-actuators, we characterized each primitive's range, rate and reversibility as a function of pH value. pH solutions were made using food-grade materials to ensure safety and accessibility: citric acid ($H_3Cit$), an acid derived from citrus fruits; sodium citrate (NaHCitrate), a common food additive; sodium bicarbonate (NaHCO), also known as baking soda; sodium hydroxide (NaOH) or lye, commonly used for food preparation; and deionized water ($H_2O$). The concentrations we used comply with the Federal Food and Drug Administration's (FDA) Generally Recognized as Safe (GRAS) listing. The solutions were tested and verified using the Oakton pH5+ EW-35613-52 pH meter, as well as pHydrion litmus strips.

### Color as a Function of pH

Our color-changing samples were prepared using 1.5%w/v kappa-carrageenan in deionized water doped with 0.1% w/v anthocyanin, purchased from Modernist Pantry and Enasco respectively. We tested samples with our pH 2-10 solutions. The samples were sprayed uniformly with pH solution, allowed to dry, and an X-Rite CMUNPH spectrophotometer was used to find a CIE L*a*b* color value for each sample.

*Range and Spectrum of Color Change*

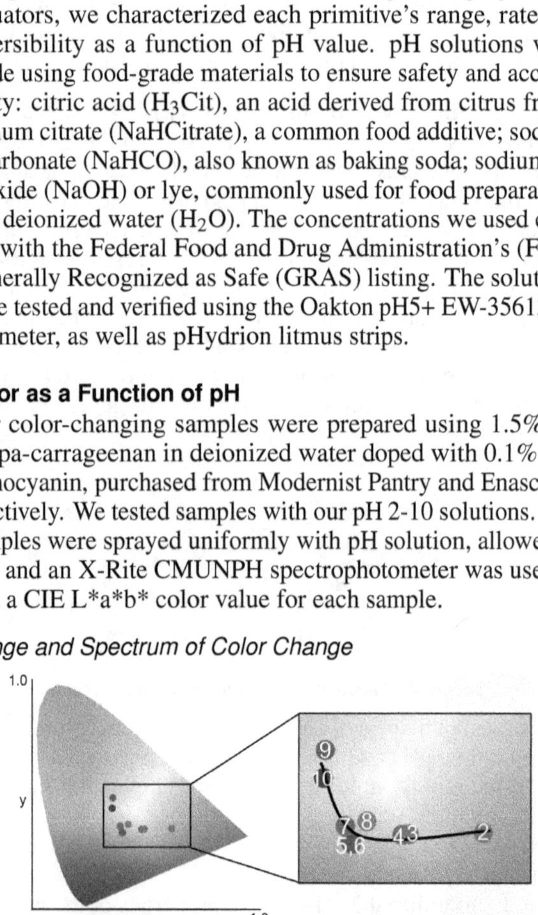


**Figure 5. CIE L*A*B* color space of color change ranges of Organic Primitive sample made with 1.5%w/v kappa-carrageenan doped with 0.1%w/v anthocyanin.**

Depending on pH, the sample color ranges from redder tones to green (figure 5). Materializing anthocyanin into a solid-state film with our selected biopolymer does not negatively affect its responsiveness.

*Rate of Color Change*

The speed of the color change was determined by filming the color primitives and applying pH 2-10. The results were qualitatively assessed as it is difficult to define specific start and stop times. Color noticeably begins to change within 11 milliseconds after solution is applied. They reached their final color between 50 to 90 seconds. Acidic pH's 2-4 are appear to be more rapid than 7-10. pH 5 and 6 were the slowest amongst all the samples. This is consistent with the different ion concentrations in the test solutions.

*Reversibility of Color Change*

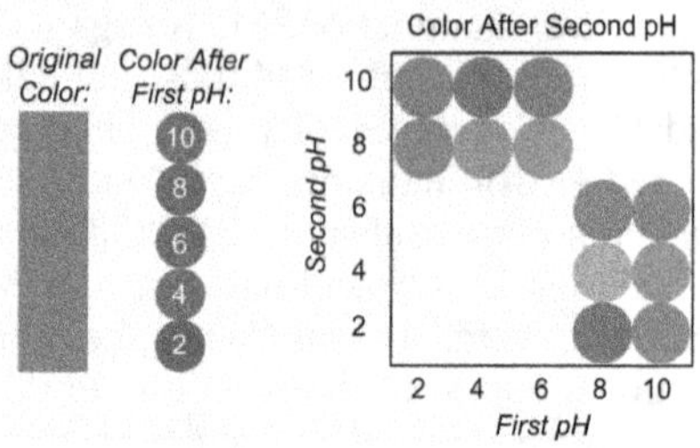


**Figure 6. The reversible effects of layering pH.**

In this study, the samples were sprayed with the first pH solution, given an hour to equilibrate and then documented. The dry sample was then sprayed with the second pH solution. After an hour, RGB values were extracted from digital photographs taken under a lighting hood. Results from figure 6 show that only certain pH responses can be reversed. This is due to the constraints of the substrate biopolymer contained in this primitive, as anthocyanin color changes in fluid are entirely reversible reactions. We hypothesize that this incomplete reversibility is due to slower diffusion rates in solid materials and buffering effects of the polymer.

### Odor as a function of pH

Our odor-changing samples were prepared by dissolving 1 g vanillin (Sigma Aldrich) in 10 mL 200-proof alcohol to create a vanillin stock solution. We then made a solution of 0.12% v/v vanillin stock and 1.5% w/v sodium alginate in deionized water. Immediately before pouring, the sodium alginate was cross-linked by adding 15 parts calcium sulfate to 100 parts vanillin-sodium alginate solution. Samples were tested with the same pH 2-10 solutions as previous trials. To evaluate the human perception of our odor-changing films, we conducted a user study with 14 subjects, 4 male and 10 female. We had participants rearrange nine 1" x 1" samples of pH-activated odor material from pH 2-10, based on odor intensity.

*Range of Odor Strengths*

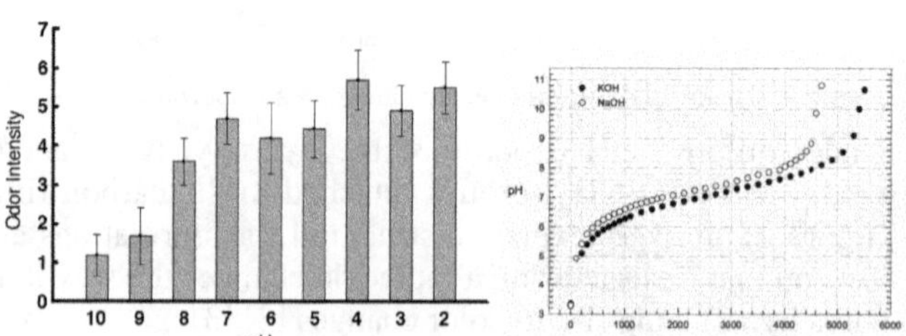


**Figure 7. Odor rearrangement results (left) where error bar represents standard error. Titration curve (right) by Frenkel, showing vanillin molecule response to pH.**

In figure 7, our results show that users can clearly distinguish the on-off switching behavior of the odor material based on pH. pH 9 and 10 were ranked as odors with no smell or low intensity, whereas samples with low pH generated a stronger odor perception. The user's sample arrangements for odor intensity correlated with Frenkel's titration curve and response of vanillin molecule to pH [7].

*Rate of Odor Change*

Two independent researchers qualitatively assessed the rates of odor change using a timer. Vanillin films as prepared above were cut into nine 1" x 1" samples and 640uL of each pH solution 2-10 were applied to a film. pH 2-8 exhibited a sweet odor released within 1-5 seconds of depositing solution. After 30 or more seconds, the odor intensified over the course of hours and maintained its smell after dried. With pH 9-10, approximately 30 seconds after a pH solution is deposited, users were able to establish that the material had no smell. Within the first 30 seconds, the material possessed a faint vanillin smell. Our preliminary study exhibits that each applied pH results in a different time-intensity relationship. This phenomena will be better examined in future studies, using olfactometry test methods as defined by the American Society of Testing and Materials ASTM E679 and E544 [28] and quantitative analysis with headspace gas chromatography.

*Reversibility of Odor Change*

Based on qualitative assessments, we found that our odor materials could be activated from a low pH (smell on) to a high pH (smell off). However, after a high pH change, the material was unable to reactivate in its smell. We hypothesize that due to the low concentration of vanillin in our materials, each time it is activated by pH solution the odor molecules are consumed by evaporation into the air.

### Shape as a Function of pH

Chitosan samples were prepared with 4% w/v chitosan powder (Spectrum) dissolved in 3% v/v acetic acid (Sigma Aldrich). After drying, the film was cut into 20 x 7.5 mm strips, and tested using pH solutions of 2, 4, 6, 8, and 10. For each pH, five 0.75 uL droplets of the pH solution were applied across the sample's 7.5 mm centerline with a micropipette, forming a hinge. The sample bent along this line over a period of approximately 10 minutes. Samples were filmed and a still image for each sample was taken from the footage 4, 7, and 10 minutes after the droplets were applied. The software ImageJ was used to quantify the bend angle of the hinge. Results are the average of two identical trials.

*Range of Angle Change*

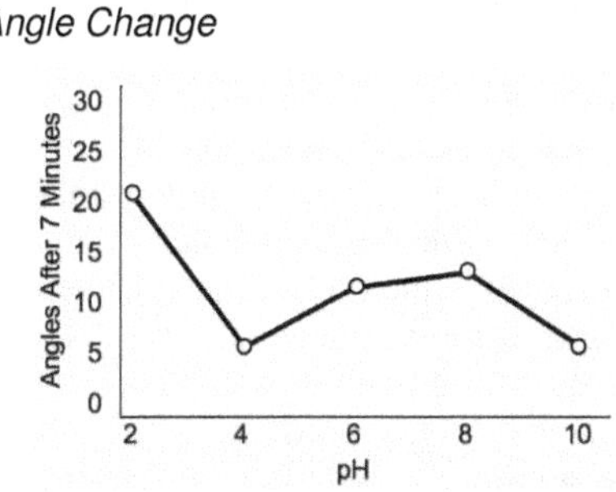


**Figure 8. Angle change 7 minutes after droplets are applied to a 4% w/v chitosan film. The bimodal trend matches literature results [ 6].**

Our results as shown in figure 8 reveal a bimodal relationship between bend angle and pH within the range of pH 2-10. Mahdavinia et al. found a similar relationship in their study, with swelling maxima at pH 3 and 8. Decreased swelling at middle pHs may be attributed to cross-linking [ 6].

*Rate of Angle Change*

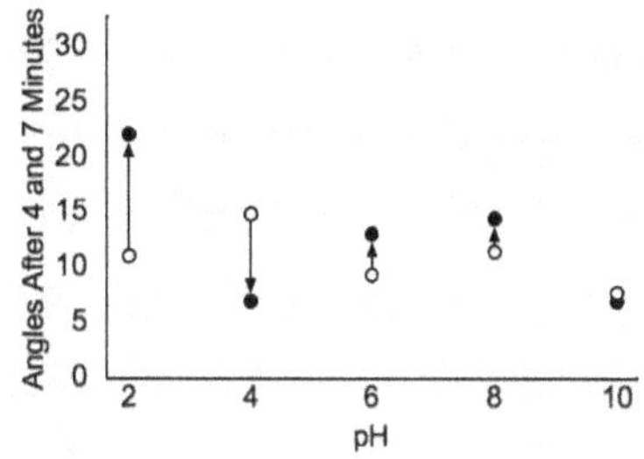


**Figure 9. Changes in bend angle for 4% w/v chitosan films between 4 and 7 minutes after pH solution is added. Upward arrows indicate an increase in bend angle.**

Regarding time evolution, the two pHs corresponding to angle minima, 4 and 10, decreased in angle between 4 and 7 minute measurements (figure 9). The other pH solutions had an increase in angle. It may be that interaction with any solution causes the chitosan to swell approximately the same amount, and then after some time the swelling becomes pH-dependent.

*Reversibility of Angle Change*

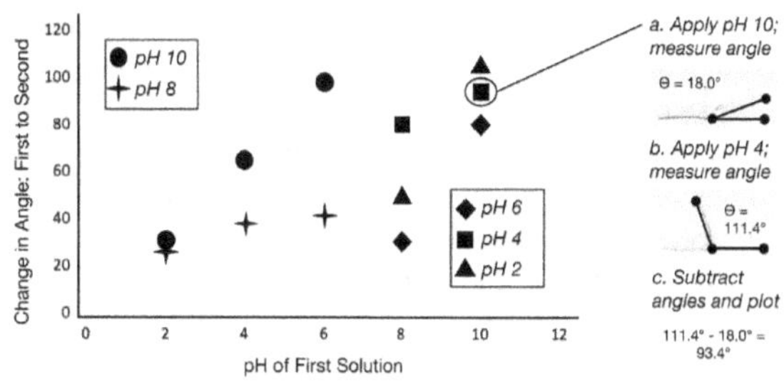


**Figure 10. Reversibility graph of layering different solutions.**

For this study, five 0.75 uL drops of the first pH solution were applied across the center of the sample. The film was given an hour to reach its final angle, measured with ImageJ (a). After the hour, droplets were applied again with a second pH solution on top of the first solution(b). Figure 10 shows that the more the second solution differs in strength from the first, the greater the change in angle is going to be. This preliminary study is promising for shape reversibility, as the bend angle of the film can be predictably manipulated by applying high and low pH solutions on the same material.

### ACTIVATION AND CONTROL

Material activation generally fall into one of three categories of control—global, local or discrete, as shown in image a, b, and c of figure 11. As shown in figure 11, global control utilizing atomizers and nozzles can activate a large area of the material. Local control can be developed by fabricating pipes and channels into the material. Discrete control can be implemented by designing specified outlets in fluidic circuits. Computational control can enable temporal control of a primitive's output by sequentially defining specific pH values deposited.

### Coupling and Decoupling pH Inputs and Outputs

Fluid inputs from natural contexts as well as fabricated solutions can be used to activate material outputs. Natural inputs

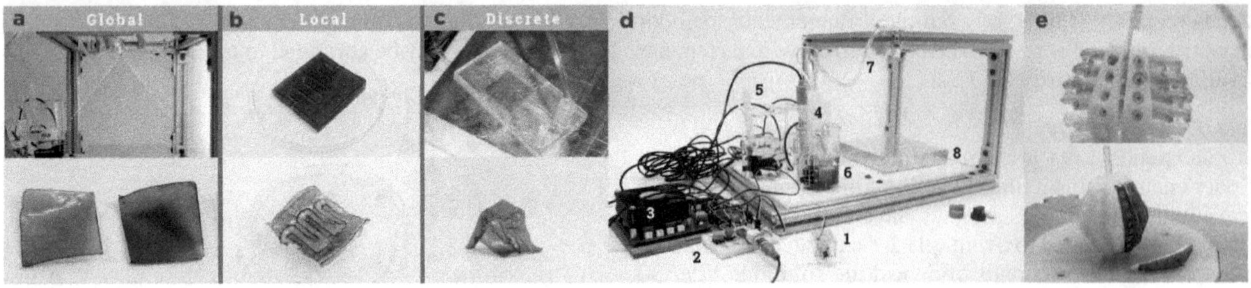


**Figure 11. Techniques for activation and control of the material primitives: a) Global activation involves pH solution sprayed onto the entirety of a material in an instance b) Local activation actuates a stream of solution in a channel c) Discrete activation triggers a single droplet in a precise position to actuate d) Hydraulic system for global and sequential activation e) Bionic fruit device deposits material primitives for use as edible films.**

include rain drops, ocean water, body fluids, food sources, and organismic excretions from plants and microbes. Fabricated inputs using prepared acid-base solutions can offer designers a wider output range while yielding more precise outputs. Fabricated pH solutions can be integrated with mechanical and electronic systems to develop machine-mediated inputs, as shown in image d of figure 11.

### Computational Activation

While it is not required in order to achieve an input-output response, electromechanical systems can be integrated for activation (figure 11-d) or deposition(e). The apparatus in image d is a platform which computationally generates a desired pH solution for global activation of an *Organic Primitive* as shown in image a. It can be used to control the outputs in a particular sequence, to enable the material to animate and perform a series of behaviors, similar to figure 15. It possesses 2 reservoirs of solution - pH 2 and pH 10, and outputs any desired pH these values. Using a series of hydraulic pumps and a pH sensor to complete the closed loop control of the system, we can continually adjust the pH value as we measure with a digital pH meter. A microcontroller with a potentiometer enables a user to select the desired pH by rotating the knob(d-4), initiating the pumps to draw fluids from pH 2 and pH 10 reservoirs(d-5) into a microfluidic mixer(d-4). Once the desired pH value is reached, the user can deposit the pH solution through the nozzle (d-7) to activate a material on the platform (d-8). The nozzles we used were adopted from off-the-shelf spray paint tops, offering a low-cost and versatile device. For deposition, image e shows a bionic fruit which deposits primitives on the surface of a 3D printed fruit for user interaction. Further elaboration is in figure 26.

Local activation (image b of figure 11) is created by casting hollow channels with the material primitives. A number of fluidic logic can be implemented to transcend the capabilities of the primitives from mere sensor-actuators, as illustrated in figure 18 and 19. Discrete activation (image c of figure 11) can be achieved by adapting our apparatus in image d to connect to a microfluidic device instead of the nozzle. The microfluidic device was fabricated from acrylic with a lasercutter to achieve 600 micron channels. It contains outlets which deposit pH solution to the material in small droplets. By depositing discrete droplets of pH solution onto a shape-color changing material, it can output a complex structure, as shown in image C of figure 11.

## DESIGN IMPLICATIONS

A limitation in these pH-reactive primitives is that they require liquid to be actuated. This presents novel design constraints, such as the ability to utilize natural inputs like rain water or prepared fluid inputs that are computationally activated. For a particular color, shape and odor state to be actuated, inputs are coupled with a pH value. Researchers should specify whether they would like coupled input-outputs such as use of natural input of saliva at pH 6, or decoupled input-outputs where prepared pH solutions generate output designs where input value can be arbitrary. Utilizing natural inputs at pH 6 to output property ranges that do not correspond to their specific value is possible, but requires researchers to develop new composite structures with the primitives to support this. Currently, the material primitives offer a range of color outputs, shape deformations and states in odor strengths but does not compute. Researchers can utilize the Design Space to integrate fluidic logic with the material primitives, for creating nonlinear feedback loops for computation.

### Multi-Property Outputs

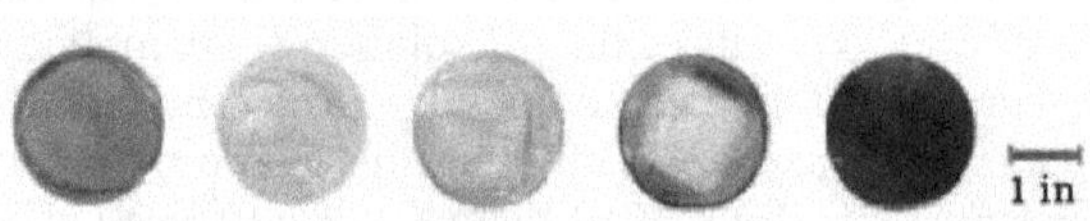


**Figure 12. Composites with optimal performance (left to right): layering of color-on-odor; the paneling of shape-in-odor, odor-in-shape, odor-in-color; and the mixing of color-odor.**

In order to produce multi-property outputs within a single material, we have systematically evaluated the combinability of the three primitives. We have classified three ways the material primitives can be composited: they can be mixed into a homogeneous solution before pouring, layered on top of each other, or synthesized side-by-side so that only the edges mix. We have tested the full combinatory range of composites made with these three methods. Figure 12 depicts the various combinations of primitive composites we determined perform most optimally. A composite was considered successful if it was (i) reactive as intended, (ii) structurally sound, and (iii) reactive within a human-perceptible timescale. These materials exhibit different behaviors when patterned by way of layering, paneling, or mixing the *Organic Primitives* together in various combinations.

### Output Design Parameters

Designers working with the shape primitive must consider its bimodal pH response. Activating the material with pH 2 will create the most pronounced shape change, while pHs 4 and 10 give more subtle changes. If rate of change is a consideration, more basic pHs result in faster equilibration. The scent-changing material gives a maximum scent response when activated with pH 4, and the scent can be suppressed with pHs 9 or 10. Using pHs greater than 9 to activate the material creates a range of intensities, though perception of these intensities vary between different users. Of the three primitives, the color-changing material had the most linear pH response. pH 2 creates a vivid and instantaneous response. However, the response to very acidic or basic pHs cannot be reversed. If the desired application requires changing color repeatedly, pHs closer to neutral (ie. 6 and 8) should be used.

### Form Factors

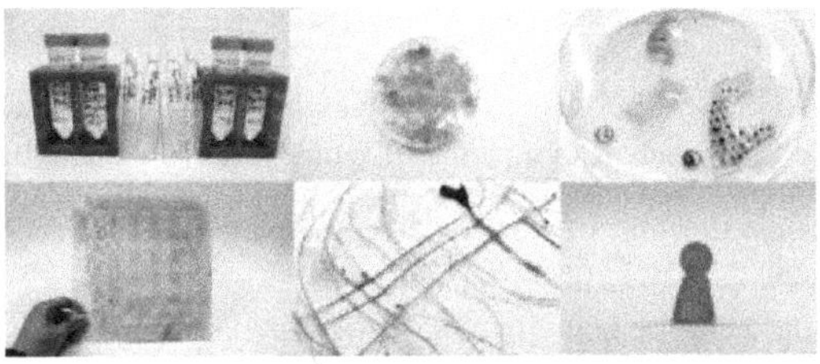

**Figure 13. (left to right clockwise) liquid based *Organic Primitives*; odor-color changing gel; color-shape changing films; color changing 3D form; odor-color changing fiber; odor-color-shape changing sheets.**

The biopolymer substrates selected for developing the material primitives allows designers to create a range of forms without a drastic alteration in processing techniques. These include fibers, films, sheets, liquids, gels, and solids, as shown in figure 13. pH-reactive color-odor fiber was fabricated using a syringe tube to extrude a formulation of anthocyanin and vanillin within sodium alginate into a calcium chloride solution. The resulting polymer fiber was ionically cross-linked. Thin color-shape changing films and color-odor-shape changing sheets were synthesized by drop-casting molecule-biopolymer solutions atop a sheet of sanded aluminum under a fan. Solid 3D and 2.5D dimensional forms can be made by casting and molding from acrylate or other materials. Primitive subsets can yield diverse properties by creating co-polymers with agar, pectin, gelatin, and other polymers.

## DESIGN SPACE FOR ORGANIC PRIMITIVES

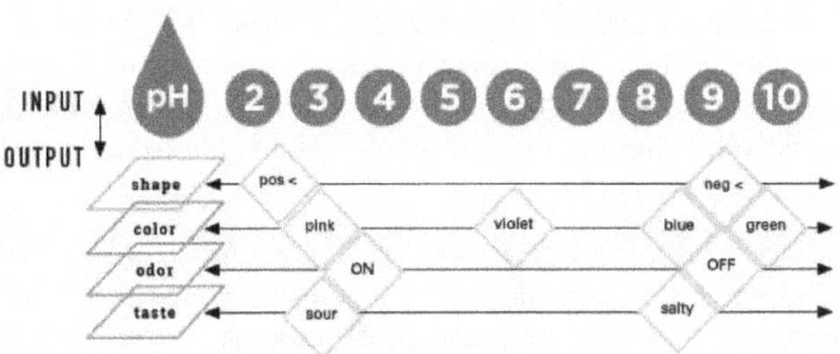


**Figure 14. Diagram of pH inputs and outputs from pH 2 - 10.**

Here, we showcase examples and techniques for developing more complex systems using the output properties enabled by *Organic Primitives*, as shown in figure 14.

### Animating Properties though Temporal Sequencing

Sequential and temporal depositions of pH solutions can yield capabilities for physically animating a material's output for color, shape, odor or combinatory changes.

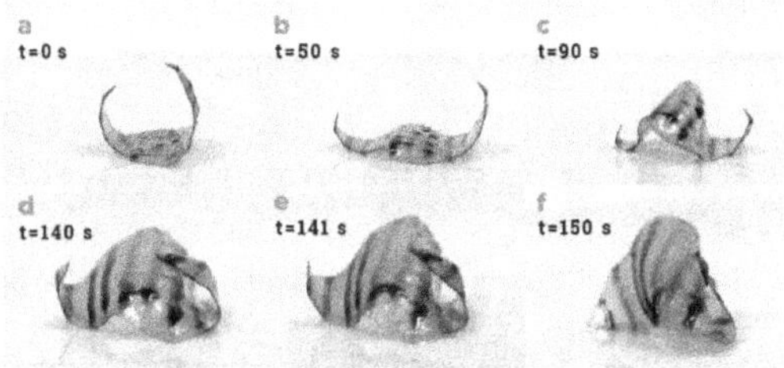


**Figure 15. Patterned shape changing primitive activated through temporal sequencing of different pH solutions. Top row was globally activated at pH 8 and bottom row at pH 2.**

Beyond sequential and temporal methods, form factor can also enable specific animation capabilities through relative diffusion rates of non-uniform thickness distributions, as shown in figure 16 and figure 15.

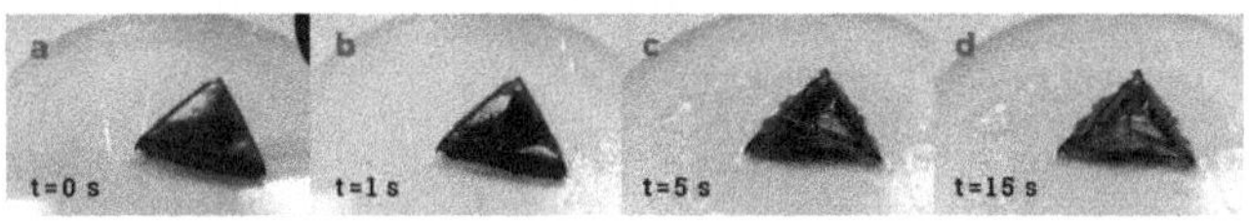


**Figure 16. Response of color-odor material molded into triangular 2.5D form to pH 2 solution.**

### Encoding Behavior through Patterning

We describe how multi-property outputs can be achieved through composites and patterning techniques through several examples we have implemented.

#### *Patterning with Multiple Organic Primitives*

Figure 17 shows a patterned odor-color primitive utilizing hydrophobic fluids such as olive oil for masking particular areas, enabling a globally activated material to possess discrete output patterns. This process termed *cloaking*, can be used to encode hidden information with multiple output properties.

**Figure 17. Example of cloaking and disguising information through patterned Odor-Color Organic Primitive.**

#### *Patterning with liquid dopants & pH Solution*

Depending upon how a material is synthesized, fabricated and patterned, activation methods can be interchanged. Instead of using pH solutions as an input to activate the material property changes, they can also be used to pattern and spatially define responsive regions in the material. Figure 15 illustrates how by patterning a shape changing primitive with liquid dopant at pH 10, we can achieve a color-shape changing material.

### Fluidic Logic

Integrating fluidics with *Organic Primitives* can enable information processing and activation through passive flow or digital control [34] [41] [43]. In this section we highlight different approaches for activation, as shown in figure 11, where different geometry is used to activate and create time-telling and titration devices.

### *Ticker for Time-telling*

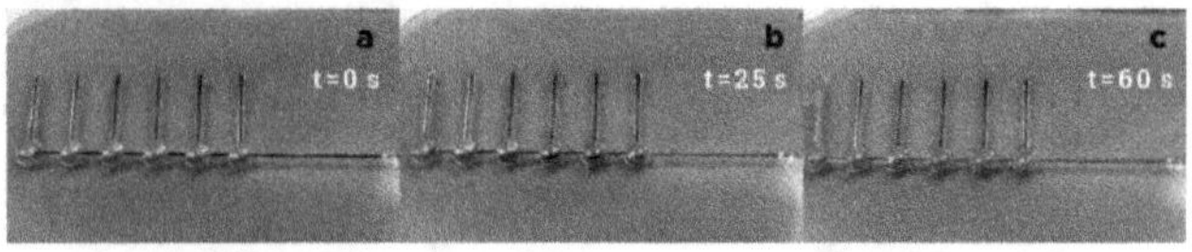


**Figure 18. Passive diffusion based time-telling device color-odor material composite.**

Through diffusion rates of Organic Primitives with pH solutions, we developed a material-based "clock" (figure 18) which changes color to mark specific time increments. The time duration can be tuned by changing the shape, length, or diameter of the channels.

### *Gradiator for Titrations*

**Figure 19. Fluidic channels molded then flowed through with pH 2 and pH 10 as inputs to generate a titrated gradient.**

Gradiators (figure 19) can be used to titrate solutions by inputting two values, such as pH 2 and pH 10, to create a material with equal values between the endpoints. This can be used to create arrays of flavor, intensities of color, and/or odor strengths.

## APPLICATIONS

Utilizing *Organic Primitives*, we explore molecular design interactions with edibles, cosmetics, environments, and interspecies. The applications shown in this section are working prototypes which illustrate the capabilities of the *Organic Primitives* toolbox. However, in order for them to be functional in the wild, further evaluation will be required. The prototypes were constructed by tuning the concentrations of the sensor-actuators and integrating specific additives.

### *Hacking Materiality of Objects*

The information displayed on interfaces about our bodies, food, environment, and organisms are often divorced from the actual systems themselves. By utilizing pre-existing objects as sensor-actuator platforms, we can take advantage of the contextual information they embody and design new relationships with the systems they represent. Figure 20 in the applications section shows an example of how *Organic Primitives* can enable an additional layer of information on objects, transforming an ordinary objects to encode meaning beyond its initial function.

### *Sensory Augmentation*

An everyday object can gain significant expressiveness if given the ability to share information about itself through its materiality. The material primitives can be used for sensory augmentations through odor, color, shape, and taste change, where novel outputs can be encoded into every day objects. Figure 21 highlights how odor-changing utensils can be used to simulate a sweet perception of food, without sugar added.

## Edible

The pH of food varies across a range of pH 2-8. For example soda has a pH of around 2.5 and many fermented foods such as pickles and cheese, range between pH 3-6. Milk and vegetables are more alkaline and range from 6-8. Oral supplements can range from pH 2-10, with vitamin C oral supplement being pH 2.4 and milk of magnesia at pH 10.5. In this section, we explore food-based experiences through the use of *Organic Primitives*.

### *Apple Sensor-Display*

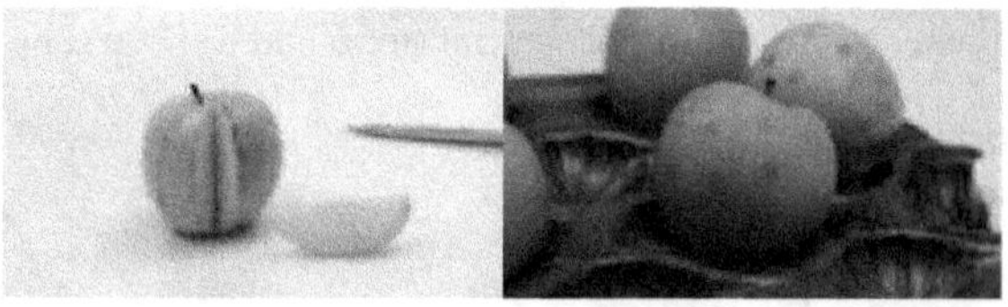

**Figure 20. Prototype of a patterned edible film coated onto the surface of an apple transforming into a sensor-display. (left) Apple displaying marks showing kids where to cut. (right) Spotted patterns communicate contaminated fruit.**

An apple can be transformed into a display by patterning color primitives tuned with methylcellulose MethocelF50 deposited onto edible starch paper. When a user washes the apple, it can display information about itself such as - where to cut for kids; recipe information (ie. required apples for pie); and more advanced application for sensing environmental contaminants during transport for food safety, as illustrated in figure 20.

### *Biodegradable Smart Utensils*

**Figure 21. Prototype of utensils at varying levels of degradability. (right) Fully edible and biodegradble utensil. (left) Before and after image of dip-coated, 3D-printed fluidic utensil.**

We explored multiple methods of creating responsive utensils at different levels of degradability, as shown in figure 21. The first is a fully biodegradable utensil using odor-color changing material primitives that serve to augment the taste and smell of food by releasing a sweet smell instead of adding sugar. The second utensil is partially degradable, where the primitive was dip-coated onto the prong end of a 3D-printed utensil with embedded fluidic channels. The fluidic channels serve as a passive time telling mechanism for pacing the food intake for a user, by changing color.

### *Shape Programmable Pasta*

Chitosan biopolymer derived from crustacean shells have been explored as dietary fiber and edible coating the food industry [11]. In figure 22, we prototype a dynamic food which enables chefs to alter shape of the pasta to enable different levels of flavor retention and sensory augmentation in pasta. The shape-changing pasta was made through patterning specific areas to define shape deformations. Other form factors for dynamic food can be used as on-plate communication and embellishments to incorporate condiments as input for simultaneous control of flavor, texture, and appearance. While not implemented in this example, we envision dynamic foods which can change based on user preferences and dietary constraints.

**Figure 22. Prototype of dynamic food that alters in shape based on pH of associated sauces.**

## Body Care and Cosmetics

### *Expressive Cosmetic Display*

Figure 23 exhibits how our molecular sensor-actuators can be used as components for cosmetic applications, by integrating primitives for dynamic makeup or for leverage pH data exerted from human body fluids.

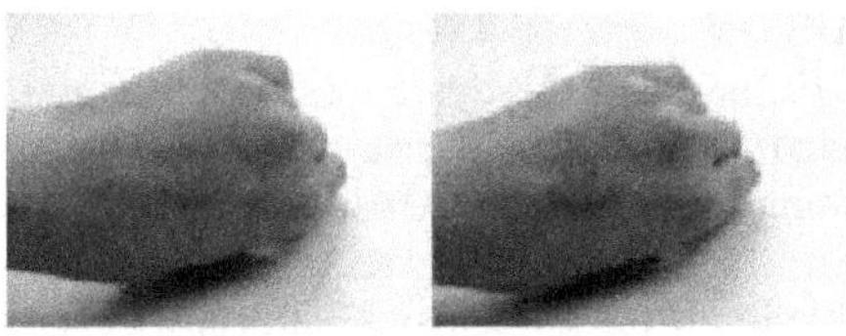

**Figure 23. Interaction prototype of cosmetics displaying hidden information by tuning color-odor primitive with vegetable glycerin.**

Depending upon the area, which they determine to be applied, the material can sense and output based on natural inputs defined by creation of body fluid. For example, applied under the eye directs sensing of tears to change color of eye-makeup. Applied throughout the back can implicate sensing of lactic acid in sweat produced by skin microflora to activate an odor release. Personal care products can also be used as inputs for designing interactions activated by household chemicals such as soaps, typically spanning between pH 8-12. Cosmetics have typically been used to accentuate facial features and communicate character. Dynamic cosmetics can be used to alter human appearances for theater and performance since character progressions tend to change rapidly. Further investigation is needed to bring this into fruition.

### *Saliva sensing for oral health*

**Figure 24. Toothbrush with modular, interchangeable *Organic Primitive* bristles.**

pH is an important factor for maintaining oral health as certain bacteria contribute to fluctuations. Prolonged periods of acidic oral environment leads to cavities. The oral environment of the mouth maintains an average of pH 6 in the mouth. Figure 24 is an illustrative example of material primitives integrated to create a responsive toothbrush where the bristles can sense and survey the pH of a user's oral environment.

## Interspecies

Plants, microbes, insects and animals utilize chemical signals for communication. In this section, we explore interactions with other species with pH-reactive *Organic Primitives*.

### *Augmenting Plant Aesthetics & Fragrance*

Gardens of flowers are often used to enhance the aesthetic environment. Gardeners often monitor and alter the pH of plants to manipulate the way they grow.

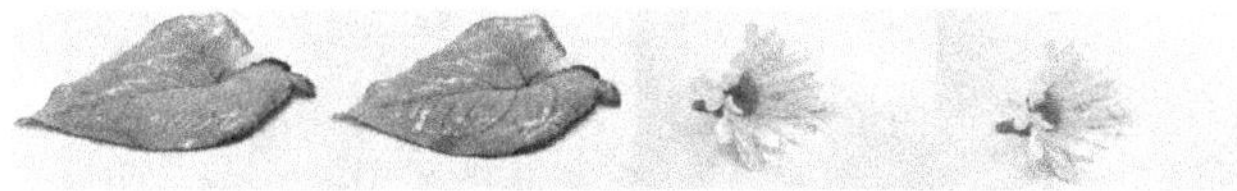

**Figure 25. Odor-color changing *Organic Primitives* coated on the surfaces of leaves (top row) and flower pedals (bottom row).**

Figure 25 shows an implementation of color and smell-changing leaves and flowers. These can be used for household decor, fostering human-plant and human-microbial interactions when users water the plant using different pH solutions.

### *Bionic Fruit for Fermentation*

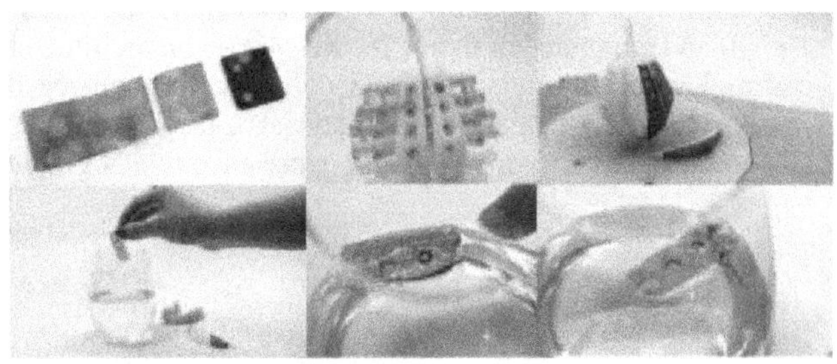

**Figure 26. Prototype of Fructus, a bionic fruit with a fluidic 3D printed core which electromechanically deposits edible pH-reactive sensor-actuators onto its surface.**

Fructus is a bionic fruit prototype which generates skins of dynamic edible films, pictured in figure 26. A microcontroller with syringes of the three primitives are set in the table below. The device deposits the materials into the 3D printed fluidic core of the bionic fruit, through a syringe pump mechanism driven by a stepper motor. The outlet of the fluidics draws the materials to coat the surfaces of the "fruit" slices. When dried, users can peel off to use as condiment, flavoring, embellishment, or integrate in non-food applications. Future work can offer these as tools for chefs to communicate to their guests by remotely triggering Fructus to synthesize different flavors, textures, and tastes in the form of dynamic edible films.

## Environment

In natural systems, chemical exchanges represent the communication pathways between micro- and macro-scale ecosystems. On a macro scale, pH values can be an indicator of environmental issues from ocean acidification to acid rain. In this section, we explore how to enable users to form more engaged relationships with the environment by using rain as an input and carrier of environmental information for sensory augmentation and display.

### *Bleeding Umbrella*

Fossil fuel combustion from automobile and industrial manufacturing generates emissions of sulfur dioxide and nitrogen oxide which contribute to rainfall acidity and environmental pollution. We developed a bleeding umbrella prototype shown in figure (figure 27), using *Organic Primitives* to sense the rain and display red streaks on the surface "as if the sky was bleeding", in the presence of acid rain. This provides the user with visceral information from the sky, creating a contextual connection between the contents of rain water and environmental contaminants.

**Figure 27. Before and after image of umbrella utilizing *Organic Primitives* for acid rain sensing and display.**

### *Architectural Material to Augment Smell of the Rain*

The smell of rain on a rural landscape is often romanticized by poets and artists. Within an urban environment, the smell of the rain is a byproduct of hydration of materials such as asphalt and concrete. In figure 28, we created an architectural material which outputs odor and color by augmenting the smell of different places. These materials can give architects an additional sensory medium and experience to design with.

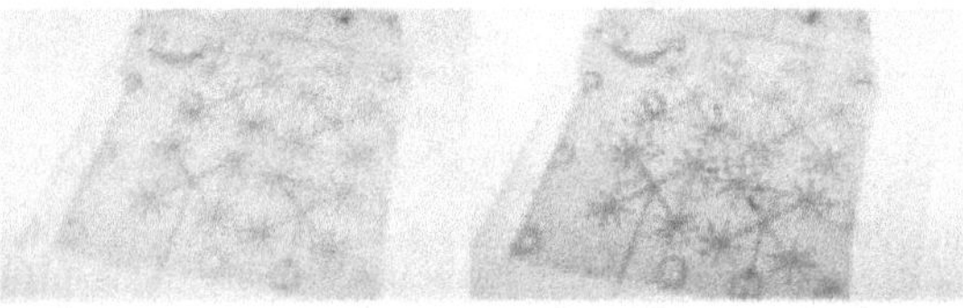

**Figure 28. Odor and color changing architectural material for rain augmentation.**

## DISCUSSION AND FUTURE WORK

Our use of the term *organic* is rooted in the carbon-based compounds that our sensor-actuator materials are built from, as distinguished from non-flat displays in organic user interfaces (OUI). Although the material primitives do not require a computer or wires to operate, they serve as sensors and actuators which offer researchers a method for interfacing with information within fluids. This approach of synthesizing color, odor and shape changing material sensor-actuators enables a variety of advantages and design opportunities as these systems: (i) have self-contained functionality as a sensor, actuator and energy source; (ii) can be manifested in different form factors and states of matter, from liquid to solid to vapor; (iii) can be integrated into both biological and electronic systems; (iv) are biocompatible, biodegradable, and edible; (v) are compact, soft, muted, and unobtrusive; (vi) open up additional modalities including taste and smell. Through this research, we hope to encourage other work in this non-traditional HCI landscape.

### Offloading Design Parameters to Software Tools

Data generated from our material characterization and evaluation serve as our design parameters in our material system. This nonlinear and multi-dimensional data can be integrated into software design tools which incorporate specific material formulations, recipes and fabrication conditions as digital and material design processes. Furthermore, the synthesis and printing of these materials can be automated onto printing platforms.

### Expanding the library of Organic Primitives

While pH serves as a starting point in this body of work, we envision a library of material primitives which can facilitate designers to interact with a variety of organic systems, across a range of signals. Primitives which can transduce molecular signals such as glucose, eH, $pCO_2$, sodium, magnesium, calcium, potassium, hormones and dioxins, can further enrich possibilities for human scale interaction with organic systems. The methods introduced in this paper can be used to develop sensor-actuators that are responsive to any number of chemical and biological stimuli. As the library of primitives expand, material robotics which can sense and output a multiplicity of behaviors can be possible. This can be achieved by utilizing the introduced techniques from the design space with multiple molecular I/O dopants, to build complex logic and behavior.

## CONCLUSION

*Organic Primitives* offer designers a toolbox to create multimodal actuation to "hack" the materiality of everyday objects - transforming them into both sensors and information displays. Because of the biocompatible nature of our sensor-actuators, we are able to utilize fluids from raindrops, ocean water, body fluids, food sources, and plant/microbe excretions as natural inputs to activate the output properties of the primitives. Our approach of employing organic compounds as molecular I/O offers a method to leverage an object's contextual meaning to enable novel sensory experiences by augmenting its material properties.

## ACKNOWLEDGMENTS

This paper was made possible by the support of Neri Oxman, Joi Ito, Linda Peterson, Jake Bernstein, Ivan Sysoev, and members of the Mediated Matter Group. We thank Laia Mogas, Judith Amores, Dhruv Jain, Yujie Hong, Chikara Inamura, Hershel Macaulay, Jifei Ou, Udayan Umapathi, Philipp Schoessler, Felix Heibeck, Basheer Tome, Nick Barry and Xiao Xiao for their insight and ideation. We are grateful for the generous feedback provided by David Kong from MIT Lincoln Laboratory, Niels Holten-Andersen from MIT Materials Science and Engineering, Manu Prakash from Stanford University and Pia Sorensen from Harvard University, at different stages of this research. We appreciate the tools provided by the MIT Center for Bits and Atoms and Ike Feitler for the spectrophotometer.

## REFERENCES

1. Soft Robotics Toolkit. (2013). `http://softroboticstoolkit.com` Accessed: 2016-03-30.
2. Zohreh Amoozgar, Joonyoung Park, Qingnuo Lin, and Yoon Yeo. 2012. Low Molecular-Weight Chitosan as a pH-Sensitive Stealth Coating for Tumor-Specific Drug Delivery. *Molecular Pharmaceutics* (2012).
3. Anthony Ananga, Vasil Georgiev, Joel Ochieng, Bobby Phills, and Violeta Tsolova. 2013. Production of Anthocyanins in Grape Cell Cultures: A Potential Source of Raw Material for Pharmaceutical, Food, and Cosmetic Industries. *The Mediterranean Genetic Code - Grapevine and Olive* (2013), 247–287.

4. Monya Baker. 2015. Irreproducible biology research costs put at 28 billion per year. (2015).
5. Kurt Bauer, Dorothea Garbe, and Horst Surburg. 2005. *Common Fragrance and Flavor Materials.*
6. Robert Boyle. 1664. *Experiments and Considerations Touching Colours.* Project Gutenberg. 1–157 pages.
7. Daphna Havkin-Frenkel Chaim Frenkel. 2006. The Physics and Chemistry of Vanillin. *Perfumer and Flavorist* 31 (2006), 28–36.
8. Cira, N J, Benusiglio, A, and Prakash, M. 2016. Vapour-mediated sensing and motility in two-component droplets. *Nature* 519, 7544 (Jan. 2016), 446–450.
9. Laura Devendorf, Joanne Lo, Noura Howell, Jung Lin Lee, Nan-Wei Gong, M. Emre Karagozler, Shiho Fukuhara, Ivan Poupyrev, Eric Paulos, and Kimiko Ryokai. 2016. "I Don't Want to Wear a Screen": Probing Perceptions of and Possibilities for Dynamic Displays on Clothing. In *Proceedings of the 2016 CHI Conference on Human Factors in Computing Systems (CHI '16).* ACM, 6028–6039.
10. M Dubinin. 1966. *Chemistry and Physics of Carbons.* Marcel Dekker, Inc. 51 pages.
11. Maher Z. Elsabee and Entsar S. Abdou. 2013. Chitosan based edible films and coatings: A review. *Materials Science and Engineering* 33 (2013), 1819–1841.
12. G.R. Mahdavinia et al. 2004. Modified chitosan 4. Superabsorbent hydrogels from poly(acrylic acid-co-acrylamide) grafted chitosan with salt- and pH-responsiveness properties. *European Polymer Journal* 40 (2004), 1399–1407.
13. Nicholas M. Farandos, Ali K. Yetisen, Michael J. Monteiro, Christopher R. Lowe, and Seok Hyun Yun. 2015. Contact lens sensors in ocular diagnostics. *Advanced Healthcare Materials* 4 (2015), 792–810.
14. Guo-Liang Yan Na-Na Liang Qiu-Hong Pan Jun Wang Malcolm J. Reeves Chang-Qing Duan Fei He, Lin Mu. 2010. Biosynthesis of anthocyanins and their regulation in colored grapes. *Molecules* 15 (2010), 9057–9091.
15. Mark N. Flair and William N. Setzer. 1990. An olfactory indicator for acid-base titrations: A laboratory technique for the visually impaired. *Journal of Chemical Education* 67 (1990), 795.
16. Wyss Institute for Biologically Inspired Engineering. Manufacturing a solution to planet-clogging plastics. (2014). http://wyss.harvard.edu/viewpressrelease/144/manufacturing-a-solution-to-planetclogging-plastics- Accessed: 2016-03-30.
17. Leonard P Freedman, Iain M Cockburn, and Timothy S Simcoe. 2015. The economics of reproducibility in preclinical research. *PLoS Biol* (2015).
18. Jian He and M Monica Giusti. 2010. Anthocyanins: Natural Colorants with Health-Promoting Properties. (2010).
19. Felix Heibeck, Basheer Tome, Clark Della Silva, and Hiroshi Ishii. 2015. uniMorph - Fabricating Thin-Film Composites for Shape-Changing Interfaces. In *Proceedings of the SIGCHI Conference on Human Factors in Computing Systems.* ACM, 233–242.
20. Benedetto Marelli et al Hu Tao, Suk-Won Hwang. 2014. Silk-based resorbable electronic devices for remotely controlled therapy and in vivo infection abatement. In *Proceedings of the National Academy of Sciences of the United States of America.*
21. Hiroshi Ishii, Dávid Lakatos, Leonardo Bonanni, and Jean-Baptiste Labrune. 2012. Radical Atoms: Beyond Tangible Bits, Toward Transformable Materials. *interactions* 19 (2012), 38–51.
22. Viirj Kan, Katsuya Fujii, Judith Amores, Chang Long Zhu Jin, Pattie Maes, and Hiroshi Ishii. 2015. Social Textiles: Social Affordances and Icebreaking Interactions. In *Proceedings of the 9th International Conference on Tangible, Embedded, and Embodied Interaction - TEI '15.* ACM, 619–624.
23. Cindy Hsin-Liu Kao, Ermal Dreshaj, Judith Amores, Sang-won Leigh, Xavier Benavides, Pattie Maes, Ken Perlin, and Hiroshi Ishii. 2015. Clayodor: Retrieving Scents Through the Manipulation of Malleable Material. In *Proceedings of the Ninth International Conference on Tangible, Embedded, and Embodied Interaction (TEI '15).*
24. Julie Legault. 2015. Amino: a domestic system for synthetic biology and continuous culturing. (2015).
25. Xin Liu, Katia Vega, Pattie Maes, and Joe A. Paradiso. 2016. Wearability Factors for Skin Interfaces. In *Proceedings of the 7th Augmented Human International Conference 2016 (AH '16).*
26. J F Mano. 2008. Stimuli-Responsive Polymeric Systems for Biomedical Applications. *Advanced Engineering Materials* 10, 6 (June 2008), 515–527.
27. M. A. McEvoy and N. Correll. 2015. Materials that couple sensing, actuation, computation, and communication. *Science* 347 (2015).
28. Charles M. McGinley. Standardized Odor Measurement Practices for Air Quality Testing. (2012). http://www.fivesenses.com Accessed: 2016-09-01.
29. Laia Mogas-Soldevila, Jorge Duro-Royo, Daniel Lizardo, Markus Kayser, William Patrick, Sunanda Sharma, Steven Keating, John Klein, Chikara Inamura, and Neri Oxman. 2015. Designing the Ocean Pavilion: Biomaterial Templating of Structural, Manufacturing, and Environmental Performance. In *Proceedings of the International Association for Shell and Spatial Structures.* IASS.
30. Majken K. Rasmussen, Esben W. Pedersen, Marianne G. Petersen, and Kasper Hornbæk. 2012. Shape-changing Interfaces: A Review of the Design Space and Open Research Questions. In *Proceedings of the SIGCHI Conference on Human Factors in Computing Systems (CHI '12).*
31. Diego T. Santos Rodrigo N. Cavalcanti and Maria Angela A Meireles. 2011. Non-thermal stabilization mechanisms of anthocyanins in model and food systems-An overview. *Food Research International* 44 (2011), 499–509.
32. Kim Lachance Shadrow. Swallow this "Password" Pill to Unlock Your Digital Devices. (2014). http://www.entrepreneur.com/article/231182 Accessed: 2016-03-30.
33. Christina D Smolke. 2009. Building outside of the box: iGEM and the BioBricks Foundation. *Nature Biotechnology* 27, 12 (2009), 1099–1102.
34. Sebastian J Maerkl Todd Thorsen and Stephen R Quake. 2002. Microfluidic large-scale integration. *Science* 298 (2002), 580–584.
35. Katia Vega and Hugo Fuks. 2013. Beauty Technology As an Interactive Computing Platform. In *Proceedings of the 2013 ACM International Conference on Interactive Tabletops and Surfaces (ITS '13).* ACM, 357–360.
36. Cor J Vink, Pierre Paquin, and Robert H Cruickshank. 2012. Taxonomy and Irreproducible Biological Science. *BioScience* 62, 5 (2012), 451–452.
37. John M Walker. 1994. The Bicinchoninic Acid (BCA) Assay for Protein Quantitation. In *Basic Protein and Peptide Protocols*, John M Walker (Ed.). Humana Press, Totowa, NJ, 5–8.
38. Stephen Warrenburg. 2005. Effects of fragrance on emotions: Moods and physiology. *Chemical Senses 30 SUPPL. 1* (2005), 248–249.
39. Martin Weigel, Tong Lu, Gilles Bailly, Antti Oulasvirta, Carmel Majidi, and Jürgen Steimle. 2015. iSkin: Flexible, Stretchable and Visually Customizable On-Body Touch Sensors for Mobile Computing. In *Proceedings of the 33rd Annual ACM Conference on Human Factors in Computing Systems (CHI '15).*
40. Mark Weiser. 1999. The Computer for the 21st Century. *SIGMOBILE Mob. Comput. Commun. Rev.* (1999), 3–11.
41. George M Whitesides. 2006. The origins and the future of microfluidics. *Nature* 442 (2006), 368–373.
42. A Wirsen X Qu and A.C. Albertsson. 1972. Enzymatische Oxidation von Vanillin. *Chimiu* 26 (1972), 343–354.

43. Sheng Xu, Yihui Zhang, Lin Jia, Kyle E. Mathewson, Kyung-In Jang, Jeonghyun Kim, Haoran Fu, Xian Huang, Pranav Chava, Renhan Wang, Sanat Bhole, Lizhe Wang, Yoon Joo Na, Yue Guan, Matthew Flavin, Zheshen Han, Yonggang Huang, and John A. Rogers. 2014. Soft Microfluidic Assemblies of Sensors, Circuits, and Radios for the Skin. *Science* 344, 6179 (2014), 70–74. DOI: http://dx.doi.org/10.1126/science.1250169

44. Kang De Yao, Tao Peng, M. F. A. Goosen, Ji Mei Min, and Yu Yin He. 1993. pH-sensitivity of hydrogels based on complex forming chitosan: Polyether interpenetrating polymer network. *Journal of Applied Polymer Science* 48, 2 (1993).

45. Lining Yao, Jifei Ou, Chin-Yi Cheng, Helene Steiner, Wen Wang, Guanyun Wang, and Hiroshi Ishii. 2015. bioLogic: Natto Cells As Nanoactuators for Shape Changing Interfaces. In *Proceedings of the 33rd Annual ACM Conference on Human Factors in Computing Systems (CHI '15)*.

46. Xiahong Zhang, Sisi Lu, and Xi Chen. 2014. A visual pH sensing film using natural dyes from Bauhinia blakeana Dunn. *Sensors and Actuators B: Chemical* 198 (2014), 268–273.

# Flexibles: Deformation-Aware 3D-Printed Tangibles for Capacitive Touchscreens

**Martin Schmitz[1], Jürgen Steimle[2], Jochen Huber[3], Niloofar Dezfuli[1], Max Mühlhäuser[1]**

[1] Technische Universität Darmstadt
Hochschulstraße 10,
64289 Darmstadt, Germany
{schmitz,dezfuli,max}@tk.tu-darmstadt.de

[2] Saarland University
Saarland Informatics Campus,
66123 Saarbrücken, Germany
steimle@cs.uni-saarland.de

[3] Synaptics
Zug, Switzerland
jochen.huber
@synaptics.com

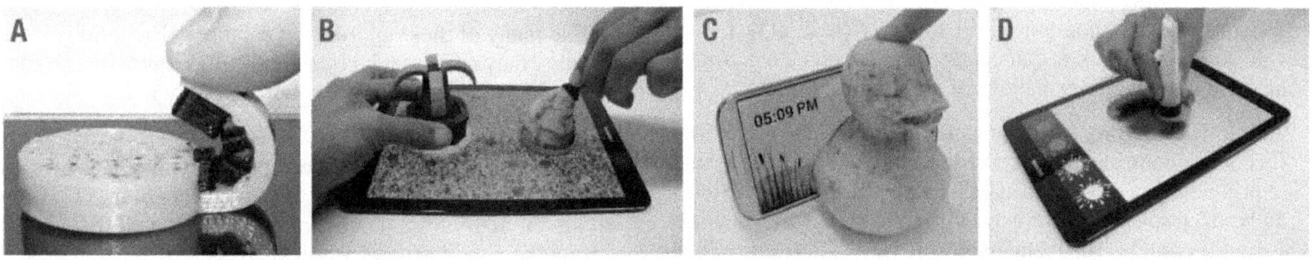


**Figure 1. Flexibles are 3D-printed deformation-aware tangibles that operate on capacitive touchscreens. By exploiting capacitive effects, new mechanisms enable the touchscreen to sense continuous bend (A & B), pressure (C), and squeeze input (D) at custom locations on the 3D object.**

## ABSTRACT

We introduce *Flexibles*: 3D-printed flexible tangibles that are deformation-aware and operate on capacitive touchscreens. Flexibles add expressive deformation input to interaction with on-screen tangibles. Based on different types of deformation mapping, we contribute a set of 3D-printable mechanisms that capture pressing, squeezing, and bending input with multiple levels of intensities. They can be integrated into 3D printed objects with custom geometries and on different locations. A Flexible is printed in a single pass on a consumer-level 3D printer without requiring further assembly. Through a series of interactive prototypes, example applications and a technical evaluation, we show the technical feasibility and the wide applicability of Flexibles.

### Author Keywords

3D printing; digital fabrication; rapid prototyping; printed electronics; capacitive sensing; input; deformation; touch

### ACM Classification Keywords

H.5.2 Information Interfaces and Presentation: User Interfaces – Input devices and strategies.


ACM ISBN 978-1-4503-4655-9/17/05 ...$15.00.
DOI: http://dx.doi.org/10.1145/3025453.3025663

## INTRODUCTION

Today's capacitive touch interaction on smartphones, tablets, and tabletops is often criticized as lacking haptic experience. To mitigate this, researchers propose interactive tangible objects that, when placed on a screen, enable physical control of on-screen contents [34, 18].

A large body of research focuses on enhancing tangible interaction on capacitive touchscreens. It has been shown that the capacitive touch sensor itself can be used to identify the location and orientation of a tangible object [34, 21, 7, 52]. Moreover touch input on an object's surface [7, 40, 20] or the configuration of mechanical controls with moving parts [7] can be detected. These approaches work with passive objects, which do not contain any electronics and therefore can be produced at low cost.

Moving beyond interaction with rigid objects, deformations are explored as a promising new input modality. Deformation is a very common and intuitive interaction in everyday life, such as bending a handle, squeezing a tube, or folding a sheet of paper. Prior approaches capture deformation input using camera-based touch tracking [12, 9], but require a stationary tracking solution in contrast to the now more commonplace and mobile capacitive touchscreens. Recent approaches utilize resistive [44, 49, 36, 1], capacitive [28], or pneumatic [50] sensing, but require an active object with embedded or tethered electronics and a power supply. This makes them less attractive for use as tangible objects on today's capacitive touchscreens.

We contribute to this stream of research by adding *deformation-awareness* to passive objects on capacitive touchscreens. *Flexibles* are 3D-printed tangible objects that recognize the deformations pressing, squeezing, and bending for tangible interaction on capacitive touch sensing hardware. They consist of deformable parts and embedded conductive sensing structures. Both are laid out in specific geometries to capture deformations and forward them to the capacitive touch sensor via capacitive coupling [34]. A Flexible can be fabricated in custom geometries using an off-the-shelf dual-extrusion 3D printer in a single print pass. It does neither require any embedded electronics nor any further assembly steps.

We introduce two principles for sensing deformations on capacitive touch sensors. On this basis, we present a set of mechanisms for capturing various forms of pressing, squeezing, and bending input. We also demonstrate how multiple mechanisms can be combined in an object. Results of technical evaluation studies show that changes in capacitance readings can be mapped to deformations of varying intensities.

With this new approach for sensing deformations of tangible objects, we contribute to the vision of interactive devices that are printed at once rather than being assembled [56]. Flexibles can be used to enrich interactions via physical manipulation of digital content, for instance, to provide faster, more fine-grained, or eyes-free input control on capacitive touchscreens. Also, they enable engaging interactions with customized 3D-printed tangible objects that are controlled by a smartphone without any additional power supply. We demonstrate these benefits with three interactive example applications.

The main contributions of this paper are:

- Two principles of mapping deformations in 3D-printed objects using commodity capacitive touch sensing hardware.
- 3D-printable mechanisms to capacitively detect multiple levels of pressing, squeezing, and bending input on passive 3D objects. Mechanisms can be combined in an object.
- Results from technical experiments investigating the accuracy of deformation sensing and example applications validating the practical feasibility of the approach.

## RELATED WORK

This paper is situated in the areas of tangibles on interactive surfaces, deformation sensing, and fabrication of interactive 3D objects.

### Tangibles On Interactive Surfaces

A body of research has investigated how optical approaches can be used to detect tangible objects on a touchscreen [2, 55]. More recent work is investigating how to detect tangibles using the now commonplace capacitive touchscreens. Many works apply variations of capacitance tags [34]. By embedding conductive material or by adding electronics to the tangible object, the capacitive touch sensor can detect presence and location of tangible objects [57, 52, 51], combinations of multiple objects [7], or forward touch on the object onto the touchscreen [7, 19, 20]. Other approaches utilize magnetic hall sensor grids to identify objects [25] and detect their posture above a screen [24].

While these approaches propose promising ways of interacting on capacitive touchscreens, they are restricted to rigid, non-deformable objects, and require additional hardware that needs to be assembled manually.

### Deformation Sensing

Prior works also explore deformations as a powerful and engaging input modality. Deformation sensing can be achieved by embedding sensors into objects [27, 47, 53, 49, 30, 48] or using optical sensing [12, 9, 46, 45, 33, 54]. Other approaches employ resistive [44, 10, 1], capacitive [28], or piezoelectric [35, 36] sensing.

While many of these approaches capture deformations in high fidelity, they are either incompatible with commonplace capacitive touchscreens, or require built-in, tethered, or stationary hardware.

Probably most closely related to our approach is work by Slyper et al. [44] and more recently Bächer et al. [1]. Slyper et al. embed wires inside manually fabricated soft silicone objects of varied geometry to resistively or magnetically sense versatile interactions, including bending, twisting, pressing, and stretching. Moreover, Bächer et al. contribute a computational approach to design and reconstruct complex deformations in 3D-printed objects by using resistive sensing. For both, objects have to be equipped with wires, need to be actively powered and read out using a dedicated microcontroller to which the object needs to be permanently tethered. In contrast, our untethered and passive approach uses capacitive coupling with a multi-touch sensor, therefore demanding a different set of requirements.

### Fabricating Interactive 3D Objects

Embedding or attaching components to non-interactive objects through *post-assembly* is one approach to add interactive capabilities to 3D objects. This can be accomplished by attaching capacitive [37] or acoustic [29] sensors, or embedding cameras [38] or accelerometers [14]. Even though these approaches require only a few components, they imply additional effort or work only with objects that are hollow and can be opened after printing.

Recently, an emerging stream of research investigates how to embed *customized interactive elements* in 3D-printed objects. This includes adding interactive input and output functionalities in 3D-printed objects through light pipes [56, 5], by filling internal pipes with media post-print [39], or via pipes that transmit sound [22]. It has also been shown how to embed interactive structures that can be deformed on-demand [11]. Other approaches print interactive objects by means of conductive spray [17] or conductive plastic [23, 40, 41, 6, 20]. 3D printing is also explored for fine-grained design of deformation behavior of non-interactive flexible objects [32, 43, 31, 4] or to fabricate soft interactive objects [15]. Vazquez et al. contribute 3D-printed pneumatic controls that can capture deformation, but require air-tightly attached hardware [50].

Adding to this body of research, Flexibles are 3D-printed in a single pass without any additional assembly and operate on commodity capacitive touch sensing hardware.

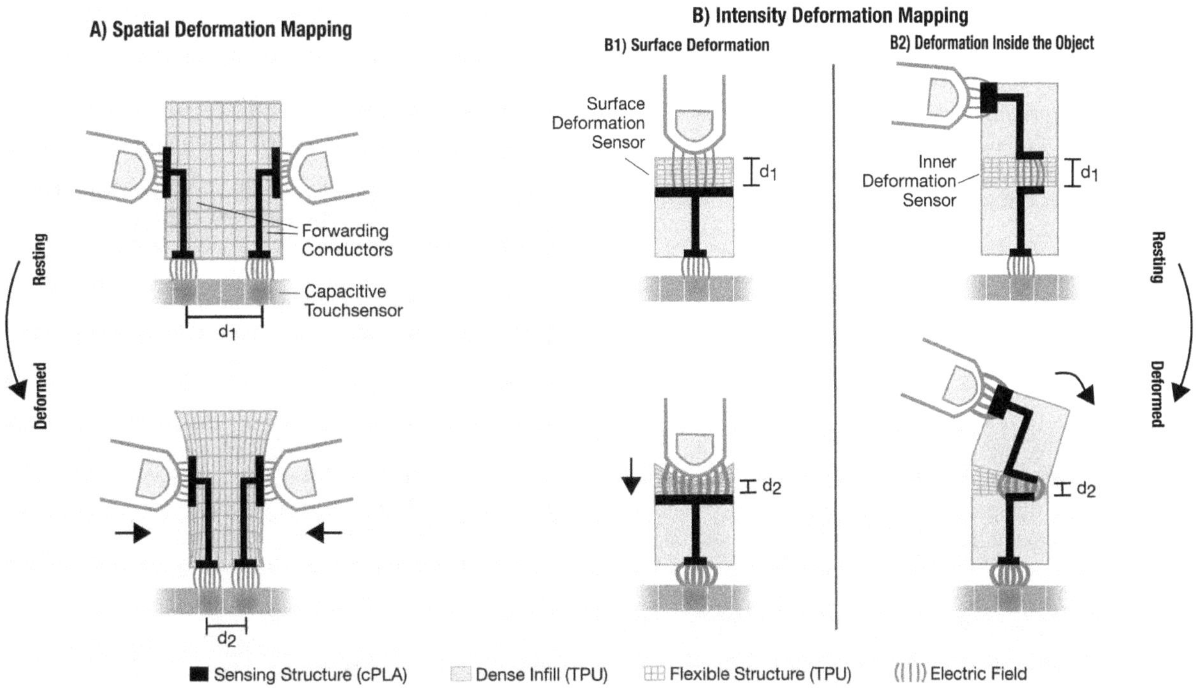


**Figure 2. Detecting deformations of a Flexible on a capacitive touchscreen via spatial (A) or intensity (B) deformation mapping.**

## FLEXIBLES

This section introduces the sensing principle that underlies Flexibles and presents the overall fabrication approach.

### Basic Principle

Most commodity multi-touch controllers perform a variant of mutual capacitance sensing [58]: A voltage is consecutively applied to unconnected rows and columns of a conductive grid, creating a uniform electric field at each intersection of the grid. When a conductor, such as a finger, gets close, it alters the electric field at the corresponding grid location. This can be measured as a change in capacitance.

Based on this general scheme, Rekimoto [34] proposed capacitive tags as a means to detect tangible objects on capacitive touchscreens. The tangible object contains a conductor that reaches from the location where it is touched to the location where it is placed on the capacitive touchscreen. When the user touches the object, the conductor capacitively couples the finger to the touch sensor. This results in a detectable change in capacitance used to detect the presence and location of the object. Informally speaking, the touch on the object is "forwarded" to the on-screen location. We thus call such a conductor a *forwarding conductor*, or in short, *forwarder*. This approach extends upon this principle by employing one or multiple forwarders along with specific 3D-printed geometries in order to detect deformations with capacitive touchscreens.

A Flexible is a 3D-printed material composite, which consists of two main functional structures (see Figure 2):

1. The *sensing structure* is embedded within the 3D-printed object and is used to recognize deformations by forwarding them onto the touchscreen. It is made of a conductive polymer.
2. The *flexible structure* is printed near the sensing structure to allow the 3D-printed object to deform at specific locations. It is made of a deformable dielectric elastomer.

Both structures can have a custom size and 3D shape. Multiple sensing and flexible structures can be embedded within a 3D-printed object. The remainder of the object is made of denser flexible material with higher solidity.

We propose two principles to detect object deformations with a capacitive touchscreen: *spatial deformation mapping*, considering the spatial location of forwarders on the touchscreen, and *intensity deformation mapping*, considering the intensity of the capacitance.

### Spatial Deformation Mapping

In spatial mapping, a deformation of the object is sensed by capturing the location of forwarders on the touchscreen (see Figure 2A). The 3D object is made of a flexible structure that allows it to deform in one or multiple dimensions. At least two forwarders need to be embedded inside this flexible structure. When the object is deformed, they change their relative position on the sensor grid.

Using this technique, fine-grained deformations that are oriented parallel to the touchscreen's surface can be detected, thanks to the touchscreen's high spatial resolution. However, it is not directly applicable to out-of-plane deformations.

### Intensity Deformation Mapping

The second approach, intensity deformation mapping, enhances the forwarder inside the object in a specific way, such that it modifies the intensity of the capacitance reading depending on deformation (see Figure 2B).

### Surface Deformation

Deformations that occur at the surface of the object, where the user is touching it, can be captured with a structure that we call *surface deformation sensor* (illustrated in Figure 2B1): the forwarder is overlaid with a flexible structure that acts as a deformable dielectric. When a user applies force, the flexible structure is compressed and the finger gets closer to the conductor.

Following the plate capacitor model [3], a variation in distance $d$ results in a change in capacitance, i.e. $C \propto A/d$ where $A$ refers to the cross-sectional area of the capacitor's plates. Based on the assumption that a distance variation relates to the amount of force exerted onto the flexible structure, we are able to infer deformations from variations in capacitance that are captured by the touchscreen. As will be shown in the evaluation section below, this principle allows to detect multiple intensities for specific deformations using commodity capacitive touch sensing hardware.

### Deformation Inside the Object

Many deformations do not primarily occur at the surface location where the user is touching the object. To capture deformation at interior locations within a volumetric object, we propose a structure that we call *inner deformation sensor* (illustrated in Figure 2B2). At the interior location where a deformation shall be captured, the forwarder is interrupted by a 3D-printed capacitor. The capacitor consists of two parallel plates. A flexible dielectric in-between the plates deforms when the object is deformed. This alters the distance or the angle between the plates of the capacitor and thereby modifies its capacitance, as well as the overall capacitance of the entire sensing structure.

## Implementation

### 3D Design and Fabrication

Flexible and sensing structures are combined in mechanisms that allow to detect different types of deformations. Multiple of these mechanisms can be integrated into the digital model of the object. For our prototypes, we manually designed the geometry using Blender and OpenSCAD. In future implementations, this could be automatized by computationally generating both structures to fit a given 3D model (c.f. [40]). We have already started to automatize this process by creating reusable scripts in OpenSCAD which allow generating sensing structures depending on adjustable parameters (e.g. size and thickness of conductors).

We decided to implement Flexibles using commonly available 3D printers. This makes the approach accessible to a wide audience. We used a standard dual-extrusion FDM 3D printer (Ultimaker Original with dual extrusion kit), and commercially available printing materials.

The sensing structure consists of carbon-doped Proto-pasta Conductive PLA (cPLA) with a volume resistivity of 30 – $115\Omega cm$. We printed cPLA with a 0.8 mm thick nozzle at a temperature of 220 ° C. We used the cooling fan and retraction of 5 mm (speed 20 mm/s).

The flexible structure is printed with NinjaFlex TPU, a Polyurethane composition (material shore hardness 85A). We printed the flexible structure with a 0.4 mm thick nozzle at a temperature of 230 ° C with a retraction of 12 mm and the cooling fan turned off (speed 30 mm/s).

The flexible structure's infill and density are important factors when fabricating deformation-aware objects because the composite of air chambers and flexible material both affect the dielectric properties required for capacitive sensing and the object's deformability. Unfortunately, most infill patterns are primarily designed to maximize stability and minimize material usage. We tested common infill patterns and found that the 3D Honeycomb pattern is best suited because the inherent 3D structure of each honeycomb allows for equal deformations in each direction (see Figure 3). We experienced an infill density of 25%, i.e. deformability of up to 1/4 of the original length, to result in an adequate sensing performance. This optimizes the deformability and dielectric constant of the flexible structure, i.e. the material between the sensing structure and the user's finger.

Designers may want to reduce the density to increase the deformability. However, as shown by [26], a smaller infill density would reduce the overall dielectric constant of the flexible structure due to the dielectric constant of NinjaFlex TPU being twice as high compared to air. As a consequence, the sensitivity of the capacitive sensor would be reduced.

For infill densities up to 100%, the flexible material nearly exhibits the properties of a solid material. Designers may use this effect to adjust the object's haptic or avoid unintentional deformations. Moreover, multiple infill densities for varying parts of the object can be achieved by splitting the object's 3D model into multiple parts and assigning each a specific density.

### Capacitive Sensing

Capacitance raw data was obtained from a regular smartphone (Samsung Galaxy S4) and tablet (Samsung Galaxy Tab S2) equipped with a standard touch controller (Synaptics S5000B). By rooting the Android phone and activating Synaptics debug mode, we obtained the capacitive values from the sensor as an 8-bit raw image with a resolution of 28x16 at 9 FPS. Up to 30 FPS are possible (c.f. [13]).

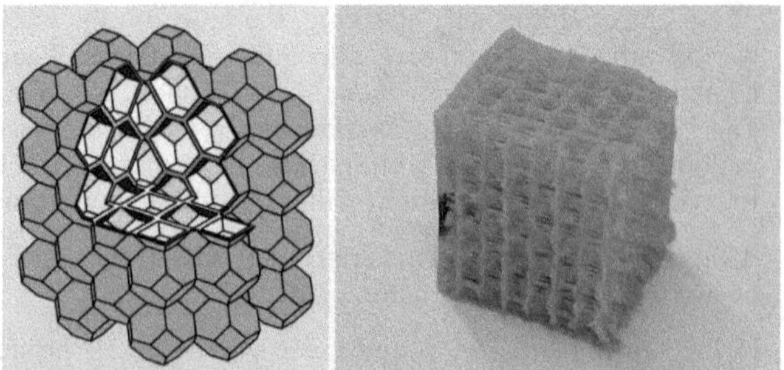

**Figure 3. Illustration of the 3D Honeycomb infill pattern as a rendering (left) and as a 3D-printed flexible TPU cube (right).**

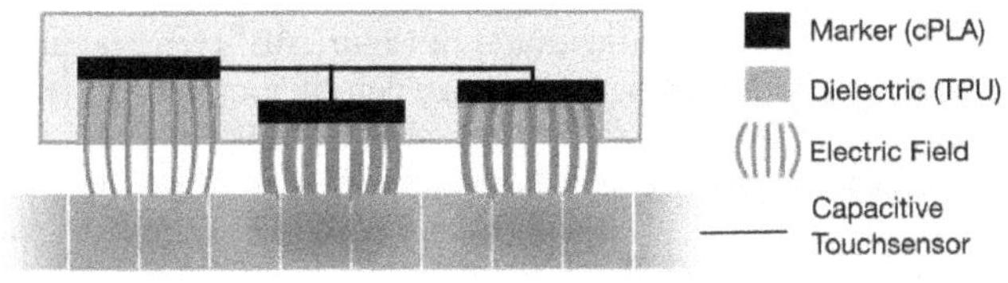


**Figure 4. Flexibles are identified and localized by varying the thickness of a dielectric between a marker and the touchsensor, resulting in a measurable difference in capacitance.**

### *Identifying and Localizing Flexibles*

Flexibles are identified and localized on the touchscreen via unique rotation-variant point patterns (c.f. [7, 21, 51]). These patterns are made of conductive material and are directly 3D-printed into the object's contact area. We improve over prior work by increasing the number of states that a single capacitive point can encode, leveraging the opportunities of 3D printing combined with capacitance measurements. By varying the amount of dielectric material that is printed between a capacitive point and the touchscreen, the intensity of the capacitance can be controlled (see Figure 4).

In our experiments, we could reliably distinguish three different states of a point. To differentiate Flexibles, we then consider the relative strength of all points in the pattern to each other. Once an object is recognized, the respective capacitive values inside the contact area (known from the 3D model) are used to recognize deformations. We have implemented a library that can be used by Android apps on a device that provides access to raw capacitances. It sends events when a Flexible was detected, its position or orientation changed, or a deformation was detected.

### *Calibration*

A Flexible needs to be manually calibrated once before use. To that end, the user places the object onto the touchscreen and holds it without deforming it. The system records a series of capacitance values and stores the mean as the value for minimal deformation. Then, the user deforms the object as much as possible. The system again records a series of values and stores the mean as the maximal deformation. Using these values, the minimum and maximum of an empirically-derived mapping function are adjusted to take variations in printing quality and human capacitance into account. We detail on such mapping functions in the evaluation section below.

## DEFORMATION-AWARE MECHANISMS

Based on spatial and intensity deformation mapping, deformation-aware mechanisms can be created that detect various types of deformations. We cover pressing, squeezing, and bending deformations. For each type of deformation, we first present a basic mechanism that capacitively senses the basic deformation with varying intensity. Second, we extend the basic mechanisms to also capture the on-object location where the force was applied or the direction of the deformation.

### Pressure Deformations

Pressure input on the surface of the object can be captured using intensity deformation mapping with a surface deformation sensor, as introduced above and illustrated in Figure 2B1.

### *Press*

To detect pressing, a surface deformation sensor is placed inside the object. Its flexible structure allows the user's finger to press into the object (see Figure 5A and B).

The main challenge is to find a suitable geometry for the sensor's conductor and to preserve deformability of the flexible structure at the same time. We explored different types of geometries and found that the best strategy consists of designing the conductor in a 3D geometry that mimics the outer shape of the 3D object at the location where it is to be pressed. Similar to the original design of a plate capacitor, this geometry maximizes the cross-sectional area between the user's finger and the conductor and also ensures a constant thickness of the dielectric flexible structure.

The designer defines this geometry by selecting an area of interest around an arbitrary location on the object's surface in the 3D CAD model. The selected area is downscaled by the required thickness of the flexible structure and translated in the normal direction to lie under the object's surface. The volume between the object's surface and the conductor is then filled with the flexible structure.

For our prototypes shown in Figure 5A and B, both surface deformation sensors (cross-sectional size of 10x10 mm²) are placed inside the object with 4 mm of flexible structure overlaid. Moreover, both are connected to the underside of the object using a forwarder with a size of 5x5 mm² at the contact face, such that the touchscreen can capture the capacitance.

The connection does not have to be straight. A slightly modified conductor routing allows for forwarding press input to an arbitrary location on the touchscreen. For instance, this makes it possible to capture press input that occurs besides the touchscreen (e.g. Figure 5B) or on objects with overhangs.

### *Localized Press*

The mechanism for pressure input can be extended to not only capture a single pressure value but also to estimate the 1D or 2D location where the press occurs on the object's surface. To that end, the surface deformation sensor is spatially replicated into multiple distinct sensors, which each connects to different

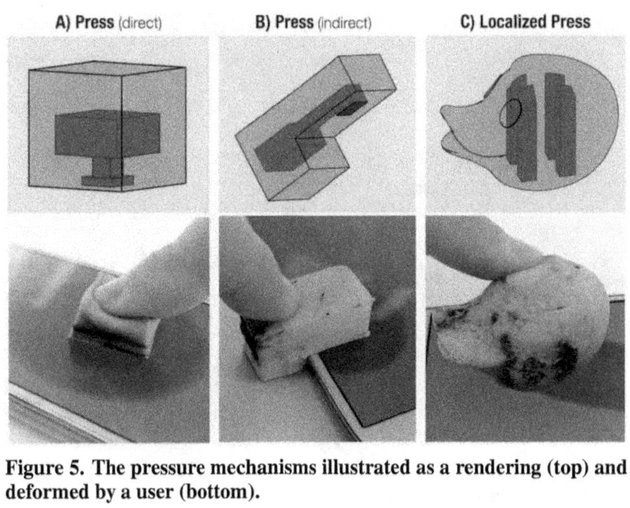


**Figure 5. The pressure mechanisms illustrated as a rendering (top) and deformed by a user (bottom).**

areas on the touchscreen. Hence, their capacitance values can be read out separately. This allows for simultaneously measuring pressure input on various distinct locations on the object. By using bilinear interpolation between all values, the location of the press on the surface can be estimated.

One of our prototypes is shown in Figure 5C. Here, a duck's head is equipped with four distinct surface deformation sensors. They are laid out in a 2x2 grid of 18x18 mm² (4x4 mm² per sensor) with 7 mm of flexible overlay. By using bilinear interpolation, we experienced that 3x3 locations can be robustly identified with this 2x2 grid.

### Squeeze Deformations

Next, we investigate how to capture squeezing. In contrast to pressing, squeezing is characterized by a *bilateral* compression from two sides pointing inside the object. Like for sensing of pressure, surface deformation sensors can be employed to capture squeezing.

#### *Squeeze*

Similar to pressure input, our tests revealed that the most suitable geometry for a squeeze-aware surface deformation sensor is mimicking the object's outer shape.

One of our prototypes is shown in Figure 6A. Here, an object is equipped with a surface deformation sensor (cross-sectional size of 10x10 mm²) with 7 mm of overlying flexible structure to both sides of the object's surface. The sensor is connected to the underside of the object using a forwarder with a size of 3x3 mm² at the contact face.

#### *Localized Squeeze*

Besides the amount of squeezing, the location of the fingers on the object's surface can be of interest (e.g. distinguishing a squeeze from left-to-right or front-to-rear). Similar to the localized pressure mechanism, the surface deformation sensor can be spatially replicated into multiple sensors, each facing a different direction. The rough squeeze input location is then identified from the pair of opposite sensors that have the highest value. By using interpolation between adjacent sensors, the resolution can be improved further.

This mechanism is illustrated in Figure 6B. Here, a cube is equipped with four distinct surface deformation sensors (cross-sectional size of 10 x 10 mm²), aligned in 90° angles. Each sensor's forwarder connects to the touchscreen with a contact size of 3x3 mm². The sensors are placed at 7 mm distance from the respective faces of the cube.

#### *In-Plane Squeeze*

Utilizing spatial deformation mapping, the following mechanism is able to infer squeeze deformations in the touchscreen's plane. For this mechanism, four forwarders are placed at the outer edges on the underside of the object. Pairs of two forwarders are connected with the object's upper surface, to ensure capacitive coupling between the user's finger and the touchscreen. The remainder of the object consists of a flexible structure, which allows squeezing the object.

When the object is deformed, the on-screen locations of the forwarders at the object's bottom change. If a threshold for all four forwarders is exceeded, their respective distances on the screen are used to approximate a contour of the object, allowing to compute the intensity of the squeeze deformation. This mechanism utilizes the higher spatial resolution of the touchscreen to sense more fine-grained squeezing. However, it is limited to squeeze deformations that are performed in parallel to the touchscreen.

A prototype is illustrated in Figure 6C. Here, a cuboid is equipped with four forwarders (contact size of 5x5 mm²). Each two are connected to each other by a conductor of size 30 x 10 mm² and separated by 30 mm of flexible structure in between.

### Bend Deformation

Bend deformations inside an object can be detected using intensity deformation mapping, as illustrated by Figure 2B.

#### *Binary Bend*

We present a binary bend mechanism that uses intensity deformation mapping to detect whether it is bent or not (see Figure 7A). It consists of one forwarder at the object's contact face and a series of inner deformation sensors at its deformable tail (see Figure 7A). The user can grab the object at the outer

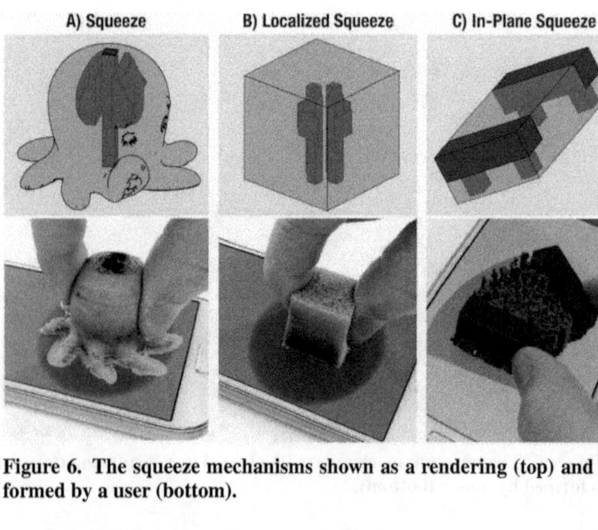


**Figure 6. The squeeze mechanisms shown as a rendering (top) and deformed by a user (bottom).**

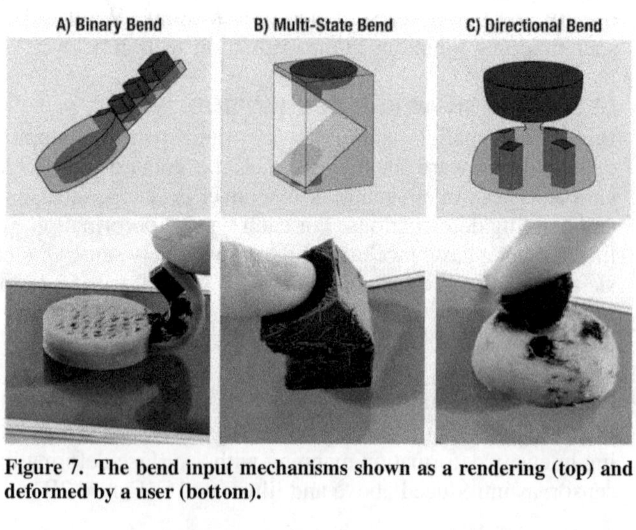


**Figure 7. The bend input mechanisms shown as a rendering (top) and deformed by a user (bottom).**

end of its tail and deform the bendable structure. Multiple separate forwarders laid out at regular intervals on the bendable structure act as inner deformation sensors: they form a capacitive bridge that is closed as soon as the object is strongly bent. Bending utilizes inner deformation sensors because a bend cannot be directly inferred from the distance of a user's finger to a conductor.

One of our prototypes, shown in Figure 7A, utilizes a circular forwarder on the touchscreen (diameter of 12 mm). The forwarder connects to two inner deformation sensors (each with a size of 4x2 mm²), which end with a conductor for coupling with the user's finger (size of 4x5 mm²). We employ air as the dielectric material in-between the inner deformation sensors (separated by 3 mm), which makes it easier to print. The capacitance significantly changes when all conductors are physically connected. Thus, this mechanism is well suited to detect binary bends but does not allow to infer a bending angle. In addition to bending, the mechanism may also be used to capture folding, since it can be printed in slim geometries.

#### *Multi-State Bend*

Increasing in complexity, the multi-state bend mechanism detects multiple bending states in a fixed direction, which is pre-defined by the designer. It utilizes an inner deformation sensor that consists of multiple parts: The upper half of the sensor connects via a forwarder to the user's finger and the lower half of the sensor connects via a forwarder to the touchscreen. By bending, the user reduces the distance between the upper and the lower forwarder. Hence, a capacitance change is induced on the screen. As will be shown in the evaluation section below, this mechanism is able to distinguish between four bending states.

One of our prototypes is shown in Figure 7B. It utilizes a circular upper forwarder (diameter of 17 mm) combined with a circular lower forwarder (diameter of 5 mm) separated by 7 mm of flexible structure in between.

#### *Directional Bend*

Two-dimensional bending of a flexible object becomes possible if two volumetric parts are connected to each other by a thinner structure. For instance, the head of a figurine is connected to its torso by a thinner neck, allowing the head to be bent around two axes (see Figure 7C). We focus on this type of bending in the following.

To that end, the multi-state bend mechanism is spatially replicated to cover a broader range of 2D directions, similar to a 2D ball joint: The upper half of the mechanism consists of a forwarder and a thin connecting dielectric structure, printed with high density to strengthen the connection. At the same time, the lower half forms multiple distinct forwarders arranged in a circular way that connect to the touchscreen. Together with the upper forwarder, they form inner deformation sensors. When the object is bent in one direction, the upper forwarder gets closer to one or two of the lower forwarders, while it gets more distant from the remaining forwarders. This results in capacitance changes that can be measured by the touchscreen. Using this technique, a bending direction between 0° and 360° can be estimated by interpolating between the capacitance of adjacent lower forwarders.

Figure 7C illustrates one of our prototypes. It utilizes a circular upper forwarder (diameter of 24 mm) mounted on a thin dielectric structure (diameter of 3 mm). The lower half consists of four distinct forwarders (contact size of 5 x 5 mm²) connecting independently to the touchscreen. We successfully tested the mechanism for up to eight forwarders placed at the lower half of the object.

### Touch Contact Input

Of note is, that all these mechanisms are also suited to sense touch contact, i.e when the user's finger is touching the forwarder with minimal force. This results in a measurable increase of capacitance, which can be clearly differentiated from no touch contact, but which is considerably weaker than when a deformation occurs.

### Combining Mechanisms

Despite deformation-aware mechanisms by themselves offer rich expressivity, they can also be combined inside of one object in parallel, resulting in various configurations that provide even greater possibilities. To that end, their forwarders are laid out such that they lead to distinct locations at the underside of the object. Hence, their values can be read out independently and simultaneously by the touchscreen.

A sufficient spacing between conductors is required. In our tests, a spacing of 5 mm between forwarders was satisfactory to ensure independent sensing performance. As an example, Figure 9 illustrates two mechanisms in a single object routed onto the contact area to simultaneously sense press and squeeze input.

## EXAMPLE APPLICATIONS

To demonstrate the practical feasibility and the potential of our approach, we developed three interactive example applications.

### Angry Trees

The first example is a tangible game, inspired by Angry Birds (see Figure 8). Users can play against each other by using two Flexibles: a palm tree and a Christmas tree. By bending and then releasing a tree, virtual fruits (either coconuts or Christmas balls) are thrown at the opponent. The on-screen

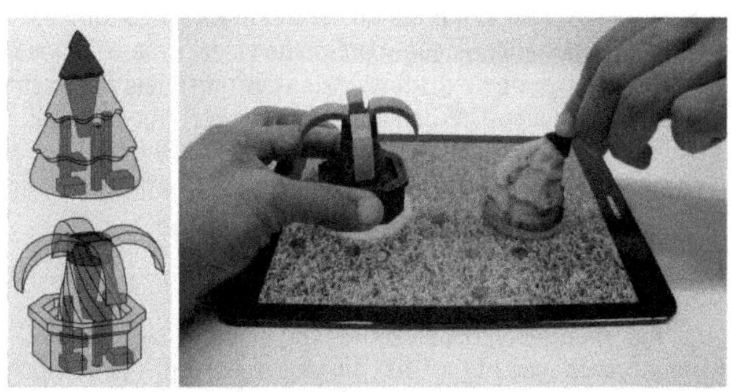

**Figure 8. Interactive board game: two angry trees throw their fruits at each other.**

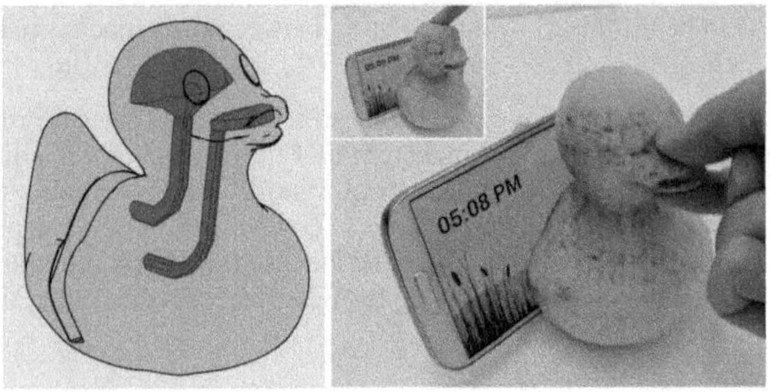


Figure 9. The alarm clock reacts to a squeeze or press (top left).

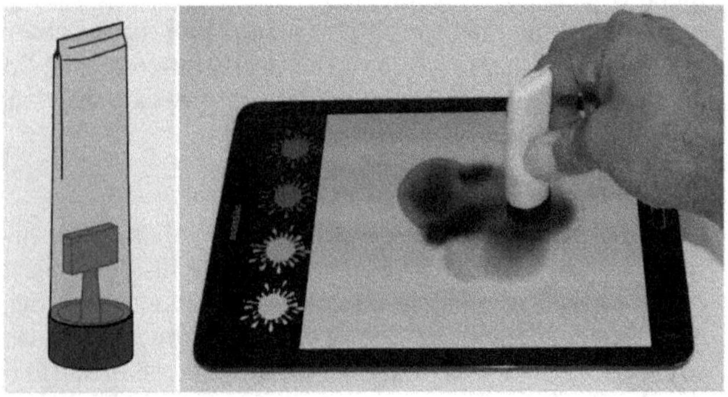

Figure 10. Mixing colors by squeezing them out of a deformable tube.

trajectory of the fruits takes into account the current position and rotation of the tree on the screen. Using a simple physics simulation, the amount of bending defines how far the fruits are thrown on the screen. By squeezing a tree, all fruits are thrown. If a tree has no fruits left, they can be picked up again by squeezing.

### Alarm Duck

To demonstrate the use of Flexibles for interactive devices, we implemented a docking station, shaped like a rubber duck, that operates as an alarm clock (see Figure 9). It enhances a smartphone with deformation-aware controls. The system launches an alarm clock application when a user docks the smartphone at the back of the duck. The user sets the alarm time by squeezing the duck's beak until the desired wake-up time is displayed on the smartphone. By squeezing more firmly, the time on the display changes more quickly.

At night, the user can press on the top of the duck for easy-to-reach functionality. A slight press shows the time left to sleep on the smartphone's display. A harder press lets the system read the time aloud. When the alarm goes off, the smartphone plays a chirping sound. The user can squeeze the beak to turn on snoozing. The length of the snoozing time depends on how firmly the user squeezes.

### Squeezy Tube

In this example, a squeezable tube is used together with a touchscreen (see Figure 10). In analogy to a physical pipette, users can select elementary colors by placing the tube onto a color on the display and then squeeze the tube. The color can then be dispensed by placing the tube on another screen location and squeezing it. Depending on the amount of squeezing, more or less color is dispensed, which allows for mixing of colors. This opens up a broad range of tangible applications in education (c.f. [42]), for instance to more directly combine different amounts of virtual fluids.

## EVALUATION

We conducted technical experiments to evaluate the accuracy of the press, squeeze, and multi-state bend input mechanisms with users.

### Accuracy of Pressure Input

First, we tested the press mechanism with the object shown in Figure 5B. To compare the actual force with which the object is being pressed to capacitance, we mounted a force sensing resistor (FSR) inside the object, in-between the flexible dielectric and the conductor of the surface deformation sensor. As the object is being pressed, force is exerted onto both the FSR and the press mechanism. We logged analog-to-digital (ADC) readings from the FSR and raw ADC readings from the capacitive touchscreen controller simultaneously by wiring them to the same computer. Five participants had the task to each press onto the object with a continuously increasing normal force, from no force to pressing firmly. This generated 500 data points. By conducting the study with users instead of a mechanical apparatus, we account for the inter-individual differences in users' capacitive responses.

As shown in Figure 11, the press mechanism is capable of sensing multiple intensities of pressure. For very small forces (<30), the capacitance increases without considerable effect on the measured force. This is the phase when the finger slightly touches the object with an increasing contact surface. This is followed by a quite linear mapping between capacitance measurements and applied force. For large forces (>300), the flexible structure reaches its limits in elasticity and the mapping is non-linear. This behavior can be modeled with a nonlinear least squares model based on a sigmoid. With this, we can compute a mapping function from capacitance to

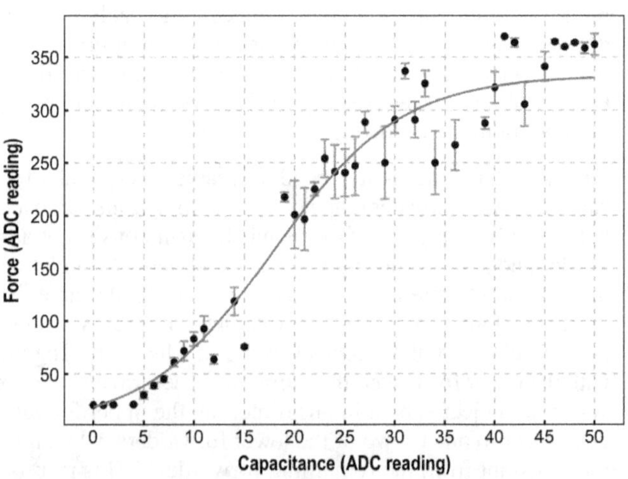


Figure 11. Mean forces (with standard deviations) for measured capacitances for press input. The mapping function is shown in red.

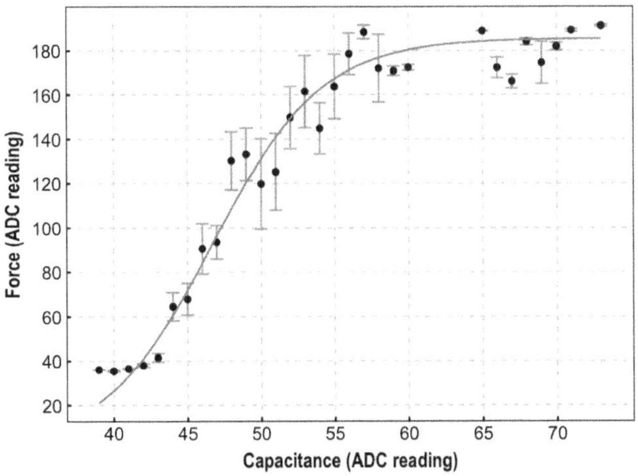


**Figure 12. Mean forces (with standard deviations) for measured capacitances for squeeze input. The mapping function is shown in red.**

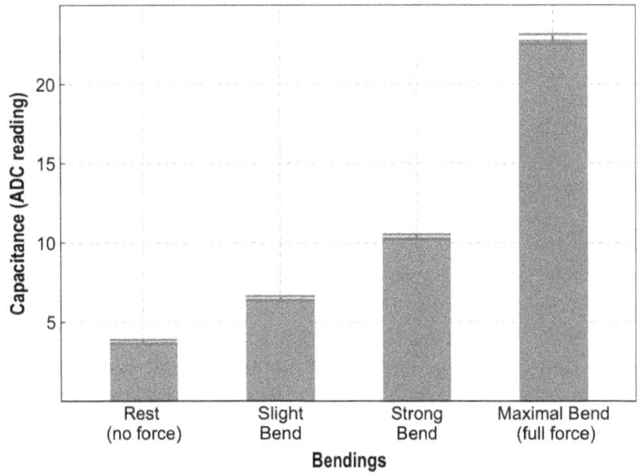


**Figure 13. Mean capacitances (with standard deviations) for four pre-defined bend states.**

force $f(C) = a/(1+exp(-b*(C-c)))$ with a = 332.73 (SD 5.92), b = 0.16 (SD 0.007), and c = 17.89 (SD 0.50) with a residual standard error of 43.8.

An object's response may differ due to variations in the printing process or individual properties of the user. As discussed, this needs to be compensated by adjusting the minimum and maximum of the mapping function via calibration. The mapping function is specific to the mechanism's geometry.

### Accuracy of Squeeze Input

We next tested the accuracy of the squeeze mechanism. Similar to the task above, we collected 500 samples with five study participants who had to squeeze an object with varying force.

Figure 12 illustrates, that this mechanism is able to measure multiple intensities of squeezing. We can fit a nonlinear least squares model based on a sigmoid. With this, we can compute an approximation of the function $f(C) = a/(1+exp(-b*(C-c)))$ with a = 185.56 (SD 4.38), b = 0.27 (SD 0.02), and c = 46.71 (SD 0.32) with a residual standard error of 42.1. Similar to the results for pressure input, the gradient is smaller for small ($<40$) and bigger forces ($>160$).

### Accuracy of Bend Input

For the multi-state bend mechanism (see Figure 7B), we recorded raw capacitive ADC readings for four pre-defined bend states: rest state (with no force applied), slight bend, strong bend, maximal bend (with maximal force applied). Participants had to deform the object to match a given bend state. In each trail, an image was displayed on a computer screen that showed a photograph of the object in the target state. For each condition, capacitance data was recorded. In total, we collected 1200 samples (for 5 users).

Across all samples, the mean values were 3.77 (SD 2.1) for rest state, 6.51 (SD 2.23) for slight bend, 10.37 (SD 2.55) for strong bends, and 22.81 (SD 5.5) for maximal bends (see Figure 13). The results show, that at least four different bend states can be reliably distinguished across different users.

## DISCUSSION AND LIMITATIONS

This paper presents first results on how to leverage capacitive coupling between a touchscreen and a 3D-printed object to sense specific pre-defined deformations. However, Flexibles have limitations that must be considered during design, fabrication, and sensing.

### Set of Deformations and Resolution

In general, a flexible object can be deformed in many complex ways. This paper explores a basic and widely used set of deformations. More complex deformations (e.g. twisting) or continuous, high-resolution deformation input are not covered. The main reason is that the electrical properties of today's flexible conductive printing materials are interference-prone (see appendix of [1]).

Despite these restrictions, we demonstrated that multiple intensity levels of pressing, squeezing and bending can be captured, alongside information about the location or direction of the deformation.

### Material Fatigue and Latency

We found no evidence of material fatigue after repeatedly deforming the object (more than 500 times). This is in line with Ion et al. [16] who demonstrate that the same TPU material can be deformed 5000 times without noticeable degradation.

Also, the approach does not rely on deforming the conductive material; only non-conductive parts are deformed. This avoids latency known from flexible conductors, such as eTPU, whose resistance is dependent on both history and rate of deformations performed over time [1].

### Scalability and Geometries

Scalability is an important issue, as the size of a Flexible and of the capacitive touchscreen may vary from small (e.g. smartphones) to very large (e.g. wall-sized displays). The mechanisms presented in this paper use sensing structures that are optimized for the size of a fingertip (16-20mm [8]). Hence the results apply only to deformations that are performed with fingers. Also, the approach requires a volumetric object inside which conductors can be routed. Therefore, geometries with thin structures, high curvatures, or cavities remain challenging.

The minimal size of a mechanism is limited by the rather low resolution and the high nozzle diameter of today's commodity 3D printers. Using our print setup, the minimal cross-sectional size of the sensing structure's conductor is 3x3 $mm^2$. A second limit to miniaturizing mechanisms relates to the flexible structure. If shrunk, the sensing resolution will be reduced because the flexible structure is deformable to a lesser extent. For very thin objects (<4 mm), the sensors will not function properly because there is no space for compressing the flexible structure. Future printers and materials, which can be extruded with smaller nozzles, are likely to alleviate these restrictions.

Designers may increase the cross-sectional size of the sensing structure's conductor to enhance its sensitivity or to better match a larger body part for interaction (e.g. hands). However, the maximum size of a sensing structure is not only limited by the printer's print volume (for our setup 21 x 21 x 20 cm). It is also limited by the rather low conductivity of the conductive material and by environmental stray capacitance. We successfully tested lengths of a forwarder up to 15 cm without noticing an influence on sensing performance. We recommend that designers construct conductors only as large as necessary for their use case. It is also possible to increase the thickness of the flexible structure, to enable greater deformations. However, an increasing thickness of the flexible structure weakens the capacitive effect. Therefore, the size of the sensing structure should be increased accordingly. We found a thickness of 4 mm to 10 mm to be a good trade-off between the sensor's sensitivity and the deformability of the material.

### Movement of Objects

When object movement is detected, the software maintains the last known deformation state. Hence, deformation sensing and object movement can only occur sequentially. As the spatial resolution of touch grids is limited, the forwarders of a Flexible are not always perfectly aligned with one intersection point of the grid. In that case, the capacitance splits up into different intersection points, which affects the sensor readings. Uninterrupted sensing could be implemented by using a specialized kernel with bilinear interpolation of readings from adjacent intersection points.

Flexibles printed with TPU at their lowermost layer exhibit a higher stiction and friction compared to PLA on touchscreen glass. Nevertheless, we observed that TPU objects were easily moved by our participants. Depending on the application, designers may want to increase or decrease the stiction or friction of a Flexible. This can be achieved by varying the ratio of PLA and TPU in the object's lowermost layer. In contrast to our print setup, this would require a 3D printer that can handle at least three materials (cPLA, TPU, and PLA).

### Unintentional Input

Capacitive measurements could be affected by capacitive effects when the user is unintentionally touching another location. Likewise, capacitive cross-talk between adjacent conductors could influence the sensor readings. To minimize these effects, designers should consider the following aspects: (1) The cross-sectional area of a surface deformation sensor should be much larger than of the remaining forwarders inside the object. (2) Any forwarder should be located rather in the center of the object than close to its outer sides unless the forwarder is designed to be touched by users for capacitive coupling. A forwarder should be as thin as possible and distant from other forwarders. The specific dimensions depend on the printer's resolution and the conductivity of the material. We experienced that adjacent forwarders should maintain a minimal distance of at least 5 mm. (3) The infill density at non-interactive locations should be increased to avoid accidental deformations.

Due to the rather low resolution of today's 3D printers, the larger cross-sectional area of wires is a reason for cross-talk between conductors that are routed in parallel. This is a noteworthy issue in objects with many spatially replicated forwarders or combined mechanisms, which require many forwarders. Future printers are likely to mitigate this issue due to increased resolution.

### Commodity Touch Sensing Hardware

Despite using unmodified commodity touch sensing hardware, the approach uses a debug interface to capture raw capacitance data. Open access to such data would require a modified driver which could be supplied by OEMs.

## CONCLUSION

This paper has presented 3D-printed flexible tangibles, called *Flexibles*, that add deformation-awareness to passive tangibles on standard capacitive touch sensing hardware. Flexibles enable many new possibilities for interaction with on-screen tangibles. We contributed two deformation mapping principles and a set of 3D-printable mechanisms that capture press, squeeze, and bend input. They can be integrated within custom geometries and on many custom locations on the tangible object. A Flexible itself is completely passive and 3D-printed in a single pass on a consumer-level 3D printer without further modifications.

With advances in 3D printing technology, we believe that deformation-aware tangible objects will become an important part of interaction with capacitive touchscreens. Based on the mechanisms presented in this paper, future work should investigate how to ease the fabrication process with automated design tools and how to apply auto-generation of deformation sensing mechanisms in order to support more complex geometries.

## ACKNOWLEDGMENTS

We thank David Fischer, Sebastian Günther, Alexander Hendrich, Daniel Kauth, Jens Krüger, Andreas Leister, Andre Pfeifer, and Max Stachalski for their valuable support. We also thank the anonymous reviewers for their valuable comments and suggestions. This work has been funded by the ICT R&D program of MSIP/IITP [B0101-16-1292, Development of Smart Space to promote the Immersive Screen Media Service], the DFG-Cluster of Excellence on Multimodal Computing and Interaction, and the German Federal Ministry of Education and Research SWC Printeract (01IS12054).

## REFERENCES


1. Moritz Bächer, Benjamin Hepp, Fabrizio Pece, Paul G Kry, Bernd Bickel, Bernhard Thomaszewski, and Otmar Hilliges. 2016. DefSense: Computational Design of Customized Deformable Input Devices. In *Proceedings of the 2016 CHI Conference on Human Factors in Computing Systems - CHI '16*. ACM Press, New York, New York, USA, 3806–3816. DOI: http://dx.doi.org/10.1145/2858036.2858354
2. Patrick Baudisch, Torsten Becker, and Frederik Rudeck. 2010. Lumino: Tangible Blocks for Tabletop Computers Based on Glass Fiber Bundles. In *Proceedings of the 28th international conference on Human factors in computing systems - CHI '10*. ACM Press, New York, New York, USA, 1165. DOI: http://dx.doi.org/10.1145/1753326.1753500
3. L K Baxter. 1996. Capacitive Sensors: Design and Applications, vol. 1 of IEEE Press Series on Electronics Technology. (1996).
4. Bernd Bickel, Moritz Bächer, Miguel a. Otaduy, Hyunho Richard Lee, Hanspeter Pfister, Markus Gross, and Wojciech Matusik. 2010. Design and Fabrication of Materials with Desired Deformation Behavior. *ACM Transactions on Graphics* 29, 4 (jul 2010), 1. DOI: http://dx.doi.org/10.1145/1833351.1778800
5. Eric Brockmeyer, Ivan Poupyrev, and Scott Hudson. 2013. PAPILLON: Designing Curved Display Surfaces with Printed Optics. In *Proceedings of the 26th annual ACM symposium on User interface software and technology - UIST '13*. ACM Press, New York, New York, USA, 457–462. DOI: http://dx.doi.org/10.1145/2501988.2502027
6. Jesse Burstyn, Nicholas Fellion, and Paul Strohmeier. 2015. *PrintPut: Resistive and Capacitive Input Widgets for Interactive 3D Prints*. Lecture Notes in Computer Science, Vol. 9296. Springer International Publishing, Cham. 332–339 pages. DOI: http://dx.doi.org/10.1007/978-3-319-22701-6
7. Liwei Chan, Stefanie Müller, Anne Roudaut, and Patrick Baudisch. 2012. CapStones and ZebraWidgets: sensing stacks of building blocks, dials and sliders on capacitive touch screens. In *Proceedings of the 2012 ACM annual conference on Human Factors in Computing Systems - CHI '12*. ACM Press, New York, New York, USA, 2189–2192. DOI: http://dx.doi.org/10.1145/2207676.2208371
8. Kiran Dandekar, Balasundar I Raju, and Mandayam a Srinivasan. 2003. 3-D Finite-Element Models of Human and Monkey Fingertips to Investigate the Mechanics of Tactile Sense. *Journal of Biomechanical Engineering* 125, 5 (2003), 682. DOI: http://dx.doi.org/10.1115/1.1613673
9. Kentaro Go, Katsutoshi Nonaka, Koji Mitsuke, and Masayuki Morisawa. 2012. Object shape and touch sensing on interactive tables with optical fiber sensors. In *Proceedings of the Sixth International Conference on Tangible, Embedded and Embodied Interaction - TEI '12*. ACM Press, New York, New York, USA, 123. DOI: http://dx.doi.org/10.1145/2148131.2148158
10. Nan-wei Gong, Jürgen Steimle, Simon Olberding, Steve Hodges, Nicholas Edward Gillian, Yoshihiro Kawahara, and Joseph A. Paradiso. 2014. PrintSense: A Versatile Sensing Technique to Support Multimodal Flexible Surface Interaction. In *Proceedings of the 32nd annual ACM conference on Human factors in computing systems - CHI '14*. ACM Press, New York, New York, USA, 1407–1410. DOI: http://dx.doi.org/10.1145/2556288.2557173
11. Daniel Gröger, Elena Chong Loo, and Jürgen Steimle. 2016. HotFlex: Post-print Customization of 3D Prints Using Embedded State Change. In *Proceedings of the 2016 CHI Conference on Human Factors in Computing Systems - CHI '16*. ACM Press, New York, New York, USA, 420–432. DOI: http://dx.doi.org/10.1145/2858036.2858191
12. Fabian Hennecke, Franz Berwein, and Andreas Butz. 2011. Optical Pressure Sensing for Tangible User Interfaces. In *Proceedings of the ACM International Conference on Interactive Tabletops and Surfaces - ITS '11*. ACM Press, New York, New York, USA, 45. DOI: http://dx.doi.org/10.1145/2076354.2076362
13. Christian Holz, Senaka Buthpitiya, and Marius Knaust. 2015. Bodyprint: Biometric User Identification on Mobile Devices Using the Capacitive Touchscreen to Scan Body Parts. *Proceedings of the ACM CHI'15 Conference on Human Factors in Computing Systems* 1 (2015), 3011–3014. DOI: http://dx.doi.org/10.1145/2702123.2702518
14. Jonathan Hook, Thomas Nappey, Steve Hodges, Peter Wright, and Patrick Olivier. 2014. Making 3D Printed Objects Interactive Using Wireless Accelerometers. In *Proceedings of the extended abstracts of the 32nd annual ACM conference on Human factors in computing systems - CHI EA '14*. ACM Press, New York, New York, USA, 1435–1440. DOI: http://dx.doi.org/10.1145/2559206.2581137
15. Scott E. Hudson. 2014. Printing Teddy Bears: A Technique for 3D Printing of Soft Interactive Objects. In *Proceedings of the 32nd annual ACM conference on Human factors in computing systems - CHI '14*. ACM Press, New York, New York, USA, 459–468. DOI: http://dx.doi.org/10.1145/2556288.2557338
16. Alexandra Ion, Johannes Frohnhofen, Ludwig Wall, Robert Kovacs, Mirela Alistar, Jack Lindsay, Pedro Lopes, Hsiang-ting Chen, and Patrick Baudisch. 2016. Metamaterial Mechanisms. In *Proceedings of the 29th Annual Symposium on User Interface Software and Technology - UIST '16*. ACM Press, New York, New York, USA, 529–539. DOI: http://dx.doi.org/10.1145/2984511.2984540

17. Yoshio Ishiguro and Ivan Poupyrev. 2014. 3D Printed Interactive Speakers. In *Proceedings of the 32nd annual ACM conference on Human factors in computing systems - CHI '14*. ACM Press, New York, New York, USA, 1733–1742. DOI: http://dx.doi.org/10.1145/2556288.2557046

18. Hiroshi Ishii and Brygg Ullmer. 1997. Tangible Bits: Towards Seamless Interfaces Between People, Bits and Atoms. In *Proceedings of the SIGCHI conference on Human factors in computing systems - CHI '97*, Vol. 39. ACM Press, New York, New York, USA, 234–241. DOI: http://dx.doi.org/10.1145/258549.258715

19. Kunihiro Kato and Homei Miyashita. 2015. ExtensionSticker: A Proposal for a Striped Pattern Sticker to Extend Touch Interfaces and its Assessment. In *Proceedings of the 33rd Annual ACM Conference on Human Factors in Computing Systems - CHI '15*, Vol. 1. ACM Press, New York, New York, USA, 1851–1854. DOI: http://dx.doi.org/10.1145/2702123.2702500

20. Kunihiro Kato and Homei Miyashita. 2016. 3D Printed Physical Interfaces that can Extend Touch Devices. In *Proceedings of the 29th Annual Symposium on User Interface Software and Technology - UIST '16 Adjunct*. ACM Press, New York, New York, USA, 47–49. DOI: http://dx.doi.org/10.1145/2984751.2985700

21. Sven Kratz, Tilo Westermann, Michael Rohs, and Georg Essl. 2011. CapWidgets: Tangible Widgets versus Multi-Touch Controls on Mobile Devices. In *Proceedings of the 2011 annual conference extended abstracts on Human factors in computing systems - CHI EA '11*. ACM Press, New York, New York, USA, 1351. DOI: http://dx.doi.org/10.1145/1979742.1979773

22. Gierad Laput, Eric Brockmeyer, Scott E. Hudson, and Chris Harrison. 2015. Acoustruments: Passive, Acoustically-Driven, Interactive Controls for Handheld Devices. In *Proceedings of the 33rd Annual ACM Conference on Human Factors in Computing Systems - CHI '15*. ACM Press, New York, New York, USA, 1935–1944. DOI: http://dx.doi.org/10.1145/2702123.2702414

23. Simon J Leigh, Robert J Bradley, Christopher P Purssell, Duncan R Billson, and David a Hutchins. 2012. A Simple, Low-Cost Conductive Composite Material for 3D Printing of Electronic Sensors. *PLoS ONE* 7, 11 (nov 2012), e49365. DOI: http://dx.doi.org/10.1371/journal.pone.0049365

24. Rong-Hao Liang, Kai-Yin Cheng, Liwei Chan, Chuan-Xhyuan Peng, Mike Y. Chen, Rung-Huei Liang, De-Nian Yang, and Bing-Yu Chen. 2013. GaussBits: Magnetic Tangible Bits for Portable and Occlusion-Free Near-Surface Interactions. In *Proceedings of the SIGCHI Conference on Human Factors in Computing Systems - CHI '13*. ACM Press, New York, New York, USA, 1391. DOI: http://dx.doi.org/10.1145/2470654.2466185

25. Rong-Hao Liang, Han-Chih Kuo, Liwei Chan, De-Nian Yang, and Bing-Yu Chen. 2014. GaussStones : Shielded Magnetic Tangibles for Multi-Token Interactions on Portable Displays. In *Proceedings of the 27th annual ACM symposium on User interface software and technology - UIST '14*. ACM Press, New York, New York, USA, 365–372. DOI: http://dx.doi.org/10.1145/2642918.2647384

26. S Moscato, R Bahr, T Le, M Pasian, M Bozzi, L Perregrini, and M M Tentzeris. 2016. Infill-Dependent 3-D-Printed Material Based on NinjaFlex Filament for Antenna Applications. *IEEE Antennas and Wireless Propagation Letters* 15 (2016), 1506–1509. DOI: http://dx.doi.org/10.1109/LAWP.2016.2516101

27. Tamotsu Murakami and Naomasa Nakajima. 1994. Direct and intuitive input device for 3-D shape deformation. In *Conference companion on Human factors in computing systems - CHI '94*. ACM Press, New York, New York, USA, 233–236. DOI: http://dx.doi.org/10.1145/259963.260449

28. Simon Olberding, Sergio Soto Ortega, Klaus Hildebrandt, and Jürgen Steimle. 2015. Foldio: Digital Fabrication of Interactive and Shape- Changing Objects With Foldable Printed Electronics. In *Proceedings of the 28th Annual ACM Symposium on User Interface Software & Technology - UIST '15*. ACM Press, New York, New York, USA, 223–232. DOI: http://dx.doi.org/10.1145/2807442.2807494

29. Makoto Ono, Buntarou Shizuki, and Jiro Tanaka. 2013. Touch & Activate: Adding Interactivity to Existing Objects using Active Acoustic Sensing. In *Proceedings of the 26th annual ACM symposium on User interface software and technology - UIST '13*. ACM Press, New York, New York, USA, 31–40. DOI: http://dx.doi.org/10.1145/2501988.2501989

30. M Pakanen, A Colley, and J Häkkilä. 2014. Squeezy Bracelet - Designing a Wearable Communication Device for Tactile Interaction. In *Proceedings of the 8th Nordic Conference on Human-Computer Interaction Fun, Fast, Foundational - NordiCHI '14*. ACM Press, New York, New York, USA, 305–314. DOI: http://dx.doi.org/10.1145/2639189.2639238

31. Julian Panetta, Qingnan Zhou, Luigi Malomo, Nico Pietroni, Paolo Cignoni, and Denis Zorin. 2015. Elastic Textures for Additive Fabrication. *ACM Transactions on Graphics* 34, 4 (2015), 135:1–135:12. DOI: http://dx.doi.org/10.1145/2766937

32. Jesús Pérez, Bernhard Thomaszewski, Stelian Coros, Bernd Bickel, José A. Canabal, Robert Sumner, and Miguel A Otaduy. 2015. Design and Fabrication of Flexible Rod Meshes. *ACM Transactions on Graphics* 34, 4 (jul 2015), 138:1–138:12. DOI: http://dx.doi.org/10.1145/2766998

33. Parinya Punpongsanon, Daisuke Iwai, and Kosuke Sato. 2015. Projection-based visualization of tangential deformation of nonrigid surface by deformation estimation using infrared texture. *Virtual Reality* 19, 1 (mar 2015), 45–56. DOI: http://dx.doi.org/10.1007/s10055-014-0256-y

34. Jun Rekimoto. 2002. SmartSkin: An Infrastructure for Freehand Manipulation on Interactive Surfaces. In *Proceedings of the SIGCHI conference on Human factors in computing systems Changing our world, changing ourselves - CHI '02*. ACM Press, New York, New York, USA, 113. DOI: http://dx.doi.org/10.1145/503376.503397

35. Christian Rendl, Patrick Greindl, Michael Haller, Martin Zirkl, Barbara Stadlober, and Paul Hartmann. 2012. PyzoFlex: Printed Piezoelectric Pressure Sensing Foil. In *Proceedings of the 25th annual ACM symposium on User interface software and technology - UIST '12*. ACM Press, New York, New York, USA, 509. DOI: http://dx.doi.org/10.1145/2380116.2380180

36. Christian Rendl, Michael Haller, Shahram Izadi, David Kim, Sean Fanello, Patrick Parzer, Christoph Rhemann, Jonathan Taylor, Martin Zirkl, Gregor Scheipl, and Thomas Rothländer. 2014. FlexSense: A Transparent Self-Sensing Deformable Surface. In *Proceedings of the 27th annual ACM symposium on User interface software and technology - UIST '14*. ACM Press, New York, New York, USA, 129–138. DOI: http://dx.doi.org/10.1145/2642918.2647405

37. Munehiko Sato, Ivan Poupyrev, and Chris Harrison. 2012. Touché: Enhancing Touch Interaction on Humans, Screens, Liquids, and Everyday Objects. In *Proceedings of the 2012 ACM annual conference on Human Factors in Computing Systems - CHI '12*. ACM Press, New York, New York, USA, 483. DOI: http://dx.doi.org/10.1145/2207676.2207743

38. Valkyrie Savage, Colin Chang, and Björn Hartmann. 2013. Sauron: Embedded Single-camera Sensing of Printed Physical User Interfaces. In *Proceedings of the 26th annual ACM symposium on User interface software and technology - UIST '13*. ACM Press, New York, New York, USA, 447–456. DOI: http://dx.doi.org/10.1145/2501988.2501992

39. Valkyrie Savage, Ryan Schmidt, Tovi Grossman, George Fitzmaurice, and Björn Hartmann. 2014. A Series of Tubes: Adding Interactivity to 3D Prints Using Internal Pipes. In *Proceedings of the 27th annual ACM symposium on User interface software and technology - UIST '14*. ACM Press, New York, New York, USA, 3–12. DOI: http://dx.doi.org/10.1145/2642918.2647374

40. Martin Schmitz, Mohammadreza Khalilbeigi, Matthias Balwierz, Roman Lissermann, Max Mühlhäuser, and Jürgen Steimle. 2015. Capricate: A Fabrication Pipeline to Design and 3D Print Capacitive Touch Sensors for Interactive Objects. In *Proceedings of the 28th annual ACM symposium on User interface software and technology - UIST '15*. ACM Press, New York, New York, USA, 253–258. DOI: http://dx.doi.org/10.1145/2807442.2807503

41. Martin Schmitz, Andreas Leister, Niloofar Dezfuli, Jan Riemann, Florian Müller, and Max Mühlhäuser. 2016. Liquido: Embedding Liquids into 3D Printed Objects to Sense Tilting and Motion. In *Proceedings of the 2016 CHI Conference Extended Abstracts on Human Factors in Computing Systems - CHI EA '16*. ACM Press, New York, New York, USA, 2688–2696. DOI: http://dx.doi.org/10.1145/2851581.2892275

42. Bertrand Schneider, Megan Strait, Laurence Muller, Sarah Elfenbein, Orit Shaer, and Chia Shen. 2012. Phylo-Genie: Engaging Students in Collaborative 'Tree-Thinking' through Tabletop Techniques. In *Proceedings of the 2012 ACM annual conference on Human Factors in Computing Systems - CHI '12*. ACM Press, New York, New York, USA, 3071–3080. DOI: http://dx.doi.org/10.1145/2207676.2208720

43. Christian Schumacher, Bernd Bickel, Jan Rys, Steve Marschner, Chiara Daraio, and Markus Gross. 2015. Microstructures to Control Elasticity in 3D Printing. *ACM Transactions on Graphics* 34, 4 (2015), 136:1–136:13. DOI: http://dx.doi.org/10.1145/2766926

44. Ronit Slyper, Ivan Poupyrev, and Jessica Hodgins. 2011. Sensing Through Structure: Designing Soft Silicone Sensors. In *Proceedings of the fifth international conference on Tangible, embedded, and embodied interaction - TEI '11*. ACM Press, New York, New York, USA, 213–220. DOI: http://dx.doi.org/10.1145/1935701.1935744

45. Jürgen Steimle, Andreas Jordt, and Pattie Maes. 2013. Flexpad: Highly Flexible Bending Interactions for Projected Handheld Displays. In *Proceedings of the SIGCHI Conference on Human Factors in Computing Systems - CHI '13*. ACM Press, New York, New York, USA, 237–246. DOI: http://dx.doi.org/10.1145/2470654.2470688

46. Yuta Sugiura, Masahiko Inami, and Takeo Igarashi. 2012. A Thin Stretchable Interface for Tangential Force Measurement. In *Proceedings of the 25th annual ACM symposium on User interface software and technology - UIST '12*. ACM Press, New York, New York, USA, 529–536. DOI: http://dx.doi.org/10.1145/2380116.2380182

47. Yuta Sugiura, Gota Kakehi, Anusha Withana, Calista Lee, Daisuke Sakamoto, Maki Sugimoto, Masahiko Inami, and Takeo Igarashi. 2011. Detecting Shape Deformation of Soft Objects Using Directional Photoreflectivity Measurement. In *Proceedings of the 24th annual ACM symposium on User interface software and technology - UIST '11*. ACM Press, New York, New York, USA, 509. DOI: http://dx.doi.org/10.1145/2047196.2047263

48. Giovanni Maria Troiano, Esben Warming Pedersen, and Kasper Hornbæk. 2015. Deformable Interfaces for Performing Music. In *Proceedings of the 33rd Annual ACM Conference on Human Factors in Computing Systems - CHI '15*. ACM Press, New York, New York, USA, 377–386. DOI: http://dx.doi.org/10.1145/2702123.2702492

49. Karen Vanderloock, Vero Vanden Abeele, Johan A.K. Suykens, and Luc Geurts. 2013. The Skweezee System: Enabling the Design and the Programming of Squeeze Interactions. In *Proceedings of the 26th annual ACM symposium on User interface software and technology - UIST '13*. ACM Press, New York, New York, USA, 521–530. DOI: http://dx.doi.org/10.1145/2501988.2502033

50. Marynel Vázquez, Eric Brockmeyer, Ruta Desai, Chris Harrison, and Scott E. Hudson. 2015. 3D Printing Pneumatic Device Controls with Variable Activation Force Capabilities. In *Proceedings of the 33rd Annual ACM Conference on Human Factors in Computing Systems - CHI '15*. ACM Press, New York, New York, USA, 1295–1304. DOI: http://dx.doi.org/10.1145/2702123.2702569

51. Simon Voelker, Christian Cherek, Jan Thar, Thorsten Karrer, Christian Thoresen, Kjell Ivar Øvergrd, and Jan Borchers. 2015. PERCs: Persistently Trackable Tangibles on Capacitive Multi-Touch Displays. In *Proceedings of the 28th annual ACM symposium on User interface software and technology - UIST '15*. ACM Press, New York, New York, USA, 351–356. DOI: http://dx.doi.org/10.1145/2807442.2807466

52. Simon Voelker, Kosuke Nakajima, Christian Thoresen, Yuichi Itoh, Kjell Ivar Øvergrd, and Jan Borchers. 2013. PUCs: Detecting Transparent, Passive Untouched Capacitive Widgets on Unmodified Multi-touch Displays. In *Proceedings of the 2013 ACM international conference on Interactive tabletops and surfaces - ITS '13*. ACM Press, New York, New York, USA, 101–104. DOI: http://dx.doi.org/10.1145/2512349.2512791

53. Johnty Wang, Nicolas Alessandro, Sidney Fels, and Bob Pritchard. 2011. SQUEEZY: Extending a Multi-touch Screen with Force Sensing Objects for Controlling Articulatory Synthesis. In *Proceedings of the International Conference on New Interfaces for Musical Expression*. Oslo, Norway, 531–532. http://www.nime.org/proceedings/2011/nime2011_531.pdf

54. Chihiro Watanabe, Alvaro Cassinelli, Yoshihiro Watanabe, and Masatoshi Ishikawa. 2014. Generic Method for Crafting Deformable Interfaces to Physically Augment Smartphones. In *Proceedings of the extended abstracts of the 32nd annual ACM conference on Human factors in computing systems - CHI EA '14*. ACM Press, New York, New York, USA, 1309–1314. DOI: http://dx.doi.org/10.1145/2559206.2581307

55. Cary Williams, Xing Dong Yang, Grant Partridge, Joshua Millar-Usiskin, Arkady Major, and Pourang Irani. 2011. TZee: Exploiting the Lighting Properties of Multi-touch Tabletops for Tangible 3D Interactions. In *Proceedings of the 2011 annual conference on Human factors in computing systems - CHI '11*. ACM Press, New York, New York, USA, 1363. DOI: http://dx.doi.org/10.1145/1978942.1979143

56. Karl Willis, Eric Brockmeyer, Scott Hudson, and Ivan Poupyrev. 2012. Printed Optics: 3D Printing of Embedded Optical Elements for Interactive Devices. In *Proceedings of the 25th annual ACM symposium on User interface software and technology - UIST '12*. ACM Press, New York, New York, USA, 589–598. DOI: http://dx.doi.org/10.1145/2380116.2380190

57. Neng-Hao Yu, Polly Huang, Yi-ping Hung, Li-Wei Chan, Seng-yong Yong Lau, Sung-Sheng Tsai, I-Chun Hsiao, Dian-je Tsai, Fang-i Hsiao, Lung-pan Cheng, and Mike Chen. 2011. TUIC: Enabling Tangible Interaction on Capacitive Multi-touch Display. In *Proceedings of the 2011 annual conference on Human factors in computing systems - CHI '11*. ACM Press, New York, New York, USA, 2995. DOI: http://dx.doi.org/10.1145/1978942.1979386

58. Thomas G. Zimmerman, Joshua R. Smith, Joseph a. Paradiso, David Allport, and Neil Gershenfeld. 1995. Applying Electric Field Sensing to Human-Computer Interfaces. In *Proceedings of the SIGCHI conference on Human factors in computing systems - CHI '95*. ACM Press, New York, New York, USA, 280–287. DOI: http://dx.doi.org/10.1145/223904.223940

# Towards Personality-driven Persuasive Health Games and Gamified Systems

**Rita Orji [1 2], Lennart E. Nacke [2], Chrysanne Di Marco [1]**
[1] Cheriton School of Computer Science, University of Waterloo, Waterloo, ON, Canada
[2] HCI Games Group, Games Institute, University of Waterloo, Waterloo, ON, Canada
rita.orji@uwaterloo.ca, lennart.nacke@acm.org, cdimarco@uwaterloo.ca

## ABSTRACT
Persuasive games and gamified systems are effective tools for motivating behavior change using various persuasive strategies. Research has shown that tailoring these systems can increase their efficacy. However, there is little knowledge on how game-based persuasive systems can be tailored to individuals of various personality traits. To advance research in this area, we conducted a large-scale study of 660 participants to investigate how different personalities respond to various persuasive strategies that are used in persuasive health games and gamified systems. Our results reveal that people's personality traits play a significant role in the perceived persuasiveness of different strategies. Conscientious people tend to be motivated by *goal setting*, *simulation*, *self-monitoring and feedback*; people who are more open to experience are more likely to be demotivated by *rewards*, *competition*, *comparison*, and *cooperation*. We contribute to the CHI community by offering design guidelines for tailoring persuasive games and gamified designs to a particular group of personalities.

### Author Keywords
Persuasive game; personality; personalization; persuasive strategies; gamified design; behavior change; risky health behavior; serious games.

### ACM Classification Keywords
H.5.m. Information interfaces and presentation (e.g., HCI): Miscellaneous. K.8.0 Games

## INTRODUCTION
There is growing evidence that persuasive games and gamified systems are effective tools for motivating behavior change, influencing people, and promoting learning using various persuasive strategies [24,25,51]. Therefore, designing digital games for purposes other than entertainment has been a focus for many HCI and game researchers[18,52]. Persuasive games and gamified systems for *health*—which are designed as interventions with the primary purpose of changing a user's behavior or attitude [16,50] have attracted the attention of researchers, physicians, and health practitioners. Research has shown that persuasive games and gamified systems can be strategically designed to motivate desirable behavior change; for example, to help people overcome addictive behaviors such as substance abuse [28,29,37], promote personal wellness, manage diseases, engage in preventive behaviors [13,20,50] and avoid risky behaviors [28–30,61].


*CHI 2017, May 06-11, 2017, Denver, CO, USA*
 ISBN 978-1-4503-4655-9/17/05…$15.00
DOI: http://dx.doi.org/10.1145/3025453.3025577

Despite this growing interest and investment in persuasive games and gamified systems, current persuasive games suffer a major limitation: Most persuasive games adopt a non-tailored approach to their design [27]. However, recent research shows that this approach may not be effective because different types of people are motivated by different persuasive strategies [48,50], and a persuasive strategy that worked well with one group of people may demotivate a different group [10,35,50]. Consequently, there is an increasing demand for persuasive games, especially those targeted at health behaviors to be tailored to the target users' motivation [6,50,53]. Research has shown that tailoring persuasive games and gamified systems can increase their efficacy in motivating the desired behavior change compared to the non-tailored systems [49]. However, there is little knowledge about how persuasive games and gamified systems can be tailored to individuals of various personality traits. Personality has been shown to play significant roles in many areas of Human-Computer Interaction (HCI) including user interface design [45], persuasive messages [23,26], and gamification [32,62].

To investigate how to tailor persuasive games and gamified systems, we conducted a large-scale study of 660 participants that examined how people of different personalities (as identified by the Big-Five Personality [57]) respond to various persuasive strategies (*competition*, *simulation*, *self-monitoring and feedback, goal setting and suggestion*, *customization*, *reward, social comparison*, *cooperation*, *punishment*, and *personalization* [21]) that are widely used in persuasive health games and gamified systems. We employed Structural Equation Modeling [58] to develop models showing how people of different personalities respond to or prefer various persuasive strategies represented in storyboards. Our results reveal that people's personality traits play a significant role in the perceived persuasiveness of different strategies. For example, conscientious people tend to be motivated by *goal setting*, *simulation*, *self-monitoring*, and *feedback*; people who are more open to experience (openness) are more likely to be demotivated by *rewards*, *competition*, *comparison*, and *cooperation*. The results highlight the need to tailor persuasive games and gamified systems based on people's personality. Our findings can help designers to make decisions about which persuasive strategy to use and which to avoid when designing persuasive games and gamified systems that are targeting people of different personalities.

Our work offers two main contributions to the field of gameful design and persuasive design in HCI. First, we show the importance of *tailoring* persuasive games and gamified systems by revealing that people of divergent personalities respond differently to dissimilar persuasive strategies. Second, we validate and compare the perceived effectiveness of individual strategies and show that the strategies differ significantly in their overall effectiveness for motivating risky health behavior change. Based on our findings, we offer design guidelines for persuasive games and gamified systems that appeal to both a broad audience and a particular group of personalities.

## RELATED WORK

In this section, we present a brief overview of persuasive strategies and game-based interventions employing the strategies. We conclude with a summary of research efforts toward tailoring persuasive games for health.

### Persuasive Strategies

A fundamental feature of persuasive games and gamified systems is persuasion, an attempt to influence or reinforce behaviors, attitudes, feelings, or thoughts [16]. Persuasion is often achieved using various persuasive strategies. Persuasive strategies are techniques that can be employed in persuasive games and gamified systems design to promote desirable behaviors or attitudes. Over the years, a number of persuasive strategies have been developed. For example, Fogg [8] developed seven persuasive strategies, and Oinas-Kukkonen [21] developed 28 persuasive strategies.

According to the previous studies, *Competition*, *Simulation*, *Self-monitoring and Feedback*, *Goal Setting and Suggestion*, *Customization*, *Reward*, *Social Comparison, Cooperation*, *Punishment*, and *Personalization* are the 10 commonly employed strategies in persuasive games and gamified systems design [40,53], see Table 1.

### Persuasive Games and Gamified Interventions.

Researchers have designed and applied games as digital interventions in many domains including binge drinking prevention [28,29,37], drug and substance use prevention [38], smoking cessation [36], energy conservation [4], healthy eating [1,49,52], and physical activity [6,17]. Among all the domains of applications, the use of persuasive games and gamified systems in the health domain has received special attention. The definitions of the persuasive strategies is presented in Table 1.

Several persuasive games and gamified systems have employed the persuasive strategies highlighted above to

| |
|---|
| **Competition:** Allows users to compete with each other to perform the desired behavior. |
| **Simulation:** Provides the means for a user to observe the cause-and-effect linkage of their behavior. |
| **Self-monitoring and Feedback:** Allows people to track thei own behaviors, providing information on both past and current states. |
| **Goal Setting and Suggestion:** Requires users to set a clear behavior goal and recommend certain actions (for achieving the desired goal to users during system use). |
| **Customization:** Provides users an opportunity to adapt a system's content and functionality to their needs and choices |
| **Reward:** Offers virtual rewards to users for performing the target behavior. |
| **Comparison:** Provides a means for the user to view and compare their performance with the performance of other user(s). |
| **Cooperation:** Requires users to cooperate (work together) to achieve a shared objective and rewards them for achieving their goals collectively. |
| **Personalization:** Offers system-tailored contents and service to its users, tailoring content and functionality to a particular user's need based on a user's characteristics. |
| **Punishment:** Penalizes the user for not performing the desired behavior or reaching their goal (such as removing acquired rewards, other cherished possessions from the user.) |

**Table 1: Definitions of the persuasive strategies**

motivate risky health behavior change. For example, *N-Squad Web Adventure* [37] is a role-playing game employing *reward*, *simulation*, *personalization*, and *cooperation* to impact knowledge about the consequences of alcohol consumption and hence discourage risky drinking behaviors. The game simulated the consequences of alcohol intake and reflected its impact on the digestive, circulatory, and nervous systems: *simulation*. To increase relevance, players are presented with a tailored effect of alcohol on young adults of their age: *personalization.* The game requires that players work as part of a team to resolve the game challenge: *cooperation.* Finally, to incentivize players, they receive points for correct responses to the game quizzes: *reward.* For a detailed review of persuasive strategies and how they are employed in alcohol and other risky health behavior see Lehto and Oinas-Kukkonen [40].

Despite these past studies there is still little knowledge about the efficacy of individual strategies and how the strategies can be tailored to people of different personalities. Our study fills this gap.

### Personality Theory and HCI

Over the years, researchers have attempted to develop models for assessing and classifying individuals into various personality types. Among them is the Big Five Factor Model (FFM) of personality [19]. The FFM is currently the leading and most widely accepted model of personality because it establishes a common taxonomy that is capable of predicting variance in individuals' behaviors, thoughts, feelings, and actions [43]. The FFM highlights five personality traits: *Extraversion*, *Openness*, *Neuroticism*, *Conscientiousness, Agreeableness,* and see Table 2. The FFM has been used by several HCI and game researchers, e.g., to understand gameplay motivation [31,33,54] and game preference [56,65]; to understand the effect of different game controller [7], game elements [32], and need fulfillment in an online game.

Despite this wide adoption of personality traits by HCI researchers, there is limited research on how to tailor persuasive technologies and persuasive games in particular to various personalities. Hirsh et al. [26] examined whether the effectiveness of persuasive messages could be increased by tailoring the message to the recipient's personality. Their results suggested that tailoring persuasive messages to the FFM was an effective way of increasing the effectiveness. Along these lines, Arteaga et al. [3] tailored persuasive mobile games to various users' personalities. User's personality information was used to inform the choice of game recommended to the users. Arteaga's study suggests some possible relationships between personality traits and persuasive games preference [2] and hence, the need for further exploratory study into the relationships.

| Traits | The five traits represent the tendency to... |
|---|---|
| Extraversion | ... be outgoing, expressiveness, seek out new opportunities, and ambitious |
| Conscientiousness | ...be self-discipline, actively plan, goal-oriented, dependable, and organized |
| Openness | ...be curious, imaginative, hold unconventional values, and creative |
| Agreeableness | ...be considerate, cooperative, tolerant, friendly, caring, and helpful |
| Neuroticism | ...be nervous, fearful, sensitive, distrustful, and emotionally unstable |

**Table 2. Definition of the Big Five factors personality**

## STUDY DESIGN AND METHODS

Our study was designed to investigate the relations between the FFM personalities (*openness*, *conscientiousness*, *extraversion*, *agreeableness*, and *neuroticism* [57]) and perceived persuasiveness of the 10 strategies (*customization*, *simulation*, *self-monitoring and feedback*, *goal-setting and suggestion*, *personalization*, *simulation*, *punishment*, *reward*, *comparison*, *competition*, and *cooperation*) for motivating change in risky healthy behavior (especially change of unhealthy alcohol behavior).

### Measurement Instrument

To collect data for our study, we follow the approach described in our earlier study [53] which investigated the appeal of persuasive strategies to various gamer types and found that the persuasiveness of the strategies vary depending on the gamer type. Specifically, we represented each persuasive strategy in a storyboard about a persuasive game for promoting change of unhealthy alcohol behaviors. The 10 storyboards were drawn by an artist and were based on storyboard design guidelines by Truong et al. [64]. Implementing the strategies in storyboards makes it easier to elicit responses from diverse populations because storyboards provide a common visual language that individuals from diverse backgrounds can read and understand [41]. Storyboards have been shown to be effective at depicting strategies in previous research [9,53]. The storyboards show a character and their interactions with gamified persuasive systems for promoting change of unhealthy alcohol behavior. We evaluated and iteratively refined the storyboards following three expert discussions: the first two with HCI and persuasive technology experts and the last one with an expert in rhetoric and narrative in games. After the expert evaluations, we conducted an online user evaluation of 10 participants with the sole purpose of ensuring that our storyboards accurately depicted the strategies. The user evaluation led to some minor refinements. Figure 1 shows an example of one of the storyboards illustrating the reward strategy. All the storyboards can be found in the supplementary material.

To elicit feedback on the persuasiveness of the strategies, each storyboard was followed by a validated scale for assessing perceived persuasiveness. The scale was adapted from Drozd et al. [15] and has been used in other persuasive research investigations [9,49,53]. The scale consists of four questions: i) *"The system would influence me."*; ii) *"The system would be convincing."*; iii) *"The system would be personally relevant for me."*; iv) *"The system would make me reconsider my alcohol drinking habits."* The questions were measured using participant agreement with a 7-point Likert scale ranging from "1 = Strongly disagree" to "7 = Strongly agree". We included an open-ended question allowing participants to provide comments to justify their ratings of each strategy. Prior to assessing the persuasiveness of the strategies, we ensured that the participants understood the strategy depicted in each storyboard by asking them two comprehension questions—first, to identify the illustrated strategy from a list of 10 different strategies (*"What strategy does this storyboard represent"*); and second, to describe what is happening in the storyboard in their own words (*"In your own words, please describe what is happening in this storyboard"*). We also included 10-item personality inventory for assessing the FFM personality traits [57]; questions for assessing the participants' demographic information, and drinking behavior were also included.

### Data Collection

We recruited participants for this study using Amazon's Mechanical Turk (AMT). We used AMT for two main reasons: First, AMT has become an accepted method of gathering users' responses [26,32,53]; and secondly, we needed a large participant sample and diverse audience for our study. AMT allows access to a global audience at a

**Figure 1: Storyboard illustrating the *Reward* persuasive strategies**

relatively low cost, and ensures efficient survey distribution, and high quality results [8,44].

To eliminate possible bias due to the ordering of the storyboards we used the page randomization functionality provided by SurveyMonkey which rotates the position of the storyboard and varies their ordering for each participant. Before the main study, we conducted two pilot studies. The first pilot study was conducted on 10 random students recruited from a Canadian University and the second on 10 participants from AMT to test the validity of our study instruments.

### Participants' Demographic Information

A total of 660 responses was included in this analysis, after filtering out incomplete responses and incorrect responses to comprehension and attention-determining questions [44]. All our participants were at least 15 years of age at the time of data collection, consumed or had consumed alcohol at some time, and read and understand English well. The participants received a small monetary compensation in compliance with the study ethics approval. In general, we had a relatively diverse population in terms of gender, age, education level attained, see Table 3. Our participants came from the USA, India, Canada, Mexico, and other countries.

## DATA ANALYSIS

The main aim of this paper is to examine the relations between the FFM personality traits and the persuasiveness of 10 commonly employed persuasive game design strategies. To achieve this, we used several well-known analytical tools and procedures. We summarize the various steps taken to analyze our data in this section.

1. We validated that our storyboards correctly depicted the intended strategy using a chi-squared test [23].
2. We determined the suitability of our data for analysis using the Kaiser-Meyer-Olkin (KMO) sampling adequacies and the Bartlett Test of Sphericity [34].
3. To examine and compare the persuasiveness of the strategies, we computed the average score for each strategy and conducted a Repeated-Measure ANOVA (RM-ANOVA) followed by pairwise comparison, after validating for the ANOVA assumptions.

| **Total Participants = 660** | |
|---|---|
| Gender | Females (51%), Males (48%), Trans* (1%), Others (0%). |
| Age | 15-25 (23%), 26-35 (41%), 36-45 (22%), Over 45 (14%). |
| Education | Less than high school (1%), High school graduate (23%), College diploma (12%), Bachelor's degree (40%), Master's degree (20%), Doctorate degree (2%), Others (2%). |
| Ethnicity | Black/Non-Hispanic (7%), Native American/American Indian (1%), Asian/Pacific Islander (19%), Hispanic (7%), Caucasian (64%), Multi-Ethnic (2%). |

**Table 3: Participants' demographic information**

4. Next, we employed the Partial Least Square (PLS) Structural Equation Modeling (SEM) (PLS-SEM) [58] to create models showing the relations between the personality traits and the persuasiveness of the strategies, Figure 2. SEM is a recommended approach for modeling of relationships between variables [39]. Specifically, we used SmartPLS 3 [58].

### Storyboard Validation

To ensure that participants understood the strategy depicted in each of the storyboards, we ran chi-squared tests on the participants' responses to the multiple-choice questions that required them to identify the represented strategy for each of the storyboards. The results for all the strategies were significant at $p < 0.01$, which indicates that the storyboards were understood by the participants and that the storyboards successfully depicted the intended persuasive strategies[53].

### Measurement Validation

We determined the suitability of our data for further analysis using the Kaiser-Meyer-Olkin (KMO) sampling adequacies and the Bartlett Test of Sphericity. Our results showed that the KMO was 0.966, well above the recommended value of 0.6. The Bartlett Test of Sphericity was statistically significant ($\chi^2$ (780)=40073.2, $p < 0.0001$). These results show that our data were suitable for further analysis [39, 45].

We report here the common set of indices for model validity and reliability in PLS-SEM. Indicator reliability can be assumed because Cronbach's α and the composite reliability that analyze the strength of each indicator are all higher than their threshold value of 0.7 [11]. The data was checked for both convergent and discriminate validity and all the required criteria for the PLS-SEM validity and reliability were satisfied. All constructs have an AVE (which represents the average variance extracted by the variables from its indicator items) above the recommended threshold of 0.5 [11]. The heterotrait-monotrait ratio of correlations (HTMT) were all below the recommended limit of 0.9. The measurement models yielded an acceptable value of all indices for PLS-SEM model validity or reliability.

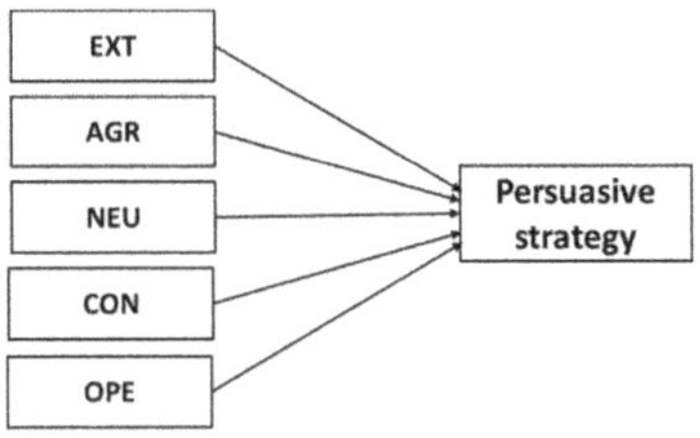


**Figure 2: PLS-SEM model structure**

## RESULTS

In this section, we first present the results showing and comparing the overall persuasiveness of the strategies, this is followed by the results showing the relationship between the five FFM personality traits and the strategies.

### Comparing the Persuasiveness of the Strategies Overall

The results of the RM-ANOVA show significant main effects of strategy type ($F_{7.37,\ 4852.224} = 62.535$, $p \approx .000$) on persuasiveness. This means that there are significant differences between the strategies with respect to their persuasiveness overall. In general, *Personalization*, *Simulation*, *Goal Setting* and *Suggestion*, *Self-monitoring* and *Feedback*, and *Social Comparison* (listed in decreasing order of persuasiveness) emerged as the most persuasive of all the strategies (significantly different from other strategies as shown by the Bonferonni-corrected pairwise comparisons). Our participants have least preference for *Punishment* and *Customization* (also significantly different from all others). The rest of the strategies (*Competition*, *Cooperation*, and *Reward*) were in the middle, with *Competition* leading the group. Figure 3 shows the notch boxplots of the strategies. The notch represents the 95% confidence interval of the median. In general, our participants perceived *Personalization*, *Goal Setting* and *Suggestion*, *Self-monitoring* and *Feedback*, and *Social Comparison*, *Competition*, and *Cooperation* as persuasive, with persuasiveness score significantly higher than neutral median rating of 4 ($p<.001$), indicated by the horizontal line in Figure 2. *Punishment* has significantly lower persuasiveness score than the neutral rating, (see Figure 2).

### The Structural Model

The structural models determine the relations between the people's personality traits and the persuasiveness of individual strategies, Figure 2. An important criterion to measure the strength of relationships between variables in structural models is to calculate the level of the path coefficient (*β*) and the significance of the path coefficient (*p*) [22]. Path coefficients measure the influence of a variable on another. The individual path coefficients (*β*) and their corresponding level of significance (*p*) obtained from our models are summarized in Table 4.

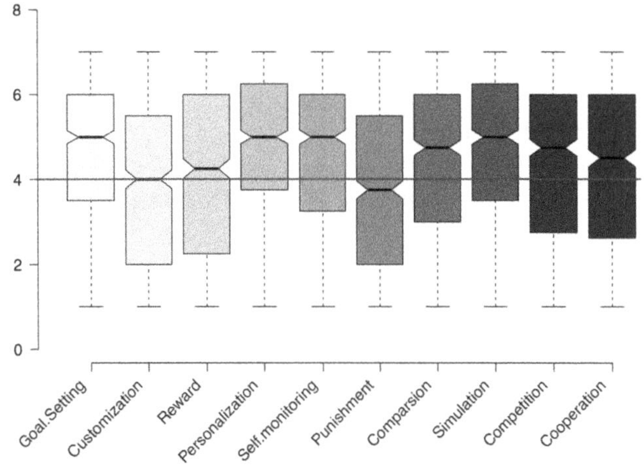


**Figure 3: A boxplot showing the overall persuasiveness (y-axis) of the 10 persuasive strategies on a scale ranging from 1 to 7. Higher numbers indicate higher persuasiveness. The horizontal line indicates a neutral rating of 4.**

| Factors | EXT | AGR | NEU | CON | OPE |
|---|---|---|---|---|---|
| Personalization | **.14** | .10 | - | .11 | .10 |
| Cooperation | .12 | **.19** | - | - | **-.12** |
| Simulation | .11 | **.14** | - | **.15** | - |
| Self-monitoring and Feedback | **.14** | .12 | - | .09 | -.09 |
| Comparison | **.18** | .12 | - | - | **-.13** |
| Punishment | **.15** | **.19** | - | - | -.09 |
| Goal Setting and Suggestion | **.16** | - | - | **.16** | - |
| Customization | .10 | **.14** | - | - | -.12 |
| Competition | **.15** | **.14** | - | - | **-.14** |
| Reward | **.14** | **.15** | - | - | **-.13** |
| EXT = Extraversion, AGR = Agreeableness, NEU = Neuroticism, CON = Conscientiousness, OPE= Openness | | | | | |

**Table 4. Standardized path coefficients and significance of the relationships. Bolded coefficients are p<.001, non-bolded are p<.05, and '-' represents non-significant coefficients.**

### Relationships between Personality Traits and Persuasive Strategies

The results from the structural model show that people's personalities influence the persuasiveness of individual strategies, Table 4. In this section, we discuss and compare the persuasiveness of the strategies for people of different personality traits.

#### *Competition*

The *competition* strategy, which leverages the power of social influence, builds on the assumption that most people are competitive and would strive to outperform their opponents [47]. Persuasive games and gamified systems designers believe that providing means for users to compete with other users would motivate them to perform the desired behavior [16]. Our results however show that *competition* is likely to motivate behavior only for people who are high in extraversion, agreeableness, and who are less open to experience ($\beta$=.15, $p$<.001), ($\beta$= .14, $p$<.001), ($\beta$= -.14, $p$<.001) respectively. These findings are supported by qualitative comments from the participants to justify their ratings. For example, participants who are high in extraversion and agreeableness have this to say about the competition strategy:

*"I am highly competitive, this is a good strategy to* ***motivate*** *me and keep me* ***committed****"*[1] [P51]. *"Winning gives a great feeling of* ***accomplishment!***" [P80].

The findings suggest that participants are motivated by competition because it *challenges them, makes them committed,* and *gives a feeling of accomplishment.* On the other hand, competition could demotivate behavior for people who are more open to experience (openness) ($\beta$= -.14, $p$<.001) and could have no significant impact on people who are high in neuroticism and conscientiousness. Some of the reasons given for the low preference for competition for this group include its *tendency to discourage* and *stress people*:

*"I do not like the competition aspect of this system, I think it could be very* ***discouraging*** *if you are constantly on the* ***losing*** *end"* [P519]. *"Interesting idea for competitive people, though I think that this would be* ***stressful*** *for me"* [P12].

Other reasons against competition are that participants may feel that living a healthy lifestyle is a personal goal and should not be turned into competition as illustrated by the comment, *"Living a healthy life is a* ***personal goal****. One's personal use of alcohol cannot be in competition with another person's. It is a competition against oneself. Competing to improve to be better than my previous self should be the strategy"* [P6]. The result is in line with previous research that found that users were uncomfortable with using competition to motivate healthy behavior [21,63], and may even become demotivated if they lose [5].

### Personalization and Customization

***Personalization*** and ***Customization*** represent two different methods of tailoring systems [53]. *Customization* is often user-controlled while *personalization* is mostly system-controlled. It has been argued that tailoring is more effective if users are allowed to do it for themselves, because it imbues users with a strong sense of personal agency and control, by allowing them to individualize their preference or request compared to when users are provided with automatic system-tailored contents [53,60]. Our results show that these two strategies are perceived differently by our participants. *Customization* is preferred by people with higher levels of extraversion and agreeableness ($\beta$=.10, $p$<.01) and ($\beta$= .14, $p$<.001) respectively, while it is perceived as negative by people who are high in openness ($\beta$= -.12, $p$<.01) (see Table 4). Some of reasons for the high preference for customization from the comments include the fact *that it increases system relevance, user confidence in the system, gives sense of personal touch, gives sense of freedom and control,* and *makes people feel connected to the system*, as shown:

*"Customization is good to make the* ***system relevant*** *to me"* [P25]. *"Because I customized it, I have more* ***confidence*** *on its efficacy"* [P255]. *"It would be cool to have a* ***personal touch*** *to the system..."* [P18]. *"Customization could help to make people* ***feel more connected*** *to the system"* [P75]. *"It gives me* ***freedom*** *and* ***control****"* [P29].

Some reasons given to justify the low preference for customization include it not being directly helpful in achieving behavior and that customization is difficult:

*"Customization is* ***not important*** *for me at all, it doesn't help me achieve the good behavior"* [P201]. *"I sometimes find customizing* ***difficult*** *to do..."* [P39].

On the other hand, *personalization* is a significant motivator for all the personality traits except for people who are emotionally unstable (neuroticism) that shows no significant association. As shown in Table 4, extraversion, agreeableness, conscientiousness, and openness perceive personalization as positive ($\beta$=.14, $p$<.001), ($\beta$=.10, $p$<.05), ($\beta$=.11, $p$<.01), and ($\beta$= 10, $p$<.05) respectively. In fact, personalization is the only strategy that is positively associated with people who are more open to experience.

Some reasons given to justify the high preference for personalization include its potential to make the system less abstract; increase users' confidence in their ability; and provide more relevant and helpful contents:

*"The good thing is that it is* ***less abstract*** [P13]. *"The information is based on me, it's far more* ***useful****"* [61]. *"I like this feature a lot. Assuming I'm already motivated, the personalized practicable information on the amount I could drink would be very* ***helpful****, and increase my* ***confidence*** *that I could change my behavior"* [P394].

The last comment from P394 suggests that personalization is useful but may work better for people who are already motivated and therefore should be used alongside other motivational strategies. This is also supported by other comments: *"Personalization is very* ***helpful****, but would need to be paired with some form of reinforcement to be effective..."* [P16]. *"It's a great concept, pretty convincing, but could be* ***boring*** *if used alone"* [P503].

### Cooperation

"A system can motivate users to adopt a target behavior by leveraging human beings' natural drive to co-operate."[46] Our results show that *cooperation* is a significant motivator for people high in agreeableness and extraversion, and those who are less open to experience ($\beta$= .19, $p$<.001), ($\beta$= .12, $p$<.01), ($\beta$= -.12, $p$<.01) respectively. Some reasons for

[1] Quotes from participants are included verbatim throughout the paper, including spelling and grammatical mistakes.

this high preference for cooperation include its potential to provide *opportunities for people to stay accountable, responsible, offer mutual help and encouragement,* and *make friends*, as can be seen from the sample comments:

*"I would be motivated because I'll be* ***harming*** *someone else if I miss my goal, not just myself"* [1]. *"I would* ***enjoy helping*** *another person reach their goals. It would be a positive experience for me that would boost my own efforts"* [P205]. *"The* ***buddying*** *idea is much more powerful than the competition idea"* [P69]. *"It's easier to meet goals when you're held* ***accountable*** *by others or you know others are checking your progress"* [9].

On the other hand, cooperation is not a significant motivator for high conscientious and emotionally unstable people. Some of the reasons for this low preference include *the tendency of cooperation to create unnecessarily tension, be tedious, stressful,* and *to possibly jeopardize relationships and privacy:*

*"It would be* ***tedious*** *for me to convince someone, I would rather work on my own personal goals"* [P357]. *"It can create* ***tension*** *between people and create opportunity for* ***negative criticism****"* [P56]. *"It would not work for me; I'd get upset with my friend if he fails! I may not want to* ***risk my relationship*** *him"* [P19]. *"...I may not use it because it seems like an* ***invasion of privacy"*** [P78].

### Simulation

An application can motivate people to change their behavior by providing a way for people to observe the cause and effect linkage of their behaviors[16]. In line with this assumption, our results show that *simulation* is one of the strategies that is not perceived by people with any personality trait as negative. Specifically, simulation is a significant motivator for people who are high in conscientiousness, agreeableness, and extraversion ($\beta$= .15, $p$<.001), ($\beta$= .14, $p$<.001), and ($\beta$= .11, $p$<.01) respectively. Some reasons given to justify this high preference for simulation include that it offers users' the opportunity to see short and long-term consequences of their behaviors, it is simple, and provides concrete and realistic information as can be seen from sample comments:

*"Allowing me to see the* ***short*** *and* ***long-term consequences*** *of heavy drinking is very educational, it'll motivate me"* [P3]. *"This's the best! It takes me on a step by step journey of alcohol consumption and the possible* ***repercussions in long and short term****"* [P209]. *"I like that this app actually shows some* ***concrete risks*** *about what can happen if I continue to drink like I have been. It's* ***real****"* [P603].

Simulation is not a significant motivator for people who are high in neuroticism and openness. Some reasons for the low preference for simulation is its tendency to scare people by showing them the consequences of their behaviors.

*"It might deter people who are more susceptible to* ***fear*** *factor of behaviors"* [P625]. *"The application shows real-life consequences and it's* ***frightening****..." "It makes me feel* ***crappy*** *and* ***scared"*** [P127].

### Self-monitoring and Feedback

This strategy builds on the human needs for awareness. Our results show that *self-monitoring and feedback* is significantly associated with all personality traits (although to different degrees and direction) except for people who are high in neuroticism. Self-monitoring and feedback isa significant motivator for people who are high in extraversion, agreeableness, conscientiousness, and for people who are less open to experience ($\beta$= .14, $p$<.001), ($\beta$= .12, $p$<.01), ($\beta$= .09, $p$<.05), and ($\beta$= -.09, $p$<.05) respectively. Some reasons given to justify the high preference for self-monitoring and feedback include that it is engaging, offers useful feedback, and could guide users and allow them compare progress:

*"I like that I would be able to see my past behavior and* ***get feedback*** *on how I can do better in the future"* [P78]. *"Keeping track of behavior is* ***engaging****. The best strategy!"* [P315]. *"Being able to* ***view*** *and* ***compare progression*** *from day to day is a greater motivator"* [P241]. *"It's a good idea, there would probably need to be some sort of* ***positive reinforcement*** *to engage people"*[P4]. The main negative comment against self-monitoring and feedback strategy is its *tendency to be tedious*:

*"User tracking would be* ***tedious*** *and not* ***fun*** *without rewards. Ideally I would like to see some way to easily track alcohol intake with a wearable device"* [P641].

The last two comments suggest that self-monitoring and feedback should be used alongside other strategies such as rewards to incentivize users and motivate behavior.

### Social Comparison

*Social Comparison* provides an opportunity for users to view and compare their performance with the performance of other users. Unlike competition, social comparison does not involve an overt competition since there is no winning or losing involved. Our results show that social comparison is a significant motivator for people high in extraversion, agreeableness, and for people that are less open to experience ($\beta$= .18, $p$<.001), ($\beta$= .12, $p$<.01), and ($\beta$= -.13, $p$<.001) respectively. Some reasons given to justify this high preference include:

*"I think a little comparison could help me by not wanting my friends to see that I am drinking more than them along with giving me good milestones"* [P529]. *"I would really* ***prefer a subtle comparison*** *with my friends than making it a competition* "[P235].

Social comparison is not a significant motivator for people with high level of neuroticism and conscientiousness and could demotivate people who are open to experience. The main negative comment against social comparison is its tendency to be *invasive, backfire, reduce self-confidence, and interfere with an individual's privacy:*

*"Seems a bit* ***invasive*** *to have your performance displayed for all your friends to see. As a comparison method, I would prefer to compare my average overall daily performance, not my friends - keep it* ***private!****"* [P471]. *"This type of*

*game could go **both ways**...if I drink less than my friends, it may make me drink more. So it basically comes down to what type of friends one is comparing with and if they promote drinking or not"* [P394]. *"It's not relevant to me due to not having a social circle, and due to prior addiction I think **shame** and **depression** would kick in more. I will lose my **confidence**"* [P68].

### Goal Setting and Suggestion

In line with the goal setting theory[42], the ***Goal setting*** and ***Suggestion*** strategy requires users to set a goal or target performance and recommend certain behaviors (for achieving the desired goal to users during system use). Our results show that goal setting is a significant motivator for people high in extraversion and conscientiousness ($\beta$= .16, $p$<.001) and ($\beta$= .16, $p$<.001) respectively. Some reasons given to justify this high preference score include the fact that it *provides useful information* and *challenges people*:

*"I like setting goals, because I **strive** to reach them. I also like that it **advises** and **encourage** me to keep moving forward the next day"* [P41]. *"Not as fun, however it has **useful information** and make me to really **challenge** myself in a good way. It may work **better with incentives**, doesn't have to be tangible, a badge or ranking system would likely do. If not, it would be useful for people who are motivated already"* [P208]. *"Goal setting is great, however without any true **incentive** to meet my goals, I would not worry quite as much about whether I actually met them"* [P411].

The last two comments suggest that goal setting and suggestion, similar to personalization, self-monitoring and feedback should be used alongside other incentive-oriented strategies such as rewards and competition to engage users and motivate behavior change.

### Reward

In line with the reinforcement theory [59], our results show that participants high in agreeableness, extraversion, and those who are less open to experience found reward as a significant motivator ($\beta$= .15, $p$<.001), ($\beta$= .14, $p$<.001), and ($\beta$= -.13, $p$<.001) respectively. Some reasons given to justify this high preference score include that *it provides additional incentive, and it is fun* and *appealing*:

*"Well, being able to quit alcohol is a reward by itself but getting an **additional reward** sounds even better"* [P257]. *"I am a big fan of playing games that give the points that you can use for in-game purchases. This kind of system would be **very appealing** to me"* [P311]. *"It is **fun** to be rewarded"* [P515].

Reward is not a significant motivator for people high in neuroticism and conscientiousness. Some explanations to justify the low preference for reward include its tendency to *trivialize the benefit of behavior* and *that it is childish*:

*"...why should someone turn a **serious issue** with health consequences into a game by offering rewards?"* [P6]. *"Childish, it seems geared toward really young people"* [P8]. *"The rewards would have to be **immediate** and really **worthwhile** like being able to cash those points in for things like an Amazon Gift Card, payment to PayPal account, or a free meal to a restaurant to motivate"* [P300].

This last comment suggests that the motivational appeal of reward could be dependent on what the reward is worth. This supports previous research that suggests that using reward as an incentive to motivate behavior may redirect the intention of a particular activity [12].

### Punishment

In contrast to rewards, some persuasive games and gamified system offer some kind of ***punishment*** (for not performing the behavior) to reinforce desired behaviors. Although it has been suggested that punishment might not be as effective for motivating behavior change as reward [14], our results show however that punishment is a significant motivator for people high in agreeableness, extraversion, and for people who are less open to experience ($\beta$= .19, $p$<.001), ($\beta$= .15, $p$<.001), and ($\beta$= -.09, $p$<.05) respectively. Some reasons given to justify this high preference include the potential of punishment to *be fun, challenging, engaging, encouraging,* and *to reveal some consequences.*

*"I enjoy this sort of game; the risks of losing stuff would encourage me to do well. It would be **fun** and **challenging**" [P19]. "This would be very beneficial to me as I do not like **disappointing** others, especially myself"* [P508]. *"I will be always up for reaching goals to avoid being punished. Great, this system is more **engaging**"* [P615]

Punishment is not a significant motivator for people high in neuroticism and conscientiousness traits. Some reasons to justify their low preference for punishment include its perception as being *awful, silly, childish, discouraging, depressing, boring, harsh,* and *demoralizing.*

*"It seems a little **harsh**"* [P93], *"This is a bit **childish**"* [P4]. *"Seems **silly** to punish"* [P18], *"This is **awful**"* [P432]. *"This system **creates negativity** which is not a good way of encouraging a positive type of behavior..."* [P41].

## Summary of Personality and Persuasive Strategies

In summary, extraversion and agreeableness emerged as the personality traits that are most responsive to the persuasive strategies overall. Openness and neuroticism emerged as the least responsive, with openness being negatively associated with most of the strategies while neuroticism shows no significant relation with any of the strategies.

## DISCUSSION

In this section, we discuss how our findings can be applied in designing persuasive games and gamified systems to appeal to both a broader audience and to be tailored to a particular user group based on their personality.

## Designing to Appeal to a Broad Audience

Our results show that *personalization* is the most persuasive of all the strategies. It is perceived as positive by all the personalities (extraversion, agreeableness, openness, and conscientiousness) except neuroticism. However, it does not negatively influence neuroticism. Therefore, to appeal to a broad user population, persuasive games and gamified systems **should tailor their contents (using automated system tailoring as opposed to user customization) to an individual's preference**. Game elements such as *cascading information theory*, *epic meaning*, and *privacy*[2] could be used to create a sense of personalized contents and personal relevance. There are ways that personalization can be deployed as a general strategy. For example, including the participant's name in system messages or considering general color preferences for cultural or age groups [53].

Similarly, *simulation* is perceived as positive by extraversion, agreeableness, and conscientiousness and does not negatively impact other personality types. *Simulation* is also one of the highly-rated strategies. Therefore, to appeal to a broad audience, persuasive games and gamified systems **should be designed to show the cause-and-effect linkage and projected outcome of an individual's health behavior**. Game elements such as *status*, *appointments*, *leaderboards*, *achievements*, *epic meaning*, *behavior momentum*, *blissful productivity*, and *urgent optimism* that structure play and give players an idea of how their behavior will impact their lives could be used to create a simulated experience of the real-world behavior within the context of play.

Our results also show that *goal setting* and *suggestion* is a significant motivator of behavior for extraverted and conscientious individuals and does not negatively impact other personality types. *Goal setting* and *suggestion* are also one of the highly preferred strategies overall. Therefore, to appeal to a broad user population, persuasive games and gamified systems **should be designed to allow users to set their own goals and offer suggestions on both how to set effective goals and how to reach the goals.** Game elements such as *quest*, *appointments*, *status*, *level*, *reward schedule*, and *countdown* that structure play around target task and time-required-to-complete-them could be used to set clear goals about the real-world behavior and offer suggestions on how to achieve them.

From the qualitative comments, participants expressed a common concern about the three strategies *personalization*, *simulation*, and *goal setting* and *suggestion.* They are perceived as "not fun", "boring", "not engaging" and, "not incentivizing" enough. Therefore, **we recommend that designers should apply *personalization, simulation,* and *goal setting and suggestion* strategies together with fun and incentive-oriented strategies such as *rewards* (badges, points, bonuses), *competition,* and *comparisons* (ranking, status, leaderboard, envy) to reinforce them.**

### Designing for Users with a Specific Personality Type

Although designing for the broadest possible audience is a common practice, tailoring persuasive experiences to individual users or user groups has been advocated [35,49,50]. Our results reveal opportunities where personalizing game experience by tailoring the strategies based on users' personality is highly desirable.

Our results show that *personalization* (system tailoring as opposed to user customization) is the only strategy that is perceived as positive by people who are very open to experience. However, people who are less open to experience are more likely to prefer customization. These findings mean that people who are more open to experience are more likely to be motivated using *system-controlled* tailoring (personalization) while people who are less open are more likely to be motivated by *user-controlled* tailoring (customization). A possible explanation is that people who feel threatened by losing control and those who are conscious about privacy tend to be more influenced by the affordance of agency in customization and tend to explore all customizable features provided by a system [53]. Individuals who are less open to experience fall into this category. On the other hand, people who are more persuaded by system relevance (and care less about control) of the resulting content tend to use only the default features [60] and hence prefer personalization — more openness to experience people belong to this category. Therefore, **we suggest that when designing to specifically appeal to people who are more open to experience, designers should personalize the system using system-controlled tailoring**. However, **when designing to specifically appeal to people who are less open to experience, designers should employ user-controlled tailoring.**

For people high in conscientiousness, our results show that they have strong preference for *goal setting and suggestion, simulation, personalization, and self-monitoring* and *feedback* and therefore are more likely to be motivated by systems employing these strategies. Therefore, when designing **to specifically appeal to people high in conscientiousness, designers should employ *goal setting and suggestion, simulation, personalization, and self-monitoring* and *feedback.*** This may demotivate behavior for people low in conscientiousness. **Therefore, designers should avoid using these strategies for this group.**

Surprisingly, our findings show that neurotic individuals are less likely to be motivated to adopt healthy behaviors using any of the strategies studied. One possible explanation is that most commonly employed persuasive strategies are not suitable for neuroticism personality traits. Therefore, **persuasive games and gamified systems should explore neuroticism-oriented persuasive strategies.** Another possible reason is that persuasion may not work for everyone, there is a limit to what and who can be persuaded to adopt healthy behavior using the persuasive strategies. Therefore, **for neuroticisms, persuasion may not be an effective approach for motivating behavior change.**

Finally, our findings reveal that extraversion, agreeableness, and openness are the three personality traits that predict most of the variability in the effectiveness of

[2] For detailed definitions of the game elements and the mapping of the persuasive strategies to some common game mechanics see Orji et al. [53].

persuasive strategies. Extraversion and agreeableness are significantly and positively associated with most strategies while openness is negatively associated with most strategies. Therefore, **to achieve personality-driven tailoring, it is necessary to differentiate participants based on these traits (at least)**.

There are many ways in which persuasive games and gamified systems could be tailored based on our results, we have highlighted a few here as examples. Table 4 details the relations between the strategies and personality traits which could guide design choices for tailoring persuasive games and gamified systems.

### Other Design Implications

Socially-oriented persuasive strategies such as competition, comparison, and cooperation are among the most frequently employed strategies both in persuasive and gamified systems and other online support systems because of their ability to leverage the power of social influence to motivate behavior change. Our findings reveal that these socially-oriented strategies are likely to demotivate people who are introverted, open to experience, and less agreeable. Our qualitative results show that this group of people perceive these strategies as *invasive*, *less privacy preserving*, and *has a high potential of harming friendship*. A participant noted that she would compete if it did not require disclosing her personal data. Therefore, we suggest that **to target these group of people, designers should include mechanisms that allow users to hide their identity or use nicknames. Designers should also make it possible for individuals to work with strangers that cannot possibly identify them.**

The qualitative comments show that socially-oriented strategies (competition, comparison, and cooperation) have the potential of being counterproductive by demotivating behaviors if not strategically implemented. As highlighted by the comment *"This type of game could go* ***both ways****...if I drink less than my friends, it may make me drink more. So it basically comes down to what type of friends one is comparing with and if they promote drinking or not"* [P394]. Therefore**, care should be taken when employing these strategies to reduce the possibility of downward comparison**. Designers can pre-screen and redistribute users across groups to ensure effective social circle for comparison. Designers can also include mechanism that allow for both within and between-group comparisons.

## LIMITATIONS

First, our study presents the self-reported persuasiveness of various strategies implemented in storyboards, but the actual persuasiveness of the strategies may differ when implemented in a specific game. Therefore, we plan to examine the persuasiveness of the recommended strategies deployed in an actual gamified persuasive system. Secondly, while our work has benefited from the large-scale study of persuasiveness of the strategies with respect to unhealthy alcohol behavior change and we can claim applicability in other health behavior domains (due to the high level nature of the storyboard depicting the strategies), our results may not generalize to other behavior domains and therefore should be applied with caution in these domains.

## CONCLUSION AND FUTURE WORK

The current study investigates the relations between personality and persuasive strategies as highlighted by the Persuasive Systems Design Framework for the first time in the literature. Specifically, the paper contributes to the HCI community by advancing understanding on how an individual's personality traits determine their preference and responsiveness to various persuasive strategies that are widely used in persuasive games and gamified systems. As a secondary objective, we validated the persuasiveness of the strategies and showed their comparative persuasiveness with respect to their ability to motivate risky health behavior change. Our results show that people's personality traits play significant roles in their responsiveness and preference for various persuasive strategies. Through the study, we exposed the limitations of the untailored approach and presented design opportunities for designing persuasive games and gamified systems that appeal both to a broad audience and can be tailored to a particular personality trait. Our findings indicate that *extraversion*, *agreeableness*, and *openness* are the three personality traits that predict most of the variance in the effectiveness of the persuasive strategies. In general, *personalization*, *simulation*, *goal setting* and *suggestion*, *self-monitoring and feedback*, and *social comparison* are the most persuasive of all the strategies while *punishment* and *customization* are the least persuasive. Our results could guide designers in making informed choices on the strategies to employ and those to avoid when designing persuasive games and gamified systems tailored to various users' personalities.

Although this study showed many interesting and significant findings, it also opens up many areas for further examination. Future research should compare the effectiveness of the strategies in actual persuasive games. Again, our results should be validated in other health behavior domains (e.g., discouraging drug use, risky sexual behavior, and smoking) to investigate possible changes in the persuasiveness of the strategies. Our results highlight differences in relations between the personality traits and the 10 persuasive strategies—this suggests a need for a persuasion profile comprised of a comprehensive list of strategies to motivate different personalities.

## ACKNOWLEDGMENTS

The authors would like to thank the NSERC Banting Fellowship and the University of Waterloo for supporting Dr. Rita Orji's research. We also thank the anonymous reviewers and study participants for insightful comments; George Ross, Mariam Ganaba, and Gustavo Tondello for their help with reviewing and refining the storyboard. All studies complied with the research ethics guidelines provided by the University of Waterloo.

## REFERENCES


1. Atif Alamri, Mohammad Mehedi Hassan, M. Anwar Hossain, Muhammad Al-Qurishi, Yousuf Aldukhayyil, and M Shamim Hossain. 2014. Evaluating the impact of a cloud-based serious game on obese people. *Computers in Human Behavior* 30: 468–475. http://doi.org/10.1016/j.chb.2013.06.021
2. Sonia M. Arteaga, Víctor M. González, Sri Kurniawan, and Raquel a. Benavides. 2012. Mobile games and design requirements to increase teenagers' physical activity. *Pervasive and Mobile Computing* 8, 6: 900–908. http://doi.org/10.1016/j.pmcj.2012.08.002
3. Sonia M. Arteaga, Mo Kudeki, and Adrienne Woodworth. 2009. Combating obesity trends in teenagers through persuasive mobile technology. *ACM SIGACCESS Accessibility and Computing*, 94: 17–25. http://doi.org/10.1145/1595061.1595064
4. Magnus Bang, Carin Torstensson, and Cecilia Katzeff. 2006. The PowerHhouse: A Persuasive Computer Game Designed to Raise Awareness of Domestic Energy Consumption. *Persuasive Technology*: 123–132. http://doi.org/http://dx.doi.org/10.1007/11755494_33.
5. Marek Bell, Matthew Chalmers, Louise Barkhuus, et al. 2006. Interweaving mobile games with everyday life. *Proceedings of the {SIGCHI} conference on Human Factors in computing systems*, ACM, 417–426. http://doi.org/10.1145/1124772.1124835
6. Shlomo Berkovsky, Mac Coombe, Jill Freyne, Dipak Bhandari, and Nilufar Baghaei. 2010. Physical activity motivating games: virtual rewards for real activity. *Proceedings of the International Conference on Human Factors in Computing Systems*, ACM, 243–252. http://doi.org/10.1145/1753326.1753362
7. Max Birk and Regan L. Mandryk. 2013. Control your game-self. *Proceedings of the SIGCHI Conference on Human Factors in Computing Systems - CHI '13*, ACM Press, 685. http://doi.org/10.1145/2470654.2470752
8. M Buhrmester, T Kwang, and Gosling S. D. 2011. Amazon's Mechanical Turk A New Source of Inexpensive, Yet High-Quality, Data? *Perspectives on Psychological Science* 6, 1: 3–5. http://doi.org/doi: 10.1177/1745691610393980
9. Marc Busch, E. Mattheiss, M. Reisinger, R. Orji, P. Fröhlich, and M. Tscheligi. 2016. *More than sex: The role of femininity and masculinity in the design of personalized persuasive games.* http://doi.org/10.1007/978-3-319-31510-2_19
10. Marc Busch, Elke Mattheiss, Wolfgang Hochleitner, et al. 2016. Using Player Type Models for Personalized Game Design - An Empirical Investigation. *International Journal on Interaction Design & Architecture(s)* Accepted f.
11. Wynne W. Chin. 1998. The Partial Least Squares Approach to Structural Equation Modeling. *Modern Methods for Business Research* 292, 2: 298–336.
12. Nathalie Colineau and Cécile Paris. 2011. Can beneficial habits be induced through reflection. *Workshop on User Models for Motivational Systems, held in conjunction with the User Modeling, Adaptation and Personalization Conference.* Retrieved from http://www.ict.csiro.au/staff/nathalie.colineau/publications/Colineau-Paris_WorkshopUM4Motivation.pdf
13. Sunny Consolvo, David W McDonald, and James A Landay. 2009. Theory-driven design strategies for technologies that support behavior change in everyday life. *Proceedings of the international conference on Human factors in computing systems*, ACM, 405–414. http://doi.org/10.1145/1518701.1518766
14. Aubrey C. Daniels. 2000. *Bringing Out the Best in People: How to Apply the Astonishing Power of Positive Reinforcement.* McGraw-Hill.
15. Filip Drozd, Tuomas Lehto, and Harri Oinas-Kukkonen. 2012. Exploring perceived persuasiveness of a behavior change support system: A structural model. *Lecture Notes in Computer Science (including subseries Lecture Notes in Artificial Intelligence and Lecture Notes in Bioinformatics)*, 157–168. http://doi.org/10.1007/978-3-642-31037-9_14
16. Brian J. Fogg. 2003. *Persuasive Technology: Using Computers to Change What We Think and Do.* Morgan Kaufmann. http://doi.org/10.1145/764008.763957
17. Yuichi Fujiki, Konstantinos Kazakos, Colin Puri, Pradeep Buddharaju, Ioannis Pavlidis, and James Levine. 2008. {NEAT-o-Games:} blending physical activity and fun in the daily routine. *Computers in Entertainment* 6, 2: 1–22. http://doi.org/10.1145/1371216.1371224
18. Kathrin M Gerling, Regan L Mandryk, Max Birk, Matthew Miller, and Rita Orji. The Effects of Embodied Persuasive Games on Player Attitudes Toward People Using Wheelchairs. http://doi.org/10.1145/2556288.2556962
19. Lewis. R Goldberg. 1993. The structure of phenotypic personality traits. *American Psychologist* 48, 1: 26–34. http://doi.org/10.1037/0003-066X.48.1.26
20. Andrea Grimes, Vasudhara Kantroo, and Rebecca E Grinter. 2010. Let's play!: mobile health games for adults. *Proceedings of the 12th ACM international conference on Ubiquitous computing*: 241–250. http://doi.org/10.1145/1864349.1864370
21. Andrea Grimes, Desney Tan, and Dan Morris. 2009. Toward technologies that support family reflections on health. *Proceedings of the {ACM} 2009 international conference on Supporting group work*, ACM, 311–320. http://doi.org/10.1145/1531674.1531721
22. Joe F. Hair, Christian M. Ringle, and Marko Sarstedt. 2011. PLS-SEM: Indeed a Silver Bullet. *Journal of Marketing Theory and Practice* 19, 2: 139–152. http://doi.org/10.2753/MTP1069-6679190202
23. Sajanee Halko and Julie A Kientz. 2010. Personality and persuasive technology: An exploratory study on health-promoting mobile applications. *Persuasive Technology*, Springer, 150–161. http://doi.org/10.1007/978-3-642-13226-1_16
24. Juho Hamari, Jonna Koivisto, and Tuomas Pakkanen. 2014. Do Persuasive Technologies persuade ? - A review of empirical studies. *Proceedings of Persuasive'14, LNCS 8462*, Springer International Publishing Switzerland, 118–136.
25. Juho Hamari, Jonna Koivisto, and Harri Sarsa. 2014. Does gamification work? - A literature review of empirical studies on gamification. *Proceedings of the Annual Hawaii International Conference on System Sciences*, JANUARY: 3025–3034. http://doi.org/10.1109/HICSS.2014.377
26. Jacob B Hirsh, Sonia K Kang, and Galen V Bodenhausen.

2012. Personalized persuasion: tailoring persuasive appeals to recipients' personality traits. *Psychological science* 23, 6: 578–81. http://doi.org/10.1177/0956797611436349

27. Marc Busch, Mattheiss Elke, Rita Orji, Marczewski, Andrzej, Wolfgang Hochleitner, Michael Lankes, Lennart E. Nacke, Tscheligi, Manfred. 2015. Personalization in serious and persuasive games and gamified interactions. *CHI PLAY 2015 - Proceedings of the 2015 Annual Symposium on Computer-Human Interaction in Play*: 811–816. http://doi.org/10.1145/2793107.2810260
28. Astrid Jander, Rik Crutzen, Liesbeth Mercken, Math Candel, and Hein de Vries. 2016. Effects of a Web-Based Computer-Tailored Game to Reduce Binge Drinking Among Dutch Adolescents: A Cluster Randomized Controlled Trial. *Journal of medical Internet research* 18, 2: e29. http://doi.org/10.2196/jmir.4708
29. Astrid Jander, Rik Crutzen, Liesbeth Mercken, and Hein De Vries. 2014. A Web-based computer-tailored game to reduce binge drinking among 16 to 18 year old Dutch adolescents: development and study protocol. *BMC Public Health* 14: 1054. http://doi.org/10.1186/1471-2458-14-1054
30. John B. Jemmott, Loretta Sweet Jemmott, and Geoffrey T. Fong. 1992. Reductions in HIV risk-associated sexual behaviors among black male adolescents: effects of an AIDS prevention intervention. *American Journal of Public Health* 82, 3: 372–377. http://doi.org/10.2105/AJPH.82.3.372
31. Shih-Ping Jeng and Ching-I Teng. 2008. Personality and motivations for playing online games. *Social Behavior and Personality: an international journal* 36, 8: 1053–1060. http://doi.org/10.2224/sbp.2008.36.8.1053
32. Yuan Jia, Bin Xu, Yamini Karanam, and Stephen Voida. 2016. Personality,targeted/Gamification: A Survey Study on Personality Traits and Motivational Affordances. *Proceedings of the SIGCHI Conference on Human Factors in Computing Systems*. http://doi.org/10.1145/2858036.2858515
33. Daniel Johnson and John Gardner. 2010. Personality, Motivation and Video Games. *Proceedings of the 22nd Conference of the Computer-Human Interaction Special Interest Group of Australia on Computer-Human Interaction - OZCHI '10*, 276. http://doi.org/10.1145/1952222.1952281
34. Henry F. Kaiser. 1970. A second generation little jiffy. *Psychometrika* 35, 4: 401–415. http://doi.org/10.1007/BF02291817
35. Maurits Kaptein, Boris De Ruyter, Panos Markopoulos, and Emile Aarts. 2012. Adaptive Persuasive Systems. *ACM Transactions on Interactive Intelligent Systems* 2, 2: 1–25. http://doi.org/10.1145/2209310.2209313
36. Rilla Khaled, Ronald Fischer, James Noble, and Robert Biddle. 2008. A qualitative study of culture and persuasion in a smoking cessation game. *Proceedings of the Third International Conference on Persuasive Technology for Human Well-Being*, Springer Berlin Heidelberg, 224–236. http://doi.org/10.1007/978-3-540-68504-3-20
37. Yvonne Klisch, Leslie M Miller, Margaret E Beier, and Shu Wang. 2012. Teaching the biological consequences of alcohol abuse through an online game: Impacts among secondary students. *CBE Life Sciences Education* 11, 1: 94–102. http://doi.org/10.1187/cbe.11-04-0040
38. Yvonne Klisch, Leslie M Miller, Shu Wang, and Joel Epstein. 2012. The Impact of a Science Education Game on Students' Learning and Perception of Inhalants as Body Pollutants. *Journal of Science Education and Technology* 21, 2: 295–303. http://doi.org/10.1007/s10956-011-9319-y
39. Emil Kupek. 2006. Beyond logistic regression: structural equations modelling for binary variables and its application to investigating unobserved confounders. *BMC medical research methodology* 6, 1: 13. http://doi.org/10.1186/1471-2288-6-13
40. Tuomas Lehto and Harri Oinas-Kukkonen. 2011. Persuasive features in web-based alcohol and smoking interventions: a systematic review of the literature. *Journal of medical Internet research* 13, 3: e46. http://doi.org/10.2196/jmir.1559
41. Corrie Lelie. 2005. The value of storyboards in the product design process. *Personal and Ubiquitous Computing* 10, 2–3: 159–162. http://doi.org/10.1007/s00779-005-0026-7
42. Edwin Locke and Gary Latham. 1994. Goal-setting theory.
43. Salvatore R. Maddi. 1989. *Personality theories: A comparative analysis, 5th ed.* Dorsey Press.
44. Winter Mason and Siddharth Suri. 2012. Conducting behavioral research on Amazon's Mechanical Turk. *Behavior research methods* 44, 1: 1–23. http://doi.org/10.3758/s13428-011-0124-6
45. Oded Nov and Ofer Arazy. 2013. Personality-targeted design: theory, experimental procedure, and preliminary results. *Proceedings of the 2013 conference on Computer ...*, 977–984. http://doi.org/10.1145/2441776.2441887
46. Harri Oinas-kukkonen and Marja Harjumaa. 2008. A Systematic Framework for Designing and Evaluating Persuasive Systems. *PERSUASIVE*, Springer, 1–5. http://doi.org/10.1007/978-3-540-68504-3
47. Harri Oinas-kukkonen and Marja Harjumaa. 2009. Persuasive Systems Design : Key Issues , Process Model , and System Features Persuasive Systems Design : Key Issues , Process Model , and System Features. *Communications of the Association for Information Systems* 24, 1: 28.
48. Rita Orji, Regan L. Mandryk, and Julita Vassileva. 2015. *Gender, age, and responsiveness to cialdini's persuasion strategies*. http://doi.org/10.1007/978-3-319-20306-5_14
49. Rita Orji. 2014. Design for Behaviour Change: A Model-driven Approach for Tailoring Persuasive Technologies. PhD Thesis: 1–257. Retrieved from http://hdl.handle.net/10388/ETD-2014-06-1555
50. Rita Orji, Regan L. Mandryk, Julita Vassileva, and Kathrin M. Gerling. 2013. Tailoring persuasive health games to gamer type. *Proceedings of the SIGCHI Conference on Human Factors in Computing Systems - CHI '13*, ACM Press, 2467–2476. http://doi.org/10.1145/2470654.2481341
51. Rita Orji and Karyn Moffatt. 2016. Persuasive technology for health and wellness: State-of-the-art and emerging trends. *Health Informatics Journal* 1: 7–9. http://doi.org/10.1177/1460458216650979
52. Rita Orji, Julita Vassileva, and Regan L. Mandryk. 2012. LunchTime: a slow-casual game for long-term dietary behavior change. *Personal and Ubiquitous Computing* 17, 6: 1211–1221. http://doi.org/10.1007/s00779-012-0590-6
53. Rita Orji, Julita Vassileva, and Regan L. Mandryk. 2014. Modeling the efficacy of persuasive strategies for different

gamer types in serious games for health. *User Modeling and User-Adapted Interaction* 24, 5: 453–498. http://doi.org/10.1007/s11257-014-9149-8

54. Jowon Park, Yosep Song, and Ching-I Teng. 2011. Exploring the links between personality traits and motivations to play online games. *Cyberpsychology, Behavior, and Social Networking* 14, 12: 747–51. http://doi.org/10.1089/cyber.2010.0502
55. Jr. Paul T. Costa and Robert R. McCrae. 1992. *NEO Personality Inventory–Revised (NEO-PI-R) and NEO Five-Factor Inventory (NEO-FFI) Professional Manua.* Psychological Assessment Resources, Odessa, FL.
56. Nicole Peever, Daniel Johnson, and John Gardner. 2012. Personality & video game genre preferences. *Proceedings of The 8th Australasian Conference on Interactive Entertainment Playing the System - IE '12*: 1–3. http://doi.org/10.1145/2336727.2336747
57. Beatrice Rammstedt and Oliver P. John. 2007. Measuring personality in one minute or less: A 10-item short version of the Big Five Inventory in English and German. *Journal of Research in Personality* 41, 1: 203–212. http://doi.org/10.1016/j.jrp.2006.02.001
58. Christian M. Ringle, S Wende, and J Becker. smartpls.de - next generation path modeling. Retrieved August 29, 2012 from http://www.smartpls.de/forum/contact.php
59. Burrhus F. Skinner. 1953. *Science And Human Behavior*. Simon and Schuster. http://doi.org/10.1037/h0052427

60 Shyam S. Sundar and Sampada S. Marathe. 2010. Personalization versus Customization: The Importance of Agency, Privacy, and Power Usage. *Human Communication Research* 36, 3: 298–322. http://doi.org/10.1111/j.1468-2958.2010.01377.x

61. R Thomas, J Cahill, and L Santilli. 1997. Using an Interactive Computer Game to Increase Skill and Self-Efficacy Regarding Safer Sex Negotiation: Field Test Results. *Health Education and Behavior* 24, 1: 71–86. http://doi.org/10.1177/109019819702400108
62. Gustavo F Tondello, Rina R Wehbe, Lisa Diamond, Marc Busch, Andrzej Marczewski, and Lennart E Nacke. The Gamification User Types Hexad Scale. http://doi.org/10.1145/2967934.2968082
63. Tammy Toscos, Anne Faber, Shunying An, and Mona Praful Gandhi. 2006. Chick clique: persuasive technology to motivate teenage girls to exercise. *{CHI} '06 extended abstracts on Human factors in computing systems*, ACM, 1873–1878. http://doi.org/10.1145/1125451.1125805
64. Khai N Truong, Gillian R Hayes, and Gregory D Abowd. 2006. Storyboarding: An Empirical Determination of Best Practices and Effective Guidelines. *DIS '06 Proceedings of the 6th conference on Designing Interactive systems, ACM New York, NY, USA*, 12–21. http://doi.org/10.1145/1142405.1142410
65. Veronica Lorena Zammitto. 2010. Gamers' Personality and their Gaming Preferences. *School of Interactive Arts and Technology M.Sc Thesi*. Retrieved April 10, 2014 from http://summit.sfu.ca/item/11349

# Is Difficulty Overrated? The Effects of Choice, Novelty and Suspense on Intrinsic Motivation in Educational Games

J. Derek Lomas[1,2], Ken Koedinger[2], Nirmal Patel[2], Sharan Shodhan[2], Nikhil Poonwala[2], Jodi L. Forlizzi[2]

The Design Lab[1]
UC San Diego
dereklomas@gmail.com

HCI Institute[2]
Carnegie Mellon
{krk,forlizzi}@cs.cmu.edu

## ABSTRACT

Many game designers aim to optimize difficulty to make games that are "not too hard, not too easy." However, recent experiments have shown that even moderate difficulty can reduce player engagement. The present work investigates other design factors that may account for the purported benefits of difficulty, such as choice, novelty and suspense. These factors were manipulated in three design experiments involving over 20,000 play sessions of an online educational game.

The first experiment (n=10,472) randomly assigned some players to a particular level of difficulty but allowed other players to freely choose their difficulty. Moderately difficult levels were most motivating when self-selected; yet, when difficulty was blindly assigned, the easiest games were most motivating. The second experiment (n=5,065) randomly assigned players to differing degrees of novelty. Moderate novelty was optimal, while too much or too little novelty reduced intrinsic motivation. A final experiment (n=6,511) investigated the role of suspense in "close games", where it was found to be beneficial. If difficulty decreases motivation while novelty and suspense increase it, then an implication for educational game designers is to make easy, interesting games that are "not too hard, not too boring."

### Author Keywords

Learning; Education; Games; Intrinsic Motivation; Challenge; Difficulty; Novelty; Suspense; Theory; Experiments; Flow; Near Win; A/B testing;

### ACM Classification Keywords

H.5.m. Information interfaces and presentation (e.g., HCI): Miscellaneous.


*CHI 2017, May 06-11, 2017, Denver, CO, USA*
 ISBN 978-1-4503-4655-9/17/05...$15.00
DOI: http://dx.doi.org/10.1145/3025453.3025638

## INTRODUCTION

It is almost a truism that good games shouldn't be too hard or too easy. It isn't surprising that games can be too hard: after all, a core objective in HCI is minimizing user difficulty and maximizing ease-of-use [20,40]. That makes it much more surprising that games can be too easy. Can games really be too easy? Or just too boring?

The evidence is mixed: in some studies [4,18,1], difficulty is good for intrinsic motivation and in other studies it is not [33,44]. To clarify this issue for educational game designers and others, we ran three controlled experiments to test how various design factors modulate the role of difficulty on player intrinsic motivation.

### The Inverted U-Shaped Curve Theory

To make it easier to make learning fun, Malone and Lepper [38] organized a "Taxonomy of Intrinsic Motivations for Learning": ~30 theoretically grounded principles for designing intrinsically motivated instruction. The taxonomy's opening claim states, "The activity should provide a continuously optimal (intermediate) level of difficulty for the learner." This claim was based on Csikszentmihalyi's theory of "Flow" [10], a theory that is now the basis of many contemporary theories of game enjoyment [51,48]. Formalized, Flow theory describes the relationship between difficulty and enjoyment as an inverted U-shaped curve [1].

> The notion that we most enjoy optimally challenging activities that are not too easy or too difficult implies a curvilinear, inverted U-shaped relation between difficulty and enjoyment, so that increases in difficulty should lead to increases in enjoyment up to an optimal level (i.e., the apex of the curve), after which further increases in difficulty lead to decreases in enjoyment. (p. 318)

### Difficulty vs Challenge

Difficulty, as a theoretical construct, has an established history; in psychometrics, it is measured as a test item's average error rate in the population of test takers [27]. In other words, more difficult items have a greater probability of being answered incorrectly. Similarly, if a game is more difficult, one has a greater probability of losing [3]. While the quote above [1] uses difficulty and challenge interchangeably, this paper will use the term *difficulty* to mean, precisely, "the probability of task failure" and will abstain from defining *challenge*, which we believe is a more nuanced and complex concept.

### Observing the Inverted-U Theory in Online Chess

To test the theory that difficulty has an inverted-U effect on enjoyment, Abuhamdeh and Csikszentmihalyi [1] conducted an empirical investigation of thousands of online chess players. They measured difficulty as the difference between the ELO chess ranking of two players (two players with the same ELO score have a 50% chance of winning). Enjoyment of games was measured via self-report immediately after each game. The result? Players most enjoyed games when they had an 80% chance of losing. These players liked hard games—but not too hard.

A few factors cloud these results. First, it is noteworthy that players had an incentive to play against harder players: winning against a higher-ranked player increases one's own ELO chess rank. Secondly, players were not blindly or randomly assigned to their opponents; instead, players could choose their opponents based on their chess rank. This gave players the ability to control their expected game difficulty. The ranking incentives and awareness of difficulty may have affected the results if certain types of players self-selected more difficult opponents. Would the results be different if ran as a controlled experiment?

### Testing the Inverted-U with Random Assignment

Several years ago, we sought to replicate this inverted-U effect using a controlled experiment in the educational game "Battleship Numberline" [33]. We hoped to identify the optimal level of game difficulty by randomly assigning hundreds of different game versions to >50,000 online players. Gameplay data revealed the difficulty (average items failed divided by total items attempted) and the intrinsic motivation (duration of voluntary play) of each game variation.

Our results were surprising, as the optimal level of difficulty seemed to be "as easy as possible." Nearly all increases in game difficulty reduced player intrinsic motivation. For both high and low ability players, easier games were consistently played longer, even when the failure rate was less than 10%. This was particularly surprising in light of previous work that indicated intrinsic motivation would be maximized when the difficulty (failure rate) of the game was between 80%-50% [1, 4].

Although our results weren't predicted by the inverted-U theory [1], they do seem to be supported by other theories of intrinsic motivation. Consider that, by definition, increased difficulty increases the rate of task failure. These failures produce negative feedback that can reduce intrinsic motivation by reducing expectations for future successes [17], reducing perceived task value [17] and reducing self-perceptions of competence [11]. Moreover, more difficult tasks are more effortful: increased effort increases fatigue and increased fatigue increases rates of task switching [31, 21]. Indeed, fatigue may be the psychological reason why harder games cause players to disengage faster [33]. In any case, these theories imply that the failure accompanying difficulty will not improve intrinsic motivation.

Still, there is plenty of evidence that challenge is enjoyable and motivating [10], particularly with success [18]. Might the positive aspects of challenge come from factors other than difficulty? For instance, when one advances through a game, the new game levels are often more difficult – but they are also new. When games introduce greater difficulty, they often also introduce interesting new design elements. Perhaps games that are "too easy" don't suffer from a lack of difficulty, but a lack of interestingness.

### Research Question

Our research aims to clarify the current situation regarding difficulty optimization in games. As Flow Theory strongly predicts an inverted-U relationship between challenge and intrinsic motivation, what other factors of challenge, apart from difficulty, might produce this inverted-U shape?

In the following three experiments, we investigate three different factors associated with challenge: player choice of difficulty, novelty and suspense. In the first experiment we use the same experimental design as the chess study [1] and show that letting players self-select their difficulty can produce an inverted-U shaped curve. In a second experiment, we randomly assigned players to different degrees of novelty and find that a moderate degree of novelty maximizes motivation. This evidence supports the idea that the motivational nature of challenge may stem from the novelty found in challenge as much as from the difficulty. In a third experiment, we randomly assign players to different criteria for winning, in order to dissociate player skill from their likelihood of winning. Our results show that players are motivated by the suspense of a close game, which tends to occur when the difficulty is matched to the player's skill. In total, this paper tests six hypotheses, provided below for convenience

> **H1.1:** Providing a choice of difficulty will produce an inverted U-shaped relationship between difficulty and engagement.
>
> **H1.2:** Player choices will resemble an inverted U-shaped curve, with most players choosing moderately difficult levels.
>
> **H1.3:** Higher skilled players will self-select themselves into more difficult game levels.
>
> **H1.4:** Knowing that game levels are "very easy" will decrease player persistence relative to players who don't know the difficulty of the level.
>
> **H2:** A moderate degree of novelty will maximize player motivation.
>
> **H3:** The closer the game, the greater the suspense and the greater the intrinsic motivation.

### Battleship Numberline Game Design

*Battleship Numberline* [33,34] is a simple online game where players attempt to explode targets by estimating numbers on a number line. In subsequent experiments, players were presented with numbers that indicating the location of a hidden submarine between two endpoints (e.g., "submarine spotted at ½" between the end points of 0-1). When a player clicks on a location along the line to indicate their estimate, a bomb falls at that location and the hidden submarine then becomes visible as feedback. If the bomb hits the target, there is a satisfying explosion and a gold star is released, incrementing the player's star count in the scoreboard. If the player misses, the bomb splashes in the water. There is no final "winning" or "losing" state in the game – instead, players can continue to play as long as they wish. Additionally, there are no leaderboards or other mechanisms that allow players to directly compare status.

**Figure 1: The *Battleship Numberline* game screen. From left to right we show the "Hard" and "Very Easy" game level. The game is easier when the target is larger because players can make more inaccurate estimates and yet still be successful.**

### Participants

*Battleship Numberline* was made available on the *GameUp* platform on Brainpop.com, a popular site for grade 4-8 classrooms. Data from experimental game sessions were collected, largely during school hours, with large drop offs during weekends and holidays (suggesting that the games were primarily played in a classroom).

The educational game site offers dozens of free games and teachers have little control over their student's activities. Thus, the decision of how long to play a particular game appears to be largely up to the student. Subjects were completely anonymous and data was collected only for a single game session (no longitudinal collection).

## DIFFICULTY CHOICE EXPERIMENT

In the chess study [1], players freely chose their opponent with full knowledge of their chess rank. Essentially, this means that players were able to choose the difficulty of their game. In contrast, the study of *Battleship Numberline* [33] involved blindly and randomly assigning players to different levels of difficulty.

Why would knowing the difficulty of a game affect a player's motivation? Knowing the difficulty of a task is likely to affect a player's causal interpretation of their performance. According to Bernard Weiner's attribution theory of motivation [50, 15], this interpretation can have big motivational outcomes.

Weiner identified three dimensions of attribution: causality (internal or external), controllability and stability. For instance, if a person attributes their poor performance to low effort (an internal, controllable and unstable cause) they are likely to feel guilty – an emotion that is linked to *increases* in future motivation [50]. In contrast, if they attribute their performance to low ability (which is an internal, uncontrollable and stable cause), they are likely to feel ashamed – an emotion linked to *decreases* in future motivation. Attribution theory provides a theoretical basis for why tasks that are labeled "very easy" might be less motivating than tasks labeled "moderately difficult." If a person is told that a game is "very easy", one is expected to be less proud of their successes, relative to another person who was told that the game was "difficult". Lower pride in one's successes over the course of a game is likely to lower overall task enjoyment. Furthermore, any failure during a "very easy" game might be especially shameful – and shame decreases motivation.

Thus, the inverted-U effect of lowered motivation during tasks labeled "very easy" might be a result of less pride during successes and more shame during failures. According to this theory, the inverted-U in the chess study might have occurred because players generally find it less enjoyable to beat a player they know is weak than to beat a player they know is strong.

### Experimental Design: Difficulty Choice Experiment

The primary goal of this experiment is to determine whether giving players a choice of difficulty produces an inverted-U relationship between difficulty and motivation in *Battleship Numberline*. As player choices can be used as a measure of population preferences, we also sought to test whether their pattern of choices resembled an inverted-U shape.

To create five different game levels of difficulty, we used data from a previous experiment [33] and used a regression model to manipulate factors predicted to vary in difficulty from very easy to very hard. We varied several design factors, including Error Tolerance (target size), Time Limit (amount of time players have to make their selection) and Item Sets (items presented).

We randomly assigned players to one of four conditions in a 2x2 between-subjects experiment, as shown in Table 1. Players either received a choice of difficulty, a choice of arbitrary game levels with no information about difficulty, a random level with labeled difficulty, or they were blindly assigned a random level with unlabeled difficulty. Prior to this assignment, players were given a 4-item in-game pretest, which predicts player ability to estimate numbers on a number line, as discussed in [33]. A game session began when players started the game and ended when players exited the game, played more than 80 trials or made no further actions after a time-out. The data presented comes from 10,472 game sessions collected.

| | **Information about difficulty** (Feedforward) | **No Information about difficulty** |
|---|---|---|
| **Choice** |   Difficulty Choice |   Arbitrary Choice |
| **No Choice** | 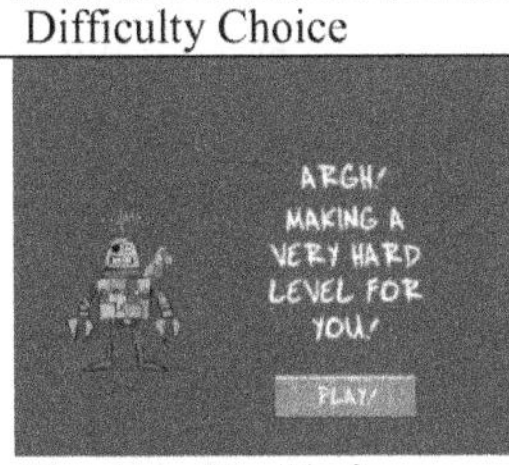  Random, No Choice |   Blind, Random |

**Table 1: The four conditions in the Difficulty Choice Experiment.**

*Operational Measures*

*Difficulty:* The average failure rate of a game level or experimental condition.

*Engagement:* The average of the number of trials played in the game level or condition (total trials divided by total players). A trial is one number line estimate attempt. Engagement, here, is equivalent with intrinsic motivation as there are no extrinsic motivators and players can choose to play another game at any time.

*Preference:* The tendency for players to select a particular choice (# choices for option X divided by total # choices).

*Persistence:* Persistence refers to the tendency for players to keep playing the game in the face of failure. Thus, if two students of the same ability were failing at the same rate but one played for longer, we would call the longer playing student more persistent. We measure persistence as a player's actual number of trials minus the predicted number of trials they were expected to play, given their failure rate. A negative persistence score means that players disengaged earlier than the average player.

### Results: Difficulty Choice Experiment

To investigate H1.1 ("Providing a choice of difficulty will produce an inverted U-shaped relationship between difficulty and engagement"), we plotted the effect of game difficulty on the duration of player engagement (Figure 2). The inverted U-shaped curve was significant only for players with a choice of difficulty, confirming **Hypothesis 1.1**.

It is notable that, while difficulty choice did produce an inverted-U shape, it did so by depressing motivation on the easy and hard levels, rather than increasing motivation on the moderately difficult levels. This foreshadows the confirmation of **Hypothesis 1.4**, that knowledge of "very easy" and "very hard" levels reduces persistence, and accounts for the inverted-U shape.

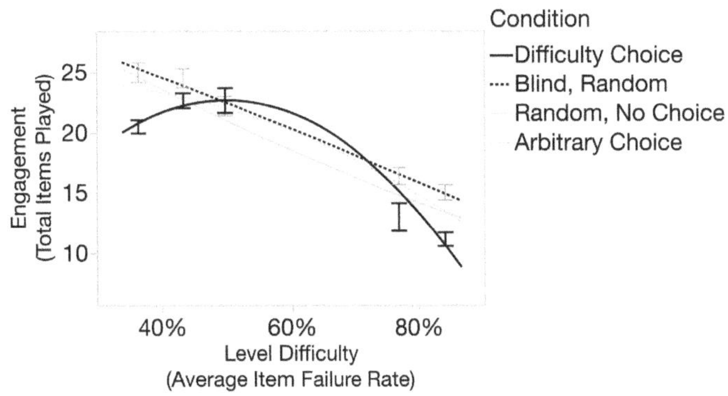


**Figure 2: The "Inverted U relation" between difficulty and player motivation is only seen when players can choose their own difficulty condition (solid black line). In comparison to the blind random assignment (dotted black), motivation in the very easy and very hard levels was depressed. Moderate difficulty did not increase motivation, even when self-selected. In all other conditions, the easiest levels were most motivating. The X-axis shows mean failure rate of each of the 5 levels of difficulty, where levels to the right are harder. The Y-axis is a measure of intrinsic motivation (the total number of items players completed). Error bars (standard error) allow for comparison of the means between blind assignment and difficulty choice.**

Following [1], our statistical test for an "inverted U-shape" was the significance of the quadratic term (difficulty squared). A squared term in a linear regression tests for curvature in the line of fit; when this term is significant, it indicates significant curvature. We used a response surface regression model of engagement, involving terms for experimental condition, level difficulty, level difficulty squared (the quadratic term) and all interactions. We found that the interaction between condition and level difficulty squared was highly significant ($p<0.0001$), indicating that the experimental condition caused the curvature of the observed inverted-U. Only the difficulty choice condition had significant curvature.

Figure 3 shows that **Hypothesis 1.2** was not supported ("player choices will resemble an inverted U-shaped curve, with most players choosing moderately difficult levels"). If anything player preference more resembled a U than an inverted U. Players seemed to distinctly prefer the easiest and hardest levels. It is noteworthy, however, that players did not consistently choose to play the easiest games, as might be predicted by the easier is better hypothesis. Figure 3 shows that players preferred the easiest level of play only 32% of the time.

Figure 3 also confirms **Hypothesis 1.3** ("Higher skilled players will self-select themselves into more difficult game levels"). To test this, we first used pretest scores to break players into two equal groups: high and low ability. Players with a high pretest score (i.e., above the median) tended to choose harder levels than players with a low pretest.

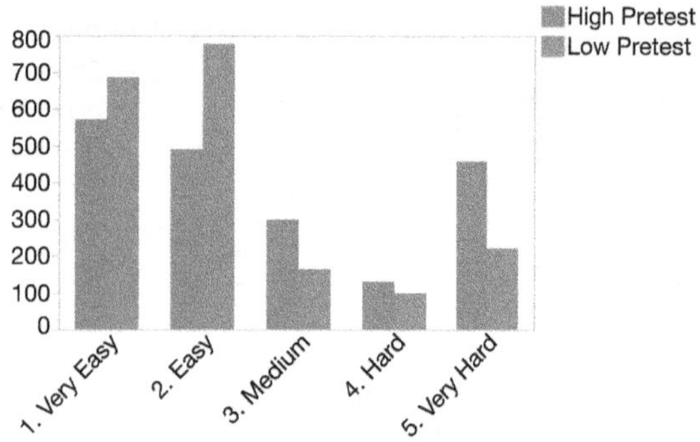


**Figure 3: Total count of choices (Y-axis) made for each of the 5 different levels of difficulty, among all players in the Difficulty Choice Condition. The relationship between level difficulty (X-axis) and player preference is not an inverted-U shape – if anything, it is a U shape. Data are evenly split between players with high and low pretest scores.**

To test Hypothesis 1.4 ("knowing that game levels are "very easy" will decrease player persistence relative to players who don't know the difficulty of the level they are playing"), we first needed to measure the effect of design variations on persistence, which was defined as how much more or less students were engaged in the face of difficulty. We calculated persistence as the difference between each player's actual engagement (# trials played) and the engagement predicted by a population-level model of the effects of failure on engagement. This linear regression model used data from all players to predict total items played using only their failure rate (total failed items divided by total attempted items).

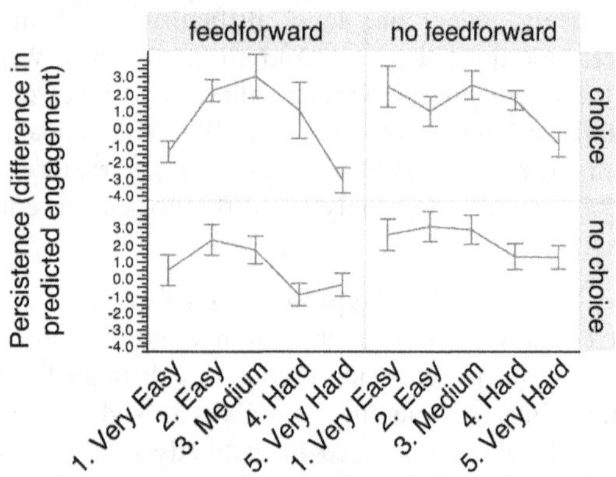


**Figure 4: There is reduced player persistence in "Very Easy" and "Very Hard" levels in the "feedforward" conditions (where players know the difficulty). The mere act of labeling levels reduced how long players played, relative to how long they'd be expected to play, given the level's difficulty. Error bars are Standard Error of the Mean.**

Figure 4 shows how level difficulty and experimental conditions interacted to affect player persistence. Interestingly, players in the two feedforward conditions (where they were told the level of difficulty) were much less persistent in the "very easy" levels, relative to players who weren't told how easy the levels were, supporting **Hypothesis 1.4**.

### Discussion: Difficulty Choice Experiment

When we randomly and blindly assigned difficulty, easier levels were consistently more engaging. But when players were given a choice of difficulty, there was inverted-U relation between difficulty and engagement. Interestingly, this inverted-U was not produced by raising the mid part of the graph, but by lowering the end parts of the graph.

Why might a choice of difficulty make moderately difficult games more motivating? One possibility is that the difficulty and the player's ability are better matched [10]. Another is that increased autonomy improves intrinsic motivation [44,11,13]. A final possibility is that moderately difficult levels *attracted* the most motivated players. It is a limitation of this study that we can't disambiguate these effects. However, this would require mild deception (randomly assigning difficulty irrespective of the choice made by players), which we sought to avoid in the present studies.

Strikingly, players who chose moderately difficult levels did not play longer than players who were blindly assigned to the same moderately difficult levels. For this reason, we suggest that the inverted-U shape emerges due to the predictions of Weiner's Attribution theory of motivation [50]: when players know they are playing a "very easy" game, they get less pride from their successes and more shame from their failures. This leads to less intrinsic motivation (they choose to play fewer items) when doing tasks described as "very easy." This effect appears to depress motivation on games that are known to be very easy – which would otherwise be motivating to players that are unaware of the difficulty level.

One key limitation of these results is that our measure of intrinsic motivation, voluntary engagement (the number of trials players choose to complete), is different from the self-report measure of enjoyment in [1]. While we assume that players choose to play longer because they are enjoying themselves, we can't rule out other reasons. An alternative behavioral measure of enjoyment is preference. Hypothesis 1.2 predicts an inverted U relation between population-level preferences (the choices made by players) and difficulty. As the behavioral choices that people make are indicative of what they enjoy doing, this served as a variation of the inverted-U hypothesis described in [1]. This hypothesis was not supported, as we found that very easy and very hard levels were disproportionately chosen.

Why might this be? One possibility is that primacy and recency effects have influenced the results. This is due to the fact that "Very Easy" was listed at the top and "Very Hard" was listed at the bottom. Murphy *et al.* [39] found that the first item in a list tends to be clicked 19% more than the second item and that the last item in the list tends to be clicked 12% more than the second to last item. Even considering this primacy effect, the preference for very hard levels is still surprisingly strong. Another possibility is that students were just curious about the nature of the very hard difficulty and wanted to explore. Supporting this, other studies have found that interest is a better predictor of student choice of difficulty than player's ability [32].

This first experiment tested whether the non-experimental design used in [1] would produce an "apparent" inverted-U shape in our population. This was confirmed. Note that this experiment was not intended to conclusively show that moderately difficult games cause an increase in player motivation or that they simply attract more motivated players via selection bias. Distinguishing between these two possible reasons for the inverted-U shape would have required an experimental design that involved some level of deceit — we would have had to tell players that they were playing easy levels or hard levels when they weren't. It is notable, however, that the players who were blindly assigned difficulty did not show increased motivation when playing moderately difficult levels.

In summary, when players are randomly assigned game difficulty, easier is better for motivation. When players have a choice of difficulty, moderate levels of difficulty produce the greatest motivation, possibly due to self-selection. Labeling difficulty has the effect of reducing intrinsic motivation for playing very easy games: in the absence of labels, players tend to persist longer in easier games. Finally, the shape of player choices of difficulty is not an inverted U.

### *Status of the Difficulty Inverted-U Shape*

Our evidence does not disprove the inverted-U effect found in the chess study. Perhaps, for instance, our results are idiosyncratic and limited to *Battleship Numberline,* or to educational games, or to games played by novices. These are important limitations. Yet, our evidence is sufficient to question the "truism" that a good game should be neither too hard nor too easy. However, another design factor—novelty—may help explain the face-value importance of a good challenge in a good game.

## NOVELTY EXPERIMENT

In the original *Battleship Numberline* study described in the introduction [33], we found just one design factor that increased both difficulty and motivation at the same time: the total number of items presented. A game level that had a small number of easy items was less motivating than a harder game level that had a large number of items. As the small number of items would repeat endlessly, we surmised that the factor of repetition, or its inverse, "novelty", might play an important role in player motivation.

Berlyne [6] conducted a large number of studies on novelty in the 1960s. These studies presented items of varying design (shape, color, size, etc) at various frequencies; the more often items were presented, the more familiar they were—they had less novelty. In general, Berlyne found that subjects increased their rating of pleasantness and interestingness with increased novelty. While these studies dealt with the novelty of individual items, an experience (such as a game) can be said to have more novelty when the design varies more frequently and in more ways. For a recent review of novelty, see [5].

A challenge often combines difficulty with other factors, like novelty. Games with too much difficulty may be frustrating. But is the lack of difficulty, itself, boring? The ratio of positive to negative feedback in most games likely exceeds 10 to 1. Perhaps making games easy is not the cause of the boringness; instead, perhaps easy games fail when they are too repetitive and uninteresting.

A 2016 experiment [26] randomly assigned players to play one of three conditions of "Left 4 Dead 2". In the balanced condition, the number and strength of zombies was normal, in the overloaded condition they were radically increased and in the boredom condition they were decreased to zero. In support of the inverted U effect [1], players reported that the balanced condition was most enjoyable. Additionally, the overloaded condition was significantly more enjoyable than the boring condition. Was the boredom condition less enjoyable because it was so easy (low failure rare) or because there were so few interesting or novel elements in the experience? For instance, when clips of the overloaded condition were shown at CHI16, the audience broke into laughter (there were a LOT of zombies). Perhaps if players had been randomly assigned to simply watch the overloaded condition, despite the lack of difficulty, the condition would still be rated as more enjoyable than the boredom condition.

Interestingly, the construct of "novelty" has also been predicted to create an inverted-U effect on motivation. From The Art of Game Design [46]: "It is impossible to overestimate the importance of novelty as motivation in the realm of game design...Keep in mind, however, that there is such a thing as being too novel." (p.154). This clearly states a testable hypothesis, that a moderate level of novelty will maximize player motivation (Hypothesis 2).

### Experimental Design: Novelty Experiment

How to manipulate novelty? Games often introduce novel design changes when players pass into a new "game level". Games with short game levels have a higher frequency of change than games with long levels. When the game itself is controlled, increasing the frequency of change (shorter levels) should increase the rate of experienced novelty.

The following experiment manipulates the frequency of change to deliver different amounts of novelty (frequency of task variation). This is implemented by randomly assigning players to different length game levels. For example, players assigned to game levels that are only 2 items long will have a higher frequency of change than players assigned to game levels that change every 20 items. In this way, we can test the theory that novelty produces an inverted U-shape effect on player engagement, as predicted by game designers and psychologists [46, 49].

In a new version of *Battleship Numberline,* 5,065 players were randomly assigned to six different frequencies of change as six different game level lengths. Players received a new game level after completing a level of 1, 2, 4, 10, 20 or 100 items. The term "game level" refers to a set of trials with a fixed game design (i.e., same time limit, same ship size, etc). Every time a player completed the items in the level, the game declared "Level Up!" and the player received one of 24 randomly selected game configurations, which varied the size of the estimation target, the time limit and the type of target (submarine or ship [33]). After players chose the game, they were presented with a choice of instruction (decimals, fractions or whole numbers). All players then were presented with the 4-item embedded pretest, as discussed in the previous experiment. Any player attempting more than 100 estimation trials was brought back to the menu screen.

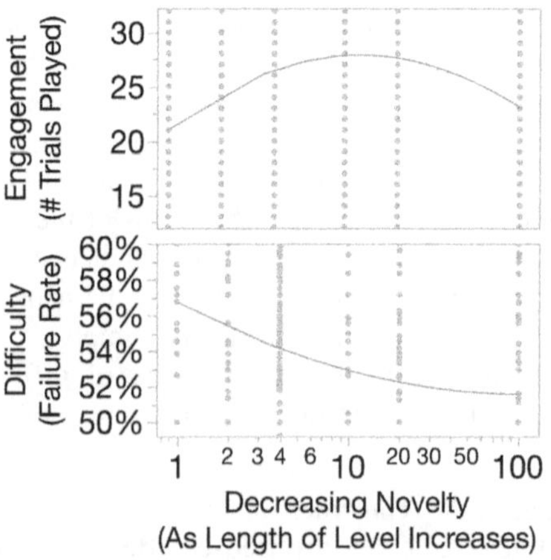


**Figure 5: The top graph shows how a change in novelty produces a clear inverted U relation with voluntary engagement (intrinsic motivation measured as number of items played). The X-axis represents decreasing novelty from left to right, as the length of game levels increases (logarithmic scale). The significance of the curvature in this quadratic regression plot is p<0.0001. The lower graph shows how difficulty decreases modestly (p=0.08) as novelty decreases.**

### Results: Novelty Experiment

Based on the shape seen in Figure 5, the game's novelty (frequency of change) appears to have an inverted-U shape relationship to player engagement (the number of trials they played). Figure 5 shows two quadratic regression plots that model the effects of level length (frequency of change) on the number of trials played and game difficulty. We present the x-axis on a logarithmic scale as that reflects the spacing of the level lengths that we tested (i.e., levels changing every 1 item, 2 items, 4 items, 10 items, 20 items, or 100 items). The quadratic term (level length * level length) is used in order to test the significance of the inverted-U shape [as discussed in 1]. The quadratic of level length was significant ($p$<0.0001), indicating significant curvature. Therefore, it appears that a moderate level of novelty produces the greatest level of player engagement. Changes in difficulty were not significant ($p$=0.8).

### Discussion: Novelty Experiment

In this experiment, we found that the amount of novelty (task variation) in the game had an inverted U-shaped relationship with player engagement. In other words, our evidence confirms **Hypothesis 2**, the hypothesis that moderate novelty (frequency of change) maximizes player engagement (intrinsic motivation). Berlyne's novelty research [6] found that simple stimuli were more pleasing when novel, but more complex stimuli became more pleasant with more familiarity. Thus, the positive effects of increasing game novelty may depend upon the overall complexity of the game; the novelty effects may be particularly beneficial for simple games. A further limitation of this study design was that it did not independently manipulate novelty and difficulty. As the highest level of novelty is associated with the highest level of difficulty, the negative effects of difficulty may be reducing the observed benefits of novelty. Novelty and difficulty will often be associated with each other, but future work might identify approaches for dissociating novelty and difficulty.

## SUSPENSE EXPERIMENT

In the original chess study [1], the researchers identified another factor besides difficulty that generated enjoyment. They found that games were most enjoyable when they were "close games" (the difference between each player's final score was near zero). The authors identified the factor of dramatic suspense (uncertainty [16]) for producing this effect. They noted that sports games where one team beats the other by a wide margin are much less enjoyable for observers than close games. The researchers then followed up on their finding in a separate experiment that manipulated player experience so all participants could experience close games and blow out wins. They again found a considerable effect of the suspense of close games. Given the strength of evidence for suspense, we sought to replicate their findings in our educational gaming context.

### Experimental Design: Suspense Experiment

The following experiment investigates the theory that the suspense of a close game will produce an inverted U-shape effect on player motivation, as predicted by [1]. To factor out the role of a player's success/failure, we randomly assigned 6,511 players to receive different standards for winning: players either needed 40%, 60%, 80% or 100% correct in the game level to "win". The present analysis deals with a subset of a larger experiment involving 52,262 play sessions, discussed in [36].

In previous experiments with *Battleship Numberline*, there was no discrete winning or losing state. Players could only succeed at individual tasks (estimating numbers on the number line); there was no explicit "end" of the game or evaluative scorecard.

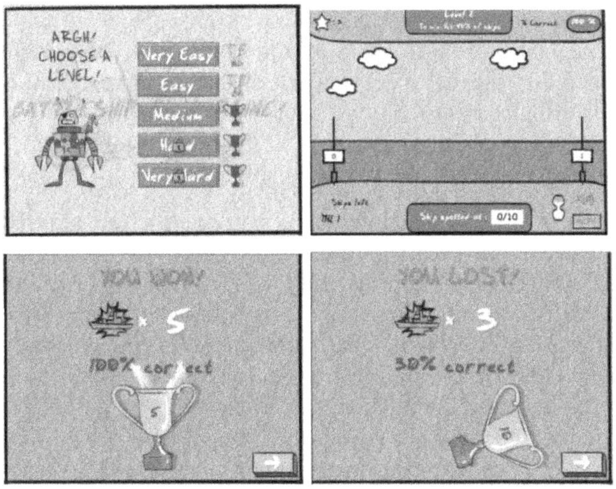


**Figure 6: Screens added to support the suspense of winning and losing. The top left screen shows the locking and achievement mechanisms, the top right shows where the goals were displayed to the player and the bottom two screens show the animated screens displaying the winning or losing state.**

For this experiment, we added several design elements to a new version of *Battleship Numberline.* First, players were presented with a menu of 5 levels, labeled from Very Easy to Very Hard (as in experiment 1). All levels were locked except for the first. During gameplay, the goal criteria for the level was written at the top of the screen ("to win, hit x% of ships"). After completing either 5 or 10 items, players were shown a scorecard where their score was shown and then they were told if they won or lost. If they won, fireworks were shown. If they lost, the trophy fell over. After pressing continue, players were shown the menu again. If they had won the level, the next level was unlocked and a trophy was shown next to the first level.

### Results: Suspense Experiment

To get a measure of the "closeness" of games, we subtracted the game's goal criteria (40%, 60%, 80% or 100%) from the player's success rate. When this closeness was zero or positive, it represented a win; when it was negative, it represented a loss.

Figure 7 shows how this "closeness of game" significantly affects a player's continuing motivation after a win/loss event ("remaining items" refers to the number of items played after the win/loss). Players with the highest positive goal difference score had the highest success rates in the game, however, they were not as motivated to continue playing as players who had barely won. This can be contrasted with all previous experiments, where higher success rates consistently lead to higher engagement (more items played). Figure 7 illustrates the idea that players tend to play for longer when they have a close game in their early levels. Note that a close loss is almost as motivating for continuing play as a blow-out win.

For a statistical test of hypothesis 3, we compared the slope of the line on either side of "0". The "winning" slope was calculated using the distance from 0 (goal difference) as well as the player's actual success rate as factors in a linear regression model. Even after factoring out the player's success rate, the model showed that additional hits beyond what was required to win significantly reduced further play ($p<0.002$); 0.64 fewer items for each 10% increase of score over the win. The same model was then applied to players who lost. In this case, the closer players were to winning, the more they played; 2.3 fewer items less for each 10% decrease in score ($p<0.0001$). As the above slopes are both significant but have opposite valence (-0.64 slope for winners and 2.3 for losers), this is strong statistical evidence for an inverted U-shaped curve—in support of **Hypothesis 3**.

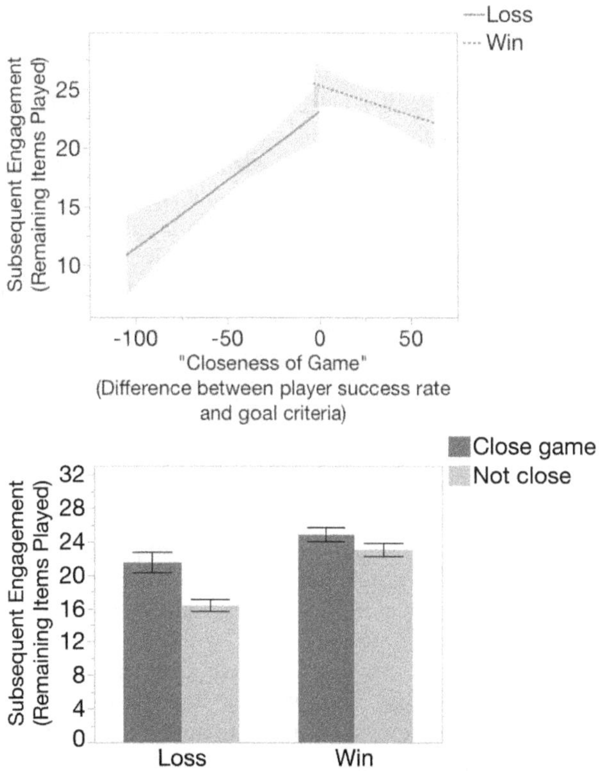


**Figure 7: Close games increase player motivation to play, as indicated by the inverted U-shaped curve (top). The X-Axis shows the closeness of the game, or the difference between a player's success rate in the level and the level's goal criteria. Players were randomly assigned to a goal criteria of 40%, 60%, 80% or 100%. Negative closeness indicates that players lost the game. The Y-axis shows the number of items that a player played following the win/loss event ("Remaining Items"). Players with a "blow out win" played significantly fewer additional items than players with a close win. The bottom graph also shows that players experiencing a close loss continued to play almost as many items as players who won.**

### Discussion: Suspense Experiment

This experimental design attempts to dissociate the effects of winning/losing from the effects of skill. We kept the task difficulty the same over all conditions and only varied, through random assignment, different criteria for winning.

This as successful, in so far as individual player failure rate was not significant in our model of continuing play, yet game "closeness" was. This suggests that the "suspense" of having a close game was the factor creating the inverted U effect seen in Figure 7, rather than the moderate level of difficulty, per se.

Varying the goal criterion is, in a way, similar to varying the difficulty of a task. Thus, are we merely finding that moderately difficult goals create suspense? We suggest that suspense is a different from difficulty and dissociable at either the task or goal level. Suspense can occur at the level of an individual game task or a set of tasks (i.e., a game level). Beyond the suspense of winning, *Battleship Numberline* uses suspense at a task level by providing a slight delay between making an estimate and dropping a bomb at that estimate. This small detail was an explicit part of the original design in order to produce a feeling of suspense by giving the player enough time to wait and discover whether their estimate was successful or not. At a similar task level, Khajah observed that the suspense of a platform-jumping task was dissociable from difficulty, which could be moderated through "covert assistance" [25]. If suspense is a dissociable factor from difficulty, then our findings indicate that there are no motivational benefits from increasing difficulty.

There are several limitations to this study. Ideally, the study design would randomly assign players to win or lose, however this would have involved deception. Instead, we randomly assigned the criteria for winning. However, this means that a "blow-out win" is not possible when the winning criterion is 100%. Furthermore, we reported findings from players during their first attempt at the first level ("Very Easy"). Losing players will necessarily be playing the same level again. This has an unknown effect on their motivation: these players will experience less subsequent difficulty, which can increase motivation, but they will also repeat what they've already done (less novelty), which is expected to decrease their motivation.

## GENERAL DISCUSSION

What other factors of challenge, apart from difficulty, might produce an inverted-U shape? We identified three design factors that can generate an inverted-U shaped curve effect: player choice, novelty and suspense. In our three experiments, these three factors appear to be independent from difficulty, suggesting that some of the purported motivational benefits of difficulty may be conflated with other, commonly associated factors.

What is the underlying meaning of the inverted-U shape? Over the years, there have been many descriptions of inverted U-shapes in psychology [reviewed by 49], where a moderate level of some thing (e.g., negative feedback, reward, anxiety, difficulty, complexity, novelty, coffee, etc.) has the effect of maximizing some other outcome (e.g., learning, performance, memory or motivation). To account for these observations, neuroscientist Donald Hebb [19] proposed a general mechanism: he claimed that different situational attributes (such as novelty) could produce an inverted-U shaped effect on performance to the extent that the attributes contributed to *arousal* in the brainstem. Too much or too little arousal will reduce performance; a moderate level of arousal is optimal.

Both novelty and difficulty could potentially affect arousal. However, the present evidence suggests that increased difficulty does not improve motivation. Does an increase in difficulty ever increase intrinsic motivation? To the extent that it does, future work can investigate whether the novelty introduced by the increased difficulty is the primary cause of the increased motivation. For instance, many games get progressively more difficult over time; this is typically viewed as an approach to maintain an optimal level of difficulty as the player's skill increases. An alternative hypothesis is that the changes in difficulty simply help maintain the novelty of the gameplay. According to this hypothesis, the appeal of challenge is more determined by optimal novelty than optimal difficulty.

### *Limitations*

There are a number of important limitations across these experiments. Our findings are specific to a simple, single player, educational, casual game for kids in school; the generalization of these findings to other contexts is, as with all experiments, unknown. The game, *Battleship Numberline*, has the advantage of being simple, which makes it easy to manipulate. However, this simplicity may produce different outcomes (as mentioned in the discussion of the Novelty experiment). Our context, Brainpop.com, has the advantage of being an ecologically valid setting for optimizing player engagement. However, in this context we can only measure the duration of a single session, rather than measuring student progress over multiple sessions. Recent work suggests that difficulty may produce more motivation over a longer time frame [43], which we cannot measure. Our context also does not give us qualitative information about student experience. Another limitation is that our online measures have not been psychometrically validated like other psychological survey instruments, such as the Intrinsic Motivation Inventory [12]. We assume that the measure of "player's total trials attempted" typically reflects a player's free choice to continue the game and not quit. However, we recognize that some data may come from classrooms where children are "forced" to play for instrumental purposes (e.g., a grade). This "noise", however, should not significantly interfere with our results as a whole, due to the random nature of the assignment. We used total trials attempted as a behavioral measure of intrinsic motivation because the use of total time (in seconds) has many more extreme outliers and the process of removing these outliers is prone to introduce bias. Better instrumentation could resolve this in future experiments.

We recognize that large-scale "real-world" environments will produce much noisier data than laboratory experiments.

One effect of this scale and noise is that data can be easily manipulated to show different effects. We encourage healthy skepticism. In this paper, we aimed to present simple data stories, tried to avoid complex statistical techniques and took the approach that our findings should be robust in the face of different approaches to analyses (e.g., with different data filters). One final measurement limitation of this work is that we did not analyze learning curves across conditions. Previous work has found that faster learning occurs with more difficult conditions [33], though this effect is questionable [43]. Thus, the findings here can only inform theories regarding the relationship between difficulty and motivation, not the subsequent effects on student learning, which remains for future work.

### Additional Future Work

All data sets are available for secondary analysis at the PSLC Datashop [28]. Our findings are primarily directed at the design of educational games, but future work can extend to entertainment games. Tom Malone's seminal work with game design factor analysis [35] is a model for future online game experiments; the entire taxonomy of intrinsic motivations for learning [38] represents testable hypotheses. Future work can deconstruct game challenges into their underlying functional factors, such as novelty, difficulty and others. As some games (e.g., Dark Souls and Flappy Bird) engage users primarily through excessive failure, it may be productive to explain these unusual failure-oriented games with the hypothesis that excessive difficulty is used a mechanism for providing novel player experiences.

### Design Implications

While the notion of challenge has many positive connotations, "difficulty" directly refers to the potential for task failure [27,33]. These two terms are useful to distinguish. Our evidence implies that early game experiences should minimize difficulty and provide a moderate degree of novelty. This does not mean designers should avoid challenge. Instead, designers should ensure that novice players receive significant amounts of positive feedback during challenges. When playing something new, players generally like to feel successful and competent. Task repetition causes fatigue and should be accompanied by a regular drip of novelty. After a time, difficulty itself can provide this source of novelty. Both low and high performance players benefit from a feeling of suspense during a close game. In general, challenge appears to be fun because it is interesting. Keeping games easy and interesting may be more important than "balancing difficulty." For this reason, we suggest the maxim "not too hard, not too easy" might be restated as "not too hard, not too boring."

## CONCLUSION

Our three experiments investigated how different challenge factors (difficulty, choice, novelty and suspense) affected intrinsic motivation. Our goal was to identify conditions where these factors of challenge might produce an inverted U-shaped effect on intrinsic motivation, as predicted by Flow Theory [10]. In summary, we found that providing players with a choice of difficulty produced an inverted-U shaped relationship between difficulty and motivation, primarily by depressing motivation on very easy levels. We also found that suspense (close games) and balanced novelty increased player motivation. However, none of our experiments showed that difficulty, by itself, actually *caused* improved motivation. Within our experimental context, our evidence indicates that increasing difficulty consistently reduces motivation, when other motivational factors are controlled. Recognizing the richness of the concept of challenge and its role in game design, these other components of challenge may provide the motivational benefits long attributed to difficulty.

We note that motivational theory does not always generalize from the laboratory to the real world. How can we identify and develop theories with strong external validity and the capacity to broadly generalize? Massive online experiments may be useful for searching the space of circumstances under which a theory will or will not apply [29]. Whether or not a scientific theory will generalize to different types of games or different types of players will always be an empirical question.

There seems to be a vast scientific and practical benefit that can be realized from running large-scale experiments inside of real products. As practitioners become increasingly comfortable running A/B tests to evaluate different designs [30], we encourage designers of popular games (educational or otherwise) to conduct more experiments designed to produce generalizable findings. This kind of basic research can benefit designers [35] by improving design theory.

The sheer scale of online gaming, which involves millions of diverse participants, could be a source for experiments that could significantly inform our scientific understanding of human motivation and design. It is promising to consider that game design patterns [7], principles [46,14] and exemplars embody hundreds of implicit and explicit hypotheses about human motivation. The sciences of motivation and design might be rapidly advanced if these design patterns were linked to psychological theory and systematically tested online.

## ACKNOWLEDGMENTS

Special thanks to BrainPop and Allison Levy for their support and encouragement! The research was supported by Carnegie Mellon's Program in Interdisciplinary Education Research (PIER) funded by grant number R305B090023 from the US Department of Education and the Institute of Education Sciences through GrantR305C100024 to WestEd and by DARPA ONR N00014-12-C-0284. Additional thanks to the UCSD Design Lab community, Mike Mozer, Mohammad Khajah, Jesse Schell, Gary and Judy Olson, the HCIC community, Scott Klemmer, Don Norman, Erik Harpstead, Bob Kraut, Playpower Labs and Kishan Patel.

## REFERENCES


1. Abuhamdeh, S. and Csikszentmihalyi, M. (2012) The Importance of Challenge for the Enjoyment of Intrinsically Motivated, Goal-Directed Activities. *Personality and Social Psychology Bulletin 38*, 3, 317–330.
2. Andersen,E.,Liu,Y.,Snider,R.,Szeto,R.,and Popovic, Z. (2011) Placing a value on aesthetics in online casual games. *ACM CHI.*
3. Aponte, M., Levieux, G., & Natkin, S. (2011). Measuring the level of difficulty in single player video games. *Entertainment Computing*, *2*(4), 205–213.
4. Atkinson, J. (1958) Towards Experimental Analysis of Human Motivation in Terms of Motives, Expectances, and incentives. In J. Atkinson, ed., *Motives in fantasy, action and society*. Van Nostrand, Princeton, NJ, 288–305.
5. Barto, A., Mirolli, M., & Baldassarre, G. (2013). Novelty or surprise? *Frontiers of Psychology*, 4
6. Berlyne, D. E. (1970). Novelty, complexity, and hedonic value. *Perception & Psychophysics*, *8*(5), 279-286.
7. Bjork, S., & Holopainen, J. (2004). *Patterns in game design*.
8. Chase, C.C. (2012). The interplay of chance and skill: Exploiting a common game mechanic to enhance learning and persistence. *Proceedings of the 2012 International Conference of the Learning Sciences.*
9. Cordova, D. I., & Lepper, M. R. (1996). Intrinsic motivation and the process of learning: Beneficial effects of contextualization, personalization, and choice. *Journal of Educational Psychology*, *88*(4), 715.
10. Csikszentmihalyi, M., & Csikszentmihalyi, I. S. (Eds.). (1992). *Optimal experience: Psychological studies of flow in consciousness*. Cambridge University Press.
11. Deci, E. L., & Ryan, R. M. (2000). The "what" and "why" of goal pursuits: Human needs and the self-determination of behavior. *Psychological Inquiry, 4,* 227–268.
12. Deci, E. L., & Ryan, R. M. (2003). Intrinsic motivation inventory. *Self-Determination Theory*, *267*.
13. Deci, E. L., Koestner, R., & Ryan, R. M. (1999). A meta-analytic review of experiments examining the effects of extrinsic rewards on intrinsic motivation. *Psychological bulletin*, *125*(6), 627.
14. Dickey, M.D. (2005) Engaging by design: How engagement strategies in popular computer and video games can inform instructional design. *Educational Technology Research and Development 53*, 2, 67–83.
15. Eccles, J.S. and Wigfield, A. Motivational beliefs, values, and goals. *Annual review of psychology 53*, (2002), 109–32.
16. Ely, J., Frankel, A., & Kamenica, E. (2015). Suspense and surprise. *Journal of Political Economy*, *123*(1), 215-260.
17. Fishbach, A. and Finkelstein, S. How feedback influences persistence, disengagement and change in goal pursuit. In A. Elliot and H. Aarts, eds., *Goal-directed behavior*. Psychology Press, 2012, 1–53.
18. Harter, S. (1978a) Pleasure derived from challenge and the effects of receiving grades on children's difficulty level choices. *Child Development 49*, 3 788–799.
19. Hebb, D. O. (1955) Drives and the C.N.S. (Conceptual Nervous System) *Psychological Review*, *62*, 243-254
20. Van der Heijden, H. (2004). User acceptance of hedonic information systems. *MIS Quarterly*, *28*(4), 695–704.
21. Hockley, R. (2013) *The Psychology of Fatigue: Work, Effort and Control.* Cambridge University Press.
22. Hong, Y., Chiu, C., Dweck, C.S., Lin, D.M.-S., and Wan, W. Implicit theories, attributions, and coping: A meaning system approach. *Journal of Personality and Social Psychology 77*, 3 (1999), 588–599.
23. Hunicke, R., & Chapman, V. (2004). AI for dynamic difficulty adjustment in games. *Challenges in Game Artificial Intelligence AAAI*, 91–96.
24. Kashdan, T. B., & Silvia, P. J. (2009). Curiosity and interest: The benefits of thriving on novelty and challenge. *Oxford handbook of positive psychology*, *2*, 367-374.
25. Khajah, M. M., Roads, B. D., Lindsey, R. V, & Mozer, M. C. (2016). Designing Engaging Games Using Bayesian Optimization. *ACM CHI.*
26. Klarkowski, M., Johnson, D., Wyeth, P., McEwan, M., Phillips, C., & Smith, S. (2016). Operationalising and Evaluating Sub-Optimal and Optimal Play Experiences through Challenge-Skill Manipulation. *ACM CHI.*
27. Kline, P. (2014). *The new psychometrics: Science, psychology and measurement*. Routledge. p.79
28. Koedinger, K. R., Baker, R. S., Cunningham, K., Skogsholm, A., Leber, B., & Stamper, J. (2010). A data repository for the EDM community: The PSLC DataShop. *Handbook of educational data mining*, *43*.

29. Koedinger, K. R., Booth, J. L., Klahr, D. (2013) Instructional Complexity and the Science to Constrain It *Science*. 22 November 2013: Vol. 342 no. 6161 pp. 935- 937

30. Kohavi, R., Longbotham, R., Sommerfield, D., and Henne, R.M. (2008) Controlled experiments on the web: survey and practical guide. *Data Mining and Knowledge Discovery 18*, 1 140–181.

31. Kurzban, R., Duckworth, A., Kable, J.W., and Myers, J. An opportunity cost model of subjective effort and task performance. *The Behavioral and brain sciences 36*, 6 (2013), 661–79.

32. Inoue, N. (2007). Why face a challenge?: The reason behind intrinsically motivated students' spontaneous choice of challenging tasks. *Learning and Individual Differences*, *17*(3), 251–259.

33. Lomas, D., Patel, K., Forlizzi, J. L., & Koedinger, K. R. (2013) Optimizing challenge in an educational game using large-scale design experiments. *ACM CHI*

34. Lomas, D., Forlizzi, J., Poonwala, N., Patel, N., Shodhan, S., Patel, K., Koedinger, K., and Brunskill, E. (2016). Interface Design Optimization as a Multi-Armed Bandit Problem. *ACM CHI.*

35. Lomas, D. (2015) Accelerating Theory Development with Large Online Experiments: Towards an Interaction Design Science. *HCIC*

36. Lomas, J. D. (2014). *Optimizing motivation and learning with large-scale game design experiments* (Doctoral dissertation, Carnegie Mellon University).

37. Malone, T. (1981) Toward a theory of intrinsically motivating instruction. *Cognitive Science 5*, 4, 333-369.

38. Malone, T. W., & Lepper, M. R. (1987). Making learning fun: A taxonomy of intrinsic motivations for learning. *Aptitude, learning, and instruction*, *3*(1987), 223-253.

39. Murphy, J., Hofacker, C. and Mizerski, R. (2006) *Primacy and recency effects on clicking behavior.* Journal of Computer Mediated Communication, 11 (2).

40. Norman, D. A. (2013). *The design of everyday things: Revised and expanded edition.* Basic books.

41. O'Rourke, E. and Haimovitz, K. (2014) Brain points: a growth mindset incentive structure boosts persistence in an educational game. *ACM CHI.*

42. Papoušek, J., & Pelánek, R. (2015) Impact of Adaptive Educational System Behaviour on Student Motivation. AIED

43. Pelánek, R., Rihák, J., & Papoušek, J. (2016). Impact of data collection on interpretation and evaluation of student models. In *Proceedings of the Sixth International Conference on Learning Analytics & Knowledge* (pp. 40-47). ACM.

44. Shalley, C. E., & Oldham, G. R. (1985). Effects of goal difficulty and expected external evaluation on intrinsic motivation: A laboratory study. *Academy of Management Journal*, *28*(3), 628-640.

45. Shapira, Z. (1989) Task choice and assigned goals as determinants of task motivation and performance. *Org. Behavior & Human Dec. Proc.* 44, 2, 141–165.

46. Schell, J. (2008) *The Art of Game Design.* Morgan Kaufmann

47. Schmierbach, M., Chung, M., Wu, M., & Kim, K. (2014). No One Likes to Lose: The Effect of Game Difficulty on Competency, Flow, and Enjoyment. *Journal of Media Psychology*, *26*(3), 105–110.

48. Sweetser, P. and Wyeth, P. (2005) GameFlow: a model for evaluating player enjoyment in games. *Computers in Entertainment (CIE) 3*, 3, 1–24.

49. Teigen, K. (1994) Yerkes-Dodson: A Law for all Seasons *Theory & Psychology* 4:525-547,

50. Weiner, B. An attributional theory of achievement motivation and emotion. *Psychological review 92*, 4 (1985), 548–73.

51. Yannakakis, G.N., Denmark, S., and Hallam, J. (2007) Towards optimizing entertainment in computer games, 933-971

52. Yerkes, R. M., & Dodson, J. D. (1908). The relation of strength of stimulus to rapidity of habit-formation. *Journal of comparative neurology and psychology*, *18*(5), 459-482.

# Why is This Happening to Me? How Player Attribution can Broaden our Understanding of Player Experience

**Ansgar E. Depping and Regan L. Mandryk**
Department of Computer Science, University of Saskatchewan
Saskatoon, SK, S7N 5C9, Canada
{firstname.lastname}@usask.ca

## ABSTRACT
Games user research (GUR) measures the performance and preference of digital game players, and interprets these measurements in the context of theories that explain human behavior. There are many validated approaches for measuring player experience that are grounded in psychological theories on motivation and emotion. Attribution theory explains how people assign causes to events and how these attributions affect peoples' emotional reactions and motivations. In this paper we argue that attribution theory can provide additional value to the existing suite of GUR tools; however, there are currently no validated tools to assess player attribution in the context of games. This paper describes the conceptualization of player attribution based on literature, presents the development and validation of a scale to assess player attribution in games, and discusses the implications of adding player attribution to the toolbox of methods for the design and evaluation of digital games.

### Author Keywords
Attribution theory; Game user research; Scale development.

### ACM Classification Keywords
K.8.0 [Personal Computing]: General - Games.

## INTRODUCTION
The digital games industry continues to grow worldwide – with estimates suggesting that it will surpass \$100b in the next few years [38]. As such, researchers and practitioners are invested in improving game design and development [46], understanding the implications of gameplay on well-being (e.g., [41]), and developing new methods to understand and model players and their game experiences (e.g., [5,9]). Games user research (GUR) focuses on understanding, measuring, analyzing, and designing novel game experiences. Drawing from foundations in human-computer interaction (HCI) and psychology, GUR provides researchers and practitioners with a range of tools to answer questions about why players behave in the ways that they do. Many of the salient constructs used to describe gamer behaviors and preferences are grounded in psychological constructs that help researchers understand, describe, and predict human behavior, thoughts, and beliefs. For example, the concept of flow [8] has long been included in how games user researchers talk about game design. As such, game-specific tools to measure flow have been created [49]. Similarly, Ryan et al. introduced the Player Experience of Need Satisfaction (PENS) scale [45] based on Self-Determination Theory (SDT) [44] to explain and measure how our basic psychological needs of competence, autonomy, and relatedness can be satisfied through games. The same group also applied the Intrinsic Motivation Inventory [35] to games to describe and measure how good games foster enjoyment and invested effort [45]. And in terms of describing player motivations, De Grove et al. [9] use social cognitive theory to create a framework and scale to describe the individual motives for playing digital games.


DOI: http://dx.doi.org/10.1145/3025453.3025648

These contributions are not just about creating game-specific scales, but rather in furthering our theoretical understanding of player experience. While the scores on these scales can help researchers predict in-game behavior, the theoretical constructs measured provide deep insights into how a player experiences a game and how they feel about themselves while playing it. The concepts of flow, psychological need satisfaction, and intrinsic motivation are deeply grounded in decades of research on the psychology of motivation in many different life situations. It is therefore not surprising that psychological constructs have been shown to be very relevant in understanding why and how players enjoy games (e.g., [4,49,45]).

Even with the application of several foundational psychological theories to GUR, there are still many aspects of player experience that we don't understand. Consider a player who gives up after the first experience of failure versus one who keeps trying in the face of frustration. Or consider a player who feels pride after beating one game, but apathy after beating another. A lot of the variance in player experiences is still a mystery to game user researchers. In this paper, we argue that causal beliefs about achievements strongly shape emotional and motivational reactions to digital games. Enduring failure could be linked to beliefs about how much control the player has over their performance. Emotional reactions to achievements such as pride or apathy could be linked to beliefs about the internal or external nature of the cause that lead to success (skill or luck). The process by which players ascribe causes to events is called attribution [52]; as demonstrated in these examples, understanding player attribution in games can provide value for games user research. Although attribution theories could provide additional value to the suite of tools already available to games user researchers, there are no validated tools to assess player attribution in the context of games. This paper describes the process of conceptualizing the construct of player attribution based on previous literature, and developing and validating a scale to assess player attribution along its four dimensions (internality, stability, controllability, globality) in games user research. We make the following three contributions:

Our first contribution is theoretical. We introduce attribution theory and argue its relevance in the context of understanding player experience.

Our second contribution is methodological. We iteratively develop and validate a scale to measure player attribution in games (the Game-Specific Attribution Questionnaire, GSAQ) through several steps.

1. We created and refined a pool of items in collaboration with expert gamers and games user researchers.
2. Using factor analyses, we refined the included items to create the GSAQ that separately assesses the four dimensions of attribution theory.
3. We validated the GSAQ, testing for invariance, reliability, discriminant validity, and convergent validity.

Our third contribution is applied. We interpret the results of a study using the GSAQ and situate them within theories of player experience, demonstrating the added value that player attribution provides. Finally, we discuss the implications for game design and evaluation.

Causal attributions answer questions of "why" [19]. When we succeed or fail in a task, when we are welcomed or excluded in a group, or when our ideas are valued or rejected by our peers, these events cause us to ask ourselves a simple question: why is this happening to me? In this paper, we argue that this question is just as important to ask in the context of digital game play. Including player attributions in the digital games research toolbox can broaden our understanding of players and their experiences.

## ATTRIBUTION THEORY

Having ideas about causality helps people understand and predict events in their lives. Psychologists call this process *attribution*. In this section we introduce attribution, discuss it in the context of emotions and game play, and present ways in which it has been measured.

### Introducing Attribution

Attribution theories try to explain how people assign causes to events and how these attributions affect emotional reactions and motivations (e.g., [52,22,1]). For example, when a student fails an exam, they can choose from a range of causes that might be responsible for this event. They could attribute this failure to causes such as not being smart enough, not having studied hard enough, unfair questions, a bad teacher, the flu they had the week before, test anxiety, or bad luck. Most of these causes are specific to the situation of a failed exam, e.g., a bad teacher or unfair questions. A lost basketball match offers a different list of possible causes than the failed exam, and yet the emotional and motivational responses to these different causal attributions can be the same. Research on attribution theory attempts to identify the basic properties, characteristics, or dimensions of causes. Describing causal beliefs on abstract dimensions allows us to classify and quantify otherwise qualitative descriptions. Attribution research has identified four abstract characteristics that describe causes [52,22,1]: *internality* (generally called locus of control) – i.e., whether the cause is internal to the agent or due to outside forces; *stability* – i.e., how stable or present the cause is over time; *controllability* – i.e., how much the cause can be volitionally altered; and *globality* – i.e., whether the cause applies across multiple situations or circumstances.

#### *Internal vs. External*

Internality has been the most embraced characteristic of causes in literature (e.g., [55,22,19]). This dimension – often called locus of control – [52] describes whether the achievement is caused by the agent (internal) or outside forces, such as the situation or another person (external). Success at a sports game because of height, success on an exam because of intelligence, and securing a date because of personality are similar attributions in that the causes lie within the person. On the other hand, success at sports because of a weak opponent, success at an exam because of a good teacher, or being accepted for a date because the other person feels lonely are similar attributions because the causes lie outside of the person [52,22,19].

#### *Stability*

The second fundamental property of causal attributions is the causal stability or causal permanence. This dimension describes causes based on how stable or present they are over time [52]. Failure or success in sports and academics due to bad luck or not enough effort are similar attributions given the unstable nature of these causes. Luck and effort are both causes that can change over time. Therefore, the next sporting event, exam, or social interaction could go differently. On the other hand, if achievements in sport are attributed to general aptitude or academic success attributed to intelligence, future events will be expected to have the same outcome due to the stable nature of these causes (e.g., [52,53,54,55]). The causal characteristic of stability is closely related to expectancies of future experiences, and is therefore linked to motivation as well as emotional responses such as confidence, hope or helplessness [19,54,55]. The dimension of stability is conceptualized as being orthogonal to the dimension of internality. Achievement attributions can be internal and stable (e.g., aptitude), internal and unstable (e.g., effort), external and stable (e.g., a teacher) or external and unstable (e.g., luck) [52,53,19].

#### *Controllability*

The dimension of controllability describes the extent that a cause can be altered or controlled. It expresses the capability of the agent to volitionally alter the cause [52]. For example, if failure has been attributed to a lack of effort, the agent can invest more effort in the future. An athlete can try harder at the next match and a student can study more for the next exam. On the other hand, if failure has been attributed to an uncontrollable cause like aptitude, the agent has no reason to believe that they can change the outcome for future events. The dimension of control is closely related to the concept of responsibility [19,54,55]. If an agent is believed to have control over what caused their achievement, they are more likely to be held accountable for it because they could have volitionally altered the outcome of the event. Thus, emotional responses to questions of responsibility such as guilt, shame, remorse, or sympathy are presumed to be closely linked to beliefs about causal controllability [19,54,55]. While internality and stability are assumed to be conceptually orthogonal, causal controllability is confounded with internality and stability. Internal causes can either be controllable (e.g., effort) or uncontrollable (e.g., aptitude). However, it is reasonable to assume that all external causes are also uncontrollable for the agent [55]. Therefore, the dimensions of internality and controllability are closely connected. Similarly, a controllable cause seems inherently unstable because the agent can alter it. Despite being conceptually distinct, causal control is assumed to overlap with both internality and stability and is not empirically orthogonal to these dimensions [55].

#### *Globality*

The final dimension, proposed by Abramson et al. [1], pertains to the global vs. specific nature of causes. Causal globality describes whether the cause for an achievement is important in all aspects of the agent's life or is specific to a situation or circumstance. If an occurrence of failure or success is attributed to a global cause, such as general intelligence or likability, the agent has reason to believe that similar outcomes can be expected in other life situations. On the other hand, given a specific cause, such as having a good day, a talent for math, or a coincidence, the agent is less likely to assume their achievement is predictive for other life situations. However, while Abramson and Seligman found support for globality, Weiner [52] questions the relevance of describing the globality of causal beliefs. As a result, globality has not always been included in attribution measurements [22].

Attribution theory has already been applied in non-game contexts to understand how people react to failure and success. Achievement attribution has been linked to emotional reactions and motivational consequences. In the next section, we present some of these findings and apply these findings to game user research.

### Attribution, Emotion, Motivation, and Games

Throughout the past decades, multiple studies have tied attribution to emotional and motivational responses. The link between attribution and emotional response is based on the assumption that feelings are determined by thoughts, and specifically by beliefs about causality [19,55]. This connection between cognition and emotion has long been acknowledged by theories regarding the genesis of emotions. It is well established that an emotional response to a stimulus is highly dependent on how that stimulus is appraised by the subject [17]. Similarly, it can be assumed that the emotional reaction of a player to a game event is dependent on that player's appraisal, i.e., attribution, of the event. A player who experiences success in a game can attribute this success to various causes (e.g., aptitude, effort, luck, strong team members), which in turn affects how the players feels about their success (e.g., confidence, pride, surprise, gratitude). In turn, motivational consequences of achievement attribution are closely linked to how someone feels about an event. For example, confidence and pride would impact future behavior differently than apprehension and surprise [54,21,55]. We next describe some achievement-linked emotions that have been empirically linked to attribution. We will also demonstrate how these findings relate to the experience of playing digital games.

#### *Pride and Admiration*

Pride for one's own success seems to build on the belief that the cause for the achievement lies within oneself (internal). Similarly, admiration for someone else's success seems to depend on an internal causal belief for that person's achievement. Attribution literature suggests internal attribution to be an antecedent of pride and admiration [19,21,55]. This relationship appears to be independent of perceived controllability of a cause. One can feel pride or admiration for both controllable (effort) and uncontrollable (aptitude) causes [55]. In games, pride in personal triumph is one of the feelings that game designers try to elicit when they think about designing challenges like boss fights or puzzles [31]. Attribution can explain why players experience more pride when they believe their success to be due to skill and good decision making rather than an easy level.

Admiration is an emotion that game designers try to elicit when it comes to status symbols within a multiplayer game [11]. Rankings or badges or skins are status symbols that are more rewarding for the receiving player when others respond to these symbols with admiration. A high ranking in a game that requires skill and dedication (internal) might elicit more admiration among other players than a high ranking in a game in which rank is less indicative of skill and dedication (e.g., pay-to-win or luck-based games).

#### *Confidence and Apprehension*

Confidence and apprehension are two emotions connected to uncertainty about future events. Research on attributional styles suggests that confidence and apprehension are connected to causal stability [52,55]. Agents may be more inclined to assume the event will repeat itself if the cause is believed to be stable than if the cause is believed to be unstable. Success that has been attributed to a stable cause (e.g., intelligence, work ethic) can lead to an expectation of future success, and thus evoke confidence. On the other hand, a success that is attributed to an unstable cause (e.g., luck) would more likely lead to uncertainty about future outcomes, thus evoking apprehension [55,19].

In games, uncertainty in the outcome is an essential tool to keep a game interesting [46]. While many games aim to make players feel competent and in control, most games also include mechanics that ensure a degree of uncertainty in the outcome. These uncertainty mechanics often include elements of chance (unstable), while confidence-evoking mechanics emphasize skill (stable). Game designers could use the concept of perceived causal stability as a framework for game mechanics when designing the balance between confidence and apprehension.

*Sympathy and Contempt*
Sympathy and contempt are two emotional reactions that are closely connected to pro- and antisocial behaviors [21,54,55]. Sympathy is experienced when the misfortune of another is ascribed to an uncontrollable cause. Contempt is assumed to be generated by the belief that another agent is responsible for a transgression and that they could have done otherwise [21]. Research on attribution has indicated that if someone is in need (e.g., poverty) and the need is attributed to a controllable cause (e.g., lack of effort), agents are inclined to react with anger towards them and withhold help. When the cause for the need is believed to be uncontrollable (e.g., disability), agents are more inclined to react with sympathy and offer help [21,55].

In games, attribution could be helpful in understanding antisocial behavior in multiplayer games. While most multiplayer games try to inspire prosocial (e.g., helpful) behavior, antisocial (e.g., toxic) behavior is still a big problem in online communities. In multiplayer team games, toxic behavior can be easily triggered when another team member performs poorly [15]. According to attribution theory, the causal beliefs of other team members regarding that poor performance will influence their reaction. If the underperforming player is believed to have no control over the failure (e.g., due to an unfairly matched opponent or high network latency), teammates should be more likely to react with sympathy and offer help. If the cause for failure is believed to be controllable, team members might be more likely to react with anger and thus engage in toxic behavior.

Attribution can contribute insight into when players behave antisocially and when they behave pro-socially. Based on attribution research, game designers could aim to inspire sympathy rather than anger by addressing the players' beliefs about causal control when a teammate underperforms.

*Shame and Guilt*
While sympathy and anger are emotions directed at another person, shame and guilt are assumed to arise from self-blame (internal attributions) [21,55]. The two emotions can be difficult to distinguish. However the underlying difference between them can be described by causal controllability [21,55]. Shame is triggered by failure that is attributed to an uncontrollable characteristic (e.g., low height, low intelligence). Guilt is triggered by failure that is attributed to a controllable characteristic (e.g., not having tried hard enough). After a failure, the agent's belief about how much volitional control they had can explain their emotional reaction. Building on this idea, Weiner [55] further contends that shame leads to inhibition of achievement striving and social withdrawal. Guilt on the other hand, is assumed to enable change and progression.

Game designers could examine failure in games from the perspective of controllability to further their understanding of what makes players give up versus endure when faced with failure. Successful games already suggest high controllability of the player to motivate progress and strengthen player resilience to failure [46].

### Previous Attribution Measures

As research on attribution theory became more prominent, measurements of attributional styles were developed. The Attributional Style Questionnaire (ASQ) [39], the Children's Attributional Style Questionnaire (CASQ) [48] and the Causal Dimension Scale (CDS) [26] are trait measures of attribution, measuring an agent's general attributional style across life situations. There are also more domain-specific questionnaires like the Academic Attributional Style Questionnaire (AASQ) [40], Organizational Attributional Style Questionnaire (OASQ) [27], or the Relationship Attribution Measure (RAM) [7]. All of these questionnaires measure attribution by presenting a number of hypothetical positive and negative scenarios. Participants were asked to name a cause they think would be responsible had that event happened to them. The participant then rated the cause on the four attributional dimensions.

Attributional measurements contribute valuable insight to many domains. People who make internal, stable and global attributions of negative events tend to exhibit more signs of depression [1,48]. Similarly, students who attribute academic failure to internal, stable and global causes tend to do more poorly in classes [40]. And in romantic partnerships, attributing negative partner behavior to internal, stable, and global causes decreased relationship satisfaction [7]. Furthermore, attributional styles in the workplace are able to predict work-related motivation and performance [27].

Despite their predictive qualities, these questionnaires have been criticized for their low reliability, and factor analyses indicated that there was little consistency between the hypothetical situations [22]. They measure attribution as a stable personality trait, assuming that within a domain (e.g., relationships, academia), attribution is cross-situationally consistent. Current literature has proposed that attributional styles may in fact not be consistent over domains or even situations[22]. The trend has therefore been to measure domain specific attributional styles (e.g. relationships, work) as the concept of the general, trait like attribution style (e.g. ASQ) does not seem to be the best empirical model. Based on these findings, a game-specific attribution questionnaire is necessary to understand player attribution, and it should measure attribution in a given situation– not as a general personality trait. Another problem is the role of controllability. While the construct of causal control is conceptually distinct from internality, they are not orthogonal, which often leads to correlations between these two dimensions.

## MEASURING GAME-SPECIFIC ATTRIBUTION

Our goal was to create and validate a game-specific attribution questionnaire (GSAQ) that measures how players attribute their in-game achievements. The following section describes the process of creating and validating our scale. We describe the process of creating the GSAQ in four steps: first, the creation and refinement of the item pool; second, the studies conducted to gather data; third, the creation of an adequate measurement model; and fourth, the quantitative assessment of the GSAQ.

### 1. Creating and Refining the Item Pool

The first step was to create a large pool of items. The four-person team that created the item pool consisted of experienced games user researchers as well as experienced gamers. The item creation was informed by the literature review on previous attributional measures in other fields. We also conducted unstructured interviews with 8 participants who considered themselves gamers to help us generate further items. Respondents were asked to remember instances of success and failure in different games and describe what they thought was responsible for those instances. The result was an item pool of 43 items, the majority of which (30 items) were designed to measure internality and controllability because these two constructs were expected to be the most difficult to empirically distinguish. We then qualitatively tested the items on a sample of 8 participants to specifically identify phrasing issues, ambiguities and difficult-to-understand items. We also asked our test subjects to cluster the items into groups they thought belonged together. This process allowed us to identify items that might not be eligible to distinguish between internality and controllability. Based on our findings, we rephrased 7 items resulting in the final refined item pool of 43 items (complete item pool of 43 items can be seen in Table 6 in the appendix).

### 2. Gathering Data

Our next goal was to gather response data we could use to create and validate a measurement model. To achieve this goal, we conducted two studies in which the only difference was the game played. Testing our items on two games allowed us to test for invariance over different games.

#### *Measures*

We included all 43 items in a randomized sequence in one questionnaire. First, we collected the GSAQ. Second, we collected player experience of need satisfaction (PENS scale) [45], which measures how much an activity satisfied a user's need for competence, autonomy and relatedness. Because we were looking at single player experience (as opposed to multiplayer), we excluded the relatedness subscale. The PENS scale also includes two constructs specific to interacting with virtual environments – intuitive control and immersion. Third, we collected intrinsic motivation using the Intrinsic Motivation Inventory (IMI), which assesses participants' interest/enjoyment, perceived competence, effort/ importance, and tension/pressure while performing a given activity [14]. In order to avoid overlap, we did not measure the competence subscale because competence is also measured by PENS. Fourth, we gathered the positive affect/ negative affect scale (PANAS), which measures positive and negative affect by asking participants to rate their agreement with a series of adjectives describing their present emotional state [50]. As we wanted to investigate how player attribution is linked to player characteristics, we also used two personality trait scales: The Big Five Inventory (BFI) [24,25], which measures personality on five dimensions (extraversion, agreeableness, conscientiousness, neuroticism and openness), and has been shown to moderate play experience [5]; and the Rosenberg self-esteem scale (RSS) [43], which measures self-esteem and which has been shown to predict game experience [4]. All items were rated on a 7-point Likert scale.

#### *Participants*

We conducted the study on the crowdsourcing platform Mechanical Turk. Mechanical Turk has been shown to be robust for conducting user studies [29,34]. The first study was conducted with 120 participants. Sixteen participants were eliminated from further analyses due to lack of compliance [34], which was indicated by failed control items in the questionnaires (e.g., "please select "agree" if you are reading this question"), as well as unrealistically quick responses to items in our attribution scale (i.e., average response time per item below 2 seconds). After this elimination process, 104 viable participants (female = 38 (36.5%), male = 66 (63.5%); Age: m= 33.00, SD = 9.81) remained. The second study was also conducted with 120 participants, of which 13 were eliminated due to lack of compliance [15], leaving 107 viable participants (female = 46 (41.5%), male = 61 (57.5%); Age: m= 32.86, SD =10.08). How frequently participants played games was measured with a descriptive 8-point scale ranging from 'every day' (8) to 'Not at all' (1). On average they played 'A few times per week' (M= 6.9, SD= 1.3).

#### *Procedure*

In both studies, participants were first asked to provide informed consent, fill out the personality questionnaires (BFI, RSS), and then play a game for 5 minutes. In the first study, participants played the match-3 type game. In the second study, they played a whack-a-mole game for 5 minutes. We chose an alignment-puzzle game and a reaction time game because we wanted two different primary mechanics that represented popular game genres. After the game, the participants were asked to fill out our Game-Specific Attribu-

| Sub-scale | Item | Factor 1 | Factor 2 | Factor 3 | Factor 4 |
|---|---|---|---|---|---|
| I | The reasons underlying my performance in this game lie within me. | **0.74** | -0.01 | 0.13 | 0.03 |
| | How well I did in this game was completely due to me. | **0.88** | 0.00 | -0.06 | -0.12 |
| | My effort determined how well I did in this this game. | **0.68** | 0.03 | 0.02 | 0.13 |
| | In this game, my performance was determined by my abilities. | **0.74** | -0.02 | 0.08 | 0.03 |
| S | The reasons for my performance in this game will stay the same in future games. | 0.01 | **0.78** | -0.01 | -0.10 |
| | Whatever affected my performance will continue to affect me in future games. | -0.14 | **0.77** | 0.08 | 0.12 |
| | The cause for my performance in this game will always be present. | 0.12 | **0.63** | -0.05 | -0.01 |
| G | The reason for my performance is something that affects other areas of my life. | -0.01 | -0.02 | **0.88** | 0.03 |
| | My performance in this game is typical for my general abilities in other areas of life. | 0.24 | 0.25 | **0.51** | -0.04 |
| | Whatever caused my score in this game is only important in the context of games. (R) | 0.01 | -0.16 | **-0.61** | 0.05 |
| C | Players have very little influence over their score in this game. (R) | -0.29 | -0.04 | 0.15 | **-0.53** |
| | It is in a player's power to become better at this game. | 0.38 | -0.01 | 0.04 | **0.81** |
| | Players are responsible for their performance in this game. | 0.23 | 0.11 | 0.03 | **0.63** |

**Table 1: EFA performed with principal axis factoring. Direct Oblimin rotation. Fixed to 4 factors. Factor loadings > .5 are printed in bold. Reverse-coded items marked with "(R)". (I = Internality, S = Stability, G = Globality, C = controllability)**

tion Questionnaire along with the other player experience measures and a final demographic survey. In total, participants filled out 115 items. On average they took 16 min to complete the study for which they received 2$ as compensation.

### 3. Creating the Measurement Model

Our next goal was to pick the best possible items out of our item pool to create a measurement model that reliably measured the four attributional dimensions We describe this process in three steps: First, we performed a preliminary analysis of the individual items to assess the item quality and remove items that performed poorly. Second, we performed exploratory and confirmatory factor analyses to assess the quality of our measurement model and to further refine it. Third, we tested if our measurement model is invariant over different games.

*Preliminary Assessment of Item Quality*

Before assessing the four dimensions of attribution using factor analyses, we inspected individual items to identify poorly-performing items. This process acted as a preliminary filter to make subsequent steps easier. As recommended [9], items were removed when a combination of several factors was present: extreme means (below 2 or above 6), limited variance (below 0.9), low squared multiple correlation (below 0.4), a low item whole correlation (below 0.4), and significant improvement of Cronbachs's alpha when removed. After this process, 28 of 43 items remained.

*Creating a Good Measurement Model*

Our scale items were designed based on a theoretical model. We therefore already had expectations about the latent factors the items were loading on. To confirm these assumptions, we performed an exploratory factor analysis (EFA) and a subsequent confirmatory factor analysis (CFS). The EFA with all 28 remaining items was performed using principal axis factoring (PAF) with Oblimin rotation. Based on our conceptual framework, factor extraction was fixed to 4 factors. With a Kaiser-Meyer-Olkin (KMO) index of .89 and a significant Bartlett's test of sphericity ($\chi^2$= 2680, p < .001), sampling adequacy was considered good. The total variance explained amounted to 45.6%. To further increase the quality of our measurement model, items were removed based on two criteria. First, on psychometric grounds: items with low factor loadings and low squared multiple correlations were candidates for removal to improve the model fit [9,32]. Second, on theoretical grounds: items that were similar in phrasing to better-performing items were removed. In an attempt to conceptually distinguish the four constructs, we removed items that were, on a content level, too similar to other constructs. Items were also removed despite performing well in an effort to increase parsimony of the model. This trade-off between goodness-of-fit and parsimony was accepted to avoid an unnecessarily long questionnaire [9,12]. Through this process, 15 items were removed. The final model included a total of 13 items measuring internality (4 items), controllability (3 items), stability (3 items), and globality (3 items). A final EFA with the remaining 13 items was run (PAF, Oblimin rotation). The sampling adequacy was good (KMO = .86, $\chi^2$= 1059, p < .001) and 59.6% of the variance was explained. All items loaded highly (> .5) and uniquely on their intended factors (see Table 1 for the final item set and the factor loadings). To test the quality of our measurement model, we conducted a CFA using AMOS. There are multiple measures that can be used to assess the goodness-of-fit for a specific model. The model fit indices for this measurement model can be seen in Table 2 along with the thresholds as recommended by Hu and Bentler [23]. The model for our Game-Specific Attribution Questionnaire shows a good fit with our data. $\chi^2$/df is good, and the significant p-value was expected due to sample size [23,9]. The CFI, TLI, RMSEA and PCLOSE values all indicate a good to great model fit.

| | Overall Model | Game 1 Model | Game 2 Model | Thresholds |
|---|---|---|---|---|
| $\chi^2$/df | 1.69 | 1.72 | 1.42 | < 3 good |
| p-value | 0.01 | 0.01 | 0.03 | < .05 |
| CFI | 0.96 | 0.95 | 0.96 | >.95 great; >.90 traditional |
| TLI | 0.96 | 0.92 | 0.94 | >.95 great; >.90 traditional |
| RMSEA | 0.06 | 0.08 | 0.06 | <.05 great <.10 acceptable |
| PCLOSE | 0.26 | 0.06 | 0.25 | >.05 |

**Table 2: Model Fit for Overall Model and Invariance Tests**

*Testing for Invariance*

Because we want our scale to measure player attribution in many different games, the CFA has to validate that the factor structure and loadings are sufficiently equivalent across games. We tested our model comparing data from the match-3 game with data from whack-a-mole. For both games, the measurement model is still sufficient, as can be seen in Table 2. The slight decrease in model fit is mainly due to the sample size that is low for a CFA once the data set is split by game [56]. Because both models still show a sufficient fit, we can assume configural invariance of our Game-Specific Attribution Questionnaire [9,32]. In addition to configural invariance, the model also has to be metrically invariant. In order to test differences in the model between games, we used a multi-group moderation test using the critical ratio differences in AMOS [32]. For all subscales, the differences in critical ratios were *not* significant indicating that our scale is also metrically invariant over different games. Stability across games for both the model fit and factor-loading suggests psychometric and theoretical soundness of the instrument [9].

## 4. Quantitative Assessment of the GSAQ

With the final items selected, we have a good measurement model for the GSAQ. We tested the scale for reliability, convergent validity, discriminant validity, and criterion-related validity.

*Reliability*

Composite reliability (CR) and Cronbach's alpha values were good for internality, controllability and stability (CR > .70, α > .75). The globality scale's CR value marginally misses the threshold of >.7 (CR = .69) and its Chronbach's α is low but still acceptable (α = .70) [9,12] (see Table 3).

*Convergent Validity*

The Average Variance Extracted (AVE) for each of the subscales is above 0.50, suggesting a good convergent validity (see Table 3). Good convergent validity indicates that the items measuring one factor are strongly related to one another, supporting the idea that they are conceptually measuring the same latent construct [9,12].

| | CR | Cronbach's α | AVE | MSV |
|---|---|---|---|---|
| Internality | 0.87 | 0.86 | 0.62 | 0.86 |
| Controllability | 0.75 | 0.75 | 0.51 | 0.86 |
| Stability | 0.77 | 0.77 | 0.53 | 0.34 |
| Globality | 0.69 | 0.70 | 0.53 | 0.34 |

**Table 3: Composite reliability, Cronbach's α, Average Variance Extracted and Maximum Shared Variance for the GSAQ**

*Discriminant Validity*

The Maximum Shared Variance (MSV) scores for internality and controllability are higher than their AVE scores, which is an indicator for low discriminant validity [32] (see Table 3). As already discussed, conceptually it is to be expected that the sense of control is strongly confounded with the locus of that control – i.e., internality. The two constructs can therefore be statistically similar due to high correlation (Table 5), but still be theoretically distinct. Nevertheless, the relationship between these constructs must be acknowledged when interpreting player attribution results.

*Criterion-Related Validity*

Until now we have only demonstrated the quality of the measurement for player attribution. The more interesting questions are if attribution can help us understand how players experience a game and how attribution is linked to player personality.

The GSAQ shows a few interesting relationships with both player characteristics and player experience. Table 4 shows a correlation matrix between attribution and player personality and experience. The player's self-esteem correlates significantly with both controllability and internality but not with stability and globality. Of the personality constructs, extraversion and agreeableness reveal no significant correlations. Conscientiousness is the tendency towards self-discipline and to control and regulate impulses [24,25]. The subscale is correlated with internality and controllability. Neuroticism is the tendency towards experiencing negative emotions, such as anxiety or depression [24,25]. The subscale is negatively correlated with internality. Openness to experience describes a willingness to engage in new experiences or imaginative activities [24,25]. The subscale is positively correlated with controllability.

While player attribution is partially linked to player personality, the attribution scales have an even stronger link to player experience measurements (i.e., PENS, IMI). This is not surprising as attribution and experience were both measured as states. Competence measures players' perceptions that "the game provided a challenging but not overwhelmingly difficult experience and enhanced efficacy" [44,45]. Internality, controllability, stability, and globality all correlated with competence. Autonomy measures "the degree to which participants felt free, and perceived opportunities to do activities that interested them" [44,45]. Autonomy significantly correlates with internality, controllability, and globality. Immersion measures how physically

| | Internality | Controllability | Stability | Globality |
|---|---|---|---|---|
| Self-esteem | **.212**** | **.156*** | .033 | .052 |
| Extraversion | .062 | .019 | .027 | .032 |
| Agreeableness | .019 | .03 | -.077 | -.125 |
| Conscientiousness | **.231**** | **.243**** | .096 | .018 |
| Neuroticism | **-.149*** | -.093 | .003 | -.038 |
| Openness | .066 | **.142*** | .053 | .085 |
| Competence | **.564**** | **.430**** | **.285**** | **.383**** |
| Autonomy | **.380**** | **.242**** | .056 | **.271**** |
| Immersion | **.214**** | .006 | -0.03 | **.282**** |
| Intuitive Controls | **.315**** | **.305**** | **.289**** | **.167**** |
| Interest | **.272**** | **.231**** | .059 | **.213**** |
| Effort | **.280**** | **.277**** | **.240**** | **.146*** |
| Pressure | **-.215**** | -.135 | -.041 | -.053 |
| Positive affect change | **.189**** | **.194**** | .028 | .119 |
| Negative affect change | **-.177*** | **-.201**** | -.052 | -.045 |
| Performance | **.233**** | **.185**** | **.206**** | **.170*** |

**Table 4: Attribution scales correlation with player personality and player experience (*p <= .05, **p <= .01)**

and emotionally present the player felt in the game environment [45], and is significantly correlated with internality and globality. Intuitive controls indicates how easily the players were able to control movement or action in the game [45], which is significantly correlated with internality, controllability, stability, and globality.

Interest/enjoyment measures how much a player enjoyed playing a game and is often interpreted as a self-report measure for intrinsic motivation [35,45]. Interest is significantly correlated with internality, controllability, and globality. Effort/importance measures how much work a player invested in the game [35,45], and significantly correlates with internality, controllability, stability, and globality. Pressure/tension measures the amount of tension and duress the player felt while playing [35,45], and as one would expect, it is negatively correlated with internality. Positive affect change [50] is significantly correlated with internality and controllability. Negative affect change [50] is negatively correlated with internality, and controllability. Finally, performance is the standardized value of in-game performance based on the game score. Game performance is significantly correlated with internality, controllability, stability, and globality. We interpret the correlations between player attribution and player experience in the next section.

## DISCUSSION

The goal of this paper was to demonstrate the value of Attribution Theory in games user research and to introduce a scale to measure player attribution in games. We have demonstrated in theory how player attribution as a construct

| | Internality | Controllability | Stability | Globality |
|---|---|---|---|---|
| Internality | - | | | |
| Controllability | .720** | - | | |
| Stability | .323** | .251** | - | |
| Globality | .303** | .154** | .362** | - |

**Table 5: GSAQ correlation matrix (*p <= .05, **p <= .01)**

could contribute to our understanding of player experience. We have also introduced the Game-Specific Attribution Questionnaire as a reliable and valid measurement tool. In the following section, we will interpret our findings, propose possible applications in games user research, and discuss the limitations of our study and how future research can address them.

### Interpretation of Results

Through the process of careful item creation, selection and scale validation, we have come up with a reliable and valid scale to measure player attribution. Our analysis indicates a good model fit, reliability and convergent validity [9]. As expected, internality and controllability are strongly correlated. These issues replicate previous findings [22]. In line with previous literature, we acknowledge the statistical connection between the two constructs while still viewing them as conceptually distinct.

The correlations between player attribution and other personality and experience measures revealed several interesting results. First, the positive connection between self-esteem and internality and controllability as well as the negative connection between neuroticism and internality replicate established connections between attributional styles and self-esteem and a tendency toward negative emotions [16,39,48]. Second, the positive relationship between game performance and all player attribution measures can be explained by well-established patterns of self-enhancing biases. Research on attribution has repeatedly shown a tendency towards attributing success as more internal, controllable, stable and global, and failure as more external, uncontrollable, unstable, and specific [6].

Third, the initial results show a strong link connecting player attribution to need satisfaction of autonomy and especially competence. We can't draw conclusions about causality based on these correlations, but a reasonable hypothesis is that a player's causal beliefs are antecedents of feelings of competence and autonomy (e.g., internal and controllable causes for success are more likely to evoke feelings of competence). Fourth, high internality, controllability and globality beliefs appear to be connected with higher interest and enjoyment of a game. How much effort the player is willing to invest is linked to all four attribution dimensions. Similar to need satisfaction, one explanation for these relationships is that a player's causal beliefs (e.g., high controllability or globality) might lead to higher interest and effort.

Finally, internality as well as controllability are positively associated with positive affect change and negatively associated with negative affect change. These findings support the ideas stated above, that causal beliefs of players can impact their emotional reaction to a gaming experience.

### Application in Digital Games Research

Our results demonstrate how attribution can be relevant in the context of player experience – providing additional explanatory value to existing measures of player experience common in games user research. We describe two ways in which the GSAQ can provide value to academic researchers and industry practitioners: by providing explanatory power and by guiding design.

#### *Improving Understanding using the GSAQ*

The GSAQ gives researchers a tool to explain differences observed in other measures of player experience. For example, Gerling et al. [18] created a system that allowed players to use a wheelchair as input to a Dance Dance Revolution clone, and a difficulty balancing technique that allowed people in wheelchairs to compete against able-bodied players. The authors suggested that if players in wheelchairs think they are only winning because of the system's aid, competence would not be fostered and self-esteem could be harmed. Assessing internality using the GSAQ for different multiplayer balancing schemes would provide value in addition to measuring the standard constructs, such as competence and self-esteem.

Recently, researchers have started using broad concepts of causal beliefs to better understand player experience. Work on dynamic difficulty adjustment has investigated the effect of overt or covert assistance in multiplayer games [10]. Overt assistance did not seem to detract from the players' perceived competence and the authors use the well-established concept of self-serving attribution biases to explain that players attribute their performance internally despite knowing they were being assisted. In another example, attribution theory was used to explain the difference between players being frustrated as an intended experience "in" the game or as a negative reaction "at" the game [36]; the authors argue that causal beliefs about internality and controllability are constructs that help us understand the nature of frustration during game play that results in a motivating or disheartening experience.

In another example, the GSAQ gives researchers a tool to further investigate aggressive (toxic) behavior in multiplayer online games. One of the most successful online multiplayer games (League of Legends, Riot) is struggling to prevent players from verbally abusing each other [15,28]. Research has shown that 48% of these toxic team conflicts arise after one team member makes a mistake that results in the death of another [15]. Escalating conflicts often contain comments like "report noob" or "stop feeding" [28]. Players can "report" other players after a game and the average number of reports per match is highest for "intentional feeding" (intentionally dying) and "assisting the enemy" [28]. Toxic behavior in these cases seems to partially stem from the belief that an underperforming team member *should* and (more importantly) *could* have done better. As such, the toxic player might be characterized by the assumption that team members control their own performance, whether or not it is appropriate or true. The GSAQ could provide insight into the idea that toxic players suffer from an attributional fallacy of overestimating causal controllability in other players. The scale could also investigate the assumption that lower controllability in other players will lead to sympathy and a willingness to help.

These examples are not an exhaustive list of all application possibilities of attribution theory, but merely serve as illustrations of how attribution theory and the GSAQ can be used to further understand player experience.

#### *Guiding Game Design*

In addition to promoting understanding, the GSAQ can also help guide designer decisions.

For example, consider a designer of an educational game who wishes to evaluate two different methods of providing feedback in their game. Attribution theory suggests that internal attribution of performance translates into pride [55]. Using the GSAQ to evaluate how different achievement badge implementations affect internality should help designers create badges that foster a sense of pride and inspire further progress in the game.

Or consider the designer of a persuasive game intended to help players learn a language. Feelings of stability resulting from the game would differentiate between a player experiencing confidence (the improvements will last) and apprehension (the improvements will go away) in using the skills learned in the game [55]. Evaluating the stability of different designs in an iterative process could help to improve the efficacy of the game during development.

Finally, consider a game intended to help players overcome a fear of public speaking by helping the player practice and apply techniques in private. Evaluating how globally players attribute progress over various designs may help determine whether players will feel that they can apply the learned in-game skills to the public speaking context.

### Limitations and Future Work

On a theoretical level, we have shown the value that attribution theory can contribute to research in digital games. Our results indicate strong links of player attribution to player personality as well as player experience. However, these initial results only hint at the insights our scale can contribute to digital games research. Further studies now have to investigate the specifics of how player attribution affects player experience. Another limitation is the relatively small sample size we used. For a CFA, a larger sample size would have been valuable [9]. Given the parameters of our model (four factors, factor loadings greater than .65, 211 participants) and no missing values in our data, we can still be confident in our interpretation of our results [56].

Our study was conducted on Amazon's Mechanical Turk, which is a crowdsourcing platform for people who want to earn money doing online work. This means that our participants were engaging with the games in a professional capacity with the extrinsic motivation of getting paid. It could be argued that the professional, experimental setting of the game experience contradicts the usual volitional, hedonistic and playful characteristic of gaming [46]. Applying our scale to volitional and playful gaming in the future will ensure that it is valid across contexts.

Both the match-3 game, and the whack-a-mole game were casual games, and these games were played for a short duration, limiting the generalizability of our results. In order to truly understand player attribution, the scale should be tested in different game genres, different levels of engagement, and in longer game sessions.

Although we show interesting correlations with player experience measures, the causal paths and relationships between attribution and need satisfaction or intrinsic motivation should be further explored to better define the role of player attribution in player experience. Is internality an antecedent of competence? Does controllability mediate the known relationship between autonomy and effort [5]? Future research should strive to further our understanding of how player attribution explains player experience. The specific relationships of causal beliefs determining emotional reactions (e.g., pride, confidence, shame, sympathy) of game users should also be explored.

## CONCLUSIONS

Research in player experience of digital games has long been using methods that are grounded in motivational psychology to further understand how a player experiences a game and how they feel about themselves while playing it. We believe that attribution theory is a valuable addition to the box of tools game researchers and designers have at their disposal. In this paper we have applied findings in attributional research from other fields to games to argue its potential value in understanding emotional and motivation reactions to games. We have also introduced the GSAQ as a tool for game research and design. A vast amount of empirical research on causal beliefs has demonstrated the effects of attribution on emotion, motivation, and behavior. We are confident that causal beliefs will provide valuable insights into game user experience. "Why is this happening to me?" is an important question in many life situations – we argue that this question is just as relevant in our understanding of how, when, and why people play digital games.

## ACKNOWLEDGMENTS

We thank Jason Bowey, Colby Johanson, and the Interaction Lab for support and NSERC SWaGUR for funding.

## APPENDIX

|  |
|---|
| My performance in this game was completely due to other people or circumstances. (R)(I) |
| The reasons underlying my performance in this game lie within me. (I) |
| **The reasons underlying my performance in this game lie outside of me. (R) (I)** |
| The score of the game was caused mostly by things other than myself. (R)(I) |
| **How well I did in this game was completely due to me. (I)** |
| How well I did in this game reflects on me. (I) |
| I currently have the capacity to do well in this game. (I) |
| My performance in this game can be used to make assessments about me. (I) |
| Performance in this game is indicative of a player's attributes. (I) |
| Something other than me influenced my performance. (R)(I) |
| I controlled my performance in this game. (I) |
| **My effort determined how well I did in this this game. (I)** |
| My performance in this game reflects directly on my skill. (I) |
| **In this game, my performance was determined by my abilities. (I)** |
| The score of the game would have been the same no matter how hard I tried. (R)(I) |
| My aptitude affects how well I do in this game. (I) |
| The cause for performance in this game can be controlled. (C) |
| Players can affect the cause of their performance in this game. (C) |
| Whatever influenced performance in this game is out of the player's hands. (C) |
| It is up to the player how well they do in this game. (C) |
| **Players have very little influence over their score in this game. (R)(C)** |
| Performance in this game is completely under the player's control. (C) |
| Players have control over their success in future rounds of this game. (C) |
| **It is in a player's power to become better at this game. (C)** |
| If a player wanted to, they could perform poorly in this game. (C) |
| Players can allow others to perform better than themselves in this game. (C) |
| Through practice, players can become better at this game. (C) |
| Players cannot change anything to be become better at this game. (R)(C) |
| **Players are responsible for their performance in this game. (C)** |
| Poor performance in this game can be blamed on the player. (C) |
| The causes for my performance in this game are stable. (S) |
| **The reasons for my performance in this game will stay the same in future games. (S)** |
| Whatever affected my performance will not change in future games. (S) |
| **Whatever affected my performance will continue to affect me in future games. (S)** |
| My performance in the game could be completely different the next time I play. (R)(S) |
| **The cause for my performance in this game will always be present. (S)** |
| The cause for my performance in this game will never be present again. (R)(S) |
| Whatever affected my performance is variable over time. (R)(S) |
| It is easy to predict how well I will perform in future rounds of the game. (S) |
| **The reason for my performance is something that affects other areas of my life. (G)** |
| **Whatever caused my score in this game is only important in the context of games. (R)(G)** |
| **My performance in this game is typical for my general abilities in other areas of life. (G)** |
| My performance in this game is only representative of my game-related abilities. (R)(G) |

**Table 6 (continued): Initial item pool of 43 items. Reversed items marked with "(R)". Final items in bold. (I = Internality, S= Stability, G = Globality, C = controllability)**

## REFERENCES


1. Lyn Y. Abramson, Martin E. Seligman, and John D. Teasdale. 1978. Learned helplessness in humans: Critique and reformulation. *Journal of Abnormal Psychology* 87, 1 (1978), 49--74. http://dx.doi.org/10.1037/0021-843x.87.1.49
2. Craig A. Anderson and Alice L. Riger. 1991. A Controllability Attributional Model of Problems in Living: Dimensional and Situationa
3. l Interactions in the Prediction of Depression and Loneliness. *Social Cognition* 9, 2 (jun 1991), 149--181. http://dx.doi.org/10.1521/soco.1991.9.2.149.
4. Max V. Birk, Regan L. Mandryk, Matthew K. Miller, and Kathrin M. Gerling. 2015. How Self-Esteem Shapes our Interactions with Play Technologies. In *Proceedings of the 2015 Annual Symposium on Computer-Human Interaction in Play* (CHI PLAY '15). ACM, New York, NY, USA, 35-45. http://dx.doi.org/10.1145/2793107.2793111
5. Max V. Birk, Dereck Toker, Regan L. Mandryk, and Cristina Conati. 2011. Modeling Motivation in a Social Network Game using Player-Centric Traits and Personality Traits. In *Proceedings of the 23rd Conference on User Modelling, Adaptation, and Personalization - UMAP '11*. Dublin, Ireland, 18-30. http://dx.doi.org/10.1007/978-3-319-20267-9_2
6. Gifford W. Bradley. 1978. Self-serving biases in the attribution process: A reexamination of the fact or fiction question. *Journal of Personality and Social Psychology* 36, 1 (1978), 56--71. http://dx.doi.org/10.1037/0022-3514.36.1.56
7. Thomas N. Bradbury and Frank D. Fincham. 1990. Attributions in marriage: Review and critique. *Psychological Bulletin* 107, 1 (1990), 3--33. http://dx.doi.org/10.1037/0033-2909.107.1.3.
8. Mihaly Csikszentmihalyi. 1988. The flow experience and its significance for human psychology. In *Psychological studies of flow in consciousness*, Mihaly Csikszentmihalyi and Isabella Selega Csikszentmihalyi (Eds.). Cambridge University Press (CUP), 15--35. http://dx.doi.org/10.1017/cbo9780511621956.002.
9. Frederik De Grove, Verolien Cauberghe, and Jan Van Looy. 2014. Development and Validation of an Instrument for Measuring Individual Motives for Playing Digital Games. *Media Psychology* (jun 2014), 1--25. http://dx.doi.org/10.1080/15213269.2014.902318
10. Ansgar E. Depping, Regan L. Mandryk, Chengzhao Li, Carl Gutwin, and Rodrigo Vicencio-Moreira. 2016. How Disclosing Skill Assistance Affects Play Experience in a Multiplayer First-Person Shooter Game. *Proceedings of the 2016 CHI Conference on Human Factors in Computing Systems*. (ACM), 3462-3472.
11. Sebastian Deterding. 2012. Gamification: designing for motivation. *interactions,19*(4), 14-17.
12. Robert F DeVellis. 2012. *Scale development: Theory and applications*. Vol. 26. Sage publications.
13. Christopher Dring, 2015, June 14th. More money is spent on games than movies and music combined, says HIS. Retrieved from www.mcvuk.com/news/read/more-money-is-spent-on-games-than-movies-and-music-combined-says-ihs/0151059
14. Edward McAuley, Terry Duncan, and Vance V. Tammen. 1989. Psychometric Properties of the Intrinsic Motivation Inventory in a Competitive Sport Setting: A Confirmatory Factor Analysis. Research Quarterly for Exercise and Sport 60, 1 (mar 1989), 48--58. http://dx.doi.org/10.1080/02701367.1989.10607413.
15. Josefine Fahlström, Emma Matson. 2014. Preventing Toxic Behaviour through Game Mechanics.
16. Gordon Fitch. 1970. Effects of self-esteem, perceived performance, and choice on causal attributions. Journal of Personality and Social Psychology 16, 2 (1970), 311--315. http://dx.doi.org/10.1037/h0029847.
17. Susan Folkman, Richard S. Lazarus, Rand J. Gruen, and Anita DeLongis. 1986. Appraisal, coping, health status, and psychological symptoms. Journal of Personality and Social Psychology 50, 3 (1986), 571--579. http://dx.doi.org/10.1037/0022-3514.50.3.571.
18. Kathrin Maria Gerling, Matthew Miller, Regan L. Mandryk, Max Valentin Birk, and Jan David Smeddinck. 2014. Effects of balancing for physical abilities on player performance, experience and self-esteem in exergames. In Proceedings of the 32nd annual ACM conference on Human factors in computing systems - CHI 14. Association for Computing Machinery (ACM). http://dx.doi.org/10.1145/2556288.2556963
19. Sandra Graham. 1991. A review of attribution theory in achievement contexts. Educational Psychology Review 3,1(mar1991),5--39. http://dx.doi.org/10.1007/bf01323661
20. Grüsser, S. M., Thalemann, R., & Griffiths, M. D. (2006). Excessive computer game playing: evidence for addiction and aggression?. CyberPsychology & Behavior, 10(2), 290-292.
21. Shlomo Hareli and Bernard Weiner. 2002. Social Emotions and Personality Inferences: A Scaffold for a New Direction in the Study of Achievement Motivation. Educational Psychologist 37, 3 (sep 2002), 183--193. http://dx.doi.org/10.1207/s15326985ep3703_4
22. Robert M. Hessling, Craig A. Anderson, and Daniel W. Russell 2,002. Attributional styles. *Encyclopedia of psychological assessment*, 116-120.
23. Li tze Hu and Peter M. Bentler. 1999. Cutoff criteria for fit indexes in covariance structure analysis: Conventional criteria versus new alternatives. *Structural Equation Modeling: A Multidisciplinary Journal* 6, 1 (jan 1999), 1--55. http://dx.doi.org/10.1080/10705519909540118
24. E. Tory Higgins. 1987. Self-discrepancy: A theory relating self and affect. *Psychological Review* 94, 3 (1987), 319--340. http://dx.doi.org/10.1037/0033-295x.94.3.31

25. Oliver P. John, Laura P. Naumann, and Christopher J. Soto, 2008. Paradigm shift to the integrative big five trait taxonomy. *Handbook of personality: Theory and research, 3*, 114-158.
26. Dan, Russell. 1982 The Causal Dimension Scale: A measure of how individuals perceive causes. *Journal of Personality and social Psychology* 42, 6, 1982: 1137.
27. Kent, Russell L. 1991. *The development and evaluation of a scale to measure organizational attributional style.*
28. Haewoon Kwak, Jeremy Blackburn, and Seungyeop Han. 2015. Exploring Cyberbullying and Other Toxic Behavior in Team Competition Online Games. In *Proceedings of the 33rd Annual ACM Conference on Human Factors in Computing Systems - CHI 15*. Association for Computing Machinery (ACM). http://dx.doi.org/10.1145/2702123.2702529
29. Aniket Kittur, Ed H. Chi, and Bongwon Suh. 2008. Crowdsourcing user studies with Mechanical Turk In *Proceedings of the SIGCHI Conference on Human Factors in Computing Systems* (CHI '08). ACM, New York, NY, USA, 453-456. http://dx.doi.org/10.1145/1357054.1357127
30. William W. Lambert and Richard S. Lazarus. 1970. Psychological Stress and the Coping Process. *The American Journal of Psychology* 83, 4 (dec 1970), 634. http://dx.doi.org/10.2307/1420698
31. Nicole Lazzaro, 2008. Fun keys: Testing emotions and player experiences. *Game Usability: Advice from the Experts for Advancing the Player Experience. Morgan Kaufmann, San Francisco, CA.*
32. Paul Benjamin Lowry and James Gaskin. 2014. Partial Least Squares (PLS) Structural Equation Modeling (SEM) for Building and Testing Behavioral Causal Theory: When to Choose It and How to Use It. *IEEE Trans. Profess. Commun.* 57, 2 (jun 2014), 123--146. http://dx.doi.org/10.1109/tpc.2014.2312452
33. Mark Martinko. 1995.*Attribution theory: An organizational perspective.* CRC Press
34. Winter Mason, and Siddharth Suri. 2012. Conducting behavioral research on Amazon's Mechanical Turk. *Behavior Research Methods,* 44(1), 1-23. http://dx.doi.org/10.3758/s13428-011-0124-6
35. Edward McAuley, Terry Duncan, and Vance V. Tammen. 1989. Psychometric properties of the Intrinsic Motivation Inventory in a competitive sport setting: A confirmatory factor analysis. *Research Quarterly for Exercise and Sport*, 60(1), 48-58. http://dx.doi.org/10.1080/02701367.1989.10607413
36. Matthew K. Miller, and Regan L. Mandryk. 2016. Differentiating in-Game Frustration from at-Game Frustration using Touch Pressure. *Proceedings of the 2016 ACM Conference on Interactive Surfaces and Spaces.* (ACM), 225-234.
37. Lennart E. Nacke, Chris Bateman, and Regan L. Mandryk, 2014. BrainHex: A neurobiological gamer typology survey. *Entertainment computing, 5*(1), 55-62.
38. Newzoo. 2015 Global Games Market Report, https://newzoo.com/solutions/revenues-projections/global-games-market-report/
39. Christopher Peterson, Amy Semmel, Carl von Baeyer, Lyn Y. Abramson, Gerald I. Metalsky, and Martin E. P. Seligman. 1982. The attributional Style Questionnaire. *Cognitive Therapy and Research* 6, 3 (sep 1982), 287--299. http://dx.doi.org/10.1007/bf01173577
40. Christopher Peterson and Lisa C. Barrett. 1987. Explanatory style and academic performance among university freshman. *Journal of Personality and Social Psychology* 53, 3 (1987), 603--607. http://dx.doi.org/10.1037/0022-3514.53.3.603.
41. Andrew K Przybylski, Netta Weinstein, Richard M Ryan, and C Scott Rigby. 2009. Having to versus wanting to play: Background and consequences of harmonious versus obsessive engagement in video games. *CyberPsychology & Behavior* 12(5), 485-492. http://dx.doi.org/10.1089/cpb.2009.0083
42. Rocío Fernández-Ballesteros, ed. 2002. *Encyclopedia of psychological assessment.* Sage
43. Morris Rosenberg, 1965. Society and the adolescent self-image. *Social Forces* 44, 2 (dec 1965), 255. http://dx.doi.org/10.2307/2575639.
44. Richard M. Ryan and Edward L. Deci. 2000. Self-determination theory and the facilitation of intrinsic motivation, social development, and well-being. *American Psychologist* 55, 1 (2000), 68--78. http://dx.doi.org/10.1037/0003-066x.55.1.68
45. Ryan, Richard M., C. Scott Rigby, and Andrew Przybylski. "The motivational pull of video games: A self-determination theory approach." *Motivation and emotion* 30, no. 4 (2006): 344-360.
46. Katie Salen, and Eric Zimmerman, 2004. *Rules of play: Game design fundamentals.* MIT press. http://dx.doi.org/10.1162/leon.2004.37.5.414
47. Klaus R Scherer, Angela Schorr, and Tom Johnstone, eds. 2001. *Appraisal processes in emotion: Theory, methods, research.* Oxford University Press
48. Martin E Seligman and et al. 1984. Attributional style and depressive symptoms among children. *Journal of Abnormal Psychology* 93, 2 (1984), 235--238. http://dx.doi.org/10.1037/0021-843x.93.2.235
49. Penelope Sweetser and Peta Wyeth. 2005. GameFlow. *Comput. Entertain.* 3, 3 (jul 2005), 3. http://dx.doi.org/10.1145/1077246.1077253
50. David Watson, and Lee Anna Clark. 1999. The PANAS-X: Manual for the positive and negative affect schedule-expanded form.
51. Bernard Weiner. 1979. A theory of motivation for some classroom experiences. *Journal of Educational Psychology* 71, 1 (1979), 3--25. http://dx.doi.org/10.1037/0022-0663.71.1.3.
52. Bernard Weiner. 1985. An attributional theory of achievement motivation and emotion. *Psychological*

*Review* 92, 4 (1985), 548--573. http://dx.doi.org/10.1037/0033-295x.92.4.548

53. Bernard Weiner. 1986. *An Attributional Theory of Motivation and Emotion*. Springer Science Business Media. http://dx.doi.org/10.1007/978-1-4612-4948-1
54. Bernard Weiner. 2001. Intrapersonal and Interpersonal Theories of Motivation from an Attribution Perspective. In *Student Motivation*. Springer Science Business Media, 17--30. http://dx.doi.org/10.1007/978-1-4615-1273-8_2
55. B. Weiner. 2014. The Attribution Approach to Emotion and Motivation: History, Hypotheses, Home Runs, Headaches/Heartaches. *Emotion Review* 6, 4 (sep 2014), 353--361. http://dx.doi.org/10.1177/1754073914534502
56. E. J. Wolf, K. M. Harrington, S. L. Clark, and M. W. Miller. 2013. Sample Size Requirements for Structural Equation Models: An Evaluation of Power, Bias, and Solution Propriety. *Educational and Psychological Measurement* 73, 6 (jul 2013), 913--934. http://dx.doi.org/10.1177/0013164413495237.

# Keeping Users Engaged through Feature Updates: A Long-Term Study of Using Wearable-Based Exergames

**Zhao Zhao, Ali Arya, Anthony Whitehead, Gerry Chan, S. Ali Etemad**
Carleton University
Ottawa, Canada
{zhao.zhao, ali.arya, anthony.whitehead, gerry.chan, ali.etemad}@carleton.ca

## ABSTRACT
Gamification and exergames in particular have been broadly employed in health and fitness as an attempt to promote exercise and more active life styles. Motivated by popularity and availability of wearable activity trackers, we present the design and findings of a study on the motivational effects of using activity tracker-based games to promote daily exercise. Furthermore, we have investigated user behaviors, usage patterns, engagement, and parameters that affect them. An exergame was developed with an accompanying wearable device, for which different variations of application updates were pushed out periodically over a 70-day period. The results of this long-term study show that the usage of wearable activity trackers during exercise, even when gamified for increased entertainment, sees a consistent decline over time. This decline, however, is observed to be reversible with periodic updates to the game. This work, we believe, can make a significant contribution to solving the user retention problem of wearable-based exergames.

### Author Keywords
Gamification; fitness; exercise; wearable device; motivation; game sustainability; exergames.

### ACM Classification Keywords
H.5.2 [User Interfaces]: Input Devices and Strategies; K.8.0 [Personal Computing]: Games

## INTRODUCTION
Gamification (utilizing game thinking and game mechanics in non-game context [7]) in exercise and fitness has rapidly emerged over the past years as a tool to promote health and wellness [2, 6, 12, 24, 29, 33, 35]. It helps users to achieve certain fitness goals and increase engagement by adding game features to physical activity.

This work is supported by Social Sciences and Humanities Research Council of Canada through IMMERSE Network.



*CHI 2017, May 06-11, 2017, Denver, CO, USA*
© 2017 ACM. ISBN 978-1-4503-4655-9/17/05...$15.00
DOI: http://dx.doi.org/10.1145/3025453.3025982

In recent years, there has been a proliferation of physical activity tracking devices, such as Fitbit, Jawbone, Garmin, etc., and these wearable devices, along with their associated applications have proven to be popular platforms for promoting health and fitness due to their wide adaption, ease of use, and continuous proximity to the users [25].

Consequently, previous research [36] suggests that off-the-shelf wearable devices have considerable potential to be utilized in gamification of exercise and fitness. In our previous work, we utilized this concept through the design and implementation of a smartphone game application, which used wearable devices as input systems [36]. Short-term studies were conducted with combinations of different exercises and types of wearable devices to evaluate the usability and motivations of our system. The results showed that based on existing technologies and user needs, the idea of employing wearable activity trackers for gamification of exercise and fitness is feasible, motivating, and engaging.

In this paper, we extend the application with more diverse features and scenarios, followed by a 70-day long-term user study, to further investigate the motivational effects of using our system for promoting and sustaining exercise engagement. In order to have people maintain a constant habit or routine, applications should be designed with not only desirable usability but also sustainability, to provide users with sustainable motivation and engagement over time [4]. We designed the application to update regularly by adding new features to enable us to evaluate the effect of such time-based updates. Our research question is whether game features and their release system can improve engagement over time. We aimed to verify the hypothesis that gradually releasing game features will improve user retention over a longer period. Therefore, we divided our participants into three groups where the first group received the game with only very basic features, the second group received a more comprehensive set of various features such as customization and multiplayer mode. The third group started from only basic features but had different features gradually unlocked every 10 days. The behavioral patterns of all three groups were monitored by tracking users' activities as well as collecting their objective experiences through questionnaires both before and after the study.

This paper continues by covering related work, followed by the application design and implementation. It continues with the description of user study design, followed by the study results and analysis. Finally, some conclusions will be drawn to summarize our findings, as well as introduce some potential directions for future work.

## RELATED WORK

Studies have shown that gamification in the area of health and fitness could motivate users to become more active [23]. The advantage of gamified exercise over traditional forms of exercise is that it is not just a physical activity, but also a form of entertainment. For example, exergames such as Just Dance (and other Wii or Kinect based exergames) offer participants a much higher level of engagement compared to regular exercise, which could reduce the level of perceived exertion. As a result, the level of motivation to stick with the game is also much higher than with traditional exercise [1]. Exergames can not only make exercise seem more enjoyable [35], but can also help improve overall well-being of older adults [17]. However, exergames may not be able to maintain long term interest in exercise [30] and some exergames are not intense enough to contribute toward the recommended daily amount of exercise for children because these games do not require as much energy expenditure as the actual sport [12]. To ensure the effectiveness of exergames, designers must consider two core issues for promoting adequate energy expenditure: 1) rewards for encouraging long term motivation and 2) better physical benefits which involves full body movements [33].

The smart phone game Zombies Run (https://zombiesrungame.com) was a successful example of gamified exercise where headphones were used to interact with users during running. This approach proved to have a positive and motivational effect [26] in promoting people to be more active. Göbel et al. [9] proposed a set of personalized exergames which combine the concepts of serious games and sensor technologies. It added customized features to the gameplay and result show that it enhances users' motivation toward the gameplay. Campbell et al. [4] discussed the concept of everyday fitness games and suggested that for applications that people frequently use in their everyday lives, designs need to be fun and sustainable, as well as adapt to behavioral changes. Wylie [34] indicated that with the use of smart phones, gamified components such as a leaderboard, achievements and challenge amongst friends are effective ways of motivating and encouraging users to reach their personal goals and track their physical fitness activities. Hamarji and Kovisto [13] investigated how social factors affect users' intention to continue using the gamified system, and their results also indicated that social factors are strong predictors for game motivation. Schwenk et al. [27] implemented a virtual reality (VR) game–based system prototype for balance rehabilitation, in which wearable sensors and interactive user interface were involved for real-time visual feedback. Findings support that real-time feedback is an important factor that could affect user's in-game experience.

In addition, Smeddinck et al. [28] conducted a 5-week study comparing exergames with traditional therapy. Results showed that a significant increase on the measure of functional reach when training with exergames. Macvean and Robertson [21] reported a 7-week study on user's physical activity, motivation and behavioral patterns on using exergames, and suggested that longitudinal studies are necessary for evaluating motivational effects, since it ensures that the intensity of a user's behavior is appropriate and sustained.

According to our literature review, game elements such as customization, social factors, as well as real-time feedback have been found to be important features of a gamified fitness application, and thus, we make use of these ideas in the design and implementation of our gamified exercise system to be evaluated over a long-term study.

To the best of our knowledge, no previous work has specific parameters of our study, i.e.: (1) combining a game with an activity tracker, (2) long-term continuous observation, (3) comparing 3 feature update methods. Gouveia et al. [11] conducted a long-term study, but users were randomly joining throughout the period; a game was not used; and updates were limited to different feedback messages/goals., In contrast, we invited those who are not very active but want to be more active, updated app features periodically, and used a game. We have followed up and improved on their suggestions of focusing on "intermediate stage", playful goals, and updated feedback. Other researchers [e.g.: 14, 20, 22] have also suggested similar strategies with no study, or have done studies with no app/game or update process.

## APPLICATION DESIGN AND IMPLEMENTATION

An iOS game created by the authors for a short-term study [36] is used as the basis for this work. However, we have added a series of new features to the original single-user single-level game, as shown in Table 1. These added game features were designed to provide users with choices of customization, to enhance real-time game experience, as well as to incorporate social factors.

| | |
|---|---|
| Customization features | Customized bird color |
| | Customized background color |
| Real-time game features | Bird nets (in level 2) |
| | Thunderstorm (in level 3) |
| Social features | Leaderboard |
| | Achievement |
| | Challenge box |

**Table 1. List of features added in the new application**

The iOS application communicates with wearable activity trackers (TI Sensortag [32]) in real-time and utilizes the data received from its inertial measurement units (IMU) as inputs to the game. Players can play the games with three exercises: running, cycling or rope skipping to control the movements of the game character in real-time. For running and cycling we have a phone mounted in front of the user on the treadmill/bicycle while they exercising, and for rope skipping we casted the phone screen to a TV to make sure users can easily see the screen while jumping. (see Figure 1) The story of the game is based on a bird that has fallen behind its flock. The objective is to regroup with the flock before time runs out and before the flock reaches its destination. There are also physical and environmental parameters that may affect the movement behavior of the bird and flock, for example a bird net may appear to catch the bird and the player has to reach a certain speed in order to break the net. Another example is a thunderstorm that may occur and threaten the flock. The game features a mission-based structure and point-based system. Higher levels can be unlocked when missions have been achieved. The achievement system is also designed to encourage players during the gameplay. Multiplayer mode brings in leaderboard and challenge boxes that allows players to compete with each other. Figure 2 presents several screens from the application. Additionally, the ability to customize character and background colors was implemented in the application (see Figure 3). We used HockeyApp [14] to distribute different versions of our application to participants, and to receive user feedback.

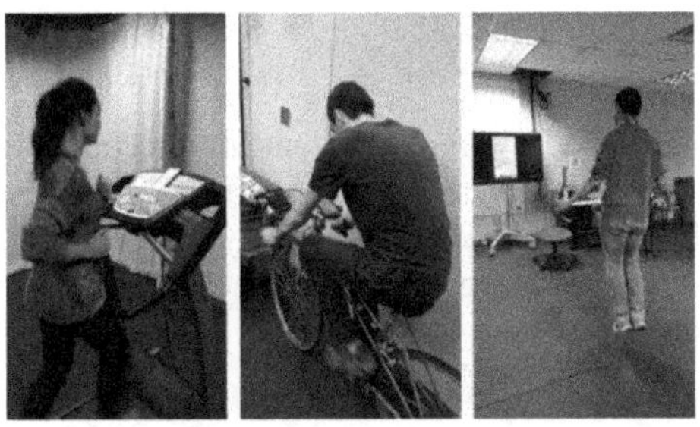

**Figure 1. The three types of exercises in our user study: running, cycling, and rope skipping.**

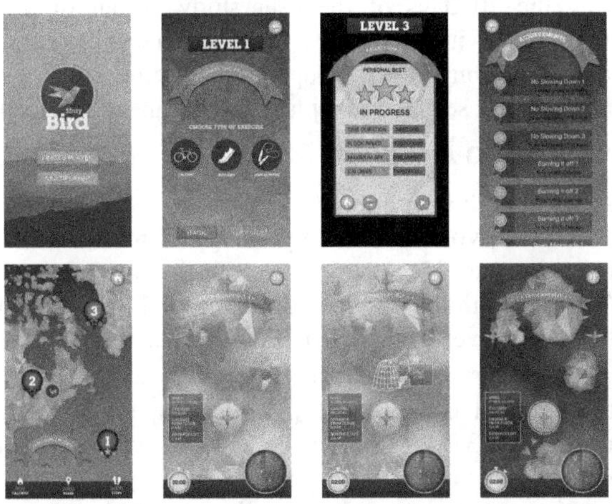


**Figure 2. Screen shots from our original application. From left to right, row one: choice of player mode, choice of exercises, result screen, achievement screen; row two: landing screen, level 1 view, level 2 view, and level 3 view.**

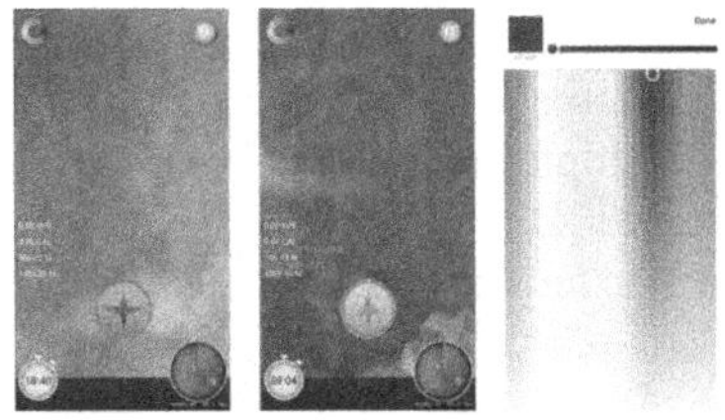

**Figure 3. Screen shots from our updated application. From left to right: customized bird color for level1, customized background color for level 2, color picker panel view.**

## USER STUDY DESIGN

### Participants and Updating Schedule

Our user study was designed to verify the hypothesis that adding different game features and gradually releasing them can positively affect the user engagement and retention. 36 participants were recruited from Carleton University by posters for our study. 30 were recruited as main subjects and 6 as backups who would replace any of the original 30 participants if they quit the study during the 70-day duration of the experiment. The backup participants started and participated in the experiments as others. Each participant was provided with a TI Sensortag [32] wearable device (see Figure 4) to take home. The wearable could be worn on the wrist or ankle (depending on the exercise they choose; for example, for cycling the sensor would be worn on the ankle). The wearable then connects to the game application that we distributed to the users. No particular set of instructions was provided, and users were allowed to explore the system on their own.

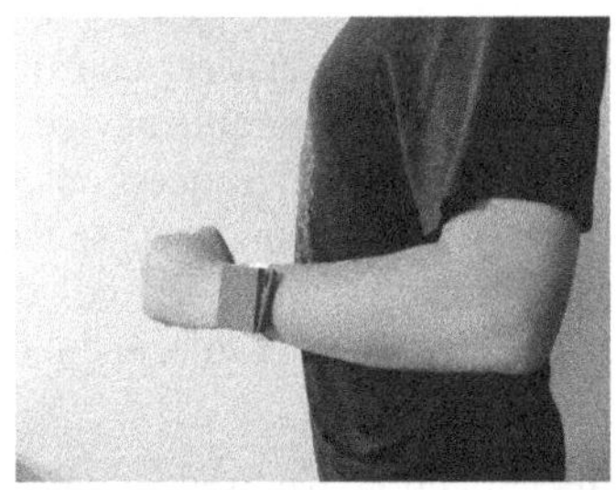

**Figure 4. The wearable device used in this study (TI Sensortag).**

| | |
|---|---|
| Basic Group | Basic features: single level, single player. |
| Full Group | Basic feature plus all the features introduced in Table 1. |
| Updating Group | Start with basic feature (same as the Basic Group), with other features gradually added (as described in Table 3). |

**Table 2. List of different features that each group received.**

The participants were then randomly divided into three equal groups of 12 (10 as main and 2 as backup). To users in the first group (referred to as Basic Group), we only provided very basic features of the game such as a single level (level 1) version of the game, as well as single player mode. Users in the second group (referred to as Full Group) were provided the full version of the application, including the ability to customize colors, as well as all 3 levels of the game, and multiplayer mode with leaderboard and challenge box, etc. Users in the third group (referred to as Updating Group) started with the same application as those in the Basic Group, but periodically received updates (once every 10 days), until after 70 days they ended up with an application that was identical to those in the Full Group. Users were told in Updating group about receiving updates every 10 days. On each update, we used push notification to let them know about new feature. The different features each group had received are summarized in Table 2 below, and the update schedule for the Updating Group is shown in Table 3.

| Day | Updates |
|---|---|
| Day 1 | Single level, single player |
| Day 11 | Add customized bird color |
| Day 21 | Add multiplayer leaderboard and challenge-box |
| Day 31 | Add level 2 (with bird net) |
| Day 41 | Add customized background color |
| Day 51 | Add achievements |
| Day 61 | Add level 3 (with thunderstorm) |

**Table 3. Automatic updates schedule used for the Updating Group.**

### Procedure and Data Collection

*Pre-study*

We asked participants to answer questionnaires upon receiving and returning the wearable device. The pre-study questionnaire asked demographic questions including age, gender, height, weight, the hours they spend per week in exercising, any wearables owned, and the types and duration of video games (PC, console, and mobile) played.

*In-game data*

For in-game data collection, we used Google Analytics API [10] to track users' comprehensive behavior data, including screen views and tapped events with associated timestamp, exercise sessions, performance, scores, and feedback and comments. We also asked users about their level of encouragement through a 5-point Likert question (from 1 = highly discouraged to 5 = highly encouraged) after each completed session they have exercised.

*Post-study*

A post-study questionnaire was conducted to comprehensively evaluate participants' experience during the study. We firstly asked three general questions to measure participants' overall motivation, satisfaction and preference based on their experience with the game:

1) I find this kind of application motivation for exercise;
2) I was overall satisfied with this application;
3) I prefer using this type of application for exercise over regular exercises.

We included parts of Intrinsic Motivation Inventory (IMI) [15] measurement to assess participants' subjective experience related to the game experience. The detail questions are attached in Appendix for reference. Since the goal of this research project is to encourage continuous participation in exercise, IMI was selected as a measure of motivation because it evaluates a person's experience while performing an activity based on criteria such as enjoyment, effort, and competence [15]. In exergames, an enjoyable game experience is associated with greater amount of energy expenditure [20] and player achievement predicts feelings of autonomy, competence, presence, enjoyment and continued motivation to play [19]. If participants report high levels on these criteria, it is likely they are intrinsically motivated and enjoy what they were doing, and will continue doing it.

In the post-study questionnaire, participants used a 7-point Likert scale (from 1 = strongly disagree to 7 = strongly agree) to rate the game-play experience, followed by some open-ended questions. Note that compared to the question regarding encouragement we asked in-game after each complete session, here we switched from 5-point to 7-point because for the in-game question (encouragement) we kept a consistent scale with our previous work [36] with a 5-point Likert scale, but because of our interest in the intrinsic motivation in this current study, we employed the IMI [15] which recommends the use of a 7-point scale.

We also included some open-ended questions regarding their preferred exercise and game mode, suggestions on both software and hardware of the system, as well as their opinion on how the game could be more engaging based on their game experience.

Ethics approval was received from the Carleton University Ethics committee. Participants received a $10 honorarium gift card to thank them for their participation in the study. During the 70 days of the user study, 4 out of the 30 participants withdrew for different reasons, and 4 participants from the back-ups of the same study group were randomly selected to replace the original participants.

## RESULTS AND ANALYSIS

### Demographic information

Out of the 30 volunteers who participated in this study, 19 were males and 11 were females. Their average age was 24.71 years with the standard deviation of 4.23 years. Their self-reported average hours of exercise per week was 3.81 hours with a standard deviation of 2.83 hours, while the self-reported average hours per week spent on playing games was 6.33 for pc/console games (with a standard deviation of 9.51) along with a 4.73 hours per week spent on playing smart-phone games (with a standard deviation of 6.33). 11 out of 30 participants (36.7%) previously (or currently) owned an activity tracking wearable device.

### In-game Data

Figure 5 shows participants' choice of exercise among the three classes enabled during our study (from in-game data monitoring), where running is the most popular, followed by cycling. This result matches the subjective results we collected from the post-study questionnaire, where the vast majority preferred running as well. Figure 6 shows the feedback that we collected during the study (after each completed session) using a 5-point Likert scale (from 1 = highly discouraged to 5 = highly encouraged) for regarding the level of encouragement by the system towards more exercise. A total of 322 answers were collected, 47 from the Basic Group, 105 from the Full Group and 170 from the Updating Group. We can see that most of the users felt positively regarding this gamified exercise experience. The Full Group felt most encouraged (with 82% of participants choosing options higher than "no difference", followed closely by the Updating (80%) and Basic Groups (70%).

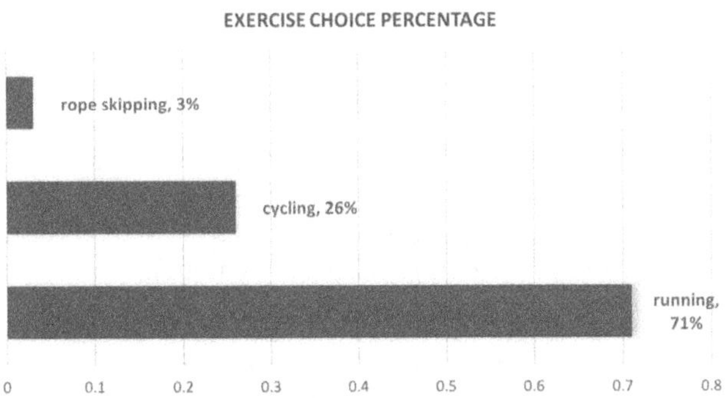


**Figure 5. Choice of exercise (from in-game data monitoring).**

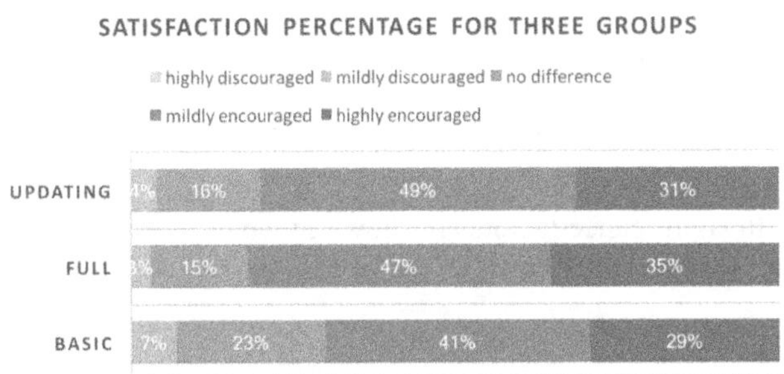


**Figure 6. Level of encouragement for three groups (asked after each completed workout session).**

### Overall Motivation, Satisfaction and Preference

A one-way between-groups analysis of variances (ANOVA) and Post-Hoc Tukey-Kramer HSD test [16] was conducted to analyze the main effects between three groups. The alpha was set at 0.05 for all statistical tests.

Figure 7 shows the average and standard deviations of the scores for question 1 to 3. Please note that the subscript B represents the Basic Group, F represents the Full Group and U represents the Updating Group. For motivation, $M_B$ = 3.80 and $SD_B$ = 0.79, $M_F$ = 5.30 and $SD_F$ = 0.95, $M_U$ = 5.50 and $SD_U$ = 0.92. There was a significant effect at the $p < 0.05$ level for the three groups [$F(2, 27) = 10.50$, $p = 0.0042$]. For preference, $M_B$ = 3.90 and $SD_B$ = 1.49, $M_F$ = 5.7 and $SD_F$ = 0.82, $M_U$ = 5.6 and $SD_U$ = 0.66. There was a significant effect at the $p < 0.05$ level for the three groups [$F(2, 27) = 12.42$, p = 0.00014]. For preference over regular exercise, $M_B$ = 3.90 and $SD_B$ = 1.49, $M_F$ = 5.70 and $SD_F$ = 0.82, $M_U$ = 5.60 and $SD_U$ = 0.66. ANOVA shows no significant effect between groups [$F(2, 27) = 3.17$, $p = 0.0581$]. The Tukey-Kramer HSD post-hoc test results for significant factors are shown in Table 4 below and the pairwise comparison significance are also marked in Figure 7. The output of the Tukey test shows the average difference, a confidence interval as well as whether we should reject the null hypothesis for each pair of groups at the given significance level, in which "True" indicates there is a significance between the two groups.

| | group1 | group2 | meandiff | lower | upper | reject |
|---|---|---|---|---|---|---|
| Motivation | B | F | 1.5 | 0.4947 | 2.5053 | True |
| | B | U | 1.7 | 0.6947 | 2.7053 | True |
| | F | U | 0.2 | -0.805 | 1.2053 | False |
| Satisfaction | B | F | 1.9 | 0.8613 | 2.9387 | True |
| | B | U | 1.7 | 0.6613 | 2.7387 | True |
| | F | U | -0.2 | -1.239 | 0.8387 | False |

**Table 4. Multiple Comparison of Means (general question) - Tukey HSD, FWER=0.05**

From the results, we can see that the Full Group and the Updating Group show significantly higher motivation and satisfaction compared to the Basic Group. This suggests that the number and types of features are the main factor affecting users' overall motivation and satisfaction. No significant effect in preference over regular exercise, suggests that all participants, even in Basic group, still prefer using the gamified exercise experience over regular exercises.

### Feature Importance Level

Only the Full Group and the Updating Group were asked to answer the second section of the questionnaire regarding the different game features (the Basic Group had only received a basic version of the game without any features for evaluation). We used statements such as: "Leaderboard was important in my game experience." to evaluate the importance level of each separate game feature. The results are shown in Figure 8, in which feature 1 to 7 represent:

1) Customized bird color,
2) Customized background color,
3) Bird nets (in level 2),
4) Thunderstorm (in level 3),
5) Leaderboard,
6) Achievements,
7) Challenge box.

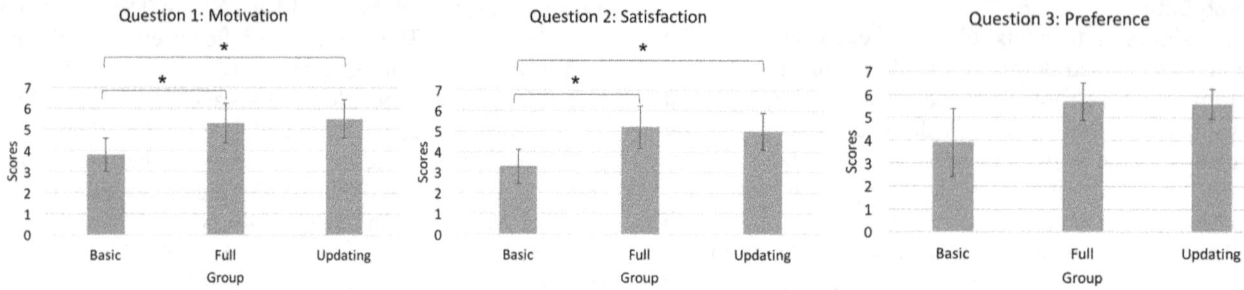


**Figure 7. Result for post-study question 1, 2 and 3. From left to right: overall motivation, overall satisfaction, and overall preference over regular exercise.**

Results on the importance level of different game features show that social factors including Leaderboard ($M_F$ = 5.71 and $SD_F$ = 0.82, $M_U$ = 5.04 and $SD_U$ = 1.05) and Achievements ($M_F$ = 5.78 and $SD_F$ = 0.79, $M_U$ = 5.34 and $SD_U$ = 1.16) are playing important roles in game experience. However, also being one of the social factors, challenge box is considered less important. A possible reason leading to this result could be the lack of real-life relationships between our participants. We believe a closer relationship between users could strengthen the importance level of challenge box. We did not add invitation feature to this study since we need to keep a consistent user group, but adding such ability in future can potentially add to the social value. Also, we found the scores of Full Group are relatively higher than the Updating group in most of the game features except for customized bird color. This might because the customized bird color was the first updating feature that the Updating Group had received, so that it became more impressive compared to other features, although this is not conclusive.

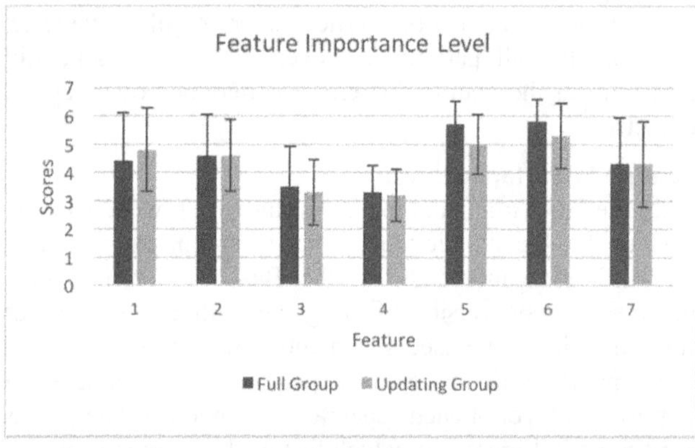


**Figure 8. Impact of different features for the Full Group and the Updating Group**

## IMI sub-scales

A reliability analysis is conducted because we modified the original IMI scale to better fit the concept of game. A Cronbach's alpha value of 0.878 ($\alpha = 0.878$) is obtained (a commonly accepted rule is that an alpha of 0.7 indicates acceptable reliability and 0.8 or higher indicates good reliability. [31])

As shown in Figure 9, for interest and enjoyment ($\alpha$ = 0.862), $M_B$ = 3.83 and $SD_B$ = 1.34, $M_F$ = 5.17 and $SD_F$ = 1.049, $M_U$ = 5.56 and $SD_U$ = 0.80. There was a significant effect at the $p < 0.05$ level for the three groups [$F(2, 27)$ = 29.43, $p$ = 1.65e-07].

For perceived competence ($\alpha$ = 0.887), $M_B$ = 4.05 and $SD_B$ = 1.32, $M_F$ = 5.18 and $SD_F$ = 1.03, $M_U$ = 5.36 and $SD_U$ = 0.80. There was a significant effect at the $p < 0.05$ level for the three groups [$F(2, 27)$ = 25.15, $p$ = 6.82e-07].

For effort/importance ($\alpha$ = 0.848), $M_B$ = 2.70 and $SD_B$ = 0.76, $M_F$ = 3.44 and $SD_F$ = 0.84, $M_U$ = 3.80 and $SD_U$ = 0.78. There was a significant effect at the $p < 0.05$ level for the three groups [$F(2, 27)$ = 12.94, $p$ = 0.0001].

For pressure/tension ($\alpha$ = 0.904), $M_B$ = 5.64 and $SD_B$ = 0.63, $M_F$ = 6.27 and $SD_F$ = 0.65, $M_U$ = 5.98 and $SD_U$ = 0.65. There was no significant effect at the $p < 0.05$ level for the three groups [$F(2, 27)$ = 2.69, $p$ = 0.086].

Finally, for value/usefulness ($\alpha$ = 0.925), $M_B$ = 3.56 and $SD_B$ = 0.86, $M_F$ = 5.15 and $SD_F$ = 0.97, $M_U$ = 5.13 and $SD_U$ = 0.88. There was a significant effect at the $p < 0.05$ level for the three groups [$F(2, 27)$ = 28.98, $p$ = 1.90e-07].

The Tukey-Kramer HSD test results for those sub-scales with significance factors are shown in table 5 below and the pairwise comparison significance are also marked in Figure 9.

| | group1 | group2 | meandiff | lower | upper | reject |
|---|---|---|---|---|---|---|
| **Interest/ enjoyment** | B | F | 1.3429 | 0.7565 | 1.9292 | True |
| | B | U | 1.7286 | 1.1422 | 2.3149 | True |
| | F | U | 0.3857 | -0.201 | 0.9721 | False |
| **Perceived competence** | B | F | 1.1333 | 0.6347 | 1.6319 | True |
| | B | U | 1.3167 | 0.8181 | 1.8153 | True |
| | F | U | 0.1833 | -0.315 | 0.6819 | False |
| **Effort/ importance** | B | F | 0.74 | 0.1934 | 1.2866 | True |
| | B | U | 1.1 | 0.5534 | 1.6466 | True |
| | F | U | 0.36 | -0.187 | 0.9066 | False |
| **Value/ usefulness** | B | F | 1.6 | 1.0037 | 2.1963 | True |
| | B | U | 1.5714 | 0.9752 | 2.1677 | True |
| | F | U | -0.029 | -0.063 | 0.5677 | False |

**Table 5. Multiple Comparison of Means (IMI sub-scales) - Tukey HSD, FWER=0.05**

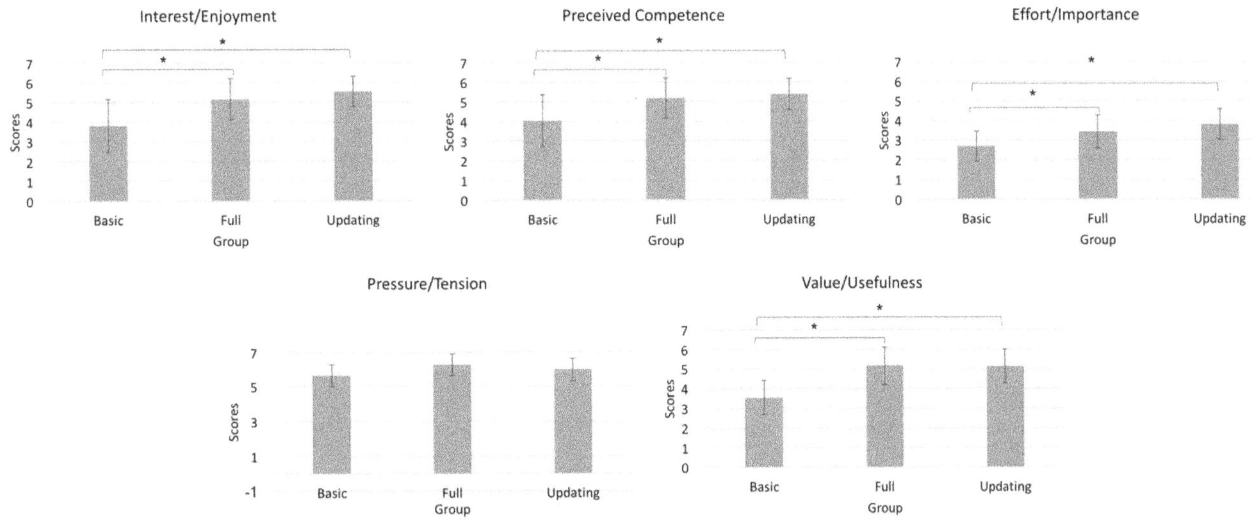


**Figure 9. Average and Standard deviation of IMI: Interest/Enjoyment, Perceived Competence, Effort/Importance, Pressure/Tension and Value/Usefulness.**

From the result, we can see that the number and diversity of game features could have impacts on user's motivation towards the gamified exercise system, because there are significant effects between the Basic Group and the Full Group, as well as between the Basic Group and the Updating Group. On the other hand, gradual updating does not take away from motivation, since there is no significant effect between the Full Group and the Updating Group. This indicates that by pushing out gradual updates, we can benefit from the advantages of the approach, namely increased engagement and retention, while not negatively impact motivation.

### Daily Active Users and Workout Sessions

Figure 10 shows the change of active users of all three groups during the 70 days. We can see for active users, there is an overall descent trend appears as time grows for all three groups, while the Basic Group declines the fastest. The waves of the Full Group were basically caused by weekends. The large variance in the Updating Group was caused by the regular updating plus the weekend. Figure 11 shows the accumulated activate users for three groups with regression line, in which the slope of the Basic Group is 1.75, for the Full Group is 3.23, and for the Updating Group is 4.30. Figure 12 shows the total started workout sessions and complete sessions of all three groups, from which we noticed a basically same trend as the active users. The decline of Basic Group is the fastest, and the Full Group is mostly affected by weekends when people have more time for exercise, as in Figure 14 shows the participants' overall completed sessions by time of day. The Updating Group maintains a relatively higher value both in started and completed sessions, which indicates the gradually updating not only brings back users to check the updates, but actually promotes engagement towards the actual behavior of exercise. Figure 13 shows accumulated completed sessions with regression line, in which the slope of the Basic Group is 1.18, for the Full Group is 2.33, and for the Updating Group is 3.26. Compared to Figure 11, we found the accumulated complete sessions are overall rise slower compared to active users. This indicates there are circumstances that participants only either open the application to check updates or play around with it, without actually accomplishing any exercise session. This made us realize that despite the elements we considered important regarding exercise experience, other features that not directly linked to gameplay may also affect user retention and the application's life cycle.

Users received notifications (through Apple Push Notification service) when updates were available for the application. It was observed that many users returned to the application to check the updates. This contributed to the number of completed workout sessions being increased. Since the Updating Group contains the most active users and completed sessions, we can conclude that the gradual releasing of updates can not only attract users to interact more with the application, but also motivate them to complete gamified exercise sessions. The total in-game workout time of the Basic Group was 439 minutes (4.3 minutes per session on average), the total time for the Full Group was 1073 minutes (an average 6.1 minutes per session), and for the Updating Group the total was 1322 minutes (an average of 5.7 minutes per session). The reason that average time for the Updating Group is slightly lower than the Full Group is that we released the second and third level at the beginning to the Full Group but in the middle of the study to the Updating Group, and higher levels are longer in duration. We can see that both in Figure 8 and Figure 10, at the start of the study, the Full Group accumulated more active users and completed sessions, but roughly after the second update, the accumulated numbers of the Updating Group exceeded the Full Group and kept a higher slope till the end of the study. We can conclude that user's curiosity towards new features can make the game more sustainable over the long run, resulting in relatively higher user retention rate. When we asked participants which exercise (running, cycling or rope skipping) they preferred, 69% chose running, 24% chose cycling, and 7% chose rope skipping. This answer was consistent with the data acquired for gameplay. For the question of which game mode (single or multi-player) they preferred, 73% chose multiplayer while 27% chose single player. We collected 122 pieces of feedback from participants by in-game pop-up question asked after each complete workout session (23.9% of the total completed sessions). The most popular comment (56 of 122) suggested they would like this kind of application to support outdoor activities, and some of them (25 of 122) stated they would prefer real-time competition mode. Additional comments were received regarding including more in-game interactions, more rewards, and more social factors (such as allowing to share to social networks).

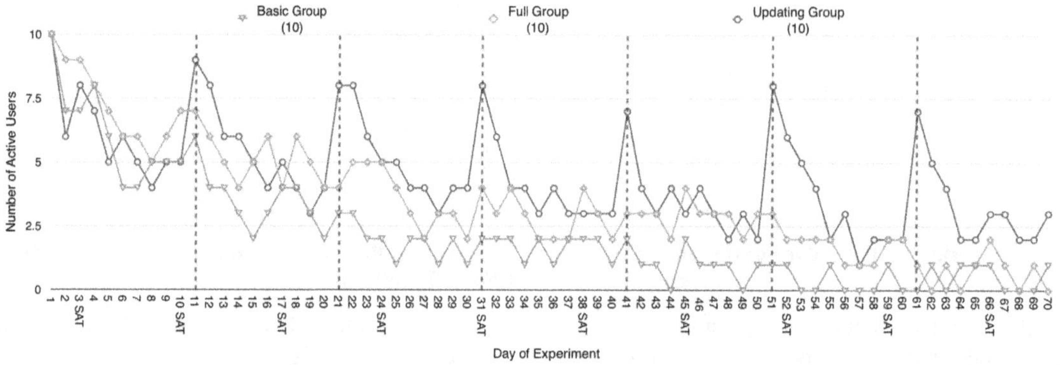


**Figure 10: Number of active users for each group is depicted per day (dotted vertical lines indicate the application update days).**

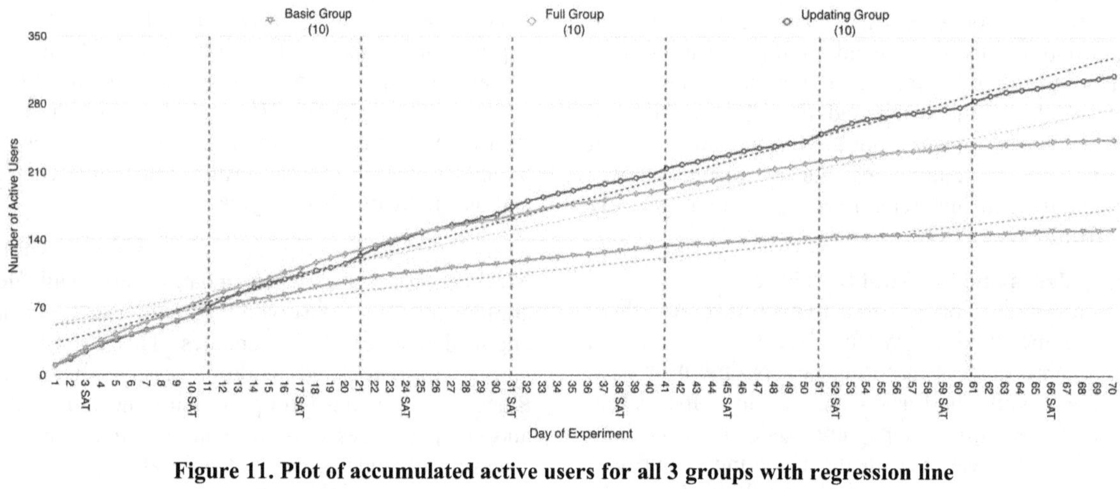


**Figure 11. Plot of accumulated active users for all 3 groups with regression line**

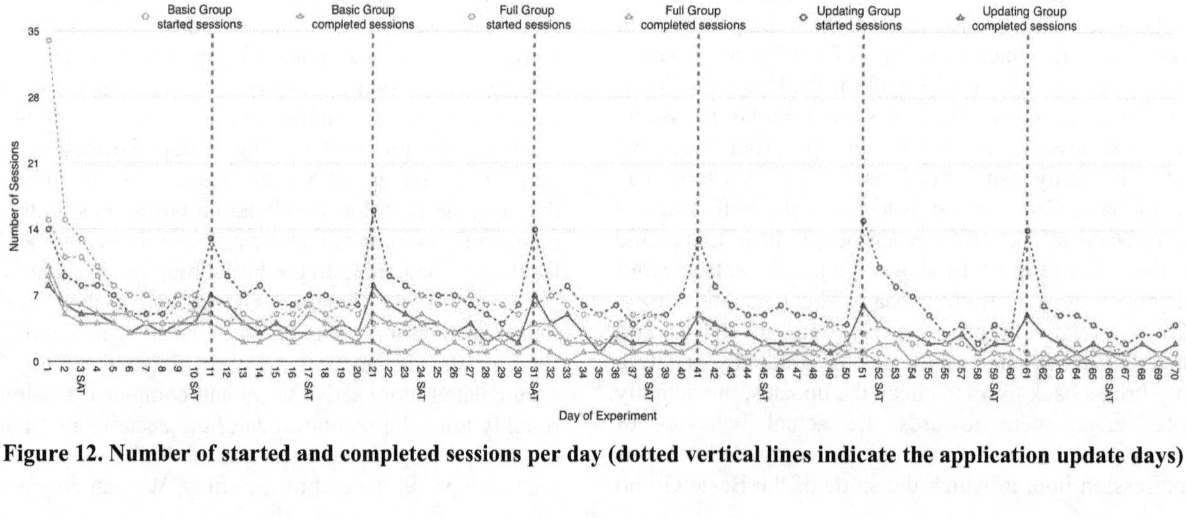


**Figure 12. Number of started and completed sessions per day (dotted vertical lines indicate the application update days)**

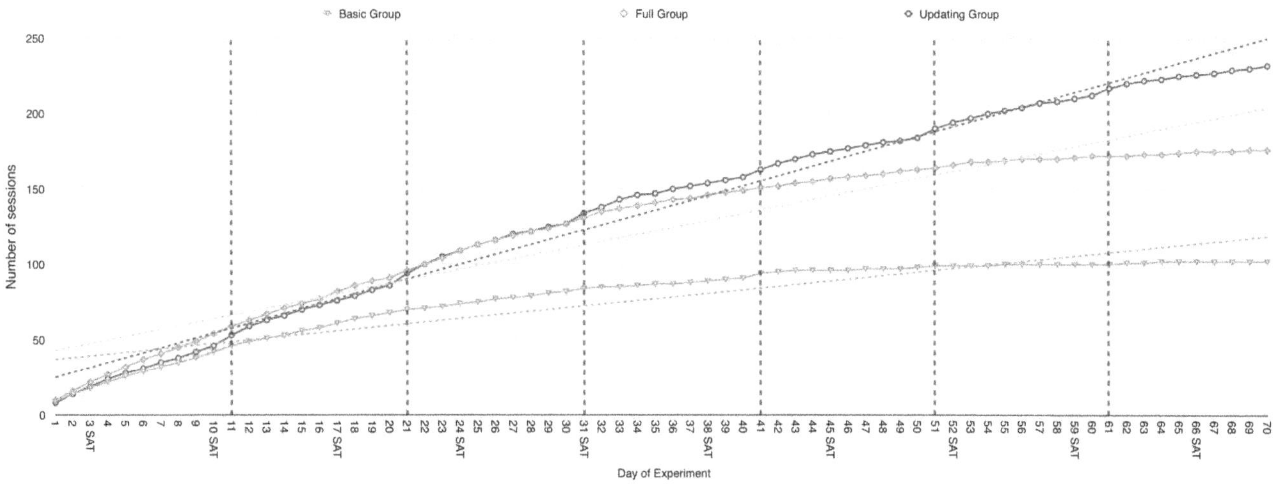


**Figure 13. Accumulated completed sessions for all 3 groups with regression line**

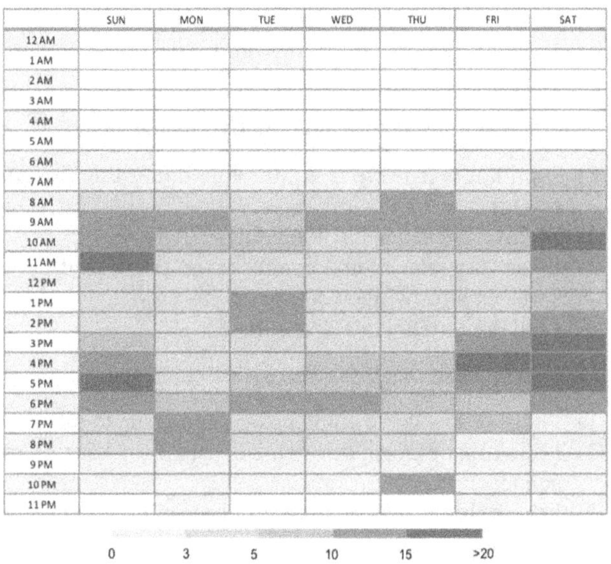


**Figure 14. Total sessions by time of day.**

## DISCUSSION

Overall in this 70-day user study, the evaluation on motivation showed that more and diverse features could increase user motivation toward the gamified exercise system, and the gradual release of game features does not negatively affect user motivation. The analysis on game sustainability showed that while there was a decline in activity level in all groups, the gradual release of features improved the sustainability to a certain extent which verifies our hypothesis that various game features and the way they are released will influence user retention.

In this study we invited intermediate stage subjects and selected them randomly. However, they had a slightly higher initial exercise rate. Looking at the results from the 5 subjects with the least self-reported exercise rates, we see that the pattern reported in the paper still exists, even stronger (higher performance in Updating group). Among them, 2 were from the Basic (total in-game workout time 1.9 and 3.0; group average 2.8), 2 from the Updating (4.2 and 6.4; group average 5.3), and 1 from the Full (3.9 vs. average 3.9).

While the Basic and Full feature groups started to asymptotically level off within the 10-week study (in weeks 5 and 9 respectively), this was not apparent in the Updating group (see Figure 13). This suggests that minor feature updates can have the effect of increasing sustainability over the long term. We further believe that a combination of minor and major updates will likely have an even longer effect on sustainability.

It can be seen in Figure 12 that sometimes the notification of new features only brings people back to check updates but without completing workouts. This increases the number of minutes of engagement with the game, not the number of actual exercises. One of the participants indicated that changes such as customized color did not create enough interest to complete a session. However, addition of the leaderboard significantly increased the motivation to complete sessions with improved results. Accordingly, we can see that different users were motivated by different features, and this can be considered as the main cause of some incomplete sessions. Player modeling techniques can determine the types of features and updates that can motivate different users. Therefore, customized feature updates may help improve workout completion rates, which is part of our future work.

The results of this study also show that participants in all groups preferred the gamified exercise experience over regular exercises; features related to social factors played a relatively more important role in this game experience, followed by customization features; and participants spent more time interacting with the system on weekends, especially during 9:00 AM to 11:00 AM, and 3:00 PM to 6:00 PM.

There are some limitations regarding this work. One limitation is with respect to participant characteristics. The participants consisted only of university students, which limits the generalizability of the results. Future research may replicate this study by recruiting participants of various age groups, gamer types (e.g.: gamer vs. non-gamers) and people with different exercise goals (e.g.: leisure vs. fitness). People of different age or who have different exercise goals could have different motivations for using the system. It is important to understand what these goals are and continue to redesign and redevelop game features to keep players engaged in the game and exercise. Another limitation of this study was data collection. We used Google Analytics in this work, which contains less than 1.5% missing data. While this is considered acceptable by most standards [3], the accuracy of the results is reduced nonetheless. Thus, a future study could employ more accurate analytical tools/software for obtaining better results.

## CONCLUSION

In this study, we extended an existing gamified exercise application with a set of more diverse features to evaluate the motivational impacts and game sustainability of a wearable-based gamified exercise and fitness system. The results of this long-term (70-day) user study shows that engagement and game-play are highly linked, and the number of game features could have impacts on user motivation towards the gamified exercise system. Moreover, consistent updates (gradual addition of new features) not only resulted in an increased usage of the application, but also had positive impacts on the actual amount of workout activity.

Finally, the feedback collected from the participants indicated a few potential paths for future work, such as the addition of support for outdoor activities, addition of real-time multiplayer modes, and others. In our future work, we will also focus on utilizing player modelling techniques to better understand users from different perspectives, and to make adaptive adjustments to the game. A comprehensive gamified fitness advisor and recommendation system can be further developed. A key follow-up to this study may be a longer study (over many months) to see how sustainability can be better understood and impacted.

## APPENDIX

The Intrinsic Motivation Inventory [15]:

Interest/Enjoyment was measured by seven sentences:

1) I enjoyed playing this game very much;
2) This game was fun to play;
3) I thought this was a boring game (reverse coded);
4) This game did not hold my attention at all (reverse coded);
5) I would describe this game as very interesting;
6) I thought this game was quite enjoyable;
7) While I was playing this game, I was thinking about how much I enjoyed it.

Perceived Competence was measured by six sentences:

1) I think I am pretty good at this game;
2) I think I did pretty well at this game, compared to other players;
3) After playing this game for a while, I felt pretty competent;
4) I am satisfied with my performance at this time;
5) I was pretty skilled at this game;
6) This was a game that I couldn't do very well (reverse coded).

Effort/Importance was measured by five sentences:

1) I put a lot of effort into this game;
2) I didn't try very hard to do well at this game (reverse coded);
3) I tried very hard at this game;
4) It was important to me to do well at this game.
5) I didn't put much energy into this game (reverse coded).

Pressure/Tension was measured by five sentences:

1) I did not feel nervous at all while doing this (reverse coded);
2) I felt very tense while doing this activity;
3) I was very relaxed in doing these (reverse coded);
4) I was anxious while working on this task;
5) I felt pressured while doing these.

Value/Usefulness was measured by 7 statements;

1) I believe this game could be of some value to me;
2) I think that playing this game is useful for keeping me active;
3) I think this is important to do because it can motivate me to engage in exercise;
4) I would be willing to lay it again because it has some value to me;
5) I think playing this game could help me to exercise more often;
6) I think playing this game could be beneficial to me;
7) I think this is an important game.

## REFERENCES


1. Riikka Ahola, et al. 2013. Gamified physical activation of young men: A multidisciplinary population-based randomized controlled trial (MOPO study). *BMC Public Health* 13, 32: 1–8.
2. Marie-Louise Bird, Brodie Clark, Johanna Millar, Sue Whetton, and Stuart Smith. 2015. Exposure to "exergames" increases older adults' perception of the usefulness of technology for improving health and physical activity: A pilot study. *JMIR Serious Games* 3, 2: e8. doi: 10.2196/games.4275.
3. Blast Analytics & Marketing. 2013. *Can You Trust Your Google Analytics Data?* Retrieved September 5

2016 from http://www.blastam.com/blog/can-you-trust-your-google-analytics-data

4. Taj Campbell, Brian Ngo, and James Fogarty. 2008. Game design principles in everyday fitness applications. *Proceedings of the 2008 ACM Conference on Computer Supported Cooperative Work, ACM2008*, 249–252.
5. James Clawson, Jessica A. Pater, Andrew D. Miller, Elizabeth D. Mynatt, and Lena Mamykina. 2015. No longer wearing: investigating the abandonment of personal health-tracking technologies on craigslist. In *Proceedings of the 2015 ACM International Joint Conference on Pervasive and Ubiquitous Computing*, 647–658.
6. Amanda J. Daley. 2009. Can exergaming contribute to improving physical activity levels and health outcomes in children? *Pediatrics,* 124, 2: 763–771.
7. Sebastian Deterding, Dan Dixon, Rilla Khaled, and Lennart Nacke. 2011. From game design elements to gamefulness: defining gamification. *Proceedings of the 15th International Academic MindTrek Conference: Envisioning Future Media Environments*. ACM2011.
8. Daniel A. Epstein, Monica Caraway, Chuck Johnston, An Ping, James Fogarty, and Sean A. Munson. 2016. Beyond abandonment to next steps: Understanding and designing for life after personal informatics tool use. In *Proceedings of the 2016 CHI Conference on Human Factors in Computing Systems*. 1109–1113.
9. Stefan Göbel, Sandro Hardy, Viktor Wendel, Florian Mehm, and Ralf Steinmetz. 2010. Serious games for health: Personalized exergames. *Proceedings of the 18th ACM international conference on Multimedia*, ACM2010, 1663–1666.
10. Google.com. 2016. *Google Analytics - Mobile, Premium and Free Website Analytics – Google*. Retrieved September 5 2016 from https://www.google.com/analytics
11. Rúben Gouveia, Evangelos Karapanos, and Marc Hassenzahl. 2015. How do we engage with activity trackers? A longitudinal study of Habito. In *Proceedings of the 2015 ACM International Joint Conference on Pervasive and Ubiquitous Computing*. 1305–1316.
12. Lee Graves, Gareth Stratton, N. D. Ridgers, and N. T. Cable. 2008. Energy expenditure in adolescents playing new generation computer games. *British journal of sports medicine* 42, 7: 592–594.
13. Juho Hamari and Jonna Koivisto. 2013. Social motivations to use gamification: An empirical study of gamifying exercise. In *ECIS* 2013, 105.
14. Hockeyapp.net. 2016. *HockeyApp - The Platform for Your Apps*. Retrieved August 5, 2016 from https://www.hockeyapp.net
15. Intrinsic Motivation Inventory. 2016. Self-Determination Theory. http://selfdeterminationtheory.org/intrinsic-motivation-inventory/
16. James Jaccard, Michael A. Becker, and Gregory Wood. 1984. Pairwise multiple comparison procedures: a review. *Psychological Bulletin,* 96, 3: 589–596.
17. Younbo Jung, et al. 2009. Games for a better life: effects of playing Wii games on the well-being of seniors in a long-term care facility. *Proceedings of the Sixth Australasian Conference on Interactive Entertainment*. ACM2009.
18. Evangelos Karapanos. 2015. Sustaining user engagement with behavior change tools. *Interactions,* 22, 4: 48–52.
19. Anthony M. Limperos and Mike Schmierbach. 2016. Understanding the relationship between exergame play experiences, enjoyment, and intentions for continued play. *Games for Health Journal,* 5, 2: 100–107.
20. Elizabeth J. Lyons, Deborah F. Tate, Dianne S. Ward, Kurt M. Ribisl, J. Michael Bowling, and Sriran Kalyanaraman. 2014. Engagement, enjoyment, and energy expenditure during active video game play. *Health Psychology,* 33, 2: 174–181.
21. Andrew Macvean and Judy Robertson. 2013. Understanding exergame users' physical activity, motivation and behavior over time. *Proceedings of the SIGCHI Conference on Human Factors in Computing Systems*. ACM.
22. Edward McAuley, Terry Duncan, and Vance V. Tammen. 1989. Psychometric properties of the Intrinsic Motivation Inventory in a competitive sport setting: A confirmatory factor analysis. *Research Quarterly for Exercise and Sport*, *60*, 1: 48–58.
23. Florian 'Floyd' Mueller, Firaz Peer, Stefan Agamanolis, and Jennifer Sheridan. 2011. Gamification and exertion. *Proceedings of the Workshop on Gamification at the Conference on Human Factors in Computing Systems*. ACM.
24. Huynh Van Nguyen, et al. 2016. Double-edged sword: The effect of exergaming on other forms of exercise; a randomized controlled trial using the self-categorization theory. *Computers in Human Behavior,* 62: 590–593.
25. Lukasz Piwek, et al. 2016. The rise of consumer health wearables: promises and barriers. *PLoS Med.,* 13, 2: e1001953.
26. Positive Gaming. 2016. The Benefits of Exergaming. Retrieved September 5, 2016 from

http://www.positivegaming.com/positivegaming/benefits/exergaming-benefits

27. Michael Schwenk, Gurtej S. Grewal, Bahareh Honarvar, Stefanie Schwenk, Jane Mohler, Dharma S. Khalsa, and Bijan Najafi. 2014. Interactive balance training integrating sensor-based visual feedback of movement performance: a pilot study in older adults. *Journal of Neuroengineering and Rehabilitation*, 11, 1: 1.
28. Jan David Smeddinck, Marc Herrlich, and Rainer Malaka. 2015. Exergames for physiotherapy and rehabilitation: A medium-term situated study of motivational aspects and impact on functional reach. *Proceedings of the 33rd Annual ACM Conference on Human Factors in Computing Systems*. ACM.
29. Amanda E. Staiano and Sandra L. Calvert. 2011. Exergames for physical education courses: Physical, social, and cognitive benefits. *Child development perspectives,* 5, 2: 93–98.
30. Haichun Sun. 2013. Impact of exergames on physical activity and motivation in elementary school students: A follow-up study. *Journal of Sport and Health Science,* 2, 3: 138–145.
31. Mohsen Tavakol and Reg Dennick. 2011. Making sense of Cronbach's alpha. *International Journal of Medical Education*, 2: 53–55.
32. Ti.com. 2016. *Simplelink SensorTag - TI.com*. Retrieved September 5, 2016 from http://www.ti.com/ww/en/wireless_connectivity/sensortag2015/?INTC=SensorTag&HQS=sensortag
33. Anthony Whitehead, Hannah Johnston, Nicole Nixon, and Jo Welch. 2010. Exergame effectiveness: what the numbers can tell us. *Proceedings of the 5th ACM SIGGRAPH Symposium on Video Games* ACM. 55–62.
34. Justin Wylie. 2010. Fitness gamification: concepts, characteristics, and applications. Retrieved from: http://www.justintwylie.com/wp-content/uploads/2014/12/JUSTIN-WYLIE-Fitness-Gamification.pdf
35. Jeffrey Yim and T. C. Nicholas Graham. 2007. Using games to increase exercise motivation. *Proceedings of the 2007 conference on Future Play*. ACM2007.
36. Zhao Zhao, S. Ali Etemad, Ali Arya, and Anthony Whitehead. 2016. Usability and motivational effects of a gamified exercise and fitness system based on wearable devices. In *International Conference of Design, User Experience, and Usability*, Springer International Publishing, 333–344.

# Supporting the Self-Management of Chronic Pain Conditions with Tailored Momentary Self-Assessments

Phil Adams[1], Elizabeth L. Murnane[1], Michael Elfenbein[1], Elaine Wethington[2,3], Geri Gay[1,4]
[1]Information Science, [2]Human Development, [3]Sociology, [4]Communication, Cornell University
{pja22, elm236, mse56, ew20, gkg1} @ cornell.edu

## ABSTRACT
To better support the self-management of chronic pain, this paper investigates how those living with the condition prefer to self-assess their pain levels using smartphones. Our work consists of three stages: design ideation and review, an in-lab user study with 10 participants resulting in nine candidate interfaces, and a 3 week field trial of two further honed measures with 12 participants. This research firstly yields a better understanding of participants' strong and sometimes contrasting preferences regarding their self-assessment of pain intensity. We additionally contribute two novel interfaces that support accurate, quick, and repeated use along with other participant-valued interactions (e.g., familiar, relatable, and highly usable). In particular, we focus on designing tailored measures that both enhance respondent motivation as well as minimize the difficulty of meaningful self-assessment by supporting the cognitive effort in translating a subjective experience into a single numerical value.

### ACM Classification Keywords
H.5.m Information Interfaces and Presentation (e.g., HCI): Miscellaneous; J.3 Life and Medical Sciences: Health

### Author Keywords
Smartphone; Pain Assessment; Questionnaire Design

## INTRODUCTION
Chronic pain, defined as recurrent or long-lasting pain, affects an estimated 20% of adults globally [27] and 30.7% of adults in the United States [39]. Chronic pain is more common in women than in men [24], and prevalence increases with age (more than 50% of older adults and as many as 80% of older adults living in nursing homes experience chronic pain [23, 33]) — groups that are also at a greater risk of inadequate treatment, along with racial and ethnic minorities [64]. Indicators of poor socioeconomic status are also significantly correlated with chronic pain conditions [39].


*CHI 2017, May 6-11, 2017, Denver, CO, USA.*

ACM ISBN 978-1-4503-4655-9/17/05 ...$15.00.
http://dx.doi.org/10.1145/3025453.3025832

Still, chronic pain impacts a wide range of disease, demographic, and socioeconomic groups [27] and additionally takes a substantial economic toll. In the United States, the cost of chronic pain is as high as $635 billion a year — more than the annual costs for cancer, diabetes, and heart disease [26]; and the economic burden of pain is similarly greater than most other health conditions around the world [55].

Common chronic pain conditions include osteoarthritis, rheumatoid arthritis, lower back pain, and headaches or migraines as well as repetitive stress disorders or other conditions resulting from injury or physical trauma. Patients with chronic pain are frequently severely debilitated, with significant limitations in their ability to function or work. Indeed, pain consistently ranks as a leading cause of years lost to disability (YLD) worldwide [75]. Chronic pain is also associated with depression, fatigue, sleep disturbances, decreased cognitive and physical abilities, and reduced quality of life overall [3].

As pain is a subjective experience, self-report is considered essential to assessing and, in turn, treating it. However, this can be a challenge both for instruments administered during doctor visits and for at-home methods. During doctor visits, pain intensity is commonly measured according to patient recall using one of several standard pen-and-paper or verbal self-report measures. However, such instruments that rely on retrospective reporting can have low test-retest reliability and be inaccurate due to recall bias, particularly for individuals with memory or other cognitive impairments [15]. These measures are also insensitive to the fluctuating nature of pain intensity over time, which can vary considerably from moment to moment and change depending on activities or other contextual factors [38].

At-home methods, which are typically diary-based, permit more frequent and in-situ assessment; but they can suffer from poor adherence and misreporting, especially if the instrument is cumbersome to use or doesn't suit a number of individually-variable reporting needs and preferences [8]. Attributes such as gender, ethnic and educational background, personality, visual ability, and the presence of affective or cognitive disorders can all influence pain measurement [25], as can pain sensitivity, which also varies dramatically between individuals [51].

This motivates a need for pain self-assessment tools that (1) provide accurate measurement, (2) can be deployed in-situ, (3) are low burden and pleasant enough to promote recurrent use, and (4) are tailored to a particular user's attributes and needs.

In this paper, we present two novel measures for the self-report of pain intensity designed to meet each of these requirements. Each measure was developed through an iterative, user-centered design process involving chronic pain sufferers and was deployed in a field trial to establish validity and usability. Both measures also fulfill a series of design goals including high usability, sensitivity to potentially delicate content, and the cognitive translation process from subjective experience to quantified data point.

The specific contributions of this paper are:

- A series of design constraints identified as important to consider and satisfy when designing pain assessment interfaces.
- Nine candidate and two refined measures for the self-report of pain intensity using a mobile device, together with the results of in-lab and field study evaluations.
- A characterization of the ways in which individuals prefer to self-report pain, along with perceived benefits and challenges of this self-monitoring.

## RELATED WORK

### Pain and Its Assessment

Pain is often understood to consist of two dimensions. The labels most commonly used today are "pain intensity" and "pain interference", though the terminology used to refer to these two dimensions does vary (e.g., "pain intensity" and "reaction to pain" [6], "sensory-discriminative" and "attitudinal" [11], and "sensory" and "reactive" [12]). Pain intensity goes beyond the presence of pain to measure its severity, and pain interference describes the degree to which pain interferes with functioning (emotionally, physically, socially) and the distress it causes [13]. Pain intensity is considered the most salient dimension of pain [71] and is therefore the one we focus on measuring in this paper.

Self-report scales for pain intensity have been present in the literature since at least the 1940s [40]. Today, pain patients are usually asked to use one or more of the Visual Analog Scale (VAS) [35, 62, 76], the Numerical Rating Scale (NRS) [22], or a version of the Faces Pain Scale (FPS) [7] or Faces Pain Scale–Revised (FPS-R) [34]. Each of these is a unidimensional measure typically anchored with text descriptors at the extreme ends of the scale. These descriptors, as well as instructions for use, vary widely in the literature although the endpoints "no pain" and "pain as bad as it could be" are not uncommon.

These instruments offer several advantages such as brief and simple administration, easy scoring, and being understandable to most patients [25]. The main limitation relates to these unidimensional measures' questionable ability to capture the subjective and multidimensional aspects of pain [50], and studies do sometimes find mixed results in terms of retest reliability and sensitivity to measuring changes in pain levels [5]. These tools can also face well-known challenges related to inconsistent completion and retrospective recall, especially in their paper-based forms; though overall, the reliability of such measures is generally found to be sufficient to be practically and clinically useful [16].

### Pain Measurement in the mHealth Age

"mHealth" is an abbreviation for "mobile health" and refers to the use of mobile technologies to support healthcare. mHealth represents an opportunity to greatly improve the self-management of pain through self-assessments that are accessible, accurate, and effective and can support long-term, in-situ monitoring [59].

Today, 72% of U.S. adults already own smartphones [57], and up to 80% of adults worldwide are anticipated to own a smartphone by 2020 [21]. Further, though probability of smartphone ownership declines with increasing age, that trend is changing over time. Given this pervasive nature of smartphones and their embeddedness into daily life [42], methods such as Experience Sampling (ESM) [32] or Ecological Momentary Assessment (EMA) [63] are promising means of administering frequent, low-burden self-assessments in natural settings. Such approaches also sidestep recall and other biases [67], promote continued use [37], and are associated with a variety of positive health outcomes such as an improved ability to cope with pain [31].

Recognizing this opportunity, researchers have begun investigating the use of mobile devices for the self-report of pain intensity. The smartphone apps "ePAL" [2] and "Painometer" [19] use the mobile medium to deliver standard, validated pain intensity scales such as NRS and FPS-R. "Pain Squad", an iPhone app developed to support pain management for adolescents with cancer, provides an electronic pain diary of 20 questions of various types (e.g., VAS scales, body-maps, multiple choice, selectable words, and free-text) adapted from an arthritis diary to be cancer-specific [65].

Several commercial mobile apps are now available for self-assessing pain as well [60]. Studies have found that using these smartphone-based tools for pain reporting and intervention can improve pain management [72] and adherence [49] as well as prevent increases in emotional distress and symptom levels [45]. However, the number of randomized controlled trials conducted on these apps is relatively small, and more thorough evaluation is still necessary [18, 47, 58]. Further, the adoption of mHealth apps can be hindered by perceived barriers such as the need for interfaces to better address users' functional limitations (e.g., visual deficits) [54].

In particular, we see a need for more work to understand individual differences in the receptivity and use of pain assessment measures in order to enable the design of instruments that better meet users' potentially diverse attributes and preferences.

### Designing Tailored Self-Report Instruments

In completing a self-report measure, there are four basic cognitive components: *comprehension* (the respondent's ability to identify the question focus and interpret the intended meaning of the question); *retrieval* (the respondent searches his or her memory for all question-related information, recalls generic and specific memories, and fills in missing details); *judgment* (the respondent summarizes and integrates the retrieved information, draws inferences, and makes assessments); and *response* (the respondent maps their judgments onto a response category or value, editing the response as necessary) [70].

To achieve optimal response quality, measures should therefore both maximize respondent motivation to answer accurately as well as minimize the difficulty of responding by making it easy to interpret questions, retrieve and integrate relevant information from memory into a judgment, and report that judgment [73]. Specifically regarding pain self-report, four features have been outlined for the usability for self-reporting pain intensity on a mobile device: an interface must be learnable and easy to start using, reporting must be and feel efficient, a measure should be tested for usability errors, and an interface should be as satisfying and even pleasurable to use as possible [66].

Of course, different measures may maximize motivation and minimize difficulty in reporting for different people, who may also have varying reactions to the design of a measure. Indeed, personalized N-of-1 style medicine emphasizes that a one-size-fits-all approach is not appropriate for the self-management of chronic conditions in mHealth [69]; and rejecting the idea that biological responses are standard, some researchers have even called for a moratorium on randomized controlled trials [41]. Considering that individuals experience and process pain in idiosyncratic ways, it thus is important to design and deploy self-report measures that consider — even embrace — their participants' individuality in these respects.

## METHOD

This study draws the above ideas together via an iterative user-centered research-through-design approach. Specifically, the research consists of three stages: design ideation and review, an in-lab user study with N=10 participants of nine candidate interfaces, and a 3 week N=12 participant field trial of two refined measures. The Cornell Institutional Review Board approved all procedures. We describe methodological details in the following subsections.

### Design Ideation and Review

We drew on the self-report and usability literatures reviewed earlier as well as our own experience developing and deploying experience sampling systems in order to ideate a large number of potential interfaces. We identified and tried to meet several design constraints:

- *Design to be highly usable.* Considering variations in psychomotor and perceptual capabilities (particularly age-related changes, as one target population is older adults), any reporting interface should use large touch-target regions, simple interactions, low manipulability given potential hand or wrist pain, and readable fonts and font sizes.
- *Design for the smartphone medium.* The smartphone affords various interaction modalities (e.g. touch, reactive displays, memory of past reports, animations) that expand the range of ways through which individuals can express their pain. Which are the most appropriate for this context and preferred by individual users?
- *Design for in-situ use.* End-users would be using self-report measures at home but also potentially at work, in social situations, or in public. The interface should be usable on the go.
- *Design for repeated use.* These interfaces would be used regularly, perhaps over years. A measure usable *enough* to complete once or occasionally can become incredibly frustrating when engaged with more often. How should the interfaces change over time and with repeated use?
- *Design to support cognitive translation processes.* Can an interface support the effort of translating a complex subjective experience into a reportable value, perhaps by way of abstract representations that convey pain or its manifestations in a "legible" way?
- *Design to elicit reports about sensitive content.* Focusing on pain might make pain experiences more salient or increase anxiety, among other potential negative effects [77]. Could interfaces abstract away or ameliorate this process?

We were additionally informed by fundamental human-computer interaction design principles [52] as well as the design thinking around microinteraction — a small piece of functionality that supports a user in completing a single task [61]. Figure 1 shows an example of one of our early sketches.

Through team discussion and review with designers, we combined and refined elements of the sketched interfaces to produce a set of designs aimed at meeting these constraints and principles (e.g., the slider of SuperVAS+ was intended to satisfy the highly usable constraint, while PhotosNature aimed to address the constraints regarding cognitive translation and sensitive content by supplying metaphorical representations of pain that could convey even intense levels but without disturbing content that might upset a user).

We also added designs for well-established pain assessment instruments mentioned earlier: usability-improved versions of the Visual Analogue Scale for Pain (VAS-P) [30]; the 11-point numeric rating scale for pain (NRS-11) [48]; and with permission from the creators, the Sydney Animated Facial Expressions (SAFE) scale [10], which is a computer animation of the Faces Pain Scale (FPS) [7] that has been deployed in a laptop version where pain is reported with the left/right arrow keys [28]. VAS-P, NRS-11, and FPS have all shown good usability and acceptability characteristics when deployed in a mobile app [19].

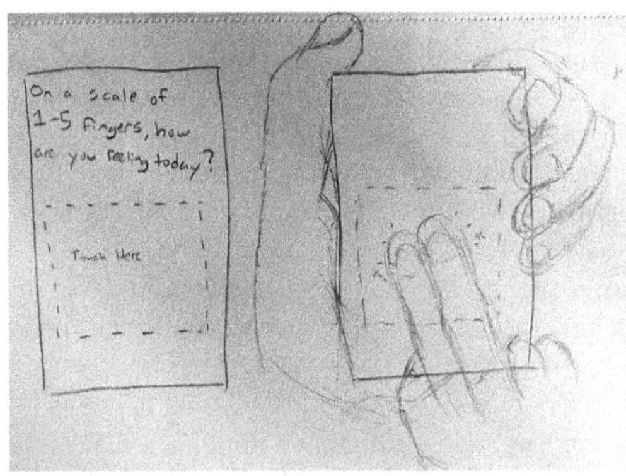


**Figure 1. Example of a pain-assessment interface that was sketched during the ideation phase and aimed to meet design constraints as well as support microinteraction principles.**

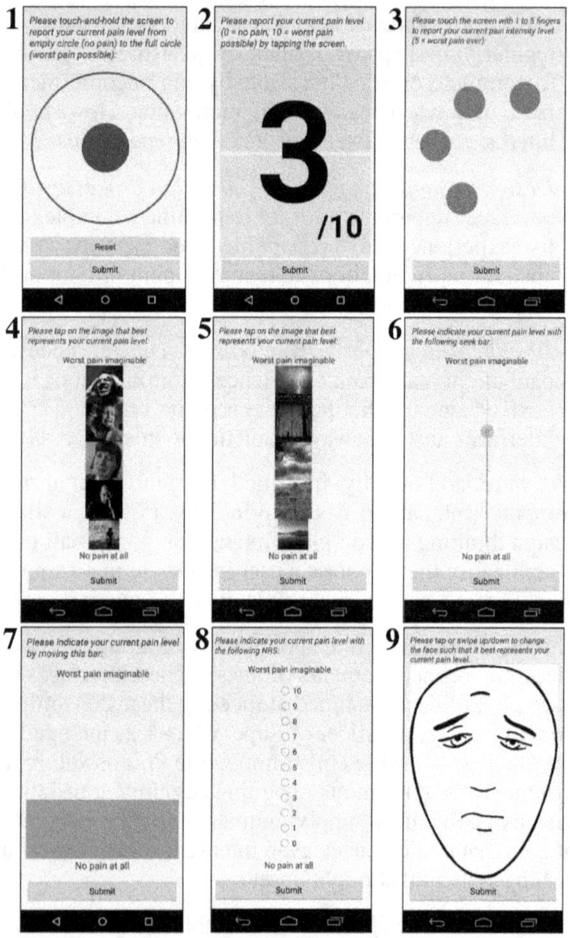


**Figure 2. Our nine candidate measures for smartphone-based pain self-assessment resulting from our iterative design cycle.**

The resulting nine measures were prototyped for the Android operating system as custom Views[1]. They can be seen in Figure 2 and are summarized as follows.

1. **Suureta**: An empty circle that slowly fills with color when any part of the interface is touched and held. Suureta can be completed by resting a knuckle, nose, or chin on the screen.

2. **TapTap**: An oversized number picker widget for reporting on a numerical 0–10 range. The currently selected value is displayed in a very large font on the screen. Tapping anywhere on the top half of the screen increments the value; tapping anywhere on the bottom decrements it.

3. **ManyFingers**: Respondents report their level of pain by touching the screen with a certain number of fingers simultaneously. Figure 1 shows the design's early-stage sketch.

4. **PhotosPeople**: A vertical five-item NRS that displays pain levels using photographs of faces instead of numbers. To generate a set of photos that portray varying levels of pain, we harvested photos from Flickr tagged with 18 words describing degrees and qualities of pain, following a protocol described in prior work [56].

5. **PhotosNature**: Same as PhotosPeople but with pain levels conveyed via abstract and landscape images (e.g., of a lightning bolt or a serene lake) rather than faces.

6. **SuperVAS**: Standard VAS-P with vertical orientation, using a custom seekbar widget.

7. **SuperVAS+**: VAS-P with vertical orientation but using a custom seekbar widget that dramatically increases the target touch region.

8. **NRS-11**: Standard NRS-11 with vertical orientation, using native radio buttons.

9. **SAFE**: A version of SAFE where the user can smoothly transition across the face images by tapping on the screen between the two anchors or by sliding a finger up or down the screen. This interaction is more natural for the smartphone medium and also avoids the practical issue of simultaneously displaying multiple face images on a small screen.

[1] https://developer.android.com/reference/android/view/View.html

### In-Lab User Studies

Through campus mailing lists, on-site physiotherapy center flyers, and snowball sampling we recruited 10 participants, each of whom experienced some form of waxing and waning chronic pain. We refer to these participants as P1–P10. Participants' recent experiences with pain ranged from low-level recurring joint pain or injury recovery up through severe arthritis or back and neck pain from a recent car accident.

Nine participants were female, though gender skew is not uncommon in smaller-scale pain studies (e.g., 51 of 78 participants were female in recent related work [29]), and chronic pain is more common in women than men [24]. Half our participants were 55 years of age or older, and nine were reasonably to very comfortable with smartphones; the other owned a smartphone but used it only as an emergency device and map.

The 40–60 minute lab session had three portions. During the first portion, we asked questions about the participant, any recent experience(s) with pain, how the person had reported pain in any setting in the past, self-tracking practices (if any), and familiarity with smartphones. In the second portion, the participant interacted with each of the nine candidate measures, used them to report current pain level, and provided feedback. We also recorded observational notes. The final portion was a reflective compare-and-contrast, where the participant qualitatively compared measures as well as used ordinal rankings across four usability dimensions to rank preferences. An opportunity was also offered to provide any additional free response. Each participant was compensated $10.

### Field Trial Evaluation

Balancing design guidelines outlined in prior work [52, 61, 66] with feedback from the in-lab study (described further in the Results section), we selected, combined, and refined elements from the candidate interfaces. For instance, participants largely did not enjoy using photo-realistic images to report pain levels

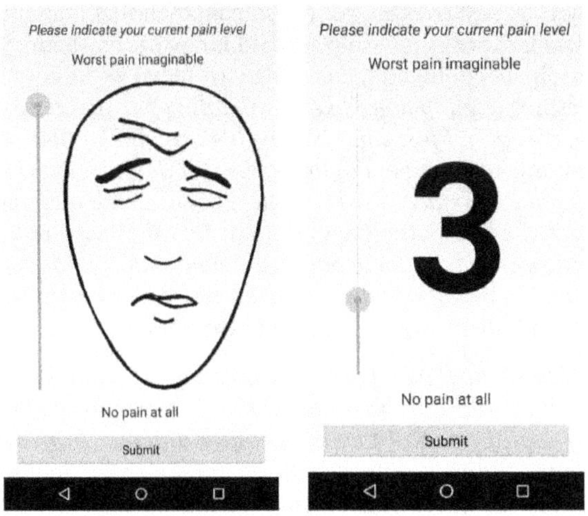


**Figure 3. Our two novel pain reporting measures, SAFESlider (left) and SuperVASNumbered (right), designed based on our in-lab study results and deployed in a 3 week field trial.**

(as employed in PhotosPeople), encouraging us to move in the more abstract direction of SAFE. Participants liked the oversized display of TapTap but thought tapping to report was time consuming, and the small touch targets NRS-11 often led to misreports. Given the importance of quick and accurate reporting, we therefore used SuperVAS's standard slider widget, which participants considered more intuitive than SuperVAS+; though the latter's large target region was appreciated and so we incorporated a generous touch area.

Figure 3 illustrates our two resultant measures: **SAFESlider** and **SuperVASNumbered**. Both had dual interaction modes; the user could either tap anywhere on the screen (as if underneath the screen lie a standard NRS-11 or VAS-P with low pain at the bottom through high pain at the top) or swipe anywhere on the screen to control the slider on the side.

We deployed these two new measures in an ESM-style field trial lasting 3 weeks (a length of time comparable to deployments of related mHealth pain assessment apps [65] and sufficient to capture declines in quality of data reporting, according to the ESM literature [68]). Campus mailing lists, on-site physiotherapy center flyers, and snowball sampling were again used to recruit another set of 12 participants, who were required to be experiencing some form of chronic pain and be Android smartphone users since our measures were developed to work on that operating system. We refer to these participants as P11–P22. Nine participants were female, four were 50 or older, and all reported being comfortable with their smartphones. Participants' current experiences with pain ranged from low-level pain through severe arthritis, compartment syndrome, or fibromyalgia.

Participants installed two applications onto their smartphones: Meter[2], a custom-developed app that housed our two measures (SAFESlider and SuperVASNumbered) as well as Ohmage[3], an open-source participatory sensing platform that allowed us to administer our measures together with a set of survey questions listed below. Specifically, participants were prompted via a notification from Ohmage to complete a short 1–3 minute survey twice a day, once in the morning and once in the evening. Each survey consisted of four questions:

1. Self-reported pain level using a version of NRS built into Ohmage
2. Self-reported pain level using one of our two measures (SAFESlider or SuperVASNumbered)
3. Subjective usability rating of that measure on a 5-point Likert scale
4. Unstructured feedback about the interface (optional)

At the end of 3 weeks, all but 2 participants also completed a 30–40 minute semi-structured interview about their experiences during the field trial. Participants were compensated $10 for each week of survey responses and $10 for the interview, for a possible total of $40.

## RESULTS

This section provides usage statistics from the field trial followed by a description of qualitative themes from both the in-lab study and the field trial.

### Usage Statistics

Our 12 field trial participants (P11–P22) completed a total of 453 surveys over the course of the study's 3 weeks, for an overall response rate of 90%. Participants completed SAFESlider 242 times (96% response rate) and SuperVASNumbered 211 times (84% response rate).

SAFESlider took a median of 5.0 seconds to complete, and the mean pain intensity value reported using SAFESlider was 2.74 on a range of 0 (no pain) to 10 (worst pain imaginable). The SuperVASNumbered measure was a bit faster to complete — taking a median of 3.6 seconds, and the mean pain intensity reported using SuperVASNumbered was also lower — a mean of 2.17 on on the same 0–10 range. Table 1 shows per-participant metrics when reporting with SAFESlider (abbreviated "*SS*") and SuperVASNumbered (abbreviated "*SVN*").

| Participant ID | Response Rate | | Response Time (seconds) | | Pain Level (0–10) | |
|---|---|---|---|---|---|---|
| | *SS* | *SVN* | *SS* | *SVN* | *SS* | *SVN* |
| P11 | 95% | 57% | 3.95s | 2.97s | 4.0 | 3.0 |
| P12 | 90% | 71% | 3.03s | 2.34s | 1.0 | 1.0 |
| P13 | 95% | 95% | 4.81s | 2.74s | 2.0 | 2.0 |
| P14 | 100% | 81% | 3.23s | 2.45s | 2.0 | 2.0 |
| P15 | 100% | 95% | 5.27s | 5.92s | 4.0 | 4.0 |
| P16 | 86% | 81% | 8.93s | 3.45s | 2.0 | 1.0 |
| P17 | 100% | 81% | 9.86s | 5.60s | 6.0 | 4.0 |
| P18 | 95% | 86% | 3.30s | 3.67s | 2.0 | 1.0 |
| P19 | 100% | 100% | 5.05s | 2.90s | 4.5 | 3.5 |
| P20 | 71% | 76% | 5.62s | 4.26s | 1.0 | 1.0 |
| P21 | 100% | 90% | 7.23s | 4.81s | 1.0 | 2.0 |
| P22 | 90% | 86% | 9.62s | 4.64s | 1.0 | 1.5 |

**Table 1. Per-participant metrics when completing SAFESlider (*SS*) and SuperVASNumbered (*SVN*). Response time and pain level are both median values within each participant.**

[2]https://play.google.com/store/apps/details?id=edu.cornell.idl.meter
[3]http://ohmage.org

| Measure | Very easy | Somewhat easy | Neither difficult nor easy | Somewhat difficult | Very difficult |
|---|---|---|---|---|---|
| *SS* | 39.2% | 36.8% | 12% | 12% | 0% |
| *SVN* | 61.6% | 29.8% | 8.1% | 0.5% | 0% |

**Table 2. Percentage of usability reports that assessed SAFESlider (*SS*) and SuperVASNumbered (*SVN*) measures across levels of ease of use.**

Though SuperVASNumbered aligned slightly better, pain reports from both measures strongly correlated with pain reported using the standard NRS (Pearson's $r = 0.93$, $p < 0.0001$) for SAFESlider and Pearson's $r = 0.98$, $p < 0.0001$ for SuperVASNumbered), indicating their validity.

Both measures were generally found to be somewhat or very easy to use according to 242 and 211 usability reports for SAFESlider and SuperVASNumbered, respectively, though participants found SuperVASNumbered somewhat easier. Table 2 provides the aggregated breakdowns about reported usability for both measures.

Importantly, we found that usability perceptions were not unanimous across participants or even within the same participant across different reporting sessions — which encourages a deeper look into what factors, both stable and temporary, might impact such reception and use of pain assessment instruments and how designs might be tailored accordingly. Toward this goal, we next present our qualitative themes that emerged from our semi-structured interviews with individuals that participated in both the in-lab study as well as the field trial.

### Thematic Analysis

To qualitatively analyze the data from the in-lab user study and the field trial, we conducted a thematic analysis [9] wherein the researchers reviewed the dataset to identify initial themes, which were shared, discussed, and iteratively refined. We found no strong correlations between the themes that emerged and demographics, level of pain, or type of pain experienced.

Overall, participants were diverse in the ways they thought about and wanted to report their pain. We believe our findings surface important topics and serve to suggest directions for advancing the development of tailored pain self-assessment measures that enhance patient experiences.

#### *Reporting Pain with Faces*

Participants had (often very) strong feelings either for or against the use of faces for reporting pain levels (e.g., via PhotosPeople, SAFE, or SAFESlider). Those who valued reporting with faces were able to connect with the people and expressions displayed (e.g., *"I can definitely imagine feeling the way this person looks"* – P2; *"I can kind of imagine him [SAFE] feeling what I feel, feeling more than just the sterile measure"* – P3). Such individuals also thought using faces to express their pain felt more natural and intuitive, e.g.:

> *"With the numbers, my brain needs to actually think more about the body part and the pain sensation explicitly and somehow try to map that onto a number. Face is a different translation channel that goes through emotion and feeling, though the underlying component is still my pain."* (P3)

However, just over half of participants felt that mapping pain to facial expressions simply could not work for them. Several participants doubted the accuracy of facial expression based measures (e.g., *"I don't like coordinating pain to facial expressions because I just can't believe it's accurate"* – P4) or had a hard time reading pain in faces (e.g., *"I don't know what pain looks like on a face"* – P7). PhotosPeople and SAFE were also rejected when participants did not feel the faces resembled their own (e.g., *"I am in pain, but I don't look like any of these people"* – P4) or could not connect those faces' expression of pain with their own self-image or experience:

> *"I think the [SAFE] person was enough of a blank canvas that I could express myself through it, but these [PhotosPeople] are real people who are different from me — that's a disconnect. When the person in the picture is different from me, and I can't connect it with myself individually, it's harder to pick that one, even if it's the right degree in the scale."* (P3)

One specific issue underlying an inability to identify with face-based interfaces was a difference between the gender of the participant and that of the face (e.g., *"I wonder if the male/female thing is a problem. You know, if I'm a female, I won't choose the male pictures"* – P4). Two participants suggested that using photos of their own faces to report pain would be more useful instead.

Several participants had quite visceral responses to PhotosPeople or even SAFE during in the in-lab sessions and reported feeling uncomfortable with images of humans (or representations of humans) in pain (e.g., *"Okay this I really don't like. I don't like seeing people in pain"* – P5). Others were not incapable of using the measure but did have a negative affective response (e.g., *"I don't have a problem reporting pain with people's faces, but I feel sad for the sadness of these people's faces"* – P6).

It is quite possible that beyond individual preferences — or perhaps correlated with preference — there are individual differences regarding the ability to make sense of the levels of pain expressed by a face in these interfaces. In fact, there is growing evidence that in non-clinical populations, capabilities in facial expression processing can vary considerably across people [53].

#### *"Numbers People"*

Analysis clearly revealed that about half the participants had a strong preference for reporting with numbers. Such participants were often self-described "numbers people", e.g.:

> *"I tend to be a numbers person, so I like [reporting with] numbers. I relate to them."* (P5)

In some cases, this was due to being familiar with using this sort of representation for self-reporting, which participants felt had become ingrained over time (e.g., *"Everywhere you're taught to think in: one to ten, what's your pain level"* – P4). Such participants made observations about how their personal predilections toward numeric scales would typically lead them to attempt to quantify their pain-assessments even when presented with a more abstract or qualitative reporting interface. For example:

> *"I always think of a number out of 0 to 10 initially. So I mentally compute '3' and then try to use the interface to map [my 3] onto that measure."* (P3)

The other half of participants rejected the number-oriented interfaces and strongly preferred the more qualitative instruments (e.g., *"It's hard to put a numerical value on something like discomfort"* – P9) or at least something they could play with and tune to their own subjective experience. These participants explained that the more abstract measures enabled them to be more descriptive and in turn more accurate in capturing their true pain levels. One participant described a sense that numbers might be better suited to scientific applications but are too sanitary and impersonal to reflect non-objective feelings like pain for all end-users:

> *"Numbers might make more sense for a health professional, but I'm not sure they do for me. No-numbers is somehow more descriptive. I think it's just got to be easier for a patient to do that, than try to put a number on it."* (P4)

### Pliable Interactions

Whether they were numbers people or favored more qualitative interfaces, multiple participants valued being able to adjust their reported score in order to "dial in" to a pain level that seemed correct (e.g., *"You've got the ability to move up and down while you think about it, until it [SuperVASPlus] kind of feels right"* – P8).

This type of tuning was afforded by the slider-based interactions we used in some interfaces (e.g., SuperVAS+, SAFESlider, SuperVASNumbered). Participants reported appreciating the flexible, modifiable nature of the slider (e.g., *"I can change my mind because I can go up and down"* – P2), which was seen as easier to use than instruments that provided a restricted set of choices (e.g., *"It's just nice to be able to move things up and down without having to hit a whole bunch of different buttons [like in NRS-11]"* – P10).

That said, selecting a value through a single-tap was still preferred by others (e.g., *"I like filling in the dots"* – P8), sometimes precisely because the array of options was constrained:

> *"This [SuperVAS] is more fine-grained than I need. Jeez, I don't know, I don't know! [NRS-11] with 10 [11] options is a relief, vs. having to finagle with an unlimited number [in SuperVAS]."* (P3)

These quotes also speak to preferences around reporting resolution and ranges. For most participants, 0–5 was too small a range (e.g., *"There's not a lot of variance from 1 to 5"* – P7; *"I would want to report 4.5/5. There's such a gap between 4 and 5"* – P8) and 0–100 was too wide, while 0–10 hit the spot. In addition, nearly all participants felt that the low end of the scale in particular offered too little resolution, especially for NRS-11 and SAFE-based interfaces (e.g., *"[NRS-11] should also have better resolution at the low end of the scale, like not 0 or 1 but .5 and 1.5 too"* – P7; *"There's a lot of 'being in pain' faces, but there could be a wider low-pain range"* – P2). Such responses also reflect the importance many individuals placed on being able to report (celebrate) no or very minimal pain levels. For example:

> *"I want it to go happier too! If I had no pain, I'd be grinning ear to ear!"* (P2)

### Designing for Delight

We aimed to make our interfaces pleasant to use, and many participants expressed that they did genuinely enjoy interacting with our measures. One noted reason was the attention we gave to aesthetics, which participants explained made instruments more alluring and encouraged their usage (e.g., *"The visual is more attractive to me, rather than [NRS-11]"* – P10).

A perceived element of playfulness was particularly appreciated (e.g., *"It's not just about giving me information, or giving me good information — it should be fun to do"* – P9). Participants explained that this enjoyability-factor strongly motivated them to use our measures, especially when considering usage over an extended period of time (e.g., *"If it's something you'd use every day, it has to be a little fun, not boring"* – P2).

In addition, participants provided a variety of helpful feedback on more traditional usability issues, ranging from the size of text and images (e.g., bigger is better), to expectations that a user should be able to tap on a scale's anchors in order to report extreme values. (We drew on such information when creating our two deployed measures, SAFESlider and SuperVASNumbered). It also became clear through observation during the in-lab study that many participants do not read scale instructions or anchor texts, even when explicitly prompted to do so (e.g., *"I just assumed that the lower end.... did it say no pain?"* – P2). Such findings helped us recognize the need to ensure users are well-acquainted with the scales they will be using — something straightforward for us to do with our field trial participants but potentially challenging if measures are deployed more broadly or outside of clinical or otherwise overseen circumstances.

### No Evidence of Negative Reactivity

The literature makes conflicting claims as to whether frequent self-report of pain intensity might result in positive, negative, or neutral outcomes [1, 32]. Some evidence finds that recalling pain and coping strategies can lead to positive outcomes such as an increased sense of control over the pain [31]. However, other findings of particular concern suggest that repeated self-assessment of such a difficult and potentially traumatic experience draws more attention to and foregrounds that negative perception of being in pain — thereby making the subjective lived experience worse [43].

We therefore found it encouraging that among our participants, not a single one reported such negative consequences from repeatedly reporting pain levels. Participants experiencing a subjectively lower degree of pain than other participants conjectured that others in more pain might experience such negative effects; however, those participants with high pain levels did not find this to be the case.

Rather, several of the participants with high pain levels explained that the act of reporting in and of itself sometimes helped to diminish pain they would be fully aware of anyway. For example:

> *"On the '7' [out of 10 pain level] days, it almost felt like the scales were an outlet for me, in a way. Like, I'm feeling bad, but it almost felt like I could report it in the thing [phone or measure] and maybe compartmentalize it. In a sort of a sense, it's maybe like the way I might vent if I'm upset. Somehow reporting it — externalizing it — actually eased it. When I'm at 7 or 8, it's not like the system is going to remind me I'm in pain — I'm not going to forget that!"* (P13)

Participants explained other positive aspects to the mindfulness that self-reporting promoted, such as adhering to pain treatments (e.g., *"I've been doing PT [physical therapy] at home... This reminder and filling out the measure didn't make my perception of the pain different, but it kept it on my mind so I would do things about it [like PT]"* – P17). Similarly, P19 found that while reporting with our measures did not increase any negative preoccupation with her pain, it did help her think about and understand her pain differently — for example, by becoming more cognizant of the potential effects of contextual factors like weather (e.g., during one very cold week of the field trial). While outside the scope of this paper, such findings suggest the value in considering how future systems might further support individuals in reflecting on, acting on, or otherwise engaging with their collected data, detected patterns, or other synthesized feedback a system might provide.

## DISCUSSION

Modern technology is primed to improve pain measurement and management, and ensuring usability and relevance for both patients and clinicians is a foremost challenge [4]. Our aim in this research was to improve upon current instruments for pain assessment that are typically lab-based, burdensome, and/or generic, in order to not only increase the accuracy and adherence of such methods but also to enhance patient experiences. Our approaches and findings are relevant to designers, researchers, and practitioners working in the domain of pain.

In exploring the needs and preferences of a diverse set of individuals dealing with a variety of pain conditions, we developed an assortment of reporting interfaces. Each was intended to meet a series of design constraints that we outlined as particularly important to consider in this context, such as the need for interfaces to promote repeated use through pleasant interactions, support decoding a personal perception into a quantifiable and comparable output, and be highly usable including during periods when pain may compromise one's dexterity and ability to complete a self-report.

Through an in-lab study and a 3 week deployment, we evaluated our measures, which demonstrated reliability based on comparisons with an established, validated pain assessment instrument (the Numerical Rating Scale, NRS). Equally importantly, our measures saw high adherence rates and usability scores and were well-received by participants. Notable reactions fell into several themes related to feelings toward face-based vs. numerical interfaces, appreciation for flexible and playful reporting experiences, and a sense that measures helped alleviate rather than aggravate pain perceptions.

Some findings were universal across all participants. In general, participants found playful interactions and aesthetic interfaces to be highly enjoyable and motivating to use including over extended periods of time, which is crucial given that chronic pain requires indefinite management. In addition, we did not observe any negative outcomes from self-monitoring pain using our tools (e.g., any increased preoccupation with pain or exacerbated symptoms); rather, our measures seemed to provide an outlet for participants that actually helped to alleviate pain perceptions in some cases.

However, many reactions were not unanimous. For instance, some participants strongly preferred a more qualitative form of reporting and favored instruments involving abstracted or face-based representations of pain. Others disliked interfaces involving faces, either because such measures did not personally resonate with a participant's own experiences and self-image or because it was upsetting to view a person (even a drawn face) in pain. Self-described "numbers people" also struggled with such measures and preferred more familiar, numerical scales (e.g., 0–10 Likert scales). In addition, some participants preferred slider-based interfaces that provided a seemingly unlimited range of malleable values that could be tweaked and tuned, while such boundless scales significantly bothered other individuals, who preferred a more scoped set of numeric values from which to choose. These rich yet sometimes contradictory findings demonstrate the need to move toward more personalized pain assessment approaches.

### Tailoring Self-Assessment

Our findings highlight that there is no one-size-fits-all solution for pain assessment. Across individuals, an array of variables can differ such as the type and severity of the pain condition, current activities and other situational circumstances, and personal preferences. Such idiosyncrasy necessitates the development of tailored assessment tools that better support diverse patient needs. In turn, these personalized interfaces can minimize difficulty and inadherence while optimizing response quality, accuracy, and user experience [73].

Our results similarly indicate that supporting these preferences lowers response burden and increases respondent motivation. Beyond external motivations, which can include a sense of accountability or an understanding of why reporting is important, motivation can further be enhanced by ensuring that completing the measure — potentially tens, hundreds, or thousands of times — is not only brief and unobtrusive but also enjoyable or even delightful.

One method of tailoring a measure to an individual and increasing the pleasurability of response is to allow each respondent to approach and engage with that measure's options differently. We do this in two ways. First, both our measures, SAFESlider and SuperVASNumbered, contain a VAS-style slider widget that can be appropriated to suit personal preferences (e.g., to accommodate spatial thinkers or optimize for more numerical, precision-based reporting). Second, these interfaces afford a tap-to-report interaction and also respond to swipes and drags, allowing users either to report with one tap or to "dial in" their pain level and adjust the reported value in real-time until it "feels right".

Another way to tailor the measure to a particular user is to provide more than one measure and let the individual choose the one that best suits his or her preferences, present circumstances, and overall needs. Our measure SuperVASNumbered very explicitly speaks more to "numbers people" through its large numeric display while our SAFESlider measure is based on facial expressions and enables a response that feels more qualitative. Using different measures in within-subject studies is not a problem assuming each measure demonstrates construct and content validity; and if user ratings correlate well between scales, then it is acceptable to make between-subject comparisons or even allow users to choose which scale they use for each momentary measurement as long as normalization steps are taken [14].

Such tailoring techniques better fit with a respondent's cognitive process for recall and self-assessment, make questions more interpretable, and support the mapping of a self-assessment to the intended report — be it numeric value, face, or slider position. Each measure is further designed to optimize for meaningful responses by enhancing motivation to report, for example by being playful, which can also reduce respondent burden and fatigue. In our study, participants appreciated this playfulness and commonly reported that they genuinely enjoyed interacting with SAFESlider.

Overall, tailoring measures to an individual can thus have several positive outcomes. First, given that response burden is down, motivation to report is up, and the reporting interface is not exactly the same all the time, we anticipate participants will maintain their reporting habits longer. Second, tailoring recognizes a person's uniqueness and preferences — but also encourages systems (and care providers) to consider those consequential individual differences more explicitly. Finally, we expect satisficing (compromising standards and exerting less effort in responding in order to reduce reporting burdens [46]) will be far less common.

### Augmenting Manual Self-Report with Passive Sensing

Advances to relieve the burdens of self-report would be particularly beneficial in the context of pain assessment given that pain can severely interfere with the ability to perform daily tasks — including recurrent self-report activities [17]. One strategy is augmenting and integrating actively collected data with passively captured information pertinent to treatment regimens. Beyond enabling the deployment of more accessible self-report tools, smartphone technology facilitates precisely this: the near-continuous measurement of condition-relevant factors in ecologically valid settings, without requiring active user interaction [20].

Specifically, pain and related symptoms (e.g., fatigue or depressed mood) often affect various functional behaviors that can be assessed using well-established smartphone-based passive sensing techniques, for instance according to activity and location data [74]. As an example, data from a phone's accelerometer, barometer, GPS, and WiFi signals could be used to evaluate the difficulty and required energy of a taken walking route and in turn infer functional capabilities and likely pain levels [4]. Further, machine learning algorithms could tune measurement and modeling to each patient based on their routines, attributes, and preferences in order to accommodate idiosyncratic experiences and manifestations of pain.

However, at the same time, self-report is an essential aspect of chronic pain management due to pain's subjective nature. In addition, the act of self-report can be beneficial in and of itself [44] — as we saw from our own participants who expressed that using our measures helped promote mindfulness and self-reflection, instill a sense of self-accountability, and provide an outlet that externalized and even eased pain perceptions. Care must thus be taken to strike a balance between relieving the intrusions, burdens, and limitations associated with pain self-report while augmenting such data with automated sensing strategies that preserve — rather than undermine — the positive aspects linked with more deliberate, manual forms of self-tracking.

### Future Work

Finally, we point out potential limitations of the research presented in this paper and outline room for future work.

#### *Target Populations*

To begin, individual differences in the experience of pain can vary dramatically, as mentioned. While our participants represent a wide range of ages and deal with a variety of pain conditions, a larger-scale study with a more diverse sample (e.g., especially with respect to gender) would therefore be desirable in order to further expand our understanding of possible patient needs and appropriate tailoring techniques. Participants could also be offered a greater amount and variety of pain measures from which to choose in order to further evaluate patient choices at a larger scale.

In particular, though chronic pain affects all populations regardless of age, gender, ethnicity, income, or geographic location [27], prevalence rates are higher for older adults, yet these individuals are more likely to receive inadequate treatment [64]. Approximately half of our sample did include older adults, but an important next step is to even further target this at-risk and underserved age group.

Our findings specifically suggest the need to examine the requirements of elderly patients suffering from pain alongside dementia, as pointed out by one of our three participants who reported caring for an elderly relative. Without interviewer prompting, this participant also reflected on the older family member's anticipated reactions to our interfaces, suggesting the promise of applying our approaches to this target case:

> *"I've just gone through this extended illness with my mother, and they were always asking what's your pain level. She was never able to put things into words, especially as she got dementia. I really wonder if she had a scale to move her finger...and push the little ball up and down [SuperVAS], that might really be helpful with older patients. She [mother] would have been able to do that and be pretty accurate."* (P4)

### Temporal Considerations

Similarly, given that pain is a chronic condition requiring ongoing management with symptoms that can potentially change over time, conducting longer term deployments is essential in order to evaluate the acceptance, engagement, and suitability of our measures over the long haul. Prolonged evaluation would also allow examination of behavioral and psychological impacts (both positive and negative) that may accompany extended self monitoring. For instance, with time, individuals can learn personal coping strategies and modify behavior in a way to minimize symptoms after gaining an increased understanding and sense of control over their pain condition [31]. However, repeated assessments can also lead people to become unusually aware of their behaviors or state and fixate on negative experiences. It is also possible that repeatedly reporting on the same construct may influence recall or self-appraisal.

Additionally, there is value in further experimentation on the time(s) of day at which momentary pain assessments are administered. We delivered prompts to our participants twice a day, in the morning and evening, but since pain can fluctuate widely over the course of a day [38], this temporal coverage should be expanded going forward. It is also important to consider the individually-suitable timing and frequency of prompts in order to minimize any sense of intrusiveness and annoyance as well as the lag between when a self-report prompt is received and actually answered.

### Integration with Clinical Care

High-quality pain management requires physicians to follow their patients' subjective experience of pain along with activities, psychological well-being, and additional traditional medical indicators. It is therefore necessary to investigate how the measures we have developed for this study — and more generally, our design process used to create these measures — fit with clinical practice. Similarly, there are additional stakeholders to consider such as other caregivers or family members who may also play a key role in a person's pain management, especially in severe cases.

Going forward, there is value in engaging with doctors in order to determine the potential impacts of our research on clinical workflows and to ensure such novel measures and outputs are relevant and useful to medical decision-making. The fact that half of our participants took issue with using numbers for self-report — the standard technique found in a doctor's office — could mean that integrating our measures with existing care practices may be a challenge. Nonetheless, our findings indicate the need to pursue development of pain-assessment methods (both on devices as well as perhaps face-to-face) that meet the diverse requirements of patients and other involved parties.

### Novel Assessment Modalities

Finally, in this study, we focused on developing pain assessment tools specifically designed for a smartphone, given the aforementioned advantages of this medium (e.g., ubiquity of ownership, portability and accessibility throughout daily life, and interaction affordances that can support the cognitive translation process from pain to report). Still, it would be worthwhile to explore alternative interfaces for the self-report of pain, especially considering the potential difficulty in manipulating devices during a pain episode.

Particularly promising directions include the development of tangible user interfaces that do not rely on visual prompts and allow the report of pain through more natural touching or squeezing actions, much the same way a person experiencing pain might grasp a nearby object or loved one's hand [4]. This sort of reporting interface is also more unobtrusive and supports reporting in a more private manner, which can be particularly important to pain patients given the stigma many attach to their condition [36]. Going forward, we encourage others to continue investigating novel approaches and modalities to support the assessment of idiosyncratic, subjective pain experiences in a reliable, personalized, and sensitive manner.

## CONCLUSION

Self-assessment is integral to measuring the subjective experience of pain — a prevalent, debilitating, and economically burdensome condition. In this research, we set out to develop novel smartphone-based assessment tools that not only support reliable, repeated, in-situ measurement in a broadly deployable manner but are also pleasant to use and tailored to personal preferences. We focused on designing visual interfaces for the self-report of pain intensity on smartphone screens given the interactions smartphones afford and their embeddedness into daily life and, in turn, the opportunities they provide for more personalized, ecologically valid assessment.

Through an iterative, user-centered design approach, we demonstrated how individuals' receptivity of a measure can be strongly impacted by design features — in particular, when it comes to abstract or qualitative interfaces vs. numeric reporting, perceived "sweet spots" in the resolution and range of reporting scales, and playful, aesthetically appealing interactions. Importantly, our studies found that participants' preferences were strong and idiosyncratic — and not always unanimous, highlighting a need for measures that can better accommodate such individual differences. Our work indicates that supporting these preferences lowers response burden and increases respondent motivation, including over long periods of time, which is critical when monitoring a lifelong condition such as chronic pain.

Such tools that are practically and personally effective for self-assessing pain could have significant impacts on both societal and personal levels by cutting treatment costs, empowering patients in their self-care, and overall, improving daily life for the millions of individuals experiencing chronic pain.

## ACKNOWLEDGMENTS

This work was supported by the National Science Foundation Directorate for Computer and Information Science and Engineering (grant number 1344587), by the National Institute on Aging (grant 3 P30 AG022845), and by the National Science Foundation Graduate Research Fellowship Program (grant DGE-1144153).

## REFERENCES


1. Leslie A Aaron, Judith A Turner, Lloyd Mancl, Heather Brister, and Craig N Sawchuk. 2005. Electronic diary assessment of pain-related variables: is reactivity a problem? *The Journal of Pain* 6, 2 (2005), 107–115.
2. Stephen Agboola, Mihir Kamdar, Clare Flanagan, Meghan Searl, Lara Traeger, Joseph Kvedar, and Kamal Jethwani. 2014. Pain management in cancer patients using a mobile app: study design of a randomized controlled trial. *JMIR research protocols* 3, 4 (2014).
3. Michael A Ashburn and Peter S Staats. 1999. Management of chronic pain. *The Lancet* 353, 9167 (1999), 1865–1869.
4. Min Aung, Faisal Alquaddoomi, Cheng-Kang Hsieh, Mashfiqui Rabbi, Longqi Yang, JP Pollak, Deborah Estrin, and Tanzeem Choudhury. 2014. Leveraging Multi-Modal Sensing for Mobile Health: a Case Review in Chronic Pain. (2014).
5. Mordechai Averbuch and Meyer Katzper. 2004. Assessment of visual analog versus categorical scale for measurement of osteoarthritis pain. *The Journal of Clinical Pharmacology* 44, 4 (2004), 368–372.
6. Henry Knowles Beecher. 1959. *Measurement of subjective responses: quantitative effects of drugs.* Oxford University Press.
7. Daiva Bieri, Robert A Reeve, G David Champion, Louise Addicoat, and John B Ziegler. 1990. The Faces Pain Scale for the self-assessment of the severity of pain experienced by children: development, initial validation, and preliminary investigation for ratio scale properties. *Pain* 41, 2 (1990), 139–150.
8. Niall Bolger, Angelina Davis, and Eshkol Rafaeli. 2003. Diary methods: Capturing life as it is lived. *Annual review of psychology* 54, 1 (2003), 579–616.
9. Richard E Boyatzis. 1998. *Transforming qualitative information: Thematic analysis and code development.* Sage.
10. GD Champion, CL von Baeyer, JDH Trieu, and B Goodenough. 1997. Sydney Animated Facial Expressions (SAFE). (1997). Randwick, NSW, Australia: Pain Research Unit, Sydney Children's Hospital.
11. W Crawford Clark and Joseph C Yang. 1983. Applications of sensory decision theory to problems in laboratory and clinical pain. *Pain measurement and assessment* (1983), 15–25.
12. CS Cleeland. 1989. Measurement of pain by subjective report. *Advances in pain research and therapy* 12 (1989), 391–403.
13. CS Cleeland and KM Ryan. 1994. Pain assessment: global use of the Brief Pain Inventory. *Annals of the Academy of Medicine* 23, 2 (1994), 129–138.
14. Dan Cosley, Shyong K Lam, Istvan Albert, Joseph A Konstan, and John Riedl. 2003. Is seeing believing?: how recommender system interfaces affect users' opinions. In *Proceedings of the SIGCHI Conference on Human Factors in Computing Systems*. ACM, 585–592.
15. Steven S Coughlin. 1990. Recall bias in epidemiologic studies. *Journal of clinical epidemiology* 43, 1 (1990), 87–91.
16. AD Craig, JO Dostrovsky, PD Wall, and R Melzack. 1999. Textbook of pain. *Oxford: University of Printing House* (1999).
17. EJ Dansie and Dennis C Turk. 2013. Assessment of patients with chronic pain. *British journal of anaesthesia* 111, 1 (2013), 19–25.
18. Rocío de la Vega and Jordi Miró. 2014. mHealth: a strategic field without a solid scientific soul. A systematic review of pain-related apps. *PloS One* 9, 7 (2014), e101312.
19. Rocío de la Vega, Roman Roset, Elena Castarlenas, Elisabet Sánchez-Rodríguez, Ester Solé, and Jordi Miró. 2014. Development and Testing of Painometer: A Smartphone App to Assess Pain Intensity. *The Journal of Pain* 15, 10 (2014), 1001–1007.
20. Deborah Estrin and Ida Sim. 2010. Open mHealth architecture: an engine for health care innovation. *Science* 330, 6005 (2010), 759–760.
21. Benedict Evans. 2013. Mobile is eating the world. *Benedict Evans Blog* (2013).
22. John T Farrar, James P Young, Linda LaMoreaux, John L Werth, and R Michael Poole. 2001. Clinical importance of changes in chronic pain intensity measured on an 11-point numerical pain rating scale. *Pain* 94, 2 (2001), 149–158.
23. BA Ferrell, BR Ferrell, and L Rivera. 1995. Pain in cognitively impaired nursing home patients. *Journal of pain and symptom management* 10, 8 (1995), 591–598.
24. Roger B Fillingim, Christopher D King, Margarete C Ribeiro-Dasilva, Bridgett Rahim-Williams, and Joseph L Riley. 2009. Sex, gender, and pain: a review of recent clinical and experimental findings. *The Journal of Pain* 10, 5 (2009), 447–485.
25. Stephen A Flaherty. 1996. Pain measurement tools for clinical practice and research. *AANA journal* (1996).
26. Darrell J Gaskin and Patrick Richard. 2012. The economic costs of pain in the United States. *The Journal of Pain* 13, 8 (2012), 715–724.
27. Daniel S Goldberg and Summer J McGee. 2011. Pain as a global public health priority. *BMC public health* 11, 1 (2011), 1.
28. Belinda Goodenough, T Piira, CL Von Baeyer, K Chua, E Wu, JDH Trieu, and GD Champion. 2005. Comparing six self-report measures of pain intensity in children. *The Suffering Child* 8 (2005), 1–25.

29. Jamie Guillory, Pamara Chang, Charles R Henderson Jr, Rouzi Shengelia, Sonam Lama, Marcus Warmington, Maryam Jowza, Seth Waldman, Geri Gay, and M Carrington Reid. 2015. Piloting a Text Message-based Social Support Intervention for Patients With Chronic Pain: Establishing Feasibility and Preliminary Efficacy. *The Clinical journal of pain* 31, 6 (2015), 548–556.

30. Gillian A Hawker, Samra Mian, Tetyana Kendzerska, and Melissa French. 2011. Measures of adult pain: Visual Analog Scale for Pain (VAS-Pain), Numeric Rating Scale for Pain (NRS-Pain), McGill Pain Questionnaire (MPQ), Short-Form McGill Pain Questionnaire (SF-MPQ), Chronic Pain Grade Scale (CPGS), Short Form-36 Bodily Pain Scale (SF-36 BPS), and Measure of Intermittent and Constant Osteoarthritis Pain (ICOAP). *Arthritis Care & Research* 63, S11 (2011), S240–S252.

31. Jennifer A Haythornthwaite, Lynette A Menefee, Leslie J Heinberg, and Michael R Clark. 1998. Pain coping strategies predict perceived control over pain. *Pain* 77, 1 (1998), 33–39.

32. Joel M Hektner, Jennifer A Schmidt, and Mihaly Csikszentmihalyi. 2007. *Experience sampling method: Measuring the quality of everyday life*. Sage.

33. Robert D Helme and Stephen J Gibson. 2001. The epidemiology of pain in elderly people. *Clinics in geriatric medicine* 17, 3 (2001), 417–431.

34. Carrie L Hicks, Carl L von Baeyer, Pamela A Spafford, Inez van Korlaar, and Belinda Goodenough. 2001. The Faces Pain Scale–Revised: toward a common metric in pediatric pain measurement. *Pain* 93, 2 (2001), 173–183.

35. EC Huskisson. 1974. Measurement of pain. *The Lancet* 304, 7889 (1974), 1127–1131.

36. Jean E Jackson. 2005. Stigma, liminality, and chronic pain: Mind–body borderlands. *American ethnologist* 32, 3 (2005), 332–353.

37. Robert N Jamison, Stephen A Raymond, Jonathan G Levine, Ellen A Slawsby, Srdjan S Nedeljkovic, and Nathaniel P Katz. 2001. Electronic diaries for monitoring chronic pain: 1-year validation study. *Pain* 91, 3 (2001), 277–285.

38. Mark P Jensen and Candace A McFarland. 1993. Increasing the reliability and validity of pain intensity measurement in chronic pain patients. *Pain* 55, 2 (1993), 195–203.

39. Catherine B Johannes, T Kim Le, Xiaolei Zhou, Joseph A Johnston, and Robert H Dworkin. 2010. The prevalence of chronic pain in United States adults: results of an Internet-based survey. *The Journal of Pain* 11, 11 (2010), 1230–1239.

40. KD Keele. 1948. The pain chart. *The Lancet* 252, 6514 (1948), 6–8.

41. Rodger Kessler and Russell E Glasgow. 2011. A proposal to speed translation of healthcare research into practice: dramatic change is needed. *American journal of preventive medicine* 40, 6 (2011), 637–644.

42. Predrag Klasnja and Wanda Pratt. 2012. Healthcare in the pocket: mapping the space of mobile-phone health interventions. *Journal of biomedical informatics* 45, 1 (2012), 184–198.

43. Annika Kohl, Winfried Rief, and Julia Anna Glombiewski. 2013. Acceptance, cognitive restructuring, and distraction as coping strategies for acute pain. *The Journal of Pain* 14, 3 (2013), 305–315.

44. William J Korotitsch and Rosemery O Nelson-Gray. 1999. An overview of self-monitoring research in assessment and treatment. *Psychological Assessment* 11, 4 (1999), 415.

45. Ólöf Birna Kristjánsdóttir, Egil A Fors, Erlend Eide, Arnstein Finset, Tonje Lauritzen Stensrud, Sandra van Dulmen, Sigrid Hørven Wigers, and Hilde Eide. 2013. A smartphone-based intervention with diaries and therapist-feedback to reduce catastrophizing and increase functioning in women with chronic widespread pain: randomized controlled trial. *Journal of Medical Internet Research* 15, 1 (2013), e5.

46. Jon A Krosnick. 1991. Response strategies for coping with the cognitive demands of attitude measures in surveys. *Applied cognitive psychology* 5, 3 (1991), 213–236.

47. Chitra Lalloo, Lindsay A Jibb, Jordan Rivera, Arnav Agarwal, and Jennifer N Stinson. 2015. "There's a Pain App for That": Review of Patient-targeted Smartphone Applications for Pain Management. *The Clinical journal of pain* 31, 6 (2015), 557–563.

48. Margo McCaffery and Alexandra Beebe. 1993. *Pain: Clinical Manual for Nursing Practice*. Baltimore: V.V. Mosby Company.

49. Catherine B McClellan, Jeffrey C Schatz, Eve Puffer, Carmen E Sanchez, Melita T Stancil, and Carla W Roberts. 2009. Use of handheld wireless technology for a home-based sickle cell pain management protocol. *Journal of pediatric psychology* 34, 5 (2009), 564–573.

50. DB McGuire. 1987. The multidimensional phenomenon of cancer pain. *Cancer pain management* (1987), 1–20.

51. Christopher S Nielsen, Roland Staud, and Donald D Price. 2009. Individual differences in pain sensitivity: measurement, causation, and consequences. *The Journal of Pain* 10, 3 (2009), 231–237.

52. Donald A Norman. 2013. *The design of everyday things: Revised and expanded edition*. Basic books.

53. Romina Palermo, Kirsty B O'Connor, Joshua M Davis, Jessica Irons, and Elinor McKone. 2013. New tests to measure individual differences in matching and labelling facial expressions of emotion, and their association with ability to recognise vocal emotions and facial identity. *PloS One* 8, 6 (2013), e68126.

54. Samantha J Parker, Sonal Jessel, Joshua E Richardson, and M Cary Reid. 2013. Older adults are mobile too! Identifying the barriers and facilitators to older adults' use of mHealth for pain management. *BMC geriatrics* 13, 1 (2013), 1.

55. Ceri J Phillips. 2009. The cost and burden of chronic pain. *Reviews in Pain* 3, 1 (2009), 2.

56. John P Pollak, Phil Adams, and Geri Gay. 2011. PAM: A Photographic Affect Meter for Frequent, In Situ Measurement of Affect. In *Proceedings of the SIGCHI Conference on Human Factors in Computing Systems.* ACM, 725–734.

57. Jacob Poushter. 2016. Smartphone Ownership and Internet Usage Continues to Climb in Emerging Economies. *Pew Research Center: Global Attitudes & Trends* (2016).

58. Charmian Reynoldson, Catherine Stones, Matthew Allsop, Peter Gardner, Michael I Bennett, S José Closs, Rick Jones, and Peter Knapp. 2014. Assessing the Quality and Usability of Smartphone Apps for Pain Self-Management. *Pain Medicine* 15, 6 (2014), 898–909.

59. Joshua E Richardson and M Carrington Reid. 2013. The promises and pitfalls of leveraging mobile health technology for pain care. *Pain Medicine* 14, 11 (2013), 1621–1626.

60. Benjamin A Rosser and Christopher Eccleston. 2011. Smartphone applications for pain management. *Journal of telemedicine and telecare* 17, 6 (2011), 308–312.

61. Dan Saffer. 2013. *Microinteractions: designing with details.* " O'Reilly Media, Inc.".

62. Jane Scott and EC Huskisson. 1976. Graphic representation of pain. *Pain* 2, 2 (1976), 175–184.

63. Saul Shiffman, Arthur A Stone, and Michael R Hufford. 2008. Ecological momentary assessment. *Annual Review of Clinical Psychology* 4 (2008), 1–32.

64. Lee S Simon. 2012. Relieving pain in America: A blueprint for transforming prevention, care, education, and research. *Journal of Pain & Palliative Care Pharmacotherapy* 26, 2 (2012), 197–198.

65. Jennifer N Stinson, Lindsay A Jibb, Cynthia Nguyen, Paul C Nathan, Anne Marie Maloney, L Lee Dupuis, J Ted Gerstle, Benjamin Alman, Sevan Hopyan, Caron Strahlendorf, and others. 2013. Development and testing of a multidimensional iPhone pain assessment application for adolescents with cancer. *Journal of Medical Internet Research* 15, 3 (2013), e51.

66. Jennifer N Stinson, Tricia Kavanagh, Janet Yamada, Navreet Gill, and Bonnie Stevens. 2006. Systematic review of the psychometric properties, interpretability and feasibility of self-report pain intensity measures for use in clinical trials in children and adolescents. *Pain* 125, 1 (2006), 143–157.

67. Arthur A Stone and Joan E Broderick. 2007. Real-Time Data Collection for Pain: Appraisal and Current Status. *Pain Medicine* 8, s3 (2007), S85–S93.

68. Arthur A Stone, Ronald C Kessler, and Jennifer A Haythomthwatte. 1991. Measuring daily events and experiences: Decisions for the researcher. *Journal of personality* 59, 3 (1991), 575–607.

69. Silvia Torsi, Nasrin Nasr, Peter C Wright, Sue J Mawson, and Gail A Mountain. 2009. User-centered design for supporting the self-management of chronic illnesses: an interdisciplinary approach. In *Proceedings of the 2nd International Conference on Pervasive Technologies Related to Assistive Environments.* ACM, 43.

70. Roger Tourangeau, Lance J Rips, and Kenneth Rasinski. 2000. *The psychology of survey response.* Cambridge University Press.

71. Dennis C Turk and Ronald Melzack. 2011. *Handbook of pain assessment.* Guilford Press.

72. Catherine E Vanderboom, Ann Vincent, Connie A Luedtke, Lori M Rhudy, and Kathryn H Bowles. 2014. Feasibility of interactive technology for symptom monitoring in patients with fibromyalgia. *Pain Management Nursing* 15, 3 (2014), 557–564.

73. David L Vannette and Jon A Krosnick. 2014. A Comparison of Survey Satisficing and Mindlessness. *The Wiley Blackwell Handbook of Mindfulness* (2014), 312.

74. Jeanine A Verbunt, Ivan PJ Huijnen, and Henk AM Seelen. 2012. Assessment of physical activity by movement registration systems in chronic pain: methodological considerations. *The Clinical Journal of Pain* 28, 6 (2012), 496–504.

75. Theo Vos, Ryan M Barber, Brad Bell, Amelia Bertozzi-Villa, Stan Biryukov, Ian Bolliger, Fiona Charlson, Adrian Davis, Louisa Degenhardt, Daniel Dicker, and others. 2015. Global, regional, and national incidence, prevalence, and years lived with disability for 301 acute and chronic diseases and injuries in 188 countries, 1990–2013: a systematic analysis for the Global Burden of Disease Study 2013. *The Lancet* 386, 9995 (2015), 743–800.

76. JM Woodfore and H Merskey. 1971. Correlation between verbal scale and visual analogue scale and pressure algometer. *J. Psychosom. Res.* 16 (1971), 173–178.

77. Jarred Younger, Rebecca McCue, and Sean Mackey. 2009. Pain outcomes: a brief review of instruments and techniques. *Current pain and headache reports* 13, 1 (2009), 39–43.

# Supporting Self-Care of Adolescents with Nut Allergy Through Video and Mobile Educational Tools

Neil Davidson[1, 2, 3], John Vines[4], Tom Bartindale[1], Selina Sutton[4], David Green[4], Rob Comber[1], Madeline Balaam[1], Patrick Olivier[1], Gillian Vance[2, 3]

[1] Open Lab, Newcastle University, Newcastle upon Tyne, UK, neil.davidson@ncl.ac.uk
[2] School of Medical Education, Newcastle University, Newcastle upon Tyne, UK
[3] Great North Children's Hospital, Newcastle upon Tyne, UK
[4] Northumbria University, Newcastle upon Tyne, UK

## ABSTRACT

Anaphylaxis is a life-threatening allergic reaction which is rapid in onset. Adolescents living with anaphylaxis risk often lack the knowledge and skills required to safely manage their condition or talk to friends about it. We designed an educational intervention comprising group discussion around videos of simulated anaphylaxis scenarios and a mobile application containing video-based branching anaphylaxis narratives. We trialed the intervention with 36 nut allergic adolescents. At 1-year follow-up participants had improved adrenaline auto-injector skills and carriage, disease- and age-specific Quality of Life and confidence in anaphylaxis management. At 3-year follow-up adrenaline carriage improved further and confidence remained higher. Participants expressed how the education session was a turning point in taking control of their allergy and how the app facilitated sharing about anaphylaxis with others. We contribute insights regarding design of mobile self-care and peer-support applications for health in adolescence, and discuss strengths and limitations of video-based mobile health interventions.

### Author Keywords

Adolescents; anaphylaxis; health; food allergy; patient education; mixed methods; video; mobile health.

### ACM Classification Keywords

J.3. Life and Medical Sciences: Health; H.5.m. Information interfaces and presentation (e.g., HCI): Miscellaneous;

## INTRODUCTION

Food allergy occurs when the immune system responds to food inappropriately and causes adverse health effects [60]. Food allergy is common, with almost 6% of Europeans reporting that they are allergic to one or more foodstuffs (half of these have convincing symptoms and test results) [43]. Symptoms of food allergy can include tingling of the mouth, rashes, swelling and more severe reactions. Anaphylaxis is a severe, potentially life-threatening allergic reaction that is rapid in onset and may cause death through airway, breathing or cardiovascular collapse [42]. Anaphylaxis prevalence is estimated at 0.3% in Europe [49] and up to 1.6% in the US [75], suggesting over 2 million Europeans and 5 million Americans are affected. Rates of anaphylaxis are increasing, with a 615% rise in hospital admissions for anaphylaxis in the United Kingdom over a 20-year period. Fatal food-triggered reactions peak in the second and third decades of life [68]. Those living with anaphylaxis risk must vigilantly avoid triggers to a severe reaction (allergens) [20], but accidental exposures may occur [44]. Prompt and effective administration of adrenaline using an auto-injector device is a key step in management of reactions [56]. However, gaps in the education and self-care of those living with anaphylaxis can lead to reactions and, in the severest of cases, death, with adolescents at particular risk [10, 42].

In recent years there has been a surge in interest in the potential for mobile applications to support people in the management of health conditions [1, 8, 28]. This has been equally so for food allergy, with prior work exploring apps to support food journaling practices [5, 14], meal decision making [32] and to identify allergen friendly eateries [26]. However, little research has addressed the role of technology as a preventative and educational measure for those with food allergy. Research in this space is even sparser in relation to adolescence, which is surprising given the specific risks of this age group [10, 54]. As such, with increasing ownership of smartphones among this age group [45, 47], mobile interventions could play an important role as part of educational programmes and self-care practices.

In this paper we report on the evaluation of React, an educational intervention that was part group session, part mobile application. React used video-based anaphylaxis narratives to illustrate to young people that different self-management choices may have different consequences. We conducted a study of React with 36 nut allergic adolescents, each of whom participated in an initial group session and were provided the React mobile application to use in their


CHI 2017, May 06-11, 2017, Denver, CO, USA
ACM 978-1-4503-4655-9/17/05.
http://dx.doi.org/10.1145/3025453.3025680

daily lives. We conducted pre and post (at 3-4 and 12 month) measures for quality of life, anaphylaxis knowledge and skills in the use of auto-injector devices. Additionally, we conducted pre and post measures of confidence around allergy management and carriage of auto-injectors (at 3-4, 12 and 36 months). We conducted focus groups (at 30 months) and individual interviews (at 37 months). We offer two contributions to HCI research. First, we highlight the potential that mobile educational packages have for improving self-care and management around potentially life-threatening health conditions. Second, we demonstrate how video can be used as a tool for reinforcing age-appropriate education for adolescents with chronic illnesses which, when combined with mobile platforms, can support the sharing of knowledge with peers to support healthy practices.

## BACKGROUND

The World Health Organization defines adolescence as the period between childhood and adulthood, from 10 to 19 years of age [76]. Adolescence is a critical phase in human development, characterised by rapid growth, biological and psychosocial changes [76]. Outcomes for long-term health conditions are poorer in adolescence than in childhood and adolescents are high users of health services [17, 73]. Self-management behaviours for long-term conditions are largely initiated during adolescence [58]. Individuals take over management of such conditions from their parents during adolescence and there is evidence that patterns of health behaviours established during adolescence are maintained through adult life [55]. Adolescence is thus an important period to influence the trajectories of health conditions throughout later life [17]. However, adolescents remain an unusually under-researched population in healthcare and age-appropriate services remain lacking [17, 55].

Food allergy affects an estimated 2.3% of adolescents, with peanut and tree nuts the most frequent triggers [51]. A recent estimate [72] suggests that there are now over 11 times more anaphylaxis episodes reported in adolescents than there were in the 1990s [20]. Living with food allergy and anaphylaxis risk has a profound impact on the quality of life and psychological distress of adolescents [4, 15]. The need to be constantly aware of avoiding triggering foodstuffs impacts on daily life and activities. Emotional quality of life [21, 52] and quality of school life [36] are also known to be adversely affected, with food allergic schoolchildren twice as likely to be bullied as their non-allergic peers [41].

The health and care literature notes important self-care strategies for adolescents who have nut allergy and who are at risk of anaphylaxis. Diligent avoidance of the nuts (and other triggers) that they are allergic to is the first stage of avoiding a reaction. However, nuts are frequently found in foods that are consumed socially and inadvertent exposure can occur [44]. In the event of an allergic reaction it is essential that an individual promptly identifies that they are having a reaction, how severe that reaction is and what treatment is most appropriate. Mild reactions are treated with antihistamines; symptoms of wheeze or shortness of breath require inhaled bronchodilators; whereas severe symptoms suggestive of anaphylaxis require prompt administration of adrenaline via an auto-injector device. These steps of avoidance, recognition of and response to reactions formed the basis of the educational package described herein.

However, evidence suggests that adolescents at risk of anaphylaxis are not adequately equipped to follow these self-care steps. Gallagher et al. highlighted that, despite receiving training by allergy specialists in clinic, adolescents remain inadequately prepared for anaphylaxis emergencies [24]. Issues included adolescents not carrying adrenaline at all times; failing to identify anaphylactic reactions; not knowing when to use adrenaline and inability to demonstrate correct administration of adrenaline [24]. It is of note that similar issues are found to be causes of deaths from anaphylactic reactions (e.g. adrenaline used too late in reaction; adrenaline not carried at time of reaction) [10, 54]. Monks et al. observed that adolescents demonstrate risk-taking behaviour when managing food allergies, which may contribute to their increased anaphylaxis mortality [38]. Such behaviours included intentional consumption of food that may have contained their triggering allergens and non-carriage of adrenaline. Additionally, Monks et al. describe how adolescents wish that their classmates and peers were more aware or educated about their allergies, as this would make allergy management simpler and risk taking less likely. The adolescent participants also felt that education that was frank about the consequences of a reaction would be helpful, perhaps using films of what happens during a reaction.

Given these challenges, effective educational strategies are required to address this population's gaps in self-care skills and behaviours and to potentially improve their quality of life. Kirk et al. reviewed self-care interventions for children and young people with a variety of chronic health conditions and reported that interventions that were group-based or involved technology were associated with improved knowledge and well-being [34]. Jones et al. demonstrated a correlation between good adherence to self-care behaviours and having a written anaphylaxis management plan or being a member of a patient support group [33]. However, only 41% of Jones' cohort reported carrying their adrenaline auto-injector at all times. While further interventions have been trialled, they target parents and carers of affected children or adults with allergies, not affected adolescents [12, 61, 70].

Thus, adolescents living with anaphylaxis risk often lack the knowledge and skills to safely manage their condition. This is a crucial time in their development, as they transition from parental control to self-care. Current education is inadequate and interventions target parents of children with allergies or adults living with anaphylaxis risk, but not adolescents themselves. Our research aims to address this gap.

### Mobile Health and Allergy in HCI

Smartphone and mobile application use among teenagers and young adults has grown rapidly in western countries, now reaching 85% in the US [45] and 90% in the UK [48]. The general proliferation in ownership of smartphones has been accompanied by interest in supporting the health of users through apps targeting specific conditions and care practices [1, 8, 28]. This provides an opportunity to explore how mobile-based interventions could be used to deliver health education and self-care support to young people with chronic health conditions [65, 74]. Indeed, young people use health information websites, social media and health apps as important sources of information and these have potential to modify their health behaviours [39, 62]. The short-term utility of mobile apps in clinical management has been demonstrated for adolescents with health conditions such as diabetes, with gamification of blood glucose measurements leading to improved frequency of measurements [13] and photo-based food diaries helping young people to better visualize important self-care strategies [23]. Similarly, there is great potential for mobile technology to support positive self-care behaviours in those living with anaphylaxis risk. However, regulators and clinicians require such technology to deliver lasting clinical benefit [35] and evidence is lacking for the long-term impact of many health applications [1, 28].

In the specific area of food allergy there is prior work exploring the role technology may play in a number of contexts. Prototype apps and models have been proposed to detect and warn users about the risk of ingesting foods that they are allergic to using situation awareness [18]; to assist those with dietary restrictions make safe meal choices [32]; and to match user's requirements to suitable restaurants [16]. Such automated systems could potentially alleviate some of the burden of constant vigilance that those with severe allergies live with, however, these systems have not yet led to consumer products and have not been trialled in real-world settings by people with allergies. Others have examined the potential of smartphone-based food diaries, demonstrating they can make it easier to capture what users or their children eat [14, 30] and to aid in the diagnosis of food allergy [5, 69]. One important design insight from such work is that it is crucial that such technology is simple to use and does not become an additional burden to families and individuals already living with considerable stress due to their allergies [30]. The "Anaphylaxis" app was developed by Anderson et al. and constitutes a digital version of a written anaphylaxis management plan [2]. Users enter details of their allergies and medication and the app contains written information about anaphylaxis symptoms and emergency response. Finally, Garbett et al. describe the NutFree app in one of the case studies of their App Movement paper [26]. Developed with people living with allergies, NutFree supports users in both searching for and providing their own location-based reviews of the nut allergy friendliness of restaurants. However, while all of these offer great potential, there has been no testing of implementation of these apps or assessment of their effectiveness. Furthermore, none of these explicitly address issues related to educational support.

### Video as an Educational and Support Tool

Compared with other educational media, interventions using video have been shown to be effective at modifying health behaviours, particularly when focusing on what can be gained from complying with recommended self-care [67]. Interactivity in video-based learning can enhance the learning experience [19]. Video has been shown to enhance knowledge and promote improved self-care in health fields as diverse as sunscreen use [6]; treatment decision making in skin cancer [37]; and sexually transmitted disease and attitudes towards condoms [9]. In particular, Armstrong highlights that video-based learning is more effective than written materials and may be particularly useful for learning new concepts or practical techniques [6]. There are no published video-based interventions for adolescents with allergy. Previous work has identified that adolescents do not find written information as helpful as others do [25]. Video may offer an age-appropriate solution to this. Video has been used in interaction design with adolescents to empower young people to participate in HCI research and as a means of accessing adolescents' everyday lives [53]. Other work has shown that video (health vlogs) can help develop social support for those with chronic diseases through intimate personal connection and the flexibility of the medium [31].

### Summary

Despite the work to date in health, care and HCI literature, there are still no interventions described in the field of allergy that demonstrate long-term impact on the knowledge, skills or self-care behaviours of those living with anaphylaxis—either in general, or adolescents in particular. Video and mobile technology have the potential to address gaps in both the literature and in the care of these young people.

## DESIGNING THE REACT INTERVENTION

In this research we were interested in exploring novel education for adolescents with nut allergy who were living with the risk of anaphylaxis. Our design process involved an interdisciplinary team including a consultant paediatric allergist; a paediatrician with interests in allergy and adolescent health, a team of interaction design researchers (one of whom lives with severe nut allergy) and film makers.

The Health Belief Model suggests that to effect change we must ensure that individuals recognise that they are susceptible to a health problem which is serious (perceived threat) and believe that there is a benefit to following a particular course of action (outweighing any barriers) that will reduce the perceived threat [57]. This model was used in the development of the intervention.

Drawing on the evidence presented above, personal and clinical experience, we developed a two-stage intervention involving: (i) a short peer group education session in which videos of simulated anaphylaxis scenarios would be shown to prompt discussion; and (ii) a smartphone application to continue providing education beyond the single session and share information with participants' friends and families.

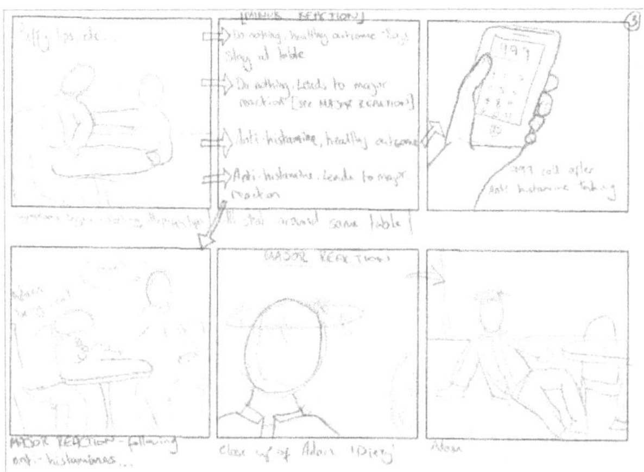

**Figure 1 – An example storyboard from the development of the anaphylaxis scenario videos, demonstrating decision points and branching outcomes (indicated by arrows).**

### Videos of Simulated Anaphylactic Reactions

The anaphylaxis scenarios reflect likely situations in which young people might be inadvertently exposed to nuts, involving the consumption of food in social settings (perceived threat). Two scenarios were scripted for friends going to the cinema and to a café. In each scenario the young person experiencing an anaphylactic reaction was uncertain how to manage the reaction and their friend was a supportive influence, showing concern and prompting them to use appropriate treatment. Scripts were designed to offer narrative branch points at which decisions made by the protagonists would lead to different outcomes (e.g. recognizing reaction was severe or not; using antihistamine treatment or adrenaline treatment) (see Figure 1).

Once completed, the scripts were filmed using young actors from a local theatre company. All possible permutations of each scenario were filmed so that an interactive branching narrative could be created. Videos were then overlaid with animations illustrating symptoms that young people watching the videos should watch out for (e.g. dizziness, shortness of breath) and treatment steps (e.g. correct way to hold adrenaline auto-injector and site to administer it). These animations were designed in a comic book style that matched the style used in the React app (see Figure 2). Practical steps were highlighted and ideal behaviour modelled to help participants acquire skills effectively [6]. Positive outcomes from successful management were emphasised to focus on potential gains from appropriate action [57, 67].

### Education Session

The education session was designed around the three critical stages of anaphylaxis self-care: (i) avoidance of allergens, (ii) recognition of allergic reaction and its severity, and (iii) appropriate response to reactions. The education session was designed to be practical to deliver within a single 90-minute session. Throughout the session we encouraged peer interaction and the sharing of personal experiences. While waiting for the session to start, participants completed an ice-breaker activity in which they matched pictures of nuts with their names and shared answers with each other. The React

**Figure 2 – React videos of simulated anaphylaxis scenarios were overlaid with animations to highlight symptoms (e.g. dizziness) and treatment steps (e.g. correct was to hold adrenaline auto-injector and correct delivery)**

videos were then shown to the group, using scenarios in which the protagonists made mistakes in reaction management. These were used as discussion prompts and again, peer interaction was encouraged. The group were then shown alternative sequences of video in which correct management decisions were made. Subsequently, the group split into 3 and rotated through 3 tasks: (i) nut recognition (food packaging and social situations), (ii) reaction severity and response (including hands-on practice with trainer auto-injector devices), and (iii) an introduction to the React app (encouraged to access app and shown features). The session closed with a check of participants' knowledge and skills.

### Mobile Application

React is a web-based app, compatible with any mobile device with Internet connectivity (i.e. smartphone or tablet). The app is comprised of four main components:

1) 'Start a Story' mode incorporates the anaphylaxis scenario videos within an interactive decision-making tool. Choices made by users determine the outcome of each scenario and include recognition of the severity of the reaction and specific steps in auto-injector use. The narrative branches depending on user choice, leading to numerous potential outcomes. Following the Health Belief Model [57], the branching narrative aims to enhance adolescents' understanding of clues to the severity of a reaction. By selecting different options on repeated progress through scenarios, users see which actions have beneficial outcomes.

2) 'How to use Auto injector' mode, contains training video and animations for different adrenaline devices.

3) 'About Me' page, to record allergies and the type of adrenaline auto-injector device that they carry.

4) Users can share the app using an app-generated Quick Response Code. This provides a "friend" version of React

**Figure 3 – The React mobile application enables the user to record details about their allergies and share the app with friends and family members using a QR code.**

containing the sharing user's allergy and auto-injector information (see Figure 3), as well as the first two components so that friends and family members can become similarly skilled in recognition and response to reactions.

## FIELD TRIAL

This was a single centre, pre- post-intervention study with long-term follow-up employing quantitative and qualitative methods. Participants were recruited from a paediatric allergy clinic in the UK between November 2012 and July 2013. Participants were aged 11-16 years at recruitment, had clinician-diagnosed peanut and/or tree nut allergy and were prescribed an adrenaline auto-injector for use in the event of anaphylaxis. Participants (and parents/guardians if under 16) gave informed consent to take part in the study. Favourable opinions were received from Research Ethics Committees for both the quantitative and qualitative phases of the study.

### Educational Intervention

Participants attended the education session in groups of up to 9. Participants were free to choose whether to continue to use the React app or not after the education session.

### Quantitative Assessment Measures

A number of measures (anaphylaxis knowledge, auto-injector skill and carriage, disease- and age-specific quality of life and confidence in anaphylaxis management) were made at baseline and at follow-up appointments at 3-4 (FU1) and 12 months (FU2) after the education session. Knowledge and skill were also measured at the end of the education session. Confidence and auto-injector carriage were additionally measured during a survey (postal and electronic) sent to participants 36 months after the intervention.

Anaphylaxis knowledge was assessed using a validated 15-item quiz [61]. Questions related to self-care strategies, recognition of reactions and correct management steps. There were 3 auto-injector devices available to participants at the time of the study (EpiPen®, EpiPen® II (Meda), Jext® (ALK-Abelló)). Auto-injector skill was measured for each device using 7-item checklists based on manufacturers' guidelines on correct device usage. Correct auto-injector administration required: (i) device recognition; (ii) removal of safety cap; (iii) selection of correct injection site; (iv) selection of correct end of device for injection; (v) use of correct injection technique; (vi) holding device in place for ≥10 seconds; and (vii) massaging injection site for ≥10 seconds. Disease- and age-specific quality of life was measured using the validated Food Allergy Quality of Life Questionnaire-Teenager Form (FAQLQ-TF) [22]. This assesses the impact of food allergy on quality of life across three subscales: Allergen Avoidance and Dietary Restriction, Emotional Impact (of food allergy on their quality of life) and Risk of Accidental Exposure. FAQLQ-TF scores range from 1 (minimal impairment in quality of life) to 7 (maximal impairment) [71]. Confidence in anaphylaxis management was rated on a 5-point (140mm) Likert scale. Participants were asked to rate "How confident do you feel about managing a severe allergic reaction (anaphylaxis)?" Self-reported adrenaline auto-injector carriage was reported as "always", "often", "occasionally" or "never".

### Qualitative methods

Questionnaires were completed at FU1 and FU2 including free text responses about auto-injector carriage and app use. Focus groups (FG) were held with participants 30 months after the education session. Purposeful sampling [50] was used to hold one group with those that had identified themselves as React app users at 12-month follow-up and the other with those who did not. Groups had 4 participants in each, lasted 60-90 minutes [29] and explored participants' views about the education session and app and experiences of living with allergy. Initial data analysis assisted in the development of the survey (S) sent to participants at 36 months. The survey included questions about who was in control of their allergy and why; peer relationships and participants' reasons for non-carriage of adrenaline. Data from the survey and focus groups informed the development of an interview schedule. Semi-structured, in-depth interviews (I) were held with 3 participants to explore emerging themes in more depth, more broadly understand the lived experience of being an adolescent with nut allergy and design opportunities around this. Focus groups and interviews were audio recorded and transcribed for analysis.

### Analysis

Paired t-tests were used to compare changes over time within groups and un-paired t-tests to compare differences between groups (continuous variables and scale data [46]). Equivalent non-parametric tests (McNemar / chi-square) were used for categorical data. Data were analysed with SPSS v22. A value of $p<0.05$ was considered significant.

An inductive thematic analysis was conducted on qualitative data (treating the data as a single corpus), using methods described by Braun and Clarke [11]. Data was read and re-read before coding at the level of sentences to paragraphs (Nvivo v10). Codes were collapsed and modified before drawing out themes from the data.

### Participants

At recruitment there were 40 nut allergic adolescents (19 females), mean age 13.8 years (S.D. 1.5, range 11.1-16.4). Peanut allergy was reported by 34 (85%), tree nut allergy by 26 (65%) and other food allergies by 13 (32.5%). Mean age

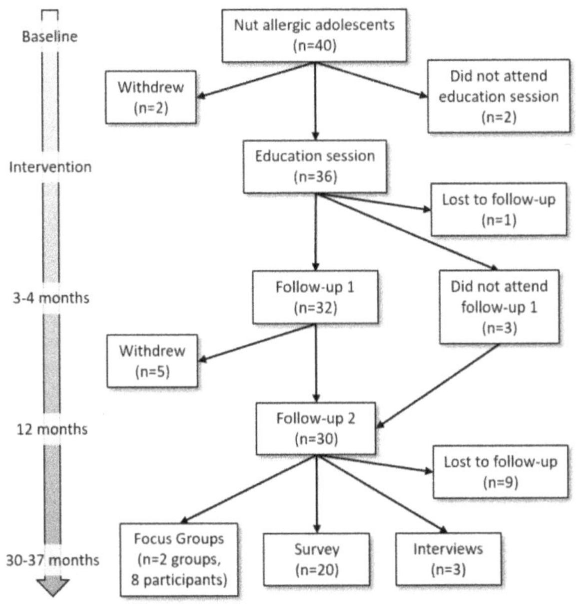


**Figure 4 – Flow of participants through study (2 participants withdrew after initial recruitment and a further 2 did not attend the education session).**

at first allergic reaction was 4.8 years (S.D. 3.6, range 0.3-12.0) and 20 (50%) reported a history of anaphylaxis. Figure 4 shows the movement of participants through the study.

## RESULTS

### Quantitative Findings

The mean knowledge scores of participants increased after the education session (10.2 (S.D. 2.3) to 11.8 (1.9), t=-4.65, p<0.001), but fell by FU2 at 12 months, with no significant change from baseline (10.8 (2.2), t=1.21, p=0.234).

At baseline only 4/40 (10%) participants completed all 7 steps of auto-injector deployment correctly. Mean auto-injector skill score rose after the education session (5.2 (1.0) to 6.3 (0.8), t=-5.29, p<0.001) and more completed all 7 steps correctly (20/36 (55.6%), p<0.001). Mean skill score fell by FU2, but remained significantly better than baseline (5.7 (0.9), t=-2.19, p=0.037) and 7/30 completed all 7 deployment steps correctly (17.5%).

There was an improvement in quality of life, as shown by a fall in the mean FAQLQ-TF scores of the participants by FU2 (4.2 (1.5) to 3.7 (1.3), t=2.25, p=0.033). The Emotional Impact subscale showing the largest improvement (4.4 (1.3) to 3.8 (1.1), t=2.57, p=0.015).

Confidence of the participants rose after the education session (71.2 (35.7) to 116.8 (23.6), t=-8.03, p<0.001) and remained up compared with baseline at all subsequent time points, including 36-month follow-up (75.0 (35.8) to 103.3 (28.9), t=-3.38, p=0.003).

At baseline, 5 participants had been prescribed their auto-injector for the first time, so could not comment on their carriage of the device. Of the remaining 35, 4 (11.4%) reported carrying their devices "always", 14 (40.0%)

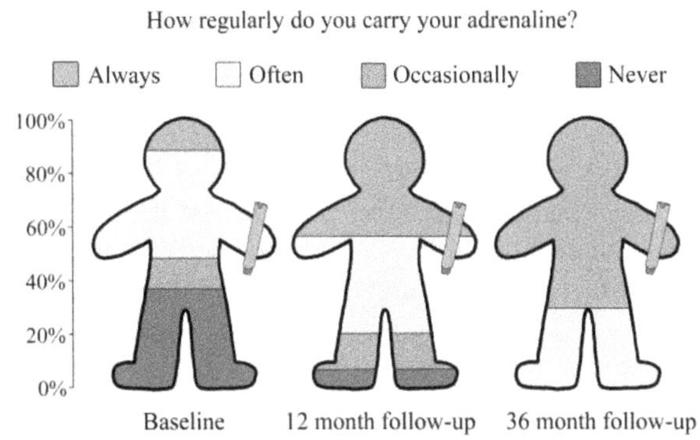


**Figure 5 – Adrenaline auto-injector carriage over the study period. Half of the participants reported carrying their device occasionally or never at baseline, with only 11% reporting always carrying it. At 3 years after the education session 70% reported carrying it at all times (p<0.001).**

"often", 4 (11.4%) "occasionally" and 13 (37.1%) "never" (see Figure 5). Over the course of the study the proportion of participants carrying their device "always" increased from 4/35 (11.4%) to 14/20 (70%, p<0.001).

#### *The React App*

At FU2, 14 of the 30 participants reported using the React app (46.7%), 10/14 (71.4%) reported that the app was helpful and 11/14 (78.6%) completed the survey at 36 months. Analytic data was limited but indicated the app had been accessed 196 times in the local region by 52 unique users by 12-month follow-up. The extra users may have been those with whom the participants had shared the app. At FU2 app users had better knowledge scores than non-users (users 11.7 (1.6), non-users 10.0 (2.4), t=2.29, p=0.030). Confidence in anaphylaxis management was greater in app users than non-users at the 36-month survey (users 114.6 (22.6), non-users 89.4 (30.9), t=2.10, p=0.050).

### Qualitative Findings

Four overriding themes were identified from the qualitative analysis: *taking control*; *individual and shared experiences; educating others; and risk taking and forgetfulness.*

#### *Taking Control*

Participants frequently discussed aspects of control related to allergy. Most explained that they felt responsible for being vigilant about potential nut exposures. Checking food they ate was free from nuts was a large part of the burden of living with nut allergy: *"I'm always checking, even though some things definitely don't have nuts in I will still want to check."* (P37, S). Participants were often reluctant to allow others to manage this aspect of living with allergy for them, trusting their own skills over even their parents: *"Even family and parents try and do it to me and it still ticks me off. At the end of the day, I will have to read it anyway. I won't feel safe until I've read it."* (P04, I).

Critically important to these young people was that they were experiencing a taking over of control of the management of their condition from their parents. Some shared control over their allergies with their parents and were happy to surrender control to them in particular settings:

*"Over the years it's got more and more my responsibility. I think it's just slowly happened without us even realising that it's happened."* (P21, I)

*"If I'm alone, for example going out with my friends, I have sole responsibility but at home my parents watch what I eat."* (P14, S)

It was clear that this was a two-way process. Parents needed to feel that their child was both competent enough and confident enough to take over control from them:

*"I think my parents mostly [ask about nuts in restaurants], but sometimes they say, 'Oh, you ask, because you need to get the confidence of when you're out on your own to say.'"* (P14, FG)

*"My mum used to nag me quite a lot about making sure I was carrying an Epipen with me [...] but now I'm a bit more independent."* (P31, FG)

Notably, at follow-ups many participants reported that the educational intervention was a turning point for them in them taking control over from their parents. This was, in part, due to it giving them an increased sense of confidence in their knowledge and skills. For example, they found the React videos and app helped sensitise them to potentially risky situations: *"the app was helpful in seeing a potentially real life situation wherein an allergic reaction could occur."* (P09, S). But it was also partly due to their parents feeling that they were better able to self-care:

*"It might actually partially have been due to this [the study], the fact that they know I've been learning about it, and so [my parents] trust me to do more with it, instead of just them having to do that."* (P33, FG)

*"I knew roughly what to do beforehand because it's got it on the Epipen but [the education session] just made me be like, 'Right, okay, I've got this.'"* (P21, I)

The app's branching videos enhanced users' decision-making ability through reflecting on and testing choices in different situations: *"I like the scenarios it gave you and made you decide what to do in certain situations."* (P05, FU1). *"[The app] was good because it taught you what to do."* (P11, FU1). The usefulness of the intervention even led to one participant describing how it had helped her to remotely assist a friend safely through managing their own allergic reaction:

*"[My friend] had a reaction. He was messaging saying, 'I don't know what to do.' And I actually talked him through what to do, and it really helped him. I think that without [the intervention], I wouldn't have had the knowledge of what to do."* (P37, FG).

The process of taking control of one's self-care from parents is a critical transition in growing up with nut allergy. Our participants were given confidence in their own knowledge and skills through this educational package, which seems to have given their parents the green light to let their children take over the day-to-day management of their allergy.

### Individual and Shared Experiences

Although many participants found the overall intervention helpful, some contested that a "generic" app and series of videos, could not capture the diversity and personal nature of allergies and reactions: *"I think [the videos] were sort of a bit stereotypical, like, of what definitely would happen, because anyone's reaction could be so different."* (P14, FG).

In part, however, it appeared that the concerns around the individualization of allergy was a result of a lack of contact with other people with allergies. Indeed, despite nut allergy being common, the intervention had been the first time many participants had discussed allergies with peers who also had allergies. Prior to this, participants had perceived themselves as isolated or alone and found discussing their issues with those their own age helpful:

*"I remember the videos the most. But I think the best thing was [...] seeing other people the same age as me with allergies because a lot of the time what I find difficult with my allergy is when I'm in public I feel like people won't understand [...] But when I realised there's lots of other people with the allergies it makes me feel a bit more confident about telling people."* (P31, FG)

*"We were with like people of similar age groups who also had similar problems involved in at the same time, it helped me remember a lot more."* (P22, FG)

*"It was better with other people the same sort of age. I think it's easier to remember it when you learn it with other people who are similar to you, than it is when you're [...] one-to-one being shown what to do."* (P33, FG)

During the group sessions the sense that nut allergy was unique to each individual started to break down as participants shared stories and personal experiences. There were a number of specific points of commonality. For example, eating out of the family home was a great source of anxiety and frustration for most participants:

*"I really don't enjoy going to [new restaurants] [...] I'll ask them, 'What can I eat?' and they'll say, 'We can't guarantee,' because that's what most places say [...] I just stay, like, perpetually really uncomfortable and nervous throughout the entire meal. I'm like, 'What if there's peanuts in something someone's eating? What if they're too close to me? What if it makes me sick? What if I start having a severe reaction to it?'"* (P04, I)

Feeling isolated from peers who did not have nut allergy was common, particularly when socialising around food: *"Everyone has a Chinese Thursday and I'm like, 'Okay, I'll just go to Greggs.'* (P21, I). *"One of the annoyances is the smug looks from your friends when they've got a cake and you don't."* (P33, FG). A further point of commonality across the participants related to problems they faced explaining their allergies to their peers. At one end of the spectrum, participants felt their non-allergic peers did not take their allergies seriously or appreciate the risks they lived with on a daily basis:

*"Half the people in the class don't believe that I could have such a severe allergic reaction. They just think I'm lying."* (P07, FG)

*"I've read so many stories of people dying purely because they were too sick to take their adrenaline and no one around them knew how to do it. [...] [Allergy is] this massive, massive thing that makes you really isolated from other people."* (P04, I)

At the other end of the spectrum participants reported being bullied, sometimes dangerously so, for having allergies:

*"I have a friend who is also allergic to nuts and jokingly one of my friends was eating nuts that he was allergic to [...] He was eating them and one of my friends took one and ran off and apparently he gave it to an upper 6th member and told him to put it down his back [...] So he went over and put it down his back [...] people don't really understand how serious things like that can be."* (P22, FG)

While stories like this were more extreme, feelings of being isolated from those who do not understand the daily anxieties of living with severe food allergy were common and clearly felt as a great burden for many participants. However, in having an unusual opportunity to meet with others with common experience they were able to exchange such stories, seek solace in one-another and share strategies for managing their condition and dealing with peer and family attitudes.

### Educating Others

A protective factor against the sorts of misunderstandings and deliberate attacks described above was having a supportive peer network. Several participants described the comfort they drew from understanding friends and people around them who knew what to do in the event of a reaction:

*"I know a lot of my friends, when they found out I had an allergy they've gone out and researched it and looked into it and stuff like that because, you know, they wanted to know what they could and couldn't do. My partner [...] Googled it and he was like, 'Is it safe to eat peanuts if my girlfriend's allergic to them?' The general consensus was 'no' so he's just stopped eating them."* (P04, I)

*"I had one friend a while ago [...] I taught him [about anaphylaxis] [...] we went to the cinema a few years ago, and pretty much the first thing he did when we got there was say, 'I just want to check. What do I do if you have a reaction of some kind?'"* (P33, FG)

However, telling friends about anaphylaxis did not come easily to all. Many felt their friends were not as well-informed as they should be. It was felt that it *"takes a lot of effort to teach all my friends. Some of my friends know how to use the injector though."* (P01, S). Another noted that their friends *"know the basics but probably forgot the technicalities"* (P07, S). In response to these issues, several participants expressed that the React app had been a useful tool to help them share about anaphylaxis with their peers and had facilitated the development of these protective support networks: *"The React app was easy to use and understand, it was an easier way of teaching my friends."* (P10, S). Others went on to explain:

*"I think it was good how it had videos of a live anaphylactic shock, so [...] if you didn't know what you were doing, you could see how to deal with it in different scenarios."* (P37, FG)

*"It was good that it helped me explain to people how to use my EpiPen [...] You'll be like, 'You don't need to take someone's trousers off.' for instance. They don't believe me. They think that I'm just being shy or something. [...] having an actual official looking app that told them you don't need to take people's pants off, that helped [...] I feel like people trust an application more than they trust me, which sounds really bad but it's true."* (P04, I)

Participants explained they would use the videos on the app as a way of visually talking through with their friends how to recognise a reaction, how to use an auto-injector device and then informally 'test' them on this knowledge. Often, this was done by showing them the videos via the participants' mobile phone. However, some participants referred to the sharable design of the React app and how this was valued as then friends could take this "knowledge" with them:

*"React was easy to share with people [...] they all had like their phones and like QR Readers on it so they're, 'Oh, we'll have a look.' [...] Check it every now and again so they could remind themselves [...] it's like easier than having to carry like the training [auto-injector] round and saying, 'This is what you have to do with it.' It would be a bit easier for them to be able to see like on their phones what they have to do."* (P15, FG)

Though a difficult process for many, building a supportive peer network is very important for adolescents living with nut allergy. Our education package gave participants tools to share important messages about their condition with their peers. The app in particular was a source of portable information that friends would trust and use to learn about their condition, with video an important component of this.

### Risk Taking and Forgetfulness

Participants reported that living risk free with nut allergy was not possible, or perhaps even desirable. Managing risk was a cornerstone of day-to-day life with allergy. Indeed, despite going through the educational intervention (and with many continuing to occasionally access the app), participants explained how they would engage in risk taking behaviours, such as deliberately not always carrying their adrenaline. One reported that in the past she had done this out of a need to reject her auto-injector as a talisman of her allergy:

*"I was, you know, 'I'm super independent. I want to go out on my own, I don't want to take my EpiPen with me because I'm sick to death of the sight of it.' [...] Luckily, the few times I managed to get out the house without it, I did not have a reaction and die."* (P04, I)

However, for most there was a considered risk assessment into whether they felt there was a need to carry their adrenaline for a particular situation and whether this outweighed the inconvenience of having to carry the device:

*"Yes. Occasionally, like if I'm going to a friend's house, I might trust them and I know they're not going to give me something that they know would be bad, then I might leave it at home."* (P33, FG)

Participants also described managed risk taking when it came to deciding whether or not to consume certain products. They explained that if one was to refuse to eat anything that packaging suggested "may contain nuts" then that would result in a severely restricted diet and was not necessary:

*"It's not really risking it, but I'll normally eat stuff if it says, 'may contain traces of nuts' [...] if it says something like 'may contain traces of peanuts' or if it's got peanuts in it it's just like, 'Nope. Will not.'"* (P04, I)

*"Unless it specifically says 'peanuts', then the likelihood is I'll eat it."* (P14, FG)

Participants described the React app as a safe place to explore risk taking and the outcomes of such behaviour: *"Tried getting [the app scenarios] wrong a few times just to see."* (P09, FU2). While these examples highlight situations where participants explicitly engaged in risk taking, there was also an admission by many that they often just forgot to take their adrenaline devices with them. This included when going out with friends, or going to school or college, situations that might include high risk of exposure to nuts:

*"I can count [...] the number of times this week I've gone out without it [...] I always forget."* (P15, FG)

*"I've forgotten it one or two times to school if I've swapped them round. If [...] I've swapped it into my weekend bag and I've then*

*forgotten to put it in my school bag on the way to school. Then I'm like, 'Don't come near me. Everyone stay away.'"* (P21, I)

However, participants found that *"[React was helpful] for refreshing my memory"* (P39, S) and the app was, *"a resource that you can turn to"* (P36, FU1). One participant remarked that the app *"helped remind me to bring my EpiPen."* (P22, FU2).

Managed risk taking is a feature of life with severe allergy for adolescents. Our education package helped the participants to feel informed about the risks that they face daily and to manage these risks safely. For those that used it, the app was an ever-present resource that could remind them of ideal self-management behaviours. However, there remain areas of risk that are unintentional, such as forgetting to carry their adrenaline auto-injectors. This highlights the need for systems to assist adolescents with remembering to carry their adrenaline, as education may not be enough to close this gap.

## DISCUSSION

This is, to our knowledge, the only field study of an educational intervention with adolescents living with the risk of anaphylaxis from nut allergy. Our findings demonstrate that our approach has long-lasting impact on the confidence and auto-injector carriage of this population. Additionally, those participants that reported using the React app had better anaphylaxis knowledge at 12 months and confidence at 36 months compared to baseline and to those who did not use the app. In the following we reflect on our findings and consider why the intervention, and the React app specifically, were so successful.

### Video-based Education and Sharing

Young people living with nut allergy must learn how to control their environment to protect themselves from nut exposure. However, not all adolescents can remember the last severe allergic reaction they had, as their last reaction may have been many years ago and parents are likely to keep the home as a protected environment. The React videos helped open their eyes to their susceptibility to a potentially severe condition [57] by showing them what a reaction might look like and how to respond appropriately to it. Repeated exposure to branching video-based narratives in the React app may have enhanced users' anaphylaxis knowledge by allowing them to see the outcomes of different management approaches, leading to better confidence. By framing the videos within peer group discussion we were able to encourage the young people to share personal experiences of living with allergy and helped them to see that there were others living with the same issues. Furthermore, the videos were engaging, memorable and, through the app, a convenient method of educating friends about anaphylaxis. Participants developed well-informed and supportive peer networks that understood the potential severity of anaphylaxis and were equipped to assist in an emergency.

### Reducing Burden Through Confidence and Networking

We know food allergy has a considerable effect on the quality of life of adolescents [4]. Adolescents with greater responsibility for self-care of their food allergy may have greater anxiety [3]. One concern on embarking on this project was that in the process of making participants more aware of their allergy we would negatively impact their psychological well-being. While our study did not measure anxiety directly, our participants' measured quality of life improved, they reported an improved sense of control over their allergy and better confidence in managing reactions. The quality of life improvement was most marked in the Emotional Impact subscale of the FAQLQ-TF (items relate to fear of consuming allergens, fear of reactions and the burden of carrying adrenaline). By increasing participants' belief in their own capabilities we may have improved their self-efficacy [7], reducing the emotional burden of their allergy. The Health Belief Model suggests that we may have assisted this change through participants better appreciating the risks of their illness and understanding ideal responses to reduce these risks [57]. It was also clear from our qualitative work that many of the participants felt better equipped to share the burden of their allergy with friends, using the app to demonstrate to them what an anaphylactic reaction looks like, how to use their auto-injector devices and through sharing their personal allergy information. Thus, the React app and their improved knowledge and skills, may also have contributed to the observed improvement in quality of life.

### Adrenaline Auto-injector Carriage

Unlike other described systems to support those living with allergies [16, 18, 32], React (and the associated education session) aimed to improve adolescents' ability to self-care by empowering them to make more informed risk assessments. As well as supporting feelings of greater awareness and self-care, our intervention improved carriage of auto-injectors. As noted, non-carriage of these devices is known to be a factor in deaths from anaphylaxis [10] and evidence shows that not just knowledge, but also perceived risk and confidence influence adolescents' decision making when deciding to carry adrenaline [33]. Few previous interventions have shown an improvement in auto-injector carriage [64], with previously described rates in adolescents of less than 50% "always" carrying their devices [33]. We have shown a highly significant improvement in participants' auto-injector carriage, which may be related to an increased sense of the need to carry it and a perceived reduction in the burden of doing so. However, some participants still forget to carry adrenaline. We do not think that the observed improvement in carriage is a natural part of growing older with allergy as other work suggests that <30% of at risk adults carry auto-injectors [63]. Other work by this study group (manuscript in review) suggests that similar adolescents not receiving our intervention do not show the same improvement in auto-injector carriage over time.

### Limitations

There are limitations to our work. The React videos did not resonate with all our participants and were unable to capture the full variety of anaphylaxis presentations and responses to treatment. By framing the videos within group discussion we were able to address some concerns, but this is not possible for the videos in the app. One solution would be to create videos with a wider variety of presentations. This would be time consuming, resource-intensive and potentially still leave challenges with resonance with personal experiences. The uptake of the app was just under 50% of those seen at 12-month follow-up. This was partly due to technical limitations of our approach. Some adolescents did not have mobile data plans so had to rely on Wi-Fi, which was not available in all situations. The web-based app allowed multiple brands of device to access it, but participants did not remember how to access it when changing phones or after a factory reset. Furthermore, there were a number of participants lost to follow-up over the course of the study, with just over 50% captured in the survey. It is possible that there is loss to follow-up bias, with those more likely to perform well more likely to continue study engagement. Additionally, compared with other work [40], we have a lack of detailed app usage analytics. This is partly due to ethical constraints but would need to be addressed in future work.

### Design Opportunities

While being overall successful, our findings also highlight a number of further opportunities for designing technology to support adolescents at risk of anaphylaxis, and young people living with chronic health conditions more generally.

First, our work highlights the potential for video-based educational interventions. Memorable video narratives that draw on literature, clinical and personal experience may have similar impact in conditions such as asthma and diabetes (where emergency treatment must be carried and used appropriately). The novel app-based branching narratives used in this work allowed participants to explore safely the outcomes of different self-management steps, reinforcing key messages and essential behaviours. However, we also saw how such video content can reproduce assumptive and stereotypical situations and experiences. One direction for future design work might therefore be to support the creation of user-generated videos and media that layer on top of videos like those produced for our intervention [59]. This might promote opportunities for young people to 'react' to videos, to share their own version of similar events, and scaffold wider diversity and multiplicity in the types of experiences represented in interventions like these.

Second, the React app contained a simple method of sharing with friends. By working through the anaphylaxis narratives on the app, participants could help their friends to explore how they could help them both day to day and in a crisis. Unlike, for example, an online support network, using the app to physically interact with those close to them helped our participants to build up local support networks of understanding and informed peers. This resonates with work by Glasemann et al. with young people living with diabetes [27], in which the authors suggest that mobile health technology may have a role in promoting a social learning experience. Further opportunity exists to explore how peer support may enhance self-care, using systems to share knowledge beyond the group education session [26]. As such, as recent work has highlighted [66], opportunities exist here to bridge the physical peer support group with those supported by online environments and mobile technologies. We might imagine these could be supported in ways particular to anaphylaxis. For example, to address issues about forgetting adrenaline auto-injectors, Bluetooth technology could be used to pair devices with their owner's smartphone and provide sensitive reminders to carry adrenaline to the phone or send prompts to the peer network, who could then encourage them to carry their device.

Finally, there are opportunities to empower adolescents with nut allergy to change not only their own behaviour but the attitudes and behaviour of the general public. Many of our participants reported how negative attitudes of others caused them distress or were, in the worst cases, endangering them. This cohort of young people are now experts in their own condition and it is important to explore how they could be supported to put pressure on the food industry (and the public in general) to be more considerate and considered in their approach to allergies. Tools like NutFree [26] are important here, but only if they support changes in environment and attitude towards those with these life-threatening conditions.

## CONCLUSIONS

Our research has shown that adolescents living with severe nut allergy can learn how to better self-care through a peer group-based intervention involving video narrative and a mobile application. This has had long-term effects that are likely to persist into adulthood and improve the safety of this population. Further work is needed to explore how adolescents can be empowered to harness supportive peer networks and influence general public and industry attitudes to severe allergies. Working with young people who live with the burden of anaphylaxis has shown us that this burden should be shared not only by families and friends, but that wider society has a crucial role to play too.

## ACKNOWLEDGEMENTS

Thanks to Dermot McNaney for the creation of the React films and to Louise Michaelis and Lisa Salter for help with facilitation of the education sessions. This research was financially supported by: the Anaphylaxis Campaign (who coordinated funding provided by Meda Pharmaceuticals, ALK-Abelló Ltd & Allergy Therapeutics plc.); the National Institute for Health Research (Doctoral Research Fellowship, Dr Neil Davidson, DRF-2014-07-131); and the Engineering and Physical Sciences Research Council (award number EP/M023001/1). The views expressed in this publication are those of the author and not necessarily those of the NHS, the National Institute for Health Research or the Department of Health. Data supporting this publication is not openly available due to ethical considerations. Access may be possible under appropriate agreement. Additional metadata record at http://dx.doi.org/10.17634/141304-8. Please contact Newcastle Research Data Service at rdm@ncl.ac.uk for further information or access requests.

## REFERENCES


1. Afshin, A., Babalola, D., Mclean, M., Yu, Z., Ma, W., Chen, C.Y., Arabi, M., and Mozaffarian, D., 2016. Information Technology and Lifestyle: A Systematic Evaluation of Internet and Mobile Interventions for Improving Diet, Physical Activity, Obesity, Tobacco, and Alcohol Use. *Journal of the American Heart Association 5*, 9, e003058. DOI= http://doi.org/10.1161/jaha.115.003058.
2. Anderson, J.K. and Wallace, L.M., 2015. Applying the Behavioural Intervention Technologies model to the development of a smartphone application (app) supporting young peoples' adherence to anaphylaxis action plan. *BMJ Innovations 1*, 2, 67-73. DOI= http://doi.org/10.1136/bmjinnov-2014-000016.
3. Annunziato, R.A., Rubes, M., Ambrose, M., Caso, N., Dillon, M., Sicherer, S.H., and Shemesh, E., 2015. Allocation of food allergy responsibilities and its correlates for children and adolescents. *Journal of Health Psychology 20*, 6, 693-701. DOI= http://doi.org/10.1177/1359105315579798.
4. Antolín-Amérigo, D., Manso, L., Caminati, M., De La Hoz Caballer, B., Cerecedo, I., Muriel, A., Rodríguez-Rodríguez, M., Barbarroja-Escudero, J., Sánchez-González, M.J., Huertas-Barbudo, B., and Alvarez-Mon, M., 2016. Quality of life in patients with food allergy. *Clinical and Molecular Allergy 14*, 1, 1-10. DOI= http://doi.org/10.1186/s12948-016-0041-4.
5. Arens-Volland, A., Feidert, F., Herbst, R., Mösges, R., and Rösch, N., 2011. Use of electronic patient diaries supports diagnosis of food allergy and diet management. *Clin Transl Allergy 1*, Suppl 1, O38-O38. DOI= http://doi.org/10.1186/2045-7022-1-S1-O38.
6. Armstrong, A.W., Idriss, N.Z., and Kim, R.H., 2011. Effects of video-based, online education on behavioral and knowledge outcomes in sunscreen use: A randomized controlled trial. *Patient Education and Counseling 83*, 2, 273-277. DOI= http://doi.org/10.1016/j.pec.2010.04.033.
7. Bandura, A., 1997. *Self-Efficacy in Changing Societies*. Cambridge University Press, Cambridge.
8. Bert, F., Giacometti, M., Gualano, M.R., and Siliquini, R., 2014. Smartphones and Health Promotion: A Review of the Evidence. *Journal of Medical Systems 38*, 1, 1-11. DOI= http://doi.org/10.1007/s10916-013-9995-7.
9. Besera, G.T., Cox, S., Malotte, C.K., Rietmeijer, C.A., Klausner, J.D., O'donnell, L., Margolis, A.D., and Warner, L., 2016. Assessing Patient Exposure to a Video-Based Intervention in STD Clinic Waiting Rooms: Findings From the Safe in the City Trial. *Health Promotion Practice 17*, 5, 731-738. DOI= http://doi.org/10.1177/1524839916631537.
10. Bock, S.A., Munoz-Furlong, A., and Sampson, H.A., 2007. Further fatalities caused by anaphylactic reactions to food, 2001-2006. *Journal of Allergy and Clinical Immunology 119*, 4, 1016-1018. DOI= http://doi.org/10.1016/j.jaci.2006.12.622.
11. Braun, V. and Clarke, V., 2006. Using thematic analysis in psychology. *Qualitative Research in Psychology 3*, 2, 77-101. DOI= http://doi.org/10.1191/1478088706qp063oa.
12. Brockow, K., Schallmayer, S., Beyer, K., Biedermann, T., Fischer, J., Gebert, N., Grosber, M., Jakob, T., Klimek, L., Kugler, C., Lange, L., Pfaar, O., Przybilla, B., Rietschel, E., Rueff, F., Schnadt, S., Szczepanski, R., Worm, M., Kupfer, J., Gieler, U., Ring, J., For the Working Group on Anaphylaxis, T., and Education, 2015. Effects of a structured educational intervention on knowledge and emergency management in patients at risk for anaphylaxis. *Allergy 70*, 2, 227-235. DOI= http://doi.org/10.1111/all.12548.
13. Cafazzo, J.A., Casselman, M., Hamming, N., Katzman, D.K., and Palmert, M.R., 2012. Design of an mHealth app for the self-management of adolescent type 1 diabetes: a pilot study. *J Med Internet Res 14*, 3, e70. DOI= http://doi.org/10.2196/jmir.2058.
14. Cordeiro, F., Bales, E., Cherry, E., and Fogarty, J., 2015. Rethinking the Mobile Food Journal: Exploring Opportunities for Lightweight Photo-Based Capture. In *Proceedings of the Proceedings of the 33rd Annual ACM Conference on Human Factors in Computing Systems* (Seoul, Republic of Korea), ACM, 3207-3216. DOI= http://doi.org/10.1145/2702123.2702154.
15. Cummings, A.J., Knibb, R.C., King, R.M., and Lucas, J.S., 2010. The psychosocial impact of food allergy and food hypersensitivity in children, adolescents and their families: a review. *Allergy 65*, 8, 933-945. DOI= http://doi.org/10.1111/j.1398-9995.2010.02342.x.
16. Daraghmi, E.Y. and Yuan, S.M., 2013. PMR: Personalized Mobile Restaurant system. In *Computer Science and Information Technology (CSIT)*, Amman, Jordan, 275-282. DOI= http://doi.org/10.1109/CSIT.2013.6588792.
17. Davies, S.C. 2013. Annual Report of the Chief Medical Officer 2012, Our Children Deserve Better: Prevention Pays. Available: https://www.gov.uk/government/uploads/system/uploads/attachment_data/file/255237/2901304_CMO_complete_low_res_accessible.pdf.
18. De Moura Quevedo, N.M., Da Costa, C.A., Da Rosa Righi, R., and Rigo, S.J., 2016. A food allergy risk detection model based on situation awareness. *Journal of Applied Computing Research 5*, 1, 32-43. DOI= http://doi.org/10.4013/jacr.2016.51.03.
19. Delen, E., Liew, J., and Willson, V., 2014. Effects of interactivity and instructional scaffolding on learning: Self-regulation in online video-based environments. *Computers & Education 78*, 312-320. DOI= http://doi.org/10.1016/j.compedu.2014.06.018.

20. Dinakar, C., 2012. Anaphylaxis in Children: Current Understanding and Key Issues in Diagnosis and Treatment. *Curr Allergy Asthma Rep 12*, 6, 641-649. DOI= http://doi.org/10.1007/s11882-012-0284-1.
21. Ferro, M.A., Van Lieshout, R.J., Ohayon, J., and Scott, J.G., 2016. Emotional and behavioral problems in adolescents and young adults with food allergy. *Allergy 71*, 4, 532-540. DOI= http://doi.org/10.1111/all.12829.
22. Flokstra-De Blok, B.M.J., Dunngalvin, A., Vlieg-Boerstra, B.J., Oude Elberink, J.N.G., Duiverman, E.J., Hourihane, J.O.B., and Dubois, A.E.J., 2008. Development and validation of the self-administered Food Allergy Quality of Life Questionnaire for adolescents. *Journal of Allergy and Clinical Immunology 122*, 1, 139-144, 144.e131-132. DOI= http://doi.org/10.1016/j.jaci.2008.05.008.
23. Froisland, D.H., Arsand, E., and Skarderud, F., 2012. Improving diabetes care for young people with type 1 diabetes through visual learning on mobile phones: mixed-methods study. *J Med Internet Res 14*, 4, e111. DOI= http://doi.org/10.2196/jmir.2155.
24. Gallagher, M., Worth, A., Cunningham-Burley, S., and Sheikh, A., 2011. Epinephrine auto-injector use in adolescents at risk of anaphylaxis: a qualitative study in Scotland, UK. *Clinical and Experimental Allergy 41*, 6, 869-877. DOI= http://doi.org/10.1111/j.1365-2222.2011.03743.x.
25. Gallagher, M., Worth, A., Cunningham-Burley, S., and Sheikh, A., 2012. Strategies for living with the risk of anaphylaxis in adolescence: qualitative study of young people and their parents. *Primary Care Respiratory Journal 21*, 4, 392-397. DOI= http://doi.org/10.4104/pcrj.2012.00072.
26. Garbett, A., Comber, R., Jenkins, E., and Olivier, P., 2016. App Movement: A Platform for Community Commissioning of Mobile Applications. In *Proceedings of the Proceedings of the 2016 CHI Conference on Human Factors in Computing Systems* (Santa Clara, California, USA), ACM, 26-37. DOI= http://doi.org/10.1145/2858036.2858094.
27. Glasemann, M., Kanstrup, A.M., and Ryberg, T., 2010. Making chocolate-covered broccoli: designing a mobile learning game about food for young people with diabetes. In *Proceedings of the Proceedings of the 8th ACM Conference on Designing Interactive Systems* (Aarhus, Denmark), ACM, 1858219, 262-271. DOI= http://doi.org/10.1145/1858171.1858219.
28. Hamine, S., Gerth-Guyette, E., Faulx, D., Green, B.B., and Ginsburg, A.S., 2015. Impact of mHealth chronic disease management on treatment adherence and patient outcomes: a systematic review. *J Med Internet Res 17*, 2, e52. DOI= http://doi.org/10.2196/jmir.3951.
29. Heary, C.M. and Hennessy, E., 2002. The Use of Focus Group Interviews in Pediatric Health Care Research. *Journal of Pediatric Psychology 27*, 1, 47-57. DOI= http://doi.org/10.1093/jpepsy/27.1.47.
30. Henricksen, K. and Viller, S., 2012. Design of software to support families with food-allergic and food-intolerant children. In *Proceedings of the Proceedings of the 24th Australian Computer-Human Interaction Conference* (Melbourne, Australia), ACM, 194-203. DOI= http://doi.org/10.1145/2414536.2414571.
31. Huh, J., Liu, L.S., Neogi, T., Inkpen, K., and Pratt, W., 2014. Health Vlogs as Social Support for Chronic Illness Management. *ACM Trans. Comput.-Hum. Interact. 21*, 4, 1-31. DOI= http://doi.org/10.1145/2630067.
32. Iizuka, K., Okawada, T., Matsuyama, K., Kurihashi, S., and Iizuka, Y., 2012. Food menu selection support system: considering constraint conditions for safe dietary life. In *Proceedings of the Proceedings of the ACM multimedia 2012 workshop on Multimedia for cooking and eating activities* (Nara, Japan), ACM, 53-58. DOI= http://doi.org/10.1145/2390776.2390786.
33. Jones, C.J., Llewellyn, C.D., Frew, A.J., Du Toit, G., Mukhopadhyay, S., and Smith, H., 2015. Factors associated with good adherence to self-care behaviours amongst adolescents with food allergy. *Pediatric Allergy and Immunology 26*, 2, 111-118. DOI= http://doi.org/10.1111/pai.12333.
34. Kirk, S., Beatty, S., Callery, P., Gellatly, J., Milnes, L., and Pryjmachuk, S., 2013. The effectiveness of self-care support interventions for children and young people with long-term conditions: a systematic review. *Child: Care, Health and Development 39*, 3, 305-324. DOI= http://doi.org/10.1111/j.1365-2214.2012.01395.x.
35. Klonoff, D.C., 2013. The Current Status of mHealth for Diabetes: Will it Be the Next Big Thing? *Journal of Diabetes Science and Technology 7*, 3, 749-758. DOI= http://doi.org/10.1177/193229681300700321.
36. Lin, A. and Sharma, H.P., 2014. Teasing and Bullying Among Adolescents With Food Allergy. *Journal of Allergy and Clinical Immunology 133*, 2, AB288. DOI= http://doi.org/10.1016/j.jaci.2013.12.1020.
37. Love, E.M., Manalo, I.F., Chen, S.C., Chen, K.-H., and Stoff, B.K., 2016. A video-based educational pilot for basal cell carcinoma (BCC) treatment: A randomized controlled trial. *Journal of the American Academy of Dermatology 74*, 3, 477-483.e477. DOI= http://doi.org/10.1016/j.jaad.2015.10.014.
38. Monks, H., Gowland, M.H., Mackenzie, H., Erlewyn-Lajeunesse, M., King, R., Lucas, J.S., and Roberts, G., 2010. How do teenagers manage their food allergies? *Clinical and Experimental Allergy 40*, 10, 1533-1540. DOI= http://doi.org/10.1111/j.1365-2222.2010.03586.x.
39. Moorhead, S.A., Hazlett, D.E., Harrison, L., Carroll, J.K., Irwin, A., and Hoving, C., 2013. A New

Dimension of Health Care: Systematic Review of the Uses, Benefits, and Limitations of Social Media for Health Communication. *J Med Internet Res 15*, 4, e85. DOI= http://doi.org/10.2196/jmir.1933.

40. Morrison, C. and Doherty, G., 2014. Analyzing Engagement in a Web-Based Intervention Platform Through Visualizing Log-Data. *J Med Internet Res 16*, 11, e252. DOI= http://doi.org/10.2196/jmir.3575.

41. Muraro, A., Polloni, L., Lazzarotto, F., Toniolo, A., Baldi, I., Bonaguro, R., Gini, G., and Masiello, M., 2014. Comparison of bullying of food-allergic versus healthy schoolchildren in Italy. *Journal of Allergy and Clinical Immunology 134*, 3, 749-751. DOI= http://doi.org/10.1016/j.jaci.2014.05.043.

42. Muraro, A., Roberts, G., Worm, M., Bilò, M.B., Brockow, K., Fernández Rivas, M., Santos, A.F., Zolkipli, Z.Q., Bellou, A., Beyer, K., Bindslev-Jensen, C., Cardona, V., Clark, A.T., Demoly, P., Dubois, A.E.J., Dunngalvin, A., Eigenmann, P., Halken, S., Harada, L., Lack, G., Jutel, M., Niggemann, B., Ruëff, F., Timmermans, F., Vlieg–Boerstra, B.J., Werfel, T., Dhami, S., Panesar, S., Akdis, C.A., Sheikh, A., The, E.F.A., and Anaphylaxis Guidelines, G., 2014. Anaphylaxis: guidelines from the European Academy of Allergy and Clinical Immunology. *Allergy 69*, 8, 1026-1045. DOI= http://doi.org/10.1111/all.12437.

43. Muraro, A., Werfel, T., Hoffmann-Sommergruber, K., Roberts, G., Beyer, K., Bindslev-Jensen, C., Cardona, V., Dubois, A., Dutoit, G., Eigenmann, P., Fernandez Rivas, M., Halken, S., Hickstein, L., Høst, A., Knol, E., Lack, G., Marchisotto, M.J., Niggemann, B., Nwaru, B.I., Papadopoulos, N.G., Poulsen, L.K., Santos, A.F., Skypala, I., Schoepfer, A., Van Ree, R., Venter, C., Worm, M., Vlieg–Boerstra, B., Panesar, S., De Silva, D., Soares-Weiser, K., Sheikh, A., Ballmer-Weber, B.K., Nilsson, C., De Jong, N.W., Akdis, C.A., The, E.F.A., and Anaphylaxis Guidelines, G., 2014. EAACI Food Allergy and Anaphylaxis Guidelines: diagnosis and management of food allergy. *Allergy 69*, 8, 1008-1025. DOI= http://doi.org/10.1111/all.12429.

44. Nguyen-Luu, N.U., Ben-Shoshan, M., Alizadehfar, R., Joseph, L., Harada, L., Allen, M., St-Pierre, Y., and Clarke, A., 2012. Inadvertent exposures in children with peanut allergy. *Pediatric Allergy and Immunology 23*, 2, 133-139. DOI= http://doi.org/10.1111/j.1399-3038.2011.01235.x.

45. Nielsen. 2014. Mobile Millennials: over 85% of generation Y owns smartphones. Available: http://www.nielsen.com/us/en/insights/news/2014/mobile-millennials-over-85-percent-of-generation-y-owns-smartphones.html [Accessed 20/11/2015].

46. Norman, G., 2010. Likert scales, levels of measurement and the "laws" of statistics. *Advances in Health Sciences Education 15*, 5, 625-632. DOI= http://doi.org/10.1007/s10459-010-9222-y.

47. Ofcom. 2015. The Communications Market Report. Available: http://stakeholders.ofcom.org.uk/binaries/research/cmr/cmr15/CMR_UK_2015.pdf [Accessed 20/11/2015].

48. Ofcom. 2016. The Communications Market Report. Available: http://stakeholders.ofcom.org.uk/binaries/research/cmr/cmr16/uk/CMR_UK_2016.pdf [Accessed 03/09/2016].

49. Panesar, S.S., Javad, S., De Silva, D., Nwaru, B.I., Hickstein, L., Muraro, A., Roberts, G., Worm, M., Bilò, M.B., Cardona, V., Dubois, A.E.J., Dunn Galvin, A., Eigenmann, P., Fernandez-Rivas, M., Halken, S., Lack, G., Niggemann, B., Santos, A.F., Vlieg-Boerstra, B.J., Zolkipli, Z.Q., Sheikh, A., The, E.F.A., and Anaphylaxis, G., 2013. The epidemiology of anaphylaxis in Europe: a systematic review. *Allergy 68*, 11, 1353-1361. DOI= http://doi.org/10.1111/all.12272.

50. Patton, M.Q., 2002. *Qualitative Research & Evaluation Methods*. SAGE Publications, Thousand Oaks, CA.

51. Pereira, B., Venter, C., Grundy, J., Clayton, C.B., Arshad, S.H., and Dean, T., 2005. Prevalence of sensitization to food allergens, reported adverse reaction to foods, food avoidance, and food hypersensitivity among teenagers. *Journal of Allergy and Clinical Immunology 116*, 4, 884-892. DOI= http://doi.org/10.1016/j.jaci.2005.05.047.

52. Polloni, L., Lazzarotto, F., Bonaguro, R., Toniolo, A., Celegato, N., and Muraro, A., 2015. Psychological care of food-allergic children and their families: an exploratory analysis. *Pediatric Allergy and Immunology 26*, 1, 87-90. DOI= http://doi.org/10.1111/pai.12325.

53. Poole, E.S. and Peyton, T., 2013. Interaction design research with adolescents: methodological challenges and best practices. In *Proceedings of the Proceedings of the 12th International Conference on Interaction Design and Children* (New York, New York, USA), ACM, 2485766, 211-217. DOI= http://doi.org/10.1145/2485760.2485766.

54. Pumphrey, R.S. and Gowland, M.H., 2007. Further fatal allergic reactions to food in the United Kingdom, 1999-2006. *Journal of Allergy and Clinical Immunology 119*, 4, 1018-1019. DOI= http://doi.org/10.1016/j.jaci.2007.01.021.

55. Resnick, M.D., Catalano, R.F., Sawyer, S.M., Viner, R., and Patton, G.C., 2012. Seizing the opportunities of adolescent health. *The Lancet 379*, 9826, 1564-1567. DOI= http://doi.org/10.1016/S0140-6736(12)60472-3.

56. Resuscitation Council (Uk). 2012. Emergency treatment of anaphylactic reactions: Guidelines for healthcare providers. Available: http://www.resus.org.uk/pages/reaction.pdf.

57. Rosenstock, I.M., Strecher, V.J., and Becker, M.H., 1988. Social Learning Theory and the Health Belief

Model. *Health Education Quarterly 15*, 2, 175-183. DOI= http://doi.org/10.1177/109019818801500203.

58. Sawyer, S.M., Drew, S., Yeo, M.S., and Britto, M.T., 2007. Adolescents with a chronic condition: challenges living, challenges treating. *The Lancet 369*, 9571, 1481-1489. DOI= http://doi.org/10.1016/S0140-6736(07)60370-5.
59. Schofield, G., Bartindale, T., and Wright, P., 2015. Bootlegger: Turning Fans into Film Crew. In *Proceedings of the Proceedings of the 33rd Annual ACM Conference on Human Factors in Computing Systems* (Seoul, Republic of Korea), ACM, 767-776. DOI= http://doi.org/10.1145/2702123.2702229.
60. Sicherer, S.H. and Sampson, H.A., 2014. Food allergy: Epidemiology, pathogenesis, diagnosis, and treatment. *Journal of Allergy and Clinical Immunology 133*, 2 (2//), 291-307.e295. DOI= http://doi.org/10.1016/j.jaci.2013.11.020.
61. Sicherer, S.H., Vargas, P.A., Groetch, M.E., Christie, L., Carlisle, S.K., Noone, S., and Jones, S.M., 2012. Development and validation of educational materials for food allergy. *J Pediatr 160*, 4, 651-656. DOI= http://doi.org/10.1016/j.jpeds.2011.09.056.
62. Skinner, H., Biscope, S., Poland, B., and Goldberg, E., 2003. How adolescents use technology for health information: implications for health professionals from focus group studies. *J Med Internet Res 5*, 4, e32. DOI= http://doi.org/10.2196/jmir.5.4.e32.
63. Song, T.T., Worm, M., and Lieberman, P., 2014. Anaphylaxis treatment: current barriers to adrenaline auto-injector use. *Allergy 69*, 8, 983-991. DOI= http://doi.org/10.1111/all.12387.
64. Spina, J.L., Mcintyre, C.L., and Pulcini, J.A., 2012. An intervention to increase high school students' compliance with carrying auto-injectable epinephrine: a MASNRN study. *Journal of School Nursing 28*, 3, 230-237. DOI= http://doi.org/10.1177/1059840511431459.
65. Squire, K. and Dikkers, S., 2012. Amplifications of learning: Use of mobile media devices among youth. *Convergence: The International Journal of Research into New Media Technologies 18*, 4, 445-464. DOI= http://doi.org/10.1177/1354856511429646.
66. Tixier, M. and Lewkowicz, M., 2016. "Counting on the Group": Reconciling Online and Offline Social Support among Older Informal Caregivers. In *Proceedings of the Proceedings of the 2016 CHI Conference on Human Factors in Computing Systems* (Santa Clara, California, USA), ACM, 3545-3558. DOI= http://doi.org/10.1145/2858036.2858477.
67. Tuong, W., Larsen, E.R., and Armstrong, A.W., 2014. Videos to influence: a systematic review of effectiveness of video-based education in modifying health behaviors. *Journal of Behavioral Medicine 37*, 2, 218-233. DOI= http://doi.org/10.1007/s10865-012-9480-7.
68. Turner, P.J., Gowland, M.H., Sharma, V., Ierodiakonou, D., Harper, N., Garcez, T., Pumphrey, R., and Boyle, R.J., 2015. Increase in anaphylaxis-related hospitalizations but no increase in fatalities: An analysis of United Kingdom national anaphylaxis data, 1992-2012. *Journal of Allergy and Clinical Immunology 135*, 4, 956-963.e951. DOI= http://doi.org/10.1016/j.jaci.2014.10.021.
69. Twomey, N., Temko, A., Hourihane, J.O.B., and Marnane, W.P., 2011. Allergy detection with statistical modelling of HRV-based non-reaction baseline features. In *Proceedings of the Proceedings of the 4th International Symposium on Applied Sciences in Biomedical and Communication Technologies* (Barcelona, Spain), ACM, 1-5. DOI= http://doi.org/10.1145/2093698.2093832.
70. Umasunthar, T., Procktor, A., Hodes, M., Smith, J.G., Gore, C., Cox, H.E., Marrs, T., Hanna, H., Phillips, K., Pinto, C., Turner, P.J., Warner, J.O., and Boyle, R.J., 2015. Patients' ability to treat anaphylaxis using adrenaline autoinjectors: a randomized controlled trial. *Allergy 70*, 7, 855-863. DOI= http://doi.org/10.1111/all.12628.
71. Van Der Velde, J.L., Flokstra-De Blok, B.M., Vlieg-Boerstra, B.J., Oude Elberink, J.N., Schouten, J.P., Dunngalvin, A., Hourihane, J.O., Duiverman, E.J., and Dubois, A.E., 2009. Test-retest reliability of the Food Allergy Quality of Life Questionnaires (FAQLQ) for children, adolescents and adults. *Quality of Life Research 18*, 2, 245-251. DOI= http://doi.org/10.1007/s11136-008-9434-2.
72. Vetander, M., Protudjer, J.L.P., Lilja, G., Kull, I., Van Hage, M., Bergström, A., Östblom, E., and Wickman, M., 2015. Food-induced anaphylaxis among a population of adolescents – Report from the BAMSE survey. *Clin Transl Allergy 5*, Suppl 3, O25-O25. DOI= http://doi.org/10.1186/2045-7022-5-S3-O25.
73. Viner, R.M., Coffey, C., Mathers, C., Bloem, P., Costello, A., Santelli, J., and Patton, G.C., 2011. 50-year mortality trends in children and young people: a study of 50 low-income, middle-income, and high-income countries. *The Lancet 377*, 9772, 1162-1174. DOI= http://doi.org/10.1016/S0140-6736(11)60106-2.
74. Wartella, E., Rideout, V., Zupancic, H., Beaudoin-Ryan, L., and Lauricella, A. 2015. Teens, Health, and Technology. *Report of the Center on Media and Human Development* [Online]. Available: http://cmhd.northwestern.edu/wp-content/uploads/2015/05/1886_1_SOC_ConfReport_TeensHealthTech_051115.pdf.
75. Wood, R.A., Camargo, C.A., Jr., Lieberman, P., Sampson, H.A., Schwartz, L.B., Zitt, M., Collins, C., Tringale, M., Wilkinson, M., Boyle, J., and Simons,

F.E.R., 2014. Anaphylaxis in America: The prevalence and characteristics of anaphylaxis in the United States. *Journal of Allergy and Clinical Immunology 133*, 2, 461-467. DOI= http://doi.org/10.1016/j.jaci.2013.08.016.

76. World Health Organization. 2014. Health for the World's Adolescents: A second chance in the second decade. Available: http://apps.who.int/adolescent/second-decade/.

# AVUI: Designing a Toolkit for Audiovisual Interfaces

**Nuno N. Correia**
Madeira-ITI, U. Madeira
Funchal, Portugal
nuno.correia@staff.uma.pt

**Atau Tanaka**
Goldsmiths, University of London
London, UK
a.tanaka@gold.ac.uk

## ABSTRACT
The combined use of sound and image has a rich history, from audiovisual artworks to research exploring the potential of data visualization and sonification. However, we lack standard tools or guidelines for audiovisual (AV) interaction design, particularly for live performance. We propose the AVUI (AudioVisual User Interface), where sound and image are used together in a cohesive way in the interface; and an enabling technology, the ofxAVUI toolkit. AVUI guidelines and ofxAVUI were developed in a three-stage process, together with AV producers: 1) participatory design activities; 2) prototype development; 3) encapsulation of prototype as a plug-in, evaluation, and roll out. Best practices identified include: reconfigurable interfaces and mappings; object-oriented packaging of AV and UI; diverse sound visualization; flexible media manipulation and management. The toolkit and a mobile app developed using it have been released as open-source. Guidelines and toolkit demonstrate the potential of AVUI and offer designers a convenient framework for AV interaction design.

### ACM Classification Keywords
H.5.2 User Interfaces: Auditory (non-speech) feedback; H.5.2 User Interfaces: Graphical user interfaces (GUI); H.5.2 User Interfaces: Prototyping; H.5.2 User Interfaces: User-centered design

### Author Keywords
User interface; toolkit; interface builder; audiovisual; crossmodal interaction; prototyping; participatory design; interaction design; hackathons.

## INTRODUCTION
The combination of audio with image has a long tradition, from color organs used by the composer Scriabin in the early 20th century [27] to the pioneering computer graphics explorations of John Whitney in the 1960s [26]. The advent of powerful personal computers for media manipulation, from the 1990s, gave further impulse to audiovisual (AV) performance [32].


*CHI 2017*, May 06 – 11, 2017, Denver, CO, USA.

ACM 978-1-4503-4655-9/17/05...$15.00
DOI: http://dx.doi.org/10.1145/3025453.3026042

These artistic explorations mirror how the brain deals with multi-sensorial information. Research on sensory substitution has explored how the brain replaces functions of one sense by another [1]. The perception of flashing lights can be manipulated by sound: a single flash of light can be seen as consisting of two flashes if displayed simultaneously with multiple sound signals [34]. In the McGurk effect, the perception of an auditory phoneme changes depending on the image [24]. An important factor for crossmodality is congruency – non-arbitrary associations between different modalities. A congruent AV display can result in better performance and higher engagement than arbitrary associations between sound and image [25].

Sound and image have been studied in HCI in different application areas, including accessibility in assistive displays [11], improvement of task accuracy in driving [31], enjoyability and performance in games [5, 25]. Despite the potential for facilitating usability and engagement, there is a lack of design guidelines and standard tools for AV interaction design. Specifically, current solutions for AV performance that facilitate UI integration with content are laborious to implement, and lack aesthetic concerns regarding coherence of UI and visuals. Interface design for AV performance is mostly subjective, and there are no established best practices. These best practices would benefit performers, audience, software developers, interaction designers, researchers and students.

We propose the AVUI (AudioVisual User Interface) where the interaction of sound and image in the interface extends the concept of GUIs. We seek to 1) leverage practices in AV performance for sketches and prototypes, using participatory design methods; 2) implement best practices into a consolidated prototype; 3) propose guidelines and a software toolkit to allow designers to easily integrate sound and image in the UI of future systems and products.

This paper reports on the multi-stage design, development, release and evaluation of a software toolkit, ofxAVUI. We present related work; the participatory design and qualitative methods used; and their results; followed by AVUI guidelines proposed, discussion and conclusions.

## RELATED WORK

### AV Performance and Tools
AV performance combines live manipulation of sound and image [4]. This distinguishes it from VJing (Video Jockey performance), where a visual performer accompanies a musician [8]. A number of artists are concerned with creating interfaces and systems for AV performance. Levin developed

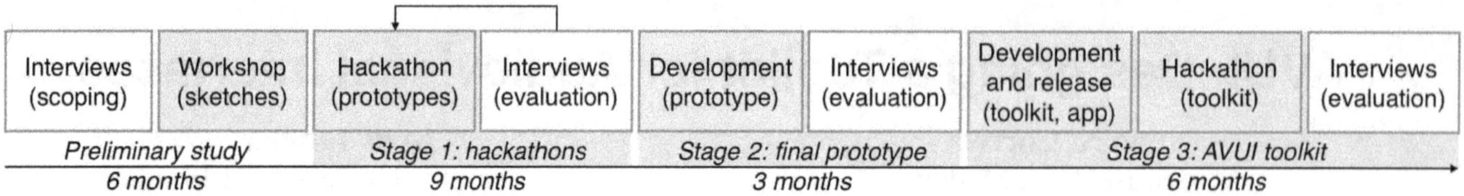


**Figure 1. Summary of the four cycles of the research: preliminary study; stages 1, 2 and 3. Workshops and hackathons in blue, interviews in white and development phases in orange. Stage 1 had two iterations**

painterly interfaces for audiovisual performance [20]. Magnusson uses abstract GUIs to represent musical structures [23]. Iwai creates playful pieces, crossing genres between game, installation and performance [29].

Most commercial VJ software, such as Modul8 (`http://www.modul8.ch`), focus on video playback and manipulation, with limited generative graphics capabilities, and only "fairly low-level musical features" [33]. AV performers "often rely on building their own systems" [33] with coding frameworks such as openFrameworks (OF) (`http://openframeworks.cc`). Therefore, an important element of VJing and AV performance is the use of Do It Yourself (DIY) tools [32]. This requires "a high level of technical ability on the part of the user" [33].

Solutions such as Processing (`http://processing.org`) offer sound toolkits, which contain visualization modules (ex: Minim), and also offer GUI modules (ex: Control P5). Similar examples could be given for other creative coding environments. But although these UI and sound/visualization modules can be combined, this is laborious, and they are not integrated out of the box, neither functionally nor aesthetically. They do not offer easy ways to implement an "AV+UI" solution, nor a GUI designed to be integrated with visuals. We aim to provide an ease of implementation, and high level of integration.

### AV Systems and Interaction Design

Schofield et al. created Cinejack for "directing narrative video through live musical performance" [33], in collaboration with artists. In MelodicBrush, a user-centered design approach is adopted to design a tabletop AV system linking calligraphy and music [15]. Wiethoff and Gehring created an interactive media façade system through an iterative approach: key data collection; user research; data analysis; design concepts; and experience concepts [35]. These studies have used multi-stage, user-centered approaches, which we adopted in our work. However, they each only evaluated one system, making generalization difficult. We apply these methods to evaluate a large number of projects in order to glean design insights across multiple systems.

The New Interfaces for Musical Expression (NIME) community has been active in studying the combination of visuals, sound and interaction design. The work of Jordà, such as FMOL and Reactable, is relevant due to the interplay of interaction and sound visualization strategies [17]. The authors of residUUm, one of the prototypes resulting from the current research, have presented their performance approaches for AV generation and audience visibility [30]. Rouages is another AV project that is concerned with audience understanding [2].

Hook has developed an interface for VJ performances, Waves [14]. He also studied VJing from the viewpoint of the performer [13] and identified three main themes: *aspirational*, *live* and *interaction*. Within *interaction*, he identifies the following sub-themes: *constraining interactions*; *haptically direct*; *parallel interaction*; *immediacy*; *manipulable media*; *reconfigurable interfaces*; and *visible interaction*. While he focuses on video content, he recognizes the need for generative media tools. We will use Hook's framework for our study, strengthening the potential generalizability of the work by building upon prior qualitative findings.

## METHODS

The research took place over a 2-year period and involved a preliminary study and three main stages (Figure 1): Pre) scoping interviews and brainstorming workshop; 1) hackathons for prototype development; 2) a "consolidation prototype" gathering best practices and expert evaluation; 3) creation of a software development toolkit for facilitating integration of AV with UI. The toolkit was released as open-source, tested in a hackathon and with internet users, and further tested by rebuilding the final prototype from Stage 2 as a publicly released product using the toolkit. The iterative cycle enabled "a dynamic process of invention, distributed across events" [9]. Hackathons and interviews (and subsequent thematic analysis) were used as methods throughout the studies.

### Hackathons

Hackathons are coding events in DIY communities where "small teams produce working software prototypes in a short time period" and these events are often centered around a common theme or technology [18]. The hackathon challenge is an important part of the method. It sets a common task in a motivating way to participants, making a hackathon "a moment of design" [16]. In a hackathon, solutions are "conceived in response to those challenges" [21]. These elements make it a fun, easy to understand technique for participatory design and code development.

### Thematic Analysis

We conducted thematic analyses of interviews in the three studies, based on techniques in [3]. We coded the responses based on emerging patterns and issues arising, then collated the codes into potential themes. We used Hook's themes as a basis for our coding. We complemented this theoretic analysis approach with an inductive analysis independent of any pre-existing coding frame. This allowed us to build on prior work, contribute our new insights, and achieve a balanced, thorough and inclusive structure of main themes and sub-themes.

## PRELIMINARY STUDY: INTERVIEWS, BRAINSTORMING

In our preliminary study [7], we conducted interviews with 12 audiovisual performers, asking them about their practice, their tools, and their needs and desires as performers. The analysis of the interviews brought forth a series of key issues: modularity, flexibility and reconfigurability; ease of hardware/software integration; instrument-like expressivity and fluidity; integration of environmental elements; generative capabilities and diversity; communication of process to the audience; reliability and speed. These concepts on the whole match and confirm the issues identified by Hook under the theme *interaction*. Generative capabilities and diversity connects to their forward looking theme of *aspiration*, and the need for a visual equivalent to sound synthesizers. The 12 interviewees provided us with a group of experts that we would consult throughout the different studies of the research – the evaluators of Stages 1 and 2 were from this same group.

The ideas from the interviews then informed a brainstorming workshop, with 19 participants (including two from the previous interview stage). The one-day workshop structure was comprised of two parts: the first one adopting the "bootlegging" idea generation technique [12]. For part 2, we extended this with a more focused, structured re-examination of ideas from part 1, which we called "Re-boot".

The five breakout groups produced five sketches (storyboards and wireframes) of procedural audiovisual performance tools. Two sketches, *Gestural Touchscreen* and *Meta/Vis*, were particularly successful in addressing the challenges set out in the workshop. Both rely on the expressive potential of multitouch interaction, employing different solutions for reconfigurability: the former allows for loading and manipulating vector graphics, and the latter adopts a simplified data-flow mechanism. Project descriptions and sketches are seen at `http://www.gen-av.org/sketches/`.

## STAGE 1: PARTICIPATORY DESIGN OF PROTOTYPES

### Hackathon and Hack Challenge

Using the key themes and the sketches from the preliminary study as input and inspiration, we ran two hackathons in an iterative cycle, Gen.AV 1 and Gen.AV 2. The objective was to leverage knowledge from AV performers into prototypes combining AV and UI, where best practices could be adopted in a future AVUI toolkit. We sent out a call for participation, with coding knowledge as prerequisite, and interviewed applicants. Each hackathon took place over two days.

Both Gen.AV 1 and 2 followed the same structure: 1) Introduction: a presentation on the previous stages of the study and results achieved so far, goals and structure of the workshop; 2) Conceptualization and sketching; and 3) Software development. 23 participants took part in Gen.AV 1 (five female and 18 male ). Gen.AV 2 had 13 participants (two female and 11 male), three of whom had taken part in Gen.AV 1. We divided participants into five (Gen.AV 1) and six (Gen.AV 2) groups, distributing prior programming experience evenly across groups.

We created hack challenges based on key conclusions (*in parenthesis*) from the preliminary study [7]. They were: 1) computer-generated sound and visuals (*generative capabilities and diversity*); 2) powerful and fluid manipulation – "like an instrument" (*instrument-like expressivity and fluidity*); 3) single-screen – what the performer sees is what the audience sees (*communication of process to the audience*); and 4) possibility to reconfigure the interface (*modularity, flexibility and reconfigurability*). The resulting projects were presented in two public performances. Five projects were showcased in the Gen.AV 1 performance, and six in Gen.AV 2. Each group produced a 10 minute performance.

### Projects

We present the five projects from Gen.AV 1. *ABP* is an animation engine and sound visualizer, where the user can define color, geometry and animation parameters. In *drawSynth*, a GUI allows controlling sound and image – users can draw vector shapes and select colors, which are sonified by a synthesis engine. *Esoterion Universe* consists of a 3D space that can be filled with planet-like audiovisual objects, each containing a GUI to modify their visual and sonic properties. *GS.avi* is an instrument that generates continuous spatial visualizations and music from the gestural input of a performer. *Modulant* allows for drawing images, using paintbrush type of tools, which are then sonified.

Six projects were built during Gen.AV 2. *Butterfly* is an audio visualizer which allows for the combination and control of four audio synthesizers, by means of manipulating icons distributed in four XY pads on the screen. *Cantor Dust* generates, displays, and sonifies Cantor set type fractals as sound and visuals. *EUG* further develops *Esoterion Universe* from Gen.AV 1, adding 3D gestural control with a Leap motion sensor. *OnTheTap* plays with the tactile, analog feel of tapping surfaces as interaction input, captured as audio. *residUUm* allows for the creation and manipulation of AV particles, with a variable lifespan, by clicking and dragging on the screen. *Wat* creates a chaotic 3D texture based on cellular automata (Figure 2). All the projects were uploaded to GitHub for download or source-code modification, accessible from `http://www.gen-av.org`. In addition to the code, the project descriptions are available from the same link, facilitating running and replicating the projects.

### Expert Interviews

After the performances, the projects were tested for ease of installation and robustness. Six projects were chosen: *Esoterion Universe*, *GS.avi* and *Modulant* from Gen.AV 1; and *Butterfly*, *residUUm* and *Wat* from Gen.AV 2. These were evaluated by expert reviewers, established audiovisual artists who had taken part in the preliminary study interviews. Each expert was given two projects for review, and at least one week time to practice with the software. Thus, each project was evaluated twice (project evaluators E1 and E2). We then conducted semi-structured interviews with the reviewers, lasting an average of 15 minutes per project. They served to follow up on the key issues emerging from the preliminary stage. The questions addressed: 1) the AV content and the relationship between sound and image; 2) ease of use of the software; 3) fluidity, AV manipulability and behavior as an "instrument"; 4) flexibility and reconfigurability of the interface; 5) potential usefulness for other artists and performers.

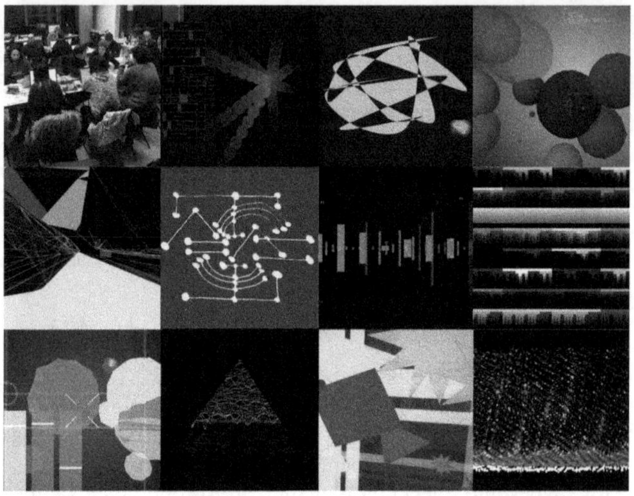

**Figure 2. Stage 1: Projects from the hackathons – left to right, then top to bottom: hackathon, ABP, drawSynth, Esoterion Universe, GS.avi, Modulant, Butterfly, Cantor Dust, EUG, OnTheTap, residUUm, Wat.**

We conducted a thematic analysis of the interviews. From this analysis, three main themes emerged: *Experience*, *Interfaces* and *Media*. We retained these themes for our analyses of the different stages of the research. Our starting point were Hook's themes related to *interaction*: *constraining interactions* (importance of constraints and focus); *haptically direct* (physical connection); *parallel interaction* (simultaneous control of multiple parameters); *immediacy* (immediate response from the software); *manipulable media* (powerful and varied manipulation of media); *reconfigurable interfaces* (reorganize controls to fit a particular performance); and *visible interaction* (make interaction visible to an audience) [13]. *Immediacy* was a pre-requisite for the selection of the projects. *Constraining interaction* was not detected. We decided to merge *haptically direct* and *parallel interaction*, as they would appear combined in our data. We split *interaction* into two new main themes: *experience* and *interface*. Additional themes related to content emerged, originating the new main theme *media*.

### *Experience*

*Visible interaction:* Two of the evaluators, in their own practice, prefer not to convey the interface to the audience, and wish to have a separate screen with the GUI for the performer (GS.avi, E1; Modulant, E2), for three main reasons: 1) the visual output could be re-routed without GUI to other software for additional manipulation (GS.avi, E2); 2) the interface is something the audience may not want to see; and 3) having a separate screen would allow for a more complex interface for the performer (Wat, E2). Another evaluator is interested in showing the UI to the audience and "conveying the performer's control on-screen" as part of the experience (residUUm, E2). Taking that approach would allow for "visually reflecting that agency onto the screen", making it understandable for an audience (Butterfly, E2).

*Haptic and parallel:* The reviewers confirmed the desire for interaction that "provides a sensation akin to being in direct contact or touching and molding media" [13]. The projects did not allow for either haptic or parallel interaction. Multitouch tablets and hardware controllers were mentioned as means to achieve a parallel interaction. Compatibility with hardware controllers and tablets is desired to achieve parallel interaction: controllers would allow for the physicality and "flexibility of an instrument" (Esoterion Universe, E1) and interaction "in a tracking pad on the computer is confusing", with a tablet-based approach being suggested (GS.avi, E2).

*Object-oriented:* When auditory and visual domains are combined, audiovisual objects can emerge, if simultaneity and a plausible common cause occur [19]. Three projects followed an object-oriented approach, by grouping audio and visual content into distinguishable entities (*Esoterion Universe*, *Butterfly* and *residUUm*). In the first two cases, a GUI was overlaid on the visuals for continuous manipulation. In the third project the opportunity for manipulation occurs only at the genesis of the object. The object approach was considered as being fruitful (Esoterion Universe, E2).

### *Interface*

*Reconfigurable interfaces:* The reconfiguration of UI becomes possible only by editing the code, which requires specific technical knowledge (Esoterion Universe, E1). Some projects organized the code in order to make it easier to reconfigure: "it's very easy to add your own synths" (Butterfly, E1).

*Interface mappings:* In some instances, a complex one-to-many mapping of interface to media parameters was considered successful (Butterfly, E2). Evaluators felt that more parameters should be controlled from the UI, resulting in insufficient mapping (Butterfly, E2; Wat, E2). Scalability of layout is desired, as it would allow for additional UI elements (Butterfly, E1).

*Interface clarity:* The lack of a parameter space in UI elements – an indication of the parameter range, and the current status – was considered problematic in some projects (residUUm, E2).

*Interface aesthetics:* The gestural aspect of one project was seen as innovative and appealing (GS.avi, E1). It was suggested that it could become more integrated in the visuals by visualizing the gestures (GS.avi, E1). The visual design of the interface is considered to be even more important when conveyed to an audience. In some cases, this design was considered to be unappealing to be shown (Modulant, E2). One reviewer considers that the UI itself should be dynamic, animated in response to the sound (Butterfly, E2). One of the projects adopts a logic of interactive quadrants with XY pads, which was considered to be original and clear (Butterfly, E1).

### *Media*

*Manipulable media:* Some projects were considered to produce outcomes with a narrow range of diversity (Esoterion Universe, E2; Butterfly, E1). In several cases, the projects rely on 2D or 3D spatial metaphors. There is a desire for an expandable canvas or scene where the media can be presented in and navigated through. This is considered to be missing on one project (Modulant, E2) and praised for its implementation on another (Wat, E1, E2). The satisfactory manipulation possibilities of some projects lead them to be considered "instruments" because of their fluidity (Wat, E1; Modulant, E1).

*Generative media:* Different evaluators appreciated different degrees of randomness. The generative aspect of some projects was considered to be too chaotic (GS.avi, E1; residUUm, E2). In the balance between generative elements and control, the latter is seen as the priority. But a certain degree of randomness is desirable, and considered to be missing in some cases (Modulant, E1).

*Media management:* The option to load files in some of the projects is appreciated (GS.avi, E2; Modulant, E1). Runtime loading of content is desired (GS.avi, E1). Real-time sharing of media between applications in the same device, using utilities such as Syphon (`http://syphon.v002.info`) is wished for (Esoterion Universe, E1). The possibility of accessing networked content is also suggested (Esoterion Universe, E2).

### Audience Study

In order to study audience understanding of the performers' actions, we asked audience members of the two performances to fill in a questionnaire about the different projects from Gen.AV 1 and 2 (with the exception of *DrawSynth*, a last minute addition). Respectively 45 and 34 respondents answered the questionnaire. The question asked was: "Did you find the connection between the performer's actions and the audiovisual result understandable?", on a scale of 1 to 5. Projects *Esoterion Universe* and *Modulant* from Gen.AV 1, and *Butterfly*, *EUG* and *residUUm* from Gen.AV 2 obtained the best results (*Modulant* with a median of 5, the others with a median of 4). The five projects that achieved the best results make visible both the interface and the parameter space. *Cantor Dust* and *OnTheTap*, both with a median of 3, implement only one of these aspects (visibility of parameter space in *Cantor Dust*) or only temporarily show them (*OnTheTap*). The remaining projects, with a median of 2, employ neither. These observations informed our design principles.

## STAGE 2: AV ZONES CONSOLIDATION PROTOTYPE

### Prototype Design

The results from Stage 1 fed into design guidelines for a final prototype, an iPad app for AV performance entitled *AV Zones*. It has been released as open-source (`https://github.com/AVUIs/AVZones-beta`). It adopts the object-oriented concept of "zones": rectangular areas that incorporate UI elements producing and manipulating sound, and a visualization of that sound. The app has three vertical zones, each with three XY pads for audio manipulation, controlling: pitch shift, delay and filter. Each zone has a sequencer, which can record touch information and visualize it. There are nine sounds available per zone, which can be switched at runtime, and replaced in the code. Different touch inputs create different results: tapping for triggering sounds; touch movement for manipulating the sound; two-finger tap to switch on and off; and double tap to trigger special function – menu or sequencer (Figure 3). The app was developed using the OF environment and the Maximilian audio library (`https://github.com/micknoise/Maximilian`). Both are open-source and cross-platform.

### Initial Tests - Performances

We tested *AV Zones* in "real world" settings: four public performances and two demos in conferences. In a performance, only an iPad is used for audiovisuals. What the performer sees is also what is projected to the audience. The interface is shown on the screen, with touch points being represented by white circles. We made minor improvements between performances. For example, a sequencer was added due to the difficulty of interacting simultaneously with the three zones, and the need to automate some of the processes by recording them.

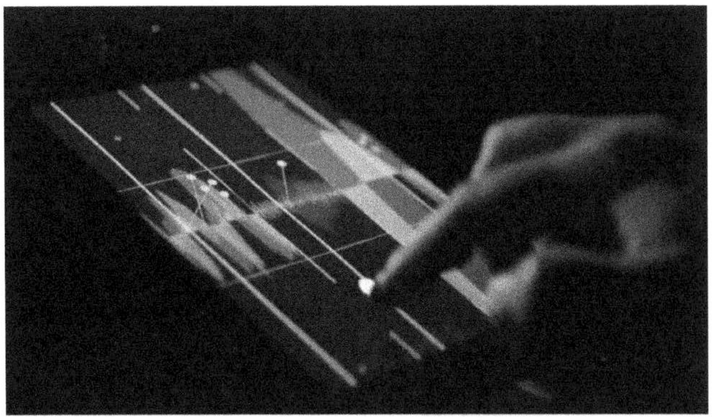

**Figure 3. Stage 2: AV Zones prototype.**

### Expert Interviews

We followed a similar evaluation procedure than in Stage 1: we installed *AV Zones* in iPads and handed them to three evaluators (E1, E2, E3) from our initial expert group. The interviewees tried the app for at least one week. We then ran semi-structured interviews lasting on average 30 minutes. We used the same questions as Stage 1. We ran a thematic analysis, maintaining the three main themes: *media*, *interface* and *experience*. More sub-themes emerged: *sound visualization* (within *media*); *constraining interaction* – a theme that had existed in Hook's analysis but had not appeared in Stage 1; and *playfulness* (within *experience* main theme).

#### *Experience*

*Constraining interaction:* Two evaluators were satisfied with the prototype's design constraints and minimalism, stating that "it's nice to have limitations", having a "minimal simplicity" was pleasing, and its "reduced nature" made it "very appropriate for a live tool" (E1, E3).

*Visible interaction:* One evaluator would like to be able to hide the UI, completely or partially, and added that by separating what the audience and the performer see, more UI elements could be added on the performer side (E1). Another respondent is satisfied that the audience can see what the performer is doing, as touch points are highlighted with white circles, and would like to see more interactions visualized, such as sound effect manipulation (E2).

*Haptic and parallel:* One respondent was satisfied with the number of zones and simultaneous control elements (E2), whereas others would like to add an external hardware MIDI controller (E1) or another tablet, creating a dual setup (E3).

*Object-oriented:* One respondent was pleased with the notion of zones and the way they operate, stating that it was a good concept and design (E2).

*Playfulness:* The application was considered to be playful – one respondent mentioned multiple times that he enjoyed playing with it, that it was "fun" (E1).

### *Interface*

*Interface aesthetics:* One evaluator was very pleased with the interface aesthetics of the sequencer functionality, stating that it looks like a "visual music composition" (E1). Another respondent considers that more work could be done in terms of visualizing additional processes in the software, such as loading or choosing sounds (E2).

*Interface clarity:* The prototype suffers from hidden discoverability issues. Several of the functionalities are activated by different types of touch interaction, not apparent in the UI. Testers had problems activating these, despite the documentation provided (E1, E2, E3). Evaluators complained that it was hard to understand what to do next (E2) leading to getting occasionally stuck (E1).

*Reconfigurable interfaces:* One respondent in particular was interested in adding reconfigurability options, such as allowing for extending functionalities with software "plugins" that others could build. Another suggestion was having the possibility of grouping zones and nesting them - this would facilitate scaling of zones without overcrowding the screen (E1). One of the respondents suggested adding a back end with substantial configuration options (E3).

### *Media*

*Manipulable media:* One respondent considers that the software is "a really useful live tool" (E3). The two audio effects, delay and filter, were considered well chosen, and having three simultaneous sounds allows for "enough scope" to maintain a performance (E3). The sequencer is considered an important element for this, as it allows to automate one zone while interacting with others (E1, E2, E3). The prototype is considered to allow for "a different way of approaching sound", less "musical" and "kind of weird" (E1). To have a broader and more musical appeal, two evaluators consider that a stricter timing or "clock" would be important (E1, E3). Having "more authorship and a sense of control" (E1) over the sound is desired. On the visual side, respondents would also like to have greater control. Only one visualization type, with "very little visual configurability" (E3) is considered insufficient. Evaluators would like to be able to have other visualizations and be able to make more choices about them (E1, E2).

*Media management:* All evaluators would like to be able to load sound files. Although this is possible, it requires modifying the code and re-installing the app, which is inconvenient. The possibility to record sounds is also desired (E2). One evaluator would like to be able to route the visuals to other software for further processing (E1).

*Sound visualization:* One evaluator considers that the approach followed, to visualize the amplitude levels of the audio buffer, was "fascinating" and "very responsive", particularly at slower speeds (E1). The other two consider this approach to be simplistic, as it does not help to "understand anything about the sound" (E2). They would rather have a "perceptually motivated approach" that would bring it closer to the state of the

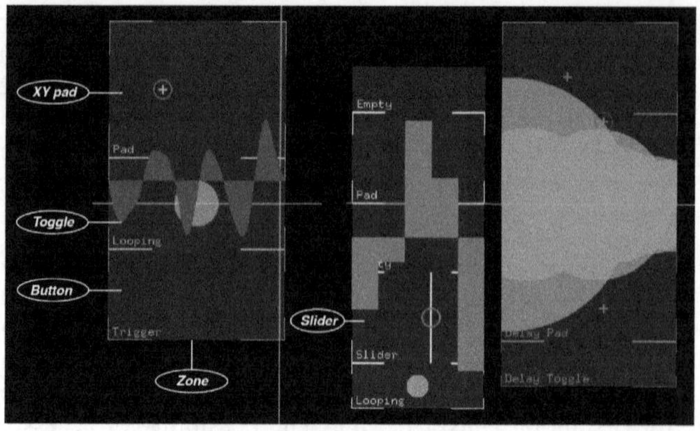


**Figure 4. Stage 3: Example of AVUI built with the toolkit, using three zones, with different UI elements and visualizations (explanatory labels in white).**

art (E2) and a two-way interaction between sound and image: not just sound visualization, but also visual sonification (E3).

## STAGE 3: THE OFXAVUI TOOLKIT

### Tookit Design and Development

To assist in making the development of AV work more streamlined, to better integrate interfaces in AV performances, and to make interaction more understandable for audiences, we have developed a toolkit for combining UI with AV content. We generalized knowledge gained from the previous stages in the development of ofxAVUI, a modular, reusable software toolkit to facilitate the production of audiovisual user interfaces. The evaluation of the 11 Stage 1 prototypes and the app from Stage 2 were distilled into a set of design insights, which in turn contributed to the definition of the feature set of our toolkit. This led to a technical specification and software architecture. The design specifications for the toolkit were, divided by main themes: 1) experience – allow for parallel and visible interaction; integrate sound, image and UI following an object-oriented approach; 2) interface – enable reconfigurable interfaces, with flexible mappings; ensure both clarity and aesthetic appeal of interface, harmonized with visuals; 3) media – allow for powerful media manipulation, with procedural content; and adopt a flexible media management. Full design specifications, and their connection with previous stages of the research can be found at `http://www.gen-av.org/avui-design-tables/`.

For the development of the toolkit, we again used OF and Maximilian. We organized the code into three groups of class files: audio, visuals and UI. Each of the three groups has a base class, making it easy to extend and to create a new audio process, a new visualization and a new UI type. The style of the UI is centralized in one class, facilitating the customization of its appearance. It was released as an "add-on" (plug-in for OF), allowing to be integrated in other OF projects by developers. We released the add-on in versions for personal computer and mobile multitouch devices. ofxAVUI was released as open source in our GitHub repository (`https://github.com/AVUIs/ofxAVUI`). As is customary with OF add-ons, we included examples, extensively commented the source code, and adopted the "ofx" prefix. It is now part of the main directory for OF add-ons, in the UI category: `http://ofxaddons.com/categories/1-gui`.

We kept the object-oriented notion of zones from the app in Stage 2, as an organization structure for combining AV and UI. Each zone has only one sound and one visualization, to reinforce its individuality and its objecthood. Different UI elements can be added to a zone: buttons, toggles, XY pads, sliders, range sliders, drop-down menus and labels. The number of zones can be defined, as well as their: size; position; color palette; UI elements. Any parameter from the UI can be rerouted to any audio feature of the zone, or any other aspect of the software (for example, any graphic on the screen). We kept the minimal UI aesthetics of the prototype. Visualization is an important link between sound and image, therefore we added two visualizations, with more configuration options. We also facilitated the creation of new visualizations, making the visualization module extensible. We incorporated the Syphon protocol, so that media could be channeled, with or without UI, to other applications (Figure 4). These design elements, core to the definition of an AVUI, are exposed to the OF developer through high level function calls, making integration into an OF project straightforward.

As an example of ease of ofxAVUI implementation, only three lines of code are needed to create and configure an AV zone with a button that triggers a sound and associated visualization. UI and visualization inherit the aesthetic properties configured for the zone.

## Evaluation

For a first, internal validation of ofxAVUI, we built a general release version of our Stage 2 prototype using the add-on. This new version allowed us to address areas to improve in *AV Zones* identified during Stage 2: interface clarity, media manipulation, and media management. In terms of interface clarity, we separated the multiple functions of the XY pad into dedicated toggles and buttons (on/off toggle, sequencer toggle, sound file drop-down menu). Regarding media manipulation, the sequencer can now record and visualize additional interactions. As for media management, users can add and manage sound files via the Apple iTunes interface, a standard for iOS apps. This final version of *AV Zones* has been released as open source on GitHub (`https://github.com/AVUIs/AVZones-ofxAVUI`), and can be loaded into an iOS device using Apple's Xcode software. The ofxAVUI add-on allowed us to easily and quickly redevelop our prototype and solve issues detected in Stage 2 (Figure 5).

To evaluate the add-on with other developers, we organized a one-day hackathon to look at its ease of use and effectiveness of development. A call was circulated using the same channels as the Stage 1 hackathons. Eight participants took part in the hackathon (five male, three female). Their profile was similar to the previous participants: audiovisual performers and developers. Four of the participants managed to complete a small project during the one-day event. The projects were: *FFT/MFCC*, audio frequency analyzers and visualizers; *Step Sequencer* for creating rhythmic patterns; *Background Image*, for customizing zones; and *Lisajous and Grid*, two additional visualizers. These projects expand the toolkit and were added to the ofxAVUI online repository (Figure 6).

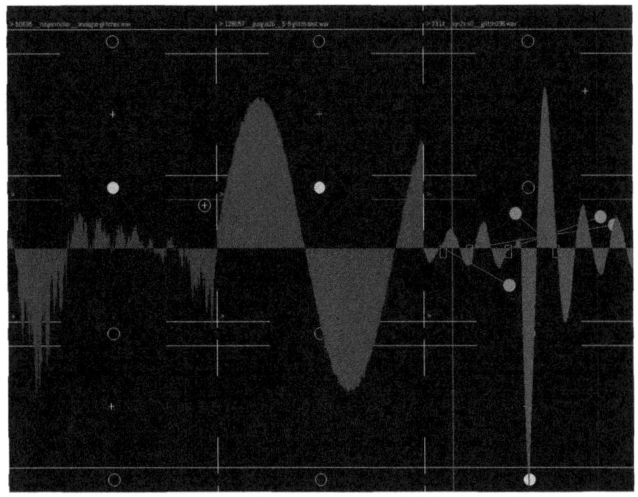

**Figure 5. Stage 3: AV Zones, rebuilt with ofxAVUI.**

In order to obtain further feedback, we reached out to ofxAVUI users on GitHub. Although software downloads are anonymous, 12 individuals had "starred" the repository – a form of following the repository and its updates on GitHub. Of those 12, eight had contact information in their GitHub profiles and were contacted by us. We sent an email asking if they would like to participate in a study. We obtained four replies, and two developers agreed to participate. They developed two projects: a four-zone *Multisampler* and *ShaderUI*, an implementation of sound-responsive shaders. They were also added to our repository.

We conducted face-to-face interviews with the participants in the hackathon (E1-8), and Skype interviews with the two online developers (E9, E10). Interviews lasted on average 30 minutes. The semi-structured interviews addressed: 1) ease of development with ofxAVUI; 2) its usefulness; 3) the appeal of its design; 4) results achieved and satisfaction with those; 5) potential for future use of the add-on.

In our thematic analysis of the interviews, a new main theme emerged: *development*, related to observations on programming and code. From this, three sub-themes were considered: *organization and architecture of code*, *speed and ease of development*, and *patching and building*. This main theme preempted the *reconfigurable interfaces* theme of the previous studies. One additional theme emerged: *scenarios*, under the *experience* main theme.

### Development

*Organization and architecture of code:* Most respondents considered that the code was well organized, with "everything nicely in their respective categories" (E1), and that it was easy to see "how the objects related to each other" (E9). Some evaluators mentioned that the code was easy to extend, as every category has a base class (E3, E10). One respondent highlighted the flexibility in mapping UI parameters to other

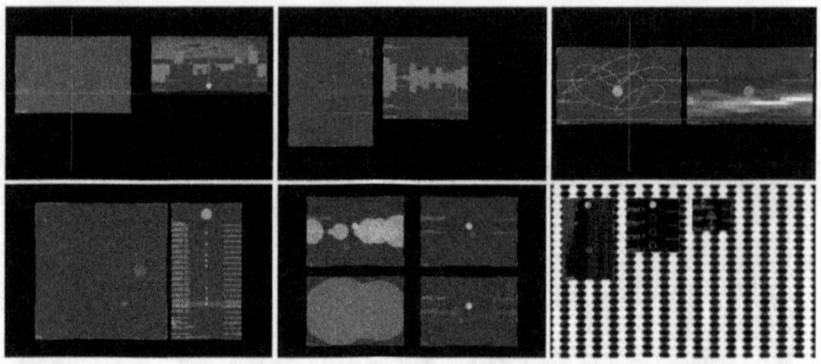

**Figure 6. Stage 3: Projects from the ofxAVUI hackathon (first four) and online evaluators (last two) – left to right, then top to bottom: *Background Image, FFT/MFCC, Lisajous and Grid, Step Sequencer, Multisampler* and *ShaderUI*.**

zones. Different from other UI toolkits, ofxAVUI is, according to our users, designed "to reuse bits and pieces in particular ways to invent new stuff" (E10). Three respondents wanted more abstraction in the code (E2, E8, E9): flexibility regarding multiple types of input (for example, touchscreen or sensors), and to be able to "switch audio engines at will" (E9). One evaluator could not finish the project on time because the toolkit did not support PureData (`https://puredata.info`) as audio engine (E8). Two evaluators felt that the UI could have taken advantage from the existing ofxGUI toolkit (E1, E3).

*Speed and ease of development:* ofxAVUI was considered easy to work with by respondents (E3, E4, E7, E9, E10), not just because of its organization and architecture, but also because "it already has the minimum package of sound, UI and visual" built in (E3). One of the respondents considers ofxAVUI easier to use than the two main UI toolkit for OF, ofxUI and ofxGUI (E10). This evaluator considers it easier and faster to prototype with than using related tools, and that "it fills a gap", providing "interesting opportunities that would not be as easily possible previously". Two respondents thought that the add-on could be better documented (E1, E10).

*Patching and building:* Three respondents would like to have a top-level environment that facilitates the creation of UIs, with a simplified coding language (E1, E3, E7), or by drag-and-drop, as in visual interface builders (E1). Two evaluators expressed interest in having a "master controller" (E5, E10) that could switch zones on and off, and reroute information between them. Another was interested in integrating zones and patching them (E3). Yet another suggested having multiple visualizations per zone, stacked in layers, visualizing different parameters (E5). Two respondents are interested in the implementation of the OSC protocol (`http://opensoundcontrol.org`) to control other applications and devices (E6, E10), with one stating that it was faster to build a OSC controller with ofxAVUI than with Lemur, a popular tablet controller builder app (E10).

### *Experience*

*Visible interaction:* In a use case that involves showing ofxAVUI to an audience, such as a performance or a demo, most respondents (E1, E3, E5, E6, E8, E10) consider that revealing the UI is important, making the software "engaging" and "easy to understand". It creates "a more cohesive experience", by showing "the beauty of the internals of the system" (E3). One respondent considers that showing an UI would depend on the use case, and that revealing it "challenges how you interact" in order to "find ways to make audience aware of what's happening" (E5).

*Scenarios:* Two evaluators considered ofxAVUI well suited to teach sound and visualization (E2, E8). One respondent considered ofxAVUI adequate for game development, particularly pedagogical games (E2). He also suggested that ofxAVUI could be used in more generic applications, for highlighting important tasks. Another evaluator stated that the adoption of OF makes the toolkit more suited to artistic applications, but if made more "portable, or not relying on OF" it could be used for more "day-to-day software development" (E9).

### *Interface*

*Interface clarity:* Two evaluators requested more visual feedback for changes of state in the UI (E2, E6), such as hovering.

*Interface aesthetics:* Several respondents liked the minimalist "bare bones" aesthetics of the UI elements (E1, E3, E9). One evaluator wanted to customize UI elements and implement UI "themes", and developed a project for adding background images to zones (E1). One respondent mentioned that the large size of the UI elements "seems more applicable to a touch interface than a mouse interface" (E10).

### *Media*

*Sound visualization:* One respondent wanted to have more possibilities for audio analysis, and created a project in that direction, based on frequency visualizers. He suggested that more audio information retrieval techniques and 3D visualizations could be added (E2). One respondent wanted to have not only sound visualization, but also visual sonification (E1). Another considered that the visualizations should be used not just for sound, but to visualize other data (E10).

*Media manipulation:* One evaluator (E4) showed interest in having live audio input. Another respondent (E5) wanted to synthesize sound from an image and its color information. One respondent was interested in rhythmical and quantized aspects of sound, and developed a step sequencer (E3).

## AVUI GUIDELINES

The best practices identified in our research allow us to propose the following design guidelines for AVUIs, for use by designers who wish to implement AVUIs, either using ofxAVUI or a different approach. They may be useful for designers who wish to use sound and image together in the interface, either by using ofxAVUI or by using different technologies. These guidelines are divided into three topics, which match the three main themes across the different stages:

### 1) Maximizing AV Experience

a) Develop AVUIs that can be implemented across multiple platforms and interaction modalities – multitouch interaction seems particularly suited, as it allows for the synaesthetic illusion of touching and molding the audiovisuals;
b) Consider the potential of AVUIs for facilitating visualization of interaction when sharing/showing a screen;
c) Adopt an object-oriented approach, for a harmonious,

coherent and interrelated convergence of audio, image and UI;
d) Facilitate different types of display, allowing for different performer-audience display configurations and hardware.

**2) Optimizing Interface Functionality and Aesthetics**
a) Use reconfigurable interfaces, possibly with a back-end, that allow to re-map elements of the UI to different sonic features and visual properties; that can also change how the sound is visualized; and that can have an extensible architecture in order to better allow for customization;
b) Explore not simply one-to-one but also one-to-many mappings between UI, audio and visual features;
c) Adopt a minimalist interface aesthetics that integrates well with the visuals, namely regarding color, shape and movement, and that does not detract from the visuals;
d) Reinforce interface clarity by ensuring visibility of all UI elements, their state, parameter space and current position to it; and verify that the visualizations do not detract from this;
e) Allow for hierarchical interfaces, with the possibility of a master control, and communication between modules.

**3) Media Strategies**
a) Allow for powerful manipulation of sound and image: different forms of media generation, such as different forms of sound and visual synthesis and sampling; multiple audio and visual effects; and experiment with mappings between UI, audio and visuals across different properties;
b) Make use of generative media, due to its variety, flexibility and economy of resources;
c) Try different visualization and sonification approaches, using information retrieval techniques from audio and image;
d) Visualization should reflect not only audio but also the multiple interactions afforded by the UI;
e) Leverage powerful media management features, such as networked content (for example, streamed audio or visuals), audio and visual input, and content sharing between applications in the same device.

## DISCUSSION

Our multi-stage research produced a range of concrete outcomes: prototypes by us as well as by participants; a software plug-in toolkit; and an app built with that plug-in. This process allowed us, in an iterative user-centric manner, to gain insight on AVUI design, summarized as a set of AVUI design guidelines above, with implications for design discussed here.

### *Comparison with Existing Solutions*

Since ofxAVUI is built in C++ and with the popular openFrameworks toolkit, it can be easily adopted by digital artists and designers, and embedded in other C++ code (without having to resort to OSC, although it also supports it). Stage 3 evaluators were very positive regarding speed and ease of development with ofxAVUI, compared to other solutions (such as ofxUI and ofxGUI), and most of them consider it easy to use. One of the main trade-offs of ofxAVUI versus other solutions is, due to its inherent pre-packaging of AV and UI, it is not as flexible as using assorted graphics and sound toolkits to build a solution from scratch. On the other hand, it is quicker, and already establishes a harmonization of UI with content.

### *Object-oriented Integration of Interface with AV*

In an AVUI as we propose, sound, visualization and user interface are integrated, functionally and aesthetically, into the same entity. This relates to the concept of audiovisual objects in cognitive science [19]. The results from our studies confirm the appeal of an object-oriented approach to AV interaction design [6]. By analyzing sound and representing it visually in real-time, sound and image are harmonized, synchronous and coherent. Audiovisual congruency is ensured, making use of the identified benefits of crossmodal congruency regarding task accuracy and engagement [5, 11, 25, 31]. This object-oriented approach to AVUI design is apt to situations where the display and interaction plane are fused, as in multitouch displays, allowing for "a sensation akin to being in direct contact or touching and molding media" [13].

### *Visibility of Interaction*

The visibility of interaction is inherent in an AVUI: an interaction triggers either a visual or a sound, which is visualized. An AVUI can be particularly suited for use cases where there are benefits from representing user interaction, such as: performances (our case-study); remote collaboration and telepresence; presentations and demos. However, we have detected different profiles of users regarding visible interaction: some prefer to visually reflect agency onto the screen, "making it understandable for an audience" (Butterfly, E2), others consider that audiences do not necessarily want to see agency on the screen. In functional applications, this will be determined by the task at hand. For creative applications, this can be a matter of taste, as we noted with our expert evaluators in Stage 1. In either case, the AVUI allows the developer to merge visual content with interface elements.

### *Reconfigurable Interfaces and Flexible Mappings*

One of the identified strong points of ofxAVUI was its modularity and reconfigurability: it is designed to recombine UI and media in different configurations and mappings, providing "interesting opportunities that would not be as easily possible previously" (user E10). In ofxAVUI, being able to easily route any UI parameter to any aspect within a zone (sound, visuals, other UI elements) or outside the zone (for example, any graphic on the screen) was considered by our users as innovative with respect to other UI toolkits. Flexibility of mappings between UI, sound and image, and ways to manage that flexibility, are fundamental qualities of an AVUI, and important features in enabling technologies for them to be useful to interaction designers across a range of application domains.

### *Design Constraints and Speed of Development*

User E3 appreciated that ofxAVUI provides the core necessary functionality in sound, UI, and visuals. This is considered an advantage for some: one evaluator considers that he can "prototype a certain part of my process faster" with ofxAVUI, and that it is easier to use than other UI toolkits (E10). For others, ofxAVUI is too constrained precisely because it is tied to specific packages of sound, UI and visuals. These evaluators would like more abstraction, to be able to replace certain elements of the toolkit (for example, the audio library).

Some evaluators would like ofxAVUI to be simpler to use, for example by adding a GUI layer that would allow users to build AVUIs by dragging and dropping elements, as in traditional interface builders. Therefore, there seems to be a desire for both higher level ease of use, and lower level flexibility. A better balance could be pursued in the future between ease of use by pre-packaging elements, and allowing for more architectural flexibility. Having been built with OF is a constraint in itself – OF is popular in media art and design, but not used as much for more generic development. The toolkit could be ported to other frameworks to facilitate its adoption for more generic use cases.

### *Participatory Design and Hackathons*

Our participatory design approach enabled us to leverage artistic knowledge in audiovisual performance from a range of practitioners into a generic software toolkit. AV performers are specialists in sound visualization and visual sonification – audiovisual crossmodal interactions. We believe that their AV design skills were an important contribution to this research that benefited the design of the ofxAVUI technology. Additionally, these users make high demands for an AV system in terms of media manipulation and interaction design: they can be considered super-users, who are regularly performing in front of an audience, and need powerful, fluid and responsive manipulation of AV media through a robust interface.

We used hackathons as a motivating, productive way to connect with our users. Hackathons were employed from two different perspectives. In Stage 1, two hackathons were used for the rapid prototyping of AV performance systems by AV artists. In Stage 3, the hackathon aimed to test in a short period of time the ease of implementation of our toolkit. Participants were asked to develop a project with it, which could be added to our toolkit repository, as an extension of its functionality or a demonstration of a new use case. We also reached out to the community of interaction designers and developers following our GitHub repository website. In this sense, we complemented the "local" perspective of the hackathons with the "global" community of GitHub users, adapting, albeit on a smaller scale, the approach followed in [28].

### *Multi-stage Approach*

Informed by related multi-stage studies [33, 35], we adopted a three-stage approach to the development of the ofxAVUI toolkit. This could be used for the development of other technologies. It can be summarized as *explore-consolidate-abstract* approach: 1) explore and gather multiple views via participatory design process, and evaluate results with other users; 2) design a prototype that consolidates best practices detected in the previous study, and evaluate with users; 3) develop a general technology based on the evaluation of the prototype, convert and abstract positive aspects of it into a toolkit, and run an additional participatory design and evaluation session for testing. This approach, with a participatory stage based on hackathons, allowed us to iteratively develop both our AVUI Guidelines and the ofxAVUI toolkit. Conclusions from each study were converted into design specifications for the following one. Conclusions from each stage fed into design specifications for the following one, with the last stage informing a set of general design guidelines.

### *AVUI as Parallel to Crossmodality in the Real World*

Our interactions with the world are multi-sensorial. Opening a door handles produces auditory and visual feedback. Some of these interactions, such as pouring water into a glass, give us audiovisual feedback regarding dimensional data. In these interactions, audio and visual information are related in a congruent way. The concept of auditory icons aims to "to use sound in a way that is analogous to the use of visual icons to provide information," providing a a natural way to represent dimensional data as well as conceptual objects [10]. AVUI extends Gaver's pragmatic concept by proposing a crossmodal approach that incorporates UI elements, sonic feedback and congruent visualization in a way that aesthetic content and interface become one. The integrated audio and visualization reflect the status of UI elements, recalling a functional simplicity of the sort encouraged by John Maeda [22].

## CONCLUSION

We have introduced the concept of AudioVisual User Interface (AVUI), a type of interface where UI, audio and visualization are interconnected and integrated. By combining UI with interrelated sound and image, the proposed concept of AVUI (and ofxAVUI toolkit in particular) can help leverage the identified benefits of audiovisual crossmodal interaction, such as improvements in performance and engagement.

We presented an iterative multi-stage process of design, prototyping, development and evaluation of ofxAVUI, an enabling software toolkit to facilitate development of AVUIs. The toolkit has been released as open-source, and is multi-platform, aiming to facilitate its adoption. Participatory design methods were used, centered around three hackathons. This process also allowed us to incorporate expert and practitioner insight into a series of generic guidelines for the design of AVUIs. The toolkit and guidelines will be of interest to interaction designers who wish to create compelling products and systems which integrate sound and image in the interface. By extending Hook's existing theoretical framework to study a large number of AV systems, we believe that the findings have a strong generalizability that the previous studies do not.

We believe that the AVUI concept and the ofxAVUI technology have potential for application in a number of use cases where a screen and interaction is shown to an audience, and for and multimodal interaction. The crossmodal linkages that an AVUI facilitate could be useful for engagement in VR and AR interactive environments. This form of interaction which fuses sensing modalities, function and content, can be compelling for a number of domains: not only areas where engagement is important, such as art, education and games, but also assistive and accessible technologies.

## ACKNOWLEDGEMENTS

We would like to thank all who collaborated in this research: workshop and hackathon participants; evaluators and interviewees; colleagues; and in particular Borut Kumperščak for programming assistance and Alessandro Altavilla for documentation. This work was supported by the EU Marie Curie fellowship FP7 REA grant 627922 and also partly by FCT/MCTES LARSyS (UID/EEA/50009/2013 (2015-2017)).

## REFERENCES


1. Paul Bach-y Rita. 1987. Brain Plasticity as a Basis of Sensory Substitution. *Neurorehabilitation and Neural Repair* 1, 2 (June 1987), 67–71. DOI: http://dx.doi.org/10.1177/136140968700100202

2. Florent Berthaut, Mark T. Marshall, Sriram Subramanian, and Martin Hachet. 2013. Rouages: Revealing the Mechanisms of Digital Musical Instruments to the Audience. In *Proceedings of New Interfaces for Musical Expression (NIME)*. Daejeon, Seoul. http://nime.org/proceedings/2013/nime2013_51.pdf

3. Virginia Braun and Victoria Clarke. 2006. Using thematic analysis in psychology. *Qualitative Research in Psychology* 3, 2 (2006), 77–101. DOI: http://dx.doi.org/10.1191/1478088706qp063oa

4. Ana Carvalho and Cornelia Lund (Eds.). 2015. *The Audiovisual Breakthrough*. Fluctuating Images, Berlin. http://www.ephemeral-expanded.net/audiovisualbreakthrough/

5. Karen Collins and Peter J. Taillon. 2012. Visualized sound effect icons for improved multimedia accessibility: A pilot study. *Entertainment Computing* 3, 1 (Jan. 2012), 11–17. DOI: http://dx.doi.org/10.1016/j.entcom.2011.09.002

6. Nuno N. Correia. 2013. *Interactive Audiovisual Objects*. Doctoral thesis. Aalto ARTS Books, Helsinki. https://www.taik.fi/kirjakauppa/product_info.php?cPath=26&products_id=269&language=en

7. Nuno N. Correia and Atau Tanaka. 2014. User-Centered Design of a Tool for Interactive Computer-Generated Audiovisuals. In *Proc. 2nd ICLI*. Lisbon. http://www.liveinterfaces.org/proceedings2014.html

8. Bram Crevits. 2006. The Roots of VJing. In *VJ: Audio-Visual Art and VJ Culture*, Michael Faulkner (Ed.). Laurence King Publishing, London, 14–19.

9. Carl DiSalvo and Melissa Gregg. 2013. Issue-Oriented Hackathons. (2013). http://carldisalvo.com/posts/issue-oriented-hackathons/

10. William W. Gaver. 1986. Auditory Icons: Using Sound in Computer Interfaces. *Hum.-Comput. Interact.* 2, 2 (June 1986), 167–177. DOI: http://dx.doi.org/10.1207/s15327051hci0202_3

11. F. Wai-ling Ho-Ching, Jennifer Mankoff, and James A. Landay. 2003. Can you see what i hear?: the design and evaluation of a peripheral sound display for the deaf. In *Proc. CHI'03 (CHI '03)*. ACM, New York, NY, USA, 161–168. DOI: http://dx.doi.org/10.1145/642611.642641

12. Lars Erik Holmquist. 2008. Bootlegging: Multidisciplinary Brainstorming with Cut-ups. In *Proceedings of the Tenth Anniversary Conference on Participatory Design 2008 (PDC '08)*. Indiana University, Indianapolis, IN, USA, 158–161. http://dl.acm.org/citation.cfm?id=1795234.1795260

13. Jonathan Hook, David Green, John McCarthy, Stuart Taylor, Peter Wright, and Patrick Olivier. 2011. A VJ centered exploration of expressive interaction. In *Proc. CHI'11 (CHI '11)*. ACM, New York, NY, USA, 1265–1274. DOI: http://dx.doi.org/10.1145/1978942.1979130

14. Jonathan Hook, John McCarthy, Peter Wright, and Patrick Olivier. 2013. Waves: exploring idiographic design for live performance. In *Proceedings of the SIGCHI Conference on Human Factors in Computing Systems (CHI '13)*. ACM, New York, NY, USA, 2969–2978. DOI: http://dx.doi.org/10.1145/2470654.2481412

15. Michael Xuelin Huang, Will W. W. Tang, Kenneth W. K. Lo, C. K. Lau, Grace Ngai, and Stephen Chan. 2012. MelodicBrush: A Novel System for Cross-modal Digital Art Creation Linking Calligraphy and Music. In *Proceedings of the Designing Interactive Systems Conference (DIS '12)*. ACM, New York, NY, USA, 418–427. DOI: http://dx.doi.org/10.1145/2317956.2318018

16. Lilly Irani. 2015. Hackathons and the Making of Entrepreneurial Citizenship. *Science, Technology & Human Values* (April 2015), 1–26. DOI: http://dx.doi.org/10.1177/0162243915578486

17. Sergi Jordà. 2003. Sonigraphical Instruments From FMOL to the reacTable*. In *NIME03*. Montreal. http://www.nime.org/proceedings/2003/nime2003_070.pdf

18. M. Komssi, D. Pichlis, M. Raatikainen, K. Kindstrom, and J. Jarvinen. 2015. What are Hackathons for? *IEEE Software* 32, 5 (Sept. 2015), 60–67. DOI: http://dx.doi.org/10.1109/MS.2014.78

19. Michael Kubovy and Michael Schutz. 2010. Audio-Visual Objects. *Review of Philosophy and Psychology* 1, 1 (March 2010), 41–61. DOI: http://dx.doi.org/10.1007/s13164-009-0004-5

20. Golan Levin. 2000. *Painterly Interfaces for Audiovisual Performance*. Ph.D. Dissertation. M.Sc. Dissertation. Massachusetts Institute of Technology, Cambridge, MA. http://acg.media.mit.edu/people/golan/thesis/thesis300.pdf

21. Thomas James Lodato and Carl DiSalvo. 2016. Issue-oriented hackathons as material participation. *New Media & Society* (Feb. 2016), 1461444816629467. DOI: http://dx.doi.org/10.1177/1461444816629467

22. John Maeda. 2006. *The Laws of Simplicity*. The MIT Press, Cambridge, MA.

23. Thor Magnusson. 2006. Affordances and Constraints in Screen-based Musical Instruments. In *Proceedings of the 4th Nordic Conference on Human-computer Interaction: Changing Roles (NordiCHI '06)*. ACM, New York, NY, USA, 441–444. DOI: http://dx.doi.org/10.1145/1182475.1182532

24. Harry Mcgurk and John Macdonald. 1976. Hearing lips and seeing voices. *Nature* 264, 5588 (Dec. 1976), 746–748. DOI: http://dx.doi.org/10.1038/264746a0

25. Oussama Metatla, Nuno N. Correia, Fiore Martin, Nick Bryan-Kinns, and Tony Stockman. 2016. Tap the ShapeTones: Exploring the Effects of Crossmodal Congruence in an Audio-Visual Interface. In *Proceedings of the 2016 CHI Conference on Human Factors in Computing Systems (CHI '16)*. ACM, New York, NY, USA, 1055–1066. DOI: http://dx.doi.org/10.1145/2858036.2858456

26. William Moritz. 1997a. Digital Harmony: The Life of John Whitney, Computer Animation Pioneer. 2.5 (Aug. 1997). http://www.awn.com/mag/issue2.5/2.5pages/2.5moritzwhitney.html

27. William Moritz. 1997b. The Dream of Color Music, And Machines That Made it Possible. *Animation World Magazine* 2.1 (April 1997). http://www.awn.com/mag/issue2.1/articles/moritz2.1.html

28. Alistair Morrison, Donald McMillan, Stuart Reeves, Scott Sherwood, and Matthew Chalmers. 2012. A Hybrid Mass Participation Approach to Mobile Software Trials. In *Proceedings of the SIGCHI Conference on Human Factors in Computing Systems (CHI '12)*. ACM, New York, NY, USA, 1311–1320. DOI: http://dx.doi.org/10.1145/2207676.2208588

29. Paul Nagle. 2008. Yamaha Tenori-On Review. *Sound On Sound* Feb. 2008 (2008). http://www.soundonsound.com/sos/feb08/articles/yamahatenorion.htm

30. I. Olowe, G. Moro, and M. Barthet. 2016. residUUm: user mapping and performance strategies for multilayered live audiovisual generation. In *Proceedings of International Conference on New Interfaces for Musical Expression (NIME)*. Brisbane. http://www.nime.org/proceedings/2016/nime2016_paper0053.pdf

31. Shin'ichi Onimaru, Taro Uraoka, Naoyuki Matsuzaki, and Michiteru Kitazaki. 2008. Cross-modal information display to improve driving performance. In *Proc. ACM symposium on Virtual reality software and technology (VRST '08)*. ACM, New York, NY, USA, 281–282. DOI: http://dx.doi.org/10.1145/1450579.1450653

32. Chris Salter. 2010. *Entangled: Technology and the Transformation of Performance*. MIT Press, Massachusetts.

33. Guy Schofield, David Green, Thomas Smith, Peter Wright, and Patrick Olivier. 2014. Cinejack: Using Live Music to Control Narrative Visuals. In *Proceedings of the 2014 Conference on Designing Interactive Systems (DIS '14)*. ACM, New York, NY, USA, 209–218. DOI: http://dx.doi.org/10.1145/2598510.2598520

34. Ladan Shams, Yukiyasu Kamitani, and Shinsuke Shimojo. 2000. Illusions: What you see is what you hear. *Nature* 408, 6814 (Dec. 2000), 788–788. DOI: http://dx.doi.org/10.1038/35048669

35. Alexander Wiethoff and Sven Gehring. 2012. Designing Interaction with Media Façades: A Case Study. In *Proceedings of the Designing Interactive Systems Conference (DIS '12)*. ACM, New York, NY, USA, 308–317. DOI: http://dx.doi.org/10.1145/2317956.2318004

# Suggesting API Usage to Novice Programmers with the Example Guru

**Michelle Ichinco, Wint Yee Hnin, and Caitlin L. Kelleher**
Washington University in St. Louis
St. Louis, MO, USA
{michelle.ichinco, hnin, ckelleher}@wustl.edu

## ABSTRACT

Programmers, especially novices, often have difficulty learning new APIs (Application Programming Interfaces). Existing research has not fully addressed novice programmers' unawareness of all available API methods. To help novices discover new and appropriate uses for API methods, we designed a system called the Example Guru. The Example Guru suggests context-relevant API methods based on each programmer's code. The suggestions provide contrasting examples to demonstrate how to use the API methods. To evaluate the effectiveness of the Example Guru, we ran a study comparing novice programmers' use of the Example Guru and documentation-inspired API information. We found that twice as many participants accessed the Example Guru suggestions compared to documentation and that participants used more than twice as many new API methods after accessing suggestions than documentation.

## ACM Classification Keywords

H.5.2 [User Interfaces]: Evaluation/method

## Author Keywords

APIs; novice programming; programming support; examples

## INTRODUCTION

Research has shown that programmers often struggle to learn and use Application Programming Interfaces (APIs) [47]. These issues learning APIs stem from a variety of causes, including insufficient resources, confusing API structure, lack of programming experience, and unawareness of API methods [46]. This paper will focus primarily on API method unawareness. While unawareness of API methods affects all programmers, those with less programming experience, such as children learning programming or end-user programmers, often find barriers to learning APIs insurmountable [28].

We are unaware of existing research in API support or computer science education that has fully addressed the awareness problem in learning APIs. Instead, researchers have created systems for helping experienced programmers use APIs that improve: code completion [26], search [50], and available documentation [49]. These support systems require users to query a method of interest, so they do not help programmers identify new applicable API methods or incorrect usages of API methods.

To illustrate why using a large and unfamiliar API can be especially challenging for non-expert programmers, imagine an end-user programmer, Julie, who needs to analyze data from a biology study quickly. She decides to use Ruby to write a CSV file of results, but does not realize that an API method exists to automatically format an array correctly with commas [8]. Instead, she loops through her data, adding commas where they seem appropriate. Existing commas within her data make this task even more complex. Imagine instead that while Julie writes her array output code, her IDE offers a tip that introduces Julie to the method used for array formatting along with examples that illustrate its use.

In this paper, we introduce a system called the Example Guru, and evaluate its impact on API exploration and use. The Example Guru is designed to suggest relevant API information while programmers work on their own projects. The Example Guru uses a set of static rules to automatically check novice programs for opportunities to suggest API information. When it finds opportunities to do so, the Example Guru offers quick suggestions of relevant API methods. The user can expand the suggestions to view two contrasting executable code examples and support for finding and adding relevant code elements. To evaluate the effectiveness of the Example Guru at encouraging new API use by novice programmers, we ran a study comparing the Example Guru's suggestions to an in-application API documentation condition designed to capture the current best practice for supporting API use. Results show that twice as many novice programmers using the Example Guru accessed suggestions as accessed the in-application documentation in the control condition. Novice programmers also used over twice as many new API methods after accessing suggestions than after accessing documentation. Overall, we found that our suggestions helped broaden novice programmers' use of a new API. This paper has two contributions: 1) a system that motivates use of new API methods through context-relevant suggestions and contrasting examples, and 2) a study demonstrating increased exploration and use of API methods over best practice in-application documentation.



*CHI 2017*, May 06-11, 2017, Denver, CO, USA



DOI: http://dx.doi.org/10.1145/3025453.3025827

## RELATED WORK

This section focuses on how related systems recommend support to programmers and users of complex software. Complex software systems are related because large numbers of available commands create problems similar to those that programmers face when learning new APIs. In the System Design section, we will discuss how the design of the interface and examples compare to similar systems. Here, we will place the Example Guru within the context of work on recommending support based on: 1) the behaviors of communities of users, 2) the ways individuals program and use complex software, and 3) the errors users encounter.

### Recommending support based on communities of users

Existing systems support novices in learning APIs, programming, and complex software by leveraging: 1) overall community usage, and 2) community example repositories.

*Overall command usage*

Some API and software support uses community data to recommend commonly used commands. Systems provide recommendations with ranked lists based on common usages in a variety of ways, such as: lists of API methods in a programming environment [19], lists of commands within software [35], or by emphasizing more commonly used API methods in documentation [49]. Some recommendation tools use collaborative filtering algorithms, which classify a user's behavior within community usage data in order to recommend API methods [37, 44] or software commands [35, 30].

*Recommending from sets of community examples*

Research has also leveraged communities of users to find examples, Q&A information, and code completion methods related to a user's program. Systems work to improve example code retrieval for supporting programmers in using APIs. They do this by comparing users' code against repositories [20], mining patterns of APIs often used together [54], looking for related words to find code examples for similar types of functionality [2], or using input and output types [50, 33]. For more project-specific examples in open-source projects, recommendations have been based on the program history and types of tasks [10, 32]. Other than examples, systems also use community resources to inform relevant Q&A recommendation [9], code completion [5, 26], and parameter completion [1, 53].

The Example Guru also uses information about how a community of users commonly uses API methods, but it uses that information along with the context of the code. Because the Example Guru aims to improve the API unawareness issue, it suggests examples, rather than improving the ease of searching for examples. Furthermore, when the Example Guru suggests examples, the suggestions present new API methods that the programmer may want to learn, rather than examples about what the user is already doing.

### Recommending support based on individual usage

Some systems provide recommendations for effective programming, APIs, or software commands based on either the user's behavior or the artifact they are working on.

*Behavior*

Research has used current or past behavior to recommend support to users of complex software and APIs. AmbientHelp recommends information based on the commands a user is working with at any point in time [34]. Similarly, CoDis suggests unfamiliar commands based on command patterns and the time since the user's last activity [55]. Another tool bases API recommendations on the user's programming history [45].

*Artifacts*

Some systems use just the artifact the user is creating to recommend help for APIs, programming, and commands in complex software. Tools for recommending APIs consider the structure of code to recommend API methods, such as by looking for redundant code [25] or using identifiers from a class's abstract syntax tree [18]. Documentation recommendations can also rely on artifacts, like by connecting method invocations to documentation [11], or by relating software interface elements to documentation [27]. Systems also recommend commands to users in sketching software based on the drawing artifacts that users create [14, 22, 40].

These systems are the most similar to the Example Guru because the Example Guru also makes suggestions based on the programmer's code. However, these systems primarily focus on recommending commands, while the Example Guru also focuses on the user's motivation to access the suggestions. To do this, the Example Guru suggests unknown or incorrectly used API usages in order to both introduce new API methods, as well as to improve the output of the programmer's code. Results-oriented programmers like novice and end-user programmers will likely be more motivated by suggestions that explicitly connect new API methods to the output of their code.

### Recommending support based on errors

Software systems and programming environments also suggest information to users based on errors. Tools for non-expert programmers recommend information to try to help users who have hit a barrier in completing a code task [23] or who have errors in their code [17]. Two specific scenarios where recommendations based on errors can be especially useful are: in pasting and adapting code examples [12], and in complex software systems where commands are easily mistaken for each other [29]. While these systems effectively suggest examples to help resolve errors, they do not necessarily introduce new skills and require that the user has hit a problem in order to know what to suggest. Instead, the Example Guru suggests context-relevant API methods based on programmers' code in order to help them use new API methods or use API methods correctly.

## THE EXAMPLE GURU

This section will first give an overview of how the Example Guru works, followed by the rationales for the interface design and the content the Example Guru suggests.

### System Overview

The Example Guru suggests API usages to novice programmers based on their code in Looking Glass [31], a blocks-based programming environment for creating 3D animations designed for children aged 10-15 (see Figure 1). Looking Glass users are similar to end-user programmers in that they are motivated by the output of their code, which in this case is an animation. The Looking Glass API is unique from many other common blocks-based APIs because it has methods such as 'walk,' 'resize,' and 'setTransparency' that perform operations on 3D graphics. We chose to implement the Example Guru within Looking Glass for three reasons: we wanted to address novice API use, Looking Glass users generally work on open-ended projects which was our target context, and we needed an unfamiliar API to introduce, so we could not use the more widely known blocks programming environments.

The Example Guru has two main features: 1) rules, which parse code, looking for opportunities to suggest API methods, and 2) suggestions, which include textual tips, contrasting code examples, and the 'show me' capability that demonstrates where to find an API method block in the interface. In essence, each rule asks a yes or no question about the presence of specific code elements in a program and triggers suggestions if the required code elements exist. For example, one rule checks for a character turning to face another character. The suggestion for that rule introduces joint movements, which allow a character to turn just their head to face something, rather than their whole body. The Example Guru uses rules to check programs each time a programmer executes their code. It then makes a suggestion to the user based on a triggered rule. The system will only make a suggestion for one rule at a time, so it uses an established priority if multiple suggestions arise at once. We provide more details about the suggestion priority in the system design section.

## System design

In order to design the Example Guru we used two methods: 1) formative studies, and 2) program analysis. For the Example Guru interface and suggestions, we used an iterative design process in a formative study with 48 participants aged 10-15. To design the rules and suggestions, we used two sets of programs not created for this study. One set contained 107 programs created by Looking Glass API experts. The second set contained 600 programs shared to the Looking Glass website by non-experts [31].

### *Rules*

For this study, we designed and implemented the rules by hand. In the discussion, we address how a system could automate this process in order for it to apply to other and larger APIs. Our process had three main steps: 1) compare novice and expert API use to select the API methods to suggest and the priority order, 2) consider the types of animations experts created with specific API methods and find simpler or related animations novices make where new API methods could be useful, and 3) author the rules within the system.

In order to select which API methods to suggest and the priority with which to suggest them, we compared our sets of novice and expert programs. We wanted to suggest API methods that novices were likely to be unfamiliar with, but also that they were likely to find useful. The set of API methods the Example Guru suggests contains API methods that experts used more often than novices and that experts used more than 5% of the time. These API methods are likely unfamiliar, but also used frequently enough by experts to be useful. Selecting the API methods to suggest based on expert usage helps to prevent the suggestions from over-fitting to the first hour of programming. Since the Example Guru only presents one suggestion at a time, we designed a priority ordering for selecting one of the triggered rules to suggest. Rules suggesting ways to correct API usages have the highest priority. The Example Guru then suggests API methods with the largest difference in expert and novice use and that experts used more often. The lowest priority suggestions are for API methods that experts and novices used with similar frequencies or that experts rarely used.

The design of rules is similar to code smells [13] and anti-patterns [23], but instead of focusing on checking for poorly composed code, most of the rules in the Example Guru look for opportunities to introduce new concepts. Essentially, rules recommend ways to improve animations through the use of previously unused API methods. Our formative work showed that it is important for the rules to find opportunities to improve novices' animations because suggestions that only improved the code quality were less exciting to novices creating animations. This is because novices in Looking Glass are focusing primarily on their animations, rather than on trying to learn new programming concepts. In order to decide when to recommend a particular unused API method, we manually checked how experts used API methods for complex animations. In many cases, novices create similar, more basic animations with more commonly used API methods. For instance, one rule checks programs for characters turning multiple rotations, as the programmer may be attempting to make characters dance. The rule has a suggestion that demonstrates how to animate joints to make a more realistic dancing animation. Each rule has an associated suggestion that introduces the API usage to the programmer.

Finally, we implemented the rules within the Example Guru. Rules contain a specification of how to parse code for opportunities to improve. Specifications use an internal API designed to simplify querying the abstract syntax tree.

### *Suggestions*

We designed the suggestion presentation and examples through an iterative process with one-on-one study sessions.

We designed the suggestion presentation with the following goals: 1) to not interrupt or overwhelm the user, 2) to be easily accessible, and 3) to demonstrate the relevance of the suggestion to the code. Formative user testing indicated that programmers were most open to new ideas and improvements around the time they decide to test their code, so the Example Guru presents new suggestions after code execution. A list of suggestions allows the user to return to a suggestion at any point (see Figure 1-A), while the code annotations connect suggestions to the relevant code (see Figure 1-B). Hovering over a suggestion in the suggestion list provides a preview of the example and hovering over an annotation in the code shows a text description of the suggestion. These previews provide a hint of what the suggestion would show if opened, similar to surprise, explain, reward [51].

The examples presented within suggestions differ from those in other systems [17, 23, 41] in two critical ways: 1) they emphasize how the API method works using two contrasting

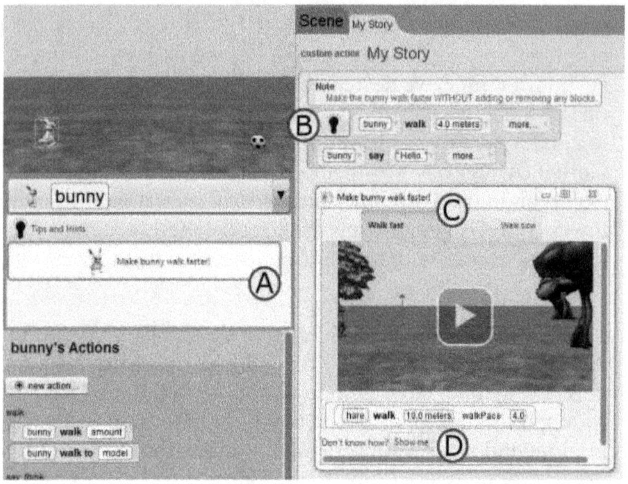

**Figure 1. The Example Guru implemented within Looking Glass. (A) List of all suggestions. (B) Code annotation button to open the most recently added suggestion. (C) Contrasting examples such as 'walk fast' and 'walk slow'. (D) 'Show me' button that users can click to see the location of the suggested block.**

examples (see Figure 1-C), and 2) they provide support for finding the relevant code block in the interface (see Figure 1-D). We developed the idea for contrasting examples through formative testing, where participants often did not know which argument values to use in blocks of code. The two contrasting examples either show different values or two API methods that work similarly in order to highlight the differences. The goal of the contrasting examples was to encourage novices to perform self-explanation, which has been shown to be effective for learning [7]. Within a blocks environment, understanding how a block works does not necessarily mean a novice can use it. Formative and related work indicated that novices sometimes have trouble finding a code block from an example [21]. One study [16] found that providing a 'show me' button that, when clicked, highlighted the location of the block in the programming environment, helped programmers find necessary blocks (see Figure 1-D). In the results, we answer whether participants used the features provided in our design. Table 1 details designs we tested and found to be ineffective.

## EVALUATION

We ran a study to evaluate the effectiveness of the Example Guru's suggestions in encouraging new API method use by comparing them to an in-application documentation control condition. We will call the two conditions the 'suggestions' condition and the 'documentation' condition. In working towards reducing the unawareness problem for novice programmers learning new APIs, we tested the following two hypotheses:

H1: Novice programmers will access suggestions more frequently than documentation. We hypothesize that the suggestions will expose novice programmers to API methods that they likely would not have realized existed.

H2: Novice programmers using suggestions will improve their API usage more as a result of suggestions than novice programmers will from API documentation. Here, we want to compare the number and type of API methods participants add to their code after accessing suggestions or documentation.

| Design | Issue |
|---|---|
| Suggestions appeared alongside the execution view. | Users did not focus on suggestions while executing their code, but instead returned to the code before considering what to do next. |
| Suggestions only appeared as buttons next to the code. | Users did not always want to access suggestions immediately, but displaying many suggestions crowded the editor. |
| Suggestions only contained one example. | Users did not understand the impact of argument values relative to their code. |
| Examples had text along with the code to explain how the example worked. | The text made the example view crowded and made it hard for users to focus on the critical elements. Users rarely read the text. |

**Table 1. Unsuccessful design attempts in formative testing**

### Documentation Condition

Currently, the best practice for supporting use of unfamiliar API methods is providing easy-to-access documentation containing example code. A few systems use suggestions within a programming context, but focus on violations of proper programming. Errors provide natural motivation to use suggestions, but in the case of API use, we cannot assume that novices will be motivated to apply a nonessential suggestion. We believe comparing to the best practice, documentation, is an appropriate first step toward evaluating the Example Guru.

We designed the documentation based on two common forms of API support: online API documentation and code completion. We wanted the documentation to have full information like online documentation, while making it easily accessible like code completion. Thus, the user can access a doc (documentation for a specific API method) by clicking a '?' button beside the code block the user is interested in (see Figure 2-A). Upon opening a doc, the user can view descriptions and examples of how the API method works, along with all of the available parameters for that API method (see Figure 2).

### Participants

We recruited participants who had never used Looking Glass because this study investigates novice programmers exploration and use of the Looking Glass API. We recruited 81 participants aged 10 to 15 from a local STEM mailing list. Two participants had used Looking Glass in the past and a third skipped the first phase of the study, so we analyzed the data from the remaining 78 participants. The 78 participants had an average age of 11.8 (SD= 1.6), were 46.2% female, 52.6% male, and 1.2% unspecified gender. We compensated each participant with a \$10 gift card to Amazon.com.

### Methods

We created materials in order to measure API information access, API usage, and participant features that could influence how participants use API information.

#### *API information access and usage*

In order to evaluate whether participants accessed suggestions more than documentation, we needed to ensure two things:

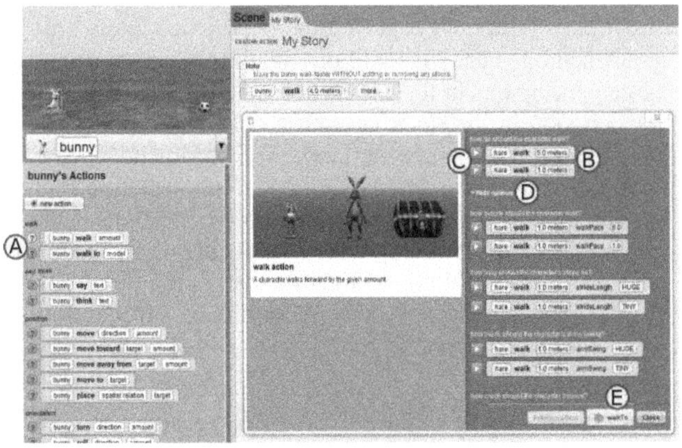

Figure 2. In-application API Documentation condition. (A) Users can access documentation using the '?' button available beside APIs. (B) Examples with different values and the description. (C) The play button can be used to execute the code. (D) Button to expand or collapse the parameters information. (E) Users can navigate to other doc using these buttons.

1) that participants were equally familiar with the API information formats, and 2) that participants actually received suggestions while working on open-ended programs. In order to familiarize participants with the API information, we created two training tasks. For the first training task, participants had to make a bunny walk faster by adding an optional argument value to a 'walk' action. For the second, they had to make a shark swim around an island by adding an optional argument value to a 'turn' code block. We provided instructions on a sheet of paper that directed participants to use the API information provided.

In order to improve the odds that participants would receive suggestions during open-ended programming, we created and tested scenes with props and characters for participants to use in creating their animations. For instance, complex movements and rotations trigger suggestions, so one scene was designed for a Seaworld show animation. This scene often motivated novice programmers to try to create complex animations with dolphins, which sometimes triggered suggestions. We selected five scenes for this study based on popular scenes from formative work because children were most excited to create animations with those scenes.

### *Participant features*

In designing the Example Guru, we wanted novice programmers to benefit from suggestions regardless of their age, gender, or programming experience. Because the suggestions are context-relevant, we hypothesized that the suggestions would interest users with very little programming experience, as well as novices with more exposure. In order to capture information about programming experience, participants filled out a demographic and computing history survey.

We also thought that the way participants like to learn might affect how they use API documentation and explore new API methods. In order to capture this, participants also filled out an exploring and learning technology survey on paper before the study, modeled after the survey about trying new technology in [6]. Additionally, to better understand participants' motivations in using new API methods, we created dynamic surveys for participants to fill out on-screen after completing open-ended programs during the study. The surveys asked questions about why participants used new API methods for the first time and why they used or did not use API information during the just-completed program.

## Study Procedures

There were three phases of this study: 1) baseline open-ended, 2) training, and 3) supported open-ended. The study was between subjects with two conditions: suggestions and documentation. Because work has demonstrated that gender plays into exploration and learning in software [6], we randomly assigned participants to either use suggestions or documentation keeping gender balanced. Participants worked individually on all tasks and were allowed to move onto the next task if they felt they had completed the current one.

### *Baseline open-ended phase*

We wanted to know how participants would use the API without any support, so participants first created an animation without API support for up to 15 minutes. Because some participants had no programming experience, the instructions for the first phase gave information about how to drag blocks into animations and execute the animations. This phase involved open-ended programming, which means that there was no correct or incorrect answer and that participants were allowed to freely create their animations. We assigned participants a specific scene for this task and balanced the assignments of scenes across participants to limit any effect of specific scenes on API usage. In order to find out more about why participants added new API methods, participants completed an on-screen survey at the end of this task that asked about: 1) one new API method participants added and executed, and 2) one that they added, executed and deleted, if these existed. Due to space constraints, we will not discuss this survey in this paper.

### *Training phase*

Due to time constraints for a controlled study, we wanted participants to become quickly comfortable with using either suggestions or documentation. To do this, we had all participants complete two training tasks. In both cases, the instructions showed how to access the suggestion or documentation that would help them complete the task. The researchers checked the participants' code to make sure they successfully completed the task and helped participants if needed. If participants completed a task without a suggestion or documentation, the researcher demonstrated how they could have used it to ensure that all participants were exposed to suggestions or documentation.

### *Supported open-ended phase*

Finally, we wanted to evaluate how participants used the API information and API methods when working on their own projects. During the supported open-ended phase, participants created open-ended animations with either suggestions or documentation available to them. We first asked participants to create a program based on the idea of a Seaworld show. The purpose of providing an idea was to give participants a goal to work towards, but not to constrain what code they should use. Next, participants were assigned a scene in which they could create any animation or use a provided story prompt if they did not have an idea. Participants had up to fifteen minutes to work on each of the two animations. If participants finished early, they could select a scene they had not yet used and create another animation. At the end of each of these animations, participants also typed answers to questions onscreen about why they added or removed certain API methods and why they accessed or did not access API information.

### Data Collection & Analysis

We logged all actions participants took and survey answers to analyze suggestion, documentation, and API usage.

#### *Time on task*

We did not require participants to spend the full amount of time provided on each task, so some participants spent less than the standard amount of time. Most participants (76%) spent the full amount of time on the baseline (15 min.) and supported open-ended (30 min.) phases. We stopped analyzing participants' data after 30 minutes in supported open-ended. We will report the results for the set of participants who spent the full amount of time (59 participants), as well as the results for all participants.

#### *Accessing API information and API usage*

We analyzed logs in order to measure which suggestions and documentation participants accessed, meaning that they clicked to open the API information. To determine whether participants used new methods from the API information in their programs, we measured which API methods participants inserted into their programs for the first time after accessing related API information. When comparing the number of accesses and API usage, we used t-tests to compare the aggregate numbers because participants received different numbers of suggestions. Additionally, participants in the API documentation condition could access docs many more times than the number of suggestions available. We use Cohen's d to measure effect size (small: .3, medium: .5, large: .8). We also report the percentages of participants who accessed API information and used API methods and compare this using Chi-squared tests. We use the odds ratio to measure effect size (small: 1.5, medium: 3.5, large: 9).

For both API information access and API usage, we describe the kinds of API methods participants were accessing information for and inserting into their programs. We believe the best way to do this is to group the API methods based on how much novice programmers generally use them. We base the frequency of novice use on the set of 600 non-expert programs described earlier. We will discuss the API methods in terms of 4 groups: those that the Example Guru did not suggest, APIs suggested that were used least frequently by novices (the bottom third of usage frequency), those suggested that were sometimes used (the middle third), and those suggested that were most often used by novices (the top third of API method usage frequency).

#### *Participant qualities*

We analyzed participant qualities to try to understand the types of novice programmers who will benefit from suggestions or documentation. We collected gender, age, programming experience, and learning style data from the surveys. We captured programming experience using two survey questions: 'Have you programmed before?' and 'Have you programmed for more than 3 hours in your whole life?' Those who had less than 3 hours of programming experience likely only programmed once or twice without much instruction or practice. Nine participants in the suggestion condition (23%) and eight participants in the documentation condition (21%) had 0-3 hours of programming experience. We also intended to capture personal preferences about using API documentation using the on-screen end-of-task surveys for both conditions. Due to a technical error, the survey questions asking participants about why they did or did not access documentation did not appear for the study participants, so we report quotes from pilot users who completed the same study and received these questions.

## RESULTS

We hypothesized that participants who received suggestions would: 1) access suggestions, and 2) use API methods from the suggestions more frequently than participants would access and use in-application documentation. In this section, we first explore these two hypotheses and then delve into how different participants used the API information and the features they used.

### Access and use of suggestions and documentation

Ideally, suggestions should encourage API exploration when novice programmers are pursuing their own projects. We evaluated this through the number of times participants accessed API information and how many new API methods they used after accessing API information.

#### *Accessing suggestions and documentation*

We found that more participants accessed suggestions than accessed documentation: 82% of suggestion participants and 41% of documentation participants accessed at least one entry. The difference in the number of participants who accessed suggestions verses documentation was significant with a medium effect size ($\chi^2(1) = 12.19, p < 0.001$, odds ratio = 6.4). Participants in both conditions described using suggestions and documentation to gain additional information about API methods that seemed potentially relevant. A participant in the documentation condition described opening an API method that changed a character's appearance because: "... I wondered what it was. It turned out to change Alice." One participant in the suggestion condition sought additional information about a new method based on the tip offered as part of the suggestion: "I opened the tip for 'setTransparency' because I thought it was good way to make an object disappear".

We found that participants accessed more total suggestions, on average, than documentation. For all 78 participants, participants accessed significantly more suggestions (M=3.3, SD=2.7) than documentation (M=1.4, SD=2.7), $t(76) = 31, p < 0.01$, $d = 0.69$. Since some participants spent less than the full task time, we also confirmed that this difference existed for the set of participants who used the whole task time. The results were very similar: participants accessed suggestions (M=3.0, SD= 2.7) significantly more than documentation (M= 1.1, SD = 1.7) with a large effect size ($t(50) = 3.3, p < 0.01, d = 0.85$). Simply accessing more suggestions is a potential benefit to novice programmers because the suggestions expose them to broader range of API methods that may be useful either immediately or in the future. In this study, we could not measure whether a participant used a suggestion based on reading the tip without opening it, but survey responses indicate that some participants did this: Participant S33 did not need to access a suggestion because reading it was enough: "I did not open the tip for Turn to Face because I read the outline for the Tip and used it in my code." Similarly, participant S70 said: "I did not open the tip because I saw it from the outside and felt like I could figure it out and I think I did."

Our goal was to encourage novice programmers to use API methods they would not necessarily use on their own. To evaluate this, we analyzed the information access and API use based on how often novice programmers in our sample set of programs used API methods. We split the API use based on one group of API methods that the Example Guru did not suggest and three groups that the Example Guru did suggest: the top third of methods that novices generally use most frequently, the middle third, the bottom third. The set that was not suggested includes API methods that novices use more than experts or that experts use in less than 5% of programs. In all three groups of API methods, the API information was accessed and used more frequently by participants in the suggestion condition (see Figure 3). While the largest use of suggestions was for API methods novices generally use the most, increasing use is beneficial because the average percentage of novices using those API methods is less than 50%. Furthermore, only participants with suggestions accessed information for the least used API methods.

The survey results provide additional insight into the reasons participants chose to access or not access API content. Due to a technical failure, participants in the documentation condition did not receive questions about their documentation access or use. Since questions about usage might encourage some users to increase their API usage, we looked for an increase in suggestion access and usage following the survey, which was administered after the first supported open-ended animation. However, we see little evidence of this. Ten participants used suggestions only during the first open-ended animation, an additional seventeen accessed suggestions throughout, and only five participants accessed zero suggestions during the first open-ended task, but one or more in the following animations. Thus, we do not believe that the survey questions influenced suggestion use.

Overall, participants described accessing suggestions to gain additional information about API methods that seemed potentially relevant. For example, one participant received a suggestion about setting the color of the sky, which they thought they could use: "The dark sky was sooo boring, so I looked at the tip and used it." Overall, participants opened 33% of the suggestions offered. For some participants, decisions not to open suggestions indicated lack of interest in those suggestions. In other cases, participants wanted to open all of the suggestions, but had not yet done so, like one participant: "I didn't open all of the tips yet." Finally, some participants were focused on other suggestions and missed ones that would have been of interest. One participant described missing a suggestion "because I was looking at other tips and didn't realize there was a tip [to] make only alien's head turn."

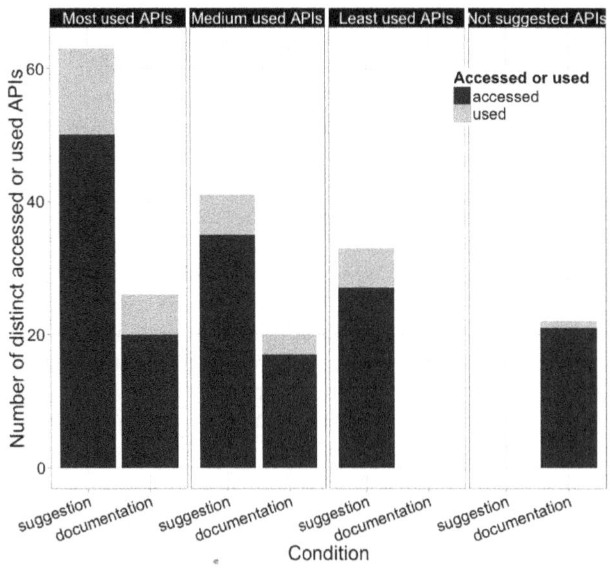


**Figure 3. API information accessed and used grouped by frequency of API use by novice programmers.**

Participants in the documentation condition similarly described a desire for additional information as a motivation for opening documentation: "I wanted to know what it was and I used it because I thought it would be pretty cool to begin and end abruptly." We unfortunately cannot report on their decisions around documentation they did not access.

### *Using suggestions and documentation*

Since increased access to API information may help to support the use of a new API method, we also wanted to explore the use of new API methods after information access. We found that more participants used new API methods after accessing suggestions than after accessing documentation. About three times as many participants in the suggestions condition used an API method after accessing the API information as in the documentation condition, 38% vs. 12.8% ($\chi^2(1) = 5.4466, p < 0.05$, odds ratio = 4.17). Additionally, participants added more new API methods after accessing the suggestions (M= .59, SD=.82) than after accessing the documentation (M= 0.15, SD = 0.43). This was significant for all 78 participants ($t(57.6) = 2.94 p < 0.01, d = 0.67$) and for the 59 participants who used the full task time ($t(49.3) = 2.2, p < 0.05, d = 0.55$).

In addition to frequency of use, it is interesting to explore the diversity of methods participants choose to use. In particular, we designed our rules and suggestions with the goal of introducing API methods that experts use more frequently than novices. Participants in both conditions used more new API methods from the group of API methods that are most commonly used by novices than the other groups. However, we note that participants using suggestions used more new methods from the middle and low use categories combined (see Figure 3). Finally, we looked at API methods for which we did not create suggestions. While some participants in the documentation group accessed information about these methods, very few were actually added. This provides some support for our method of selecting API methods for suggestions.

Our survey results suggest that participants in the suggestions condition decided to use an API method based on its potential to improve their animation. One participant explained "I just thought that changing the posture of the dolphins created a more natural feel than just moving its entire body." In contrast, participants in the documentation condition more often cited goals of understanding. For example, one participant using documentation stated, "I opened it and chose to use it so I could see what it looked like." We see a similar dichotomy around participants' explanations for non-use. A participant in the suggestions condition chose not to use an accessed suggestion because it did not mesh with her vision for her story: "I wanted to have the dolphin to go different distances showing they each do a little more than the last dolphin." A participant in the documentation condition explained accessing but not using documentation for a duration parameter because "...I wanted to see how it worked."

**Do participants' demographics affect how they used suggestions and documentation?**

In the design of the Example Guru, we hoped to support participants regardless of age, programming experience, and gender. By having suggestions relate to the context of the program and API methods that the programmer had not yet used, we hypothesized that the suggestions should continue to be relevant to programmers as they become familiar with more of the API. Previous studies have found a correlation between age and programming success with the same age range of children [15]. These differences in performance could result from the developmental changes that impact children's abilities to understand abstraction around the ages of 11-12 [42]. We hoped that the context-relevant approach would support novice programmers of differing ages. We also hypothesized that suggestions might better support participants who liked to learn by accessing information, rather than by tinkering, since suggestions do not require the user to seek out new API methods and documentation. Since females have been shown to be less likely to learn through exploration in some cases [3], it seemed as though the suggestions might provide better support for female novice programmers.

*Age and Programming Experience*

Our results did not show a relationship between age and accessing and using either suggestions or documentation. Specifically, we found no significant correlation between age and suggestion access($t(37) = -0.5, p = 0.62, r = -0.08$) nor between age and documentation access ($t(37) = 0.37, p = 0.71, r = 0.06$). Similarly, we found no significant correlation between age and the number of API methods used after accessing suggestions ($t(37) = -0.92, p = 0.36, r = -0.15$), nor between age and the number of API methods used after accessing documentation ($t(37) = -0.22, p = 0.83, r = -0.04$). These results suggest that both documentation and suggestions are used similarly by children ranging in age from ten to fifteen.

Programming experience played a larger role in how much participants accessed and used API information. Those with less than three hours of programming experience were the most likely to access both suggestions (100%) and documentation (75%). Participants with little programming in both conditions added new API methods after accessing them at similar rates: 44% of those in the suggestions condition and 38% of those in the documentation condition added API methods. However, among those with more than three hours of programming experience, we see a trend towards more use of suggestions. Of the participants in the suggestions condition, 77% accessed a suggestion and 40% added a new API method after accessing its suggestion. For participants in the documentation condition, only 32% accessed API information and 6.5% used a new API method after accessing its documentation. This trend suggests significant promise in the use of context-relevant API suggestions to help programmers continue to explore new API methods.

*Gender and Learning Style*

When considering how gender might relate to participants' use of API information, we explored use by reported gender, as well as learning style based on a survey.

We found that both males and females accessed and used the suggestions at higher rates than the documentation. However, male participants accessed suggestions more often than female participants: males accessed an average of 4.3 suggestions as compared to 2.2 suggestions for females ($t(33.5) = -2.7, p < 0.05, d = .83$). Male participants also accessed a larger percentage of the suggestions they received, so the larger number of suggestions accessed by males was not due to a larger number of suggestions received ($t(34.3) = -2.7, p < 0.05, d = 0.84$). While not significant, we note that female participants accessed documentation more often than male participants, averaging 1.9 documentation accesses as compared to 1.05 for males, as shown in Table 2. Overall, male participants opened more suggestions, but both genders accessed suggestions. The significant difference in terms of the number of suggestions accessed represents an important avenue for additional research. While suggestions performed better than documentation for both male and female participants, the lower usage by female participants has the potential to create an educational inequity.

One of the main personality traits that often correlates with gender differences in programming is the programmer's learning style: whether they like to learn by tinkering and exploring or using a step-by-step approach, so we also wanted to compare the way participants desired to learn and their behaviors. We created a survey based on the survey in [6] in order to try to determine whether participants were more likely to explore and tinker as a way of exploring the API or whether they were more reliant on information like tutorials or books. Unfortunately, the survey only had a reliability of $\alpha = 0.65$ for the questions about learning through exploring, and $\alpha = 0.5$ for the questions about learning using process-oriented information, both of which are less than the accepted reliability for surveys (0.7), so we will not report results for the survey.

**Do participants take advantage of API information features?**

This section presents results on how participants used features in the suggestions and documentation. Due to the structure of this study, we cannot evaluate the impact of specific features, so instead we explore three questions about feature use to provide insight into the value of the system design: 1) how did participants access information, 2) how much did they execute

| Condition | Action | <3 hours prog. | 3+ hours prog. | p | Male | Female | p |
|---|---|---|---|---|---|---|---|
| Suggestions | Accessed | 100%<br>M=3.8 SD=2.3 | 77%<br>M=3.2 SD=2.9 | | 86%<br>M=4.3 SD=3.0 | 78%<br>M=2.2 SD=1.8 | <.05 |
| | Added API call | 44%<br>M=.56 SD=.72 | 40%<br>M=.6 SD=.86 | | 48%<br>M=.67 SD=.86 | 33 %<br>M=.5 SD=.79 | |
| Documentation | Accessed | 75%<br>M=3.4 SD=4.0 | 32%<br>M=.94 SD =2.0 | .07 | 30%<br>M=1.05 SD=2.8 | 56%<br>M=1.9 SD=2.7 | |
| | Added API call | 38%<br>M=.5 SD=.76 | 6.5%<br>M=.06 SD=.25 | .08 | 10%<br>M=0.1 SD=.31 | 17%<br>M=0.22 SD=.5 | |

**Table 2. Participant characteristics and information access and API usage.**

examples, and 3) how much do they use contrasting examples and the 'show me' button?

We expected participants to access the suggestions and documentation using all of the mechanisms provided, which we found to be true, as shown in Table 3. For the most part, participants accessed suggestions from the suggestion list (see Figure 1-A) and '?' buttons (see Figure 2-A), which were both in or near the palette where users drag code blocks from. The list of suggestions was designed to help participants return to suggestions, which participants did: "I opened the tip [suggestion] because I had forgotten how to do it."

We found that the majority of participants who accessed API information also executed examples in both conditions, but did so more with suggestions: 81.3% of participants who accessed suggestions executed an example at least once, while 68.8 % of participants who accessed documentation executed at least one example. Executing examples may suggest that participants wanted to engage more deeply with the information in order to find out more about it. Participants who executed examples from suggestions executed on average 4.7 examples (SD = 3.5), while participants executed examples an average of 9.7 times from documentation (SD= 9). This may be because suggestions only provided two examples, while documentation often showed eight examples.

Because we designed suggestions specifically to provide contrasting examples and a button to help novices find code blocks, we measured how much they used those features. 44% of participants who accessed suggestions used contrasting examples and accessed the contrasting example for 1.8 suggestions on average (SD= 1.2). 38% of participants who accessed suggestions used the 'show me' button, and on average, clicked it 3.2 times (SD= 2.5). Since participants likely will not need these features for every suggestion, having over 30% usage

| Condition | Way of accessing | % of accesses |
|---|---|---|
| Suggestions | Suggestion Panel | 86.5% |
| | Code Annotation | 11.1% |
| | Preview from Panel | 2.4% |
| Documentation | '?' Button | 45.1% |
| | Expanding Parameters | 29.4% |
| | 'More Examples' | 17.6% |
| | Next/Previous Buttons | 7.8% |

**Table 3. Participants accessed the API information all of the different ways in both conditions**

and having participants return to use these features multiple times seems to indicate that participants found the features useful.

## DISCUSSION AND FUTURE WORK

Given that programmers across a broad range of skill sets describe learning or attempting to learn using 'just-in-time' strategies, effective situated support for API learning has the potential to improve programmer success and efficiency, particularly for novices. The results of our study suggest that the Example Guru approach has the potential to better support learning of APIs during open-ended programming. Yet, there are places where further work is needed. First, our results found that females used fewer suggestions than males, leading to a potential learning inequity. Second, we hand-coded our rules for this study. To enable approaches like the Example Guru to be used more broadly will require readily scalable approaches to generating effective rules.

### Learning APIs

To achieve mastery of a new API, novice programmers must continue to develop their skills over time. Yet, existing research suggests that novices reach a plateau in which they quickly learn to use a subset of the available capabilities within the system and then stop learning new skills [52, 48]. One recent paper [36] found an increase in the number of API methods used with experience. However, the increase was small after the initial period. Although measures of API method use cannot tell us whether the novice programmers actually have a full understanding of how the API methods work, programmers must first gain exposure and experience with the API methods. Thus, this work begins to address issues in API learning by improving the number of API methods that novice programmers explore and use.

We believe that some of the plateau effect may be due to a lack of appropriate learning mechanisms. While users may consult tutorials and similar materials when getting started with a new system or API, the use of them tends to drop off in favor of open-ended programming and just-in-time learning [4]. Yet, just-in-time approaches to learning often require that programmers know the right method to query for information. The Example Guru approach shows promise in introducing novice programmers to a broader selection of API methods as they work on their own projects. Rather than requiring that they know what methods to search for, the Example Guru observes their code and offers potentially relevant information. Participants accessed suggestions and used API methods from suggestions more frequently than documentation, creating more potential learning opportunities. It is important to note that participants accessed suggestions for API methods novices rarely use in common practice, while users in the documentation condition chose to explore mostly commonly used methods. Over a longer period, the increased exposure to and use of API information could lead to substantial learning gains.

Finally, our results suggest the potential for continued usage by those with varying skill levels. In both the documentation and suggestion conditions, participants with fewer than three hours of programming experience accessed and used API information more frequently than those with more than three hours of experience. The difference is much more dramatic in the documentation condition where only 32% of participants with more programming experience accessed the API information at all. In contrast, 77% of those with more than three hours of programming experience accessed the suggestions. Yet, there is still room for improvement. While 40% of the more experienced novices in our sample engaged with API methods from suggestions, 60% did not.

### Gender and the Example Guru

Our results showed different usage patterns among male and female participants. Specifically, male participants accessed more suggestions than female participants, averaging 4.3 versus 2.2 suggestions accessed. This is a potentially troubling difference, as over time this can lead to an educational inequity. Based on the results of this study, we have little information about the reasons for this difference. Previous work suggests that females may prefer learning using step-by-step instructions, rather than through tinkering and exploring [24] and that females have a tendency toward comprehensive information processing versus males' tendency toward selective information processing [38, 39]. However, we note that this difference occurs based solely on the tip describing the suggestion and before users are in a position to do much information processing. This is an area where future work is needed in order to understand and address this difference.

### Rules and suggestions at scale

The manual approach that we took to create rules and suggestions is a labor intensive one, so a natural direction for future work is to explore ways to partially or fully automate this process. Generalizing this work requires the ability to perform two processes at a larger scale: 1) generating the rules, and 2) creating interactive examples.

We authored our rules by hand, which involved manually considering how expert API usage could improve novice programs. We could reduce the amount of human effort necessary through automatic search of program corpora to identify patterns of API use. By incorporating positive and negative labels from resources like Stack Overflow, a system could likely make a reasonable decision about the correct ways experts use APIs and when an API method might be useful. However, some human intuition will likely be necessary to curate the final rules.

We designed our example code based on expert usages of API methods. A system could select example code automatically from online forum code with labels or a large corpus of expert code. We also need ways to automatically select contrasting examples and enable users to visualize examples. Contrasting examples could be automatically generated in some cases by changing parameter values. In other cases, API methods mentioned in forum threads may be relevant as contrasting API methods. This might be another area where a small amount of expert human opinion may be necessary, but a system could simplify this process by presenting a list of possible contrasting examples to let an expert quickly choose. Most example code, when run, will not automatically provide a visualization to help novices understand how it works. Approaches like those used in Python Tutor [43] and algorithm animation could provide visualizations of non-visual code.

### Limitations

There are two limitations to this study: the population we picked and the length of the study.

We recruited participants from a mailing list focused on STEM which draws from a sample of more interested and self-motivated learners than the general population. This may have meant that participants were more interested in technology and excited to explore the API than the norm. Furthermore, 94% of participants had programming experience of some form, including 82% who had been taught programming, which is above the norm for middle school children in the US.

While the results from this initial study are exciting, it is important to note that this study focused on a relatively short period of time and on API use, rather than learning. While the patterns of use suggest the potential for improved longer term learning, it will be important to explore how novice programmers engage with the Example Guru over a longer period. We need further studies to understand whether the Example Guru improves novices' comprehension of the API methods.

## CONCLUSION

Programmers at all levels prefer to learn while working on their own projects, but most existing tools provide API help using method names. We introduce the Example Guru, a system that suggests context-relevant API methods to programmers while they work on open-ended projects. Our study comparing suggestions and in-application documentation found that participants in the suggestion condition accessed and used information about the API methods more often than participants in the documentation condition. Further, the suggestions introduced participants to a greater diversity of methods. API learning is a fundamental part of programming activity today. Over time, this pattern of suggestion use could result in more efficient and higher quality use of unfamiliar APIs.

## ACKNOWLEDGMENTS

This material is based upon work supported by the National Science Foundation under Grant Nos. 1054587 & 1440996. We would like to thank Kyle Harms, Dennis Cosgrove, and Randall Brachman for their feedback on this paper.

## REFERENCES

1. Muhammad Asaduzzaman, Chanchal K Roy, and Kevin A Schneider. 2015. PARC: Recommending API methods parameters. In *Software Maintenance and Evolution (ICSME), 2015 IEEE International Conference on*. IEEE, 330–332.

2. Sushil K Bajracharya, Joel Ossher, and Cristina V Lopes. 2010. Leveraging usage similarity for effective retrieval of examples in code repositories. In *Proceedings of the eighteenth ACM SIGSOFT international symposium on Foundations of software engineering*. ACM, 157–166.
3. Laura Beckwith, Cory Kissinger, Margaret Burnett, Susan Wiedenbeck, Joseph Lawrance, Alan Blackwell, and Curtis Cook. 2006. Tinkering and gender in end-user programmers' debugging. In *Proceedings of the SIGCHI conference on Human Factors in computing systems*. ACM, 231–240.
4. Joel Brandt, Philip J. Guo, Joel Lewenstein, Mira Dontcheva, and Scott R. Klemmer. 2009. Two studies of opportunistic programming: interleaving web foraging, learning, and writing code. In *Proceedings of the SIGCHI Conference on Human Factors in Computing Systems*. ACM, 1589–1598.
5. Marcel Bruch, Martin Monperrus, and Mira Mezini. 2009. Learning from examples to improve code completion systems. In *Proceedings of the the 7th joint meeting of the European software engineering conference and the ACM SIGSOFT symposium on The foundations of software engineering*. ACM, 213–222.
6. Margaret Burnett, Scott D. Fleming, Shamsi Iqbal, Gina Venolia, Vidya Rajaram, Umer Farooq, Valentina Grigoreanu, and Mary Czerwinski. 2010. Gender differences and programming environments: across programming populations. In *Proceedings of the 2010 ACM-IEEE international symposium on empirical software engineering and measurement*. ACM, 28.
7. Michelene TH Chi, Miriam Bassok, Matthew W. Lewis, Peter Reimann, and Robert Glaser. 1989. Self-explanations: How students study and use examples in learning to solve problems. *Cognitive science* 13, 2 (1989), 145–182.
8. Class : CSV (Ruby 1.9.3,) 2016. `http://ruby-doc.org/stdlib-1.9.3/libdoc/csv/rdoc/CSV.html`. (2016). Accessed: 2016-09-20.
9. Joel Cordeiro, Bruno Antunes, and Paulo Gomes. 2012. Context-based recommendation to support problem solving in software development. In *2012 Third International Workshop on Recommendation Systems for Software Engineering (RSSE)*. IEEE, 85–89.
10. Davor Cubranic and Gail C Murphy. 2003. Hipikat: Recommending pertinent software development artifacts. In *Software Engineering, 2003. Proceedings. 25th International Conference on*. IEEE, 408–418.
11. Uri Dekel and James D Herbsleb. 2009. Improving API documentation usability with knowledge pushing. In *Proceedings of the 31st International Conference on Software Engineering*. IEEE Computer Society, 320–330.
12. Christian Dörner, Andrew R Faulring, and Brad A Myers. 2014. EUKLAS: Supporting copy-and-paste strategies for integrating example code. In *Proceedings of the 5th Workshop on Evaluation and Usability of Programming Languages and Tools*. ACM, 13–20.
13. Martin Fowler and Kent Beck. 1999. *Refactoring: Improving the Design of Existing Code*. Addison-Wesley Professional.
14. C Ailie Fraser, Mira Dontcheva, Holger Winnemöller, Sheryl Ehrlich, and Scott Klemmer. 2016. DiscoverySpace: Suggesting Actions in Complex Software. In *Proceedings of the 2016 ACM Conference on Designing Interactive Systems*. ACM, 1221–1232.
15. Kyle James Harms, Jason Chen, and Caitlin L. Kelleher. 2016. Distractors in Parsons Problems Decrease Learning Efficiency for Young Novice Programmers. In *Proceedings of the 2016 ACM Conference on International Computing Education Research*. ACM, 241–250.
16. Kyle J. Harms, Dennis Cosgrove, Shannon Gray, and Caitlin Kelleher. 2013. Automatically generating tutorials to enable middle school children to learn programming independently. In *Proceedings of the 12th International Conference on Interaction Design and Children*. ACM, 11–19.
17. Björn Hartmann, Daniel MacDougall, Joel Brandt, and Scott R Klemmer. 2010. What would other programmers do: suggesting solutions to error messages. In *Proceedings of the SIGCHI Conference on Human Factors in Computing Systems*. ACM, 1019–1028.
18. Lars Heinemann, Veronika Bauer, Markus Herrmannsdoerfer, and Benjamin Hummel. 2012. Identifier-based context-dependent API method recommendation. In *Software Maintenance and Reengineering (CSMR), 2012 16th European Conference on*. IEEE, 31–40.
19. Reid Holmes and Robert J Walker. 2008. A newbie's guide to Eclipse APIs. In *Proceedings of the 2008 international working conference on Mining software repositories*. ACM, 149–152.
20. Reid Holmes, Robert J Walker, and Gail C Murphy. 2006. Approximate structural context matching: An approach to recommend relevant examples. *IEEE Transactions on Software Engineering* 32, 12 (2006), 952–970.
21. Michelle Ichinco and Caitlin Kelleher. 2015. Exploring novice programmer example use. In *Visual Languages and Human-Centric Computing (VL/HCC), 2015 IEEE Symposium on*. IEEE, 63–71.
22. Takeo Igarashi and John F Hughes. 2001. A suggestive interface for 3D drawing. In *Proceedings of the 14th annual ACM symposium on User interface software and technology*. ACM, 173–181.
23. Will Jernigan, Amber Horvath, Michael Lee, Margaret Burnett, Taylor Cuilty, Sandeep Kuttal, Anicia Peters, Irwin Kwan, Faezeh Bahmani, and Andrew Ko. 2015. A principled evaluation for a principled Idea Garden. In *Visual Languages and Human-Centric Computing (VL/HCC), 2015 IEEE Symposium on*. IEEE, 235–243.
24. M. Gail Jones, Laura Brader-Araje, Lisa Wilson Carboni, Glenda Carter, Melissa J. Rua, Eric Banilower, and Holly Hatch. 2000. Tool time: Gender and students' use of

tools, control, and authority. *Journal of Research in Science Teaching* 37, 8 (2000), 760–783.

25. David Kawrykow and Martin P Robillard. 2009. Improving API usage through automatic detection of redundant code. In *Proceedings of the 2009 IEEE/ACM International Conference on Automated Software Engineering*. IEEE Computer Society, 111–122.
26. Muhammad Asaduzzaman Chanchal K Roy Kevin and A Schneider Daqing Hou. 2014. CSCC: simple, efficient, context sensitive code completion. (2014).
27. Md Adnan Alam Khan, Volodymyr Dziubak, and Andrea Bunt. 2015. Exploring personalized command recommendations based on information found in Web documentation. In *Proceedings of the 20th International Conference on Intelligent User Interfaces*. ACM, 225–235.
28. Andrew Jensen Ko, Brad A. Myers, and Htet Htet Aung. 2004. Six learning barriers in end-user programming systems. In *Visual Languages and Human Centric Computing, 2004 IEEE Symposium on*. IEEE, 199–206.
29. Benjamin Lafreniere, Parmit K Chilana, Adam Fourney, and Michael A Terry. 2015. These Aren't the Commands You're Looking For: Addressing False Feedforward in Feature-Rich Software. In *Proceedings of the 28th Annual ACM Symposium on User Interface Software & Technology*. ACM, 619–628.
30. Wei Li, Justin Matejka, Tovi Grossman, Joseph A. Konstan, and George Fitzmaurice. 2011. Design and evaluation of a command recommendation system for software applications. *ACM Transactions on Computer-Human Interaction (TOCHI)* 18, 2 (2011), 6.
31. Looking Glass Community 2016. `https://lookingglass.wustl.edu/`. (2016). Accessed: 2013-02-24.
32. Yuri Malheiros, Alan Moraes, Cleyton Trindade, and Silvio Meira. 2012. A source code recommender system to support newcomers. In *2012 IEEE 36th Annual Computer Software and Applications Conference*. IEEE, 19–24.
33. David Mandelin, Lin Xu, Rastislav Bodík, and Doug Kimelman. 2005. Jungloid mining: helping to navigate the API jungle. In *ACM SIGPLAN Notices*, Vol. 40. ACM, 48–61.
34. Justin Matejka, Tovi Grossman, and George Fitzmaurice. 2011. Ambient help. In *Proceedings of the SIGCHI Conference on Human Factors in Computing Systems*. ACM, 2751–2760.
35. Justin Matejka, Wei Li, Tovi Grossman, and George Fitzmaurice. 2009. CommunityCommands: command recommendations for software applications. In *Proceedings of the 22nd annual ACM symposium on User interface software and technology*. ACM, 193–202.
36. J. Nathan Matias, Sayamindu Dasgupta, and Benjamin Mako Hill. 2016. Skill Progression in Scratch Revisited. In *Proceedings of the 2016 CHI Conference on Human Factors in Computing Systems*. ACM, 1486–1490.
37. Frank McCarey, Mel O Cinneide, and Nicholas Kushmerick. 2006. A recommender agent for software libraries: An evaluation of memory-based and model-based collaborative filtering. In *Proceedings of the IEEE/WIC/ACM international conference on Intelligent Agent Technology*. IEEE Computer Society, 154–162.
38. Joan Meyers-Levy. 1986. *Gender differences in information processing: A selectivity interpretation*. Ph.D. Dissertation. Northwestern University.
39. Joan Meyers-Levy and Durairaj Maheswaran. 1991. Exploring differences in males' and females' processing strategies. *Journal of Consumer Research* 18, 1 (1991), 63–70.
40. Sundar Murugappan, Subramani Sellamani, and Karthik Ramani. 2009. Towards beautification of freehand sketches using suggestions. In *Proceedings of the 6th Eurographics Symposium on Sketch-Based Interfaces and Modeling*. ACM, 69–76.
41. Stephen Oney and Joel Brandt. 2012. Codelets: linking interactive documentation and example code in the editor. In *Proceedings of the SIGCHI Conference on Human Factors in Computing Systems*. ACM, 2697–2706.
42. Jean Piaget. 1972. Intellectual evolution from adolescence to adulthood. *Human development* 15, 1 (1972), 1–12.
43. Python Tutor 2017. Python Tutor - Visualize Python, Java, JavaScript, TypeScript, Ruby, C, and C++ code execution. `http://pythontutor.com/`. (2017).
44. Luisa Fernanda Hernández Ramírez and others. 2016. API recommendation system in Software Engineering. (2016).
45. Romain Robbes and Michele Lanza. 2008. How program history can improve code completion. In *Automated Software Engineering, 2008. ASE 2008. 23rd IEEE/ACM International Conference on*. IEEE, 317–326.
46. Martin P. Robillard. 2009. What makes APIs hard to learn? Answers from developers. *IEEE software* 26, 6 (2009), 27–34.
47. Martin P. Robillard and Robert Deline. 2011. A field study of API learning obstacles. *Empirical Software Engineering* 16, 6 (2011), 703–732.
48. Christopher Scaffidi and Christopher Chambers. 2012. Skill progression demonstrated by users in the Scratch animation environment. *International Journal of Human-Computer Interaction* 28, 6 (2012), 383–398.
49. Jeffrey Stylos, Andrew Faulring, Zizhuang Yang, and Brad A Myers. 2009. Improving API documentation using API usage information. In *2009 IEEE Symposium on Visual Languages and Human-Centric Computing (VL/HCC)*. IEEE, 119–126.
50. Suresh Thummalapenta and Tao Xie. 2007. ParseWEB: a programmer assistant for reusing open source code on the web. In *Proceedings of the twenty-second IEEE/ACM international conference on Automated software engineering*. ACM, 204–213.

51. Aaron Wilson, Margaret Burnett, Laura Beckwith, Orion Granatir, Ledah Casburn, Curtis Cook, Mike Durham, and Gregg Rothermel. 2003. Harnessing curiosity to increase correctness in end-user programming. In *Proceedings of the SIGCHI conference on Human factors in computing systems*. ACM, 305–312.
52. Benjamin Xie and Hal Abelson. 2016. Skill Progression in MIT App Inventor. *Visual Languages and Human-Centric Computing (VL/HCC), 2016 IEEE Symposium on* (2016).
53. Cheng Zhang, Juyuan Yang, Yi Zhang, Jing Fan, Xin Zhang, Jianjun Zhao, and Peizhao Ou. 2012. Automatic parameter recommendation for practical API usage. In *Proceedings of the 34th International Conference on Software Engineering*. IEEE Press, 826–836.
54. Hao Zhong, Tao Xie, Lu Zhang, Jian Pei, and Hong Mei. 2009. MAPO: Mining and recommending API usage patterns. In *European Conference on Object-Oriented Programming*. Springer, 318–343.
55. Sedigheh Zolaktaf and Gail C Murphy. 2015. What to learn next: recommending commands in a feature-rich environment. In *2015 IEEE 14th International Conference on Machine Learning and Applications (ICMLA)*. IEEE, 1038–1044.

# Toward Everyday Gaze Input: Accuracy and Precision of Eye Tracking and Implications for Design

Anna Maria Feit[1,2] Shane Williams[2] Arturo Toledo[2,3] Ann Paradiso[2]
Harish Kulkarni[2] Shaun Kane[2,4] Meredith Ringel Morris[2]
[1]Aalto University [2]Microsoft Research [3]Toledo Design [4]University of Colorado

## ABSTRACT

For eye tracking to become a ubiquitous part of our everyday interaction with computers, we first need to understand its limitations outside rigorously controlled labs, and develop robust applications that can be used by a broad range of users and in various environments. Toward this end, we collected eye tracking data from 80 people in a calibration-style task, using two different trackers in two lighting conditions. We found that accuracy and precision can vary between users and targets more than six-fold, and report on differences between lighting, trackers, and screen regions. We show how such data can be used to determine appropriate target sizes and to optimize the parameters of commonly used filters. We conclude with design recommendations and examples how our findings and methodology can inform the design of error-aware adaptive applications.

### ACM Classification Keywords

H.5.m. Information Interfaces and Presentation : Misc.

### Author Keywords

Eye tracking; gaze filters; sensor noise; adaptive interfaces.

## INTRODUCTION

Eye tracking has become an easily available and relatively cheap modality to enhance interaction with a computer. Remote (as opposed to head-mounted) video-based eye trackers are available for under $200 [43, 45]. They are unobtrusive and can be mounted on a display or built into laptops [28]. As a result, there is increasing interest in using information about eye gaze not only as a research instrument, but to enhance our everyday interaction with computers. Gaze-enabled applications and interaction techniques range from explicit gaze input, such as pointing [22, 49] or gaze gestures [8, 16, 33] to attentive applications that use gaze to make inferences about the user's intentions [13, 29, 38] and improve input with other modalities [37].

Surprisingly, little work has been done to understand the requirements of such applications as they integrate into our everyday computer use. There is no common standard or framework for designers and developers to rely on to develop easy-to-use and robust gaze-enabled applications. As when designing applications for other input modalities, such as touch or mouse, they have to face basic questions such as:
*Which region of the screen is easiest to interact with? How accurate can we expect the user's input to be? What is the minimum usable size of an interactive element?*

Prior work has found that tracking quality deviates from the numbers obtained in manufacturers' labs [5, 11, 30, 31] and that tracking *accuracy* (the offset from the true gaze point) and *precision* (the spread of the gaze points) vary widely across different tracking conditions and users. However, few efforts have been made to draw any formal conclusions that could inform the design of gaze-enabled applications; if so, they concentrate on specific applications or interaction techniques (e.g. [18, 32]) Research studies typically try to keep variation as small as possible by carefully controlling tracking conditions, user positioning, frequently recalibrating the eye tracker, and excluding participants that do not track well. While this is reasonable for research, it is not feasible in practice.

To illustrate the extent of this problem in everyday use of gaze input, we conducted an informal survey among five expert users of gaze applications (people with ALS who rely on gaze-based AAC for communication). We found that they have to recalibrate their eye tracker between three and ten times per day, even though devices are mounted to their wheelchairs and their movement in front of the screen is limited due to their motor disabilities. Despite this frequent recalibration, they reported that they typically fail to interact with an application several times per day as the application cannot account for differences in tracking quality.

To establish eye gaze as part of our everyday interaction with computers, we need to understand the characteristics and limitations of eye tracking in practice and derive standards for the design of gaze-enabled applications that take into account that accuracy and precision can vary widely across different tracking conditions. Toward this end, we collected calibration-style eye tracking data from 80 participants in a controlled but practical setup, using two different trackers in two lighting conditions. In contrast to many eye tracking studies, we did not exclude any participant due to insufficient tracking quality and only calibrated once at the beginning. Our findings offer several contributions for the design and development of gaze-enabled applications:

1. We report **accuracy and precision ranges** overall and for different parts of the screen that characterize the large variation across different tracking conditions.


*CHI 2017*, May 06–11, 2017, Denver, CO, USA

ISBN 978-1-4503-4655-9/17/05...$15.00
DOI: http://dx.doi.org/10.1145/3025453.3025599

2. We provide a formal way to derive **appropriate target sizes** from measures of accuracy and precision. Based on our data we give recommendations for the minimum size of gaze-aware regions to allow robust interaction.
3. We present an approach to find optimal parameters for any filter that minimizes target size and signal delay. We compare five commonly used **filtering techniques** and provide optimized parameters.
4. We show our vision of **error-aware adaptive applications** and show how our results and methodology can be utilized in the design and operating principle of such applications.

Our methods can be re-applied to future hardware versions or in other contexts to derive updated measurements as technology and use scenarios evolve.

## BACKGROUND AND RELATED WORK

There are various technologies that can be used to capture eye gaze (see e.g. [11] for an overview). We focus on remote video-based eye tracking, in which an eye-tracking camera is attached to or integrated in a device's screen.

### Computer Interaction by Eye Gaze

Eye trackers deliver information about where on the screen the user is looking. Applications can use this data for *explicit eye input* that requires conscious control by the user, or can use it as an implicit source of information, often in combination with other input modalities (*attentive user interfaces*) [26]. In the following, we use the term *gaze-enabled* to refer to any application that reacts to the changing gaze of the user. In this paper, we concentrate on estimation of gaze points by remote, video-based eye trackers. They capture the gaze location of the user in screen coordinates at regular intervals, depending on the recording frequency (commonly 30–60 Hz). Optionally, the system can apply filters to smooth the signal, and algorithms to detect events. The application then processes the signal and responds accordinglyNote that each processing step must happen in real-time and cannot rely on information from future gaze points without delaying the application.

The most important gaze events for interactive applications are *fixations* and *saccades*. A fixation denotes a period of time (from less than 100 ms up to several seconds [11, 25]) for which the gaze location is static within a small region. A saccade is the rapid and ballistic movement between fixations; they take about 30–80 ms [11] and can be 2° or larger [26]. While there are other gaze events — including smooth pursuit, microsaccades or glissades [11] — fixations and saccades are essential to describe how the attention of the user changes and can be recognized most reliably [11]. Table 1 overviews interactions performed in various gaze-enabled applications, ranging from explicit eye input to attentive user interfaces, with several in-between these two ends of the continuum (this list is not exhaustive, but represents exemplars of common interaction styles). The second column shows the gaze events on which the interaction relies. Independent of the conscious level of control, the applications mainly use the same gaze events to extract information about the user's intention: single gaze points, fixations, and saccades, with a few exceptions

| | Explicit or implicit interaction by eye gaze | Gaze event | Ref #'s |
|---|---|---|---|
| ● | Gaze pointing | Fixation or gaze point | [7, 22, 49] |
| ● | Gaze gestures | Sequence of fixations | [8, 16, 23, 33, 47] |
| ● | Dwell-based selection | Fixation over min. time | [17, 24] |
| ◐ | Multimodal selection | Fixation or gaze point | [17, 20] |
| ◐ | Selection by following a moving object | Smooth pursuit | [35] |
| ● | Drag and drop | Fixation or gaze point | [17, 20] |
| ● | Rotary control and sliders | Smooth pursuit | [40] |
| ◐ | Switching windows | Gaze point | [10] |
| ◐ | Image annotation | Fixation | [10] |
| ○ | Reading | Fixation or gaze point | [42] |
| ○ | Focus of attention | Fixation or gaze point, saccade | [9, 15, 27, 29, 37] |

**Table 1. An overview of interactions performed in gaze-enabled applications. Circles mark the degree of explicit control from full control (●) to no conscious control (○). Most interactions rely on the detection of fixations and saccades, while a few utilize smooth pursuit of a target.**

using smooth pursuit. This work concentrates on applications that use saccades and fixations for computer interaction.

### Accuracy and Precision of Gaze Tracking

The (spatial) quality of the tracked gaze can be measured in terms of precision and accuracy. Accuracy denotes the offset between the true gaze position and the recorded position, whereas precision measures the dispersion of recorded gaze points during a fixation (i.e. , the gaze points' standard deviation). We measure accuracy and precision separately in the $x$- and $y$-directions. Accuracy is often reported by manufacturers to be $< 0.5°$. However, in particular for remote eye trackers, offset from the true gaze point is often found to be larger than 1° [5, 30], even in controlled environments.

#### *Factors that influence tracking quality*

The tracking method considered in this paper relies on pupil and corneal reflection tracking, the most common method for estimating the gaze location [11]. The image in Figure 1 shows a user's eyes and the location of the pupil and corneal reflection, as estimated by the SMI REDn scientific. The heavy mascara, thick frames of glasses, and reflections shown in the image could potentially impair the quality of the captured gaze. In general, tracking quality is influenced by the interplay of various factors related to properties of the user's eye, the tracking environment, the tracking method, as well as the calibration procedure (e.g. [11, 30]). Such properties include glasses or contact lenses, varying eye physiologies, different levels of sunlight, properties of artificial lighting, and the resolution and focus of the camera, among others. In the resulting signal, four different types of noise have been recognized: system inherent, physiological, optic artifacts, and data loss [11]. Artifacts and data loss impact the interaction, but can be detected and removed from the data stream (at the cost of signal delay), whereas the detection of physiological and system generated noise relies on filtering by the system.

#### *Algorithmic approaches to robust interaction*

Various algorithmic methods have been proposed to filter or correct the estimated gaze point (see [11] for a review), but many rely on post-hoc processing that introduces high latency, making them unsuitable for real-time interaction. We extend

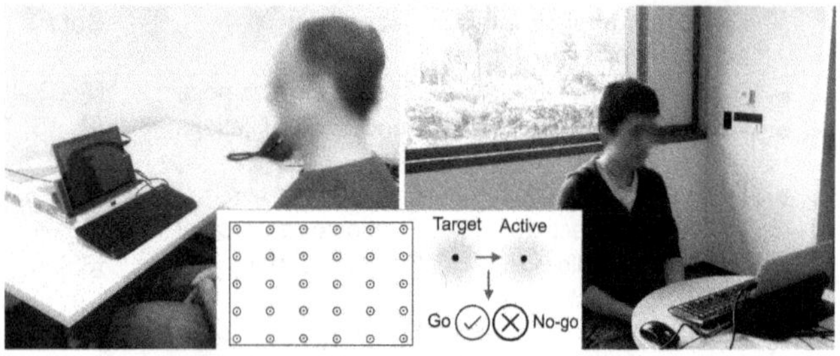


**Figure 1. Image of the study setup. Left: in a room with no windows illuminated by artificial light. Right: in a room with large windows facing the tracker, recorded on a cloudy day. Inset: design of targets and go/no-go symbols and their distribution over the screen.**

prior work [39] by evaluating several real-time filtering techniques for interactive applications based on our collected data, and propose an approach to choose optimal parameters. Recent efforts model and predict the error when estimating the gaze position on head-worn eye tracking glasses [2, 3]. Such models are the first step towards adaptive and personalized user interfaces for gaze interaction that adapt to the quality of the tracked gaze. However, at this stage, they are complex to train and implement, and it is unclear how they perform under less controlled conditions. Our focus is on remote eye tracking rather than head-mounted systems.

### *Design approaches to robust interaction*

Several interaction methods and design approaches have been proposed to deal with poor accuracy and precision. One obvious approach is to enlarge targets. However, this is not always feasible as the overall size of the interface is limited. Space-efficient techniques, such as hierarchical menus, can facilitate interaction with large targets, but slow down performance, as they require more steps for selection. Dynamic approaches, such as zooming or fisheye lenses [1, 4, 9] can make selection more robust, but may visually distract the user. Gaze gestures [8, 16, 33, 47] have been found to be more robust against noise in comparison to target-based selections, but may require unnaturally large saccades to overcome tracking problems and may be hard to learn. Smooth pursuit [35, 40, 46] shows promise as a robust selection technique, but requires a moving stimulus that the eye can follow which is often not suitable for many traditional user interfaces. Requiring longer dwell times in dwell-based gaze selection is another approach to avoiding accidental target selection, though this slows down interaction times; expert users may be able to reliably select targets with dwell times near 300 ms, but only if target sizes are appropriate for the tracking quality [24]. Our findings can inform the design of many of the applications shown in Table 1 to optimally adapt to the tracking quality at a given time.

## DATA COLLECTION

We collected gaze data across a broad range of people, using two different eye trackers in two environments with different lighting. We controlled important factors to be the same throughout the study, such as position of the user relative to the tracker, but kept the setup as natural as possible to capture how much accuracy and precision of eye tracking can vary in tracking conditions similar to those in practice.

| | | | | | |
|---|---|---|---|---|---|
| **Age** | 18–24 | 25–34 | 35–44 | 45–54 | 55–64 |
| | 12 | 45 | 14 | 8 | 1 |
| **Eye color** | Blue | Green | Hazel | Dark brown | |
| | 11 | 9 | 10 | 50 | |
| **Ethnicity** | Asian or Pac. Isl. | Black or Afr. Am. | Hispanic | White | Other or Mixed |
| | 23 | 7 | 9 | 34 | 7 |
| **Experience** | Never used eye tracking | | | Has used eye tracking | |
| | 52 | | | 28 | |

**Table 2. Study participants' demographic information**

**Participants:** 81 participants took part in the experiment (62 male, 19 female). When advertising the study, we explicitly encouraged people to take part even if they wore glasses or contact lenses, or had experienced problems using eye tracking before. Table 2 shows demographic information. The calibration process failed for only one participant (male) for whom no data could be collected, and which is excluded in Table 2. Participants were compensated with a $5 lunch coupon.

**Eye trackers:** We collected gaze data with 2 different eye trackers: Tobii EyeX [45] and SMI REDn scientific [14], both at 60 Hz. The first is an affordable tracker developed for consumer use, the second is sold for scientific purposes and is more expensive. The trackers have a similar form factor and can be attached to the bottom of screens up to 27". They operate at a similar tracking range, not restricting the user in their natural movement. SMI reports an accuracy of $0.4°$ and a spatial resolution (root mean square) of 0.05. No such values are available for the Tobii EyeX [44]. Participants were assigned randomly to use one of the eye trackers.

**Tracking Environment:** We collected data in two different lighting environments, shown in Figure 1. The *artificial* environment was a room with no windows; light was from halogen MR16 spot lights and two fluorescent 40-watt Biax lamps in $2\times2$ fixtures. The *daylight* environment was a room with large windows facing the tracker; additional lighting came from the same fluorescent lights used in the artificial setup. Data was collected on a cloudy day. While both conditions do not provide the optimal lighting recommended for an eye tracking lab [11], they allow us to capture the noise induced by external lighting that may be encountered in practice in end users' homes, offices, etc. Participants were assigned randomly to one environment.

**Setup:** The equipment setup was the same in both environments. We used a Microsoft Surface Pro 3 with an Intel Core i5-4300U 1.9 GHz and 4 GB memory. The application was shown on the 12" screen at a resolution of $1440\times960$ pixel (144 DPI). Both trackers were magnetically affixed to a horizontal bar at the bottom of the Surface's docking station with the material provided by the manufacturers. We placed the display on a table at the same height in both environments. To compensate for different participant heights, we tilted the docking station towards the user to adapt the gaze angle between the user's eyes and the eye tracker, until the manufacturer's calibration software showed a good tracking position. Participants were positioned at 65 cm from the screen. They were told to try to stay still, but that they could move their head naturally. With this setup, a visual angle of $1°$ corresponds to a movement of ca. 1.1 cm on the screen.

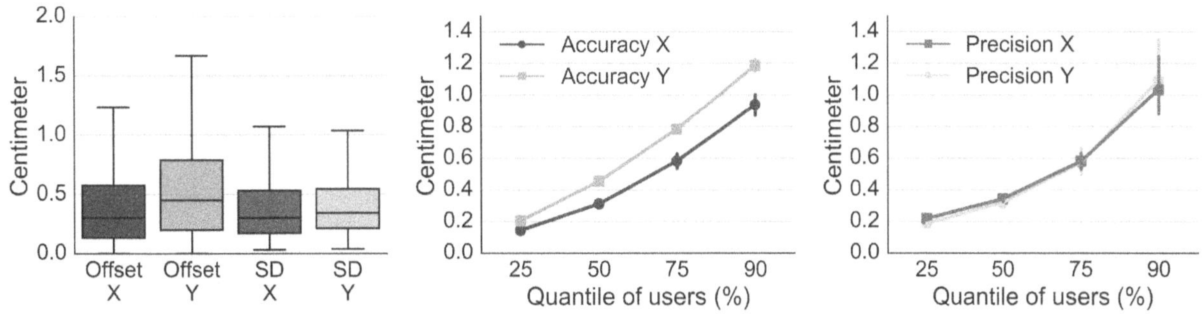


**Figure 2. Left: box plot of the accuracy (offset) and precision (standard deviation) over all target fixations. Center and right: different percentiles, averaged over all targets, show that accuracy and precision vary largely in practical tracking conditions.**

**Task and Procedure:** The participants' task was to look at targets randomly presented on the screen for about two seconds each. If the target turned into a checkmark, they were instructed to press the spacebar as quickly as possible; if it turned into a cross, they should wait for the next target. This go/no-go task was used to keep the participants' attention on the target [12]. Thirty targets were shown in random order, distributed over the screen as shown in Figure 1, with a vertical distance of 214 pixel (3.32°, 3.77 cm), and a horizontal distance of 267 pixel (4.14°, 4.71 cm) between neighboring targets. Each target's (invisible) activation area was a circular region of 500 pixel diameter (8.8 cm, 7.7°). When the participant's gaze was inside the target for 500 ms, it was activated and its color turned cyan. After 1250 ms the go/no-go task started. If a target could not be activated after 5 s (because the tracked gaze was too noisy), the next target appeared. Figure 1 shows the targets and the go/no-go icons. Before the task started, we calibrated the eye trackers with a 7-point calibration method provided by the manufacturers. The study started with a demographic questionnaire. After that, the instructions for the go/no-go task were displayed, and then the task began.

**Data Collection and Preprocessing:** All gaze points were recorded as an (x,y) position in screen coordinates, as given by the API of the respective tracker, with filtering turned off. For each target, we extracted the gaze points of a 1 s window (60 frames) during which the participant looked at the target. We did not use a fixation detection algorithm, which cannot reliably distinguish between saccades and noise artifacts, but extracted the data in one of two ways: (1) *Online:* A target was activated if the gaze of the user stayed within a 250 pixel radius from the target for 500 ms. Gaze points were extracted for the next 1000 ms and saved if the gaze was still within that region after that time; otherwise, the activation was reset. The go/no-go task was only shown if we could extract the gaze points. (2) *Offline:* If a target could not be activated for 5 s, the next one was shown. From the recorded data we extracted 1 s during which we could be sure that the participant looked at the target. Therefore, we chose a 1 s window for which on average the gaze points were closest to the target. This post-processing had to be done for 11% of the fixations

For each fixation, we then excluded the gaze points where no eyes could be tracked (reported as such by the eye tracker). If this was more than 2/3 of the gaze points, we excluded this fixation from the analysis.

## ANALYSIS AND RESULTS

The analyzed dataset consists of 2,343 fixations from 80 users looking at 30 targets (2.4% of fixations were excluded, as described above). By "target fixation" we simply denote the data recorded while a user was looking at a target. No algorithmic method was involved to extract fixation events. In the following analysis, we first compute aggregate measures for each target. Where not denoted differently, we then average across the 30 targets for each user to account for the fact that fixations by the same participant are not independent observations.

### Data Loss and Distribution of Gaze Points

Data loss occurs when the eye tracker cannot estimate the gaze position. On average, each target fixation consists of 55.6 gaze points recorded over 1 s (ca. 60 frames). The average data loss is 7.9% of frames. A two-way ANOVA shows significantly higher loss for the Tobii tracker than for the SMI: gaze position could not be estimated for 13.1% versus 2.8% of points per target ($F(1,79) = 18$, $p < 0.01$). No such difference was found for the tracking environments (8.1% in artificial versus 7.8% in daylight) and there was no interaction effect. For 1,450 fixations (62%) no data was lost. For the remaining 38%, tracking was lost on average 11 times during the 1 s fixation, for an average of 1.5 frames.

We performed normality tests on the gaze points of each target fixation, separately in the x- and y-directions (D'Agostino and Pearson's test as implemented by Python's SciPy package [7, 20] with a significance level of $p < .01$). They showed that on average gaze points are normally distributed in the x-direction for 71% of the fixations, and in the y-direction for 74%.

### Precision and Accuracy

For all gaze points during a target fixation we compute accuracy and precision separately in the $x$- and $y$-direction. Accuracy denotes the absolute offset between the fixated target and the mean of the estimated gaze points. Precision is computed as the standard deviation (SD) of the gaze points.

Table 3 shows an overview of the results. Values are averaged across users and given for different conditions. We also show average accuracy and precision values for different percentiles of users fixating each target, e.g. only the best 25%. Standard deviations are given in brackets. We used multivariate ANOVA to test for significant differences in accuracy and precision between the tracker and light conditions. We report

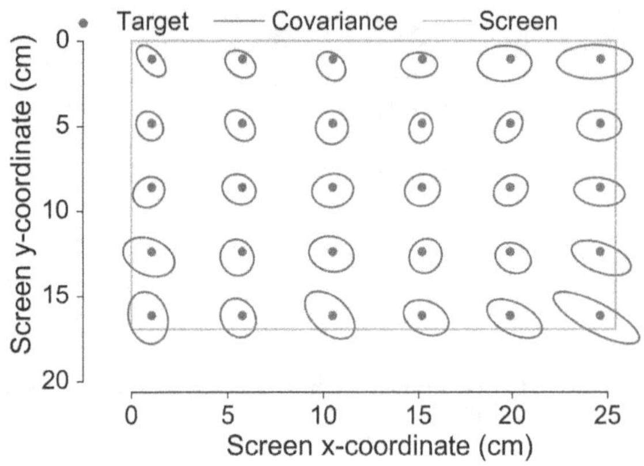


**Figure 3. Precision of the estimated gaze points over the different targets. Covariance ellipses show the contour of the 2D Gaussian, fitted to the gaze points corresponding to all fixations of the same target.**

| | Accuracy (cm) | | Precision (cm) | |
|---|---|---|---|---|
| | X | Y | X | Y |
| **Overall** | 0.47 (0.64) | 0.57 (0.52) | 0.52 (0.73) | 0.5 (0.56) |
| **Percentile** | | | | |
| 25% | 0.15 | 0.2 | 0.19 | 0.22 |
| 50% | 0.31 | 0.45 | 0.32 | 0.32 |
| 75% | 0.58 | 0.78 | 0.57 | 0.58 |
| 90% | 0.93 | 1.19 | 1.1 | 1.04 |
| **Tracker** | | | | |
| SMI REDn | 0.58 (0.75) | 0.66 (0.57) | 0.51 (0.91) | 0.51 (0.64) |
| Tobii EyeX | 0.36 (0.5) | 0.48 (0.45) | 0.53 (0.44) | 0.48 (0.44) |
| **Light** | | | | |
| Artificial | 0.51 (0.75) | 0.65 (0.6) | 0.6 (0.87) | 0.56 (0.68) |
| Daylight | 0.42 (0.51) | 0.5 (0.42) | 0.44(0.56) | 0.44 (0.4) |

**Table 3. Average accuracy and precision across all users, across different percentiles of each target, and for different tracker and light conditions (lower values are better). Standard deviations are given in brackets. An extended table with degrees is provided in the supplementary material.**

values in cm, which is independent of screen resolution. For space reasons, we do not report the values in degrees of visual angle, but refer to the supplementary material for an extended version of the table. Our results should not be seen as absolute properties of the tested eye trackers or tracking environments, but show how much we can expect accuracy and precision to vary as eye tracking is used in everyday computer interaction.

### *Variation over all conditions*

Figure 2 shows how much accuracy and precision can vary over all collected data. Table 3 gives the corresponding results. A paired samples t-test showed that on average, accuracy is worse in the y-direction by about 0.1 cm ($t(1,79) = 2.8, p < .01$). The middle and right plot in Figure 3 visualize how accuracy and precision increase over different percentiles. No significant difference between the $x$- and the $y$-direction was found for precision ($t(1,79) = 1.0.3$, $p = 0.3$).

The middle and right plots in Figure 2 visualize how accuracy and precision become worse for different percentiles of users. The results given in Table 3 are average values over the corresponding percentiles of each target. Very accurate fixations (25th percentile) are only 0.15 cm in the $x$- and 0.2 cm in the $y$-direction offset from the target. On the other hand, inaccurate fixations (90th percentile) can be as far offset as 0.93 cm in the $x$- and 1.19 cm in the $y$-direction, a more than six-fold difference. Similar for the spread of the gaze points.

### *Comparison between tracking conditions*

Two-way MANOVA found a significant difference between the eye trackers used in the study ($F(1,79) = 7.7$, $p < .01$). Follow-up univariate testing showed that the Tobii EyeX tracker was more accurate than the SMI REDn scientific in both the $x$-direction ($F(1,79) = 9.4$, $p < .01$) and $y$-direction ($F(1,79) = 10.6$, $p < .01$), whereas no significant difference was found for precision. This stands in contrast to our previous finding that the Tobii EyeX has significantly more data loss than the SMI REDn, in which case it cannot track the gaze position at all. As shown in Table 3, tracking in the daylight condition was consistently better by about 0.1-0.15cm. However, this difference was not found to be significant($F(1,79) = 1.7$, $p = 0.16$) by the two-way MANOVA. Also there was no significant interaction effect.

### *Comparison between screen regions*

The precision of the estimated gaze for each target is worse toward the right and bottom edge of the screen, as shown in Figure 3. The ellipses represent the covariance matrix computed over all gaze points from all 80 users. Multivariate ANOVA and follow-up univariate analysis with TukeyHSD tests found that the precision of the bottom row was significantly worse compared to all other rows at the $p < .05$ (adjusted) significance level in both $x$- and $y$-direction. In contrast, there was no significant difference for accuracy between any of the rows.

Significant differences between columns were only found for precision in the $x$- direction. Precision was significantly worse for the right-most (6th) column in comparison to all other columns at the $p < .01$ (adjusted) significance level. In the supplementary material we provide exact accuracy and precision values for rows and columns.

### *Comparison over time*

The tracking quality did not significantly change for the same participant during the experiment. MANOVA found no difference for either accuracy or precision between the first and last target fixation of each user ($F(1,158) = 0.9$, $p = 0.46$).

## FROM ACCURACY AND PRECISION TO TARGET SIZE

Once we know the tracking accuracy and precision, we can derive appropriate target sizes. A target denotes any region in a user interface that should recognize if the user's gaze falls inside its borders in order to trigger a functionality. This can be an explicitly controlled button, the words and lines in an attentive reading application, the active recognition region for gaze gestures, or the area of interest in a research experiment.

When a user fixates the center of a target, we assume that the captured gaze points are normally distributed in the x and y directions around a mean with offset $O_{x/y}$ (accuracy) from the target center and a standard deviation $\sigma_{x/y}$(precision). For robust and smooth interaction, we suggest that at least 95% of gaze points should fall inside the target regions; this means we can derive the target width and height as:

$$S_{w/h} = 2\,(O_{x/y} + 2\,\sigma_{x/y}) \tag{1}$$

We multiply $\sigma_{x/y}$ by 2, as about 95% of values lie within two standard deviations of the mean for normally distributed data.

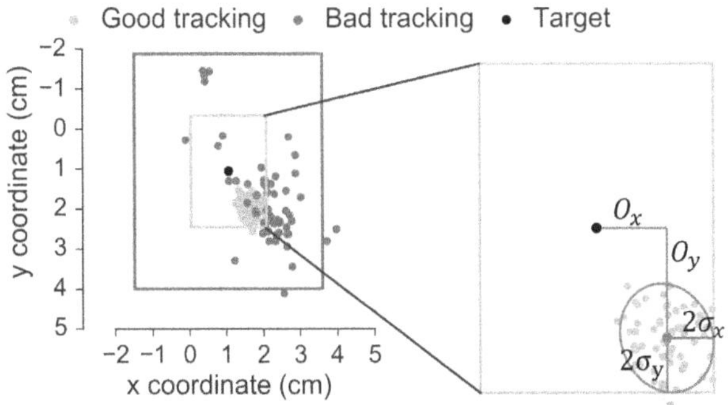


**Figure 4. Given the accuracy and precision, target size is computed based such that 95% of gaze points fall inside the target. The plot shows example target sizes based on two different fixations of the same target, one with good and one with bad tracking quality.**

An error rate of more than 5% (every 20th point) slows down performance and leads to errors that are often hard to recover from.However, if an interaction technique can be used reliably with a smaller percentage of points, Equation 1 can be easily modified by replacing the multiplier with the corresponding value from the standard normal table.

Figure 4 visualizes the computation of the target size based on the offset and SD of the raw gaze points and shows two example targets based on the gaze points of two fixations with good and bad tracking quality. Although Equation 1 is a simplification and not a statistical assessment of the distribution of the gaze points, it can be used to quickly compute appropriate target sizes based on precision and accuracy values. When we check this formula based on our collected data, we get that for each target fixation on average 94.9% of gaze points fall inside a target of width and height as computed by Equation 1. Table 5 shows the resulting average target sizes computed based over all target fixations, and over different percentiles of users for each target. Sizes can vary from 0.94×1.24 cm for users that track well, up to 5.96×6.24 cm if we want to allow robust interaction for nearly all users in our dataset. These target sizes are based on unfiltered data; next, we discuss filtering techniques and derive similar values based on filtered data.

## PARAMETER OPTIMIZATION FOR FILTERS

Filters can significantly improve the precision of the tracked gaze by removing noise artifacts and reducing signal dispersion. Several filters have been proposed for real-time systems; however, developers implementing these filters must choose parameters that control their performance. This is often done suboptimally based on prior experience or heuristics. We describe an easy-to-implement procedure to optimize the parameters of any filter for minimum target size and minimum delay, based on calibration-style data as collected in our study. We then compare five different types of filters with three different kernel functions, and evaluate their effect on precision and accuracy in comparison to the unfiltered data.

### Filters for Interactive Gaze Applications

In interactive gaze-enabled applications, no post-processing of the data is possible, and any filtering must be done in real-time. This limits the ability to detect outliers and artifacts, which introduce a delay of several frames. For most applications there are two main states that need to be recognized: fixations and saccades. Eye tremor, microsaccades, and noise should be filtered in order to stabilize the signal and improve precision. The quick and sudden change between those states must be accounted for by the filter. This makes commonly used methods, such as moving average, Kalman filter, and Savytzki-Golay, filter less useful [6, 39]. Based on prior work [39] and our own experience, we tested five different types of filters. They are summarized in Table 4 and described in the following.

| Filter | Parameter | Ranges |
|---|---|---|
| Weighted Average (WA) [19, 48] | Window size N | 2–40 frames |
| WA + saccade detection [39] | Saccade threshold $s$<br>Max. window size $N$ | 1–4 cm (à .05)<br>2–40 frames |
| WA + saccade detection<br>+ 1-sample outlier correction | Saccade threshold $s$<br>Max. window size $N$ | 1–4 cm (à .05)<br>2–40 frames |
| 1€ filter [6] | Adaption rate $\beta$ Cut-off frequency $f_{c_{min}}$ | 0–1.5 (à .01)<br>0.4–6.5 (à .1) |
| Stampe filter [41] | – | – |

**Table 4. Filtering techniques for which we optimize parameters and that we evaluate based on our collected data. Ranges denotes the parameter ranges considered in the grid search.**

**The Stampe filter** [41] is commonly used to remove outliers from the tracked gaze signal. It uses a two-step procedure that detects one- and two-frame deviations from a continuously increasing or decreasing signal and corrects them according to the surrounding points. This introduces a delay of up to two frames. No parameters are necessary.

**Weighted average (WA)** [19, 48] or finite impulse response filter (FIR) computes the filtered point $\hat{X}_t$ at time $t$ as the weighted average over the last $N$ points:

$$\hat{X}_t = \sum_{i=0}^{N} \frac{w_i}{\sum_j w_j} \cdot X_{t-i} \quad (2)$$

where $X_{t-i}$ is the point observed at time $t-i$ , and $w_i$ is the corresponding (normalized) weight. The only parameter for a WA filter is the window size $N$. The function defining the weight for each point in the averaging window, is called the kernel function. We test three different kernel functions:

1. A *Linear kernel* corresponds to a simple average of the last N points, $w_i = 1$.
2. A *triangular kernel* [21, 48] assigns a weight of 1 to the least recent point ($N$), 2 to the next point ($N-1$), and so on, $w_i = N-i+1$.
3. A *Gaussian kernel* function [19] assigns weights according to a Gaussian function, where the variance is chosen such that no point in the averaging window is assigned a weight smaller than 0.05 [39], $w_i = e^{-\frac{(i-1)^2}{2\sigma^2}}$

**Saccade detection** can be used to extend the WA filter [36]. Similar to the identification by dispersion threshold algorithm [34], commonly used for fixation detection in offline processing [11], it defines a threshold $s$ that is used to detect saccades. As long as the distance between successive gaze points is smaller than $s$, they are assumed to belong to the same fixation. The filtered gaze point is computed as the weighted average over the last $N$ points of the same fixation. If the distance exceeds the threshold, a saccade is detected and

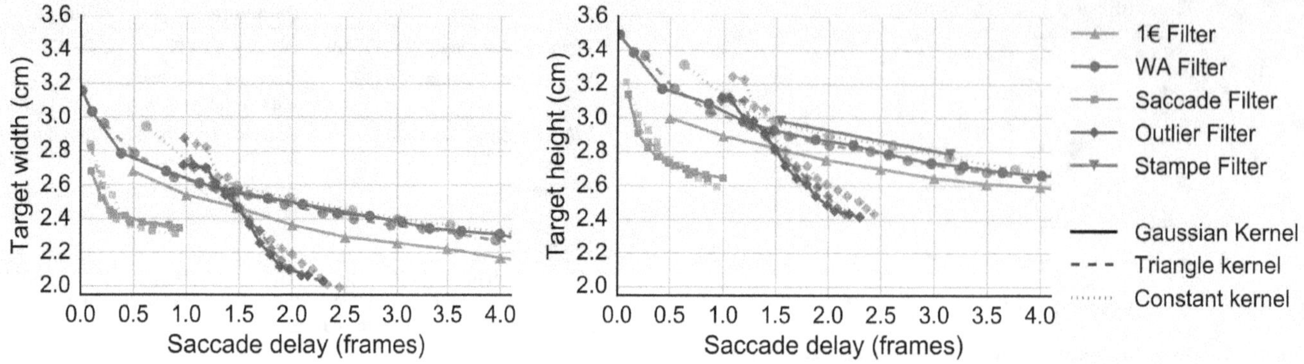


**Figure 5. Pareto front of optimal parameter settings for each tested filter. Filters are evaluated based on the resulting target size and average delay in detecting a saccade. Corresponding parameters are given in the supplementary material. Depending on the application, appropriate parameters can be chosen that yield the desired trade-off between target size and signal delay.**

no filter is applied. The new gaze point is the first of a new fixation. We test the same kernel functions as described above. In addition to the window size $N$, the filter requires to set the saccade threshold $s$.

**Outlier correction** further extends the WA filter [21]. It detects and removes single outliers that would be detected as two successive saccades by the previous filter. If the distance between successive gaze points exceeds the saccade threshold $s$, the new gaze point is saved as the start of a potential new fixation. The algorithm waits for the next observation to confirm the detection of a saccade. If the next gaze point is closer to the previous fixation, the potential fixation is discarded as an outlier. Otherwise, a new fixation is started. This introduces a one-frame delay. Points belonging to the same fixation are filtered by a WA filter, as before. The parameters are the size $N$ of the averaging window and the saccade threshold $s$.

**The 1€ filter** [6] has been proposed for filtering the signal obtained from human motion tracking. It uses a low-pass filter but adapts the cut-off frequency depending on the movement speed. At low speeds, the signal is heavily smoothed, at the cost of responsiveness to signal changes. As speed increases, the cut-off frequency is increased, thus the filter is less effective but more responsive to the fast changes in the signal. This principle makes the 1€ filter potentially well-suited for eye tracking, where static fixations alternate with very fast saccades. To our knowledge it has not been applied to eye tracking data before. It has two parameters to control smoothness and responsiveness of the filter: the cut-off frequency $f_{c_{min}}$ and the adaption rate $\beta$.

## Parameter Optimization

Most of these filters require the choice of one or more parameters, which determine the effectiveness of the filter. We propose an approach to optimize parameters based on data collected through a calibration-style study such as the one described earlier in this paper. In a grid search, we instantiate a filter with each possible parameter, apply it to the data, and evaluate its effect on two criteria: the resulting *target size* and the *delay in following a saccade*. For each possible parameter, the following steps are performed separately in the $x$- and $y$-direction:

1. **Target size:** For each target fixation in the data set, apply the filter, compute the accuracy and precision of the filtered gaze, and derive the corresponding target size according to Equation 1. Compute the target size $S_{75\%}$ over all fixations as the 75th percentile of all target sizes. This represents a target size that allows for robust interaction, where for 75% of fixations at least 95% of gaze points fall inside the target.
2. **Saccade simulation:** Simulate saccades between two neighboring targets of size $S_{75\%}$. For each target fixation, simulate a second fixation by shifting each gaze point by $S_{75\%}$ cm and append it to the original fixation. The resulting signal simulates a fixation-saccade-fixation sequence. Create a second sequence by shifting the original points by $-S_{75\%}$ cm in the negative direction.
3. **Saccade delay:** Apply the filter to the constructed sequences. For each filtered sequence, compute saccade delay as number of frames from the start of the second fixation until the signal first exceeds the lower target bound of the second target. Adjust the delay by any delay the unfiltered signal may have due to signal noise.

In this way, for each potential set of parameters, we compute the target size necessary for robust interaction and the average signal delay the filter would lead to when used in a gaze-enabled application. In order to decide on the best parameters, we have to trade off these two opposing criteria. Therefore, we identify the Pareto optimal solutions by discretizing the delay, and then for each delay, determining the parameters that yield the minimum target size without exceeding this delay.

Figure 5 shows the resulting Pareto fronts for applying each filter in the x- and y-direction. Each point denotes a parameter setting that yields the minimum target size for the corresponding delay. The *Weighted Average filter* can be seen as a baseline. Its only parameter, the size of the averaging window, determines the trade-off between small target size and short delays. The *Gaussian and Triangle kernel* perform slightly better than the *Constant kernel.* They give a higher weight to more recent points, thus allowing for a larger averaging window at the same signal delay than the Constant kernel. In practice the *Stampe filter* yields a larger delay than expected from its construction. The two points in the plot represent the first and second step during which one- and two-frame outliers

| | Target width (cm) | | | Target height (cm) | | |
|---|---|---|---|---|---|---|
| | Raw | Filt. | Diff | Raw | Filt. | Diff |
| **Overall** | 3.0 | 2.02 | 33% | 3.14 | 2.19 | 30% |
| **Percentile** | | | | | | |
| 25% | 0.94 | 0.58 | 38 % | 1.24 | 0.8 | 35% |
| 50% | 1.8 | 1.12 | 38 % | 2.26 | 1.48 | 35% |
| 75% | 3.28 | 1.9 | 42 % | 3.78 | 2.35 | 38% |
| 90% | 5.96 | 3.9 | 35 % | 6.24 | 4.24 | 32% |

**Table 5. Recommended target sizes for robust and smooth interaction by eye gaze, and a comparison between sizes computed based on raw data and filtered data. Percentiles show how much target sizes varies for different levels of tracking quality.**

are corrected, in theory yielding one- and two-frame delays. However, depending on the noise structure, the Stampe filter may detect saccades as outliers, thus yielding a larger delay. In practice, this leads to similar or worse performance than the weighted average filter. The *1€ filter* performs better than the WA filter, due to the dynamic adjustment of the cut-off frequency. However, in practice this adjustment is not enough for the filter to react to the sudden and large signal jumps corresponding to a saccade. Moreover, the cut-off frequency is also adjusted to noise artifacts that show similar dynamics as saccades. The *Saccade filter* performs best for a delay up to one frame (16 ms with a 60 Hz tracker). While in theory, it does not introduce any delay, in practice a saccade may not be detected, in which case a strong averaging filter is applied. On the other hand, choosing a small saccade threshold ensures minimal delay, but increases the number of outliers wrongly detected as saccades, thus yielding a larger target size. A similar trade-off applies to the *Outlier filter*. The construction of the filter introduces a minimum delay of one frame. However, stronger filtering is achieved if we increase the saccade threshold and thus take into account larger delays if a saccade is not recognized, on average up to about 2.5 frames.

The supplementary material contains corresponding parameter settings for each filter. Developers can use these results to choose the best filter settings appropriate for their application. If a different setup is used or as technology develops, the presented approach and metrics can be used to derive optimal parameters for any given filter based on data obtained from simple target fixations.

### Effect on Accuracy and Precision

Based on our comparison, we choose to filter our data with the Outlier filter with a Gaussian kernel, which extends weighted averaging with saccade detection and outlier correction. According to our optimization, we choose a saccade threshold of 1.45 cm in x- and 1.65 cm in the y-direction, and a window size of 36 and 40 frames respectively. In practice, this would yield a delay of about two frames (32 ms with a 60 Hz tracker).

Figure 6 shows the resulting average target sizes based on the filtered and unfiltered data of each target fixation. Table 5 compares the average sizes based on the raw and filtered data. The first row shows the average overall data. Precision has improved from 0.53 cm to 0.29 cm in the x-direction and from 0.51 to 0.27 cm in the y-direction, while accuracy has approximately stayed the same. The other rows show the variation of target size for different percentiles of target fixations. They

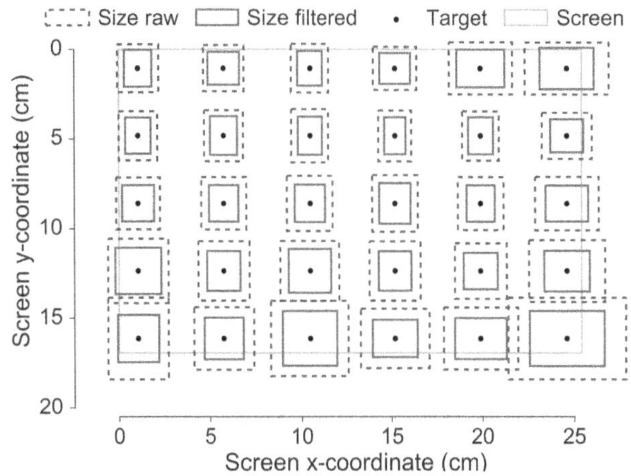


**Figure 6. Appropriate target sizes for different screen positions, computed based on the raw and the filtered data.**

are computed based on the corresponding percentile for each target and averaged over all targets. The optimized Outlier filter reduces the target size by up to 42%. However, the filter can only improve the precision of the data, not its accuracy.

## IMPLICATIONS FOR GAZE-ENABLED APPLICATIONS

We can use our findings to derive implications for the design of gaze-enabled applications that are used by a broad range of users under varying tracking conditions. Such implications are useful for designers and developers, but also for researchers who want to minimize the risk of having to exclude users from their study or who want to conduct studies in more natural environments.

**Target size and distances**: Gaze-enabled regions should be designed slightly larger in height than in width, since we observed consistently larger standard deviations in the *y*-direction. According to our data, target sizes of at least 1.9×2.35 cm allow for reliable interaction for at least 75% of users if optimal filtering is used. If no filter is implemented, this should be enlarged to 3.28×3.78 cm. Targets of this size can be placed directly next to each other. Note that the size only denotes the region that is reactive to the eye gaze; this can be invisible to the user and the corresponding UI elements can be smaller, in which case the distance between graphical elements must then take into account the larger tracking area.

**Screen regions**: Avoid placing gaze-enabled elements towards the bottom or right edge of the screen, for which accuracy and precision was found to be significantly worse.

**Filtering**: Use a weighted average filter with a Gaussian or Triangular kernel and saccade detection. If the application can account for a two-sample delay, additional outlier correction (Kumar et al. 2008) can improve precision further and reduce recognition of false saccades. In this work, we obtained best results with the following parameters: window size of 36/40 frames, saccade threshold of 1.45 cm/1.65 cm in x-/y-direction. The latter one could be further adapted to the specific applications, for example when targets are far apart and expected saccades thus larger. Therefore, the supplementary material provides optimized parameters.

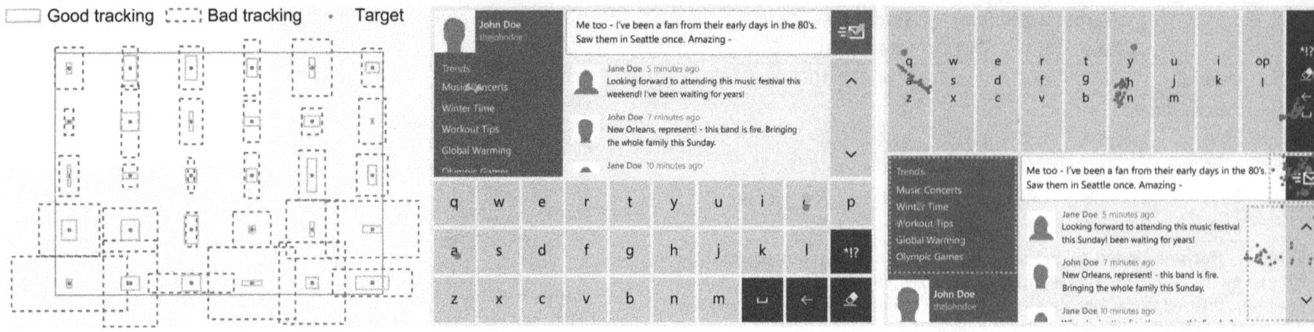


**Figure 7. Example case that shows how the design of a gaze-controlled social network application can be adapted to the changing tracking quality. Left: Target sizes for good and bad tracking, based on data from two users. Middle: UI for good tracking quality. Right: UI adapted to bad tracking. The keyboard has moved up where tracking is best and letters are grouped to account for vertical offset and spread of gaze points. Green lines show that the active gaze region of the buttons is actually larger than the graphical UI element, accounting for bad tracking near the bottom of the screen.**

## Error-Aware and Adaptive Applications

Our findings open up a new set of questions, setting the stage for research in future areas such as adaptive UIs. We share the vision of other researchers (e.g. [2, 3, 36]) that applications should be aware of uncertainty in the input signal and adapt their interface and functionality accordingly. However, eye tracking poses a challenge in that the error of the estimated gaze point varies substantially depending on the interplay of many factors and thus is hard to predict and correct. Therefore, we envision applications consisting of flexible modules that adapt their graphical representation and functionality to variations in accuracy and precision of the tracked gaze. The results and methods presented in this paper are an important step towards the the design of such adaptive modules. To exemplify this, we sketch an example application in Figure 7. We show how the user interface of a social network application can be adapted based on example data of two different users from our data set. We envision the application to adapt to the changes in tracking quality by going through the following steps:

**1. Collect information about tracking accuracy and precision** by analyzing target fixations during calibration and usage. Utilize the data to compute appropriate target sizes as shown in Equation 1. The left plot in Figure 7 shows example target sizes based on data from two different users. Yellow denotes "good" and blue "bad" tracking quality.

**2. Choose optimal filter parameters**, trading off signal response and precision based on the characteristics of the application. For example, if error corrections are costly, a more aggressive filter could be chosen if signal quality drops, taking into account delayed response of user actions for a more robust interaction. Optimal parameters for a range of acceptable delays are given in the supplementary material.

**3. Adapt functionality and design** of the UI to account for the changes in tracking quality, either as predefined or optimized in real-time. This is exemplified in Figure 7. The middle part shows a UI designed for good tracking quality: it has a full keyboard placed on the bottom of the screen (as familiar from mobile interfaces); links and buttons can be selected individually. The UI on the right is adapted to poor tracking. The keyboard is moved to the top where tracking is relatively best, and letters are grouped to account for the vertical offset and spread of gaze points (grouped-key text entry may then be disambiguated algorithmically using text prediction, or combined with a secondary input action to select individual characters). The links under "Trends" are merged into one gaze target, while keeping them visually as before; if activated, an alternative pointing technique like zooming [4, 10] or fish-eye lenses [1] could be applied. Similarly, the scroll buttons are kept as before, but their active gaze region expands beyond the screen and toward the static message window.

**4. Optimize when to adapt the UI**, by monitoring changes in tracking and predicting the potential gain. In order for adaptive interfaces to be usable, the system needs to take into account the cost for the user to adapt to the new UI. To determine the best changes the system trades off criteria such as interaction cost, learning time, or user preference in interaction with the user. Toward this end, future work is needed to develop appropriate user models and optimization methods.

Other types of applications could benefit from information about accuracy and precision. For example, the more accurate and precise the estimated gaze points, the more complex and small the **gaze gestures** that can be used. During runtime, a gesture system could adapt to loss of tracking quality and encourage the user to perform larger gestures, or provide different gesture sets for different levels of tracking quality. Recognition algorithms could also take into account the quality of the tracked gaze to better differ between noise in the signal and noise in the gesture performance. **Attentive reading applications** (e.g. [13, 38]) could adapt their font size and word spacing for better recognition of fixations during reading. Visualizing tracking quality to the end user could be useful, for example in **remote collaborative settings** where information about collaborators' gaze can be a useful communication tool, but a noisy signal can be confusing [7].

## DISCUSSION

We showed how eye tracking precision and accuracy can vary under tracking conditions similar to those encountered in practice. Our work underscores the importance of error-aware applications that adapt to variations in tracking quality, and we suggested several opportunities for how our results can inform the design of such applications. In the following, we discuss the generalizability of our findings to applications used in-the-wild and opportunities for further work.

### Generalizability of Results

To assess the generalizability of our results to gaze input in everyday computer interaction, we have replicated our data collection with six experienced eye tracking users (people with ALS who rely on gaze-based AAC for communication), in environments and setups in which they use their eye trackers in practice. The task was the same as described in the Study section, but we only used the Tobii EyeX tracker, and mounted it on a rolling stand (rather than table) for wheelchair accessibility. Compared to the first study, gaze points were tracked with a similarly large variation in precision; multivariate ANOVA found no difference for precision in either the $x$- or the $y$-direction. However, accuracy of the gaze points varied even more, ranging from 0.16 cm and 0.21 cm in the $x$- and $y$-direction if tracking was good (25th percentile) to 1.32 cm and 1.67 cm in the $x$- and $y$-direction for poor tracking (90th percentile). Multivariate ANOVA and follow-up univariate testing found the difference in accuracy to the first study significant ($F(1,86) = 2.6$, $p = 0.04$). Further analysis showed, that in comparison to the first study, there were more outliers for which offset was over 1 cm. A Mood's median test found no significant difference in accuracy between the two studies.

This shows that the conditions created in our study closely resemble those that we can expect in practice. However, when applying our findings designers should keep in mind that in particular the accuracy can vary even more, suggesting that designers should be conservative in their design of targets.

### Limitations and Opportunities for Future Work

Several characteristics of our study design may lead to even larger variations in-the-wild. We computed target sizes with the assumption that users look at the center of a target. If the user's gaze changes within a small region, accuracy and precision will likely stay the same but more gaze points will land outside a target as the gaze gets close to its border. It is a separate research question how the visual design of targets (label shape, color, etc.) changes the focus of a user.

Our study was short, thus we did not find differences in accuracy or precision between a user's first and last fixation. In practice, we expect that accuracy and precision further decrease over time (due to movement, fatigue, etc.).

We found that accuracy and precision become worse toward the bottom and right edge of the screen. However, both tested trackers can be used with screens up to 27", which is larger than the 12" screen we used. We expect tracking to also get worse toward the left and top edges as targets are placed closer to the spatial limits of the tracker; however, a similar study on a larger screen is necessary to confirm this expectation.

We used two commercially-available remote, IR eye trackers under two lighting setups. The specific accuracy and precision measures we report may vary under other environmental conditions and/or with different equipment. However, our study reveals that in practical conditions, tracking quality is much more affected by differences between individual users than trackers or lighting. Using mixed linear regression to model the accuracy and precision of our data, we found that on average differences in lighting and tracker only account for up to 8.3% of the deviation in tracking quality, whereas differences between users account for up to 32.8%. Thus, it is reasonable to assume that data collected under similar conditions with other eye trackers are likely to show a similarly large variation in tracking accuracy and precision; formally investigating this would be a valuable direction for future research. For applications to be usable in practice, it is important to account for these large variations in tracking quality, regardless of the source. But in order to generate updated measurements as use scenarios and eye tracking devices evolve, other researchers can use the experimental and analytic methodologies we described in this paper.

## CONCLUSION

Eye tracking has the potential to revolutionize how we interact with computers. Attentive applications seamlessly integrate gaze input into existing interaction paradigms and explicit gaze control opens new design spaces for HCI. While researchers have developed many interaction techniques and applications that use gaze information, there was a gap in understanding the requirements of such applications as they are released to consumers. Toward this end, our work provides important contributions for developers and designers of gaze-enabled applications, as well as researchers using eye tracking:

1. We showed that there is **large variability in accuracy and precision** when eye tracking is used in more practical conditions. Differences between users can be more than six-fold, and we analyzed variations of trackers and screen regions.
2. We propose a way of formally going from measures of accuracy and precision to **target sizes**. We provide look-up tables for appropriate target sizes and discuss the best screen regions. Our findings can be directly used by people developing gaze-enabled applications.
3. We **optimize and evaluate filters** that work for eye tracking data in practical conditions. We propose an optimization approach to find parameters that minimize target size and signal delay, given calibration-style data. Developers can directly use our results to choose the filter and parameters appropriate for their application, while researchers can follow our approach as they develop new filters.
4. We outline our vision of **error-aware gaze application**, that adapt their design and interaction techniques to the current tracking quality. We discuss several examples and provide a walkthrough how our findings can be used to inform the design of such applications.

For eye tracking to become a ubiquitous part of our everyday interaction with computers, it is important to more systematically explore the question of "What is good design?' for gaze input, with the goal of establishing standards and frameworks for robust, usable gaze applications. The presented findings are an important step toward this goal, and our methods can be re-applied to future hardware versions or in other contexts to derive updated measurements as technology evolves.

## ACKNOWLEDGMENTS

We thank Mike Bennett, Ed Cutrell, Shahram Eivazi, and Antti Oulasvirta for their insightful comments. We also thank our PALS and study participants, and the MSR Enable team.

## REFERENCES


1. Michael Ashmore, Andrew T. Duchowski, and Garth Shoemaker. 2005. Efficient eye pointing with a fisheye lens. In *Proceedings of Graphics Interface 2005*. Canadian Human-Computer Communications Society, Waterloo, 203–210.
2. Michael Barz, Andreas Bulling, and Florian Daiber. 2016a. Computational Modelling and Prediction of Gaze Estimation Error for Head-mounted Eye Trackers DFKI Technical Report. (2016).
3. Michael Barz, Florian Daiber, and Andreas Bulling. 2016b. Prediction of gaze estimation error for error-aware gaze-based interfaces. In *Proceedings of the Ninth Biennial ACM Symposium on Eye Tracking Research & Applications - ETRA '16*. ACM Press, New York, New York, USA, 275–278. DOI: http://dx.doi.org/10.1145/2857491.2857493
4. Richard Bates and Howell Istance. 2002. Zooming interfaces!: enhancing the performance of eye controlled pointing devices. In *Proceedings of the fifth international ACM conference on Assistive technologies - Assets '02*. ACM Press, New York, New York, USA, 119. DOI: http://dx.doi.org/10.1145/638249.638272
5. Pieter Blignaut, Kenneth Holmqvist, Marcus Nyström, and Richard Dewhurst. 2014. Improving the Accuracy of Video-Based Eye Tracking in Real Time through Post-Calibration Regression. In *Current Trends in Eye Tracking Research*. Springer International Publishing, Cham, 77–100. DOI: http://dx.doi.org/10.1007/978-3-319-02868-2_5
6. Géry Casiez, Nicolas Roussel, and Daniel Vogel. 2012. 1€ filter: a simple speed-based low-pass filter for noisy input in interactive systems. In *Proceedings of the 2012 ACM annual conference on Human Factors in Computing Systems - CHI '12*. ACM Press, New York, New York, USA, 2527. DOI: http://dx.doi.org/10.1145/2207676.2208639
7. Sarah D'Angelo and Darren Gergle. 2016. Gazed and Confused: Understanding and Designing Shared Gaze for Remote Collaboration. In *Proceedings of the 2016 CHI Conference on Human Factors in Computing Systems - CHI '16*. ACM Press, New York, New York, USA, 2492–2496. DOI: http://dx.doi.org/10.1145/2858036.2858499
8. Heiko Drewes and Albrecht Schmidt. 2007. *Interacting with the computer using gaze gestures*. Springer-Verlag. 475–488 pages.
9. Andrew T Duchowski, Nathan Cournia, and Hunter Murphy. 2004. Gaze-contingent displays: a review. *Cyberpsychology & behavior : the impact of the Internet, multimedia and virtual reality on behavior and society* 7, 6 (dec 2004), 621–34. DOI: http://dx.doi.org/10.1089/cpb.2004.7.621
10. David Fono and Roel Vertegaal. 2005. EyeWindows: evaluation of eye-controlled zooming windows for focus selection. In *Proceedings of the SIGCHI conference on Human factors in computing systems - CHI '05*. ACM Press, New York, New York, USA, 151. DOI: http://dx.doi.org/10.1145/1054972.1054994
11. Kenneth Holmqvist, Marcus Nyström, Richard Andersson, Richard Dewhurst, Halszka Jarodzka, and Joost de Weijer. 2011. *Eye tracking: A comprehensive guide to methods and measures*. OUP Oxford.
12. Yu-Chun Huang and Fong-Gong Wu. 2015. Visual and manual loadings with QWERTY-like ambiguous keyboards: Relevance of letter-key assignments on mobile phones. *International Journal of Industrial Ergonomics* 50 (2015), 143–150. DOI: http://dx.doi.org/10.1016/j.ergon.2015.08.002
13. Aulikki Hyrskykari, Päivi Majaranta, Antti Aaltonen, and Kari-Jouko Räihä. 2000. Design issues of iDICT: A Gaze-Assisted Translation Aid. In *Proceedings of the symposium on Eye tracking research & applications - ETRA '00*. ACM Press, New York, New York, USA, 9–14. DOI: http://dx.doi.org/10.1145/355017.355019
14. SensoMotoric Instruments. 2016. SMI REDn Scientific – Specifiactions. (2016). http://www.smivision.com/fileadmin/user
15. Howell Istance and Aulikki Hyrskykari. 2011. Gaze-Aware Systems and Attentive Applications. In *Gaze Interaction and Applications of Eye Tracking*. Vol. 58. IGI Global, 175–195. DOI: http://dx.doi.org/10.4018/978-1-61350-098-9.ch013
16. Howell Istance, Aulikki Hyrskykari, Lauri Immonen, Santtu Mansikkamaa, and Stephen Vickers. 2010. Designing gaze gestures for gaming: an Investigation of Performance. In *Proceedings of the 2010 Symposium on Eye-Tracking Research & Applications - ETRA '10*. ACM Press, New York, New York, USA, 323. DOI: http://dx.doi.org/10.1145/1743666.1743740
17. Robert J. K. Jacob. 1991. The use of eye movements in human-computer interaction techniques: what you look at is what you get. *ACM Transactions on Information Systems* 9, 2 (Apr 1991), 152–169. DOI: http://dx.doi.org/10.1145/123078.128728
18. Shahram Jalaliniya and Diako Mardanbegi. 2016. Eyegrip: Detecting targets in a series of uni-directional moving objects using optokinetic nystagmus eye movements. In *Proceedings of the 2016 CHI Conference on Human Factors in Computing Systems*. ACM, 5801–5811.
19. J Jimenez, D Gutierrez, and P Latorre. 2008. Gaze-based Interaction for Virtual Environments. *Journal of Universal Computer Science 14* 19 (2008), 3085–3098. http://giga.cps.unizar.es/
20. Manu Kumar, Tal Garfinkel, Dan Boneh, and Terry Winograd. 2007. Reducing shoulder-surfing by using gaze-based password entry. In *Proceedings of the 3rd symposium on Usable privacy and security - SOUPS '07*. ACM Press, New York, New York, USA, 13. DOI: http://dx.doi.org/10.1145/1280680.1280683

21. Manu Kumar, Jeff Klingner, Rohan Puranik, Terry Winograd, and Andreas Paepcke. 2008. Improving the accuracy of gaze input for interaction. In *Proceedings of the 2008 symposium on Eye tracking research & applications - ETRA '08*. ACM Press, New York, New York, USA, 65. DOI: http://dx.doi.org/10.1145/1344471.1344488

22. Manu Kumar, Andreas Paepcke, and Terry Winograd. 2007. EyePoint: practical pointing and selection using gaze and keyboard. In *Proceedings of the SIGCHI conference on Human factors in computing systems - CHI '07*. ACM Press, New York, New York, USA, 421. DOI: http://dx.doi.org/10.1145/1240624.1240692

23. Andrew Kurauchi, Wenxin Feng, Ajjen Joshi, Carlos Morimoto, and Margrit Betke. 2016. EyeSwipe: Dwell-free Text Entry Using Gaze Paths. In *Proceedings of the 2016 CHI Conference on Human Factors in Computing Systems - CHI '16*. ACM Press, New York, New York, USA, 1952–1956. DOI: http://dx.doi.org/10.1145/2858036.2858335

24. Päivi Majaranta, Ulla-Kaija Ahola, and Oleg Špakov. 2009. Fast gaze typing with an adjustable dwell time. In *Proceedings of the 27th international conference on Human factors in computing systems - CHI 09*. ACM Press, New York, New York, USA, 357. DOI: http://dx.doi.org/10.1145/1518701.1518758

25. Päivi Majaranta, Hirotaka Aoki, Mick Donegan, Dan Witzner Hansen, and John Paulin Hansen. 2011. *Gaze Interaction and Applications of Eye Tracking: Advances in Assistive Technologies*. Information Science Reference - Imprint of: IGI Publishing.

26. Päivi Majaranta and Andreas Bulling. 2014. Eye Tracking and Eye-Based Human-Computer Interaction. Springer London, 39–65. DOI: http://dx.doi.org/10.1007/978-1-4471-6392-3_3

27. Michael Mauderer, Simone Conte, Miguel A. Nacenta, and Dhanraj Vishwanath. 2014. Depth perception with gaze-contingent depth of field. In *Proceedings of the 32nd annual ACM conference on Human factors in computing systems - CHI '14*. ACM Press, New York, New York, USA, 217–226. DOI: http://dx.doi.org/10.1145/2556288.2557089

28. Msi. 2016. msi GT72S G TOBII (6TH GEN) (GTX 980M). (2016). https://us.msi.com/Laptop/GT72S-G-Tobii-6th-Gen-GTX-980M.html

29. Cuong Nguyen and Feng Liu. 2016. Gaze-based Notetaking for Learning from Lecture Videos. In *Proceedings of the 2016 CHI Conference on Human Factors in Computing Systems - CHI '16*. ACM Press, New York, New York, USA, 2093–2097. DOI: http://dx.doi.org/10.1145/2858036.2858137

30. Marcus Nyström, Richard Andersson, Kenneth Holmqvist, and Joost van de Weijer. 2013. The influence of calibration method and eye physiology on eyetracking data quality. *Behavior Research Methods* 45, 1 (mar 2013), 272–288. DOI: http://dx.doi.org/10.3758/s13428-012-0247-4

31. Kristien Ooms, Lien Dupont, Lieselot Lapon, and Stanislav Popelka. 2015. Accuracy and precision of fixation locations recorded with the low-cost Eye Tribe tracker in different experimental set-ups. *Journal of Eye Movement Research* 8, 1 (2015). DOI: http://dx.doi.org/10.16910/JEMR.8.1.5

32. Håkon Raudsandmoen and Børge Rødsjø. 2012. Empirically Based Design Guidelines for Gaze Interaction in Windows 7. (2012). http://urn.kb.se/resolve?urn=urn:nbn:no:ntnu:diva-19544

33. David Rozado, Javier S. Agustin, Francisco B. Rodriguez, and Pablo Varona. 2012. Gliding and saccadic gaze gesture recognition in real time. *ACM Transactions on Interactive Intelligent Systems* 1, 2 (jan 2012), 1–27. DOI: http://dx.doi.org/10.1145/2070719.2070723

34. Dario D. Salvucci and Joseph H. Goldberg. 2000. Identifying fixations and saccades in eye-tracking protocols. In *Proceedings of the symposium on Eye tracking research & applications - ETRA '00*. ACM Press, New York, New York, USA, 71–78. DOI: http://dx.doi.org/10.1145/355017.355028

35. Simon Schenk, Philipp Tiefenbacher, Gerhard Rigoll, and Michael Dorr. 2016. SPOCK: A Smooth Pursuit Oculomotor Control Kit. In *Proceedings of the 2016 CHI Conference Extended Abstracts on Human Factors in Computing Systems - CHI EA '16*. ACM Press, New York, New York, USA, 2681–2687. DOI: http://dx.doi.org/10.1145/2851581.2892291

36. Julia Schwarz, Scott Hudson, Jennifer Mankoff, and Andrew D. Wilson. 2010. A framework for robust and flexible handling of inputs with uncertainty. In *Proceedings of the 23nd annual ACM symposium on User interface software and technology - UIST '10*. ACM Press, New York, New York, USA, 47. DOI: http://dx.doi.org/10.1145/1866029.1866039

37. Baris Serim and Giulio Jacucci. 2016. Pointing while Looking Elsewhere: Designing for Varying Degrees of Visual Guidance during Manual Input. *Proceedings of the 2016 CHI Conference on Human Factors in Computing Systems* (2016), 5789–5800. DOI: http://dx.doi.org/10.1145/2858036.2858480

38. John L. Sibert, Mehmet Gokturk, and Robert A. Lavine. 2000. The reading assistant: eye gaze triggered auditory prompting for reading remediation. In *Proceedings of the 13th annual ACM symposium on User interface software and technology - UIST '00*. ACM Press, New York, New York, USA, 101–107. DOI: http://dx.doi.org/10.1145/354401.354418

39. Oleg Špakov. 2012. Comparison of eye movement filters used in HCI. In *Proceedings of the Symposium on Eye Tracking Research and Applications - ETRA '12*. ACM Press, New York, New York, USA, 281. DOI: http://dx.doi.org/10.1145/2168556.2168616

40. Oleg Špakov, Poika Isokoski, Jari Kangas, Deepak Akkil, and Päivi Majaranta. 2016. PursuitAdjuster: an exploration into the design space of smooth pursuit-based widgets. In *Proceedings of the Ninth Biennial ACM Symposium on Eye Tracking Research & Applications - ETRA '16*. ACM Press, New York, New York, USA, 287–290. DOI: http://dx.doi.org/10.1145/2857491.2857526

41. Dave M Stampe. 1993. Heuristic filtering and reliable calibration methods for video-based pupil-tracking systems. *Behavior Research Methods, Instruments, & Computers* 25, 2 (1993), 137–142.

42. Thomas Templier, Kenan Bektas, and Richard H.R. Hahnloser. 2016. Eye-Trace: Segmentation of Volumetric Microscopy Images with Eyegaze. In *Proceedings of the 2016 CHI Conference on Human Factors in Computing Systems - CHI '16*. ACM Press, New York, New York, USA, 5812–5823. DOI: http://dx.doi.org/10.1145/2858036.2858578

43. The Eye Tribe. 2016. Eye Tribe Tracker Pro. (2016). https://theeyetribe.com/products/

44. Tobii Technology. 2016a. EyeX controller accurary and precision test report, tobii developer zone. (2016). http://developer.tobii.com/community/forums/topic/eyex-controller-accurary-and-precision-test-report/

45. Tobii Technology. 2016b. Tobii EyeX Controller – Specifications. (2016). http://www.tobii.com/xperience/products/

46. Mélodie Vidal, Andreas Bulling, and Hans Gellersen. 2013. Pursuits: Spontaneous Interaction with Displays based on Smooth Pursuit Eye Movement and Moving Targets. In *Proceedings of the 2013 ACM international joint conference on Pervasive and ubiquitous computing - UbiComp '13*. ACM Press, New York, New York, USA, 439. DOI:http://dx.doi.org/10.1145/2493432.2493477

47. Jacob O. Wobbrock, James Rubinstein, Michael W. Sawyer, and Andrew T. Duchowski. 2008. Longitudinal evaluation of discrete consecutive gaze gestures for text entry. In *Proceedings of the 2008 symposium on Eye tracking research & applications - ETRA '08*. ACM Press, New York, New York, USA, 11. DOI: http://dx.doi.org/10.1145/1344471.1344475

48. Erroll Wood and Andreas Bulling. 2014. EyeTab: model-based gaze estimation on unmodified tablet computers. In *Proceedings of the Symposium on Eye Tracking Research and Applications - ETRA '14*. ACM Press, New York, New York, USA, 207–210. DOI: http://dx.doi.org/10.1145/2578153.2578185

49. Shumin Zhai, Carlos Morimoto, and Steven Ihde. 1999. Manual and gaze input cascaded (MAGIC) pointing. In *Proceedings of the SIGCHI conference on Human factors in computing systems the CHI is the limit - CHI '99*. ACM Press, New York, New York, USA, 246–253. DOI: http://dx.doi.org/10.1145/302979.303053

# Heat-Nav: Using Temperature Changes as Navigational Cues

**Jordan Tewell**
City, University of London
London, United Kingdom
jordan.tewell.1@city.ac.uk

**Jon Bird**
City, University of London
London, United Kingdom
jon.bird@city.ac.uk

**George R. Buchanan**
University of Melbourne
Melbourne, Australia
george.buchanan@unimelb.edu.au

## ABSTRACT
HCI is increasingly exploring how temperature can be used as an interaction modality. One challenge is that temperature changes are perceived over the course of seconds. This can be attributed to both the slow response time of skin thermoreceptors and the latency of the technology used to heat and cool the skin. For this reason, thermal cues are typically used to communicate single states, such as an emotion, and then there is a pause of tens of seconds to allow the skin to re-adapt to a neutral temperature before sending another signal. In contrast, this paper presents the first experimental demonstration that continuous temperature changes can guide behaviour: significantly improving performance in a 2D maze navigation task, without having to return to a neutral state before a new signal is sent. We discuss how continuous thermal feedback may be used for real world navigational tasks.

### Author Keywords
Thermal feedback; thermal haptics; navigation

### ACM Classification Keywords
H.5.2. User Interfaces – Haptic IO.

## INTRODUCTION
HCI research has primarily investigated whether or not thermal cues can communicate single states, for example, an emotion, activity level or social distance [4][15][9]. In these studies, the temperature is usually reset back to neutral for tens of seconds before sending a new thermal cue, a process referred to commonly as 're-adaptation'. This is necessary as the skin slowly habituates to temperature, which can undermine how strongly the participant can detect a new stimulus. There is an open question about the usefulness of thermal feedback for guiding behaviour if it is necessary to pause for tens of seconds before a new thermal cue is presented.


*CHI 2017, May 06-11, 2017, Denver, CO, USA*
© 2017 ACM. ISBN 978-1-4503-4655-9/17/05…$15.00
DOI: http://dx.doi.org/10.1145/3025453.3025965

The limitations of human physiology and technology present other challenges for using thermal cues to guide behaviour. The cutaneous sense of temperature is carried on nerve endings that have slow response times [6]. Non-linear interactions between these neurons result in sensory illusions such as 'synthetic heat', as illustrated by placing a hand on interlaced warm and cool bars, which results in a burning sensation [2]. Furthermore, thermal signals need to be sufficiently intense, otherwise it can be difficult for users to perceive them correctly, if at all [16]. As well as these human factors, there are also the limitations of thermal electric coolers (TECs), the technology used to deliver thermal feedback in most research. TECs typically have high power consumption, slow rates of change, and large heat dissipation.

However, these limitations do not render thermal feedback useless. There remains an opportunity to use this channel of communication for tasks that require feedback only every few seconds. With their low resolution and slow refresh rate, a potential advantage of thermal displays is that they do not require significant focused attention from the user and can present information in an ambient manner [17]. This paper's contribution is to experimentally demonstrate that temperature feedback can effectively guide on-going behaviour. We developed a Thermal Array Display (TAD), consisting of three TECs worn on the arm, which can display patterns of warm, cool, and neutral temperatures [11]. This paper presents a laboratory-based experiment that demonstrates how continuous thermal feedback provided by the TAD can improve user performance in a navigation task. Unlike previous research, we did not reset the TECs to a neutral temperature prior to sending the thermal signals.

## BACKGROUND
User preferences for feedback modality can vary by location and situation. While vibrotactile feedback (VTF) is effective in many situations, it is not appropriate in noise-sensitive environments, such as libraries, and is also less effective in loud and bumpy environments, like trains [3]. Thermal feedback can be silent, depending on the technology used [14], and does not require users' full attention. An in-situ evaluation of PocketNavigator [10] further identified a number of issues using VTF for navigation. Participants often found VTF irritating and they had to learn how to interpret the VTF cues. Although distraction was reduced, participants still looked frequently at their mobile displays: "our results confirm that distraction is a challenge" (pp. 7-8).

Researchers have proposed that temperature cues could also be used to guide navigation. Wettach *et al.* argued that temperature could be a good interaction modality for 'calm technologies' that provide ambient signals, particularly in the domain of navigation, as thermal cues can provide "a rough clue about the intensity of a certain signal or entity" [13 p.2]. However, no outcomes were reported from their study other than "the user was able to find her way to the destination…" [p.2]. No controlled studies have been carried out on other thermal navigation prototypes that have been developed. Lécuyer *et al.* [5] proposed a device indicating sun direction to visually impaired users, but did not evaluate the potential of using both heat and cool cues to guide navigation. Quido [1] used both thermal and VTF to guide participants towards a goal in a 2D maze. While their results showed that performance improved over time, they did not investigate the relative contribution of the two modalities to guide behaviour. Hiya-Atsu [8] investigated a spatial navigation task where users searched for an object on a computer display with a temperature augmented mouse. While all participants found the hidden objects, no details were reported about how the device was evaluated. Our aim was to address the limitations of previous research by investigating the efficacy of temperature changes to guide navigation in a controlled laboratory experiment.

## HARDWARE OVERVIEW

The Thermal Array Display, or TAD, is shown in Fig. 1. It is worn on the arm and consists of three stimulators, each one comprising a TEC device (MCPE1-01708NCS, Multicomp), a thermistor (MC65F103A, Amphenol Sensors), a 6V DC fan, and a heatsink. The TECs are controlled by a Proportional-Integral-Derivative (PID) controller on an Arduino Mega 2560 micro-controller. The PID reads the thermistor and sets the output temperature by varying the voltage and direction. Voltage is powered from a 6V, 10A mains supply and is varied using a 490 Hz Pulse Width Modulated signal and smoothed using a choke inductor. A motor driver (MC33926, Pololu) controls the direction, allowing both sides of the TEC to warm up or cool down. This system enables reliable detection of smaller temperature differences than with a single TEC as it both improves error rate and degree of error significantly [11].

**Figure 1. The Thermal Array Display (TAD) consists of three stimulator units, one positioned on the wrist, one under the elbow and the other between them.**

## EXPERIMENT DESIGN

In the children's game 'Hot-and-Cold', a temperature metaphor is used to guide players towards the location of a hidden object. We hypothesised that actual temperature changes on the skin could provide similar proximity information in a navigation task: increasing heat could indicate getting closer to a goal; conversely, increasing cold could let a user know they are moving further away. To test this hypothesis, we developed a 2D maze navigation task and in a controlled experiment compared user navigation performance with and without thermal feedback.

A participant is represented by a red dot in a 2D maze displayed on a computer display (Fig. 2). They control their position by moving from one path block to an adjacent one using the keyboard arrow keys. Participants were instructed to make as few moves as possible and to try and find the goal within a time limit of ten minutes. The goal, represented by a green dot on the screen, was hidden somewhere inside the maze, and only the local area around the player's current position was visible, the rest of the maze being blacked out. Fig. 2 shows a 3x3 block section of a maze visible to the user on screen, with the surrounding area left semi-transparent in the image—rather than blacked out—to show the maze.

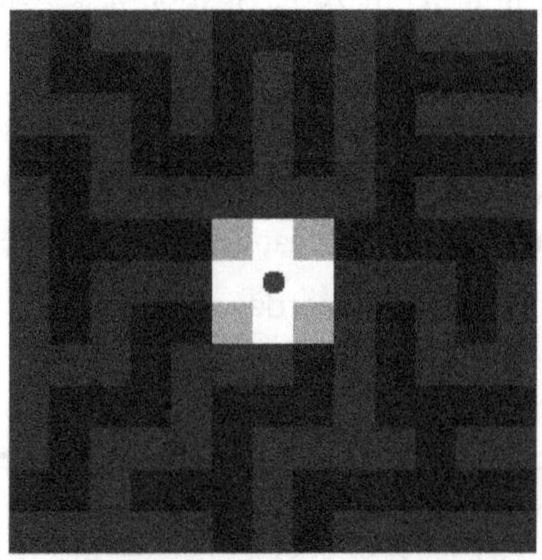

**Figure 2. Participants (represented by a red dot) could only see the maze in the immediate area around their current position and the rest of the maze was blacked out (left semi-transparent in this image to show the underlying maze design).**

### Thermal Feedback Design

Wilson *et al.* used a temperature range of 22°C-38°C [15], a safe and comfortable zone of temperatures appropriate for thermal feedback. As our apparatus has a rate of change of about 1°C/sec, we chose feedback stimuli in the narrower range of 29°C - 35°C to minimize time taken for the TECs to reach the desired temperature.

To design effective thermal feedback for maze navigation, different techniques for correlating temperature changes with a participant's location relative to the goal were explored in pilot studies. We experimented with both *what* was being signalled and *how* it was mapped to temperature changes. We initially tried signalling the current distance from the *global* shortest path between the start and end goal. Pilot study participants found this hard to interpret and often got stuck in a region of the maze. Even if participants did get onto the globally shortest path, they would sometimes head towards the start rather than the goal.

It was more useful to signal distance from the *current* shortest path, recalculated each turn, based on the current position using breadth-first search. We experimented mapping distance from the path to a range of temperatures, with feedback getting colder the further they moved away. However, pilot study participants found these subtle temperature changes and slow rate of change confusing.

It was more effective to use only two temperatures: very warm (35°C) to indicate the participant was on the current shortest path, and very cool (29°C) for when they left the current shortest path. If the user remained on the path, feedback stayed very warm and a change in temperature only occurred if they left the path. The TAD took 6 seconds to cool from 35°C to 29°C given the latency of the TECs, but participants in the pilot usually noticed the cooling and reacted before the minimum temperature was reached. We were interested in determining whether, even with the high latency, lack of re-adaptation, and ambient style feedback, temperature changes would improve navigation in a controlled experiment using 2D mazes.

### Maze Design

Several maze designs were explored to determine an appropriate size and complexity: the number of maze junctions that lead to different paths and number of moves needed to go direct from start to finish. We choose mazes of 40x40 blocks, where each block is a single move up, down, left or right. These dimensions were chosen based on the average length of time it took pilot participants to complete a maze without thermal feedback (317.8s, std. dev. 167.9s), meaning we could expect our participants to complete four mazes within an hour session. Four mazes were designed by hand, assisted by an on-line generator: http://www.billsgames.com/mazegenerator/. Each maze design consisted of the same number of junctions, contained no loops, and had a single path from the start point to the goal (global shortest path) of 245 moves.

## PROCEDURE

The experiment used a within-subjects design and the order that participants experienced control and thermal feedback conditions was counterbalanced. 12 participants, 9 males and 3 females, all students in the engineering school of a UK university (mean age 31.7 years, std. dev. 6.3 years), were split into two groups. Group 1 wore the device for the first two mazes (feedback condition) and then removed it for the other two (the control condition). Group 2 did not wear the device for the first two mazes and wore it for the last two. In the control condition, a participant had to reach the goal location without any guidance; in the feedback condition, they were provided with thermal cues that informed them whether they were on (very warm) or off (very cool) the local shortest path. Mazes were completed in a pre-determined, randomized order, unique to each participant.

Before navigating any mazes, participants were given written and oral instructions to ensure they understood what the thermal feedback signified and how the controls worked. Participants wore earplugs due to audible sounds from the inductors, as confirmed in the pilots. Before each of the two mazes in the feedback condition started, their skin was re-adapted to a neutral temperature (32°C). However, re-adaptation only occurred before participants started each maze and not while they were navigating the maze.

The time taken to reach the goal and the number of moves made were recorded for each maze. If a participant did not complete the maze within the time limit, they were 'timed out' and a cap time of 10 minutes was used. Every move was logged so that we could generate heat maps of participants' behaviour with and without thermal feedback. After the four mazes were completed, each participant was interviewed about their experience with the thermal feedback.

## RESULTS

The mean time to complete mazes with thermal feedback was 249.0s, (std. dev. 115.6s); in the control condition, it was 358.5s, (std. dev. 165.3s). The mean number of moves taken with feedback was 593.5 (std. dev. 321.4); the control condition mean was 1396.0 (std. dev. 577.7). Participants tended to slow down when using thermal cues: on average 2.4 moves per second (mps) were made in the feedback case, whereas 3.9 mps were made in the control condition.

As the data were non-normal, we used a Mann-Whitney non-parametric test to compare performance in the two conditions. This produced $U_a$=413.5, z=-2.58, p=0.0049 (one sided) when comparing times. Applying the same test to the number of turns taken produced $U_a$=537, z=-5.12, p<0.0001 (one-sided). Thermal feedback, while of relatively long latency, strongly reduced maze solution time. The low time-out rate across the two conditions did not permit a valid statistical comparison, but the relative counts of 5 (control) versus 1 (thermal) are consistent with the improved performance of using thermal feedback.

In interviews, every participant reported that they understood the thermal feedback and found it easier to find the target with temperature cues: "the temperature feedback helped me to predict where the target was" [P11]; "it's like a guide to the right path" [P6]. All participants reported that the temperatures were comfortable, P12 said "it was at a level that lets you just feel it". Participants used temperature changes, rather than the absence or presence of feedback to guide their navigation: P3 reporting "it's not too hot or cold but there's enough of a difference to tell them apart." Some participants emphasised it had taken time to learn the feedback, P5 saying "once I got used to it, I went a bit slower". There is statistical evidence of a learning effect between the first and second maze. Discarding all pairs that include an unsuccessful attempt (timed out), the average time using thermal feedback fell from 248.2s to 198.0s (std. dev. 75.0s); in the control condition, performance was 355.3s vs 337.3s. The latter was not significant. Improvement with thermal guidance was normally distributed and a pair-wise t-test proved significant (p=0.01, t=2.65, df=2).

Fig. 3 shows 'heat maps' for Maze #2: the start position is bottom right and the target is bottom left. The left image shows P6's moves without thermal feedback, using a strategy they described as, "just try all available paths – some of the paths, I visited them 3 or 4 times". Seven participants reported using this 'exploration' strategy in the control condition. Two reported that they did this systematically—e.g. always turning the same direction at a junction—while others admitted they were more random. Three users said they tried to memorise the maze, but P5 admitted, "I tried to remember the junctions but it was too difficult". Fig. 3 (middle) shows P4 navigating with thermal feedback and it can be compared to the global shortest path shown in blue (right). Thermal feedback reduced exploration of the maze, indicating when participants left the path and thereby reduced their exploration of blind alleys. However, some participants still turned in the wrong direction at some junctions and took some time to return to the correct path. P8 said "sometimes I couldn't distinguish the difference so I had to continue further to understand is it cold or warm". Participants had to learn to adapt to the latency of the feedback, by slowing their rate of movement and seeing how the temperature changed when they took a certain path. P10 expressed frustration that they "had to keep turning around" and expressed a preference for navigation cues that more actively guided them, rather than feedback after the path was left. P1 was more comfortable with the ambient feedback, saying "[you] can't always rely just on temperature – it's more of a complementary hint – I still need to trace the maze in my head".

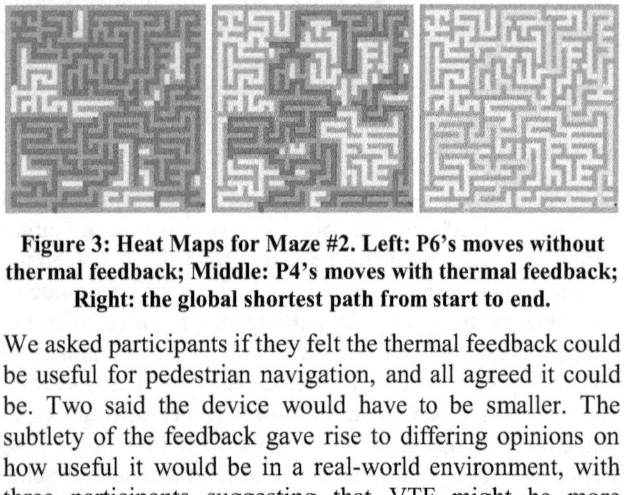

**Figure 3: Heat Maps for Maze #2. Left: P6's moves without thermal feedback; Middle: P4's moves with thermal feedback; Right: the global shortest path from start to end.**

We asked participants if they felt the thermal feedback could be useful for pedestrian navigation, and all agreed it could be. Two said the device would have to be smaller. The subtlety of the feedback gave rise to differing opinions on how useful it would be in a real-world environment, with three participants suggesting that VTF might be more effective and one stating that, "with this system you will be able to look around" [P3].

## DISCUSSION

Given the high latency of the feedback provided to participants, how were they able to use temperature information to improve navigation? First, the feedback was simple to understand, using a warm temperature to inform participants that they were on the right path and a decrease in temperature only when they left the shortest local path. Second, though it took six seconds for the TAD to change between the warmest and the coolest temperature, most participants detected the temperature change before the extremes were reached. Participants all found the feedback useful, but they needed to initially learn how to interpret the temperature changes.

The feedback is similar to a method previously used to successfully guide a complex real-time behaviour using VTF, specifically the bowing action of children learning the violin, who were 'buzzed' when their bow left the desired trajectory [7]. A key difference is that participants reported using both the thermal cues to navigate, rather than relying on the absence or presence of feedback. Future work can explore how the TAD could provide more complex thermal signals to indicate direction as well as the distance from the optimal path.

Our results are particularly relevant for the design of mobile interfaces for pedestrian navigation. Continuous thermal feedback could provide ambient cues for pedestrian exploration of urban areas. It could indicate both a route to follow and the presence of points of interest while tourists can focus on their environment, rather than their mobiles, and make serendipitous discoveries [12]. Given the slower speed that people walk compared to the rate at which participants could move around the maze, the high latency of the feedback may be less of an issue for real-world pedestrian navigation. Temperature could also potentially provide anticipatory navigation cues for drivers, as some drivers' seats and steering wheels already have heating elements built in, although it's not currently clear whether they would be suitable for communicating salient temperature cues. Future work will investigate whether our findings will transfer to noisy and challenging real world environments [16].

More generally, the interview data suggests the potential of using temperature to convey ambient information - a sensory channel that stays in the periphery of a users' attention and only shifts to the centre of attention when necessary. Whether thermal cues are less distracting than other feedback modalities needs verification, but our participants reported barely feeling them.

## CONCLUSION

Our controlled study demonstrates the effectiveness of continuous thermal feedback for guiding behaviour, without having to pause between signals to re-adapt the skin. In contrast to previous work that only demonstrated the potential of using temperature feedback for navigation, we provide the first experimental evaluation of simple thermal cues for guiding navigation in a 2D maze. Given the latency of the thermal feedback and lack of re-adaptation between signals, it was not clear whether it would be effective, but our results show thermal feedback enhances navigation performance in a 2D maze task, compared to when there is no feedback.

## REFERENCES


1. Jan Balata, Katerina Prazakova, Anna Kutikova, Miroslav Macik, and Zdenek Mikovec. Quido: arcade game with thermo-haptic feedback." In *IEEE 4rd international conference on cognitive infocommunications* (CogInfoCom 2013), 923-924.
2. A. D. Craig and M.C. Bushnell. 1994. The thermal grill illusion: unmasking the burn of cold pain. *Science* 256, 5169: 252-255.
3. Eve Hoggan, Andrew Crossan, Stephen A. Brewster, and Topi Kaaresoja. 2009. Audio or tactile feedback: which modality when?. In *Proceedings of the SIGCHI Conference on Human Factors in Computing Systems* (CHI '09). ACM, New York, NY, USA, 2253-2256.
4. Ken Iwasaki, Takashi Miyaki, and Jun Rekimoto. 2010. AffectPhone: a handset device to present user's emotional state with warmth/coolness. In *Proceedings of the 1st International Workshop on Bio-inspired Human-Machine Interfaces and Healthcare Applications*, 83-88.
5. Anatole Lécuyer, Pascal Mobuchon, Christine Mégard, Jérôme Perret, Claude Andriot, and Jean-Pierre Colinot. 2009. HOMERE: a multimodal system for visually impaired people to explore virtual environments. In *Virtual Reality Proceedings IEEE*, 251-258.
6. Michael W. Levine and Jeremy M. Shefner. 2000. *Fundamentals of Sensation and Perception* (3rd. ed.). Oxford University Press.
7. Janet Van Der Linden, Erwin Schoonderwaldt, Jon Bird and Rose Johnson (2011). Musicjacket—combining motion capture and vibrotactile feedback to teach violin bowing. *IEEE Transactions on Instrumentation and Measurement*, 60(1), 104-113.
8. Mutsuhiro Nakashige, Minoru Kobayashi, Yuriko Suzuki, Hidekazu Tamaki, and Suguru Higashino. 2009. "Hiya-Atsu" media: augmenting digital media with temperature. In *Extended Abstracts on Human Factors in Computing Systems* (CHI EA '09), 3181-3186.
9. Takuji Narumi, Akagawa Tomohiro, Young Ah Seong, and Michitaka Hirose. 2009. Characterizing the Space by thermal feedback through a wearable device. In *Virtual and Mixed Reality*, Randall Shumaker (ed.). Springer Berlin Heidelberg, 355-364.
10. Martin Pielot, Benjamin Poppinga, and Susanne Boll. 2010. PocketNavigator: vibro-tactile waypoint navigation for everyday mobile devices. *In Proceedings of the 12th international conference on Human computer interaction with mobile devices and services* (MobileHCI '10). ACM, New York, NY, USA, 423-426.
11. Jordan Tewell, Jon Bird, and George Buchanan. 2017. The Heat is On: A Temperature Display for Conveying Affective Feedback. *In Proceedings of the 35th Annual ACM Conference on Human Factors in Computing Systems* (CHI' 17).
12. Martin Traunmueller and Ava Fatah gen. Schieck. 2013. Introducing the space recommender system: how crowd-sourced voting data can enrich urban exploration in the digital era. *In Proceedings of the 6th International Conference on Communities and Technologies* (C&T '13). ACM, New York, NY, USA, 149-156.
13. Reto Wettach, Christian Behrens, Adam Danielsson, and Thomas Ness. 2007. A thermal information display for mobile applications. In *Proceedings of the 9th international conference on Human computer interaction with mobile devices and services* (MobileHCI '07), 182-185.
14. Graham Wilson, Stephen Brewster, Martin Halvey, and Stephen Hughes. 2013. Thermal Feedback Identification in a Mobile Environment. In *Revised Selected Papers of the 8th International Workshop on Haptic and Audio Interaction Design - Volume 7989* (HAID 2013), Ian Oakley and Stephen Brewster (Eds.), Vol. 7989. Springer-Verlag New York, Inc., New York, NY, USA, 10-19.
15. Graham Wilson, Gavin Davidson, and Stephen A. Brewster. 2015. In the heat of the moment: subjective interpretations of thermal feedback during interaction. In *Proceedings of the 33rd Annual ACM Conference on Human Factors in Computing Systems* (CHI' 15), 2063-2072.
16. Graham Wilson, Martin Halvey, Stephen A. Brewster, and Stephen A. Hughes. 2011. Some like it hot: thermal feedback for mobile devices. In *Proceedings of the SIGCHI Conference on Human Factors in Computing Systems* (CHI '11), 2555-2564.
17. Craig Alexander Wisneski. 1999. *The design of personal ambient displays*. Ph.D Dissertation. Massachusetts Institute of Technology, Cambridge, MA.

# CodePilot: Scaffolding End-to-End Collaborative Software Development for Novice Programmers

**Jeremy Warner**
UC Berkeley
Berkeley, CA, USA
jeremy.warner@berkeley.edu

**Philip J. Guo**
UC San Diego
La Jolla, CA, USA
pg@ucsd.edu

## ABSTRACT

Novice programmers often have trouble installing, configuring, and managing disparate tools (e.g., version control systems, testing infrastructure, bug trackers) that are required to become productive in a modern collaborative software development environment. To lower the barriers to entry into software development, we created a prototype IDE for novices called CodePilot, which is, to our knowledge, the first attempt to integrate coding, testing, bug reporting, and version control management into a real-time collaborative system. CodePilot enables multiple users to connect to a web-based programming session and work together on several major phases of software development. An eight-subject exploratory user study found that first-time users of CodePilot spontaneously used it to assume roles such as developer/tester and developer/assistant when creating a web application together in pairs. Users felt that CodePilot could aid in scaffolding for novices, situational awareness, and lowering barriers to impromptu collaboration.

## ACM Classification Keywords

H.5.m. Information Interfaces and Presentation (e.g. HCI): Miscellaneous

## Author Keywords

novice programmers; pair programming; collaborative IDE

## INTRODUCTION

Learning to code is now a popular activity around the world due in part to the abundance of software engineering job opportunities [12]. Enrollments within university computer science departments, coding bootcamps, and programming-based Massive Open Online Courses have been skyrocketing. The majority of programming courses (both in-person and online) focus on the actual mechanics of writing code. However, to become a productive professional software engineer, novices need to learn much more than how to write code properly. They need to also get accustomed to working within a modern collaborative software development environment – coordinating with their teammates using tools such as version control systems, testing infrastructure, and bug/issue trackers [1, 3, 10]. Although in theory anyone can install, configure, and manage a plethora of free open-source tools for all of these purposes, in practice the logistical overhead of learning to manage these tools can be extremely daunting to novices who are already expending large amounts of effort learning the mechanics of programming itself [2]. To lower the barriers to entry for novices to get acquainted with collaborative software development, we created a prototype IDE called *CodePilot*.

CodePilot enables multiple programmers to coordinate in real time throughout several major phases of modern software development – writing, running, and testing code, generating bug reports, managing the bug/issue tracker, and managing the version control system – with no required external software setup or configuration. It serves as convenient "training wheels" for novices to quickly get practice with techniques such as pair programming [13, 14] and test-driven development [7], which have been shown to improve productivity, software quality, and knowledge sharing. For instance, when a novice is paired up with an expert (e.g., a tutor or teaching assistant in a course), they can learn by serving as an apprentice and watching the expert work alongside them within CodePilot.

An eight-subject exploratory study found that novice students were able to use CodePilot to spontaneously assume roles such as developer/tester and developer/assistant when creating a web application together in pairs. Users felt that CodePilot could aid in scaffolding for novices, situational awareness, and lowering barriers to impromptu collaboration.

This paper contributes a novice-oriented IDE that scaffolds collaborative development activities such as pair programming, testing, bug reporting, and version control management.

## RELATED WORK

To our knowledge, CodePilot is the first attempt to integrate real-time collaborative coding, testing, bug reporting, and version control management into a unified system. Prior real-time collaboration tools for software development are focused only on writing code itself rather than on the end-to-end development process. These are available as plug-ins for existing IDEs (e.g., CollabVS for Visual Studio [9] and ATCoPE for Eclipse [5]) and in web-based Google Docs-like collaborative editors such as Cloud9 (`https://c9.io/`), MadEye (`https://madeye.io/`), and Collabode [6]. Another class of real-time software collaboration tools (e.g,. FASTDash [1], Saros [11], Syde [8]) provides situational awareness by informing developers of what development tasks, files, and code


*CHI 2017*, May 06–11, 2017, Denver, CO, USA

ACM 978-1-4503-4655-9/17/05...$15.00
DOI: http://dx.doi.org/10.1145/3025453.3025876

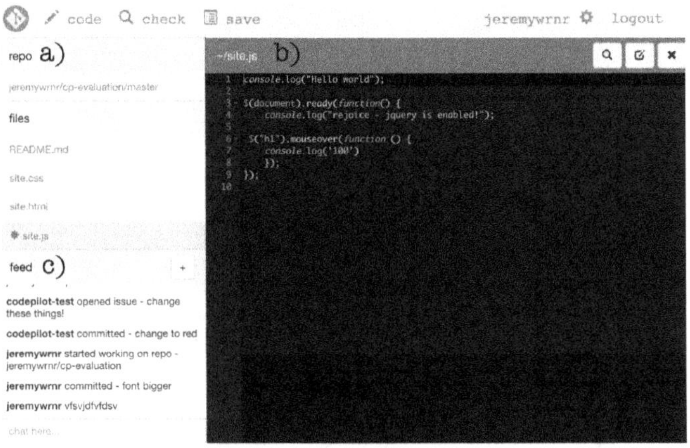


Figure 1. CodePilot is a web-based IDE designed for novices. Multiple users can connect to a shared session via a URL. a) The file selector enables each user to add, delete, and edit files. b) The code editor pane is a multi-user text editor similar to Google Docs. c) The activity feed shows all users' activities and enables inline text chat.

Figure 2. When the user clicks the "test" icon in Figure 1b, the code editor pane is replaced with a testing pane. This testing pane renders the user's current HTML/CSS/JavaScript code in the browser, along with a JavaScript console (top) and an editable task queue linked to GitHub's issue tracker for the project (bottom). Clicking the "report issue" button at the upper right pops up the bug reporting tool shown in Figure 3.

edits their partners are working on in real time. These tools directly inspired CodePilot's activity feed feature (Figure 1c).

## FORMATIVE OBSERVATIONS AND DESIGN GOAL

We were motivated to create CodePilot after spending a semester observing students at our university's weekly student hacking (i.e., hobby coding) group meetings. One recurring barrier we noted from observations and interviews with novice attendees was the intimidating logistical overhead of setting up disparate development tools such as testing infrastructure, bug/issue trackers, and version control repositories, especially when doing so involved intricate knowledge of command-line and configuration file tweaking. As a result of this setup overhead, novices were often reluctant to "dive in" to work on more substantive projects that involved collaboration, testing, and version control; instead, they often lingered in the background and watched passively while the more experienced students worked on their projects during group meetings.

Based on these observations, we wanted to create an IDE to get these novices started with collaborative software development without the discouraging overhead of external tool setup. Production-grade web IDEs such as Cloud9 offer intricate configuration options and debugging mechanisms, but setting these up can also serve as a deterrent for novice programmers. Thus, our main design goal for CodePilot was to embed scaffolding for these tools into a simple unified interface, sacrificing advanced power-user features for a streamlined novice-friendly workflow. Even though we were directly motivated by in-person use cases we observed in the university computer lab, we designed CodePilot to work equally well in remote online settings such as Massive Open Online Courses.

## CODEPILOT SYSTEM DESIGN AND USAGE SCENARIO

CodePilot is a web-based IDE (integrated development environment) where multiple users can connect to a collaborative software development session via a single URL. Project repositories can be imported from `GitHub`, a popular Git repository hosting platform. Once imported, users collaborate on the project in real time, and can then commit and push any of their changes back to GitHub. CodePilot is implemented using MeteorJS, employs Firebase/Firepad for document synchronization, the Ace web editor, and GitHub's Developer API. It is open-sourced under the MIT License at `https://github.com/jeremywrnr/codepilot`. The authors also host a running instance of CodePilot at `http://codepilot.xyz`.

We illustrate the features and design rationale of CodePilot using an example usage scenario. Alice and Bob are two students working together to create a HTML/CSS/JavaScript web application. Alice first logs into CodePilot with her GitHub account and creates empty HTML, CSS, and JavaScript files for her new project. She then emails Bob the unique URL of her CodePilot session. When Bob visits that session URL, both see the IDE interface shown in Figure 1.

### Writing Code

Alice and Bob can each write code in any project file just like in a regular IDE (Figure 1b). If they are editing the same file concurrently, their changes are synchronized in real-time like in Google Docs, using Firepad to synchronize edits. They gain situational awareness [1, 8, 11] and can coordinate via the *activity feed* (Figure 1c), which shows a real-time stream of events (e.g., "Alice created issue X", "Bob committed changes to GitHub") and allows inline text chat. Alice and Bob can now engage in pair programming [13, 14] where both work on the same file at once or in side-by-side programming [4] where each works on their own file while coordinating via inline chat. The Ace web-based text editor provides language-specific syntax highlighting and code auto-completion. CodePilot supports an arbitrary number of concurrent collaborating users subject to network and CPU limitations.

**Figure 3. When the user clicks the "report issue" button in the testing pane, a pop-up appears that allows the user to highlight parts of the rendered webpage for emphasis and to black out private data prior to taking a screenshot. Then the user can write a textual bug report and CodePilot submits it to GitHub's issue tracker along with that screenshot and a snapshot of the current code, to facilitate reproducibility.**

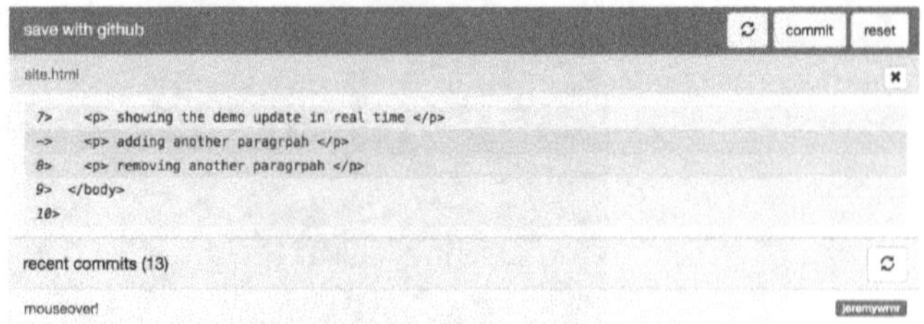


**Figure 4. Before performing a commit, users are shown a visual diffing interface inside CodePilot, which provides affordances similar to `git status` and `git reset` by summarizing changes since the last commit and providing a mechanism to reset the file's content to its last committed version.**

### Running, Testing, and Debugging Code

Let's say Alice is the primary software developer on their project, and Bob is serving as her tester. As Alice writes new code, Bob can click the "test" button in Figure 1b at any time to save a snapshot of their code and enter a testing pane shown in Figure 2, which overlays over the editor pane in Figure 1b.

CodePilot's testing pane renders the snapshot of the HTML/CSS/JavaScript code that Bob just saved and includes an inline JavaScript console to support `console.log` print debugging. Using this pane, Bob can check that the HTML/CSS is rendering as expected and that dynamic JavaScript events are behaving appropriately. Note that Alice's new code edits will *not* be incorporated into the testing pane until Bob clicks the "reload" button to explicitly pull in new changes. This design enables Bob to test a known code snapshot without risking it invisibly changing without his knowledge.

For our current prototype, we created and evaluated a testing pane for HTML/CSS/JS web applications, but one could imagine creating other testing panes for different kinds of apps or platforms. With additional engineering effort, it is also feasible to hook CodePilot into external testing services, such as a class grading platform like Gradescope (`https://gradescope.com/`) or a continuous integration testing service like TravisCI (`https://travis-ci.org/`).

Bob can chat with Alice in the activity feed to give feedback, provide documentation links, and add tasks such as feature requests to an asynchronous queue for Alice to address later. This queue is synced with GitHub's issue tracking system so that teammates can see tasks on the GitHub website, even when not logged into CodePilot. Existing GitHub issues are also automatically imported into CodePilot, so all issues can be opened or closed from both platforms.

### Generating Bug Reports

If Bob finds a bug when he is testing, he can click the "report issue" button in the testing pane, which pops up the bug reporter (Figure 3). Using this tool, Bob can highlight areas on the webpage for emphasis and black out private information that he does not wish to share as a screenshot in his bug report. In Figure 3, Bob highlights the cat image for emphasis and then writes a full textual report describing the bug he found.

When Bob submits his bug report, CodePilot creates a new GitHub issue (using its issue tracker) containing his report text, screenshot with highlights/blackouts, and a snapshot of the underlying code that Bob was testing. This way, anyone can reproduce this bug by checking out that code snapshot. Alice now gets notified of Bob's new bug report in her activity feed. At her convenience, she can switch over to her own testing pane to see the contents of Bob's report and check out his snapshot to reproduce and investigate the bug herself.

The main design consideration in the bug reporter was to collect as much relevant information inline as possible so that a tester such as Bob can quickly report bugs without context switching. Additionally, this graphical selection method of debugging was chosen because it is intuitive for web interface designs, which are inherently visual and therefore often will have bugs that can be recognized visually.

### Managing the Bug/Issue Tracker

CodePilot integrates tightly with GitHub, leveraging it as both a bug/issue tracker and a Git-based version control system. Alice and Bob can use the testing pane (Figure 2) to directly add, edit, and resolve issues on GitHub, and they can use the version control pane (Figure 4) to check out, commit, visually diff, and revert code versions in Git.

GitHub integration makes it possible for Alice and Bob to write code, test code, report bugs, and commit changes to version control entirely within CodePilot while coordinating via the activity feed. Without this feature, they would need to use external apps such as the Git command-line client or the GitHub website to manage the bug/issue tracker and version control system. Having all of these workflow phases unified into one IDE also makes it easy for other teammates to join this project by visiting a URL, as long as they have a GitHub account and the proper access permissions.

### Managing the Version Control System

CodePilot's fully-synchronous nature prompted some design compromises and us choosing sensible defaults with regards to how to best interface with GitHub's API for asynchronous-style collaboration. Each commit serves as a complete snapshot, so if code is checked out at a specific commit with CodePilot, users can append to the existent history on GitHub, but cannot rewrite it. CodePilot loads all the code of the chosen commit, which by default is the HEAD of the active branch. Then, when committing back to GitHub, the new commit is simply stacked on top of the HEAD of the active branch.

One immediately apparent problem occurs when trying to collaborate with users outside of CodePilot, as the repository histories diverge. In an educational setting to train novices, we recommend for everyone to work within CodePilot. But to ameliorate this problem when it does come up, CodePilot allows for the current state and history to be manually pulled in from GitHub, but in the process overwrites any uncommitted changes with the newest commit. It also separates versions of code by branch, so users working on different branches in CodePilot do not interfere with each other's work. New branches can be created from those inside CodePilot, allowing for multiple tracks of development inside a single project.

When creating a new commit, there can be only a single author; to attribute work done by others, one workaround is for the commit author to explicitly include who they worked with in the commit message. Before committing, users are shown a visual summary of changes (Figure 4) and given the chance to undo any changes they do not want to save. There is no option to commit a subset of files though, as we opted to keep the simpler model of saving the entire project as a snapshot rather than confusing users with partially-committed directories.

CodePilot also features the ability to fork any GitHub repository accessible to the current user. For example, with a team assignment skeleton repository in a class, students can easily fork it and immediately begin working together, avoiding the initial hassle of environment setup while gaining the additional benefits of version control and real-time collaboration.

Finally, there is no notion of explicitly 'git-pushing' one's code back to GitHub when working within CodePilot. Instead, GitHub serves as a simple reference log of project snapshots, so whenever a commit is made, it automatically gets added to the HEAD of the current active branch. This abstracts away a fair deal of the networking complexity and distributed system management that are often error-prone for novice Git users.

## EXPLORATORY STUDY OF NOVICE PAIR PROGRAMMING

To gauge novice perceptions of CodePilot, we ran an exploratory user study where four pairs of students (all first-time users) used it to collaboratively build a simple web application.

We recruited 8 computer science students from our university with low to moderate levels of web programming experience (6 male, 2 female). We paired them up randomly and gave each

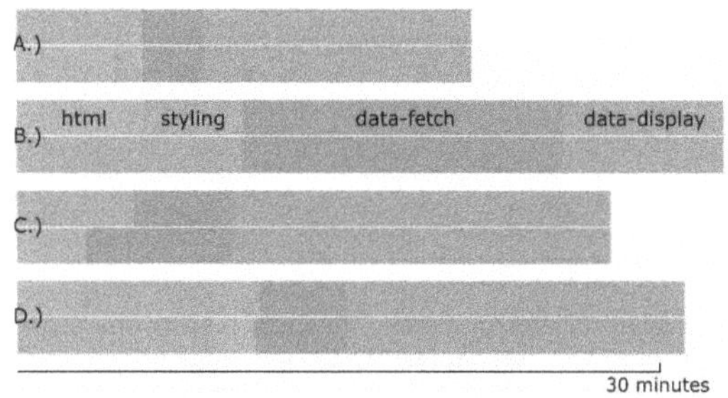


**Figure 5. The amount of time that each pair of programmers spent on each component of the web programming task using CodePilot. Each bar is a pair, split into two halves, one for each programmer in the pair.**

pair 30 minutes to build a simple weather display app with four components – `html`: create a template for the weather display, `styling`: style it according to CSS specifications, `data-fetch`: use JavaScript to fetch JSON data from an online weather data source, `data-display`: dynamically parse, format, and display the fetched data on the webpage. We set up CodePilot's code editor pane with three skeleton files (HTML, CSS, JS) that participants had to fill in, and we began each session with a 10-minute tutorial on CodePilot's features.

Using pilot tests (CodePilot pilots!) we refined this task to both resemble a realistic web app and one that can be implemented in 30 minutes. We recorded participants' monitors and conducted 15-minute semi-structured follow-up interviews to assess their perceptions of CodePilot and how it compared to software development tools they have used in the past.

We let each pair work however they wanted within CodePilot so that we could observe what kinds of interactions emerge naturally. As expected, pairs varied in how much they worked collaboratively and also how much time they took to complete the task. No pair quit the study before completion.

Figure 5 shows how each pair split their time. In general, participants worked separately on the simpler `html` and `styling` components and then joined together to complete the more challenging `data-fetch` and `data-display` parts. Since each pair was co-located to make it easier for the research team to observe them working together (and to replicate the in-person student hacking club experience that motivated us to develop CodePilot), they always coordinated verbally. However, in follow-up interviews, several mentioned that they could have easily used text chat if necessary.

Figure 6 shows a detailed timeline of activities that each pair engaged in, with five types of events – *view*: looking at a source code file (HTML, CSS, or JavaScript) in the code editor, *edit*: actively editing a file in the editor, *test*: testing the app in the testing pane, *docs*: reading documentation webpages in the browser, *git*: managing version control pane. We told each pair to make at least one Git commit when they finished, but some made additional commits to save intermediate progress.

Analyzing temporally co-occurring events in Figure 6 reveals that participants were able to use CodePilot to spontaneously assume well-known collaborative software development roles without any prompting by the research team. The most common role was ***traditional pair programming*** where both par-

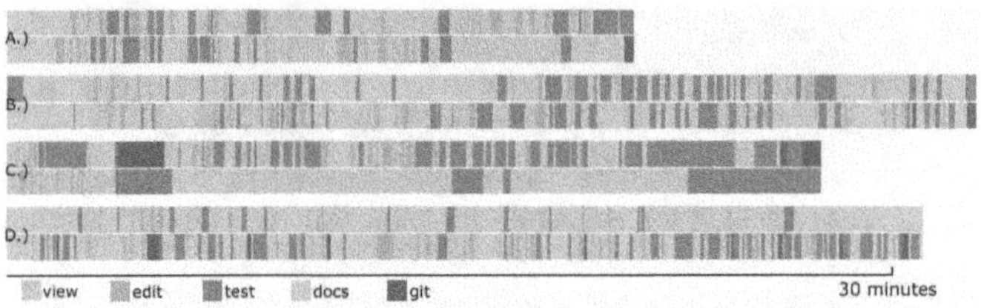


**Figure 6. The amount of time that each pair spent on activities such as viewing code, editing code, testing, reading documentation, and managing the Git version control system. Each horizontal bar represents a pair and is split into two halves, one for each programmer in the pair.**

ticipants were viewing and editing the same file at the same time in the code editor pane. This occurred during 23% of the total time, aggregating over all 4 sessions. The second most common role was ***developer/tester*** [7] where one person was in the code editor while their partner was in the testing pane, which occurred during 21% of the time. The third most common role was ***developer/assistant*** where one person would be coding while the other would be looking up documentation on the web to help out their partner, which occurred during 19% of the time. Other roles included both partners looking up documentation (9%) and both in the testing pane (7%).

Pair C was unique since the second partner (bottom half of Pair C in Figures 5 and 6) had significantly less programming experience. Thus, after completing the HTML, they served as a ***dedicated assistant*** the entire rest of the session and made no more code edits (no pink lines). They supported their partner's coding by testing, looking up documentation, and acting as a second pair of eyes on the code. Thus, CodePilot enabled collaboration even between people of widely varying skills.

## DISCUSSION

Our exploratory study showed that novices can in fact use CodePilot to successfully work together in common collaborative roles on a simple yet realistic web programming project, unencumbered by many of the costs of starting up a collaborative software development session. We found three main themes from analyzing the qualitative data of user perceptions of CodePilot in post-study interviews:

***Scaffolding for novices***: Participants reported that as relative newcomers to programming, they found it hard to learn the nuances of Git at the same time as learning core programming concepts, which made them often neglect version control entirely in their own projects. They pointed out how CodePilot's integrated visual Git interface could be a useful instructional scaffold to gently introduce novices to version control concepts before seeing full-fledged command-line tools. They also said that experts would still prefer the flexibility of command-line tools, but that CodePilot can quickly get novices onboarded and working alongside their more experienced peers.

***Situational awareness***: Participants preferred using CodePilot over working side-by-side on separate computers using regular IDEs due to the extra situational awareness provided by the activity feed and concurrent editing in the CodePilot editor. Even without talking to one another, they could see what their partner was doing at each moment so that they did not work on something redundant or contradictory. In one instance, both partners of Pair B attempted to use JavaScript to parse the fetched data using different algorithms, but they saw the contradiction right away in the shared editor and talked to each other about how to proceed. Participants also appreciated not having to deal with unexpected Git merge conflicts that would have arisen if they had collaborated asynchronously.

***Lower the barriers to impromptu collaboration***: Even though some participants still preferred the power-user features of command-line tools, they appreciated how easy it was to jump into a new CodePilot session and to send a URL for their teammates to join as well. They mentioned how this tool could encourage more impromptu collaboration amongst developers, especially for prototyping, since it was so simple to get started using it. Being university students, our participants mainly expressed excitement about using CodePilot for class projects, hobby projects, and hackathons, but they also felt that it could be useful in their future jobs in the technology industry. Specifically, they mentioned that CodePilot could encourage coworkers to work together more due to lower barriers to collaboration, and it may also benefit system administrators and I.T. support personnel at software development organizations. Instead of wrangling employees to constantly install, upgrade, and manage multiple versions of disparate tools, I.T. staff can maintain a single up-to-date CodePilot web application that all developers use. Having a unified end-to-end environment also makes it easier for system administrators to debug configuration issues that stifle developers (e.g., "Why is my version control system acting so slow today?").

Although these initial results are encouraging for eliciting first impressions from novices and generating future design ideas, further studies are needed to more rigorously quantify CodePilot's effects on collaboration, productivity, and learning.

## CONCLUSION AND FUTURE DIRECTIONS

As more people learn to code both in person and online, it is important to foster good collaborative software development habits. CodePilot takes one step toward this goal by unifying the collaborative development workflow into a single IDE and thus lowering the barrier to entry for novices. More broadly, as remote and distributed software development grow more prevalent in the coming years, it becomes ever more important to build in collaboration as a core design consideration in the next generation of IDEs. Our CodePilot prototype points toward a future where anyone can quickly jump into a software project and start making meaningful contributions.

In the future, we can extend CodePilot to cover additional phases of software development such as requirements gathering, project planning, design, and user testing. We also hope to support parallel prototyping and fork/branch-based models of development so that collaborators can easily explore alternatives without needing to work on only one version of the code. We can also investigate how to replay the recorded traces of collaborative development sessions to train novices offline. Even more broadly, CodePilot can serve as a research platform: If it were instrumented with fine-grained opt-in logging and deployed at scale, then software engineering researchers could mine that data and conduct controlled experiments to gain insights about how developers collaborate and learn.

## ACKNOWLEDGMENTS

This work was supported in part by the National Science Foundation under grant NSF CRII IIS-1463864, by the Donald M. Barnard Scholarship, and by the University of Rochester GEAR Scholarship and University Research Award. Also, thanks to Dan Hassin for his valuable insights.

## REFERENCES

1. Jacob T. Biehl, Mary Czerwinski, Greg Smith, and George G. Robertson. 2007. FASTDash: A Visual Dashboard for Fostering Awareness in Software Teams. In *Proceedings of the SIGCHI Conference on Human Factors in Computing Systems (CHI '07)*. ACM, New York, NY, USA, 1313–1322. DOI: http://dx.doi.org/10.1145/1240624.1240823
2. Yan Chen, Steve Oney, and Walter S. Lasecki. 2016. Towards Providing On-Demand Expert Support for Software Developers. In *Proceedings of the 2016 CHI Conference on Human Factors in Computing Systems (CHI '16)*. ACM, New York, NY, USA, 3192–3203. DOI: http://dx.doi.org/10.1145/2858036.2858512
3. Laura Dabbish, Colleen Stuart, Jason Tsay, and Jim Herbsleb. 2012. Social Coding in GitHub: Transparency and Collaboration in an Open Software Repository. In *Proceedings of the ACM 2012 Conference on Computer Supported Cooperative Work (CSCW '12)*. ACM, New York, NY, USA, 1277–1286. DOI: http://dx.doi.org/10.1145/2145204.2145396
4. Prasun Dewan, Puneet Agarwal, Gautam Shroff, and Rajesh Hegde. 2009. Distributed Side-by-side Programming. In *Proceedings of the 2009 ICSE Workshop on Cooperative and Human Aspects on Software Engineering (CHASE '09)*. IEEE Computer Society, Washington, DC, USA, 48–55. DOI: http://dx.doi.org/10.1109/CHASE.2009.5071410
5. Hongfei Fan, Chengzheng Sun, and Haifeng Shen. 2012. ATCoPE: Any-time Collaborative Programming Environment for Seamless Integration of Real-time and Non-real-time Teamwork in Software Development. In *Proceedings of the 17th ACM International Conference on Supporting Group Work (GROUP '12)*. ACM, New York, NY, USA, 107–116. DOI: http://dx.doi.org/10.1145/2389176.2389194
6. Max Goldman, Greg Little, and Robert C. Miller. 2011. Real-time Collaborative Coding in a Web IDE. In *Proceedings of the 24th Annual ACM Symposium on User Interface Software and Technology (UIST '11)*. ACM, New York, NY, USA, 155–164. DOI: http://dx.doi.org/10.1145/2047196.2047215
7. Max Goldman and Robert C. Miller. 2010. Test-driven Roles for Pair Programming. In *Proceedings of the 2010 ICSE Workshop on Cooperative and Human Aspects of Software Engineering (CHASE '10)*. ACM, New York, NY, USA, 13–20. DOI: http://dx.doi.org/10.1145/1833310.1833313
8. Lile Hattori and Michele Lanza. 2010. Syde: A Tool for Collaborative Software Development. In *Proceedings of the 32Nd ACM/IEEE International Conference on Software Engineering - Volume 2 (ICSE '10)*. ACM, New York, NY, USA, 235–238. DOI: http://dx.doi.org/10.1145/1810295.1810339
9. R. Hegde and P. Dewan. 2008. Connecting Programming Environments to Support Ad-Hoc Collaboration. In *Proceedings of the 2008 23rd IEEE/ACM International Conference on Automated Software Engineering (ASE '08)*. IEEE Computer Society, Washington, DC, USA, 178–187. DOI: http://dx.doi.org/10.1109/ASE.2008.28
10. James D. Herbsleb. 2007. Global Software Engineering: The Future of Socio-technical Coordination. In *2007 Future of Software Engineering (FOSE '07)*. IEEE Computer Society, Washington, DC, USA, 188–198. DOI: http://dx.doi.org/10.1109/FOSE.2007.11
11. Stephan Salinger, Christopher Oezbek, Karl Beecher, and Julia Schenk. 2010. Saros: An Eclipse Plug-in for Distributed Party Programming. In *Proceedings of the 2010 ICSE Workshop on Cooperative and Human Aspects of Software Engineering (CHASE '10)*. ACM, New York, NY, USA, 48–55. DOI: http://dx.doi.org/10.1145/1833310.1833319
12. Patrick Thibodeau. 2013. India to overtake U.S. on number of developers by 2017. http://www.computerworld.com/article/2483690/it-careers/india-to-overtake-u-s--on-number-of-developers-by-2017.html. (2013). Accessed: 2016-09-13.
13. Laurie Williams, Robert R. Kessler, Ward Cunningham, and Ron Jeffries. 2000. Strengthening the Case for Pair Programming. *IEEE Software* 17, 4 (July 2000), 19–25. DOI: http://dx.doi.org/10.1109/52.854064
14. Laurie Williams, Charlie McDowell, Nachiappan Nagappan, Julian Fernald, and Linda Werner. 2003. Building Pair Programming Knowledge Through a Family of Experiments. In *Proceedings of the 2003 International Symposium on Empirical Software Engineering (ISESE '03)*. IEEE Computer Society, Washington, DC, USA, 143–. http://dl.acm.org/citation.cfm?id=942801.943642

# Crowdsourcing GO: Effect of Worker Situation on Mobile Crowdsourcing Performance

**Kazushi Ikeda**
KDDI Research, Inc.
Fujimino, Japan
kz-ikeda@kddi-research.jp

**Keiichiro Hoashi**
KDDI Research, Inc.
Fujimino, Japan
hoashi@kddi-research.jp

### ABSTRACT
The increasing popularity of mobile crowdsourcing platforms has enabled crowd workers to accept jobs wherever/whenever they are, and also provides opportunity for task requesters to order time/location specific tasks to workers. Since workers on mobile platforms are working on the go, the situation of the workers is expected to influence their performance. However, the effects of mobile worker situations to task performance is an uninvestigated area. In this paper, our research question is, "*do worker situations affect task completion, price and quality on mobile crowdsourcing platforms?*" We draw on economics and psychology research to examine whether worker situations such as busyness, fatigue and presence of companions affect their performance. Our three-week between-subjects field experiment revealed that worker busyness caused 30.1% relative decrease of task completion rate. Mean accepted task price increased by 7.6% when workers are with companions. Worker fatigue caused 37.4% relative decrease of task quality.

### Author Keywords
Crowdsourcing; mobile crowdsourcing; situational effect; worker performance.

### ACM Classification Keywords
H.5.3 Information interfaces and presentation (e.g., HCI): Group and Organization Interfaces.

### INTRODUCTION
Mobile Crowdsourcing have gained popularity, where workers use their mobile phones to work on location and time specified tasks. Increasing number of research focus on mobile crowdsourcing such as restaurant recommendations for specific locations [4], and news article generation by requesting photos and videos from on-site workers [52]. Some commercial service platforms have emerged including Gigwalk [2] and Field Agent [1] that mainly deal with mobile crowdsourcing tasks. Push notification is a key function to actively ask workers for contribution who meet the task conditions such as location and time. Unlike conventional crowdsourcing platforms, where workers do tasks at their convenient time, workers on mobile crowdsourcing platforms may receive task requests via push notifications in situations when they are not suitable for doing tasks. However, the effect of worker situation on mobile crowdsourcing performance has not been investigated well.

In this paper, we set a research question: "*does worker situation affect task completion rate, accepted task price and task quality on mobile crowdsourcing platforms?*" Drawing behavioral economic research on crowdsourcing has successfully highlighted an effective incentive method from potential alternatives [29]. By following the idea, we draw on the economics and psychological literatures to derive critical worker situations that are expected to affect mobile crowdsourcing performance. First, the idea of *opportunity cost*, i.e., a concept where someone obtains something by giving up others [47], is referred to extract the busyness factor. When a worker feels busy, he has something more worth of doing than the crowdsourcing task, which may result in lower task completion rate or require higher price to complete the same task. Second, from biological psychology, we hypothesize the effect of mental fatigue. Namely, we expect that mental fatigue of workers decreases their motivation and affects their work quality [10]. Third, we focus on the existence of companions. In the presence of companions, e.g., family members, friends, etc., touching mobile phone or even putting it on the desk can increase mental barriers for task completion [42]. In other words, crowd workers may feel rude to do task in the presence of companions.

This study aims to examine whether these worker situations, i.e., degree of busyness, degree of fatigue, and presence of companions, affect worker performance on mobile crowdsourcing platforms. Verifying the validness of these three hypotheses for mobile crowdsourcing is not a trivial issue, since the existing studies in the economic and psychology domain do not assume the mobile environment. For example, mental fatigue has been reported to decrease worker performance in continuous tasks, but its applicability to a one-time task on mobile crowdsourcing must be investigated thoroughly. We conduct between-subjects field


*CHI 2017*, May 6–11, 2017, Denver, CO, USA.

ACM ISBN 978-1-4503-4655-9/17/05...$15.00.
DOI: http://dx.doi.org/10.1145/3025453.3025917

experiment with time-limited mobile crowdsourcing tasks. The task includes questionnaires that collect worker situation during their task completion. Content of tasks are unchanged throughout the experimental period. Task price is changed per task request, and controlled so that it would be uniformly distributed with a fixed median price. Workers tend to decline cheaper price tasks. If workers tend to decline more frequently in a specific situation, the mean task price for that situation increases. In order to evaluate task quality for each situation, we used gold standard, or known answer task.

Results of the experiment indicate that task completion rate was most affected by the degree of busyness. Compared to low busyness worker, high busyness worker showed 30.1 % relative decrease in task completion rate ($p < .001$). Mean accepted task price was most affected by the presence of companions. Workers with companions had a higher mean accepted task price by 7.6% ($p < .001$) compared to workers without companions. Task quality was most affected by the degree of fatigue. Compared to lowly fatigued workers, workers with high fatigue showed 37.4% relative decrease in task quality, measured by the accuracy (F-measure) of completed tasks ($p < .05$). Subjective opinions collected after the experiment also supported our hypotheses.

The rest of the paper is organized as follows. We first review related work on crowdsourcing performance, mobile crowdsourcing and notification to mobile devices. Second, we develop our research question and hypotheses by drawing theories in economics and psychology. We then introduce the experimental design of our field experiment and present quantitative and qualitative results. Finally, we describe limitations and future work.

## RELATED WORK

### Crowdsourcing Performance

Studies for improving performance on crowdsourcing platforms such as incentives and worker motivation have attracted much attention. Most of these studies focus on task completion, task price and task quality. Task completion and task price have strong relations with each other. Regardless of their motivations, microtask crowd workers seek to earn money [5]. They seek out tasks that maximize their expected earnings [26]. The simplest approach to increase task completion is to pay more: this was one of the first widely-cited results in crowdsourcing research [40]. Some existing studies realize higher task completion without task price increase. Participants increase their effort when the system reminds them of the uniqueness of their contribution [8]. Stimulating worker curiosity keeps longer participation on micro task crowdsourcing [36]. Introducing a method for shortening task completion time is effective to reduce task price. A framework for managing paid experts on the crowdsourcing platform has successfully reduced both the task completion time and the task price in relatively large projects, such as animation movie creation and development of software [46]. In order to minimize the cost of micro tasks, a new interface has been proposed to drastically accelerate labeling tasks by allowing workers to make errors [35].

Task quality is also an important measure to evaluate crowdsourcing platform performance. Accepting the task only when workers agree with each other improves the accuracy of the task [49]. Offerings to train workers and give feedback can improve quality [54, 17]. Including known answers as gold standard has also improved individual worker precision, and aggregated task accuracy [37]. Simply offering higher payment does not increase quality [40]. The order of consequence tasks affects task accuracy [12].

### Mobile Crowdsourcing and Notification

Mobile crowdsourcing technologies are increasingly gaining attention [39, 15]. Various types of applications and tasks have been developed on mobile crowdsourcing platforms. Simple transcription task of hand written text is provided by utilizing mobile phones as portable interfaces [23]. Recent advances in mobile technologies have also allowed for more intricate and creative tasks. For instance, location-based distribution of crowdsourcing tasks has allowed workers to perform highly context specific tasks. Some examples of this include giving location-aware recommendations for restaurants [4], and authoring news articles by requesting photographs or videos of certain events from workers [52]. An investigations of situated crowdsourcing has been reported, where kiosk devices located on a university campus are used to reveal the relationships among task completion, location, time and incentives [27]. Some of these applications require to push tasks to workers on specific location and time. However, worker situation has not been investigated well on mobile crowdsourcing platforms.

In HCI research, various notification methods for mobile devices have been proposed, which consider user situation estimated from sensed information on their mobile devices. Several researchers have investigated the effect of interruption caused by notification under various situations [3, 7, 34]. Relevance of information to the workers' situation is a key factor to avoid notification from being noisy [16]. Even though many users are frustrated with notifications, they prefer to keep using notification systems for information delivery, instead of checking for new information manually [30]. Wearable devices have also been used to notify information in the timing of activity switch [25]. Psychological approaches help to understand human behavior towards notifications. Psycho-physiological states of users under interruptive notifications have been investigated [56]. The influence of task interruption on individual decision making has been investigated to quantitatively evaluate the effects of overloaded notifications [50].

## SITUATIONAL EFFECT ON WORK PERFORMANCE

### Research Question

Existing studies on notifications mainly focus on increasing response rate, and targeting notifications of new information or advertisements on mobile devices. However, these techniques are not suitable for improving the performance of mobile crowdsourcing platform, such as task completion rate, task price and task quality. Existing work has shown that physical location of workers affects their decision of accepting task prices on mobile crowdsourcing [43]. Furthermore, qualitative studies based on worker interview for the motivation on the mobile crowdsourcing have also indicated that situational factors can affect worker motivation [51, 14]. Despite such efforts, effects of workers' situations on the task has not been quantitatively investigated well. This observation motivates our research question:

RQ: *Does worker situation affect task completion rate, accepted task price and task quality on mobile crowdsourcing platforms?*

### Hypothesis

In order to develop reasonable hypotheses of worker situations that affect mobile crowdsourcing performance, we draw on economics and psychology literature. There is a rich history of research in economics and psychology that can help us to understand how human internal factors such as economic sense and mental status affect worker performance. This section presents a review of studies in economics and psychology, in order to establish the hypotheses of this research.

In economic theory, the opportunity cost of a resource is referred as the value of the next-highest-valued alternative use of that resource. Generally, the opportunity cost of time is measured by wages or income [38, 20]. The value of time for individuals without income, such as house workers, has been estimated by indirect approaches [22, 55]. Variety of human activities such as shopping [41] and leisure [32] have been explained by opportunity cost, and have been priced based on alternatives. So far, few studies have discussed the applicability of opportunity cost to the situation of workers in crowdsourcing. When a worker is busy, s/he is required to give up many alternatives to complete a mobile crowdsourcing task. We assume the opportunity cost of a task is relatively higher under busyness. Therefore, our first hypothesis is,

*H1: Task completion rate on mobile crowdsourcing platforms decreases, and the accepted task price increases when workers are feeling busy.*

Mental fatigue is a very common phenomenon that applies major consequences for everyday task performance. Fatigued people often experience difficulties in concentration and appear to be more easily distractible [11]. Mental fatigue also affects worker motivation and productivity [10]. Existing studies mainly focus on continuous tasks such as driving a car. For example, driving errors such as large speed variations and even running off the road have observed to be increasingly frequent in correlation to driver's fatigue [13]. Mental fatigue also affects more simple tasks such as recognizing letters on the monitor, where continuous work has increased error rate [18]. Based on such existing studies, we assume that fatigue caused by external situations may affect worker performance on mobile crowdsourcing tasks, which leads to our second hypothesis:

*H2: Task quality on mobile crowdsourcing platform decreases when workers feel fatigue.*

The presence of mobile devices can increase mental barriers for face-to-face communication. In a field experiment, 100 couples discuss a randomly assigned topic together. Some participants held their mobile device in their hand or placed it on the table. The conversations were self-rated by the participants. Conversations without mobile devices were rated as significantly superior compared with those in the presence of a mobile device [42]. Some workers may feel rude to work on their mobile devices while talking or being with companions. In addition, multi-tasking sometimes decreases productivity by causing more errors and slowing task completion. In a university class, the professor asked students to use laptops during the lecture, which resulted in lack of students' concentration and significant decrease in the examination score [24]. More simply, watching television while remembering sets of digits or while doing homework resulted in poorer performance than when focusing on a single task [6, 45]. Based on these literature, we derive our third hypothesis as follows. Note that the previous literature do not directly evaluate the effect of the presence of companions on task performance.

*H3: Task completion rate on mobile crowdsourcing platforms decreases, task price increases, and task quality decreases when workers are with companions.*

## EXPERIMENTAL DESIGN

To investigate whether the worker situations of busyness, fatigue and the presence of companions affect worker performance on mobile crowdsourcing platforms, we have conducted a between-subjects experiment in August 2016. In the experiment, we recruit participants to install a mobile crowdsourcing application that sends tasks intermittently throughout the day. Workers are allowed to accept or ignore the tasks according to their situation. A different task price is set per each task request, and controlled so that it would be uniformly distributed with a fixed median price. A known answer task (gold standard) is used to evaluate task accuracy for each situation. Workers are asked to answer their situation of degree of busyness, degree of fatigue, presence of companions along with their task completion. We also periodically send additional questionnaire to collect worker situations when workers ignore the task. The task completion rate, mean accepted task price and task quality are measured for each situation.

### Participants

We recruited participants (N=50, 58.0% female, aged 20–58, mean age=37.5, std. dev=9.1) through email advertisements sent to approximately 1,000 staff working for a recruiting company in Japan. Their living and working location

| Task | Quality of service survey |
|---|---|
| Notification | 27 times/day (7AM-8:30PM) |
| Required time | 216 sec (median) / task |
| Incentive price | 10~50 yen/task with 5-yen basis (uniform distribution with mean of 30 yen) |
| Measurement | Task completion rate, mean task acceptance price and task quality |
| Participants | 50 |
| Duration | 3 weeks from Aug 8 to Aug 28, 2016 |

**Table 1. Summary of experimental settings. We evaluated task completion rate, mean accepted task price and task quality in different worker conditions.**

expands over the whole country of Japan. Participants must have an Android or iPhone smartphone to participate. Other than that, there were no restrictions applied to the participants by their demographics, and assume that no factor was concerned to cause bias in worker demographics.

### Method

Since there is no mobile crowdsourcing platform service available in Japan (e.g., Gigwalk) which support push notification, the experiment was conducted on our own crowdsourcing platform. The platform is capable of providing tasks to workers based on specific location and time. All participants installed an application for this experiment on their phones, and the task was branded as a quality-of-service survey from the telecommunications company. It is notable that mobile network monitoring is common task on mobile crowdsourcing platforms [19, 33].

We periodically send task notifications to workers. Workers can select whether s/he accept the task or not after confirming the task price for each notification. Existing studies about interruption determine the availability of users based only on their response to notifications. In mobile crowdsourcing, we must consider not just the workers' availability, but also their current situations and task conditions (e.g. task price). Thus, we categorize workers' response to the following 3 categories: (1) Unavailable (No response to notification), (2) Decline (Confirm notification but choose not to complete task), and (3) Accept (Complete task). These categories can be distinguished from the experiment log data

Table 1 summarizes the experimental conditions. The application notifies tasks to workers approximately every 30 minutes, 27 times per day. Since tasks are location dependent, the invitation expires five minutes after notification. After confirming the task, the completion deadline is set to 15 minutes. The median of task completion time was 216 sec. The task price is randomly decided every time between ¥10 yen ($1.5/hr) and ¥50 ($7.5/hr) by ¥5 basis with a uniform distribution of ¥30 median ($4.5/hr). The experiment was conducted for a three-week period.

In the task, workers are asked to watch a three-minute streaming video and answer the questionnaire about the quality of the video and their situations. Evaluating Quality of Experience (QoE) for video streaming by crowd workers under various network performance is a famous crowdsourcing application [28]. Table 2 describes the detail of the questionnaire. After watching the video, workers are asked to answer the number of suspended times of the streaming and the number of noise appeared on the screen due to low communication service quality (an example frame extracted from a typical noisy video is shown to workers). Workers are also asked to answer their situation that affects communication quality, such as their current location and moving status (Q. 2-1, 2-2). Finally, workers are asked about their degree of busyness, degree of fatigue, and presence of companions (Q. 2-3, 2-4, 2-5).

**Q. 1** Please answer the following questions after watching the video.
**Q. 1-1** How many times did the video suspend?
(a) None (b) Once (c) Twice (d) Three times (e) Four times or more (f) Suspend and never resume (after 15 sec passed)
**Q. 1-2** How many times did you find noise in the video?
(a) None (b) Once (c) Twice (d) Three times (e) Four times or more

**Q. 2** Please answer about your situation.
**Q. 2-1** What are you doing now? (Select one for each)
(a) Moving (b) Staying in one place
(a) on the Train (b) Outdoors (c) Indoors
**Q. 2-2** Please describe details of your location (Free text)
e.g. "I'm at station [X] on the [Y] line"
**Q. 2-3** How busy did you feel before starting this task?
(a) Very busy (b) Moderately busy
(c) Moderately not busy (d) Not busy at all
**Q. 2-4** How much fatigue did you feel before starting this task?
(a) Very high (b) Moderately high
(c) Moderately low (d) Not at all
**Q. 2-5** Describe currently present companions
(a) Alone (b) Family (c) Friends (d) Colleagues
(e) Others (free text)

**Table 2. Task description (translated from Japanese).**

Although the content of streaming video is the same for every task, we randomly assign noisy video with a 25% probability to evaluate task accuracy. We prepare five types of noisy video, by inserting 15 sec of noise in different parts of the three-minute video. In order to avoid cases where the streaming quality actually degrades due to low quality communication service, the application buffers the entire streaming video. In case the playing time within the video catches up with the end of the buffered video, the streaming video is paused and never resumes (workers answer (f) in Q. 1-1 in such cases). This mechanism allows us to distinguish the gold standard from actual degradation of communication service quality.

### Conditions

In the experiment, we evaluate three types of worker situations; busyness, fatigue, and presence of companions, with three measurements of crowdsourcing performance; task completion rate, mean accepted price and task quality. The three types of worker situations are collected by the questions from Q. 2-3 to Q. 2-5 in Table 2. We ask busyness and fatigue of worker with four graded questions and grouped into two categories, respectively. Namely, we asked workers to select one from the four degrees of busyness: "very busy", "moderately busy", "moderately not busy" and "not busy at all". The former two options are grouped into high busyness (HB), whereas the latter two options are grouped into low busyness (LB). In the same manner, the four degrees of fatigue are grouped into high fatigue (HF) and low fatigue (LF). The presence of companion is grouped into "with someone" (WS) and "alone" (AL).

In order to examine task completion rate, we also need to collect worker situations when workers do not complete tasks. For this purpose, we send additional (out-of-task) questionnaire every three hours, inquiring the situation of workers (Q 2-3 to Q 2-5) during the last 3 hours. This questionnaire enables exhaustive data collection in all situations, regardless of task completion.

### Measures

We evaluate task completion rate, mean accepted task price and task quality across all situations. In order to collect worker situations, we used the out-of-task questionnaire to evaluate task completion rate, and the in-task questionnaire was used to evaluate mean accepted task price and task quality of completed tasks.

Task completion rate is defined for each situation as follows.

*Task completion rate = number of completed tasks / number of notified tasks*

Mean accepted task price is calculated for each situation only from the completed (accepted) tasks. The price of all notified tasks are uniformly distributed with the median of ¥30, thus, if workers tend to decline cheaper tasks (like ¥10) more frequently in a specific situation, the mean accepted task price for that situation increases.

We evaluate task quality using noisy videos as the gold standard. We can check how carefully workers pay attention to the task by analyzing the detection performance of the noisy videos. We used recall, precision, F-measure and accuracy as evaluation criteria. These criteria are defined as follows using TP (True Positive), TN (True Negative), FP (False Positive) and FN (False Negative), where the noisy videos are positive.

$$Recall = TP / ( TN + TP ),\ Precision = TP / ( FP + TP )$$

$$F\text{-}measure = 2 / ( 1 / Recall + 1 / Precision)$$

$$Accuracy = ( TP + FN ) / ( TP + TN + FP + FN )$$

In the task, workers are required to answer the questionnaire after watching a three-minute video. Therefore, tasks completed earlier than three minutes are considered to be invalid, or cheated. We evaluate the average completion time and the ratio of invalid (shorter than three minutes) tasks as intermediate criteria for estimating task quality.

Finally, we asked the participants for subjective opinions about the relationship between their situations and performance. Namely, we asked three questions: "In which situation do you feel the most difficult to accept the task?" "In which situation do you feel the most difficult to concentrate on the task?" and "Have you declined low price tasks?" along with their reasons.

### Method of Analysis

To determine whether worker situations affect their performance, we conducted statistical tests. All worker situations are grouped into two categories, as previously described. Namely, busyness and fatigue are grouped into high and low (HB, LB, HF and LF defined in the Condition section). The presence of companions is grouped into "with someone" (WS) or "alone" (AL). Therefore, condition groups consist of two unpaired groups. Since task completion rate and task accuracy are binominal data, i.e., tasks completed or not, accurate or not, we used Chi-square test to compare the significance of the difference. As for mean accepted task price and task completion time, we can assume normality in their distribution. Therefore, we used t-test to compare the differences between the condition groups.

## RESULTS

The recruited 50 participants received 27 notifications per day, 567 notifications in total during the three-week experimental period. A total of 47 participants out of 50 participants completed at least three tasks during the period. The total number of completed tasks was 3,596. The response rate of the out-of-task questionnaire was 36%. Table 3 shows the number of worker situations answered in the in-task and out-of-task questionnaire. The quantity of answers in each situation are sufficient for statistical analysis, and are relatively evenly distributed among the situations. In the experiment, we used the number of tasks for the statistical test. The coincidence of worker situations for the same time exceeded 90% between in-task and out-of-task questionnaires, which indicates that workers were able to accurately recall their situations for specific times of day that were selected in the out-of-task questionnaires.

### Task Completion

First, we examine the relationship between worker situation and task completion. In order to compare task completion rate among worker situations, we need to collect the situation of workers when they have ignored the task. We used the out-of-task questionnaire for this purpose. Table 4 shows the task completion rate for each situation, absolute and relative difference of task completion rate, and p value of Chi-square test of the differences within each situation.

| Situation | in-task | out-of-task |
|---|---|---|
| HB | 1340 | 3727 |
| LB | 2256 | 4486 |
| HF | 1829 | 4200 |
| LF | 1767 | 4013 |
| WS | 1879 | 5366 |
| AL | 1717 | 2847 |

**Table 3. The number of worker situations answered in the in-task and out-of-task questionnaire. The numbers of each situation were large enough for statistical analysis, and were free from large deviation among the situations.**

| Situation | Task Completion (%) | Difference Abs. / Rel. (%) | p value |
|---|---|---|---|
| HB | 25.7 | 7.74 / 30.1 | .0000 |
| LB | 33.4 | | *** |
| HF | 29.7 | 2.28 / 7.72 | .7554 |
| LF | 30.1 | | |
| WS | 28.2 | 5.03 / 17.9 | .0000 |
| AL | 33.2 | | *** |

**Table 4. Task completion rate across worker situations. Workers with high busyness (HB) decreased task completion rate by 30.1% relative compared to workers with low busyness (LB) (p<.001).**

When workers are busy, the task completion rate has decreased by 7.74% (30.1 % relative decrease) compared to when workers are not busy. Our Chi-square test with Yates' continuity correction reveal that the difference is significant ($\chi^2(1, N=8213) = 57.8$, $p < .001$, $\varphi = 0.084$). As for fatigue, no significant difference between the task completion rates for high fatigued workers and low fatigued workers is observed. When workers are accompanied with someone, task completion rate has decreased by 5.03% (17.9 % relative decrease) compared to when workers are alone, The Chi-square test reveals that this difference is also significant ($\chi^2(1, N=8213) = 22.2$, $p < .001$, $\varphi = 0.052$). From these results, it can be concluded that task completion rate greatly decreases when workers are busy or with other people.

### Task Price

We measured mean accepted task price to analyze the relationship between worker situations and task price. Since task price is uniformly distributed from ¥10 to ¥50 with a median of ¥30 yen, if workers tend to decline cheaper tasks (like ¥10) more frequently in a specific situation, the mean task price of that situation increases. Unlike task completion rate, calculation of mean accepted task price requires only the information of completed task data. Therefore, we used only the worker situations collected by in-task questionnaire. Table 5 shows mean accepted task price for each situation, difference of mean accepted task price, and p value of t-test for the difference.

| Situation | Mean accepted task price (yen) | Difference (%) | p value |
|---|---|---|---|
| HB | 32.8 | 5.95 | .0050 |
| LB | 30.9 | | ** |
| HF | 32.2 | 4.02 | .0543 |
| LF | 31.0 | | |
| WS | 32.8 | 7.67 | .0003 |
| AL | 30.5 | | *** |

**Table 5. Mean accepted task price across worker situations. Workers with someone else (WS) increased mean accepted task price by 7.67% compared to workers alone (AL) (p<.001).**

When workers are busy, the mean accepted task price has increased by 5.95%, compared to when workers are not busy, where a Welch's t-test reveals that the difference is significant ($t(2808) = 2.29$, $p < .001$). The mean accepted task price has increased 4.02% for fatigued workers compared to when workers do not feel fatigue, but the difference is not statistically significant according to the t-test ($t(3592) = -0.09$, $p = .0543 > .05$). When workers are with someone, mean accepted task price has increased by 7.67% compared to when workers are alone. The t-test reveals that the difference is significant ($t(3561) = 3.43$, $p < .001$). These results indicate that when workers are busy or with someone else, they decline lower priced tasks more frequently.

Based on the above results, we conclude that workers' busyness and the presence of companions cause significant differences in both task completion rate and mean accepted task price. This result can be explained by the findings in prior work [40], where task completion and task price have strong relations with each other.

### Task Quality

We examine the relationship between worker situation and task quality. In the task, workers are asked to watch three-minute streaming video, and answer the questionnaire about quality of communication service. We assigned videos which contain intentional noise as the gold standard with a 25% probability. The direct measurements for evaluating task quality are recall, precision, F-measure and accuracy for detecting noisy video, as explained in the Experimental Design section. As an indirect measurement, we evaluate the task completion time. We compare average task completion time across the worker situations. The tasks that were completed shorter than three minutes are considered to be invalid. We also measure the rate of invalid tasks. Table 6 shows mean and median of task completion time, the invalid task rate, and p value of t-test for the difference in the mean task completion time.

When workers are either busy, fatigued or with someone, mean task completion time is significantly shorter ($p < .001$) compared to when workers are not busy, not fatigued or alone, respectively. Particularly, when workers feel fatigued, mean task completion time is 20.1% shorter compared to

| Situation | Mean (sec) | Median (sec) | Invalid (%) | p value |
|---|---|---|---|---|
| HB | 177 | 192 | 49.0 | .0000 |
| LB | 202 | 225 | 33.5 | *** |
| HF | 171 | 152 | 51.3 | .0000 |
| LF | 215 | 229 | 26.8 | *** |
| WS | 179 | 208 | 46.6 | .0000 |
| AL | 208 | 224 | 31.3 | *** |

**Table 6. Mean and median of task completion time, the invalid task rate, and p value of t-test for the difference in mean task completion time. Workers feeling high fatigue (HF) decreased mean task completion time by 20.1%, and roughly doubled the invalid task rate, compared to workers feeling low fatigue (LF).**

when workers don't feel fatigued. The rate of invalid task of fatigued workers is approximately two times larger than that of workers without fatigue. On crowdsourcing platforms, some lazy workers do not complete tasks in the expected manner. Without introducing techniques to control task quality, 30% of tasks can contain poor results [9]. The results of our experiment indicate that, similar to prior work, about 30% of tasks are invalid when workers are not busy, not fatigued or alone. However, when workers feel high fatigue and busyness, or are with someone else, the invalid task rate significantly increases, which results in the increase of low quality tasks.

Table 7 shows the relationship between worker situations and task quality measured by recall, precision, F-measure and accuracy. We designed this task assuming that telecommunication companies utilize the collected information to detect low quality areas of communication services. In such scenarios, criteria such as recall, precision and F measure are considered to be important. On the other hand, since recall and precision are in a trade-off relation, applying the statistical test is inappropriate. Thus, we applied Chi-square test to the accuracy measure to examine whether the detection accuracy of noisy video differs across worker situations.

We assigned videos containing 15 sec noise during the 3 min video as the gold standard with the probability of 25%. Due to the low probability of noise appearance, and highly demanding task design where workers are required to concentrate on the mobile phone screen for three minutes, the task was so difficult that the F-measure ranges around 0.2 to 0.4. Significant differences were observed in the accuracy across worker situations. On the basis of the F-measure, HB, HF and WS was lower compared to LB, LF and AL, respectively.

When workers feel high fatigue, both the recall and the precision has decreased compared to when workers feel low fatigue. F-measure has decreased from 0.364 to 0.265 (37.4% relative decrease), which was the largest decrease among all the worker situations. Our Chi-square test with Yates' continuity correction revealed that the difference in

| Situation | Precision | Recall | F measure | Accuracy | p value |
|---|---|---|---|---|---|
| HB | 0.567 | 0.188 | 0.282 | 0.742 | .7193 |
| LB | 0.461 | 0.261 | 0.333 | 0.748 | |
| HF | 0.478 | 0.184 | 0.265 | 0.730 | .0379 |
| LF | 0.500 | 0.287 | 0.364 | 0.761 | * |
| WS | 0.449 | 0.191 | 0.268 | 0.733 | .0730 |
| AL | 0.529 | 0.277 | 0.364 | 0.759 | |

**Table 7. Recall, precision, F measure and accuracy of the tasks across the conditions. Workers feeling high fatigue (HF) significantly decreased the accuracy of the tasks compared to the workers feeling low fatigue (LF).**

the accuracy is significant ($\chi^2(1, N=3596) = 4.31$, $p < .05$, $\varphi = 0.035$). This result indicates that workers under fatigue could not concentrate on the task because fatigue decreases their productivity and causes errors, as described in our hypothesis. Similar to worker fatigue, when workers are with someone else, the precision, the recall and the F-measure have also decreased. This result indicates that workers have failed to concentrate on the tasks, either due to the distraction from their companions, or by attempting to complete the task as quickly as possible so that they will not keep the companions waiting. However, the p value of the Chi-square test was 0.073, which does not show significant difference in the accuracy of the task. As for busyness, high busyness increased the precision but decreased the recall. This is probably because workers did not check the detail of the video in busy situations, thus were able to detect only explicitly apparent noise, and ignored minor noise.

### Subjective Opinion

After the experiment, we asked the participants for their subjective opinions about the relationship between worker situation and performance. Regarding task completion and task quality, we asked in which situations they feel difficulties to accept tasks, and in which situations they feel difficulties to concentrate on tasks, along with their respective reasons. Of the 50 participants who participated in the experiment, 42 participants (84%) answered the questionnaire. Table 8 shows the number and the rate of answered situations where workers feel difficulties to accept tasks. Table 9 shows the number and the rate of answered situations where workers feel difficulties to concentrate on tasks.

In Table 8, busyness was selected as the most significant factor which applies difficulty to workers to accept tasks. The second most significant factor was companions. These results are consistent with the results of the quantitative evaluation, where the task completion rate was the lowest when workers are busy, and was the second lowest when workers are with someone else. Common reasons why busy workers feel difficult to accept the tasks are, *"I couldn't check the notification of my private phone while I'm at my office"* and *"I couldn't find three minutes on my busy schedule."* Common reasons why workers with someone feel difficult to accept the tasks was, *"I felt it rude to watch the*

| Situation | # of answers | % of answers |
|---|---|---|
| High busyness | 21 | 50.0 |
| High fatigue | 4 | 9.5 |
| With someone | 10 | 23.8 |
| Others | 7 | 16.7 |

**Table 8. The number and ratio of situations where workers feel difficulties to accept tasks. Many workers answered that busyness and companions make them difficult to accept tasks.**

| Situation | # of answers | % of answers |
|---|---|---|
| High busyness | 21 | 50.0 |
| High fatigue | 4 | 9.5 |
| With someone | 15 | 35.7 |
| Others | 2 | 4.8 |

**Table 9. The number of ratio of situations where workers feel difficulties to concentrate on tasks. Similar to the result in Table 8, many workers answered that busyness and companions make them difficult to concentrate on tasks.**

*video when I was with someone."* These opinions indicate that the experiment of Misra [42] that we referred for the establishment of our hypothesis is also valid for mobile crowdsourcing platforms.

Table 9 indicates the busyness is the largest, and the presence of companions is the second largest factor to apply difficulties to workers to concentrate on the task. However, the results of the previous quantitative experimental results show that workers most lost their concentration when they were feeling high fatigue. This result indicates that workers' feelings and their actual behavior are different. The main reason why busy workers feel difficult to concentrate on the tasks is, *"I couldn't keep my eyes on my mobile phone due to the busyness."* The common reason of workers who selected companions was, *"I cared about my companions and tried to complete the task as quickly as possible."* These opinions are considered to be the cause of decrease in task quality. Although only a few workers selected fatigue as the reason, one of the workers commented that *"I was too sleepy to keep watching the video until the end."* This indicates that it may be difficult for workers to notice the reduction of task quality caused by their own fatigue.

## DISCUSSION

Our research question in this paper is, "*does worker situation affect task completion rate, accepted task price and task quality on mobile crowdsourcing platforms?*" By drawing economics and psychology literature, we established three hypotheses about worker situations (busyness, fatigue and the presence of companions). We begin our discussion by highlighting whether these hypotheses are supported by our experiments. Table 9 shows the correspondence matrix of our hypotheses and experimental results.

Table 10 illustrates that most of our hypotheses are supported by the experimental results. The only hypothesis that was not able to be confirmed was the decrease of task quality of

| Situation | Completion | Price | Quality |
|---|---|---|---|
| Busyness | Supported | Supported | NA |
| Fatigue | NA | NA | Supported |
| Companion | Supported | Supported | Not supported |

**Table 10. Correspondence matrix of hypotheses and experimental results about the relationships between worker situations and task performance. In most part of the matrix, our hypotheses are supported by experimental results, but the task quality reduction with companions was not supported.**

workers with companions, since the Chi-square test did not show a significant difference with p value of 0.067 (> .05). We will discuss the details of the effect of worker situations on task completion rate, accepted task price and task quality, as follows.

For task completion rate, existing studies on notifications to mobile devices mainly focus on reducing the burden of interruption caused by the notification, and increasing the response rate toward the notification. By analyzing the log data of mobile devices, momentary situations like switching applications on the phone are detected as a suitable timing for notification [44]. However, results from such existing work cannot be applied to mobile crowdsourcing platforms because workers consider the amount of time necessary to complete a task before deciding whether or not to accept it. In the experiment, we assumed a task which requires more than three minutes to complete. As some participants have reported, we observe that workers hesitate to accept tasks when they are busy or with someone else, because they are unconfident to complete the task under such situations.

Existing studies report that task completion and task price have strong relations with each other [40]. We were also able to observe such results in our experiments, that busyness and the presence of companions both affect task completion rate and mean accepted task price. When workers are busy, they have many alternatives that increase the opportunity cost of the mobile crowdsourcing task. Workers are supposed to regard the time with companions as one of such valuable alternatives. After the experiment, we asked workers whether they have declined low price tasks. As the result, 50% of workers answered yes, and 50% answered no. One of the common reasons of workers who answered yes for this question was that the task was not cost effective. One of the subjects was clearly conscious about the idea of opportunity cost, mentioning that *"I prioritize the ¥50 task even when I am busy, but I prioritize other things for the ¥10 task."* Contrarily, typical reasons of workers who answered no for this question were, *"I accepted the task even with low price because it increases my income"* and *"I decided whether I accept the task or not only based on my situation."* These opinions indicate that worker situations affect their decisions on the acceptance of low priced tasks.

For the task quality, mental fatigue has been reported to increase errors in continuous tasks [11]. However, we haven't found any studies on the relationship between worker fatigue and task quality on mobile crowdsourcing platforms, where small tasks are separately pushed to workers. Our experimental results indicate that worker fatigue affects task quality even for one-time tasks.

Let us discuss how the findings from our experiments can be leveraged in practical situations. The experimental results show that worker situations affect mobile crowdsourcing performance of task completion rate, task price and task quality. In order to utilize worker situation on practical mobile crowdsourcing platforms, new technologies which can accurately obtain worker situations are required. Development of such technologies, such as sensor devices and methods to analyze signals from these sensors, and also their implementation to smartphones is expected to make this possible in the near future.

We present our analysis to explore the possibility to leverage our results currently, i.e., without the anticipation of future technology developments. First, we summarize the degree of busyness, degree of fatigue, and the presence of companions obtained from out-of-task questionnaire. Figure 1 shows the ratio of workers in HB (High Busyness), HF (High Fatigue) and WS (With Someone) situations defined in the Experimental Design section, grouped by weekdays, weekends, and time of day. According to Figure 1, the ratios of busy workers and fatigued workers, and the ratio of workers with someone are lower in the morning of both weekdays and weekends. These times of day are considered suitable for requesting tasks. The ratio of workers with someone increases around noon on weekday but relatively decreases on weekends. Figure 1 shows the summary of the situations of all workers, but life styles are different for each worker, such as working days and hours. We can optimize task completion rate, task price and task quality by requesting tasks for workers with suitable situations obtained from their activity logs. The lower part of Figure 1 shows the mean accepted task price for each time of day on weekdays and weekends. From the figure, there seems to be a correlation between worker situations and task price. The correlation coefficient between the rate of busy workers and the mean accepted task price was 0.58 on weekdays, and 0.50 on weekends, which indicates a moderately positive correlation. This finding indicates that requesters can save the cost of mobile crowdsourcing by requesting tasks in time slots when workers are not busy.

The rest of this section discusses the limitations of this research. First, we focus on the representativeness of the mobile crowdsourcing platform and the task used in the study. We conducted the experiment on our own mobile crowdsourcing platform, mainly because there were no commercial mobile crowdsourcing platforms in Japan which support push notifications like Gigwalk. Our platform operates similarly to Gigwalk and others, in that it is capable of providing tasks to workers based on specific location and time. We believe that the findings from this platform can be generalized to other mobile crowdsourcing platforms that support push notification to workers. However, the applicability to each mobile crowdsourcing platform should be examined accordingly.

We used a survey task to evaluate the quality of communication service, where workers are asked to watch a video and answer a set of questionnaires. There are several reasons to think this task can be generalized to other mobile crowdsourcing tasks. First, there are many labeling tasks for video contents on crowdsourcing platforms. Second, "survey" is one of the top twenty keywords on Amazon Mechanical Turk [31]. Third, information sensing tasks such as reporting weather and measuring amount of traffic are all popular ways of use for mobile crowdsourcing platforms [53]. We designed the task so that workers require more than three minutes to complete the task, because workers would accept all tasks without paying attention to the task price if we set a short completion time. In our experiment, workers were required to use up to several tens of seconds to confirm the notification on their mobile phone and check the price of the task, prior to task acceptation. The switching cost for suspending current activity is also large. If we set the task completion time to one minute, the additional time cost to accept the task will exceed time necessary to complete the task, which is calculated as sunk cost. As the result, workers would accept all tasks or decline all tasks regardless of the task price. We designed the three-minute task to avoid this problem. As a result, 50% of workers decided whether they accept the task or not after confirming the task price, which shows that our experimental design worked well.

In this paper, we have asked the degrees of busyness and fatigue, and the presence of companions as typical worker situations. Analyzing worker situations in more detail is our future work. For example, categorizing the reasons of busyness, the cause of fatigue and the conversational content with the companion would be helpful to deeply understand the effect of worker situations on their performance. Existing study about interruptibility shows that conversation context affects response rate toward notifications from mobile devices [48], indicating the importance of such effects.

Another remaining question is, *"Are there any other situations that affect worker performance?"* We do not think that our three hypotheses cover all possible situations which affect mobile worker performance. Many alternative situations can be listed, e.g., extrinsic factors such as weather and social events, and physical conditions such as means of transportation and indoor/outdoor. Contributions of this paper are the definition of the three hypotheses drawn from economics and psychology studies, and the examination of their actual effect to improve performance on mobile crowdsourcing platforms. The evaluation of other worker situations is our future work.

Another limitation is the validness of our hypotheses for tasks that are more excessively associated with worker movement, e.g., field surveys, which are also popular on mobile crowdsourcing platforms. In these tasks, more

| Day | Situation | 7 | 8 | 9 | 10 | 11 | 12 | 13 | 14 | 15 | 16 | 17 | 18 | 19 | 20 |
|---|---|---|---|---|---|---|---|---|---|---|---|---|---|---|---|
| Weekday | HB | 0.378 | 0.426 | 0.488 | 0.516 | 0.534 | 0.566 | 0.581 | 0.535 | 0.515 | 0.518 | 0.548 | 0.628 | 0.612 | 0.618 |
| | HF | 0.394 | 0.384 | 0.401 | 0.447 | 0.486 | 0.544 | 0.548 | 0.568 | 0.560 | 0.599 | 0.635 | 0.688 | 0.678 | 0.718 |
| | WS | 0.550 | 0.595 | 0.635 | 0.656 | 0.674 | 0.716 | 0.721 | 0.688 | 0.674 | 0.637 | 0.668 | 0.692 | 0.623 | 0.509 |
| Weekend | HB | 0.215 | 0.252 | 0.289 | 0.252 | 0.291 | 0.333 | 0.351 | 0.387 | 0.367 | 0.356 | 0.406 | 0.471 | 0.526 | 0.444 |
| | HF | 0.363 | 0.339 | 0.341 | 0.358 | 0.409 | 0.458 | 0.477 | 0.544 | 0.541 | 0.586 | 0.558 | 0.563 | 0.603 | 0.651 |
| | WS | 0.549 | 0.566 | 0.610 | 0.614 | 0.615 | 0.678 | 0.690 | 0.668 | 0.700 | 0.671 | 0.685 | 0.697 | 0.744 | 0.683 |

| Day | Task Price | 7 | 8 | 9 | 10 | 11 | 12 | 13 | 14 | 15 | 16 | 17 | 18 | 19 | 20 |
|---|---|---|---|---|---|---|---|---|---|---|---|---|---|---|---|
| Weekday | | 28.7 | 30.2 | 30.9 | 31.2 | 32.2 | 31.6 | 30.3 | 27.4 | 30.8 | 30.1 | 30.5 | 31.7 | 32.5 | 32.9 |
| Weekend | | 29.3 | 30.7 | 28.6 | 30.6 | 31.8 | 29.7 | 32.6 | 30.1 | 29.8 | 29.8 | 31.7 | 32.1 | 34.5 | 28.8 |

**Figure 1: The ratio of workers in HB (High Busyness), HF (High Fatigue) and WS (With Someone) situations (upper table) and mean accepted task price (lower table) grouped by weekdays, weekends and time of day. Worker situations and mean accepted task price differ depending on the time and day.**

sophisticated worker situations (for example, staying inside or outside) are considered to affect worker performance. In related papers. We limited the scope of tasks into those which do not require physical movement, in order to simplify the research issue. However, since tasks associated with worker movement are one of the major tasks on mobile crowdsourcing platforms, evaluation of the effect of worker situations for these tasks is an interesting area to explore in the future.

We have conducted the experiment without the existence of other crowdsourcing tasks. On commercial mobile crowdsourcing services, many tasks are available at the same time. Evaluation of the relationship between worker situations and their task selection under multiple task conditions is also another interesting direction of future work.

## CONCLUSION

In this paper, we have investigated the effect of worker situations such as busyness, fatigue and the presence of companions on task completion rate, task price and task quality on mobile crowdsourcing platforms. In order to develop reasonable hypotheses of worker situation that affect mobile crowdsourcing performance, we draw on economics and psychology literature. We conducted a between-subjects experiment with 50 participants using a mobile crowdsourcing app to examine our hypotheses. The experimental results show that task completion rate decreased by 30.1% in relative value when workers are busy. Mean accepted task price increased by 7.6 % when workers are with companions. Task quality decreased by 37.4% in relative value of F-measure when workers feel fatigue. Subjective opinions obtained after the experiment also supported our hypotheses in that workers feel difficult to accept the tasks when they are busy and with someone else.

On mobile crowdsourcing platforms, there are strong demands from task requesters to complete time/location-specific tasks with quick response and higher quality. Our experiment show a possibility to solve these requesters' demands from the observation of the effect of worker situations on task completion rate and task quality. As a practical method to collect worker situations, we show that worker situations differ depending on the time and day. In the near future, technical advances in sensor devices and analytics of human activity will realize more highly accurate estimation of worker situations. At that time, we believe our study will greatly contribute to increase mobile crowdsourcing performance.

We summarize the contributions of our study as follows:

- We have established hypotheses about the effect of worker situations on mobile crowdsourcing performance by drawing economics and psychology literature.
- We have carried out a mobile crowdsourcing field experiment with 50 participants and investigated valid worker situations in quantitative and qualitative ways.
- We have shown a practical use scenario to apply worker situations on mobile crowdsourcing by showing the difference of worker situations depending on the time and day.

So far, we have investigated our hypotheses with a quality of communication service survey task. In order to expand our findings to the tasks associated with worker movement and multi-task conditions, we plan to establish hypotheses about the factors that affects worker performance and behavior in those settings.

## ACKNOWLEDGEMENTS

We would like to thank Michael S. Bernstein of Stanford HCI group for valuable discussion about research design. We would like to thank Yasuyuki Nakajima, Toshiaki Tanaka, Hajime Nakamura, Tsuzuki Tojo, Yasuhiro Takishima and Kazunori Matsumoto of KDDI Research, Inc. for supporting the study. We also thank all of the participants in our experiment.

## REFERENCES


1. Field Agent, https://www.fieldagent.net/
2. Gigwalk, http://www.gigwalk.com/
3. Adamczyk, P. D. and Bailey, B. P. If not now, when?: the effects of interruption at different moments within task execution. In Proc. CHI, 2004, 271-278.
4. Alt, F., Shirazi, A., Schmidt, A., Kramer, U. and Nawaz, Z. Location-based crowdsourcing: extending crowdsourcing to the real world. In Proc. NordiCHI 2010, 13-22.
5. Antin, J. and Shaw, A. Social desirability bias in reports of motivation for US and India workers on Mechanical Turk. In Proc. CSCW, 2011.
6. Armstrong, G. B. and Sopory, P. Effects of background television on phonological and visuo-spatial working memory. Communication Research, 24, 5, 1997, 459-480.
7. Bailey, B. P. and Konstan, J. A. On the need for attention-aware systems: Measuring effects of interruption on task performance, error rate, and affective state. Computers in Human Behavior, 22, 4, 2006, 685-708.
8. Beenen, G., Ling, K., Wang, X., Chang, K., Frankowski, D., Resnick, P. and Kraut, R. Using social psychology to motivate contributions to online communities. In Proc. CSCW, 2004, 212-221.
9. Bernstein, M. S., Little, G., Miller, R. C., Hartmann, B., Ackerman, M. S., Karger, D. R., Crowell, D. and Panovich, K. Soylent: a word processor with a crowd inside. Communications of the ACM, 58, 8, 2015, 85-94.
10. Boksem, M. A., Meijman, T. F. and Lorist, M. M. Mental fatigue, motivation and action monitoring. Biological psychology, 72, 2, 2006, 123-132.
11. Boksem, M. A., Meijman, T. F. and Lorist, M. M. Effects of mental fatigue on attention: an ERP study. Cognitive brain research, 25, 1, 2005, 107-116.
12. Cai, C. J., Iqbal, S. T. and Teevan, J. Chain reactions: The impact of order on microtask chains. In Proc. CHI, 2016.
13. Campagne, A., Pebayle, T. and Muzet, A. Correlation between driving errors and vigilance level: influence of the driver's age. Physiology and Behavior, 80, 2004, 515-524.
14. Chang Y. J., Paruthi G. and Newman M. W. A field study comparing approaches to collecting annotated activity data in real-world settings. In Proc. UbiComp, 2015, 671-682.
15. Chatzimilioudis, G., Konstantinidis, A., Laoudias, C. and Zeinalipour-Yazti, D. Crowdsourcing with smartphones. IEEE Internet Computing, 16, 5, 2012, 36-44.
16. Czerwinski, M., Cutrell, E. and Horvitz, E. Instant messaging: Effects of relevance and timing. In Proc. HCI, 2000, 71-76.
17. Dow, S., Kulkarni, A., Klemmer, S. and Hartmann, B. Shepherding the crowd yields better work. In Proc. CSCW, 2012, 1013-1022.
18. Faber, L. G., Maurits, N. M. and Lorist, M. M. Mental fatigue affects visual selective attention. PLOS one, 7, 10, 2012, e48073.
19. Faggiani, A., Gregori, E., Lenzini, L., Luconi, V. and Vecchio, A. Smartphone-based crowdsourcing for network monitoring: Opportunities, challenges, and a case study. IEEE Communications Magazine, 52, 1, 2014, 106-113.
20. Goldman, A. and Johansson, J. K. Determinants of search for lower prices: An empirical assessment of the economics of information theory. Journal of Consumer Research, 5, 3, 1978, 176-186.
21. Gould, S., Brumby, D., Cox, A., Gonz´alez, V., Salvucci, D. and Taatgen, N. Multitasking and interruptions: a sig on bridging the gap between research on the micro and macro worlds. In Proc. CHI, 2012, 1189-1192.
22. Gronau, R. The intrafamily allocation of time: The value of the housewives' time. The American Economic Review, 63, 4, 1973, 634-651.
23. Gupta, A., Thies, W., Cutrell, E. and Balakrishnan, R. mClerk: enabling mobile crowdsourcing in developing regions. In Proc. CHI, 2012, 1843-1852.
24. Hembrooke, H., and Geri G. The laptop and the lecture: The effects of multitasking in learning environments. Journal of computing in higher education, 15, 1, 2003, 46-64.
25. Ho, J. and Intille, S. S. Using context-aware computing to reduce the perceived burden of interruptions from mobile devices. In. Proc. CHI, 2005, 909-918.
26. Horton, J. J., and Chilton, L. B. The labor economics of paid crowdsourcing. In Proc. of the 11th ACM conference on Electronic commerce, 2010, 209-218.
27. Hosio, S., Goncalves, J., Lehdonvirta, V., Ferreira, D. and Kostakos, V. Situated crowdsourcing using a market model. In Proc. UIST, 2014, 55-64.
28. Hoßfeld, T., Seufert, M., Hirth, M., Zinner, T., Tran-Gia, P. and Schatz, R. Quantification of YouTube QoE via crowdsourcing. In Multimedia, In Proc. ISM, 2011, 494-499.
29. Ikeda, K. and Bernstein, M. S. Pay It Backward: Per-Task Payments on Crowdsourcing Platforms Reduce Productivity. In Proc. CHI, 2016, 4111-4121.
30. Iqbal, S. T. and Horvitz, E. Notifications and awareness: A field study of alert usage and preferences. In Proc. CSCW, 2010, 27-30.

31. Ipeirotis, P. G. Analyzing the amazon mechanical turk marketplace. XRDS: Crossroads, the ACM Magazine for Students, 17, 2, 2010, 16-21.
32. Johnson, M. B. Travel time and the price of leisure. Economic Inquiry, 4, 2. 1966, 135-145.
33. Kaup, F., Jomrich, F. and Hausheer, D. Demonstration of NetworkCoverage–A Mobile Network Performance Measurement App. In Proc NetSys, 2015.
34. Kreifeldt, J. G. and McCarthy, M. E. Interruption as a test of the user-computer interface. In Proc. the 17th Annual Conference on Manual Control, 1981, 655-667.
35. Krishna, R., Hata, K., Chen, S., Kravitz, J., Shamma, D. A., Fei-Fei, L. and Bernstein, M. S. Embracing error to enable rapid crowdsourcing. In Proc. CHI, 2016.
36. Law, E., Yin, M., Joslin Goh, K. C., Terry, M. and Gajos, K. Z. Curiosity killed the cat, but makes crowdwork better. In Proc. CHI, 2016.
37. Le, J., Edmonds, A., Hester, V. and Biewald, L. Ensuring quality in crowdsourced search relevance evaluation: The effects of training question distribution. In Proc. CSE, 2010, 21-26.
38. Lippman, S. A. and McCall, J. The economics of job search: A survey. Economic inquiry, 14, 2, 1976, 155-189.
39. Liu, Y., Lehdonvirta, V., Alexandrova, T. and Nakajima, T. Drawing on Mobile Crowds via Social Media. Case UbiAsk: Image Based Mobile Social Search Across Languages. Multimedia Systems, 18, 1, 2012, 53-56.
40. Mason, W. and Watts, D. J. Financial incentives and the "performance of crowds". In Proc. HCOMP, 2009, 77-85.
41. Marmorstein, H., Grewal, D. and Fishe, R. P. The value of time spent in price-comparison shopping: Survey and experimental evidence. Consumer Research, 19, 1, 1992, 52-61.
42. Misra, S., Cheng, L., Genevie, J. and Yuan, M. The iPhone effect: the quality of in-person social interactions in the presence of mobile devices. Environment and Behavior, 48, 2, 2016, 275-298.
43. Musthag, M. and Ganesan, D. Labor dynamics in a mobile micro-task market. In Proc. CHI, 2013, 641-650.
44. Okoshi, T., Ramos, J., Nozaki, H., Nakazawa, J., Dey, A. K. and Tokuda, H. Attelia: Reducing user's cognitive load due to interruptive notifications on smart phones. In Proc. PerCom, 2015, 96-104.
45. Pool, M. M., Koolstra, C. M. and Van der Voort, T. H. Distraction effects of background soap operas on homework performance: An experimental study enriched with observational data. Educational Psychology, 23, 4, 2003, 361-380.
46. Retelny, D., Robaszkiewicz, S., To, A., Lasecki, W. S., Patel, J., Rahmati, N., Doshi, T. Valentine, M. and Bernstein, M. S. Expert crowdsourcing with flash teams. In Proc. UIST, 2014, 75-85.
47. Roberts, R. Getting the most out of life: The concept of opportunity cost. The Library of Economics and Liberty, 5, 2007.
48. Schulze, F. and Groh, G. Conversational context helps improve mobile notification management. In Proc. Mobile HCI, 2016, 518-528.
49. Shaw, A. D., Horton, J. J. and Chen, D. L. Designing incentives for inexpert human raters. In Proc. CSCW 2011, 275-284.
50. Speier, C., Valacich, J. S. and Vessey, I. The influence of task interruption on individual decision making: An information overload perspective. Decision Sciences, 30, 2, 1999, 337-360.
51. Teodoro, R., Ozturk, P., Naaman, M., Mason, W. and Lindqvist, J. The motivations and experiences of the on-demand mobile workforce. In Proc. CSCW, 2014, 236-247.
52. Vaataja, H., Vainio, T., Sirkkunen, E. and Salo, K. Crowdsourced news reporting: supporting news content creation with mobile phones. In Proc. MobileHCI, 2011, 435-444.
53. Vaish, R., Wyngarden, K., Chen, J., Cheung, B. and Bernstein, M. S. Twitch crowdsourcing: crowd contributions in short bursts of time. In Proc. CHI, 2014, 3645-3654.
54. Yu, L., André, P., Kittur, A. and Kraut, R. A. Comparison of social, learning, and financial strategies on crowd engagement and output quality. In Proc. CSCW 2014, 967-978.
55. Zick, C. D. and Bryant, W. K. Alternative strategies for pricing home work time. Home Economics Research Journal, 12, 2, 1983, 133-144.
56. Zijlstra, F. R., Roe, R. A., Leonora, A. B. and Krediet, I. Temporal factors in mental work: Effects of interrupted activities. Occupational and Organizational Psychology, 72, 2, 1999, 163-185.

# Understanding "Death by GPS": A Systematic Study of Catastrophic Incidents Associated with Personal Navigation Technologies

**Allen Yilun Lin*, Kate Kuehl**, Johannes Schöning†, Brent Hecht***
*Northwestern University, **University of Minnesota, †University of Bremen
allen.lin@eecs.northwestern.edu, kuehl088@umn.edu, schoening@uni-bremen.de,
bhecht@northwestern.edu

## ABSTRACT
Catastrophic incidents associated with GPS devices and other personal navigation technologies are sufficiently common that these incidents have been given a colloquial nickname: "Death by GPS". While there is a significant body of work on the use of personal navigation technologies in everyday scenarios, no research has examined these technologies' roles in catastrophic incidents. In this paper, we seek to address this gap in the literature. Borrowing techniques from public health research and communication studies, we construct a corpus of 158 detailed news reports of unique catastrophic incidents associated with personal navigation technologies. We then identify key themes in these incidents and the roles that navigation technologies played in them, e.g. missing road characteristics data contributed to over 24% of these incidents. With the goal of reducing casualties associated with personal navigation technologies, we outline implications for design and research that emerge from our results, e.g. advancing "space usage rule" mapping, incorporating weather information in routing, and improving visual and audio instructions in complex situations.

### Author Keywords
GPS; SatNav; personal navigation technologies; map apps

### ACM Classification Keywords
H.5.m. Information interfaces and presentation (e.g., HCI): Miscellaneous;

## INTRODUCTION
A tourist drives his rental car across a beach and directly into the Atlantic Ocean [16]. A person in Belgium intending to drive to a nearby train station ends up in Croatia [46]. A family traveling on a dirt road gets stranded for four days in the Australian outback [45]. These incidents all have one major factor in common: playing a key role in each incident was a personal navigation technology, i.e. a GPS device, a mobile map app (e.g. Google Maps, Apple Maps) or a "SatNav".

Catastrophic incidents associated with personal navigation technologies are sufficiently common that they have come to be associated with a colloquial name: "Death by GPS" [34]. While thankfully not all of these incidents involve the loss of life, it is not uncommon to see media reports of people endangering themselves or others and/or causing extensive property damage due in part to their interaction with a personal navigation technology.

It is tempting to blame these incidents on users and users alone. Indeed, reports of these incidents are often peppered with comments from witnesses and observers inquiring as to why drivers "wouldn't question driving into a puddle that doesn't seem to end" [34] and did not notice "multiple-language traffic signs" [46]. However, it is our responsibility as HCI researchers to design better systems that help people avoid making "user errors" [36], especially when these errors involve such extensive human and financial costs.

The geographic human-computer interaction ("GeoHCI") [17] literature includes a relatively large body of work that examines how people use GPS-based navigation technologies in standard scenarios and in the course of their everyday lives (e.g. [7,18,21,27,28]). However, no work has focused on the increasingly large number of catastrophic incidents associated with these technologies. In other words, the "Death by GPS" phenomenon has yet to be studied in a rigorous fashion.

This paper seeks to begin the process of addressing this gap in the literature. As has been pointed out in the work on typical interactions with GPS devices [7], a major obstacle to the systematic analysis of "Death by GPS" incidents is that no database of these incidents exists. Additionally, methods that have been used to study interaction with GPS devices in the past (e.g. lab studies, field studies) are not valid for this type of analysis.

To overcome these obstacles, we turned to an unlikely source of data: news articles. This approach is adapted from the public health literature, where news articles are used as sensors when the research topic is of sufficient significance but no authoritative dataset is available. Using rigorous best practices for building a minimally biased-corpus of news


*CHI 2017, May 06-11, 2017, Denver, CO, USA*
ACM 978-1-4503-4655-9/17/05.
http://dx.doi.org/10.1145/3025453.3025737

stories and expert-led qualitative coding, we collected and analyzed a dataset of 158 news stories about unique catastrophic incidents associated with personal navigation technologies.

In our analyses of this corpus, we had two cascading research goals:

**Goal 1**: Identify the *patterns* that characterize catastrophic incidents associated with personal navigation technologies.

**Goal 2:** Use the identified patterns to generate *implications for research and design* that can help *build safer personal navigation technologies.*

More specifically, for our first goal, we sought to ascertain themes in both the basic properties of these incidents (e.g. Who was involved? What happened?) and themes in the roles that navigation technologies played in the incidents (i.e. How did the navigation technology specifically fail the user?). Based on the identified patterns, our second research goal involved outlining a series of concrete steps that researchers and practitioners can take to prevent the reoccurrence of common types of catastrophic incidents (and save lives).

We find, for instance, that a large number of "Death by GPS" incidents are single-vehicle collisions (likely far more than accidents caused by other factors), that stranding events were the next most common type of incident, and that distraction by a navigation device was significantly associated with more serious incidents. With regard to the roles of technology, we observed that missing road characteristics attributes (e.g. road surface types and current condition) had a substantial effect, as did the failure to correctly infer routing preferences (among a series of other factors).

The implications for research and design that emerge from our findings span the spectrum of "GeoHCI" topical domains. For example, we discuss how our results highlight the importance of (1) incorporating vehicle type and weather information into routing algorithms, (2) improving navigation guidance in the face of complex geographies, and (3) developing separate interfaces for tourists and locals. More generally, our results show that navigation devices can be more intelligent about safety than their current state-of-the-art: telling users to pay attention to their environment when the device is turned on. Blanket warnings like these are known to be ineffective in HCI [35], and our results show a path forward towards improved approaches.

In summary, this paper makes the following contributions:

1. We perform the first research that systematically characterizes catastrophic incidents associated with personal navigation technologies and the role that these technologies played in these incidents. We identify major themes in the incidents themselves and in the roles played by technology.
2. With the goal of preventing the patterns we identified in these catastrophic incidents from reoccurring, we outline a series of implications for research and design that can help us develop safer personal navigation technologies.

To further research on this topic, we are also releasing the core dataset we developed for this paper[1]. This dataset consists of the complete corpus of 158 news stories along with all the codes we applied to each story in the process described below. To make our findings more accessible, we are also releasing an interactive web map version of the corpus, which allows users to see the approximate location of each incident and further information about the incident[2].

**A Note on Terminology:** The subject of this research resulted in several terminological challenges. The core technologies of interest to this paper – GPS devices, SatNav devices, and mobile map applications like Google Maps and Apple Maps – are often referred to using the term "GPS". This term ignores the diverse positioning techniques (e.g. Wi-Fi positioning), routing algorithms, and cartography built into these technologies, so we felt it was imprecise to use this more casual language given the nature of this paper. As such, we use the term "personal navigation technology" (sometimes shortened to "navigation technology" or "navigation device"). Similarly, given the diversity of the types of incidents in our corpus, assigning this class of incidents a formal name was not straightforward. We chose the term "catastrophic incidents" in accordance with the "extremely unfortunate or unsuccessful" definition of "catastrophic" [50].

## RELATED WORK

This work's core motivation primarily emerges from two areas in the "GeoHCI" literature: (1) work that has examined the use of personal navigation technologies in standard scenarios and (2) research that has looked at the long-term behavioral and cognitive effects of using these technologies.

### Navigation Technologies in Standard Scenarios

Researchers began to investigate HCI issues associated with in-car navigation systems almost as soon as these technologies were first commercialized [10,11,48]. This thread of research covers a diverse set of topics including attention demands [11,23,48], cartography [27,33,42], different modes of output [9,21] and age-related variation [2], all with a focus on *everyday usage scenarios*. For instance, Kun et al. [23] conducted a lab simulation study and found that graphical GPS interfaces distracted users from the primary task of driving. Medenica et al. [33] coupled augmented reality with in-car GPS navigators and showed that this combination reduced drivers' distractions. Jensen et

1 The dataset can be downloaded here: https://goo.gl/8vE14V

2 The interactive map is available here: https://goo.gl/jlQ8S4

al. [21] compared different interaction modes of in-car GPS navigators and concluded that the combination of audio-visual output is preferred by drivers, but did not significantly reduce device-related distractions.

The projects in this research thread that most directly motivated our work are those of Hipp et al. [18] and Brown and Laurier [6]. Both studies considered the "troubles" drivers encountered with in-car GPS devices in typical driving situations. Hipp et al. [18] conducted a traditional user interface evaluation to compare the performances of different types of in-car navigation systems on the same route. They identified unexpressed routing preferences, failure to understand intentional detours from planned routes, and the lack of real-time traffic information as the common interaction weakness of commercial navigators (with the latter now being fixed in most modern navigation technologies). Brown and Laurier [7] carried out an interaction analysis in which they observed and interviewed drivers about their daily uses of in-car GPS to understand their navigation practices. They outlined five types of "normal troubles" of using in-car GPS navigators in everyday driving: destination, routing, maps and sensors, timing of instructions and inflexibility of the technology.

This work is distinguished from that above in that instead of studying the use of personal navigation technologies in standard scenarios, we focus on catastrophic incidents that involved these technologies. Some of the roles that these technologies play in catastrophic incidents are similar to those identified in the literature on standard scenarios, and other roles are new to the literature (as are the resulting design implications). We discuss the relationship between our findings and the findings from prior work in detail below.

### Long-term Impact of Navigation Technology Use

Another class of relevant research focuses on understanding the behavioral and cognitive changes produced by personal navigation technologies. For instance, Leshed et al. [28] conducted an ethnography-based study and showed that drivers using GPS-based navigation technologies are disengaged from their surrounding environment. Aporta and Higgs [3] examined the long-term impact of navigation technology at a larger scale, arguing that the adoption of navigation technologies has alienated many Inuit hunters from the traditional wayfinding skills they have depended on for thousands of years. Other studies have looked at the cognitive impact of navigation systems. For instance, Gardony et la. [13] conducted a lab-based simulation study and demonstrated that these devices may impair users' ability to record information about the environment and their spatial orientation. The findings of this line of work inform this paper's research and design implications, specifically those related to the multifaceted relationships between a navigation technology, its user, and the environment.

## METHODS

Although catastrophic incidents associated with personal navigation technologies are sufficiently noteworthy to have been given a moniker – "Death by GPS" – no authoritative dataset of these incidents exists. The high stakes of these incidents make them worthy of study, but the lack of available data and relative rarity of these incidents make it difficult to analyze them. Additionally, lab experiments or other simulations are not currently well-suited to this research area.

Fortunately, the domain of public health has significant experience studying phenomena with the same core properties as "Death by GPS" incidents, i.e. relatively rare phenomena of media interest for which no authoritative dataset is available and for which simulations are not currently tractable. Specifically, to examine these phenomena, researchers in this domain have followed a two-step pipeline: (1) build a corpus of news stories describing these incidents and (2) analyze the corpus using expert-led qualitative coding techniques. For example, in the absence of a national surveillance system for homicide-suicide in the United States, Malphurs and Cohen [31] collected and coded related news articles from 191 national newspapers to identify the number and subtypes of such incidents. This approach of relying on newspapers to summarize the characteristics of homicide-suicide incidents has also been applied in the Netherlands [29] and Italy [40]. Similarly, to study the collisions between wheelchairs and motor vehicles, a type of accident that is not distinguished in police reports, LaBan and Nabity [24] gathered 107 news articles using LexisNexis. They analyzed this corpus to understand gender incidence ratios, proportion of different types of motor vehicles, the time of incidents, and other characteristics of these incidents.

In this paper, we adopt this approach from the public health literature. To do so, we first verified that no relevant authoritative dataset exists by contacting several local police departments and national agencies, including the Minneapolis Police Department (USA), the Aachen Police Department (Germany), National Transportation Safety Board (USA) and National Highway Traffic Safety Administration (USA). We then implemented the pipeline from public health, using the process described in more detail below.

### Phase 1: Corpus Development

One of the key challenges in the public health-based approach is gathering the corpus of news articles. Most prior work has relied on one of two methods: (1) an exhaustive search in the local newspaper of a specific study site (e.g. [5,38]) or (2) unstructured but extensive querying of news search engines (e.g. [24,31]). Since our work is not well-suited to a specific study site, we implemented a more robust version of the latter approach using best practices from communication studies for sampling news stories with minimal bias [25,44].

The first step in this minimal bias sampling approach involves leveraging prior research in this space (i.e. the literature covered in the Related Work section) to seed a set of keywords, which is then grown using a variety of structured strategies (e.g. synonym generation). These keywords are then used to iteratively query a news database (in our case LexisNexis), with the set of keywords refined at each step. Achieving acceptable precision for one's keywords is particularly important given that these databases often have strict limits on the total number of news stories that can be returned for a given query (e.g. LexisNexis's is set to 1000 stories). We were able to achieve a precision of 40.8%, which is within acceptable parameters [44]. This left us with 408 articles that were related to catastrophic incidents associated with personal navigation technologies. We note that we restricted our search to stories published in 2010 or later to ensure that our findings are relevant to modern personal navigation technologies (e.g. smartphone map apps) rather than early-generation devices. Additionally, due to language constraints with respect to the database and the coders, we only searched for stories written in English, a subject we cover in more detail in the limitation section.

Two challenges remained before we could begin the next stage of the pipeline. First, many of the articles were opinion columns about the "Death by GPS" phenomenon and did not describe specific incidents. Second, some incidents were described by two different journalists in two different publications. To remove these articles from our dataset, two researchers conducted an exhaustive search, reading each article and evaluating its validity for our study and matching duplicates (we kept the more detailed of any two stories on the same incident; disagreements were resolved through discussion).

In the end, we were left with a corpus that contains 158 news stories, each describing a unique catastrophic incident associated with personal navigation technologies. For replication purposes and for researchers who may want to apply this method in other contexts, we have included additional detail about how we implemented our corpus-building procedure in the documentation of our coded dataset. We also discuss the one minor change we had to make to the standard procedure to adapt it to the goals of our research project: we could not simply use the keywords from prior research on interaction with navigation technologies because these only focused on standard scenarios. As such, we used a slightly more iterative keyword generation method in which researchers identified keywords from small samples of actual relevant news stories.

### Phase 2: Expert-led Coding

The second stage of the public health pipeline involves employing a relatively standard qualitative coding procedure with an important exception: coders are domain experts. This expertise enables coders to map properties of incidents reported in news articles to pre-existing topics in the literature of interest, or to new challenges when relevant. In our case, our two coders (members of our research team) had extensive expertise in both geography and HCI, the two fields most associated with our research questions. More specifically, each coder had both a Masters' degree in geography or geoinformatics and a Masters' degree in computer science (with a focus on HCI).

The specifics of the coding process were as follows: using a small seed corpus, knowledge of our research goals, and expertise in the research domain, our coders jointly established a series of coding dimensions. Next, using a random sample of 10 articles, the coders jointly developed a list of codes for each dimension and developed a corresponding codebook (this is included in our dataset). Both coders then evaluated a set of 40 overlapping articles to assess each dimension for interrater reliability. Importantly, when it was not possible to assess an article for a particular coding dimension, coders left the value blank.

The Cohen's Kappa of coders' results on all dimensions ranged from 0.69 to 0.95, which indicates "substantial agreement" [26]. Of particular note, we achieved a Cohen's Kappa of 0.79 for the *Technological Cause* dimension, which is the basis for a set of key findings below. As the Cohen's Kappa was sufficiently high for all dimensions, coders evaluated the remaining articles on an individual basis.

Beyond *Technological Cause*, other major coding dimensions that were considered included the *Seriousness* of the incident (e.g. Was death involved?), the *Incident Type* (e.g. Was it a single-vehicle collision? Did a vehicle get stranded?), *Weather*, *Road Surface* (e.g. Was it on a dirt road or a paved road?), whether *Distraction* was explicitly noted as an issue in the article and whether the driver was a *Local Driver* or Non-local Driver to the area of the incident. A complete list of dimensions and their corresponding specific codes is included in our public dataset. For the major coding dimensions, coders were able to assign codes for over 90% of incidents with the exception of *Local Driver,* in which 37% of incidents could not be coded.

### Interpretation of Results

As described above, there is a consensus (e.g. [22,24,29,31,38,40]) in the public health literature that when no authoritative data is available, the news article-based pipeline we employ here can provide valuable early insight about a phenomenon of interest. However, news article-derived data has its share of limitations, as is the case with many datasets considered in public health (e.g. even authoritative crime datasets have been criticized for potentially strong racial biases [39], an issue the computing community has been facing in association with predictive policing technologies [20]). To the best of our knowledge, our use of news article-derived data is novel to the HCI literature. As such, we believe that highlighting the known limitations of this type of data early in the paper is important so that our results can be interpreted in proper context.

The most significant limitation of news article-derived data is a risk of "newsworthiness" bias, or an overrepresentation of incidents that are in alignment with the incentive structures of news organizations. While at least one study has found no such bias (e.g. [38]), others have found newsworthiness bias to manifest as an overrepresentation of (1) accidental incidents (e.g. fewer suicides, more unusual events) or (2) more fatal incidents (e.g. more murders, fewer assaults) [12]. All incidents that we examine are accidental in nature, making the accidental bias less relevant [12,38]. However, a potential bias towards fatal incidents is important to consider when examining our results below.

To minimize further risk of bias, we employ robust statistical tests when making comparisons between types of incidents. In most cases, we are able to simply use Pearson's Chi-squared test of independence. However, in circumstances where the assumptions of Chi-squared distribution are violated due to relatively small sample size, we used a likelihood ratio G test of independence, a best practice suggested by [1,32]. All $p$-values reported in the paper have been subject to Bonferroni correction.

Newsworthiness bias mainly affects proportional results (i.e. comparisons between incident types), which are a small percentage of the results we present below. The bulk of our results are either qualitative descriptions of incidents or absolute values (e.g. raw counts of incidents of certain types). Our absolute results should be interpreted in the context of a limited understanding of the size of the incident population, i.e. we do not know what share of catastrophic incidents associated with personal navigation technologies are included in our news corpus. However, even if the incidents in our sample are close to the entire population, the aggregate devastation to blood and treasure of just these incidents make them worthy of analysis and discussion in the HCI literature, which does not often examine such high-cost interactions with technology. In order to add additional context and further this discussion, we provide qualitative descriptions of incidents wherever space allows.

## RESULTS

In this section, we provide an overview of the major results that emerged from our coding process. In doing so, we seek to address our first research goal: characterizing patterns in catastrophic incidents associated with personal navigation technologies. We organize our thematic findings into two groups (1) themes in the basic properties of these incidents and (2) themes in the technological causes of these incidents. We discuss each group of findings in turn below.

### Basic Properties

#### *Many People Have Died in Incidents Associated with Personal Navigation Technologies*

Table 1 shows the results of our coding for the *Seriousness* of the incidents with respect to human and financial cost. Clear in Table 1 is that navigation technologies have been associated with some truly tragic events: our corpus describes the deaths of 52 people in total, including two children. These deaths occurred across 45 incidents, or 28% of our corpus. Additionally, our corpus contains 23 incidents (15%) that resulted in significant bodily harm, but not death.

| **Seriousness of Incidents** | **#** | **%** |
|---|---|---|
| Major (deaths) | 44 | 28% |
| Major (injuries) | 23 | 15% |
| Medium (e.g. property damage, legal consequences) | 52 | 33% |
| Low (e.g. significant inconvenience) | 39 | 25% |

**Table 1. Distribution of the *Seriousness* of incidents.**

Although the proportion of fatal incidents in our corpus may be exaggerated due to the aforementioned newsworthiness bias, the absolute number of deaths (and injuries) associated with navigation technologies that we have identified is alarming. GPS devices, mobile maps, and other navigation technologies provide us with tremendous benefits, but these results indicate that they also have a set of costs that had not yet been systematically enumerated. These results also highlight the importance of better understanding catastrophic incidents like those studied here, as well as using this understanding to design safer technologies.

Table 1 also shows that "Death by GPS" is not the ideal term to describe incidents associated with navigation technologies that have serious implications. Over 50% of the incidents in our corpus did not involve death or significant injury, with the damage in these cases being primarily of a financial or other nature. Examples of these incidents include a group of skiers who intended to go to La Plagne, a famous ski resort in the Alps, but ended up arriving at Plagne, a town in southern France that is 715 km away (article #46[3]). Another example involved five men who drove onto a nuclear power plant's property at the behest of their navigation device and were suspected of terrorism (article #95).

#### *The Most Common Incident Type is a Single-Vehicle Crash, but There is Substantial Incident Type Diversity*

Table 2 depicts the results of our coding for *Incident Type* and shows that the most common type of incident in our corpus is car crashes. However, the table also shows that crashes are far from the only type of incident we encountered. For instance, almost 20% of incidents resulted in cars being stranded in very rural areas and over 15% involved people going on substantial detours. We were also surprised by the number of reports (7) of people driving on the wrong side of the road for an extended distance. Such examples include a person who drove 48km on the wrong side of a highway after following her device's instructions to enter the wrong freeway ramp (article #90) and a 37-year-old man who was caught driving the wrong way on an Australian

[3] News article numbers refer to the index in our released dataset.

| Types of Incidents | # (%) |
|---|---|
| Trespass (violate space usage rules) | 5 (3%) |
| Wrong way (opposite side) | 7 (4%) |
| Detour (e.g. wrong address) | 25 (16%) |
| Stranded/stuck (e.g. in the wildness, on railroad tracks) | 31 (20%) |
| Crashes | 90 (57%) |
| Crashes with pedestrians/bikes | 13 (8%) |
| Crashes with vehicles | 26 (17%) |
| Single-vehicle collisions | 51 (32%) |

**Table 2. Distribution of *Incident Types*.**

highway for more than 10 km and attributed the error to his navigation device (article #12).

In Table 2, we also show subtypes of the Crashes incident type. We found that single-vehicle collisions comprised the majority of crashes (51 cases, 32% of overall incidents), with crashes with other vehicles (26 cases, 17%) and crashes with pedestrians and bikes (13 cases, 8%) making up the remainder of crash incidents. To understand single-vehicle collisions in more detail, we did an additional round of coding to identify more detailed themes (this was done by a single expert coder). Here we found that vehicles colliding with buildings, walls, and guardrails due to excessively narrow roads were the most common type of single-vehicle incident. Crashing with low overhead bridges is another common occurrence in our corpus, with a diverse array of other objects in the environment being the subject of the remainder of the single-car crashes.

#### *Personal Navigation Technology-related Crashes Appear to Be Proportionally Different Than Typical Crashes*

To put the above results in context, we utilized The National Automotive Sampling System General Estimates System (NASS GES) dataset from the U.S. National Highway Traffic Safety Administration [49]. The NASS GES dataset contains a representative sample of vehicle crashes of all types as reported by police. While not directly comparable to our corpus, the NASS GES can provide a sense of whether personal navigation technology-related crashes are distributionally similar to the population of car crashes, or whether the role played by navigation technology manifests in different types of crash outcomes.

Our results suggest that the latter is the case: crashes associated with personal navigation technologies appear to be different in type relative to typical crashes. For instance, only 15% of car crashes in the NASS GES dataset are single-vehicle collisions, whereas the same type accounts for 57% of crashes in our corpus (Table 2). Moreover, crashes associated with building/walls/guardrails and overhead bridges are much less common in the NASS GES dataset, comprising less than 2% of crashes overall, while in our corpus they account for 42% of all crashes. Among other implications, this result provides further evidence that simply adopting standard recommendations from traditional traffic safety research will not be able to address the safety concerns associated with personal navigation technologies.

#### *Unfamiliarity with One's Surroundings Plays a Key Role*

A substantial percentage of the incidents in our corpus occurred when users of personal navigation technologies were outside of their home region. Specifically, 78% percent of the incidents involved non-locals and only 22% percent involved locals. Some examples of incidents involving non-locals include one story in which a person drove her car into a swamp (article #23). The driver was quoted as saying "This was the road it told me to take ... I don't know the area at all, so I just thought it was okay". Another incident consisted of a driver hitting and killing a pedestrian, with the corresponding news article reporting that "the driver was unfamiliar with the area and was adjusting her GPS navigational system" (article #71).

While the use of navigation technologies likely increases outside of one's home region, this result does suggest that user interfaces for navigation technologies may want to encourage more caution and support users in different ways when they are in their home region and when they are traveling. We discuss these implications for design in more detail below.

#### *Distraction Leads to More Serious Incidents*

We identified a significant association between our *Distraction* coding dimension and our *Seriousness* dimension, with distraction leading to many deadly incidents ($\chi^2(2) = 19.2,\ p < .05$). Examining the 21 deadly incidents that involved distraction in more detail, we found that in five cases, people were using non-critical features of their navigation device. For instance, a driver killed a cyclist while "using the zoom-in function" (article #33) and another driver from Springfield injured a bicyclist while "looking for place to eat on GPS" (article #40).

#### *Stranding Risk Increases with Dirt Roads, Bad Weather, and Especially Both at the Same Time*

We observed significant associations between our *Road Surface* coding dimension and our *Incident Type* dimension. In particular, if vehicles were traveling on a dirt road, there were more than the expected number of stranding incidents ($G^2(12) = 53.0,\ p < .05$). This was especially the case when weather was a factor. Examples include a medical student from Quebec who followed GPS and got stranded on a logging road for three days in the snow (article #4) and a British couple and their children who were stranded for four days on an unsealed road that was made muddy by torrential rain (article #115). Interestingly, the latter family thought that their in-car GPS device was suggesting a significant shortcut and followed its instructions as a result, a point we return to later.

More generally, we found significant interaction between disaster type dimension and the weather dimension ($G^2(4) = 21.1,\ p < .05$). Specifically, there are more than the expected

| Technological Causes | # (%) |
|---|---|
| Missing or incorrect geographic objects | 5 (4%) |
| Geocoding (i.e. associating toponym and its coordinates) | 7 (6%) |
| Incorrect toponym disambiguation (i.e. select similar but wrong destination) | 8 (7%) |
| Instructions/visualization | 18 (16%) |
| Non-transparent/wrong route preference | 18 (16%) |
| Missing or incorrect attributes | 64 (53%) |
| Physical characteristics of the road (e.g. road surface, road widths) | 30 (25%) |
| Clearance height | 17 (14%) |
| Traffic rules (e.g. no left turn) | 5 (4%) |
| Temporary blockage | 3 (3%) |
| Geopolitical boundary (e.g. country border) | 2 (2%) |
| Private area | 2 (2%) |
| Ferry line as road | 3 (3%) |
| Bridge limitation | 2 (2%) |

**Table 3. Distribution of *Technological Cause*. Note: The # does not add up to 158 because coders did not enter a code when there was not enough information in given news story to make a certain type of assessment.**

number of stranding incidents under severe weather, as one might anticipate.

## Technological Causes

Table 3 shows the results of our coders assessing each article for its *Technological Cause*. In this section, we discuss the themes in the distribution of these results, as well as the findings from a more detailed coding that we conducted to understand important trends.

### *Attributes that are Missing or Incorrect Are a Major Problem*

Geographic information, like that which is used in routing for personal navigation technologies, consists of two components: spatial information and attributes of that spatial information [14]. Broadly speaking, in a routing context, the spatial information is the location of a road and the attributes consist of key properties of the road (e.g. the speed limit).

Our results in Table 3 suggest that missing and incorrect attributes play a major role in the catastrophic incidents in our corpus, being in part responsible for 64 (53%) of these incidents. To better understand the types of attributes involved, one expert conducted a second round of coding to determine the types of attributes that were most often missing or incorrect and the results are also included in Table 3. The physical characteristics of the road (e.g. width, surface) (30 incidents) and clearance height (17 incidents) were by far the most common type of attributes that were missing or incorrect. Indeed, stories about routing algorithms neglecting the road characteristics and the heights of overpasses are pervasive in our corpus. For example, as noted above, failure to incorporate road surface information led multiple sedans to be stranded on unpaved roads (often in a very dangerous fashion) (e.g. article #4, #115) and multiple trucks ran into serious trouble due to low-clearance roads (e.g. article #6, #34, #36). Indeed, we found trucks were more susceptible to suffer from attribute related issues due to this problem as evidenced by the significant interaction between our *Vehicle Type* coding dimension and the *Technological Cause* dimension ( $G^2(15) = 67.4$, $p < .05$).

Another theme present in the attribute types in Table 3 is the notion of "space usage rules" (SURs) [41], or regulations associated with the use of a certain area (in this case, a road). For instance, in one incident, a truck that traveled on truck-prohibited road killed a father and a daughter in a sedan (article #27). In another, an in-car GPS device guided a driver up a private driveway, and the driver ended up in a physical confrontation with the owners of the property (article #102).

### *Cartographic and Audio Instructions Are Not Capable of Handling Complex Geographic Contexts*

Table 3 shows that almost 18 incidents involved an issue with routing guidance, either in visual (cartographic) or audio form. Past work on the use of GPS devices in standard scenarios identified that excessive instructions are a significant problem with GPS usability [2,7]. While we did observe this problem in our corpus, many of the incidents given this code by our experts related to a different issue: the inability of the personal navigation technology to help drivers navigate *complex geographic contexts*.

For example, in one story in our corpus, a person who was driving at night was faced with a freeway on-ramp that was immediately parallel to a railroad track (article #146). Figure 1 shows a Street View image of the exact location of the incident. When the driver's navigation device asked him to turn right, the driver turned onto the railroad tracks as the instructions were ambiguous. Ten kilometers later, the driver's car was destroyed by an oncoming train, but fortunately the driver survived by jumping out of the car. Similarly, article #66 tells a tragic story in which a bicyclist was hit by a driver who ignored a "Yield" sign at a non-typical intersection because the driver's navigation device screen simply instructed her to "go straight". Wrong-way driving was particularly (and significantly; $G^2(24) = 100.1$, $p < .05$ ) associated with cartographic and navigation instruction issues, and complex geographies were common in these cases. For instance, one report in our corpus (article #39) describes the story of a driver who followed her navigation device's instructions to "take the first left turn" at a roundabout. However, the actual first left turn (not the first *legal* left turn) was the exit ramp of a freeway, and the driver – who was on the road at night – entered the freeway driving in the wrong direction. This driver sadly lost her life.

### *Standard Scenarios versus Catastrophic Incidents*

As noted above, past work has done a rigorous job of identifying and categorizing problems encountered by users

**Figure 1. A Google Street View image depicting the complex geography of the location of the incident in article #146.**

of personal navigation technologies in standard usage scenarios. While the issues discussed above have not been highlighted in prior work, one additional contribution of the results in Table 3 is to add gravity to many of the previously-identified issues. For instance, in a study of challenges encountered in standard GPS device usage, Brown and Laurier [7] found that route preferences, out-of-date spatial data, the timing of navigation guidance, and positioning errors were key sources of user frustration. Some of these issues appear in Table 3, meaning that they were in part responsible for a number of catastrophic incidents in addition to more everyday usability issues.

Of particular note are Brown and Laurier's findings with respect to route preference. Route preference issues played a role in 18 (16%) of the news stories in our corpus, indicating they are a significant issue in catastrophic incidents as well as everyday usage scenarios. However, the route selection issues present in our corpus are of a substantially different character than those identified by Brown and Laurier. Specifically, while participants in Brown and Laurier's study wanted more route choice, people in our corpus were given too many choices (i.e. at least one was dangerous). For example, in one incident a Canadian couple got lost in rural Nevada after selecting the "shortest path" route option suggested by their navigation device, which included a little-maintained road. They were stranded in Nevada for 49 days, during which time the husband sadly lost his life (article #9). We return to this case and the issue of strict "shortest path" routing and route selection in the implications section.

With respect to prior work, it is also interesting to examine Table 3 for what is not common or present at all in our corpus. It appears that some issues with everyday use of navigation technologies do not play a role in catastrophic incidents associated with these technologies. For instance, positioning inaccuracies and the lack of adaptability to intentional "detours" were the sources of major usability challenges in the work of Brown and Laurier. However, neither appeared in our corpus. Similarly, missing spatial data was not a major issue in our corpus – it played a role in only 5 (4%) of incidents – but has been identified as a significant issue in standard usage scenarios. For catastrophic incidents, the issue appears to be attributes rather than the spatial data itself, a subject we discuss immediately below.

## IMPLICATIONS FOR RESEARCH AND DESIGN

In this section, we turn our attention to our second research goal: helping to identify solutions to the problems we found in our results section by enumerating a series of implications for both research and design. Some of these implications suggest improvements to the design of existing systems, while other present important new challenges for the GeoHCI research community. We have organized these implications into two high-level categories corresponding to two broad areas of the GeoHCI research space: implications related to *spatial computing* (e.g. routing algorithms, missing attributes) and implications related *user interaction* issues.

### Spatial Computing Implications

#### *Geometries without Attributes Can Be Dangerous*

A major finding above is that missing attributes play a substantial role in the catastrophic incidents in our corpus. This suggests that road network geometries may be "getting ahead" of the corresponding attributes. That is, data providers are adding road segments to their networks faster than they are adding the attributes to those segments that are necessary to facilitate safe routing.

These results suggest that data providers may not want to integrate road segments into their networks unless those segments have high-quality data for a core set of attributes. Based on our findings, these attributes should include the type of the road (e.g. dirt, asphalt) and the clearance height of the road (as defined by any overpasses, tunnels, and other obstacles) at minimum.

#### *Incorporate Vehicle Type into Routing Decisions*

Even when high-quality attributes are included, however, they must be used intelligently by routing algorithms. Returning to Table 3, a key theme emerges in this respect: many of the incidents included in this table could have been prevented if routing algorithms can understand the limitations of the vehicle that they are routing. For instance, it is often not safe for sedans to drive down rough country roads, and trucks should not drive down roads with low clearance heights. Coupled with good coverage of attributes, incorporating vehicle type information would be a straightforward and effective way to maintain good coverage of possible routes (e.g. allowing SUVs to drive down rough country roads), while at the same time increasing safety.

#### *Extend Space Usage Rule Mapping Efforts to Road Networks*

We identified that the lack of space usage rules (i.e. usage regulations) is a common missing attribute associated with the catastrophic incidents in our corpus. Space usage rules (SURs) have been a topic of growing interest in the GeoHCI research community in the past few years (e.g. [19,41,43]), but this literature has focused on mapping rules associated with regions rather than roads. For example, a common research challenge in SUR mapping is identifying regions in which smoking is legal or illegal [41].

Our research suggests that more effort should be spent on the identification of SURs for road networks. In particular, improving data related to the maximum clearance of roads, whether roads are public or private, and improved recognition of traffic rules are particularly important. Fortunately, unlike many SUR mapping challenges that require multifaceted approaches (e.g. natural language processing, crowdsourcing), it is likely that much of the work here can be done using computer vision (CV) approaches. The automated detection of traffic rules in this fashion is already underway [4]. It is likely that private property signs would present unique challenges for CV algorithms due to their diversity, but this is a contained problem that can likely be at least partially addressed with current state-of-the-art CV techniques.

#### *The Weather Matters When Routing*

Our results suggest that routing algorithms should consider weather information when generating routes, and should do so in concert with vehicle type information. A substantial number of the stranding incidents in our corpus would have been avoided with relatively straightforward weather- and vehicle-aware routing approaches. For instance, if it has rained 20 centimeters in the past day, routing algorithms should not send drivers of sedans down dirt roads. Similarly, if it has snowed 20 centimeters and it has stayed below freezing, routing algorithms should recommend that sedan drivers stick to main thoroughfares, which are plowed more quickly and more often (and should perhaps consider increasingly available information in many cities about which roads have been plowed since the last major snow).

#### *The Downsides of Map Matching*

We observed in our corpus that map matching techniques [15] can backfire. These techniques are designed to mitigate GPS noise by "snapping" vehicle locations to the closest road network geometry. However, they were likely involved in the three incidents in which a person drove on a train track parallel to a road (article #17, #32, #116) and also a few incidents in which people drove on the wrong side of the divided road (e.g. article #12, #90) (all cases happened in evening). In these cases, map matching algorithms likely "snapped" the driver's position to the nearest or the correct side of the road, making the driver believe that they were on right track (which may be difficult to assess at night).

Although more work is needed to understand this issue in detail, one potential improvement is to make map matching algorithms more error-sensitive in situations in which the distance between geometries is smaller than the error tolerance. Specifically, when an algorithm notices that there are multiple parallel linear geometries (e.g. a divided highway or a railroad parallel to a road), it can reduce the tolerance of its map matching radius. When observing a small, persistent mismatch for a short period, GPS devices could immediately prompt users about this mismatch and ask the driver to look at the environment to confirm that the vehicle is on a legal road.

### User Interaction Implications

#### *Route Preference Must Be Accompanied with Adequate Information to Make an Educated Choice*

Past research on the use of navigation technology in standard scenarios has advocated for providing greater route preference for users. Our results suggest that this preference must be accompanied with adequate information for users to make safe decisions. Current navigation devices often offer multiple routing preferences such as "fastest", "shortest", or "eco mode". At the very least, these technologies should warn users that certain choice may involve traversing unsafe territory, as was the case with the Canadian couple that chose the "shortest path" through Nevada without understanding the consequences of doing so.

As mentioned above, in addition to the usability problem of excessive instructions with bad timing found by previous studies, we identified a new type of guidance-related problem: instructions that are too simple for the spatial decisions that the user has to make. Two research challenges emerge from this issue: (1) automatically detecting complex geographies and (2) developing interfaces to better support users in these contexts. With regard to the first challenge, public crash datasets (e.g. [49]) can provide ground truth information to help develop regression models that assess the complexity of a routing context based on the topology of the surrounding road network (and likely other information, such as railroads). The second challenge might be at least partially addressed through the use of image-based navigation, i.e. by annotating Street View imagery with arrows and labels. Image-based navigation is known to have benefits over most other approaches [47] but needs to be updated frequently to reflect any potential changes in the environment..

#### *Local Mode and Non-Local Mode*

Our results suggest that non-local drivers are at substantially greater risk for catastrophic incidents associated with navigation technologies than local drivers. These findings advocate for the development of customized features for each of these populations, i.e. a "local mode" and a "non-local mode". For instance, neuroscience research has shown that more attention is required when driving in an unfamiliar environment [30]. As such, designers should investigate strategies for reducing interaction with drivers when drivers are outside their home region(s). Additionally, routing algorithms could provide non-local drivers with an "easiest" route that prioritizes highways and avoids complex intersections to minimize the turn-by-turn instructions and general information load. Similarly, GPS devices could disable non-essential functionality (e.g. searching for local restaurants) while in unfamiliar territory and re-enable those functions only when drivers come to a complete stop (or return to their home areas).

## DISCUSSION

In this paper, we provided the first characterization of the patterns in catastrophic incidents associated with the use of personal navigation technologies. We have also outlined a series of implications for design and research that emerge from these patterns. Below, we highlight several discussion points associated with this research.

First, it is interesting to reflect on the design implications in the context of automated vehicles. Some of the implications will clearly become moot if a human is not behind the wheel (e.g. those related to improved instructions), as will be the case for many of the core functionalities of navigation devices [6]. However, other implications may become significantly more important. For instance, adding attribute information to geometries, improving understanding of space usage rules and incorporating weather information will be critical to helping automated cars avoid dangerous navigation decisions. The same would likely apply in the nearer term with semi-automated cars, as recent work suggests that there may be excessive deference to automated routing approaches given the attentional challenges of partial automation [37]. Similarly, the research community has pointed out the need to keep drivers engaged when behind the wheel of a mostly-automated vehicle. Prompting users in the case of persistent map matching issues and engaging them in other difficult navigation-related tasks may be one way to accomplish this goal.

Second, the news article-based pipeline we use here may be able to help HCI researchers examine other difficult-to-study phenomena. As noted above, our public health-based approach is best suited to phenomena that share three properties: (1) no authoritative dataset is available, (2) instances are too rare to observe in large numbers in the wild and cannot be replicated in a lab setting, and (3) instances are frequently covered by journalists. Some additional HCI phenomena that share these properties include criminal events in the sharing economy and safety concerns related to location-based games like Pokémon GO [8]. To make it easier for researchers to employ our methodology, we have provided a step-by-step description of our approach in the documentation that is included with our coded dataset.

It is important to note that our coded dataset contains much more data than we could fully describe in this paper. While we have highlighted what we as researchers in the geographic HCI domain believe to be the most important themes in our results, other researchers may benefit from examining our data from a different perspective. One particularly interesting avenue of exploration that we are working to investigate is using the spatial locations of each incident (available in the dataset) to try to develop predictive models of the types of areas in which the use of navigation technologies might be particularly risky.

While we believe it is important for the HCI community to examine and learn from catastrophic incidents associated with the use of computing technologies, it is also important to put the relative incidence of these catastrophes in context. While we identified that GPS devices and related technologies played a role in at 158 catastrophic incidents involving 52 deaths, these technologies have also likely played a role in saving the lives of many people (e.g. guiding people to emergency resources, preventing people from getting lost). With this in mind, the design and research suggestions we make above are careful to be augmentative of existing navigation technology functionality rather than substantially altering current functionality.

### Limitations

In addition to the drawbacks of the news article-based pipeline discussed above, this paper is also subject to several additional limitations. For instance, while our incident corpus is the first agglomeration of its type of any scale, future work should seek to increase this size by either finding more news stories or collecting data on incidents that are not reported in the news. With respect to identifying unreported incidents, crowdsourcing has been proven effective for building databases of technology failures in the domain of aviation [51]. This may be an approach that is feasible in this domain as well. Similarly, a related limitation of our dataset is that it that 97% of our articles came from either the U.S., the U.K., Canada, New Zealand, or Australia (due to the focus on English articles). It is reasonable to assume that patterns in other countries might be different, and future work should examine these patterns.

The issue of survivor bias should also be considered. It is likely that navigation technologies have played a role in a significant number of deadly accidents for which there was no witness or exogenous information to identify the role of the technology (the 44 deadly incidents considered here had one or both of these). Interestingly, survivor bias could counteract the fatality bias discussed above.

## CONCLUSION

In this paper, we have extended prior work on user interaction with navigation technologies to consider catastrophic incidents associated with these technologies. We have characterized key patterns that exist in these incidents and enumerated implications for research and design that emerge from these patterns. This research increases our understanding of how the navigation technologies that we design cause serious harm, as well as provides a path towards developing safer navigation technologies.

## ACKNOWLEDGEMENTS

We would like to thank our colleagues in GroupLens and our anonymous reviewers for their feedback. This work was funded in part by the U.S. National Science Foundation (IIS-1421655, CAREER IIS-1552955) and by the Volkswagen Foundation through a Lichtenberg Professorship.

## REFERENCES

1. Alan Agresti. 1996. *An introduction to categorical data analysis*. Wiley New York.

2. Abdullah Al Mahmud, Omar Mubin, and Suleman Shahid. 2009. User experience with in-car GPS navigation systems: comparing the young and elderly drivers. 1. https://doi.org/10.1145/1613858.1613962
3. Claudio Aporta and Eric Higgs. 2005. Satellite Culture: Global Positioning Systems, Inuit Wayfinding, and the Need for a New Account of Technology. *Current Anthropology* 46, 5: 729–753. https://doi.org/10.1086/432651
4. Vahid Balali, Armin Ashouri Rad, and Mani Golparvar-Fard. 2015. Detection, classification, and mapping of U.S. traffic signs using google street view images for roadway inventory management. *Visualization in Engineering* 3, 1: 15. https://doi.org/10.1186/s40327-015-0027-1
5. J. Baullinger, L. Quan, E. Bennett, P. Cummings, and K. Williams. 2001. Use of Washington State newspapers for submersion injury surveillance. *Injury Prevention* 7, 4: 339–342. https://doi.org/10.1136/ip.7.4.339
6. David Beattie, Lynne Baillie, Martin Halvey, and Roderick McCall. 2015. Adapting SatNav to meet the demands of future automated vehicles. In *CHI 2015 Workshop on Experiencing Autonomous Vehicles: Crossing the Boundaries between a Drive and a Ride*. Retrieved June 14, 2016 from http://strathprints.strath.ac.uk/52245/
7. Barry Brown and Eric Laurier. 2012. The Normal Natural Troubles of Driving with GPS. In *Proceedings of the SIGCHI Conference on Human Factors in Computing Systems* (CHI '12), 1621–1630. https://doi.org/10.1145/2207676.2208285
8. Ashley Colley, Jacob Thebault-Spieker, Yilun Lin, Jonna Häkkilä, Nuno Nunes, Dirk Wenig, Kate Kuehl, Benjamin Fischman, Valentina Nisi, Nina Runge, Donald Degraen, Brent Hecht, and Johannes Schöning. 2017. The Geography of Pokémon GO: Beneficial and Problematic Effects on Places and Movement. In *Proceedings of the SIGCHI Conference on Human Factors in Computing Systems*.
9. P. Dalton, P. Agarwal, N. Fraenkel, J. Baichoo, and A. Masry. 2013. Driving with navigational instructions: Investigating user behaviour and performance. *Accident Analysis & Prevention* 50: 298–303. https://doi.org/10.1016/j.aap.2012.05.002
10. Thomas A. Dingus and Melissa C. Hulse. 1993. Some human factors design issues and recommendations for automobile navigation information systems. *Transportation Research Part C: Emerging Technologies* 1, 2: 119–131. https://doi.org/10.1016/0968-090X(93)90009-5
11. Thomas A. Dingus, Melissa C. Hulse, Jonathan F. Antin, and Walter W. Wierwille. 1989. Attentional demand requirements of an automobile moving-map navigation system. *Transportation Research Part A: General* 23, 4: 301–315. https://doi.org/10.1016/0191-2607(89)90013-7
12. Philip R. Fine, Chester S. Jones, J. Michael Wrigley, J. Scott Richards, and Matthew D. Rousculp. 1998. Are newspapers a viable source for intentional injury... *Southern Medical Journal* 91, 3: 234.
13. Aaron L. Gardony, Tad T. Brunyé, Caroline R. Mahoney, and Holly A. Taylor. 2013. How Navigational Aids Impair Spatial Memory: Evidence for Divided Attention. *Spatial Cognition & Computation* 13, 4: 319–350. https://doi.org/10.1080/13875868.2013.792821
14. Michael F. Goodchild. 2001. A Geographer Looks at Spatial Information Theory. In *Spatial Information Theory*, Daniel R. Montello (ed.). Springer Berlin Heidelberg, 1–13. https://doi.org/10.1007/3-540-45424-1_1
15. Joshua S. Greenfeld. 2002. Matching GPS observations to locations on a digital map. In *Transportation Research Board 81st Annual Meeting*.
16. Hilary Hanson. 2012. GPS Leads Japanese Tourists To Drive Into Australian Bay. *The Huffington Post*. Retrieved September 12, 2016 from http://www.huffingtonpost.com/2012/03/19/gps-tourists-australia_n_1363823.html
17. Brent Hecht, Johannes Schöning, Thomas Erickson, and Reid Priedhorsky. 2011. Geographic Human-computer Interaction. In *CHI '11 Extended Abstracts on Human Factors in Computing Systems* (CHI EA '11), 447–450. https://doi.org/10.1145/1979742.1979532
18. Markus Hipp, Florian Schaub, Frank Kargl, and Michael Weber. 2010. Interaction Weaknesses of Personal Navigation Devices. In *Proceedings of the 2Nd International Conference on Automotive User Interfaces and Interactive Vehicular Applications* (AutomotiveUI '10), 129–136. https://doi.org/10.1145/1969773.1969796
19. Konstantin Hopf, Florian Dageförde, and Diedrich Wolter. 2015. Identifying the Geographical Scope of Prohibition Signs. In *Spatial Information Theory*, Sara Irina Fabrikant, Martin Raubal, Michela Bertolotto, Clare Davies, Scott Freundschuh and Scott Bell (eds.). Springer International Publishing, 247–267. https://doi.org/10.1007/978-3-319-23374-1_12
20. White House. 2016. Big Data: A Report on Algorithmic Systems, Opportunity, and Civil Rights. *Washington, DC: Executive Office of the President, White House*.
21. Brit Susan Jensen, Mikael B. Skov, and Nissanthen Thiruravichandran. 2010. Studying Driver Attention and Behaviour for Three Configurations of GPS Navigation in Real Traffic Driving. In *Proceedings of the SIGCHI Conference on Human Factors in Computing Systems* (CHI '10), 1271–1280. https://doi.org/10.1145/1753326.1753517
22. John D. Kraemer and Connor S. Benton. 2015. Disparities in road crash mortality among pedestrians using wheelchairs in the USA: results of a capture–recapture analysis. *BMJ Open* 5, 11: e008396. https://doi.org/10.1136/bmjopen-2015-008396

23. Andrew L. Kun, Tim Paek, Željko Medenica, Nemanja Memarović, and Oskar Palinko. 2009. Glancing at Personal Navigation Devices Can Affect Driving: Experimental Results and Design Implications. In *Proceedings of the 1st International Conference on Automotive User Interfaces and Interactive Vehicular Applications* (AutomotiveUI '09), 129–136. https://doi.org/10.1145/1620509.1620534
24. Myron M. LaBan and Thomas S. Nabity. 2010. Traffic Collisions Between Electric Mobility Devices (Wheelchairs) and Motor Vehicles: Accidents, Hubris, or Self-destructive Behavior? *American Journal of Physical Medicine & Rehabilitation* 89, 7: 557–560. https://doi.org/10.1097/PHM.0b013e3181d8a346
25. Stephen Lacy, Brendan R. Watson, Daniel Riffe, and Jennette Lovejoy. 2015. Issues and Best Practices in Content Analysis. *Journalism & Mass Communication Quarterly*: 1077699015607338. https://doi.org/10.1177/1077699015607338
26. J. Richard Landis and Gary G. Koch. 1977. The Measurement of Observer Agreement for Categorical Data. *Biometrics* 33, 1: 159–174. https://doi.org/10.2307/2529310
27. Talia Lavie, Tal Oron-Gilad, and Joachim Meyer. 2011. Aesthetics and usability of in-vehicle navigation displays. *International Journal of Human-Computer Studies* 69, 1–2: 80–99. https://doi.org/10.1016/j.ijhcs.2010.10.002
28. Gilly Leshed, Theresa Velden, Oya Rieger, Blazej Kot, and Phoebe Sengers. 2008. In-car Gps Navigation: Engagement with and Disengagement from the Environment. In *Proceedings of the SIGCHI Conference on Human Factors in Computing Systems* (CHI '08), 1675–1684. https://doi.org/10.1145/1357054.1357316
29. M. C. A. Liem and F. Koenraadt. 2007. Homicide-suicide in the Netherlands: A study of newspaper reports, 1992 - 2005. *Journal of Forensic Psychiatry & Psychology* 18, 4: 482–493. https://doi.org/10.1080/14789940701491370
30. Mandy Mader, André Bresges, Reyhan Topal, Alexander Busse, Michael Forsting, and Elke R. Gizewski. 2009. Simulated car driving in fMRI—Cerebral activation patterns driving an unfamiliar and a familiar route. *Neuroscience Letters* 464, 3: 222–227. https://doi.org/10.1016/j.neulet.2009.08.056
31. Julie E. Malphurs and Donna Cohen. 2002. A newspaper surveillance study of homicide-suicide in the United States. *The American Journal of Forensic Medicine and Pathology* 23, 2: 142–148.
32. Mary L. McHugh. 2013. The Chi-square test of independence. *Biochemia Medica* 23, 2: 143–149. https://doi.org/10.11613/BM.2013.018
33. Zeljko Medenica, Andrew L. Kun, Tim Paek, and Oskar Palinko. 2011. Augmented Reality vs. Street Views: A Driving Simulator Study Comparing Two Emerging Navigation Aids. In *Proceedings of the 13th International Conference on Human Computer Interaction with Mobile Devices and Services* (MobileHCI '11), 265–274. https://doi.org/10.1145/2037373.2037414
34. Greg Milner. 2016. *Pinpoint: How GPS Is Changing Technology, Culture, and Our Minds*. W. W. Norton & Company.
35. Jakob Nielsen. 2001. Error message guidelines. *Nielsen Norman Group*: 06–24.
36. Donald A. Norman. 2013. *The Design of Everyday Things: Revised and Expanded Edition*. Basic Books.
37. Stephen M. Casner Norman Edwin L. Hutchins, Don. The Challenges of Partially Automated Driving. Retrieved December 21, 2016 from http://cacm.acm.org/magazines/2016/5/201592-the-challenges-of-partially-automated-driving/fulltext
38. David Y. Rainey and Carol W. Runyan. 1992. Newspapers: a source for injury surveillance? *American journal of public health* 82, 5: 745–746.
39. Robert M. Regoli and John D. Hewitt. 2008. *Exploring Criminal Justice*. Jones & Bartlett Learning.
40. Paolo Roma, Antonella Spacca, Maurizio Pompili, David Lester, Roberto Tatarelli, Paolo Girardi, and Stefano Ferracuti. 2012. The epidemiology of homicide–suicide in Italy: A newspaper study from 1985 to 2008. *Forensic Science International* 214, 1–3: e1–e5. https://doi.org/10.1016/j.forsciint.2011.06.022
41. Pavel Andreevich Samsonov, Xun Tang, Johannes Schöning, Werner Kuhn, and Brent Hecht. 2015. You Can'T Smoke Here: Towards Support for Space Usage Rules in Location-aware Technologies. In *Proceedings of the 33rd Annual ACM Conference on Human Factors in Computing Systems* (CHI '15), 971–974. https://doi.org/10.1145/2702123.2702269
42. Julia Schreiber. 2009. Bridging the gap between useful and aesthetic maps in car navigation systems. In *Proceedings of the 11th International Conference on Human-Computer Interaction with Mobile Devices and Services*, 51. Retrieved September 19, 2016 from http://dl.acm.org/citation.cfm?id=1613922
43. Marcus Soll, Philipp Naumann, Johannes Schöning, Pavel Samsonov, and Brent Hecht. 2016. Helping Computers Understand Geographically-Bound Activity Restrictions. 2442–2446. https://doi.org/10.1145/2858036.2858053
44. Jo Ellen Stryker, Ricardo J. Wray, Robert C. Hornik, and Itzik Yanovitzky. 2006. Validation of Database Search Terms for Content Analysis: The Case of Cancer News Coverage. *Journalism & Mass Communication Quarterly* 83, 2: 413–430. https://doi.org/10.1177/107769900608300212
45. By Bonnie Malkin in Sydney. 2010. Britons stranded in Australian Outback for four days after satnav error. Retrieved September 12, 2016 from http://www.telegraph.co.uk/news/worldnews/australiaandthepacific/australia/7925649/Britons-stranded-in-Australian-Outback-for-four-days-after-satnav-error.html

46. Bruno Waterfield. 2013. GPS failure leaves Belgian woman in Zagreb two days later. Retrieved September 12, 2016 from http://www.telegraph.co.uk/news/worldnews/europe/belgium/9798779/GPS-failure-leaves-Belgian-woman-in-Zagreb-two-days-later.html
47. Dirk Wenig, Alexander Steenbergen, Johannes Schöning, Brent Hecht, and Rainer Malaka. 2016. ScrollingHome: Bringing Image-based Indoor Navigation to Smartwatches. In *Proceedings of the 18th International Conference on Human-Computer Interaction with Mobile Devices and Services* (MobileHCI '16), 400–406. https://doi.org/10.1145/2935334.2935373
48. Walter W. Wierwille, Jonathan F. Antin, Thomas A. Dingus, and Melissa C. Hulse. 1988. Visual Attentional Demand of An In-car Navigation Display System. Retrieved September 13, 2016 from https://trid.trb.org/view.aspx?id=927088
49. *Traffic Safety Facts 2014: A Compilation of Motor Vehicle Crash Data from the Fatality Analysis Reporting System and the General Estimates System.* National Highway Traffic Safety Administration. Retrieved from https://crashstats.nhtsa.dot.gov/Api/Public/ViewPublication/812261
50. Definition of Catastrophic. Retrieved from https://www.google.com/search?q=catastrophic+incidents&ie=utf-8&oe=utf-8#q=catastrophic
51. *Aviation Safety Reporting System.* NASA. Retrieved from http://akama.arc.nasa.gov/ASRSDBOnline/QueryWizard Filter.aspx.

# The Effect of Population and "Structural" Biases on Social Media-based Algorithms – A Case Study in Geolocation Inference Across the Urban-Rural Spectrum

**Isaac Johnson*, Connor McMahon†, Johannes Schöning‡, Brent Hecht***
*Northwestern University, Evanston, USA
†GroupLens Research, University of Minnesota, Minneapolis, USA
‡University of Bremen, Bremen, Germany
isaacj@u.northwestern.edu, mcmahon250@umn.edu,
schoening@uni-bremen.de, bhecht@northwestern.edu

## ABSTRACT
Much research has shown that social media platforms have substantial population biases. However, very little is known about how these population biases affect the many algorithms that rely on social media data. Focusing on the case study of geolocation inference algorithms and their performance across the urban-rural spectrum, we establish that these algorithms exhibit significantly worse performance for underrepresented populations (i.e. rural users). We further establish that this finding is robust across both text- and network-based algorithm designs. However, we also show that some of this bias can be attributed to the design of algorithms themselves rather than population biases in the underlying data sources. For instance, in some cases, algorithms perform badly for rural users even when we substantially overcorrect for population biases by training exclusively on rural data. We discuss the implications of our findings for the design and study of social media-based algorithms.

### Author Keywords
Algorithmic accountability; geolocation inference; population bias; social media.

### ACM Classification Keywords
H.5.m. Information interfaces and presentation (e.g., HCI): Miscellaneous;

## INTRODUCTION
As social media adoption has increased dramatically, research that takes advantage of this publicly-available, real-time stream of information has also become quite prevalent. In addition to facilitating new discoveries about human behavior in the social sciences and related fields (e.g., [1,12,13]), social media has also been a major catalyst in the development of new intelligent algorithms. For instance, researchers have used social media to develop new recommender systems (e.g., [38,59]), summarize the character of cities (e.g., [9,66]), and infer the location of Internet users (e.g., [34,41,45]), among other applications (e.g., [4,30,49]).

Recently, concerns about population bias in social media have been the subject of much discussion (most notably in *Science* [55]). Social media population bias, or the notion that different demographic groups may participate in social media platforms at different rates, has been found to be endemic to most social media datasets. Much work has gone into quantifying and understanding these biases, with significant biases being found along gender (e.g., [51]), age (e.g., [39]), race (e.g., [46]), income (e.g., [44]), education (e.g., [39]), and urban/rural lines (e.g., [28]).

Many researchers who use social media to understand human behavior have recognized the importance of correcting for social media population biases in their studies (e.g., [14,55]). They have also begun the critical work of developing best practices for doing so (e.g., [55]). However, the same is not true in literature on social media-based algorithms: even though it has been hypothesized for several years that population bias would affect social media-based algorithms (e.g., [28,46]), little research has been done to investigate this hypothesis (let alone identify remediating measures).

The goal of this paper is to help address this gap in the literature. Since the space of social media-based algorithms and social media population biases is extensive, we initiated our exploration with a focused but important case study: examining the performance of Twitter geolocation inference algorithms across the U.S. urban-rural spectrum. Due to the rising import of geographic information, geolocation inference algorithms – usually focusing on Twitter data – have attracted widespread interest across computer science and related fields (e.g., [10,15,23,25,33,45,52]). The aim of these algorithms is to predict the location of a Twitter user or her tweets using implicit signals. This is typically done by examining the content of the user's tweets and/or the geographic configuration of her explicitly encoded social ties.


*CHI 2017*, May 06-11, 2017, Denver, CO, USA
ACM 978-1-4503-4655-9/17/05.
http://dx.doi.org/10.1145/3025453.3026015

Similarly, U.S. rural-urban biases in social media have also attracted a growing amount of attention in the literature (e.g., [22,28,31,67]). This is likely in part due to the relatively large effect sizes involved: people who live in rural areas often participate in social media at a fraction of the rate of their urban counterparts and contribute orders of magnitude less content. Twitter is no exception to this trend (e.g., [31,61,67]). The urban-rural population-bias effect sizes are of particular interest given the significant size of the rural population: over 46 million people live in rural counties in the United States (close to double the population of 18-24 year-olds) [36].

Rather than focusing on a single geolocation algorithm to assess the effect of urban/rural population bias on algorithm effectiveness, we study two well-known geolocation inference algorithms: that of Priedhorsky et al. [52] and that of Jurgens [33]. We chose these two algorithms because they span the range geolocation inference algorithm design, allowing us to more robustly evaluate the effect of population bias. Priedhorsky et al.'s and Jurgens' algorithms fundamentally differ in two key ways: methodological paradigm and problem definition. With respect to paradigm, Priedhorsky et al.'s algorithm is representative of text-based approaches to geolocation inference (e.g., [6,27,37,43,52,53]) while Jurgens' is representative of network-based approaches (e.g., [3,10,33,45,54]). Similarly, Priedhorsky et al.'s algorithm seeks to solve the "geolocate a tweet" version of the problem, while Jurgens' algorithm addresses the "geolocate a user" version of the problem.

As we will describe below, we find that regardless of methodological paradigm or problem definition, geolocation algorithms underperform for rural users. In some cases, the effect sizes are dramatic. For instance, the text-based algorithm is able to geolocate urban tweets within 100km of their true location at a rate 2.3x greater than is the case for rural tweets.

However, a major result in this paper is that population bias is not the only driver of population-variable accuracy in social media-based algorithms. Rather, we find evidence that design choices in social media-based algorithms can also have a powerful biasing effect. That is, our results suggest that algorithmic bias is a function to a large degree of both population bias in the underlying social media dataset and *structural bias* that arises from algorithmic design choices. We also observe early evidence that text-based algorithms may be more liable to structural bias than network-based algorithms. In particular, we found that when population bias was removed through balanced resampling and oversampling, our network-based algorithm showed much improved performance on rural users, but the same methods were less effective in our text-based algorithm.

This paper has several implications for those who develop and study social media-based algorithms. For instance, our research provides additional weight to calls (e.g., [57]) to consider the design of algorithms rather than just the output of these algorithms when evaluating intelligent technologies for bias. In other words, our results directly motivate further research on algorithmic design decisions that avoid structural bias. Moreover, as we will discuss, our results point to specific solutions to structural bias in the geographic algorithm domain. Similarly, our results also highlight the dangers of global evaluation metrics for social media-based algorithms, providing a data point that shows that these metrics can hide poor performance for certain populations and establish perverse incentives to reduce performance for these populations even further when they are minorities.

In addition to showing that both population and structural bias can result in uneven performance by social media algorithms, this research also makes more specific contributions to the large body of research on geolocation inference algorithms. Namely, by demonstrating that these algorithms' performance is geographically variable in a systemic fashion, we show that it is likely that these algorithms have introduced additional bias into the studies and systems that have used their output. This raises the stakes for quickly identifying solutions and establishing best practices. It also suggests that researchers who use these algorithms should be careful to audit their output as we have done here prior to incorporating them into their larger systems.

Finally, it is important to note before continuing that while we find important biases that are robust across two separate algorithms, this is a case study on Twitter geolocation inference rather than an exhaustive survey of population bias's effect on all social media-based algorithms. Given their import, identifying potential biases in social media-based algorithms is a serious matter, as is developing means of addressing them. However, because our findings our limited to a single algorithm family (albeit an important one), our findings should be interpreted as an important preliminary step in these directions rather than the definitive answer to the associated questions.

## RELATED WORK

This work builds on research in three main areas: 1) characterization of population bias in social media, 2) social media-based geolocation algorithms, and 3) the literature on algorithmic accountability. We discuss these areas and their relationship to our work below.

### Population Bias in Social Media

Population bias is a well-studied issue in social media. Since 2005, the Pew Research Center has conducted annual surveys of social media usage in the United States. These surveys [51] show that social media participation rates vary extensively across gender, race, education, socioeconomic status, and urban-rural lines.

Augmenting the Pew findings, many researchers have investigated this problem by analyzing the geographic distribution of posts across social media sites and making demographic inferences from census data or from users' self-reported information. The demographic dimension of analysis we choose for our study – the urban-rural spectrum – has been the focus of some of this work. For instance, Hecht and Stephens [28] studied Foursquare, Flickr, and Twitter and found a consistent pro-urban bias (e.g., there are 3.5 times more Twitter users per capita in urban areas than rural areas). Similarly, Malik et al. [44] demonstrated that there are higher densities of tweets in urban, young, and rich areas. Gilbert, Karahalios, and Sandvig [21] found substantial differences in behavior between urban and rural users in Myspace. Many other papers have studied population bias issues across other geographies, platforms, and demographics, and, to our best knowledge, some form of population bias has consistently appeared in all of this work.

A few researchers have attempted to explicitly account for population bias in their own studies. Culotta [14] demonstrated that tweet-based models of public health indicators saw improved performance when their Twitter dataset was balanced for race and gender by county. Landeiro and Culotta [37] examined how to control for shifts in the magnitude of population bias within input data to classification algorithms. Finally, Pavalanathan and Eisenstein [50] have explored how people of different ages and genders tweet differently and how this relates to performance in geolinguistic algorithms. They balanced their tweet samples based on the total population by county but did not find that this significantly impacted their algorithm.

We are motivated by the above work and the questions that it raises. While Culotta saw improved precision when controlling for specific population biases, Pavalanathan and Eisenstein did not when controlling for more general population density, but still found vast disparities in performance of the algorithm across age and gender. These divergent results raise the question of how algorithmic bias arises and is manifest in social media-based algorithms as well as the relationship between algorithmic bias and population bias in social media. Our results explain the conflicting findings in this motivating work by delineating the concept of structural bias and showing how it can counteract or exacerbate population bias. Moreover, by also examining network-based algorithms in our research, we are able to speak more broadly to social media-based algorithms in general and not just a single class of algorithms.

### Geolocation Inference Algorithms

A large portion of the research and applications associated with Twitter data has a geographic component. However, this research is limited by the fact that only 1-2% of tweets are geolocated [10]. As a result, geolocation inference algorithms for Twitter, which attempt to uncover tweet and user locations that have not been explicitly disclosed, have become a very common direction of study [18]. Similar algorithms have been developed for other social media platforms as well (e.g., Flickr [19] and Tumblr [11])

There are two main classes of Twitter geolocation inference algorithms [34]: text-based, which predict the location of a tweet based on its content, and network-based, which predict a home location for a user based on their connections to other users.

Text-based geolocation algorithms rely on the tendency for language usage to vary as a function of geography (e.g., [65]). By extracting lexical features and concepts local to an area from the text during a training phase (e.g., sports teams, regional vernacular, a town name), these algorithms can build models that predict the geographic location of a new tweet based on its content. These algorithms generally either attempt to model text features as an explicitly spatial process (e.g., [52,53,64]) or treat the geolocation problem as a classification problem among administrative units (e.g., cities) (e.g., [8,25,43]).

Network-based geolocation algorithms rely on the social network in which social media posts are typically embedded. In these algorithms, explicitly encoded network ties or user interactions are used to build an egocentric social network for the user whose location is desired. Any known locations of the user's neighbors are combined to predict the location of the user [34]. This approach leverages a fundamental principle in human geography that, in general, interaction decreases with distance (e.g., [24]), meaning that connected users are likely close geographically [3].

Though our goal is to probe algorithmic bias within social media-based algorithms in general, selecting geolocation algorithms as our case study has two additional benefits: both text-based (e.g., [6,27,37,43,52,53]) and network-based (e.g., [3,10,33,45,54]) geolocation inference have been a major area of interest in the past few years, and our work can help lead to more equal and effective approaches in the future. Second, because of this robust literature on both text- and network-based approaches, we are able to explore bias in social-media based algorithms that draw on two of the most prominent methodological paradigms, improving generalizability and affording cross-paradigmatic comparisons.

### Algorithmic Accountability

Our research builds on the growing literature on algorithmic accountability (e.g., [2,56,57]), in which algorithms are probed for discrimination or other societally undesirable outcomes. Our work extends the accountability literature to include well-known geolocation inference algorithms (and the rural-urban divide). Additionally, much of the algorithmic accountability literature has focused on detecting algorithmic bias when faced with a black-box system (e.g. [7,35,60,63]). Our research focuses on algorithms with a published description, open-source code, and accessible data, enabling us to investigate biases at a more detailed level, determine the potential causes of these biases with more certainty, and begin to learn how to mitigate these biases. In the discussion section, we highlight how our findings related to structural bias emphasize the importance of lower-level analyses (as per Sandvig et al. [57]) and open-source implementations in understanding and reducing algorithmic bias.

## METHODS AND DATA

In this section, we describe our two focus geolocation inference algorithms and the datasets they use in more detail. In general, our approach to working with these algorithms was to replicate the choices and approach taken in the corresponding papers. In the few cases when this was not possible, we deferred to other best practices in the geolocation literature as is explained below.

### Text-based Algorithm

We selected the text-based algorithm from Priedhorsky et al. [52] for our analysis. We chose this algorithm because it is representative of many text-based algorithms in its general approach (e.g., it calculates a geographic layer for each term and utilizes a standard set of Twitter text and metadata fields), has made an impact since it was published (e.g., [25]), and its source code has been made available by its authors[1], which minimizes the risk of implementation error and provides us with full control over the algorithm and its inputs.

The algorithm is trained on a set number of tweets with known locations and builds Gaussian mixture models (GMMs) for tokens in the text of the tweet, its user's time-zone, self-reported location field, and specified language. The GMMs capture the probability that a given token originated from an area based on the training data. A prediction for a given tweet is made by tokenizing it, weighting and combining the individual GMMs for each token in the tweet, and making a prediction based on the highest probability area in the resulting GMM.

### Network-based Algorithm

We selected the algorithm by Jurgens [33] for our network-based algorithm. We chose this algorithm because its performance is in line with other state-of-the-art approaches [34]. Additionally, like Priedhorsky et al.'s algorithm, code for Jurgens' algorithm has been provided by the author[2], minimizing implementation risk and allowing for direct manipulation.

Jurgens' algorithm builds a bi-directional mention network by generating an edge between two users only when both users have mentioned each other in a tweet. A mention occurs when a user includes another user's username in a tweet using the "@" notation (e.g., "President @barackobama will be speaking tonight"). Starting with a training set of users with known locations, Jurgens' algorithm iteratively propagates the location of the known users to any of their neighbors who have not been successfully located, inferring the location of a newly located user in each iteration as the median of their previously located neighbors. Jurgens repeats this process for five iterations and we do the same in our analyses.

### Social Media Datasets

We built our tweet dataset for our text-based algorithm following standard practices in the text-based geolocation inference community (e.g. [6,16,37]). More specifically, we utilized the Twitter Streaming API with a bounding box configured to the contiguous United States, which, like many geographic studies of geotagged content in the U.S. (e.g. [39,47])[3], was the geographic extent of our analyses. In line with prior work (e.g. [6,16,37]), we left open our tweet collector for one month. Only tweets with coordinates in the contiguous United States were retained, resulting in a dataset of 51.2 million tweets from 1.6 million unique users from October 2014. All of these tweets are explicitly geotagged with the latitude-longitude coordinates from where the tweet originated, which is necessary to provide ground truth of the algorithm. One important exception to our approach relative to that of Priedhorksy et al. was that we used geographically bounded version of the Streaming API rather than the random Streaming API. We made this exception for a simple reason: we required a much larger dataset in our study region in order to have sufficient data in rural areas for our experiments.

Network-based approaches utilize different techniques to collect data than text models and, as such, it was important to collect a separate dataset to be in accordance with standard practices in the network-based domain. To gather data for our network model, we adopted the methodology used by Jurgens et al. [34], which involved building a mention network from a dataset of randomly collected tweets (our dataset started with 99 million tweets from 26 million users from August and September 2015). We further restricted this dataset to only consider tweets from users we could geolocate to the United States, which narrowed our dataset down to 3.2 million tweets from 1.2 million users as described below, of which 113K comprised the ground truth of our final mention network (see below for more information about ground truth development). Though this is smaller than that used by Jurgens et al., it is in line with other network-based algorithm studies [34].

### Ground Truth Data

As noted above, we selected the urban-rural divide as our focus demographic dimension because it corresponds to a well-studied population bias that exists in most forms of social media [28]. To categorize locations along the urban/rural spectrum for our second demographic variable, we follow standard practice in the literature that looks at urban/rural issues in online communities [28,32].

[1] https://github.com/reidpr/QUAC

[2] https://github.com/networkdynamics/geoinference

[3] Geographic methods often assume a contiguous region, and this is the case for the methods we employ here. Moreover, given their populations, it is highly unlikely that the inclusion of Alaska and Hawaii would have significant altered our results.

Specifically, we utilize the U.S. National Center for Health Statistics' Urban-Rural Classification Scheme for Counties [29], which assigns each county in the United States an ordinal code from 1 (most urban) to 6 (most rural).

Using these codes, it is straightforward to obtain urban/rural data for our text-based algorithm's ground-truth dataset. Namely, since this dataset consists entirely of geotagged tweets in the contiguous United States, we simply perform a reverse geocoding operation that labels each tweet with the county in which it is located. We then assign each county's urban/rural code to the tweet.

While text-based algorithms predict the location of each tweet individually, as noted above, network-based approaches typically seek to locate a given user (and assign all of that user's tweets to that "home" location). There are two methods used in the literature for determining a user's home location for use as ground truth in these algorithms (see Johnson et al. [31] for a complete overview of ground truth identification techniques). Jurgens [33] and McGee, Caverlee, and Cheng [45] respectively define a user's home location as the geometric median of their tweets given a minimum of five (three) geotagged tweets within 30 kilometers (50 miles) of each other. The other method takes advantage of the user's self-reported location field. This method has the drawback of being quite noisy [27] and though Jurgens et al. [34] found the location field to lead to lower overall precision, it is a method that has been used routinely in the literature [40,54]

We first evaluated the geometric median method for our dataset but found the resultant dataset to be prohibitively small, with only 20,000 users and a miniscule number of rural users. As such, we turned instead to geocoding the location field through an approach that has been shown to significant reduce the noise in this data source (albeit with reduced recall) [26]: using a Wikipedia-based geocoder. We leveraged the geocoder in WikiBrain [58], which resulted in a much larger dataset of 1.2 million users from which we built our mention network.

In line with previous results on population bias, we found that, relative to our census data, the most urban users (NCHS class 1) were highly overrepresented in our datasets (130% and 210% relative to their proportion in the overall population for the text-based and network-based datasets respectively). The most rural users (NCHS class 6) were accordingly underrepresented (45% and 24% relative proportion for the text-based and network-based datasets respectively). Lastly, it is important to note that rural/urban labels were used for evaluation purposes only and are not provided to the algorithm with training or testing data.

### Evaluation Framework

When evaluating the two algorithms, we followed the procedure outlined by the two corresponding papers as closely as possible to measure the bias present in typical performance. We use five-fold validation for each network-based model. For the text model, we build and test five models for each condition. We constrain the test tweets in each text-based model to those from the days following the dates of the tweets that comprise the training data, ensure no overlap in users between training and testing phases, and use training set sizes (30,000) equal to those used by Priedhorsky et al. However, because we were limited to the Streaming API rather than the higher-volume "gardenhose" API for collecting our Twitter data, we limited the size of our network model training datasets to 24,000 users (selected anew for each fold out of the 113,000 who comprised our ground truth data), which is smaller than that used by Jurgens. We examined training datasets up to 40,000 for our baseline model though and found similar trends.

In all cases, we define algorithm precision as the percentage of predictions within 100km of the actual location. We tested different values for the distance (20km, 50km, 200km, 500km) as well as defining a true positive as a prediction lying within the same county as the ground truth (much research aggregates tweets to counties in order to leverage census data). All of these definitions led to similar patterns of results. We also tested the text-based algorithm with a similar dataset of tweets from June 2015 and saw similar trends. We only report recall (the percentage of users or tweets for which an algorithm could provide a location) for the network-based models because the recall was consistently around 100% for the text-based models.

In line with the NCHS classifications [29], we combine data from counties with NCHS codes of 1 and 2 ("large metropolitan counties") into one "urban" class and counties from NCHS codes of 5 and 6 ("nonmetropolitan counties") into one "rural" class. We use these definitions of urban and rural for the rest of the paper. We restrict our reporting and discussion to just these urban and rural classes, though the results for NCHS categories 3 and 4 generally fell between those for the urban and rural classes.

## RESULTS

We structured our exploration of the effect of population bias on social media-based algorithms by asking three cascading research questions. Our first question was whether the two geolocation algorithms exhibit biased performance in favor of urban areas (**RQ1: Is there an algorithmic bias in the direction of the population bias?).** Our next step was to inquire whether any identified bias was due to population bias (**RQ2: Is any bias due to population bias?**). We did this by examining the change in algorithmic bias when we adjusted the training dataset so that it contained a representative urban/rural sample of the general population.

Finally, given a positive answer to RQ2, we planned a third research question whose objective was to investigate whether any remaining bias could be eliminated by training solely on the algorithmically disadvantaged population (**RQ3: Can any remaining underperformance for a specific population be fixed by training solely on data from that population?**). This is equivalent to building a

| | % of Training Data | | Precision (Recall) | | |
|---|---|---|---|---|---|
| **Text-Based Models** | **Urban** | **Rural** | **Urban** | **Rural** | **Overall** |
| Typical (Baseline) | 63.8% | 9.0% | 23.0 ± 3.0% | 9.9 ± 0.4% | 20.6 ± 1.9% |
| Population Bias Balanced | 55.3% | 15.0% | 22.1 ± 1.5% | 10.5 ± 0.6% | 20.4 ± 1.1% |
| Urban Boosted | 100% | 0% | 27.6 ± 3.0% | 4.9 ± 0.3% | 19.5 ± 2.0% |
| Rural Boosted | 0% | 100% | 5.0 ± 0.5% | 17.9 ± 1.5% | 6.8 ± 0.6% |
| **Network-Based Models** | **Urban** | **Rural** | **Urban** | **Rural** | **Overall** |
| Typical (Baseline) | 75.0% | 5.2% | 25.7 ± 0.4% (13.1%) | 20.6 ± 1.7% (8.1%) | 25.0 ± 0.4% (12.3%) |
| Population Bias Balanced | 55.3% | 15.0% | 20.6 ± 0.8% (12.4%) | 39.2 ± 5.2% (9.5%) | 22.2 ± 0.8% (11.9%) |
| Urban Boosted | 100% | 0% | 27.0 ± 3.9% (13.3%) | 5.0 ± 1.9% (9.0%) | 22.3 ± 3.2% (11.6%) |
| Rural Boosted* | 0% | 100% | 1.0 ± 0.3% (4.6%) | 59.2 ± 5.3% (8.4%) | 3.8 ± 0.4% (4.5%) |

**Table 1. Urban-rural results for typical training data as well as various population bias manipulations. Precision: confidence intervals for percentage of predictions within 100 km of true location. Recall: values in parentheses, except the text-based models which had recall always around 100%. *The network-based rural-boosted model was trained on 6000 tweets due to lack of data.**

separate algorithm customized (trained) specifically for rural users and tweets and another for urban users and tweets. The goal of RQ3 was to identify whether any bias that remained after adjusting for any population imbalances was inherent to the algorithm.

Below, we use our three research questions to structure our discussion of our results. To determine the significance of changes in precision of the algorithm, we adopt the methods used by Compton et al. [10], which set confidence intervals as the average precision ±1.5 times the interquartile range for the folds. Comparisons are only made when confidence intervals do not overlap unless otherwise noted.

### RQ1: Is there algorithmic bias?

Examining the precision of each algorithm in urban and rural contexts (Table 1, rows labeled "Typical (Baseline)"), a clear pattern of bias emerges. Both algorithms perform worse for rural users than for urban users, with the magnitude of the bias being greatest in the text-based algorithm: this algorithm is able to accurately locate urban users within 100km at a rate approximately 2.3 times greater than that for rural users. The equivalent precision number for the network model is 1.3x, and recall is 1.6x better for urban users than rural users in the network model as well.

Figure 1 on the following page shows the precision of the text-based algorithm by county in the contiguous United States. It demonstrates the depth of this bias – almost all high precision clusters center in urban areas around cities.

In addition to motivating further inquiry as to whether this algorithmic bias arises from population bias in the underlying dataset or other factors (i.e. our RQ2 and RQ3), this result has important implications in and of itself. Namely, geolocation inference algorithms have served as inputs to systems and studies and our results establish for the first time that the use of these well-known geolocation inference algorithms from the literature will inject further population bias into any geographically referenced dataset of Twitter users. For instance, in the case of the text-based algorithm, 2.3x more urban users than rural users will be "put on the map" correctly. We return to this point in the discussion section.

### RQ2: Is the observed bias due to population bias?

The cells in the "Typical (Baseline)" rows and "% of Training Data" column in Table 1 indicate that, as noted above and in line with a number of previous studies on Twitter, our unadjusted training data has significant underlying population biases. For instance, we can see that 63.8% of our text-based urban/rural ground-truth dataset can be classified as urban according to our definition, but only 9.0% of our dataset can be classified as rural. The actual census proportions would be 55.3% and 15.0% respectively, indicating a strong urban bias in our dataset.

Our goal with this research question was to determine whether correcting for this population bias in the training datasets is the primary cause of the biases we observed in our RQ1 analyses. As pointed out by Pavalanathan and Eisenstein [50] and Burger et al. [5], more data about a group in prediction tasks generally improves accuracy of the algorithm. Therefore, we expect that by adjusting for population bias, we can induce greater and perhaps equal performance for underrepresented populations (i.e. rural populations). Though rural areas still would have a much lower number of tweets even within a population-balanced dataset, maintaining a consistent number of tweets per person in an area as training data should capture an equal percentage of an area's location-indicative words (to use Han, Cook, and Baldwin's [25] vocabulary).

To answer our second research question, we performed a simple modification of the datasets on which we trained each algorithm: instead of resampling the datasets at random for each fold of training the algorithm as we did in RQ1, we resampled them such that they were representative of the demographics of the general population with respect to the rural/urban divide. In other words, we generated training

**Figure 1. Text-based geolocation baseline precision by county (percentage of tweets originating from each county correctly geolocated to within 100km of each tweet's true location).**

datasets without population bias. We did not adjust how we sampled data for testing each fold (i.e. it remained random).

The results of the evaluation of each algorithm under this population-balanced condition can be found in Table 1 in the rows labeled "Population Bias Balanced". These rows tell a relatively straightforward story: while using a representative sample of the general population significantly changed the results for the network-based model with respect to the urban/rural divide, balancing the population had only a negligible effect on the text-based model. In other words, the text-based model remained significantly urban-biased, even when using a training set that removes population bias in the underlying Twitter dataset. On the other hand, the network-based model was significantly less biased when trained on a population-balanced dataset.

Like was the case for RQ1, this result both motivates the investigation of our subsequent research question (RQ3) and has implications on its own. Whereas there is evidence that addressing the effects of demographic bias in social media-based social science research can be done by simply resampling the underlying dataset [14], our findings suggest the same cannot be said for social media-based algorithms, at least in the case of our text-based model. This is another subject to which we attend below.

### RQ3: Can we fix biases through oversampling?

Even when the representation of rural Twitter users has been boosted to match that of the general population, rural users still make up a much smaller relative proportion of the training set and therefore have a much smaller corresponding absolute number of training samples. In this experiment, we sought to see if this imbalance in absolute number of tweets can explain the algorithmic bias we observed above.

We did this by training and testing on each demographic group separately (i.e. separate models for rural and for urban). If separate models perform equally well (e.g., rural precision is as high as urban precision), then we would know that the algorithmic bias in our algorithm arises solely from population characteristics of the input dataset. If bias still exists even in separate models, then we would know that there are structural biases within the algorithms that prevent equal performance for these demographics, no matter their representation in the training dataset.

The results of this experiment can be seen in the rows labeled "Urban Boosted" and "Rural Boosted" in Tables 1. Of particular note is the performance of the text-based algorithm. Even when training and testing solely on tweets from rural users, the text-based model cannot geolocate these tweets as well as it can for tweets from urban users when using a simple random sample or population-adjusted training set (let alone using an only-urban model). While we do see a large and significant improvement in the rural case, performance still falls short of that of urban tweets for all of our models that contained any urban training data at all. We also note that we tried boosting the absolute number of training samples by up to two times the number used in Priedhorsky et al., and the results were consistent: the rural-only model still had a precision less than the random and population-adjusted urban precision. In other words, no matter the training data, there appears to be something in the design of the text-based algorithm that prevents it from performing well for rural users relative to urban users.

The story for the network-based model is different, with it appearing to also suffer from structural biases, but not to the same degree as the text-based model. With respect to precision, the model trained only on rural users actually outperforms the model trained only on urban users. However, the recall remains lower than any of the urban models.

These results have important implications for the design and application of social media-based algorithms. We begin our Discussion section below by highlighting these implications.

## DISCUSSION

### Algorithmic Bias = Population Bias + Structural Bias + ε

The results to our second and third research questions suggest a nuanced understanding of the mechanisms behind algorithmic bias. Namely, while we saw that some algorithmic bias could be explained by population bias in the underlying training sets (e.g., the gap in performance between urban and rural users in the network-based algorithm), not all of it could. In fact, in the case of the text-based algorithm, even dramatically overcorrecting for population bias by training solely on rural users did not make the algorithm perform as well as it typically does for urban users.

These findings support the notion that algorithmic bias must be understood as a function of both population bias and structural bias inherent to the algorithm's design (as well as other factors that have yet to be discovered). In other words, there is something about the nature of some algorithms that inherently biases them towards lower performance for certain populations.

### A Closer Look at Structural Bias

Examining the structure of the two algorithm families under consideration, a number of hypotheses emerge for their differing amounts of structural bias along urban/rural lines. Network-based algorithms build an egocentric network, so a prediction for a given user is affected directly by her/his social network neighbors and potentially indirectly by other nearby users (e.g. neighbors of neighbors) through multiple stages of inference. This means that addition or subtraction of users in one part of the network largely does not impact a given user elsewhere in the network even though it can boost precision and recall amongst their more immediate social network neighbors. Indeed, within our mention network, we find very high homophily: 90% of edges between users with known ground-truth locations are of the same type (i.e. for a user known to be in an rural class 6 county, there is a 90% chance that any of their social network neighbors whose location is known a priori are also in rural class 6 counties) Boosting data for rural users therefore greatly increases the likelihood that a rural user in the testing dataset will have neighbors that are located without affecting most urban users because they would not be closely linked through the network to the rural users.

Text-based algorithms, on the other hand, see much greater dependencies between users. Toponyms and language that have broad usage across the country will be skewed towards being located in urban areas with their higher density of users. Furthermore, when examining the average number of words per tweet that can be identified as geographic Wikipedia concepts (i.e., words tied directly to place) through wikification algorithms implemented by Sen et al. [58], we see that the most urban tweets (NCHS code = "1") have 25% more "wikifiable" words per tweet than the most rural tweets (NCHS code = "6"). Since location-specific words such as these are key to how the text-based algorithm operates, some of the urban advantage may come from differing language patterns and topics of conversation in tweets across urban-rural lines [16].

Another common design decision in text-based algorithms that could be a cause of structural urban/rural bias relates to the fixed distance parameters central to many of these algorithms' low-level functionality. These distance parameters, which manifest as grid-cell sizes or geographic probability distribution ranges, fail to take into account the varying distances at which the use of a term is predictive in urban versus rural areas. For instance, when someone tweets a name of a high school mascot in an urban area, that name is predictive for a smaller area than the same situation in a rural area (i.e. rural areas have significantly larger school districts by area). This problem can be understood in geostatistics terms: the use of a fixed-distance parameter assumes a fixed range of spatial autocorrelation for tweet usage, which likely is not true across urban/rural lines. In more general terms, this means that employing fixed distance parameters will fail to capture the full predictive power of each rural tweet in text-based algorithms, and rural areas already have fewer tweets per capita to begin with.

### Achieving Parity

Though lower overall recall and precision is a barrier to implementation of network-based algorithms, our work indicates that it may be easier to achieve parity within network-based algorithms by boosting data collection efforts around underrepresented populations. Although more work should be done to confirm this effect in other types of social media algorithms, researchers and designers for whom equity is a top priority may want to consider utilizing network-based methods when doing Twitter-based geolocation.

It is also important to note that the contribution of structural bias to algorithmic bias we have identified here adds weight to the argument of Sandvig et al. [57] and others (e.g., [62]) that algorithmic accountability work needs to consider algorithms at levels deeper than simply inputs and outputs and that algorithmic accountability research teams have people with "algorithmic skills that allow a facility with the relevant [algorithmic] ideas" [57]. These skills will be necessary to identify and address bias at the structural level.

Similarly, the notion of structural bias highlights the importance of open-source implementations of algorithms. Open-source affords the ability to understand and design fixes for these algorithmic biases because we are able to examine and manipulate how these algorithms function. Our results show that we cannot rely solely on adjusting the data going into the algorithm to achieve parity.

### A Tradeoff Between Equity and Effectiveness

There is one column in Table 1 that we have yet to discuss in detail: the "Overall" column. This column indicates the performance on the entire randomized population (i.e. data in an unmodified proportion of users and tweets). In other words, the "Overall" column reports the precision (and recall) a researcher or developer would expect to achieve if she were to apply the model listed in each row to all of Twitter.

There is a clear trend in the "Overall" column: for models in which rural performance is better, the performance on overall population gets worse. From the perspective of a researcher or developer, this means that in order to improve rural accuracy, one has to reduce overall accuracy. Furthermore, for the text-based algorithm, we also tested a wider variety of urban-rural training data proportions to understand the responsiveness of the algorithm to smaller shifts in data. In doing so, we found that peak performance (21.0% overall precision at 100 km) came in a model that removed a quarter of the rural training data and boosted urban accordingly. Rural users performed very poorly in this model (6.8% precision), but the slight increase in precision for urban users (23.5% precision) along with their inherently higher proportions in the testing data was sufficient to boost the overall precision.

Our results demonstrate that, at least in the case of Twitter geolocation, that there is a clear trade-off between equity and effectiveness, a result for which there is evidence in other algorithmic accountability contexts as well (e.g., [35,48]). An important corollary to this tradeoff is that using single measures of precision and recall for an algorithm can gloss over very real, non-random variation in algorithmic performance for different groups of people. Until better algorithms can be developed that do not compromise equity (or equality) for effectiveness (e.g., by addressing structural bias), algorithm designers should conduct and report a more thorough examination of performance across different populations as has been advocated by many in the algorithmic accountability community, especially when past work has suggested that there may be population bias or structural bias.

### Privacy

We have conducted this research with the assumption that higher precision and recall is a desirable outcome for a given population. While this is a valid assumption in an application of geolocation like public health tracking, this is not always the case for social media-based algorithms and for geolocation specifically. It is important to note that in this light, there may be benefits to being "disadvantaged" by geolocation algorithms: our results suggest that rural users are harder to "find" in an automated fashion, preserving privacy. Geolocation inference is already employed by at least some social surveillance firms, locating tweets based on the language and metadata [17]. An interesting direction of research (e.g. [25]) is to invert the goals of this paper and attempt to find ways reduce the "geolocatability" of a person or a population (i.e. defend against "inference attacks" [42]).

## LIMITATIONS AND FUTURE WORK

In this paper, we necessarily binned users into categories along the urban and rural spectrum. There is without a doubt a tremendous amount of diversity in the people and behaviors present within each of these categories, and further research may want to address this. Categorizing users based on behavior and content as opposed to demographic labels could provide additional insight into who is likely to be affected by these algorithmic biases.

Following best practices in the Twitter geolocation literature (e.g. [27,33,34,52]), for our ground truth data, we depended on explicitly geotagged tweets for our text-based algorithm (i.e. tweet location) and a very conservative (i.e. precision-focused rather than recall-focused) geocoding of the location field for our network-based algorithm (i.e. user home location). While doing so was critical to our goal of evaluating bias in the algorithms as they were published, it is possible that these mechanisms may disproportionally remove people of one demographic relative to another demographic. Although developing a ground truth through other means (e.g. a survey) would be a major research project in its own right, examining Twitter geolocation algorithms through this lens would be a useful addition to the literature.

Another area of future work would be expanding the focus of this study (the contiguous United States) to other cultures and geographic contexts. It is known that different cultures use social media differently (and have their own population biases) so it is not clear how our results would extend to these areas. Furthermore, building on our understanding of how different populations use social media (e.g., variation of the use of mentions across cultures [20]) will enable better prediction of where algorithmic biases might arise. Along the same lines, we sought to choose representative algorithms, but different algorithms may perform differently and introduce their own structural biases.

Finally, now that this paper has established the role of structural bias, a very important direction of future work is finding ways to reduce or eliminate it in important algorithms. We expect that doing so could lead to an interesting and fruitful line of work.

## CONCLUSION

This research improves our understanding of algorithmic biases in social media-based algorithms. We demonstrated the degree to which these algorithmic biases arise from both population biases in the training data and structural biases inherent to the algorithms themselves. Through the implementation of both a text-based and a network-based algorithm for geolocation inference, we found that network-based approaches may be less susceptible to structural biases. We also discussed the implications of our findings for designers and users of social-media based algorithms. These implications include (1) the need for more work developing algorithms that avoid the structural biases we observed here and (2) that global evaluation metrics can mask significant underperformance for certain populations in these algorithms.

## ACKNOWLEDGEMENTS

We would like to thank our colleagues at GroupLens at the University of Minnesota for their support and brainstorming time. This project was funded in part by the U.S. National Science Foundation (CAREER IIS-1552955 and IIS-1526988), the Volkswagen Foundation, and a University of Minnesota College of Science and Engineering Graduate Fellowship.

## REFERENCES

1. Saeed Abdullah, Elizabeth L. Murnane, Jean M.R. Costa, and Tanzeem Choudhury. 2015. Collective Smile: Measuring Societal Happiness from Geolocated Images. In *CSCW*. https://doi.org/10.1145/2675133.2675186
2. Mike Ananny, Karrie Karahalios, Christian Sandvig, and Christo Wilson. 2015. Auditing Algorithms from the Outside: Methods and Implications. In *ICWSM*.
3. Lars Backstrom, Eric Sun, and Cameron Marlow. 2010. Find me if you can: improving geographical prediction with social and spatial proximity. In *WWW*.
4. Saeideh Bakhshi, David A. Shamma, and Eric Gilbert. 2014. Faces Engage Us: Photos with Faces Attract More Likes and Comments on Instagram. In Proceedings of the 32nd Annual ACM Conference on Human Factors in Computing Systems (CHI '14), 965–974. https://doi.org/10.1145/2556288.2557403
5. John D. Burger, John Henderson, George Kim, and Guido Zarrella. 2011. Discriminating gender on Twitter. In *EMNLP*.
6. Miriam Cha, Youngjune Gwon, and H. T. Kung. 2015. Twitter Geolocation and Regional Classification via Sparse Coding. In *ICWSM*.
7. Le Chen, Alan Mislove, and Christo Wilson. 2015. Peeking Beneath the Hood of Uber. 495–508. https://doi.org/10.1145/2815675.2815681
8. Zhiyuan Cheng, James Caverlee, and Kyumin Lee. 2010. You Are Where You Tweet : A Content-Based Approach to Geo-locating Twitter Users. *CIKM*. https://doi.org/10.1145/1871437.1871535
9. Zhiyuan Cheng, James Caverlee, Kyumin Lee, and Daniel Z. Sui. 2011. Exploring Millions of Footprints in Location Sharing Services. *ICWSM* 2011.
10. Ryan Compton, David Jurgens, and David Allen. 2014. Geotagging one hundred million twitter accounts with total variation minimization. In *IEEE BigData*.
11. Ryan Compton, Craig Lee, Jiejun Xu, Luis Artieda-moncada, Tsai-ching Lu, Lalindra De Silva, and Michael Macy. 2013. Using publicly visible social media to build detailed forecasts of civil unrest. 1–11.
12. Justin Cranshaw, Jason I Hong, and Norman Sadeh. 2012. The Livehoods Project : Utilizing Social Media to Understand the Dynamics of a City. *ICWSM*: 58–65.
13. Aron Culotta. 2014. Estimating county health statistics with twitter. In *JSM Proceedings*, 1335–1344. https://doi.org/10.1145/2556288.2557139
14. Aron Culotta. 2014. Reducing Sampling Bias in Social Media Data for County Health Inference. *JSM Proceedings*.
15. Mark Dredze, Michael J. Paul, Shane Bergsma, and Hieu Tran. 2013. Carmen: A twitter geolocation system with applications to public health. In *AAAI Workshop: HIAI*.
16. Jacob Eisenstein, Brendan O'Connor, Noah A. Smith, and Eric P. Xing. 2010. A latent variable model for geographic lexical variation. *EMNLP*. https://doi.org/10.1038/nrm2900
17. Benjamin Elgin and Peter Robison. 2016. How Despots Use Twitter to Hunt Dissidents. *Bloomberg Technology*. Retrieved from https://www.bloomberg.com/news/articles/2016-10-27/twitter-s-firehose-of-tweets-is-incredibly-valuable-and-just-as-dangerous
18. David Flatow, Mor Naaman, Ke Eddie Xie, Yana Volkovich, and Yaron Kanza. 2015. On the Accuracy of Hyper-local Geotagging of Social Media Content. In *WSDM*. https://doi.org/10.1145/2684822.2685296
19. Andrew Gallagher, Devashree Joshi, Jie Yu, and Jiebo Luo. 2009. Geo-location inference from image content and user tags. In *Computer Vision and Pattern Recognition Workshops, 2009. CVPR Workshops 2009. IEEE Computer Society Conference on*, 55–62.
20. Ruth Garcia-Gavilanes, Daniele Quercia, and Alejandro Jaimes. 2013. Cultural dimensions in twitter: Time, individualism and power. *ICWSM* 13.
21. Eric Gilbert, Karrie Karahalios, and Christian Sandvig. 2008. The Network in the Garden : An Empirical Analysis of Social Media in Rural Life. *CHI*: 1603–1612.
22. Eric Gilbert, Karrie Karahalios, and Christian Sandvig. 2010. The Network in the Garden: Designing Social Media for Rural Life. *American Behavioral Scientist* 53, 9: 1367–1388. https://doi.org/10.1177/0002764210361690
23. Mark Graham, Scott A. Hale, and Devin Gaffney. 2014. Where in the World Are You? Geolocation and Language Identification in Twitter. *The Professional*

*Geographer* 0, 0: 1–11. https://doi.org/10.1080/00330124.2014.907699
24. T. Hagerstrand. 1968. Innovation diffusion as a spatial process. 334 pp.
25. Bo Han, Paul Cook, and Timothy Baldwin. 2014. Text-based twitter user geolocation prediction. *Journal of Artificial Intelligence Research*: 451–500.
26. Brent Hecht and Darren Gergle. 2010. On the "localness" of user-generated content. *CSCW*: 229. https://doi.org/10.1145/1718918.1718962
27. Brent Hecht, Lichan Hong, Bongwon Suh, and Ed H. Chi. 2011. Tweets from Justin Bieber's heart: the dynamics of the location field in user profiles. In *CHI.*
29. Brent Hecht and Monica Stephens. 2014. A Tale of Cities: Urban Biases in Volunteered Geographic Information. In Eighth International AAAI Conference on Weblogs and Social Media.
29. DD Ingram and SJ Franco. 2014. 2013 NCHS urban-rural classification scheme for counties. *Vital Health Statistics* 2, 166.
30. Yushi Jing, David Liu, Dmitry Kislyuk, Andrew Zhai, Jiajing Xu, Jeff Donahue, and Sarah Tavel. 2015. Visual Search at Pinterest. In *Proceedings of the 21th ACM SIGKDD International Conference on Knowledge Discovery and Data Mining* (KDD '15), 1889–1898. https://doi.org/10.1145/2783258.2788621
31. Isaac L. Johnson, Subhasree Sengupta, Johannes Schöning, and Brent Hecht. 2016. The Geography and Importance of Localness in Geotagged Social Media. In *2016 CHI Conference on Human Factors in Computing Systems*, 515–526. https://doi.org/10.1145/2858036.2858122
32. Isaac Johnson, Yilun Lin, Toby Jia-Jun Li, Andrew Hall, Aaron Halfaker, Johannes Schöning, and Brent Hecht. 2016. Not at Home on the Range: Peer Production and the Urban/Rural Divide. *CHI.*
33. David Jurgens. 2013. That's What Friends Are For: Inferring Location in Online Social Media Platforms Based on Social Relationships. *ICWSM* 13: 273–282.
34. David Jurgens, Tyler Finethy, James McCorriston, Yi Tian Xu, and Derek Ruths. 2015. Geolocation prediction in twitter using social networks: A critical analysis and review of current practice. In *ICWSM.*
35. Matthew Kay, Cynthia Matuszek, and Sean A. Munson. 2015. Unequal Representation and Gender Stereotypes in Image Search Results for Occupations. In *Proceedings of the 33rd Annual ACM Conference on Human Factors in Computing Systems* (CHI '15), 3819–3828. https://doi.org/10.1145/2702123.2702520
36. Lorin D. Kusmin. 2016. *Rural America At A Glance: 2015 Edition*. United States Department of Agriculture. Retrieved from http://www.ers.usda.gov/media/1952235/eib145.pdf
37. Virgile Landeiro and Aron Culotta. 2016. Robust text classification in the presence of confounding bias. In *Thirtieth AAAI Conference on Artificial Intelligence.* Retrieved May 17, 2016 from http://www.aaai.org/Conferences/AAAI/2016/Papers/02Landeiro12445.pdf
38. Géraud Le Falher, Aristides Gionis, and Michael Mathioudakis. 2015. Where Is the Soho of Rome? Measures and Algorithms for Finding Similar Neighborhoods in Cities. In *ICWSM.*
39. Linna Li, Michael F. Goodchild, and Bo Xu. 2013. Spatial, temporal, and socioeconomic patterns in the use of Twitter and Flickr. *Cartography and Geographic Information Science* 40, 2: 61–77. https://doi.org/10.1080/15230406.2013.777139
40. Rui Li, Shengjie Wang, Hongbo Deng, Rui Wang, and Kevin Chen-Chuan Chang. 2012. Towards social user profiling: unified and discriminative influence model for inferring home locations. In *SIGKDD.*
41. Xutao Li, Tuan-Anh Nguyen Pham, Gao Cong, Quan Yuan, Xiao-Li Li, and Shonali Krishnaswamy. 2015. Where You Instagram?: Associating Your Instagram Photos with Points of Interest. In *Proceedings of the 24th ACM International on Conference on Information and Knowledge Management* (CIKM '15), 1231–1240. https://doi.org/10.1145/2806416.2806463
42. J. Lindamood, R. Heatherly, M. Kantarcioglu, and B. Thuraisingham. 2009. Inferring Private Information Using Social Network Data. In *WWW '09: 2009 International World Wide Web Conference.*
43. Jalal Mahmud, Jeffrey Nichols, and Clemens Drews. 2014. Home Location Identification of Twitter Users. *ACM TIST* 5, 3: 1–21. https://doi.org/10.1145/2528548
44. Momin M. Malik, Hemank Lamba, Constantine Nakos, and Jürgen Pfeffer. 2015. Population Bias in Geotagged Tweets. In *ICWSM.*
45. Jeffrey McGee, James Caverlee, and Zhiyuan Cheng. 2013. Location prediction in social media based on tie strength. In *CIKM*, 459–468. https://doi.org/10.1145/2505515.2505544
46. Alan Mislove, Sune Lehmann, Yong-yeol Ahn, Jukka-pekka Onnela, and J Niels Rosenquist. Understanding the Demographics of Twitter Users. *ICWSM*: 554–557.
47. Lewis Mitchell, Morgan R Frank, Kameron Decker Harris, Peter Sheridan Dodds, and Christopher M Danforth. 2013. The geography of happiness: connecting twitter sentiment and expression, demographics, and objective characteristics of place. *PloS one* 8, 5: e64417. https://doi.org/10.1371/journal.pone.0064417
48. Cathy O'Neil. 2016. *Weapons of Math Destruction: How Big Data Increases Inequality and Threatens Democracy*. Crown, New York.
49. Aditya Pal, Amac Herdagdelen, Sourav Chatterji, Sumit Taank, and Deepayan Chakrabarti. 2016. Discovery of Topical Authorities in Instagram. In *WWW.*
50. Umashanthi Pavalanathan and Jacob Eisenstein. 2015. Confounds and Consequences in Geotagged Twitter Data. *EMNLP.*

51. Andrew Perrin. 2015. Social Media Usage: 2005-2015. *Pew Research Center*.
52. Reid Priedhorsky, Aron Culotta, and Sara Y. Del Valle. 2014. Inferring the Origin Locations of Tweets with Quantitative Confidence. *CSCW* 29: 997–1003.
53. Stephen Roller, Michael Speriosu, Sarat Rallapalli, Benjamin Wing, and Jason Baldridge. 2012. Supervised text-based geolocation using language models on an adaptive grid. In *EMNLP-CoNLL*.
54. Dominic Rout, Kalina Bontcheva, Daniel Preoţiuc-Pietro, and Trevor Cohn. 2013. Where's@ wally?: a classification approach to geolocating users based on their social ties. In *Hypertext*, 11–20.
55. Derek Ruths and Jürgen Pfeffer. 2014. Social media for large studies of behavior. *Science* 346, 6213: 1063–1064. https://doi.org/10.1126/science.346.6213.1063
56. Christian Sandvig, Kevin Hamilton, Karrie Karahalios, and Cedric Langbort. 2014. Auditing algorithms: Research methods for detecting discrimination on internet platforms. *Data and Discrimination*.
57. Christian Sandvig, Kevin Hamilton, Karrie Karahalios, and Cedric Langbort. 2015. Can an Algorithm be Unethical? In *65th Annual Meeting of the International Communication Association*.
58. Shilad Sen, Toby Jia-Jun Li, WikiBrain Team, and Brent Hecht. 2014. WikiBrain: Democratizing Computation on Wikipedia. In *OpenSym* (OpenSym '14), 27:1–27:10. https://doi.org/10.1145/2641580.2641615
59. Börkur Sigurbjörnsson and Roelof Van Zwol. 2008. Flickr tag recommendation based on collective knowledge. In *WWW*.
60. Gary Soeller, Karrie Karahalios, Christian Sandvig, and Christo Wilson. 2016. MapWatch: Detecting and Monitoring International Border Personalization on Online Maps. In *Proceedings of the 25th International Conference on World Wide Web* (WWW '16), 867–878. https://doi.org/10.1145/2872427.2883016
61. Monica Stephens. 2013. Gender and the GeoWeb: divisions in the production of user-generated cartographic information. *GeoJournal* 78, 6: 981–996. https://doi.org/10.1007/s10708-013-9492-z
62. Suresh Venkatasubramanian. 2016. Algorithmic Fairness: From social good to a mathematical framework. Retrieved September 17, 2016 from https://algorithmicfairness.wordpress.com/2016/04/15/keynote-at-icwsm/
63. Jacob Thebault-Spieker, Loren G. Terveen, and Brent Hecht. 2015. Avoiding the South Side and the Suburbs: The Geography of Mobile Crowdsourcing Markets. In *Proceedings of the 18th ACM Conference on Computer Supported Cooperative Work & Social Computing* (CSCW '15), 265–275. https://doi.org/10.1145/2675133.2675278
64. Benjamin P. Wing and Jason Baldridge. 2011. Simple supervised document geolocation with geodesic grids. In *ACL*.
65. Wilbur Zelinsky. 1980. North America's Vernacular Regions. *Annals of the Association of American Geographers* 70, 1: 1–16. https://doi.org/10.1111/j.1467-8306.1980.tb01293.x
66. Danning Zheng, Tianran Hu, Quanzeng You, Henry Kautz, and Jiebo Luo. 2015. Towards Lifestyle Understanding: Predicting Home and Vacation Locations from User's Online Photo Collections. In *ICWSM*.
67. Kathryn Zickuhr and Aaron Smith. 2011. 28% of American Adults Use Mobile and Social Location-Based Services. *Pew Internet and American Life Project*.

# The Geography of Pokémon GO: Beneficial and Problematic Effects on Places and Movement

**Ashley Colley[1*], Jacob Thebault-Spieker[2*], Allen Yilun Lin[3*], Donald Degraen[4], Benjamin Fischman[2], Jonna Häkkilä[1], Kate Kuehl[2], Valentina Nisi[5], Nuno Jardim Nunes[5], Nina Wenig[6], Dirk Wenig[6], Brent Hecht[3**], Johannes Schöning[6**]**

*Indicates co-First Authors, **Indicates co-Principal Investigators

[1]University of Lapland (Finland), [2]University of Minnesota (USA), [3]Northwestern University (USA), [4]Saarland University (Germany), [5]Madeira-ITI (Portugal), [6]University of Bremen (Germany)

Contact e-mails: ashley.colley@ulapland.fi, thebault@cs.umn.edu, allen.lin@eecs.northwestern.edu, bhecht@northwestern.edu, schoening@uni-bremen.de

## ABSTRACT

The widespread popularity of Pokémon GO presents the first opportunity to observe the geographic effects of location-based gaming at scale. This paper reports the results of a mixed methods study of the geography of Pokémon GO that includes a five-country field survey of 375 Pokémon GO players and a large scale geostatistical analysis of game elements. Focusing on the key geographic themes of places and movement, we find that the design of Pokémon GO reinforces existing geographically-linked biases (e.g. the game advantages urban areas and neighborhoods with smaller minority populations), that Pokémon GO may have instigated a relatively rare large-scale shift in global human mobility patterns, and that Pokémon GO has geographically-linked safety risks, but not those typically emphasized by the media. Our results point to geographic design implications for future systems in this space such as a means through which the geographic biases present in Pokémon GO may be counteracted.

## Author Keywords

Location-based games, geography, Pokémon GO, augmented reality, algorithmic bias, GeoHCI

## ACM Classification Keywords

H.5.m. Information interfaces and presentation (e.g., HCI): Miscellaneous;

## INTRODUCTION

One of the most visible HCI developments of 2016 was the widespread success of the location-based game Pokémon GO. While the HCI community has studied location-based gaming for over a decade, Pokémon GO represents the true democratization of this domain. With a peak popularity defined by more active users than Twitter and more engagement than Facebook [68], it is likely that Pokémon Go catalyzed the first meaningful experience with location-based gaming for tens of millions of people around the world.



*CHI 2017, May 06-11, 2017, Denver, CO, USA*

ACM 978-1-4503-4655-9/17/05.

http://dx.doi.org/10.1145/3025453.3025495

When a topic that is well-known in the literature undergoes widespread popularization, it is frequently an exciting opportunity to address open questions about the topic and its broader implications. Indeed, the success of Pokémon GO presents a number of compelling research opportunities in location-based gaming and related areas (e.g. augmented reality, computer vision, game mechanics). We expect that researchers will rapidly begin to leverage these opportunities in the near future.

In this paper, we focus on an important but targeted subset of questions about location-based gaming that are raised by Pokémon GO: those related to Pokémon GO*'s geography*. The geographic HCI ("GeoHCI") [24,25] literature and the location-based gaming literature have both hypothesized that the democratization of a technology like Pokémon GO would have substantial geographic effects, particularly effects related to *movement* and *places* [6,11,16,17,54] (two of the "five themes of geography" [69,70]). In this research, we utilized the unprecedented opportunity presented by Pokémon GO to investigate these broad hypotheses. Focusing on the themes of movement and places, we ask two high-level questions:

- **RQ1:** How has the **movement** of people changed as a result of Pokémon GO?
- **RQ2:** Which types of **places** are advantaged and disadvantaged by Pokémon GO?

A key component of the successful execution of this research was its rapid mobilization. With the goal of seizing a potentially rare opportunity to peek into a geographic future in which location-based games are an everyday phenomenon, we collected data at or near the peak of Pokémon GO's popularity. The race to study rapidly emerging topics, however, can sometimes lead researchers to sacrifice rigor for expediency. In an attempt to avoid making such a sacrifice, we designed a mixed-methods approach that was comprised of two studies that each addressed our research questions from a different angle. First, coordinating with a team in Europe and in the United States, we conducted in-the-wild field surveys of 375 Pokémon GO players across five countries. Second, focusing on the United States, we executed a large-scale geostatistical analysis of the distribution of a fundamental game element in Pokémon GO: "PokéStops". This analysis included the application of a technique called *spatial Durbin modeling*, a recently established best practice for controlling for spatial autocorrelation (an essential concern when examining many geographic datasets).

The combination of these two studies allowed us to gain both a broader and a deeper understanding of the geography of Pokémon GO than either would have alone, helping us to answer our two research questions with significantly more robustness. More specifically, we identified a set of five core findings across both our field survey and spatial modeling exercises. These findings point to a relatively cohesive story about Pokémon GO's effect on movement and places. Namely, we found that Pokémon GO causes people to visit new locations at a remarkable scale (and spend money while they are there), although this movement is associated with some degree of distraction-related risk. Critically, however, while people visit novel places, these places tend to be in areas with significant pre-existing advantages: our results strongly suggest that *the design of Pokémon GO heavily advantages urban places with few minorities and the people who live in these areas*.

The effect sizes we identify with respect to race, ethnicity and the urban/rural spectrum are substantial and troubling. In the United States, people who live in predominately white non-Hispanic urban areas have extensive advantages in the game relative to people who live in urban areas with large minority populations and to people who live in rural areas. For instance, we find evidence that predominately white non-Hispanic neighborhoods in urban areas in the United States have 20 more PokéStops per square kilometer than urban areas with very large minority populations, with 20 PokéStops per square kilometer being approximately 4 times the overall mean density. The effect sizes across the rural and urban spectrum are even larger: in core urban counties, PokéStop density is *over 95 times greater* on average than in entirely rural counties.

Our results lead to implications for the geographic design of location-based games. For instance, we discuss below how game designers can avoid introducing the racial, ethnic, and urban bias present in Pokémon GO (and even work to counteract them) through the use of alternative geographic design strategies. Our results also point to ways to make movement safer for players by helping them avoid distraction-related safety risks.

## BACKGROUND AND RELATED WORK

### Geographic Human-Computer Interaction

This research was motivated by prior work in both disciplines associated with the "geographic HCI" community [24,25]: geography and HCI. While not focused specifically on location-based gaming, geographers have examined the geographic effects in the highly-related area of augmented reality (Pokémon GO is often described as "augmented reality" rather than a location-based game, e.g. [62]). These geographers have argued from a critical perspective that data and code that "augments" reality can remake place, often in a fashion that reinforces preexisting power structures (e.g. [14,16,17,34]). This work helped to motivate the decision to put pre-existing advantages and disadvantages at the center of our research question about place.

This paper was also motivated by work within the HCI community that examines geographic crowdsourcing processes like the efforts in Wikipedia to describe all notable locations (e.g. [15,19,23,50]) and OpenStreetMap's efforts to map the world (e.g. [47,66,67]). Broadly speaking, across nearly all this work, researchers have identified that these processes lead to advantaged areas having better coverage than disadvantaged areas. For instance, researchers found that rural areas have lower-quality content than urban areas in Wikipedia and OpenStreetMap (e.g. [30,37,66,67]); that geotagged tweets and photos are more common in well-educated areas (e.g. [33]); and that these biases have carried over into the crowd processes of the sharing economy (e.g. [49,56]). This paper adds location-based gaming to this unfortunate list, but our work also suggests solutions that can be employed in future location-based games, and perhaps geographic crowdsourcing more generally.

### Location-based Gaming

As noted above, while Pokémon GO is the first blockbuster success in the area, the HCI community has studied location-based gaming for over a decade (e.g. [8,40,42,63,65]). Well-known contributions include (but are certainly not limited to) Bell et al.'s work on their *Feeding Yoshi* game, which introduced the notion of seamful design to location-based games and provided the first longitudinal, qualitative view on location-based gaming [3], and *Pirates!* [4], which highlighted the potential social impact of such games. Overviews of research on location-based games – which are also known by other names such as "pervasive games" and "augmented reality games" – can be found in the survey papers by Montola et al. [43], Avouris and Yiannoutsou [2] and Magerkurth et al. [35].

While the vast majority of location-based games research examines this domain through a lens other than geography (e.g. technical implementation, game mechanics, narrative, health benefits, social dimensions), several games have been designed as geographic data collection tools (e.g. [39,46]) and others have taken a geographic perspective in their analyses. For instance, Gentes et al. examines the relationship between space, place, and several other dimensions (e.g. infrastructure) in the context of location-based gaming [11], a discussion that relates to that of the work in geography mentioned above. Additionally, geographic factors are often emergent themes in location-based gaming research, and some of these factors relate to our findings below. For instance, Bell et al. [3] noticed that movement was more difficult while playing Feeding Yoshi due to the distraction associated with playing the game. This and a series of related results [5,22,32,57] motivated us to inquire about this issue in Pokémon GO.

The location based game *Ingress* (also developed by Pokémon GO's developer Niantic) presents perhaps the closest prior art to Pokémon GO. As is the case with location-based gaming work more generally, research looking at *Ingress* (e.g. [6,28,71]) has largely adopted non-geographic perspectives. However, this research has led to a few relevant geographic results, particularly related to movement. For instance, Chess [6] highlights that *Ingress* players become both more active in their local physical space, but at the same time become part of the global virtual game space. Moreover, a blog post [71] reporting on in a survey of *Ingress* players found that 56% of players play within a radius of 11-100 km and, importantly, 88% of players have visited previously unvisited locations whilst playing. These results helped to motivate our question related to movement. Because a large body of literature tells us that people tend to be sedentary and their mobility patterns are highly predictable when they do move (e.g. [54]), if these patterns extended to the broader audience Pokémon GO, it could represent a significant change in human movement behavior. Through our research question associated with movement, we sought to see if this was the case, as well as to elucidate more details about other changes to movement behavior related to Pokémon GO.

### Pokémon GO Background

#### *Overview*

Pokémon GO is a free-to-play, location-based game developed by Niantic, Inc. for iOS and Android devices. It was initially released in selected countries in July 2016. In the game, players use a mobile device's positioning capability to locate, capture, and battle virtual creatures, called Pokémon, who appear on the screen as if they were in the same real-world location as the player.

There are 151 different Pokémon in the game at the time of writing, spread across 15 different types, such as normal, water, ground, grass and ghost types. Individual Pokémon appear (*'spawn'*) temporarily at a location, during which time they can be caught by players at that location. Catching Pokémon is one primary way players progress in the game.

In this paper, we focus extensively on "PokéStops", virtual game features that are assigned to fixed locations in the physical world. When players visit PokéStops, they receive benefits in the game (e.g. Poké Balls which are used to catch Pokémon, Potions which are used to heal Pokémon after battles at "Gyms", and experience points). Additionally, in certain game conditions (e.g. using a lure), PokéStop locations have a high frequency of spawning Pokémon. PokéStops can be revisited, but players must wait at least five minutes before doing so. In general, as we will discuss, the higher the PokéStop density in a region, the better for the player.

Niantic established the locations of PokéStops by drawing from the locations of "portals" in its earlier location-based game Ingress [72]. Portal locations were initially seeded with crowdsourced historical markers [27], as well as with churches, parks, monuments, and public art mined from geotagged images [72]. This dataset was then expanded using a much larger crowdsourcing process that invited Ingress players to submit portal locations [72]. This crowdsourcing system has since been closed, drawing the ire of the community (this shuttering is considered to be the least popular 'game feature' of Ingress [73]).

As part of Pokémon GO's gameplay, players are provided with a limited amount of information regarding the detailed algorithms underlying the game. Additionally, the map view in the game's mobile app only gives players visibility of PokéStop and gym locations within an approximately 3 km radius of their current location.

## METHODS

In this work, we take a mixed methods approach, focusing on two primary approaches for understanding the geography of Pokémon GO. First, we deployed a multi-national field survey and interviewed Pokémon GO players at or near the peak of Pokémon GO's launch-related popularity. Second, we augment our findings in the field study with a geostatistical analysis of the distribution of PokéStops in the United States. As we hypothesized, the integration of these two studies allowed us to gain a broader and deeper understanding of the geography of Pokémon GO than either alone. Below, we discuss each of these studies in turn.

### Field Survey

We designed our survey to address both our research question about place and our research question about movement. After making basic inquiries as to demographics and Pokémon GO experience, the survey contained a series of questions targeted at better understanding the role of place and movement in Pokémon GO. For instance, with regard to place, we asked respondents to describe a place they found "boring" (disadvantage) or "exciting" (advantage) with respect to the game. At the time of survey development, a series of news stories [74–76] had emerged describing Pokémon GO players being victimized in "dangerous places", with the notion of such places having a long literature in geography (e.g. [38]). As such, we also inquired as to whether participants had experienced any related incidents. For movement, we inquired as to whether participants had visited any new locations as a result of the game (and to describe these locations), as well as the means by which they engaged in Pokémon GO movement (i.e. mode of transportation, awareness of environment).

The field study took place during two weeks from July 22, 2016 to August 5, 2016 in five different countries (USA,

| **Background** | |
|---|---|
| Gender | Male 65%, Female 33%, Other 2% |
| Age * | $M = 25.1$ years, $SD = 8.0$. $Min = 11$, $Max = 56$ |
| Platform | iOS 45%, Android 55% |
| Mobile gaming | Do not usually play games on smartphone 48% |
| Geospatial gaming | Played a geospatial game 27%, heard of Ingress 52%, played Ingress 11% |
| Pokémon history | Previous fans 79% (TV shows, Gameboy games, trading cards) |
| **Pokémon GO Gameplay** | |
| Total playing time ** | $M = 20.8$ days, $SD = 8.2$ |
| Daily playing time | $Mdn = 2$ hours (< 1 h = 11%, 1 - 2 h = 35%, 2 - 4 h = 37%, > 4 h = 17%) |
| Session length | $M = 78$ minutes, $SD = 87$ |
| Trainer level | $Mdn = 17$ (1st quartile = 13, 3rd quartile = 21) |
| Group play | Friends 72%, family 29%, exclusively alone 12%, sometimes alone 30% |

* Note that we were not allowed by IRB of the US university participating in this research to approach people under 18 years.

** Typically, players started playing in the same week as the game was launched in their country.

**Table 1. Background data from field interviews (n = 375)**

Germany, Portugal, Finland, Belgium). Background data from the respondents is presented in Table 1. The time period of the study roughly corresponded with a timeframe of 2-4 weeks after the launch of the game in each country, which aligned well with Pokémon GO's popularity peak [77].

All the interviewers (half male and half female) had local knowledge and selected the locations for interviews as those places where they had previously observed people playing Pokémon GO. At each selected location, the interviewer spent a minimum of one hour. Subsequent interview locations were chosen to be at least 1km from previous locations. Interviewers visually identified Pokémon GO players based on their behavior and approached and interviewed consenting players, resulting in 375 valid interviews. The distribution of interview responses by country was: Germany: 103, USA: 95, Belgium: 68, Portugal: 59 and Finland: 50.

Respondents' free text responses were analyzed using an open coding approach: A single coder defined the codebook, and two coders evaluated each response. A third researcher then arbitrated disagreements between the coders. Answers were coded such that an individual answer could produce codes in multiple categories, however multiple mentions in the same category were counted as only a single code.

### Geostatistical Analyses

While there are many geographic data streams in Pokémon GO that could help augment our field survey, we focused on the geographic distribution of PokéStops. Specifically, we examined the metric *PokéStop density* (PokéStops per square kilometer) as our core dependent variable.

Broadly speaking, PokéStop density can be thought of as a proxy for advantage in Pokémon GO. That is, the game advantages players who live in areas with high PokéStop density over those who do not. This inequality manifests itself in several ways. Most importantly, moving in search of spawned Pokémon is a core element of gameplay (see below), and in regions with high PokéStop density, there will always be a PokéStop nearby, ensuring resource availability as needed (PokéStops provide Poké Balls to catch Pokémon and Potions to heal players' Pokémon injured during Gym battles). Additionally, people in regions with high PokéStop densities are more likely to have a PokéStop closer to them at all times than would be the case in regions with low density (subject to the ecological fallacy). Finally, players in high-density regions have an additional nuanced but important capability: they can continuously loop between PokéStops, substantially reducing the negative effect of the five-minute revisit restriction on PokéStops (i.e. the benefits of PokéStop density do not increase linearly).

There are two other geographic elements of the game that could have been used as proxies for advantage, but both had important drawbacks. First, we could have analyzed the distribution of spawned Pokémon, but the geography of this spawning is highly variable, and collecting these data would not have been possible under the ethical constraints described below. Second, Pokémon Gyms are an interesting geographic element that, like PokéStops, are fixed in physical space. However, Gyms are not nearly as fundamental to the game. A player could play the game without battling in Gyms, but the resources PokéStops provide are necessary (unless the player wishes to spend their own money to purchase resources, a possibility in the game, but clearly a disadvantage). Below, we discuss (1) how we collected PokéStop data, (2) the types of places we examined and (3) our geostatistical methods.

#### *PokéStop Data*

We collected PokéStop data directly from Niantic using a customized data collection program. The program is based on two open source projects – pgoapi [58], a popular third-party Pokémon GO python API, and PokémonGo-Map [78], a Pokémon GO visualization app. At a high level, our program takes as input the minimum bounding rectangle of a U.S. county and captures geographic locations of all PokéStops present in that county.

At the time of our analysis, it was unclear whether our use of PokéStop data was permitted under Niantic's terms of service. Because of this ambiguity and the fact that SIGCHI is currently undergoing a review of its ethics protocol related to terms of service and has not yet published its guidelines [51], we took as conservative an approach as possible. Specifically, we reduced our impact to the Pokémon GO servers to an absolute minimum and collected only data essential to our research questions. This ensured that the benefits of our collection program (e.g. identifying racial and ethnic bias in Pokémon GO) outweighed any costs.

To minimize our impact on the server, we issued requests to the server as infrequently as possible while still being able to collect the minimum amount of data to achieve our goals. This amounted to issuing a request once every ten seconds and pausing the collector for one minute after every 15 requests. We also maximized the geographic extent of each request to minimize the overall number of requests.

Because our access to PokéStop data was significantly restricted by the speed of our data collector, we focused our geostatistical analyses on specific regions. For our urban vs. rural comparison, we randomly selected 20 U.S. counties in each of six government-defined classes along the urban-rural spectrum, with these classes explained in detail below. For our race and ethnicity analyses, we focused on two metropolitan areas: Chicago and Detroit. We also motivate the choice of these cities below. More generally, these focus regions mean that the conclusions of our geostatistical analyses are restricted to the United States (and in some cases, may be restricted to just Chicago and Detroit). While the conclusions may apply more globally and the restriction of focus to a single country (and even a single metropolitan area) is common in related work in the GeoHCI space (e.g. [66,67]), future work should investigate these phenomenon using a more international perspective.

### Demographic Datasets

As noted above, the GeoHCI community has identified that geographic systems can be prone to significant geographically-linked demographic biases when they rely on crowdsourced datasets like Pokémon GO does with PokéStops. Two of the most significant biases that have been observed occur along the urban-rural spectrum (e.g. [12,13,26,30]) and across ethnic/racial lines (e.g. [30,33,49]). As such, when examining places for advantage and/or disadvantage, we do so through the lenses defined by the urban-rural spectrum and race and ethnicity. That is, we ask (1) Do places of a specific racial and ethnic make-up have advantages in Pokémon GO? and, similarly, (2) Do more urban areas have advantages over more rural areas?

Following prior work, we make use of specific U.S. government sources for our demographic data. With regard to race and ethnicity, we utilize the percentage of the population that is white and non-Hispanic[1], a variable from the U.S. Census [59] that is commonly used to assess the percentage of the population that identifies as a racial and/or ethnical minority in the United States (e.g. [21,55]). For urban/rural data, like prior work (e.g. [26]), we turn to the National Center for Health Statistics' (NCHS) urban-rural ordinal classifications [79], which assigns each U.S. county a rating from "1" ("large central metro") to "6" ("noncore", or not part of any metro- or micropolitan area).

For our urban/rural analyses, we randomly selected 20 counties from each NCHS class. For our race and ethnicity analyses, we focused on Chicago and Detroit. We selected Chicago because it has been used in prior related work on geographic crowdsourced systems (e.g. [56]). We added Detroit because it is a poorer metropolitan area with a large minority population.

### Geostatistical Modeling

The nature of our datasets required that we use different approaches for our urbanness question and our race and ethnicity question. With regard to the former, due to the lack of spatial autocorrelation (see below) in our random sets of 20 counties, we were able to use straightforward descriptive statistics to analyze PokéStop density across each NCHS class on the rural and urban spectrum.

Looking at race and ethnicity within urban areas, however, requires significantly different methods because of the presence of spatial autocorrelation. Spatial autocorrelation is a complex topic and is discussed in an HCI context in several recent papers (e.g. [30,36]). However, in our particular study, the presence of spatial autocorrelation means that the demographics of one area of a city might affect both the PokéStop density in that area and *in neighboring areas* (among other spatial relationships). Indeed, as described below, people in our field study reported traveling non-trivial distances in search of PokéStops, which makes accounting for these spatial dependence relationships critical to our analysis.

While autocorrelation was ignored in HCI and related fields for many years, this is increasingly no longer the case. However, the methods that have been used to control for autocorrelation in HCI thus far – spatial error and spatial lag models – do not capture the spatial relationship between the demographics in one area and the PokéStop density nearby. *Spatial Durbin models*, an emerging best practice in the geostatistics literature, do capture this type of dependence, which is fundamental to our analysis. As cross-region relationships between dependent and independent variables like those in our analysis (more formally, "exogenous spatial relationships") are quite common in spatial data studied in HCI, spatial Durbin models will likely prove useful for HCI research questions outside the context of this paper. Overviews of spatial Durbin modeling can be found in Yang et al. [64] and Elhorst [7].

We applied spatial Durbin models to census tracts (a standard U.S. Census spatial unit) within Chicago and Detroit. Our primary independent variable was the percent of each tract's population that identifies as non-Hispanic white. We also included as a control the population density of each tract, an important consideration given prior work on the urban-rural spectrum. We log-scaled this variable to account

[1] The U.S. Census treats race (e.g. "White", "Black" "American Indian and Alaskan Native") as orthogonal to ethnicity ("Hispanic"). Most people of Hispanic ethnicity report their race white, hence the need for a "non-Hispanic white" variable. [59]

for a long-tail distribution of population densities. Our dependent variable was PokéStop density measured in PokéStops per square kilometer (note that spatial Durbin models also include a "lag" term for each independent and dependent variable).

Spatial Durbin models are interpreted somewhat differently than standard regression models. Interpretation of the model hinges on the *direct effects* and *indirect effects*. Thus, we do not report the coefficients fit by the model, as they are not commonly interpreted (e.g. Yang et al. [64]). Direct effects describe the relationship between an independent variable (e.g. % non-Hispanic white) and the dependent variable (e.g. PokéStop density) *within a tract*. Indirect effects describe the relationship between the *average independent variable value of a tract's neighbors* and the dependent variable in that tract. More generally, like in a traditional regression, a positive effect (either direct or indirect) between our race and ethnicity variable (% non-Hispanic white) and PokéStop density would indicate that white non-Hispanic regions have an advantage in the game. Conversely, if no significant direct or indirect effect is found, no relationship between PokéStop Density and race or ethnicity would have been identified.

## RESULTS

In this section, we present the results of our field survey and geostatistical analyses. We organize this section into 5 high-level findings that emerge across both analyses, with results from the survey supporting the geostatistics and vice versa.

### Finding #1: Existing geographic advantages are reinforced (Places)

The results of both our survey and our geostatistical analyses suggest that the design of Pokémon GO follows and reinforces existing geographic contours of advantage and disadvantage. More specifically, we find that people who live in urban places with small minority populations (and to a lesser extent richer places) have distinct advantages over people who live in other areas, where PokéStop density is substantially lower. Moreover, the game incentivizes movement towards these advantaged areas and away from rural places and places with larger minority populations, a problem that we will see has important financial implications. Below, we discuss these findings in detail.

#### *The Urban-Rural Spectrum*

Our findings suggest that rural places and the people who live in them are substantially disadvantaged in Pokémon GO. The effect sizes in this respect are considerable. Figure 1 shows the results of our randomized county-level analysis. The figure shows a dramatic decrease in PokéStops per square kilometer as counties become more rural. While there are approximately 2.9 PokéStops per square kilometer in core urban counties, the equivalent number in rural "class 6" counties is 0.03 PokéStops per square kilometer. This difference is significant ($t(19)=4.2$, $p < 0.001$). Put another way, the most urban counties have, on average, approximately 97 times more PokéStops per square kilometer than the most rural counties. Moreover, this result also means that Pokémon GO incentivizes people to move away from rural areas and towards urban areas, where they can much more easily find dense regions of PokéStops. As we will see below, this has an effect on travel patterns, money flows, and other factors.

The results of our survey indicate that rural disadvantage is so significant as to make the game somewhat unplayable in rural areas. When asked if there were any places that they had been in which playing Pokémon Go was boring, 15 percent of respondents reported rural areas, e.g. "Countryside, outside the cities, no game content there" (#44, Belgium) and "In the woods; nothing is happening [there]" (#271, USA). A number of participants responded to this question by explicitly saying that "rural areas" or the "countryside" were boring places to play Pokémon GO.

#### *Race and Ethnicity*

Our results also strongly suggest that the geographic distribution of PokéStops substantially advantages areas with large white (non-Hispanic) populations. Consider Table 2, which shows the outcome of our spatial Durbin modeling analyses in the cities of Chicago and Detroit. In both cases, we see a significant and substantial positive direct or indirect

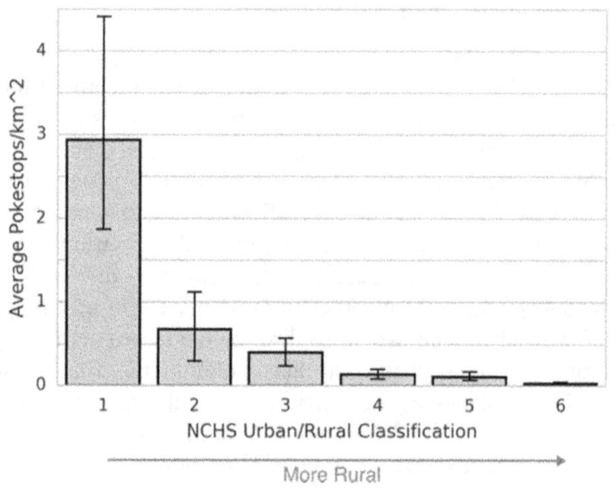


**Figure 1. Average PokéStops per square kilometer for counties across the urban-rural spectrum. Density in entirely rural counties (class 6) is orders-of-magnitude smaller than density in urban core counties (class 1).**

| **Chicago Effects** | | | | |
|---|---|---|---|---|
| | *Direct* | *p-value* | *Indirect* | *p-value* |
| % non-Hispanic white | 7.55 | 0.1 | 21.66 | 0.007 |
| $\log_2$[population/km$^2$] | 1.55 | < 0.001 | 10.20 | < 0.001 |
| **Detroit Effects** | | | | |
| | *Direct* | *p-value* | *Indirect* | *p-value* |
| % non-Hispanic white | 26.80 | <0.001 | 11.79 | *n.s.* |
| $\log_2$[population/km$^2$] | 0.76 | 0.05 | -2.58 | 0.15 |

**Table 2. Results of spatial Durbin models**

effect for the percentage of the population that is white non-Hispanic on PokéStop density. Put simply, this means that as the share of the population that is African American, Hispanic, and other minorities increases, the number of PokéStops per square kilometer decreases, often by a significantly margin.

Unpacking Table 2 in more detail, we see in the "Direct" column that if a census tract in Detroit were to go from 0% to 100% white non-Latino, the PokéStop density would increase by 26.8 PokéStops/km$^2$. For context, the mean overall PokéStop density for tracts in Detroit is 5.7. A similar trend can be seen for Chicago's "Indirect" column: the value here means that if a census tract's neighbors were to go from 0% to 100% white non-Latino, the census tract would see an increase in PokéStop density of 21.6 PokéStops/km$^2$. The relative size of this effect is smaller, though: Chicago has a mean density of 17.6.

The trends in Table 2 can be seen cartographically in Figure 2, which depicts PokéStop density in Chicago next to a map of the percent of the population that is non-Hispanic white. The mostly non-minority northeastern areas are replete with PokéStops, as is the central business district and nearby touristic areas. However, the largely African-American and Hispanic "South Side" and "West Side" have much lower densities, usually between 0 and 11 PokéStops/km$^2$.

Many coverage bias studies of GeoHCI systems consider income in addition to or instead of race/ethnicity as the two are dismayingly correlated in the U.S. and in many other countries. In keeping with this trend, we examined our results with an income lens and found a somewhat surprising result: PokéStop density seems much more linked to race and ethnicity than income, even though income and race and ethnicity are strongly associated in our study areas. At a city-wide-scale, there is some indication that poorer places have fewer PokéStops: Chicago has a median household income that is almost twice as high as that of Detroit [80] and the mean PokéStop density in Chicago is over three times higher than in Detroit. Detroit is also significantly less white non-Hispanic (7.8%) than Chicago (31.7%) [80], so, as is typical in coverage bias work, the disadvantage experienced by low-income areas is one-and-the-same with the disadvantage experienced by areas predominately populated by minorities.

However, looking at a more local scale within cities, we see a decoupling of this disadvantage, with PokéStop density lower in minority neighborhoods but not necessarily in low-income neighborhoods. We re-ran our Durbin models using income instead of percent white non-Hispanic and found a surprising result: despite strong associations between income and race/ethnicity in our study areas, we did not detect the same effects for income as we did for race. In fact, we detected no significant results for income in either city, and the trends were much smaller (e.g. around 4 PokéStops per sq. km.). Examining our data in more detail, we observed a few interesting examples of middle-class, minority neighborhoods that experience very low PokéStop density. For instance, this is the case for census tracts in the far south of Chicago, which tend to be higher income, but unlike areas further north, are almost exclusively African American.

#### Finding #2: Pokémon GO can be a rare catalyst for large-scale destination choice change (Movement)

Humans rarely change their movement patterns. A large body of work (e.g.[31,45,61]), including recent research in

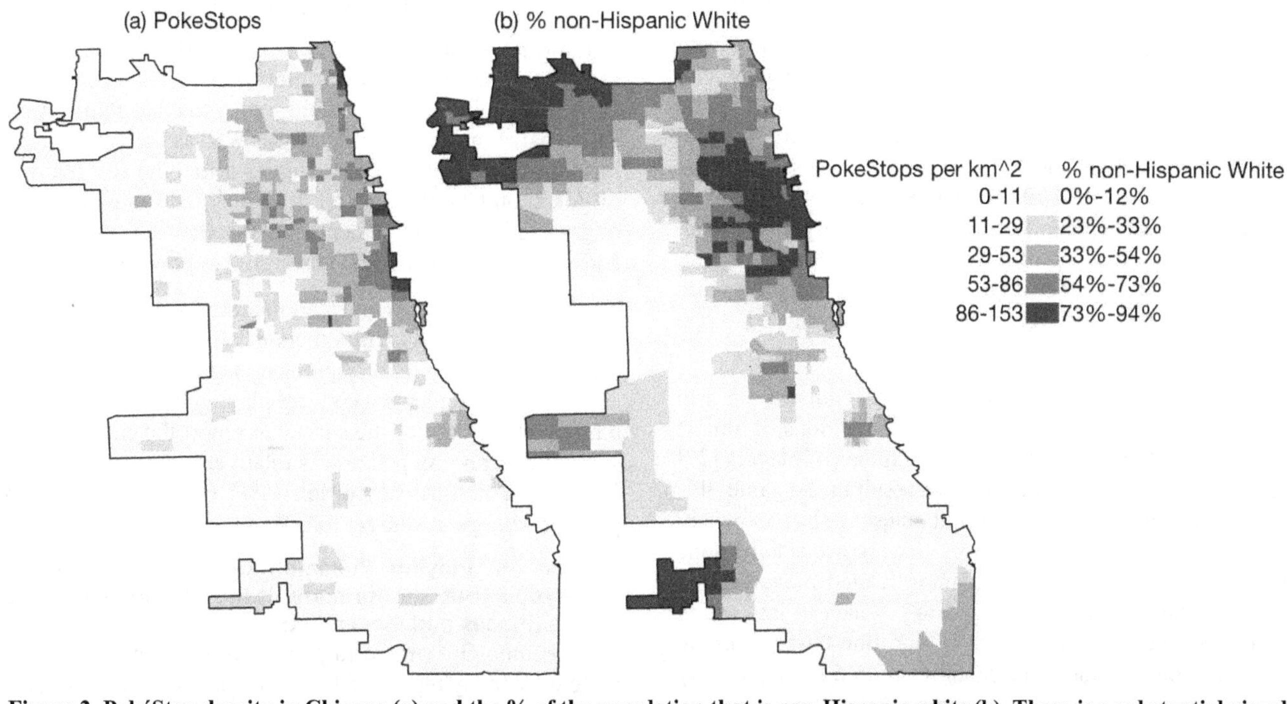


**Figure 2. PokéStop density in Chicago (a) and the % of the population that is non-Hispanic white (b). There is a substantial visual correlation that bears out in our Durbin models. Data classification (colors) were defined by QGIS's natural breaks algorithm.**

*Science* [54], has established that human mobility is highly predictable, with most people moving between home, work, and a few other fixed locations (e.g. coffee shop, grocery store, daycare, religious institutions). However, prior work in the location-based gaming space suggests that Pokémon GO might be successfully incenting people to do something they rarely do: substantially change where they choose to go (i.e. alter their "destination choice" or "trip distribution" in transportation science parlance [41]). Moreover, given the popularity of Pokémon GO, the game may be encouraging people to go to new places at a tremendous scale.

Our results suggest that this hypothesis is supported. Two data points from our field survey stand out in this respect. First, we asked respondents if they had ever previously visited the survey location prior to their present visit. Only 83% had visited the location before, meaning that for 17% of players, Pokémon GO caused them to visit the survey location for the very first time.

This finding is substantiated by a second finding from our survey: almost 60% of respondents indicated that they had visited at least one new place while playing Pokémon GO. The types of newly-visited locations were highly heterogeneous and defined by the types of POIs at which PokéStops were placed. This included parks (mentioned by 22% of respondents who had been to a new location), POIs like soccer/football stadiums and castles (14%) and water features (11%). Our data suggests that most of these new locations are likely within a moderate (but not small) distance from respondents' homes or workplaces: the median distance respondents reported travelling to the survey location was 3km. However, 9% of respondents did indicate visiting an entirely new town/city because of Pokémon GO.

It is interesting to note that the 3km finding is concordant with Figure 2, in which areas of high PokéStop density tend to be both in and *near* areas with a very large non-Hispanic white population. This is captured in the indirect effects in the Chicago spatial Durbin model, where we see that the average non-Hispanic white population of a tract's neighbors has a substantial effect on the PokéStop density in the tract. We did not see a significant indirect effect in Detroit, however, and it may be that Pokémon GO movement is more concentrated there owing to the fact that areas with large non-minority populations are very concentrated.

More generally, given the tremendous regularity in trip destination choice [54] under standard conditions, if almost two-thirds of Pokémon GO's tens of millions of players [77] visited at least one new location as a result of the game, this would represent a substantial and unusual shift in where humans choose to go. Although more work needs to be done to understand location-based gaming-related movement in more detail, this finding may have interesting interdisciplinary implications. If location-based gaming continues to grow and if our mobility-related findings apply in other location-based gaming contexts, it will be important to consider game-incentivized movement in the many models in domains ranging from urban planning to epidemiology that require movement data.

It is also important to consider this higher-level finding in the context of this paper's other findings. Most notably, given our results related to PokéStop distribution, to the extent that demographic contours are crossed in Pokémon GO-related movement, the movement likely involves mostly people from disadvantaged areas going to advantaged areas, rather than the other way around. As we shift into discussing the economic geography of Pokémon GO below, the flow from disadvantaged to advantaged becomes even more notable.

**Finding #3: Pokémon GO plays a role in where people spend money (Movement)**

Geographic studies related to movement are interested not only in the movement of people, but also in the movement of goods and resources (e.g. [9,10,20,52]). As such, in our field survey, we inquired as to whether people had spent money at locations they had visited while playing Pokémon GO. This question also has important implications related to the monetization of location-based games, around which there has been much discussion [81–83].

Almost half of interviewees (46%) had purchased something at a venue they were near because of Pokémon GO-related movement. Typically, these were foodstuffs (25% mentioned purchasing drinks and 23% food). We also found evidence that, for some players, Pokémon GO was a driver for a day's outing, e.g. visiting the cinema after playing was mentioned by several participants (e.g. "A bar to have a drink and cinema to watch a movie"; #46, Belgium)). The purchase of alcohol was specifically mentioned by 11% of participants (terms such as alcohol, beer, pub, bar, liquor), e.g. "Fast food and drinks in a beer garden" (#110, Germany).

**Finding #4: Pokémon GO is associated with group, not individual, movement (Movement)**

One clear finding from our field survey that has implications the social computing community as well as the GeoHCI and location-based gaming communities is that the vast majority of Pokémon GO players appear to play (and move) in pairs or groups. 70% of respondents said that they never play alone and only 12% indicated that they always play alone.

The respondents who indicated that they at least sometimes played Pokémon GO with others mostly did so with friends (72% percent of overall respondents) and family (29%). We also asked respondents who were playing Pokémon GO with a group at the time of the survey to report the current group size. The mean group size was relatively small at 2.7 ($SD$ = 1.9), but a non-trivial portion (7%) of respondents were playing with groups larger than five.

**Finding #5: Playing Pokémon Go can be somewhat dangerous, but the primary issue is movement not places (Places and Movement)**

As Pokémon GO surged in popularity following its launch, there were many reports in the press about risks to health and safety associated with the game. These reports fell into two categories, each associated with one of the two geographic themes that are the focus of this paper: places and movement. The bulk of the press reports (e.g. [81–83]) related to places and revolved around players wandering into "areas that they should be avoiding" [75] a type of report that has been shown to have an important negative effect on people's "platial" mental maps in their home regions [38]. The reports associated with movement described incidents in which Pokémon GO players, distracted from their surroundings and immersed in the game on their smartphones, encountered an environmental hazard (e.g. a car [60,76], a cliff [84]).

We asked respondents several questions that inquired as to any risks to their health or safety associated with movement or places they had experienced while playing Pokémon GO. Our results suggest that the danger associated with movement is much more widespread than that associated with places. Over one-third of respondents (33%) reported some form of near miss or actual collision with an object in their environment. Players mostly reported bumping into signs, poles and other people (as in Bell et al. [3]).

The most serious implication of players' reduced environmental awareness is when they come into conflict with road traffic. In this respect, 11% of participants recalled situations in which they had put their personal safety at risk by, for example, crossing the street without looking. e.g., "I wasn't paying attention and my boyfriend had to prevent me from stepping into the street" (#330, USA). While such risks are also present in other uses of smartphones (e.g. [5,57]), the excitement of gameplay may intensify the risk.

With regard to place-related danger, only 1 of our 375 respondents reported an incident similar to those reported in the media (though a degree less serious). This respondent (#182, Finland) reported being threatened with a knife. Thirteen percent of our respondents did, however, report feeling unsafe in a place while playing Pokémon GO. In some cases, these participants specifically referred to their mental maps as the reason for their discomfort, e.g. "[I was in the] inner city" (#45, Germany) and "Being in Dinkytown late at night with my cell phone out" (#36, USA).

## DISCUSSION

In this section, we first explicate several design implications that emerge from the five findings above. We then continue with more general discussion about our results.

### Implications for Design

#### *"Geotechnical Design" for Location-based Gaming*

Our findings related to the relatively severe bias present in Pokémon GO are very likely not endemic to location-based gaming in general. Instead, they are likely emergent from Pokémon GO's geographic design (i.e. "geotechnical design"), specifically the manner in which PokéStops were geographically distributed.

As discussed in the Related Work section, the GeoHCI research community has established through a large literature that datasets that are the product of organic geographic crowdsourcing processes tend to have significant coverage biases. These biases are nearly always demographically linked, providing advantages for already-advantaged demographics (e.g. [18,29,30,48]). By relying heavily on data submitted from Ingress players, Niantic used an organic geographic crowdsourcing process to distribute PokéStops. As such, it is not a surprise that Pokémon GO is a game that advantages urban, white, non-Hispanic people.

Fortunately, alternative geographic design approaches can likely lead to much more desirable outcomes. For instance, some reasonable approaches might be:

- Making the reuse of game elements in undercovered areas more advantageous than in more heavily covered areas (e.g. reducing the cooldown time for PokéStops or increasing spawn rates for rare Pokémon).
- Supplementing crowdsourced data in underrepresented areas with the locations of all public spaces. This can be done with OpenStreetMap data, among other techniques.
- Using non-geographic crowdsourcing (i.e. Mechanical Turk) to search through Street View imagery to identify adequate locations for game elements. Computer vision approaches can likely be used to partially automate this process once a training set has been developed.
- Identifying new types of suitable game element locations for rural areas (e.g. road pull-outs) and dramatically increasing the density of game elements in the small populated places that exist in these areas.
- Adding features for groups of co-located players that have lower geographical dependence, e.g. if five players are co-located, a PokéStop type element is created dynamically.

Interestingly, bias in location-based games is probably an easier problem to address than bias in other geographic datasets important to the GeoHCI literature. For instance, to resolve the urban biases in Wikipedia and OpenStreetMap, the corresponding communities will likely have to engage in content creation and recruiting efforts at a massive scale. For location-based game designers, once a solution is identified, it can likely be scaled with minimal effort. It takes a lot of work to write a good Wikipedia article about an undercovered place; adding a PokéStop is quite a bit simpler.

Finally, and more generally, our results suggest that location-based game designers should at minimum audit the geographic distributions of important game elements. To do so, they can employ the exact same geostatistical approaches that we have in this paper (e.g. spatial Durbin modeling).

#### *Reducing Movement-associated Risks*

Although the general risks of using a smartphone while walking in urban environments has been widely reported [44], few actual solutions to address the problem have been proposed. In the scope of location-based gaming and Pokémon GO, we believe the following approaches to improving player safety could be explored:

- Avoid game content appearing across a road from the player's location, reducing the desire to rush to cross a potentially busy street (although doing so would involve interesting challenges at the intersection of spatial computing and game mechanics).
- Whilst the game already requires players travelling at high speed to acknowledge that they are passengers rather than drivers, this feature could be extended to prevent aspects of gameplay in a moving vehicle that could result in rapid route deviations.
- Have the system notify the user, e.g. by freezing the UI, when they are in dangerous areas, e.g. near busy roads.

### Capturing a Moment in Time Using Mixed Methods

For those that study location-based gaming and geographic technologies, Pokémon GO's dramatic rise to prominence was a fascinating phenomenon to observe. When the game became a global blockbuster, we were struck by the democratization of location-based gaming that was occurring but, like others in the field [40,63,65], we anticipated that that its mass popularity would be short-lived.

As such, in order to understand as much about this phenomenon as quickly possible, we developed a mixed methods approach that folded a research agenda that would likely occur in serial under normal conditions into a single project conducted in parallel. Our hypothesis was that our two methods would reinforce each other in the same fashion as if the projects were conducted in serial.

This hypothesis turned out to be supported. The results of our field study substantially helped to shape our geostatistical analyses, e.g. contributing to the motivation to use spatial Durbin models (given the movement range from Finding #2) and to use PokéStop density as our dependent variable (due to the number of people that visited the survey locations for PokéStops). Conversely, the findings of the geostatistical analysis provided critical context to our survey results. For instance, without the geostatistical analysis, our results about people spending money and visiting new places while playing Pokémon GO are a uniformly positive story. With the geostatistical analyses, it becomes a story at least partially about the reinforcing of existing advantages. Moreover, as expected, since the time of our survey the global interest in Pokémon GO has waned [77] (although by no means dissolved entirely [1,53,85]). Many of the survey locations, for instance, now have many fewer players than they did during the period of the survey.

### Limitations and Future Work

While our field survey considered five countries, our geostatistical analyses focused only on specific regions of the United States. Future work should seek to expand the geographic reach of these analyses to more areas of the U.S. and, critically, to different countries. While many countries have challenges associated with race, ethnicity, and equality similar to those in the U.S., they tend to have different geographic structures and histories than their American versions. The same is true with regard to the relationships between urban and rural areas. While we expect that the phenomena we observed generalize internationally at least in part, it is would be interesting to see the extent of the validity of this generalization. Additionally, expanding our field survey to more countries would have similar benefits.

Selecting interview locations using interviewers' local knowledge of active Pokémon GO player locations was the likely only feasible approach to gain insights from a large number of players quickly. However, the use of more formal geographic sampling strategies to survey a representative group of Pokémon GO players would have been preferred if more time were available. We note, however, that we observed relatively little geographic variation in our survey results: besides local differences in geographical structures (e.g. suburbs are predominantly a US concept), we found little difference in reported playing and geographical movement behaviors across the 5 countries surveyed.

Another important limitation and direction of future work relates to the breadth of the concepts of movement and places. This paper asked two specific questions: how has movement *changed* and which types of places are *advantaged or disadvantaged*. However, there are a number of other questions one could ask about these concepts in relationship to Pokémon GO and location-based gaming. For instance: How does Pokémon GO alter the senses of place of players in places both previously known and unknown to them? How does the visible extent available to players affect movement? What types of people are involved in Pokémon GO-related "migration"? Do players revisit locations they first discover in Pokémon GO? More broadly, while this paper began the study of the geography of Pokémon GO, we have a lot more to learn about the geographic dimension of Pokémon GO and location-based gaming more generally.

### Data Sharing

We are releasing our complete survey results so that other researchers may conduct additional analyses using this data (url: https://git.io/vMY7R).

## CONCLUSION

The paper provided the first detailed snapshot of the geography of a widely democratized location-based game. While we expect that some of our findings will not generalize beyond Pokémon GO and very similar games, others provide early insight into the geography a world in which location-based gaming and related technologies are more widespread. In several important cases, these insights are "canaries in the coal mine", providing warnings that can inform the design of safer and less racially- and ethnically-biased technologies.

## ACKNOWLEDGEMENTS

We wish to thank GroupLens Research for their feedback, especially Daniel Kluver and Loren Terveen. This research was supported in part by Tekes –the Finnish Funding Agency for Innovation as part of 'The Naked Approach' program and the Volkswagen Foundation through a Lichtenberg Professorship.

## REFERENCES


1. Jennifer Allen. The past and future of location based AR games like Pokemon Go. Retrieved January 4, 2017 from http://www.gamasutra.com/view/news/277331/The_past_and_future_of_location_based_AR_games_like_Pokemon_Go.php
2. Nikolaos M. Avouris and Nikoleta Yiannoutsou. 2012. A review of mobile location-based games for learning across physical and virtual spaces. *J. UCS* 18, 15: 2120–2142.
3. Marek Bell, Matthew Chalmers, Louise Barkhuus, Malcolm Hall, Scott Sherwood, Paul Tennent, Barry Brown, Duncan Rowland, Steve Benford, Mauricio Capra, and Alistair Hampshire. 2006. Interweaving mobile games with everyday life. In *Proceedings of the SIGCHI conference on Human Factors in computing systems* (CHI '06), 417–426. https://doi.org/10.1145/1124772.1124835
4. Staffan Björk, Jennica Falk, Rebecca Hansson, and Peter Ljungstrand. 2001. Pirates! Using the physical world as a game board. In *In Proceedings of Interact 2001*, 9–13.
5. Katherine W. Byington and David C. Schwebel. 2013. Effects of mobile Internet use on college student pedestrian injury risk. *Accident Analysis & Prevention* 51: 78–83.
6. Shira Chess. 2014. Augmented regionalism: Ingress as geomediated gaming narrative. *Information, Communication & Society* 17, 9: 1105–1117.
7. J. Paul Elhorst. 2010. Applied Spatial Econometrics: Raising the Bar. *Spatial Economic Analysis* 5, 1: 9–28. https://doi.org/10.1080/17421770903541772
8. Martin Flintham, Steve Benford, Rob Anastasi, Terry Hemmings, Andy Crabtree, Chris Greenhalgh, Nick Tandavanitj, Matt Adams, and Ju Row-Farr. 2003. Where on-line meets on the streets: experiences with mobile mixed reality games. In *Proceedings of the SIGCHI conference on Human factors in computing systems* (CHI '03), 569–576. https://doi.org/10.1145/642611.642710
9. Robin Flowerdew and Murray Aitkin. 1982. A method of fitting the gravity model based on the Poisson distribution. *Journal of regional science* 22, 2: 191–202.
10. Ruth García-Gavilanes, Yelena Mejova, and Daniele Quercia. 2014. Twitter ain't without frontiers: economic, social, and cultural boundaries in international communication. In *Proceedings of the 17th ACM conference on Computer supported cooperative work & social computing* (CSCW '14), 1511–1522. https://doi.org/10.1145/2531602.2531725
11. Annie Gentes, Aude Guyot-Mbodji, and Isabelle Demeure. 2010. Gaming on the move: urban experience as a new paradigm for mobile pervasive game design. *Multimedia systems* 16, 1: 43–55.
12. Eric Gilbert, Karrie Karahalios, and Christian Sandvig. 2008. The network in the garden: an empirical analysis of social media in rural life. In *Proceedings of the SIGCHI Conference on Human Factors in Computing Systems* (CHI '08), 1603–1612. https://doi.org/10.1145/1357054.1357304
13. Eric Gilbert, Karrie Karahalios, and Christian Sandvig. 2010. The Network in the Garden: Designing Social Media for Rural Life. *American Behavioral Scientist* 53, 9: 1367–1388. https://doi.org/10.1177/0002764210361690
14. Mark Graham, Stefano De Sabbata, and Matthew A. Zook. 2015. Towards a study of information geographies: (im)mutable augmentations and a mapping of the geographies of information. *Geo: Geography and Environment* 2, 1: 88–105. https://doi.org/10.1002/geo2.8
15. Mark Graham, Bernie Hogan, Ralph K. Straumann, and Ahmed Medhat. 2014. Uneven Geographies of User-Generated Information: Patterns of Increasing Informational Poverty. *Annals of the Association of American Geographers* 104, 4: 746–764. https://doi.org/10.1080/00045608.2014.910087
16. Mark Graham and Matthew Zook. 2013. Augmented realities and uneven geographies: exploring the geolinguistic contours of the web. *Environment and Planning A* 45, 1: 77 – 99. https://doi.org/10.1068/a44674
17. Mark Graham, Matthew Zook, and Andrew Boulton. 2013. Augmented reality in urban places: contested content and the duplicity of code. *Transactions of the Institute of British Geographers* 38, 3: 464–479. https://doi.org/10.1111/j.1475-5661.2012.00539.x
18. Mordechai Haklay. 2010. How good is volunteered geographical information? A comparative study of OpenStreetMap and Ordnance Survey datasets. *Environment and planning B: Planning and design* 37, 4: 682–703.
19. Scott A. Hale. 2015. Cross-language Wikipedia Editing of Okinawa, Japan. In *Proceedings of the 33rd Annual ACM Conference on Human Factors in Computing Systems* (CHI '15), 183–192. https://doi.org/10.1145/2702123.2702346
20. Darren Hardy, James Frew, and Michael F. Goodchild. 2012. Volunteered geographic information production as a spatial process. *International Journal of Geographical Information Science* 26, 7: 1191–1212.
21. Eszter Hargittai. 2007. Whose Space? Differences Among Users and Non-Users of Social Network Sites. *Journal of Computer-Mediated Communication* 13, 1: 276–297. https://doi.org/10.1111/j.1083-6101.2007.00396.x
22. Rami Hashish, PhD, D. P. T. Principal, and National Biomechanics Institute. 400AD. Pokémon GO... And Get Injured? | Huffington Post. *The Huffington Post.* Retrieved September 18, 2016 from

http://www.huffingtonpost.com/rami-hashish/pokemon-goand-get-injured_b_11437770.html
23. Brent Hecht and Darren Gergle. 2010. The Tower of Babel Meets Web 2.0: User-Generated Content and Its Applications in a Multilingual Context. In *CHI '10: 28th International Conference on Human Factors in Computing Systems* (CHI '10), 291–300. https://doi.org/10.1145/1753326.1753370
24. Brent Hecht, Johannes Schöning, Licia Capra, Afra Mashhadi, Loren Terveen, and Mei-Po Kwan. 2013. 2013 Workshop on Geographic Human-Computer Interaction. In *CHI '13 EA: Extended Abstracts of the 31st CHI Conference on Human Factors in Computing Systems*.
25. Brent Hecht, Johannes Schöning, Thomas Erickson, and Reid Priedhorsky. 2011. Geographic human-computer interaction. In *CHI '11 EA: 29th ACM Conference on Human Factors in Computing Systems (Extended Abstracts)* (CHI EA '11), 447–450. https://doi.org/10.1145/1979742.1979532
26. Brent Hecht and Monica Stephens. 2014. A Tale of Cities: Urban Biases in Volunteered Geographic Information. In *ICWSM '14: Eight International AAAI Conference on Weblogs and Social Media*.
27. Christopher Huffaker. 2016. There are fewer Pokemon Go locations in black neighborhoods, but why? *bnd*. Retrieved September 21, 2016 from http://www.bnd.com/news/nation-world/national/article89562297.html
28. Nathan Hulsey and Joshua Reeves. 2014. The gift that keeps on giving: Google, Ingress, and the gift of surveillance. *Surveillance & Society* 12, 3: 389.
29. Isaac Johnson and Brent Hecht. 2015. Structural Causes of Bias in Crowd-derived Geographic Information: Towards a Holistic Understanding. Retrieved September 17, 2016 from http://www-users.cs.umn.edu/~joh12041/Publications/StructuralCausesBiases_aaaispring2016.pdf
30. Isaac Johnson, Yilun Lin, Toby Li, Andrew Hall, Aaron Halfaker, Johannes Schöning, and Brent Hecht. 2016. Not at Home on the Range: Peer Production and the Urban/Rural Divide. In *CHI '16: 34th International Conference on Human Factors in Computing Systems*.
31. Ryuichi Kitamura and Toon Van Der Hoorn. 1987. Regularity and irreversibility of weekly travel behavior. *Transportation* 14, 3: 227–251.
32. Sheila G. Klauer, Feng Guo, Bruce G. Simons-Morton, Marie Claude Ouimet, Suzanne E. Lee, and Thomas A. Dingus. 2014. Distracted driving and risk of road crashes among novice and experienced drivers. *New England journal of medicine* 370, 1: 54–59.
33. Linna Li, Michael F. Goodchild, and Bo Xu. 2013. Spatial, temporal, and socioeconomic patterns in the use of Twitter and Flickr. *Cartography and Geographic Information Science* 40, 2: 61–77. https://doi.org/10.1080/15230406.2013.777139
34. Tony Liao and Lee Humphreys. 2015. Layar-ed places: Using mobile augmented reality to tactically reengage, reproduce, and reappropriate public space. *New Media & Society* 17, 9: 1418–1435. https://doi.org/10.1177/1461444814527734
35. Carsten Magerkurth, Adrian David Cheok, Regan L. Mandryk, and Trond Nilsen. 2005. Pervasive games: bringing computer entertainment back to the real world. *Computers in Entertainment (CIE)* 3, 3: 4–4.
36. Momin M. Malik, Hemank Lamba, Constantine Nakos, and Jürgen Pfeffer. 2015. Population Bias in Geotagged Tweets. In *ICWSM 2015 Working on Standards and Practices in Large-Scale Social Media Research*.
37. Afra Mashhadi, Giovanni Quattrone, and Licia Capra. 2013. Putting ubiquitous crowd-sourcing into context. In *CSCW '13: 2013 ACM Conference on Computer Supported Cooperative Work*, 611–622.
38. Sorin Matei, Sandra J. Ball-Rokeach, and Jack Linchuan Qiu. 2001. Fear and misperception of Los Angeles urban space a spatial-statistical study of communication-shaped mental maps. *Communication Research* 28, 4: 429–463.
39. Sebastian Matyas, Christian Matyas, Christoph Schlieder, Peter Kiefer, Hiroko Mitarai, and Maiko Kamata. 2008. Designing location-based mobile games with a purpose: collecting geospatial data with CityExplorer. In *Proceedings of the 2008 international conference on advances in computer entertainment technology* (ACE '08), 244–247. https://doi.org/10.1145/1501750.1501806
40. Frans Mäyrä. Note on Pokémon Go: fantasy of collecting and exploring "urban nature." Retrieved September 17, 2016 from https://fransmayra.fi/2016/07/16/note-on-pokemon-go-fantasy-of-collecting-and-exploring-urban-nature/
41. Michael G. McNally. 2007. The four step model. *Handbook of transport modelling* 1: 35–41.
42. Keith Mitchell, Duncan McCaffery, George Metaxas, Joe Finney, Stefan Schmid, and Andrew Scott. 2003. Six in the city: introducing Real Tournament-a mobile IPv6 based context-aware multiplayer game. In *Proceedings of the 2nd workshop on Network and system support for games*, 91–100. https://doi.org/10.1145/963900.963909
43. Markus Montola, Jaakko Stenros, and Annika Waern. 2009. *Pervasive games: theory and design*. Morgan Kaufmann Publishers Inc.
44. Jack L. Nasar and Derek Troyer. 2013. Pedestrian injuries due to mobile phone use in public places. *Accident Analysis & Prevention* 57: 91–95.
45. Anastasios Noulas, Salvatore Scellato, Renaud Lambiotte, Massimiliano Pontil, and Cecilia Mascolo. 2012. A tale of many cities: universal patterns in human urban mobility. *PloS one* 7, 5: e37027.
46. Catia Prandi, Valentina Nisi, Paola Salomoni, and Nuno Jardim Nunes. 2015. From gamification to

pervasive game in mapping urban accessibility. In *Proceedings of the 11th Biannual Conference on Italian SIGCHI Chapter*, 126–129. https://doi.org/10.1145/2808435.2808449

47. Giovanni Quattrone, Licia Capra, and Pasquale De Meo. 2015. There's No Such Thing as the Perfect Map: Quantifying Bias in Spatial Crowd-sourcing Datasets. In *Proceedings of the 18th ACM Conference on Computer Supported Cooperative Work & Social Computing*, 1021–1032.
48. Giovanni Quattrone, Afra Mashhadi, and Licia Capra. 2014. Mind the Map: The Impact of Culture and Economic Affluence on Crowd-mapping Behaviours. In *Proceedings of the 17th ACM Conference on Computer Supported Cooperative Work & Social Computing* (CSCW '14), 934–944. https://doi.org/10.1145/2531602.2531713
49. Giovanni Quattrone, Davide Proserpio, Daniele Quercia, Licia Capra, and Mirco Musolesi. 2016. Who Benefits from the "Sharing" Economy of Airbnb? In *Proceedings of the 25th International Conference on World Wide Web* (WWW '16), 1385–1394. https://doi.org/10.1145/2872427.2874815
50. Shilad W. Sen, Heather Ford, David R. Musicant, Mark Graham, Oliver S.B. Keyes, and Brent Hecht. 2015. Barriers to the Localness of Volunteered Geographic Information. In *Proceedings of the 33rd Annual ACM Conference on Human Factors in Computing Systems* (CHI '15), 197–206. https://doi.org/10.1145/2702123.2702170
51. SIGCHI Ethics Working Group. 2016. ACM SIGCHI Research Ethics. Retrieved September 18, 2016 from https://www.facebook.com/groups/866225810172460/
52. Chris Smith, Daniele Quercia, and Licia Capra. 2013. Finger on the pulse: identifying deprivation using transit flow analysis. In *Proceedings of the 2013 conference on Computer supported cooperative work* (CSCW '13), 683–692. https://doi.org/10.1145/2441776.2441852
53. Mike Sonders. 2016. Pokémon GO daily revenue: On the decline, but there's still good news. *SurveyMonkey Intelligence*. Retrieved January 4, 2017 from https://www.surveymonkey.com/business/intelligence/pokemon-go-revenue/
54. Chaoming Song, Zehui Qu, Nicholas Blumm, and Albert-László Barabási. 2010. Limits of Predictability in Human Mobility. *Science* 327, 5968: 1018–1021. https://doi.org/10.1126/science.1177170
55. Fred Stutzman and Jacob Kramer-Duffield. 2010. Friends Only: Examining a Privacy-enhancing Behavior in Facebook. In *Proceedings of the SIGCHI Conference on Human Factors in Computing Systems* (CHI '10), 1553–1562. https://doi.org/10.1145/1753326.1753559
56. Jacob Thebault-Spieker, Loren G. Terveen, and Brent Hecht. 2015. Avoiding the South Side and the Suburbs: The Geography of Mobile Crowdsourcing Markets. In *Proceedings of the 18th ACM Conference on Computer Supported Cooperative Work & Social Computing* (CSCW '15), 265–275. https://doi.org/10.1145/2675133.2675278
57. Leah L. Thompson, Frederick P. Rivara, Rajiv C. Ayyagari, and Beth E. Ebel. 2013. Impact of social and technological distraction on pedestrian crossing behaviour: an observational study. *Injury prevention* 19, 4: 232–237.
58. tjado@maecke.de. *pgoapi - a pokemon go api lib in python*. Retrieved from https://github.com/tejado/pgoapi
59. U.S. Census Bureau. 1999. Explanation of Race and Hispanic Origin Categories. Retrieved September 15, 2016 from https://www.census.gov/population/estimates/rho.txt
60. Alice G. Walton. Pokémon GO Is Actually A Health Hazard, Study Finds. *Forbes*. Retrieved September 21, 2016 from http://www.forbes.com/sites/alicegwalton/2016/09/16/pokemon-go-is-actually-a-health-hazard-study-finds/
61. Yingzi Wang, Nicholas Jing Yuan, Defu Lian, Linli Xu, Xing Xie, Enhong Chen, and Yong Rui. 2015. Regularity and conformity: location prediction using heterogeneous mobility data. In *Proceedings of the 21th ACM SIGKDD International Conference on Knowledge Discovery and Data Mining*, 1275–1284. https://doi.org/10.1145/2783258.2783350
62. Nick Wingfield and Mike Isaac. 2016. Pokémon Go Brings Augmented Reality to a Mass Audience. *The New York Times*. Retrieved September 20, 2016 from http://www.nytimes.com/2016/07/12/technology/pokemon-go-brings-augmented-reality-to-a-mass-audience.html
63. D. Yvette Wohn. Why Pokemon Go is Popular: Maybe Not The Reasons You Think. Retrieved September 17, 2016 from https://yvettewohn.com/2016/07/17/why-pokemon-go-is-popular-maybe-not-the-reasons-you-think/
64. Tse-Chuan Yang, Aggie J. Noah, and Carla Shoff. 2013. Exploring Geographic Variation in US Mortality Rates Using a Spatial Durbin Approach: Mortality and Spatial Durbin. *Population, Space and Place* 21, 1: 18–37. https://doi.org/10.1002/psp.1809
65. Lana Yarosh. Notes from the Field: Pokémon GO! Retrieved September 16, 2016 from http://lanayarosh.com/2016/07/notes-from-the-field-pokemon-go/
66. Dennis Zielstra, Hartwig H. Hochmair, and Pascal Neis. 2013. Assessing the Effect of Data Imports on the Completeness of OpenStreetMap – A United States Case Study. *Transactions in GIS* 17, 3: 315–334. https://doi.org/10.1111/tgis.12037
67. Dennis Zielstra and Alexander Zipf. 2010. A comparative study of proprietary geodata and volunteered geographic information for Germany. In *AGILE '10*.

68. Pokémon Go tops Twitter's daily users, sees more engagement than Facebook. *TechCrunch*. Retrieved September 15, 2016 from http://social.techcrunch.com/2016/07/13/pokemon-go-tops-twitters-daily-users-sees-more-engagement-than-facebook/
69. Five themes of geography. *Wikipedia, the free encyclopedia*. Retrieved September 20, 2016 from https://en.wikipedia.org/w/index.php?title=Five_themes_of_geography&oldid=739269546
70. The Five Themes of Geography. Retrieved September 20, 2016 from http://maps.unomaha.edu/workshops/career/fivethemes.html
71. The Demographics of Ingress. Retrieved September 15, 2016 from http://simulacrum.cc/2013/01/23/the-demographics-of-ingress/
72. How the gurus behind Google Earth created "Pokémon Go." *Mashable*. Retrieved September 16, 2016 from http://mashable.com/2016/07/10/john-hanke-pokemon-go/
73. The results are in: Your favourite Ingress feature of 2015. *Edinburgh Enlightened*. Retrieved September 20, 2016 from http://blog.enl-ed.uk/2016/01/04/the-best-and-the-worst-new-ingress-feature-of-2015/
74. Pokemon Go - the world's most dangerous game? *Mail Online*. Retrieved September 21, 2016 from http://www.dailymail.co.uk/news/article-3684228/Is-world-s-dangerous-game-terrifying-Pokemon-app-craze-killed-one-person-make-children-easy-prey-PAEDOPHILES-s-coming-Britain-soon.html
75. How "pokemon Go" Is Taking Tech Into Dangerous, Uncharted Waters. *FoxNews.com*. Retrieved September 17, 2016 from http://www.foxnews.com/tech/2016/07/22/how-pokemon-go-is-taking-tech-into-dangerous-uncharted-waters.html
76. Girl hit by car while playing "Pokemon Go," blames the game. *WESH*. Retrieved September 17, 2016 from http://www.wesh.com/video/now-this/girl-hit-by-car-while-playing-pokemon-go-blames-the-game/40722578
77. These Charts Show That Pokemon Go Is Already in Decline. *Bloomberg.com*. Retrieved September 17, 2016 from http://www.bloomberg.com/news/articles/2016-08-22/these-charts-show-that-pokemon-go-is-already-in-decline
78. PokemonGoMap/PokemonGo-Map. *GitHub*. Retrieved September 21, 2016 from https://github.com/PokemonGoMap/PokemonGo-Map
79. National Center for Health Statistics Urban Rural Classification Scheme for Counties. Retrieved September 11, 2013 from http://www.cdc.gov/nchs/data_access/urban_rural.htm
80. Population estimates, July 1, 2015, (V2015). Retrieved September 17, 2016 from //www.census.gov/quickfacts/table/PST045215/2622000,1714000
81. How "Pokémon GO" Can Lure More Customers To Your Local Business. *Forbes*. Retrieved September 17, 2016 from http://www.forbes.com/sites/jasonevangelho/2016/07/09/how-pokemon-go-can-lure-more-customers-to-your-local-business/
82. The monetization promise and pitfalls of Pokémon Go. *TechCrunch*. Retrieved September 17, 2016 from http://social.techcrunch.com/2016/08/26/the-monetization-promise-and-pitfalls-of-pokemon-go/
83. An Alternative Way To Monetize Pokémon Go. *Wall Street Journal*. Retrieved September 18, 2016 from http://blogs.wsj.com/moneybeat/2016/07/29/an-alternative-way-to-monetize-pokemon-go/
84. Men fall from cliff playing Pokémon Go. *CNN*. Retrieved September 17, 2016 from http://www.cnn.com/2016/07/15/health/pokemon-go-players-fall-down-cliff/index.html
85. How Niantic Labs Plans to Follow Pokemon Go's Crushing Success | Inc.com. Retrieved January 4, 2017 from http://www.inc.com/bartie-scott/niantic-labs-2016-company-of-the-year-nominee.html

# Empirical Analysis of the Subjective Impressions and Objective Measures of Domain Scientists' Visual Analytic Judgments

**Aritra Dasgupta, Susannah Burrows, Kyungsik Han, Philip J. Rasch**
Pacific Northwest National Laboratory
Richland, USA
{aritra.dasgupta, susannah.burrows, kyungsik.han, philip.rasch}@pnnl.gov

## ABSTRACT
Scientists often use specific data analysis and presentation methods familiar within their domain. But does high familiarity drive better analytical judgment? This question is especially relevant when familiar methods themselves can have shortcomings: many visualizations used conventionally for scientific data analysis and presentation do not follow established best practices. This necessitates new methods that might be unfamiliar yet prove to be more effective. But there is little empirical understanding of the relationships between scientists' subjective impressions about familiar and unfamiliar visualizations and objective measures of their visual analytic judgments. To address this gap and to study these factors, we focus on visualizations used for comparison of climate model performance. We report on a comprehensive survey-based user study with 47 climate scientists and present an analysis of: i) relationships among scientists' familiarity, their perceived levels of comfort, confidence, accuracy, and objective measures of accuracy, and ii) relationships among domain experience, visualization familiarity, and post-study preference.

## ACM Classification Keywords
H.5.m. Information Interfaces and Presentation (e.g. HCI)

## Author Keywords
Information visualization; visual comparison; climate; familiarity; trust; preference; Taylor plot; slope plot

## INTRODUCTION
Domain experts' analytical workflow often comprises a set of conventional methods for data analysis and presentation. Since experts are highly familiar with these methods, they tend to inherently have greater confidence in their outputs than in those of new, unfamiliar methods. At the same time, conventional data visualization methods used by practitioners might not be in sync with visualization best practices [9]. However, there is little empirical analysis of the relative effectiveness of familiar and unfamiliar visualization techniques, compared with domain scientists' subjective impressions (e.g., confidence, preference, etc.) or with objective performance measures.

To fill this gap, we contribute a user study with climate scientists, focusing on the common task of comparing and assessing similarities and differences in model fidelity across multiple simulations. We report on three related contributions in this paper. *First*, through a problem characterization phase, we developed a shared understanding of the important visualization tasks for model fidelity comparison, and identified visualization techniques that are currently widely used for these tasks. By applying visualization design principles, we collaboratively developed and selected two sets of visualizations: familiar visualizations modified for more effective visual comparison, and unfamiliar visualizations that had the potential to be more effective than the familiar ones. *Second*, using these two sets we conducted a user study with 47 climate scientists, where we recorded their objective task responses, their subjective impressions [4], such as their perceived levels of comfort, confidence, accuracy when carrying out analysis tasks using a particular visualization, and their preferred visualization as indicated at the close of the study. *Third*, we analyzed study results for understanding the relationships among scientists' domain experience, familiarity, and objective measures of their analytical judgments, the discrepancies between their familiarity and preference levels for each visualization, and also the discrepancies between their subjective impressions and objective performance measures.

## PROBLEM AND TASK CHARACTERIZATION
The work reported here results from a *six*-month long collaboration between two climate scientists (co-authors of this paper) and visualization researchers. Following the nested model approach [21], there were four distinct stages in our collaboration: i) characterization of the model fidelity analysis problem, ii) a shared understanding of the visualization tasks, iii) analysis of the state-of-the-art in visualizations used by climate scientists, and iv) participatory design of prototypes. We had frequent face-to-face discussions for facilitating all of these stages, and the outcome of this collaborative design process helped us select appropriate tasks and visualizations, calibrated by experts' degree of familiarity, for the user study. In this section we describe the model fidelity analysis problem and characterize the relevant visualization tasks.

**Model Fidelity Analysis:** Climate model fidelity is measured by the degree of consistency between models and observations for specific model output variables or features. Scientists


*CHI 2017*, May 06 - 11, 2017, Denver, CO, USA

ACM 978-1-4503-4655-9/17/05 $15.00
DOI http://dx.doi.org/10.1145/3025453.3025882

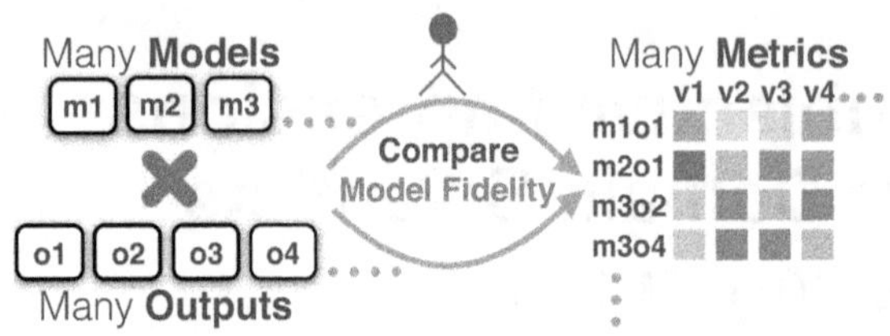


**Figure 1. Illustrating the multi-model, multi-output comparison problem where scientists have to visually reconcile similarities and differences with respect to many models, outputs, and metrics. The visualization challenge is twofold: i) scale up to the different *levels* of the categories, e.g., models $m1$, $m2$, $m3$, etc., and outputs $o1$, $o2$, $o3$, $o4$, etc. and ii) at the same time provide visual cues for similarity and dissimilarity based on the values for many metrics ($v1$, $v2$, $v3$, $v4$, etc.).**

frequently summarize aspects of the model's *fidelity*, using statistical metrics such as (but not limited to) the root-mean-square error, correlation, and relative variance of the model output variables compared to observations of the same variable [12]. Because a credible climate simulation requires reasonable simulations of many different physical processes and state variables, it is typically not sufficient to evaluate models on a single metric, instead, models must be compared across a suite of such metrics, leading to a more complex analysis situation. In addition, identifying models that exhibit similar or dissimilar patterns of performance across a suite of metrics may lead to important insights into model behaviors. Frequently, trade-offs occur between different aspects of model fidelity, with models that perform better in one area performing worse in another, so scientists must perform nuanced analysis to understand subtle similarities and differences in fidelity with respect to multiple metrics.

**Multi-Way Visual Comparison Tasks:** Model fidelity analysis is typically supported by visual comparison of multiple metrics across simulations derived from multiple models. We term these tasks *multi-way visual comparison* tasks (Figure 1), since they involve comparison across different dimensions: among models and output variables, their combinations, and across different metrics. The comparison tasks are simpler when evaluating a single model using a single type of statistical metric, e.g. comparing model-observation correlation for temperature and precipitation fields; or when comparing the performance of multiple models for a single variable and type of metric, e.g. identifying the model that produces the lowest root-mean-square-error for cloud extent. However, in reality, when evaluating overall model fidelity, scientists often need to compare across many models (10–15 or more), many output variables (10–15), and more than one metric (e.g. root-mean-square error, global mean bias, correlation, and variance).

As illustrated in Figure 1, a major visualization design challenge in multi-way visual comparison tasks stems from the need to simultaneously express similarity and dissimilarity based patterns across multiple categorical variables (e.g., types of models, output variables, etc.) and numerical variables (e.g., fidelity metrics). Visualizations of model fidelity metrics should enable an expert user to efficiently and accurately perform tasks such as: i) assess and compare the overall fidelity of models across a range of metrics, and ii) identify groups of models that exhibit similar or different patterns of behavior across multiple metrics. In this work, our main motivation was to understand how scientists' analytical judgment for comparison of fidelity across different combinations of models, model outputs and metrics is impacted by different visualization techniques.

## RELATED WORK

Our contributions combine two areas of visualization research: i) visual comparison approaches, and ii) evaluation of the user experience of domain experts using visualizations.

### Alternative Approaches for Visual Comparison

The design space of visual comparison using data sets that contain a mix of numerical and categorical attributes can be described based on three different approaches. In the first approach, multiple visual variables [2], like shape, color, or symbols, can be used for representing different categorical variables. Such visualizations are popular in the climate science domain [24]. But they do not scale well to the number of levels in a categorical variable, as the number of discriminatory steps using color or shape is limited. The second approach is to use small multiples [29], where depending on the task, a scatter plot or bar chart can be instantiated for each categorical variable. The number of small multiples can be a problem when there are many categories or many levels in a category, and might not scale well for visual comparison. In a third approach, several researchers have proposed alternative representations of categorical data [10]. Researchers have also looked at different interestingness measures for encoding multivariate relationships in mixed data sets [1] and using analytical methods like multiple correspondence analysis [5]. In this work, we focus on model fidelity visualization techniques used in the climate science community. Two popular choices are the Taylor plots [28] and heat maps [24]. We analyzed their merits and demerits, proposed alternatives by modifying these familiar visualizations to suit the visual comparison tasks, and introduced unfamiliar yet potentially optimal visualizations that could lead to better analytical judgment.

### Evaluating Domain Experts' Visualization Experience

Previous research has demonstrated that visualization researchers and domain experts often disagree about the efficacy of visualization designs [3] . This can be for two reasons: domain experts tend to trust and prefer familiar analysis methods over new ones [27], and there is a general lack of awareness of visualization best practices and available alternatives [9]. In human-machine relationships, as in human-human relationships, familiarity breeds trust [11], and analysts tend to have more trust in familiar means and mediums. However, some conventional methods that are widely used for model performance visualization may scale poorly to more complex data. Novel approaches may offer better support for complex comparisons of model fidelity across multiple models and variables. To investigate how much domain scientists trust and prefer different visualization techniques, we followed the strategy in McAllister's survey [20], which was subsequently adapted for evaluating domain experts' trust in cyber security interfaces [27] and in complex dynamic systems [30]. We adopt a relevant subset of these questions for our evaluation.

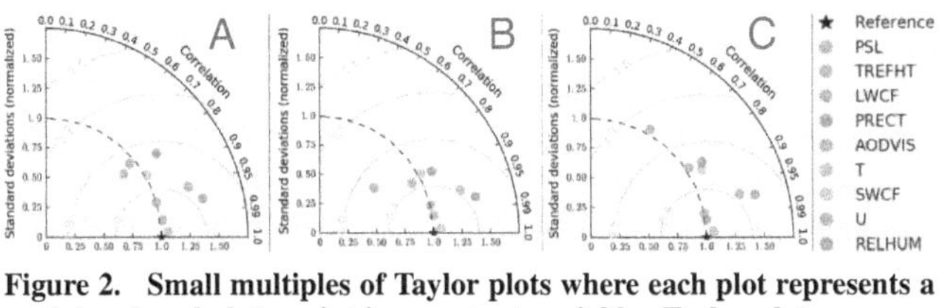


**Figure 2. Small multiples of Taylor plots where each plot represents a model and each data point is an output variable. Taylor plots are popularly used for model fidelity comparison. Since the default layout with many symbols is less effective for comparison across many ($\geq 3$) models and many ($\geq 3$) variables, we designed this small multiple version, which our collaborators rated positively and was eventually used in the study.**

Domain experts' trust in and preference for visualization systems is an emerging area of research [26]. In our work, we focus exclusively on the efficacy of alternative visualization designs and how they can inspire comfort, confidence, and preference in climate scientists.

## VISUALIZATION DESIGN ALTERNATIVES

The multi-way visual comparison tasks abstracted during the problem characterization phase were utilized for analyzing the merits and demerits of different model fidelity visualization techniques. This was done through a review of the literature and discussions with two climate scientists (co-authors on this paper), one of whom has more than 30 years of experience in climate modeling. In the course of our discussions we narrowed down on a subset of such tasks that climate scientists most frequently perform as part of their analysis routine. By applying visualization design principles in the context of model comparison [9], we found that familiar visualizations such as the Taylor plots, heat maps, and bar charts, that are used for such tasks, might not be the optimal choice. These led us to propose design alternatives by modifying familiar visualizations and introducing new ones. In this section, we describe their design rationale.

### Modification of Familiar Visualizations

We collaboratively critiqued the familiar visualizations by analyzing if they effectively communicate similarity in model fidelity and if that information can be recovered by scientists accurately and efficiently. Based on our analysis, we proposed the use of improved versions of the familiar visualizations.

**Small Multiples of Taylor Plots**: A Taylor plot [28] graphically summarizes how closely a pattern (or a set of patterns) matches observations. The similarity between two patterns is quantified in terms of their correlation, their centered, normalized root-mean-square difference and their variability (represented by their standard deviations). These plots are especially useful in evaluating multiple ($< 3$) output variables of complex models or in gauging the relative skill of many different models for a small number of output variables ($< 3$). As shown in the Taylor plot in Figure 2, each circle represents a model output. The light gray contours show the centered normalized RMSE, which is proportional to the distance from the reference point (1, 1). The angular axis indicates the correlation with respect to the observational data. The radial axis indicates the variance ratio, i.e. the ratio of the model's standard deviation to the standard deviation of the observations, which was not used in this study.

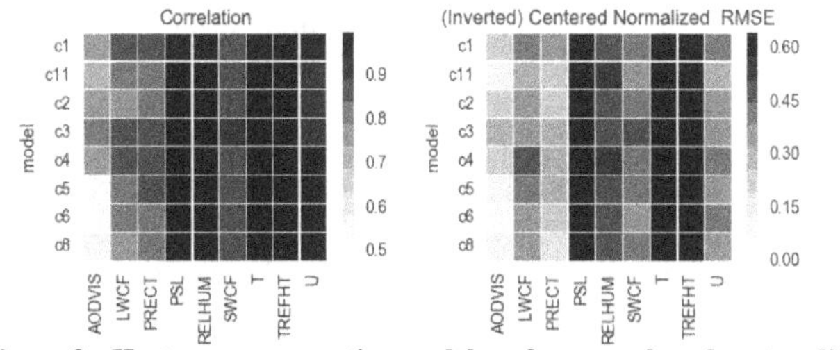


**Figure 3. Heatmaps representing model performance based on two different metrics provide a quick overview of overall differences and variability. To help in distinguishing among small differences, we use a segmented color scheme. Using of color to express quantitative differences can lead to less accurate judgment.**

When a single Taylor plot [28] is used to summarize many ($> 3$) variables across many ($> 3$) models, information can be obscured by overlap and clutter. In such plots, multiple visual variables are used to represent the different levels within categorical variables, which can reduce the accuracy and efficiency of visual analysis. We addressed this problem by using small multiples of Taylor plots [29]. In the small multiples used in this study, each Taylor plot (Figure 2) represents a different model, while color is used to encode different output variables. This encompasses both superposition (for variables) and juxtaposition (for models) categories for visual comparison [13]. Similar to identifying shapes in scatter plots, one can compare the shapes of point clouds in these Taylor plots for a multi-way comparison among models and variables. This small multiple approach can suffer from two limitations: visual scalability when the number of models is greater than four or five, and difficulty in comparing across different output variables using their relative positions on the small multiple plots. Other strategies for using Taylor plots are possible, but each strategy we considered suffers from similar difficulties in comparing many models. We feel Taylor plots are most useful when comparing a few ($< 3$) models for multiple output variables, or multiple models for a few ($< 3$) output variables.

**Variants of Heat Maps and Bar Charts**: A heat map is one of the most widely-used visualizations for comparing model outputs or model performance [6]. We designed a heat map with a continuous color scheme [14] where yellow indicated bad performance while blue indicated good performance. We used two heat maps for representing two different performance metrics. In the heat maps, all models and variables are represented within a *large single* plot [31], in contrast to the *small multiples* used for the Taylor plots. By using color to represent variables, heat maps can support an efficient comparison of model fidelity and aid identification of similarities and dissimilarities by visual pattern recognition, but the use of color might limit the accuracy of quantitative comparisons [33].While similarity metrics could be used to sort variables in heat maps in a more meaningful fashion, we chose to use alphabetical sorting because of its common use in the climate science literature, and to ease comparison of the same variables across multiple heat maps, where different orderings for each heat map can lead to high comparison complexity.

We found bar charts to be a very familiar visual representation for climate scientists, which are often used to examine relative distributions among variables, but not necessarily for multi-way comparison tasks. We also found variants of bar chart representations in the climate science literature, including stacked bar charts, with different stacks representing different categories [24]. By using spatial position along a common axis to encode information, bar charts can support accurate estimation and comparison of small differences in quantitative values [33]. To support visual comparison among multiple models, we used a small multiple approach where each small multiple represents a model, and in order to encode multiple metrics, two sets of bar charts are provided, where each set represents a metric. While bar charts enable quantitatively accurate evaluations, comparison across multiple bar charts for many models and variables may be difficult and inefficient.

### Design of Unfamiliar Visualizations: Slope Plots

We introduced the slope plots (Figure 4), a variant of the slopegraph proposed by Tufte [29], to our collaborators as an alternative, yet potentially unfamiliar, solution for multi-way visual comparison. Our aim was to overcome the following shortcomings of the existing visualizations. i) The original Taylor plots do not scale for many models and variables ii) The small multiples of Taylor plots and bar charts may not support optimal comparison amongst multiple (10) models and multiple (10) variables. iii) The heat map, with a large single approach, supports efficient comparison, but because it uses color to represent quantities, may reduce accuracy. With the slope plot, we also followed the large single approach, but with a position-based encoding and explicit cues of similarity/dissimilarity, we aimed at making the comparison tasks. more accurate and efficient. We describe the design rationale and implementation in detail below.

**Slope plots** encode one numerical variable (representing a metric) in a single plot, while multiple such plots can be juxtaposed for multi-way visual comparison. The main rationale behind the slope plot was to allow comparison by both superposition and juxtaposition [13], so that scientists can assess variability among both output variables and models quickly and accurately.

The layout of the slope plot is inspired by the parallel coordinates visualization [17]. Slope plots have an intentional horizontal layout to avoid confusion with line plots with time on the horizontal axis. In the slope plot (Figure 4), each horizontal axis represents the same numerical variable, correlation on the left plot and centered RMSE on the right. The axis can be discretized based on the number of levels in a category, which in this case are the different models, represented by color. The number of axes is equal to the number of levels in another categorical variable, in this case, the model outputs.

Polylines connecting the axes represent different models and their slopes are not indicative of functional relationships among the outputs. Relative slopes indicate the similarities and differences among the models. By linking different points, we added Gestalt effects of connectivity [18] and similarity, where parallelism or non-parallelism of lines (representing models) will give visual cues of overall similarity [7] or dissimilarity with respect to both models and variables. The spread of the points on the horizontal axis indicates variability across models. The advantage of slope plots over the other

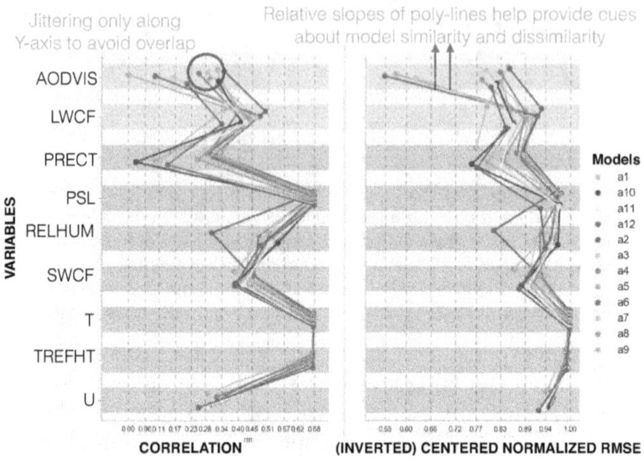


**Figure 4. The slope plot was designed as an alternative to the existing model fidelity visualization techniques. Each polyline represents a model and their relative slopes indicate similarities and dissimilarities with respect to different output variables, which are represented on the horizontal axes. This design offers an efficient way to look at variability across both models (polylines) and variables (rows). Jitter is added along the Y-axis to avoid over-plotting.**

visualizations is that it scales well to the association among multiple levels of two categorical variables (i.e., models and outputs) while at the same time preserving the perceptual cues about similarity and dissimilarity.

One of the problems with spatial encoding is the over-plotting of multiple data points. To minimize such over-plotting, we introduced jitter along the vertical axis. This does not distort the values as the vertical axis is categorical, and due to the jitter lines do not overlap and can be precisely identified.

## STUDY DESIGN

We conducted a within-subjects study to evaluate climate scientists' subjective and objective measures of analytical judgment using the familiar and potentially unfamiliar visualization techniques. The study was divided into three sections.

In the first section, we asked participants questions regarding their demographic characteristics and years of domain experience, and provided training on the tasks and visualizations that would be used for the study. For this study, it was important to isolate any domain-specific bias from the assessment of the visualizations. Climate scientists, when comparing models across multiple metrics, may at times assign different weights to different output variables, depending on the importance of those variables to the analytical task. Our instructions made it clear that for the purposes of the study, participants should treat all variables and metrics as equally important. We also emphasized that the goal of this study was not to *identify the best model*, but to assess the *effectiveness of the analysis methods*, namely, the different visualization techniques.

In the second section, participants were asked to perform three tasks for each visualization they were shown. These tasks were designed to be relevant for scientists in developing an understanding of the information contained in multiple fidelity metrics across multiple model simulations.

In the third section, we selected a set of questions that assessed scientists' subjective experience of the visualizations with respect to different dimensions of trust (e.g., perceived accuracy, efficiency, comfort, confidence) and to their preference for a particular visualization technique. We describe the different aspects of our study design in detail below.

### Data and Visualization Generation

We discuss the data and visualization generation based on the performance metric outputs.

**Models and Outputs:** We used simulation output from a number of variants of version 5 of the Community Atmosphere Model (CAM5, [23]), the atmosphere component of the Community Earth System Modeling (CESM) project [16]; and descendants of that model developed for a variety of projects supported with funding from the U.S. Department of Energy (DOE) Earth System Model Program, which we call generically "CAM5" variants hereafter. We selected output variables that participate in many important ways in the climate system. These variables play important roles in the Earth's radiation budget and cloud features (LWCF, SWCF, RELHUM, AOD-VIS), the hydrologic cycle (PRECT), and general circulation features (T, TREFHT, and U).

**Fidelity Metrics:** The model performance metrics selected here are amongst the metrics that are commonly and widely used in the climate modeling community [22]. These metrics, the correlation and the normalized standard variance, are straightforward to calculate and interpret. The two metrics relate to two different aspects of model performance: the correlation is a measure of *pattern matching*, while the normalized standard variance is a measure of how well the magnitude of the variability of the model agrees with the variability of observations. The model-observation agreement is often evaluated in a climatological sense, i.e., an average January from the model simulation is compared with an average observed January, or an average is computed for a three-month period identified as a season. In keeping with that practice, the visualizations presented in this study represent fidelity metrics computed for each of those seasons. We used two data sets from two seasons as a repeated measure.

*Normalization and Variability*: A higher correlation score indicates *good* model performance, as the output is highly correlated with the observation. A higher nRMSE score on the other hand signifies *poor* model performance. Therefore for semantic equivalence between a plot for correlation and a plot for nRMSE, where high values represent *good* performance, we invert the nRMSE scores by subtracting each value from the maximum value in the data set. Within each pair of plots in the study, one indicates the correlation and the other indicates the inverted nRMSE score. In order to ensure a reasonable amount of variability among the fidelity scores for both the metrics, we selected data set pairs where the average standard deviation across the models for a pair was the highest.

**Visualizations:** We selected four visualizations for the study, based on our understanding of scientists' familiarity. These were small multiples of Taylor plots, heatmaps, small multiples of bar charts, and slope plots, as discussed earlier. We expected the slope plot to be the least familiar visualization.

For ordering the rows and columns in heat maps and slope plots, and for organizing the layout of the small multiples, we selected a default alphabetical order and did not perform any layout optimization. This was for two reasons: First, for the small multiple approach, each multiple will have a different ordering and it could be hard to trace model names across many of them. Second, since the tasks were about similarity and dissimilarity (all performed together), any optimization would be based on a pairwise distance metric. Sorting or laying out small multiples based on a pairwise distance metric is non-trivial and may lead to visual complexity. Therefore, for the sake of consistency, we did not optimize the layout for any of the plots. Further, we controlled for the following factors: i) *Ordering*: The visualizations were randomly ordered across participants. To minimize the recall effect, for the same kind of visualization across two data sets, the left and right orders were swapped. For example, we had two instantiations of juxtaposed heatmaps: one where the right metric was correlation and the left one was nRMSE, whereas in the second data set, it was the reverse. ii) *Scales*: The ranges on the axes of the plots were scaled based on the minimum and maximum value of the data; small differences could be highlighted by not scaling between a global minimum and global maximum. ii) *Resolution*: The degree of numerical resolution possible in each visualization was dependent on the visualization type. Heat maps use the lowest resolution defined by the number of color levels, but all other visualizations use spatial encoding, with their effective resolution depending on spatial locations. Equivalence in resolution between visualizations was supported by holding the interval spacing of axis ticks constant across all spatial visualizations. Pilot studies also helped us fine-tune the resolution and reduce clutter.

### Questionnaire and Task Selection

In this section, we discuss the questions posed to participants and the tasks they had to perform during the study for each of the three sections. Participants were required to respond to all items in the study for their response to be considered complete, and they were not allowed to skip questions.

**Section 1. Demographics, Experience, and Familiarity:** In this section, we asked scientists to report their age, gender, years of domain experience, and their primary role as a climate scientist (i.e., global model user, global model developer, regional model user, or regional model developer). These questions were followed by the introduction of all visualizations by showing an example of each visualization, using real data, and describing each visualization in the context of the tasks. Before starting the task performance section, we first asked participants to rate their *familiarity* with each of the four visualizations, and their *frequency of use* of each visualization as part of their analysis routine. By normalizing and averaging their responses on these two questions, we derived a familiarity score for each participant for a particular visualization technique.

**Section 2. Analytical Tasks:** For the study, we focused on the comparison-based tasks that we derived through our initial discussions about climate scientists' analytical workflow. We conducted pilot tests to evaluate suitable comparative analysis tasks that could be performed using all four visualization types and the associated difficulty levels of the tasks, and accordingly distilled these into the following three tasks that were posed for each visualization:

**Task A**: "Identify two models, which are most similar in their correlation and normalized RMSE metrics across most of the output variables."

**Task B**: "Which two output variables show the highest variability in their correlation and normalized RMSE across all models?"

**Task C**: "Identify the two models that disagree the most in their correlation and normalized RMSE metrics across most of the output variables."

For each of these tasks, participants were asked to rate their confidence and comfort level with each visualization, on a 5 point Likert scale. The **difficulty level** of Tasks A and C was greater than that of Task B as in the case of the latter, only a few output variables showed significantly greater variability than others. This was easier to detect visually as compared with the subtle similarities and differences among multiple models.

**Section 3. Subjective Impressions Rating:** At the end of the task performance section, participants were asked to record their subjective impressions of the visualizations they used. We recorded two types of responses: **i) Perceived accuracy, efficiency, comfort, confidence, and preference**: To analyze participants' perceptions about using a particular visualization, they were asked to record, on a Likert scale, their perceived accuracy, efficiency, comfort, confidence, and preference for each visualization. These questions were a subset of the trust-related questions used in McAllister's survey [20], and later adopted by Takayama et al [27] for evaluating analysts' trust in user interfaces for system administrators. Note the redundancy in asking about perceived confidence and comfort levels, for each task, and also amongst post-completion questions. This intentional redundancy allowed us to assess the consistency between participant's subjective perceptions after completion of each task, compared with their post-study, overall evaluations of each visualization. **ii) Preference Ranking**: This was a ranking on a scale of 1 (highest) to 4 (lowest), where participants assigned a rank to their preferred visualization. Preference is a strong indicator of potential adoption of a visualization technique. Following the recommendations of Lam et al. [19] for assessing user experience with visualizations, we also asked participants to comment on the advantages and barriers they perceived in using each visualization. By analyzing these comments we could potentially find the reason behind scientists' strong or weak preference for a visualization.

### Participants

Participants were recruited anonymously through different mailing lists that involve collaborations among universities and research laboratories. No personal identifiers about participants were recorded. We only recorded their IP addresses, to ensure that duplicate responses were not submitted from the same machine.Overall, there were 47 participants with a self-reported background in climate modeling. The study participants comprised a very experienced group of climate scientists with a median domain experience of 12 years, and a majority of participants rating themselves as *very familiar* or *extremely familiar* with modeling. Each participant performed three tasks (Task A,B,C) for each of the four visualization types, where two data sets were used as a repeated measure. The total number of trials was thus $47 \times 4 \times 2 = 376$.

### Settings

The experiments reported in this study were all web-based. This remotely-based study setting was necessary because the participants in the study were climate scientists spread across different academic institutions and research labs across the United States, Europe, and South America. In our experimental set-up we took several measures to ensure reliability and minimize bias in the results that could arise from the web-based setting. First, to minimize the risk that a participant might not understand the question or be ready for the test, we trained participants about the visualizations and allowed them to them quit the study if they did not understand a question. Participants could not return to previous tasks to compare their responses across multiple visualizations.If a participant stopped the study and returned to it later, they reentered the study from the point where they had left off, preventing unintentional repetition of the tasks by a participant.

The trials were randomized across participants, and they sequentially performed all three analytic tasks using one particular visualization before being presented with the next visualization, reflecting the general analytical workflow of scientists. We asked participants if they had any known color vision deficiency (color-blindness), as the ability to distinguish among colors, was needed to interpret most of the visualizations used in the study. We filtered out results from one participant who self-identified as color-blind.

### Hypotheses

**Objective Accuracy of Task Performance**. Given our design rationale for slope plots, we expected them to support greater objective accuracy in task performance. But we also expected task complexity, the length of domain experience and degree of familiarity with particular visualizations to affect performance accuracy. These expectations led to the following hypotheses: **H1a)** Overall, participants will report a greater level of accuracy with slope plots. **H1b)** Tasks A and C will result in greater differences in performance than Task B due to the greater complexity of these tasks **H1c)** Longer domain experience and greater familiarity with particular visualizations will lead to more accurate performance.

**Perceived Confidence, Comfort, Accuracy and Efficiency**: We know that familiarity with an analytical tool increases trust and confidence in that tool among users [11]. This led to the following hypothesis:**H2)** Participants with longer domain experience will report higher average confidence and comfort levels for familiar visualizations than for relatively unfamiliar visualizations, such as the slope plots. Given the position based encoding of slope plots, we hypothesized that: **H3a)**

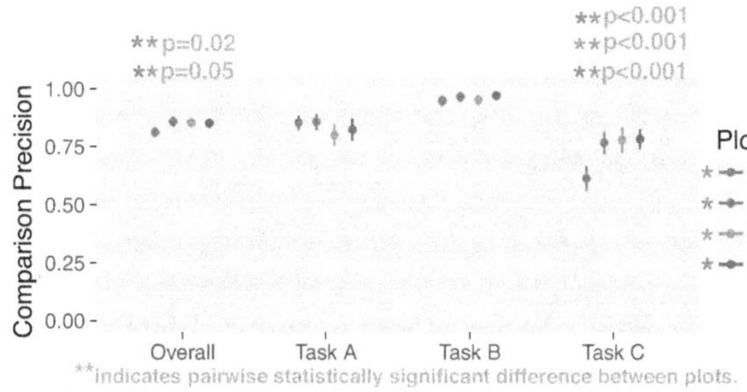


**Figure 5. Objective accuracy based on the comparison precision metric. Error bars represent 95% confidence intervals. Overall, the heat map and slope plot showed the highest level of accuracy, with a significant difference with respect to the Taylor plot ($p$ <0.05). While comparison precision values for Tasks A and B were similar, for Task C, we observe that the heat map, slope plot, and bar chart were significantly more accurate than the Taylor plot ($p$ <0.05).**

Participants will report greater perceived accuracy with slope plots as compared to heat maps. **H3b)** Participants will appreciate the utility of slope plots, and that will be reflected in their comparable or higher average ranking in terms of perceived accuracy and efficiency than more familiar plots such as Taylor plots, heat maps, and bar charts.

**Familiarity Vs Preference**: Recent visualization studies with domain experts have also demonstrated that carefully and collaboratively designed visualizations and interfaces can convince experts of their utility and may inspire trust and preference [3, 9]. This led to: **H4a)** Overall, participants will exhibit a level of preference for slope plots that is comparable with that of familiar visualizations. We expected the effect of familiarity on preference to be weaker in participants with fewer years of domain experience as they might be more open to novel approaches. This led to: **H4b**) Participants with greater domain experience will exhibit a stronger preference for familiar visualizations, while participants with less experience will be most likely to report a post-study preference for less familiar visualizations that are of similar or greater perceived effectiveness for completing the tasks.

**Objective Accuracy Vs Perceived Accuracy, Preference, Familiarity**: Regarding the discrepancy between subjective impressions and precision of scientists' judgment, we have seen in past studies that self-calibrated levels of trust correlate with greater accuracy in task performance [30]. This led to the following hypotheses: **H5a)** Participants' perceived accuracy will match their objective performance accuracy. **H5b)** Participants' familiarity and preference ranking for different visualizations will match with the ranking of the visualizations derived from their objective accuracy.

### Metrics

**Comparison Precision**: In Tasks A and C, participants were asked to identify the two most similar and dissimilar models, respectively. To compute an objective metric characterizing the correctness of each participants' response, we used the the following method: First, we computed the root mean squared difference (RMSD) between each pair of models for a given metric, and then calculated the average between the two RMSD values for each of the two metrics. Next we ranked the model pairs based on the average RMSD values. The correct

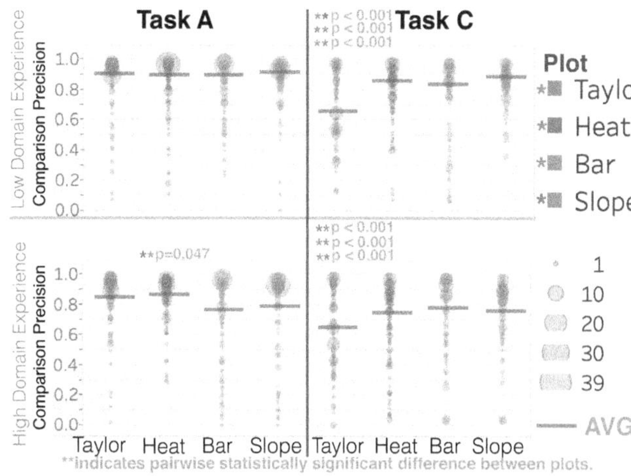


**Figure 6. Distributions of comparison precision scores for Tasks A and C for the high and low experience groups. Task A resulted in comparable levels of accuracy across both experience groups except for the significant difference in accuracy between heat map and bar chart for the high experience group. For Task C, we can observe consistently lower accuracy levels for Taylor plots across both experience groups.**

response to Task A and to Task C is the pair of models that exhibits the highest or lowest RMSD , respectively.

In Task B, participants were asked to identify the two models with the greatest variability in their fidelity scores. To identify these two models, we first calculated the standard deviation of the variables with respect to the individual metrics and then averaged them for a net variability score. Next we ranked the models by their net variability.

Because the fidelity scores used in this study differ only subtly between models, the differences among the RMSD and variability scores computed for different models were also modest. Hence, instead of categorizing each participant's response as true or false, we developed a combined "comparison precision" metric derived from the relative ranks of the models for the similarity score (Task A), dissimilarity score (Task C) and average variability score (Task B). *Comparison precision* is given by $C_p = \frac{(n-r)}{n}$ where $n$ is the total number of models and $r$ is the rank of the model based on any given individual score,and where the first two models (i.e., the correct answers) are assigned a rank 0, so that the correct response has a precision of 1. We therefore have a $C_p$ score for each of the tasks and for an overall comparison we compute an average of the three scores across all the tasks.

**Discrepancy**: We computed the discrepancy between how scientists actually performed and their perceptions about their performance and the visualizations using the difference between the rankings of visualizations derived from *comparison precision* scores and their subjective impression ratings, by normalizing them to a common scale. For each participant, by using their average comparison precision score across all the tasks, we rank ordered the visualizations on a scale of 1 (best) to 4 (worst), and compared this ranking with their preference and familiarity based rankings. Next we derived an average discrepancy between the rankings (ΔAccPreference, ΔAccFamiliarity) by computing the difference between them and averaging that across all participants. For analyzing the discrepancy between objective and perceived accuracy, we rescaled the responses for perceived accuracy to span the range from 0 to 1, by converting $(0,1,2,3,4,5)$ to (0, 0.25, 0.5, 0.75 and 1). We rescaled the objective accuracy ranks, ranging from 1 to 4, using a similar transformation, that is, converting $(1,2,3,4)$ to $(1.0,0.66,0.33,0)$, giving higher weight to higher ranked models. We then obtained the discrepancy (ΔObjSubjAccuracy) by subtracting the rescaled subjective impression scores from those of objective accuracy. A greater difference indicates that the rankings of scientists' performance and their self-rated impression of their own performance did not match: they either overestimated or underestimated their performance accuracy.

**Participant grouping criteria**: We grouped participants into *high* and *low* groups based on self-reported domain experience. Participants were asked to rate their degree of familiarity (on a 5-point Likert scale) and the number of years of experience in climate modeling. These two measured variables had different scales, so we first normalized them by dividing by the maximum value for each category and calculated the average of the two normalized values. We then assigned 25 participants to the high group (above the average) and 22 to the low group (below the average).

## RESULTS

We report the study results by comparing participants' objective accuracy with subjective impressions and analyzing the effects of experience and familiarity. Uncertainty in all results is reported as 95% confidence intervals, estimated by bootstrapping, reflecting the range of uncertainty in the mean value. The fixed effects (i.e., independent variables) were the two climate modeling experience groups (i.e., high and low experience), three tasks (i.e., Task A, B, and C), and four visualization types (e.g., Taylor plot, heat map, bar chart, and slope plot). Confidence and comfort level were assessed using a repeated measures design :participants were exposed to multiple treatment conditions (i.e., visualization tasks) and answered the same set of questions for each condition. To analyze these variables, we fit a mixed effects analysis of variance (ANOVA) model [32], with a normal conditional distribution, and random effects for repeated measures to account for the non-independent nature of the data. We adjusted the $p$-values for analyses involving multiple comparisons using the Bonferroni correction [15].

**Objective Accuracy**: By applying the average comparison precision metric, we found that overall, participants were more precise in their judgments using heat maps (Mean: 0.864, Confidence Interval: $[0.841, 0.886]$) and slope plots (0.860, $[0.837, 0.882]$) with significant differences from Taylor plots (0.806, $[0.784, 0.828]$) at $p < 0.05$ (Figure 5), thereby partially supporting our hypothesis **H1a**. By looking at the taskwise breakdown, we can see that: i) for Task A, performances using heat maps (0.857, $[0.818, 0.896]$) and Taylor plots (0.852, $[0.813, 0.891]$) were slightly more accurate than for bar charts (0.800 $[0.761, 0.839]$) and slope plots (0.823, $[0.784, 0.862]$), ii) for Task B, all plots exhibited comparable levels of accuracy, and participants were more accurate than for Tasks A and C, thus supporting **H1b**; and iii) for Task C, heat maps (0.768, $[0.729, 0.806]$), slope plots (0.784, $[0.745, 0.823]$) and

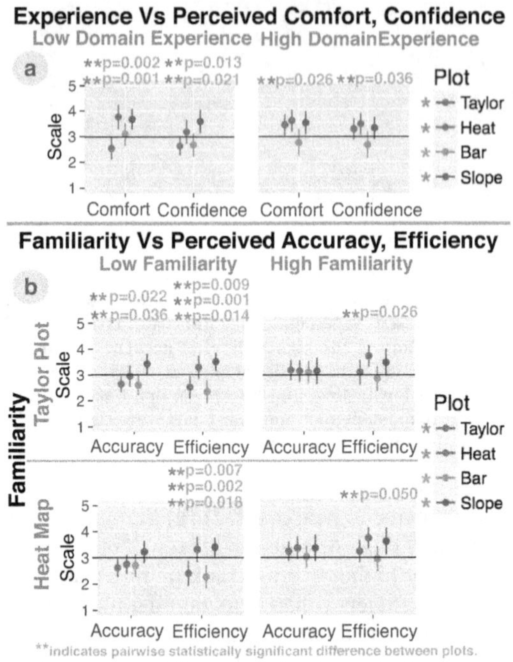


**Figure 7. Experience and Familiarity Vs Subjective Impressions. Error bars represent 95% confidence intervals. Significant results ($p < 0.05$) annotated on the plots show that low experienced participants were less comfortable and confident with Taylor plots as opposed to slope plots. Across different familiarity groups, slope plots show comparable, if not higher perceived accuracy and efficiency ratings, as opposed to more familiar plots.**

bar charts (0.780, $[0.741, 0.818]$) led to significantly greater accuracy than Taylor plots (0.615, $[0.576, 0.654]$). Across all tasks, we failed to find an overall effect of familiarity on performance accuracy. By analyzing the effect of domain experience, we found different trends for Task A and Task C. For Task A we found that that performances were comparable across all visualizations in both experience groups except for participants with greater domain experience were more accurate with heat maps (Mean = 0.86) than the bar charts (Mean = 0.76). But f For Task C, we found that across both experience groups, participants performed significantly better using slope plots, heat maps and bar charts, than the Taylor plots. Therefore we found limited support for **H1c**.

**Perceived Comfort, Confidence, Accuracy and Efficiency**: Figure 7a shows confidence and comfort levels for all four visualizations. The low experience group rated the slope plot highest in comfort (Mean: 3.61, Confidence Interval: $[3.43, 3.80]$) and confidence (3.56, $[3.37, 3.74]$), with significant differences from the Taylor plot for comfort (2.91, $[2.72, 3.10]$; $p < 0.05$) and confidence (2.97, $[2.79, 3.16]$; $p < 0.05$). For the high domain experience group, the perceived levels of comfort and confidence were comparable across the Taylor plot, heat map, and slope plot, with significant differences only with respect to the bar chart. We therefore did not find evidence to support **H2**. Participants tended to rate the slope plot and heat map significantly higher ($p < 0.05$) in perceived accuracy and efficiency, compared to the Taylor plot and bar chart. We however could not find support for **H3a**, as perceived accuracy for heat maps and slope plots was comparable. We created low and high familiarity groups for both the Taylor plot and heat map, using the familiarity rankings assigned by the partici-

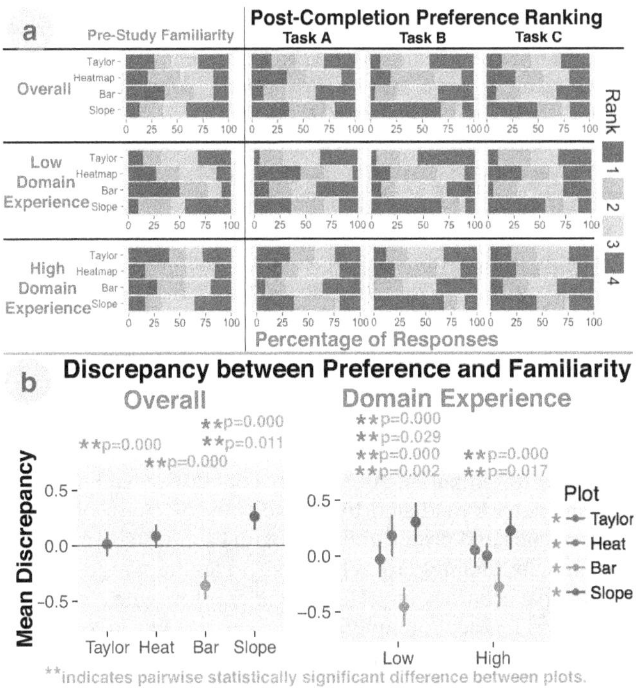

Figure 8. Post-completion preference rankings and the discrepancy between rankings based on familiarity and preference. Error bars represent 95% confidence intervals. We can that irrespective of experience many participants tended to have a high preference for the relatively unfamiliar slope plots.

pants. These two visualizations that had a sufficient number of participants in each category to achieve statistical significance. As shown in Figure 7, we found that participants with greater familiarity with a plot type perceived that visualization to have higher accuracy and efficiency. However, for the high familiarity groups we can observe that participants' perceived levels of accuracy and efficiency with slope plots were comparable to either Taylor plots or heat maps. For both the low familiarity groups, in most cases participants expressed greater levels of perceived accuracy and efficiency with the slope plots. These findings supported our hypothesis **H3b**.

**Familiarity and Preference**: Figure 8a shows the distribution of the familiarity and preference rankings for each visualization. The slope plot clearly ranks much lower in familiarity, being ranked first or second for familiarity by the fewest participants (27%), followed by the Taylor plot (48%), heat map (52%), and bar chart (74%). As observed in Figure 8a, participants' preference rankings differed substantially from their pre-study familiarity rankings for slope plots. Overall, the slope plot was ranked first for Task B and Task C, which both involved dissimilarity identification, and was ranked second for Task A, which involved similarity identification. When identifying their overall most-preferred visualization, 33% of participants selected the slope plot, which is only 4% less than the heat map. Thus our findings did not support **H4a**. We compared the pre-study familiarity and post-study preference rankings using the discrepancy metric. A greater or positive discrepancy score indicates a high preference for a relatively less familiar visualization, while a lower or negative discrepancy score is associated with a low preference for a relatively more familiar visualization. As we observe in Figure 8b, slope plots (0.264, [0.153, 0.376]) attained the greatest positive discrepancy, with significant differences from the Taylor plot (0.011, [−0.100, 0.123]) overall ($p < 0.05$) and for low domain experience group ($p < 0.05$) (thus supporting **H4b**), and from heat map for high domain experience group ($p < 0.05$).

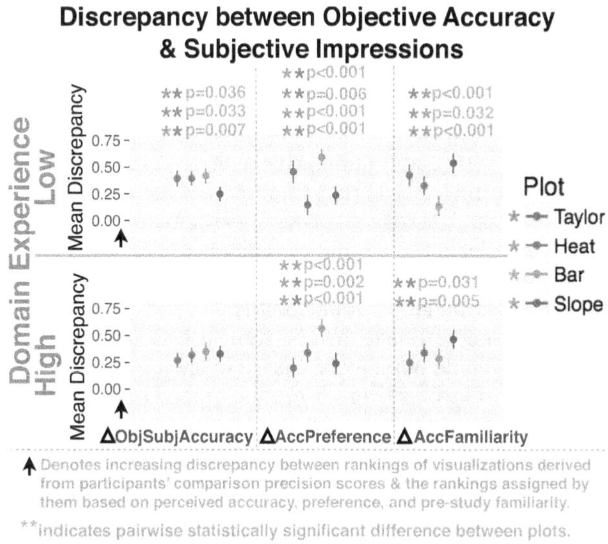

Figure 9. Discrepancy between rankings derived from objective accuracy and perceived accuracy, preference, and familiarity. Error bars represent 95% confidence intervals. The low experience group was least discrepant about their accuracy using slope plots as evidenced by the least mean discrepancy score. Slope plots also showed: i) consistently low discrepancy levels between objective accuracy and preference across both experience groups, signifying that preference for slope plots also matched performance accuracy, and ii) consistently high discrepancy levels between objective accuracy and familiarity, signifying that lack of familiarity was not a barrier in accurate performance using slope plots.

**Discrepancy between Objective Accuracy and Subjective Impressions**: We found that the discrepancy between objective and perceived accuracy (ΔObjSubjAccuracy) was lower for more experienced participants, and that within the high experience group, there was less variability in the discrepancy scores across all visualizations. As shown in Figure 9,for less experienced participants, slope plots (0.247, [0.175, 0.320]) were the least discrepant, with significant differences from all other visualizations, Taylor plots (0.392, [0.319, 0.465]), heat maps (0.393, [0.321, 0.466]), and bar charts (0.418, [0.345, 0.491]), at ($p < 0.05$). We therefore did not find evidence to support **H5a** as there were significant discrepancies. We also found limited support for **H5b**: across both experience groups, there was significantly high discrepancy between objective accuracy-based ranking and subjective preference-based rankings for bar charts ($p < 0.05$). For the low experience group we observed a similarly high discrepancy for the Taylor plots (0.455, [0.362, 0.548]), with significant differences from heat maps (0.146, [0.053, 0.239]) and slope plots (0.235, [0.142, 0.328]). The discrepancy between familiarity and objective accuracy for slope plots (Figure 9) was the highest for both experience groups, implying that irrespective of participants' experience, slope plots ranked lower with respect to familiarity, but ranked higher relative to more familiar visualizations for performance accuracy.

## DISCUSSION

In this section, we reflect on our key findings and analyze participants' comments provided at the end of the study.

**Effect of Experience and Familiarity:** We found that domain experience and familiarity with visualizations did not drive performance accuracy (Figure 5, 6) for multi-way comparison tasks. Across all groups, participants reported similarly high levels of comfort, confidence, accuracy, and efficiency with the relatively unfamiliar slope plots (Figure 7). On the other hand, we found that less experienced scientists tended to underestimate their performance accuracy for Taylor plots. This could possibly be caused by their lower confidence and comfort ratings (Figure 7a) due to the visual complexity of Taylor plots or the associated learning curve involved in their interpretation for scientists who have less experience with this visualization. From previous research, we know high perceived accuracy, comfort, and confidence are antecedents of human-machine trust [20]. These findings lead us to an intuition that using visualization design best practices can improve accessibility, potentially overcome the barrier of low familiarity, and inspire trust in domain experts for use in deriving analytical insights [8].

**Implications for Model Fidelity Visualization:** In their final comments almost all participants (44 out of 47) mentioned that the slope plot was useful for easily comparing models and variables and for identifying variability across models. Examples of the answers include: *"It's much easier to compare many models on this plot. The other plots I had to compare pairwise in order for it to make sense to me; here, we get many models all at once which is more efficient (P33).".* We also found that the use of small multiples (Taylor plots, bar charts) or large singles (heat maps, slope plots) [31] did not seem to have an effect on objective accuracy. Small multiples of bar charts were as accurate with the large single approach of slope plots for Task C, while the large single approaches were as accurate than other visualizations for Task A. Further research is needed to explore the relative advantages and disadvantages of these approaches in the context of visual comparison tasks. In the context of subjective impressions, however, there was a stronger preference for the large single approach for comparing many models and many variables as small multiples entail significant comparison complexity. This was implied by the following observation by one of the participants: "Seeing simultaneous patterns in many/many models/variables takes a lot of concentration on shapes of distributions of dots and corresponding colors of the dots - challenging!". Several participants with longer domain experience, however, commented that for a smaller number of output variables and models, they might still prefer Taylor plots or bar charts.

**Adoption of Unfamiliar Visualization:** Overall, we found that most participants had a high degree of preference for the slope plots irrespective of their familiarity with other plots or experience, which is indicative of potential adoption [25] by scientists in the future. Many participants mentioned the slope plot may complement other visualization approaches, or be well-suited to particular tasks. One participant commented that the *"[s]lope plot does not give an immediate intuitive understanding of the performance of a particular model, as the heatmap does. I would use it in combination with a heatmap as a more accurate but less intuitive visualization with strength in showing variability of variables (P10)." "This is probably the best visualization for looking at the spread amongst models with regards to a specific variable (P4).", etc.* In keeping with this sentiment, our collaborators have begun to adopt the slope plots as part of their workflow, and we are currently planning follow-up research on how different similarity-based visualizations (slope plots, heat maps) can be combined for exploring model fidelity patterns at different levels of detail.

## CONCLUSION AND FUTURE WORK

We have presented a comprehensive analysis of objective and subjective measures of the efficacy of alternative visualization designs for climate model fidelity comparison and how these measures are mediated by the scientists' length of domain experience and prior familiarity with each visualization. Our significant findings are as follows: i) Familiarity did not drive objective accuracy or self-reported comfort with, confidence in, or preference for any visualization. ii) Objective accuracy on all tasks was similar across all visualizations, except that scientists, irrespective of the length of their domain experience, were less accurate in identifying dissimilar models using Taylor plots compared to other visualizations. iii) Scientists with greater domain experience were generally less discrepant about their perceived accuracy than less experienced scientists, while the latter group was least discrepant about their perceived accuracy with the unfamiliar slope plots. iv) The unfamiliar slope plot was the most frequently preferred visualization for the tasks presented in this study, and exhibited comparable or higher levels of objective accuracy with respect to familiar visualizations, for both highly experienced and less experienced scientists. An appreciation and preference for the slope plot were also expressed in many of the written comments submitted by the participants. This suggests that collaborative design of optimal visualizations, adapted to scientific tasks, can potentially lead to a broader acceptance and adoption of new designs within a scientific community.

In the future, we would like to extend these findings to other domains, and determine whether greater comfort and confidence levels also lead to greater scientific consensus. Especially in climate modeling, a recurring problem is the lack of well-defined consensus on the features that characterize good or bad models. We believe that effective visualizations can aid scientists in more objectively identifying patterns of model fidelity and their causes, leading to greater consensus regarding model fidelity, and improved efficiency in model calibration and assessment activities. This will ultimately contribute to improved understanding of global climate change patterns.

## ACKNOWLEDGMENT

We thank Daniel Tompkins for his assistance in the metrics calculations and plotting. This research was funded by the Laboratory Directed Research and Development Program (LDRD) at the Pacific Northwest National Laboratory, which is operated by Batelle for the U.S. Department of Energy (DOE) under contract DE-AC05-76RLO01830.

## REFERENCES


1. Jürgen Bernard, Martin Steiger, Sven Widmer, Hendrik Lücke-Tieke, Thorsten May, and Jörn Kohlhammer. 2014. Visual-interactive Exploration of Interesting Multivariate Relations in Mixed Research Data Sets. In *Computer Graphics Forum*, Vol. 33. Wiley Online Library, 291–300.
2. Jacques Bertin. 1983. *Semiology of graphics: diagrams, networks, maps*. University of Wisconsin press.
3. Matthew Brehmer, Jocelyn Ng, Kevin Tate, and Tamara Munzner. 2016. Matches, Mismatches, and Methods: Multiple-View Workflows for Energy Portfolio Analysis. *IEEE Transactions on Visualization and Computer Graphics* 22, 1 (2016), 449–458.
4. Sabrina Bresciani and Martin J Eppler. 2009. The benefits of synchronous collaborative information visualization: Evidence from an experimental evaluation. *IEEE transactions on visualization and computer graphics* 15, 6 (2009), 1073–1080.
5. Bertjan Broeksema, Alexandru C Telea, and Thomas Baudel. 2013. Visual Analysis of Multi-Dimensional Categorical Data Sets. In *Computer Graphics Forum*, Vol. 32. Wiley Online Library, 158–169.
6. Curt Covey, Krishna M AchutaRao, Michael Fiorino, Peter J Gleckler, Karl E Taylor, and Michael F Wehner. 2002. *Intercomparison of climate data sets as a measure of observational uncertainty*. UCRL.
7. Aritra Dasgupta and Robert Kosara. 2010. Pargnostics: Screen-Space Metrics for Parallel Coordinates. *Transactions on Visualization and Computer Graphics* 16, 6 (2010), 1017–26.
8. Aritra Dasgupta, Joon-Yong Lee, Ryan Wilson, Robert A Lafrance, Nick Cramer, Kristin Cook, and Samuel Payne. 2017. Familiarity Vs Trust: A Comparative Study of Domain Scientists' Trust in Visual Analytics and Conventional Analysis Methods. *IEEE Transactions on Visualization and Computer Graphics* 23, 1 (2017), 271–280.
9. Aritra Dasgupta, Jorge Poco, Yaxing Wei, Robert Cook, Enrico Bertini, and Claudio T. Silva. 2015. Bridging Theory with Practice: An Exploratory Study of Visualization Use and Design for Climate Model Comparison. *IEEE Transactions on Visualization and Computer Graphics* 21, 9 (2015), 996–1014.
10. Michael Friendly and SAS Institute. 2000. *Visualizing categorical data*. Sas Institute Cary, NC.
11. David Gefen. 2000. E-commerce: the role of familiarity and trust. *Omega* 28, 6 (2000), 725–737.
12. Peter J Gleckler, Karl E Taylor, and Charles Doutriaux. 2008. Performance metrics for climate models. *Journal of Geophysical Research: Atmospheres* 113, D6 (2008).
13. Michael Gleicher, Danielle Albers, Rick Walker, Ilir Jusufi, Charles D. Hansen, and Jonathan C. Roberts. 2011. Visual comparison for information visualization. *Information Visualization* 10, 4 (2011), 289–309.
14. Mark Harrower and Cynthia A Brewer. 2003. ColorBrewer. org: an online tool for selecting colour schemes for maps. *The Cartographic Journal* 40, 1 (2003), 27–37.
15. Yosef Hochberg. 1988. A sharper Bonferroni procedure for multiple tests of significance. *Biometrika* 75, 4 (1988), 800–802.
16. James W. Hurrell, M.M. Holland, P. R. Gent, S. Ghan, J. E. Kay, P. J. Kushner, J.-F. Lamarque, W.G. Large, D. Lawrence, K. Lindsay, W. H. Lipscomb, M. C. Long, N. Mahowald, D. R. Marsh, R. B. Neale, P. J. Rasch, S. Vavrus, M. Vertenstein, D. Bader, W.D. Collins, J.J. Hack, J. Kiehl, and S. Marshall. 2013. The Community Earth System Model: A Framework for Collaborative Research. *Bulletin of the American Meteorological Society* (2013), 1339–1360.
17. Alfred Inselberg and Bernard Dimsdale. 1990. Parallel Coordinates: A Tool for Visualizing Multi-Dimensional Geometry. In *IEEE Visualization*. IEEE CS Press, 361–378.
18. Kurt Koffka. 2013. *Principles of Gestalt psychology*. Vol. 44. Routledge.
19. Heidi Lam, Enrico Bertini, Petra Isenberg, Catherine Plaisant, and Sheelagh Carpendale. 2012. Empirical studies in information visualization: Seven scenarios. *IEEE Transactions on Visualization and Computer Graphics* 18, 9 (2012), 1520–1536.
20. Daniel J McAllister. 1995. Affect-and cognition-based trust as foundations for interpersonal cooperation in organizations. *Academy of management journal* 38, 1 (1995), 24–59.
21. T. Munzner. 2009. A nested process model for visualization design and validation. *IEEE Transactions on Visualization and Computer Graphics* 15, 6 (2009), 921–928.
22. Allan H Murphy. 1988. Skill scores based on the mean square error and their relationships to the correlation coefficient. *Monthly Weather Review* 116, 12 (1988), 2417–2424.
23. R B. Neale, C. C. Chen, A. Gettelman, P. H. Lauritzen, S. Park, D. L. Williamson, A. J. Conley, R. Garcia, D. Kinnison, J-F. Lamarque, D. Marsh, M. Mills, A. K. Smith, S. TIlmes, F. Vitt, H. Morrison, P. Cameron-Smith, W. D. Collins, M. J. Iacono, R. C. Easter, S. J. Ghan ans X. Liu, P. J. Rasch, and M. Taylor. 2012. *Description of the NCAR Community Atmosphere Model: CAM5.0*. Technical Report NCAR/TN-486+STR. National Center for Atmospheric Research, Boulder, Colorado, USA. 268 pp., URL = `http://www.ccsm.ucar.edu/models/atm-cam`.
24. Intergovernmental Panel on Climate Change. 2015. *Climate Change 2014: Mitigation of Climate Change*. Vol. 3. Cambridge University Press.

25. Catherine Plaisant. 2004. The challenge of information visualization evaluation. In *Proceedings of the working conference on Advanced visual interfaces*. ACM, 109–116.
26. Dominik Sacha, Hansi Senaratne, Bum Chul Kwon, Geoffrey Ellis, and Daniel A Keim. 2016. The role of uncertainty, awareness, and trust in visual analytics. *IEEE Transactions on Visualization and Computer Graphics* 22, 1 (2016), 240–249.
27. Leila Takayama and Eser Kandogan. 2006. Trust as an underlying factor of system administrator interface choice. In *CHI'06 extended abstracts on Human factors in computing systems*. ACM, 1391–1396.
28. Karl E Taylor. 2001. Summarizing multiple aspects of model performance in a single diagram. *Journal of Geophysical Research: Atmospheres* 106, D7 (2001), 7183–7192.
29. Edward R. Tufte. 2001. *The Visual Display of Quantitative Information* (2nd ed.). Graphics Press.
30. Ananth Uggirala, Anand K Gramopadhye, Brain J Melloy, and Joe E Toler. 2004. Measurement of trust in complex and dynamic systems using a quantitative approach. *International Journal of Industrial Ergonomics* 34, 3 (2004), 175–186.
31. Stef van den Elzen and Jarke J van Wijk. 2013. Small multiples, large singles: A new approach for visual data exploration. In *Computer Graphics Forum*, Vol. 32. Wiley Online Library, 191–200.
32. Edward Vonesh and Vernon M Chinchilli. 1996. *Linear and nonlinear models for the analysis of repeated measurements*. CRC press.
33. C. Ware. 2004. *Information visualization: Perception for Design*. Morgan Kaufmann.

# A Cognitive Model of How People Make Decisions Through Interaction with Visual Displays

**Xiuli Chen**
School of Psychology,
University of Birmingham,UK
chenxy@bham.ac.uk*

**Sandra Dorothee Starke**
Electronic, Electrical and
Systems Engineering,
University of Birmingham,UK
s.d.starke@bham.ac.uk

**Chris Baber**
Electronic, Electrical and
Systems Engineering,
University of Birmingham,UK
c.baber@bham.ac.uk

**Andrew Howes**
School of Computer Science,
University of Birmingham,UK
HowesA@bham.ac.uk*

## ABSTRACT
In this paper we report a cognitive model of how people make decisions through interaction. The model is based on the assumption that interaction for decision making is an example of a Partially Observable Markov Decision Process (POMDP) in which observations are made by limited perceptual systems that model human foveated vision and decisions are made by strategies that are adapted to the task. We illustrate the model by applying it to the task of determining whether to block a credit card given a number of variables including the location of a transaction, its amount, and the customer history. Each of these variables have a different validity and users may weight them accordingly. The model solves the POMDP by learning patterns of eye movements (strategies) adapted to different presentations of the data. We compare the model behavior to human performance on the credit card transaction task.

## ACM Classification Keywords
H.1.2 User/Machine Systems: Human factors, Human information processing

## Author Keywords
cognitive modeling; visual search; eye movements; Markov Decision Process; reinforcement learning; decision making.

## INTRODUCTION
Decision makers interact with computer systems in order to gather information and evaluate options. In particular, they sometimes use information visualizations that are designed to aggregate large amounts of information into readily perceptible representations of multi-dimensional data. An important research question is how do these representations help human decision making?


CHI 2017, May 06-11, 2017, Denver, CO, USA
ACM 978-1-4503-4655-9/17/05.
http://dx.doi.org/10.1145/3025453.3025596

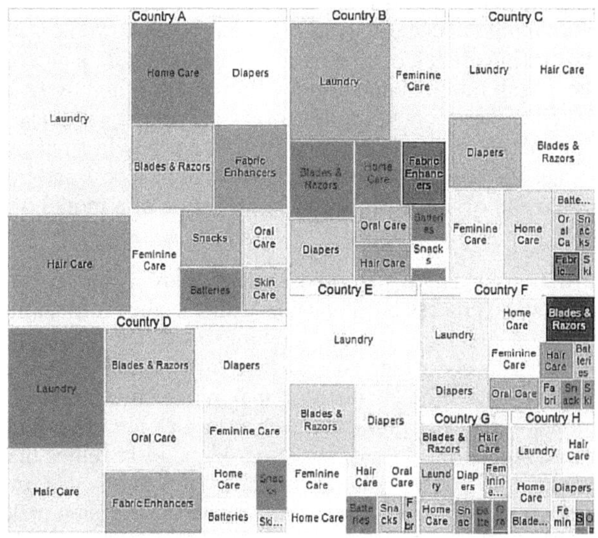


**Figure 1. A color-map used by Procter & Gamble to show where their products stand in their respective markets. It shows markets in which products compete and their relative share (red indicating low market share and green indicating high market share). The color-map is used to help managers understand what is going on in the business, and to decide what to do about it. Figure from Harvard Business Review (`https://hbr.org/2013/04/how-p-and-g-presents-data`).**

An example of a typical decision problem is deciding where and whether to make business investments. One of the visualizations that might be employed to support such a task is the color-map visualization illustrated in Figure 1. This visualization represents the relative share of Proctor and Gamble products in a range of markets in which they compete; market size is represented by the size of the rectangle and market share is represented by color (red indicating low market share and green indicating high market share). The visualization is designed with the goal of helping managers make better and faster decisions [9]. Later in the paper we describe another decision task that involves spotting potential frauds in credit card data.

Why might one expect such visualizations to be effective? We might suppose that visualizations support the recognition of complex patterns across cues; or they may offer an intuitive encoding of meaning (e.g. green indicates a good market share); or it may be that certain colors attract attention and these can be used to highlight important features. In general, the visualization is intended to enable users to directly perceive patterns in the data and this *direct perception* is assumed to result in faster and more accurate decisions. Color-map visualizations epitomize the goal of designing visualization technologies that support higher level decision making by taking advantage of human perceptual mechanisms.

Foundational work in Human-Computer Interaction developed models of the cost structure of sensemaking [37] and focused on how the design of visualizations impacts the cost of data extraction. There are likely to be differences in extraction costs (e.g. decision time) for different visualizations. In related work in intelligence analysis [1], it has been shown how users engage in parallel, overlapping explorations of data and often work with minimal and sketchy frames to explain these data. Together these contributions suggest that people will make use of a subset of the available information, partly in an effort to reduce the cost associated with information access and partly as a result of the incremental construction of a model of the data.

In the current paper, we propose an integrative cognitive model of how the process of interaction with visualizations supports decision making. It is an attempt to explain how display design can contribute to reducing information access cost and therefore efficient decision making. A key feature of the model is that the predicted user strategies are an emergent consequence of the cost structure of the task, rather than a model assumption. The model builds on a number of recent threads in Human-Computer Interaction and decision making research. These threads are described below.

1. *Partially Observable Markov Decision Processes* (POMDP). A POMDP is a mathematical framework for modeling sequential decision problems in which (1) only incomplete observations of the state of the world can be made, and (2) the transitions between states are stochastic. These properties are important for modeling interactive decision making because of the partial and stochastic nature of human information gathering. For example, using the visualization in Figure 1 to acquire information about large markets, or markets with low share, requires multiple fixations to bring high resolution foveated vision to bear on areas of interest. Each fixation retrieves only a little (partial) information and it does so with some frequency of error (see *Active Vision* below) and is therefore stochastic.

2. *Active vision*. While foveated vision is very accurate, peripheral vision is much less so [23]. As a consequence there is uncertainty as to which, and whether, objects in peripheral vision are detected. This uncertainty limits the extent to which visualizations in HCI can support direct perception. As a consequence multiple eye movements and fixations are often required to build a belief about what is on the display that is sufficient to guide action. Eye movements are, therefore, actively recruited in order to solve the user's decision task, not to build a complete model of the display. Recent work shows how color, shape, and size have different consequences for visual search of displays [23]. We used the constraints proposed in [23] to define the POMDP's observation function.

3. *Machine learning*. Human eye movements can be predicted by solving a POMDP, bounded by a model of human vision, with machine learning [6, 7]. Machine learning is used to find a strategy for choosing actions given each belief about the state of the world, where beliefs about the world are built through repeated fixations. For any POMDP there are one or more optimal strategies that choose the actions that maximize the average utility of interaction. In interactive decision tasks, the problem is to find a strategy for moving the eyes so as to generate good estimates of the task-relevant displayed state and, therefore, best possible decisions. We might expect that good visualizations facilitate efficient strategies by increasing the rate or reliability with which the human eye gathers information.

4. *Decision strategies*. Behavioral evidence suggests that people use simple but general rules (e.g., search rules, stopping rules and decision rules) in order to make good decisions quickly [16, 15, 14]. Other evidence suggests that people acquire decision strategies that are highly adapted to the cost structure of the task [19, 17]. The use of machine learning to derive strategies allows us to explore the extent to which *heuristics* are an emergent consequence of adaptation to the decision task specified in the POMDP and, therefore, the limits of the specified cognitive-perceptual mechanisms [20, 25].

Below, we first report the integrative model and then report a comparison of the model's behavior to human data. The data were collected using a laboratory study of human participants performing an ecologically determined task requiring a decision about whether a credit card payment might be fraudulent. In order to do this, participants were provided with information about various card transaction cues (e.g. transaction history, amount etc.) that were presented using one of two types of display. In one type of display, the information was presented numerically, and in the other, a color-map was used. We hypothesized that the color-map would enhance the human capacity to encode information using peripheral vision in accordance with the constraints investigated by [23]. Moreover, we used the model to predict the decision time, accuracy and number of fixations used for each interface. In addition, the study manipulated the cost of accessing each cue. In one condition, cues were always present on the display and in the other they were covered until individually revealed by a mouse click.

The contribution of the work is in providing a new model and empirical validation of how people make decisions through interaction with visualizations such as color-maps. The model shows how decision making behavior is an emergent consequence of adaptation to display design. Critically, the model does not make any priori assumptions about decision strategy, rather the strategy is calculated using a machine learning algorithm. Detailed comparisons between the model's behavior and human performance metrics (including performance time and eye movements) are provided.

## BACKGROUND

In this section we further review the background to the four threads (introduced above) that contribute to our work.

### Partially Observable Markov Decision Process

It has been suggested by a number of authors that human visual search can be understood as the solution to a Partially Observable Markov Decision Process (POMDP) [6, 32, 7]. As we have said, the POMDP provides a mathematical framework that captures the interaction between an agent and the stochastic environment that it inhabits [22]. Specifically, the complete state of the environment is not known to the agent. Instead, the agent receives observations that are bounded by the limits of human perception and must make a decision based on partial information. Framing the model as a POMDP allows for the calculation of the optimal strategy given a theory of the human visual system.

For example, a target localization task was framed as a POMDP problem by [6]. In their task, a visual target was present in one position in a grid. To find the target, the agent used a series of fixations, one at each time step, each on one of the points in the grid. The information received at each time step was from the fixated point (with high reliability) and surrounding points (with lower reliability). The authors showed how the optimal strategy can generate human like behavior without assuming ad-hoc heuristics such as inhibition-of-return to previous locations. They also found that the optimal policy can contradict accepted ideas by sometimes preferring to look just to the side of the target, rather than directly at it, so as to gather more information with peripheral vision.

A random dots motion discrimination task was framed as a POMDP problem by [32]. In this task, primates were shown a visual display containing a group of moving dots. A fraction of the dots moved in one of two fixed directions (left or right) and other dots moved in random directions. The primates were rewarded for determining the direction in which the majority of dots moved, where the number of random dots was manipulated. Rao's (2010) model showed that primate decision times could be modeled as the solution to a POMDP that determined the threshold for switching from information gathering to decision.

### Active vision

Studies of visual perception show that perceiving a pattern such as that in Figure 1 involves a complex sequence of eye movements to gather information and maximize the utility of the decision [42, 40, 18, 29]. This is a process of active vision. People move their eyes to seek out items within a visual scene that are relevant to the task or question they are engaged in. Eye movements are necessary since foveated vision covers only 1-2 degrees visual angle; the fovea has the highest density of daylight/color vision receptor cells. With increasing eccentricity, there is a sharp drop off in the density of these cells, and hence vision becomes rapidly blurred. The periphery, covering a much larger area than the fovea, still contains useful information despite the reduced acuity. It is well known that peripheral vision plays a key role in guiding eye movements during visual search [13] and that color, shape and size have different acuity functions [23].

### Machine learning (for POMDP solutions)

The POMDP formalism is very general to a diverse range of problems [39, 26]. Unfortunately, the generality of POMDPs entails high computational cost to derive the control policy; research in the field of POMDP is mainly focused on approximate solutions [39]. For example, recent work has shown that Deep Q-Networks are capable of learning human-level control policies on a variety of different Atari 2600 games [26]. Simpler tasks can be solved with a combination of Bayesian inference for state estimation and Q-learning [47] for policy learning.

### Decision strategies

The study of decision strategies has, in large part, been the study of decision heuristics. One prominent decision heuristic has received much attention: the take-the-best (TTB) heuristic [16]. The TTB heuristic consists of a set of rules concerning the most important aspects of information gathering and decision making: the search rule, the stopping rule and the decision rule. These requires knowing the validity of cues. Validity is the probability that the information represented by a cue will lead an observer to the correct decision. A person using TTB searches from the most useful information (with the highest validity) to the information with the lowest validity (the search rule). Crucially, information search terminates once a cue discriminates between the considered options or once all cues have been examined (the stopping rule); at which point the heuristic would choose the option favored by the discriminating cue (the decision rule).

Following [15] seminal work, showing how Take-The-Best (TTB) can describe human information gathering and decision making behaviors, a number of articles offered empirical investigations into which heuristics people choose [27, 28, 4, 3, 24]. A particular concern in this research has been whether people use Take-The-Best (TTB), which uses information highly selectively, or a heuristic such as Weighted-ADDitive (WADD) that integrates all information [36, 35]. While this debate has been conducted in the psychology literature, it is highly relevant to understanding how information visualizations are used by people, and therefore to how visualizations should be designed. If people use TTB and not WADD then they may make use of a much smaller part of the displayed information than if they use WADD. Also, it is possible that use of these heuristics integrates with the visualization design.

## TASK

Before introducing our theory of decision making through interaction with visualizations, we briefly described a task, the credit card fraud detection task, which will be used to illustrate the theory.

The task is motivated by a real-world scenario that is known to be extremely difficult for people. Credit card fraud detection analysts attempt to identify fraudulent patterns in transaction data-sets, often characterized by a large number of samples, many dimensions and online updates [8]. Despite the use of automated detection algorithms, there continue to be key roles for people to play in the analysis process. These roles range from defining and tuning the algorithms that automatic systems deploy, to triaging and screening recommendations from such systems, to contacting customers (either to query a transaction or to explain a decision). In terms of triaging and screening, we assume that an automated detection process is running and that this process has flagged a given transaction (or set of transactions) as suspicious and a user will engage in some form of investigation to decide how to respond to the flag. Based on pilot interviews and discussions with credit card fraud analysts and organizations, we believe that there are several ways in which the investigation could be performed. In some instances, the investigation could involve direct contact with the card-holder, in which the caller follows a pre-defined script and protocols that do not involve investigative capabilities. In some cases, these are passed to the analyst who needs to make a decision as to whether or not the credit card is blocked (this is the approach assumed in this paper). In this instance, the analyst would take a more forensic approach to the behavior of the card holder and the use of the card, relative to some concept of normal activity. In some cases, investigation could be at the level of transactions, in which the analyst seeks to identify patterns of criminal activity involving several cards. In this instance, the analysis would be looking for evidence of stolen details or unusual patterns of use of several cards, say multiple transactions in different locations within a short time-frame. Other functions that people can perform in the fraud detection process include: risk prioritization, fast closure of low risk cases, documentation of false positives [30], and identification of risk profiles and fraud patterns [38, 21].

In this study, we use a simplified version of fraud detection in which the task is to decide whether a transaction should be blocked (prevented from being authorized) or allowed. As shown in Figure 2, participants are provided with 9 sources of information (cues) and these are presented using one of 4 display designs (visualizations). The cues differ in the reliability with which they determine whether or not a transaction is a fraud and the participants must discover these validities with experience and decide which cues are worth using to make a decision. Further details are provided in the Experiment section.

The visualizations presented in Figure 2 do not have the full richness and complexity of the visualization used in Figure 1. In particular, our experimental interfaces did not use size to represent a dimension of the data. Our focus on color is partly to enable simple experimental designs and also because color is known to be more detectable with peripheral vision than shape [23].

## THEORY AND MODEL

The theoretical claim made in this paper is that decision strategies are an emergent consequence of both the statistical properties of the environment (the experienced cue validities, different time cost for extracting information) and of the constraints imposed by human perceptual mechanisms. For a visualization task, this theory can be written precisely by formulating the decision problem as a POMDP for active vision and solving this problem with machine learning to find an optimal decision strategy (emergent heuristics).

In the resulting model, eye movement strategies and stopping rules, are an emergent consequence of the visualization and the limits of human vision [7, 43, 6]. The assumption is that people choose which cues to look at and when to stop looking at cues informed by the reward/cost that they receive for the decisions they make. Better decisions will receive higher rewards, which will reinforce good eye movement strategies.

In the following paragraphs, we report the problem formulation and model, followed by human data that tests the model predictions.

### Problem formulation

We assume that the problem faced by a decision analyst can be modeled as a Partially Observable Markov Decision Process (POMDP) [22]. On each time step, the environment is in one of the possible states that is not directly observed. Instead, by interacting with the environment (taking actions), observations and reward (cost if the value is negative) are received from it. That is, the environment is partially observable. This action-observation-reward sequence happens in cycles indexed by $t = 1, 2, 3, \ldots$. Because the environment's state is not directly observed, actions are taken under uncertainty of the true environment state. On each time step, an action is chosen from the action space including both information gathering actions and decision actions. The action selection is dependent on the history of observations and actions.

To be more specific, the action-observation sequence is used to update the estimate of the underlying true state (call *'belief state'* below) using Bayesian inference. Q-learning [47] is then used to learn which action to do next (e.g., to gather more information or to make a decision) given the current belief state, so as to maximize the expected future reward. It does so by learning the belief-action values through simulated experience. Belief-action values are updated incrementally (learned) as reward and cost feedback is received from the interaction during the simulated experience. For example, if the model looks at cue A in a certain belief state and subsequently makes an incorrect decision, then the value of the action (look at cue A) at this belief state will decrease. With enough simulation trials, the optimal strategy will emerge and the model will take the best actions given the beliefs.

In the following sections more detail is provided about how the belief estimate and action selection work. A procedure for the computer simulation is provided in box Algorithm 1.

A formal description of our task as a POMDP is given in the following [22].

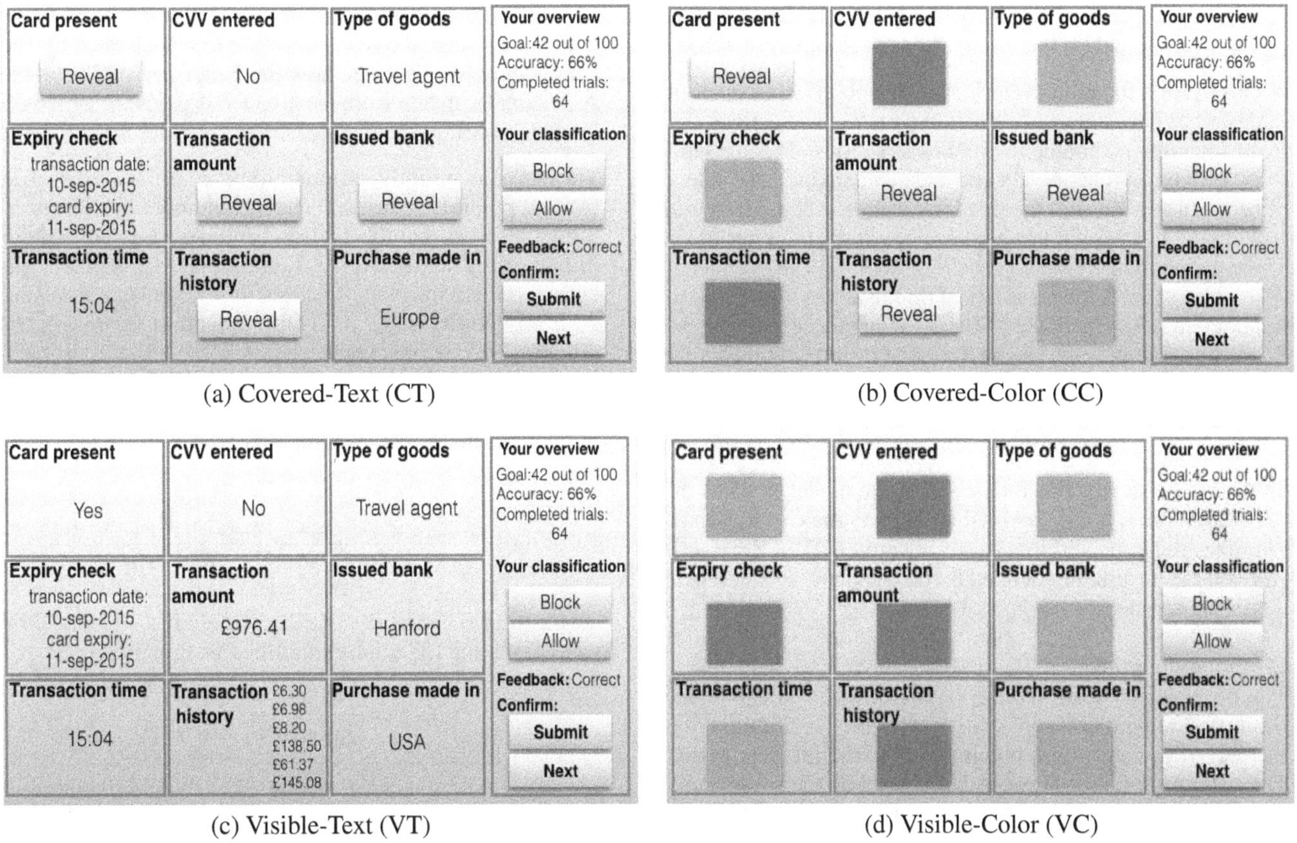


**Figure 2. Four interface variants for credit card fraud detection. The information cues are represented with text (left panels) or color (right panels) and the information is either immediately available (bottom panels) or revealed by clicking the 'Reveal' buttons (top panels).**

- State space $S$: At any time step $t$, the environment is in a state $s_t \in S$. A state represents a true information pattern presented on the user interface. As shown in Figure 2, nine cues associated with credit card transactions are presented on the interface. The value of each cue was discretized into two levels, representing 'fraudulent (F)' and 'normal (N)' respectively. Therefore, for example, one of the states is a 9-element vector [F,N,N,F,F,F,N,F,N], each item of which represents the value for one of the cues ('F' for fraudulent and 'N' for normal). Hence, the size of the state space is $2^9 = 512$.
- Action space $A$: An action is taken at each time step, $a_t \in A$. The action space, $A$, consists of both the information gathering actions (i.e., which cue to fixate) and decision making actions (i.e., Block/Allow transaction). Therefore, the size of the action space is 11 (9 cues plus 2 decision actions).
- Reward function $r(S,A)$: At any moment, the environment (in one of the states $s$) generates a reward (cost if the value is negative), $r(s,a)$, in response to the action taken $a$. For the information gathering actions, the reward is the time cost (the unit is seconds). The time cost includes both the dwell time on the cues and the saccadic time cost of traveling between cues. More detail regarding the time cost is provided in subsection 'Time Cost' below. In the experiment to be modeled (described below), the participants were asked to complete 100 *correct* trials as quickly as possible, so that errors were operationalized as time cost. In the model, the cost for incorrect decisions is based on participants' average time cost (Seconds) for a trial (CT:$17 \pm 15$; CC:$24 \pm 7$;VT:$20 \pm 8$; VC:$13 \pm 3$). That is, the penalty of an incorrect trial is the time cost for doing another trial.
- Transition function $T(S_{t+1}|S_t,A_t)$: In addition to the reward, another consequence of the action is that the environment switches to a new state according to the transition function. In the current task the states (i.e. displayed information patterns) stay unchanged across time steps within one trial. Therefore, $T(S_{t+1}|S_t,A_t)$ equals to 1 only when $S_{t+1} = S_t$. $T(S_{t+1}|S_t,A_t)$ equals 0 otherwise. That is, the state transition matrix is the identity matrix.
- Observation space $O$: After transitioning to a new state, a new observation is received. The observation, $o_t \in O$, is defined as the information gathered at the time step $t$. An observation is a 9-element vector, each element of which represents the information gathered for one of the cues. Each element of the observation has three levels, F (fraudulent), N (normal) and U (unknown). For example, one observation

might be represented as [F,N,U,F,U,U,U,N,N]. Therefore the upper bound on the observation space is $3^9 = 19683$.

- Observation function $p(O_t|S_t,A_t)$: The observation function describes how states (information patterns) and actions (fixate locations) combine to yield observations. The availability of information about a cue is dependent on the distance between this cue and the fixation location (eccentricity). In addition, it is known that an object's color is more visible in the periphery than the object's text label [23]. In our model, the observation model is based on the acuity functions reported in [23], where the visibility of an object is dependent on, for example, the object size, the object feature (color or text), and the eccentricity. The observational model is explained in more details in subsection 'Observation Model' below.
- Discount rate $\gamma$: At each time step $t$, the model receives the reward $r(s_t,a_t)$. The optimal strategy is the one that maximizes the expected long-term reward: $E[\sum_{t=0}^{\infty}\gamma^t r(s_t,a_t)]$ given the uncertainty defined by the elements above, where $\gamma$ is a discount rate, $0 \leq \gamma < 1$.

### Observation Model

The observation obtained is constrained by a theory of the limits on the human visual system. Our model assumed that the text information was obtained only when it was fixated. The color information was obtained based on the color acuity function reported in [23]. This function was used to determine the availability of the color information for each cue given the distance between the cues and the fixated location (called *eccentricity*), and the size of the item. Specifically, on each fixation, the availability of the color information was determined by the probabilities defined in Equation (1).

$$P(available) = P(size + X > threshold) \quad (1)$$

where *size* is the object size in terms of visual angle in degrees; $X \sim \mathcal{N}(size, v \times size)$; $threshold = a \times e^2 + b \times e + c$; $e$ is eccentricity in terms of visual angle in degrees. In the model, the function were set with parameter values of v=0.7, b=0.1, c=0.1, a=0.035 as in [23].

### Time Cost

The time cost of the information gathering actions consisted of two factors. One is the saccade duration: the time for traveling between cues. The other is the dwell duration: the time for extracting information from cues.

The saccade duration $D$ (in milliseconds) was determined with the following equation from [2]:

$$D = 37 + 2.7A \quad (2)$$

where $A$ is the amplitude (in terms of visual angle in degrees) of the saccade between two successive fixations.

The dwell durations used in the model were determined from experimental data (see below).

### Bayesian belief update

At each time step, the environment is in a state, which is not directly observed. The model maintains a belief $b$ about the state given the information observed so far. Every time the agent takes an action $a$ and observes $o$, $b$ is updated by Bayes' rule. Below we describe how the belief update is computed. An example update from $t = 0$ to $t = 1$ is given, which could be generalized to the update from $t$ to $t+1$.

The belief is initially assumed to be an uniform distribution over all possible states, $b_0$. That is, without any evidence, the model believes that the environment is equally possible to be in one of the states. At $t = 1$, an action, $a_1$, is taken, which causes the environment to transition from state $s$ to state $s'$ with probability $T(s' \mid s, a)$ (the transition function). After reaching $s'$, one observation,$o_1$, is received with probability $p(o_1 \mid s', a_1)$ (the observation function). The belief state, $b_1$, is obtained given the action $a_1$, the observation $o_1$, and the previous belief $b_0$, as in Equation (3) below.

$$b_1(s') = \frac{\sum_{s\in S} b_0(s) \times T(s' \mid s,a_1) \times p(o_1 \mid s',a_1)}{\sum_{s'\in S} p(o_1 \mid s',a_1) \sum_{s\in S} T(s' \mid s,a_1) b_0(s)} \quad (3)$$

As mentioned above $T(s'|s,a_1) = 1$ only if $s' = s$, and 0 otherwise, Equation (3) can be simplified as Equation (4):

$$b_1(s) = \frac{b_0(s) \times p(o_1 \mid s,a_1)}{\sum_{s\in S} p(o_1 \mid s,a_1) b_0(s)} \quad (4)$$

At each time $t$, a belief $b_t$ vector consists of a probability for each of the states, $b_t(s_i)$, where $i \in 1,2,3,...N_s$ and $N_s$ is the number of the states. In our model, the probabilities of the states were rounded to two decimal places. $b_t$ was then used as a prior for next update when $a_{t+1}$ and $o_{t+1}$ is receiving (Equation (5)).

$$b_{t+1}(s_i) = \frac{b_t(s_i) \times p(o_{t+1} \mid s_i,a_{t+1})}{\sum_{s_i\in S} p(o_{t+1} \mid s_i,a_{t+1}) b_t(s_i)} \quad (5)$$

### Learning

The control knowledge is represented as a mapping between the beliefs and actions, which is learned with Q-learning [47]. Further details of the algorithm can be found in any standard Machine Learning text (e.g.[47, 41]). Here, a summarized procedure for the computer simulation is provided in box Algorithm 1.

Before learning, an empty Q-table was assumed in which the values (i.e., Q-values) of all belief-action pairs were zero. The model therefore started with no control knowledge and action selection was entirely random. The model was then trained through simulated experience until performance plateaued (requiring about $5 * 10^6$ trials). The model explored the action space using an $\varepsilon$-greedy exploration based on the Q-table. This means that it exploited the greedy/best action with a probability $1 - \varepsilon$, and it explored all the actions randomly with probability $\varepsilon$. $\varepsilon$ was set to 0.05 in our model. Q-values of the encountered belief-action pairs were adjusted according to the reward and cost feedback, as shown in the equations in line 10 and line 13. Q(b,a) is the Q-value for one belief-action pair $(b,a)$; $r$ is the immediate reward/cost obtained while the action $a$ is taken (based on the reward function defined); $\alpha$ is called learning rate, which is set to 0.1; $\gamma$ is called discounted factor,

**Algorithm 1** Pseudocode for the simulation

```
Initialize Q(B,A) = 0;
for each simulating trial
    Initialize b to be uniform across all the states
    terminal=FAULT;
    while terminal= FAULT do
        choose a from b (using ε-greedy).
        Take action a, observe o, receive r.
        if a ≠ BLOCK and a ≠ ALLOW then
            Belief update b'
            Update Q(b,a):
Q(b,a) ← Q(b,a) + α[r + γmax_a'(Q(b',a') − Q(b,a))]
            b ← b'
        else
            Update Q(b,a):
            Q(b,a) ← Q(b,a) + α[r − Q(b,a))]
            terminal=TRUE
        end if
    end while
end for
```

which is set to 0.9. The idea is that, these Q-values are learned (or estimated) by simulated experience of the interaction tasks. The true Q-values are estimated by the sampled points encountered during the simulations. The optimal policy acquired through this training was then used to generate the predictions described below (last 1000 trials of the simulation)[1]

## EXPERIMENT: CREDIT CARD FRAUD DETECTION

### Subjects

Sixteen participants (age: $31.6 \pm 7.5$; 11 males ) from staff and students at University of Birmingham voluntarily participated in the experiment. No financial or other incentives were given. Participants were equally and randomly assigned to four experimental groups which are detailed below.

### Apparatus

A customized user interface was created in Matlab (The MathWorks). The participants were seated in front of a 22 inch screen instrumented with an eye tracker (X2-60, Tobii, Sweden) recording gaze data at 60 Hz. The eye tracker was operated through Matlab using the Tobii SDK and Matlab binding.

### Design

The participants were asked to take on the role of a credit card fraud analyst at a bank. The task was to decide whether a given transaction should be blocked (prevented from being authorized) or allowed. As shown in each panel of Figure 2, nine information sources were laid out in a $3 \times 3$ grid. An operation panel was presented on the right side of the interface, including Block/Allow decision buttons and a feedback window.

The nine cues, as shown in Table 1, were selected as relevant to the detection of credit card fraud based on the literature and discussions with domain experts from FICO, FeedZai and the UK Cards Association. Each cue was presented in binary terms based on rules for fraudulent and non-fraudulent behavior (as shown in Table 1); rules were provided to the

[1]The model was implemented in Matlab and can be downloaded on request from the first author (Email: xxx.xxx@gmail.com).

| Cue | Normal | Fraudulent | Validity |
|---|---|---|---|
| #1: Transaction Amount | $\leq 500$ | $> 510$ | 0.60 |
| #2: Transaction History | 3 small amounts in a row | N/A | 0.70 |
| #3: Card Present | YES | NO | 0.65 |
| #4: CVV Entered | YES | NO | 0.55 |
| #5: Card Issued Bank* | Hanford | NorthWest | 0.60 |
| #6: Purchase Made in* | Europe | USA | 0.85 |
| #7: Card Expiry Check | $\geq 5$ days | $\leq 4$ days | 0.55 |
| #8: Transaction Time | 6:00-20:00 | 20:00-6:00 | 0.60 |
| #9: Type of Goods* | Travel agent | Electrical goods | 0.55 |

**Table 1. Information used for the 9 cues. Starred cues (*) were counterbalanced across participants.**

participants. The cues had *validities* [0.85, 0.70, 0.65, 0.60, 0.60, 0.60, 0.55, 0.55 and 0.55], where validity was defined as the probability that the cue indicated fraud given that the ground truth of the transaction is fraudulent. Validities were arbitrarily assigned to the nine cues and reflected the observation that high quality cues are relatively rare in many tasks. The location of each cue on the interface was assigned randomly for each participant and stayed constant across all trials. Participants were asked to complete 100 correct trials as quickly as possible. As trials in which an error was made (e.g. blocking a non-fraudulent transaction) did not reduce the total number of correct trials required, errors resulted in time costs.

The experiment was a $3 \times 2 \times 2$ design. The independent factors were *validity*, *format* and *availability*. *Validity* had 9 levels (grouped into high, medium, and low levels of validity). *Format* had two levels: text vs. color. *Availability* had two levels: visible vs. covered. Format and availability give four user interfaces 2.

- Covered-Text (CT) condition (Figure 2a): The cue information was presented in covered text. In order to check each cue, the participants had to click on the associated button on each cue and wait for 1.5 seconds while a blank screen was shown.
- Covered-Color (CC) condition (Figure 2b): The cue information was presented by color (green for possibly normal, red for possibly fraudulent). As with CT, the information was covered until clicked.
- Visible-Text (VT) condition (Figure 2c): The cue information was presented in text. The information was visible immediately (no mouse-click was required).
- Visible-Color (VC) condition (Figure 2d): The cue information was presented in color and no mouse-click was required to reveal it.

### Procedure

Participation in the study started with reading and signing the information sheet and consent form, followed by reading the detailed written study instructions. After eye-tracker calibration, the participants then worked through the first transaction with the opportunity to ask any clarifying questions. After this, participants worked through transactions at their own pace.

The workflow for evaluating a transaction was as follows. On each trial, participants were told to use as much information as

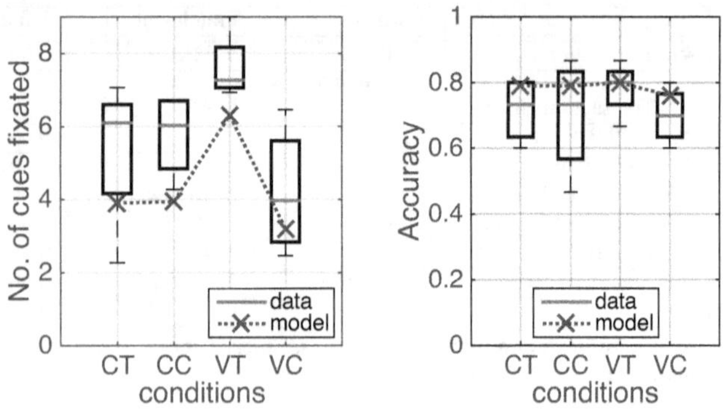


**Figure 3. The number of cues (left) and accuracy (right) predicted by the model across 4 experimental conditions (x-axis). Model predictions (blue crosses) are plotted with the participant's data (boxplots). The figure shows that the model predicts that an elevated number of cues will be used by participants in the Visible-Text condition.**

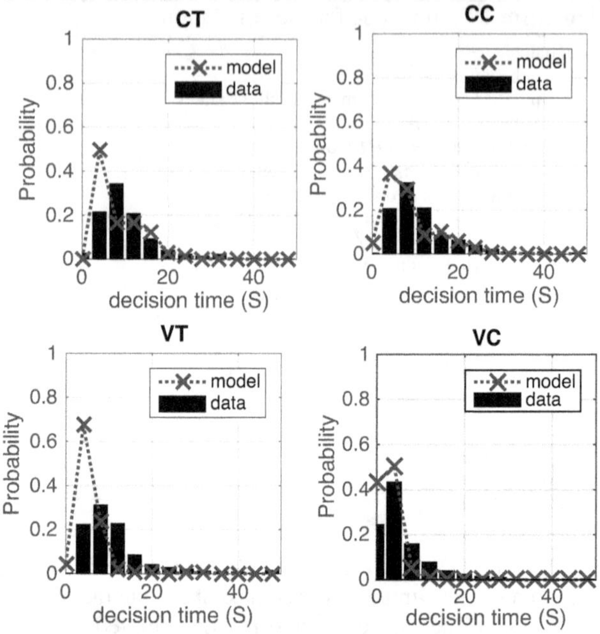


**Figure 4. The decision time distributions. The bin centers for the histograms are 0,4,8,12,...48. For human data, the decision time is the time between clicking the 'next transaction' button to clicking 'Allow/Block' decision button. For the model, the decision time includes the saccade time across panels (including information panels and operational panels) and the dwell duration on the panels as described in the 'Time Cost' section.**

they see fit (up to 9) by clicking the 'reveal' buttons or by fixating depending on the condition they were assigned to. They then indicated their decision in the right panel by clicking the 'Allow' or 'Block' button. Following this, participants clicked on the cues that they based their decision on (for later cross-validation not reported here) and then confirmed their decision by pressing a 'submit' button. Participants then received feedback regarding the correctness of the decision. The next trial was shown after clicking the button 'next transaction'. This button was placed in the top right corner of the display above the operational panel so as not to confound initial gaze data on the cues. At intervals of 15 minutes, participants were offered the opportunity to take a short break.

## RESULTS AND DISCUSSION

On average participants made $43.88 \pm 15.68$ errors on their way to completing 100 correct trials. In accordance with our theory, we were interested in participant performance once they were adapted to the task. For this reason we analyzed the last 15 trials completed by each participant. The analyzed trials included both correct and error trials. The model results reported below were generated by modeling each individual participant and aggregating.

### Information cues fixated and accuracy

As we stated above, the model's dwell times were calibrated to the empirical data for each cue. On average the calibrated dwell time was $0.66 \pm 0.10$ seconds across the cues.

Having calibrated the model, we were then able to predict how many cues should be fixated in each condition. This prediction and the human data are shown in Figure 3. The model correctly predicts that participants should fixate on more cues in the Visible-Text condition (VT: $6.21 \pm 1.32$) than in the other three conditions. It also correctly predicts that participants should fixate fewer cues in the Visible-Color condition (Visible-Color: $3.08 \pm 1.32$) and it learns to be relatively economical in the 'covered' conditions (Covered-Text: $3.95 \pm 1.97$; Covered-Color: $3.84 \pm 1.21$).

Intuitively, these findings can be explained in terms of adaptation to information cost and limits of peripheral vision. In the Visible-Text condition, information is cheap and foveated vision is required to read text, therefore more cues are used. In contrast, in the covered conditions (Covered-Text and Covered-Color) information access is expensive reducing the number of cues used. Lastly, in the Visible-Color condition, peripheral vision, rather than only foveated vision, can be used to access information and it appears that as a consequence fewer cues are used, at least by being directly fixated.

A visual comparison of the human data and model predictions (Figure 3) shows that the model accurately predicts the qualitative pattern of results, although the model predicts fewer cues on average (about 1.5 cues fewer).

While participants fixated on more cues in the Visible-Text condition, they did so without significant increase in accuracy (boxplots in the right panel of Figure 3). Participants achieved about 74% accuracy (CT:0.75, CC:0.70, VT:0.78, VC:0.75), which our analysis suggests is close to optimal given the cost of action, the validity of the cues and task of completing 100 tasks as quickly as possible. The model achieved about 79% accuracy across the four conditions (CT:$0.79 \pm 0.03$, CC:$0.79 \pm 0.01$, VT:$0.79 \pm 0.02$, VC:$0.76 \pm 0.05$). The model predicts the same level of accuracy achieved in all conditions (Figure 3).

The variance explained by the model's prediction of the number of cues fixated was $R^2 = 0.72$ with $RMSE = 1.64$. The variance explained by the accuracy prediction was $R^2 = 0.71$ with $RMSE = 0.05$.

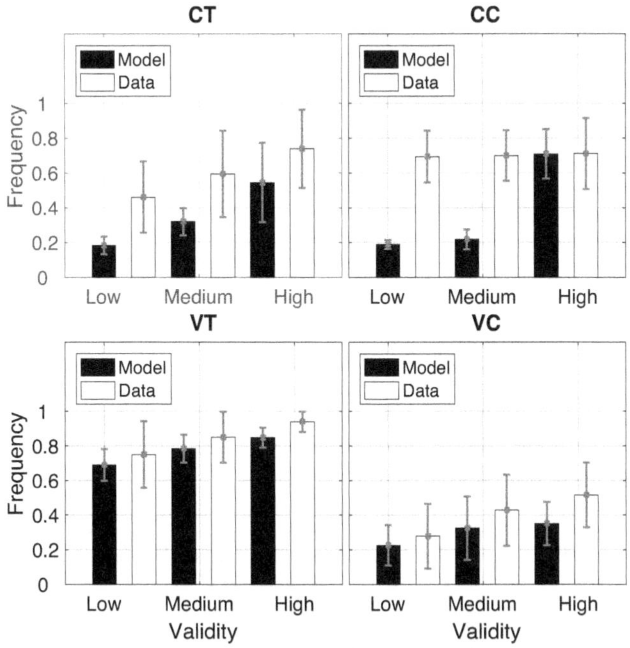


**Figure 5. The frequency that the model used cues split by condition and validity. For human data, 'Frequency' (y-axis) represents the frequency that each cue were used by participants in the last 15 trials.**

### Decision time distribution

It is well known that long-tail left-skewed distributions are a signature of human decision duration (e.g. a review in [10, 5]). Changes in difficulty of decisions produce changes in their spread but very little change in their shape [33, 34]. Figure 4 (black bars) shows that human decision time in our experiment is also long-tailed and left-skewed. The decision-time distributions for the model (Figure 4) show the same shape, although faster than the human data. The distributions are interesting because despite the fact that no skewed distributions are built into the model, they emerge as a consequence of adaptation to the constraints.

The variance explained by the model's decision time prediction for each of the four conditions was (CC) $R^2 = 0.73$, $RMSE = 0.06$; (CT) $R^2 = 0.53$, $RMSE = 0.09$; (VC) $R^2 = 0.87$, $RMSE = 0.07$; (VT) $R^2 = 0.41$, $RMSE = 0.14$. The low $R^2$ values for the text conditions, CT and VT, are a consequence of the overly fast model performance, which gives a more skewed distribution than for humans.

### Effects on frequency of cue fixation

A $2 \times 2 \times 3$ mixed effects ANOVA was used to test the effect of *format* (text vs. color), *availability* (visible vs. covered), and *validity* (low, medium, high) on the frequency of cues fixated. So as to conduct this analysis we first grouped the 9 levels of validity into 3 levels. These were: high validity ([0.85,0.7,0.65], medium validity [0.6, 0.6, 0.6], and low validity [0.55,0.55,0.55]. This grouping reflects the planned structure of the materials but was also necessary to ensure sufficient data in each cell for the analysis (an analysis across all 9 levels proved inconclusive due to high variance). There was

| Availability/Format/Validity | Mean ± Std (Data) | Mean ± Std (Model) |
|---|---|---|
| covered/text/low | 0.46 ± 0.22 | 0.18 ± 0.03 |
| covered/text/medium | 0.59 ± 0.31 | 0.32 ± 0.04 |
| covered/text/high | 0.74 ± 0.24 | 0.54 ± 0.04 |
| covered/color/low | 0.69± 0.10 | 0.19 ± 0.01 |
| covered/color/ medium | 0.70± 0.04 | 0.22 ± 0.06 |
| covered/color/high | 0.71± 0.26 | 0.71 ± 0.02 |
| visible/text/low | 0.75 ± 0.19 | 0.70 ± 0.12 |
| visible/text/ medium | 0.85 ± 0.16 | 0.78 ± 0.10 |
| visible/text/high | 0.94 ± 0.05 | 0.85 ± 0.05 |
| visible/color/low | 0.28 ± 0.24 | 0.23 ± 0.11 |
| visible/color/medium | 0.43 ± 0.24 | 0.33 ± 0.12 |
| visible/color/high | 0.52 ± 0.07 | 0.35 ± 0.06 |

**Table 2. Cue fixation frequency in each condition for both Data and Model (also see Figure 5)**

a significant main effect of validity F(2,24)=4.91, p=0.016, $\eta^2 = 0.29$. There was a significant main effect of format F(1,12)=5.32, p=0.04, $\eta^2$=0.31. There was no main effect of availability F(1,12)=0.10, p=0.76, $\eta^2 = 0.008$. There was an interaction between format and availability F(1,12)=13.94, p=0.003, $\eta^2 = 0.54$. There were no other significant interactions.

We also compared the human cue use frequencies to those of the model (Figure 5 and Table 2). The model was not fitted to these data but, rather, provided zero-free parameter predictions given the earlier calibration to dwell times. It is clear from the figure that although the model consistently uses fewer cues than the participants, it does capture the trend for higher frequency use of high validity cues. For the model, this was true irrespective of condition, whereas for the humans it was only true in conditions CT, VT and VC. With the covered-color (CC) interface, participants exhibited a high use of cues irrespective of validity, suggesting, perhaps, that this condition was hardest to learn.

In addition, to capturing the effect of validity, it can also be seen that the model partially captures the effect of format as text cues were fixated more frequently than color cues in both participants and model; VT (highest frequency), CT (next highest) and VC (lowest frequency).

### Implications for decision strategies

The analysis above suggests that participants were strategically adapting their use of cues both to the validity of the cues and simultaneously to the structure of the interface and visualisation. Participants chose to use more high validity cues and chose to fixate on more textual cues than color cues, possibly because the color cues could be perceived with peripheral vision. The use of peripheral cues is most evident in that the lowest frequency of fixation on cues was in the Visible Colour condition.

The analysis also provides evidence about the use of decision heuristics such as Take-the Best (TTB) and Weighted Additive (WADD). TTB would be indicated by the participants selecting just the very best cue (which in our interface always discriminates) and then making a Block/Allow decision. However, it can be seen Figure 5 that participants did not only use the highest validity cue. Further, WADD would be indicated by the participants using all of the available cues. However, it is clear that this is not happening, with participants preferring to use only a subset of the best cues. While there is plenty of evidence in other tasks that people use TTB, they do not seem to do so in our task, and may not do so exclusively.

## DISCUSSION

We have reported a new theory of how people use interaction to make decisions in which strategies for information gathering and choice are an emergent consequence of the capacity to make partial observations of a display. This theory can be written precisely by formulating the decision problem as a POMDP for interaction and solving this problem with machine learning to find an optimal decision strategy. Further, we applied the model to different types of information visualization and showed that when color-map visualizations were made available, more use should be made of peripheral vision to gather information. This result is a consequence of the fact that strategies for information gathering can take advantage of the different human acuity functions associated with color and with text; whereas color information can be obtained from the periphery, text must be foveated to be understood.

In addition, the model predicts that people will not make exclusive use of TTB (or WADD). These strategies have been extensively studied in the human decision making literature, but more recent work has suggested that people exhibit a more flexible range of strategies. Instead of assuming TTB or WADD, our model derived the optimal strategy given a POMDP problem formulation; this optimal strategy involved using a weighted integration of the best cues. These cues provide information that optimizes the trade-off between time and accuracy imposed in the experiment. This result is consistent with work that emphasises the adaptation of strategies to a cognitive architecture in interaction with a local task [17, 19, 31]. Further work is required to determine whether TTB emerges as a consequence of different task scenarios.

Also, while not explored in the empirical analysis above, the model makes predictions that are consistent with previously reported strategies. One of the most well-known strategies is called *center-of-gravity* (also called *averaging saccades* or *the global effect*) [12, 46, 44, 45], which refers to the fact that people frequently land saccades on a region of low-interest that is surrounded by multiple regions of high-interest. Figure 6 shows that this 'center-of-gravity' effect is an emergent effect of our model.

The fact that the model is able to predict the *strategies* that people use is a departure from models that are programmed with strategies so as to fit performance time. This is important because it suggests that the theory might be easily developed in the future so as to rapidly evaluate the usability of a broader range of visualizations for a more extensive range of decision tasks. For example, in the near future we wish to consider multidimensional visualizations that not only make use of color, but also size, shape, grouping etc. It should be possible to increment the observation functions, for example with a shape detection capacity, and then use the learning algorithm to find new strategies for the new visualizations.

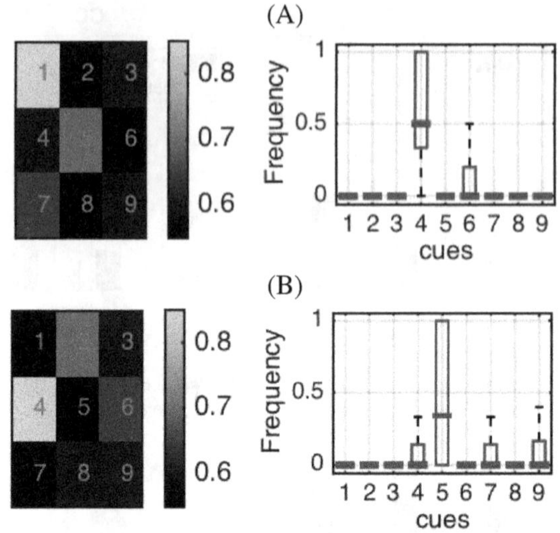


**Figure 6. In each row of the figure, the frequency of the model's cue fixations (right panel) is shown for a different spatial arrangement of cue validities (left panel). The validity of ROIs in the left panels is represented as a heat map (high validity is a lighter color). The frequency of model fixations is represented as a box plot. The column numbers in the box plot correspond to the numbers of the ROIs (1..9). In the top row, ROI number 4 has a low validity but is surrounded by relatively high validity ROIs (1,5 and 7). In contrast, in the bottom row, ROI number 5 has a low validity and surrounding ROIs 2, 4 and 6 have high validity. In both rows, the model fixates frequently on the ROI that is surrounded by high validity ROIs. This is known as a centre-of-gravity effect.**

Lastly, while we have chosen not to state design implications of our work, we anticipate that there will in the long-term, be design implications. We anticipate that these will derive from future work that is informed by the deeper understanding of interactive decision making that we have provided. This belief is founded on the abundant evidence of the value of theoretical work that can be found in the HCI literature. In fact, some of the field's most influential work has also been some of its most theoretical; see the work of Pirolli and Card on information foraging or the work of Russell et al. (1993) on sensemaking [37]. More generally, we note the potential harm that a focus on design implications may have if it leads to the exclusion of theoretical work [11]. We argue that staying at the cutting edge of interaction theory will help provide a means to improve the efficiency of more applied work by explaining the underlying processes involved in interaction. It is possible that researchers and practitioners who understand the causal structure of interaction are more likely to generate genuinely novel design interventions.

In conclusion, we have reported the first model of how people make decisions through interaction in which strategies for information gathering and decision are derived given a specification of a Partially Observable Markov Decision Process with human-like perceptual observation functions. The model makes predictions that are validated by human data.

## ACKNOWLEDGMENTS

This research was supported by the EU-funded SPEEDD project (FP7-ICT 619435).

## REFERENCES


1. Chris Baber, Simon Attfield, Gareth Conway, Chris Rooney, and Neesha Kodagoda. 2016. Collaborative sense-making during simulated Intelligence Analysis exercises. *International Journal of Human-Computer Studies* 86 (2016), 94–108.
2. Robert W Baloh, Andrew W Sills, Warren E Kumley, and Vicente Honrubia. 1975. Quantitative measurement of saccade amplitude, duration, and velocity. *Neurology* 25, 11 (1975), 1065.
3. Arndt Bröder and Wolfgang Gaissmaier. 2011. *Heuristics: The foundations of adaptive behavior*. Oxford University Press.
4. Arndt Bröder and Stefanie Schiffer. 2006. Adaptive flexibility and maladaptive routines in selecting fast and frugal decision strategies. *Journal of Experimental Psychology: Learning, Memory, and Cognition* 32, 4 (2006), 904.
5. Jerome R Busemeyer and James T Townsend. 1993. Decision field theory: a dynamic-cognitive approach to decision making in an uncertain environment. *Psychological review* 100, 3 (1993), 432.
6. Nicholas J. Butko and Javier R. Movellan. 2008. I-POMDP: An infomax model of eye movement. In *2008 IEEE 7th International Conference on Development and Learning, ICDL*. 139–144.
7. Xiuli Chen, Gilles Bailly, Duncan P. Brumby, Antti Oulasvirta, and Andrew Howes. 2015. The Emergence of Interactive Behavior: A Model of Rational Menu Search. *Proceedings of the ACM CHI'15 Conference on Human Factors in Computing Systems* 1 (2015), 4217–4226.
8. Andrea Dal Pozzolo, Olivier Caelen, Yann-Aël Le Borgne, Serge Waterschoot, and Gianluca Bontempi. 2014. Learned lessons in credit card fraud detection from a practitioner perspective. *Expert systems with applications* 41, 10 (2014), 4915–4928.
9. Thomas H. Davenport. 2013. How P&G Presents Data to Decision-Makers. *Harvard Business Review* (2013).
10. Fermin del Prado Martin. 2008. A theory of reaction time distributions. (dec 2008).
11. Paul Dourish. 2006. Implications for design. *SIGCHI Conference on Human Factors in Computing Systems (CHI'06)* (2006), 541–550. DOI: http://dx.doi.org/10.1145/1124772.1124855
12. John M. Findlay. 1982. Global visual processing for saccadic eye movements. *Vision Research* 22, 8 (1982), 1033–1045.
13. Wilson S Geisler. 2011. Contributions of ideal observer theory to vision research. *Vision research* 51, 7 (2011), 771–781.
14. Gerd Gigerenzer and Wolfgang Gaissmaier. 2011. Heuristic decision making. *Annual review of psychology* 62 (2011), 451–482.
15. Gerd Gigerenzer and Daniel G Goldstein. 1996. Reasoning the fast and frugal way: models of bounded rationality. *Psychological review* 103, 4 (1996), 650.
16. Gerd Gigerenzer and Peter M Todd. 1999. *Fast and frugal heuristics: The adaptive toolbox*. Oxford University Press.
17. Wayne D Gray, Chris R Sims, Wai-Tat W-T Fu, and Michael J Schoelles. 2006. The soft constraints hypothesis: a rational analysis approach to resource allocation for interactive behavior. *Psych Review* 113, 3 (2006), 461.
18. Mary Hayhoe and Dana Ballard. 2014. Modeling Task Control of Eye Movements. *Current Biology* 24, 13 (2014), R622—-R628.
19. Andrew Howes, Geoffrey B Duggan, Kiran Kalidindi, Yuan-Chi Tseng, and Richard L Lewis. 2015. Predicting Short-Term Remembering as Boundedly Optimal Strategy Choice. *Cognitive Science* 40, 5 (2015), 1192–1223.
20. Andrew Howes, Richard L. Lewis, and Alonso Vera. 2009. Rational adaptation under task and processing constraints: implications for testing theories of cognition and action. *Psychological review* 116, 4 (2009), 717–751. DOI: http://dx.doi.org/10.1037/a0017187
21. Sanjeev Jha and J Christopher Westland. 2013. A Descriptive Study of Credit Card Fraud Pattern. *Global Business Review* 14, 3 (2013), 373–384.
22. L Kaelbling, Michael L. Littman, and Ar Cassandra. 1998. Planning and Acting in Partially Observable Stochastic Domains. *Artificial Intelligence* 101, 1-2 (1998), 99–134.
23. David E. Kieras and Anthony J. Hornof. 2014. Towards accurate and practical predictive models of active-vision-based visual search. In *Proceedings of the SIGCHI Conference on Human Factors in Computing Systems*. ACM, 3875–3884.
24. Michael D Lee and S A Zhang. 2012. Evaluating the coherence of Take-the-best in structured environments. *Judgment and Decision Making* 7, 4 (2012).
25. Richard L. Lewis, Andrew Howes, and Satinder Singh. 2014. Computational rationality: linking mechanism and behavior through bounded utility maximization. *Topics in Cognitive Science* 6, 2 (2014), 279–311.
26. Volodymyr Mnih, Koray Kavukcuoglu, David Silver, Alex Graves, Ioannis Antonoglou, Daan Wierstra, and Martin Riedmiller. 2013. Playing atari with deep reinforcement learning. *arXiv preprint arXiv:1312.5602* (2013).
27. Ben R Newell and David R Shanks. 2003. Take the best or look at the rest? Factors influencing" one-reason" decision making. *Journal of Experimental Psychology: Learning, Memory, and Cognition* 29, 1 (2003), 53.

28. Ben R Newell, Nicola J Weston, and David R Shanks. 2003. Empirical tests of a fast-and-frugal heuristic: Not everyone "takes-the-best". *Organizational Behavior and Human Decision Processes* 91, 1 (2003), 82–96.
29. Jose Nunez-Varela and Jeremy L. Wyatt. 2013. Models of gaze control for manipulation tasks. *ACM Transactions on Applied Perception (TAP)* 10, 4 (2013), 20.
30. Manoj Pandey. 2010. Operational risk forum: A model for managing online fraud risk using transaction validation. *Journal of Operational Risk* 1 (2010), 49.
31. Stephen J. Payne and Andrew Howes. 2013. Adaptive interaction: A utility maximization approach to understanding human interaction with technology. *Synthesis Lectures on Human-Centered Informatics* 6, 1 (2013), 1–111.
32. Rajesh P N Rao. 2010. Decision making under uncertainty: a neural model based on partially observable markov decision processes. *Frontiers in computational neuroscience* 4, November (2010), 146.
33. Roger Ratcliff. 2002. A diffusion model account of response time and accuracy in a brightness discrimination task: fitting real data and failing to fit fake but plausible data. *Psychonomic bulletin {&} review* 9, 2 (jun 2002), 278–291.
34. Roger Ratcliff and Philip L Smith. 2010. Perceptual discrimination in static and dynamic noise: the temporal relation between perceptual encoding and decision making. *Journal of experimental psychology. General* 139, 1 (feb 2010), 70–94.
35. Jörg Rieskamp and Ulrich Hoffrage. 2008. Inferences under time pressure: How opportunity costs affect strategy selection. *Acta psychologica* 127, 2 (2008), 258–276.
36. Jörg Rieskamp and Philipp E Otto. 2006. SSL: a theory of how people learn to select strategies. *Journal of Experimental Psychology: General* 135, 2 (2006), 207.
37. Daniel M Russell, Mark J Stefik, Peter Pirolli, and Stuart K Card. 1993. The cost structure of sensemaking. In *Proceedings of the INTERACT'93 and CHI'93 conference on Human factors in computing systems*. ACM, 269–276.
38. Daniel Sánchez, M A Vila, L Cerda, and José-Mar\'\ia Serrano. 2009. Association rules applied to credit card fraud detection. *Expert Systems with Applications* 36, 2 (2009), 3630–3640.
39. Guy Shani, Joelle Pineau, and Robert Kaplow. 2013. A survey of point-based POMDP solvers. *Autonomous Agents and Multi-Agent Systems* 27, 1 (2013), 1–51.
40. Nathan Sprague, Dana Ballard, and Al Robinson. 2007. Modeling embodied visual behaviors. *ACM Transactions on Applied Perception (TAP)* 4, 2 (2007), 11.
41. R.S. Sutton and A.G. Barto. 1998. Reinforcement Learning: An Introduction. *IEEE Transactions on Neural Networks* 9, 5 (1998), 1054–1054.
42. Julia Trommershäuser, Paul W Glimcher, and Karl R Gegenfurtner. 2009. Visual processing, learning and feedback in the primate eye movement system. *Trends in Neurosciences* 32, 11 (2009), 583–590.
43. Yuan-Chi Tseng and Andrew Howes. 2015. The adaptation of visual search to utility, ecology and design. *International Journal of Human-Computer Studies* 80 (2015), 45–55.
44. S Van der Stigchel and T C Nijboer. 2011. The global effect: what determines where the eyes land? *Journal of Eye Movement Research* 4, 2 (2011), 1–13.
45. Dustin Venini, Roger W. Remington, Gernot Horstmann, and Stefanie I. Becker. 2014. Centre-of-gravity fixations in visual search: When looking at nothing helps to find something. *Journal of Ophthalmology* 2014, June (2014).
46. Françoise Vitu. 2008. About the global effect and the critical role of retinal eccentricity: Implications for eye movements in reading. *Journal of Eye Movement Research* 2, 3 (2008), 1–18.
47. C Watkins and Peter Dayan. 1992. Q-Learning. *Machine Learning* 8 (1992), 279–292.

# Building with Data: Architectural Models as Inspiration for Data Physicalization

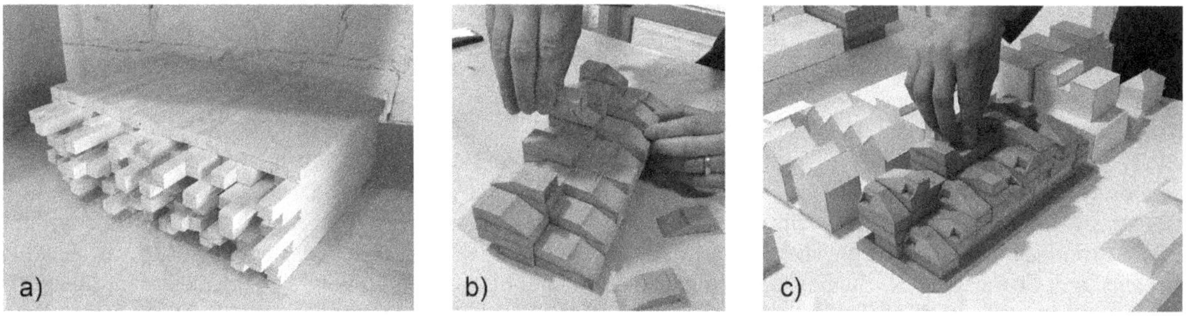

**Figure 1. a) Concept Model. b) Working Model. c) Working Model in Context Model. All Images: MoDA Architecture.**


**Carmen Hull**
University of Calgary
Calgary, Canada
carmen.hull@ucalgary.ca

**Wesley Willett**
University of Calgary
Calgary, Canada
wj@wjwillett.net



## ABSTRACT

In this paper we analyze the role of physical scale models in the architectural design process and apply insights from architecture for the creation and use of data physicalizations. Based on a survey of the architecture literature on model making and ten interviews with practicing architects, we describe the role of physical models as a tool for exploration and communication. From these observations, we identify trends in the use of physical models in architecture, which have the potential to inform the design of data physicalizations. We identify four functions of architectural modeling that can be directly adapted for use in the process of building rich data models. Finally, we discuss how the visualization community can apply observations from architecture to the design of new data physicalizations.



### Author Keywords

Data Visualization; Data Physicalization; Architectural Models; Embodied Interaction; Design Process

### ACM Classification Keywords

H.5.m. Information interfaces and presentation





*CHI 2017, May 06 - 11, 2017, Denver, CO, USA*





ACM 978-1-4503-4655-9/17/05…$15.00
DOI: http://dx.doi.org/10.1145/3025453.3025850


## INTRODUCTION

The tradition of building scale models has a long and well-established place in architectural practice. Models have immense popular appeal – they invite tactile exploration, facilitate collaboration, and evoke a sense of "delight in the miniature" [24]. Perhaps most importantly, physical models immediately reveal the relationships between multiple dimensions of a structure, relationships that are often not obvious in blueprints or static views. For architects, models are a unique and powerful tool which "sustains a communicable precision without narrowing the delightful cultivation of the imagination" [1].

Data physicalization, by contrast, is a relatively new field of research that has emerged within the data visualization community to find modalities beyond screen-based interactions for viewing and exploring complex data sets [17]. Jansen et al. emphasize that to create effective data physicalizations, we must better understand how they operate in practice [19]. This includes understanding which physical representations work best to engage audiences, how to encode variables in physical form, how to support interactivity, and what types of workflows can best support data physicalization.

Architecture is a rich place to look for inspiration and answers to these questions. Like data physicalization, the field of architecture is facing challenges in addressing the shortcomings of digital modeling and is rediscovering the power of physical models. Computer models lack depth, texture and a sense of materiality, despite the most advanced digital modeling and rendering software [31]. By examining methods used for centuries by architects, and how they have been adapted for contemporary digital practice, we suggest useful observations that can be directly applied to the field of data physicalization.

To explore these questions, we reviewed the architectural literature on physical models, conducted one-on-one interviews with ten architects, and examined the use of scale models in the design process. Based on our observations, we discuss the benefits that physical models provide and identify distinct types of models used for both generating and presenting ideas. In this paper we (1) characterize the process and history of model-making in architecture, (2) identify aspects of the model-making process that are relevant to data physicalization, and (3) suggest four implications for design: Exploring Spatial Relationships and Characteristics, Supporting Comparison and History, Providing Context, and Evoking Emotion.

## RELATED WORK

We begin by characterizing the use of models in architecture and its evolution over time, and consider its relationship to recent work on data physicalization.

### The History of Physical Models in Architecture

Historically, architectural models have always functioned as objects of critical engagement [27]. The earliest evidence of models is from Egyptian times when they were often buried with the owner of the building as a symbol of wealth or status [31]. The first word used to describe models, *paradeigma*, indicates the representation of patterns or information about an architectural idea rather than a scaled replica of a building [5]. Leon Battista Alberti was the first to document the benefits of physical models for architects in the 13th century – highlighting their value not only for presentation to clients but also as a conceptual device for the architect during the design process. Alberti appreciated how architects could constantly rework and modify physical models as well as iteratively share models in collaboration with builders and craftsman, eliciting their recommendations to produce better designs [21].

The invention of perspective during the Renaissance started the primacy of the image over the model and by extension, a lack of esteem for getting one's hands dirty [28]. The model became a tool representative of the lowly world of the craftsman. This professional elitism continued through the Baroque period with the discovery of descriptive geometry and other advancements in drawing techniques, until the geometric experiments of architect Antonio Gaudi in 1882. Gaudi considered ruled surfaces, specifically the hyperbolic paraboloids, to be symbols of divine perfection, but they could not be defined on paper. His hanging wire and plaster forms became the first instance of a self-generating formal system as adjustments of wires and weights could produce a diverse set of similar forms [31]. A short time later, in the first half of the twentieth century, architects such as Frank Lloyd Wright and Walter Gropius reinvigorated the model in practice. Wright credited his early experiences playing with *Froebel's gifts* (physical constructive teaching tools designed by German pedagogue Friedrich Fröbel) for his understanding of formal representation. Meanwhile, Gropius argued that the native intelligence of the hand, with the help of tools and machinery, was essential to design because "conception and visualization are always simultaneous" [27]. Gropius also saw that the abstract representations of plans and sections separated the object from reality, and required specialized training to be understood, whereas models offered an unmediated connection to the schema.

Building on the work of the Bauhaus, Mies Van der Rohe pioneered the notion that the model could serve functional roles outside of the design and construction process. His utopian glass skyscraper model suggested that a model could exist as both political statement and object of desire [27], bringing the model into the realm of a distinct art object. This notion culminated in New York in 1970 with the first exhibition devoted solely to the architectural model. In the same era, the founder of the MIT Media Lab, Nicholas Negroponte, emphasized tactile methods of exploration using models, even as digital design and computation were becoming more common within the architectural pedagogy [25]. In many offices, analog models were phased out of everyday practice in the 1980's as CAD (computer aided design) models became much cheaper and easier to produce and modify. With the introduction of BIM (building information modeling) and parametric modeling, the idea of data as a fundamental driver of the design process influenced a radically different breed of architect.

Despite these advancements, the increase of 'unbuildable' models created by parametric modeling software [31], combined with an abundance of overly 'photoshopped' renderings, has renewed appreciation of the tangible and tactile appeal of physical models [7]. Similarly, the advent of digital fabrication has made model making easier and faster [31]. There has been very little research, however, on the functions of modeling itself as an action. Albena Yaneva has studied the strategy of architects to 'scale' themselves into the various models during the design process with a case study of analog models in the design workflow of Dutch architect OMA [43]. The majority of the current discourse on models in architecture focuses on new fabrication technologies [31] or theoretical critiques of scaling and modeling [9]. However, we are not aware of any prior research that has applied these ideas to domains outside of architecture.

### Data Physicalization

Like architecture, data physicalization [19] often involves the creation and use of three-dimensional physical models. Whereas architectural models typically reflect real or imagined geometries that could be manifest in the physical world, physicalizations instead give physical form to abstract data with no direct physical analog. Despite these differences, the two share a variety of common concerns, and devote considerable attention to the physical properties, interactions, and encodings of the resulting models.

While research on the benefits of data physicalization is still sparse, initial studies [2, 17, 31] have shown that physicalizations can provide some advantages over their screen-based counterparts. For example, Jansen et al. have shown that physical 3D bar charts outperform screen-based equivalents for information extraction tasks. Specifically, they identified the importance of physical touch, as well as the visual realism of the physical objects as possible advantages [17]. Other recent research has demonstrated how physicalizations can serve as useful and accessible teaching tools [15] as well as a focus point for data-driven community dialogues.

Although many historical examples of data physicalization exist in other disciplines, researchers have only recently begun to catalog and describe them systematically using terminology from the visualization literature [6]. Vande Moere and his collaborators have categorized and discussed a wide range of emergent and artistic examples – categorizing the different degrees of physicality they exhibit the embodiment model [45] and the degree to which they are classified as symbolic, iconic and indexical [22]. Similarly, White and Feiner [40], Willett et al. [41], and Offenhuber and Telhan [26] have explored the range of ways in which physicalizations are connected to and reflective of the physical world around them. Hogan and Hornecker [13], meanwhile, identify a variety of historical and emergent examples of physicalizations in disciplines including engineering, ergonomics, and virtual reality.

Notably absent from recent discussions of data physicalization is a detailed consideration of the use of physical representations and models in architecture, despite the long and rich history of physical model making in architectural practice. However, architecture and HCI overlap in a number of different ways as information technology becomes more embedded within our existing physical, social and cultural networks. In fact, the design challenge for both fields is 'fundamentally a matter of embodiment' [20].

Some recent work on interactive physical displays for dynamic 3D visualizations – including systems like InForm [8] and EMERGE [34] – draws on a historical lineage that includes a discussion of architecture. However, few tangible computing examples after the seminal MetaDesk [36] and Urp [37] systems created at MIT in the late 1990s and early 2000s have applied metaphors or tasks from architecture directly. We address this by suggesting that the challenges faced by designers of data physicalizations are similar to those faced by architects – who also encode meaning into form in a way that allows for others to 'read' the mapping without specialized knowledge.

Our goal is not to assert that the two fields are identical, or that one maps directly to the other. Rather, we propose that the use of malleable physical representations in architecture and data physicalization share important characteristics – particularly with respect to tactile exploration and problem solving. Our work seeks to identify opportunities where data physicalization may be able to borrow from and adapt interactions and techniques that have long-demonstrated utility in architecture.

| | gender | age | occupation | yrs in field | yrs using physical models | yrs using digital models | education | design level |
|---|---|---|---|---|---|---|---|---|
| P1 | m | 35-40 | RA | 12 | 16 | 16 | 8 | senior |
| P2 | f | 30-35 | IA | 6 | 10 | 10 | 7 | intermediate |
| P3 | f | 30-35 | IA | 4 | 4 | 7 | 8 | intermediate |
| P4 | f | 30-35 | RA | 4 | 6 | 5 | 8 | intermediate |
| P5 | f | 40-45 | RA | 20 | 10 | 15 | 8 | senior |
| P6 | m | 45-50 | RA | 20 | 6 | 15 | 8 | senior |
| P7 | m | 35-40 | RA | 10 | 10 | 10 | 8 | senior |
| P8 | m | 65-70 | RA | 40 | 40 | 20 | 8 | expert |
| P9 | m | 70+ | RA | 50 | 50 | 8 | 12 | expert |
| P10 | f | 50-55 | designer | 30 | 30 | 20 | 8 | expert |

IA = intern architect RA = registered architect

**Table 1. Interview demographics.**

## EXPLORING MODEL MAKING IN ARCHITECTURE

To better understand the roles and functions that physical models play in architectural practice, we interviewed ten architects from a variety of backgrounds. During these interviews we sought to examine the range of tasks that physical models support in architectural practice. We also attempted to identify specific physical, visual, tactile, and interactive characteristics of these models that make them well-suited to these tasks. Finally, we explored the social role of models and the ways in which they facilitate interactions and exchanges between architects, their collaborators, their clients, and the general public. Throughout, we aimed to identify methods and techniques that might transfer to the design of data physicalizations.

### Methodology

We recruited architects who either presently use or have previously used physical models as part of their design practice. We wanted to get a sense of how model making has changed with the introduction of digital fabrication technologies in the last twenty years and sought to survey architects who work with both digitally fabricated and hand-made models. We selected the individuals (five females, five males) based on their specific training and experience with model building. See Table 1 for demographic details.

We conducted each interview at the architect's workplace, giving us a chance to observe physical models from their current projects. Each interview lasted roughly one hour. The interviewees were all willing to volunteer their time without remuneration. We used a semi-structured interview format, beginning with the following questions:

*Q1. What types of models do you use, and how often do you use them?*

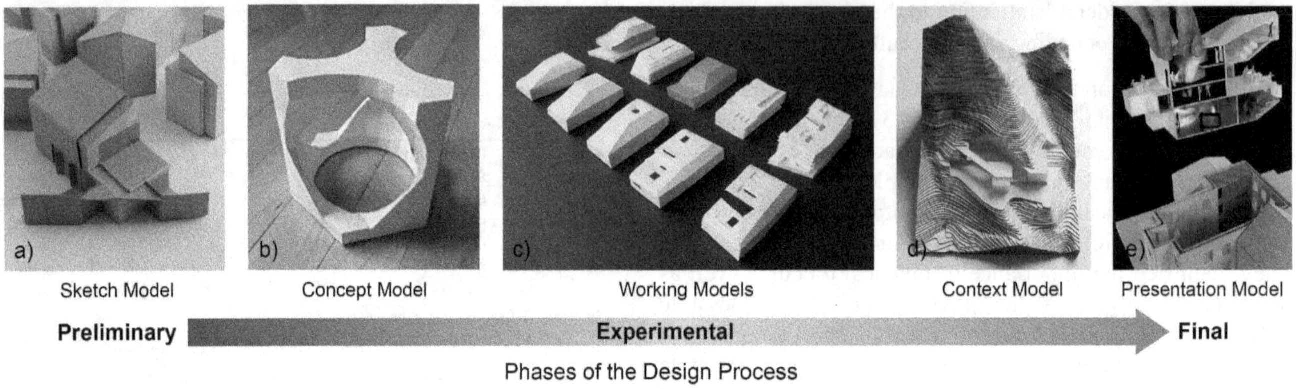


**Figure 2. Model types organized according to their position in the design process (left to right): a) Sketch model. Image: Walker Bush Architects. b) Concept model. Image: Noel Heard. c) Working Models. Image: Manifold Architecture Studio. d) Context Model. Image: Buro NY. e) Presentation Model. Image: Saša Randić + Idis Turato.**

*Q2. What specific functions or roles do physical models play during the design process?*

*Q3. What strategies do you use to evoke emotion in your models?*

*Q4. How do models function differently when used for yourself as a design tool versus as a collective tool for multiple designers or the general public?*

*Q5. How does the architect use scale in physical models? At which scales do architects create models and for what purposes?*

Building on these questions, we explored topics in model making based on each architect's individual preferences and experience. Wherever possible, we encouraged the architects to ground and illustrate their discussion using specific examples from their own current and past work. We collected audio recordings and handwritten notes from each interview for later analysis. When feasible, we also collected photos of physical models.

### Analysis

Because this study was explorative rather than evaluative, we used an iterative open-coding process. First, one researcher transcribed and segmented the interviews. Then, a pair of researchers worked together to cluster and identify emergent themes based on the physical characteristics, audience, and situations when particular models are used. All themes and functions identified in the paper resulted from this convergent process involving both researchers.

## ARCHITECTURAL MODELS

To frame these observations, we begin with a detailed description of the different types of models most commonly used by our interviewees, along with standard functions they support during the design process. We also examine the use of scale and physicality in architectural models.

### Types of Models

The architecture literature, as well as the architects we interviewed, describe numerous genres of models intended for different points in the design process and various audiences. Here, we focus on a subset of these model types that covers the entire design process from conception to presentation. While not an exhaustive list of all types of models used in architecture, this subset highlights the diversity of models used by architects as well as the functions they serve. We focused on just a few types of models where our interviews and examination suggested clear implications for the design of data physicalizations.

#### *Sketch Models*

At the beginning of a project, architects typically do not know yet what they are going to build. To help define and explore the space of high-level design options and ideas, they often use *sketch models* made with inexpensive materials like cardboard, foam blocks, or sheets of paper that can be easily modified by adding or subtracting elements. Architects use these models to quickly materialize an idea in a playful and experimental flow of ideas. For example, one architect (P7) noted using a 'basket of fun objects' or primitive shapes to quickly explore different compositions. The resulting models are intended for an internal design audience, and their rough, unfinished quality helps convey the uncertainty present at this initial stage of the design process.

One common sketching strategy involved starting with just a few known parameters or a "fuzzy approximation" of an idea. Physically elaborating on these initial ideas could then suggest possible directions for further development. As P2 put it, "*These models are very exploratory, messy. They are more 'live'*."

Our interviewees noted that quick modeling was easiest using materials that already have volume like foam or blocks. Foam can be cut or reshaped easily to adjust the form and can be modified for both amorphous and rectilinear shapes. Several also described paper as a useful medium, noting that it is inexpensive, readily available, and can be quickly folded and layered to produce a variety of different forms. Architects repeatedly cited construction speed and physicality as important characteristics when selecting sketching materials, and critiqued digital tools as lacking these traits.

> *"The feedback from a physical sketch model is quick, more of a visceral response, it's easier to understand the change in the real world than in the digital." -P2*

All of our respondents described sketch models as the primary type of model they use, and many appreciated the responsiveness and flexibility of sketch models during the earliest stages of the design process.

> *"I use the model mostly for myself, to test an idea out. With the model, it's easier to see the whole thing at once." -P3*

> *"[A model] just shows it doesn't work and you have the freedom to change." -P9*

Six of the interviewees emphasized that the manipulations they made in this stage were what provided the most insight and stressed that time spent with sketch models can be a valuable way of generating new ideas. As P10 confirmed, "*The time spent is really important, it gives you time to sit back, rethink your design and get a grip on [an idea].*"

P1 noted that the most valuable aspect within the process of working with multiple iterations of a model is that inevitable "mistakes and failures" will occur. However, "*in those mistakes or failings something really special can emerge that you didn't think of*" which isn't as discoverable in a digital model. Furthermore, P1 emphasized that "*there is something integral about the brain/tactile connection, and the way that we process information.*"

### Concept Models

A *concept model* distills the core idea of the project, focusing on its most fundamental formal and material relationships. P3 described her interpretation of the concept model as "*a physical manifestation of an artistic ideal.*" It represents "*the essential idea that is taken into material relationships, spatial relationships, across all scales.*" Similarly, P10 described the *concept model* as a "*driver for the design.*" P1 uses these kinds of models to express "*the visceral ideas. How you incorporate light, space, or the mixing of two systems.*" He also stressed that this step was an essential aspect of his work that allowed him to address critical ideas before thinking about a physical building.

Although differences in materiality exist across all types of models, concept models most clearly emphasize the use of materials and visual variables to evoke an emotional response. The architects we surveyed all noted the choice of materials as the primary strategy they used to influence viewers' response to the model.

> *"The materiality is the most important aspect of a model. Even an amazing plastic 3D printed model doesn't have the appeal of a rich wooden model." -P6*

Several architects even described choosing materials to represent specific feelings and bodily sensations.

> *"Materials have a grounded or heavy feel to them – a visual mass not related to actual weight necessarily, although most people understand this relationship. Concrete can be heavy or light, depending on the treatment. Glass is lightness and clarity." -P5*

All of the architects agreed on the implicit social conventions around certain materials and forms which elicit different emotions. For example, P7 acknowledged that "you wouldn't use a cold material like steel if you wanted people to feel a sense of warmth." Another architect (P2) highlighted the use of illumination which has the ability to "breathe life into the model."

### Working Models

As the design process continues, architects often use *working models* to refine and compare variations of the current design. These models can then be used as the focus for discussion with other members of the design team like engineers or investors. Each successive iteration resolves and refines the interplay of all design elements as the model becomes more precise and communicates finer details. P6 described how he would "*make a bunch of little variations and then pick the best two and keep working on those.*" Each time the architects make a decision or change, they instantiate the update via new model and consider the implications of this change on the design as a whole. Each successive model contains and fuses more data within the material and geometric properties, adding more complexity and detail.

Working models are typically constructed from malleable materials like foam or balsa, allowing architects to make changes by physically cutting or adding to the model. This malleability supports rapid exploration and iteration of a design. However, more dramatic changes may require the construction of entirely new models that can be compared directly to the previous versions. Generally, the level of detail included in working models increases over time as the architects' focus shifts from the overall structure to finer grained aspects of the design. Models will often increase in size as a result, allowing greater resolution and detail.

As work progresses, the collection of working models produced by the team serves as a visual record of the process. Each model exists as a snapshot of a particular moment, or as a record of a particular line of inquiry that can be referenced later. Architects often reported physically placing models within their studio or office to support comparison and recall. These design alternatives could be grouped or analyzed together or used to compare different examples of design modifications. Ultimately, collections of working models create a physical and visible record of past decisions and design options that support both individual reflection and coordination within a design team.

Architects also reported that working models played a social role, supporting collaboration within their studios and with outside stakeholders. P9, an architect with 50 years of experience, indicated that he showed working models to show his clients on almost every project. stating that:

> *"Most people, even geotechnical engineers, will understand the model only. The models are the common language. The people are part of it; they are all over it. They can move stuff around. They are with you instead of against you." -P9*

Several mid-career architects (P1 and P6) made similar points, noting that working models provided concrete checkpoints that were accessible to both to their clients and to their collaborators.

> *"It is easy to hide mistakes in a digital model when you are presenting to the client, and so the physical reality of the model is a sort of forcing function to resolve the design fully. The details get lost on the computer, but when it is all out in front of you it is easy to catch errors." -P6*

P5 also noted that she felt models played a major role in supporting a collaborative culture within her studio.

> *"Working on a computer is a solitary event and people don't interrupt. When I am working on a model, my colleagues will come up to me and talk about the project, which almost always results in a change for the better. There is a distance to virtual things which isn't really a good thing" -P5*

### *Context Models*

Architects also discussed creating *context models* to study the relationship between a design and the surrounding landscape or urban conditions. A deeper consideration of context will include an analysis of the external systems that a project taps into – be they social, cultural, environmental, economic, technological, etc. The context model describes the relationship of an object to its environment on all of these levels.

Several of the architects stressed the importance of using physical context models, rather than drawings or digital designs. In particular, they emphasized that physical models can make the shape and profile of the surrounding terrain clear, allowing viewers (and even the architects themselves) to accurately assess variations in slope and elevation.

> *"Even contour lines don't really show the terrain. You get a stronger reaction because of the materiality. Our brains still focus on form. Even in our office we see immediately if it works or not." -P9*

Architects also emphasized how context models can provide an overview of the totality of a site that is hard to achieve even from an in-person visit. In fact, context models can often provide a unique bird's eye view of the site, allowing architects to physically examine sight lines, symmetries, and spatial relationships that may be impossible to see from on the ground. Moreover, context models can visually encode information about the surrounding environment –such as the age of surrounding buildings or the presence of affordable housing – that is simply not available in-situ.

Context models can also serve as a platform for physical design explorations and experiments, in which architects interactively test possible designs by placing them at different locations on a site model (Figure 1c). P7 described a modeling exercise where his team used blocks representing different programmatic functions (for example, the administration, classrooms, and services for a school). They could test relationships between the context and the general locations of each activity before designing the building itself.

Finally, as one interviewee (P3) noted, context models can be necessary for international and remote projects, where the architects have limited and infrequent access to the actual site. In these situations, detailed models can serve as a stand-in for the actual site, providing architects with much of the contextual information they need in order to situate their designs.

### *Presentation Models*

In contrast to *working models*, which have lower fidelity and support iterative discussions throughout the design process, *presentation models* are intended to showcase the final design to an audience of primarily non-designers. As a result, the craftsmanship of these models is much more refined, using high quality materials and finishes. In contemporary studios, presentation models are often made with digital fabrication tools that can cut or shape precise geometry with clearly articulated details at all scales.

Because of their high cost and complexity, presentation models are almost exclusively a tool for public engagement. Surprisingly, we found that presentation models were the type of model least used by the architects we interviewed – as they found these detailed models costly and time-consuming to build, even with digital fabrication. Only one architect (P10) continues to make a final presentation model for her projects noting that, "*if the project is less than $1 million, it just doesn't make sense economically*." Despite this drawback, every architect we interviewed marveled at the power these models had to engage people – noting that they produced a sense of fascination that drawings could never achieve.

> *'The clients feel as though they have a part in the project when we show them a model that doesn't occur with drawings. It makes the project seem more real to them, and more connected to them, they immediately want to touch it. -P9*

## Scale

Generally, the size and complexity of models tend to increase as designs become more fully defined. However, architects still described creating models at a variety of different scales – even within the same phases of the design process. The appropriate scale for a model was often determined based on a number of factors, including the scope of the project, the available workspace to construct the model, and time and money available. The level of detailing also determined an appropriate scale since smaller models tend to focus on basic geometric forms, while larger models are more useful for exploring fine details. P5 mentioned that scale is also determined by the "*inherent characteristics*" of the modeling medium. For example, wood with a large grain is poorly-suited for small models, as it can "*distort the sense of scale.*"

Architects also noted a relationship between scale and formality. Small models tend to be considered more casual or abstract, whereas a larger model with finer detailing implies a more finished product. This aspect can be substantial when presenting ideas to clients or stakeholders.

> *"The client will see a more polished and refined model as a finished product, so we would never make the model more detailed than necessary in the beginning stages of the project to make it clear that this was a work in progress." -P5*

Reiterating this notion, P2 remarked that "*a higher level of detail makes things less abstract, less open to imagination.*" Similarly, P3 commented that "*larger models have more impact – it makes people really excited*" while P4 noted that, "*it's easier for the layman to understand a larger model because it's closer to their size.*"

### Physicality and Tangibility

All of the ten architects interviewed highly valued physical models because of their tangible characteristics, which they believed made them easier to understand than drawings or on-screen models. Most also praised physical models' accessibility for large groups in collaboration.

Several specifically noted that the three-dimensionality of physical models make them well-suited to illustrate the complexities of a project to non-designers.

> *"Models are only abstract to one degree (shrinking) whereas drawing was abstracting in two degrees (size and dimensionality)." -P4*

P7 explained that his clients also preferred 3D physical models because they removed technical barriers implicit in 2D drawings and on-screen renderings. Clients examining physical models do not need to understand the language of blueprints, or the interactions necessary to examine or manipulate a digital model.

> *"Models have a lot of the information stripped away that refines an idea to a salient point – simplification helps people to understand the kinds of spaces. You might simplify it down to surface areas and transparent areas, focusing on openings in the building. Textural qualities, very simple and refined down to the basic idea. A hierarchy of materials within a project." -P7*

Two intern architects, who both have artistic backgrounds as well as industry experience making models for clients, remarked on the ability of the model to engage the imagination of their clients. P4 noted that, "*It's the intermediate step between the abstract ideas of a building and the reality. They can still project their own ideas on how it's going to be.*"

In the same vein, P8, an architect with over 40 years of experience building models, notes that with digital models, "*there is almost invariably a disconnect. There is no interaction. With physical models, it's the tactility. It's real, and you shrink yourself to fit in the model.*"

The second most mentioned advantage of physical models was the ability to circumnavigate the model freely to view the project in its' entirety. P8 and P9 both highlighted models' accessibility to large groups:

> *"A model is accessible to everyone equally, unlike a monitor or paper drawings. In a physical model, you move around to see the angle you want to see, you're in control. Clients would often move back and forth around the model, leaning in for a closer look and then taking in the project as a whole." -P8*

> *"[Groups] jump on it. Even a walkthrough video did not have the same impact." -P9*

Some of the most engaging models are those made to be investigated by an audience, with movable parts that can be lifted off or moved to the side so as to see the interior spaces of a project. Several interviewees speculated that the viewers' enjoyment of the model may be linked to childhood and the pleasure of learning through play.

> *"There is some connection to childhood. You want to grab the little car and drive it." -P8*

Interviewees also speculated that the physicality of the models might improve their memorability.

> *"In every school in [region] there was a relief map of the province - 8 foot, huge, painted plaster. Once you touched that mountain you understood it and remembered it your entire life." -P8*

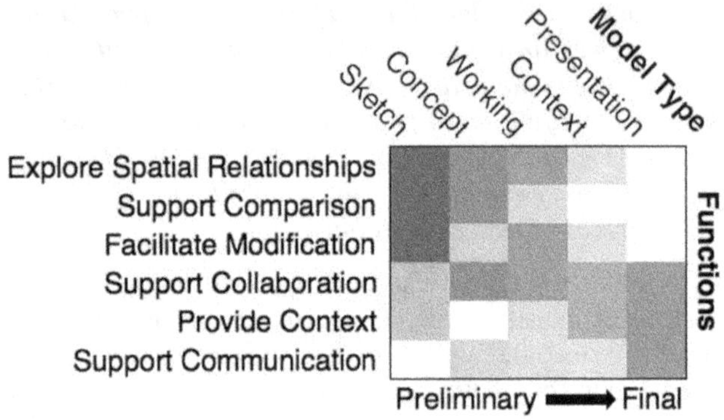


**Table 2.** Types of Models and Related Functions. The color scheme is the same as the one used in Figure 2.

This suggestion aligns with recent work by Stusak et al. [32] which indicates that physicality can improve the memorability of data representations.

## DISCUSSION

While architects use a number of distinct genres of physical models as part of their craft, each of these types can still serve multiple and sometimes overlapping functions (see Table 2). These common, low-level functions underscore the specific points during the process of conceptualizing and designing a structure where physical models are particularly valuable. Moreover, each of the shared functions highlights material properties, manipulation strategies, and use cases that we believe can prove useful for data physicalizations more generally.

Building on the models and applications discussed in the previous section, we outline a set of four specific functions of physical models that can serve as inspiration for the design and development of future physicalization systems.

### 1. Exploring Spatial Relationships and Characteristics

Early stage sketch and concept models provide architects with a physical means of testing, exploring, and iteratively modifying the physical characteristics of a design, often via manual construction and manipulation. Architects often use these kinds of models early in their design process because they provide a quick and adaptable way of creating and comparing design alternatives.

This need to rapidly create and assess possible design alternatives is analogous in many ways to the challenges faced by visualization designers and analysts early in the data analysis process, as they seek to understand and craft appropriate representations for new datasets. While both visualization experts and novices often use "data sketching" [38] as a way to make sense of data on paper or in 2D tools, few mechanisms exist for supporting this kind of rapid, iterative data exploration in the physical world.

Recent work on "constructive visualization" – in which authors manually assemble representations of data using discrete physical tokens or building blocks [15] – provides one potential model for facilitating this kind of exploration. Like many approaches to sketch modeling in architecture, constructive visualization can be playful, accessible, and supports dynamic refinement of representations. However, this line of research has tended to emphasize the pedagogical, rather than practical, benefits of construction – in part because the process of additively assembling physicalizations token-by-token can be an arduous affair.

Architectural sketch modeling, by contrast, often employs non-additive and non-discrete construction methods like subtractive construction using foam and other easily-manipulable materials. Purely manual subtractive techniques may be less valuable when creating data physicalizations, where the resulting physical representations generally need to reflect a precise encoding of the underlying data. However, computer-assisted tools for handheld subtractive fabrication like Zoran and Paradiso's FreeD [46] suggest that simple data-driven tools could easily enable these kinds of physical data sketching or "data excavation."

Similarly, early-stage model-making in architecture often leverages assembly techniques like bricolage in which models are created by piecing together existing objects and physical components. This practice, sometimes called "junk prototyping," is also common in product design and interaction design [10]. Bricolage is valuable because it provides a fast, accessible, and social mechanism for exploring new ideas, while building on the existing complexity and texture of the component objects (rather than simpler primitives like tokens). We believe that bricolage-style techniques may also have value for data physicalization, particularly in social settings where their tangibility and composability can help ground discussions. For example, a collection of simple physical time series could serve as composable building blocks for examining and comparing possible forecast models or concretely illustrating and discussing imaginary policy scenarios. In contrast to the simple tokens used in constructive visualization, these components might include more realistic variability, trends, and other data features (peaks, outliers, etc.) that could be readily assembled to create plausible time series and facilitate deeper conversations.

### 2. Supporting Comparison and History

Physical models serve as forms of external memory for architects throughout the design process, and their physical nature often permits rearrangement and reconfiguration to support various design tasks. For example, architects may place sets of working models alongside one another to support direct comparison between several design choices or possible building materials. In a studio setting, architects may also position or distribute models on shelves and tables, creating a physical record of the design process that can prompt continued awareness of past experiments and possible alternatives.

Work in information visualization has long recognized the importance of visual representations as forms of external memory [3]. To this end, both visualization and visual

**Figure 3.** SweatAtoms artifacts support the physical comparison of a series of different athletic activities. Image: R.A. Khot.

analytics research has explored the value of visual histories of the analysis process [12] and visually organizing analysis results to support efficient sense-making [42]. However, mechanisms for comparing on-screen visualizations and analysis histories are limited by the amount of screen real estate. Only a few tools support direct interactive comparisons between multiple representations [16] or attempt to recreate the sense of a large, persistent work environment that supports shared spatial memory and analysis history [14].

Data physicalizations, on the other hand, lend themselves readily to the kinds of direct, physical comparison and rearrangement we see with architectural models. Early research has demonstrated that small handheld physicalizations can be easier to compare and manipulate than their on-screen counterparts [18]. However, our experience with architectural models suggests that the ability to sort, order, and organize larger numbers of physicalizations across a workspace may bring additional benefits – improving awareness of previous exploration and making it easier to revisit and juxtapose analyses. Increased use of persistent data physicalizations as part of their everyday analysis practice could eventually allow knowledge workers to reclaim some of the spatial and tangible value often attributed to more traditional architecture and design studio spaces [30]. For example, Stusak et al. [33] discuss how collections of SweatAtoms– 3D printed physicalizations showing athletes' activity over individual workouts – can be arranged to create "memory landscapes" highlighting longer-term activity (Figure 3).

The idea of spatially distributing analytic views and markers of analysis history also has promising implications for the design of virtual- and augmented-reality analysis environments [4]. While not strictly physical, augmented reality visualizations created with modern headsets could easily be rendered at unique and reconfigurable locations relative to a viewer or their surroundings. Such systems could potentially capitalize on many of the benefits of physical models, without the cost or complexity of physical fabrication or mechanical actuation.

### 3. Providing Context

When designing a structure or environment architects always need to consider the interplay between structures and their surrounding environment. While it is valuable to visit a site and examine the physical landscape in person, the vast majority of the work exploring the relationship between the design and its surroundings happens in the studio. Context models that include not only the structure being designed but also its surroundings provide a valuable tool for contextualizing new designs. Physically modeling the surrounding environment at smaller scales allows architects to more readily examine and manipulate buildings, topography, and environmental conditions in ways that are difficult or impossible in the real world. Similarly, when creating models, architects can select and emphasize important elements of a scene like nearby buildings, vegetation, property boundaries, or rights-of-way, while de-emphasizing less important details.

A growing body of visualization work has also begun to recognize the value of context when presenting and interpreting data. However, this work has tended to emphasize the value of situating visualizations in real-world environments [40], embedding data representations in close proximity to relevant people, objects, and locations [41], or altering environments to make important phenomena visible in-place [26]. As a result, much of the work has focused on using augmented reality tools to render representations of data directly at relevant locations.

Our discussions with architects, however, suggest that embedding or situating data within small-scale physical facsimiles of real environments may also have considerable value for data analysis. For example, by providing context about the area, physical scale models of a large field site could help analysts more easily examine and make sense of relationships between samples or specimens collected there. In contrast to on-screen GIS tools, more detailed physical context models could allow analysts to use physical locomotion, tangibility, and direct manipulation to explore the data, while also providing rich information about the original environment.

Tangible computing systems like Urp [37] and Piper et al.'s Illuminating Clay [29] have demonstrated how dynamic physical models and projection can be combined to support planning and urban design tasks. Despite this, tools that would allow data analysts to quickly create and utilize context models as part of their own data analysis practice remain largely unexplored. Fortunately, recent advances in 3D scanning and digital fabrication [44] seem poised to streamline the process of creating models from existing objects and locations. Widespread interest in content capture for virtual reality headsets also promises to make it easier to create virtual context models for a variety of visualization applications.

**Figure 4.** Blip: A Year of Travel. Image: Cemre Güngör.

### 4. Evoking Emotion

Architects rely on a rich palette of materials when constructing models. This is particularly true for concept models and presentation models, which – like the buildings they envision – are often intended to evoke an emotional response. In practice, aesthetic, material, and construction choices can have a strong influence on how viewers perceive, react to, and choose to interact with models.

For example, Cemre Güngör's 'Blip' (Figure 4), uses transparent acrylic to represent the feeling of '*looking into one's past*' and to allow for viewing from all angles [11]. In this case, the designer used his choice of material properties expressly to influence the emotional response of the viewer in a way that suited his feelings about the data set.

While information visualization has long considered the perceptual implications of low-level visual encodings such as shape and color in data graphics [3], the perceptual characteristics of the materials used in data physicalizations remain unexplored. Moreover, very little work has sought to systematically characterize the emotional impact or visual appeal of different information graphics [23]. In practice, the question of aesthetics is often treated as a distraction by much of the visualization research community, where discussion of extreme aesthetics and visual embellishments [2] are often rebutted with appeals to Tuftean minimalism [35]. However, for data physicalizations – which must ultimately be constructed from real-world materials rather than pixels – these questions of aesthetics become more difficult to sidestep.

Many informal social conventions exist around the use of material and light (brushed metal implies seriousness, foam is "sketchy", LEGO is playful, etc.). However, little practical guidance exists for designers looking to create either perceptually affective or emotionally provocative data physicalizations. While initial perceptual studies of physical variables like size are ongoing [20] more work is needed to develop a nuanced understanding of the practical and aesthetic tradeoffs associated with different construction techniques. There are no de facto 'style guides' for architects to guide material choices, however, existing work on model-making and materiality in architecture [39] could provide a practical starting point for physicalization designers looking to understand the interplay between material form and emotional response.

## CONCLUSION & FUTURE WORK

Architectural models are a versatile visual and physical tool for exploring complex spatial relationships. By identifying the characteristics and functions of physical models in architecture, we highlight opportunities for new kinds of physical representations that support the analysis, exploration, and presentation of a much wider variety of data. Specifically, our work details four functions of physical models that can serve as inspiration for building physical data systems. We describe low-level functions that underscore the specific points during the process of conceptualizing and designing a structure where physical models are particularly valuable. Our initial discussion also highlights material properties, manipulation strategies, and use cases that each point to potentially valuable research areas for physicalization. As the field of data physicalization grows, we hope that the traditions of architectural model-making can provide inspiration for imaginative and precise representations of data that inform the mind as much as they engage the senses.

## ACKNOWLEDGEMENTS

We wish to thank our colleagues Charles Perin, Sowmya Somanath, Jennifer Payne, Lora Oehlberg and Aura Pon for their valuable feedback, as well as all of our interviewees who generously donated their time.

## REFERENCES

1. Emily Abruzzo and Eric Ellingsen (eds.). 2008. *Models*. Princeton Architectural Press.
2. Scott Bateman, Regan L Mandryk, Carl Gutwin, Aaron Genest, David Mcdine, and Christopher Brooks. 2010. Useful Junk? The Effects of Visual Embellishment on Comprehension and Memorability of Charts. *Human Factors*: 2573–2582. http://doi.org/10.1145/1753326.1753716
3. Stuart Card and Jock Mackinlay. 1997. The structure of the information visualization design space. *Information Visualization, 1997.*: 92–99. http://doi.org/10.1109/INFVIS.1997.636792
4. Tom Chandler, Maxime Cordeil, Tobias Czauderna, et al. 2015. Immersive Analytics. *2015 Big Data Visual Analytics (BDVA)*, IEEE, 1–8. http://doi.org/10.1109/BDVA.2015.7314296
5. John James. Coulton. 1977. *Ancient Greek Architects at Work : Problems of Structure and Design*. Cornell University Press.
6. Pierre Dragicevic and Yvonne Jansen. List of Physical Visualizations. Retrieved September 15, 2016 from http://dataphys.org/list/

7. Nick Dunn. 2010. *Architectural Modelmaking*. Laurence King.

8. Sean Follmer, Daniel Leithinger, Alex Olwal, Akimitsu Hogge, and Hiroshi Ishii. 2013. inFORM: dynamic physical affordances and constraints through shape and object actuation. *UIST '13 Proceedings*: 417–426. http://doi.org/10.1145/2501988.2502032

9. Marco Frascari, Jonathan Hale, and Bradley Starkey (eds.). 2007. *From Models to Drawings: Imagination and representation in architecture*. Routledge.

10. Nancy Frishberg. 2006. Prototyping with junk. *Interactions* 13, 1: 21–23. http://doi.org/http://dx.doi.org/10.1145/1109069.1109086

11. Cemre Gungor. Blip: A Year of Travel. *2011*. Retrieved September 12, 2016 from http://dataphys.org/list/blip-a-year-of-travel/

12. Jeffrey Heer, Jock D Mackinlay, Chris Stolte, and Maneesh Agrawala. 2008. Graphical Histories for Visualization : Supporting Analysis , Communication , and Evaluation. 14, 6: 1189–1196.

13. Trevor Hogan and Eva Hornecker. 2012. How Does Representation Modality Affect User-Experience of Data Artifacts? *Proceedings of Haptic and Audio Interaction Design* 7468: 141–151. http://doi.org/10.1007/978-3-642-32796-4_15

14. Seth Hunter, Pattie Maes, Stacey Scott, and Henry Kaufman. 2011. MemTable : An Integrated System for Capture and Recall of Shared Histories in Group Workspaces. *Social Work*: 3305–3314. http://doi.org/10.1145/1978942.1979432

15. Samuel Huron, Sheelagh Carpendale, Alice Thudt, Anthony Tang, and Michael Mauerer. 2014. Constructive visualization. *Proceedings of the 2014 conference on Designing interactive systems*, ACM Press, 433–442. http://doi.org/10.1145/2598510.2598566

16. Petra Isenberg and Sheelagh Carpendale. 2007. Interactive tree comparison for Co-located collaborative information visualization. *IEEE Transactions on Visualization and Computer Graphics* 13, 6: 1232–1239. http://doi.org/10.1109/TVCG.2007.70568

17. Yvonne Jansen and Pierre Dragicevic. 2013. An interaction model for visualizations beyond the desktop. *IEEE Transactions on Visualization and Computer Graphics* 19, 12: 2396–2405. http://doi.org/10.1109/TVCG.2013.134

18. Yvonne Jansen, Pierre Dragicevic, and Jean-Daniel Fekete. 2013. Evaluating the efficiency of physical visualizations. *Proceedings of the SIGCHI Conference on Human Factors in Computing Systems*: 2593. http://doi.org/10.1145/2470654.2481359

19. Yvonne Jansen, Pierre Dragicevic, Petra Isenberg, et al. 2015. Opportunities and Challenges for Data Physicalization. *Proceedings of the SIGCHI Conference on Human Factors in Computing Systems*: 3227–3236. http://doi.org/10.1145/2702123.2702180

20. Yvonne Jansen and Kasper Hornbaek. 2016. A Psychophysical Investigation of Size as a Physical Variable. *IEEE Transactions on Visualization and Computer Graphics* 22, 1: 479–488. http://doi.org/10.1109/TVCG.2015.2467951

21. Criss Mills. 2000. *Designing with Models : a Studio Guide to Making and Using Architectural Design Models*. John Wiley.

22. Andrew Vande Moere and Stephanie Patel. 2010. The Physical Visualization of Information: Designing Data Sculptures in an Educational Context. *Visual Information Communication*, 1: 1–23. http://doi.org/10.1007/978-1-4419-0312-9_1

23. Andrew Vande Moere, Martin Tomitsch, Christoph Wimmer, Boesch Christoph, and Thomas Grechenig. 2012. Evaluating the effect of style in information visualization. *IEEE Transactions on Visualization and Computer Graphics* 18, 12: 2739–2748. http://doi.org/10.1109/TVCG.2012.221

24. Mark Morris. 2006. *Models : Architecture and the Miniature*. Wiley-Academy.

25. Nicholas Negroponte. 1971. Aspects of Living in an Architecture Machine. *Design Research Society Conference Proceedings*: 63–67.

26. Dietmar Offenhuber and Orkan Telhan. 2015. Indexical visualization—the data-less information display. In *Ubiquitous Computing, Complexity and Culture*, Jay David Bolter, Lily Diaz, Morten Søndergaard and Maria Engberg (eds.). Routledge, 288–303.

27. Ansgar Oswald. 2008. *Architectural Models*. DOM Publishers.

28. Juhani Pallasmaa. 2013. Hapticity and Time. In *Encounters 1 - Architectural Essays*. Rakennustieto Publishing.

29. Ben Piper, Carlo Ratti, and Hiroshi Ishii. 2002. Illuminating Clay : A Tangible Interface with potential GRASS applications. *Proceedings of the SIGCHI Conference on Human Factors in*

*Computing Systems*: 355–362. http://doi.org/10.1145/503376.503439

30. Donald A. Schön. 1985. *The design studio : an exploration of its traditions and potentials*. RIBA Publications for RIBA Building Industry Trust.

31. Milena Stavric, Predrag Sidanin, and Bojan Tepavcevic. 2013. *Architectural Scale Models in the Digital Age: Design, Representation and Manufacturing*. Springer.

32. Simon Stusak, Jeannette Schwarz, and Andreas Butz. 2015. Evaluating the Memorability of Physical Visualizations. *Proceedings of the SIGCHI Conference on Human Factors in Computing Systems*: 3247–3250. http://doi.org/10.1145/2702123.2702248

33. Simon Stusak, Aurelien Tabard, Franziska Sauka, Rohit Ashok Khot, and Andreas Butz. 2014. Activity sculptures: Exploring the impact of physical visualizations on running activity. *IEEE Transactions on Visualization and Computer Graphics* 20, 12: 2201–2210. http://doi.org/10.1109/TVCG.2014.2352953

34. Faisal Taher, John Hardy, Abhijit Karnik, et al. 2015. Exploring Interactions with Physically Dynamic Bar Charts. *Proceedings of the SIGCHI Conference on Human Factors in Computing Systems*: 3237–3246. http://doi.org/10.1145/2702123.2702604

35. Edward Tufte. 1983. *The Visual Display of Quantitative Information*. Graphics Press.

36. Brygg Ullmer and Hiroshi Ishii. 1997. The metaDESK: models and prototypes for tangible user interfaces. *UIST '97 Proceedings*: 223–232. http://doi.org/10.1145/263407.263551

37. John Underkoffler and Hiroshi Ishii. 1999. Urp: A luminous-tangible workbench for urban planning and design. *Proceedings of the SIGCHI Conference on Human Factors in Computing Systems*: 386–393. http://doi.org/http://doi.acm.org/10.1145/302979.303114

38. Jagoda Walny, Samuel Huron, and Sheelagh Carpendale. 2015. An Exploratory Study of Data Sketching for Visual Representation. *Computer Graphics Forum* 34, 3: 231–240. http://doi.org/10.1111/cgf.12635

39. Megan Werner. 2011. *Model Making*. Princeton Architectural Press.

40. Sean White and Steven Feiner. 2009. SiteLens: Situated Visualization Techniques for Urban Site Visits. *Proceedings of the 2009 ACM CHI Conference on Human Factors in Computing Systems*: 1117–1120. http://doi.org/10.1145/1518701.1518871

41. Wesley Willett, Yvonne Jansen, and Pierre Dragicevic. 2017. Embedded Data Representations. *IEEE Transactions on Visualization and Computer Graphics* 23, 1: 461–470. http://doi.org/10.1109/TVCG.2016.2598608

42. William Wright, David Schroh, Pascale Proulx, Alex Skaburskis, and Brian Cort. 2006. The Sandbox for analysis: concepts and methods. *Proceedings of the SIGCHI Conference on Human Factors in Computing Systems*: 801–810. http://doi.org/10.1145/1124772.1124890

43. Albena Yaneva. 2005. Scaling Up and Down: Extraction Trials in Architectural Design. *Social Studies of Science* 35, 6: 867–894. http://doi.org/10.1177/0306312705053053

44. Longyu Zhang, Haiwei Dong, and Abdulmotaleb El Saddik. 2016. From 3D Sensing to Printing: A Survey. *Acm Transactions on Multimedia Computing Communications and Applications* 12, 2. http://doi.org/10.1145/2818710

45. Jack Zhao and Andrew Vande Moere. 2008. Embodiment in data sculpture. *DIMEA '08 Proceedings*, ACM Press, 343. http://doi.org/10.1145/1413634.1413696

46. Amit Zoran and Ja Paradiso. 2013. Freed: a freehand digital sculpting tool. *Proceedings of the SIGCHI Conference on Human Factors in Computing Systems*: 2613–2616. http://doi.org/10.1145/2470654.2481361

# Author Index

# NOTES

# NOTES

# NOTES

# NOTES

# NOTES

# NOTES

# NOTES

# NOTES

# NOTES

# NOTES

## NOTES

# NOTES

# NOTES

## NOTES

# NOTES

# NOTES

# NOTES

# NOTES

# NOTES

# NOTES

# NOTES

# NOTES

www.ingramcontent.com/pod-product-compliance
Lightning Source LLC
LaVergne TN
LVHW082006200926
848481LV00010B/2811